Use and enjoy this in
the best of health, sweetheart
Always —
Dave

12-94

The Art of the Personal Essay

A *Teachers & Writers Collaborative* Book

A N C H O R ⚓ **B O O K S**

D O U B L E D A Y

New York London Toronto Sydney Auckland

The Art of the Personal Essay

An Anthology from the Classical Era to the Present

Selected and with an
Introduction by

Phillip Lopate

AN ANCHOR BOOK
PUBLISHED BY DOUBLEDAY
a division of Bantam Doubleday Dell Publishing Group, Inc.
1540 Broadway, New York, New York 10036

ANCHOR BOOKS, DOUBLEDAY, *and the portrayal of an anchor are trademarks of*
Doubleday, a division of Bantam Doubleday Dell Publishing Group, Inc.

A *Teachers & Writers Collaborative* Book

Book Design by Cheryl L. Cipriani

Library of Congress Cataloging-in-Publication Data

The Art of the personal essay : an anthology from the classical era to the present
  / selected and with an introduction by Phillip Lopate.
      p.   cm.
    "A Teachers & Writers Collaborative book."
    Includes bibliographical references (p.   ).
    1. Essays.   2. Essays—Translations into English.   I. Lopate, Phillip,
  1943–   .   II. Teachers & Writers Collaborative.
PN6141.A78   1994
808.84—dc20   *94-29708*
                                                                                         CIP

ISBN 0-385-42298-9

CONTENTS

III
The Rise of the English Essay

Contents

Contents [ix]

BY THEME

BY FORM

Prose Poem and Reverie

Reportage

Valediction

ACKNOWLEDGMENTS

The editor and publisher are grateful for permission to include the following copyrighted material in this volume.

James Baldwin, "Notes of a Native Son" from *Notes of a Native Son* by James Baldwin. Copyright © 1955, renewed 1983 by James Baldwin. Reprinted by permission of Beacon Press. "Alas, Poor Richard" from *Nobody Knows My Name*, Copyright © 1961 by James Baldwin. Copyright renewed. Published by Vintage Books. Reprinted by arrangement with the James Baldwin Estate.

Roland Barthes, "Leaving the Movie Theater" from *The Rustle of Language* by Roland Barthes, translated by Richard Howard. Translation copyright © 1986 by Farrar, Straus & Giroux, Inc. Reprinted by permission of Hill and Wang, a division of Farrar, Straus & Giroux, Inc.

Max Beerbohm, "Going Out for a Walk" and "Laughter" are reprinted by permission of Mrs. Eva Reichmann.

Robert Benchley, "My Face" from *The Benchley Roundup* by Robert Benchley, selected by Nathaniel Benchley. Copyright 1938 by Robert Benchley. Reprinted by permission of HarperCollins Publishers, Inc.

Walter Benjamin. "Unpacking My Library" from *Illuminations* by Walter Benjamin. Copyright © 1955 Suhrkamp Verlag, Frankfurt am Main, English translation by Harry Zohn copyright © 1968 by Harcourt Brace & Company, reprinted by permission of Harcourt Brace & Company. "Hashish in Marseilles" from *Reflections, Essays, Aphorisms, Autobiographical Writings* by Walter Benjamin, translated by Edmund Jephcott, English translation copyright © 1978 by Harcourt Brace & Company, reprinted by permission of the publisher.

Wendell Berry, "An Entrance to the Woods" from *Recollected Essays, 1965–1980* by Wendell Berry. Copyright © 1971, 1981 by Wendell Berry. Reprinted by permission of North Point Press, a division of Farrar, Straus & Giroux, Inc.

Jorge Luis Borges, "Blindness" by Jorge Luis Borges from *Seven Nights*. Translated by Eliot Weinberger. Copyright © 1980 by Fondo de Cultura Economica. Reprinted by permission of New Directions Publishing Corp.

Hubert Butler, "Aunt Harriet" from *The Subprefect Should Have Held His Tongue*, an Allan Lane selection, which was originally taken from *The Children of Drancy*, first published by The Lilliput Press in Ireland in 1988. Copyright by the literary estate of Hubert Butler. Reprinted by permission of the Lilliput Press.

E. M. Cioran, "Some Blind Alleys: A Letter" by E. M. Cioran. Copyright © 1956 by Editions Gallimard. Translation copyright © 1968 by Quadrangle Books, Inc. Reprinted from *The Temptation to Exist* by E. M. Cioran, translated from the French by Richard Howard, published by Seaver Books, New York, New York.

Joan Didion, "Goodbye to All That" from *Slouching Towards Bethlehem* by Joan Didion. Copyright © 1967, 1968 by Joan Didion. "In Bed" from *The White Album* by Joan Didion. Copyright © 1979 by Joan Didion.

Annie Dillard, "Seeing" from *Pilgrim at Tinker Creek* by Annie Dillard. Copyright © 1974 by Annie Dillard. Reprinted by permission of HarperCollins Publishers, Inc.

M. F. K. Fisher, "Once a Tramp, Always . . ." from *With Bold Knife and Fork* by M. F. K. Fisher. Copyright © 1969 by M. F. K. Fisher. Reprinted by permission of the Putnam Publishing Group.

F. Scott Fitzgerald, "The Crack-Up" from *The Crack-Up* by F. Scott Fitzgerald. Copyright 1945 by New Directions Publishing Corp. Reprinted by permission of New Directions Publishing Corp.

Carlos Fuentes, "How I Started to Write" from *Myself with Others* by Carlos Fuentes. Copyright © 1988 by Carlos Fuentes. Reprinted by permission of Farrar, Straus & Giroux, Inc.

Natalia Ginzburg, "He and I" by Natalia Ginzburg. Copyright © 1962 by Giulio Einaudi editore s.p.a. Translation copyright © 1985 by Dick Davis. Reprinted from *The Little Virtues* by Natalia Ginzburg, published by Seaver Books, New York, New York, and by Carcanet Press Limited, Manchester, England.

Edward Hoagland, "The Courage of Turtles" and "The Threshold and the Jolt of Pain" by Edward Hoagland. Reprinted by permission of Lescher & Lescher.

Ou-yang Hsiu, "Pleasure Boat Studio" from *The Literary Works of Ou-Yang Hsiu*, translated by Ronald Egan. Reprinted with the permission of Cambridge University Press.

Kenko, "Essays in Idleness" by Kenko and translated by Donald Keene. Copyright © 1967 by Columbia University Press, New York. Reprinted with the permission of the publisher.

Seymour Krim, "For My Brothers and Sisters in the Failure Business" by Seymour Krim. Reprinted from *What's This Cat's Story? The Best of Seymour Krim* by permission of the Estate of Seymour Krim.

Phillip Lopate, "Against Joie de Vivre" by Phillip Lopate. Copyright © 1989 by Phillip Lopate. Reprinted by permission of Poseidon Press, a division of Simon & Schuster, Inc.

Mary McCarthy, "My Confession" by Mary McCarthy. Reprinted by permission of The Mary McCarthy Literary Estate.

H. L. Mencken, "On Being an American" by H. L. Mencken. Reprinted by permission of Enoch Pratt Free Library in accordance with the terms of the will of H. L. Mencken.

Michel de Montaigne, "Of Books," "Of a Monstrous Child," and "On Some Verses of Virgil" by Michel de Montaigne. Reprinted from *The Complete Essays of Montaigne*, translated by Donald M. Frame, with the permission of Stanford University Press. Copyright © 1958 by the Board of Trustees of the Leland Stanford Junior University.

George Orwell, "Such, Such Were the Joys" from *Such, Such Were the Joys* by George Orwell. Copyright 1952 and renewed 1980 by Sonia Brownell Orwell, reprinted by permission of Harcourt Brace & Company.

Gayle Pemberton, "Do He Have Your Number, Mr. Jeffrey?" from *The Hottest Water in Chicago* by Gayle Pemberton. Copyright © 1992 by Gayle Pemberton. Reprinted by permission of Faber and Faber, Inc.

Plutarch, "Consolation to His Wife" by Plutarch, translated by Moses Hadas. Reprinted by permission of the estate of Elizabeth C. Hadas.

Adrienne Rich, "Split at the Root: An Essay on Jewish Identity" reprinted from *Blood, Bread, and Poetry, Selected Prose 1979–1985*, by Adrienne Rich, by permission of the author and W. W. Norton & Company, Inc. Copyright © 1986 by Adrienne Rich.

Richard Rodriguez, "Late Victorians," from *Days of Obligation* by Richard Rodriguez. Copyright © 1992 by Richard Rodriguez. Used by permission of Viking Penguin, a division of Penguin Books U.S.A., Inc.

Scott Russell Sanders, "Under the Influence" by Scott Russell Sanders. Copyright © 1989 by *Harper's Magazine*. All Rights Reserved. Reprinted from the November 1989 issue by special permission.

Richard Selzer, "The Knife" by Richard Selzer. Copyright © 1974, 1975, 1976, 1987 by Richard Selzer. Reprinted by permission of Simon & Schuster, Inc.

Seneca, "On Noise" and "Asthma" by Seneca, translated by Robin Campbell. "Scipio's Villa" and "Slaves" by Seneca, translated by Moses Hadas. Reprinted by permission of the estate of Elizabeth C. Hadas.

Sei Shonagon, "Hateful Things" by Sei Shonagon from *The Pillow Book*, translated by Ivan Morris. Copyright © 1967 by Columbia University Press, New York. Reprinted by permission of the publisher.

Sara Suleri, "Meatless Days" by Sara Suleri. Copyright © 1989 by The University of Chicago. All Rights Reserved. Reprinted by permission of The University of Chicago Press.

Junichiro Tanizaki, "In Praise of Shadows" by Junichiro Tanizaki. Translated by Thomas J. Harper and Edward G. Seidensticker. Published by Leete's Island Books, Inc., Box 3131, Stony Creek, Conn. 06405.

James Thurber, "The Secret Life of James Thurber" by James Thurber. Copyright 1945 by James Thurber. Copyright © 1973 by Helen Thurber & Rosemary A. Thurber. From *The Thurber Carnival*, published by Harper & Row.

Ivan Turgenev, "The Execution of Tropmann" by Ivan Turgenev from *Turgenev's Lit-*

erary Reminiscences, translated by David Magarshack. Copyright © 1958 by Farrar, Straus & Cudahy. Copyright renewed 1986 by Elsie D. Magarshack. Reprinted by permission of Farrar, Straus & Giroux, Inc.

Gore Vidal, "Some Memories of the Glorious Bird and an Earlier Self" from *Matters of Fact and of Fiction* by Gore Vidal. Copyright © 1973, 1974, 1975, 1976, 1977 by Gore Vidal. Reprinted by permission of Random House, Inc.

E. B. White, "Once More to the Lake" and "The Ring of Time" from *Essays of E. B. White* by E. B. White. Copyright 1941 by E. B. White. Copyright © 1956 by E. B. White. Reprinted by permission of HarperCollins Publishers, Inc.

Virginia Woolf, "Street Haunting" and "The Death of the Moth" from *The Death of the Moth and Other Essays* by Virginia Woolf, copyright 1942 Harcourt Brace & Company and renewed 1970 by Marjorie T. Parsons, Executrix, and reprinted by permission of the publisher.

INTRODUCTION

T HIS BOOK ATTEMPTS to put forward and interpret a tradition: the personal essay. Though long spoken of as a subcategory of the essay, the personal essay has rarely been isolated and studied as such. It should certainly be celebrated, because it is one of the most approachable and diverting types of literature we possess.

The hallmark of the personal essay is its intimacy. The writer seems to be speaking directly into your ear, confiding everything from gossip to wisdom. Through sharing thoughts, memories, desires, complaints, and whimsies, the personal essayist sets up a relationship with the reader, a dialogue—a friendship, if you will, based on identification, understanding, testiness, and companionship.

At the core of the personal essay is the supposition that there is a certain unity to human experience. As Michel de Montaigne, the great innovator and patron saint of personal essayists, put it, "Every man has within himself the entire human condition." This meant that when he was telling about himself, he was talking, to some degree, about all of us. The personal essay has an implicitly democratic bent, in the value it places on experience rather than status distinctions. "And on the loftiest throne in the world we are still sitting only on our own rump," wrote Montaigne.

Let us get certain worrisome distinctions out of the way. The traditional division in the essay has been between formal and informal essays. Not being good at definitions, I will take the easy way out and quote Holman and Harmon's *A Handbook to Literature.* The formal (sometimes called impersonal) essay is characterized by "seriousness of purpose, dignity, logical organization, length. . . . The technique of the formal essay is now practically identical with that of all factual or theoretical prose writing in which literary effect is secondary to serious purpose." The informal essay, in contrast, is characterized by "the personal element (self-revelation, individual tastes and experiences, confidential manner), humor, graceful style, rambling structure, unconventionality or novelty of theme, freshness of form, freedom from stiffness and affectation, incomplete or tentative treatment of topic."

The personal essay is a subset of the informal essay, or, as *A Handbook of Literature* defines it, "a kind of informal essay, with an intimate style, some autobiographical content or interest, and an urbane conversational manner." To make things more confusing, another subset of the informal essay is the familiar essay, which sounds rather like the personal essay: "The more personal, intimate type of informal essay. It deals lightly, often humorously, with personal experiences, opinions, and prejudices, stressing especially the unusual or novel in attitude and having to do with the varied aspects of everyday life." I have never seen a strong distinction drawn in print between the personal essay and the familiar essay; maybe they are identical twins, maybe close cousins. The difference, if there is any, is one of nuance, I suspect. The familiar essay values lightness of touch above all else; the personal essay, which need not be light, tends to put the writer's "I" or idiosyncratic angle more at center stage.

The personal essay has an open form and a drive toward candor and self-disclosure. Unlike the formal essay, it depends less on airtight reasoning than on style and personality, what Elizabeth Hardwick called "the soloist's personal signature flowing through the text."

The Conversational Element

In its preference for a conversational approach, the personal essay shows its relationship to the dialogue, an ancient form going back to Plato. Both forms acknowledge the duality, or rather multiplicity, of selves that human beings harbor. "It is natural to enter into dialogues and disputes with others," writes the critic Stuart Hampshire, "because it is natural to enter into disputes with oneself. The mind works by contradiction." Personal essayists converse with the reader because they are already having dialogues and disputes with themselves.

Montaigne may not have been, as he claimed, the first writer to take himself as his subject, but he was perhaps the first to talk to himself convincingly on the page. Reading him, we seem to be eavesdropping on a mind in solitude. He chatters, pen in hand, and keeps putting questions to himself when the essay threatens to flag.

Still, this talky manner is not entirely original. If we go back to Seneca, as Montaigne did, we see the same tendency to reproduce the give-and-take of conversation. I'm not speaking of Seneca's formal essays, which employ the full machinery of classical oratory, but his letters, which come much closer to being personal essays in the modern mode. By using the device of a letter to a friend, Seneca was able to incorporate conversational throat-clearings, feints, rhetorical questions, and replies, talking past his alleged correspondent to the general reader. He will pop in a phrase such as "This is all very well, you might say, but isn't it sometimes a lot simpler . . . ?" Seneca examines his own doubts by placing objections in the mouth of the reader. His prose is thorny, abrupt like conversation, and it leaves a sort of dry almond taste from all those chewy aphorisms.

The personal essay has historically sought to puncture the stiffness of formal discourse with language that is casual, everyday, demotic, direct. William Hazlitt, one of the giants of the form, took Dr. Johnson to task for always using big words and Latinate syntax. Hazlitt defined his own ideal, the familiar style, as the following: "To write a genuine familiar or truly English style, is to write as any one would speak in common conversation who had a thorough command and choice of words, or who could discourse with ease, force, and perspicuity, setting aside all pedantic and oratorical flourishes." The conversational dynamic—the desire for contact —is ingrained in the form, and serves to establish a quick emotional intimacy with the audience.

Honesty, Confession, and Privacy

Let us say that the writer has caught the reader's attention with a frank, conversational manner. In effect, a contract between writer and reader has been drawn up: the essayist must then make good on it by delivering, or discovering, as much honesty as possible.

The struggle for honesty is central to the ethos of the personal essay. "I want to be an honest man and a good writer," James Baldwin put it, in that order. Yet the personal essayist often admits that few of us can remain honest for long, since humans are incorrigibly self-deceiving, rationalizing animals. Ironically, it is this skepticism that uniquely equips the personal essayist for the difficult climb into honesty. So often the "plot" of a personal essay, its drama, its suspense, consists in watching how far the essayist can drop past his or her psychic defenses toward deeper levels of honesty. One may speak of a vertical dimension in the form: if the essayist can delve further underneath, until we feel the topic has been handled as honestly, as *fairly* as possible, then at least one essential condition of a successful personal essay has been met. (The others, such as pleasurable literary style, formal shapelessness, and intellectual sustenance, still await consideration.) If, however, the essayist stays at the same flat level of self-disclosure and understanding throughout, the piece may be pleasantly smooth, but it will not awaken that shiver of self-recognition—equivalent to the frisson in horror films when the monster looks at himself in the mirror—which all lovers of the personal essay await as a reward.

There is a certain strictness, or even cruelty at times, in the impulse of the personal essayist to scrape away illusions. In "On the Pleasure of Hating," Hazlitt describes friends getting together to analyze their mutual acquaintances: "We regarded them no more in our experiments than 'mice in an air-pump:' or like malefactors, they were regularly cut down and given over to the dissecting-knife. We spared neither friend nor foe. We sacrificed human infirmities at the shrine of truth. The skeletons of character might be seen, after the juice was extracted, dangling in the air like flies in cobwebs."

Often the rough handling begins with oneself. "We must remove the mask," says Montaigne. For Wendell Berry, in "An Entrance to the Woods," the mask is human nature itself, and the wilderness alone can help him shed its false lendings: "And so, coming here, what I have done is strip away the human facade that usually stands between me and the universe."

The spectacle of baring the naked soul is meant to awaken the sympathy of the reader, who is apt to forgive the essayist's self-absorption in return for the warmth of his or her candor. Some vulnerability is essential to the personal essay. Unproblematically self-assured, self-contained, self-satisfied types will not make good essayists. There is, of course, such a thing as a rhetoric of sincerity, and the skilled essayist can fake a vulnerable tone. But if this is done too often, the skilled reader will turn away in disgust. "There is one thing the essayist cannot do—he cannot indulge himself in deceit or in concealment, for he will be found out in no time," wrote E. B. White.

The personal essayist must above all be a reliable narrator; we must trust his or her core of sincerity. We must also feel secure that the essayist has done a fair amount of introspective homework already, is grounded in reality, and is trying to give us the maximum understanding and intelligence of which he or she is capable. A dunderhead and a psychotic killer may be sincere, but that would not sufficiently recommend them for the genre.

Part of our trust in good personal essayists issues, paradoxically, from their exposure of their own betrayals, uncertainties, and self-mistrust. Their sincerity issues from an awareness of their potential for insincerity— see Max Beerbohm's telling aside, "But (it seems that I must begin every paragraph by questioning the sincerity of what I have just said)"—and it gives them a doubled authority.

In focusing on the honesty of personal essayists, I do not mean to imply that they are relentlessly exposing dark secrets about themselves. We learn more about their habits of thought than about the sorts of abuses and crimes that spice our afternoon TV talk shows: incest, date-rape, addictions. The sins that make these essayists cringe in retrospect usually turn out to be an insensitivity that wounded another, a lack of empathy, or the callowness of youth.

Is it a paradox that personal essayists are often excruciatingly frank, yet protective of their privacy? Richard Rodriguez, for instance, is a master of the confessional tone, yet he tells us that his family calls him "Mr. Secrets," and he plays a hide-and-seek game of revealing himself. We learn very little about the actual circumstances of Max Beerbohm's life from his writings. How he managed to make ends meet, with whom he had affairs, whether his was a difficult or an easy marriage—these celebrity tidbits are never volunteered by the gentlemanly Max. Yet few writers have limned so quirky and recognizable a self-portrait. Chronic Beerbohm readers come to feel as close to him as if they were behind the wheel of a video arcade game, seeing how the world comes at him and recognizing the exact moment at which his tenderness is likely to swerve into mischief.

How the world comes at another person, the irritations, jubilations, aches and pains, humorous flashes—these are the classic building materials of the personal essay. We learn the rhythm by which the essayist receives, digests, and spits out the world, and we learn the shape of his or her privacy. "If you wish to preserve your secret," wrote Alexander Smith of Montaigne, "wrap it up in frankness."

The Contractions and Expansions of the Self

Personal essayists are adept at interrogating their ignorance. Just as often as they tell us what they know, they ask at the beginning of an exploration of a problem what it is they don't know—and why. They follow the clue of their ignorance through the maze. Intrigued with their limitations, both physical and mental, they are attracted to cul-de-sac: what one doesn't understand, or can't do, is as good a place as any to start investigating the borders of the self. So Natalia Ginzburg tells us that she can never remember the names of even the most famous actors; Charles Lamb confides that he has no musical ear; Max Beerbohm analyzes his failure to grasp philosophy.

Also common to the genre is a taste for littleness. This includes self-belittlement. In "Of Greatness," Abraham Cowley, after quoting Horace's "The gods have done well in making me a humble and small-spirited fellow," goes on to say slyly, "I confess I love littleness almost in all things.

A little convenient estate, a little cheerful house, a little company, and a very little feast; and, if I were to fall in love again (which is a great passion, and therefore, I hope, I have done with it), it would be, I think, with prettiness, rather than with majestical beauty."

Natalia Ginzburg's collection of essays is entitled *The Little Virtues.* We see operating here a form of inverse boasting: in exchange for lack of stature or power in the world, the personal essayist claims unique access to the small, humble things in life. And this taste for the miniature becomes a strong suit of the form: the ability to turn anything close at hand (Charles Lamb's ears, Virginia Woolf's moth, Samuel Johnson's boarding house) into a grand meditational adventure.

Just as the personal essayist is able to make the small loom large, so he or she simultaneously contracts and expands the self. This is done first by finding the borders, limits, defects, and disabilities of the particular human package one owns, then by pointing them out, which implies at least a partial surmounting through detachment. The personal essay is the reverse of that set of Chinese boxes that you keep opening, only to find a smaller one within. Here you start with the small—the package of flaws and limits—and suddenly find a slightly larger container, insinuated by the essay's successful articulation and the writer's self-knowledge. The personal essayist is a Houdini who, having confessed his sins and peccadilloes and submitted voluntarily to the reader's censuring handcuffs, suddenly slips them off with malicious ease by claiming, *I am more than the perpetrator of that shameful act; I am the knower and commentator as well.*

If tragedy is said to ennoble people and comedy to cut people down to size, then the personal essay, with its ironic deflations, its insistence on human frailty, tilts toward the comic. Montaigne (like his predecessor and fellow humanist Erasmus) was at pains to show *Homo sapiens* as a fickle, conceited fool whose vanity needed pulling down. However, by drawing attention to so many strands of inconsistency in human behavior, he could not help but create the opposite impression: a humanity enlarged by complexity. The fulsome confession of limit carries the secret promise of an almost infinite opening-out.

Personal essayists from Montaigne on have been fascinated with the changeableness and plasticity of the materials of human personality. Starting with self-description, they have realized they can never render all at once the entire complexity of a personality. So they have elected to follow an additive strategy, offering incomplete shards, one mask or persona after another: the eager, skeptical, amiable, tender, curmudgeonly, antic, somber. If "we must remove the mask," it is only to substitute another mask. The hope is that in the end, when an essayist's lifework has been accumulated, all these personae will add up to a genuine unmasking.

In the meantime, the personal essayist tries to make his many partial selves dance to the same beat—to unite, through force of voice and style, these discordant, fragmentary personae so that the reader can accept them as issuing from one coherent self. Sometimes a persona is literally artificial, as in Charles Lamb's "Elia," a lightly fictionalized stand-in for himself. Lamb comically exploits the supposed differences between his narrator and himself while getting away with a fair amount of autobiography. Unless the essayist forces the issue, the reader is often not aware of the discontinuities among his personae, so strong is the illusion of cohesive selfhood in the voice of a writer we admire.

The harvesting of self-contradiction is an intrinsic part of the personal essay form. Often, seeing two samples of an essayist's work allows us to grasp this principle of multiple personae in action. The Edward Hoagland we meet in "The Courage of Turtles," a gentle naturalist stroking a turtle's belly, is both contradicted and extended by Hoagland's confession of spanking women in "The Threshold and the Jolt of Pain." If some readers are repelled by a writer's behavioral contradictions, this is quite all right, because the personal essayist is not necessarily out to win the audience's unqualified love but to present the complex portrait of a human being.

This spectacle is offered up in sections, which makes autobiographies and personal essays, for all their overlapping aspects, fundamentally different. A memoirist is entitled to move in a linear direction, accruing extra points of psychological or social shading from initial set-ups, like a novelist, the deeper he or she moves in the narrative. There is no need to keep explaining who the narrator or the narrator's father or mother are at the beginning of each chapter. The personal essayist, though, cannot assume that the reader will ever have read anything by him or her before, and so must reestablish a persona each time and embed it in a context by providing sufficient autobiographical background. This usually means having to repeat basic circumstances of his life materials over and over—a wildly wasteful procedure, from the standpoint of narrative economy. Far better, you would think, for the essayist to get it over with once and for all and simply write his life story in a linear fashion. But for one thing, he may, in a fit of modesty, feel that his life story is not worth telling in toto, even if a portion of it seems to be. And for another, the essay form allows the writer to circle around one particular autobiographical piece, squeezing all possible meaning out of it, while leaving the greater part of his life story available for later milking. It may even be that the personal essayist is more temperamentally suited to this circling procedure, diving into the volcano of self and extracting a single hot coal to consider and shape, either because of laziness or because of an aesthetic impulse to control a smaller frame.

The Role of Contrariety

It is often the case that personal essayists intentionally go against the grain of popular opinion. They raise the ante, as it were, making it more difficult for the reader to identify frictionlessly with the writer. The need to assert a quite specific temperament frequently leads the essayist into playing the curmudgeon, for there is no quicker way to demonstrate idiosyncracy and independence than to stand a platitude on its head (see Dr. Johnson on solitude in the country), to show a prickly opposition to what the rest of humanity views as patently wholesome (Beerbohm on "Going Out for a Walk"), or to find merits in what the community regards as loathsome (Hazlitt's "On the Pleasure of Hating"). The touchy sensibility of a Hazlitt, Beerbohm, or Cioran, ever on the alert for an opportunity to bristle, makes us follow them with amused suspense: what will they think to object to next?

Behind these contrarieties is a fear of staleness and cliché, or, to put the matter more positively, a compulsion toward fresh expression. To assert that all men are brothers, that prejudice and racism are bad, and that nature should not be despoiled may win a writer points in heaven, but it is doubtful that these pronouncements will quicken the reader's pulse. The novice essayist often errs by taking a strong moralistic stand and running it into the ground, with nowhere to go after two paragraphs. Here the personal essayist will open up a new flank, locating a tension between two valid, opposing goals, or a partial virtue in some apparent ill, or an ambivalence in his own belief-system. I am not saying that an essayist should become an immoralist just for the sake of originality, but that he should be alert for contradictions that open up new ways of looking at old subjects.

The enemy of the personal essay is self-righteousness, not just because it is tiresome and ugly in itself, but because it slows down the dialectic of self-questioning, what Cioran calls "thinking against oneself." Of course, personal essayists may write from powerful moral or political conviction, so long as they are also willing to render a frank, shaded account of their own feelings. Mary McCarthy, describing in "My Confession" how she became a staunch anti-Stalinist, is unafraid to tell the less than noble part that vanity, laziness, and stubbornness played in this conversion. George Orwell uncovers the proper little fascist in himself as a schoolboy in "Such, Such Were the Joys . . . ," and elsewhere *(The Road to Wigan Pier)* is honest enough to admit that he sometimes found himself recoiling at the smell of the workers he was otherwise so keen to defend. James Baldwin's moral passion is all the more credible once we know about his struggles with his father and his admissions of irrational rage and opportunism.

The conscience of the personal essay arises from the author's examination of his or her prejudices. Essayists must be able to pass judgment, or else their work will be toothless; but this right should extend from an awareness of their own potential culpability, if only through mental temptation. The idea is to implicate first oneself and then the reader in a fault that seems initially to belong safely elsewhere. The essayist is someone who lives with the guilty knowledge that he is "prejudiced" (Mencken called his essay collections *Prejudices*) and has a strong predisposition for or against certain everyday phenomena. It then becomes his business to attend to these inner signals, these stomach growls, these seemingly indefensible intuitions, and try to analyze what lies underneath them, the better to judge them. As Georg Lukacs wrote, "The essay is a judgment, but the essential, the value-determining thing about it is not the verdict (as is the case with the system) but the process of judging."

The Problem of Egotism

Thoreau justifies his use of "I" on the opening page of *Walden:* "In most books the *I,* or first person, is omitted; in this it will be retained; that, in respect to egotism, is the main difference. We commonly do not remember that it is, after all, always the first person that is speaking." Still, it takes a fair amount of ego to discourse on one's private affairs and offer judgments about life. This can make the writer, let alone the reader, uneasy. Most people are brought up to think it is impolite to talk much about themselves; in academic papers, scholars are discouraged from using the first person singular. Surely one of the reasons for the self-deprecating air that many personal essayists adopt is to ward off potential charges of vanity or self-absorption.

E. B. White confronted this problem head-on when he wrote:

> I think some people find the essay the last resort of the egoist, a much too self-conscious and self-serving form for their taste; they feel that it is presumptuous of a writer to assume that his little excursions or his small observations will interest the reader. There is some justice in their complaint. I have always been aware that I am by nature self-absorbed and egoistical; to write of myself to the extent I have done indicates a too great attention to my own life, not enough to the lives of others. I have worn many shirts, and not all of them have been a good fit. But when I am discouraged or downcast I need only fling open the door of my closet, and there, hidden behind everything else, hangs the mantle of Michel de Montaigne, smelling slightly of camphor.

Since White was one of the most self-effacing personal essayists, it is interesting that even he was stung with guilt about egotism. His temporary solution—wrapping himself in the mantle of Montaigne—is also interesting, as though only the personal essay tradition could validate his self-involvement.

The nineteenth-century English writer Alexander Smith drew some helpful distinctions between pleasurable and irritating egotism in essayists: "The speaking about oneself is not necessarily offensive. A modest, truthful man speaks better about himself than about anything else, and on that subject his speech is likely to be most profitable to his hearers. . . . If he be without taint of boastfulness, of self-sufficiency, of hungry vanity, the world will not press the charge home. If a man discourses continually of his wines, his plate, his titled acquaintances, the number and quality of his horses, his men-servants and maid-servants, he must discourse very skillfully indeed if he escapes being called a coxcomb."

Smith reassures us that "it is this egotism, this perpetual reference to self, in which the charm of the essayist resides. If a man is worth knowing at all, he is worth knowing well." In a similar vein, Logan Pearsall Smith wrote that "the amused observation of one's own self is a veritable gold mine whose surface has hardly yet been scratched." While personal essayists as a rule share that conviction, all have occasionally had to wrestle with what might be called the stench of ego. A person can write about himself from angles that are charmed, fond, delightfully nervy; alter the lens just a little and he crosses over into gloating, pettiness, defensiveness, score settling (which includes self-hate), or whining about his victimization. The trick is to realize that one is not important, except insofar as one's example can serve to elucidate a more widespread human trait and make readers feel a little less lonely and freakish.

Cheek and Irony

Closely allied to these seesaws of modesty and egotism, universality and touchy eccentricity, is the penchant of the personal essayist for outbreaks of mischievous impudence. The conversational address to the reader is frequently the signal for such cheeky liberties, as though the rebellious, clever servant-author were tweaking the nose of the dull-witted master-reader. Cheekiness is a way of keeping readers alert. It cuts through the pious and commonplace.

Such cool impertinence often takes the form of a self-reflexive moment, which punctures the argument by drawing attention to the stage machinery of essayistic discourse. Montaigne launched this habit by impishly and preemptively criticizing his essays ("some excrements of an aged mind").

Beerbohm's "Laughter" begins, "M. Bergson, in his well-known essay on the theme, says . . . well, he says many things; but none of these, though I have just read them, do I clearly remember, nor am I sure that in the act of reading I understand any of them." This is an example of how the facetiously self-reflective confession of an inadequacy can have the perverse effect of cheek. When Walter Benjamin ends "Unpacking My Library" by saying about the true collector, "So I have erected one of his dwellings, with books as the building stones, before you, and now he is going to disappear inside, as is only fitting," he is both parodying the solemnity of the learned essay and treating the reading audience like children at a puppet show.

Part of what gives personal essayists the license to be so cheeky is their suspicion that they are not performing in the central ring of the literary circus. "The essayist, unlike the novelist, the poet, and the playwright, must be content in his self-imposed role of second-class citizen," wrote E. B. White. "A writer who has his sights trained on the Nobel Prize or other earthly triumphs had best write a novel, a poem, or a play, and leave the essayist to ramble about, content with living a free life and enjoying the satisfactions of a somewhat undisciplined existence."

Georg Lukacs, in "On the Nature and Form of the Essay," specifically linked the essayist's cheeky humor and the status of the genre. Referring to "that humor and that irony which we find in the writings of every truly great essayist," he observed that the "essayist dismisses his own proud hopes which sometimes lead him to believe that he has come close to the ultimate: he has, after all, no more to offer than explanations of the poems of others, or at best his own ideas. But he ironically adapts himself to this smallness—the eternal smallness of the most profound work of the intellect in the face of life—and even emphasizes it with ironic modesty."

The Idler Figure

As part of their ironic modesty, personal essayists frequently represent themselves as loafers or retirees, inactive and tangential to the marketplace. The shiftless marginality of the essayist's persona is underscored by the titles of some of the most famous essay series: *The Idler, The Rambler* (Samuel Johnson), *The Spectator, The Tatler* (Addison and Steele). Perhaps by affecting the role of lazy scribblers, essayists make themselves out to be harmless, thereby able to poke fun at will.

Asian literature has a long tradition of the retired scholar—sometimes forced into premature exile by falling into political disfavor, like the Chinese essayist Ou-yang Hsiu—who uses his leisure to contemplate the beauties of nature and the poetic transience of life. The Japanese monk

Kenko, having withdrawn from the world for spiritual purposes, wrote a book of stream-of-consciousness mini-essays called *Essays in Idleness.* Seneca penned his letters during enforced idleness and exile. Montaigne also portrayed himself as a retired country gentleman, given over to his library and idle thoughts, when in fact he still carried on important diplomatic missions during the religious wars.

Joseph Addison wrote in his *Spectator,* "I live in the World rather as a Spectator of Mankind, than as one of the species. . . . I have acted in all the Parts of my Life as a looker-on, which is the Character I intend to preserve in this Paper." The use of the term "Character," a popular eighteenth-century literary form which broke mankind down into types, alerts us that we are getting from Addison a stylized essayistic persona rather than realistic autobiography. Addison's partner, Sir Richard Steele, similarly offers us a detached narrator, cheerfully outside the net of economic productivity. In "Twenty-four Hours in London," he follows the crowd around for a day: "It is an inexpressible Pleasure to know a little of the World, and be of no Character or Significancy in it. To be ever unconcerned, and ever looking on new Objects with an endless Curiosity, is a Delight known only to those who are turned for Speculation: Nay, they who enjoy it, must value things only as they are the Objects of Speculation, without drawing any worldly Advantage to themselves from them, but just as they are what they contribute to their Amusement, or the Improvement of the Mind."

Here the idler begins to defend himself, even to adapt a tone of superiority toward the breadwinner. Robert Louis Stevenson, in his essay "An Apology for Idlers," advances this line of argument.

> Extreme *busyness* . . . is a symptom of deficient vitality; and a faculty for idleness implies a catholic appetite and a strong sense of personal identity. There is a sort of dead-alive, hackneyed people about, who are scarcely conscious of living except in the exercise of some conventional occupation. Bring these fellows into the country, or set them aboard ship, and you will see how they pine for their desk or their study. They have no curiosity; they cannot give themselves to random provocations; they do not take pleasure in the exercise of their faculties for its own sake . . . they *cannot* be idle, their nature is not generous enough; and they pass those hours in a sort of coma, which are not dedicated to furious moiling in the gold-mill.

Substitute "essayist" for "idler" in Stevenson's passage, and you have a catalogue of the genre's virtues: curiosity; openness; appetite for pleasure; willingness to reflect, to give oneself to "random provocations," nature, beauty. All this adds up to the capacity for perception. The essayist is fascinated with perception, which provides a never-ending source of speculative material. The art of vision can take place under normal circumstances (as in Woolf's "Street Haunting") or be heightened by drugs (Benjamin's "Hashish in Marseilles"), hunger (Soyinka's "Why Do I Fast?"), ecstatic nature mysticism (Dillard's "Seeing"), or illness (Lu Hsun's "Death").

By Stevenson's logic, only the idle person is able to practice *seeing*—to perceive the little, uncommercial miracles in life. The essayist here aligns himself with what is traditionally considered a female perspective, in its appreciation of sentiment, dailiness, and the domestic. Indeed, the male personal essayist, quick to label himself an idler, also volunteers that he is something less than a virile patriarch. A somewhat celibate bachelorhood seems to hover around the Spectator, Idler, Rambler, and other stylized essayistic personae. Lamb describes his first-person surrogate, Elia, with a shrewd bit of self-analysis: "He was too much of the boy-man. The *toga virilis* never sate gracefully on his shoulders. The impressions of infancy had burnt into him, and he resented the impertinence of manhood." Stevenson, who did marry, was still chiefly known for his boys' stories and essays like "The Lantern-Bearers," which dwell lovingly on this preadult stage of life. Walter Benjamin portrayed himself as a bookworm, a nerd, a schlemiel who could never quite grow up and enter the adult world of making a living.

I must reiterate, of course, that some of this self-portraiture has a fictional slant. Many personal essayists have enjoyed alternately stripping themselves bare and creating a slightly distorted, even shabbier version of themselves, the way the comedian Jack Benny made himself out to be much stingier than he was, just for the joke of it. While the personal essayist is such a trustworthy witness, at times no one works closer to "unreliable narrator" territory. Certain high-pitched tones of Lamb, Hazlitt, Beerbohm, and others stir up unmistakable echoes of Dostoevsky's Underground Man, Ford Madox Ford's Good Soldier, and other unreliable narrators. How to account for this paradox? We should recall that the novel and the essay rose together and fed off each other as literary forms; fiction's "unreliable narrator" may have even derived initially, in part, from the mischievous candor and first-person expressiveness unleashed in personal essays.

The Past, the Local, and the Melancholy

The past is frequently and often lyrically visited by personal essayists. The retrospective glance comes naturally to the essayist: the past is an Aladdin's lamp which he or she never tires of rubbing. As Hazlitt said about his friend Lamb, "Mr. Lamb has a distaste to new faces, to new books, to new buildings, to new customs. . . . He evades the present, he mocks the future. His affections revert to, and settle on, the past, but then, even this must have something personal and local in it to interest him deeply and thoroughly."

Beerbohm, who took up Lamb's mantle a century later, also showed a fastidious, unjournalistic distaste for the topical. "Sir Max Beerbohm seems to bring with him the aroma of an age that is just past: his writings always were like that and they always will be; just not quite up to date," wrote Bonamy Dobrée, "and so, one guesses, enduring."

Another fine sifter of the past, the contemporary Irish essayist Hubert Butler, now in his nineties, remarked in "Beside the Nore," "I have always believed that local history is more important than national history." In Butler, the personal essayist's loyalty to the local and near-at-hand are intermixed with an amateur archeologist's search for traces of history. "The past comes close in disconnected fragments and I was thinking of the days when we were children and had dancing classes with the young Tighes at the Noreview Hotel in Thomastown; their mother, with my Aunt Harriet, used to run a Christian Science Reading Room opposite the Castle in Kilkenny, two spiders into whose web no fly ever came." Though Butler traveled widely, in Russia, Egypt, China, and the United States, and got swept up in the political events of his time, he wrote, "I am more inclined to apologize for writing about great events, which touched me not at all, than for tracing again the tiny snail track which I made myself." This "snail track" might be the insignia of the personal essay genre.

There is a melancholy tone in much of Butler's work, which also crops up in Montaigne, Lamb, Hazlitt, Lu Hsun, Gore Vidal, and so on. It might be called "the voice of middle age." If the personal essay frequently presents a middle-aged point of view, it may be because it is the fruit of ripened experience, which naturally brings with it some worldly disenchantment, or at least realism. With middle age also comes a taste for equilibrium; hence, that stubborn, almost unnerving calm that so often pervades the personal essay. Montaigne exemplified the melancholy, stoical balance of middle age ("I have seen the grass, the flower, and the fruit; now I see the dryness—happily since it is naturally"), which is, for better or worse, the by-product of a developed sense of selfhood.

F. Scott Fitzgerald starts "The Crack-Up" by sounding the quintessential note of middle-aged experience: "Of course all life is a process of breaking down, but the blows that do the dramatic side of the work—the big sudden blows that come, or seem to come, from outside—the ones you remember and blame things on and, in moments of weakness, tell your friends about, don't show their effect all at once. There is another sort of blow that comes from within—that you don't feel until it's too late to do anything about it, until you realize with finality that in some regard you will never be as good a man again."

While young people excel at lyrical poetry and mathematics, it is hard to think of anyone who made a mark on the personal essay form in his or her youth. The closest candidates might be James Baldwin and Joan Didion, and both adopted precociously world-weary personae while still in their twenties. Baldwin had no sooner left his brutal Harlem adolescence than he began describing it, with rueful ache and Jamesian distance, like a lost kingdom. Didion's elegiac "Goodbye to All That," written at thirty-four, is already saturated with her trademark disenchantment.

It is difficult to write analytically from the middle of confusion, and youth is a confusion in which the self and its desires have not yet sorted themselves out. A young person still thinks it is possible—there is time enough—to become all things: athlete and aesthete, soldier and pacifist, anchorite and debauchee. Later, knowing one's fate and accepting the responsibility of that uninnocent knowledge define the perspective of the form. The personal essayist looks back at the choices that were made, the roads not taken, the limiting familial and historic circumstances, and what might be called the catastrophe of personality. In literature, noted Gore Vidal, "the true confessors have been aware that not only is life mostly failure, but that in one's failure or pettiness or wrongness exists the living drama of the self." The wonder is that the personal essay can make this bitter awareness appetizing and even amusing to the reader.

Questions of Form and Style

The essay is a notoriously flexible and adaptable form. It possesses the freedom to move anywhere, in all directions. It acts as if all objects were equally near the center and as if "all subjects are linked to each other" (Montaigne) by free association. This freedom can be daunting, not only for the novice essayist confronting such latitude but for the critic attempting to pin down its formal properties.

The essay challenges formal analysis by what Walter Pater called its "unmethodical method," open to digression and promiscuous meanderings. Dr. Johnson described the essay as "a loose sally of the mind" and "an irregular, undigested piece"—which did not prevent him from undertaking a substantial involvement in the form, suggesting at least a hope that it would bring him aesthetic dividends. I take with a grain of salt those claims, by slumming lovers of the essay, that it is not really an art form, and somehow better off for being what the Spanish philosopher Eduardo Nicol called *"almost* literature and *almost* philosophy." From my perspective, there is no *almost* about it: good essays are works of literary art. Their supposed formlessness is more a strategy to disarm the reader with the appearance of unstudied spontaneity than a reality of composition.

Formally personal essays have, in one sense, a head start over other essay types, being already unified by a strong "I" perspective (either an actual first-person narrator or an implied one). Still, there is no guarantee that the personal essay will attain a shapeliness or a sense of aesthetic inevitability. The well-made short story has a recognizable arc that seems built into the genre, whereas even an essay that is "well made" seems to follow a more intuitive, groping path. The writer of the poorest sonnet is assured that in the end there will be a fourteen-line poem, whereas the essayist may be left with nothing more than a set of fragmentary notes.

The essayist attempts to surround a something—a subject, a mood, a problematic irritation—by coming at it from all angles, wheeling and diving like a hawk, each seemingly digressive spiral actually taking us closer to the heart of the matter. In a well-wrought essay, while the search appears to be widening, even losing its way, it is actually eliminating false hypotheses, narrowing its emotional target and zeroing in on it.

The essayist must be a good storyteller. This is a point rarely made, perhaps because of the classifying urge to keep the two genres neatly fenced off. True, the essayist happily violates the number-one rule of short story workshops, "Show, don't tell"; the glory of the essayist is to tell, once and for all, everything that he or she thinks, knows, and understands. Yet often it happens that a personal essay starts out in a seemingly directionless or at least open manner, with all the time in the world, only to hop onto a narrative possibility and let the storytelling momentum take it home. Addison and Steele often walk a thin line between the reflective essay and the anecdotal vignette, crossing over when it suits them; Hazlitt's "The Fight" and Lamb's "Dream Children: A Reverie" are both hybrids of essay and fictional technique; Virginia Woolf's "Street Haunting" follows a single character, the narrator, around for an evening; Turgenev organizes "The Execution of Tropmann" around his reactions to a single dramatic event; Orwell's "Such, Such Were the Joys . . ." performs in many ways like an autobiographical novella; Baldwin's personal essays push at the frontier between fiction and reportage. All good essayists make use at times of storytelling devices: descriptions of character and place, incident, dialogue, conflict. They needn't narrate some actual event to produce a narrative. Even a "pure" meditation, the track of one's thoughts, has to be shaped, given a kind of plot or urgency, if it is to communicate.

About Hazlitt's style, Ronald Blythe wrote, "Each essay shows the build-up of numerous small climaxes, such as are sometimes employed in the novel. Excitement and expectation mount." Hazlitt, trained in philosophy, tended to stay closer to a line of argument than other personal essayists do. But even when writers have deliberately shied away from developing a single thesis or line of attack, usually we can locate in their essays a buried argument. The stated subject or title of a piece may be only its pretext. Montaigne's "Of Coaches" works its way round from modes of conveyance to a ringing denunciation of European settlers' treatment of Indians in the New World. E. B. White's "The Ring of Time" begins as a description of a small circus and veers off into a commentary on racial integration. White would probably have been embarrassed to preach integration head-on, but he was less hesitant to back into it casually.

Many times the personal essayist will start to explore a subject, then set up a countertheme, and eventually braid the two. Sara Suleri's "Meatless Days," for instance, begins as an almost facetious treatment of certain organ meats, but along the way this theme is thickened with family history, cultural conflicts, gender, and grief. The personal essayist is like a cook who learns through trial and error just when to add another spice or countertaste to the stew.

Here the art of elaboration enters in. Much of what characterizes true essayists is the ability to draw out a point through example, list, simile, small variation, hyperbolic exaggeration, whatever. The great essayists have all had this gusto in fleshing out an idea, which becomes not a chore but an opportunity. An example is the opening of Charles Lamb's essay "A Chapter on Ears."

> I have no ear.—
>
> Mistake me not, reader—nor imagine that I am by nature destitute of those exterior twin appendages, hanging ornaments, and (architecturally speaking) handsome volutes to the human capital. Better my mother had never borne me.—I am, I think, rather delicately than copiously provided with those conduits; and I feel no disposition to envy the mule for his plenty, or the mole for her exactness, in those ingenious labyrinthine inlets—those indispensable side-intelligencers.
>
> Neither have I incurred, or done anything to incur, with Defoe, that hideous disfigurement, which constrained him to draw upon assurance—to feel "quite unabashed," and at ease upon that article. I was never, I thank my stars, in the pillory; nor, if I read them aright, is it within the compass of my destiny, that I ever should be.
>
> When therefore I say that I have no ear, you will understand me to mean—*for music.*

By this time, the reader will want either to strangle the author or, if he has a taste for Lamb, to laugh. The mock-solemnity with which this slender idea is elaborated, the piling-up of mules and architecture, inlets and punitive instruments and "side-intelligencers," always makes me smile. Part of the humor rests in the peculiar dictional spin Lamb puts on words. Today's readers may miss this joke, but his contemporaries knew how absurdly dusty his vocabulary was, even for the early nineteenth century. A runaway antiquarianism is one of Lamb's standard comic techniques. Another is the pretend fussy sense of dignity ("rather delicately than copiously provided"). The elegant care with which Lamb's sentences are written, the humor in his wry linguistic touches, make him a writer to savor.

Another technique of the personal essay that serves both structural and comic functions is the digression. The chief role of the digression is to amass all the dimensions of understanding that the essayist can accumulate by bringing in as many contexts as a problem or insight can sustain without overburdening it. The digression must wander off the point only to fulfill it. A kind of elaboration, it scoops up subordinate themes in passing. Some of the essayist's comic irony derives from a self-consciousness about digression, the joke being, as in *Tristram Shandy,* that the writer cannot stay on the point but must garrulously blab about everything.

Another formal technique employed by the personal essayist is the movement from individual to universal. The concrete details of personal experience earn the generalization (often an aphorism), and the generalization sends the author back for more particulars. Sometimes this spiral is aided by a modulation in pronouns: "I," "one," "we," and "you." The jump from "I" to "we" or "you" can seem presumptuous if taken too quickly (as the joke goes, "What do you mean 'we,' masked man?"). It requires preparation and timing; personal essayists must always watch their pronouns carefully.

William Hazlitt, for all his brusque lack of diplomacy, was a master of this pronominal tact. At the beginning of "On Going a Journey," he establishes a highly individuated first-person voice, proudly refusing to sue for reader empathy: "One of the pleasantest things in the world is going a journey; but I like to go by myself. I can enjoy society in a room; but out of doors, nature is company enough for me." In each of these sentences, Hazlitt's jaunty rhythms suggest a hiker swinging his arms, entirely self-sufficient: the first clause invites us in, the semicolon stops us, the second clause pushes us away. The author is celebrating his solitude: the rest of us, stay out. Yet midway down the first page, he is already declaring, "The soul of a journey is liberty, perfect liberty, to think, feel, do, just as one pleases. We go a journey chiefly to be free of all impediments and of all inconveniences; to leave ourselves behind, much more to get rid of others. It is because I want a little breathing-space . . ." and so on. In four sentences he has moved from the eccentric "I" to the mildly generalizing "one," which forms a tactical bridge to the "we" of aphorism and sweeping pronouncement; then back to "I" for more evidence-gathering based on personal experience. "You" comes in a few sentences later, at first as the actual reader who is being addressed ("if I were to explain to you"), then as a substitute for "I," which furthers the symbiosis between author and audience.

Quotation and the Uses of Learning

In the midst of Hazlitt's rhetorical amble (an essay is a kind of walkabout, which may explain why so many are written about walking), the author throws in a few scraps of poetry, unattributed. Why these quotations? Possibly to elevate the tone a few notches; possibly to poke fun at his own earnestness. But it raises the larger question, what is the stylistic function of quotation in the personal essay?

One obvious answer would seem to be to lend authority to the author's argument. Montaigne was a compulsive sprinkler of citations, and he cheerfully claimed he was doing it to get a free ride on other men's brains. In "Of Books," he talked about this quoting habit: "For I make others say what I cannot say so well, now through the weakness of my language, now through the weakness of my understanding. . . . I have sometimes deliberately not indicated the author, in order to hold in check the temerity of those hasty condemnations that are tossed at all sorts of writings. . . . I want them to give Plutarch a fillip on my nose and get burned insulting Seneca in me. I have to hide my weakness under these great authorities."

Montaigne made such a mosaic of his and others' words that quotations became a kind of baroque tilework overlaying his *Essais,* without compromising his originality. If anything, modern readers may feel that he is cutting his forebears down to size, since his own voice is so much more robust than these peeps from the ancients, which we tend to skip. Montaigne, being a Renaissance humanist, reverential toward the classical authors (who themselves used frequent quotation), would not have seen it this way. We must remember that the Renaissance essay partly grew out of the custom of keeping "commonplace books," which were filled with favorite quotations. In England, Burton's *The Anatomy of Melancholy,* a learned catch-all encrusted with citations and meditations, became a kind of mother-text inspiring the essay form.

The pleasure of knowing that we are in cultivated hands, attending to a well-stocked, liberally educated mind, is a central attraction of the personal essay. Such learning was easier to demonstrate when there was a commonly recognized body of quotable culture among the educated class. In the Renaissance, this common culture consisted largely of the ancients and the Bible; in nineteenth-century England, of the Elizabethan dramatists and great British poets.

Today, a writer's cultivation might be signaled less by quotation (what is a modern essayist to quote, without sounding pompous?) than by syntax. A complex, pretzel-shaped sentence by M. F. K. Fisher, Gore Vidal, or Mary McCarthy shows that the writer is still hearing whispers of Latin and has had an old-fashioned "good education." Indeed, now that the dictional distinction between the formal and the informal essay has been somewhat eroded, we are as likely to encounter a slightly mannered, baroque, "dressed-up" language in contemporary personal essayists (see Baldwin, Vidal, McCarthy) as in their formal counterparts.

Nevertheless, the personal essay has always striven for the ideal of "light learning," which graciously informs without humiliating or playing the pedantic schoolmaster. It has always distanced itself from the scholarly treatise. "The essay," wrote Bonamy Dobrée, ". . . claimed to put aside all pedantry, all learning crammed out of books, and merely gave you the reasonable decent man talking to you or me or anyone else of what he thought about life: or rather, the man was talking to himself and allowing anyone who cared to do so to overhear him." All personal essays are addressed to what Virginia Woolf called "the common reader," that happy, somewhat fuzzy figure who may or may not exist but who has been solicited and invited to partake.

The Personal Essay as Mode of Thinking and Being

The essay form as a whole has long been associated with an experimental method. This idea goes back to Montaigne and his endlessly suggestive use of the term *essai* for his writings. To essay is to attempt, to test, to make a run at something without knowing whether you are going to succeed. The experimental association also derives from the other fountainhead of the essay, Francis Bacon, and his stress on the empirical inductive method, so useful to the development of the physical sciences.

There is something heroic in the essayist's gesture of striking out toward the unknown, not only without a map but without certainty that there is anything worthy to be found. One would like to think that the personal essay represents a kind of basic research on the self, in ways that are allied with science and philosophy. Montaigne called himself a new type, an "accidental philosopher," expressing the mocking hope that his impromptu approach—seemingly the opposite to that of traditional philosophers, with their patient construction of logical systems—might almost by chance add up to a philosophy. In the end he got his wish; it would not be inappropriate to teach Montaigne in a moral philosophy course. But what of other personal essayists, and the essay form in general?

The modern German philosopher Theodor Adorno saw rich, subversive possibilities in precisely the "anti-systematic" properties of the essay. In our century, when the grand philosophical systems seem to have collapsed under their own weight and authoritarian taint, the light-footed, free-wheeling essay suddenly steps forward as an attractive way to open up philosophical discourse. As Adorno put it, "Luck and play are what are essential to the essay. It does not begin with Adam and Eve but with what it wants to discuss; it says what is at issue and stops where it feels itself complete—not where nothing is left to say. . . . The essay does not strive for closed, deductive or inductive construction. It revolts above all against the doctrine—deeply rooted since Plato—that the changing and ephemeral is unworthy of philosophy, against the ancient injustice toward the transitory."

Adorno's approving statement that "the essay shies away from the violence of dogma" echoes Robert Louis Stevenson's about the idler (read: essayist): "He will not be heard among the dogmatists. He will have a great and cool allowance for all sorts of people and opinions. If he finds no out-of-the-way truths, he will identify himself with no very burning falsehood." When Beerbohm apologizes in "Laughter" for never being able to retain abstract philosophy, he is also inversely speaking out for another way of thinking, taking sides in what R. Lane Kauffmann calls "the historical conflict between fragmentary and totalizing modes of thought—between essay and system."

Recent essayists, such as Roland Barthes, Joan Didion, and Richard Rodriguez, have made a virtue of fragmentation, offering it as a mirror to the unconnectable, archipelago-like nature of modern life. "The usual reproach against the essay," wrote Adorno, "that it is fragmentary and random, itself assumes the givenness of totality and . . . suggests that man is in control of totality. But the desire of the essay is not to seek and filter the eternal out of the transitory; it wants, rather, to make the transitory eternal."

Roland Barthes said toward the end of his life that he had produced "only essays, an ambiguous genre in which analysis vies with writing." The rueful tone of this statement should not distract us from its pride. In Europe, the essay has provided those with philosophic minds, such as Barthes, Benjamin, Adorno, Cioran, Simone Weil, and Jurgen Habermas, the chance to be writers as well.

The unashamed subjectivity of the personal essay makes it less suspect in a mental climate in which people have learned to mistrust the "value-free, objective" claims of scholarship and science. Another intriguing feature of the form for contemporary theorists and advocates of "process" writing is that it seems to lay bare its process as it goes along. I say "seems" because there is still a good deal of selection and art in this appearance of spontaneous process. Still, as Alexander Smith noted, "The essayist gives you his thoughts, and lets you know, in addition, how he came by them." This honoring of the thought as it pops up lends a water-colorist's freshness to the form.

Naturally, essayists who honor the flow of their thoughts may often end up contradicting themselves. But what would be a flaw in the systems-building philosopher may be an essential step for the essayist. As F. Scott Fitzgerald said, paraphrasing Keats' idea of negative capability, "The test of a first-rate intelligence is the ability to hold two opposed ideas in the mind at the same time, and still retain the ability to function." The essay's capacity for processing doubt is part of what makes it so stimulating and tonic.

This tolerance for contradiction also puts an added pressure on the essayist, according to Adorno: "The slightly yielding quality of the essay-ist's thought forces him to greater intensity than discursive thought can offer; for the essay, unlike discursive thought, does not proceed blindly, automatically, but at every moment it must reflect on itself." Here, O. B. Hardison, Jr.'s definition of the essay seems particularly apt: "The essay is the enactment of a process by which the soul realizes itself even as it is passing from day to day and from moment to moment."

The self-consciousness and self-reflection that essay writing demands cannot help but have an influence on the personal essayist's life. Montaigne confessed at one point that "in modelling this figure upon myself, I have had to fashion and compose myself so often to bring myself out, that the model itself has to some extent grown firm and taken shape. Painting myself for others, I have painted my inward self with colors clearer than my original ones. I have no more made my book than my book has made me." Thus the writing of personal essays not only monitors the self but helps it gel. The essay is an enactment of the creation of the self.

"I write what I please," stated George Orwell. Whether entirely true or not, this represents the ideal mental condition of the personal essayist, the same one enunciated by Hazlitt when he wrote, "No one has said to me, *Believe this, do that, say what we would have you;* no one has come be-tween me and my free-will; I have breathed the very air of truth and independence."

In the final analysis, the personal essay represents a mode of being. It points a way for the self to function with relative freedom in an uncertain world. Skeptical yet gyroscopically poised, undeceived but finally tolerant of flaws and inconsistencies, this mode of being suits the modern existen-tial situation, which Montaigne first diagnosed. His recognition that hu-man beings were surrounded by darkness, with nothing particularly solid to cling to, led to a philosophical acceptance that one had to make oneself up from moment to moment.

Still, we must not make excessive claims. The essay is not, for the most part, philosophy; nor is it yet science. How seriously ought we to take its claims of being experimental? It lacks the rigor of a laboratory experiment; it does not hold on to its hypotheses long enough to prove them. But it is what it is: a mode of inquiry, another way of getting at the truth.

As one pedagogic champion of the personal essay, William Zeiger, put it,

> The practice of experimenting, or trying something out, is expressed in the now uncommon sense of the verb *to prove*—the sense of "testing" rather than of "demonstrating validity." Montaigne "proved" his ideas in that he tried them out in his essays. He spun out their implications, sampled their suggestions. He did not argue or try to persuade. He had no investment in winning over his audience to his opinion; accordingly, he had no fear of being refuted. On the contrary, he expected that some of the ideas he expressed would change, as they did in later essays. Refutation represented not a personal defeat but an advance toward truth as valuable as confirmation. To "prove" an idea, for Montaigne, was to examine it in order to *find out* how true it was.

The Rationale and Arrangement of This Book

This volume is divided into five sections, which attempt to uncover the *tradition* of the personal essay. One reason to consider it a tradition is that its practitioners were often so aware of and quick to comment on one another's work. Montaigne writes about Seneca and Plutarch, Cowley and Hazlitt about Montaigne, Stevenson and Woolf about Hazlitt, Kenko about Shonagon, and so on. It is as though a like-minded tribe of writers sought each other out over the centuries, clinging to the seashell sound of intimacy, candor, and irony that corroborated their own voices.

As part of this conversation with their ancestors, the new practitioners made their own attempts at themes favored in the personal essay tradition: friendship, solitude, attachment to the past, childhood; talk, social manners, and the folly of fashion; city versus country life, walking, idleness, travel, hobbies; collecting, public spectacles, and entertainments; books, the vocation of writing, food, appetites, interior decor; illness, mortality. The list is short on war, apocalypse, zeal, the grotesque. Even in periods of extreme upheaval, the personal essayist tends to cling to the familiar and domestic, the emotional middle of the road—not necessarily because he or she is lucky enough to have been spared tragedy, but perhaps the opposite. Charles Lamb saw his sister stab their mother to death and never wrote an essay about this or any other violence, showing a marked preference for calmer subjects. Similarly, M. F. K. Fisher refrained from writing about the suicides of her brother and husband, because she could not see a way to transmute them into her kind of literature.

The customary way to view the personal essay tradition holds that its main spine extends from Montaigne to the English essayists, with continental and American extensions. True enough. But I have wanted to expand the picture by showing how this literary impulse might pop up anywhere on the globe, and what permutations it might take in different cultures.

For the first section of this book, I was determined to include something from the classical Greco-Roman world, especially as Montaigne kept insisting on his literary debt to the ancients. We know there existed a whole tradition of prose meditations, orations, *moralia,* epistles among classical writers, which might, in hindsight, fit under the rubric of the personal essay. Some commentators, like Lukacs, go further and declare Plato the first and greatest essayist. Although I think it is stretching things to call Platonic dialogues essays, clearly these two circuitous forms have certain overlaps, as noted, and in the Platonic version of the present anthology (one without size restrictions), I might be very tempted to put in a dialogue by Plato or Cicero, Leopardi or Wilde, just to watch the two forms play off each other. Finally I came down to selecting Seneca and Plutarch, both because Montaigne singled them out as *his* favorites and because I liked them best.

I was aware that Japan had a vital tradition of "I" writing that emphasized sincerity, candor, and "follow the brush" spontaneity, going back to the tenth-century notebooks of Sei Shonagon, the empress's lady-in-waiting. But these writings often took the form of journals and letters rather than fully articulated personal essays. In the end, too charmed by Shonagon and Kenko to leave them out, I rationalized that their selections represent the sort of bedrock out of which the personal essay grows: Shonagon with her temperamental, singular voice and list-making; Kenko with his free-associating, fragmented mini-essays.

As for China, preliminary researches suggest a strong tradition of personal essays, going back at least to the Tang dynasty. Essay writing was part of the examination process for officials as well as a favored form of the literati. Of the thousands that were written, however, so few have been translated, and of those, so few have been translated readably enough to pass along, that I have been hamstrung in my efforts to present more than the merest taste of this tradition. The modern essayist Lu Hsun, whom I have included in a later section, will perhaps round out the Chinese essay picture a little.

Section two, devoted to Montaigne, brings us back to the main tradition of the personal essay as it has customarily been interpreted. No explanations need be made for spotlighting this author in an essay anthology: he is the giant, the mountain of the form. I should warn, however, that he can be difficult for readers approaching him for the first time. One keeps looking for a connecting argument, a through-line, where there may not be any. Finally one just has to surrender to Montaigne, dive into the ocean of his thoughts and bob around in that undulating, fascinating mind for the sheer line-by-line reward of it.

Section three focuses on the English personal essay. It was the English, rather than Montaigne's own countrymen, who took up his challenge and extended, refined, and cultivated the essay. This may have something to do with the English tolerance for eccentricity, or with the overall predilection of English writers for comic irony. The critic John Bayley has added a further speculation about the essay's popularity in England: "Could it be that the national propensity to reserve and reticence—the more or less stiff upper lip—found a way of releasing itself in a confiding stream of well-turned but unpretending chatter, mental gossip?"

England also spawned the other great tributary of the essay form, the formal or Baconian essay. Francis Bacon and his followers had a more impersonal, magisterial, law-giving, and didactic manner than the skeptical Montaigne. But they should not be viewed as opposites; the distinction between formal and informal essay can be overdone, and most great essayists have crossed the line frequently. The difference is one of degree. Hazlitt was essentially a personal essayist, though he wrote theater and art criticism; Matthew Arnold and John Ruskin were essentially formal essayists, though they may have tried a personal essay once in a while. Personality creeps into the most impersonal of writers: it is difficult to read Bacon on friendship or having children, for instance, without suspecting he is talking about autobiographical matters. Dr. Johnson was probably more a moral essayist than a personal one, though his work has such an individual, idiosyncratic stamp that I have persuaded myself to place him in the personal camp. George Orwell seems split fifty-fifty, an essay hermaphrodite who always kept one eye on the subjective and one on the political.

The rise of the English personal essay in the eighteenth and early nineteenth centuries was directly connected to the growth of newspapers and magazines, which provided the essayist with an audience and a limited income. The influence of periodicals on the genre had mixed results, as it continues to do. The need to say everything in a limited space for a general audience reined in the form; no English periodical essayist could pursue the open, stream-of-consciousness manner of Montaigne's late writings. But if periodicals clipped the personal essay's wings, they also helped shape, sharpen, and relax the form. J. B. Priestley has remarked:

> When a man is writing regularly for one set of readers (and nearly all the essayists were regular contributors to the Press, appearing in

the same periodical at regular intervals), he tends to lose a certain stiffness, formality, self-consciousness, that would inevitably make its appearance if he were writing a whole book alone. He comes to feel that he is among friends and can afford as it were to let himself go, and the secret of writing a good essay is to let oneself go. . . . It also encourages him to focus his attention upon passing little things that he might have disdained were he not writing for the next week's paper. He is a snapper-up of unconsidered trifles, and it is his pleasure and privilege to glimpse the significance of such trifles, so that for a second we see them, surprisingly against the background of the Eternities.

Addison and Steele were perhaps the first to be star newspaper essayists. They did so in part by shrewdly focusing on manners and mores for their middle-class readers, who wanted to imitate the aristocracy. Delightful dollops of social satire and topicality were imported into the personal essay under Addison and Steele's tutelage, while a certain amount of intimacy was lost. Steele achieves it in "An Hour or Two Sacred to Sorrow," but it is rare for him, and rarer still for his blithe, dulcet-toned partner, Addison.

By the early nineteenth century, the pendulum had swung back toward vulnerability, with Hazlitt and Lamb. "Man was getting tired of considering himself as a social creature only, and was trying to rediscover himself as an individual, whose interest for others," wrote Bonamy Dobrée, "as well as for himself, lay precisely in his being different from other people." Lamb and Hazlitt brought the idiosyncratic personal essay to such a zenith of development that for a good while after them it had nowhere to go but down. The Victorian era saw a turn toward the formal essay, the so-called essay of ideas written by Carlyle, Ruskin, Arnold, Macaulay, Pater. Between Lamb and Beerbohm there was scarcely an English personal essay, with the exception of those by Robert Louis Stevenson and Thomas De Quincey. But Beerbohm seemed a happy reincarnation of the personal essayists of old. Then came Virginia Woolf, who slowly worked her way into the form, starting with unsigned book reviews and ending up with magnificent book-length personal essays (*A Room of One's Own, A Sketch of the Past*). George Orwell established a ruggedly trustworthy, straight-talking voice which became one of the most influential styles of the century.

Section four offers some examples of shapes that the personal essay has taken in other cultures around the world. In "The Execution of Tropmann," Ivan Turgenev examines his uneasy reactions to a public event in a blend of reportage, political persuasion, and personal essay. Walter Benjamin, E. M. Cioran, and Roland Barthes, as noted, give the personal essay a more philosophical, abstract twist. Hugh Butler and Natalia Ginzburg, chroniclers of parish and domicile, write from a very rooted, local perspective. By contrast, Carlos Fuentes' cosmopolitan persona is that of a citizen of the world. "How I Started to Write" is Fuentes' version of a classical personal essay theme, finding one's literary vocation. The drama of the self-created personality may also be glimpsed in Wole Soyinka's and Sara Suleri's pieces, which bring us variants from Africa and the Muslim subcontinent. Junichiro Tanizaki masterfully gives the personal essay a Japanese twist, via the linked-*haiku* logic of his transitions from topic to topic, which peel away the shadows of the Japanese house to find rich speculations about aesthetics, sexuality, and ethnicity.

The anthology's fifth and last section is devoted to the American scene. While somewhat pale imitators of the English periodical essayists existed from early on on this side of the Atlantic, the first unmistakably American notes in essay writing were struck by Emerson and Thoreau. By writing personal meditations about nature and the land, Thoreau also founded what has become a thriving, prototypically American subgenre of the essay: nature and ecological writing, represented here by Wendell Berry, Edward Hoagland, and Annie Dillard.

Another fertile training ground for the American personal essay was humor writing. Robert Benchley, James Thurber, Dorothy Parker, H. L. Mencken, Heywood Hale Broun, and Franklin P. Adams were all part of a dazzling constellation of popular columnists and humoristic commentators who held sway in the twenties and thirties. A more harrowingly confessional note, left over from those Jazz Age days, was introduced by F. Scott Fitzgerald in *The Crack-Up*. In the forties, E. B. White, A. J. Liebling, and Joseph Mitchell perfected the clean, lucid, gentlemanly essay manner that became the *New Yorker*'s house style.

Meanwhile, in magazines such as *Partisan Review* and *Commentary,* a more combative, energetic, pushy style of essay writing was coming to the fore. The postwar era saw the ascent of the essayist as public intellectual, invited to take stands on just about everything from politics to culture to the personal life. In retrospect, the oft-abused fifties now look like a golden age of American essay prose, with such writers as Mary McCarthy, Edmund Wilson, Lionel Trilling, Harold Rosenberg, Robert Warshow, Irving Howe, Elizabeth Hardwick, Alfred Kazin, Leslie Fiedler, James Baldwin, Seymour Krim, and Gore Vidal. Since then, fewer essayists have had the confidence or the nerve to offer themselves as all-purpose, generalist commentators. Some would attribute this to an erosion of the public, civic sphere. Others would point to the greater faith the public now places in experts—which may indeed account for the proliferation of essay collections by physicists, surgeons, biologists, animal trainers, and literary theorists.

When we come to the present moment, the picture gets cloudier. There is a great deal of disagreement over the status and fortunes of the American personal essay at present. Doomsayers see a long, whimpering decline since the early nineteenth century, with little chance for recovery. Optimists have boldly declared that this is "the age of the essay," though they use the term in its broadest application, to include virtually all unspecialized nonfiction, from the celebrity profile to the self-help book. What, then, is the essay's place in the literature of today?

On the one hand, the personal essay, with its predilection for equanimity and common sense, its unrepentant humanism and assertion of a cohesive self, has never been quite comfortable in a modernist aesthetic. (Indeed, the very assumption of the universality of experience would now be challenged by some literary theorists as a colonizing tactic to mute the differences between disenfranchised groups and the dominant culture.)

An added problem is that the nature of reading has changed. George Steiner has written about the decline in silence and in the unhurried, memorizing, ceremonial rites of reading. Those who speed-read for general argument may be frustrated by the personal essay, which is neither a legal brief nor an editorial. It "depends on pleasures experienced by a meditative mind free to meander leisurely in quiet moments," wrote Alexander J. Butrim, which may conflict with "the general inclination in modern popular culture for immediate satisfaction and instant entertainment."

On the other hand, the personal essay's suitability for experimental method and self-reflective process, its tolerance for the fragmentary and irresolution, make it uniquely appropriate to the present era, whether we want to label it late modernist or postmodernist. My own sense is that we are going through a cautious revival of the genre. Each year, more and more publishers are willing to bring out essay collections (albeit often disguised as single-theme meditations).

The revival is fueled partly by the appetites of periodicals for opinion and a lively point of view, and partly by an American preference for "facts" and a temporary mistrust of fictional "fabrication." The public, weaned on Oprah, seems uniquely sympathetic to the sound of authentic witnessing and hard-won experience. There is a new breed of travel essayists who specialize in misadventure, and a whole new generation of personal journalists who have carried forth the banner of the New Journalism. Certainly many journalistic pieces lack the specific gravity of true personal essays, just as much that is supposedly personal in today's essays has an undigested, shorthand quality; but for the moment, all this essayistic proliferation and diversity represents an opportunity.

Another opportunity comes from the growing awareness that the United States is a pluralistic, multicultural society, that this is our future as a society, and that we need to listen carefully to the intellectual voices of minorities and immigrants (such as Gayle Pemberton and Richard Rodriguez). The personal essay turns out to be one of the most useful instruments with which outsiders can reach the dominant culture quickly and forcefully and testify to the precise ambiguities of their situation as individuals and group members. It can also be, as Adrienne Rich's essay shows, a vehicle to analyze how often we are "split at the root" when it comes to our chosen and inherited identities.

Principles of Selection

Obviously, in a one-volume anthology, even one so hefty as this, it would be impossible to do justice to all literary cultures and all centuries. That being the case, the reader would prefer, I assume, a strongly individual editorial viewpoint, and that is what I have attempted to provide. My first criterion has been to choose essays that I fell in love with or that I could not seem to shake off. It always comes down in the end to personal taste, and I confess that mine is for the ironic over the solemn, the crusty over the sugary. Also, since I am myself a personal essayist, my taste is more that of a practitioner than of a literary scholar.

My second rule of thumb has been to stress the personal note. Though it nearly killed me to leave out Bacon and Emerson, I decided in the end that they were not really personal essayists but great formal essayists whose minds moved inexorably toward the expression of impersonal wisdom and authority, regardless of flickering references to an "I." For the same reason, I have had to omit, with a pang, many literary essayists whose work I deeply admire, such as Edmund Wilson, Lionel Trilling, Susan Sontag, and Elizabeth Hardwick.

Because of my interest in the personal essay as a self-contained art form, I have also suppressed the impulse to lift chapters from favorite autobiographies, such as Saint Augustine's *Confessions,* De Quincey's *Confessions of an Opium Eater* or *Autobiographia Literaria,* Nabokov's *Speak, Memory,* Updike's *Self-Consciousness,* Nadezhda Mandelstam's *Hope Against Hope,* and palm them off as individual essays. Even if they could have stood on their own, I did not want to muddy the waters with borrowings from another, more dominant genre.

Because I have wanted to show how different essayists have tried to solve the problem of structure in an amoebic form, I have also opted for whole pieces rather than excerpts. As a reader of anthologies, I feel frustrated by abridgements. Unfortunately, this rule has meant having to pass over some of my favorite personal essays, such as *A Room of One's Own* and "A Sketch of the Past," by Virginia Woolf, and *The Fire Next Time,* by James Baldwin, which were too long for inclusion. Whenever possible, however, I have included more than one selection by an essayist, to show how he or she handles different personae and structures.

I have also favored writers who dedicated themselves substantially to the essay form. Great writers are usually great no matter what they turn their hands to, and I do not doubt it would have been possible to assemble a first-rate collection of personal essays by major novelists such as Dickens, Dostoevsky, George Eliot, James, Lawrence, Proust, Stendhal. But I have in the main shied away from this approach and gone with the self-proclaimed essayists.

These principles constitute my reasons for consciously selecting and excluding certain writers. What of the gaps that have less to do with editorial taste than with what seems to be an objective dearth of materials? I have discovered that for different cultural reasons, not all peoples around the globe have been equally drawn to the personal essay. Historically, Africans, for instance, have had a strong oral folktale tradition, in which the storyteller conveys the group's collective wisdom rather than his or her own idiosyncratic meditation. Although autobiography has become important in African literature over the past fifty years, the vast majority of essays written in the postwar independence period have tended to be didactic or polemical. Given the serious task of developing a new African literature in times of crisis, this preference for the public over the personal voice in essays is certainly understandable.

In many countries and cultures, the "I" has been downplayed, either because of communal factors (Native Americans have viewed the tribe, not the self, as the key unit of identity) or ideological forces (in communist regimes, individualism is considered a reactionary, bourgeois concept) or spiritual traditions. The Arabist and Islamic scholars I have consulted have concurred that there is no tradition of personal essay writing as such in Arab literature. Most of the "I" sensibility tended to be expressed in poetry. The vast majority of prose from medieval Islam onward consisted of spiritual-philosophical treatises, whose authors naturally tried to assert an objective tone of authority on questions of religious interpretation; the last thing they wanted was to be subjectively personal. Even spiritual autobiographies, such as Ghazzali's *The Deliverer from Evil,* were rare, and these tended to shed vestiges of the personal as the successful mystic drowned the self in God.

Particularly in religions with mystical traditions, in both East and West, where the surrender of the ego is seen as a paramount attainment, spiritual striving and the enterprise of the personal essay seem somewhat at cross-purposes. The spiritual meditations of Donne, Traherne, and Jeremy Taylor may have had a formal influence on the development of the personal essay, but they could never themselves be personal essays, because the "I" in them is so transitional. As Simone Weil, a converted Catholic, put the matter, "The sin in me says 'I.' . . . Humility consists in knowing that in what we call 'I' there is no source of energy by which we can rise. . . . Perfect joy excludes even the very feeling of joy, for in the soul filled by the object no corner is left for saying 'I.' " The soul of the personal essayist, it would seem, neither expects nor receives perfect joy, and therefore retains plenty of room for saying "I."

The sparse representation of women in the ranks of the personal essayists before this century is not, I hope, a sexist oversight but a reflection of the facts of the situation. The initial lack of rapport between women writers and the personal essay may be attributed to several factors. In England, to give a typical example, professional women writers from Aphra Behn onward who supported themselves with their pens gravitated toward the more remunerative forms: novels, dramas, poetry. Their personal writing tended to end up in diaries and letters. What essays they did write were usually impersonal or passionately polemical, such as Mary Wollstonecraft's "A Vindication of the Rights of Women." There were no female Hazlitts and Lambs.

It may also be that belletrism was so saturated with the figure and mystique of the "man of letters" that women were discouraged from entering that particular arena. The personal essay, for all its protestations of littleness and marginality, in fact leans on a tone of easy, gentlemanly, "natural" authority which comes from being in the world—the tone precisely most difficult for women, especially those raised traditionally, to assert. There is perhaps in the very notion of the generalist amateur, comfortably talking about anything and everything, a certain masculine arrogance. Until recently, it was easier for women writers either to conceal themselves behind their characters in novels and plays or to fight against the tyranny of men in polemical treatises than to adopt the light irony or immodestly confessional self-exposure of the personal essayist.

Fortunately, the modern era has seen women writers adopting the essay form more and more, helping to revive it, transforming its concerns, and at times giving it a different sound. One has only to read Virginia Woolf or M. F. K. Fisher or Annie Dillard to realize how much more comfortable certain women essayists are than their male counterparts with sensuous description, dazzling lyricism, and a willingness to dilate the moment. However, women essayists such as Mary McCarthy, Hannah Arendt, and Adrienne Rich give no quarter when it comes to analytical toughness.

The hardest job I have had was selecting personal essays written by my contemporaries. We are too close to the present to make accurate judgments about what will last or can comfortably stand with the masters of old. My apologies to the many essayists of today whom I fully intended to include but finally could not because of space limitations; I could have easily filled another volume this size with intriguing personal essays from the past twenty years. Recent essay anthologies have, if anything, tended to be too preoccupied with the present moment and the glamour of relevance while neglecting the whole magnificent tradition that has informed the genre. As it was this neglect that I wanted most to rectify, I have concentrated on the historical grandeurs of the personal essay in this collection.

It is customary to credit all those friends, colleagues, and relatives who contributed to the merits of a book and to exonerate them from its mistakes and deficiencies. But why not blame the people whom I am about to list for not arguing more firmly against my prejudices? They should have saved me from myself.

Seriously, I am deeply indebted to the following for their knowledge and tips: Bill Holm, Victor Mair, Michael Selz, Salma Jayyusi, Wendy Lesser, Richard Tristman, Marie Ponsot, Rachel Hadas, Michael Heller, Richard Howard, Bill Zavatsky, Maura Spiegel, Michael Millman, Vivian Gornick, Seymour Kleinberg, Wesley Brown, David Shapiro, Raymond Schindler, Richard Pena, Nora Sayre, Fran Kiernan, Mike Carson, Angeline Goreau, Carol Ascher, Edward Said, Bob Pittenger, Herbert Kohl, Mikhael Iossel, Wendy Weil. At Doubleday Anchor, my first editor, Sallye Leventhal, believed in the project and got it going; Martha Levin was both enthusiastic and very instrumental in publishing the book. My second, main editor, Charlie Conrad, has been a joy to work with—full of valuable inputs and common sense. I am deeply indebted to my old friend and partner at Teachers & Writers Collaborative, Ron Padgett, who has helped me take what was a vague idea for a project and see it through all its complicated stages. Finally, my wife, Cheryl Cipriani, I thank for being, and more specifically for being my companion, adviser, salvation, and solace.

I

Forerunners

SENECA

Seneca the Younger (c. A.D. 3–65) was born in Córdoba, Spain, about the same time as Christ; his father, Seneca the Elder, was an accomplished rhetorician and writer. Seneca went to Rome to study philosophy and rhetoric and became a renowned orator and writer himself. He also took up the philosophy of Stoicism, which counseled that perfection and contentment could be reached through reason, simple living, indifference to pain and death, and social equality. To the Stoics, a wise man was one who played the cards that were dealt him, uncomplainingly and with dignity, whether a slave or a king.

Exiled by the emperor Claudius, who was said to fear the philosopher's growing popularity, Seneca was recalled eight years later in triumph to become the young Nero's tutor. His influence over Nero was, at least initially, salutary; for a while, the emperor's tutor and the military leader Burrus ruled Rome together harmoniously behind the scenes. But eventually Nero's cruel propensities revealed themselves: he killed his mother, his brother, and, after Seneca was again sent into exile, his tutor; that is, he demanded that Seneca kill himself, and the old man obliged. The nobility with which Seneca took his life was much admired, and was considered an apt demonstration of his philosophy, suicide being a Stoic virtue. However, he was often criticized for the disparity between his Stoic beliefs and his practices in other respects: he amassed enormous wealth, curried favor, and even whined at misfortune—he acted, in short, like a human being instead of a paragon of virtue.

Seneca was a prolific author of tragedies (which strongly influenced Elizabethan drama), dialogues, and orations, but his reputation as the founder of the essay rests on his letters, which both Montaigne and Bacon cited as their inspiration and which remain his most attractive and accessible work. Essays in disguise, these "moral letters," written during Seneca's last exile, were probably intended from the start for publication rather than for their ostensible recipient, a civil servant named Lucilius. Each has a homiletic, ethical, Stoic message to convey. In them, a portrait of Seneca also emerges: asthmatic, aging, wry, alternately crabby and serene, critical of hypocrisy and luxury, observant of manners and mores (we learn much from him about Roman daily life), argumentative, worldly.

In his style Seneca stressed brevity and clarity. Reacting in part against Cicero's "grand style," a beautiful but wordy, florid oratory that rounded out sentences on the basis of sound, Seneca developed a more clipped, epigrammatic manner known as the humble or familiar style, which used common language and relied more heavily on metaphor, antithesis, and wit. Since writing in Seneca's time was often read aloud and drew applause at "points" —witty turns of phrase—it tended to devolve into aphoristic series. The results can be both dazzling and fatiguing. Macauley once complained that Seneca's "works are made up of mottoes. There is hardly a sentence which might not be quoted; but to read him straightforward is like dining on nothing but anchovy sauce." The paradox of Seneca's style is that it is at once simpler, more plainspoken than Cicero's and more baroque, contorted under brevity's lash. A virtue of his jerky, abrupt manner is that it gives the impression of a mind in action—thought, counterthought, without any smoothing over the bumps. Its importance to us here is that it affected the development of the essay during the sixteenth and seventeenth centuries, when classicism had returned and the reigning academic model was the euphonious Cicero. The anti-Ciceronians, such as Bacon, Montaigne, and Lipsius, led a rebellion, taking Seneca as their model, and out of it came modern prose: quick, pungent, ironic, self-questioning, reflective of mental process. It all goes back to Seneca.

On Noise

I CANNOT for the life of me see that quiet is as necessary to a person who has shut himself away to do some studying as it is usually thought to be. Here am I with a babel of noise going on all about me. I have lodgings right over a public bathhouse. Now imagine to yourself every kind of sound that can make one weary of one's years. When the strenuous types are doing their exercises, swinging weight-laden hands about, I hear the grunting as they toil away—or go through the motions of toiling away—at them, and the hissings and strident gasps every time they expel their pent-up breath. When my attention turns to a less active fellow who is contenting himself with an ordinary inexpensive massage, I hear the smack of a hand pummelling his shoulders, the sound varying according as it comes down flat or cupped. But if on top of this some ball player comes along and starts shouting out the score, that's the end! Then add someone starting up a brawl, and someone else caught thieving, and the man who likes the sound of his voice in the bath, and the people who leap into the pool with a tremendous splash. Apart from those whose voices are, if nothing else, natural, think of the hair remover, continually giving vent to his shrill and penetrating cry in order to advertise his presence, never silent unless it be while he is plucking someone's armpits and making the client yell for him! Then think of the various cries of the man selling drinks, and the one selling sausages and the other selling pastries, and all the ones hawking for the catering shops, each publicizing his wares with a distinctive cry of his own.

"You must be made of iron," you may say, "or else hard of hearing if your mind is unaffected by all this babel of discordant noises around you, when continual 'good morning' greetings were enough to finish off the Stoic Chrysippus!" But I swear I no more notice all this roar of noise than I do the sound of waves or falling water—even if I am here told the story of a people on the Nile who moved their capital solely because they could not stand the thundering of a cataract! Voices, I think, are more inclined to distract one than general noise; noise merely fills one's ears, battering away at them while voices actually catch one's attention. Among the things which create a racket all around me without distracting me at all I include the carriages hurrying by in the street, the carpenter who works in the same block, a man in the neighbourhood who saws, and this fellow tuning horns and flutes at the Trickling Fountain and emitting blasts instead of music. I still find an intermittent noise more irritating than a continuous one. But by now I have so steeled myself against all these things that I can even put up with a coxswain's strident tones as he gives his oarsmen the rhythm. For I force my mind to become self-absorbed and not let outside things distract it. There can be absolute bedlam without so long as there is no commotion within, so long as fear and desire are not at loggerheads, so long as meanness and extravagance are not at odds and harassing each other. For what is the good of having silence throughout the neighbour-hood if one's emotions are in turmoil?

> *The peaceful stillness of the night had lulled*
> *The world to rest.**

This is incorrect. There is no such thing as "peaceful stillness" except where reason has lulled it to rest. Night does not remove our worries; it brings them to the surface. All it gives us is a change of anxieties. For even when people are asleep they have dreams as troubled as their days. The only true serenity is the one which represents the free development of a sound mind. Look at the man whose quest for sleep demands absolute quiet from his spacious house. To prevent any sound disturbing his ears every one of his host of slaves preserves total silence and those who come anywhere near him walk on tip-toe. Naturally enough he tosses from side to side, trying to snatch some fitful sleep in between the spells of fretting, and complains of having heard sounds when he never heard them at all. And what do you suppose is the reason? His mind is in a ferment. It is this which needs to be set at peace. Here is the mutiny that needs to be suppressed. The fact that the body is lying down is no reason for suppos-ing that the mind is at peace. Rest is sometimes far from restful. Hence our need to be stimulated into general activity and kept occupied and busy with pursuits of the right nature whenever we are victims of the sort of idleness that wearies of itself. When great military commanders notice indiscipline among their men they suppress it by giving them some work to do, mounting expeditions to keep them actively employed. People who are really busy never have enough time to become skittish. And there is nothing so certain as the fact that the harmful consequences of inactivity are dissipated by activity.

We commonly give the impression that the reasons for our having gone into political retirement are our disgust with public life and our dissatis-faction with some uncongenial and unrewarding post. Yet every now and then ambition rears its head again in the retreat into which we were really

---

* A fragment of Varro Atacinus' translation from the Greek of Apollonius' *Argonautica*.

driven by our apprehensions and our waning interest; for our ambition did not cease because it had been rooted out, but merely because it had tired—or become piqued, perhaps, at its lack of success. I would say the same about extravagant living, which appears on occasion to have left one and then, when one has declared for the simple life, places temptation in the way. In the middle of one's programme of frugality it sets out after pleasures which one had discarded but not condemned, its pursuit of them indeed being all the more ardent the less one is aware of it. For when they are in the open vices invariably take a more moderate form; diseases too are on the way towards being cured when once they have broken out, instead of being latent, and made their presence felt. So it is with the love of money, the love of power and the other maladies that affect the minds of men—you may be sure that it is when they abate and give every appearance of being cured that they are at their most dangerous. We give the impression of being in retirement, and are nothing of the kind. For if we are genuine in this, if we have sounded the retreat and really turned away from the surface show, then, as I was saying a little while ago, nothing will distract us. Men and birds together in full chorus will never break into our thinking when that thinking is good and has at last come to be of a sure and steady character.

The temperament that starts at the sound of a voice or chance noises in general is an unstable one and one that has yet to attain inward detachment. It has an element of uneasiness in it, and an element of the rooted fear that makes a man a prey to anxiety, as in the description given by our Virgil:

> And I, who formerly would never flinch
> At flying spears or serried ranks of Greeks,
> Am now alarmed by every breeze and roused
> By every sound to nervousness, in fear
> For this companion and this load alike.*

The earlier character here is the wise man, who knows no fear at the hurtling of missiles, or the clash of weapons against weapons in the close-packed ranks, or the thunderous noise of a city in destruction. The other, later one has everything to learn; fearing for his belongings he pales at every noise; a single cry, whatever it is, prostrates him, being immediately taken for the yelling of the enemy; the slightest movement frightens him out of his life; his baggage makes him a coward. Pick out any one of your "successful" men, with all they trail or carry about with them, and you will

---

* *Aeneid*, II:726–9. Aeneas is describing his feelings as he leads his son and carries his father out of Troy while the city is being sacked.

have a picture of the man "in fear for this companion and this load." You may be sure, then, that you are at last "lulled to rest" when noise never reaches you and when voices never shake you out of yourself, whether they be menacing or inviting or just a meaningless hubbub of empty sound all round you.

"This is all very well," you may say, "but isn't it sometimes a lot simpler just to keep away from the din?" I concede that, and in fact it is the reason why I shall shortly be moving elsewhere. What I wanted was to give myself a test and some practice. Why should I need to suffer the torture any longer than I want to when Ulysses found so easy a remedy for his companions even against the Sirens?*

Asthma

I L L   H E A L T H —which had granted me quite a long spell of leave— has attacked me without warning again. "What kind of ill health?" you'll be asking. And well you may, for there isn't a single kind I haven't experienced. There's one particular ailment, though, for which I've always been singled out, so to speak. I see no reason why I should call it by its Greek name,** difficulty in breathing being a perfectly good way of describing it. Its onslaught is of very brief duration—like a squall, it is generally over within the hour. One could hardly, after all, expect anyone to keep on drawing his last breath for long, could one? I've been visited by all the troublesome or dangerous complaints there are, and none of them, in my opinion, is more unpleasant than this one—which is hardly surprising, is it, when you consider that with anything else you're merely ill, while with this you're constantly at your last gasp? This is why doctors have nicknamed it "rehearsing death," since sooner or later the breath does just what it has been trying to do all those times. Do you imagine that

---

* Homer narrates in Book XII of the Odyssey how the hero, following the advice of Circe, stopped the ears of his crew with beeswax while they rowed past the place where the temptresses sang.

** i.e. its medical name, asthma.

as I write this I must be feeling in high spirits at having escaped this time?
No, it would be just as absurd for me to feel overjoyed at its being over—
as if this meant I was a healthy man again—as it would be for a person to
think he has won his case on obtaining an extension of time before trial.

Even as I fought for breath, though, I never ceased to find comfort in
cheerful and courageous reflections. "What's this?" I said. "So death is
having all these tries at me, is he? Let him, then! I had a try at him a long
while ago myself." "When was this?" you'll say. Before I was born. Death
is just not being. What that is like I know already. It will be the same after
me as it was before me. If there is any torment in the later state, there
must also have been torment in the period before we saw the light of day;
yet we never felt conscious of any distress then. I ask you, wouldn't you
say that anyone who took the view that a lamp was worse off when it was
put out than it was before it was lit was an utter idiot? We, too, are lit and
put out. We suffer somewhat in the intervening period, but at either end
of it there is a deep tranquillity. For, unless I'm mistaken, we are wrong,
my dear Lucilius, in holding that death follows after, when in fact it precedes as well as succeeds. Death is all that was before us. What does it
matter, after all, whether you cease to be or never begin, when the result
of either is that you do not exist?

I kept on talking to myself in these and similar terms—silently, needless
to say, words being out of the question. Then little by little the affliction in
my breathing, which was coming to be little more than a panting now,
came on at longer intervals and slackened away. It has lasted on, all the
same, and in spite of the passing of this attack, my breathing is not yet
coming naturally. I feel a sort of catch and hesitation in it. Let it do as it
pleases, though, so long as the sighs aren't heartfelt. You can feel assured
on my score of this: I shall not be afraid when the last hour comes—I'm
already prepared, not planning as much as a day ahead. The man, though,
whom you should admire and imitate is the one who finds it a joy to live
and in spite of that is not reluctant to die. For where's the virtue in going
out when you're really being thrown out? And yet there is this virtue
about my case: I'm in the process of being thrown out, certainly, but the
manner of it is as if I were going out. And the reason why it never happens
to a wise man is that being thrown out signifies expulsion from a place one
is reluctant to depart from, and there is nothing the wise man does reluctantly. He escapes necessity because he wills what necessity is going to
force on him.

—Translated by Robin Campbell

Scipio's Villa

I WRITE YOU THIS from the actual villa of Scipio Africanus. I
have just done reverence to the hero's spirit and to an altar which I
suspect is his tomb. His soul, I am convinced, has returned to the heavens
whence it came, not because he commanded great armies—mad Cambyses
did that, and exploited his madness to good effect—but because of his
singular moderation and piety. This, I think, was more remarkable when
he abandoned his country than when he defended it; it was impossible
that he continue in Rome and Rome continue free. "I have no wish to
make light of our laws and constitution," he said. "All citizens must have
equal rights. Use the service I have done you, my country, but without my
presence. I have been the cause of your liberty, and I shall be its proof. I
depart if I have grown too big to be good for you."

How could I not admire the high spirit which withdrew him into voluntary exile and so disburdened the state? A situation had come about
where either liberty must injure Scipio or Scipio liberty, and neither was
admissible. So he made way for the laws and betook himself to Liternum,
in the thought that his exile was as much a service to the state as was
Hannibal's.

I have looked at the villa built of squared blocks, the wall enclosing a
grove, towers buttressed on both sides as a bulwark for the house, a cis-
tern hidden among buildings and shrubbery which might be adequate for
an army, and a cramped bath, quite unlighted, after the old fashion; our
ancestors thought a hot bath must be dark. It afforded me great satisfaction to compare Scipio's habits with ours. In this cranny the terror of
Carthage, whom Rome had to thank that the Gallic sack was not repeated,
used to wash down a body tired out by field chores. For he used to do real
work, and himself cultivated his acres, as was the regular practice in the
old days. It was under this dingy ceiling he stood, this very ordinary floor
held his weight.

Who would tolerate such bathing nowadays? A man thinks himself
poor and slovenly if his walls are not shiny with large and costly mirrors, if
his Alexandrian marbles are not figured with slabs from Numidia, if there
is no border elaborately worked around the whole with a varied pictorial
pattern, if there is no room enclosed in glass, if there is no Thasian marble
—once a rare sight in an occasional temple—to line the pools into which

we lower our bodies when they have been reduced by a hard sweat, when the spigots for discharging the water are not silver. So far I have been speaking of ordinary establishments; what shall I say when I come to the freedmen's baths? What a quantity of statuary, what a quantity of columns that hold nothing up but are planted as extravagant ornaments! What a quantity of water, arranged to produce a series of crashing falls! We have become so dainty that we will tread only on gems.

In this bath of Scipio's there are not windows but chinks cut out of the masonry to admit light without weakening the structure. Nowadays they call baths moth-dens if they are not planned to get sun all day through spacious windows, unless they can bathe and tan simultaneously, unless they have a view of the countryside and the sea from their tubs. So it is; bathhouses which drew admiring throngs when they were dedicated are dismissed and relegated to the category of the superannuated as soon as luxury has devised some new gadget to bury itself under. Once baths were few and had no elegant trimmings. Why trim out a place meant for use, not luxury, where the admission is a penny? There were no showers in those days, nor a continuous stream as from a hot spring, and they didn't think it mattered how crystal the water to leave their dirt in was.

Good heavens, what a joy to step into that dimly lit bath, covered with an ordinary roof, in the knowledge that Cato as aedile, look you, or Fabius Maximus, or one of the Cornelii had tempered the water with his own hand! Even the noblest aediles, as part of their function, used to enter the resorts which catered to the populace and insist upon cleanliness and a moderate and healthy temperature, not the blazing heat newly introduced, so great indeed that a slave convicted of crime should be bathed alive! Now I think a man might as well say, "The bath is on fire," as, "The bath is warm."

Nowadays some people write Scipio down a yokel because he let no daylight into his sweat room, did not broil in a strong glare, or wait in his bath until he stewed. "Ah, a disaster of a man! He didn't know how to live. The water he bathed in was not filtered but often cloudy, and after heavy rains almost muddy." Baths like that did not bother Scipio; he had come to wash off sweat, not perfume. And what kind of remark do you suppose this will elicit? "I don't envy Scipio; a man who bathed that way was really living in exile." If you must know, he didn't bathe every day. Writers who have recorded the manners of our old Romans tell us that they washed their arms and legs every day—these, of course, they dirtied working—and took a whole bath once a week. "I can see they were very dirty," someone will say. "How do you suppose they smelled?" Of soldiery and exertion and manliness. Men are fouler now, after baths came to be trimmed out. When Horace chooses to describe an infamous fellow, notorious for his mincing foppishness, what does he say? "Buccillus smells of pastilles" (*Sermones* 1.2.27). Show me a Buccillus today: his smell would seem goatish, like the noisome Gargonius with whom Horace contrasts Buccillus. For today it is not enough to use perfume unless you apply it two or three times a day, to keep it from evaporating on the body. And why should a man preen himself on the scent as if it were his own?

If all this strikes you as too gloomy charge it up to Scipio's house, where I learned from Aegialus, who is a frugal householder and now owns the farm, that a tree can be transplanted even if it is quite old. We old fellows need to know this, for we all plant olive orchards for others to enjoy.

Slaves

Y OUR ATTITUDE TO YOUR SLAVES is one of familiarity, as I learn from people who have been in your company. I am pleased; it is what one expects of your good sense and cultivation. "They are slaves"—no, men. "They are slaves"—no, comrades. "They are slaves" —no, humble friends. "They are slaves"—no, fellow slaves, if you remember that Fortune holds equal sway over both.

That is why I laugh at people who think it degrading for a man to dine with his slave. Why, except that conventional exclusiveness has decreed that a master must be surrounded at his dinner by a squad of slaves standing at attention? The master eats more than he can hold; his inordinate greed loads his distended belly, which has unlearned the belly's function, and the digestion of all this food requires more ado than its ingestion. But the unhappy slaves may not move their lips for so much as a word. Any murmur is checked by a rod; not even involuntary sounds—a cough, a sneeze, a choke—are exempted from the lash. If a word breaks the silence the penalty is severe. Hungry and mute, they stand through the whole night.

In consequence, when they cannot speak in the master's presence, they speak *about* him. Yet when slaves spoke not only in the master's presence but *with* him, when their lips were not sewn tight, they were ready to put their necks out for their master, to turn any danger that threatened him upon their own heads; they spoke at dinners, but under torture their lips

were sealed. But afterward the arrogance of masters gave currency to the
proverb, "So many slaves, so many enemies." We do not acquire them as
enemies, we make them such. Other cruel and inhuman treatment I pass
over: we abuse them as one does pack animals, not even as one abuses
men. When we recline at table one slave wipes up the hawking, another
crouches to take up the leavings of the drunks. One carves the costly
game, separating the portions by deft sweeps of a practiced hand—unhappy man, to live solely for the purpose of carving fowl neatly, unless the
man who teaches the trade for pleasure's sake is more wretched than the
man who learns it for necessity's! Another, who serves the wine, is got up
like a woman and must wrestle with his age; he can never escape boyhood
but is dragged back to it. His figure may now be a soldier's, but his hairs
are rubbed away or plucked out by the roots to make him smooth, and he
must divide his sleepless night between his master's drunkenness and his
lust; in the bedroom he is a man, in the dining room a boy. Another has
the assignment of keeping book on the guests; he stands there, poor fellow, and watches to see whose adulation and whose intemperance of gul-
let or tongue will get him an invitation for the following day. Add the
caterers with their refined *expertise* of the master's palate; they know what
flavors will titillate him, what table decorations will please his fancy, what
novelty might restore his appetite when he feels nauseous, what his surfeit
will scorn, what tidbit he would crave on a particular day. With slaves like
these the master cannot bear to dine; he would count it an affront to his
dignity to come to table with his own slave. Heaven forbid!

But how many of those slaves are in fact his masters! I have seen Callistus' master a suitor outside Callistus' door and have seen him shut out
while others were admitted—the master who tagged him for sale and sent
him to market with a job-lot of chattels. But the slave included in this
preliminary batch on which the auctioneer tried out his voice paid tit for
tat. He crossed Callistus' name from the roster in turn and judged him
unfit to enter his house. His master sold Callistus, but how much did
Callistus cost his master!

Remember, if you please, that the man you call slave sprang from the
same seed, enjoys the same daylight, breathes like you, lives like you, dies
like you. You can as easily conceive him a free man as he can conceive you
a slave. In the Marian disasters many men of noble birth who had entered
military service as the preliminary to a senatorial career were declassed by
Fortune and reduced to being shepherds or cottagers; now despise a man
for his condition when you may find yourself in the same even as you
despise it!

I do not wish to take up the large topic of the treatment of slaves, where
we show ourselves proud, cruel, and insulting in the highest degree. The
essence of my teaching is this: Treat your inferior as you would wish your

superior to treat you. Whenever the thought of your wide power over your slave strikes you, be struck, too, by the thought of your master's equally wide power over you. "But I have no master!" you object. All in good time; you may have one. Remember how old Hecuba was when she became a slave, or Croesus, or Darius' mother, or Plato, or Diogenes.

Treat your slave with compassion, even with courtesy; admit him to your conversation, your planning, your society. Here the genteel will protest loudly and unanimously: "Nothing could be more degrading or disgusting!" But these same people I shall catch kissing the hands of other people's slaves. Can't you see how our ancestors stripped the title of master of all invidiousness and the title of slave of all contumely? The master they called "paterfamilias" and the slaves "family"; this usage still obtains in the mimes. They instituted a festival at which masters dined with their slaves—not, of course, the only day they could do so. They allowed slaves to hold office in the household and to act as judges; the household they regarded as a miniature republic.

"What is the upshot? Am I to bring all slaves to my table?" No more than all free men. But if you imagine I would exclude some because their work is dirty, that muleteer, for example, or that cowhand, you are mistaken. I value them not by their jobs but by their character; a man gives himself his own character, accident allots his job. Have some dine with you because they are deserving, some to make them deserving. If their sordid contacts have left a taint, association with respectable people will shake it off. There is no reason to go to the forum or senate house in search of a friend, my dear Lucilius; if you pay careful heed you will find one at home. Without an artisan good material often lies unused; try it and you will find out.

A man is a fool if he looks only at the saddle and bridle and not at the horse itself when he is going to buy one; he is a greater fool if he values a man by his clothing and condition, which only swathes us like clothing. "He is a slave!" But perhaps a free man in spirit. "He is a slave!" Shall that count against him? Show me a man who is not; one is a slave to lust, another to greed, another to ambition, all to fear. I can show you a consular who is slave to a crone, a millionaire who is slave to a housemaid; I can point to young aristocrats indentured to pantomimes. Voluntary slavery is the meanest of all.

Those squeamish types should not deter you, therefore, from camaraderie with your slaves and make you proudly superior. Slaves ought to respect rather than fear you. Here someone will protest that I am now rallying slaves to the cap of liberty and toppling masters from their elevation by saying, "Slaves ought to respect rather than fear a master." "That is what he said: slaves ought to respect him, like his clients or those who pay him formal calls." The protester forgets that what is enough for a god is not too little for a master. If a man is respected he is also loved, and love cannot blend with fear.

Your own attitude is consequently as right as can be, in my judgment; you do not choose to have your slaves fear you, you use words to castigate them. A lash is to admonish dumb beasts. What offends need not wound. It is our daintiness that drives us to distraction, so that anything that does not meet our caprice provokes our wrath. We assume regal lordliness. Kings forget their own strength and others' weakness and fly into a white-hot fury as if they had really been injured, when their exalted position guarantees them complete immunity to any possibility of injury. Nor are they unaware of their immunity; by complaining, they solicit an opening for inflicting harm. They profess they have been injured in order to work injury.

I do not wish to detain you longer; you need no exhortation. Among its other traits good character approves its decisions and abides by them. Wickedness is fickle and changes frequently, not for something better but for something different. Farewell.

—Translated by Moses Hadas

PLUTARCH

Plutarch (A.D. 46?–c. 120) was born in Boetia, not far from Delphi, studied at Athens, became a valued diplomat (like Montaigne), and at the height of his worldly success retired to his native town to become a priest of the temple of Delphi and teach philosophy to the young. He is best known as the first great biographer: his Parallel Lives *paired biographies of noble Greeks and Romans, such as Alexander the Great and Julius Caesar. But it is his numerous* Moralia, *essays and dialogues on ethical, literary, and historical subjects, that influenced the development of the personal essay.*

As the classicist and translator Moses Hadas has noted, "Almost alone in the canon of Greek writers whom Europe has accepted, Plutarch can be called charming, and his charm, combined with his broad and direct knowledge, makes him the most effective intermediary between the Graeco-Roman world and our own. Unlike the austere classics, again, Plutarch is a personal writer, and in the course of his copious works he tells us of his family and friends and reveals his tastes and interests so fully that we know him more intimately than we do any other Greek writer." Plutarch put great stock on family ties and friendship and, atypically for his age, saw marriage as the closest of human bonds. "There is an unexampled reverence for womanhood," wrote Hadas, "a touching tenderness for little children, a deep sympathy for animal creation, and, so far as such a thing was possible for an aristocratic Platonist, a respect for all the disinherited of the earth. It is his humanitarianism, in large part, which made Plutarch so appealing to Montaigne and to Shakespeare."

The essay below, "Consolation to His Wife," displays all of Plutarch's sympathetic tendencies. The consolation was a well-established literary genre in antiquity (Seneca wrote several), but Plutarch's is often considered the most attractive example of the form, because of its genuineness of feeling and touching directness.

Consolation to His Wife

M Y DEAR WIFE:

The messenger you sent with tidings of the death of our little daughter apparently missed me on his road to Athens, and consequently I learned about the child only when I arrived in Tanagra. I suppose that the funeral has already taken place. I could wish that the arrangements were such as to cause you the minimum of pain, both for the present and the future. If you have omitted any ceremony which you think might lighten your grief because you wished to await my approval, do carry it out. But excesses and superstitions should be avoided; I know it is not in your character to indulge in them.

Above all, my dear wife, help us both preserve our customary composure in this affliction. I am of course very sensible of it and feel its force; but if I find your grief exceeds due measure I shall be more greatly distressed than by the misfortune itself. Neither am I "fashioned of oak or stone," as is well known to you, who have shared with me in the nurture of our several children, all of whom we have ourselves brought up at home.

After the birth of our four sons you yearned for a daughter, and I seized the opportunity of giving her your dear name: I know that she was precious to you. Peculiar poignancy attaches to tenderness for children when their presence is altogether welcome and completely untainted by ill will and reproach. The child herself possessed a marvelous cheeriness of temper and gentleness, and her responsiveness to love and eagerness to please evoked not only pleasure but an appreciation of human goodness. She would invite her nurse to offer her breast not only to other infants but even to furnishings and toys in which she took delight. It was as if, out of humane sensibilities, she invited them to her own table, to share in the good things she had; what was most delightful to her she wished all who pleased her to enjoy.

I cannot see, my dear wife, why these and similar qualities which delighted us when she was alive should now distress and confound us when we bring them to mind. Rather do I fear lest we lose those memories along with our grief, like that Clymene who said, "I hate that well-turned cornel bow; away with all exercises!" She avoided and shuddered at every reminder of her son. In general, nature avoids everything that causes distress. But in the case of our child, in the degree that she proved to us a thing most lovable to fondle and look at and hear, so the memory of her must abide with us and become part of us, and it will bring us a greater quantity and variety of joy than of sorrow. Surely some portion of the discourses I have uttered to others should prove helpful to ourselves in time of need; we must not then sink into lethargy nor conjure up the sorrows which are the price of those numerous delights.

I was told by those who were present and found your conduct remarkable that you did not put on mourning nor induce any uncomeliness or unseemliness in yourself or in your servants, that there was no preparation for extravagant solemnities at the grave, but that everything was done decently and quietly with only the family in attendance. For my part I was not surprised, for you would never prink for the theater or processions, but even for pleasurable outings thought that extravagance was useless and maintained your sensible moderation even among people who looked askance at it. It is not only in bacchic celebrations that a virtuous woman must remain uncorrupted, but in sorrow too she must remember that excess is to be avoided and that transports of emotion require to be controlled; it is not her love, as the many think, that she must fight against, but the incontinence of her soul. Upon love we bestow sorrow and respect and an abiding memory of the departed; but the insatiable yearning for lamentation which leads to wailing and beating of the breast is no less shameful than unbridled voluptuousness—though men find it venial, for it is a bitter smart rather than an agreeable sensation which is associated with the impropriety. What could be more illogical than to check excess of laughter and gaiety and then give free flow to rivers of tears and lamentations which stream from the same source? Or, as some husbands do, to quarrel with their wives over the use of perfumery and purple and then suffer them to shear their hair in mourning, to dye their garments black, to sit in unnatural attitudes and recline in uncomfortable postures? Or, what is hardest of all, to oppose their wives and prevent them if they chastise their servants or maids immoderately or unfairly, and then to overlook it when they chastise themselves unfeelingly and cruelly in trying circumstances which call for gentleness and kindliness?

But between us, my dear wife, there was never any occasion for such differences, nor, I think, will there ever be. The simplicity of your grooming and the frugality of your diet has evoked the astonishment of all the philosophers who have ever visited or associated with us. Nor is there any of our townsmen who has not remarked upon your admirable simplicity at festivals and sacrifices and theatrical performances. Upon a similar occasion in the past you demonstrated your singular steadfastness when you lost the eldest of your children; and it was the same when charming Charon left us. I remember that friends were escorting me on my way from the seashore when the news of my son's death was brought, and they together with others accompanied me to the house. When they observed perfect orderliness and quiet in the house they thought, as they afterwards confided in others, that nothing amiss had happened and that it was an empty rumor that reached me. So discreetly had you arranged your household at a juncture which offered occasion for great disorder. And yet you yourself suckled that son, and underwent surgery when your breast suffered a contusion. That is the conduct of a noble woman and a loving mother.

The majority of mothers, we observe, take their children into their arms, when others have bathed them and prinked them out, and treat them like dolls; and then, if the children die, they dissolve into empty and ungrateful grief, not out of affection, for affection is rational and dignified; but vainglory mixed with a modicum of natural feeling produces wild and unassuageable transports of grief. This phenomenon Aesop understood very well. When Zeus distributed their honors to the gods, he tells us, Grief too put in a request, and Zeus ordained that Grief should indeed receive honor, but only from those who elected and desired to bestow it. This is exactly what happens. In the beginning everyone welcomes Grief into his house, and then when it has had time to take root and has become a companion and housemate it will no longer depart when the inmates wish it to. It must therefore be resisted at the threshold and not be allowed within the citadel by way of mourning dress or shorn locks or other such tokens, which, confronting and glowering upon us daily, render our spirit petty and narrow and confined and unsmiling and timorous, so that it has no share in jollity or brightness or the kindly board, being so besieged and hard pressed by grief. Upon this evil there follows neglect of the body and aversion to anointing, bathing, and other attention to the person. The opposite should be the case; a troubled soul should itself receive support from a robust body. A great part of sorrow is blunted and relaxed, like a wave under a clear sky, when the body enjoys tranquil sailing. But where a bad regimen begets meagerness and roughness and the body transmits nothing that is beneficial or salutary to the soul but only pain and discomfort, like acrid and annoying exhalations, then it can no longer easily recover even if it wish to do so. Such are the afflictions which visit a soul that has been thus abused.

But the dreadful thing which does so much mischief in these cases I need have no fear of—I mean the visits of silly women and their cries and the continuing lamentations by which they fan and whet grief and prevent it from abating either through other causes or of itself. I know the good fight you lately fought when you supported Theon's sister and resisted the women who were charging in with wails and shrieks, simply to pile fire upon fire. When people see a friend's house aflame they extinguish it with all possible speed and strength, but when souls are ablaze they only add kindling. When a man's eyes are sore his friends do not let him finger them, however much he wishes to, nor do they themselves touch the inflammation: But a man sunk in grief suffers every chance comer to stir and augment his affliction, like a running sore; and by reason of the fingering and consequent irritation it hardens into a serious and intractable evil. Against such a contingency I know that you will be on guard.

Endeavor often to transpose yourself in imagination to the period when our child was not yet born, and yet we had no cause to reproach fortune; and then consider that our present state is a continuation of that former period, for our condition is now as it was then. If we look upon our situation in the past as freer of reproach than our present state we shall seem to be resentful that our child was ever born. The two years of her life that intervened must by no means be effaced from our memory but rather reckoned as a pleasure, for they afforded us delight and happiness. We must never consider a small good as a large evil, nor be ungrateful for what fortune has given us because it has not filled the measure as full as we expected. Always respectfulness to the divine and a cheerful and uncomplaining attitude towards fortune produces fruit that is good and sweet. In case of misfortune there is no surer means of either quenching grief entirely or diminishing its size and intensity by an admixture of opposite emotions than by calling to mind good things in the past and transposing and reshaping our reflections upon life from the gloomy and troubled to the bright and shining. Perfumes not only delight our sense of smell but are an antidote to bad odors. Similarly, recollection of good things in the midst of evil functions as a necessary remedy for such as do not avoid the memory of past blessings and do not always and everywhere upbraid fortune. It becomes us ill, inculpating our own lives, to find fault with a single blot, as in a book, when all the rest is clean and unstained.

You have oftentimes heard that happiness depends upon a correct rationale which renders a temperament steadfast, and that changes of fortune do not produce significant deviations and contribute no great weight to the direction our lives take. But even if we allow ourselves to be governed, like the majority, by external events and take into our reckoning the untoward strokes of fortune, and if we gauge our happiness by the judgment of ordinary folk, still I must caution you to take no account of the tears and lamentations of visitors who follow the tiresome custom of paying condolence calls. Rather reflect how much these people envy you for your children, your household, your way of life. It would be a perversity for you to find fault with your estate and chafe at it when others would cheerfully choose your lot even with the affliction which now distresses us. Nay, this present sting should make you sensible of our numerous blessings which remain untouched. Shall we imitate those who collect Homeric lines which are defective at beginning or end and overlook large and excellent stretches of his poetry? Shall we meticulously search out faulty passages in our lives for condemnation and cavalierly neglect the mass of our blessings? We should then be imitating mean and greedy misers who make no use of their accumulations but wail in anguish if they are lost.

If you pity the babe because she departed this life unmarried and childless, again you have the consolation of knowing that you yourself enjoyed a full share of such experiences. It is not fair to set a high value upon these matters for those who lack them and a low for those who have them. She has arrived where there is no distress; there is then no need for us to be distressed. Why should we be afflicted with grief on her account when she herself can experience no grief? The loss of treasures loses its sting when they reach a state to which the sting is no longer appropriate. It was only of little things that your Timoxena was deprived, for all she knew was little things, and in little things she took her pleasure. How can we say that she was deprived of things of which she had no knowledge, no experience, no desire?

You have often heard the assertion made—and the majority find it convincing—that the departed suffer no evil or distress whatever. You will not credit such assertions, I know, because of our ancestral doctrines and the mystic symbols of the Dionysiac initiations with which we have our intimate and shared bond. The soul is incorruptible, and you must imagine that its experience is like that of a caged bird. If it has been maintained in the body for a long time and has become habituated to this life by numerous concerns and long custom, then when it is lifted out it snuggles into the body again, as a bird in its cage, and by repeated births does not forego or cease being involved in the passions and chances of this world. Do not think that old age is vilified and abused because of wrinkles and hoary hair and bodily failure; the most grievous defect of old age is that it renders the soul forgetful of the memories of yonder world and preoccupied with the things of this world, and it is so far bent and distorted that it retains the posture into which it was forced by the body. But the soul which remains in the body but a short span and is then liberated quickly recovers its natural form, for the constraint which was put upon it was but mild and gentle. Fire which has been just quenched can be rekindled by fanning and quickly resumes its strength: and so it is with the soul which has remained but a short while in the body. It is made to pass the gates of death as quickly as possible, before it conceives too great a love for the things of this world and is rendered effeminate by the body and fused with it as by some drug.

The truth concerning these matters is emphasized in our ancient and traditional laws and usages. For those who die in infancy we do not offer the libations or other funeral rites which are customary in the case of other dead because children have no share in earth or earthly concerns. Nor do we visit their tombs and monuments or keep solemn wakes at their bodies. Our laws do not permit such practices because it is an impious thing to mourn for those who are so quickly translated to a better region and a divine lot. And now inasmuch as it is harder to reject our traditions than to trust them, let us comport ourselves outwardly as the laws prescribe, and let our inward conduct be even more untainted and pure and sensible.

—Translated by Moses Hadas

SEI SHONAGON

some approximate dates?
↓

previously unknown to me... again denoting how little life's basics change.

Sei Shonagon (exact dates unknown) was a court lady in tenth-century Japan who kept an inimitable journal recording her likes, her dislikes, and the events around her. She lived in the Heian era, a period of high culture which also produced her rival, the novelist Lady Murasaki (Tale of Genji). *Shonagon's* Pillow Book *remains fresh and delightful, partly because the author was such an unapologetic maverick—an outspoken, truly independent woman.*

In her work, she is an inveterate list-keeper: "Embarrassing Things," "Depressing Things," "Hateful Things," "Elegant Things" . . . These lists become the matrix for Shonagon's judgments: she has a perfectionist sense of how everything ought to be, down to the smallest detail. "Oxen should have very small foreheads," she declares, or "I cannot stand a woman who wears sleeves of unequal length." With her Japanese penchant for arrangement, she is attentive to all infractions of seasonal ritual. She scrutinizes the pettiest reactions of the empress for signs of shifting favoritism; she can be outrageously, comically spiteful, and, by our standards, a terrible snob. But Shonagon also has an earthy side; she is amusingly frank about bedroom behavior and secret trysts. Ivan Morris, her translator, notes, "Her attitude to men . . . was competitive to the point of overt hostility. And, partly owing to this combative spirit, her writing is free of any whining, querulous tone." Though it would be stretching things to call the Pillow Book *a personal essay, it is a book-length meditation on matters personal, and in its reclamation of the ephemera of daily life, it laid the groundwork for Japanese essay writing of the future.*

Hateful Things

ONE IS IN A HURRY TO LEAVE, but one's visitor keeps chattering away. If it is someone of no importance, one can get rid of him by saying, "You must tell me all about it next time"; but, should it be the sort of visitor whose presence commands one's best behaviour, the situation is hateful indeed.

One finds that a hair has got caught in the stone on which one is rubbing one's inkstick, or again that gravel is lodged in the inkstick, making a nasty, grating sound.

Someone has suddenly fallen ill and one summons the exorcist. Since he is not at home, one has to send messengers to look for him. After one has had a long fretful wait, the exorcist finally arrives, and with a sigh of relief one asks him to start his incantations. But perhaps he has been exorcizing too many evil spirits recently; for hardly has he installed himself and begun praying when his voice becomes drowsy. Oh, how hateful!

A man who has nothing in particular to recommend him discusses all sorts of subjects at random as though he knew everything.

An elderly person warms the palms of his hands over a brazier and stretches out the wrinkles. No young man would dream of behaving in such a fashion; old people can really be quite shameless. I have seen some dreary old creatures actually resting their feet on the brazier and rubbing them against the edge while they speak. These are the kind of people who in visiting someone's house first use their fans to wipe away the dust from the mat and, when they finally sit on it, cannot stay still but are forever spreading out the front of their hunting costume or even tucking it up under their knees. One might suppose that such behaviour was restricted to people of humble station; but I have observed it in quite well-bred people, including a Senior Secretary of the Fifth Rank in the Ministry of Ceremonial and a former Governor of Suruga.

I hate the sight of men in their cups who shout, poke their fingers in their mouths, stroke their beards, and pass on the wine to their neighbours with great cries of "Have some more! Drink up!" They tremble, shake their heads, twist their faces, and gesticulate like children who are singing, "We're off to see the Governor." I have seen really well-bred people behave like this and I find it most distasteful.

To envy others and to complain about one's own lot; to speak badly about people; to be inquisitive about the most trivial matters and to resent and abuse people for not telling one, or, if one does manage to worm out some facts, to inform everyone in the most detailed fashion as if one had known all from the beginning—oh, how hateful!

One is just about to be told some interesting piece of news when a baby starts crying.

A flight of crows circle about with loud caws.

An admirer has come on a clandestine visit, but a dog catches sight of him and starts barking. One feels like killing the beast.

One has been foolish enough to invite a man to spend the night in an unsuitable place—and then he starts snoring.

A gentleman has visited one secretly. Though he is wearing a tall, lacquered hat, he nevertheless wants no one to see him. He is so flurried, in fact, that upon leaving he bangs into something with his hat. Most hateful! It is annoying too when he lifts up the Iyo blind that hangs at the entrance of the room, then lets it fall with a great rattle. If it is a head-blind, things are still worse, for being more solid it makes a terrible noise when it is dropped. There is no excuse for such carelessness. Even a head-blind does not make any noise if one lifts it up gently on entering and leaving the room; the same applies to sliding-doors. If one's movements are rough, even a paper door will bend and resonate when opened; but, if one lifts the door a little while pushing it, there need be no sound.

One has gone to bed and is about to doze off when a mosquito appears, announcing himself in a reedy voice. One can actually feel the wind made by his wings and, slight though it is, one finds it hateful in the extreme.

A carriage passes with a nasty, creaking noise. Annoying to think that the passengers may not even be aware of this! If I am travelling in someone's carriage and I hear it creaking, I dislike not only the noise but also the owner of the carriage.

One is in the middle of a story when someone butts in and tries to show that he is the only clever person in the room. Such a person is hateful, and so, indeed, is anyone, child or adult, who tries to push himself forward.

One is telling a story about old times when someone breaks in with a little detail that he happens to know, implying that one's own version is inaccurate—disgusting behaviour!

Very hateful is a mouse that scurries all over the place.

Some children have called at one's house. One makes a great fuss of them and gives them toys to play with. The children become accustomed to this treatment and start to come regularly, forcing their way into one's inner rooms and scattering one's furnishings and possessions. Hateful!

A certain gentleman whom one does not want to see visits one at home or in the Palace, and one pretends to be asleep. But a maid comes to tell one and shakes one awake, with a look on her face that says, "What a sleepyhead!" Very hateful.

A newcomer pushes ahead of the other members in a group; with a knowing look, this person starts laying down the law and forcing advice upon everyone—most hateful.

A man with whom one is having an affair keeps singing the praises of some woman he used to know. Even if it is a thing of the past, this can be very annoying. How much more so if he is still seeing the woman! (Yet sometimes I find that it is not as unpleasant as all that.)

A person who recites a spell himself after sneezing. In fact I detest anyone who sneezes, except the master of the house.

Fleas, too, are very hateful. When they dance about under someone's clothes, they really seem to be lifting them up.

The sound of dogs when they bark for a long time in chorus is ominous and hateful.

I cannot stand people who leave without closing the panel behind them.

How I detest the husbands of nurse-maids! It is not so bad if the child in the maid's charge is a girl, because then the man will keep his distance. But, if it is a boy, he will behave as though he were the father. Never letting the boy out of his sight, he insists on managing everything. He regards the other attendants in the house as less than human, and, if anyone tries to scold the child, he slanders him to the master. Despite this disgraceful behaviour, no one dare accuse the husband; so he strides about the house with a proud, self-important look, giving all the orders.

I hate people whose letters show that they lack respect for worldly civilities, whether by discourtesy in the phrasing or by extreme politeness to someone who does not deserve it. This sort of thing is, of course, most odious if the letter is for oneself, but it is bad enough even if it is addressed to someone else.

As a matter of fact, most people are too casual, not only in their letters but in their direct conversation. Sometimes I am quite disgusted at noting how little decorum people observe when talking to each other. It is particularly unpleasant to hear some foolish man or woman omit the proper marks of respect when addressing a person of quality; and, when servants fail to use honorific forms of speech in referring to their masters, it is very bad indeed. No less odious, however, are those masters who, in addressing their servants, use such phrases as "When you were good enough to do such-and-such" or "As you so kindly remarked." No doubt there are some masters who, in describing their own actions to a servant, say, "I presumed to do so-and-so!"

Sometimes a person who is utterly devoid of charm will try to create a good impression by using very elegant language; yet he only succeeds in being ridiculous. No doubt he believes this refined language to be just what the occasion demands, but, when it goes so far that everyone bursts out laughing, surely something must be wrong.

It is most improper to address high-ranking courtiers, Imperial Advisers, and the like simply by using their names without any titles or marks of respect; but such mistakes are fortunately rare.

If one refers to the maid who is in attendance on some lady-in-waiting as "Madam" or "that lady," she will be surprised, delighted, and lavish in her praise.

When speaking to young noblemen and courtiers of high rank, one should always (unless Their Majesties are present) refer to them by their official posts. Incidentally, I have been very shocked to hear important people use the word "I" while conversing in Their Majesties' presence. Such a breach of etiquette is really distressing, and I fail to see why people cannot avoid it.

A man who has nothing in particular to recommend him but who speaks in an affected tone and poses as being elegant.

An inkstone with such a hard, smooth surface that the stick glides over it without leaving any deposit of ink.   *But "real"*

Ladies-in-waiting who want to know everything that is going on.   *ladies who are & are O.K.?*

Sometimes one greatly dislikes a person for no particular reason—and then that person goes and does something hateful.

? A gentleman who travels alone in his carriage to see a procession or some other spectacle. What sort of a man is he? Even though he may not be a person of the greatest quality, surely he should have taken along a few of the many young men who are anxious to see the sights. But no, there he sits by himself (one can see his silhouette through the blinds), with a proud look on his face, keeping all his impressions to himself.

? A lover who is leaving at dawn announces that he has to find his fan and his paper. "I know I put them somewhere last night," he says. Since it is pitch dark, he gropes about the room, bumping into the furniture and muttering, "Strange! Where on earth can they be?" Finally he discovers the objects. He thrusts the paper into the breast of his robe with a great rustling sound; then he snaps open his fan and busily fans away with it. Only now is he ready to take his leave. What charmless behaviour! "Hateful" is an understatement.

Equally disagreeable is the man who, when leaving in the middle of the night, takes care to fasten the cord of his headdress. This is quite unnecessary; he could perfectly well put it gently on his head without tying the cord. And why must he spend time adjusting his cloak or hunting costume? Does he really think someone may see him at this time of night and criticize him for not being impeccably dressed?

A good lover will behave as elegantly at dawn as at any other time. He drags himself out of bed with a look of dismay on his face. The lady urges him on: "Come, my friend, it's getting light. You don't want anyone to find you here." He gives a deep sigh, as if to say that the night has not been nearly long enough and that it is agony to leave. Once up, he does not instantly pull on his trousers. Instead he comes close to the lady and whispers whatever was left unsaid during the night. Even when he is dressed, he still lingers, vaguely pretending to be fastening his sash.

Presently he raises the lattice, and the two lovers stand together by the side door while he tells her how he dreads the coming day, which will keep them apart; then he slips away. The lady watches him go, and this moment of parting will remain among her most charming memories.

Indeed, one's attachment to a man depends largely on the elegance of his leave-taking. When he jumps out of bed, scurries about the room, tightly fastens his trouser-sash, rolls up the sleeves of his Court cloak, over-robe, or hunting costume, stuffs his belongings into the breast of his robe and then briskly secures the outer sash—one really begins to hate him.

So, she shouts: It's ME, only ME, who is important ∴ deserving of praise ···· etc etc.

totally tedious

—*Translated by Ivan Morris*

and His interest in this bully of a human ?

Another example of how little the world has changed ... if we look deeply

KENKO

Essays in Idleness *is the English title for one of the classical works of Japanese prose, the* Tsurezuregusa *of Kenko. The original Japanese name of the collection derives from the expression "with nothing better to do." These charming musings are not, strictly speaking, essays in the Western sense of the term, but fragments ranging from a line to several pages—the primary matter of essays, so to speak. Like Sei Shonagon's* Pillow Book, *observes translator Donald Keene, they employ "the random mode of composition known as* zuihitsu *(follow the brush) in Japanese. This form—or lack of form—was most congenial to Japanese writers, who turned to it perhaps because it was less 'dishonest' than creating fiction. The formlessness of the* zuihitsu *did not impede enjoyment by readers; indeed, they took pleasure not only in moving from one to another of the great variety of subjects but in tracing subtle links joining the successive episodes."*

About the author, Kenko (c. 1283–1350), little is known except that he had a function in the imperial court and a reputation as a poet. He became a Buddhist monk in 1324, after the death of the emperor whom he had served. Even without further biographical details, however, his quirky personality stands out. By his own admission, he was addicted to the past and conservatively dismayed at any falling-away from tradition. He celebrated the very Japanese idea of the beauty of impermanence. He had refined, pronounced tastes, which included a preference for the irregular and unfinished, the understated and the restrained. In his period as a Buddhist monk, he never exactly retreated from the world but retired to a city temple in Kyoto, not far from the royal court, whose status distinctions and worldly manners continued to preoccupy him.

Essays in Idleness

W HAT A STRANGE, demented feeling it gives me when I realize I have spent whole days before this inkstone, with nothing better to do, jotting down at random whatever nonsensical thoughts have entered my head.

1

It is enough, it would seem, to have been born into this world for a man to desire many things. The position of the emperor, of course, is far too exalted for our aspirations. Even the remote descendants of the imperial line are sacred, for they are not of the seed of man. Ordinary nobles of a rank that entitles them to retainers—let alone those who stand in the solitary grandeur of the chancellor—appear most impressive, and even their children and grandchildren, though their fortunes may decline, still possess a distinctive elegance. Persons of lower rank, fortunate enough to achieve some success in keeping with their station, are apt to wear looks of self-satisfaction and no doubt consider themselves most important, but actually they are quite insignificant.

No one is less to be envied than a priest. Sei Shōnagon wrote of priests that they seemed to outsiders "like sticks of wood," an apt description. The clerics impress nobody, even when they flaunt their authority and their importance is loudly proclaimed. It is easy to see why the holy man Sōga should have said that worldly fame is unseemly in priests, and that those who seek it violate the teachings of Buddha. A true hermit might, in fact, seem more admirable.

It is desirable that a man's face and figure be of excelling beauty. I could sit forever with a man, provided that what he said did not grate on my ears, that he had charm, and that he did not talk very much. What an unpleasant experience it is when someone you have supposed to be quite distinguished reveals his true, inferior nature. A man's social position and looks are likely to be determined at birth, but why should not a man's mind go from wisdom to greater wisdom if it is so disposed? What a shame it is when men of excellent appearance and character prove hopelessly inept in social encounters with their inferiors in both position and appearance, solely because they are badly educated.

A familiarity with orthodox scholarship, the ability to compose poetry and prose in Chinese, a knowledge of Japanese poetry and music are all desirable, and if a man can serve as a model to others in matters of precedent and court ceremony, he is truly impressive. The mark of an excellent man is that he writes easily in an acceptable hand, sings agreeably and in tune, and, though appearing reluctant to accept when wine is pressed on him, is not a teetotaler.

7

If man were never to fade away like the dews of Adashino, never to vanish like the smoke over Toribeyama, but lingered on forever in the world, how things would lose their power to move us! The most precious thing in life is its uncertainty. Consider living creatures—none lives so long as man. The May fly waits not for the evening, the summer cicada knows neither spring nor autumn. What a wonderfully unhurried feeling it is to live even a single year in perfect serenity! If that is not enough for you, you might live a thousand years and still feel it was but a single night's dream. We cannot live forever in this world; why should we wait for ugliness to overtake us? The longer man lives, the more shame he endures. To die, at the latest, before one reaches forty, is the least unattractive. Once a man passes that age, he desires (with no sense of shame over his appearance) to mingle in the company of others. In his sunset years he dotes on his grandchildren, and prays for long life so that he may see them prosper. His preoccupation with worldly desires grows ever deeper, and gradually he loses all sensitivity to the beauty of things, a lamentable state of affairs.

8

Nothing leads a man astray so easily as sexual desire. What a foolish thing a man's heart is! Though we realize, for example, that fragrances are short-lived and the scent burnt into clothes lingers but briefly, how our hearts always leap when we catch a whiff of an exquisite perfume! The holy man of Kume lost his magic powers after noticing the whiteness of the legs of a girl who was washing clothes; this was quite understandable, considering that the glowing plumpness of her arms, legs, and flesh owed nothing to artifice.

1 0

A house, I know, is but a temporary abode, but how delightful it is to find one that has harmonious proportions and a pleasant atmosphere. One feels somehow that even moonlight, when it shines into the quiet domicile of a person of taste, is more affecting than elsewhere. A house, though it may not be in the current fashion or elaborately decorated, will appeal to us by its unassuming beauty—a grove of trees with an indefinably ancient look; a garden where plants, growing of their own accord, have a special charm; a verandah and an open-work wooden fence of interesting construction; and a few personal effects left carelessly lying about, giving the place an air of having been lived in. A house which multitudes of workmen have polished with every care, where strange and rare Chinese and Japanese furnishings are displayed, and even the grasses and trees of the garden have been trained unnaturally, is ugly to look at and most depressing. How could anyone live for long in such a place? The most casual glance will suggest how likely such a house is to turn in a moment to smoke.

A man's character, as a rule, may be known from the place where he lives. The Gotokudaiji minister[1] stretched a rope across his roof to keep the kites from roosting. Saigyō,[2] seeing the rope, asked, "Why should it bother him if kites perch there? That shows you the kind of man this prince is." I have heard that Saigyō never visited him again. I remembered this story not long ago when I noticed a rope stretched over the roof of the Kosaka palace,[3] where Prince Ayanokōji[4] lives. Someone told me that, as a matter of fact, it distressed the prince to see how crows clustering on the roof would swoop down to seize frogs in the pond. The story impressed me, and made me wonder if Sanesada may not also have had some such reason.

1 1

About the tenth month I had the occasion to visit a village beyond the place called Kurusuno. I made my way far down a moss-covered path until I reached a lonely-looking hut. Not a sound could be heard, except for the dripping of a water pipe buried in fallen leaves. Sprays of chrysan-

---

[1] Fujiwara no Sanesada (1139–91), a poet.
[2] Saigyō (1118–90), one of the greatest Japanese poets.
[3] Another name for the Tendai temple Myōhō-in. Some scholars read the name as Osaka.
[4] The prince was a son of the Emperor Kameyama (1249–1305), and was also known by his Buddhist name, Shōe. An imperial prince still resides at Myōhō-in.

themum and red maple leaves had been carelessly arranged on the holy-water shelf. Evidently somebody was living here. Moved, I was thinking, "One can live even in such a place," when I noticed in the garden beyond a great tangerine tree, its branches bent with fruit, that had been enclosed by a forbidding fence. Rather disillusioned, I thought now, "If only the tree had not been there!"

2 2

In all things I yearn for the past. Modern fashions seem to keep on growing more and more debased. I find that even among the splendid pieces of furniture built by our master cabinetmakers, those in the old forms are the most pleasing. And as for writing letters, surviving scraps from the past reveal how superb the phrasing used to be. The ordinary spoken language has also steadily coarsened. People used to say "raise the carriage shafts" or "trim the lamp wick," but people today say "raise it" or "trim it." When they should say, "Let the men of the palace staff stand forth!" they say, "Torches! Let's have some light!" Instead of calling the place where the lectures on the Sutra of the Golden Light are delivered before the emperor "the Hall of the Imperial Lecture," they shorten it to "the Lecture Hall," a deplorable corruption, an old gentleman complained.

2 9

When I sit down in quiet meditation, the one emotion hardest to fight against is a longing in all things for the past. After the others have gone to bed, I pass the time on a long autumn's night by putting in order whatever belongings are at hand. As I tear up scraps of old correspondence I should prefer not to leave behind, I sometimes find among them samples of the calligraphy of a friend who has died, or pictures he drew for his own amusement, and I feel exactly as I did at the time. Even with letters written by friends who are still alive I try, when it has been long since we met, to remember the circumstances, the year. What a moving experience that is! It is sad to think that a man's familiar possessions, indifferent to his death, should remain unaltered long after he is gone.

3 2

About the twentieth of the ninth month, at the invitation of a certain gentleman, I spent the night wandering with him viewing the moon. He happened to remember a house we passed on the way, and, having himself announced, went inside. In a corner of the overgrown garden heavy with dew, I caught the faint scent of some perfume which seemed quite accidental. This suggestion of someone living in retirement from the world moved me deeply.

In due time, the gentleman emerged, but I was still under the spell of the place. As I gazed for a while at the scene from the shadows, someone pushed the double doors open a crack wider, evidently to look at the moon. It would have been most disappointing if she had bolted the doors as soon as he had gone! How was she to know that someone lingering behind would see her? Such a gesture could only have been the product of inborn sensitivity.

I heard that she died not long afterwards.

1 3 7

Are we to look at cherry blossoms only in full bloom, the moon only when it is cloudless? To long for the moon while looking on the rain, to lower the blinds and be unaware of the passing of the spring—these are even more deeply moving. Branches about to blossom or gardens strewn with faded flowers are worthier of our admiration. Are poems written on such themes as "Going to view the cherry blossoms only to find they had scattered" or "On being prevented from visiting the blossoms" inferior to those on "Seeing the blossoms"? People commonly regret that the cherry blossoms scatter or that the moon sinks in the sky, and this is natural; but only an exceptionally insensitive man would say, "This branch and that branch have lost their blossoms. There is nothing worth seeing now."

In all things, it is the beginnings and ends that are interesting. Does the love between men and women refer only to the moments when they are in each other's arms? The man who grieves over a love affair broken off before it was fulfilled, who bewails empty vows, who spends long autumn nights alone, who lets his thoughts wander to distant skies, who yearns for the past in a dilapidated house—such a man truly knows what love means.

The moon that appears close to dawn after we have long waited for it moves us more profoundly than the full moon shining cloudless over a thousand leagues. And how incomparably lovely is the moon, almost greenish in its light, when seen through the tops of the cedars deep in the mountains, or when it hides for a moment behind clustering clouds during a sudden shower! The sparkle on hickory or white-oak leaves seemingly wet with moonlight strikes one to the heart. One suddenly misses the capital, longing for a friend who could share the moment.

And are we to look at the moon and the cherry blossoms with our eyes alone? How much more evocative and pleasing it is to think about the

spring without stirring from the house, to dream of the moonlit night
though we remain in our room!

The man of breeding never appears to abandon himself completely to
his pleasures; even his manner of enjoyment is detached. It is the rustic
boors who take all their pleasures grossly. They squirm their way through
the crowd to get under the trees; they stare at the blossoms with eyes for
nothing else; they drink saké and compose linked verse; and finally they
heartlessly break off great branches and cart them away. When they see a
spring they dip their hands and feet to cool them; if it is the snow, they
jump down to leave their footprints. No matter what the sight, they are
never content merely with looking at it.

Such people have a very peculiar manner of watching the Kamo Festival. "The procession's awfully late," they say. "There's no point waiting in
the stands for it to come." They go off then to a shack behind the stands
where they drink and eat, play go or backgammon, leaving somebody in
the stands to warn them. When he cries, "It's passing now!" each of them
dashes out in wild consternation, struggling to be first back into the
stands. They all but fall from their perches as they push out the blinds and
press against one another for a better look, staring at the scene, determined not to miss a thing. They comment on everything that goes by, with
cries of "Look at this! Look at that!" When the procession has passed,
they scramble down, saying, "We'll be back for the next one." All they are
interested in is what they can see.

People from the capital, the better sort, doze during the processions,
hardly looking at all. Young underlings are constantly moving about, performing their masters' errands, and persons in attendance, seated behind,
never stretch forward in an unseemly manner. No one is intent on seeing
the procession at all costs.

It is charming on the day of the Festival to see garlands of hollyhock
leaves carelessly strewn over everything. The morning of the Festival, before dawn breaks, you wonder who the owners are of the carriages silently
drawn up in place, and guess, "That one is his—or his," and have your
guesses confirmed when sometimes you recognize a coachman or servant.
I never weary of watching the different carriages going back and forth,
some delightfully unpretentious, others magnificent. By the time it is
growing dark you wonder where the rows of carriages and the dense
crowds of spectators have disappeared to. Before you know it, hardly a
soul is left, and the congestion of returning carriages is over. Then they
start removing the blinds and matting from the stands, and the place, even
as you watch, begins to look desolate. You realize with a pang of grief that
life is like this. If you have seen the avenues of the city, you have seen the
festival.

I suddenly realized, from the large number of people I could recognize in the crowds passing to and fro before the stands, that there were not so many people in the world, after all. Even if I were not to die until all of them had gone, I should not have long to wait. If you pierce a tiny aperture in a large vessel filled with water, even though only a small amount drips out, the constant leakage will empty the vessel. In this capital, with all its many people, surely a day never passes without someone dying. And are there merely one or two deaths a day? On some days, certainly, many more than one or two are seen to their graves at Toribeno, Funaoka, and other mountainsides, but never a day passes without a single funeral. That is why coffin makers never have any to spare. It does not matter how young or how strong you may be, the hour of death comes sooner than you expect. It is an extraordinary miracle that you should have escaped to this day; do you suppose you have even the briefest respite in which to relax?

When you make a *mamagodate* with backgammon counters, at first you cannot tell which of the stones arranged before you will be taken away. Your count then falls on a certain stone and you remove it. The others seem to have escaped, but as you renew the count you will thin out the pieces one by one, until none is left. Death is like that. The soldier who goes to war, knowing how close he is to death, forgets his family and even forgets himself; the man who has turned his back on the world and lives in a thatched hut, quietly taking pleasure in the streams and rocks of his garden, may suppose that death in battle has nothing to do with him, but this is a shallow misconception. Does he imagine that, if he hides in the still recesses of the mountains, the enemy called change will fail to attack? When you confront death, no matter where it may be, it is the same as charging into battle.

1 4 9

You should never put the new antlers of a deer to your nose and smell them. They have little insects that crawl into the nose and devour the brain.

—*Translated by Donald Keene*

*charm + talent lead
to amusing resolutions*

OU-YANG HSIU

*Ou-yang Hsiu (1007–1072) was a Sung dynasty poet, essayist, and scholar
and is ranked as one of the so-called eight masters of Chinese classical prose.
He led a colorful life of rises and falls in imperial favor: first promoted, then
exiled for outspokenness; assigned as provincial governor to out-of-the-way
places, then recalled to the capital to serve as collator of texts in the Imperial
Library; promoted to the powerful post of policy critic, only to be slandered
for incest (with his daughter-in-law—a charge both the writer and the young
woman denied) and demoted again. With all his government positions, he
considered himself first and foremost a writer. He was a reformer in prose,
seeking to loosen the hold of the ornate, euphonic style known as "parallel
prose," which was then demanded of men who took the civil service exami-
nations. Ou-yang Hsiu advocated a more flexible prose that would stress
content and ideas over the rigidly formalized, mechanical style then required.
His work is also more boldly personal, relaxed ("letting my brush write
what it would"), and conversational than that of his predecessors—as one
can see from the playful rhetorical questions he keeps asking in "Pleasure
Boat Studio."*

*It was common practice in China to write essays that celebrated landscape
and setting, and Ou-yang Hsiu availed himself of the opportunity to show
off his descriptive skills. Other noted essays of his include "Old Drunkard's
Pavilion," "My Three Zithers," and "Farewell to Yang Shih," where he tells
how he "used to be afflicted by melancholia" but cured it by zither-playing.
Chinese essayists were also expected to explain at the end of each piece how
the composition came into being; hence the conclusion of "Pleasure Boat
Studio."*

Pleasure Boat Studio

T HREE MONTHS after I came to Hua I converted the rooms of the eastern wing of the government offices into a place for me to spend my leisure time. I named it "Pleasure Boat Studio." The studio is one room across and seven rooms long (the rooms being connected by doorways), and so to walk into my studio is just like walking into a boat. First, in a corner of the warm room I made a hole in the roof to let in light. Then on either side of the bright and open unwalled rooms I installed railings to sit on or lean against. Anyone who relaxes in my studio will find that it is just like relaxing on a boat. The craggy stone mounds and the flowering plants and trees that I arranged just beyond the eaves on both sides make it seem all the more that one is drifting down the middle of a river, with the mountains on the right facing forests on the left, all very attractive. This, then, is why I named my studio after a boat.

In the "Judgment" of the *Book of Changes,* whenever one encounters dangerous circumstances the advice is always: "Cross the river." One can see from this that the real purpose of boats is to deliver people from danger rather than to provide comfort. But now I have converted part of the government offices into a studio for relaxation and have named it after a boat—was that not a perverse thing to do? Furthermore, I myself was once banished to the rivers and lakes because of my crimes. I sailed down the Pien River, crossed the Huai, and floated along the mighty Yangtze as far as Pa Gorges. Then I turned and went up the Han-mien River. In all, I must have covered several thousand miles on water. During those wearisome travels, when I was unlucky enough to encounter sudden storms or rough waters, many times I cried aloud to the gods to spare my brief life. In one such moment, as I looked ahead and behind, I noticed that the only other people out in boats were all either merchants or government officials. I sighed as I thought to myself: except for men who are anxious for profit and those who have no choice, who would be caught out here?

By Heaven's grace, I came through all such crises alive. Moreover, today my former misdeeds have been forgiven and I have been reinstated at Court. This is why I have now come to this prefecture where I eat my fill on public food and live comfortably in government quarters. As I think back on all the mountains I passed through and all the dangers my boat was exposed to, when dragons and water-serpents surfaced around me and high waves broke and surged on all sides, it is hardly surprising that I am sometimes frightened from my sleep by nightmares. And yet now I disregard all the dangers I faced and name my studio after a boat. Can it be that I am fond of life afloat after all?

I have heard of men of antiquity who fled from the world to distant rivers and lakes and refused to their dying day to return. They must have found some source of pleasure there. If one is not anxious for profit, even at the risk of danger, or is not convicted of a crime and forced to embark; rather, if one has a favorable breeze and gentle seas and is able to rest comfortably on a pillow and mat, sailing several hundred miles in a single day, then is boat travel not enjoyable? Of course, I have no time for such diversions. But since "pleasure boat" is the designation of boats used for such pastimes, I have now adopted it as the name of my studio. Is there anything wrong with that?

My friend, Ts'ai Chün-mo (Ts'ai Hsiang) excels at large style calligraphy. His writing is quite unusual and imposing. I have decided to ask him to write out my studio's name in large characters, which I will display on a pillar. I feared, however, that some people might not understand why I chose the name I did, and so I wrote out this explanation and inscribed it on the wall.

Written on the twelfth day of the twelfth month in the Jen-wu year (January 25, 1043).

—Translated by Ronald Egan

II

Fountainhead

MICHEL de MONTAIGNE

Michel Eyquem de Montaigne (1533–1592) may well have been the greatest **yes!** *essayist who ever lived. His father's family, the Eyquems, had amassed their wealth as merchants and risen to minor landowning nobility; they built a chateau in the town of Montaigne, in the Périgord region, and Montaigne considered himself as much a son of Gascony as of France. His mother's family, the Loupes (Lopez) clan, were also rich merchants, descended from Spanish Jews. Montaigne's father, who had interesting educational notions, raised him to speak nothing but Latin the first six years of his life, thus insuring his lifelong attachment to classical literature. By his own account, Montaigne was a lazy, sensual youth indulged by his father. He studied law and until he was thirty-eight practiced dutifully in the local courts, where, as a magistrate, he learned "the capacity to sift the truth." At that point he decided to retire with his wife to the family estate and spend his remaining years studying and writing—he was not sure what. One of the precipitating factors in this retreat to his tower was the death of his best friend, Etienne de La Boétie. Indeed, it has been suggested that Montaigne began writing his book so that he could talk to someone; the reader took the place of La Boétie.*

The first Essais (French for "attempts" or "trials"), written from 1572 to 1574, were short and relatively impersonal, filled with classical quotation; Montaigne had not yet stumbled on the idea of self-study as his major subject. But his confidence rose, especially after the successful publication of the first set (Book One), and his essays grew longer and more confiding, until he announced that his mission was to put before the public a full verbal portrait of himself. He claimed he was the first to do this. Some would argue that it was Saint Augustine (whose Confessions Montaigne seems not to have known), but in any case Montaigne was "the first writer of lay introspection," in Erich Auerbach's phrase. Certainly there is a vast difference between the Confessions, which seek to uncover through narrative the pattern of Augustine's spiritual fate, and Montaigne's circling, minute self-observations, which remind one more of a cat examining its fur. What Montaigne tells us about himself is peculiarly, charmingly specific and daily: he is on the short side, has a loud, abrasive voice, suffers from painful kidney stones, scratches his ears a lot (the insides itch), loves sauces, is not sure radishes agree with him, does his best thinking on horseback, prefers glass to metal cups, moves his bowels regularly in the morning, and so on. It is as if the self were a new continent, and Montaigne its first explorer.

Of course he had a little help: the spirit of humanism was in the air, via Erasmus and others, and the classical Greek and Roman authors were being used as a Trojan horse to open the gates to a freer, more speculative and self-analytical mentality (Socrates' "Know thyself"). Rabelais' great, bawdy novel, Gargantua and Pantagruel, likewise gave Montaigne license to write in support of pleasure and an integration of mind and body. Alongside an increase in classical learning and scientific knowledge, new worlds were literally being discovered. Explorers brought back reports of exotic native customs from the Americas and the Pacific, which fueled Montaigne's relativistic bent. Skeptical, undogmatic, and curious about difference (see "Of a Monstrous Child"), Montaigne was further persuaded of the need for tolerance by the civil war between Catholics and Protestants in his own back yard.

It was Montaigne's conviction that in spite of the range of human diversity, there is a basic unity to human experience: "Each man bears the entire form of man's estate." And if such is the case, then writing about oneself is not a private, narcissistic act but will strike a chord of grateful recognition in readers everywhere. Montaigne's unique talent for communicating himself proved the point: we now have thousands of verbal self-portraits in print, and few have inspired readers to identify themselves with the writer nearly as much as Montaigne's. Part of the reason for its success was Montaigne's ability to see himself as an average human being. Of course, he was scarcely average in intelligence and literary gifts. But he regarded the ups and downs and pleasures of his daily life as typical; he chose to write not in Latin, the learned language of the time, but in conversational, vernacular French; and he minimized his singular career (a valued diplomat used by kings, and twice mayor of Bordeaux), opting instead for a tone of ironic self-deprecation. This grew partly out of his view of the human condition.

Montaigne regarded humanity as constantly in flux, vain, ashamed of itself, and contradictory. Rather than condemning people, however, he recommended a generous self-forgiveness. He preferred not to aim so high (there is little of the mystical, transcendent, or tragic in this author) but to steer a middle course. His *thought evolved from an early expression of Stoicism* (including *the concern about dying well*) *to skepticism and eventually a brand of epicureanism (giving counsel on the art of living well).*

One of the most radical of Montaigne's practices was to follow his thoughts no matter where they led him. The result *conveyed the spontaneity of mental discovery,* on the one hand, and a heedless lack of structure, on the other. In "Of Books" and elsewhere, he made a case for the common reader, *the nonscholar,* who will simply say what he or she thinks about a book. His literary preferences were for Senecan conclusions rather than windy lead-ups, for language that is to the point, not bothering with elegance but "rough and contemptuous." His *own sentences were sinewy, dry, yet succulent; they* ✗ explode like pomegranate *seeds on the tongue.* Appending afterthoughts to his old essays in succeeding editions, Montaigne let digressions swell and complicate, even undercut, his earlier idea. Since there is little that is orderly and so much that is rewarding along the way, *the best way to approach Montaigne is to surrender to his approach and saturate yourself in his mind. He is one writer who becomes much easier to read, the more you read him.*

Montaigne is not always "politically correct," but he did have the courage to try to think things out for himself. Take his audacious essay "On Some Verses of Virgil," about sexuality, a somewhat forbidden topic at the time. A case could be made for Montaigne as either a proto-feminist, ahead of his day in insisting that men and women are not so different and opposing a double standard, or a male chauvinist, with a stereotypical idea of women as licentious and a cynical view of marriage. Certainly he was a man of his time, with all its prejudices, and should be read in a historical context. But *what is moving is his effort to enter the tangle and make his way through to* ✗ *what he actually thought about it, not what he was supposed to think.*

Montaigne's insistence that we ought first to look at our own personal experience—the book of life—and try to learn from it has been a powerful model for the world ever since. Montaigne had an especially strong influence on English literature, from the Elizabethans to the flowering of the English essay. It may help to situate his achievement if we see it as a crucial link in a chain of breakthroughs in human consciousness: the Essais *came out just a few years before Shakespeare's sonnets and plays on appearance and doubt; a decade or so before Cervantes' masterpiece of comic self-reference,* Don Quixote; *and a half-century before Pascal's rigorous, aphoristic* Pensées, *written partly under the spell of and partly in reply to Montaigne's seductive book.*

Of Books

I HAVE NO DOUBT that I often happen to speak of things that are better treated by the masters of the craft, and more truthfully. This is purely the essay of my natural faculties, and not at all of the acquired ones; and whoever shall catch me in ignorance will do nothing against me, for I should hardly be answerable for my ideas to others, I who am not answerable for them to myself, or satisfied with them. Whoever is in search of knowledge, let him fish for it where it dwells; there is nothing I profess less. These are my fancies, by which I try to give knowledge not of things, but of myself. The things will perhaps be known to me some day, or have been once, according as fortune may have brought me to the places where they were made clear. But I no longer remember them. And if I am a man of some reading, I am a man of no retentiveness.

Thus I guarantee no certainty, unless it be to make known to what point, at this moment, extends the knowledge that I have of myself. Let attention be paid not to the matter, but to the shape I give it.

Let people see in what I borrow whether I have known how to choose what would enhance my theme. For I make others say what I cannot say so well, now through the weakness of my language, now through the weakness of my understanding. I do not count my borrowings, I weigh them. And if I had wanted to have them valued by their number, I should have loaded myself with twice as many. They are all, or very nearly all, from such famous and ancient names that they seem to identify themselves enough without me. In the reasonings and inventions that I transplant into my soil and confound with my own, I have sometimes deliberately not indicated the author, in order to hold in check the temerity of those hasty condemnations that are tossed at all sorts of writings, notably recent writings of men still living, and in the vulgar tongue, which invites everyone to talk about them and seems to convict the conception and design of being likewise vulgar. I want them to give Plutarch a fillip on my nose and get burned insulting Seneca in me. I have to hide my weakness under these great authorities. I will love anyone that can unplume me, I mean by clearness of judgment and by the sole distinction of the force and beauty of the remarks. For I who, for lack of memory, fall short at every turn in picking them out by knowledge of their origin, can very well realize, by measuring my capacity, that my soil is not at all capable of producing certain too rich flowers that I find sown there, and that all the fruits of my own growing could not match them.

For this I am obliged to be responsible: if I get myself tangled up, if there is vanity and faultiness in my reasonings that I do not perceive or that I am not capable of perceiving when pointed out to me. For faults often escape our eyes; but infirmity of judgment consists in not being able to perceive them when another reveals them to us. Knowledge and truth can lodge in us without judgment, and judgment also without them; indeed the recognition of ignorance is one of the fairest and surest testimonies of judgment that I find.

I have no other marshal but fortune to arrange my bits. As my fancies present themselves, I pile them up; now they come pressing in a crowd, now dragging single file. I want people to see my natural and ordinary pace, however off the track it is. I let myself go as I am. Besides, these are not matters of which we are forbidden to be ignorant and to speak casually and at random.

I should certainly like to have a more perfect knowledge of things, but I do not want to buy it as dear as it costs. My intention is to pass pleasantly, and not laboriously, what life I have left. There is nothing for which I want to rack my brain, not even knowledge, however great its value.

I seek in books only to give myself pleasure by honest amusement; or if I study, I seek only the learning that treats of the knowledge of myself and instructs me in how to die well and live well:

This is the goal toward which my sweating horse should strain.

—PROPERTIUS

If I encounter difficulties in reading, I do not gnaw my nails over them; I leave them there, after making one or two attacks on them. If I planted myself in them, I would lose both myself and time; for I have an impulsive mind. What I do not see at the first attack, I see less by persisting. I do nothing without gaiety; continuation and too strong contention dazes, depresses, and wearies my judgment. My sight becomes confused and dispersed. I have to withdraw it and apply it again by starts, just as in order to judge the luster of a scarlet fabric, they tell us to pass our eyes over it several times, catching it in various quickly renewed and repeated glimpses.

If this book wearies me, I take up another; and I apply myself to it only at the moments when the boredom of doing nothing begins to grip me. I do not take much to modern books, because the ancient ones seem to me fuller and stronger; nor to those in Greek, because my judgment cannot do its work with a childish and apprentice understanding.

Among the books that are simply entertaining, I find, of the moderns, the *Decameron* of Boccaccio, Rabelais, and *The Kisses* of Johannes Secundus, if they may be placed under this heading, worth reading for amusement. As for the Amadises and writings of that sort, they did not have the authority to detain even my childhood. I will also say this, whether boldly or rashly, that this heavy old soul of mine no longer lets itself be tickled, not merely by Ariosto, but even by the good Ovid: his facility and inventions, which once enchanted me, hardly entertain me at all now.

I speak my mind freely on all things, even on those which perhaps exceed my capacity and which I by no means hold to be within my jurisdiction. And so the opinion I give of them is to declare the measure of my sight, not the measure of things. When I feel a distaste for Plato's *Axiochus* as a work without power considering such an author, my judgment does not trust itself: it is not so stupid as to oppose itself to the authority of so many other famous ancient judgments, which it considers its tutors and masters, and with which it is rather content to err. It blames and condemns itself either for stopping at the outer bark, not being able to penetrate to the heart, or for looking at the thing by some false light. It is content with simply securing itself from confusion and disorder; as for its weakness, it readily recognizes and admits it. It thinks it gives a correct interpretation to the appearances that its conception presents to it; but these are weak and imperfect.

Most of Aesop's Fables have many meanings and interpretations. Those who take them allegorically choose some aspect that squares with the fable, but for the most part this is only the first and superficial aspect; there are others more living, more essential and internal, to which they have not known how to penetrate; this is how I read them.

But, to pursue my path, it has always seemed to me that in poetry Virgil, Lucretius, Catullus, and Horace hold the first rank by very far, and especially Virgil in his *Georgics,* which I consider the most accomplished work in poetry; in comparison with it one can easily recognize that there are passages in the *Aeneid* which the author would have brushed up still a little more if he had had the chance. And the fifth book of the *Aeneid* seems to me the most perfect. I also love Lucan and enjoy his company, not so much for his style as for his own worth and the truth of his opinions and judgments. As for the good Terence, the very refinement and charm of the Latin language, I find him admirable at representing to the life the movements of the soul and the state of our characters; at every moment our actions throw me back to him. I cannot read him so often as not to find in him some new beauty and grace.

Those who lived near Virgil's time used to complain that some compared Lucretius to him. I am of the opinion that that is in truth an unequal comparison; but I have much to do to confirm myself in this belief when I find myself fixed on one of the beautiful passages in Lucretius. If they were stung by this comparison, what would they say of the barbarous brutishness and stupidity of those who nowadays compare Ariosto to him? And what would Ariosto himself say?

O foolish and dull-witted age!

—CATULLUS

I think the ancients had still more reason to complain of those who compared Plautus to Terence (the latter savors much more of the gentleman) than of those who compared Lucretius to Virgil. It does much for the esteem and preference of Terence that the father of Roman eloquence[1] has him, and him alone of his class, so often in his mouth; and also the verdict that the first judge among the Roman poets[2] gives of his fellow.

It has often struck my mind how in our time those who set themselves to write comedies (like the Italians, who are rather happy at it) use three or four plots from Terence or Plautus to make one of their own. They pile up in a single comedy five or six stories from Boccaccio. What makes them so load themselves with material is the distrust they have of being able to sustain themselves by their own graces; they have to find a body to lean on; and not having enough of their own to detain us, they want the story to amuse us. It is quite the contrary with my author: the perfections and beauties of his style of expression make us lose our appetite for his subject. His distinction and elegance hold us throughout; he is everywhere so delightful,

Clear flowing and most like a crystal stream,

—HORACE

and so fills our soul with his charms, that we forget those of his plot.

This same consideration draws me on further. I observe that the good ancient poets avoided the affectation and the quest, not only of the fantastic Spanish and Petrarchian flights, but even of the milder and more restrained conceits that are the adornment of all the poetic works of the succeeding centuries. Yet there is no good judge who misses them in those ancients, and who does not admire incomparably more the even polish and that perpetual sweetness and flowering beauty of Catullus' epigrams than all the stings with which Martial sharpens the tails of his. This is for

---

[1] Cicero.
[2] Horace.

the same reason that I was stating just now, as Martial says of himself: *he had less need for the labor of wit, since his subject matter took the place of wit.* The former, without getting excited and without goading themselves, make themselves sufficiently felt: they have matter enough for laughter everywhere, they don't have to tickle themselves. The latter need outside help: the less wit they have, the more body they need. They mount on horseback because they are not strong enough on their legs.

Just as at our balls these men of low condition who keep dancing schools, not being able to imitate the bearing and fitness of our nobility, seek to recommend themselves by perilous leaps and other strange mountebank's antics. And the ladies can more cheaply show off their carriage in the dances where there are various contortions and twistings of the body, than in certain other formal dances where they need only walk with a natural step and display a natural bearing and their ordinary grace. As I have also seen excellent clowns, in their ordinary dress and usual face, give us all the pleasure that can be derived from their art, while the apprentices and those who are not so highly skilled need to flour their faces, dress up, and counterfeit wild movements and grimaces in order to make us laugh.

This idea of mine is easier to recognize in the comparison of the *Aeneid* and the *Orlando Furioso* than anywhere else. We see the former on outspread wings in lofty and sustained flight always pursuing his point; the latter fluttering and hopping from tale to tale as from branch to branch, not trusting his wings except for a very short hop, and alighting at every turn for fear his breath and strength should fail:

> He tries his wings in short excursions.
>
> —VIRGIL

These, then, in this sort of subjects, are the authors I like best.

As for my other reading, which mingles a little more profit with the pleasure, and by which I learn to arrange my humors and my ways, the books that serve me for this are Plutarch, since he exists in French, and Seneca. They both have this notable advantage for my humor, that the knowledge I seek is there treated in detached pieces that do not demand the obligation of long labor, of which I am incapable. Such are the *Moral Essays* of Plutarch and the *Epistles* of Seneca, which are the finest part of his writings, and the most profitable. I need no great enterprise to get at them, and I leave them whenever I like. For they have no continuity from one to the other.

These authors agree in most of the opinions that are useful and true; and so were their fortunes similar: they were born at about the same time, each tutored a Roman Emperor, both came from foreign countries, both were rich and powerful. Their teaching is the cream of philosophy, and presented in simple and pertinent fashion. Plutarch is more uniform and constant, Seneca more undulating and diverse. The latter labors, strains, and tenses himself to arm virtue against weakness, fear, and vicious appetites; the other seems not to esteem their power so much, and to disdain to hurry his step or stand on guard for them. Plutarch's opinions are Platonic, mild, and accommodated to civil society; the other's are Stoic and Epicurean, more remote from common use, but in my opinion more suitable for private life and more sturdy. In Seneca it seems that he concedes a little to the tyranny of the emperors of his time, for I hold it for certain that it is by a forced judgment that he condemns the cause of those high-minded murderers of Caesar; Plutarch is free throughout. Seneca is full of witty points and sallies, Plutarch of things. The former heats you and moves you more; the latter contents you more and pays you better. He guides us, the other pushes us.

As for Cicero, the works of his that can best serve my purpose are those that treat of philosophy, especially moral. But to confess the truth boldly (for once you have crossed over the barriers of impudence there is no more curb), his way of writing, and every other similar way, seems to me boring. For his prefaces, definitions, partitions, etymologies, consume the greater part of his work; what life and marrow there is, is smothered by his long-winded preparations. If I have spent an hour in reading him, which is a lot for me, and I remember what juice and substance I have derived, most of the time I find nothing but wind; for he has not yet come to the arguments that serve his purpose and the reasons that properly touch on the crux, which I am looking for.

For me, who ask only to become wiser, not more learned or eloquent, these logical and Aristotelian arrangements are not to the point. I want a man to begin with the conclusion. I understand well enough what death and pleasure are; let him not waste his time anatomizing them. I look for good solid reasons from the start, which will instruct me in how to sustain their attack. Neither grammatical subtleties nor an ingenious contexture of words and argumentations are any use for that. I want reasonings that drive their first attack into the stronghold of the doubt; his languish around the pot. They are good for the school, for the bar, and for the sermon, where we have leisure to nap and are still in time a quarter of an hour later to pick up the thread of the discourse. It is necessary to speak thus to judges, whom we want to win over rightly or wrongly, to children, and to the common herd, to whom we have to say everything to see what will carry.

I do not want a man to use his strength making me attentive and to shout at me fifty times *"Or oyez!"* in the manner of our heralds. The

Romans used to say in their religion *"Hoc age,"* as we say in ours *"Sursum corda".*³ these are so many words lost on me. I come fully prepared from my house; I need no allurement or sauce; I can perfectly well eat my meat quite raw; and instead of whetting my appetite by these preparations and preliminaries, they pall and weary it.

Will the license of the times excuse my sacrilegious audacity in considering that even Plato's dialogues drag and stifle his substance too much, and in lamenting the time put into these long vain preliminary interlocutions by a man who had so many better things to say? My ignorance will excuse me better in that I have no perception of the beauty of his language. In general I ask for books that make use of learning, not those that build it up.

The first two, and Pliny, and their like, have no *Hoc age;* they want to have to do with men who themselves have told themselves this; or if they have one, it is a substantial *Hoc age* that has a body of its own.

I also like to read the *Letters to Atticus,*⁴ not only because they contain a very ample education in the history and affairs of his time, but much more because in them I discover his personal humors. For I have a singular curiosity, as I have said elsewhere, to know the soul and the natural judgments of my authors. We must indeed judge their capacity, but not their character nor themselves, by that display of their writings that they expose on the stage of the world. I have regretted a thousand times that we have lost the book that Brutus had written on virtue: for it is a fine thing to learn the theory from those who well know the practice. But since the preachings are one thing and the preacher another, I am as glad to see Brutus in Plutarch as in a book of his own. I would rather choose to know truly the conversation he held in his tent with some one of his intimate friends on the eve of a battle than the speech he made the next day to his army; and what he was doing in his study and his chamber than what he was doing in the public square and in the Senate.

As for Cicero, I am of the common opinion, that except for learning there was not much excellence in his soul. He was a good citizen, of an affable nature, as all fat jesting men, such as he was, are apt to be; but of softness and ambitious vanity he had in truth a great deal. And moreover I do not know how to excuse him for having considered his poetry worth being published. It is not a great imperfection to write verses badly; but it is a lack of judgment in him not to have felt how unworthy they were of the glory of his name. As for his eloquence, it is entirely beyond comparison; I believe that no man will ever equal him.

---

³ *"Or oyez"*—"Now listen." *"Hoc age"*—"Give heed." *"Sursum corda"*—"Lift up your hearts."
⁴ By Cicero.

The younger Cicero, who resembled his father only in name, while commanding in Asia, had several strangers at his table one day, and among others Cestius, seated at the lower end, as people often push in to the open tables of the great. Cicero inquired who he was of one of his men, who told him his name. But like a man whose thoughts were elsewhere and who kept forgetting what they answered him, he asked him that again two or three more times. The servant, in order not to have the trouble of repeating the same thing so often to him, and to make him know him by some circumstance, said to him: "It is that Cestius of whom you were told that he sets no great store by your father's eloquence in comparison with his own." Cicero, suddenly stung by this, ordered them to lay hold of this poor Cestius and had him very soundly whipped in his presence. That was a discourteous host!

Even among those who, all things considered, esteemed this eloquence of his as incomparable, there were some who did not fail to note some faults in it; thus the great Brutus, his friend, used to say that it was a broken and weak-loined eloquence, *fractam et elumbem*. The orators who lived near his time also reprehended in him his sedulous care for a certain long cadence at the end of his periods, and noted the words *esse videatur*[5] which he uses so often. As for me, I prefer a cadence that falls shorter, cut into iambics. To be sure, he does sometimes mix up his rhythms quite roughly, but rarely. My ears have noted this passage: "Ego vero me minus diu senem esse mallem, quam esse senem, antequam essem."[6]

The historians come right to my forehand. They are pleasant and easy; and at the same time, man in general, the knowledge of whom I seek, appears in them more alive and entire than in any other place—the diversity and truth of his inner qualities in the mass and in detail, the variety of the ways he is put together, and the accidents that threaten him. Now those who write biographies, since they spend more time on plans than on events, more on what comes from within than on what happens without, are most suited to me. That is why in every way Plutarch is my man. I am very sorry that we do not have a dozen Laertiuses, or that he is not either more receptive or more perceptive. For I consider no less curiously the fortunes and the lives of these great teachers of the world than the diversity of their doctrines and fancies.

In this kind of study of history we must leaf without distinction through all sorts of authors, both old and new, both gibberish and French, in order to learn in them the things of which they variously treat. But it seems to me that Caesar singularly deserves to be studied, not only for the knowledge of history, but for himself, so much perfection and excellence

---

[5] "It would seem to be."
[6] "For my part, in truth, I would rather be old less long than be old before I am old."

he has above all the others, although Sallust is one of their number. Indeed I read this author with a little more reverence and respect than one reads human works: now considering him in himself by his actions and the miracle of his greatness, now the purity and inimitable polish of his language, which surpassed not only all the historians, as Cicero says, but perhaps Cicero himself. With so much sincerity in his judgments when speaking of his enemies, that except for the false colors with which he tries to cover his evil cause and the filthiness of his pestilential ambition, I think the only fault that can be found in him is that he has been too sparing in speaking of himself. For so many great things cannot have been performed by him without much more of himself having gone into them than he sets down.

I like historians who are either very simple or outstanding. The simple, who have not the wherewithal to mix in anything of their own, and who bring to it only the care and diligence to collect all that comes to their attention and to record everything faithfully without choice or discrimination, leave our judgment intact to discern the truth. Such, for example, among others, is the good Froissart, who has gone along in his undertaking with such frank simplicity that having made a mistake he is not at all afraid to recognize it and correct it at the spot where he has been made aware of it; and who presents to us even the diversity of the rumors that were current and the different reports that were made to him. This is the material of history, naked and unformed; each man can make his profit of it according to his understanding.

The really outstanding ones have the capacity to choose what is worth knowing; they can pick out of two reports the one that is more likely. From the nature and humors of princes they infer their intentions and attribute appropriate words to them. They are right to assume the authority to regulate our belief by their own; but certainly this privilege belongs to very few people.

Those in between (which are the commonest sort) spoil everything for us. They want to chew our morsels for us; they give themselves the right to judge, and consequently to slant history to their fancy; for once the judgment leans to one side, one cannot help turning and twisting the narrative to that bias. They undertake to choose the things worth knowing, and often conceal from us a given word, a given private action, that would instruct us better; they omit as incredible the things they do not understand, and perhaps also some things because they do not know how to say them in good Latin or French. Let them boldly display their eloquence and their reasonings, let them judge all they like; but let them also leave us the wherewithal to judge after them, and not alter or arrange by their abridgements and selection anything of the substance of the matter, but pass it on to us pure and entire in all its dimensions.

Most of the time, especially in these days, people are selected for this work from among the common herd for the sole consideration of knowing how to speak well; as if here we were trying to learn grammar! And having been hired only for that and having put on sale only their babble, they are right accordingly to care chiefly only about that part. Thus with many fine words they go and cook up a fine concoction of the rumors they pick up in the city squares.

The only good histories are those that have been written by the very men who were in command in the affairs, or who were participants in the conduct of them, or who at least have had the fortune to conduct others of the same sort. Such are almost all the Greek and Roman histories. For when several eyewitnesses have written about the same subject (as it happened in those days that greatness and learning usually met), if there is a mistake, it must be very slight, and on a very doubtful incident. What can you expect of a doctor discussing war, or a schoolboy discussing the intentions of princes? If we want to note the scruples the Romans had in this, we need only this example. Asinius Pollio found in the histories even of Caesar some mistake into which he had fallen through not having been able to keep his eyes on every part of his army and having believed individuals who often reported to him things insufficiently verified; or else through not having been carefully enough informed by his lieutenants about what they had done in his absence. We can see by this example whether this quest of truth is delicate, when we cannot trust the commander's knowledge of a battle his soldiers have fought, or the soldiers' knowledge of what happened near them, unless, in the manner of a judicial inquiry, we confront the witnesses and hear the objections about the evidence in the slightest details of each incident. Truly, the knowledge we have of our own affairs is much looser. But this has been sufficiently treated by Bodin, and according to my way of thinking.

To compensate a little for the treachery and weakness of my memory, so extreme that it has happened to me more than once to pick up again, as recent and unknown to me, books which I had read carefully a few years before and scribbled over with my notes, I have adopted the habit for some time now of adding at the end of each book (I mean of those that I intend to use only once) the time I finished reading it and the judgment I have derived of it as a whole, so that this may represent to me at least the sense and general idea I had conceived of the author in reading it. I want to transcribe here some of these annotations.

Here is what I put some ten years ago in my Guicciardini (for whatever language my books speak, I speak to them in my own): "He is a diligent historiographer from whom, in my opinion, one can learn the truth about the affairs of his time as exactly as from any other: and indeed in most of them he was an actor himself, and of honorable rank. There is no appearance that through hatred, favor, or vanity, he disguised things; which is attested by the free judgments he gives of the great, and especially of those by whom he had been advanced and employed in responsibilities, like Pope Clement VII. As for the part he seems to want to make most of, which is his digressions and discourses, there are some good ones and enriched with fine traits, but he is too fond of them. For by not wanting to leave anything unsaid, having a subject so full and ample and almost infinite, he becomes diffuse and smacking a bit of scholastic prattle. I have also noted this, that of so many souls and actions that he judges, so many motives and plans, he never refers a single one to virtue, religion, and conscience, as if these qualities were wholly extinct in the world; and of all actions, however fair in appearance they may be of themselves, he throws the cause back onto some vicious motive or some profit. It is impossible to imagine that among the infinite number of actions that he judges there was not a single one produced by the way of reason. No corruption can have seized men so universally that someone would not escape the contagion. This makes me fear that his taste was a bit corrupted; and it may have happened that he judged others by himself."

In my Philippe de Commines there is this: "Here you will find the language pleasant and agreeable, of a natural simplicity; the narrative pure, and the author's good faith showing through it clearly, free from vanity in speaking of himself, and of partiality ór envy in speaking of others; his ideas and exhortations accompanied more by good zeal and truth than by any exquisite capacity; and, throughout, authority and gravity, representing the man of good background and brought up in great affairs."

On the *Memoirs* of Monsieur du Bellay:[7] "It is always a pleasure to see things written by people who have experienced how they should be conducted; but it cannot be denied that there is clearly revealed in these two lords a great falling off from the frankness and freedom of writing that shine forth in the ancients of their class, such as the sire de Joinville, intimate friend of Saint Louis; Eginhard, chancellor of Charlemagne; and, of more recent memory, Philippe de Commines. This is rather a plea for King Francis against the Emperor Charles V, than a history. I will not believe that they have changed anything in the main facts; but as for turning the judgment of events to our advantage, often contrary to reason, and omitting everything that is ticklish in the life of their master, they make a practice of it: witness the disgrace of Messieurs de Montmorency and de Brion, which are forgotten; indeed the very name of Madame d'Etampes is not to be found. One may cover up secret actions; but to be silent about

---

[7] These *Memoirs,* which cover the years 1513–47 and were first published in 1569, are presented by Martin du Bellay but include three books (out of ten) by his brother Guillaume du Bellay, seigneur de Langey. This explains Montaigne's reference to "these two lords."

what all the world knows, and about things that have led to public results of such consequence, is an inexcusable defect. In short, to get a complete knowledge of King Francis and the events of his time, a man should turn elsewhere, if he takes my advice. The profit one can make here is from the detailed narrative of the battles and exploits of war at which these gentlemen were present; some private words and actions of certain princes of their time; and the dealings and negotiations carried on by the seigneur de Langey, in which there are plenty of things worth knowing, and ideas above the ordinary."

Of a Monstrous Child

THIS STORY WILL GO ITS WAY SIMPLY, for I leave it to the doctors to discuss it. The day before yesterday I saw a child that two men and a nurse, who said they were the father, uncle, and aunt, were leading about to get a penny or so from showing him, because of his strangeness. In all other respects he was of ordinary shape; he could stand on his feet, walk, and prattle, about like others of the same age. He had not yet been willing to take any other nourishment than from his nurse's breast; and what they tried to put in his mouth in my presence he chewed on a little and spat it out without swallowing. There seemed indeed to be something peculiar about his cries. He was just fourteen months old.

Below the breast he was fastened and stuck to another child, without a head, and with his spinal canal stopped up, the rest of his body being entire. For indeed one arm was shorter, but it had been broken by accident at their birth. They were joined face to face, and as if a smaller child were trying to embrace a bigger one around the neck. The juncture and the space where they held together was only four fingers' breadth or thereabouts, so that if you turned the imperfect child over and up, you saw the other's navel below; thus the connection was in between the nipples and the navel. The navel of the imperfect child could not be seen, but all the rest of his belly could. In this way all of this imperfect child that was not attached, as the arms, buttocks, thighs, and legs, remained hanging and dangling on the other and might reach halfway down his legs. The nurse also told us that he urinated from both places. Moreover the limbs of this other were nourished and living and in the same condition as his own, except that they were smaller and thinner.

This double body and these several limbs, connected with a single head, might well furnish a favorable prognostic to the king that he will maintain under the union of his laws these various parts and factions of our state. But for fear the event should belie it, it is better to let it go its way, for there is nothing like divining about things past. *So that, when things have happened, by some interpretation they are found to have been prophesied* [Cicero]. As they said of Epimenides that he prophesied backward.

I have just seen a shepherd in Médoc, thirty years old or thereabouts, who has no sign of genital parts. He has three holes by which he continually makes water. He is bearded, has desire, and likes to touch women.

What we call monsters are not so to God, who sees in the immensity of his work the infinity of forms that he has comprised in it; and it is for us to believe that this figure that astonishes us is related and linked to some other figure of the same kind unknown to man. From his infinite wisdom there proceeds nothing but that is good and ordinary and regular; but we do not see its arrangement and relationship. *What he sees often, he does not wonder at, even if he does not know why it is. If something happens which he has not seen before, he thinks it is a prodigy* [Cicero].

We call contrary to nature what happens contrary to custom; nothing is anything but according to nature, whatever it may be. Let this universal and natural reason drive out of us the error and astonishment that novelty brings us.

On Some Verses of Virgil

T O T H E E X T E N T that useful thoughts are fuller and more solid, they are also more absorbing and more burdensome. Vice, death, poverty, disease, are grave subjects and grieve us. We should have our soul instructed in the means to sustain and combat evils, and in the rules for right living and right belief, and should often arouse it and exercise it in this fine study. But for a soul of the common sort this must be done with some respite and with moderation; it goes mad if it is too continually tense.

In my youth I needed to warn and urge myself to stick to my duty: blitheness and health do not go so well, they say, with these wise and serious reflections. At present I am in another state. The conditions of old age warn me, sober me, and preach to me only too much. From an excess of gaiety I have fallen into an excess of severity, which is more disagreeable. Wherefore at this point I deliberately let myself go a bit to license and sometimes occupy my soul with youthful wanton thoughts to give it a rest. Henceforth I shall be only too sedate, too heavy, and too mature. The years lecture me every day in coldness and temperance. This body of mine flees disorder and fears it. It is my body's turn to guide my mind toward reform. It dominates in turn, and more roughly and imperiously. It does not leave me a single hour, sleeping or waking, unoccupied with instruction about death, patience, and penitence. I defend myself against temperance as I once did against sensual pleasure; for it pulls me too far back, even to the point of insensibility.

Now I want to be master of myself in every direction. Wisdom has its excesses, and has no less need of moderation than does folly. Thus, for fear I may dry up, wither, and grow heavy with prudence, in the intervals that my ills grant me—

> Lest my mind dwell too much upon its ills
>
> —OVID

—I very gently sidestep and avert my gaze from this stormy and cloudy sky that I have in front of me, which, thank God, I do indeed consider without fright, but not without effort and study, and I amuse myself in the remembrance of my past youth:

> The soul craves what it has lost,
> And wholly throws itself into the past.
>
> —PETRONIUS

Let childhood look ahead, old age backward: was not this the meaning of the double face of Janus? Let the years drag me along if they will, but backward. As long as my eyes can discern that lovely season now expired, I turn them in that direction at intervals. If youth is escaping from my blood and my veins, at least I want not to uproot the picture of it from my memory:

Our lives are two
If we can relish our past life anew.

—MARTIAL

Plato orders men to attend the exercises, dances, and games of youth, in order to rejoice in others at the suppleness and beauty of body that is no longer in themselves, and to call to mind the grace and charm of that flowering age; and he wants them to attribute the honor of victory in these sports to the young man who has most exhilarated and delighted the greatest number of them.

Once I used to mark the burdensome and gloomy days as extraordinary. Those are now my ordinary ones; the extraordinary are the fine serene ones. I am on my way to the point where I will leap for joy as at a novel favor when nothing pains me. Though I tickle myself, I can scarcely wring a poor laugh out of this wretched body any more. I am merry only in fancy and in dreams, to divert by trickery the gloom of old age. But indeed it would require another remedy than a dream: a feeble struggle, that of art against nature. It is great simplicity to lengthen and anticipate human discomforts, as everyone does. I would rather be old less long than be old before I am old. Even the slightest occasions of pleasure that I can come upon, I seize. I know indeed by hearsay several kinds of pleasures that are prudent, strong, and glorious; but opinion has not enough power over me to give me an appetite for them. I do not so much want them noble, magnificent, and ostentatious, as sweet, easy, and ready at hand. *We depart from nature; we give ourselves up to the people, who are not a good guide in anything* [Seneca].

My philosophy is in action, in natural and present practice, little in fancy. Would I might take pleasure in playing at cobnut or with a top!

He set not people's shouts before the public safety.

—ENNIUS, QUOTED BY CICERO

Pleasure is a rather unambitious quality. It thinks itself rich enough in itself without adding the prize of reputation, and prefers to be in the shade. We should take the whip to a young man who spent his time discriminating between the taste of wines and sauces. There is nothing I ever knew less or valued less than this. At present I am learning it. I am much ashamed of it, but what should I do? I am still more ashamed and vexed at the circumstances that drive me to it. It is for us to trifle and play the fool, and for the young to stand on their reputation and in the best place. They are going toward the world, toward reputation; we are coming from it. *Let them have to themselves weapons, horses, spears, clubs, ball games, swimming, and races; let them leave to us old men, out of many sports, dice and knuckle-bones* [Cicero].

The laws themselves send us home. I can do no less, on behalf of this puny condition into which my age pushes me, than furnish it with toys and pastimes, like childhood: and into that indeed we are falling back. Both wisdom and folly will have all they can do to support me and help me by their alternate services in this calamity of old age:

> *Mingle a dash of folly with your wisdom.*
>
> —HORACE

Likewise I flee the slightest pains; and those that formerly would not even have scratched me, now pierce me through and through: so easily is my habit of body beginning to apply itself to illness. *To a frail body every pain is intolerable* [Cicero].

> *And nothing that is hard can a sick mind endure.*
>
> —OVID

I have always been sensitive and susceptible to pain; now I am still more tender, and exposed on all sides:

> *Anything cracked will shatter at a touch.*
>
> —OVID

My judgment keeps me indeed from kicking and grumbling against the discomforts that nature orders me to suffer, but not from feeling them. I, who have no other aim but to live and be merry, would run from one end of the world to the other to seek out one good year of pleasant and cheerful tranquillity. A somber, dull tranquillity is easy enough to find for me, but it puts me to sleep and stupefies me; I am not content with it. If there are any persons, any good company, in country or city, in France or elsewhere, residing or traveling, who like my humors and whose humors I like, they have only to whistle in their palm and I will go furnish them with essays in flesh and bone.

Since it is the privilege of the mind to rescue itself from old age, I advise mine to do so as strongly as I can. Let it grow green, let it flourish meanwhile, if it can, like mistletoe on a dead tree. But I fear it is a traitor. It has such a tight brotherly bond with the body that it abandons me at every turn to follow the body in its need. I take it aside and flatter it, I work on it, all for nothing. In vain I try to turn it aside from this bond, I offer it

Seneca and Catullus, and the ladies and the royal dances; if its companion
has the colic, it seems to have it too. Even the activities that are peculiarly
its own cannot then be aroused; they evidently smack of a cold in the
head. There is no sprightliness in its productions if there is none in the
body at the same time.

Our masters are wrong in that, seeking the causes of the extraordinary
flights of our soul, they have attributed some to a divine ecstasy, to love, to
warlike fierceness, to poetry, to wine, but have not assigned a proper share
to health—an ebullient, vigorous, full, lazy health, such as in the past my
green years and security supplied me with now and then. The blaze of
gaiety kindles in the mind vivid, bright flashes beyond our natural capacity, and some of the lustiest, if not the most extravagant, enthusiasms.

Now then, it is no wonder if a contrary state weighs down my spirits,
nails them down, and produces a contrary effect.

> *Drooping with the body, it rises to no task.*
>
> —MAXIMIANUS

Moreover, my mind wants me to be grateful to it because, so it says, it
concedes much less to this bond than is usual with most men. At least,
while we have a truce, let us banish troubles and difficulties from our
relations:

> *So while we may, let's banish wrinkle-fronted age;*
>
> —HORACE

gloomy things should be lightened with pleasantries [Sidonius Apolinaris].

I love a gay and sociable wisdom, and shun harshness and austerity in
behavior, holding every surly countenance suspect:

> *The sullen arrogance of a gloomy face.*
>
> —BUCHANAN

> *That sad group also has its sodomites.*
>
> —MARTIAL

I heartily agree with Plato when he says that an easy or a difficult humor
is of great importance to the goodness or badness of the soul. Socrates had
a settled expression, but serene and smiling, not settled like that of old
Crassus, who was never seen to laugh. Virtue is a pleasant and gay quality.

I know well that very few people will frown at the license of my writings
who do not have more to frown at in the license of their thoughts. I

conform well to their hearts, but I offend their eyes. It is a well-ordered humor that criticizes Plato's writings and glides over his supposed relations with Phaedo, Dion, Stella, and Archeanassa. *Let us not be ashamed to say what we are not ashamed to think* [author unknown].

I hate a surly and gloomy spirit that slides over the pleasures of life and seizes and feeds upon its misfortunes: like flies, which cannot cling to a smooth and well-polished body, and attach themselves to and rest on rough and uneven places, and like leeches that suck and crave only bad blood.

Furthermore, I have ordered myself to dare to say all that I dare to do, and I dislike even thoughts that are unpublishable. The worst of my actions and conditions does not seem to me so ugly as the cowardice of not daring to avow it. Everyone is discreet in confession; people should be so in action. Boldness in sinning is somewhat compensated and bridled by boldness in confessing. Whoever would oblige himself to tell all, would oblige himself not to do anything about which we are constrained to keep silent. God grant that this excessive license of mine may encourage our men to attain freedom, rising above these cowardly and hypocritical virtues born of our imperfections; that at the expense of my immoderation I may draw them on to the point of reason. A man must see his vice and study it to tell about it. Those who hide it from others ordinarily hide it from themselves. And they do not consider it covered up enough if they themselves see it; they withdraw and disguise it from their own conscience. *Why does no one confess his vices? Because he is still in their grip now; it is only for a waking man to tell his dream* [Seneca].

The diseases of the body become clearer as they increase. We find that what we were calling a cold or a sprain is the gout. The diseases of the soul grow more obscure as they grow stronger; the sickest man is least sensible of them. That is why they must be handled often in the light of day, with a pitiless hand, be opened up and torn from the hollow of our breast. As in the matter of good deeds, so in the matter of evil deeds, mere confession is sometimes reparation. Is there any ugliness in doing wrong that can dispense us from the duty of confessing it?

It is painful for me to dissemble, so much so that I avoid taking others' secrets into my keeping, not really having the heart to disavow what I know. I can keep silent about it, but deny it I cannot without effort and displeasure. To be really secret a man must be so by nature, not by obligation. In the service of princes it is a small thing to be secret if one is not a liar to boot. If the man who was asking Thales the Milesian whether he should solemnly deny having committed adultery had asked me, I would have answered him that he should not do it, for lying seems to me even worse than adultery. Thales advised him quite differently: to swear to his innocence, so as to shield the greater fault by the lesser. However, this advice was not so much a choice as a multiplication of vices.

Whereupon let us say this word in passing, that we offer a good bargain to a man of conscience when we propose to him some difficulty as a counterpoise to vice. But when we shut him up between two vices, we put him to a rough choice, as they did to Origen: that he should either worship an idol or endure being carnally enjoyed by a big ugly Ethiopian who was brought before him. he submitted to the first condition, and sinfully, it is said. On this basis those women would not be wrong who protest to us these days, according to their error,[1] that they would rather burden their conscience with ten men than with one Mass.

If it is indiscretion to publish one's errors thus, there is no great danger that it will pass into an example and custom. For Aristo used to say that the words men fear most are those that uncover them. We must tuck up this stupid rag that covers our conduct. They send their conscience to the brothel and keep their countenance in good order. Even those who are traitors and assassins espouse the laws of ceremony and fix their duty there. Yet it is not for injustice to complain of indecorum, or malice of indiscretion. It is a pity that a wicked man is not also a fool, and that outward decency should palliate his vice. These decorative incrustations belong only to a good, healthy wall that deserves to be preserved or whitened.

In honor of the Huguenots, who condemn our private and auricular confession, I confess myself in public, religiously and purely. Saint Augustine, Origen, and Hippocrates have published the errors of their opinions; I, besides, those of my conduct. I am hungry to make myself known, and I care not to how many, provided it be truly. Or to put it better, I am hungry for nothing, but I have a mortal fear of being taken to be other than I am by those who come to know my name.

A man who does everything for honor and glory, what does he think to gain by presenting himself to the world in a mask, concealing his true being from public knowledge? Praise a hunchback for his handsome figure, and he is bound to take it as an insult. If you are a coward and people honor you as a valiant man, is it you they are talking about? They take you for another. I would just as soon have such a man find gratification in having people doff their hat to him, thinking that he is master of the troop, when he is one of the meanest of the retinue.

As Archelaus, king of Macedonia, was passing in the street, someone poured some water on him. Those with him said he should punish the man. "Yes," he said, "but he did not pour water on me, but on the man he thought I was." Socrates said to the man who informed him that people were speaking ill of him: "Not at all; there is nothing in me of what they say."

As for me, if someone praised me for being a good pilot, for being very

_____

[1] Protestantism.

modest, or for being very chaste, I would owe him no thanks. And similarly if someone called me traitor, robber, or drunkard, I would consider myself offended just as little. Those who have a false opinion of themselves can feed on false approbations; not I, who see myself and search myself to my very entrails, who know well what belongs to me. I am pleased to be less praised, provided I am better known. I might be considered wise with the kind of wisdom I consider folly.

I am annoyed that my essays serve the ladies only as a public article of furniture, an article for the parlor. This chapter will put me in the boudoir. I like their society when it is somewhat private; when public, it is without favor or savor.

In farewells we exaggerate the warmth of our affection toward the things we are leaving. I am taking my last leave of the world's pastimes; here are our last embraces. But let us come to my theme.

What has the sexual act, so natural, so necessary, and so just, done to mankind, for us not to dare talk about it without shame and for us to exclude it from serious and decent conversation? We boldly pronounce the words "kill," "rob," "betray"; and this one we do not dare pronounce, except between our teeth. Does this mean that the less we breathe of it in words, the more we have the right to swell our thoughts with it?

For it is a good one that the words least in use, least written and most hushed up, are the best known and most generally familiar. No age, no type of character, is ignorant of them, any more than of the word "bread." They impress themselves on everyone without being expressed, without voice and without form. It is also a good one that this is an action that we have placed in the sanctuary of silence, from which it is a crime to drag it out even to accuse and judge it. Nor do we dare to chastise it except roundaboutly and figuratively. A great favor for a criminal, to be so execrable that justice deems it unjust to touch and see him: free and saved by virtue of the severity of his condemnation.

Is it not the same as in the matter of books, which become all the more marketable and public by being suppressed? For my part I am going to take Aristotle at his word when he says that bashfulness serves as an ornament to youth but a reproach to old age.

These verses are preached in the ancient school, a school I adhere to much more than to the modern; its virtues seem to me greater, its vices less:

> *Those who flee Venus too much sin no less*
> *Than those who do pursue her to excess.*

> —AMYOT'S PLUTARCH

Thou, goddess, thou alone rul'st over everything;
Without thee nothing rises to the light of day;
Nothing becomes, without thee, lovable or gay.

—LUCRETIUS

I do not know who can have put Pallas and the Muses on bad terms with Venus and made them cold toward Love; but I know no deities better suited or more indebted to one another. Whoever takes away from the Muses their amorous fancies will rob them of the best subject they have and the noblest matter of their work. And whoever makes Love lose the communication and service of poetry will disarm him of his best weapons. In this way they charge the god of intimacy and affection, and the patron goddesses of humanity and justice, with the vice of ingratitude and lack of appreciation.

I have not been so long cashiered from the roll and retinue of this god as not to have a memory informed of his powers and merits:

I know the traces of the ancient flame.

—VIRGIL

There is still some remnant of heat and emotion after the fever:

In wintry years, let me not lack this heat.

—JOHANNES SECUNDUS

Dried out and weighed down as I am, I still feel some tepid remains of that past ardor:

As the Aegean, when those winds have died
Which only lately made it churn and leap,
Does not at once grow calm, or put aside
The roar and violence of the raging deep.

—TASSO

But from what I understand of it, the powers and worth of this god are more alive and animated in the painting of poetry than in their own reality,

And verses have their fingers to excite.

—JUVENAL

Poetry reproduces an indefinable mood that is more amorous than love itself. Venus is not so beautiful all naked, alive, and panting, as she is here in Virgil:

> *The goddess ceased to speak, and snowy arms outflung*
> *Around him faltering, soft fondling as she clung.*
> *He quickly caught the wonted flame; the heat well-known*
> *Entered his marrow, ran through every trembling bone.*
> *Often a brilliant lightning flash, not otherwise,*
> *Split by a thunderclap, runs through the cloudy skies.*
>   *He spoke,*
> *Gave the embraces that she craved; then on her breast,*
> *Outpoured at last, gave himself up to sleep and rest.*

—VIRGIL

What I find worth considering here is that he portrays her as a little too passionate for a marital Venus. In this sober contract the appetites are not so wanton; they are dull and more blunted. Love hates people to be attached to each other except by himself, and takes a laggard part in relations that are set up and maintained under another title, as marriage is. Connections and means have, with reason, as much weight in it as graces and beauty, or more. We do not marry for ourselves, whatever we say; we marry just as much or more for our posterity, for our family. The practice and benefit of marriage concerns our race very far beyond us. Therefore I like this fashion of arranging it rather by a third hand than by our own, and by the sense of others rather than by our own. How opposite is all this to the conventions of love! And so it is a kind of incest to employ in this venerable and sacred alliance the efforts and extravagances of amorous license, as it seems to me I have said elsewhere.[2] A man, says Aristotle, should touch his wife prudently and soberly, lest if he caresses her too lasciviously the pleasure should transport her outside the bounds of reason. What he says on account of conscience, the doctors say on account of health: that an excessively hot, voluptuous, and assiduous pleasure spoils the seed and hinders conception. They say, on the other hand, that for a languid encounter, as this one is by its nature, we should present ourselves rarely and at considerable intervals, to fill it with a just and fertile heat:

> *Athirst to take the member in and hide it deep.*

—VIRGIL

---

[2] Essays I:30, "Of Moderation."

I see no marriages that sooner are troubled and fail than those that progress by means of beauty and amorous desires. It needs more solid and stable foundations, and we need to go at it circumspectly; this ebullient ardor is no good for it.

Those who think to honor marriage by joining love to it act, it seems to me, the same as those who, to favor virtue, hold that nobility is nothing else but virtue. These are things that have a certain relationship, but there is a great difference between them. There is no point in mixing up their names and titles; we wrong one or the other by confusing them. Nobility is a fine quality, and introduced with reason. But inasmuch as it is a quality dependent on others, and which can fall to a vicious and worthless man, it is well below virtue in esteem. It is a virtue, if indeed it is one, that is artificial and visible, dependent upon time and fortune, varying in form according to countries, living and mortal, with no more source than the river Nile, genealogical and common to many, a matter of succession and resemblance, derived by inference, and a very weak inference at that. Knowledge, strength, goodness, beauty, riches, all other qualities, fall into the range of communication and association; this one is self-consuming, of no use in the service of others.

One of our kings was proposed the choice between two competitors for the same office, one of whom was a nobleman, the other was not. He ordered that they choose, without regard to this quality, the one who had the more merit; but that if the worth should be entirely equal, they should then take nobility into account. That was giving it exactly its proper place. Antigonus said to a young stranger who was asking him for the post of his father, a man of valor who had just died: "My friend, in such benefits I do not consider so much the nobility of my soldiers as I do their prowess." In truth, it should not go as it did with the functionaries of the kings of Sparta, trumpeters, minstrels, cooks, whose duties were inherited by their children, no matter how ignorant they were, in preference to the most experienced men in the trade.

The people of Calicut make of their nobles a superhuman species. Marriage is forbidden them, and every other occupation but war. Of concubines they may have their fill, and the women as many lovers, without jealousy toward one another; but it is a capital and unpardonable crime to mate with a person of another condition than their own. And they consider themselves polluted if they are so much as touched by them in passing, and, as their nobility is marvelously injured and damaged by this, they kill those who have merely approached a little too close to them; so that the ignoble are obliged to cry out as they walk, like the gondoliers in Venice at the street corners, to avoid collisions; and the nobles command them to move aside in the direction they want. Thereby the nobles avoid an ignominy that they consider perpetual; and the others, a certain death. No length of time, no princely favor, no office or virtue or riches can make a commoner become a noble. In which this custom helps, that marriages are forbidden between one trade and another. A girl from a shoemaker's family cannot marry a carpenter. And the parents are obliged to train their children exactly for the father's calling and not for any other; whereby the distinction and continuity of their fortune is maintained.

A good marriage, if such there be, rejects the company and conditions of love. It tries to reproduce those of friendship. It is a sweet association in life, full of constancy, trust, and an infinite number of useful and solid services and mutual obligations. No woman who savors the taste of it,

Whom the nuptial torch with welcome light has joined,

—CATULLUS

would want to have the place of a mistress or paramour to her husband. If she is lodged in his affection as a wife, she is lodged there much more honorably and securely. When he dances ardent and eager attention elsewhere, still let anyone ask him then on whom he would rather have some shame fall, on his wife or his mistress; whose misfortune would afflict him more; for whom he wishes more honor. These questions admit of no doubt in a sound marriage.

The fact that we see so few good marriages is a sign of its price and its value. If you form it well and take it rightly, there is no finer relationship in our society. We cannot do without it, and yet we go about debasing it. The result is what is observed about cages: the birds outside despair of getting in, and those inside are equally anxious to get out. Socrates, when asked which was preferable, to take or not to take a wife, said: "Whichever a man does, he will repent it." It is a compact to which the saying is applied most appropriately, *man* is *to man* either *a god* or *a wolf* [Cecilius, quoted by Symmachus; and Plautus]. Many qualities must come together to construct it. It is found nowadays better suited to simple plebeian souls, in which luxury, curiosity, and idleness do not disturb it so much. Men with unruly humors like me, who hate any sort of bond or obligation, are not so fit for it:

Sweeter it is to me to live with neck unyoked.

—MAXIMIANUS

Of my own choice, I would have avoided marrying Wisdom herself, if she had wanted me. But say what we will, the custom and practice of ordinary life bears us along. Most of my actions are conducted by example, not by choice. At all events, I did not really bid myself to it, I was led to it, and borne by extraneous circumstances. For not only inconvenient things, but anything at all, however ugly and vicious and repulsive, can become acceptable through some condition or circumstance: so inane is our human posture. And I was borne to it certainly more ill-prepared and contrary than I am now after having tried it. And, licentious as I am thought to be, I have in truth observed the laws of marriage more strictly than I had either promised or expected. It is no longer time to kick when we have let ourselves be hobbled. A man must husband his freedom prudently; but once he has submitted to an obligation, he must keep to it under the laws of common duty, at least make an effort to. Those who make this bargain only to behave with hatred and contempt act unjustly and harmfully. And that fine rule that I see passing from hand to hand among the women like a sacred oracle,

> *Serve your husband as your master*
> *And guard against him as a traitor,*
>
> —FRENCH; SOURCE UNKNOWN

which is to say "Behave toward him with a constrained, hostile, and distrustful reverence," a war cry and a challenge, is equally unjust and hard. I am too soft for such thorny plans. To tell the truth, I have not yet attained such perfection of cleverness and refinement of wit as to confound reason with injustice and cast into derision any order and rule that does not accord with my appetite. Because I hate superstition, I do not promptly throw myself into irreligion. If a man does not always do his duty, at least he must always love and acknowledge it. It is treachery to get married without getting wedded. Let us pass on.

Our poet represents a marriage full of harmony and well matched, in which, nevertheless, there is not much loyalty. Did he mean that it is not impossible to give in to the impact of love and nonetheless reserve some duty toward marriage, and that one may injure marriage without breaking it up completely? A servant may shoe his master's mule[3] without hating him for all that. Beauty, opportunity, destiny (for destiny has a hand in it too)

> *There is a destiny that rules*
> *The parts our clothes conceal; for if the stars abhor you,*
> *Unheard-of length of member will do nothing for you*
>
> —JUVENAL

—have attached her to a stranger; not so wholly, perhaps, that she may not have some tie left by which she still holds to her husband. Love and

---

[3] Presumably, steal from him.

marriage are two intentions that go by separate and distinct roads. A woman may give herself to a man whom she would not at all want to have married; I do not mean because of the state of his fortune, but because of his personal qualities. Few men have married their mistresses who have not repented it—even in the other world: what a bad match Jupiter made with his wife, whom he had first frequented and enjoyed in love affairs! It is the old saying: "Shit in your hat and then put it on your head."

I have seen in my time, in high place, love shamefully and dishonorably cured by marriage: the considerations are too different. We love, without conflict, two diverse and contrary things. Isocrates used to say that people liked Athens the way men like the ladies they serve for love. Everyone loved to come and wander around and pass his time there; no one loved it enough to marry it, that is to say, to reside and settle there. I have been vexed to see husbands hate their wives for the mere fact that they themselves are doing them wrong. At least we should not love them less for our own fault. Through repentance and compassion, at least, they should be dearer to us.

They are different ends, Isocrates says, and yet in some sort compatible. Marriage has for its share utility, justice, honor, and constancy: a flat pleasure, but more universal. Love is founded on pleasure alone, and in truth its pleasure is more stimulating, lively, and keen: a pleasure inflamed by difficulty. There must be a sting and a smart in it. It is no longer love if it is without arrows and without fire. The liberality of the ladies is too profuse in marriage, and blunts the point of affection and desire. Just see the pains that Lycurgus and Plato take in their laws to avoid this disadvantage.

Women are not wrong at all when they reject the rules of life that have been introduced into the world, inasmuch as it is the men who have made these without them. There is naturally strife and wrangling between them and us: the closest communion we have with them is still tumultuous and tempestuous.

In our author's opinion we treat them inconsiderately in the following way. We have discovered, he says, that they are incomparably more capable and ardent than we in the acts of love—and that priest[4] of antiquity so testified, who had been once a man and then a woman,

> To him in both aspects was Venus known.
>
> —OVID

—and besides, we have learned from their own mouth the proof that was once given in different centuries by an emperor and an empress[5] of Rome,

---

[4] Tiresias.
[5] Proculus and Messalina.

master workmen and famous in this task: he indeed deflowered in one night ten captive Sarmatian virgins; but she actually in one night was good for twenty-five encounters, changing company according to her need and liking,

> *Her secret parts burning and tense with lust,*
> *And, tired by men, but far from sated, she withdrew.*

>   —JUVENAL

We know about the dispute that occurred in Catalonia from a woman complaining of the too assiduous efforts of her husband: not so much, in my opinion, that she was bothered by them (for I believe in miracles only in matters of faith), as by way of a pretext to curtail and curb, in the very thing that is the fundamental act of marriage, the authority of husbands over their wives, and to show that the peevishness and malignity of wives extends beyond the nuptial bed and treads underfoot the very graces and sweets of Venus; to which complaint the husband, a truly brutish and perverted man, answered that even on fast days he could not do with less than ten. There intervened that notable sentence of the queen of Aragon, by which, after mature deliberation with her council, this good queen, to give for all time a rule and example of the moderation and modesty required in a just marriage, ordained as the legitimate and necessary limit the number of six a day, relinquishing and giving up much of the need and desire of her sex, in order, she said, to establish an easy and consequently permanent and immutable formula. At which the doctors cry out: "What must the feminine appetite and concupiscence be when their reason, their reformation, and their virtue are set at this rate?" Consider these varying judgments about our sexual needs, and then the fact that Solon, chief of the lawgiving school, assesses conjugal intercourse, in order to keep from failing, at only three times a month. After believing and preaching all this, we have gone and given women continence as their particular share, and upon utmost and extreme penalties.

There is no passion more pressing than this, which we want them alone to resist, not simply as a vice of its own size, but as an abomination and execration, more to be resisted than irreligion and parricide; and meanwhile we give in to it without blame or reproach. Even those of us who have tried to get the better of it have sufficiently admitted what difficulty, or rather impossibility, there was in subduing, weakening, and cooling off the body by material remedies. We, on the contrary, want them to be healthy, vigorous, plump, well-nourished, and chaste at the same time: that is to say, both hot and cold. For marriage, which we say has the function of keeping them from burning, brings them but little cooling off, according to our ways. If they take a husband in whom the vigor of youth is still boiling, he will pride himself on expending it elsewhere:

> *Bassus, for shame, or we must go to law:*
> *I bought your penis at a heavy price;*
> *You've sold it, Bassus, it is yours no more.*

—MARTIAL

The philosopher Polemon was justly brought to justice by his wife, for sowing in a sterile field the fruit that was due to the genital field. If they take one of those broken-down ones, there they are in full wedlock worse off than virgins or widows. We consider them well provided for because they have a man beside them, as the Romans considered Clodia Laeta, a Vestal, violated because Caligula had approached her, even though it was attested that he had only approached her. But on the contrary, their need is only increased thereby, inasmuch as the contact and company of any male whatever awakens their heat, which would remain quieter in solitude. And for the purpose, it is likely, of rendering their chastity more meritorious by this circumstance and consideration, Boleslaus and Kinge, his wife, the king and queen of Poland, by mutual agreement consecrated it by a vow, while lying together on their very wedding night, and maintained it in the face of marital opportunities.

We train them from childhood to the ways of love. Their grace, their dressing up, their knowledge, their language, all their instruction, has only this end in view. Their governesses imprint in them nothing else but the idea of love, if only by continually depicting it to them in order to disgust them with it. My daughter (she is the only child I have) is at the age at which the laws allow the most ardent of them to marry. She is of a backward constitution, slight and soft, and has been brought up by her mother accordingly, in a retired and private manner: so that she is now only just beginning to grow out of the naïveté of childhood.

She was reading a French book in my presence. The word *fouteau* occurred, the name of a familiar tree.[6] The woman she has to train her stopped her short somewhat roughly and made her skip over that perilous passage. I let her go ahead in order not to disturb their rules, for I do not involve myself at all in directing her: the government of women has a mysterious way of proceeding; we must leave it to them. But if I am not mistaken, the company of twenty lackeys could not have imprinted in her imagination in six months the understanding and use and all the conse-

---

[6] Beech.

quences of the sound of those wicked syllables as did this good old woman by her reprimand and interdict:

> *The ripened maid delights to learn*
> *In wanton Ionic dance to turn,*
> *And fondly dreams, when still a child,*
> *Of loves incestuous and wild.*
>
> —HORACE

Let them dispense with ceremony a bit, let them speak freely; we are but children compared with them in this knowledge. Hear them describe our wooings and our conversations, and you will realize full well that we bring them nothing that they have not known and digested without us. Could it be as Plato says, that they were once dissipated boys? My ear one day happened to be in a place where without suspicion it could snatch some of the talk they were having among themselves. If only I might repeat it! By Our Lady, I said, we make fine use of our time by going off to study the phrases of Amadis and the stories of Boccaccio and Aretino so as to seem worldly-wise! There is not a word, not an example, not a trick that they do not know better than our books: it is a teaching that is born in their veins,

> *And Venus herself inspired them,*
>
> —VIRGIL

which those good schoolmasters, nature, youth, and health, continually breathe into their souls. They have no need to learn it, they breed it:

> *Nor any more delighted is a snow-white dove,*
> *Or if there be another thing more hot for love,*
> *To keep on plucking kisses with a biting bill,*
> *Than is a woman with her many-fancied will.*
>
> —CATULLUS

If this natural violence of their desire were not somewhat held in check by the fear and honor with which they have been provided, we would be shamed. The whole movement of the world resolves itself into and leads to this coupling. It is a matter infused throughout, it is a center to which all things look. We still see some of the ordinances of wise old Rome drawn up for the service of love, and the precepts of Socrates for the instruction of courtesans:

Nor do the Stoics' little volumes hate
On silken cushions to lie in state.

—HORACE

Zeno, among his laws, also made rules for the splitting and battering operations required to deflower virgins. What was the point of the philosopher Strato's book "Of Carnal Conjunction"? And what did Theophrastus treat of in those he entitled, one "The Lover," the other "Of Love"? And Aristippus in his, "Of Ancient Delights"? What is the purpose of Plato's so extensive and vivid descriptions of the boldest amours of his time? And "The Book of the Lover" by Demetrius Phalereus? And "Clinias, or the Ravished Lover," by Heraclides Ponticus? And Antisthenes' book "Of Begetting Children, or of Weddings," and the other, "Of the Master or the Lover"? And Aristo's "On Amorous Exercises"? And Cleanthes', one "Of Love," the other "On the Art of Loving"? The "Dialogues on Love" of Sphaerus? And Chrysippus' fable of Jupiter and Juno, shameless beyond all endurance, and his fifty very lascivious Epistles? For I must leave aside the writings of the philosophers who followed the Epicurean sect.

Fifty deities were in times past assigned to this office, and there were nations where, to assuage the lust of those who came to their devotions, they kept girls and boys in the churches to be enjoyed, and it was a ceremonious act to use them before coming to service. *Doubtless incontinence is necessary for the sake of continence; a conflagration is extinguished by fire* [Tertullian].

In most parts of the world this part of our body was deified. In one and the same province some flayed off the skin in order to offer and consecrate a piece of it, the others offered and consecrated their seed. In another, the young men publicly pierced and opened it in various places between the flesh and the skin, and put skewers through these openings, the longest and thickest that they could endure; and of these skewers they afterward made a fire as an offering to their gods. They were considered deficient in vigor and chastity if they were upset by the power of this cruel pain. Elsewhere the most sacred magistrate was revered and recognized by those parts of him; and in many ceremonies an effigy of it was carried in pomp in honor of various divinities.

The Egyptian ladies, at the festival of the Bacchanals, wore a wooden one around their neck, exquisitely fashioned, big and heavy, according to each one's capacity; besides which the statue of their god displayed one which surpassed in size the rest of the body.

The married women hereabouts form a figure of one with their kerchiefs over their forehead to glory in the enjoyment they have of it; and when they come to be widows they put it down in back and hide it beneath their coifs.

The most modest matrons in Rome were honored to offer flowers and garlands to the god Priapus; and the virgins at the time of their nuptials were made to sit on his least seemly parts. And I know not but that I have seen some semblance of a like devotion in my time. What was the meaning of that ridiculous part of the breeches worn by our fathers, which is still seen on our Swiss? What is the point of the show we make even now of the shape of our pieces under our galligaskins, and what is worse, often by falsehood and imposture beyond their natural size? *sock in the crotch?*

I am tempted to believe that this sort of garment was invented in better and more conscientious ages so as not to deceive people, so that each man alike might publicly and gallantly render an account of his capacity. The simpler nations still have it somewhat corresponding to the real size. In those days the workman was taught the art, as is done in measuring the arm or the foot.

That good man who, when I was young, castrated so many beautiful ancient statues in his great city, so that the eye might not be corrupted, following the advice of that other ancient worthy—

Nude bodies shown in public lead to shameful acts

—ENNIUS, QUOTED BY CICERO

—should have called to mind that nothing was gained unless he also had horses and asses castrated, and finally all nature, just as in the mysteries of the Bona Dea[7] all semblance whatever of masculinity was excluded.

Yes, everything on earth, the race of man and beast,
Fish of the sea, and flocks, and gaily painted birds,
Rush into passionate flame.

—VIRGIL

The gods, says Plato, have furnished us with a disobedient and tyrannical member, which, like a furious animal, undertakes by the violence of its appetite to subject everything to itself. To women likewise they have given a gluttonous and voracious animal which, if denied its food in due season, goes mad, impatient of delay, and, breathing its rage into their bodies, stops up the passages, arrests the breathing, causing a thousand kinds of ills, until it has sucked in the fruit of the common thirst and therewith plentifully irrigated and fertilized the depth of the womb.

---

[7] Originally a Roman goddess of chastity.

Now my legislator should also have called to mind that it is perhaps a more chaste and fruitful practice to let them know the living reality early than to leave them to guess it according to the freedom and heat of their imagination. In place of the real parts, through desire and hope, they substitute others three times life-size. And a certain man of my acquaintance ruined his chances by exposing his in a place where he was not yet in a position to put them to their more serious use.

What mischief is not done by those enormous pictures that boys spread about the passages and staircases of palaces! From these, women acquire a cruel contempt for our natural capacity.

How do we know that Plato did not have this in mind when, imitating other well-constituted states, he ordained that men and women, young and old, should appear in one another's sight stark naked in gymnastics?

The Indian women, who see the men in the raw, have at least cooled their sense of sight. And although the women of the great kingdom of Pegu, who have nothing to cover them below the waist but a cloth slit in front and so narrow that whatever ceremonious modesty they seek to preserve, at each step they can be seen whole, may say that this is a device thought up in order to attract the men to them and divert them from their fondness for other males, to which that nation is altogether addicted, it might be said that they lose by it more than they gain and that a complete hunger is sharper than one that has been satisfied at least by the eyes.

Moreover, Livia used to say that to a good woman a naked man is no more than a statue.

The Lacedaemonian women, more virginal as wives than our women are as maidens, saw the young men of their city every day stripped at their exercises, and were not too careful themselves to cover their thighs in walking, considering themselves, as Plato says, sufficiently covered by their virtue without a farthingale.[8]

But those men of whom Saint Augustine tells us attributed to nudity a wonderful power of temptation by doubting whether at the universal judgment women will rise again in their own sex and not rather in ours, lest they tempt us still in that holy state.

In short, we allure and flesh them by every means; we incessantly heat and excite their imagination; and then we bellyache. Let us confess the truth: there is hardly one of us who is not more afraid of the shame that comes to him for his wife's vices than for his own; who does not take better care (wonderful charity) of his good wife's conscience than of his own; who would not rather be a thief and sacrilegious and have his wife be a murderess and a heretic, than not to have her be more chaste than her husband.

---

[8] In French, "de leur vertu sans vertugade."

And the women will gladly offer to go to the law courts to seek gain, and to war to seek a reputation, rather than be obliged to keep so difficult a guard in the midst of idleness and pleasures. Don't they see that there is not a merchant, or a lawyer, or a soldier who will not leave his business to run after this other—and the porter and the cobbler, all harassed and worn out as they are with work and hunger?

> *Would you give, for all Mygdonian Phrygia's gold,*
> *Or all the wealth Achaemenes possesses,*
> *Or what Arabia's full coffers hold,*
>   *One of Licinnia's tresses,*

> *While to your kisses sweet her neck so white*
> *She bends, or, cruel, tenderly denies*
> *Those in which more than you she takes delight,*
>   *And soon she'll snatch by surprise?*

> —HORACE

Iniquitous appraisal of vices! Both we and they are capable of a thousand corruptions more harmful and unnatural than lasciviousness. But we create and weigh vices not according to nature but according to our interest, whereby they assume so many unequal shapes. The severity of our decrees makes women's addiction to this vice more exacerbated and vicious than its nature calls for, and involves it in consequences that are worse than their cause.

I do not know whether the exploits of Caesar and Alexander surpass in hardship the resoluteness of a beautiful young woman brought up in our fashion, in full view of and contact with the world, assailed by so many contrary examples, keeping herself entire in the midst of a thousand continual and powerful solicitations. There is no action more thorny, or more active, than this inaction. I find it much easier to bear a suit of armor all one's life than a virginity; and the vow of virginity is the most noble of all vows, as being the hardest: *The power of the Devil is in the loins,* says Saint Jerome.

Certainly we have resigned to the ladies the most arduous and vigorous of human duties, and we leave them the glory of it. That should serve them as a singular spur to persevere in it. This is a fine occasion for them to defy us and to trample underfoot that vain preeminence in valor and virtue that we claim over them. They will find, if they take note, that they will be not only very esteemed for this but also more loved. A gallant man does not abandon his pursuit for being refused, provided the refusal is dictated by chastity rather than choice. We can swear, threaten, and complain all we like: we lie, we love them the better for it. There is no allurement like a modesty that is not heartless and surly. It is stupidity and baseness to persevere against hatred and contempt, but against a virtuous and constant resolution mingled with a grateful good will, it is the exercise of a noble and generous soul. They may recognize our services up to a certain degree, and honorably make us feel that they do not disdain us.

For that law that commands them to abominate us because we adore them and to hate us because we love them is indeed cruel, if only for its difficulty. Why shall they not hear our offers and requests so long as they keep within the duty of modesty? Why do we go surmising that they have some more licentious idea within? A queen of our time used to say shrewdly that to refuse to hear these advances was a testimony of weakness and an accusation of one's own facility; and that a lady who had not been tempted could not boast of her chastity.

The limits of honor are by no means so curtailed. It has room to relax, it can allow itself some freedom without transgressing. At its frontier there is some space that is free, indifferent, and neutral. If a man has been able to hunt it down and bring it to bay by force right in its corner and stronghold, he is a fool if he is not satisfied with his fortune. The prize of victory is estimated by its difficulty. Do you want to know what impression your service and your merit have made on her heart? Measure it by her character. Some may grant more who do not grant so much. The obligation for the benefit is entirely relative to the will of the person who grants it. The other circumstances that enter into a benefit are dumb, dead, and fortuitous. It costs her more to give that little than it costs her companion to give her all. If in anything rarity is a value, it must be in this. Do not consider how little it is, but how few have it. The value of money changes according to the coinage and the place where it is minted.

Whatever the spite and indiscretion of some men may make them say in the excess of their discontent, virtue and truth always regain their advantage. I have known women whose reputation was long unjustly damaged to restore themselves to the universal esteem of men by their constancy alone, without any effort or artifice. Everyone repents and takes back what he had believed of them; after being slightly suspect girls, they hold the first rank among ladies of virtue and honor. Someone said to Plato: "Everyone is speaking ill of you." "Let them talk," he said, "I will live in such a fashion as to make them change their tune."

Besides the fear of God and the prize of so rare a glory, which should incite women to preserve themselves, the corruption of our time forces them to; and if I were in their place, there is nothing I would not do rather than entrust my reputation to such dangerous hands. In my time the pleasure of telling about it (a pleasure which yields little in sweetness to that of the thing itself) was permitted only to those who had some faithful and unique friend. Nowadays the ordinary conversation at gatherings and at table consists of boasts of the favors received and the secret liberality of the ladies. Truly one must be abject and base in heart beyond measure to allow these tender charms to be so cruelly persecuted, pawed over, and ransacked by such ungrateful, indiscreet, and fickle persons.

This immoderate and illegitimate exasperation of ours against this vice is born of the most vain and tempestuous malady that afflicts human souls, which is jealousy.

> *Who forbids taking a light from a flaming torch?*
>
> —OVID

> *Give all they will, yet thereby nothing's lost.*
>
> —PRIAPEA 7

Jealousy and her sister envy seem to me among the most foolish of the troop. Of the latter I can scarcely speak: this passion, which is painted as being so strong and powerful, has, by its good grace, no access to me. As for the other, I know it, at least by sight. The animals have a sense of it: when the shepherd Crastis fell in love with a goat, her mate out of jealousy came and butted his head as he was asleep and crushed it. We have raised this fever to an excessive pitch, after the example of same barbarian nations. The better disciplined ones have been touched by it, which is reasonable, but not carried away:

> *Never adulterer, by sword of husband slain,*
> *Did with his purple blood the Stygian waters stain.*
>
> —JOHANNES SECUNDUS

Lucullus, Caesar, Pompey, Antony, Cato, and other brave men were cuckolds and knew it without stirring up a tumult about it. In those days there was only one fool of a Lepidus who died in anguish over it.

> *Then you will suffer the adulterer's fate:*
> *They'll spread your legs, and cram your open gate*
> *With radishes and mullets.*
>
> —CATULLUS

And the god of our poet, when he surprised one of his companions with his wife, contented himself with putting them to shame:

>   *And one merry wag among the gods,*
>   *Wished that thus he might be disgraced;*
>
>   —OVID

and, for all that, he allows himself to be warmed by the sweet caresses she offers him, complaining that it was on this account she had come to mistrust his affection:

>   *Why go seek causes from afar? Whither has gone,*
>   *Goddess, your faith in me?*
>
>   —VIRGIL

In fact she asks a favor of him for a bastard of hers—

>   *I ask for arms, a mother for her son*
>
>   —VIRGIL

—which is liberally granted her; and Vulcan speaks honorably of Aeneas,

>   *Arms for a warrior must be made,*
>
>   —VIRGIL

with a humanity truly more than human. And I will consent that this excess of goodness be left to the gods:

>   *Nor is it fair to equal men with gods.*
>
>   —CATULLUS

As for the confusion of children, not only do the most serious legislators ordain and favor it in their republics, but furthermore it does not concern the women, in whom this passion of jealousy is, I know not how, still more firmly seated:

>   *For often Juno, mistress of the gods,*
>   *Burns at her husband's daily escapades.*
>
>   —CATULLUS

When jealousy seizes these poor, weak, and unresisting souls, it is pitiful how cruelly it drags them about and tyrannizes over them. It insinuates itself into them under the title of friendship, but once it possesses them, the same causes that served as the foundation of good will serve as the foundation of mortal hatred. Of all the diseases of the mind it is the one which the most things serve to feed and the fewest things to remedy. The virtue, the health, the merit, the reputation, of the husband are the fire-brands of the wives' ill will and fury:

No hatreds are so keen as those of love.

—PROPERTIUS

This fever disfigures and corrupts all that is otherwise beautiful and good in them; and in a jealous woman, however chaste she may be and however good a housewife, there is no action that does not smack of bitterness and unpleasantness. It is a frenzied agitation, which tosses them to an extreme completely contrary to its cause. A good example was one Octavius in Rome. After he had slept with Pontia Posthumia, his affection was increased by the enjoyment, and he sought most urgently to marry her. When he was unable to persuade her, his extreme love threw him into the reactions of the most cruel and mortal hatred: he killed her. Likewise the ordinary symptoms of that other love malady are intestine hatreds, plots, conspiracies,

'Tis known what woman in a rage can do,

—VIRGIL

and a rage which is all the more fretful for being constrained to justify itself under the pretext of good will.

Now the duty of chastity is very extensive. Is it their will that we want our women to curb? That is a very supple and active faculty; it has a lot of agility if we try to immobilize it. What if dreams sometimes involve them so far that they cannot deny them? It is not in them, nor perhaps in Chastity herself, since she is a female, to keep themselves from lust and desire. If their will alone concerns us, where are we? Imagine the great rush if a man had the privilege of being borne swift as a bird, without eyes to see or tongue to tell, into the arms of each woman who would accept him.

The Scythian women put out the eyes of all their slaves and prisoners of war to make use of them more freely and secretly.

Oh, what a terrific advantage is opportuneness! If someone asked me the first thing in love, I would answer that it is knowing how to seize the right time; the second likewise, and the third too; it is a point that can accomplish anything.

I have often lacked luck, but also sometimes enterprise: God keep from harm the man who can laugh at this. These days love calls for more temerity, which our young men excuse on the pretext of ardor; but if the women considered the matter closely, they would find that temerity comes rather from contempt. I used to be scrupulously afraid of giving offense, and I am inclined to respect what I love. Besides, in these negotiations, if you take away respect you rub out the glamor. In this I like to have a man somewhat play the child and the timid slave. If not altogether in this, in other situations I have something of the stupid bashfulness that Plutarch speaks of, and the course of my life has been harmed and blemished by it in various ways: a quality very ill-suited to my nature in general—and indeed what are we but sedition and discrepancy? My eyes are tender for enduring a refusal, as they are for refusing; and it troubles me so much to be troublesome to others that on the occasions when duty forces me to test out someone's will in a doubtful matter which may cost him some trouble, I do it halfheartedly and against the grain. But if the matter affects my personal interest, though Homer truly says that bashfulness is a stupid virtue in a needy man, I ordinarily commission a third person to blush in my place. And with the same difficulty I dismiss people who want to use me; so that it has happened to me sometimes to have the wish to refuse but not the strength.

Thus it is folly to try to bridle in women a desire that is so burning and so natural to them. And when I hear them boast of having such a virginal and cold disposition, I laugh at them: they are leaning over too far backward. If it is a toothless and decrepit old woman or a dry and consumptive young one, though it is not altogether credible, at least they have some semblance of truth in saying it. But those who still move and breathe make their position worse in this way, since ill-considered excuses serve as accusation. Like a gentleman, one of my neighbors, who was suspected of impotence,

> *Whose member, feebler than a tender beet,*
> *Never rose even up to middle height,*
>
> —CATULLUS

who, three or four days after his wedding, to justify himself, went around boldly swearing that he had ridden twenty stages the night before; which was afterward used to convict him of pure ignorance and to annul his marriage. Besides, what these women say has no value, for there is neither continence nor virtue unless there is an urge to the contrary. "It is true," they should say, "but I am not ready to give myself up." The saints themselves talk that way. I mean those women who boast in good earnest of their coldness and insensibility and who, with a straight face, want to be believed. For when it is with an affected countenance, in which the eyes belie their words, and with the jargon of their profession which has its effect in reverse, I think that's fine. I am a great admirer of naturalness and freedom, but there is no help for it: unless it is completely simple and childlike, it is unbecoming to ladies and out of place in these dealings: it promptly slides into shamelessness. Their disguises and their faces deceive only fools. Lying holds an honorable place in love; it is a detour that leads us to truth by the back door.

If we cannot hold back their imagination, what do we expect of them? Deeds? There are enough of these that escape all outside communication, by which chastity may be corrupted:

> *That which he does unwitnessed, he does often.*
>
> —MARTIAL

And the deeds that we fear the least are perhaps the most to be feared; silent sins are the worst:

> *A simpler prostitute offends me less.*
>
> —MARTIAL

There are acts by which they can lose their chastity without unchastity, and, what is more, without their knowledge. *A midwife, for instance, making a manual examination of some virgin's integrity, whether through malice, unskilfulness, or accident, by inspecting it has destroyed it* [Saint Augustine]. Some have lost their maidenhead for having looked for it; some have destroyed it in sport.

We could not possibly circumscribe precisely for them the actions that we forbid them. We must formulate our rules in general and uncertain terms. The very idea that we form of their chastity is ridiculous; for among the extreme examples I know of is Fatua, wife of Faunus, who never let herself be seen by any man whatever after her wedding; and Hiero's wife, who never noticed her husband's stinking breath, thinking that this was a quality common to all men. They must become insensible and invisible in order to satisfy us.

Now let us confess that the crux in judging this duty lies principally in the will. There have been husbands who have suffered cuckoldry not only without reproach or sense of offense toward their wives but with singular obligation to and recommendation of their virtue. Some women, who loved their honor better than their life, have prostituted it to the frenzied appetite of a mortal enemy to save their husband's life, and done for him what they would not at all have done for themselves. This is not the place to extend these examples; they are too lofty and too rich to be displayed in this light; let us keep them for a nobler setting.

But for examples of more commonplace luster, are there not women every day who lend themselves for the mere profit of their husbands and by their express order and mediation? And in ancient times Phaulius of Argos offered his wife to King Philip out of ambition; just as out of civility a certain Galba, who had Maecenas to supper, seeing that his wife and his guest were beginning to conspire by glances and signs, let himself sink down on his cushion, acting like a man weighed down with sleep, to lend a hand to their understanding. And he admitted it with rather good grace; for when at this point a servant made bold to lay hands on the wine that was on the table, he shouted at him: "Don't you see, you rogue, that I am asleep only for Maecenas?"

One woman may be of loose conduct, and yet have a more reformed disposition than another who conducts herself in a more regular manner. As we see some who complain of having been vowed to chastity before the age of discretion, so I have seen some complain truthfully of having been vowed to debauchery before the age of discretion. The vice of the parents can be the cause of this, or the force of necessity, which is a rough counselor. In the East Indies, where chastity was in singular repute, nevertheless custom allowed a married woman to abandon herself to any man who presented her with an elephant, and that with some glory for having been valued at so high a price.

Phaedo the philosopher, a man of good family, after the capture of his country, Elis, made it his trade to prostitute the beauty of his youth as long as it lasted to anyone that wanted it for the price in money, so as to make a living. And Solon was the first in Greece, they say, who, by his laws, gave women the liberty to provide for the necessities of their life at the expense of their chastity, a custom which Herodotus says was accepted in many governments before his time.

And then what is the fruit of this painful anxiety? For whatever justice there may be in jealousy, it still remains to be seen whether its agitation is really useful. Is there someone who thinks to shackle women by his ingenuity?

> *Put on a lock, confine her. But then who will guard*
> *The guards themselves? Your wife is shrewd; with them*
> *she'll start.*
>
> —JUVENAL

What occasion will not be enough for them in so knowing an age?

Curiosity is vicious in all things, but here it is pernicious. It is folly to want to be enlightened about a disease for which there is no medicine that does not make it worse and aggravate it; the shame of which is increased and made public principally by jealousy; revenge for which wounds our children more than it cures us. You dry up and die in quest of a proof so obscure.

How pitifully have those men reached their goal who in my time have succeeded in this quest! If the informer does not present at the same time the remedy and relief, the information he gives is injurious and he deserves a dagger-thrust more than does a man who gives you the lie. People make no less fun of the man who takes pains to do something about it than of the man who is unaware of it. The mark of cuckoldry is indelible; once a man is stamped with it he is stamped forever; the punishment makes it public more than the fault. It is a fine thing to see our private misfortunes torn out of the shadows and doubt to be trumpeted on the tragic stage, and especially misfortunes that pinch us only by the telling. For "a good wife" and "a good marriage" are said not about those that are so, but about those that are not talked about. We have to be ingenious to avoid this annoying and useless knowledge. And the Romans had the custom, when returning from a trip, of sending someone ahead to the house to make their arrival known to their wives, in order not to surprise them. And therefore a certain nation introduced the custom that the priest open the way to the bride on the wedding day, to rid the husband of doubt and of the curiosity of investigating in this first trial whether she comes to him a virgin or damaged by another's love.

"But people talk about it." I know a hundred honorable men who are cuckolded, honorably and not very discreditably. A gallant man is pitied for it, not disesteemed. Make your virtue stifle your misfortune, make good people curse the occasion of it, make the man who wrongs you tremble at the very thought of it. And then, who is not talked about in this sense, from the smallest to the greatest?

> *Who many legions did command, and was*
> *A better man than you, poor wretch, in many ways.*
>
> —LUCRETIUS

See how many honorable men are involved in this reproach in your presence? Don't think that you are spared any more elsewhere. "But even the ladies will laugh at it." And what are they fonder of laughing at these days than a peaceful and well-settled marriage? Each one of you has made someone a cuckold: now nature is all in similarities, in compensation and tit for tat. The frequency of this accident should by this time have moderated its bitterness; it will soon have become a custom.

Miserable passion, which has also this about it, that it is incommunicable,

E'en Fortune would not lend an ear to our laments.

—CATULLUS

For to what friend do you dare entrust your griefs, who, even if he does not laugh at them, will not use them as an approach and an instruction to get a share in the quarry himself? The bitternesses of marriage, like the sweets, are kept secret by the wise. And among the other annoying conditions that are found in it, this, for a talkative man like myself, is one of the main ones: that custom makes it improper and prejudicial to communicate to anyone all that we know and feel about it.

To give women the same advice in order to disgust them with jealousy would be a waste of time. Their very essence is so steeped in suspicion, vanity, and curiosity, that one should not expect to cure them by any legitimate way. They often recover from this ailment by a form of health much more to be feared than the disease itself. For as there are enchantments that can take away the evil only by unloading it onto another, so they are apt to transfer this fever to their husbands when they lose it.

However, to tell the truth, I do not know if a man can suffer anything worse from them than jealousy. It is the most dangerous of their conditions, as the head is of their members. Pittacus used to say that everyone had his weakness, and that his was his wife's bad temper: except for that, he would consider himself happy in every respect. It is a very grievous misfortune where a man so just, so wise, so valiant, feels the whole state of his life altered by it; what are we small fry to do?

The senate of Marseilles was right to grant the request of the man who asked permission to kill himself to deliver himself from his tempestuous wife; for this is a disease which never goes away without taking everything with it, and which has no effective solution but flight or endurance, though both are very hard.

That man knew what it was all about, it seems to me, who said that a good marriage was one made between a blind wife and a deaf husband.

Let us also see to it that the great and violent rigor of this obligation that we enjoin on them does not produce two effects contrary to our purpose: that is, that it does not make the pursuers keener and the wives more ready to surrender easily. For as for the first point, by increasing the value of the place, we increase the value and desire of the conquest. May it not have been Venus herself who thus shrewdly raised the price of her merchandise by making panders of the laws, knowing how insipid a pleasure it is unless it is given value by imagination and a high cost? In short, it is all hog's flesh that is given variety by the sauce, as Flamininus' host said. Cupid is a treacherous god; he makes it his sport to wrestle with piety and justice; he glories in the fact that his power clashes with every other power and that all other rules yield to his.

> *He seeks out matter for his sin.*
>
> —OVID

And as for the second point, would we not be less cuckolded if we were less afraid to be, according to the nature of women? For prohibition incites and invites them:

> *You would, they won't; and when you won't, they will.*
>
> —TERENCE

> *They are ashamed to go by the permitted way.*
>
> —LUCAN

What better interpretation could we find for Messalina's behavior? In the beginning she made her husband a cuckold in secret, as people do; but carrying on her affairs too easily, through his stupidity, she soon disdained that practice. Now behold her making love openly, acknowledging her lovers, entertaining them and favoring them in the sight of one and all. She wanted him to feel it. When that animal could not be awakened for all that, and made her pleasures flat and insipid by the over-lax facility with which he seemed to authorize and legitimize them, what did she do? Wife of a healthy, live emperor, and in Rome, the theater of the world, at high noon, in a public festival and ceremony, and with Silius, whom she had been enjoying a long time beforehand, she got married one day when her husband was out of town.

Does it not seem as if she was on her way to becoming chaste through her husband's nonchalance, or seeking another husband who would whet her appetite by his jealousy, and who by opposing her would arouse her? But the first difficulty she encountered was also the last. The animal awoke with a start. One is often worse off with these deaf and unconscious people. I have found by experience that this extreme tolerance, when it comes apart, produces some of the harshest acts of vengeance; for the anger and fury, heaped up together, catching fire all of a sudden, explodes all its energy at the first attack,

> *And looses all the reins of wrath,*
>
> —VIRGIL

He put her to death and also a great number of those who were intimate with her, even to some who could not help it and whom she had invited to her bed with scourges.

What Virgil says of Venus and Vulcan, Lucretius had said more appropriately of a stolen enjoyment between her and Mars:

> *He who rules the savage things*
> *Of war, the mighty Mars, oft on thy bosom flings*
> *Himself; the eternal wound of love drains all his powers;*
> *Wide-mouthed, with greedy eyes thy person he devours,*
> *Head back, his very soul upon thy lips suspended:*
> *Take him in thy embrace, goddess, let him be blended*
> *With thy holy body as he lies; let sweet words pour*
> *Out of thy mouth.*
>
> —LUCRETIUS

When I ruminate that *rejicit* (flings), *pascit* (devours), *inhians* (wide-mouthed), *molli* (soft), *fovet* (fondles), *medullas* (marrow), *labefacta* (trembling), *pendet* (suspended), *percurrit* (runs through), and that noble *circumfusa* (blended), mother of the pretty *infusus* (outpoured),[9] I despise those petty conceits and verbal tricks that have sprung up since. These good people needed no sharp and subtle play on words; their language is all full and copious with a natural and constant vigor. They are all epigram, not only the tail but the head, stomach, and feet. There is nothing forced, nothing dragging; the whole thing moves at the same pace. *Their whole contexture is manly; they are not concerned with pretty little flowers* [Seneca]. This is not a soft and merely inoffensive eloquence; it is sinewy and solid, and does not so much please as fill and ravish; and it ravishes the strongest minds most. When I see these brave forms of expression, so alive, so profound, I do not say "This is well said," I say "This is well thought." It is the sprightliness of the imagination that elevates and swells the words. *It is the heart that makes a man eloquent* [Quintilian]. Our people call judgment language and fine words full conceptions.

This painting is the result not so much of manual dexterity as of having the object more vividly imprinted in the soul. Gallus speaks simply, because he conceives simply. Horace is not content with a superficial expression; it would betray him. He sees more clearly and deeply into the thing. His mind unlocks and ransacks the whole storehouse of words and figures in order to express itself; and he needs them to be beyond the commonplace, as his conception is beyond the commonplace. Plutarch says that he

---

[9] Some of these words are taken from the Virgil quotation that gives this chapter its title.

saw the Latin language through things. It is the same here: the sense illuminates and brings out the words, which are no longer wind, but flesh and bone. The words mean more than they say. Even the weak-minded feel some notion of this; for when I was in Italy I said whatever I pleased in ordinary talk, but for serious discourse I would not have dared trust myself to an idiom that I could neither bend nor turn out of its ordinary course. I want to be able to do something of my own with it.

Handling and use by able minds give value to a language, not so much by innovating as by filling it out with more vigorous and varied services, by stretching and bending it. They do not bring to it new words, but they enrich their own, give more weight and depth to their meaning and use; they teach the language unaccustomed movements, but prudently and shrewdly. And how little this gift is given to all is seen in so many French writers of our time. They are bold and disdainful enough not to follow the common road, but want of invention and of discretion ruins them. There is nothing to be seen in them but a wretched affectation of originality, cold and absurd disguises, which instead of elevating the substance bring it down. Provided they can strut gorgeously in their novelty, they care nothing about effectiveness. To seize a new word they abandon the ordinary one, which is often stronger and more sinewy.

In our language I find plenty of stuff but a little lack of fashioning. For there is nothing that might not be done with our jargon of hunting and war, which is a generous soil to borrow from. And forms of speech, like plants, improve and grow stronger by being transplanted. I find it sufficiently abundant, but not sufficiently pliable and vigorous. It ordinarily succumbs under a powerful conception. If your pace is tense, you often feel it growing limp and giving way under you, and that when it fails you Latin comes to your aid, and Greek to others.

Of some of those words that I have just picked out it is harder for us to perceive the energy, because the frequent use of them has somewhat debased and vulgarized their grace for us; as in our vernacular we encounter excellent phrases and metaphors whose beauty is withering with age and whose color has been tarnished by too common handling. But that takes away nothing of their savor to those who have a good nose, nor does it detract from the glory of those ancient authors who, as is likely, first brought these words into this luster.

Learning treats of things too subtly, in a mode too artificial and different from the common and natural one. My page makes love and understands it. Read him Leon Hebreo and Ficino:[10] they talk about him, his thoughts and his actions, and yet he does not understand a thing in it. I do

---

[10] Leon Hebreo, or Jehudah Abarbanel, a Portuguese-born Jewish scholar, published his *Dialoghi d'Amore* in Italian in 1535. Marsilio Ficino of Florence (1433–99), who sought to reconcile

not recognize in Aristotle most of my ordinary actions: they have been covered and dressed up in another robe for the use of the school. God grant these men may be doing the right thing! If I were of the trade, I would naturalize art as much as they artify nature. Let us leave Bembo and Equicola[11] alone.

When I write, I prefer to do without the company and remembrance of books, for fear they may interfere with my style. Also because, in truth, the good authors humble me and dishearten me too much. I am inclined to do the trick of that painter who, after painting a miserable picture of some cocks, forbade his boys to let any real cock come into his shop. And to give myself a little luster I would rather need the device of the musician Antinonides,[12] who, when he had to make music, arranged that either before or after him the audience should be steeped in some other bad singers.

But it is harder for me to do without Plutarch. He is so universal and so full that on all occasions, and however eccentric the subject you have taken up, he makes his way into your work and offers you a liberal hand, inexhaustible in riches and embellishments. It vexes me that I am so greatly exposed to pillage by those who frequent him.[13] I cannot be with him even a little without taking out a drumstick or a wing.

For this purpose of mine it is also appropriate for me to write at home, in a backward region, where no one helps me or corrects me, where I usually have no contact with any man who understands the Latin of his Paternoster and who does not know even less French.[14] I would have done it better elsewhere, but the work would have been less my own; and its principal end and perfection is to be precisely my own. I would indeed correct an accidental error, and I am full of them, since I run on carelessly. But the imperfections that are ordinary and constant in me it would be treachery to remove.

When I have been told, or have told myself: "You are too thick in figures of speech. Here is a word of Gascon vintage. Here is a dangerous phrase." (I do not avoid any of those that are used in the streets of France; those who would combat usage with grammar make fools of themselves.) "This is ignorant reasoning. This is paradoxical reasoning. This one is too mad. You are often playful: people will think you are speaking in earnest

---

Platonism with Christianity and in whose Latin translation Montaigne read Plato, was noted in sixteenth-century France for his version of the theory of love set forth in Plato's Symposium.

[11] Italian authors of philosophical treatises on love which appeared not long before Montaigne's time.

[12] Mentioned by Plutarch in his "Life of Demetrius." The name should be Antigenidas or Antigenides.

[13] In other words, people who borrow from Plutarch may also unconsciously be borrowing from Montaigne, since Montaigne has borrowed so much from Plutarch.

[14] Montaigne presumably means the French of Paris and the Ile-de-France.

when you are making believe." "Yes," I say, "but I correct the faults of inadvertence, not those of habit. Isn't this the way I speak everywhere? Don't I represent myself to the life? Enough, then. I have done what I wanted. Everyone recognizes me in my book, and my book in me."

Now I have an aping and imitative nature. When I used to dabble in composing verse (and I never did any but Latin), it clearly revealed the poet I had last been reading. And of my first essays, some smell a bit foreign. In Paris I speak a language somewhat different than at Montaigne. Anyone I regard with attention easily imprints on me something of himself. What I consider, I usurp: a foolish countenance, an unpleasant grimace, a ridiculous way of speaking. Vices even more: once they prick me, they stick to me and will not go away without shaking. I have been observed to swear more often by imitation than by nature.

A murderous imitation, like that of the horribly big and strong apes that King Alexander encountered in a certain region of the Indies. Otherwise it would have been hard to get the better of them, but they lent him the means of doing so by that inclination of theirs to imitate everything they saw done. For from this the hunters got the idea of putting on shoes in their sight with many knots in the laces, of rigging themselves out in headgear with running nooses, and of seeming to anoint their eyes with glue. Thus their apish nature brought these poor imprudent beasts to harm. They glued up their own eyes, hobbled their own feet, and strangled themselves.

That other faculty of ingeniously mimicking the gestures and words of another on purpose, which often brings pleasure and wonder, is not in me any more than in a stump.

When I swear in my own way, it is only "by God,"[15] which is the most straightforward of all oaths. They say that Socrates swore by the dog, Zeno by the same interjection that Italians use now, *cappari,*[16] and Pythagoras by water and air.

I so easily receive these superficial impressions without thinking of them that when I have had "Sire" or "Highness" in my mouth for three days in a row, a week later they will slip out instead of "Excellency" or "Lordship." And what I have begun to say in sport and in jest I will say seriously the next day. Wherefore in writing I am the more unwilling to accept the well-worn topics, for fear I may treat them at someone else's expense.

Any topic is equally fertile for me. A fly will serve my purpose; and God grant that this topic I have in hand now was not taken up at the command

---

[15] *Par Dieu* is much milder in French than its English equivalent.
[16] Montaigne means that Zeno swore "by the goats."

of so flighty a will! Let me begin with whatever subject I please, for all subjects are linked with one another.

But I am displeased with my mind for ordinarily producing its most profound and maddest fancies, and those I like the best, unexpectedly and when I am least looking for them; which suddenly vanish, having nothing to attach themselves to on the spot: on horseback, at table, in bed, but mostly on horseback, where my thoughts range most widely. In speech I am rather sensitively jealous of attention and silence if I am speaking in earnest: whoever interrupts me stops me. When I travel, the very necessity of the road cuts conversation short; besides, I most often travel without company fit for these protracted discussions, whereby I get full leisure to commune with myself.

It turns out as with my dreams. While dreaming I recommend them to my memory (for I am apt to dream that I am dreaming); but the next day I may well call to mind their coloring just as it was, whether gay, or sad, or strange; but as to what they were besides, the more I strain to find out, the more I plunge it into oblivion. So of these chance thoughts that drop into my mind there remains in my memory only a vain notion, only as much as I need to make me rack my brains and fret in quest of them to no purpose.

Now then, leaving books aside and speaking more materially and simply, I find after all that love is nothing else but the thirst for sexual enjoyment in a desired object, and Venus nothing else but the pleasure of discharging our vessels—a pleasure which becomes vicious either by immoderation or by indiscretion. For Socrates love is the appetite for generation by the mediation of beauty. And considering often the ridiculous titillation of this pleasure, the absurd, witless, and giddy motions with which it stirs up Zeno and Cratippus, that reckless frenzy, that face inflamed with fury and cruelty in the sweetest act of love, and then that grave, severe, and ecstatic countenance in so silly an action; and that our delights and our excrements have been lodged together pell-mell, and that the supreme sensual pleasure is attended, like pain, with faintness and moaning; I believe that what Plato says is true, that man is the plaything of the gods:

> *What savage jest is this!*
>
> —CLAUDIAN

and that it was in mockery that nature left us the most confused of our actions to be the most common, in order thereby to make us all equal and to put on the same level the fools and the wise, and us and the beasts. The most contemplative and wisest of men, when I imagine him in that position, seems to me an impostor to put on wise and contemplative airs; here are the peacock's feet that humble his pride:

Against truth said in laughing
Is there a law?

—HORACE

Those who will not allow serious ideas in the midst of games act, as someone says, like a man who is afraid to worship the statue of a saint if it is undraped.

We eat and drink as the animals do, but these are not actions that hinder the operations of our mind. In these we keep our advantage over them. But this other puts every other thought beneath its yoke and by its imperious authority brutifies and bestializes all the theology and philosophy there is in Plato; and yet he does not complain of it. In everything else you can keep some decorum; all other operations come under the rules of decency. This one cannot even be imagined other than vicious or ridiculous. Just to see this, try to find a wise and discreet way of doing it. Alexander used to say that he knew himself to be mortal chiefly by this action and by sleep. Sleep suffocates and suppresses the faculties of our mind; the sexual act likewise absorbs and dissipates them. Truly it is a mark not only of our original corruption but also of our inanity and deformity.

On the one hand Nature pushes us on to it, having attached to this desire the most noble, useful, and pleasant of all her operations; and on the other hand she lets us accuse and shun it as shameless and indecent, blush at it, and recommend abstinence. Are we not brutes to call brutish the operation that makes us?

The various nations in their religions have many conventions in common, such as sacrifices, lamps, burning incense, fasts, offerings, and, among other things, the condemnation of this action. All opinions come to this, besides the very widespread practice of cutting off the foreskin, which is a punishment of the act. Perhaps we are right to blame ourselves for making such a stupid production as man, to call the action shameful, and shameful the parts that are used for it. (At present mine are truly shameful and pitiful.)

The Essenes, of whom Pliny speaks, maintained their numbers for several centuries without nurses and without baby clothes, by the influx of foreigners who, following this fine humor, continually joined them: a whole nation risked exterminating itself rather than involve themselves in a woman's embrace, and forfeiting the continuation of mankind rather than create a man. They say that Zeno had to do with a woman only once

in his life, and then out of civility, so as not to seem too obstinately to
disdain the sex.

Everyone shuns to see a man born, everyone runs to see him die. For
his destruction we seek a spacious field in broad daylight; for his construction we hide in a dark little corner. It is a duty to hide and blush in order
to make him; and it is a glory and a source of many virtues to be able to
unmake him. One is an offense, the other an act of grace; for Aristotle says
that to benefit someone, in a certain phrase of his country, is to kill him.
The Athenians, to put the disgrace of these two actions on the same level,
when they had to purify the island of Delos and justify themselves to
Apollo, forbade both any burial and any birth within its territory. *We are
ashamed of our very selves* [Terence]. We regard our being as vice.

There are nations that cover themselves when eating. I know a lady, and
one of the greatest, who has this same opinion, that chewing is a disagreeable grimace which takes away much of women's grace and beauty; and
she does not like to appear in public with an appetite. And I know a man
who cannot bear to see anyone eat or to be seen eating, and who avoids
any company even more when he is filling than when he is emptying
himself.

In the empire of the Turk are found a great number of men who, to
outdo others, never let themselves be seen when they have their meals;
who have only one a week; who cut and mangle their face and limbs; who
never speak to anyone: all of them people who think they honor their
nature by denaturing themselves, who prize themselves for their contempt,
and think to improve themselves by their impairment. What a monstrous
animal to be a horror to himself, to be burdened by his pleasures, to
regard himself as a misfortune!

There are some who conceal their lives—

> *They change for exile their sweet homes and hearths*
>
> —VIRGIL

—and hide them from the sight of other men; who avoid health and
cheerfulness as hostile and harmful qualities. Not only many sects but
many nations curse their birth and bless their death. There are some nations in which the sun is abominated and the darkness adored.

We are ingenious only in maltreating ourselves; that is the true quarry of
the power of our mind—a dangerous tool when out of control.

> *O wretched men, who hold their joys as crimes!*
>
> —MAXIMIANUS

Alas, poor man! You have enough necessary ills without increasing them by your invention, and you are miserable enough by nature without being so by art. You have real and essential deformities enough without forging imaginary ones. Do you find that you are too much at your ease unless your ease strikes you as unpleasantness? Do you think you have fulfilled all the necessary duties to which nature obligates you, and that she is wanting and idle in you unless you take on new duties? You are not afraid to offend the universal and indubitable laws, and are proudly intent on your own laws, which are partial and fanciful: and the more particular, uncertain, and contradicted they are, the more you devote your effort to them. The positive rules of your own invention possess and bind you, and the rules of your parish; those of God and the world leave you untouched. Just run through a few examples that would illustrate this idea; your life is all made up of them.

The verses of these two poets, treating of lasciviousness as reservedly and discreetly as they do, seem to me to reveal it and illuminate it more closely. The ladies cover their bosoms with a veil, the priests many sacred things; painters put shadows in their work to bring out the light more; and it is said that the sun and wind strike harder by reflection than direct. An Egyptian made a wise answer to the man who asked him: "What are you carrying there hidden under your cloak?" "It is hidden under my cloak so that you won't know what it is." But there are certain other things that people hide only to show them.

Listen to this man, who is more open:

> *And pressed her naked body unto mine.*
>
> —OVID

I feel that he is caponizing me. Let Martial turn up Venus' skirts as high as he pleases, he will not succeed in revealing her so completely. He who says everything satiates and disgusts us; he who is afraid to express himself leads us on to think more than there is. There is treachery in this sort of modesty, and especially in half opening to us, as these do, so fair a road to the imagination. Both the action and the picture of it should smack of theft.

I like the love-making of the Spaniards and Italians, more respectful and timid, more mannered and veiled. I don't know who it was in ancient times who wanted his throat as long as a crane's neck so as to relish longer what he swallowed. That wish is more appropriate in this quick and precipitate pleasure, especially for such natures as mine, for I have the failing of being too sudden. In order to arrest its flight and prolong it in preambles, everything among them serves as a favor and a recompense: a glance, a bow, a word, a sign. If a man could dine off the steam of a roast, wouldn't that be a fine saving? This is a passion that with very little solid essence mixes in much more vanity and feverish dreams: it should be satisfied and served accordingly. Let us teach the ladies to make the most of themselves, to respect themselves, to beguile and fool us. We make our ultimate attack the first one; the French impetuosity is always there. If the ladies spin out and spread out their favors in small amounts, each man, even to miserable old age, will find there some little scrap of pleasure, according to his worth and merit.

He who has no enjoyment except in enjoyment, who must win all or nothing, who loves the chase only in the capture, has no business mixing with our school. The more steps and degrees there are, the more height and honor there is in the topmost seat. We should take pleasure in being led there, as is done in magnificent palaces, by divers porticoes and passages, long and pleasant galleries, and many windings. This arrangement would redound to our advantage; we would stay there longer and love there longer. Without hope and without desire we no longer go at any worth-while gait.

Our mastery and entire possession is something for them to fear infinitely. Once they have wholly surrendered to the mercy of our fidelity and constancy, they are in a very hazardous position. Those are rare and difficult virtues. As soon as the ladies are ours, we are no longer theirs:

> The lust of greedy mind once satisfied,
> We fear nor care for oaths once sworn, but now denied.

—CATULLUS

And Thrasonides, a young Greek, was so much in love with his love that having won his mistress' heart he refused to enjoy her, so as not to deaden, satiate, and weaken by enjoyment that restless ardor on which he prided and fed himself.

Dearness gives relish to the meat. See how much the form of salutation which is peculiar to our nation debases by its facility the charm of kisses, which Socrates says are so powerful and dangerous for stealing our hearts. It is a disagreeable custom, and unfair to the ladies, to have to lend their lips to any man who has three footmen at his heels, however unattractive he may be:

> A bluish ice, from nostrils like a dog's,
> Comes hanging down, his beard stiffens and clogs . . .
> A hundred times I'd rather kiss his ass.

—MARTIAL

And we ourselves do not gain much by it; for as the world is divided, for three beautiful women we have to kiss fifty ugly ones. And for a tender stomach, as men of my age have, one bad kiss is too high a price for one good one.

In Italy they play the part of timid suitors even with the women who are for sale, and they defend the practice thus: that there are degrees in enjoyment, and that by courting they want to obtain for themselves that which is most complete. These women sell only their bodies; the will cannot be put on sale, it is too free and too much its own master. Thus these men say that they are wooing their will; and they are right. It is the will that must be courted and solicited. I abhor the idea of a body void of affection being mine. And it seems to me that such frenzy is close to that of the boy who went and defiled out of love the beautiful statue of Venus that Praxiteles had made, or that of the frantic Egyptian hot after the carcass of a dead woman he was embalming and shrouding; which gave rise to the law that was made since then in Egypt, that the bodies of beautiful young women and of those of good family should be kept three days before being put in the hands of the undertakers. Periander behaved more monstrously when he extended his conjugal affection (more regular and legitimate) to the enjoyment of Melissa, his dead wife.

Doesn't it seem a lunatic humor in Luna, unable otherwise to enjoy her darling Endymion, to put him to sleep for several months, and take her satisfaction in enjoying a boy who stirred only in his dreams?

I say likewise that we love a body without soul or sentiment, when we love a body without its consent and desire. Not all enjoyments are alike. Some are meager and languid. A thousand causes other than good will may win us this concession from the ladies. It is not sufficient evidence of affection; there may be treachery in it as elsewhere; sometimes they go to it with only one buttock:

> *As cool as if preparing frankincense and wine . . .*
> *You'd think her absent or of marble.*
>
> —MARTIAL

I know some who would rather lend that than their coach, and who communicate only in that way. You must observe whether they like your company for yet some other purpose or for this alone, as they might that of some husky stable-boy; in what rank and at what value you are lodged there,

> *If to you alone*
> *She gives herself, and marks that day with a whiter stone.*
>
> —CATULLUS

What if she eats your bread with the sauce of a more agreeable imagination?

> *'Tis you she holds, but sighs for other, absent loves.*
>
> —TIBULLUS

What! have we not seen someone in our own time use this act for the purpose of a horrible vengeance, thereby to poison and kill, as he did, an honorable woman?

Those who know Italy will never find it strange if for this subject I do not seek examples elsewhere; for that nation may be called the teacher of the world in this. They have generally more beautiful women and fewer ugly ones than we; but in rare and outstanding beauties I think we are on a par. And I judge as much of their intellects. Of the ordinary sort they have many more, and obviously brutishness is incomparably rarer there; in unusual minds and minds of the highest stature, we concede them nothing. If I had to extend this comparison, it would seem to me I could say that on the contrary valor is more common and natural among us than among them; but in them we sometimes see it so full and vigorous that it surpasses the sturdiest examples that we have.

The marriages of that country are lame in this: their custom commonly imposes so harsh and so slavish a law on the wives that the most distant contact with a stranger is as capital an offense to them as the most intimate. The result of this law is that all approaches necessarily become substantial; and since it all comes to the same for them, they have a very easy choice. And once they have broken through these partitions, believe me, they are on fire: *Lust, like a wild beast, irritated by its chains, is then let loose* [Livy]. We must give them a little more rein:

> *Lately I saw, rebellious to the bit, a colt*
> *With stubborn mouth run like a thunderbolt.*
>
> —OVID

The desire for company is weakened by giving it a little liberty.

We run about the same chance. They are too extreme in constraint, we in license. It is a fine practice of our nation that our sons are received into good families to be brought up and trained as pages, as in a school of nobility. And it is considered a discourtesy and an affront to refuse one of noble birth. I have perceived—for so many houses, so many different styles and forms—that the ladies who have tried to give the maidens in their retinue the most austere rules have not come out any better. Moderation is needed: a good part of their conduct must be left to their own discretion; for one way or another, there is no discipline that can curb them in all directions. But it is quite true that a girl who has escaped safe, bag and baggage, from a free schooling, inspires much more confidence than one who comes out safely from a severe, prisonlike school.

Our fathers trained their daughters' faces to bashfulness and timidity (hearts and desires were the same); we, to self-assurance: we don't know what we're doing. That is for the Sarmatian women, who may not lie with a man until with their own hands they have killed another in war.

For me, who have no rights in this except through the ears, it is enough that they retain me as counsel, according to the privilege of my age. So I counsel them abstinence, as I do to us; but if this generation is too hostile to it, at least discretion and modesty. For as the story tells about Aristippus, speaking to some young men who blushed to see him enter the house of a courtesan, "The vice is in not coming out, not in entering." If she will not keep her conscience clear, let her keep her name clear; if the substance is not worth much, let the appearance be preserved.

I commend gradation and delay in the dispensation of their favors. Plato shows that in every kind of love the defenders are forbidden to yield easily and promptly. It is a trait of greediness, which they must cover up with all their art, to surrender so heedlessly, completely, and impetuously. By conducting themselves with order and measure in granting their favors, they beguile our desire much better and conceal their own. Let them always flee before us, I mean even those who intend to let themselves be caught; they conquer us better in flight, like the Scythians. Indeed, according to the law that Nature gives them, it is not properly for them to will and desire; their role is to suffer, obey, consent. That is why Nature has given them a perpetual capacity, to us a rare and uncertain one. They have their hour always, so that they may be ready for ours: *born to be passive* [Seneca]. And whereas Nature has willed that our appetites should show and declare themselves prominently, she has made theirs occult and internal, and has furnished them with parts unsuitable for show and simply for the defensive.

We must leave to Amazonian license actions like this one. When Alexander was passing through Hyrcania, Thalestris, queen of the Amazons, came to find him with three hundred warriors of her own sex, well mounted and well armed, having left the remainder of a large army that was following her beyond the neighboring mountains; and said to him, right out loud and in public, that the fame of his victories and valor had brought her there to see him, to offer him her resources and power in support of his enterprises; and that finding him so handsome, young, and vigorous, she, who was perfect in all his qualities, advised him that they should lie together, so that of the most valiant woman in the world and the most valiant man who was then alive there should be born something great and rare for the future. Alexander thanked her just the same for the rest; but to allow enough time for the accomplishment of her last request, he stopped in that place thirteen days, which he celebrated as lustily as he could in honor of so courageous a princess.

We are in almost all things unjust judges of their actions, as they are of ours. I admit the truth when it hurts me, just as when it serves me. It is an ugly aberration that pushes them so often to change and keeps them from fixing their affection on any object whatever, as we see of that goddess[17] to whom are attributed so many changes and lovers. Yet the truth is that it is contrary to the nature of love if it is not violent, and contrary to the nature of violence if it is constant. And those who are astonished at this and exclaim against it and seek out the causes of this malady in women as if it were unnatural and incredible, why don't they see how often they accept it in themselves without being appalled and calling it a miracle? It would perhaps be more strange to see any stability in it. It is not simply a bodily passion. If there is no end to avarice and ambition, neither is there any to lechery. It still lives after satiety; no constant satisfaction or end can be prescribed to it, for it always goes beyond its possession.

And furthermore, inconstancy is perhaps somewhat more pardonable in them than in us. They can allege, as we can, the inclination to variety and novelty which is common to us both; and allege secondly, as we cannot, that they buy a cat in a bag (Joanna, queen of Naples, had Andreasso, her first husband, strangled at the bars of her window with a gold and silk cord woven by her own hand, when in matrimonial duties she found that neither his parts nor his efforts corresponded well enough with the expectations she had formed of them on seeing his build, his beauty, his youth and agility, whereby she had been caught and deceived); that action involves more effort than submission; and that consequently they are always able to satisfy our needs, whereas it may be otherwise when it is up to us to satisfy theirs.

Plato for this reason wisely established in his laws that in order to decide on the suitability of a marriage the judges should see the young men who aspire to it stark naked, and the girls naked down to the girdle only. When they come to try us, they may not find us worthy of their choice:

> *Having explored his body, found his member limp*
> *As a wet thong, impossible by hand to primp,*
> *She leaves the dastard bed.*
>
> —MARTIAL

---

[17] Venus.

It is not enough that a man's will should carry straight. Weakness and incapacity legitimately break up a marriage:

> *A stronger lover elsewhere must be found*
> *By whom her virgin zone may be unbound.*
>
> —CATULLUS

Why not? And according to her standard, a more licentious and active amorous relationship,

> *If he cannot last out the pleasant task.*
>
> —VIRGIL

But is it not a great impudence to bring our imperfections and weaknesses where we desire to please and leave a good opinion and recommendation of ourselves? For the little that I need nowadays,

> *Even for one*
> *Encounter, limp,*
>
> —HORACE

I would not want to trouble a person whom I have to reverence and fear:

> *Nor ever fear*
> *A man whose life, alas, has tottered past*
> *His fiftieth year.*
>
> —HORACE

Nature should have contented herself with making this age miserable, without making it also ridiculous. I hate to see it, for one inch of wretched vigor that heats it up three times a week, bustle about and swagger with the same fierceness as if it had some great and proper day's work in its belly: a real flash in the pan. And I marvel to see such a lively and frisky flame so sluggishly congealed and put out in a moment. This appetite should belong only to the flower of beauty and youth. Just rely on age, if you want to find out, to second that indefatigable, full, constant, and great-souled ardor that is in you: it will leave you nicely in the lurch! Rather pass it on boldly to some tender, dazed, and ignorant boy, still trembling under the rod and blushing at it,

Even as Indian ivory, stained with red,
Or lilies mingled in the flower bed
With roses.

—VIRGIL

He who can await, the morning after, without dying of shame, the disdain of those fair eyes that have witnessed his limpness and impertinence,

Her silent looks made eloquent reproach,

—OVID

has never felt the satisfaction and pride of having conquered them and put circles around them by the vigorous exercise of a busy and active night. When I have seen one of them grow weary of me, I have not promptly blamed her fickleness; I have wondered whether I did not have reason rather to blame Nature. Certainly she has treated me unfairly and unkindly—

But if the penis be not long or stout enough . . .
Even the matrons—all too well they know—
Look dimly on a man whose member's small.

—PRIAPEA

—and done me the most enormous damage.

Each one of my parts makes me myself just as much as every other one. And no other makes me more properly a man than this one.

I owe a complete portrait of myself to the public. The wisdom of my lesson is wholly in truth, in freedom, in reality; disdaining, in the list of its real duties, those petty, feigned, customary, provincial rules; altogether natural, constant, and universal; of which propriety and ceremony are daughters, but bastard daughters.

We will readily take care of the vices of appearance when we have taken care of those of reality. When we have done with the latter, we will attack the others, if we find we need to attack them. For there is danger that we dream up new duties to excuse our negligence toward our natural duties and mix them up. As proof of this: we see that in places where faults are crimes, crimes are only faults; that in nations where the laws of propriety are rarer and looser, the primitive and common laws are better observed; for the innumerable multitude of so many duties smothers, weakens, and dissipates our concern. Application to trivial things draws us away from urgent ones. Oh what an easy and applauded route those superficial men take, compared with ours! These are shadows with which we comfort ourselves and pay one another off; but we do not really pay, we rather add to our debt to that great Judge who tucks up our rags and tatters from around our shameful parts and does not merely pretend to see us throughout, even to our inmost and most secret filth. Our virginal modesty would be a useful propriety if it could keep him from making this discovery.

In short, whoever would wean man of the folly of such a scrupulous verbal superstition would do the world no great harm. Our life is part folly, part wisdom. Whoever writes about it only reverently and according to the rules leaves out more than half of it. I am not making excuses to myself, and if I did, I would make excuses rather for my excuses than for any other part of me. I am making excuses to certain humors which I believe to be stronger in number than those that are on my side. In consideration of them I will further say this—for I wish to satisfy everyone, though it is a very difficult thing *for one single man to accommodate himself to so great a variety of ways, discourses, and wills* [Cicero]—that they should not properly blame me for what I quote from authorities accepted and approved for many centuries; and that it is not right that they should refuse me, because I lack rhyme, the dispensation that even churchmen, and some of the most proudly crested at that, enjoy in our time. Here are two of them:

> *May I die if your crack is more than a faint line.*
>
> —BEZA

> *A friendly tool contents and treats her well.*
>
> —SAINT-GELAIS

And what about the many others?

I like modesty, and it is not by judgment that I have chosen this scandalous way of speaking; it is nature that has chosen it for me. I do not commend it, any more than I do any forms that are contrary to accepted practice; but I excuse it, and by particular and general circumstances I make the accusation lighter. Let's get on.

Likewise whence can come that usurpation of sovereign authority that you assume over those women who grant you favors at their own expense—

> *If she gave you furtive favors in the black of night*
>
> —CATULLUS

—so that you immediately put on the rights, the coldness, and the authority of a husband? It is a free compact; why do you not keep to it as you want to hold them to it? There is no power of prescription in voluntary things.

It is contrary to form, but still it is true that in my time I have handled this business, as far as the nature of it would permit, as conscientiously as any other business and with some air of justice; and that I swore to them only what I felt about my affection, and represented to them candidly its decadence, its vigor, and its birth, its fits and its lapses. One does not always go about it at the same pace. I have been so sparing in promising that I think I have carried out more than I promised or owed. They have found me faithful even to the point of serving their inconstancy—I mean an avowed and sometimes multiplied inconstancy. I have never broken with them as long as I held to them even by a bit of thread; and whatever occasions for it they have given me, I have never broken with them to the point of scorn or hatred. For such intimacies, even when acquired on the most shameful terms, still oblige me to some good will. Anger and some-what heedless impatience I have sometimes shown them on the occasion of their ruses and evasions and our quarrels; for by my nature I am subject to sudden outbursts which, though slight and brief, often harm my affairs. If they wanted to test the freedom of my judgment, I did not shirk giving them sharp paternal advice and pinching them where they smarted. If I have left them with any reason to complain of me, it is rather for having found in me a love which, compared with modern usage, was stupidly conscientious. I have kept my word in things in which I might easily have been excused. In those days they sometimes surrendered with honor and on conditions that they readily suffered the conqueror to break. I have more than once, in the interest of their honor, made pleasure yield in its greatest stress; and when reason urged me, I have armed them against myself, so that they conducted themselves more safely and severely by my rules, when they freely relied on them, than they would have done by their own.

As much as I could, I have taken upon myself alone the risk of our assignations, to free them of it, and I have always arranged our meetings in the hardest and most unexpected ways, so that they might be less under suspicion and besides, in my opinion, more accessible. Meetings are chiefly exposed in the places people think are automatically enclosed. Things least feared are least guarded against and observed. You can more easily dare what no one thinks you will dare, which becomes easy by its difficulty.

Never was a man more impertinently genital in his approaches. This way of loving is more according to the rules; but who knows better than I how ridiculous it is to people nowadays, and how ineffectual? Yet I shall not repent of it; I have nothing more to lose there:

A votive tablet shows
I hung my dedicated clothes,
Dripping with brine,
Here in the sea-god's shrine.

—HORACE

It is time now to speak of it openly. But just as I might peradventure say
to another: "My friend, you are dreaming; love in your time has little to do
with faith and probity"—

If under reason's certain rule
You seek to bring this, all you do is add
This to your tasks: with reason to go mad

—TERENCE

—so, on the contrary, if I were to begin over again, it would certainly be
by the same method and the same procedure, however fruitless it might be
for me. Ineptitude and stupidity are praiseworthy in a blameworthy action. The further I depart from their attitude in this, the nearer I approach
my own.

For the rest, in this business I did not let myself go entirely; I took
pleasure in it, but I did not forget myself; I preserved entire the little sense
and discretion that nature has given me, for their service and mine: a little
excitement, but no folly. My conscience was also involved in it to the
point of licentiousness and dissoluteness; but to the point of ingratitude,
treachery, malignity, and cruelty, no. I did not purchase the pleasure of
this vice at all costs, but contented myself with its proper and simple cost:
No vice is self-contained [Seneca].

I hate almost equally a stagnant and sleepy idleness and a thorny and
painful busyness. The one pinches me, the other puts me to sleep. I like
wounds as much as bruises, and cutting blows as much as dry ones. I
found in this business, when I was more fit for it, a just moderation between these two extremes. Love is a sprightly, lively, and gay agitation; I
was neither troubled nor afflicted by it, but I was heated and moreover
made thirsty by it. A man should stop there; it is hurtful only to fools.

A young man asked the philosopher Panaetius whether it would be
becoming to a wise man to be in love. "Let us leave aside the wise man,"
he replied, "but you and I, who are not, let us not get involved in a thing
so excited and violent, which enslaves us to others and makes us contemptible to ourselves." He spoke truly, that we should not entrust a thing
so precipitous in itself to a soul that has not the wherewithal to withstand
its assaults and to disprove in practice the saying of Agesilaus, that wisdom and love cannot live together. It is a vain occupation, it is true,

unbecoming, shameful, and illegitimate; but carried on in this fashion, I consider it healthy, proper to enliven a heavy body and soul; and as a physician, I would prescribe it to a man of my temperament and condition as readily as any other recipe to rouse him and keep him in vigor till he is well on in years, and to keep him from the clutches of old age. While we are only in its outskirts and the pulse still beats,

> *While hair is freshly gray, old age hale and erect,*
> *While Lachesis has thread to spin, and while I stand*
> *And walk on my own feet, no staff in my right hand.*

> —JUVENAL

we need to be stimulated and tickled by some biting agitation such as this. See how much youth, vigor, and gaiety it gave back to the wise Anacreon. And Socrates, when older than I am, speaking of an object of his love, said: "When I had leaned my shoulder against his and brought my head close to his, as we were looking into a book together, I suddenly felt, without prevarication, a stinging in my shoulder like some animal's bite, and I was more than five days with it prickling, and a continual itching flowed into my heart." A touch, and an accidental one, and by a shoulder, to inflame and alter a soul cooled and enervated by age, and the first of all human souls in reformation! Indeed, why not? Socrates was a man, and wanted neither to be nor to seem anything else.

Philosophy does not strive against natural pleasures, provided that measure goes with them; she preaches moderation in them, not flight. The power of her resistance is employed against alien and bastard pleasures. She says that the appetites of the body are not to be augmented by the mind, and warns us ingeniously not to try to arouse our hunger by satiety, not to stuff instead of filling the belly, to avoid all enjoyment that brings us want and all meat and drink that makes us thirsty and hungry; as, in the service of love, she orders us to take an object that simply satisfies the body's need, that does not stir the soul, which should not make this its business but simply follow and assist the body.

But am I not right to consider that these precepts, which by the way are in my opinion still a bit rigorous, concern a body that performs its function, and that for a run-down body, as for a broken-down stomach, it is excusable to warm it up and support it by art, and by the mediation of fancy to restore appetite and blitheness to it, since by itself it has lost them?

May we not say that there is nothing in us during this earthly imprisonment that is purely either corporeal or spiritual, and that we do wrong to tear apart a living man, and that it seems somewhat reasonable that we should behave as favorably at least toward the use of pleasure as we do toward pain? Pain, for example, was vehement even to perfection in the souls of the saints, through penitence; the body naturally had a share in it by virtue of their union, and yet could have little share in the cause. Yet they were not content that it should simply follow and assist the afflicted soul; they afflicted the body itself with atrocious and appropriate torments, in order that, vying with each other, the soul and the body should plunge man into pain, the more salutary for its harshness.

In a similar case, that of bodily pleasures, is it not unjust to cool the soul toward them and say that she should be dragged to them as to some constrained and servile obligation and necessity? It is rather for her to hatch them and foment them, to offer and invite herself to them, since the authority of ruling belongs to her; as it is also for her, in my opinion, in the pleasures that are her own, to inspire and infuse into the body all the feeling their nature allows, and to strive to make them sweet and salutary to it. For it is indeed reasonable, as they say, that the body should not follow its appetites to the disadvantage of the mind; but why is it not also reasonable that the mind should not pursue its appetites to the disadvantage of the body?

I have no other passion to keep me in breath. What avarice, ambition, quarrels, lawsuits, do for others who, like me, have no assigned occupation, love would do more agreeably. It would restore to me vigilance, sobriety, grace, care for my person; would secure my countenance, so that the grimaces of old age, those deformed and pitiable grimaces, should not come to disfigure it; would take me back to sane and wise studies, whereby I might make myself more esteemed and more loved, ridding my mind of despair of itself and its employment, and reacquainting it with itself; would divert me from a thousand troublesome thoughts, a thousand melancholy moods, that idleness and the bad state of our health loads us with at such an age; would warm up again, at least in dreams, this blood that nature is abandoning; would hold up the chin and stretch out a little the muscles and the soul's vigor and blitheness for this poor man who is going full speed toward his ruin.

But I quite understand that love is a very hard commodity to recover. By weakness and long experience our taste has become more delicate and exquisite. We demand more when we bring less; we most want to choose when we least deserve to be accepted. Knowing ourselves for what we are, we are less bold and more distrustful; nothing can assure us of being loved, knowing our condition and theirs. I am ashamed to find myself amid this green and ardent youth,

> *Whose member firmer stands, in its undaunted pride,*
> *Than a young tree upon a mountainside.*

—HORACE

Why should we go offering our wretchedness amid this sprightliness?

> *That ardent youngsters may stand round and watch,*
> *Not without mocking shout,*
> *As into ashes our weak torch burns out?*

> —HORACE

They have strength and right on their side; let us make way for them, we have no hold left.

And this bud of nascent beauty does not let itself be handled by such stiff hands or be won over by purely material means. For as that ancient philosopher replied to one who mocked him for having been unable to win the good graces of a tender youth he was pursuing: "My friend, the hook will not bite into such fresh cheese."

Now this is a relationship that needs mutuality and reciprocity. The other pleasures that we receive may be acknowledged by recompenses of a different nature; but this one can be paid for only in the same kind of coin. In truth, in this delight the pleasure I give tickles my imagination more sweetly than that which I feel. Now there is no nobility in a man who can receive pleasure where he gives none; it is a mean soul that is willing to owe everything and takes pleasure in fostering relations with persons to whom he is a burden. There is neither beauty, nor grace, nor intimacy so exquisite that a gallant man should desire it at this price. If they can be kind to us only out of pity, I had much rather not live at all than live on alms. I would like to have the right to ask it of them in the style I have seen beggars use in Italy: *"Do good for your own sake";* or in the manner in which Cyrus exhorted his soldiers: "Who loves himself, let him follow me."

Rally, someone will tell me, round women of your own condition, whom company in like fortune will make easier for you. Oh what a stupid and insipid compromise!

> *I will*
> *Not pluck at a dead lion's beard.*

> —MARTIAL

Xenophon uses it as an objection and an accusation against Meno that in his love affairs he made use of persons who had passed their flower. I find more sensual pleasure in merely seeing the just and sweet union of two young beauties, or in merely considering it in imagination, than in myself making the second in a sad and ill-formed union. I resign that fantastic appetite to the Emperor Galba, who was addicted only to tough old meat, and to this poor wretch:

Would God that as I dream of you I might behold you,
And press sweet kisses on your altered locks,
Take your worn body in my arms and thus enfold you!

—OVID

And among the leading forms of ugliness I count artificial and forced beauties. Hemon, a young boy of Chios, thinking by fine attire to acquire the beauty that nature denied him, presented himself to the philosopher Arcesilaus and asked him whether a wise man could fall in love. "Yes indeed," he replied, "provided it is not with a bedecked and sophisticated beauty like yours." An avowed ugliness and old age is less old and less ugly to my taste than another that is painted and glossed over.

Shall I say it, provided no one takes me by the throat for it? Love does not seem to me properly and naturally in its season except in the age next to childhood:

If you should place him in a troop of girls,
With his ambiguous face and flowing curls,
A thousand sharp onlookers could be wrong
And fail to pick him out amid the throng.

—HORACE

Nor beauty either. For when Homer makes beauty last until the chin begins to show a shadow, Plato himself remarks that such a flower is rare. And it is well known why the sophist Dion so humorously called the downy hairs of adolescence Aristogeitons and Harmodiuses.[18] In manhood I find it already out of place; not to speak of old age:

For pitiless past the withered oaks
Love flies.

—HORACE

And Margaret, queen of Navarre, like a woman, prolongs the advantage of women very far, ordaining that at thirty it is time for them to change the title of "beautiful" to "good."

The shorter the possession we give Love over our life, the better we are. Look at his bearing: he is a beardless boy. Who does not know how in his school they proceed contrary to all order? Study, exercise, practice, are ways leading to incapacity; the novices there give the lessons: *Love knows*

---

[18] Because these hairs deliver lovers of the boys who grow them from the tyranny of love, as Harmodius and Aristogeiton delivered Athens from tyranny.

no rule [Saint Jerome]. Certainly Love's conduct has much more style when it is mingled with heedlessness and confusion; mistakes and misadventures give it point and grace. Provided it is sharp and hungry, it matters little whether it is prudent. See how he goes reeling, tripping, and wantonly playing; you put him in the stocks when you guide him by art and wisdom, and you constrain his divine freedom when you subject him to those hairy and callous hands.

Moreover, I often hear women portray this relationship as wholly spiritual and disdain to place in consideration the interest that the senses have in it. Everything contributes to it. But I may say that I have often seen us excuse the weakness of their minds in favor of their bodily beauties; but I have never yet seen that for the sake of our beauty of mind, however wise and mature that mind may be, they were willing to grant favors to a body that was slipping the least little bit into decline. Why is not one of them seized with desire for that noble Socratic exchange of body for soul, buying a philosophical and spiritual intelligence and generation at the price of her thighs, the highest price to which she can raise them? Plato ordains in his *Laws* that whoever has performed some signal and useful exploit in war, regardless of his ugliness or old age, may not for the war's duration be refused a kiss or other amorous favor from whomever he wants. What he finds so just in recommendation of military worth, may it not also be so in recommendation of some other kind of worth? And why is not one of them seized with desire to gain before her sisters the glory of this chaste love? And I do mean chaste,

> *For if it comes to love's encounter,*
> *Like fire in straw, mighty in size, with little power,*
> *They spend their rage in vain.*
>
> —VIRGIL

The vices that are stifled in thought are not the worst.

To conclude this notable commentary, which has escaped from me in a flow of babble, a flow sometimes impetuous and harmful—

> *And as an apple, secret present from her love,*
> *Falls out from the chaste bosom of the maid,*
> *Where she has quite forgot it, hid beneath her robe,*
> *When at her mother's step she starts, afraid;*
> *As she rises it falls, rolls off at a swift pace;*
> *A guilty blush spreads o'er her downcast face*
>
> —CATULLUS

—I say that males and females are cast in the same mold; except for education and custom, the difference is not great. Plato invites both without discrimination to the fellowship of all studies, exercises, functions, warlike and peaceful occupations, in his commonwealth. And the philosopher Antisthenes eliminated any distinction between their virtue and ours. It is much easier to accuse one sex than to excuse the other. It is the old saying: The pot calls the kettle black.

—Translated by Donald M. Frame

III

The Rise *of* the English Essay

Johnson was accurate about and Cowley seems so tidy ... so personal ... A relief from much pomposity

ABRAHAM COWLEY

Abraham Cowley (1618–1667), the son of a grocer, studied at Cambridge and showed precocious literary talent. A supporter of the Royalists, he went to France as a result of the Puritan uprising and remained with the royal family for twelve years. After the Restoration, he returned and took a medical degree. A poet of the English metaphysical school, he wrote verse that is full of elaborate conceits and is no longer read much, but his personal essays continue to impress with their naturalness and simplicity. He is considered one of the earliest masters of a clear and easy English prose style. Samuel Johnson, in his Lives of the Poets, *praised Cowley for his essays: "His thoughts are natural, and his style has a smooth and placid equability, which has never yet obtained its due commendation. Nothing is far-sought, or hard-laboured; but all is easy without feebleness, and familiar without grossness."*

Cowley followed the intention of Montaigne (rather than Bacon) in trying to convey an intimate moment of personal reflection on whatever subject was uppermost in his mind. A modern admirer, Bonamy Dobrée, has made the case for him: "Cowley is, perhaps, [England's] first really friendly essayist; he never pretends to be more enlightened or more exquisite in feeling than the average man." His insights "are personal, not abstract. . . . Thus when he writes so charmingly about the delight of gardens, one knows that he himself is a gardener, whereas one is pretty certain that Bacon had never plied a hoe. Moreover Cowley is such pleasant reading because wherever he can he uses the homely image; he doesn't challenge your thought or argue with you, but makes you feel all the time how pleasant it is to agree with him."

Of Greatness

"SINCE we cannot attain to greatness," says the Sieur de Montaigne, "let us have our revenge by railing at it": this he spoke but in jest. I believe he desired it no more than I do, and had less reason; for he enjoyed so plentiful and honorable a fortune in a most excellent country, as allowed him all the real conveniences of it, separated and purged from the incommodities. If I were but in his condition, I should think it hard measure, without being convinced of any crime, to be sequestrated from it, and made one of the principal officers of state. But the reader may think that what I now say is of small authority, because I never was, nor ever shall be, put to the trial: I can therefore only make my protestation:

> *If ever I more riches did desire*
> *Than cleanliness and quiet do require:*
> *If e'er ambition did my fancy cheat,*
> *With any wish, so mean as to be great,*
> *Continue, Heaven, still from me to remove*
> *The humble blessings of that life I love.*

I know very many men will despise, and some pity me, for this humor, as a poor-spirited fellow; but I am content, and, like Horace, thank God for being so.

> *"Di bene fecerunt, inopis me quodque pusilli,*
> *Finxerunt animi."*[1]

I confess I love littleness almost in all things. A little convenient estate, a little cheerful house, a little company, and a very little feast; and, if I were to fall in love again (which is a great passion, and therefore, I hope, I have done with it), it would be, I think, with prettiness, rather than with majestical beauty. I would neither wish that my mistress, nor my fortune, should be a *bona roba,* nor, as Homer uses to describe his beauties, like a daugh-

---

[1] Horace, Sat. I. iv. 17: "The gods have done well in making me a humble and small-spirited fellow."

ter of great Jupiter, for the stateliness and largeness of her person; but, as Lucretius says,

"Parvula, pumilio, Χαρίτων μία, tota merum sal."

Where there is one man of this, I believe there are a thousand of Senecio's mind, whose ridiculous affectation of grandeur Seneca the elder describes to this effect: Senecio was a man of a turbid and confused wit, who could not endure to speak any but mighty words and sentences, till this humor grew at last into so notorious a habit, or rather disease, as became the sport of the whole town: he would have no servants, but huge, massy fellows; no plate or household stuff, but thrice as big as the fashion: you may believe me, for I speak it without raillery, his extravagancy came at last into such a madness that he would not put on a pair of shoes, each of which was not big enough for both his feet: he would eat nothing but what was great, nor touch any fruit but horse-plums and pound-pears: he kept a concubine that was a very giantess, and made her walk too always in chiopins, till at last he got the surname of Senecio Grandio, which, Messala said, was not his *cognomen,* but his *cognomentum:* when he declaimed for the three hundred Lacedaemonians, who alone opposed Xerxes's army of above three hundred thousand, he stretched out his arms, and stood on tiptoes, that he might appear the taller, and cried out, in a very loud voice: "I rejoice, I rejoice"—we wondered, I remember what new great fortune had befallen his eminence—"Xerxes," says he, "is all mine own. He who took away the sight of the sea with the canvas veils of so many ships"—and then he goes on so, as I know not what to make of the rest, whether it be the fault of the edition, or the orator's own burly way of nonsense.

This is the character that Seneca gives of this hyperbolical fop, whom we stand amazed at, and yet there are very few men who are not in some things, and to some degrees, *grandios.* Is anything more common than to see our ladies of quality wear such high shoes as they cannot walk in, without one to lead them; and a gown as long again as their body, so that they cannot stir to the next room, without a page or two to hold it up? I may safely say that all the ostentation of our grandees is just like a train, of no use in the world, but horribly cumbersome and incommodious. What is all this but a spice of *grandio?* How tedious would this be if we were always bound to it! I do believe there is no king who would not rather be deposed than endure, every day of his reign, all the ceremonies of his coronation.

The mightiest princes are glad to fly often from these majestic pleasures (which is, methinks, no small disparagement to them) as it were for refuge, to the most contemptible divertisements, and meanest recreations, of the vulgar, nay, even of children. One of the most powerful and fortunate princes of the world,[2] of late, could find out no delight so satisfactory, as the keeping of little singing birds, and hearing of them, and whistling to them. What did the emperors of the whole world? If ever any men had the free and full enjoyment of all human greatness (nay, that would not suffice, for they would be gods too), they certainly possessed it: and yet one of them, who styled himself lord and god of the earth, could not tell how to pass his whole day pleasantly, without spending constantly two or three hours in catching of flies, and killing them with a bodkin, as if his godship had been Beelzebub.[3] One of his predecessors, Nero (who never put any bounds, nor met with any stop to his appetite), could divert himself with no pastime more agreeable than to run about the streets all night in a disguise, and abuse the women, and affront the men whom he met, and sometimes to beat them, and sometimes to be beaten by them: this was one of his imperial nocturnal pleasures. His chiefest in the day was to sing and play upon a fiddle, in the habit of a minstrel, upon the public stage: he was prouder of the garlands that were given to his divine voice (as they called it then) in those kind of prizes than all his forefathers were of their triumphs over nations: he did not at his death complain that so mighty an emperor, and the last of all the Caesarian race of deities, should be brought to so shameful and miserable an end; but only cried out, "Alas! what pity it is that so excellent a musician should perish in this manner!" His uncle Claudius spent half his time at playing at dice; that was the main fruit of his sovereignty. I omit the madnesses of Caligula's delights, and the execrable sordidness of those of Tiberius. Would one think that Augustus himself, the highest and most fortunate of mankind, a person endowed too with many excellent parts of nature, should be so hard put to it sometimes for want of recreations, as to be found playing at nuts and bounding-stones with little Syrian and Moorish boys, whose company he took delight in, for their prating and their wantonness?

> *Was it for this that Rome's best blood he spilt,*
> *With so much falsehood, so much guilt?*
> *Was it for this, that his ambition strove*
> *To equal Caesar, first; and after, Jove?*
> *Greatness is barren, sure, of solid joys;*
> *Her merchandise (I fear) is all in toys:*
> *She could not else, sure, so uncivil be,*
> *To treat his universal majesty,*

---

[2] Louis XIII. The Duke of Luynes, Constable of France, is said to have gained the favor of this powerful prince by training up singing birds for him.—*Anonymous.*

[3] Beelzebub signifies the Lord of Flies.—*Cowley.*

His new-created deity,
With nuts and bounding-stones and boys.

But we must excuse her for this meagre entertainment; she has not really wherewithal to make such feasts as we imagine. Her guests must be contented sometimes with but slender cates, and with the same cold meats served over and over again, even till they become nauseous. When you have pared away all the vanity, what solid and natural contentment does there remain, which may not be had with five hundred pounds a year? Not so many servants or horses; but a few good ones, which will do all the business as well: not so many choice dishes at every meal; but at several meals all of them, which makes them both the more healthy, and the more pleasant: not so rich garments, nor so frequent changes; but as warm and as comely, and so frequent change too, as is every jot as good for the master, though not for the tailor or *valet de chambre:* not such a stately palace, nor gilt rooms, or the costliest sorts of tapestry; but a convenient brick house, with decent wainscot, and pretty forest-work hangings. Lastly (for I omit all other particulars, and will end with that which I love most in both conditions), not whole woods cut in walks, nor vast parks, nor fountain or cascade gardens; but herb, and flower, and fruit gardens, which are more useful, and the water every whit as clear and wholesome as if it darted from the breasts of a marble nymph, or the urn of a river god.

If, for all this, you like better the substance of that former estate of life, do but consider the inseparable accidents of both: servitude, disquiet, danger, and, most commonly, guilt, inherent in the one; in the other, liberty, tranquillity, security, and innocence. And when you have thought upon this, you will confess that to be a truth which appeared to you before but a ridiculous paradox, that a low fortune is better guarded and attended than a high one. If, indeed, we look only upon the flourishing head of the tree, it appears a most beautiful object,

"Sed quantum vertice ad auras
Ætherias, tantum radice in Tartara tendit."

As far as up towards heaven the branches grow,
So far the roots sink down to hell below.

Another horrible disgrace to greatness is, that it is for the most part in pitiful want and distress. What a wonderful thing is this! Unless it degenerate into avarice, and so cease to be greatness, it falls perpetually into such necessities as drive it into all the meanest and most sordid ways of borrowing, cozenage, and robbery:

"Mancipiis locuples, eget aris Cappadocum rex."

This is the case of almost all great men, as well as of the poor King of Cappadocia: they abound with slaves, but are indigent of money. The ancient Roman emperors, who had the riches of the whole world for their revenue, had wherewithal to live (one would have thought) pretty well at ease, and to have been exempt from the pressures of extreme poverty. But, yet with most of them it was much otherwise; and they fell perpetually into such miserable penury, that they were forced to devour or squeeze most of their friends and servants, to cheat with infamous projects, to ransack and pillage all their provinces. This fashion of imperial grandeur is imitated by all inferior and subordinate sorts of it, as if it were a point of honor. They must be cheated of a third part of their estates; two other thirds they must expend in vanity; so that they remain debtors for all the necessary provisions of life, and have no way to satisfy those debts, but out of the succors and supplies of rapine: "As riches increase," says Solomon, "so do the mouths that devour them."[4] The master mouth has no more than before. The owner, methinks, is like Ocnus in the fable, who is perpetually winding a rope of hay, and an ass at the end perpetually eating it.

Out of these inconveniences arises naturally one more, which is, that no greatness can be satisfied or contented with itself: still, if it could mount up a little higher, it would be happy; if it could gain but that point, it would obtain all its desires; but yet at last, when it is got up to the very top of the Peak of Teneriffe, it is in very great danger of breaking its neck downwards, but in no possibility of ascending upwards into the seat of tranquillity above the moon. The first ambitious men in the world, the old giants, are said to have made an heroical attempt of scaling heaven in despite of the gods; and they cast Ossa upon Olympus, and Pelion upon Ossa: two or three mountains more, they thought, would have done their business; but the thunder spoilt all the work, when they were come up to the third story.

And what a noble plot was crossed!
And what a brave design was lost!

A famous person of their offspring, the late giant of our nation, when, from the condition of a very inconsiderable captain, he made himself lieutenant-general of an army of little Titans, which was his first mountain, and afterwards general, which was his second, and after that, absolute tyrant of three kingdoms, which was the third, and almost touched the

---

[4] Eccles. v. II.

heaven which he affected, is believed to have died with grief and discontent, because he could not attain to the honest name of a king, and the old formality of a crown, though he had before exceeded the power by a wicked usurpation. If he could have compassed that, he would perhaps have wanted something else that is necessary to felicity, and pined away for the want of the title of an emperor or a god. The reason of this is, that greatness has no reality in nature, but is a creature of the fancy, a notion that consists only in relation and comparison: it is indeed an idol; but St. Paul teaches us "that an idol is worth nothing in the world." There is, in truth, no rising or meridian of the sun, but only in respect to several places: there is no right or left, no upper hand, in nature; everything is little, and everything is great, according as it is diversely compared. There may be perhaps some village in Scotland or Ireland, where I might be a great man; and in that case I should be like Caesar (you would wonder how Caesar and I should be like one another in anything); and choose rather to be the first man of the village, than second at Rome. Our country is called Great Britainy, in regard only of a lesser of the same name; it would be but a ridiculous epithet for it, when we consider it together with the Kingdom of China. That, too, is but a pitiful rood of ground, in comparison of the whole earth besides: and this whole globe of earth, which we account so immense a body, is but one point or atom in relation to those numberless worlds that are scattered up and down in the infinite space of the sky which we behold.

ADDISON & STEELE

Ho + Hum = Is this New Yorker 400 years prior? Their readers must have been mightily bored.

In the annals of essay writing, Addison and Steele seem joined at the hip. Though they had separate careers and temperaments—Joseph Addison (1672–1719) was a successful diplomat and Whig politician who rose to the post of secretary of state; Richard Steele (1672–1729) lived a more helter-skelter, bohemian life as a journalist and playwright—it is their successful collaboration, writing and publishing two periodicals printed on newssheet, The Tatler *and* The Spectator, *that fuses them in our minds.*

The eighteenth century witnessed a phenomenal flourishing of periodicals, providing work for talented writers as well as hacks. Steele started The Tatler, *which appeared three times a week, offering witty essays, criticism, gossipy items, and news bits, and Addison, his friend from Oxford days, joined soon after. Though written in an amusing, breezy style, the essays often put forward a moral point, or they offered lessons in manners to a middle-class readership aspiring to imitate the aristocracy. Their energy often came from the topical: fashions or the talk of the town. Addison's "Nicolini and the Lions" typifies the duo's fascination with theater and public spectacle. Steele's "Twenty-four Hours in London" is an early instance of a writer's transforming random street activity into literature (Lamb's essay on beggars, Gogol's "Nevsky Prospect," Virginia Woolf's "Street Haunting," and Walter Benjamin's urban pieces are later examples). Addison and Steele also shared the period's fascination with character types, and often disguised their authorship behind humorous false personae and made-up correspondents (see "Love-Letters"). The men's club in* The Spectator *is composed of characters that would influence Dickens and other nineteenth-century novelists.*

Both The Tatler *and* The Spectator *were so popular that they were re-*

printed in full editions for centuries. Addison's smooth prose style, particularly, was held up for emulation. Samuel Johnson wrote, "His prose is the model of the middle style. . . . Whoever wishes to attain an English style, familiar but not coarse, and elegant but not ostentatious, must give his days and nights to the volumes of Addison." Today's readers may resist Addison's mellifluous polish, preferring Steele's edgier, more spontaneous and intimate tone. Both were familiar essayists more often than personal ones; "In an age when emotional modesty was part of good manners, the essayists were embarrassed to speak in their own persons," notes Robert J. Allen. Of the two, Steele seemed more inclined to bare his soul (see "An Hour or Two Sacred to Sorrow").

Nicolini and the Lions

Dic mihi, si fueris tu leo, qualis eris?—Mart.
Were you a lion, how would you behave?

T HE R E is nothing that of late years has afforded matter of greater amusement to the town than Signor Nicolini's[1] combat with a lion in the Haymarket, which has been very often exhibited to the general satisfaction of most of the nobility and gentry in the kingdom of Great Britain. Upon the first rumor of his intended combat, it was confidently affirmed, and is still believed, by many in both galleries, that there would be a tame lion sent from the Tower every opera night in order to be killed by Hydaspes.[2] This report, though altogether groundless, so universally prevailed in the upper regions of the playhouse that some of the most refined politicians in those parts of the audience gave it out in whisper that the lion was a cousin-german of the tiger who made his appearance in King William's days, and that the stage would be supplied with lions at the public expense during the whole session. Many likewise were the conjectures of the treatment which this lion was to meet with from the hands of Signor

---

[1] The Cavaliere Nicolino Grimaldi, a Neapolitan, came to London in 1708. He performed first in "Pyrrhus and Demetrius" in 1710, the last of the mongrel Anglo-Italian operas. In 1712 he left England, after gaining the name of being "the greatest performer in dramatick music that is now living, or that perhaps ever appeared on a stage" ("Spectator," 405). He is alluded to by Addison in "Spectator," 5, as acting in the opera "Rinaldo" by "Mynheer Handel."

[2] An opera by Francesco Mancini, produced at the Haymarket, 1710.

Nicolini; some supposed that he was to subdue him *in recitativo,* as Orpheus used to serve the wild beasts in his time, and afterwards to knock him on the head; some fancied that the lion would not pretend to lay his paws upon the hero, by reason of the received opinion, that a lion will not hurt a virgin. Several, who pretended to have seen the opera in Italy, had informed their friends that the lion was to act a part in high Dutch, and roar twice or thrice to a thorough bass before he fell at the feet of Hydaspes. To clear up a matter that was so variously reported, I have made it my business to examine whether this pretended lion is really the savage he appears to be, or only a counterfeit.

But before I communicate my discoveries, I must acquaint the reader, that upon my walking behind the scenes last winter, as I was thinking on something else, I accidentally jostled against a monstrous animal that extremely startled me, and, upon my nearer survey of it, appeared to be a lion rampant. The lion seeing me very much surprised told me, in a gentle voice, that I might come by him if I pleased; "for," says he, "I do not intend to hurt anybody." I thanked him very kindly, and passed by him: and in a little time after saw him leap upon the stage, and act his part with very great applause. It has been observed by several that the lion has changed his manner of acting twice or thrice since his first appearance; which will not seem strange when I acquaint my reader that the lion has been changed upon the audience three several times. The first lion was a candle-snuffer, who, being a fellow of a testy, choleric temper, overdid his part, and would not suffer himself to be killed as easily as he ought to have done; besides, it was observed of him, that he grew more surly every time that he came out of the lion; and having dropt some words in ordinary conversation, as if he had not fought his best, and that he suffered himself to be thrown upon his back in the scuffle, and that he would wrestle with Mr. Nicolini for what he pleased, out of his lion's skin, it was thought proper to discard him: and it is verily believed to this day, that had he been brought upon the stage another time, he would certainly have done mischief. Besides, it was objected against the first lion, that he reared himself so high upon his hinder paws, and walked in so erect a posture, that he looked more like an old man than a lion.

The second lion was a tailor by trade, who belonged to the playhouse, and had the character of a mild and peaceable man in his profession. If the former was too furious, this was too sheepish for his part; insomuch, that after a short modest walk upon the stage, he would fall at the first touch of Hydaspes, without grappling with him, and giving him an opportunity of showing his variety of Italian trips. It is said, indeed, that he once gave him a rip in his flesh-colored doublet: but this was only to make work for himself, in his private character of a tailor. I must not omit that it was this second lion who treated me with so much humanity behind the scenes.

The acting lion at present is, as I am informed, a country gentleman, who does it for his diversion, but desires his name may be concealed. He says very handsomely in his own excuse, that he does not act for gain, that he indulges an innocent pleasure in it; and that it is better to pass away an evening in this manner than in gaming and drinking: but at the same time says, with a very agreeable raillery upon himself, that if his name should be known, the ill-natured world might call him, "The ass in the lion's skin." This gentleman's temper is made out of such a happy mixture of the mild and the choleric that he outdoes both his predecessors, and has drawn together greater audiences than have been known in the memory of man.

I must not conclude my narrative without first taking notice of a groundless report that has been raised to a gentleman's disadvantage of whom I must declare myself an admirer; namely, that Signor Nicolini and the lion have been seen setting peaceably by one another, and smoking a pipe together behind the scenes; by which their common enemies would insinuate that it is but a sham combat which they represent upon the stage; but upon inquiry I find, that if any such correspondence has passed between them, it was not till the combat was over, when the lion was to be looked upon as dead, according to the received rules of the drama. Besides, this is what is practised every day in Westminster Hall, where nothing is more usual than to see a couple of lawyers, who have been tearing each other to pieces in the court, embracing one another as soon as they are out of it.

I would not be thought in any part of this relation to reflect upon Signor Nicolini, who in acting this part only complies with the wretched taste of his audience; he knows very well that the lion has many more admirers than himself; as they say of the famous equestrian statue on the Pont-Neuf at Paris, that more people go to see the horse than the king who sits upon it. On the contrary, it gives me a just indignation to see a person whose action gives new majesty to kings, resolution to heroes, and softness to lovers, thus sinking from the greatness of his behavior, and degraded into the character of the London 'prentice. I have often wished that our tragedians would copy after this great master of action. Could they make the same use of their arms and legs, and inform their faces with as significant looks and passions, how glorious would an English tragedy appear with that action, which is capable of giving dignity to the forced thoughts, cold conceits, and unnatural expressions of an Italian opera! In the meantime, I have related this combat of the lion, to show what are at present the reigning entertainments of the politer part of Great Britain.

Audiences have often been reproached by writers for the coarseness of their tastes, but our present grievance does not seem to be the want of a good taste, but of common sense.

—*Joseph Addison*

An Hour or Two Sacred to Sorrow

T HERE ARE THOSE AMONG MANKIND, who can enjoy no relish of their being, except the world is made acquainted with all that relates to them, and think everything lost that passes unobserved; but others find a solid delight in stealing by the crowd, and modelling their life after such a manner, as is as much above the approbation as the practice of the vulgar. Life being too short to give instances great enough of true friendship or good will, some sages have thought it pious to preserve a certain reverence for the names of their deceased friends; and have withdrawn themselves from the rest of the world at certain seasons, to commemorate in their own thoughts such of their acquaintance who have gone before them out of this life. And indeed, when we are advanced in years, there is not a more pleasing entertainment, than to recollect in a gloomy moment the many we have parted with, that have been dear and agreeable to us, and to cast a melancholy thought or two after those, with whom, perhaps, we have indulged ourselves in whole nights of mirth and jollity. With such inclinations in my heart I went to my closet yesterday in the evening, and resolved to be sorrowful; upon which occasion I could not but look with disdain upon myself, that though all the reasons which I had to lament the loss of many of my friends are now as forcible as at the moment of their departure, yet did not my heart swell with the same sorrow which I felt at the time; but I could, without tears, reflect upon many pleasing adventures I have had with some, who have long been blended with common earth. Though it is by the benefit of nature, that length of time thus blots out the violence of afflictions; yet, with tempers too much given to pleasure, it is almost necessary to revive the old places of grief in our memory; and ponder step by step on past life, to lead the mind into that sobriety of thought which poises the heart, and makes it beat with due time, without being quickened with desire, or retarded with despair, from its proper and equal motion. When we wind up a clock that is out of order, to make it go well for the future, we do not immediately set the hand to the present instant, but we make it strike the round of all its hours, before it can recover the regularity of its time. Such, thought I, shall be my method this evening; and since it is that day of the year which I dedicate to the memory of such in another life as I much delighted in when living, an hour or two shall be sacred to sorrow and their memory, while I run over all the melancholy circumstances of this kind which have occurred to me in my whole life.

The first sense of sorrow I ever knew was upon the death of my father, at which time I was not quite five years of age; but was rather amazed at what all the house meant, than possessed with a real understanding why nobody was willing to play with me. I remember I went into the room where his body lay, and my mother sat weeping alone by it. I had my battledore in my hand, and fell a-beating the coffin, and calling Papa; for, I know not how, I had some slight idea that he was locked up there. My mother caught me in her arms, and, transported beyond all patience of the silent grief she was before in, she almost smothered me in her embraces; and told me in a flood of tears, Papa could not hear me, and would play with me no more, for they were going to put him under ground, whence he could never come to us again. She was a very beautiful woman, of a noble spirit, and there was a dignity in her grief amidst all the wildness of her transport, which, methought, struck me with an instinct of sorrow, that, before I was sensible of what it was to grieve, seized my very soul, and has made pity the weakness of my heart ever since. The mind in infancy is, methinks, like the body in embryo; and receives impressions so forcible, that they are as hard to be removed by reason, as any mark with which a child is born is to be taken away by any future application. Hence it is, that good nature in me is no merit; but having been so frequently overwhelmed with her tears before I knew the cause of any affliction, or could draw defences from my own judgment, I imbibed commiseration, remorse, and an unmanly gentleness of mind, which has since ensnared me into ten thousand calamities; and from whence I can reap no advantage, except it be, that, in such a humour as I am now in, I can the better indulge myself in the softnesses of humanity, and enjoy that sweet anxiety which arises from the memory of past afflictions.

We, that are very old, are better able to remember things which befell us in our distant youth, than the passages of later days. For this reason it is, that the companions of my strong and vigorous years present themselves more immediately to me in this office of sorrow. Untimely and unhappy deaths are what we are most apt to lament; so little are we able to make it indifferent when a thing happens, though we know it must happen. Thus we groan under life, and bewail those who are relieved from it. Every object that returns to our imagination raises different passions, according to the circumstance of their departure. Who can have lived in an army, and in a serious hour reflect upon the many gay and agreeable men that might long have flourished in the arts of peace, and not join with the imprecations of the fatherless and widows on the tyrant to whose ambition they fell sacrifices? But gallant men, who are cut off by the sword, move rather our veneration than our pity; and we gather relief enough from their own contempt of death, to make that no evil, which was approached with so much cheerfulness, and attended with so much honour. But when we turn our thoughts from the great parts of life on such occasions, and instead of lamenting those who stood ready to give death to those from whom they had the fortune to receive it; I say, when we let our thoughts wander from such noble objects, and consider the havoc which is made among the tender and the innocent, pity enters with an unmixed softness, and possesses all our souls at once.

Here (were there words to express such sentiments with proper tenderness) I should record the beauty, innocence, and untimely death, of the first object my eyes ever beheld with love. The beauteous virgin! how ignorantly did she charm, how carelessly excel! Oh death! thou hast right to the bold, to the ambitious, to the high, and to the haughty; but why this cruelty to the humble, to the meek, to the undiscerning, to the thoughtless? Nor age, nor business, nor distress, can erase the dear image from my imagination. In the same week I saw her dressed for a ball, and in a shroud. How ill did the habit of death become the pretty trifler! I still behold the smiling earth — A large train of disasters were coming on to my memory, when my servant knocked at my closet-door, and interrupted me with a letter, attended with a hamper of wine, of the same sort with that which is to be put to sale on Thursday next, at Garraway's coffeehouse. Upon the receipt of it, I sent for three of my friends. We are so intimate, that we can be company in whatever state of mind we meet, and can entertain each other without expecting always to rejoice. The wine we found to be generous and warming, but with such a heat as moved us rather to be cheerful than frolicsome. It revived the spirits, without firing the blood. We commended it until two of the clock this morning; and having to-day met a little before dinner, we found, that though we drank two bottles a man, we had much more reason to recollect than forget what had passed the night before.

—Richard Steele

Twenty-four Hours in London

Sine me, Vacivom tempus ne quod duim mihi Laboris.—Ter. Heau.[1]

I T   I S   A N   I N E X P R E S S I B L E   Pleasure to know a little of the World, and be of no Character or Significancy in it. To be ever unconcerned, and ever looking on new Objects with an endless Curiosity, is a Delight known only to those who are turned for Speculation: Nay, they who enjoy it, must value things only as they are the Objects of Speculation, without drawing any worldly Advantage to themselves from them, but just as they are what contribute to their Amusement, or the Improvement of the Mind. I lay one Night last Week at *Richmond;* and being restless, not out of Dissatisfaction, but a certain busie Inclination one sometimes has, I arose at Four in the Morning, and took Boat for *London,* with a Resolution to rove by Boat and Coach for the next Four and twenty Hours, till the many different Objects I must needs meet with should tire my Imagination, and give me an Inclination to a Repose more profound than I was at that Time capable of. I beg People's Pardon for an odd Humour I am guilty of, and was often that Day, which is saluting any Person whom I like, whether I know him or not. This is a Particularity would be tolerated in me, if they considered that the greatest Pleasure I know I receive at my Eyes, and that I am obliged to an agreeable Person for coming abroad into my View, as another is for a Visit of Conversation at their own Houses.

The Hours of the Day and Night are taken up in the Cities of *London* and *Westminster* by Peoples as different from each other as those who are Born in different Centuries. Men of Six-a-Clock give way to those of Nine, they of Nine to the Generation of Twelve, and they of Twelve disappear, and make Room for the fashionable World, who have made Two-a-Clock the Noon of the Day.

When we first put off from Shoar, we soon fell in with a Fleet of Gardiners bound for the several Market-Ports of *London;* and it was the most pleasing Scene imaginable to see the Chearfulness with which those industrious People ply'd their Way to a certain Sale of their Goods. The Banks on each Side are as well Peopled, and beautified with as agreeable Plantations, as any Spot on the Earth; but the *Thames* it self, loaded with the Product of each Shoar, added very much to the Landskip. It was very

---

[1] "Don't prevent me from giving myself a holiday from work."—Terence, *The Self-Tormentor.*

easie to observe by their Sailing, and the Countenances of the ruddy Virgins who were Supercargos, the Parts of the Town to which they were bound. There was an Air in the Purveyors for *Covent-Garden,* who frequently converse with Morning Rakes, very unlike the seemly Sobriety of those bound for *Stocks-Market.*

Nothing remarkable happened in our Voyage; but I landed with Ten Sail of Apricock Boats at *Strand-Bridge,* after having put in at *Nine-Elmes,* and taken in Melons, consigned by Mr. *Cuffe* of that Place, to *Sarah Sewell* and Company, at their Stall in *Covent-Garden.* We arrived at *Strand-Bridge* at Six of the Clock, and were unloading; when the Hackney-Coachmen of the foregoing Night took their Leave of each other at the *Dark-House,* to go to Bed before the Day was too far spent. Chimney-Sweepers passed by us as we made up to the Market, and some Raillery happened between one of the Fruit-Wenches and those black Men, about the Devil and *Eve,* with Allusion to their several Professions. I could not believe any Place more entertaining than *Covent-Garden;* where I strolled from one Fruit-Shop to another, with Crowds of agreeable young Women around me, who were purchasing Fruit for their respective Families. It was almost Eight of the Clock before I could leave that Variety of Objects. I took Coach and followed a young Lady, who tripped into another just before me, attended by her Maid. I saw immediately she was of the Family of the *Vainloves.* There are a Sett of these, who of all things affect the Play of *Blindman's-Buff,* and leading Men into Love for they know not whom, who are fled they know not where. This sort of Woman is usually a janty Slattern; she hangs on her Cloaths, plays her Head, varies her Posture, and changes Place incessantly; and all with an Appearance of striving at the same time to hide her self, and yet give you to understand she is in Humour to laugh at you. You must have often seen the Coachmen make Signs with their Fingers as they drive by each other, to intimate how much they have got that Day. They can carry on that Language to give Intelligence where they are driving. In an instant my Coachman took the Wink to pursue, and the Lady's Driver gave the Hint that he was going through *Long-Acre* towards St. *James's:* While he whipped up *James-Street,* we drove for *King-Street,* to save the Pass at St. *Martins Lane.* The Coachmen took Care to meet, justle, and threaten each other for Way, and be intangled at the End of *Newport-Street,* and *Long-Acre.* The Fright, you must believe, brought down the Lady's Coach Door, and obliged her, with her Mask off, to enquire into the Bustle, when she sees the Man she would avoid. The Tackle of the Coach-Window is so bad she cannot draw it up again, and she drives on sometimes wholly discovered, and sometimes half escaped, according to the Accident of Carriages in her Way. One of these Ladies keeps her Seat in an Hackney-Coach as well as the best Rider does on a managed Horse. The laced Shooe on her Left Foot, with a careless

Gesture, just appearing on the opposite Cushion, held her both firm, and in a proper Attitude to receive the next Jolt.

As she was an excellent Coach-Woman, many were the Glances at each other which we had for an Hour and an Half in all Parts of the Town by the Skill of our Drivers; till at last my Lady was conveniently lost with Notice from her Coachman to ours to make off, and he should hear where she went. This Chase was not at an End, and the Fellow who drove her came to us, and discovered that he was ordered to come again in an Hour, for that she was a Silk-Worm. I was surprized with this Phrase, but found it was a Cant among the Hackney Fraternity for their best Customers, Women who ramble twice or thrice a Week from Shop to Shop, to turn over all the Goods in Town without buying any thing. The Silk-Worms are, it seems, indulged by the Tradesmen; for tho' they never buy, they are ever talking of new Silks, Laces and Ribbands, and serve the Owners in getting them Customers, as their common Dunners do in making them pay.

The Day of People of Fashion began now to break, and Carts and Hacks were mingled with Equipages of Show and Vanity; when I resolved to walk it out of Cheapness; but my unhappy Curiosity is such, that I find it always my Interest to take Coach, for some odd Adventure among Beggars, Ballad Singers, or the like, detains and throws me into Expence. It happened so immediately; for at the Corner of *Warwick-Street,* as I was listning to a new Ballad, a ragged Rascal, a Beggar who knew me, came up to me, and began to turn the Eyes of the good Company upon me, by telling me he was extream Poor, and should die in the Streets for want of Drink, except I immediately would have the Charity to give him Six-pence to go into the next Ale-House and save his Life. He urged, with a melancholy Face, that all his Family had died of Thirst. All the Mob have Humour, and two or three began to take the Jest; by which Mr. *Sturdy* carried his Point, and let me sneak off to a Coach. As I drove along, it was a pleasing Reflection to see the World so prettily chequered since I left *Richmond,* and the Scene still filling with Children of a new Hour. This Satisfaction encreased as I moved towards the City; and gay Signs, well disposed Streets, magnificent publick Structures, and wealthy Shops, adorned with contented Faces, made the Joy still rising till we came into the Centre of the City, and Centre of the World of Trade, the *Exchange* of *London.* As other Men in the Crowds about me were pleased with their Hopes and Bargains, I found my Account[2] in observing them, in Attention to their several Interests. I, indeed, looked upon my self as the richest Man that walked the *Exchange* that Day; for my Benevolence made me share the Gains of every Bargain that was made. It was not the least of the

---

[2] benefit.

Satisfactions in my Survey, to go up Stairs, and pass the Shops of agreeable Females; to observe so many pretty Hands busie in the Foldings of
Ribbands, and the utmost Eagerness of agreeable Faces in the Sale of
Patches, Pins, and Wires, on each Side the Counters, was an Amusement,
in which I should longer have indulged my self, had not the dear Creatures called to me to ask what I wanted, when I could not answer, only *To
look at you.* I went to one of the Windows which opened to the Area
below, where all the several Voices lost their Distinction, and rose up in a
confused Humming; which created in me a Reflection that could not come
into the Mind of any but of one a little too studious; for I said to my self,
with a kind of Punn in Thought, *What Nonsense is all the Hurry of this
World to those who are above it?* In these, or not much wiser Thoughts, I
had like to have lost my Place at the Chop-House; where every Man,
according to the natural Bashfulness or Sullenness of our Nation, eats in a
publick Room a Mess of Broth, or Chop of Meat, in dumb Silence, as if
they had no Pretence to speak to each other on the Foot of being Men,
except they were of each other's Acquaintance.

I went afterwards to *Robin's,* and saw People who had dined with me at
the Five-penny Ordinary[3] just before, give Bills for the Value of large
Estates; and could not but behold with great Pleasure, Property lodged in,
and transferred in a Moment from such as would never be Masters of half
as much as is seemingly in them, and given from them every Day they live.
But before Five in the Afternoon I left the City, came to my common
Scene of *Covent-Garden,* and passed the Evening at *Will's* in attending the
Discourses of several Sets of People, who relieved each other within my
Hearing on the Subjects of Cards, Dice, Love, Learning and Politicks. The
last Subject kept me till I heard the Streets in the Possession of the Bell-
man, who had now the World to himself, and cryed, *Past Two of Clock.*
This roused me from my Seat, and I went to my Lodging, led by a Light,[4]
whom I put into the Discourse of his private Oeconomy, and made him
give me an Account of the Charge, Hazard, Profit and Loss of a Family
that depended upon a Link, with a Design to end my trivial Day with the
Generosity of Six-pence, instead of a third Part of that Sum. When I came
to my Chamber I writ down these Minutes; but was at a Loss what Instruction I should propose to my Reader from the Enumeration of so
many insignificant Matters and Occurrences; and I thought it of great Use,
if they could learn with me to keep their Minds open to Gratification, and
ready to receive it from any thing it meets with. This one Circumstance
will make every Face you see give you the Satisfaction you now take in
beholding that of a Friend; will make every Object a pleasing one; will

[3] café.
[4] man with a lantern.

make all the Good which arrives to any Man, an Encrease of Happiness to
your self.

—*Richard Steele*

Love-Letters

Will's Coffee-house, June 17.

T HE SUSPENSION OF THE PLAYHOUSE has made me
have nothing to send you from hence; but calling here this Evening,
I found the Party I usually sit with, upon the Business of Writing, and
examining what was the handsomest Style in which to address Women,
and write Letters of Gallantry. Many were the Opinions which were immediately declared on this Subject: Some were for a certain Softness; some
for I know not what Delicacy; others for something inexpressibly Tender:
When it came to me, I said there was no Rule in the World to be made for
writing Letters, but that of being as near what you speak Face to Face as
you can; which is so great a Truth, that I am of Opinion Writing has lost
more Mistresses than any one Mistake in the whole Legend of Love. For
when you write to a Lady for whom you have a solid and honourable
Passion, the great Idea you have of her, joined to a quick Sense of her
Absence, fills your Mind with a Sort of Tenderness, that gives your Language too much the Air of Complaint, which is seldom successful. For a
Man may flatter himself as he pleases, but he will find, that the Women
have more Understanding in their own Affairs than we have, and Women
of Spirit are not to be won by Mourners. He that can keep handsomely
within Rules, and support the Carriage of a Companion to his Mistress, is
much more likely to prevail, than he who lets her see, the whole Relish of
his Life depends upon her. If possible therefore divert your Mistress,
rather than sigh to her. The pleasant Man she will desire for her own Sake;
but the languishing Lover has nothing to hope from but her Pity. To show
the Difference, I produced two Letters a Lady gave me, which had been
writ by two Gentlemen who pretended to her, but were both killed the
next Day after the Date at the Battle of *Almanza.* One of them was a
mercurial gay-humoured Man; the other a Man of a serious, but a great

and gallant Spirit. Poor *Jack Careless!* This is his Letter: You see how it is folded: The Air of it is so negligent, one might have read half of it by peeping into it, without breaking it open. He had no Exactness.

MADAM,

It is a very pleasant Circumstance I am in, that while I should be thinking of the good Company we are to meet within a Day or two, where we shall go to Loggerheads, my Thoughts are running upon a Fair Enemy in *England.* I was in Hopes I had left you there; but you follow the Camp, tho' I have endeavoured to make some of our Leaguer Ladies drive you out of the Field. All my Comfort is, you are more troublesome to my Colonel than my self: I permit you to visit me only now and then; but he downright keeps you. I laugh at his Honour as far as his Gravity will allow me; but I know him to be a Man of too much Merit to succeed with a Woman. Therefore defend your Heart as well as you can, I shall come Home this Winter irresist- ibly dressed, and with quite a new Foreign Air. And so I had like to say, I rest, but alass! I remain,

> Madam,
> Your most Obedient,
> Most Humble Servant,

John Careless.

Now for Colonel *Constant's* Epistle: you see it is folded and directed with the utmost Care.

MADAM,

I do my self the Honour to write to you this Evening, because I believe to Morrow will be a Day of Battle, and something forebodes in my Breast that I shall fall in it. If it proves so, I hope you will hear, I have done nothing below a Man who had the Love of his Country, quickened by a Passion for a Woman of Honour. If there be any Thing noble in going to a certain Death; if there be any Merit, that I meet it with Pleasure, by promising my self a Place in your Esteem; if your Applause, when I am no more, is preferable to the most glorious Life without you: I say, Madam, If any of these Considerations can have Weight with you, you will give me a kind Place in your Memory, which I prefer to the Glory of *Caesar.* I hope, this will be read, as it is writ, with Tears.

The beloved Lady is a Woman of a sensible Mind; but she has confessed to me, that after all her true and solid Value for *Constant,* she had much more Concern for the Loss of *Careless.* Those noble and serious Spirits have something equal to the Adversities they meet with, and consequently lessen the Objects of Pity. Great Accidents seem not cut out so much for Men of familiar Characters, which makes them more easily pitied, and soon after beloved. Add to this, that the Sort of Love which generally succeeds, is a Stranger to Awe and Distance. I asked *Romana,* Whether of the Two she should have chosen had they survived? She said, She knew she ought to have taken *Constant;* but believed, she should have chosen *Careless.*

—*Richard Steele*

SAMUEL JOHNSON

Samuel Johnson (1709–1784), or Dr. Johnson, as he is commonly known, is one of the heroes of Western intellectual life. Overcoming poverty, illness, and a strikingly unprepossessing appearance, he became the leading light of English literature's Augustan Age. Boswell's classic biography captures the conversational wit and lovable eccentricities of Johnson. A well-rounded man of letters, he excelled at poetry, biography (the magnificent Lives of the Poets), *drama, fiction (*Rasselas*), literary criticism (Prefaces to Shakespeare), lexicography (compiling the first full English dictionary), and, last but not least, essays.*

An admirer of Addison and Steele, Johnson started several of his own periodical essay series: The Rambler, The Adventurer, *and* The Idler. *With his penchant for moral seriousness, aphorism, and judgmental gravity, he tended to slow down the more journalistically streamlined, vigorous prose of Addison and Steele. Lady Mary Wortley Montagu said, amusingly if unfairly, that Johnson followed* The Spectator *"with the same pace a packhorse would do a hunter," and Hazlitt critiqued the oratorical, ploddingly rounded evenness of his sentences. The fact is that Johnson had more on, and in, his mind than most writers, so only a philosophical, ruminative style would do for him.*

Most critics have viewed Dr. Johnson as a moral essayist rather than a personal essayist. Still, we see him cutting a personal figure in the essay about his landlady's boarding house, and his psychologically astute pieces on the fragility of friendship and procrastination seem too keenly observed not to have been drawn from his own experience. Johnson displays a modern sense of realism; he refuses to sugar-coat things (see his skepticism about the joys of "The Solitude of the Country"). The dark side of Johnson's philoso-

phy is said to have come from a_dread of the "vacuity of life." In The
Rambler, *he analyzes most human activity as a kind of running away from
the horrified awareness of inner vacuum, a need* "to fill the vacancies of
attention, *and lessen the tediousness of time" with novelty and diversion.
Whether one agrees or not, it is hard to dispute the deep thoughtfulness of
Johnson's prose.*

The Boarding House

S IR ,

You have formerly observed that curiosity often terminates in barren
knowledge, and that the mind is prompted to study and enquiry rather by
the uneasiness of ignorance, than the hope of profit. Nothing can be of
less importance to any present interest than the fortune of those who have
been long lost in the grave, and from whom nothing now can be hoped or
feared. Yet to rouse the zeal of a true antiquary little more is necessary
than to mention a name which mankind have conspired to forget; he will
make his way to remote scenes of action thro' obscurity and contradiction,
as *Tully* sought amidst brushes and brambles the tomb of *Archimedes*.

It is not easy to discover how it concerns him that gathers the produce
or receives the rent of an estate, to know through what families the land
has passed, who is registered in the conqueror's survey as its possessor,
how often it has been forfeited by treason, or how often sold by prodigal-
ity. The power or wealth of the present inhabitants of a country cannot be
much encreased by an enquiry after the names of those barbarians, who
destroyed one another twenty centuries ago, in contests for the shelter of
woods or convenience of pasturage. Yet we see that no man can be at rest
in the enjoyment of a new purchase till he has learned the history of his
grounds from the ancient inhabitants of the parish, and that no nation
omits to record the actions of their ancestors, however bloody, savage, and
rapacious.

The same disposition, as different opportunities call it forth, discovers
itself in great or little things. I have always thought it unworthy of a wise

man to slumber in total inactivity only because he happens to have no employment equal to his ambition or genius; it is therefore my custom to apply my attention to the objects before me, and as I cannot think any place wholly unworthy of notice that affords a habitation to a man of letters, I have collected the history and antiquities of the several garrets in which I have resided:

Quantulacunque estis, vos ego magna voco.[1]

How small to others, but how great to me!

Many of these narratives my industry has been able to extend to a considerable length; but the woman with whom I now lodge has lived only eighteen months in the house, and can give no account of its ancient revolutions; the plaisterer, having, at her entrance, obliterated by his white-wash, all the smoky memorials which former tenants had left upon the ceiling, and perhaps drawn the veil of oblivion over politicians, philosophers, and poets.

When I first cheapened my lodgings, the landlady told me, that she hoped I was not an author, for the lodgers on the first floor had stipulated that the upper rooms should not be occupied by a noisy trade. I very readily promised to give no disturbance to her family, and soon dispatched a bargain on the usual terms.

I had not slept many nights in my new apartment before I began to enquire after my predecessors, and found my landlady, whose imagination is filled chiefly with her own affairs, very ready to give me information.

Curiosity, like all other desires, produces pain as well as pleasure. Before she began her narrative, I had heated my head with expectations of adventures and discoveries, of elegance in disguise, and learning in distress; and was somewhat mortified when I heard, that the first tenant was a taylor, of whom nothing was remembered but that he complained of his room for want of light; and, after having lodged in it a month, and paid only a week's rent, pawned a piece of cloth which he was trusted to cut out, and was forced to make a precipitate retreat from this quarter of the town.

The next was a young woman newly arrived from the country, who lived for five weeks with great regularity, and became by frequent treats very much the favourite of the family, but at last received visits so frequently from a cousin in *Cheapside,* that she brought the reputation of the house into danger, and was therefore dismissed with good advice.

The room then stood empty for a fortnight; my landlady began to think that she had judged hardly, and often wished for such another

---

[1] Ovid, *Amores,* III. xv. 14.

lodger. At last an elderly man of a grave aspect, read the bill, and bargained for the room, at the very first price that was asked. He lived in close retirement, seldom went out till evening, and then returned early sometimes chearful, and at other times dejected. It was remarkable, that whatever he purchased, he never had small money in his pocket, and tho' cool and temperate on other occasions, was always vehement and stormy till he received his change. He paid his rent with great exactness, and seldom failed once a week to requite my landlady's civility with a supper. At last, such is the fate of human felicity, the house was alarm'd at midnight by the constable, who demanded to search the garrets. My landlady assuring him that he had mistaken the door, conducted him up stairs, where he found the tools of a coiner; but the tenant had crawled along the roof to an empty house, and escaped; much to the joy of my landlady, who declares him a very honest man, and wonders why any body should be hanged for making money when such numbers are in want of it. She however confesses that she shall for the future always question the character of those who take her garret without beating down the price.

The bill was then placed again in the window, and the poor woman was teazed for seven weeks by innumerable passengers, who obliged her to climb with them every hour up five stories, and then disliked the prospect, hated the noise of a publick street, thought the stairs narrow, objected to a low cieling, required the walls to be hung with fresher paper, asked questions about the neighbourhood, could not think of living so far from their acquaintance, wished the window had looked to the south rather than the west, told how the door and chimney might have been better disposed, bid her half the price that she asked, or promised to give her earnest the next day, and came no more.

At last, a short meagre man, in a tarnish'd waistcoat, desired to see the garret, and when he had stipulated for two long shelves and a larger table, hired it at a low rate. When the affair was completed, he looked round him with great satisfaction, and repeated some words which the woman did not understand. In two days he brought a great box of books, took possession of his room, and lived very inoffensively, except that he frequently disturbed the inhabitants of the next floor by unseasonable noises. He was generally in bed at noon, but from evening to midnight he sometimes talked aloud with great vehemence, sometimes stamped as in rage, sometimes threw down his poker, then clattered his chairs, then sat down in deep thought, and again burst out into loud vociferations; sometimes he would sigh as oppressed with misery, and sometimes shake with convulsive laughter. When he encountered any of the family he gave way or bowed, but rarely spoke, except that as he went up stairs he often repeated,

Ὃς ὑπέοτατα δώματα ναίει.[2]

This habitant th' aerial regions boast.

hard words, to which his neighbours listened so often, that they learned them without understanding them. What was his employment she did not venture to ask him, but at last heard a printer's boy enquire for the author.

My landlady was very often advised to beware of this strange man, who, tho' he was quiet for the present, might perhaps become outrageous in the hot months; but as she was punctually paid, she could not find any sufficient reason for dismissing him, till one night he convinced her by setting fire to his curtains, that it was not safe to have an author for her inmate.

She had then for six weeks a succession of tenants, who left the house on Saturday, and instead of paying their rent, stormed at their landlady. At last she took in two sisters, one of whom had spent her little fortune in procuring remedies for a lingering disease, and was now supported and attended by the other: she climbed with difficulty to the apartment, where she languished eight weeks, without impatience or lamentation, except for the expence and fatigue which her sister suffered, and then calmly and contentedly expired. The sister followed her to the grave, paid the few debts which they had contracted, wiped away the tears of useless sorrow, and returning to the business of common life, resigned to me the vacant habitation.

Such, Mr. *Rambler,* are the changes which have happened in the narrow space where my present fortune has fixed my residence. So true is it that amusement and instruction are always at hand for those who have skill and willingness to find them; and so just is the observation of *Juvenal,*[3] that a single house will shew whatever is done or suffered in the world.

I am, Sir, &c.

---

[2] Hesiod, *Works and Days,* I. 8.
[3] *Satires,* XIII. 159–160.

The Solitude of the Country

THERE HAS ALWAYS prevailed among that part of mankind that addict their minds to speculation, a propensity to talk much of the delights of retirement; and some of the most pleasing compositions produced in every age, contain descriptions of the peace and happiness of a country life.

I know not whether those who thus ambitiously repeat the praises of solitude, have always considered, how much they depreciate mankind by declaring, that whatever is excellent or desirable is to be obtained by departing from them; that the assistance which we may derive from one another, is not equivalent to the evils which we have to fear; that the kindness of a few is overbalanced by the malice of many; and that the protection of society is too dearly purchased, by encountering its dangers and enduring its oppressions.

These specious representations of solitary happiness, however opprobrious to human nature, have so far spread their influence over the world, that almost every man delights his imagination with the hopes of obtaining some time an opportunity of retreat. Many indeed, who enjoy retreat only in imagination, content themselves with believing, that another year will transport them to rural tranquillity, and die while they talk of doing what if they had lived longer they would never have done. But many likewise there are, either of greater resolution or more credulity, who in earnest try the state which they have been taught to think thus secure from cares and dangers; and retire to privacy, either that they may improve their happiness, increase their knowledge, or exalt their virtue.

The greater part of the admirers of solitude, as of all other classes of mankind, have no higher or remoter view, than the present gratification of their passions. Of these some, haughty and impetuous, fly from society only because they cannot bear to repay to others the regard which themselves exact, and think no state of life eligible, but that which places them out of the reach of censure or controul, and affords them opportunities of living in a perpetual compliance with their own inclinations, without the necessity of regulating their actions by any other man's convenience or opinion.

There are others of minds more delicate and tender, easily offended by every deviation from rectitude, soon disgusted by ignorance or imperti-

nence, and always expecting from the conversation of mankind, more elegance, purity and truth than the mingled mass of life will easily afford.
Such men are in haste to retire from grossness, falsehood and brutality;
and hope to find in private habitations at least a negative felicity, and
exemption from the shocks and perturbations with which public scenes
are continually distressing them.

To neither of these votaries will solitude afford that content, which she
has been taught so lavishly to promise. The man of arrogance will quickly
discover, that by escaping from his opponents he has lost his flatterers,
that greatness is nothing where it is not seen, and power nothing where it
cannot be felt: and he, whose faculties are employed in too close an observation of failings and defects, will find his condition very little mended by
transferring his attention from others to himself; he will probably soon
come back in quest of new objects, and be glad to keep his captiousness
employed on any character rather than his own.

Others are seduced into solitude merely by the authority of great names,
and expect to find those charms in tranquillity which have allured statesmen and conquerors to the shades: these likewise are apt to wonder at
their disappointment, from want of considering, that those whom they
aspire to imitate carried with them to their country seats minds full
fraught with subjects of reflection, the consciousness of great merit, the
memory of illustrious actions, the knowledge of important events, and the
seeds of mighty designs to be ripened by future meditation. Solitude was
to such men a release from fatigue, and an opportunity of usefulness. But
what can retirement confer upon him, who having done nothing can receive no support from his own importance, who having known nothing
can find no entertainment in reviewing the past, and who intending nothing can form no hopes from prospects of the future: he can, surely, take
no wiser course, than that of losing himself again in the croud, and filling
the vacuities of his mind with the news of the day.

Others consider solitude as the parent of philosophy, and retire in expectation of greater intimacies with science, as Numa repaired to the
groves when he conferred with Egeria.[1] These men have not always reason
to repent. Some studies require a continued prosecution of the same train
of thought, such as is too often interrupted by the petty avocations of
common life: sometimes, likewise, it is necessary, that a multiplicity of
objects be at once present to the mind; and every thing, therefore, must be
kept at a distance, which may perplex the memory, or dissipate the attention.

But though learning may be conferred by solitude, its application must
be attained by general converse. He has learned to no purpose, that is not

---

[1] Plutarch, *Lives,* "Numa," IV; Livy, I.21.

able to teach; and he will always teach unsuccessfully, who cannot recommend his sentiments by his diction or address.

Even the acquisition of knowledge is often much facilitated by the advantages of society: he that never compares his notions with those of others, readily acquiesces in his first thoughts, and very seldom discovers the objections which may be raised against his opinions; he, therefore, often thinks himself in possession of truth, when he is only fondling an error long since exploded. He that has neither companions nor rivals in his studies, will always applaud his own progress, and think highly of his performances, because he knows not that others have equalled or excelled him. And I am afraid it may be added, that the student who withdraws himself from the world, will soon feel that ardour extinguished which praise or emulation had enkindled, and take the advantage of secrecy to sleep rather than to labour.

There remains yet another set of recluses, whose intention intitles them to higher respect, and whose motives deserve a more serious consideration. These retire from the world, not merely to bask in ease or gratify curiosity, but that being disengaged from common cares, they may employ more time in the duties of religion, that they may regulate their actions with stricter vigilance, and purify their thoughts by more frequent meditation.

To men thus elevated above the mists of mortality, I am far from presuming myself qualified to give directions. On him that appears "to pass through things temporary," with no other care than "not to lose finally the things eternal,"[2] I look with such veneration as inclines me to approve his conduct in the whole, without a minute examination of its parts; yet I could never forbear to wish, that while vice is every day multiplying seducements, and stalking forth with more hardened effrontry, virtue, would not withdraw the influence of her presence, or forbear to assert her natural dignity by open and undaunted perseverance in the right. Piety practised in solitude, like the flower that blooms in the desart, may give its fragrance to the winds of heaven, and delight those unbodied spirits that survey the works of God and the actions of men; but it bestows no assistance upon earthly beings, and however free from taints of impurity, yet wants the sacred splendor of beneficence.

Our Maker, who, though he gave us such varieties of temper and such difference of powers yet designed us all for happiness, undoubtedly intended that we should obtain that happiness by different means. Some are unable to resist the temptations of importunity, or the impetuosity of their own passions incited by the force of present temptations: of these it is undoubtedly the duty, to fly from enemies which they cannot conquer,

---

[2] Paraphrased from Corinthians, iv.18.

and to cultivate, in the calm of solitude, that virtue which is too tender to endure the tempests of public life. But there are others, whose passions grow more strong and irregular in privacy; and who cannot maintain an uniform tenor of virtue, but by exposing their manners to the public eye, and assisting the admonitions of conscience with the fear of infamy: for such it is dangerous to exclude all witnesses of their conduct, till they have formed strong habits of virtue, and weakened their passions by frequent victories. But there is a higher order of men so inspirited with ardour, and so fortified with resolution, that the world passes before them without influence or regard: these ought to consider themselves as appointed the guardians of mankind; they are placed in an evil world, to exhibit public examples of good life; and may be said, when they withdraw to solitude, to desert the station which Providence assigned them.

O.K. — it was written a very long time ago — but the idea of a relationships built on hidden motivations + false representations of attitude are totally distasteful — could not be intimate.

MARIA EDGEWORTH

Maria Edgeworth (1768–1849) was a member of the Anglo-Irish gentry known in her day for her romantic Irish stories, Castle Rackrent, The Absentee, *and* Ormond. *(Walter Scott and Turgenev both credited her handling of this material as inspiration for their tales of Scotland and Russia, respectively.) Her father was a progressive landowner and inventor who had four wives and twenty-one children. Maria was his oldest daughter, and she idolized him; he in turn carefully oversaw her education and involved her in the running of the estate. She also played an active part in raising her younger siblings, and became an educational reformer whose children's books and pedagogic writings, stressing learning by doing and independence of thought, had a wide influence on the Continent. Hubert Butler, the modern Anglo-Irish essayist (see Part IV), wrote a moving tribute to Edgeworth, noting, among other things, what contemporaries saw as her "constant flow of gaiety."*

Edgeworth's delightfully mocking "An Essay on the Noble Science of Self-Justification," first included in Letters for Literary Ladies *(1795), may be seen as a worldly woman's response to the eighteenth-century line of essay writing about manners, mores, and gender. Addison and Steele typically took a patronizing tone toward women, ridiculing their dependence on supposedly absurd new fashions and their alleged illogical and changeable natures. Edgeworth, seeming to agree at first with these male critics, actually puts the problem in a more subversive light: given the unfair disparity of power between the sexes, she suggests, "unreasonable" arguments become a logical weapon for a woman to use. According to the scholars Katherine M. Rogers and William McCarthy, "Though Edgeworth satirizes the emotional rhetoric women use to control men, her aim is not to make women subservient, but to make them rational: that is, to assert just claims and rely on rational arguments." But this may be too didactic a reading of such a mis-*

*chievous piece. That Edgeworth never married adds another dimension to
her irreverent portrayal of conjugal power struggles.*

*Edgeworth's focus here is also on that traditional essay subject, the dynam-
ics of conversation, which Montaigne, Swift, Addison and Steele, Johnson,
and Hazlitt all wrote about. She brings a special sensitivity to the nuances of
argument and accommodation in speech while reflexively underscoring the
conversational flavor of the essay form through her addresses to the reader.*

An Essay on the Noble Science of Self-Justification

> *"For which an eloquence that aims to vex,
> With native tropes of anger arms the sex."*
>
> —PARNELL

ENDOWED AS THE FAIR SEX INDISPUTABLY ARE,
with a natural genius for the invaluable art of self-justification, it may
not be displeasing to them to see its rising perfection evinced by an attempt to reduce it to a science. Possessed, as are all the fair daughters of
Eve, of an hereditary propensity, transmitted to them undiminished
through succeeding generations, to be "soon moved with slightest touch
of blame"; very little precept and practice will confirm them in the habit,
and instruct them in all the maxims of self-justification.

Candid pupil, you will readily accede to my first and fundamental ax-
iom—that a lady can do no wrong.

But simple as this maxim may appear, and suited to the level of the
meanest capacity, the talent of applying it on all the important, but more
especially on all the most trivial, occurrences of domestic life, so as to
secure private peace and public dominion, has hitherto been monopolized
by the female adepts in the art of self-justification.

Excuse me for insinuating by this expression, that there may yet be
amongst you some novices. To these, if any such, I principally address
myself.

And now, lest fired by ambition you lose all by aiming at too much, let
me explain and limit my first principle. "That you can do no wrong." You
must be aware that real perfection is beyond the reach of mortals, nor
would I have you aim at it; indeed it is not in any degree necessary to our
purpose. You have heard of the established belief in the infallibility of the
sovereign pontiff, which prevailed not many centuries ago—if man was

allowed to be infallible, I see no reason why the same privilege should not be extended to woman—but times have changed; and since the happy age of credulity is past, leave the opinions of men to their natural perversity— their actions are the best test of their faith. Instead then of a belief in your infallibility, endeavor to enforce implicit submission to your authority. This will give you infinitely less trouble, and will answer your purpose as well.

Right and wrong, if we go to the foundation of things, are, as casuists tell us, really words of very dubious signification, perpetually varying with customs and fashion, and to be adjusted ultimately by no other standards but opinion and force. Obtain power, then, by all means: power is the law of man; make it yours.

But to return from a frivolous disquisition about right, let me teach you the art of defending the wrong. After having thus pointed out to you the glorious end of your labors, I must now instruct you in the equally glorious means.

For the advantage of my subject I address myself chiefly to married ladies; but those who have not as yet the good fortune to have that common enemy, a husband, to combat, may in the meantime practice my precepts upon their fathers, brothers, and female friends; with caution, however, lest by discovering their arms too soon, they preclude themselves from the power of using them to the fullest advantage hereafter. I therefore recommend it to them to prefer, with a philosophical moderation, the future to the present.

Timid brides, you have, probably, hitherto been addressed as angels. Prepare for the time when you shall again become mortal. Take the alarm at the first approach of blame; at the first hint of a discovery that you are anything less than infallible—contradict, debate, justify, recriminate, rage, weep, swoon, do anything but yield to conviction.

I take it for granted that you have already acquired sufficient command of voice; you need not study its compass; going beyond its pitch has a peculiarly happy effect upon some occasions. But are you voluble enough to drown all sense in a torrent of words? Can you be loud enough to overpower the voice of all who shall attempt to interrupt or contradict you? Are you mistress of the petulant, the peevish, and the sullen tone? Have you practiced the sharpness which provokes retort, and the continual monotony which by setting your adversary to sleep effectually precludes reply? an event which is always to be considered as decisive of the victory, or at least as reducing it to a drawn battle—you and Somnus[1] divide the prize.

Thus prepared for an engagement, you will next, if you have not already done it, study the weak part of the character of your enemy—your hus-

---

[1] The Roman god of sleep.

band, I mean: if he be a man of high spirit, jealous of command and impatient of control, one who decides for himself, and who is little troubled with the insanity of minding what the world says of him, you must proceed with extreme circumspection; you must not dare to provoke the combined forces of the enemy to a regular engagement, but harass him with perpetual petty skirmishes: in these, though you gain little at a time, you will gradually weary the patience, and break the spirit of your opponent. If he be a man of spirit, he must also be generous; and what man of generosity will contend for trifles with a woman who submits to him in all affairs of consequence, who is in his power, who is weak, and who loves him?

"Can superior with inferior power contend?" No; the spirit of a lion is not to be roused by the teasing of an insect.

But such a man as I have described, besides being as generous as he is brave, will probably be of an active temper: then you have an inestimable advantage; for he will set a high value upon a thing for which you have none—time; he will acknowledge the force of your arguments merely from a dread of their length; he will yield to you in trifles, particularly in trifles which do not militate against his authority; not out of regard for you, but for his time; for what man can prevail upon himself to debate three hours about what could be as well decided in three minutes?

Lest amongst infinite variety the difficulty of immediate selection should at first perplex you, let me point out, that matters of *taste* will afford you, of all others, the most ample and incessant subjects of debate. Here you have no criterion to appeal to. Upon the same principle, next to matters of taste, points of opinion will afford the most constant exercise to your talents. Here you will have an opportunity of citing the opinions of all the living and dead you have ever known, besides the dear privilege of repeating continually:—"Nay, you must allow *that.*" Or, "You can't deny *this,* for it's the universal opinion—everybody says so! everybody thinks so! I wonder to hear you express such an opinion! Nobody but yourself is of that way of thinking!" with innumerable other phrases, with which a slight attention to polite conversation will furnish you. This mode of opposing authority to argument, and assertion to proof, is of such universal utility, that I pray you to practice it.

If the point in dispute be some opinion relative to your character or disposition, allow in general, that "you are sure you have a great many faults"; but to every specific charge reply, "Well, I am sure I don't know, but I did not think *that* was one of my faults! nobody ever accused me of that before! Nay, I was always remarkable for the contrary; at least before I was acquainted with you, sir: in my own family I was always remarkable for the contrary: ask any of my own friends; ask any of them; they must know me best."

But if, instead of attacking the material parts of your character, your husband should merely presume to advert to your manners, to some slight personal habit which might be made more agreeable to him; prove, in the first place, that it is his fault that it is not agreeable to him; ask which is most to blame, "she who ceases to please, or he who ceases to be pleased" —His eyes are changed, or opened. But it may perhaps have been a matter almost of indifference to him, till you undertook its defense: then make it of consequence by rising in eagerness, in proportion to the insignificance of your object; if he can draw consequences, this will be an excellent lesson: if you are so tender of blame in the veriest trifles, how impeachable must you be in matters of importance! As to personal habits, begin by denying that you have any; or in the paradoxical language of Rousseau declare that the only habit you have is the habit of having none; as all personal habits, if they have been of any long standing, must have become involuntary, the unconscious culprit may assert her innocence without hazarding her veracity.

However, if you happen to be detected in the very fact, and a person cries, "Now, now, you are doing it!" submit, but declare at the same moment—"That it is the very first time in your whole life that you were ever known to be guilty of it; and therefore it can be no habit, and of course nowise reprehensible."

Extend the rage for vindication to all the objects which the most re- motely concern you; take even inanimate objects under your protection. Your dress, your furniture, your property, everything which is or has been yours, defend, and this upon the principles of the soundest philosophy: each of these things all compose a part of your personal merit; all that connected the most distantly with your idea gives pleasure or pain to others, becomes an object of blame or praise, and consequently claims your support or vindication.

In the course of the management of your house, children, family, and affairs, probably some few errors of omission or commission may strike your husband's pervading eye; but these errors, admitting them to be er- rors, you will never, if you please, allow to be charged to any deficiency in memory, judgment, or activity, on your part.

There are surely people enough around you to divide and share the blame; send it from one to another, till at last, by universal rejection, it is proved to belong to nobody. You will say, however, that facts remain unalterable; and that in some unlucky instance, in the changes and chances of human affairs, you may be proved to have been to blame. Some stubborn evidence may appear against you; still you may prove an alibi, or balance the evidence. There is nothing equal to balancing evidence; doubt is, you know, the most philosophic state of the human mind, and it will be kind of you to keep your husband perpetually in this skeptical state.

Indeed the short method of denying absolutely all blameable facts, I should recommend to pupils as the best; and if in the beginning of their career they may startle at this mode, let them depend upon it that in their future practice it must become perfectly familiar. The nice distinction of simulation and dissimulation depends but on the trick of a syllable; palliation and extenuation are universally allowable in self-defense; prevarication inevitably follows, and falsehood "is but in the next degree."

Yet I would not destroy this nicety of conscience too soon. It may be of use in your first setting out, because you must establish credit; in proportion to your credit will be the value of your future asseverations.

In the meantime, however, argument and debate are allowed to the most rigid moralist. You can never perjure yourself by swearing to a false opinion.

I come now to the art of reasoning: don't be alarmed at the name of reasoning, fair pupils; I will explain to you my meaning.

If, instead of the fiery-tempered being I formerly described, you should fortunately be connected with a man, who, having formed a justly high opinion of your sex, should propose to treat you as his equal, and who in any little dispute which might arise between you, should desire no other arbiter than reason; triumph in his mistaken candor, regularly appeal to the decision of reason at the beginning of every contest, and deny its jurisdiction at the conclusion. I take it for granted that you will be on the wrong side of every question, and indeed, in general, I advise you to choose the wrong side of an argument to defend; whilst you are young in the science, it will afford the best exercise, and, as you improve, the best display of your talents.

If, then, reasonable pupils, you would succeed in argument, attend to the following instructions.

Begin by preventing, if possible, the specific statement of any position, or if reduced to it, use the most *general terms*, and take advantage of the ambiguity which all languages and which most philosophers allow. Above all things, shun definitions; they will prove fatal to you; for two persons of sense and candor, who define their terms, cannot argue long without either convincing, or being convinced, or parting in equal good-humor; to prevent which, go over and over the same ground, wander as wide as possible from the point, but always with a view to return at last precisely to the same spot from which you set out. I should remark to you, that the choice of your weapons is a circumstance much to be attended to: choose always those which your adversary cannot use. If your husband is a man of wit, you will of course undervalue a talent which is never connected with judgment: "for your part, you do not presume to contend with him in wit."

But if he be a sober-minded man, who will go link by link along the chain of an argument, follow him at first, till he grows so intent that he does not perceive whether you follow him or not; then slide back to your own station; and when with perverse patience he has at last reached the last link of the chain, with one electric shock of wit make him quit his hold, and strike him to the ground in an instant. Depend upon the sympathy of the spectators, for to one who can understand *reason,* you will find ten who admire *wit.*

But if you should not be blessed with "a ready wit," if demonstration should in the meantime stare you in the face, do not be in the least alarmed—anticipate the blow. Whilst you have it yet in your power, rise with becoming magnanimity, and cry, "I give it up! I give it up! La! let us say no more about it; I do so hate disputing about trifles. I give it up!" Before an explanation on the word trifle can take place, quit the room with flying colors.

If you are a woman of sentiment and eloquence, you have advantages of which I scarcely need apprise you. From the understanding of a man, you have always an appeal to his heart, or, if not, to his affection, to his weakness. If you have the good fortune to be married to a weak man, always choose the moment to argue with him when you have a full audience. Trust to the sublime power of numbers; it will be of use even to excite your own enthusiasm in debate; then as the scene advances, talk of his cruelty, and your sensibility, and sink with "becoming woe" into the pathos of injured innocence.

Besides the heart and the weakness of your opponent, you have still another chance, in ruffling his temper; which, in the course of a long conversation, you will have a fair opportunity of trying; and if—for philosophers will sometimes grow warm in the defense of truth—if he should grow absolutely angry, you will in the same proportion grow calm, and wonder at his rage, though you well know it has been created by your own provocation. The bystanders, seeing anger without any adequate cause, will all be of your side.

Nothing provokes an irascible man, interested in debate, and possessed of an opinion of his own eloquence, so much as to see the attention of his hearers go from him: you will then, when he flatters himself that he has just fixed your eye with his *very best* argument, suddenly grow absent— your house affairs must call you hence—or you have directions to give to your children—or the room is too hot, or too cold—the window must be opened—or door shut—or the candle wants snuffing. Nay, without these interruptions, the simple motion of your eye may provoke a speaker; a butterfly, or the figure in a carpet may engage your attention in preference to him; or if these objects be absent, the simply averting your eye, looking through the window in quest of outward objects, will show that your mind has not been abstracted, and will display to him at least your wish of not attending. He may, however, possibly have lost the habit of watching your eye for approbation; then you may assault his ear: if all other resources fail, beat with your foot that dead march of the spirits, that incessant tattoo, which so well deserves its name. Marvelous must be the patience of the much-enduring man whom some or other of these devices do not provoke: slight causes often produce great effects; the simple scratching of a pick-axe, properly applied to certain veins in a mine, will cause the most dreadful explosions.

Hitherto we have only professed to teach the defensive: let me now recommend to you the offensive part of the art of justification. As a supplement to reasoning comes recrimination: the pleasure of proving that you are right is surely incomplete till you have proved that your adversary is wrong; this might have been a secondary, let it now become a primary object with you; rest your own defense on it for further security: you are no longer to consider yourself as obliged either to deny, palliate, argue, or declaim, but simply to justify yourself by criminating another; all merit, you know, is judged of by comparison. In the art of recrimination, your memory will be of the highest service to you; for you are to open and keep an account-current of all the faults, mistakes, neglects, unkindnesses of those you live with; these you are to state against your own: I need not tell you that the balance will always be in your favor. In stating matters of opinion, produce the words of the very same person which passed days, months, years before, in contradiction to what he is then saying. By displacing, disjointing words and sentences, by misunderstanding the whole, or quoting only a part of what has been said, you may convict any man of inconsistency, particularly if he be a man of genius and feeling; for he speaks generally from the impulse of the moment, and of all others can the least bear to be charged with paradoxes. So far for a husband.

Recriminating is also of sovereign use in the quarrels of friends; no friend is so perfectly equable, so ardent in affection, so nice in punctilio, as never to offend: then "Note his faults, and con them all by rote." Say you can forgive, but you can never forget; and surely it is much more generous to forgive and remember, than to forgive and forget. On every new alarm, call the unburied ghosts from former fields of battle; range them in tremendous array, call them one by one to witness against the conscience of your enemy, and ere the battle is begun take from him all courage to engage.

There is one case I must observe to you in which recrimination has peculiar poignancy. If you have had it in your power to confer obligations on anyone, never cease reminding them of it: and let them feel that you have acquired an indefeasible right to reproach them without a possibility of their retorting. It is a maxim with some sentimental people, "To treat their servants as if they were their friends in distress."—I have observed that people of this cast make themselves amends, by treating their friends in distress as if they were their servants.

Apply this maxim—you may do it a thousand ways, especially in company. In general conversation, where everyone is supposed to be on a footing, if any of your humble companions should presume to hazard an opinion contrary to yours, and should modestly begin with, "I think," look as the man did when he said to his servant, "You think, sir—what business have you to think?"

Never fear to lose a friend by the habits which I recommend: reconciliations, as you have often heard it said—reconciliations are the cement of friendship; therefore friends should quarrel to strengthen their attachment, and offend each other for the pleasure of being reconciled.

I beg pardon for digressing: I was, I believe, talking of your husband, not of your friend—I have gone far out of the way.

If in your debates with your husband you should want "eloquence to vex him," the dull prolixity of narration, joined to the complaining monotony of voice which I formerly recommended, will supply its place, and have the desired effect: Somnus will prove propitious; then, ever and anon as the soporific charm begins to work, rouse him with interrogatories, such as, "Did not you say so? Don't you remember? Only answer me that!"

By-the-by, interrogatories artfully put may lead an unsuspicious reasoner, you know, always to your own conclusion.

In addition to the patience, philosophy, and other good things which Socrates learned from his wife,[2] perhaps she taught him this mode of reasoning.

But, after all, the precepts of art, and even the natural susceptibility of your tempers, will avail you little in the sublime of our science, if you cannot command that ready enthusiasm which will make you enter into the part you are acting; that happy imagination which shall make you believe all you fear and all you invent.

Who is there amongst you who cannot or who will not justify when they are accused? Vulgar talent! the sublime of our science is to justify before we are accused. There is no reptile so vile but what will turn when it is trodden on; but of a nicer sense and nobler species are those whom nature has endowed with antennae, which perceive and withdraw at the distant approach of danger. Allow me another allusion: similes cannot be crowded too close for a female taste; and analogy, I have heard, my fair pupils, is your favorite mode of reasoning.

The sensitive plant is too vulgar an allusion; but if the truth of modern

---

[2] According to tradition, the wife of the great Greek philosopher Socrates was a notorious shrew. He is said to have expressed gratitude for her because she taught him patience.

naturalists may be depended upon, there is a plant which, instead of receding timidly from the intrusive touch, angrily protrudes its venomous
juices upon all who presume to meddle with it—do not you think this
plant would be your fittest emblem?

Let me, however, recommend it to you, nice souls, who, of the mimosa
kind, "fear the dark cloud, and feel the coming storm," to take the utmost
precaution lest the same susceptibility which you cherish as the dear
means to torment others should insensibly become a torment to yourselves.

Distinguish then between sensibility and susceptibility; between the
anxious solicitude not to give offense, and the captious eagerness of vanity
to prove that it ought not to have been taken; distinguish between the
desire of praise and the horror of blame: can any two things be more
different than the wish to improve, and the wish to demonstrate that you
have never been to blame?

Observe, I only wish you to distinguish these things in your own minds;
I would by no means advise you to discontinue the laudable practice of
confounding them perpetually in speaking to others.

When you have nearly exhausted human patience in explaining, justifying, vindicating; when in spite of all the pains you have taken, you have
more than half betrayed your own vanity; you have a never-failing re-
source in paying tribute to that of your opponent, as thus:

"I am sure you must be sensible that I should never take so much pains
to justify myself if I were indifferent to your opinion. I know that I ought
not to disturb myself with such trifles; but nothing is a trifle to me which
concerns you. I confess I am too anxious to please; I know it's a fault, but
I cannot cure myself of it now. Too quick sensibility, I am conscious, is the
defect of my disposition; it would be happier for me if I could be more
indifferent, I know."

Who could be so brutal as to blame so amiable, so candid a creature?
Who would not submit to be tormented with kindness?

When once your captive condescends to be flattered by such arguments
as these, your power is fixed; your future triumphs can be bounded only
by your own moderation; they are at once secured and justified.

Forbear not, then, happy pupils; but, arrived at the summit of power,
give a full scope to your genius, nor trust to genius alone: to exercise in all
its extent your privileged dominion, you must acquire, or rather you must
pretend to have acquired, infallible skill in the noble art of physiognomy;
immediately the thoughts as well as the words of your subjects are exposed to your inquisition.

Words may flatter you, but the countenance never can deceive you; the
eyes are the windows of the soul, and through them you are to watch what
passes in the inmost recesses of the heart. There, if you discern the slight-

est ideas of doubt, blame, or displeasure; if you discover the slightest symptoms of revolt, take the alarm instantly. Conquerors must maintain their conquests; and how easily can they do this, who hold a secret correspondence with the minds of the vanquished! Be your own spies then; from the looks, gestures, slightest motions of your enemies, you are to form an alphabet, a language intelligible only to yourselves, yet by which you shall condemn them; always remembering that in sound policy suspicion justifies punishment. In vain, when you accuse your friends of the high treason of blaming you, in vain let them plead their innocence, even of the intention. "They did not say a word which could be tortured into such a meaning." No, "but they looked daggers, though they used none."[3]

And of this you are to be the sole judge, though there were fifty witnesses to the contrary.

How should indifferent spectators pretend to know the countenance of your friend as well as you do—you, that have a nearer, a dearer interest in attending to it? So accurate have been your observations, that no thought of their souls escapes you; nay, you often can tell even what they are going to think of.

The science of divination certainly claims your attention; beyond the past and the present, it shall extend your dominion over the future; from slight words, half-finished sentences, from silence itself, you shall draw your omens and auguries.

"I know what you were going to say"; or, "I know such a thing was a sign you were inclined to be displeased with me."

In the ardor of innocence, the culprit, to clear himself from such imputations, incurs the imputation of a greater offense. Suppose, to prove that you were mistaken, to prove that he could not have meant to blame you, he should declare that at the moment you mention, "You were quite foreign to his thoughts, he was not thinking at all about you."

Then in truth you have a right to be angry. To one of your class of justificators, this is the highest offense. Possessed as you are of the firm opinion that all persons at all times, on all occasions, are intent upon you alone, is it not less mortifying to discover that you were thought ill of, than that you were not thought of at all? "Indifference, you know, sentimental pupils, is more fatal to love than even hatred."

Thus, my dear pupils, I have endeavored to provide precepts adapted to the display of your several talents; but if there should be any amongst you who have no talents, who can neither argue nor persuade, who have neither sentiment nor enthusiasm, I must indeed—congratulate them; they are peculiarly qualified for the science of Self-justification: indulgent nature, often even in the weakness, provides for the protection of her crea-

---

[3] Adapted from *Hamlet* 3:2, line 402.

tures: just Providence, as the guard of stupidity, has enveloped it with the impenetrable armor of obstinacy.

Fair idiots! let women of sense, wit, feeling, triumph in their various arts: yours are superior. Their empire, absolute as it sometimes may be, is perpetually subject to sudden revolutions. With them, a man has some chance of equal sway: with a fool he has none. Have they hearts and understandings? Then the one may be touched, or the other in some unlucky moment convinced; even in their very power lies their greatest dangers—not so with you. In vain let the most candid of his sex attempt to reason with you; let him begin with, "Now, my dear, only listen to reason" —you stop him at once with, "No, my dear, you know I do not pretend to reason; I only say, that's my opinion."

Let him go on to prove that yours is a mistaken opinion—you are ready to acknowledge it long before he desires it. "You acknowledge it may be a wrong opinion; but still it is your opinion." You do not maintain it in the least either because you believe it to be wrong or right, but merely because it is yours. Exposed as you might have been to the perpetual humiliation of being convinced, nature seems kindly to have denied you all perception of truth, or at least all sentiment of pleasure from the perception.

With an admirable humility, you are as well contented to be in the wrong as in the right; you answer all that can be said to you with a provoking humility of aspect.

"Yes; I do not doubt but what you say may be very true, but I cannot tell; I do not think myself capable of judging on these subjects; I am sure you must know much better than I do. I do not pretend to say but that your opinion is very just; but I own I am of a contrary way of thinking; I always thought so, and I always shall."

Should a man with persevering temper tell you that he is ready to adopt your sentiments if you will only explain them; should he beg only to have a reason for your opinion—no, you can give no reason. Let him urge you to say something in its defense—no; like Queen Anne, you will only repeat the same thing over again, or be silent. Silence is the ornament of your sex; and in silence, if there be not wisdom, there is safety. You will, then, if you please, according to your custom, sit listening to all entreaties to explain, and speak—with a fixed immutability of posture, and a predetermined deafness of eye, which shall put your opponent utterly out of patience; yet still by persevering with the same complacent importance of countenance, you shall half persuade people you could speak if you would; you shall keep them in doubt by that true want of meaning, "which puzzles more than wit";[4] even because they cannot conceive the excess of your stupidity, they shall actually begin to believe that they

---

[4] Pope, *Moral Essays,* "Epistle II. To a Lady," line 114.

themselves are stupid. Ignorance and doubt are the great parents of the sublime.

Your adversary, finding you impenetrable to argument, perhaps would try wit:—but, "On the impassive ice the lightnings play." His eloquence or his kindness will avail less; when in yielding to you after a long harangue, he expects to please you, you will answer undoubtedly with the utmost propriety, "That you should be very sorry he yielded his judgment to you; that he is very good; that you are much obliged to him; but that, as to the point in dispute, it is a matter of perfect indifference to you; for your part, you have no choice at all about it; you beg that he will do just what he pleases; you know that it is the duty of a wife to submit; but you hope, however, you may have an *opinion* of your own."

Remember, all such speeches as these will lose above half their effect, if you cannot accompany them with the vacant stare, the insipid smile, the passive aspect of the humbly perverse.

Whilst I write, new precepts rush upon my recollection; but the subject is inexhaustible. I quit it with regret, though fully sensible of my presumption in having attempted to instruct those who, whilst they read, will smile in the consciousness of superior powers. Adieu! then, my fair readers: long may you prosper in the practice of an art peculiar to your sex! Long may you maintain unrivaled dominion at home and abroad; and long may your husbands rue the hour when first they made you promise *"to obey!"*

CHARLES LAMB

Charles Lamb (1775–1834), one of the great masters of the English essay, was born in a quiet, cloistered section of buildings in London called the Temple. His father was a servant and barrister's clerk who had seven children. Three survived: Charles, the youngest, his brother John, and his sister Mary, who helped raise him. Lamb went to Christ's Hospital school on a scholarship (and befriended the future poet Samuel Coleridge there), but because of family poverty he was forced to quit school and go to work at fourteen as a clerk at the South Sea House. A few years later he switched to the East India House, where he clerked for the rest of his life, until retired on a pension (see "The Superannuated Man").

At age twenty, Lamb witnessed a horrific family tragedy: Mary, temporarily insane, stabbed their mother to death and wounded their father. Lamb, who seized the knife out of his beloved sister's hand, soon afterward cracked under the strain and had a mental breakdown himself. Mary was spared prison by the courts and remanded to the custody of her younger brother, who took care of her (as she did him) for the rest of their lives. Periodically she would suffer relapses; a friend reports how he "met the brother and sister on one such occasion, walking hand in hand across the fields to the old asylum, both bathed in tears." Lamb remained a bachelor; his one professed love was for a blonde with blue eyes, Ann Simmons (renamed Alice W——n in the essays), who married someone else.

Lamb had a great zest for theater and wrote impressive drama criticism (Specimens of English Dramatic Poets) *and, with Mary, the children's classic* Tales from Shakespeare. *His own attempts at playwriting failed; with typical self-mockery, he joined the crowd who hooted derisively at the premiere of his lame farce,* Mr. H— *(about a gentleman trying to conceal that* his name is Hogsflesh!). He had more success moonlighting as a journalist, supplying jokes and squibs for the newspapers. In 1820, at age forty-five, he began writing the pieces that eventually became Essays of Elia for London Magazine (which also published Hazlitt, Keats, and DeQuincey). He took the name Elia from an Italian fellow clerk at South Sea House. The lightly fictionalized persona is essentially Lamb, but with playful alterations (Mary becomes "Cousin Bridget") and intentional confusions (brother John, in the wrenching conclusion to "Dream Children," is styled both "John L." and "James Elia," as if the author could not make up his mind whether to disguise or name the loss).

Just as the device of a fictional persona allowed Lamb the necessary distance to shape his autobiographical material, so the artful arrangement of Essays of Elia and its sequel, More Essays of Elia, ensured that they were not just collections but books. They can be read almost like a novel, with an irresistible, idiosyncratic, quixotic character at its center. Lamb was an astute psychologist, fascinated like Montaigne with the exasperating contradictions of character. Many of his essays are either portraits of eccentrics or wry explorations of his own ambivalences. Elia is both an individual and a type, a forerunner of those passively resistant nineteenth-century office workers who turn up in Melville's "Bartleby the Scrivener," Gogol's "The Overcoat," Dostoevsky's "The Double," and Hawthorne's "The Custom House."

Obstinately enthralled with the past, Lamb fashioned his style on English Renaissance prose writers such as Sir Thomas Browne, Robert Burton, and Sir William Temple, who were considered quaint even in his day. He loved archaic, mildewed vocabulary, which he used with solemn mockery—as he did puns, exaggerated metaphors, buffoonish catalogues—for comic effect. He was also a master of ironic shading, and could move from outrageous silliness to sincerity and pathos in a single sentence. Praised, somewhat stereotypically, for "sweetness of heart, delicacy of feeling, and indefinable charm of style," this gentle Lamb was not without claws: he had a perverse streak that could cuff the reader and rupture affability. His experiences with tragedy and death, though he rarely wrote of them specifically, may account for the melancholy cast underneath the Cheshire Cat smile.

In company, Lamb's gifts for conversation and friendship were much prized. He even managed to remain friends with the irascible William Hazlitt and to provide a stable home for the younger man to visit. "The great difference," noted Ronald Blythe, "between Lamb and Hazlitt was that the former seemed to have received the gift of perpetual early middle age and the latter, with his moodiness, his . . . hero worship, his passionate love and his general recklessness, appeared to have been cursed with everlasting youth." Together, they brought the English personal essay to its highest peak.

New Year's Eve

E VERY MAN HATH TWO BIRTH-DAYS: two days, at least, in every year, which set him upon revolving the lapse of time, as it affects his mortal duration. The one is that which in an especial manner he termeth *his.* In the gradual desuetude of old observances, this custom of solemnizing our proper birth-day hath nearly passed away, or is left to children, who reflect nothing at all about the matter, nor understand any thing in it beyond cake and orange. But the birth of a New Year is of an interest too wide to be pretermitted by king or cobbler. No one ever regarded the First of January with indifference. It is that from which all date their time, and count upon what is left. It is the nativity of our common Adam.

Of all sound of all bells (bells, the music nighest bordering upon heaven)—most solemn and touching is the peal which rings out the Old Year. I never hear it without a gathering-up of my mind to a concentration of all the images that have been diffused over the past twelvemonth; all I have done or suffered, performed or neglected—in that regretted time. I begin to know its worth, as when a person dies. It takes a personal colour; nor was it a poetical flight in a contemporary, when he exclaimed

I saw the skirts of the departing Year.

It is no more than what in sober sadness every one of us seems to be conscious of, in that awful leave-taking. I am sure I felt it, and all felt it with me, last night; though some of my companions affected rather to manifest an exhilaration at the birth of the coming year, than any very tender regrets for the decease of its predecessor. But I am none of those who—

Welcome the coming, speed the parting guest.

I am naturally, beforehand, shy of novelties; new books, new faces, new years,—from some mental twist which makes it difficult in me to face the prospective. I have almost ceased to hope; and am sanguine only in the prospects of other (former) years. I plunge into foregone visions and con-clusions. I encounter pell-mell with past disappointments. I am armour-proof against old discouragements. I forgive, or overcome in fancy, old adversaries. I play over again *for love,* as the gamesters phrase it, games, for which I once paid so dear. I would scarce now have any of those untoward accidents and events of my life reversed. I would no more alter them than the incidents of some well-contrived novel. Methinks, it is better that I should have pined away seven of my goldenest years, when I was thrall to the fair hair, and fairer eyes, of Alice W———n,[1] than that so passionate a love-adventure should be lost. It was better that our family should have missed that legacy, which old Dorrell cheated us of, than that I should have at this moment two thousand pounds *in banco,* and be without the idea of that specious old rogue.

In a degree beneath manhood, it is my infirmity to look back upon those early days. Do I advance a paradox, when I say, that, skipping over the intervention of forty years, a man may have leave to love *himself,* without the imputation of self-love?

If I know aught of myself, no one whose mind is introspective—and mine is painfully so—can have a less respect for his present identity, than I have for the man Elia. I know him to be light, and vain, and humorsome; a notorious * * *; addicted to * * * *: averse from counsel, neither taking it, nor offering it;—* * * besides; a stammering buffoon; what you will; lay it on, and spare not; I subscribe to it all, and much more, than thou canst be willing to lay at his door———but for the child Elia—that "other me," there, in the back-ground—I must take leave to cherish the remembrance of that young master—with as little reference, I protest, to this stupid changeling of five-and-forty, as if it had been a child of some other house, and not of my parents. I can cry over its patient small-pox at five, and rougher medicaments. I can lay its poor fevered head upon the sick pillow at Christ's, and wake with it in surprise at the gentle posture of maternal tenderness hanging over it, that unknown had watched its sleep. I know how it shrank from any the least colour of falsehood.—God help thee, Elia, how art thou changed! Thou art sophisticated.—I know how honest, how courageous (for a weakling) it was—how religious, how imaginative, how hopeful! From what have I not fallen, if the child I remember was indeed myself,—and not some dissembling guardian, presenting a false identity, to give the rule to my unpractised steps, and regulate the tone of my moral being!

That I am fond of indulging, beyond a hope of sympathy, in such retrospection, may be the symptom of some sickly idiosyncrasy. Or is it owing to another cause; simply, that being without wife or family, I have not learned to project myself enough out of myself; and having no offspring of my own to dally with, I turn back upon memory, and adopt my own early idea, as my heir and favourite? If these speculations seem fantastical to thee, reader—(a busy man, perchance), if I tread out of the way of thy

---

[1]Alice Winterton.

sympathy, and am singularly-conceited only, I retire, impenetrable to ridicule, under the phantom cloud of Elia.

The elders, with whom I was brought up, were of a character not likely to let slip the sacred observance of any old institution; and the ringing out of the Old Year was kept by them with circumstances of peculiar ceremony.—In those days the sound of those midnight chimes, though it seemed to raise hilarity in all around me, never failed to bring a train of pensive imagery into my fancy. Yet I then scarce conceived what it meant, or thought of it as a reckoning that concerned me. Not childhood alone, but the young man till thirty, never feels practically that he is mortal. He knows it indeed, and, if need were, he could preach a homily on the fragility of life; but he brings it not home to himself, any more than in a hot June we can appropriate to our imagination the freezing days of December. But now, shall I confess a truth?—I feel these audits but too powerfully. I begin to count the probabilities of my duration, and to grudge at the expenditure of moments and shortest periods, like miser's farthings. In proportion as the years both lessen and shorten, I set more count upon their periods, and would fain lay my ineffectual finger upon the spoke of the great wheel. I am not content to pass away "like a weaver's shuttle." Those metaphors solace me not, nor sweeten the unpalatable draught of mortality. I care not to be carried with the tide, that smoothly bears human life to eternity; and reluct at the inevitable course of destiny. I am in love with this green earth; the face of town and country; the unspeakable rural solitudes, and the sweet security of streets. I would set up my tabernacle here. I am content to stand still at the age to which I am arrived; I, and my friends: to be no younger, no richer, no handsomer. I do not want to be weaned by age; or drop, like mellow fruit, as they say, into the grave.—Any alteration, on this earth of mine, in diet or in lodging, puzzles and discomposes me. My household-gods plant a terrible fixed foot, and are not rooted up without blood. They do not willingly seek Lavinian shores. A new state of being staggers me.

Sun, and sky, and breeze, and solitary walks, and summer holidays, and the greenness of fields, and the delicious juices of meats and fishes, and society, and the cheerful glass, and candle-light, and fire-side conversations, and innocent vanities, and jests, and *irony itself*—do these things go out with life?

Can a ghost laugh, or shake his gaunt sides, when you are pleasant with him?

And you, my midnight darlings, my Folios—must I part with the intense delight of having you (huge armfuls) in my embraces? Must knowledge come to me, if it come at all, by some awkward experiment of intuition, and no longer by this familiar process of reading?

Shall I enjoy friendships there, wanting the smiling indications which point me to them here,—the recognisable face—the "sweet assurance of a look"—?

In winter this intolerable disinclination to dying—to give it its mildest name—does more especially haunt and beset me. In a genial August noon, beneath a sweltering sky, death is almost problematic. At those times do such poor snakes as myself enjoy an immortality. Then we expand and burgeon. Then are we as strong again, as valiant again, as wise again, and a great deal taller. The blast that nips and shrinks me, puts me in thought of death. All things allied to the insubstantial, wait upon that master feeling; cold, numbness, dreams, perplexity; moonlight itself, with its shadowy and spectral appearances,—that cold ghost of the sun, or Phoebus' sickly sister, like that innutritious one denounced in the Canticles:—I am none of her minions—I hold with the Persian.

Whatsoever thwarts, or puts me out of my way, brings death into my mind. All partial evils, like humours, run into that capital plague-sore.—I have heard some profess an indifference to life. Such hail the end of their existence as a port of refuge; and speak of the grave as of some soft arms, in which they may slumber as on a pillow. Some have wooed death——— but out upon thee, I say, thou foul, ugly phantom! I detest, abhor, execrate, and (with Friar John) give thee to six-score thousand devils, as in no instance to be excused or tolerated, but shunned as a universal viper; to be branded, proscribed, and spoken evil of! In no way can I be brought to digest thee, thou thin, melancholy *Privation,* or more frightful and confounding *Positive!*

Those antidotes, prescribed against the fear of thee, are altogether frigid and insulting, like thyself. For what satisfaction hath a man, that he shall "lie down with kings and emperors in death," who in his life-time never greatly coveted the society of such bed-fellows?—or, forsooth, that, "so shall the fairest face appear?"—why, to comfort me, must Alice W——n be a goblin? More than all, I conceive disgust at those impertinent and misbecoming familiarities, inscribed upon your ordinary tombstones. Every dead man must take upon himself to be lecturing me with his odious truism, that "such as he now is, I must shortly be." Not so shortly, friend, perhaps, as thou imaginest. In the meantime I am alive. I move about. I am worth twenty of thee. Know thy betters! Thy New Years' Days are past. I survive, a jolly candidate for 1821. Another cup of wine—and while that turn-coat bell, that just now mournfully chanted the obsequies of 1820 departed, with changed notes lustily rings in a successor, let us attune to its peal the song made on a like occasion, by hearty, cheerful Mr Cotton.—

THE NEW YEAR

Hark, the cock crows, and yon bright star
Tells us, the day himself's not far;

And see where, breaking from the night,
He gilds the western hills with light.
With him old Janus doth appear,
Peeping into the future year,
With such a look as seems to say,
The prospect is not good that way
Thus do we rise ill sights to see,
And 'gainst ourselves to prophesy;
When the prophetic fear of things
A more tormenting mischief brings,
More full of sore-tormenting gall,
Than direst mischiefs can befall.
But stay! but stay! methinks my sight,
Better inform'd by clearer light,
Discerns sereneness in that brow,
That all contracted seem'd but now.
His revers'd face may show distaste,
And frown upon the ills are past;
But that which this way looks is clear,
And smiles upon the New-born Year.
He looks too from a place so high,
The Year lies open to his eye;
And all the moments open are
To the exact discoverer.
Yet more and more he smiles upon
The happy revolution.
Why should we then suspect or fear
The influences of a year,
So smiles upon us the first morn,
And speaks us good so soon as born?
Plague on't! the last was ill enough,
This cannot but make better proof;
Or, at the worst, as we brush'd through
The last, why so we may this too;
And then the next in reason shou'd
Be superexcellently good:
For the worst ills (we daily see)
Have no more perpetuity,
Than the best fortunes that do fall;
Which also bring us wherewithal
Longer their being to support,
Than those do of the other sort:
And who has one good year in three,

> *And yet repines at destiny,*
> *Appears ungrateful in the case,*
> *And merits not the good he has.*
> *Then let us welcome the New Guest*
> *With lusty brimmers of the best;*
> *Mirth always should Good Fortune meet*
> *And render e'en Disaster sweet:*
> *And though the Princess turn her back,*
> *Let us but line ourselves with sack,*
> *We better shall by far hold out,*
> *Till the next Year she face about.*

How say you, reader—do not these verses smack of the rough magnanimity of the old English vein? Do they not fortify like a cordial; enlarging the heart, and productive of sweet blood, and generous spirits, in the concoction? Where be those puling fears of death, just now expressed or affected?—Passed like a cloud—absorbed in the purging sunlight of clear poetry—clean washed away by a wave of genuine Helicon, your only Spa for these hypochondries—And now another cup of the generous! and a merry New Year, and many of them, to you all, my masters!

A Chapter on Ears

I HAVE NO EAR.—

Mistake me not, reader—nor imagine that I am by nature destitute of those exterior twin appendages, hanging ornaments, and (architecturally speaking) handsome volutes to the human capital. Better my mother had never borne me.—I am, I think, rather delicately than copiously provided with those conduits; and I feel no disposition to envy the mule for his plenty, or the mole for her exactness, in those ingenious labyrinthine inlets—those indispensable side-intelligencers.

Neither have I incurred, or done anything to incur, with Defoe, that hideous disfigurement, which constrained him to draw upon assurance—

to feel "quite unabashed," and at ease upon that article. I was never, I thank my stars, in the pillory; nor, if I read them aright, is it within the compass of my destiny, that I ever should be.

When therefore I say that I have no ear, you will understand me to mean—*for music*. To say that this heart never melted at the concord of sweet sounds, would be a foul self-libel. *"Water parted from the sea"* never fails to move it strangely. So does *"In infancy."* But they were used to be sung at her harpsichord (the old-fashioned instrument in vogue in those days) by a gentlewoman—the gentlest, sure, that ever merited the appellation—the sweetest—why should I hesitate to name Mrs. S——, once the blooming Fanny Weatheral of the Temple—who had power to thrill the soul of Elia, small imp as he was, even in his long coats; and to make him glow, tremble, and blush with a passion, that not faintly indicated the day-spring of that absorbing sentiment which was afterwards destined to over-whelm and subdue his nature quite for Alice W——n.

I even think that *sentimentally* I am disposed to harmony. But *organically* I am incapable of a tune. I have been practising *"God save the King"* all my life; whistling and humming of it over to myself in solitary corners; and am not yet arrived, they tell me, within many quavers of it. Yet hath the loyalty of Elia never been impeached.

I am not without suspicion, that I have an undeveloped faculty of music within me. For thrumming, in my mild way, on my friend A.'s piano, the other morning, while he was engaged in an adjoining parlour,—on his return he was pleased to say, *"he thought it could not be the maid!"* On his first surprise at hearing the keys touched in somewhat an airy and master-ful way, not dreaming of me, his suspicions had lighted on *Jenny*. But a grace, snatched from a superior refinement, soon convinced him that some being—technically perhaps deficient, but higher informed from a princi-ple common to all the fine arts—had swayed the keys to a mood which Jenny, with all her (less-cultivated) enthusiasm, could never have elicited from them. I mention this as a proof of my friend's penetration, and not with any view of disparaging Jenny.

Scientifically I could never be made to understand (yet have I taken some pains) what a note in music is; or how one note should differ from another. Much less in voices can I distinguish a soprano from a tenor. Only sometimes the thorough-bass I contrive to guess at, from its being supereminently harsh and disagreeable. I tremble, however, for my misap-plication of the simplest terms of *that* which I disclaim. While I profess my ignorance, I scarce know what to *say* I am ignorant of. I hate, perhaps, by misnomers. *Sostenuto* and *adagio* stand in the like relation of obscurity to me; and *Sol, Fa, Mi, Re,* is as conjuring as *Baralipton*.

It is hard to stand alone in an age like this,—(constituted to the quick and critical perception of all harmonious combinations, I verily believe, beyond all preceding ages, since Jubal stumbled upon the gamut,) to remain, as it were, singly unimpressible to the magic influences of an art, which is said to have such an especial stroke at soothing, elevating, and refining the passions.—Yet, rather than break the candid current of my confessions, I must avow to you that I have received a great deal more pain than pleasure from this so cried-up faculty.

I am constitutionally susceptible of noises. A carpenter's hammer, in a warm summer noon, will fret me into more than midsummer madness. But those unconnected, unset sounds, are nothing to the measured malice of music. The ear is passive to those single strokes; willingly enduring stripes while it hath no task to con. To music it cannot be passive. It will strive—mine at least will—spite of its inaptitude, to thrid the maze; like an unskilled eye painfully poring upon hieroglyphics. I have sat through an Italian Opera, till, for sheer pain, and inexplicable anguish, I have rushed out into the noisiest places of the crowded streets, to solace myself with sounds, which I was not obliged to follow, and get rid of the distracting torment of endless, fruitless, barren attention! I take refuge in the unpretending assemblage of honest common-life sounds;—and the purgatory of the Enraged Musician becomes my paradise.

I have sat at an Oratorio (that profanation of the purposes of the cheerful playhouse) watching the faces of the auditory in the pit (what a contrast to Hogarth's Laughing Audience!) immoveable, or effecting some faint emotion—till (as some have said, that our occupations in the next world will be but a shadow of what delighted us in this) I have imagined myself in some cold Theatre in Hades, where some of the *forms* of the earthly one should be kept up, with none of the *enjoyment;* or like that

> ——*Party in a parlour*
> *All silent, and all* DAMNED.

Above all, those insufferable concertos, and pieces of music, as they are called, do plague and embitter my apprehension.—Words are something; but to be exposed to an endless battery of mere sounds; to be long a dying; to lie stretched upon a rack of roses; to keep up languor by unintermitted effort; to pile honey upon sugar, and sugar upon honey, to an interminable tedious sweetness; to fill up sound with feeling, and strain ideas to keep pace with it; to gaze on empty frames, and be forced to make the pictures for yourself; to read a book, *all stops,* and be obliged to supply the verbal matter; to invent extempore tragedies to answer to the vague gestures of an inexplicable rambling mime—these are faint shadows of what I have undergone from a series of the ablest-executed pieces of this empty *instrumental music.*

I deny not, that in the opening of a concert, I have experienced something vastly lulling and agreeable:—afterwards followeth the languor and the oppression.—Like that disappointing book in Patmos; or, like the comings on of melancholy, described by Burton, doth music make her first insinuating approaches:—"Most pleasant it is to such as are melancholy given, to walk alone in some solitary grove, betwixt wood and water, by some brook side, and to meditate upon some delightsome and pleasant subject, which shall affect him most, *amabilis insania,* and *mentis gratissimus error.* A most incomparable delight to build castles in the air, to go smiling to themselves, acting an infinite variety of parts, which they suppose, and strongly imagine, they act, or that they see done.—So delightsome these toys at first, they could spend whole days and nights without sleep, even whole years in such contemplations, and fantastical meditations, which are like so many dreams, and will hardly be drawn from them —winding and unwinding themselves as so many clocks, and still pleasing their humours, until at the last the SCENE TURNS UPON A SUDDEN, and they being now habitated to such meditations and solitary places, can endure no company, can think of nothing but harsh and distasteful subjects. Fear, sorrow, suspicion, *subrusticus pudor,* discontent, cares, and weariness of life, surprise them on a sudden, and they can think of nothing else: continually suspecting, no sooner are their eyes open, but this infernal plague of melancholy seizeth on them, and terrifies their souls, representing some dismal object to their minds; which now, by no means, no labour, no persuasions, they can avoid, they cannot be rid of, they cannot resist."

Something like this "SCENE TURNING" I have experienced at the evening parties, at the house of my good Catholic friend *Nov*——; who, by the aid of a capital organ, himself the most finished of players, converts his drawing-room into a chapel, his week days into Sundays, and these latter into minor heavens.*

When my friend commences upon one of those solemn anthems, which peradventure struck upon my heedless ear, rambling in the side aisles of the dim Abbey, some five-and-thirty years since, waking a new sense, and putting a soul of old religion into my young apprehension—(whether it be *that,* in which the Psalmist, weary of the persecutions of bad men, wisheth to himself dove's wings—or *that other,* which, with a like measure of sobriety and pathos, inquireth by what means the young man shall best cleanse his mind)—a holy calm pervadeth me.—I am for the time

> —*rapt above earth,*
> *And possess joys not promised at my birth.*

But when this master of the spell, not content to have laid a soul prostrate, goes on, in his power, to inflict more bliss than lies in her capacity to receive—impatient to overcome her "earthly" with his "heavenly,"—still

---

* I have been there, and still would go
'Tis like a little heaven below.—Dr. Watts.

pouring in, for protracted hours, fresh waves and fresh from the sea of sound, or from that inexhausted *German* ocean, above which, in triumphant progress, dolphin-seated, ride those Arions *Haydn* and *Mozart,* with their attendant Tritons, *Bach, Beethoven,* and a countless tribe, whom to attempt to reckon up would but plunge me again in the deeps,—I stagger under the weight of harmony, reeling to and fro at my wits' end;—clouds, as of frankincense, oppress me—priests, altars, censers, dazzle before me —the genius of *his* religion hath me in her toils—a shadowy triple tiara invests the brow of my friend, late so naked, so ingenuous—he is Pope,— and by him sits, like as in the anomaly of dreams, a she-Pope too,—tricoroneted like himself!—I am converted, and yet a Protestant;—at once *malleus hereticorum,* and myself grand heresiarch: or three heresies centre in my person:—I am Marcion, Ebion, and Cerinthus—Gog and Magog— what not?—till the coming in of the friendly supper-tray dissipates the figment, and a draught of true Lutheran beer (in which chiefly my friend shows himself no bigot) at once reconciles me to the rationalities of a purer faith; and restores to me the genuine unterrifying aspects of my pleasant-countenanced host and hostess.

Dream Children: A Reverie

C HILDREN LOVE TO LISTEN to stories about their elders, when *they* were children; to stretch their imagination to the conception of a traditionary great-uncle, or grandame, whom they never saw. It was in this spirit that my little ones crept about me the other evening to hear about their great-grandmother Field, who lived in a great house in Norfolk[1] (a hundred times bigger than that in which they and papa lived) which had been the scene—so at least it was generally believed in that part of the country—of the tragic incidents which they had lately become familiar with from the ballad of the Children in the Wood. Certain it is that the whole story of the children and their cruel uncle was to be seen fairly

---

[1] Blakesware, in Hertfordshire, is meant, where Lamb's grandmother, Mary Field, was housekeeper.

carved out in wood upon the chimney-piece of the great hall, the whole story down to the Robin Redbreasts, till a foolish rich person pulled it down to set up a marble one of modern invention in its stead, with no story upon it. Here Alice put out one of her dear mother's looks, too tender to be called upbraiding. Then I went on to say, how religious and how good their great-grandmother Field was, how beloved and respected by every body, though she was not indeed the mistress of this great house, but had only the charge of it (and yet in some respects she might be said to be the mistress of it too) committed to her by the owner, who preferred living in a newer and more fashionable mansion which he had purchased somewhere in the adjoining county; but still she lived in it in a manner as if it had been her own, and kept up the dignity of the great house in a sort while she lived, which afterwards came to decay, and was nearly pulled down, and all its old ornaments stripped and carried away to the owner's other house, where they were set up, and looked as awkward as if some one were to carry away the old tombs they had seen lately at the Abbey, and stick them up in Lady C.'s tawdry gilt drawing-room. Here John smiled, as much as to say, "that would be foolish indeed." And then I told how, when she came to die, her funeral was attended by a concourse of all the poor, and some of the gentry too, of the neighbourhood for many miles round, to show their respect for her memory, because she had been such a good and religious woman; so good indeed that she knew all the Psaltery by heart, ay, and a great part of the Testament besides. Here little Alice spread her hands. Then I told what a tall, upright, graceful person their great-grandmother Field once was; and how in her youth she was esteemed the best dancer—here Alice's little right foot played an involuntary movement, till upon my looking grave, it desisted—the best dancer, I was saying, in the county, till a cruel disease, called a cancer, came, and bowed her down with pain; but it could never bend her good spirits, or make them stoop, but they were still upright, because she was so good and religious. Then I told how she was used to sleep by herself in a lone chamber of the great lone house; and how she believed that an apparition of two infants was to be seen at midnight gliding up and down the great staircase near where she slept, but she said "those innocents would do her no harm;" and how frightened I used to be, though in those days I had my maid to sleep with me, because I was never half so good or religious as she —and yet I never saw the infants. Here John expanded all his eye-brows and tried to look courageous. Then I told how good she was to all her grand-children, having us to the great-house in the holydays, where I in particular used to spend many hours by myself, in gazing upon the old busts of the Twelve Caesars, that had been Emperors of Rome, till the old marble heads would seem to live again, or I to be turned into marble with them; how I never could be tired with roaming about that huge mansion, with its vast empty rooms, with their worn-out hangings, fluttering tapestry, and carved oaken panels, with the gilding almost rubbed out—sometimes in the spacious old-fashioned gardens, which I had almost to myself, unless when now and then a solitary gardening man would cross me—and how the nectarines and peaches hung upon the walls, without my ever offering to pluck them, because they were forbidden fruit, unless now and then,—and because I had more pleasure in strolling about among the old melancholy-looking yew trees, or the firs, and picking up the red berries, and the fir apples, which were good for nothing but to look at—or in lying about upon the fresh grass, with all the fine garden smells around me—or basking in the orangery, till I could almost fancy myself ripening too along with the oranges and the limes in that grateful warmth—or in watching the dace that darted to and fro in the fish-pond, at the bottom of the garden, with here and there a great sulky pike hanging midway down the water in silent state, as if it mocked at their impertinent friskings,—I had more pleasure in these busy-idle diversions than in all the sweet flavours of peaches, nectarines, oranges, and such like common baits of children. Here John slily deposited back upon the plate a bunch of grapes, which, not unobserved by Alice, he had meditated dividing with her, and both seemed willing to relinquish them for the present as irrelevant. Then in somewhat a more heightened tone, I told how, though their great-grandmother Field loved all her grand-children, yet in an especial manner she might be said to love their uncle, John L——, because he was so handsome and spirited a youth, and a king to the rest of us; and, instead of moping about in solitary corners, like some of us, he would mount the most mettlesome horse he could get, when but an imp no bigger than themselves, and make it carry him half over the county in a morning, and join the hunters when there were any out—and yet he loved the old great house and gardens too, but had too much spirit to be always pent up within their boundaries—and how their uncle grew up to man's estate as brave as he was handsome, to the admiration of everybody, but of their great-grandmother Field most especially; and how he used to carry me upon his back when I was a lame-footed boy—for he was a good bit older than me—many a mile when I could not walk for pain;—and how in after life he became lame-footed too, and I did not always (I fear) make allowances enough for him when he was impatient, and in pain, nor remember sufficiently how considerate he had been to me when I was lame-footed; and how when he died, though he had not been dead an hour, it seemed as if he had died a great while ago, such a distance there is betwixt life and death; and how I bore his death as I thought pretty well at first, but afterwards it haunted and haunted me; and though I did not cry or take it to heart as some do, and as I think he would have done if I had died, yet I missed him all day long, and knew not till then how much I had loved

him. I missed his kindness, and I missed his crossness, and wished him to
be alive again, to be quarrelling with him (for we quarrelled sometimes),
rather than not have him again, and was as uneasy without him, as he their
poor uncle must have been when the doctor took off his limb. Here the
children fell a crying, and asked if their little mourning which they had on
was not for uncle John, and they looked up, and prayed me not to go on
about their uncle, but to tell them some stories about their pretty dead
mother. Then I told how for seven long years, in hope sometimes, sometimes in despair, yet persisting ever, I courted the fair Alice W——n; and,
as much as children could understand, I explained to them what coyness,
and difficulty, and denial meant in maidens—when suddenly, turning to
Alice, the soul of the first Alice looked out at her eyes with such a reality
of re-presentment, that I became in doubt which of them stood there
before me, or whose that bright hair was; and while I stood gazing, both
the children gradually grew fainter to my view, receding, and still receding
till nothing at last but two mournful features were seen in the uttermost
distance, which, without speech, strangely impressed upon me the effects
of speech; "We are not of Alice, nor of thee, nor are we children at all.
The children of Alice call Bartrum father. We are nothing; less than nothing, and dreams. We are only what might have been, and must wait upon
the tedious shores of Lethe millions of ages before we have existence, and
a name"—and immediately awaking, I found myself quietly seated in my
bachelor armchair, where I had fallen asleep, with the faithful Bridget
unchanged by my side—but John L. (or James Elia) was gone for ever.

The Superannuated Man

Sera tamen respexit
Libertas.
      —VIRGIL.

A Clerk I was born in London gay.
      —O'KEEFE.

IF PERADVENTURE, Reader, it has been thy lot to waste the
golden years of thy life—thy shining youth—in the irksome confinement of an office; to have thy prison days prolonged through middle age
down to decrepitude and silver hairs, without hope of release or respite; to
have lived to forget that there are such things as holidays, or to remember

them but as the prerogatives of childhood; then, and then only, will you be able to appreciate my deliverance.

It is now six-and-thirty years since I took my seat at the desk in Mincing-lane. Melancholy was the transition at fourteen from the abundant playtime, and the frequently-intervening vacations of school days, to the eight, nine, and sometimes ten hours' a-day attendance at the counting-house. But time partially reconciles us to anything. I gradually became content—doggedly contented, as wild animals in cages.

It is true I had my Sundays to myself; but Sundays, admirable as the institution of them is for purposes of worship, are for that very reason the very worst adapted for days of unbending and recreation. In particular, there is a gloom for me attendant upon a city Sunday, a weight in the air. I miss the cheerful cries of London, the music, and the ballad-singers—the buzz and stirring murmur of the streets. Those eternal bells depress me. The closed shops repel me. Prints, pictures, all the glittering and endless succession of knacks and gewgaws, and ostentatiously displayed wares of tradesmen, which make a week-day saunter through the less busy parts of the metropolis so delightful—are shut out. No book-stalls deliciously to idle over—no busy faces to recreate the idle man who contemplates them ever passing by—the very face of business a charm by contrast to his temporary relaxation from it. Nothing to be seen but unhappy countenances—or half-happy at best—of emancipated 'prentices and little tradesfolks, with here and there a servant-maid that has got leave to go out, who, slaving all the week, with the habit has lost almost the capacity of enjoying a free hour; and livelily expressing the hollowness of a day's pleasuring. The very strollers in the fields on that day look anything but comfortable.

But besides Sundays, I had a day at Easter, and a day at Christmas, with a full week in the summer to go and air myself in my native fields of Hertfordshire. This last was a great indulgence; and the prospect of its recurrence, I believe, alone kept me up through the year, and made my durance tolerable. But when the week came round, did the glittering phantom of the distance keep touch with me? or rather was it not a series of seven uneasy days, spent in restless pursuit of pleasure, and a wearisome anxiety to find out how to make the most of them? Where was the quiet, where the promised rest? Before I had a taste of it, it was vanished. I was at the desk again, counting upon the fifty-one tedious weeks that must intervene before such another snatch would come. Still the prospect of its coming threw something of an illumination upon the darker side of my captivity. Without it, as I have said, I could scarcely have sustained my thraldom.

Independently of the rigours of attendance, I have ever been haunted with a sense (perhaps a mere caprice) of incapacity for business. This, during my latter years, had increased to such a degree, that it was visible in all the lines of my countenance. My health and my good spirits flagged. I had perpetually a dread of some crisis, to which I should be found unequal. Besides my daylight servitude, I served over again all night in my sleep, and would awake with terrors of imaginary false entries, errors in my accounts, and the like. I was fifty years of age, and no prospect of emancipation presented itself. I had grown to my desk, as it were; and the wood had entered into my soul.

My fellows in the office would sometimes rally me upc he trouble legible in my countenance; but I did not know that it hau raised the suspicions of any of my employers, when, on the 5th of last month, a day ever to be remembered by me, L——, the junior partner in the firm, calling me on one side, directly taxed me with my bad looks, and frankly inquired the cause of them. So taxed, I honestly made confession of my infirmity, and added that I was afraid I should eventually be obliged to resign his service. He spoke some words of course to hearten me, and there the matter rested. A whole week I remained labouring under the impression that I had acted imprudently in my disclosure; that I had foolishly given a handle against myself, and had been anticipating my own dismissal. A week passed in this manner—the most anxious one, I verily believe, in my whole life—when on the evening of the 12th of April, just as I was about quitting my desk to go home (it might be about eight o'clock), I received an awful summons to attend the presence of the whole assembled firm in the formidable back parlour. I thought now my time is surely come, I have done for myself, I am going to be told that they have no longer occasion for me. L——, I could see, smiled at the terror I was in, which was a little relief to me,—when to my utter astonishment B——, the eldest partner, began a formal harangue to me on the length of my services, my very meritorious conduct during the whole of the time (the deuce, thought I, how did he find out that? I protest I never had the confidence to think as much). He went on to descant on the expediency of retiring at a certain time of life (how my heart panted!), and asking me a few questions as to the amount of my own property, of which I have a little, ended with a proposal, to which his three partners nodded a grave assent, that I should accept from the house, which I had served so well, a pension for life to the amount of two-thirds of my accustomed salary—a magnificent offer! I do not know what I answered between surprise and gratitude, but it was understood that I accepted their proposal, and I was told that I was free from that hour to leave their service. I stammered out a bow, and at just ten minutes after eight I went home—for ever. This noble benefit—gratitude forbids me to conceal their names—I owe to the kindness of the most munificent firm in the world—the house of Boldero, Merryweather, Bosanquet, and Lacy.

Esto perpetua!

For the first day or two I felt stunned—overwhelmed. I could only apprehend my felicity; I was too confused to taste it sincerely. I wandered about, thinking I was happy, and knowing that I was not. I was in the condition of a prisoner in the old Bastile, suddenly let loose after a forty years' confinement. I could scarce trust myself with myself. It was like passing out of Time into Eternity—for it is a sort of Eternity for a man to have all his Time to himself. It seemed to me that I had more time on my hands than I could ever manage. From a poor man, poor in Time, I was suddenly lifted up into a vast revenue; I could see no end of my possessions; I wanted some steward, or judicious bailiff, to manage my estates in Time for me. And here let me caution persons grown old in active business, not lightly, nor without weighing their own resources, to forego their customary employment all at once, for there may be danger in it. I feel it by myself, but I know that my resources are sufficient; and now that those first giddy raptures have subsided, I have a quiet home-feeling of the blessedness of my condition. I am in no hurry. Having all holidays, I am as though I had none. If Time hung heavy upon me, I could walk it away; but I do *not* walk all day long, as I used to do in those old transient holidays, thirty miles a day, to make the most of them. If Time were troublesome, I could read it away; but I do *not* read in that violent measure, with which, having no Time my own but candlelight Time, I used to weary out my head and eyesight in bygone winters. I walk, read, or scribble (as now) just when the fit seizes me. I no longer hunt after pleasure; I let it come to me. I am like the man

—*That's born, and has his years come to him,*
In some green desert.

"Years!" you will say; "what is this superannuated simpleton calculating upon? He has already told us he is past fifty."

I have indeed lived nominally fifty years, but deduct out of them the hours which I have lived to other people, and not to myself, and you will find me still a young fellow. For *that* is the only true Time, which a man can properly call his own—that which he has all to himself; the rest, though in some sense he may be said to live it, is other people's Time, not his. The remnant of my poor days, long or short, is at least multiplied for me threefold. My ten next years, if I stretch so far, will be as long as any preceding thirty. 'Tis a fair rule-of-three sum.

Among the strange fantasies which beset me at the commencement of my freedom, and of which all traces are not yet gone, one was, that a vast tract of time had intervened since I quitted the Counting House. I could not conceive of it as an affair of yesterday. The partners, and the clerks with whom I had for so many years, and for so many hours in each day of the year, been closely associated—being suddenly removed from them— they seemed as dead to me. There is a fine passage, which may serve to illustrate this fancy, in a Tragedy by Sir Robert Howard, speaking of a friend's death:—

> —'Twas but just now he went away;
> I have not since had time to shed a tear;
> And yet the distance does the same appear
> As if he had been a thousand years from me.
> Time takes no measure in Eternity.

To dissipate this awkward feeling, I have been fain to go among them once or twice since; to visit my old desk-fellows—my co-brethren of the quill—that I had left below in the state militant. Not all the kindness with which they received me could quite restore to me that pleasant familiarity, which I had heretofore enjoyed among them. We cracked some of our old jokes, but methought they went off but faintly. My old desk; the peg where I hung my hat, were appropriated to another. I knew it must be, but I could not take it kindly. D——l take me, if I did not feel some remorse—beast, if I had not—at quitting my old compeers, the faithful partners of my toils for six-and-thirty years, that smoothed for me with their jokes and conundrums the ruggedness of my professional road. Had it been so rugged then, after all? or was I a coward simply? Well, it is too late to repent; and I also know that these suggestions are a common fallacy of the mind on such occasions. But my heart smote me. I had violently broken the bands betwixt us. It was at least not courteous. I shall be some time before I get quite reconciled to the separation. Farewell, old cronies, yet not for long, for again and again I will come among ye, if I shall have your leave. Farewell, Ch——, dry, sarcastic, and friendly! Do——, mild, slow to move, and gentlemanly! Pl——, officious to do, and to volunteer, good services!—and thou, thou dreary pile, fit mansion for a Gresham or a Whittington of old, stately house of Merchants; with thy labyrinthine passages, and light-excluding, pent-up offices, where candles for one-half the year supplied the place of the sun's light; unhealthy contributor to my weal, stern fosterer of my living, farewell! In thee remain, and not in the obscure collection of some wandering bookseller, my "works!" There let them rest, as I do from my labours, piled on thy massy shelves, more MSS. in folio than ever Aquinas left, and full as useful! My mantle I bequeath among ye.

A fortnight has passed since the date of my first communication. At that period I was approaching to tranquillity, but had not reached it. I boasted of a calm indeed, but it was comparative only. Something of the first flutter was left; an unsettling sense of novelty; the dazzle to weak eyes of unaccustomed light. I missed my old chains, forsooth, as if they had been some necessary part of my apparel. I was a poor Carthusian, from strict cellular discipline suddenly by some revolution returned upon the world. I am now as if I had never been other than my own master. It is natural for me to go where I please, to do what I please. I find myself at 11 o'clock in the day in Bond-street, and it seems to me that I have been sauntering there at that very hour for years past. I digress into Soho, to explore a book-stall. Methinks I have been thirty years a collector. There is nothing strange nor new in it. I find myself before a fine picture in the morning. Was it ever otherwise? What is become of Fish-street Hill? Where is Fenchurch-street? Stones of old Mincing-lane, which I have worn with my daily pilgrimage for six-and-thirty years, to the footsteps of what toil-worn clerk are your everlasting flints now vocal? I indent the gayer flags of Pall Mall. It is Change time, and I am strangely among the Elgin marbles. It was no hyperbole when I ventured to compare the change in my condition to passing into another world. Time stands still in a manner to me. I have lost all distinction of season. I do not know the day of the week or of the month. Each day used to be individually felt by me in its reference to the foreign post days; in its distance from, or propinquity to, the next Sunday. I had my Wednesday feelings, my Saturday nights' sensations. The genius of each day was upon me distinctly during the whole of it, affecting my appetite, spirits, &c. The phantom of the next day, with the dreary five to follow, sate as a load upon my poor Sabbath recreations. What charm has washed that Ethiop white? What is gone of Black Monday? All days are the same. Sunday itself—that unfortunate failure of a holiday, as it too often proved, what with my sense of its fugitiveness, and over-care to get the greatest quantity of pleasure out of it—is melted down into a week-day. I can spare to go to church now, without grudging the huge cantle which it used to seem to cut out of the holiday. I have time for everything. I can visit a sick friend. I can interrupt the man of much occupation when he is busiest. I can insult over him with an invitation to take a day's pleasure with me to Windsor this fine May-morning. It is Lucretian pleasure to behold the poor drudges, whom I have left behind in the world, carking and caring; like horses in a mill, drudging on in the same eternal round—and what is it all for? A man can never have too much Time to himself, nor too little to do. Had I a little son, I would christen him NOTHING-TO-DO; he should do nothing. Man, I verily believe, is out of his element as long as he is operative. I am altogether for the life contemplative. Will no kindly earthquake come and swallow up those accursed cotton-mills? Take me that lumber of a desk there, and bowl it down

As low as to the fiends.

I am no longer * * * * * *, clerk to the Firm of, &c. I am Retired Leisure. I am to be met with in trim gardens. I am already come to be known by my vacant face and careless gesture, perambulating at no fixed pace, nor with any settled purpose. I walk about; not to and from. They tell me, a certain *cum dignitate* air, that has been buried so long with my other good parts, has begun to shoot forth in my person. I grow into gentility perceptibly. When I take up a newspaper, it is to read the state of the opera—*Opus operatum est.* I have done all that I came into this world to do. I have worked task-work, and have the rest of the day to myself.

WILLIAM HAZLITT

William Hazlitt (1778–1830) was the son of a Unitarian minister who bounced from parish to parish (even settling for a while in America after the Revolution) because of his radical, deist views. Hazlitt inherited from his father a freethinker's love of liberty and republicanism. Studying metaphysics to become a philosopher, he fell in love with painting (a passion he never lost), but found his draftsmanship insufficient and switched to writing. His decision to write was also inspired by meeting, at nineteen, Coleridge and Wordsworth. He was instantly won over to their new style of Romantic poetry; later he became disenchanted with both men and drew devastating portraits of them in his memoir "My First Acquaintance with Poets." This sharp swing between enthusiasm and disappointment became a pattern with Hazlitt. Still, he always remained loyal to the sympathies and ideals of his youth. What he could never forgive others, such as Wordsworth, was their abandonment of progressive politics as they got older, for more conservative positions. Hazlitt remained a young man in the ardor of his likes and dislikes.

Needing money, he turned to journalism, and the combination of his wide interests (drama, politics, paintings, manners, psychology) and his ability to bring any subject alive with his strong, even violent, opinions attracted an audience. His career was launched by a controversial attack of Malthus' essay on population, and he never shrank thereafter from making an enemy in print. "Hazlitt," declared Keats, an admirer, ". . . is your only good damner, and if ever I am damn'd—damn me if I shouldn't like him to damn me." He was the first to recognize that "I am not in the ordinary sense of the term a good-natured man," and his analysis "On the Pleasure of Hating" remains a classic of spleen. But he was equally good at conveying his enjoyment of, say, boxing, in "The Fight," or walking, in "On Going a Journey." Above all else, he valued what he called "gusto"—energy of will, red-bloodedness—and he strove successfully to bring that quality to his writing.

Hazlitt is now regarded as part of the history of Romanticism—one might say he was the essayistic arm of the Romantics—and he stressed the importance of feeling in art and life. His own feelings seemed never entirely in control: he quarreled with nearly all his friends and was reckless and frustrated in matters of love. He married twice, both times unhappily; and at the age of forty-three, the same year his successful essay collection, Table Talk, appeared, he fell in love, unrequitedly and scandalously, with a pretty barmaid. His obsessional account of that disastrous infatuation, Liber Amoris, remains a fascinating piece of confessional literature. (Decades later, Robert Louis Stevenson, who had planned to write Hazlitt's biography, withdrew from the project in dismay when he discovered it.) Hazlitt's political infatuation with his idol, Napoleon, was equally misguided: he devoted years to composing a favorable three-volume history of an emperor who had been the enemy of the British, and the book, instead of bringing him the fortune he expected, bankrupted the publishing company. Hazlitt, who had already written a premature "Farewell to Essay-Writing," was forced to return to the form that had elicited his best results.

That Hazlitt was an astute student of the essay may be witnessed in his still-fresh analyses of Montaigne, Addison and Steele, Dr. Johnson, his friend Lamb, and Washington Irving. His own efforts brought a new intimacy to the personal essay, establishing as never before a conversational rapport, a dialogue with the reader. He championed vernacular language, a varied syntax, and streamlined, modern sentences. His arguments and themes were powerfully focused, displaying a philosophically trained mind. Above all, his prose is pulsing, energetic, alive. Hazlitt's very irritableness, which goaded him on like sand in an oyster, led in the end to beautifully formed pearls.

On Going a Journey

O NE OF THE PLEASANTEST THINGS in the world is going a journey; but I like to go by myself. I can enjoy society in a room; but out of doors, nature is company enough for me. I am then never less alone than when alone.

> *"The fields his study, nature was his book."*

I cannot see the wit of walking and talking at the same time. When I am in the country I wish to vegetate like the country. I am not for criticizing hedge-rows and black cattle. I go out of town in order to forget the town and all that is in it. There are those who for this purpose go to watering-places, and carry the metropolis with them. I like more elbow-room and fewer incumbrances. I like solitude, when I give myself up to it, for the sake of solitude; nor do I ask for

> *"a friend in my retreat,*
> *Whom I may whisper solitude is sweet."*

The soul of a journey is liberty, perfect liberty, to think, feel, do, just as one pleases. We go a journey chiefly to be free of all impediments and of all inconveniences; to leave ourselves behind, much more to get rid of others. It is because I want a little breathing-space to muse on indifferent matters, where Contemplation

> *"May plume her feathers and let grow her wings,*
> *That in the various bustle of resort*
> *Were all too ruffled, and sometimes impair'd,"*

that I absent myself from the town for a while, without feeling at a loss the moment I am left by myself. Instead of a friend in a post-chaise or in a Tilbury, to exchange good things with, and vary the same stale topics over again, for once let me have a truce with impertinence. Give me the clear blue sky over my head, and the green turf beneath my feet, a winding road before me, and a three hours' march to dinner—and then to thinking! It is hard if I cannot start some game on these lone heaths. I laugh, I run, I leap, I sing for joy. From the point of yonder rolling cloud I plunge into my past being, and revel there, as the sun-burnt Indian plunges headlong into the wave that wafts him to his native shore. Then long-forgotten things, like "sunken wrack and sumless treasuries," burst upon my eager sight, and I begin to feel, think, and be myself again. Instead of an awkward silence, broken by attempts at wit or dull common-places, mine is that undisturbed silence of the heart which alone is perfect eloquence. No one likes puns, alliterations, antitheses, argument, and analysis better than I do; but I sometimes had rather be without them. "Leave, oh, leave me to my repose!" I have just now other business in hand, which would seem idle to you, but is with me "very stuff of the conscience." Is not this wild rose sweet without a comment? Does not this daisy leap to my heart set in its coat of emerald? Yet if I were to explain to you the circumstance that has so endeared it to me, you would only smile. Had I not better then keep it to myself, and let it serve me to brood over, from here to yonder craggy point, and from thence onward to the far-distant horizon? I should be but bad company all that way, and therefore prefer being alone. I have heard it said that you may, when the moody fit comes on, walk or ride on by yourself, and indulge your reveries. But this looks like a breach of manners, a neglect of others, and you are thinking all the time that you ought to rejoin your party. "Out upon such half-faced fellowship," say I. I like to be either entirely to myself, or entirely at the disposal of others; to talk or be silent, to walk or sit still, to be sociable or solitary. I was pleased with an observation of Mr. Cobbett's, that "he thought it a bad French custom to drink our wine with our meals, and that an Englishman ought to do only one thing at a time." So I cannot talk and think, or indulge in melancholy musing and lively conversation by fits and starts. "Let me have a companion of my way," says Sterne, "were it but to remark how the shadows lengthen as the sun declines." It is beautifully said; but, in my opinion, this continual comparing of notes interferes with the involuntary impression of things upon the mind, and hurts the sentiment. If you only hint what you feel in a kind of dumb show, it is insipid: if you have to explain it, it is making a toil of a pleasure. You cannot read the book of nature without being perpetually put to the trouble of translating it for the benefit of others. I am for this synthetical method on a journey in preference to the analytical. I am content to lay in a stock of ideas then, and to examine and anatomise them afterwards. I want to see my vague notions float like the down of the thistle before the breeze, and not to have them entangled in the briars and thorns of controversy. For once, I like to have it all my own way; and this is impossible unless you are alone, or in such company as I do not covet. I have no objection to argue a point with any one for twenty miles of measured road, but not for pleasure. If you remark the scent of a bean-field crossing the road, perhaps your fellow-traveller has no smell. If you point to a distant object, perhaps he is short-sighted, and has to take out his glass to look at it. There is a feeling in the air, a tone in the colour of a cloud, which hits your fancy, but the effect of which you are unable to account for. There is then no sympathy, but an uneasy craving after it, and a dissatisfaction which pursues you on the way, and in the end probably produces ill-humour. Now I never quarrel with myself, and take all my own conclusions for granted till I find it necessary to defend them against objections. It is not merely that you may not be of accord on the objects and circumstances that present themselves before you—these may recall a number of objects, and lead to associations too delicate and refined to be possibly communicated to others. Yet these I love to cherish, and sometimes still fondly clutch them, when I can escape from the throng to do so. To give way to our feelings before company seems extravagance or affectation; and, on the other hand, to have to unravel this mystery of our being at every turn, and to make others take an equal interest in it (otherwise the end is not answered), is a task to which few are competent. We must "give it an understanding, but no tongue." My old friend C[oleridge], however, could do both. He could go on in the most delightful explanatory way over hill and dale a summer's day, and convert a landscape into a didactic poem or a Pindaric ode. "He talked far above singing." If I could so clothe my ideas in sounding and flowing words, I might perhaps wish to have some one with me to admire the swelling theme; or I could be more content, were it possible for me still to hear his echoing voice in the woods of All-Foxden. They had "that fine madness in them which our first poets had"; and if they could have been caught by some rare instrument, would have breathed such strains as the following:—

> "Here be woods as green
> As any, air likewise as fresh and sweet
> As when smooth Zephyrus plays on the fleet
> Face of the curled streams, with flow'rs as many
> As the young spring gives, and as choice as any;
> Here be all new delights, cool streams and wells,
> Arbours o'ergrown with woodbine, caves and dells;
> Choose where thou wilt, whilst I sit by and sing,
> Or gather rushes to make many a ring
> For thy long fingers; tell thee tales of love,
> How the pale Phoebe, hunting in a grove,
> First saw the boy Endymion, from whose eyes
> She took eternal fire that never dies;
> How she convey'd him softly in a sleep,
> His temples bound with poppy, to the steep

Head of old Latmos, where she stoops each night,
Gilding the mountain with her brother's light,
To kiss her sweetest."

—FLETCHER'S *Faithful Shepherdess.*

Had I words and images at command like these, I would attempt to wake
the thoughts that lie slumbering on golden ridges in the evening clouds:
but at the sight of nature my fancy, poor as it is, droops and closes up its
leaves, like flowers at sunset. I can make nothing out on the spot:—I must
have time to collect myself.

In general, a good thing spoils out-of-door prospects: it should be reserved for Table-talk. L[amb] is for this reason, I take it, the worst company in the world out of doors; because he is the best within. I grant,
there is one subject on which it is pleasant to talk on a journey; and that is,
what one shall have for supper when we get to our inn at night. The open
air improves this sort of conversation or friendly altercation, by setting a
keener edge on appetite. Every mile of the road heightens the flavour of
the viands we expect at the end of it. How fine it is to enter some old
town, walled and turreted, just at approach of night-fall, or to come to
some straggling village, with the lights streaming through the surrounding
gloom; and then, after inquiring for the best entertainment that the place
affords, to "take one's ease at one's inn"! These eventful moments in our
lives' history are too precious, too full of solid, heart-felt happiness to be
frittered and dribbled away in imperfect sympathy. I would have them all
to myself, and drain them to the last drop: they will do to talk of or to
write about afterwards. What a delicate speculation it is, after drinking
whole goblets of tea—

"The cups that cheer, but not inebriate,"

and letting the fumes ascend into the brain, to sit considering what we
shall have for supper—eggs and a rasher, a rabbit smothered in onions, or
an excellent veal-cutlet! Sancho in such a situation once fixed upon cow-
heel; and his choice, though he could not help it, is not to be disparaged.
Then, in the intervals of pictured scenery and Shandean contemplation, to
catch the preparation and the stir in the kitchen [getting ready for the
gentleman in the parlour]. *Procul, O procul este profani!* These hours are
sacred to silence and to musing, to be treasured up in the memory, and to
feed the source of smiling thoughts hereafter. I would not waste them in
idle talk; or if I must have the integrity of fancy broken in upon, I would
rather it were by a stranger than a friend. A stranger takes his hue and
character from the time and place; he is a part of the furniture and cos-

tume of an inn. If he is a Quaker, or from the West Riding of Yorkshire, so much the better. I do not even try to sympathise with him, and he breaks no squares. [How I love to see the camps of the gypsies, and to sigh my soul into that sort of life. If I express this feeling to another, he may qualify and spoil it with some objection.] I associate nothing with my travelling companion but present objects and passing events. In his ignorance of me and my affairs, I in a manner forget myself. But a friend reminds one of other things, rips up old grievances, and destroys the abstraction of the scene. He comes in ungraciously between us and our imaginary character. Something is dropped in the course of conversation that gives a hint of your profession and pursuits; or from having some one with you that knows the less sublime portions of your history, it seems that other people do. You are no longer a citizen of the world; but your "unhoused free condition is put into circumscription and confine." The *incognito* of an inn is one of its striking privileges—"lord of one's self, uncumber'd with a name." Oh! it is great to shake off the trammels of the world and of public opinion—to lose our importunate, tormenting, everlasting personal identity in the elements of nature, and become the creature of the moment, clear of all ties—to hold to the universe only by a dish of sweet-breads, and to owe nothing but the score of the evening—and no longer seeking for applause and meeting with contempt, to be known by no other title than *the Gentleman in the parlour!* One may take one's choice of all characters in this romantic state of uncertainty as to one's real pretensions, and become indefinitely respectable and negatively right-worshipful. We baffle prejudice and disappoint conjecture; and from being so to others, begin to be objects of curiosity and wonder even to ourselves. We are no more those hackneyed common-places that we appear in the world; an inn restores us to the level of nature, and quits scores with society! I have certainly spent some enviable hours at inns—sometimes when I have been left entirely to myself, and have tried to solve some metaphysical problem, as once at Witham-common, where I found out the proof that likeness is not a case of the association of ideas—at other times, when there have been pictures in the room, as at St. Neot's (I think it was), where I first met with Gribelin's engravings of the Cartoons, into which I entered at once, and at a little inn on the borders of Wales, where there happened to be hanging some of Westall's drawings, which I compared triumphantly (for a theory that I had, not for the admired artist) with the figure of a girl who had ferried me over the Severn, standing up in the boat between me and the twilight—at other times I might mention luxuriating in books, with a peculiar interest in this way, as I remember sitting up half the night to read *Paul and Virginia*, which I picked up at an inn at Bridgewater, after being drenched in the rain all day; and at the same place I got through two volumes of Madame D'Arblay's *Camilla.* It was on the tenth of April, 1798, that I sat down to a volume of the *New Eloise,* at the inn at Llangollen, over a bottle of sherry and a cold chicken. The letter I chose was that in which St. Preux describes his feelings as he first caught a glimpse from the heights of the Jura of the Pays de Vaud, which I had brought with me as a *bon bouche* to crown the evening with. It was my birth-day, and I had for the first time come from a place in the neighbourhood to visit this delightful spot. The road to Llangollen turns off between Chirk and Wrexham; and on passing a certain point you come all at once upon the valley, which opens like an amphitheatre, broad, barren hills rising in majestic state on either side, with "green upland swells that echo to the bleat of flocks" below, and the river Dee babbling over its stony bed in the midst of them. The valley at this time "glittered green with sunny showers," and a budding ash-tree dipped its tender branches in the chiding stream. How proud, how glad I was to walk along the high road that overlooks the delicious prospect, repeating the lines which I have just quoted from Mr. Coleridge's poems! But besides the prospect which opened beneath my feet, another also opened to my inward sight, a heavenly vision, on which were written, in letters large as Hope could make them, these four words, LIBERTY, GENIUS, LOVE, VIRTUE; which have since faded into the light of common day, or mock my idle gaze.

"The beautiful is vanished, and returns not."

Still I would return some time or other to this enchanted spot; but I would return to it alone. What other self could I find to share that influx of thoughts, of regret, and delight, the fragments of which I could hardly conjure up to myself, so much have they been broken and defaced. I could stand on some tall rock, and overlook the precipice of years that separates me from what I then was. I was at that time going shortly to visit the poet whom I have above named. Where is he now? Not only I myself have changed; the world which was then new to me, has become old and incorrigible. Yet will I turn to thee in thought, O sylvan Dee, in joy, in youth and gladness as thou then wert; and thou shalt always be to me the river of Paradise, where I will drink of the waters of life freely!

There is hardly anything that shows the shortsightedness or capriciousness of the imagination more than travelling does. With change of place we change our ideas; nay, our opinions and feelings. We can by an effort indeed transport ourselves to old and long-forgotten scenes, and then the picture of the mind revives again; but we forget those that we have just left. It seems that we can think but of one place at a time. The canvas of the fancy is but of a certain extent, and if we paint one set of objects upon it, they immediately efface every other. We cannot enlarge our conceptions, we only shift our point of view. The landscape bares its bosom to the enraptured eye, we take our fill of it, and seem as if we could form no other image of beauty or grandeur. We pass on, and think no more of it: the horizon that shuts it from our sight, also blots it from our memory like a dream. In travelling through a wild barren country I can form no idea of a woody and cultivated one. It appears to me that all the world must be barren, like what I see of it. In the country we forget the town, and in town we despise the country. "Beyond Hyde Park," says Sir Topling Flutter, "all is a desert." All that part of the map that we do not see before us is a blank. The world in our conceit of it is not much bigger than a nutshell. It is not one prospect expanded into another, county joined to county, kingdom to kingdom, lands to seas, making an image voluminous and vast;—the mind can form no larger idea of space than the eye can take in at a single glance. The rest is a name written in a map, a calculation of arithmetic. For instance, what is the true signification of that immense mass of territory and population known by the name of China to us? An inch of pasteboard on a wooden globe, of no more account than a China orange! Things near us are seen of the size of life: things at a distance are diminished to the size of the understanding. We measure the universe by ourselves, and even comprehend the texture of our being only piece-meal. In this way, however, we remember an infinity of things and places. The mind is like a mechanical instrument that plays a great variety of tunes, but it must play them in succession. One idea recalls another, but it at the same time excludes all others. In trying to renew old recollections, we cannot as it were unfold the whole web of our existence; we must pick out the single threads. So in coming to a place where we have formerly lived, and with which we have intimate associations, every one must have found that the feeling grows more vivid the nearer we approach the spot, from the mere anticipation of the actual impression: we remember circumstances, feelings, persons, faces, names that we had not thought of for years; but for the time all the rest of the world is forgotten!—To return to the question I have quitted above:

I have no objection to go to see ruins, aqueducts, pictures, in company with a friend or a party, but rather the contrary, for the former reason reversed. They are intelligible matters, and will bear talking about. The sentiment here is not tacit, but communicable and overt. Salisbury Plain is barren of criticism, but Stonehenge will bear a discussion antiquarian, picturesque, and philosophical. In setting out on a party of pleasure, the first consideration always is where we shall go to: in taking a solitary ramble, the question is what we shall meet with by the way. "The mind is its own place"; nor are we anxious to arrive at the end of our journey. I can myself do the honours indifferently well to works of art and curiosity. I once took a party to Oxford with no mean *éclat*—shewed them that seat of the Muses at a distance,

"With glistering spires and pinnacles adorn'd—"

descanted on the learned air that breathes from the grassy quadrangles
and stone walls of halls and colleges—was at home in the Bodleian; and at
Blenheim quite superseded the powdered Cicerone that attended us, and
that pointed in vain with his wand to commonplace beauties in matchless
pictures. As another exception to the above reasoning, I should not feel
confident in venturing on a journey in a foreign country without a companion. I should want at intervals to hear the sound of my own language.
There is an involuntary antipathy in the mind of an Englishman to foreign
manners and notions that requires the assistance of social sympathy to
carry it off. As the distance from home increases, this relief, which was at
first a luxury, becomes a passion and an appetite. A person would almost
feel stifled to find himself in the deserts of Arabia without friends and
countrymen: there must be allowed to be something in the view of Athens
or old Rome that claims the utterance of speech; and I own that the
Pyramids are too mighty for any single contemplation. In such situations,
so opposite to all one's ordinary train of ideas, one seems a species by
one's-self, a limb torn off from society, unless one can meet with instant
fellowship and support.—Yet I did not feel this want or craving very
pressing once, when I first set my foot on the laughing shores of France.
Calais was peopled with novelty and delight. The confused, busy murmur
of the place was like oil and wine poured into my ears; nor did the mari-
ners' hymn, which was sung from the top of an old crazy vessel in the
harbour, as the sun went down, send an alien sound into my soul. I only
breathed the air of general humanity. I walked over "the vine-covered hills
and gay regions of France," erect and satisfied; for the image of man was
not cast down and chained to the foot of arbitrary thrones: I was at no loss
for language, for that of all the great schools of painting was open to me.
The whole is vanished like a shade. Pictures, heroes, glory, freedom, all
are fled: nothing remains but the Bourbons and the French people!—
There is undoubtedly a sensation in travelling into foreign parts that is to
be had nowhere else; but it is more pleasing at the time than lasting. It is
too remote from our habitual associations to be a common topic of discourse or reference, and, like a dream or another state of existence, does
not piece into our daily modes of life. It is an animated but a momentary
hallucination. It demands an effort to exchange our actual for our ideal
identity; and to feel the pulse of our old transports revive very keenly, we
must "jump" all our present comforts and connexions. Our romantic and
itinerant character is not to be domesticated. Dr. Johnson remarked how
little foreign travel added to the facilities of conversation in those who had
been abroad. In fact, the time we have spent there is both delightful, and
in one sense instructive; but it appears to be cut out of our substantial,

downright existence, and never to join kindly on to it. We are not the same, but another, and perhaps more enviable individual, all the time we are out of our own country. We are lost to ourselves, as well as our friends. So the poet somewhat quaintly sings,

> *"Out of my country and myself I go."*

Those who wish to forget painful thoughts, do well to absent themselves for a while from the ties and objects that recall them; but we can be said only to fulfil our destiny in the place that gave us birth. I should on this account like well enough to spend the whole of my life in travelling abroad, if I could anywhere borrow another life to spend afterwards at home!

On the Pleasure of Hating

T HERE IS A SPIDER crawling along the matted floor of the room where I sit (not the one which has been so well allegorised in the admirable *Lines to a Spider,* but another of the same edifying breed); he runs with heedless, hurried haste, he hobbles awkwardly towards me, he stops—he sees the giant shadow before him, and, at a loss whether to retreat or proceed, meditates his huge foe—but as I do not start up and seize upon the straggling caitiff, as he would upon a hapless fly within his toils, he takes heart, and ventures on with mingled cunning, impudence, and fear. As he passes me, I lift up the matting to assist his escape, am glad to get rid of the unwelcome intruder, and shudder at the recollection after he is gone. A child, a woman, a clown, or a moralist a century ago, would have crushed the little reptile to death—my philosophy has got beyond that—I bear the creature no ill-will, but still I hate the very sight of it. The spirit of malevolence survives the practical exertion of it. We learn to curb our will and keep our overt actions within the bounds of humanity, long before we can subdue our sentiments and imaginations to the same mild tone. We give up the external demonstration, the *brute* violence, but cannot part with the essence or principle of hostility. We do not tread upon the poor little animal in question (that seems barbarous and pitiful!) but we regard it with a sort of mystic horror and superstitious loathing. It will ask another hundred years of fine writing and hard thinking to cure us of the prejudice, and make us feel towards this ill-omened tribe with something of "the milk of human kindness," instead of their own shyness and venom.

Nature seems (the more we look into it) made up of antipathies: without something to hate, we should lose the very spring of thought and action. Life would turn to a stagnant pool, were it not ruffled by the jarring interests, the unruly passions, of men. The white streak in our own fortunes is brightened (or just rendered visible) by making all around it as dark as possible; so the rainbow paints its form upon the cloud. Is it pride? Is it envy? Is it the force of contrast? Is it weakness or malice? But so it is, that there is a secret affinity [with], a *hankering* after, evil in the human mind, and that it takes a perverse, but a fortunate delight in mischief, since it is a never-failing source of satisfaction. Pure good soon grows insipid, wants variety and spirit. Pain is a bittersweet, which never surfeits. Love turns, with a little indulgence, to indifference or disgust: hatred alone is immortal. Do we not see this principle at work everywhere? Animals torment and worry one another without mercy: children kill flies for sport: every one reads the accidents and offences in a newspaper as the cream of the jest: a whole town runs to be present at a fire, and the spectator by no means exults to see it extinguished. It is better to have it so, but it diminishes the interest; and our feelings take part with our passions rather than with our understandings. Men assemble in crowds, with eager enthusiasm, to witness a tragedy: but if there were an execution going forward in the next street, as Mr. Burke observes, the theatre would be left empty. A strange cur in a village, an idiot, a crazy woman, are set upon and baited by the whole community. Public nuisances are in the nature of public benefits. How long did the Pope, the Bourbons, and the Inquisition keep the people of England in breath, and supply them with nicknames to vent their spleen upon! Had they done us any harm of late? No: but we have always a quantity of superfluous bile upon the stomach, and we wanted an object to let it out upon. How loth were we to give up our pious belief in ghosts and witches, because we liked to persecute the one, and frighten ourselves to death with the other! It is not the quality so much as the quantity of excitement that we are anxious about: we cannot bear a state of indifference and *ennui:* the mind seems to abhor a *vacuum* as much as ever nature was supposed to do. Even when the spirit of the age (that is, the progress of intellectual refinement, warring with our natural infirmities) no longer allows us to carry our vindictive and headstrong humours into effect, we try to revive them in description, and keep up the old bugbears, the phantoms of our terror and our hate, in imagination. We burn Guy Fawx in effigy, and the hooting and buffeting and maltreating that poor tattered figure of rags and straw makes a festival in every village in England once a year. Protestants and Papists do not now burn one another at the stake: but we subscribe to new editions of Fox's *Book of Martyrs;* and the secret of the success of the *Scotch Novels* is much the same—they carry us back to the feuds, the heart-burnings, the havoc, the dismay, the wrongs, and the revenge of a barbarous age and people—to the rooted prejudices and deadly animosities of sects and parties in politics and religion, and of contending chiefs and clans in war and intrigue. We feel the full force of the spirit of hatred with all of them in turn. As we read, we throw aside the trammels of civilization, the flimsy veil of humanity. "Off, you lendings!" The wild beast resumes its sway within us, we feel like hunting-animals, and as the hound starts in his sleep and rushes on the chase in fancy, the heart rouses itself in its native lair, and utters a wild cry of joy, at being restored once more to freedom and lawless, unrestrained impulses. Every one has his full swing, or goes to the Devil his own way. Here are no Jeremy Bentham Panopticons, none of Mr. Owen's impassable Parallelograms (Rob Roy would have spurned and poured a thousand curses on them), no long calculations of self-interest—the will takes its instant way to its object, as the mountain-torrent flings itself over the precipice: the greatest possible good of each individual consists in doing all the mischief he can to his neighbour: that is charming, and finds a sure and sympathetic chord in every breast! So Mr. Irving, the celebrated preacher, has rekindled the old, original, almost exploded hell-fire in the aisles of the Caledonian Chapel, as they introduce the real water of the New River at Sadler's Wells, to the delight and astonishment of his fair audience. *'Tis pretty, though a plague,* to sit and peep into the pit of Tophet, to play at *snap-dragon* with flames and brimstone (it gives a smart electrical shock, a lively filip to delicate constitutions), and to see Mr. Irving, like a huge Titan, looking as grim and swarthy as if he had to forge tortures for all the damned! What a strange being man is! Not content with doing all he can to vex and hurt his fellows here, "upon this bank and shoal of time," where one would think there were heartaches, pain, disappointment, anguish, tears, sighs, and groans enough, the bigoted maniac takes him to the top of the high peak of school divinity to hurl him down the yawning gulf of penal fire; his speculative malice asks eternity to wreak its infinite spite in, and calls on the Almighty to execute its relentless doom! The cannibals burn their enemies and eat them in good-fellowship with one another: meek Christian divines cast those who differ from them but a hair's-breadth, body and soul into hell-fire for the glory of God and the good of His creatures! It is well that the power of such persons is not co-ordinate with their wills: indeed, it is from the sense of their weakness and inability to control the opinions of others, that they thus "outdo termagant," and endeavour to frighten them into conformity by big words and monstrous denunciations.

The pleasure of hating, like a poisonous mineral, eats into the heart of religion, and turns it to rankling spleen and bigotry; it makes patriotism an excuse for carrying fire, pestilence, and famine into other lands: it leaves to virtue nothing but the spirit of censoriousness, and a narrow, jealous, inquisitorial watchfulness over the actions and motives of others. What have the different sects, creeds, doctrines in religion been but so many pretexts set up for men to wrangle, to quarrel, to tear one another in pieces about, like a target as a mark to shoot at? Does any one suppose that the love of country in an Englishman implies any friendly feeling or disposition to serve another bearing the same name? No, it means only hatred to the French or the inhabitants of any other country that we happen to be at war with for the time. Does the love of virtue denote any wish to discover or amend our own faults? No, but it atones for an obstinate adherence to our own vices by the most virulent intolerance to human frailties. This principle is of a most universal application. It extends to good as well as evil: if it makes us hate folly, it makes us no less dissatisfied with distinguished merit. If it inclines us to resent the wrongs of others, it impels us to be as impatient of their prosperity. We revenge injuries: we repay benefits with ingratitude. Even our strongest partialities and likings soon take this turn. "That which was luscious as locusts, anon becomes bitter as coloquintida;" and love and friendship melt in their own fires. We hate old friends: we hate old books: we hate old opinions; and at last we come to hate ourselves.

I have observed that few of those whom I have formerly known most intimate, continue on the same friendly footing, or combine the steadiness with the warmth of attachment. I have been acquainted with two or three knots of inseparable companions, who saw each other "six days in the week," that have broken up and dispersed. I have quarrelled with almost all my old friends, (they might say this is owing to my bad temper, but) they have also quarrelled with one another. What is become of "that set of whist-players," celebrated by ELIA in his notable *Epistle to Robert Southey, Esq.* (and now I think of it—that I myself have celebrated in this very volume) "that for so many years called Admiral Burney friend?" They are scattered, like last year's snow. Some of them are dead, or gone to live at a distance, or pass one another in the street like strangers, or if they stop to speak, do it as coolly and try to *cut* one another as soon as possible. Some of us have grown rich, others poor. Some have got places under Government, others a *niche* in the *Quarterly Review.* Some of us have dearly earned a name in the world; whilst others remain in their original privacy. We despise the one, and envy and are glad to mortify the other. Times are changed; we cannot revive our old feelings; and we avoid the sight, and are uneasy in the presence of, those who remind us of our infirmity, and put us upon an effort at seeming cordiality which embarrasses ourselves, and does not impose upon our *quondam* associates. Old friendships are like meats served up repeatedly, cold, comfortless, and distasteful. The stomach turns against them. Either constant intercourse and familiarity breed weariness and contempt; or, if we meet again after an interval of absence, we appear no longer the same. One is too wise, another too foolish, for us; and we wonder we did not find this out before. We are disconcerted and kept in a state of continual alarm by the wit of one, or tired to death of the dullness of another. The *good things* of the first (besides leaving stings behind them) by repetition grow stale, and lose their startling effect; and the insipidity of the last becomes intolerable. The most amusing or instructive companion is at best like a favourite volume, that we wish after a time to *lay upon the shelf;* but as our friends are not willing to be laid there, this produces a misunderstanding and ill-blood between us. Or if the zeal and integrity of friendship is not abated, [n]or its career interrupted by any obstacle arising out of its own nature, we look out for other subjects of complaint and sources of dissatisfaction. We begin to criticize each other's dress, looks, and general character. "Such a one is a pleasant fellow, but it is a pity he sits so late!" Another fails to keep his appointments, and that is a sore that never heals. We get acquainted with some fashionable young men or with a mistress, and wish to introduce our friend; but he is awkward and a sloven, the interview does not answer, and this throws cold water on our intercourse. Or he makes himself obnoxious to opinion; and we shrink from our own convictions on the subject as an excuse for not defending him. All or any of these causes mount up in time to a ground of coolness or irritation; and at last they break out into open violence as the only amends we can make ourselves for suppressing them so long, or the readiest means of banishing recollections of former kindness so little compatible with our present feelings. We may try to tamper with the wounds or patch up the carcase of departed friendship; but the one will hardly bear the handling, and the other is not worth the trouble of embalming! The only way to be reconciled to old friends is to part with them for good: at a distance we may chance to be thrown back (in a waking dream) upon old times and old feelings: or at any rate we should not think of renewing our intimacy, till we have fairly spit our spite, or said, thought, and felt all the ill we can of each other. Or if we can pick a quarrel with some one else, and make him the scape-goat, this is an excellent contrivance to heal a broken bone. I think I must be friends with Lamb again, since he has written that magnanimous Letter to Southey, and told him a piece of his mind! I don't know what it is that attaches me to H—— so much, except that he and I, whenever we meet, sit in judgment on another set of old friends, and "carve them as a dish fit for the Gods." There was L[eigh] [Hunt], John Scott, Mrs. [Montagu], whose dark raven locks make a picturesque background to our discourse,

B——, who is grown fat, and is, they say, married, R[ickman]; these had all separated long ago, and their foibles are the common link that holds us together. We do not affect to condole or whine over their follies; we enjoy, we laugh at them, till we are ready to burst our sides, *"sans* intermission, for hours by the dial." We serve up a course of anecdotes, *traits,* master-strokes of character, and cut and hack at them till we are weary. Perhaps some of them are even with us. For my own part, as I once said, I like a friend the better for having faults that one can talk about. "Then," said Mrs. [Montagu], "you will never cease to be a philanthropist!" Those in question were some of the choice-spirits of the age, not "fellows of no mark or likelihood"; and we so far did them justice: but it is well they did not hear what we sometimes said of them. I care little what any one says of me, particularly behind my back, and in the way of critical and analytical discussion: it is looks of dislike and scorn that I answer with the worst venom of my pen. The expression of the face wounds me more than the expressions of the tongue. If I have in one instance mistaken this expression, or resorted to this remedy where I ought not, I am sorry for it. But the face was too fine over which it mantled, and I am too old to have misunderstood it! . . . I sometimes go up to ——'s; and as often as I do, resolve never to go again. I do not find the old homely welcome. The ghost of friendship meets me at the door, and sits with me all dinner-time. They have got a set of fine notions and new acquaintance. Allusions to past occurrences are thought trivial, nor is it always safe to touch upon more general subjects. M. does not begin as he formerly did every five minutes, "Fawcett used to say," &c. That topic is something worn. The girls are grown up, and have a thousand accomplishments. I perceive there is a jealousy on both sides. They think I give myself airs, and I fancy the same of them. Every time I am asked, "If I do not think Mr. Washington Irving a very fine writer?" I shall not go again till I receive an invitation for Christmas Day in company with Mr. Liston. The only intimacy I never found to flinch or fade was a purely intellectual one. There was none of the cant of candour in it, none of the whine of mawkish sensibility. Our mutual acquaintance were considered merely as subjects of conversation and knowledge, not at all of affection. We regarded them no more in our experiments than "mice in an air-pump:" or like malefactors, they were regularly cut down and given over to the dissecting-knife. We spared neither friend nor foe. We sacrificed human infirmities at the shrine of truth. The skeletons of character might be seen, after the juice was extracted, dangling in the air like flies in cobwebs: or they were kept for future inspection in some refined acid. The demonstration was as beautiful as it was new. There is no surfeiting on gall: nothing keeps so well as a decoction of spleen. We grow tired of every thing but turning others into ridicule, and congratulating ourselves on their defects.

We take a dislike to our favourite books, after a time, for the same reason. We cannot read the same works for ever. Our honey-moon, even though we wed the Muse, must come to an end; and is followed by indifference, if not by disgust. There are some works, those indeed that produce the most striking effect at first by novelty and boldness of outline, that will not bear reading twice: others of a less extravagant character, and that excite and repay attention by a greater nicety of details, have hardly interest enough to keep alive our continued enthusiasm. The popularity of the most successful writers operates to wean us from them, by the cant and fuss that is made about them, by hearing their names everlastingly repeated, and by the number of ignorant and indiscriminate admirers they draw after them:—we as little like to have to drag others from their un-merited obscurity, lest we should be exposed to the charge of affectation and singularity of taste. There is nothing to be said respecting an author that all the world have made up their minds about: it is a thankless as well as hopeless task to recommend one that nobody has ever heard of. To cry up Shakespear as the god of our idolatry, seems like a vulgar national prejudice: to take down a volume of Chaucer, or Spenser, or Beaumont and Fletcher, or Ford, or Marlowe, has very much the look of pedantry and egotism. I confess it makes me hate the very name of Fame and Genius, when works like these are "gone into the wastes of time," while each successive generation of fools is busily employed in reading the trash of the day, and women of fashion gravely join with their waiting-maids in discussing the preference between the *Paradise Lost* and Mr. Moore's *Loves of the Angels.* I was pleased the other day on going into a shop to ask, "If they had any of the *Scotch Novels?*" to be told—"That they had just sent out the last, *Sir Andrew Wylie!*"—Mr. Galt will also be pleased with this answer! The reputation of some books is raw and *unaired:* that of others is worm-eaten and mouldy. Why fix our affections on that which we cannot bring ourselves to have faith in, or which others have long ceased to trouble themselves about? I am half afraid to look into *Tom Jones,* lest it should not answer my expectations at this time of day; and if it did not, I should certainly be disposed to fling it into the fire, and never look into another novel while I lived. But surely, it may be said, there are some works that, like nature, can never grow old; and that must always touch the imagination and passions alike! Or there are passages that seem as if we might brood over them all our lives, and not exhaust the sentiments of love and admiration they excite: they become favourites, and we are fond of them to a sort of dotage. Here is one:

> —*"Sitting in my window*
> *Printing my thoughts in lawn, I saw a god,*
> *I thought (but it was you), enter our gates;*

My blood flew out and back again, as fast
As I had puffed it forth and sucked it in
Like breath; then was I called away in haste
To entertain you: never was a man
Thrust from a sheepcote to a sceptre, raised
So high in thoughts as I; you left a kiss
Upon these lips then, which I mean to keep
From you for ever. I did hear you talk
Far above singing!"

A passage like this, indeed, leaves a taste on the palate like nectar, and we seem in reading it to sit with the Gods at their golden tables: but if we repeat it often in ordinary moods, it loses its flavour, becomes vapid, "the wine of *poetry* is drank, and but the lees remain." Or, on the other hand, if we call in the aid of extraordinary circumstances to set it off to advantage, as the reciting it to a friend, or after having our feelings excited by a long walk in some romantic situation, or while we

—*"play with Amaryllis in the shade,*
Or with the tangles of Neaera's hair"—

we afterwards miss the accompanying circumstances, and instead of transferring the recollection of them to the favourable side, regret what we have lost, and strive in vain to bring back "the irrevocable hour"—wondering in some instances how we survive it, and at the melancholy blank that is left behind! The pleasure rises to its height in some moment of calm solitude or intoxicating sympathy, declines ever after, and from the comparison and a conscious falling-off, leaves rather a sense of satiety and irksomeness behind it. . . . "Is it the same in pictures?" I confess it is, with all but those from Titian's hand. I don't know why, but an air breathes from his landscapes, pure, refreshing, as if it came from other years; there is a look in his faces that never passes away. I saw one the other day. Amidst the heartless desolation and glittering finery of Fonthill, there is a portfolio of the Dresden Gallery. It opens, and a young female head looks from it; a child, yet woman grown; with an air of rustic innocence and the graces of a princess, her eyes like those of doves, the lips about to open, a smile of pleasure dimpling the whole face, the jewels sparkling in her crisped hair, her youthful shape compressed in a rich antique dress, as the bursting leaves contain the April buds! Why do I not call up this image of gentle sweetness, and place it as a perpetual barrier between mischance and me?—It is because pleasure asks a greater effort of the mind to support it than pain; and we turn after a little idle dalliance from what we love to what we hate!

As to my old opinions, I am heartily sick of them. I have reason, for they have deceived me sadly. I was taught to think, and I was willing to believe, that genius was not a bawd, that virtue was not a mask, that liberty was not a name, that love had its seat in the human heart. Now I would care little if these words were struck out of the dictionary, or if I had never heard them. They are become to my ears a mockery and a dream. Instead of patriots and friends of freedom, I see nothing but the tyrant and the slave, the people linked with kings to rivet on the chains of despotism and superstition. I see folly join with knavery, and together make up public spirit and public opinions. I see the insolent Tory, the blind Reformer, the coward Whig! If mankind had wished for what is right, they might have had it long ago. The theory is plain enough; but they are prone to mischief, "to every good work reprobate." I have seen all that had been done by the mighty yearnings of the spirit and intellect of men, "of whom the world was not worthy," and that promised a proud opening to truth and good through the vista of future years, undone by one man, with just glimmering of understanding enough to feel that he was a king, but not to comprehend how he could be king of a free people! I have seen this triumph celebrated by poets, the friends of my youth and the friends of man, but who were carried away by the infuriate tide that, setting in from a throne, bore down every distinction of right reason before it; and I have seen all those who did not join in applauding this insult and outrage on humanity proscribed, hunted down (they and their friends made a byword of), so that it has become an understood thing that no one can live by his talents or knowledge who is not ready to prostitute those talents and that knowledge to betray his species, and prey upon his fellow-man. "This was some time a mystery: but the time gives evidence of it." The echoes of liberty had awakened once more in Spain, and the morning of human hope dawned again: but that dawn has been overcast by the foul breath of bigotry, and those reviving sounds stifled by fresh cries from the time-rent towers of the Inquisition—man yielding (as it is fit he should) first to brute force, but more to the innate perversity and dastard spirit of his own nature which leaves no room for farther hope or disappointment. And England, that arch-reformer, that heroic deliverer, that mouther about liberty, and tool of power, stands gaping by, not feeling the blight and mildew coming over it, nor its very bones crack and turn to a paste under the grasp and circling folds of this new monster, Legitimacy! In private life do we not see hypocrisy, servility, selfishness, folly, and impudence succeed, while modesty shrinks from the encounter, and merit is trodden under foot? How often is "the rose plucked from the forehead of a virtuous love to plant a blister there!" What chance is there of the success of real passion? What certainty of its continuance? Seeing all this as I do, and unravelling the web of human life into its various threads of meanness, spite, cowardice, want of feeling, and want of understanding, of indifference towards others, and ignorance of ourselves—seeing custom prevail over all excellence, itself giving way to infamy—mistaken as I have been in my public and private hopes, calculating others from myself, and calculating wrong; always disappointed where I placed most reliance; the dupe of friendship, and the fool of love;—have I not reason to hate and to despise myself? Indeed I do; and chiefly for not having hated and despised the world enough.

The Fight

—*"The fight, the fight's the thing,*
Wherein I'll catch the conscience of the king."

W HERE THERE'S A WILL, THERE'S A WAY. —I said so to myself, as I walked down Chancery lane, about half-past six o'clock on Monday the 10th of December, to inquire at Jack Randall's where the fight the next day was to be; and I found "the proverb" nothing "musty" in the present instance. I was determined to see this fight, come what would, and see it I did, in great style. It was my *first fight,* yet it more than answered my expectations. Ladies! it is to you I dedicate this description; nor let it seem out of character for the fair to notice the exploits of the brave. Courage and modesty are the old English virtues; and may they never look cold and askance on one another! Think, ye fairest of the fair, loveliest of the lovely kind, ye practisers of soft enchantment, how many more ye kill with poisoned baits than ever fell in the ring; and listen with subdued air and without shuddering, to a tale tragic only in appearance, and sacred to the FANCY!

I was going down Chancery lane, thinking to ask at Jack Randall's where the fight was to be, when looking through the glass-door of the *Hole in the Wall,* I heard a gentleman asking the same question *at* Mrs. Randall, as the author of *Waverley* would express it. Now Mrs. Randall stood answering the gentleman's question, with the authenticity of the lady of the Champion of the Light Weights. Thinks I, I'll wait till this person comes out, and learn from him how it is. For to say a truth, I was not fond of going into this house of call for heroes and philosophers, ever since the owner of it (for Jack is no gentleman) threatened once upon a time to kick me out of doors for wanting a mutton-chop at his hospitable board, when the conqueror in thirteen battles was more full of *blue ruin* than of good manners. I was the more mortified at this repulse, inasmuch as I had heard Mr. James Simpkins, hosier in the Strand, one day when the character of the *Hole in the Wall* was brought in question, observe— "The house is a very good house, and the company quite genteel: I have been there myself!" Remembering this unkind treatment of mine host, to which mine hostess was also a party, and not wishing to put her in unquiet thoughts at a time jubilant like the present, I waited at the door, when, who should issue forth but my friend Joe Toms, and turning suddenly up Chancery lane with that quick jerk and impatient stride which distinguishes a lover of the FANCY, I said, "I'll be hanged if that fellow is not going to the fight, and is on his way to get me to go with him." So it proved in effect, and we agreed to adjourn to my lodgings to discuss measures with that cordiality which makes old friends like new, and new friends like old, on great occasions. We are cold to others only when we are dull in ourselves and have neither thoughts nor feelings to impart to them. Give a man a topic in his head, a throb of pleasure in his heart, and he will be glad to share it with the first person he meets. Toms and I, though we seldom meet, were an *alter idem* on this memorable occasion, and had not an idea that we did not candidly impart; and "so carelessly did we fleet the time," that I wish no better, when there is another fight, than to have him for a companion on my journey down, and to return with my friend Jack Pigott, talking of what was to happen or of what did happen, with a noble subject always at hand, and liberty to digress to others whenever they offered. Indeed, on my repeating the lines from Spenser in an involuntary fit of enthusiasm,

> *"What more felicity can fall to creature,*
> *Than to enjoy delight with liberty?"*

my last-named ingenious friend stopped me by saying that this, translated into the vulgate, meant *"Going to see a fight."*

Joe Toms and I could not settle about the method of going down. He said there was a caravan, he understood, to start from Tom Belcher's at two, which would go there *right out* and back again the next day. Now I never travel all night, and said I should get a cast to Newbury by one of the mails. Joe swore the thing was impossible, and I could only answer that I had made up my mind to it. In short, he seemed to me to waver, said he only came to see if I was going, had letters to write, a cause coming on the day after, and faintly said at parting (for I was bent on setting out that moment)—"Well, we meet at Philippi!" I made the best of my way to Piccadilly. The mail coach stand was bare. "They are all gone," said I—"this is always the way with me—in the instant I lose the future—if I had not stayed to pour out that last cup of tea, I should have been just in time;"—and cursing my folly and ill-luck together, without inquiring at the coach-office whether the mails were gone or not, I walked on in despite, and to punish my own dilatoriness and want of determination. At any rate, I would not turn back: I might get to Hounslow, or perhaps farther, to be on my road the next morning. I passed Hyde park corner (my Rubicon), and trusted to fortune. Suddenly I heard the clattering of a Brentford stage, and the fight rushed full upon my fancy. I argued (not unwisely) that even a Brentford coachman was better company than my own thoughts (such as they were just then) and at his invitation mounted the box with him. I immediately stated my case to him— namely, my quarrel with myself for missing the Bath or Bristol mail, and my determination to get on in consequence as well as I could, without any disparagement or insulting comparison between longer or shorter stages. It is a maxim with me that stage-coaches, and consequently stage-coachmen, are respectable in proportion to the distance they have to travel: so I said nothing on that subject to my Brentford friend. Any incipient tendency to an abstract proposition, or (as he might have construed it) to a personal reflection of this kind, was however nipped in the bud; for I had no sooner declared indignantly that I had missed the mails, than he flatly denied that they were gone along, and lo! at the instant three of them drove by in rapid, provoking, orderly succession, as if they would devour the ground before them. Here again I seemed in the contradictory situation of the man in Dryden who exclaims,

> *"I follow Fate, which does too hard pursue!"*

If I had stopped to inquire at the White Horse Cellar, which would not have taken me a minute, I should now have been driving down the road in all the dignified unconcern and *ideal* perfection of mechanical conveyance. The Bath mail I had set my mind upon, and I had missed it, as I miss everything else, by my own absurdity, in putting the will for the deed, and aiming at ends without employing means. "Sir," said he of the Brentford, "the Bath mail will be up presently, my brother-in-law drives it, and I will engage to stop him if there is a place empty." I almost doubted my good genius; but, sure enough, up it drove like lightning, and stopped directly at the call of the Brentford Jehu. I would not have believed this possible, but the brother-in-law of a mail-coach driver is himself no mean man. I was transferred without loss of time from the top of one coach to that of the other, desired the guard to pay my fare to the Brentford coachman for me as I had no change, was accommodated with a great coat, put up my umbrella to keep off a drizzling mist, and we began to cut through the air like an arrow. The mile-stones disappeared one after another, the rain kept off; Tom Turtle, the trainer, sat before me on the coach-box, with whom I exchanged civilities as a gentleman going to the fight; the passion that had transported me an hour before was subdued to pensive regret and conjectural musing on the next day's battle; I was promised a place inside at Reading, and upon the whole, I thought myself a lucky fellow. Such is the force of imagination! On the outside of any other coach on the 10th of December, with a Scotch mist drizzling through the cloudy moonlight air, I should have been cold, comfortless, impatient, and, no doubt, wet through; but seated on the Royal mail, I felt warm and comfortable, the air did me good, the ride did me good, I was pleased with the progress we had made, and confident that all would go well through the journey. When I got inside at Reading, I found Turtle and a stout valetudinarian, whose costume bespoke him one of the FANCY, and who had risen from a three months' sick bed to get into the mail to see the fight. They were intimate, and we fell into a lively discourse. My friend the trainer was confined in his topics to fighting dogs and men, to bears and badgers; beyond this he was "quite chap-fallen," had not a word to throw at a dog, or indeed very wisely fell asleep, when any other game was started. The whole art of training (I, however, learnt from him,) consists in two things, exercise and abstinence, abstinence and exercise, repeated alternately and without end. A yolk of an egg with a spoonful of rum in it is the first thing in a morning, and then a walk of six miles till breakfast. This meal consists of a plentiful supply of tea and toast and beef-steaks. Then another six or seven miles till dinner-time, and another supply of solid beef or mutton with a pint of porter, and perhaps, at the utmost, a couple of glasses of sherry. Martin trains on water, but this increases his infirmity on another very dangerous side. The Gas-man takes now and then a chirping glass (under the rose) to console him, during a six weeks' probation, for the absence of Mrs. Hickman—an agreeable woman, with (I understand) a pretty fortune of two hundred pounds. How matter presses on me! What stubborn things are facts! How inexhaustible is nature and art! "It is well," as I once heard Mr. Richmond observe, "to see a variety." He was speaking of cock-fighting as an edifying spectacle. I cannot deny but that one learns more of what *is* (I do not say of what *ought to be*) in this desultory mode of practical study, than from reading the same book twice over, even though it should be a moral treatise. Where was I? I was sitting at dinner with the candidate for the honours of the ring, "where good digestion waits on appetite, and health on both." Then follows an hour of social chat and native glee; and afterwards, to another breathing over heathy hill or dale. Back to supper, and then to bed, and up by six again— Our hero

> "*Follows so the ever-running sun,*
> *With profitable ardour—*"

to the day that brings him victory or defeat in the green fairy circle. Is not this life more sweet than mine? I was going to say; but I will not libel any life by comparing it to mine, which is (at the date of these presents) bitter as coloquintida and the dregs of aconitum!

The invalid in the Bath mail soared a pitch above the trainer, and did not sleep so sound, because he had "more figures and more fantasies." We talked the hours away merrily. He had faith in surgery, for he had had three ribs set right, that had been broken in a *turn-up* at Belcher's, but thought physicians old women, for they had no antidote in their catalogue for brandy. An indigestion is an excellent common-place for two people that never met before. By way of ingratiating myself, I told him the story of my doctor, who, on my earnestly representing to him that I thought his regimen had done me harm, assured me that the whole pharmacopeia contained nothing comparable to the prescription he had given me; and, as a proof of its undoubted efficacy, said, that "he had had one gentleman with my complaint under his hands for the last fifteen years." This anecdote made my companion shake the rough sides of his three great coats with boisterous laughter; and Turtle, starting out of his sleep, swore he knew how the fight would go, for he had had a dream about it. Sure enough the rascal told us how the three first rounds went off, but "his dream," like others, "denoted a foregone conclusion." He knew his men. The moon now rose in silver state, and I ventured, with some hesitation, to point out this object of placid beauty, with the blue serene beyond to the man of science, to which his ear he "seriously inclined," the more as it gave promise *d'un beau jour* for the morrow, and showed the ring undrenched by envious showers, arrayed in sunny smiles. Just then, all going on well, I thought on my friend Toms, whom I had left behind, and said innocently, "There was a blockhead of a fellow I left in town, who said there was no possibility of getting down by the mail, and talked of going by a caravan from Belcher's at two in the morning, after he had written some letters." "Why," said he of the lapells, "I should not wonder if that was the very person we saw running about like mad from one coach-door to another, and asking if any one had seen a friend of his, a gentleman going to the fight, whom he had missed stupidly enough by staying to write a note." "Pray, Sir," said my fellow-traveller, "had he a plaid-cloak on?"—"Why, no," said I, "not at the time I left him, but he very well might afterwards, for he offered to lend me one." The plaid-cloak and the letter decided the thing. Joe, sure enough, was in the Bristol mail, which preceded us by about fifty yards. This was droll enough. We had now but a few miles to our place of destination, and the first thing I did on alighting at Newbury, both coaches stopping at the same time, was to call out, "Pray, is there a gentleman in that mail of the name of Toms?" "No," said Joe, borrowing something of the vein of Gilpin, "for I have just got out."

"Well!" says he, "this is lucky; but you don't know how vexed I was to miss you; for," added he, lowering his voice, "do you know when I left you I went to Belcher's to ask about the caravan, and Mrs. Belcher said very obligingly, she couldn't tell about that, but there were two gentlemen who had taken places by the mail and were gone on in a laudau, and she could frank us. It's a pity I didn't meet with you; we could then have got down for nothing. But *mum's the word.*" It's the devil for any one to tell me a secret, for it is sure to come out in print. I do not care so much to gratify a friend, but the public ear is too great a temptation to me.

Our present business was to get beds and a supper at an inn; but this was no easy task. The public-houses were full, and where you saw a light at a private house, and people poking their heads out of the casement to see what was going on, they instantly put them in and shut the window, the moment you seemed advancing with a suspicious overture for accommodation. Our guard and coachman thundered away at the outer gate of the Crown for some time without effect—such was the greater noise within;—and when the doors were unbarred, and we got admittance, we found a party assembled in the kitchen round a good hospitable fire, some sleeping, others drinking, others talking on politics and on the fight. A tall English yeoman (something like Matthews in the face, and quite as great a wag)—

"A lusty man to ben an abbot able,"—

was making such a prodigious noise about rent and taxes, and the price of corn now and formerly, that he had prevented us from being heard at the gate. The first thing I heard him say was to a shuffling fellow who wanted to be off a bet for a shilling glass of brandy and water—"Confound it, man, don't be *insipid!*" Thinks I, that is a good phrase. It was a good omen. He kept it up so all night, nor flinched with the approach of morning. He was a fine fellow, with sense, wit, and spirit, a hearty body and a joyous mind, free-spoken, frank, convivial—one of that true English breed that went with Harry the Fifth to the siege of Harfleur—"standing like greyhounds in the slips," &c. We ordered tea and eggs (beds were soon found to be out of the question) and this fellow's conversation was *sauce piquante.* It did one's heart good to see him brandish his oaken towel and to hear him talk. He made mince-meat of a drunken, stupid, red-faced, quarrelsome, *frowsy* farmer, whose nose "he moralized into a thousand similes," making it out a firebrand like Bardolph's. "I'll tell you what, my friend," says he, "the landlady has only to keep you here to save fire and candle. If one was to touch your nose, it would go off like a piece of charcoal." At this the other only grinned like an idiot, the sole variety in his purple face being his little peering grey eyes and yellow teeth; called for another glass, swore he would not stand it; and after many attempts to provoke his humorous antagonist to single combat, which the other turned off (after working him up to a ludicrous pitch of choler) with great adroitness, he fell quietly asleep with a glass of liquor in his hand, which he could not lift to his head. His laughing persecutor made a speech over him, and turning to the opposite side of the room, where they were all sleeping in the midst of this "loud and furious fun," said, "There's a scene, by G-d, for Hogarth to paint. I think he and Shakespeare were our two best men at copying life." This confirmed me in my good opinion of him. Hogarth, Shakespeare and Nature, were just enough for him (indeed for any man) to know. I said, "You read Cobbett, don't you? At least," says I, "you talk just as well as he writes." He seemed to doubt this. But I said, "We have an hour to spare: if you'll get pen, ink, and paper, and keep on talking, I'll write down what you say; and if it doesn't make a capital 'Political Register,' I'll forfeit my head. You have kept me alive to-night, however. I don't know what I should have done without you." He did not dislike this view of the thing, nor my asking if he was not about the size of Jem Belcher; and told me soon afterwards, in the confidence of friendship, that "the circumstance which had given him nearly the greatest concern in his life, was Cribb's beating Jem after he had lost his eye by racket playing."—The morning dawns; that dim but yet clear light appears, which weighs like solid bars of metal on the sleepless eyelids; the guests drop down from their chambers one by one—but it was too late to think of going to bed now (the clock was on the stroke of seven), we had nothing for it but to find a barber's (the pole that glittered in the morning sun lighted us to his shop), and then a nine miles' march to Hungerford. The day was fine, the sky was blue, the mists were retiring from the marshy ground, the path was tolerably dry, the sitting-up all night had not done us much harm—at least the cause was good; we talked of this and that with amicable difference, roving and sipping of many subjects, but still invariably we returned to the fight. At length, a mile to the left of Hungerford, on a gentle eminence, we saw the ring surrounded by covered carts, gigs, and carriages, of which hundreds had passed us on the road; Toms gave a youthful shout, and we hastened down a narrow lane to the scene of action.

Reader, have you ever seen a fight? If not, you have a pleasure to come, at least if it is a fight like that between the Gas-man and Bill Neate. The crowd was very great when we arrived on the spot; open carriages were coming up, with streamers flying and music playing, and the country-people were pouring in over hedge and ditch in all directions, to see their hero beat or be beaten. The odds were still on Gas, but only about five to four. Gully had been down to try Neate, and had backed him considerably, which was a damper to the sanguine confidence of the adverse party.

About two hundred thousand pounds were pending. The Gas says, he has lost 3000*l.* which were promised him by different gentlemen if he had won. He had presumed too much on himself, which had made others presume on him. This spirited and formidable young fellow seems to have taken for his motto the old maxim, that "there are three things necessary to success in life—*Impudence! Impudence! Impudence!*" It is so in matters of opinion, but not in the FANCY, which is the most practical of all things, though even here confidence is half the battle, but only half. Our friend had vapoured and swaggered too much, as if he wanted to grin and bully his adversary out of the fight. "Alas! the Bristol man was not so tamed!" —"This is *the grave-digger*" (would Tom Hickman exclaim in the moments of intoxication from gin and success, shewing his tremendous right hand), "this will send many of them to their long homes; I haven't done with them yet!" Why should he—though he had licked four of the best men within the hour, yet why should he threaten to inflict dishonourable chastisement on my old master Richmond, a veteran going off the stage and who has borne his sable honours meekly? Magnanimity, my dear Tom, and bravery, should be inseparable. Or why should he go up to his antagonist, the first time he ever saw him at the Fives Court, and measuring him from head to foot with a glance of contempt, as Achilles surveyed Hector, say to him, "What, are you Bill Neate? I'll knock more blood out of that great carcase of thine, this day fortnight, than you ever knock'd out of a bullock's!" It was not manly, 'twas not fighter-like. If he was sure of the victory (as he was not), the less said about it the better. Modesty should accompany the FANCY as its shadow. The best men were always the best behaved. Jem Belcher, the Game Chicken (before whom the Gas-man could not have lived) were civil, silent men. So is Cribb, so is Tom Belcher, the most elegant of sparrers, and not a man for every one to take by the nose. I enlarged on this topic in the mail (while Turtle was asleep), and said very wisely (as I thought) that impertinence was a part of no profession. A boxer was bound to beat his man, but not to thrust his fist, either actually or by implication, in every one's face. Even a highwayman, in the way of trade, may blow out your brains, but if he uses foul language at the same time, I should say he was no gentleman. A boxer, I would infer, need not be a blackguard or a coxcomb, more than another. Perhaps I press this point too much on a fallen man—Mr. Thomas Hickman has by this time learnt that first of all lessons, "That man was made to mourn." He has lost nothing by the late fight but his presumption; and that every man may do as well without! By an over-display of this quality, however, the public had been prejudiced against him, and the *knowing-ones* were taken in. Few but those who had bet on him wished Gas to win. With my own prepossessions on the subject, the result of the 11th of December appeared to me as fine a piece of poetical justice as I had ever witnessed. The difference of weight between the two combatants (14 stone to 12) was nothing to the sporting men. Great, heavy, clumsy, long-armed Bill Neate kicked the beam in the scale of the Gas-man's vanity. The amateurs were frightened at his big words, and thought they would make up for the difference of six feet and five feet nine. Truly, the FANCY are not men of imagination. They judge of what has been, and cannot conceive of any thing that is to be. The Gas-man had won hitherto; therefore he must beat a man half as big again as himself—and that to a certainty. Besides, there are as many feuds, factions, prejudices, pedantic notions in the FANCY as in the state or in the schools. Mr. Gully is almost the only cool, sensible man among them, who exercises an unbiassed discretion, and is not a slave to his passions in these matters. But enough of reflections, and to our tale. The day, as I have said, was fine for a December morning. The grass was wet, and the ground miry, and ploughed up with multitudinous feet, except that, within the ring itself, there was a spot of virgin-green closed in and unprofaned by vulgar tread, that shone with dazzling brightness in the mid-day sun. For it was now noon, and we had an hour to wait. This is the trying time. It is then the heart sickens, as you think what the two champions are about, and how short a time will determine their fate. After the first blow is struck, there is no opportunity for nervous apprehensions; you are swallowed up in the immediate interest of the scene—but

> *"Between the acting of a dreadful thing*
> *And the first motion, all the interim is*
> *Like a phantasma, or a hideous dream."*

I found it so as I felt the sun's rays clinging to my back, and saw the white wintry clouds sink below the verge of the horizon. "So, I thought, my fairest hopes have faded from my sight!—so will the Gas-man's glory, or that of his adversary, vanish in an hour." The *swells* were parading in their white box-coats, the outer ring was cleared with some bruises on the heads and shins of the rustic assembly (for the cockneys had been distanced by the sixty-six miles); the time drew near; I had got a good stand; a bustle, a buzz, ran through the crowd; and from the opposite side entered Neate, between his second and bottle-holder. He rolled along, swathed in his loose great coat, his knock-knees bending under his huge bulk; and, with a modest cheerful air, threw his hat into the ring. He then just looked round, and began quietly to undress; when from the other side there was a similar rush and an opening made, and the Gas-man came forward with a conscious air of anticipated triumph, too much like the cock-of-the-walk. He strutted about more than became a hero, sucked oranges with a supercilious air, and threw away the skin with a toss of his

head, and went up and looked at Neate, which was an act of supereroga-
tion. The only sensible thing he did was, as he strode away from the
modern Ajax, to fling out his arms, as if he wanted to try whether they
would do their work that day. By this time they had stripped, and presented a strong contrast in appearance. If Neate was like Ajax, "with
Atlantean shoulders, fit to bear" the pugilistic reputation of all Bristol,
Hickman might be compared to Diomed, light, vigorous, elastic, and his
back glistened in the sun, as he moved about, like a panther's hide. There
was now a dead pause—attention was awe-struck. Who at that moment,
big with a great event, did not draw his breath short—did not feel his
heart throb? All was ready. They tossed up for the sun, and the Gas-man
won. They were led up to the *scratch*—shook hands, and went at it.

In the first round every one thought it was all over. After making play a
short time, the Gas-man flew at his adversary like a tiger, struck five blows
in as many seconds, three first, and then following him as he staggered
back, two more, right and left, and down he fell, a mighty ruin. There was
a shout, and I said, "There is no standing this." Neate seemed like a
lifeless lump of flesh and bone, round which the Gas-man's blows played
with the rapidity of electricity or lightning, and you imagined he would
only be lifted up to be knocked down again. It was as if Hickman held a
sword or a fire in that right hand of his, and directed it against an un-
armed body. They met again, and Neate seemed, not cowed, but particularly cautious. I saw his teeth clenched together and his brows knit close
against the sun. He held out both his arms at full length straight before
him, like two sledge-hammers, and raised his left an inch or two higher.
The Gas-man could not get over this guard—they struck mutually and
fell, but without advantage on either side. It was the same in the next
round; but the balance of power was thus restored—the fate of the battle
was suspended. No one could tell how it would end. This was the only
moment in which opinion was divided; for, in the next, the Gas-man
aiming a mortal blow at his adversary's neck, with his right hand, and
failing from the length he had to reach, the other returned it with his left
at full swing, planted a tremendous blow on his cheek-bone and eye-brow,
and made a red ruin of that side of his face. The Gas-man went down, and
there was another shout—a roar of triumph as the waves of fortune rolled
tumultuously from side to side. This was a settler. Hickman got up, and
"grinned horrible a ghastly smile," yet he was evidently dashed in his
opinion of himself; it was the first time he had ever been so punished; all
one side of his face was perfect scarlet, and his right eye was closed in
dingy blackness, as he advanced to the fight, less confident, but still determined. After one or two rounds, not receiving another such remem-
brancer, he rallied and went at it with his former impetuosity. But in vain.
His strength had been weakened,—his blows could not tell at such a dis-

tance,—he was obliged to fling himself at his adversary, and could not strike from his feet; and almost as regularly as he flew at him with his right hand, Neate warded the blow, or drew back out of its reach, and felled him with the return of his left. There was little cautious sparring—no half-hits—no tapping and trifling, none of the *petit-maitreship* of the art—they were almost all knock-down blows:—the fight was a good stand-up fight. The wonder was the half-minute time. If there had been a minute or more allowed between each round, it would have been intelligible how they should by degrees recover strength and resolution; but to see two men smashed to the ground, smeared with gore, stunned, senseless, the breath beaten out of their bodies; and then, before you recover from the shock, to see them rise up with new strength and courage, stand ready to inflict or receive mortal offence, and rush upon each other "like two clouds over the Caspian"—this is the most astonishing thing of all:—this is the high and heroic state of man! From this time forward the event became more certain every round; and about the twelfth it seemed as if it must have been over. Hickman generally stood with his back to me; but in the scuffle, he had changed positions, and Neate just then made a tremendous lunge at him, and hit him full in the face. It was doubtful whether he would fall backwards or forwards; he hung suspended for a second or two, and then fell back, throwing his hands in the air, and with his face lifted up to the sky. I never saw any thing more terrific than his aspect just before he fell. All traces of life, of natural expression, were gone from him. His face was like a human skull, a death's head, spouting blood. The eyes were filled with blood, the nose streamed with blood, the mouth gaped blood. He was not like an actual man, but like a preternatural, spectral appearance, or like one of the figures in Dante's *Inferno.* Yet he fought on after this for several rounds, still striking the first desperate blow, and Neate standing on the defensive, and using the same cautious guard to the last, as if he had still all his work to do; and it was not till the Gas-man was so stunned in the seventeenth or eighteenth round, that his senses forsook him, and he could not come to time, that the battle was declared over.[1] Ye who despise the FANCY, do something to shew as much *pluck,* or as much self-possession as this, before you assume a superiority which you have never given a single proof of by any one action in the whole course of your lives!—When the Gas-man came to himself, the first words he uttered were, "Where am I? What is the matter?"—"Nothing is the matter,

---

[1] Scroggins said of the Gas-man, that he thought he was a man of that courage, that if his hands were cut off, he would still fight on with the stumps—like that of Wildrington,—

—*"In doleful dumps,*
Who, when his legs were smitten off,
Still fought upon his stumps."

Tom,—you have lost the battle, but you are the bravest man alive." And Jackson whispered to him, "I am collecting a purse for you, Tom."—Vain sounds, and unheard at that moment! Neate instantly went up and shook him cordially by the hand, and seeing some old acquaintance, began to flourish with his fists, calling out, "Ah! you always said I couldn't fight— What do you think now?" But all in good humour, and without any appearance of arrogance; only it was evident Bill Neate was pleased that he had won the fight. When it was over, I asked Cribb if he did not think it was a good one? He said, *"Pretty well!"* The carrier-pigeons now mounted into the air, and one of them flew with the news of her husband's victory to the bosom of Mrs. Neate. Alas, for Mrs. Hickman!

Mais au revoir, as Sir Fopling Flutter says. I went down with Toms; I returned with Jack Pigott, whom I met on the ground. Toms is a rattle-brain; Pigott is a sentimentalist. Now, under favour, I am a sentimentalist too—therefore I say nothing, but that the interest of the excursion did not flag as I came back. Pigott and I marched along the causeway leading from Hungerford to Newbury, now observing the effect of a brilliant sun on the tawny meads or moss-coloured cottages, now exulting in the fight, now digressing to some topic of general and elegant literature. My friend was dressed in character for the occasion, or like one of the FANCY; that is, with a double portion of great coats, clogs, and over-hauls: and just as we had agreed with a couple of country-lads to carry his superfluous wearing-apparel to the next town, we were overtaken by a return post-chaise, into which I got, Pigott preferring a seat on the bar. There were two strangers already in the chaise, and on their observing they supposed I had been to the fight, I said I had, and concluded they had done the same. They appeared, however, a little shy and sore on the subject; and it was not till after several hints dropped, and questions put, that it turned out that they had missed it. One of these friends had undertaken to drive the other there in his gig: they had set out, to make sure work, the day before at three in the afternoon. The owner of the one-horse vehicle scorned to ask his way, and drove right on to Bagshot, instead of turning off at Houns-low: there they stopped all night, and set off the next day across the country to Reading, from whence they took coach, and got down within a mile or two of Hungerford, just half an hour after the fight was over. This might be safely set down as one of the miseries of human life. We parted with these two gentlemen who had been to see the fight, but had returned as they went, at Wolhampton, where we were promised beds (an irresistible temptation, for Pigott had passed the preceding night at Hungerford as we had done at Newbury), and we turned into an old bow-windowed parlour with a carpet and a snug fire; and after devouring a quantity of tea, toast, and eggs, sat down to consider, during an hour of philosophic leisure, what we should have for supper. In the midst of an Epicurean

deliberation between a roasted fowl and mutton chops with mashed potatoes, we were interrupted by an inroad of Goths and Vandals—*O procul
este profani*—not real flash-men, but interlopers, noisy pretenders, butchers from Tothill-fields, brokers from Whitechapel, who called immediately
for pipes and tobacco, hoping it would not be disagreeable to the gentlemen, and began to insist that it was *a cross*. Pigott withdrew from the
smoke and noise into another room, and left me to dispute the point with
them for a couple of hours *sans intermission* by the dial. The next morning
we rose refreshed; and on observing that Jack had a pocket volume in his
hand, in which he read in the intervals of our discourse, I inquired what it
was, and learned to my particular satisfaction that it was a volume of the
New Eloise. Ladies, after this, will you contend that a love for the FANCY is
incompatible with the cultivation of sentiment?—We jogged on as before,
my friend setting me up in a genteel drab great coat and green silk handkerchief (which I must say became me exceedingly), and after stretching
our legs for a few miles, and seeing Jack Randall, Ned Turner, and Scroggins, pass on the top of one of the Bath coaches, we engaged with the
driver of the second to take us to London for the usual fee. I got inside,
and found three other passengers. One of them was an old gentleman with
an aquiline nose, powdered hair, and a pigtail, and who looked as if he
had played many a rubber at the Bath rooms. I said to myself, he is very
like Mr. Windham; I wish he would enter into conversation, that I might
hear what fine observations would come from those finely-turned features.
However, nothing passed, till stopping to dine at Reading, some inquiry
was made by the company about the fight, and I gave (as the reader may
believe) an eloquent and animated description of it. When we got into the
coach again, the old gentleman, after a graceful exordium, said, he had,
when a boy, been to a fight between the famous Broughton and George
Stevenson, who was called the *Fighting Coachman,* in the year 1770, with
the late Mr. Windham. This beginning flattered the spirit of prophecy
within me, and riveted my attention. He went on—"George Stevenson
was coachman to a friend of my father's. He was an old man when I saw
him some years afterwards. He took hold of his own arm and said, 'there
was muscle here once, but now it is no more than this young gentleman's.'
He added, 'well, no matter; I have been here long, I am willing to go
hence, and I hope I have done no more harm than another man.' Once,"
said my unknown companion, "I asked him if he had ever beat
Broughton? He said Yes; that he had fought with him three times, and the
last time he fairly beat him, though the world did not allow it. 'I'll tell you
how it was, master. When the seconds lifted us up in the last round, we
were so exhausted that neither of us could stand, and we fell upon one
another, and as Master Broughton fell uppermost, the mob gave it in his
favour, and he was said to have won the battle. But the fact was, that as

his second (John Cuthbert) lifted him up, he said to him, "I'll fight no more, I've had enough;" which,' says Stevenson, 'you know gave me the victory. And to prove to you that this was the case, when John Cuthbert was on his death-bed, and they asked him if there was any thing on his mind which he wished to confess, he answered, "Yes, that there was one thing he wished to set right, for that certainly Master Stevenson won that last fight with Master Broughton; for he whispered him as he lifted him up in the last round of all, that he had had enough." ' This," said the Bath gentleman, "was a bit of human nature"; and I have written this account of the fight on purpose that it might not be lost to the world. He also stated as a proof of the candour of mind in this class of men, that Stevenson acknowledged that Broughton could have beat him in his best day; but that he (Broughton) was getting old in their last rencounter. When we stopped in Piccadilly, I wanted to ask the gentleman some questions about the late Mr. Windham, but had not courage. I got out, resigned my coat and green silk handkerchief to Pigott (loth to part with these ornaments of life), and walked home in high spirits.

P.S. Toms called upon me the next day, to ask me if I did not think the fight was a complete thing? I said I thought it was. I hope he will relish my account of it.

ROBERT LOUIS STEVENSON

Robert Louis Stevenson (1850–1894) is known today chiefly for his adventure stories for youth (Treasure Island, Kidnapped) and his horror classic, The Strange Case of Dr. Jekyll and Mr. Hyde. Yet it was not so long ago that his essays were held up in the classroom as models of the form.

Born in Edinburgh and strongly identifying himself as Scottish, Stevenson suffered from fragile health all his life. Tuberculosis and curiosity goaded him to take outdoor exercise, including walking tours and canoe trips through Europe. He devoted himself to literature, contributing essays, sketches, stories, and travel writing to periodicals. In 1880, Stevenson married Frances Osbourne, an American divorcée and mother ten years his senior, and this bond brought him stability and contentment. He and his family sought a healthier environment for his tubercular condition, and traveled through America to settle eventually in Samoa, where he built his "dream" tropical estate, Vailima. There he wrote his last works and died.

Stevenson had a valetudinarian's heightened appreciation for nature, children, exotic climes—and books. Extremely well-read, a lively and intelligent literary critic, he cited his major influences as Montaigne, the New Testament, Whitman, Goethe, Wordsworth, Meredith, Thoreau, and Hazlitt. "Though we are mighty fine fellows nowadays, we cannot write like Hazlitt," he confessed. True enough: Stevenson's essays do not have Hazlitt's aggressive vigor; they speak with a gentler, milder voice, more charitable and consciously Christian, in the Victorian manner; they identify with and attempt to win over or at least placate the reader, rather than staring him down, as Hazlitt's do. But they have a sweetness, tact, and wisdom that exercise their own appeal.

As both storyteller and critic, Stevenson often defended the claims of *imaginative fantasy against the harsher realism of the Naturalist school (Flaubert, Zola). In two of the essays below, "An Apology for Idlers" and "The Lantern-Bearers," he is at pains to protect a space for dreaming and innocence, particularly in youth. The third selection, "On Marriage," is part of a once-famous suite of essays about love, sex, and wedlock, titled "Virginibus Puerisque," which analyzes the complexities and ambivalences of adulthood. Throughout his essays, Stevenson charms us with conversational smoothness, intricate prose rhythms, and developed metaphors, and an humane, good-humored, flexible narrative voice.*

The Lantern-Bearers

1

T HESE BOYS CONGREGATED every autumn about a certain easterly fisher-village, where they tasted in a high degree the glory of existence. The place was created seemingly on purpose for the diversion of young gentlemen. A street or two of houses, mostly red and many of them tiled; a number of fine trees clustered about the manse and the kirkyard, and turning the chief street into a shady alley; many little gardens more than usually bright with flowers; nets a-drying, and fisher-wives scolding in the backward parts; a smell of fish, a genial smell of seaweed; whiffs of blowing sand at the street-corners; shops with golf-balls and bottled lollipops; another shop with penny pickwicks (that remarkable cigar) and the *London Journal,* dear to me for its startling pictures, and a few novels, dear for their suggestive names: such, as well as memory serves me, were the ingredients of the town. These, you are to conceive posted on a spit between two sandy bays, and sparsely flanked with villas —enough for the boys to lodge in with their subsidiary parents, not enough (not yet enough) to cocknify the scene: a haven in the rocks in front: in front of that, a file of gray islets: to the left, endless links and sand wreaths, a wilderness of hiding-holes, alive with popping rabbits and soaring gulls: to the right, a range of seaward crags, one rugged brow beyond another; the ruins of a mighty and ancient fortress on the brink of one; coves between—now charmed into sunshine quiet, now whistling with wind and clamorous with bursting surges; the dens and sheltered hollows redolent of thyme and southernwood, the air at the cliff's edge brisk and clean and pungent of the sea—in front of all, the Bass Rock, tilted seaward like a doubtful bather, the surf ringing it with white, the solan-geese hanging round its summit like a great and glittering smoke. This choice piece of seaboard was sacred, besides, to the wrecker; and the Bass, in the eye of fancy, still flew the colours of King James; and in the ear of fancy the arches of Tantallon still rang with horse-shoe iron, and echoed to the commands of Bell-the-Cat.

There was nothing to mar your days, if you were a boy summering in that part, but the embarrassment of pleasure. You might golf if you wanted; but I seem to have been better employed. You might secrete yourself in the Lady's Walk, a certain sunless dingle of elders, all mossed over by the damp as green as grass, and dotted here and there by the stream-side with roofless walls, the cold homes of anchorites. To fit themselves for life, and with a special eye to acquire the art of smoking, it was even common for the boys to harbour there; and you might have seen a single penny pickwick, honestly shared in lengths with a blunt knife, bestrew the glen with these apprentices. Again, you might join our fishing parties, where we sat perched as thick as solan-geese, a covey of little anglers, boy and girl, angling over each other's heads, to the much entanglement of lines and loss of podleys and consequent shrill recrimination— shrill as the geese themselves. Indeed, had that been all, you might have done this often; but though fishing be a fine pastime, the podley is scarce to be regarded as a dainty for the table; and it was a point of honour that a boy should eat all that he had taken. Or again, you might climb the Law, where the whale's jawbone stood landmark in the buzzing wind, and behold the face of many counties, and the smoke and spires of many towns, and the sails of distant ships. You might bathe, now in the flaws of fine weather, that we pathetically call our summer, now in a gale of wind, with the sand scouring your bare hide, your clothes thrashing abroad from underneath their guardian stone, the froth of the great breakers casting you headlong ere it had drowned your knees. Or you might explore the tidal rocks, above all in the ebb of springs, when the very roots of the hills were for the nonce discovered; following my leader from one group to another, groping in slippery tangle for the wreck of ships, wading in pools after the abominable creatures of the sea, and ever with an eye cast backward on the march of the tide and the menaced line of your retreat. And then you might go Crusoeing, a word that covers all extempore eating in the open air: digging perhaps a house under the margin of the links, kindling a fire of the sea-ware, and cooking apples there—if they were truly apples, for I sometimes suppose the merchant must have played us off with some inferior and quite local fruit, capable of resolving, in the neighbourhood of fire, into mere sand and smoke and iodine; or perhaps pushing to Tantallon, you might lunch on sandwiches and visions in the grassy court, while the wind hummed in the crumbling turrets; or clambering along the coast, eat geans[1] (the worst, I must suppose, in Christendom) from an adventurous gean tree that had taken root under a cliff, where it was shaken with an ague of east wind, and silvered after gales with salt, and grew so foreign among its bleak surroundings that to eat of its produce was an adventure in itself.

There are mingled some dismal memories with so many that were joyous. Of the fisher-wife, for instance, who had cut her throat at Canty Bay; and of how I ran with the other children to the top of the Quadrant, and beheld a posse of silent people escorting a cart, and on the cart, bound in a chair, her throat bandaged, and the bandage all bloody—horror!—the fisher-wife herself, who continued thenceforth to hag-ride my thoughts, and even today (as I recall the scene) darkens daylight. She was lodged in the little old jail in the chief street; but whether or no she died there, with a wise terror of the worst, I never inquired. She had been tippling; it was but a dingy tragedy; and it seems strange and hard that, after all these years, the poor crazy sinner should be still pilloried on her cart in the scrap-book of my memory. Nor shall I readily forget a certain house in the Quadrant where a visitor died, and a dark old woman continued to dwell alone with the dead body; nor how this old woman conceived a hatred to myself and one of my cousins, and in the dread hour of the dusk, as we were clambering on the garden-walls, opened a window in that house of mortality and cursed us in a shrill voice and with a marrowy choice of language. It was a pair of very colourless urchins that fled down the lane from this remarkable experience! But I recall with a more doubtful sentiment, compounded out of fear and exultation, the coil of equinoctial tempests; trumpeting squalls, scouring flaws of rain; the boats with their reefed lugsails scudding for the harbour mouth, where danger lay, for it was hard to make when the wind had any east in it; the wives clustered with blowing shawls at the pier-head, where (if fate was against them) they might see boat and husband and sons—their whole wealth and their whole family—engulfed under their eyes; and (what I saw but once) a troop of neighbours forcing such an unfortunate homeward, and she squalling and battling in their midst, a figure scarcely human, a tragic Maenad.

These are things that I recall with interest; but what my memory dwells upon the most, I have been all this while withholding. It was a sport peculiar to the place, and indeed to a week or so of our two months' holiday there. Maybe it still flourishes in its native spot; for boys and their pastimes are swayed by periodic forces inscrutable to man; so that tops

---

[1] Wild cherries.

and marbles reappear in their due season, regular like the sun and moon; and the harmless art of knucklebones has seen the fall of the Roman empire and the rise of the United States. It may still flourish in its native spot, but nowhere else, I am persuaded; for I tried myself to introduce it on Tweedside, and was defeated lamentably; its charm being quite local, like a country wine that cannot be exported.

The idle manner of it was this:—

Toward the end of September, when school-time was drawing near and the nights were already black, we would begin to sally from our respective villas, each equipped with a tin bull's-eye lantern. The thing was so well known that it had worn a rut in the commerce of Great Britain; and the grocers, about the due time, began to garnish their windows with our particular brand of luminary. We wore them buckled to the waist upon a cricket belt, and over them, such was the rigour of the game, a buttoned top-coat. They smelled noisomely of blistered tin; they never burned aright, though they would always burn our fingers; their use was naught; the pleasure of them merely fanciful; and yet a boy with a bull's-eye under his top-coat asked for nothing more. The fishermen used lanterns about their boats, and it was from them, I suppose, that we had got the hint; but theirs were not bull's-eyes, nor did we ever play at being fishermen. The police carried them at their belts, and we had plainly copied them in that; yet we did not pretend to be policemen. Burglars, indeed, we may have had some haunting thoughts of; and we had certainly an eye to past ages when lanterns were more common, and to certain story-books in which we had found them to figure very largely. But take it for all in all, the pleasure of the thing was substantive; and to be a boy with a bull's-eye under his top-coat was good enough for us.

When two of these asses met, there would be an anxious "Have you got your lantern?" and a gratified "Yes!" That was the shibboleth, and very needful too; for, as it was the rule to keep our glory contained, none could recognise a lantern-bearer, unless (like the polecat) by the smell. Four or five would sometimes climb into the belly of a ten-man lugger, with nothing but the thwarts above them—for the cabin was usually locked, or choose out some hollow of the links where the wind might whistle overhead. There the coats would be unbuttoned and the bull's-eyes discovered; and in the chequering glimmer, under the huge windy hall of the night, and cheered by a rich steam of toasting tinware, these fortunate young gentlemen would crouch together in the cold sand of the links or on the scaly bilges of the fishing-boat, and delight themselves with inappropriate talk. Woe is me that I may not give some specimens—some of their foresights of life, or deep inquiries into the rudiments of man and nature, these were so fiery and so innocent, they were so richly silly, so romantically young. But the talk, at any rate, was but a condiment; and these gatherings themselves only accidents in the career of the lantern-bearer. The essence of this bliss was to walk by yourself in the black night; the slide shut, the top-coat buttoned; not a ray escaping, whether to conduct your footsteps or to make your glory public: a mere pillar of darkness in the dark; and all the while, deep down in the privacy of your fool's heart, to know you had a bull's-eye at your belt, and to exult and sing over the knowledge.

2

It is said that a poet has died young in the breast of the most stolid. It may be contended, rather, that this (somewhat minor) bard in almost every case survives, and is the spice of life to his possessor. Justice is not done to the versatility and the unplumbed childishness of man's imagination. His life from without may seem but a rude mound of mud; there will be some golden chamber at the heart of it, in which he dwells delighted; and for as dark as his pathway seems to the observer, he will have some kind of a bull's-eye at his belt.

It would be hard to pick out a career more cheerless than that of Dancer, the miser, as he figures in the "Old Bailey Reports," a prey to the most sordid persecutions, the butt of his neighbourhood, betrayed by his hired man, his house beleaguered by the impish school-boy, and he himself grinding and fuming and impotently fleeing to the law against these pin-pricks. You marvel at first that anyone should willingly prolong a life so destitute of charm and dignity; and then you call to memory that had he chosen, had he ceased to be a miser, he could have been freed at once from these trials, and might have built himself a castle and gone escorted by a squadron. For the love of more recondite joys, which we cannot estimate, which, it may be, we should envy, the man had willingly forgone both comfort and consideration. "His mind to him a kingdom was"; and sure enough, digging into that mind, which seems at first a dust-heap, we unearth some priceless jewels. For Dancer must have had the love of power and the disdain of using it, a noble character in itself; disdain of many pleasures, a chief part of what is commonly called wisdom; disdain of the inevitable end, that finest trait of mankind; scorn of men's opinions, another element of virtue; and at the back of all, a conscience just like yours and mine, whining like a cur, swindling like a thimble-rigger, but still pointing (there or thereabout) to some conventional standard. Here were a cabinet portrait to which Hawthorne perhaps had done justice; and yet not Hawthorne either, for he was mildly minded, and it lay not in him to create for us that throb of the miser's pulse, his fretful energy of gusto, his vast arms of ambition clutching in he knows not what: insatiable, in-

sane, a god with a muck-rake. Thus, at least, looking in the bosom of the
miser, consideration detects the poet in the full tide of life, with more,
indeed, of the poetic fire than usually goes to epics; and tracing that mean
man about his cold hearth, and to and fro in his discomfortable house,
spies within him a blazing bonfire of delight. And so with others, who do
not live by bread alone, but by some cherished and perhaps fantastic
pleasure; who are meat salesmen to the external eye, and possibly to themselves are Shakespeares, Napoleons, or Beethovens; who have not one
virtue to rub against another in the field of active life, and yet perhaps, in
the life of contemplation, sit with the saints. We see them on the street,
and we can count their buttons; but heaven knows in what they pride
themselves! heaven knows where they have set their treasure!

There is one fable that touches very near the quick of life: the fable of
the monk who passed into the woods, heard a bird break into song, hear-
kened for a trill or two, and found himself on his return a stranger at his
convent gates; for he had been absent fifty years, and of all his comrades
there survived but one to recognise him. It is not only in the woods that
this enchanter carols, though perhaps he is native there. He sings in the
most doleful places. The miser hears him and chuckles, and the days are
moments. With no more apparatus than an ill-smelling lantern I have
evoked him on the naked links. All life that is not merely mechanical is
spun out of two strands: seeking for that bird and hearing him. And it is
just this that makes life so hard to value, and the delight of each so incommunicable. And just a knowledge of this, and a remembrance of those
fortunate hours in which the bird has sung to us, that fills us with such
wonder when we turn the pages of the realist. There, to be sure, we find a
picture of life in so far as it consists of mud and of old iron, cheap desires
and cheap fears, that which we are ashamed to remember and that which
we are careless whether we forget; but of the note of that time-devouring
nightingale we hear no news.

The case of these writers of romance is most obscure. They have been
boys and youths; they have lingered outside the window of the beloved,
who was then most probably writing to someone else; they have sat before
a sheet of paper, and felt themselves mere continents of congested poetry,
not one line of which would flow; they have walked alone in the woods,
they have walked in cities under the countless lamps; they have been to
sea, they have hated, they have feared, they have longed to knife a man,
and maybe done it; the wild taste of life has stung their palate. Or, if you
deny them all the rest, one pleasure at least they have tasted to the full—
their books are there to prove it—the keen pleasure of successful literary
composition. And yet they fill the globe with volumes, whose cleverness
inspires me with despairing admiration, and whose consistent falsity to all
I care to call existence, with despairing wrath. If I had no better hope than

to continue to revolve among the dreary and petty businesses, and to be moved by the paltry hopes and fears with which they surround and animate their heroes, I declare I would die now. But there has never an hour of mine gone quite so dully yet; if it were spent waiting at a railway junction, I would have some scattering thoughts, I could count some grains of memory, compared to which the whole of one of these romances seems but dross.

These writers would retort (if I take them properly) that this was very true; that it was the same with themselves and other persons of (what they call) the artistic temperament; that in this we were exceptional, and should apparently be ashamed of ourselves; but that our works must deal exclusively with (what they call) the average man, who was a prodigious dull fellow, and quite dead to all but the paltriest considerations. I accept the issue. We can only know others by ourselves. The artistic temperament (a plague on the expression!) does not make us different from our fellow-men, or it would make us incapable of writing novels; and the average man (a murrain on the word!) is just like you and me, or he would not be average. It was Whitman who stamped a kind of Birmingham sacredness upon the latter phrase; but Whitman knew very well, and showed very nobly, that the average man was full of joys and full of a poetry of his own. And this harping on life's dulness and man's meanness is a loud profession of incompetence; it is one of two things: the cry of the blind eye, *I cannot see,* or the complaint of the dumb tongue, *I cannot utter.* To draw a life without delights is to prove I have not realised it. To picture a man without some sort of poetry—well, it goes near to prove my case, for it shows an author may have little enough. To see Dancer only as a dirty, old, small-minded, impotently fuming man, in a dirty house, besieged by Harrow boys, and probably beset by small attorneys, is to show myself as keen an observer as . . . the Harrow boys. But these young gentlemen (with a more becoming modesty) were content to pluck Dancer by the coat-tails; they did not suppose they had surprised his secret or could put him living in a book: and it is there my error would have lain. Or say that in the same romance—I continue to call these books romances, in the hope of giving pain—say that in the same romance, which now begins really to take shape, I should leave to speak of Dancer, and follow instead the Harrow boys; and say that I came on some such business as that of my lantern-bearers on the links; and described the boys as very cold, spat upon by flurries of rain, and drearily surrounded, all of which they were; and their talk as silly and indecent, which it certainly was. I might upon these lines, and had I Zola's genius, turn out, in a page or so, a gem of literary art, render the lantern-light with the touches of a master, and lay on the indecency with the ungrudging hand of love; and when all was done, what a triumph would my picture be of shallowness and dulness! how it would

have missed the point! how it would have belied the boys! To the ear of
the stenographer, the talk is merely silly and indecent; but ask the boys
themselves, and they are discussing (as it is highly proper they should) the
possibilities of existence. To the eye of the observer they are wet and cold
and drearily surrounded; but ask themselves, and they are in the heaven of
a recondite pleasure, the ground of which is an ill-smelling lantern.

3

For, to repeat, the ground of a man's joy is often hard to hit. It may hinge
at times upon a mere accessory, like the lantern, it may reside, like
Dancer's, in the mysterious inwards of psychology. It may consist with
perpetual failure, and find exercise in the continued chase. It has so little
bond with externals (such as the observer scribbles in his note-book) that
it may even touch them not; and the man's true life, for which he consents
to live, lie altogether in the field of fancy. The clergyman, in his spare
hours, may be winning battles, the farmer sailing ships, the banker reaping
triumph in the arts: all leading another life, plying another trade from that
they chose; like the poet's housebuilder, who, after all is cased in stone.

> *By his fireside, as impotent fancy prompts,*
> *Rebuilds it to his liking.*

In such a case the poetry runs underground. The observer (poor soul,
with his documents!) is all abroad. For to look at the man is but to court
deception. We shall see the trunk from which he draws his nourishment;
but he himself is above and abroad in the green dome of foliage, hummed
through by winds and nested in by nightingales. And the true realism were
that of the poets, to climb up after him like a squirrel, and catch some
glimpse of the heaven for which he lives. And the true realism, always and
everywhere, is that of the poets: to find out where joy resides, and give it a
voice far beyond singing.

For to miss the joy is to miss all. In the joy of the actors lies the sense of
any action. That is the explanation, that the excuse. To one who has not
the secret of the lanterns, the scene upon the links is meaningless. And
hence the haunting and truly spectral unreality of realistic books. Hence,
when we read the English realists, the incredulous wonder with which we
observe the hero's constancy under the submerging tide of dulness, and
how he bears up with his jibbing sweetheart, and endures the chatter of
idiot girls, and stands by his whole unfeatured wilderness of an existence,
instead of seeking relief in drink or foreign travel. Hence in the French, in
that meat-market of middle-aged sensuality, the disgusted surprise with

which we see the hero drift sidelong, and practically quite untempted, into every description of misconduct and dishonour. In each, we miss the personal poetry, the enchanted atmosphere, that rainbow work of fancy that clothes what is naked and seems to ennoble what is base; in each, life falls dead like dough, instead of soaring away like a balloon into the colours of the sunset; each is true, each inconceivable; for no man lives in the external truth, among salts and acids, but in the warm, phantasmagoric chamber of his brain, with the painted windows and the storied walls.

Of this falsity we have had a recent example from a man who knows far better—Tolstoi's *Powers of Darkness*. Here is a piece full of force and truth, yet quite untrue. For before Mikita was led into so dire a situation he was tempted, and temptations are beautiful at least in part; and a work which dwells on the ugliness of crime and gives no hint of any loveliness in the temptation, sins against the modesty of life, and even when a Tolstoi writes it, sinks to melodrama. The peasants are not understood; they saw their life in fairer colours; even the deaf girl was clothed in poetry for Mikita, or he had never fallen. And so, once again, even an Old Bailey melodrama, without some brightness of poetry and lustre of existence, falls into the inconceivable and ranks with fairy tales.

4

In nobler books we are moved with something like the emotions of life; and this emotion is very variously provoked. We are so moved when Levine labours in the field, when André sinks beyond emotion, when Richard Feverel and Lucy Desborough meet beside the river, when Antony, "not cowardly, puts off his helmet," when Kent has infinite pity on the dying Lear, when, in Dostoieffky's *Despised and Rejected,* the uncomplaining hero drains his cup of suffering and virtue. These are notes that please the great heart of man. Not only love, and the fields, and the bright face of danger, but sacrifice and death and unmerited suffering humbly supported, touch in us the vein of the poetic. We love to think of them, we long to try them, we are humbly hopeful that we may prove heroes also.

We have heard, perhaps, too much of lesser matters. Here is the door, here is the open air. *Itur in antiquam silvam.*

An Apology for Idlers

BOSWELL: *We grow weary when idle.*
JOHNSON: *That is, sir, because others being busy, we want company; but if we were idle, there would be no growing weary; we should all entertain one another.*

J U S T   N O W , when everyone is bound, under pain of a decree in absence convicting them of *lèse*-respectability, to enter on some lucrative profession, and labour therein with something not far short of enthusiasm, a cry from the opposite party who are content when they have enough, and like to look on and enjoy in the meanwhile, savours a little of bravado and gasconade. And yet this should not be. Idleness so called, which does not consist in doing nothing, but in doing a great deal not recognised in the dogmatic formularies of the ruling class, has as good a right to state its position as industry itself. It is admitted that the presence of people who refuse to enter in the great handicap race for sixpenny pieces, is at once an insult and a disenchantment for those who do. A fine fellow (as we see so many) takes his determination, votes for the sixpences, and in the emphatic Americanism, "goes for" them. And while such an one is ploughing distressfully up the road, it is not hard to understand his resentment, when he perceives cool persons in the meadows by the wayside, lying with a handkerchief over their ears and a glass at their elbow. Alexander is touched in a very delicate place by the disregard of Diogenes. Where was the glory of having taken Rome for these tumultuous barbarians, who poured into the Senate house, and found the Fathers sitting silent and unmoved by their success? It is a sore thing to have laboured along and scaled the arduous hilltops, and when all is done, find humanity indifferent to your achievement. Hence physicists condemn the unphysical; financiers have only a superficial toleration for those who know little of stocks; literary persons despise the unlettered; and people of all pursuits combine to disparage those who have none.

But though this is one difficulty of the subject, it is not the greatest. You could not be put in prison for speaking against industry, but you can be sent to Coventry for speaking like a fool. The greatest difficulty with most subjects is to do them well; therefore, please to remember this is an apology. It is certain that much may be judiciously argued in favour of diligence; only there is something to be said against it, and that is what, on the present occasion, I have to say. To state one argument is not necessarily to be deaf to all others, and that a man has written a book of travels in Montenegro, is no reason why he should never have been to Richmond.

It is surely beyond a doubt that people should be a good deal idle in youth. For though here and there a Lord Macaulay may escape from school honours with all his wits about him, most boys pay so dear for their medals that they never afterwards have a shot in their locker, and begin the world bankrupt. And the same holds true during all the time a lad is educating himself, or suffering others to educate him. It must have been a very foolish old gentleman who addressed Johnson at Oxford in these words: "Young man, ply your book diligently now, and acquire a stock of knowledge; for when years come upon you, you will find that poring upon books will be but an irksome task." The old gentleman seems to have been unaware that many other things besides reading grow irksome, and not a few become impossible, by the time a man has to use spectacles and cannot walk without a stick. Books are good enough in their own way, but they are a mighty bloodless substitute for life. It seems a pity to sit, like the Lady of Shalott, peering into a mirror, with your back turned on all the bustle and glamour of reality. And if a man reads very hard, as the old anecdote reminds us, he will have little time for thought.

If you look back on your own education, I am sure it will not be the full, vivid, instructive hours of truantry that you regret; you would rather cancel some lack-lustre periods between sleep and waking in the class. For my own part, I have attended a good many lectures in my time. I still remember that the spinning of a top is a case of Kinetic Stability. I still remember that Emphyteusis is not a disease, nor Stillicide a crime. But though I would not willingly part with such scraps of science, I do not set the same store by them as by certain other odds and ends that I came by in the open street while I was playing truant. This is not the moment to dilate on that mighty place of education, which was the favourite school of Dickens and of Balzac, and turns out yearly many inglorious masters in the Science of the Aspects of Life. Suffice it to say this: if a lad does not learn in the streets, it is because he has no faculty of learning. Nor is the truant always in the streets, for if he prefers, he may go out by the gardened suburbs into the country. He may pitch on some tuft of lilacs over a burn, and smoke innumerable pipes to the tune of the water on the stones. A bird will sing in the thicket. And there he may fall into a vein of kindly thought, and see things in a new perspective. Why, if this be not education, what is? We may conceive Mr Worldly Wiseman accosting such an one, and the conversation that should thereupon ensue:—

"How now, young fellow, what dost thou here?"

"Truly, sir, I take mine ease."

"Is not this the hour of the class? and should'st thou not be plying thy Book with diligence, to the end thou mayest obtain knowledge?"

"Nay, but thus also I follow after Learning, by your leave."

"Learning, quotha! After what fashion, I pray thee? Is it mathematics?"

"No, to be sure."

"Is it metaphysics?"

"Nor that."

"Is it some language?"

"Nay, it is no language."

"Is it a trade?"

"Nor a trade neither."

"Why, then, what is't?"

"Indeed, sir, as a time may soon come for me to go upon Pilgrimage, I am desirous to note what is commonly done by persons in my case, and where are the ugliest Sloughs and Thickets on the Road; as also, what manner of Staff is of the best service. Moreover, I lie here, by this water, to learn by root-of-heart a lesson which my master teaches me to call Peace, or Contentment."

Hereupon Mr Worldly Wiseman was much commoved with passion, and shaking his cane with a very threatful countenance, broke forth upon this wise: "Learning, quotha!" said he; "I would have all such rogues scourged by the Hangman!"

And so he would go his way, ruffling out his cravat with a crackle of starch, like a turkey when it spread its feathers.

Now this, of Mr Wiseman's, is the common opinion. A fact is not called a fact, but a piece of gossip, if it does not fall into one of your scholastic categories. An inquiry must be in some acknowledged direction, with a name to go by; or else you are not inquiring at all, only lounging; and the workhouse is too good for you. It is supposed that all knowledge is at the bottom of a well, or the far end of a telescope. Sainte-Beuve, as he grew older, came to regard all experience as a single great book, in which to study for a few years ere we go hence; and it seemed all one to him whether you should read in Chapter XX, which is the differential calculus, or in Chapter XXXIX, which is hearing the band play in the gardens. As a matter of fact, an intelligent person, looking out of his eyes and hearkening in his ears, with a smile on his face all the time, will get more true education than many another in a life of heroic vigils. There is certainly some chill and arid knowledge to be found upon the summits of formal and laborious science; but it is all round about you, and for the trouble of looking, that you will acquire the warm and palpitating facts of life. While others are filling their memory with a lumber of words, one-half of which they will forget before the week be out, your truant may learn some really useful art: to play the fiddle, to know a good cigar, or to speak with ease and opportunity to all varieties of men. Many who have "plied their book diligently," and know all about some one branch or another of accepted lore, come out of the study with an ancient and owl-like demeanour, and prove dry, stockish, and dyspeptic in all the better and brighter parts of life. Many make a large fortune, who remain underbred and pathetically stupid to the last. And meantime there goes the idler, who began life along with them—by your leave, a different picture. He has had time to take care of his health and his spirits; he has been a great deal in the open air, which is the most salutary of all things for both body and mind; and if he has never read the great Book in very recondite places, he has dipped into it and skimmed it over to excellent purpose. Might not the student afford some Hebrew roots, and the business man some of his half-crowns, for a share of the idler's knowledge of life at large, and Art of Living? Nay, and the idler has another and more important quality than these. I mean his wisdom. He who has much looked on at the childish satisfaction of other people in their hobbies, will regard his own with only a very ironical indulgence. He will not be heard among the dogmatists. He will have a great and cool allowance for all sorts of people and opinions. If he finds no out-of-the-way truths, he will identify himself with no very burning falsehood. His way takes him along a by-road, not much frequented, but very even and pleasant, which is called Commonplace Lane, and leads to the Belvedere of Commonsense. Thence he shall command an agreeable, if no very noble prospect; and while others behold the East and West, the Devil and the Sunrise, he will be contentedly aware of a sort of morning hour upon all sublunary things, with an army of shadows running speedily and in many different directions into the great daylight of Eternity. The shadows and the generations, the shrill doctors and the plangent wars, go by into ultimate silence and emptiness; but underneath all this, a man may see, out of the Belvedere windows, much green and peaceful landscape; many firelit parlours; good people laughing, drinking, and making love as they did before the Flood or the French Revolution; and the old shepherd telling his tale under the hawthorn.

Extreme _busyness,_ whether at school or college, kirk or market, is a symptom of deficient vitality; and a faculty for idleness implies a catholic appetite and a strong sense of personal identity. There is a sort of dead-alive, hackneyed people about, who are scarcely conscious of living except in the exercise of some conventional occupation. Bring these fellows into the country, or set them aboard ship, and you will see how they pine for their desk or their study. They have no curiosity; they cannot give themselves over to random provocations; they do not take pleasure in the exercise of their faculties for its own sake; and unless Necessity lays about them with a stick, they will even stand still. It is no good speaking to such folk: they _cannot_ be idle, their nature is not generous enough; and they pass those hours in a sort of coma, which are not dedicated to furious moiling in the gold-mill. When they do not require to go to the office, when they are not hungry and have no mind to drink, the whole breathing world is a blank to them. If they have to wait an hour or so for a train, they fall into a stupid trance with their eyes open. To see them, you would suppose there was nothing to look at and no one to speak with; you would imagine they were paralysed or alienated; and yet very possibly they are hard workers in their own way, and have good eyesight for a flaw in a deed or a turn of the market. They have been to school and college, but all the time they had their eye on the medal; they have gone about in the world and mixed with clever people, but all the time they were thinking of their own affairs. As if a man's soul were not too small to begin with, they have dwarfed and narrowed theirs by a life of all work and no play; until here they are at forty, with a listless attention, a mind vacant of all material of amusement, and not one thought to rub against another, while they wait for the train. Before he was breeched, he might have clambered on the boxes; when he was twenty, he would have stared at the girls; but now the pipe is smoked out, the snuff-box empty, and my gentleman sits bolt upright upon a bench, with lamentable eyes. This does not appeal to me as being Success in Life.

But it is not only the person himself who suffers from his busy habits, but his wife and children, his friends and relations, and down to the very people he sits with in a railway carriage or an omnibus. Perpetual devotion to what a man calls his business, is only to be sustained by perpetual neglect of many other things. And it is not by any means certain that a man's business is the most important thing he has to do. To an impartial estimate it will seem clear that many of the wisest, most virtuous, and most beneficent parts that are to be played upon the Theatre of Life are filled by gratuitous performers, and pass, among the world at large, as phases of idleness. For in that Theatre, not only the walking gentlemen, singing chambermaids, and diligent fiddlers in the orchestra, but those who look on and clap their hands from the benches, do really play a part and fulfil important offices towards the general result. You are no doubt very dependent on the care of your lawyer and stockbroker, of the guards and signalmen who convey you rapidly from place to place, and the policemen who walk the streets for your protection; but is there not a thought of gratitude in your heart for certain other benefactors who set you smiling when they fall in your way, or season your dinner with good company? Colonel Newcome helped to lose his friend's money; Fred Bayham had an ugly trick of borrowing shirts; and yet they were better people to fall among than Mr Barnes. And though Falstaff was neither sober nor very honest, I think I could name one or two long-faced Barabbases whom the world could better have done without. Hazlitt mentions that he was more sensible of obligation to Northcote, who had never done him anything he could call a service, than to his whole circle of ostentatious friends; for he thought a good companion emphatically the greatest benefactor. I know there are people in the world who cannot feel grateful unless the favour has been done them at the cost of pain and difficulty. But this is a churlish disposition. A man may send you six sheets of letter-paper covered with the most entertaining gossip, or you may pass half an hour pleasantly, perhaps profitably, over an article of his; do you think the service would be greater, if he had made the manuscript in his heart's blood, like a compact with the devil? Do you really fancy you should be more beholden to your correspondent, if he had been damning you all the while for your importunity? Pleasures are more beneficial than duties because, like the quality of mercy, they are not strained, and they are twice blest. There must always be two to a kiss, and there may be a score in a jest; but wherever there is an element of sacrifice, the favour is conferred with pain, and, among generous people, received with confusion. There is no duty we so much underrate as the duty of being happy. By being happy, we sow anonymous benefits upon the world, which remain unknown even to ourselves, or when they are disclosed, surprise nobody so much as the benefactor. The other day, a ragged, barefoot boy ran down the street after a marble, with so jolly an air that he set every one he passed into a good humour; one of these persons, who had been delivered from more than usually black thoughts, stopped the little fellow and gave him some money with this remark: "You see what sometimes comes of looking pleased." If he had looked pleased before, he had now to look both pleased and mystified. For my part, I justify this encouragement of smiling rather than tearful children; I do not wish to pay for tears anywhere but upon the stage; but I am prepared to deal largely in the opposite commodity. A happy man or woman is a better thing to find than a five-pound note. He or she is a radiating focus of goodwill; and their entrance into a room is as though another candle had been lighted. We need not care whether they could prove the forty-seventh proposition; they do a better thing than that, they practically demonstrate the great Theorem of the Liveableness of Life. Consequently, if a person cannot be happy without remaining idle, idle he should remain. It is a revolutionary precept; but thanks to hunger and the workhouse, one not easily to be abused; and within practical limits, it is one of the most incontestable truths in the whole Body of Morality. Look at one of your industrious fellows for a moment, I beseech you. He sows hurry and reaps indigestion; he puts a vast deal of activity out to interest, and receives a large measure of nervous derangement in return. Either he absents himself entirely from all fellow-ship, and lives a recluse in a garret, with carpet slippers and a leaden inkpot; or he comes among people swiftly and bitterly, in a contraction of his whole nervous system, to discharge some temper before he returns to work. I do not care how much or how well he works, this fellow is an evil feature in other people's lives. They would be happier if he were dead. They could easier do without his services in the Circumlocution Office, than they can tolerate his fractious spirits. He poisons life at the well-head. It is better to be beggared out of hand by a scapegrace nephew, than daily hag-ridden by a peevish uncle.

And what, in God's name, is all this pother about? For what cause do they embitter their own and other people's lives? That a man should publish three or thirty articles a year, that he should finish or not finish his great allegorical picture, are questions of little interest to the world. The ranks of life are full; and although a thousand fall, there are always some to go into the breach. When they told Joan of Arc she should be at home minding women's work, she answered there was plenty to spin and wash. And so, even with your own rare gifts! When nature is "so careless of the single life," why should we coddle ourselves into the fancy that our own is of exceptional importance? Suppose Shakespeare had been knocked on the head some dark night in Sir Thomas Lucy's preserves, the world would have wagged on better or worse, the pitcher gone to the well, the scythe to the corn, and the student to his book; and no one been any the wiser of the loss. There are not many works extant, if you look the alternative all over, which are worth the price of a pound of tobacco to a man of limited means. This is a sobering re-flection for the proudest of our earthly vanities. Even a tobacconist may, upon consideration, find no great cause for personal vainglory in the phrase; for although tobacco is an admirable sedative, the qualities nec-essary for retailing it are neither rare nor precious in themselves. Alas and alas! you may take it how you will, but the services of no single individual are indispensable. Atlas was just a gentleman with a pro-tracted nightmare! And yet you see merchants who go and labour them-selves into a great fortune and thence into the bankruptcy court; scrib-blers who keep scribbling at little articles until their temper is a cross to all who come about them, as though Pharaoh should set the Israelites to make a pin instead of a pyramid; and fine young men who work them-selves into a decline, and are driven off in a hearse with white plumes upon it. Would you not suppose these persons had been whispered, by the Master of the Ceremonies, the promise of some momentous destiny? and that this lukewarm bullet on which they play their farces was the bull's-eye and centrepoint of all the universe? And yet it is not so. The ends for which they give away their priceless youth, for all they know, may be chimerical or hurtful; the glory and riches they expect may never come, or may find them indifferent; and they and the world they inhabit are so inconsiderable that the mind freezes at the thought.

On Marriage

HOPE, they say, deserts us at no period of our existence. From first to last, and in the face of smarting disillusions, we continue to expect good fortune, better health, and better conduct; and that so confidently, that we judge it needless to deserve them. I think it improbable that I shall ever write like Shakespeare, conduct an army like Hannibal, or distinguish myself like Marcus Aurelius in the paths of virtue; and yet I have my by-days, hope prompting, when I am very ready to believe that I shall combine all these various excellences in my own person, and go marching down to posterity with divine honors. There is nothing so monstrous but we can believe it of ourselves. About ourselves, about our aspirations and delinquencies, we have dwelt by choice in a delicious vagueness from our boyhood up. No one will have forgotten Tom Sawyer's aspiration: "Ah, if he could only die *temporarily!*" Or, perhaps, better still, the inward resolution of the two pirates, that "so long as they remained in that business, their piracies should not again be sullied with the crime of stealing." Here we recognize the thoughts of our boyhood; and our boyhood ceased—well, when?—not, I think, at twenty; nor, perhaps, altogether at twenty-five; nor yet at thirty; and possibly, to be quite frank, we are still in the thick of that Arcadian period. For as the race of man, after centuries of civilization, still keeps some traits of their barbarian fathers, so man the individual is not altogether quit of youth, when he is already old and honored, and Lord Chancellor of England. We advance in years somewhat in the manner of an invading army in a barren land; the age that we have reached, as the phrase goes, we but hold with an outpost, and still keep open our communications with the extreme rear and first beginnings of the march. There is our true base; that is not only the beginning, but the perennial spring of our faculties; and grandfather William can retire upon occasion into the green enchanted forest of his boyhood.

The unfading boyishness of hope and its vigorous irrationality are nowhere better displayed than in questions of conduct. There is a character in the *Pilgrim's Progress,* one Mr. *Linger-after-Lust,* with whom I fancy we are all on speaking terms; one famous among the famous for ingenuity of hope up to and beyond the moment of defeat; one who, after eighty years of contrary experience, will believe it possible to continue in the business of piracy and yet avoid the guilt of theft. Every sin is our last; every 1st of

January a remarkable turning-point in our career. Any overt act, above all, is felt to be alchemic in its power to change. A drunkard takes the pledge; it will be strange if that does not help him. For how many years did Mr. Pepys continue to make and break his little vows? And yet I have not heard that he was discouraged in the end. By such steps we think to fix a momentary resolution; as a timid fellow hies him to the dentist's while the tooth is stinging.

But, alas, by planting a stake at the top of flood, you can neither prevent nor delay the inevitable ebb. There is no hocus-pocus in morality; and even the "sanctimonious ceremony" of marriage leaves the man unchanged. This is a hard saying, and has an air of paradox. For there is something in marriage so natural and inviting, that the step has an air of great simplicity and ease; it offers to bury forever many aching preoccupations; it is to afford us unfailing and familiar company through life; it opens up a smiling prospect of the blest and passive kind of love, rather than the blessing and active; it is approached not only through the delights of courtship, but by a public performance and repeated legal signatures. A man naturally thinks it will go hard with him if he cannot be good and fortunate and happy within such august circumvallations.

And yet there is probably no other act in a man's life so hot-headed and foolhardy as this one of marriage. For years, let us suppose, you have been making the most indifferent business of your career. Your experience has not, we may dare to say, been more encouraging than Paul's or Horace's; like them, you have seen and desired the good that you were not able to accomplish; like them, you have done the evil that you loathed. You have waked at night in a hot or a cold sweat, according to your habit of body, remembering, with dismal surprise, your own unpardonable acts and sayings. You have been sometimes tempted to withdraw entirely from this game of life; as a man who makes nothing but misses withdraws from that less dangerous one of billiards. You have fallen back upon the thought that you yourself most sharply smarted for your misdemeanors, or, in the old, plaintive phrase, that you were nobody's enemy but your own. And then you have been made aware of what was beautiful and amiable, wise and kind, in the other part of your behavior; and it seemed as if nothing could reconcile the contradiction, as indeed nothing can. If you are a man, you have shut your mouth hard and said nothing; and if you are only a man in the making, you have recognized that yours was quite a special case, and you yourself not guilty of your own pestiferous career.

Granted, and with all my heart. Let us accept these apologies; let us agree that you are nobody's enemy but your own; let us agree that you are a sort of moral cripple, impotent for good; and let us regard you with the unmingled pity due to such a fate. But there is one thing to which, on these terms, we can never agree:—we can never agree to have you marry.

What! you have had one life to manage, and have failed so strangely, and now can see nothing wiser than to conjoin with it the management of some one else's? Because you have been unfaithful in a very little, you propose yourself to be a ruler over ten cities. You strip yourself by such a step of all remaining consolations and excuses. You are no longer content to be your own enemy; you must be your wife's also. You have been hitherto in a mere subaltern attitude; dealing cruel blows about you in life, yet only half responsible, since you came there by no choice or movement of your own. Now, it appears, you must take things on your own authority: God made you, but you marry yourself; and for all that your wife suffers, no one is responsible but you. A man must be very certain of his knowledge ere he undertake to guide a ticket-of-leave man through a dangerous pass; you have eternally missed your way in life, with consequences that you still deplore, and yet you masterfully seize your wife's hand, and, blindfold, drag her after you to ruin. And it is your wife, you observe, whom you select. She, whose happiness you most desire, you choose to be your victim. You would earnestly warn her from a tottering bridge or bad investment. If she were to marry some one else, how you would tremble for her fate! If she were only your sister, and you thought half as much of her, how doubtfully would you entrust her future to a man no better than yourself!

Times are changed with him who marries; there are no more by-path meadows, where you may innocently linger, but the road lies long and straight and dusty to the grave. Idleness, which is often becoming and even wise in the bachelor, begins to wear a different aspect when you have a wife to support. Suppose, after you are married, one of those little slips were to befall you. What happened last November might surely happen February next. They may have annoyed you at the time, because they were not what you had meant; but how will they annoy you in the future, and how will they shake the fabric of your wife's confidence and peace! A thousand things unpleasing went on in the *chiaroscuro* of a life that you shrank from too particularly realizing; you did not care, in those days, to make a fetish of your conscience; you would recognize your failures with a nod, and so, good-day. But the time for these reserves is over. You have wilfully introduced a witness into your life, the scene of these defeats, and can no longer close the mind's eye upon uncomely passages, but must stand up straight and put a name upon your actions. And your witness is not only the judge, but the victim of your sins; not only can she condemn you to the sharpest penalties, but she must herself share feelingly in their endurance. And observe, once more, with what temerity you have chosen precisely *her* to be your spy, whose esteem you value highest, and whom you have already taught to think you better than you are. You may think you had a conscience, and believed in God; but what is a conscience to a wife? Wise men of yore erected statues of their deities, and consciously performed their part in life before those marble eyes. A god watched them at the board, and stood by their bedside in the morning when they woke; and all about their ancient cities, where they bought and sold, or where they piped and wrestled, there would stand some symbol of the things that are outside of man. These were lessons, delivered in the quiet dialect of art, which told their story faithfully, but gently. It is the same lesson, if you will—but how harrowingly taught!—when the woman you respect shall weep from your unkindness or blush with shame at your misconduct. Poor girls in Italy turn their painted Madonnas to the wall: you cannot set aside your wife. To marry is to domesticate the Recording Angel. Once you are married, there is nothing left for you, not even suicide, but to be good.

And goodness in marriage is a more intricate problem than mere single virtue; for in marriage there are two ideals to be realized. A girl, it is true, has always lived in a glass house among reproving relatives, whose word was law; she has been bred up to sacrifice her judgments and take the key submissively from dear papa; and it is wonderful how swiftly she can change her tune into the husband's. Her morality has been, too often, an affair of precept and conformity. But in the case of a bachelor who has enjoyed some measure both of privacy and freedom, his moral judgments have been passed in some accordance with his nature. His sins were always sins in his own sight; he could then only sin when he did some act against his clear conviction; the light that he walked by was obscure, but it was single. Now, when two people of any grit and spirit put their fortunes into one, there succeeds to this comparative certainty a huge welter of competing jurisdictions. It no longer matters so much how life appears to one; one must consult another: one, who may be strong, must not offend the other, who is weak. The only weak brother I am willing to consider is (to make a bull for once) my wife. For her, and for her only, I must waive my righteous judgments, and go crookedly about my life. How, then, in such an atmosphere of compromise, to keep honor bright and abstain from base capitulations? How are you to put aside love's pleadings? How are you, the apostle of laxity, to turn suddenly about into the rabbi of precision; and after these years of ragged practice, pose for a hero to the lackey who has found you out? In this temptation to mutual indulgence lies the particular peril to morality in married life. Daily they drop a little lower from the first ideal, and for awhile continue to accept these changelings with a gross complacency. At last Love wakes and looks about him; finds his hero sunk into a stout old brute, intent on brandy pawnee; finds his heroine divested of her angel brightness; and in the flash of that first disenchantment, flees forever.

Again, the husband, in these unions, is usually a man, and the wife commonly enough a woman; and when this is the case, although it makes the firmer marriage, a thick additional veil of misconception hangs above the doubtful business. Women, I believe, are somewhat rarer than men; but then, if I were a woman myself, I dare say I should hold the reverse; and at least we all enter more or less wholly into one or other of these camps. A man who delights women by his feminine perceptions will often scatter his admirers by a chance explosion of the under side of man; and the most masculine and direct of women will some day, to your dire surprise, draw out like a telescope into successive lengths of personation. Alas! for the man, knowing her to be at heart more candid than himself, who shall flounder, panting, through these mazes in the quest for truth. The proper qualities of each sex are, indeed, eternally surprising to the other. Between the Latin and the Teuton races there are similar divergences, not to be bridged by the most liberal sympathy. And in the good, plain, cut-and-dry explanations of this life, which pass current among us as the wisdom of the elders, this difficulty has been turned with the aid of pious lies. Thus, when a young lady has angelic features, eats nothing to speak of, plays all day long on the piano, and sings ravishingly in church, it requires a rough infidelity, falsely called cynicism, to believe that she may be a little devil after all. Yet so it is: she may be a tale-bearer, a liar, and a thief; she may have a taste for brandy, and no heart. My compliments to George Eliot for her Rosamond Vincy; the ugly work of satire she has transmuted to the ends of art, by the companion figure of Lydgate; and the satire was much wanted for the education of young men. That doctrine of the excellence of women, however chivalrous, is cowardly as well as false. It is better to face the fact, and know, when you marry, that you take into your life a creature of equal, if of unlike, frailties; whose weak human heart beats no more tunefully than yours.

But it is the object of a liberal education not only to obscure the knowledge of one sex by another, but to magnify the natural differences between the two. Man is a creature who lives not upon bread alone, but principally by catchwords; and the little rift between the sexes is astonishingly widened by simply teaching one set of catchwords to the girls and another to the boys. To the first, there is shown but a very small field of experience, and taught a very trenchant principle for judgment and action; to the other, the world of life is more largely displayed, and their rule of conduct is proportionately widened. They are taught to follow different virtues, to hate different vices, to place their ideal, even for each other, in different achievements. What should be the result of such a course? When a horse has run away, and the two flustered people in the gig have each possessed themselves of a rein, we know the end of that conveyance will be in the ditch. So, when I see a raw youth and a green girl, fluted and fiddled in a dancing measure into that most serious contract, and setting out upon life's journey with ideas so monstrously divergent, I am not surprised that some make shipwreck, but that any come to port. What the boy does almost proudly, as a manly peccadillo, the girl will shudder at as a debasing vice; what is to her the mere common-sense of tactics, he will spit out of his mouth as shameful. Through such a sea of contrarieties must this green couple steer their way; and contrive to love each other; and to respect, forsooth; and be ready, when the time arrives, to educate the little men and women who shall succeed to their places and perplexities.

And yet, when all has been said, the man who should hold back from marriage is in the same case with him who runs away from battle. To avoid an occasion for our virtues is a worse degree of failure than to push forward pluckily and make a fall. It is lawful to pray God that we be not led into temptation; but not lawful to skulk from those that come to us. The noblest passage in one of the noblest books of this century, is where the old pope glories in the trial, nay, in the partial fall and but imperfect triumph, of the younger hero.* Without some such manly note, it were perhaps better to have no conscience at all. But there is a vast difference between teaching flight, and showing points of peril that a man may march the more warily. And the true conclusion of this paper is to turn our back on apprehensions, and embrace that shining and courageous virtue, Faith. Hope is the boy, a blind, headlong, pleasant fellow, good to chase swallows with the salt; Faith is the grave, experienced, yet smiling man. Hope lives on ignorance; open-eyed Faith is built upon a knowledge of our life, of the tyranny of circumstance and the frailty of human resolution. Hope looks for unqualified success; but Faith counts certainly on failure, and takes honorable defeat to be a form of victory. Hope is a kind old pagan; but Faith grew up in Christian days, and early learned humility. In the one temper, a man is indignant that he cannot spring up in a clap to heights of elegance and virtue; in the other, out of a sense of his infirmities, he is filled with confidence because a year has come and gone, and he has still preserved some rags of honor. In the first, he expects an angel for a wife; in the last, he knows that she is like himself—erring, thoughtless, and untrue; but like himself also, filled with a struggling radiancy of better things, and adorned with ineffective qualities. You may safely go to school with hope; but ere you marry, should have learned the mingled lesson of the world: that dolls are stuffed with sawdust, and yet are excellent playthings; that hope and love address themselves to a perfection never realized, and yet, firmly held, become the salt and staff of life; that you yourself are compacted of infirmities, perfect, you might say, in imperfection, and yet you have a something in you lovable and worth preserving; and

---

* Browning's *The Ring and the Book*.

that, while the mass of mankind lies under this scurvy condemnation, you will scarce find one but, by some generous reading, will become to you a lesson, a model, and a noble spouse through life. So thinking, you will constantly support your own unworthiness, and easily forgive the failings of your friend. Nay, you will be wisely glad that you retain the sense of blemishes; for the faults of married people continually spur up each of them, hour by hour, to do better and to meet and love upon a higher ground. And ever, between the failures, there will come glimpses of kind virtues to encourage and console.

MAX BEERBOHM

"The incomparable Max," George Bernard Shaw called Max Beerbohm (1872–1956), and Virginia Woolf deemed him perfect in his way, envying his sleight-of-hand artistry. The praise and admiration of his contemporaries may seem at first extravagant for so lighthearted and flippant an author, but Beerbohm represents the best possible case for the determinedly minor writer. As Cynthia Ozick has noted, "A delectable preciousness (not inevitably a pejorative, if you consider Max Beerbohm), or a calculated smallness, or an unstoppable scheme of idiosyncrasy, comic or other—or simply the persnickety insistence on being minor—can claim permanence as easily as the more capacious qualities of a Proust or a Joyce."

Beerbohm's first writings and caricatures (he was a consummate cartoonist) started appearing while he was still a student at Oxford, in the Yellow Book, *the organ of the Aesthetic movement, led by Aubrey Beardsley and Oscar Wilde. Beerbohm wrote a precocious, funny apology for aesthetes, "Dandies and Dandies." Apparently a dandy in his own dress, though a self-mocking one, he was socially popular—he made people laugh. His literary parodies in* A Christmas Garland *are still hilarious, as is his zany novel,* Zuleika Dobson. *But his accomplishments in the personal essay—which he may be said to have revived single-handedly in England, after several dormant generations—have left the deepest mark.*

As Beerbohm's writing evolved, he abandoned the Edwardian contortions and formal mannerisms that he had so deftly practiced earlier for a more direct, streamlined, modern prose style. In other respects he shunned the modern, tweaking the solemn speed and spirit of the age. Beerbohm often took the role of the curmudgeon (see "Going Out for a Walk"). He exercised stunning control of a persona that veered between modesty and impu-

dence, tenderness and spite. He was above all a master of scale, not making any piece bigger or louder than it needed to be. His concise writing style achieved comic effects with the spin he put on individual words, with sudden shifts in diction and the puncturing of sentimentality. Underneath his light, playful manner there is at times considerable thoughtfulness and wisdom (see "Laughter").

Going Out for a Walk

I T   I S   A   F A C T that not once in all my life have I gone out for a walk. I have been taken out for walks; but that is another matter. Even while I trotted prattling by my nurse's side I regretted the good old days when I had, and wasn't, a perambulator. When I grew up it seemed to me that the one advantage of living in London was that nobody ever wanted me to come out for a walk. London's very drawbacks—its endless noise and bustle, its smoky air, the squalor ambushed everywhere in it—assured this one immunity. Whenever I was with friends in the country, I knew that at any moment, unless rain were actually falling, some man might suddenly say "Come out for a walk!" in that sharp imperative tone which he would not dream of using in any other connexion. People seem to think there is something inherently noble and virtuous in the desire to go for a walk. Any one thus desirous feels that he has a right to impose his will on whomever he sees comfortably settled in an arm-chair, reading. It is easy to say simply "No" to an old friend. In the case of a mere acquaintance one wants some excuse. "I wish I could, but"—nothing ever occurs to me except "I have some letters to write." This formula is unsatisfactory in three ways. (1) It isn't believed. (2) It compels you to rise from your chair, go to the writing-table, and sit improvising a letter to somebody until the walkmonger (just not daring to call you liar and hypocrite) shall have lumbered out of the room. (3) It won't operate on Sunday mornings. "There's no post out till this evening" clinches the matter; and you may as well go quietly.

Walking for walking's sake may be as highly laudable and exemplary a thing as it is held to be by those who practise it. My objection to it is that

it stops the brain. Many a man has professed to me that his brain never
works so well as when he is swinging along the high road or over hill and
dale. This boast is not confirmed by my memory of anybody who on a
Sunday morning has forced me to partake of his adventure. Experience
teaches me that whatever a fellow-guest may have of power to instruct or
to amuse when he is sitting on a chair, or standing on a hearth-rug,
quickly leaves him when he takes one out for a walk. The ideas that came
so thick and fast to him in any room, where are they now? where that
encyclopaedic knowledge which he bore so lightly? where the kindling
fancy that played like summer lightning over *any* topic that was started?
The man's face that was so mobile is set now; gone is the light from his
fine eyes. He says that A. (our host) is a thoroughly good fellow. Fifty
yards further on, he adds that A. is one of the best fellows he has ever met.
We tramp another furlong or so, and he says that Mrs. A. is a charming
woman. Presently he adds that she is one of the most charming women he
has ever known. We pass an inn. He reads vapidly aloud to me: "The
King's Arms. Licensed to sell Ales and Spirits." I foresee that during the
rest of the walk he will read aloud any inscription that occurs. We pass a
milestone. He points at it with his stick, and says "Uxminster. 11 Miles."
We turn a sharp corner at the foot of a hill. He points at the wall, and says
"Drive Slowly." I see far ahead, on the other side of the hedge bordering
the high road, a small notice-board. He sees it too. He keeps his eye on it.
And in due course "Trespassers," he says, "Will Be Prosecuted." Poor
man!—mentally a wreck.

Luncheon at the A.s, however, salves him and floats him in full sail.
Behold him once more the life and soul of the party. Surely he will never,
after the bitter lesson of this morning, go out for another walk. An hour
later, I see him striding forth, with a new companion. I watch him out of
sight. I know what he is saying. He is saying that I am rather a dull man to
go a walk with. He will presently add that I am one of the dullest men he
ever went a walk with. Then he will devote himself to reading out the
inscriptions.

How comes it, this immediate deterioration in those who go walking for
walking's sake? Just what happens? I take it that not by his reasoning
faculties is a man urged to this enterprise. He is urged, evidently, by something in him that transcends reason; by his soul, I presume. Yes, it must be
the soul that raps out the "Quick march!" to the body.—"Halt! Stand at
ease!" interposes the brain, and "To what destination," it suavely asks the
soul, "and on what errand, are you sending the body?"—"On no errand
whatsoever," the soul makes answer, "and to no destination at all. It is just
like you to be always on the look-out for some subtle ulterior motive. The
body is going out because the mere fact of its doing so is a sure indication
of nobility, probity, and rugged grandeur of character."—"Very well,

Vagula, have your own wayula! But I," says the brain, "flatly refuse to be mixed up in this tomfoolery. I shall go to sleep till it is over." The brain then wraps itself up in its own convolutions, and falls into a dreamless slumber from which nothing can rouse it till the body has been safely deposited indoors again.

Even if you go to some definite place, for some definite purpose, the brain would rather you took a vehicle; but it does not make a point of this; it will serve you well enough unless you are going *out for a walk.* It won't, while your legs are vying with each other, do any deep thinking for you, nor even any close thinking; but it will do any number of small odd jobs for you willingly—provided that your legs, also, are making themselves useful, not merely bandying you about to gratify the pride of the soul. Such as it is, this essay was composed in the course of a walk, this morning. I am not one of those extremists who must have a vehicle to every destination. I never go out of my way, as it were, to avoid exercise. I take it as it comes, and take it in good part. That valetudinarians are always chattering about it, and indulging in it to excess, is no reason for despising it. I am inclined to think that in moderation it is rather good for one, physically. But, pending a time when no people wish me to go and see them, and I have no wish to go and see any one, and there is nothing whatever for me to do off my own premises, I never will go out for a walk.

Laughter

M. BERGSON, in his well-known essay on this theme, says . . . well, he says many things; but none of these, though I have just read them, do I clearly remember, nor am I sure that in the act of reading I understood any of them. That is the worst of these fashionable philosophers—or rather, the worst of me. Somehow I never manage to read them till they are just going out of fashion, and even then I don't seem able to cope with them. About twelve years ago, when every one suddenly talked to me about Pragmatism and William James, I found myself moved by a dull but irresistible impulse to try Schopenhauer, of whom, years before that, I had heard that he was the easiest reading in the world, and the most exciting and amusing. I wrestled with Schopenhauer for a day or so, in vain. Time passed; M. Bergson appeared "and for his hour was lord of the ascendant"; I tardily tackled William James. I bore in mind, as I approached him, the testimonials that had been lavished on him by all my friends. Alas, I was insensible to his thrillingness. His gaiety did not make me gay. His crystal clarity confused me dreadfully. I could make nothing of William James. And now, in the fullness of time, I have been floored by M. Bergson.

It distresses me, this failure to keep pace with the leaders of thought as they pass into oblivion. It makes me wonder whether I am, after all, an absolute fool. Yet surely I am not that. Tell me of a man or a woman, a place or an event, real or fictitious: surely you will find me a fairly intelligent listener. Any such narrative will present to me some image, and will stir me to not altogether fatuous thoughts. Come to me in some grievous difficulty: I will talk to you like a father, even like a lawyer. I'll be hanged if I haven't a certain mellow wisdom. But if you are by way of weaving theories as to the nature of things in general, and if you want to try those theories on some one who will luminously confirm them or powerfully rend them, I must, with a hang-dog air, warn you that I am not your man. I suffer from a strong suspicion that things in general cannot be accounted for through any formula or set of formulae, and that any one philosophy, howsoever new, is no better than another. That is in itself a sort of philosophy, and I suspect it accordingly; but it has for me the merit of being the only one I can make head or tail of. If you try to expound any other philosophic system to me, you will find not merely that I can detect no flaw in it (except the one great flaw just suggested), but also that I haven't, after a minute or two, the vaguest notion of what you are driving at. "Very well," you say, "instead of trying to explain all things all at once, I will explain some little, simple, single thing." It was for sake of such shorn lambs as myself, doubtless, that M. Bergson sat down and wrote about— Laughter. But I have profited by his kindness no more than if he had been treating of the Cosmos. I cannot tread even a limited space of air. I have a gross satisfaction in the crude fact of being on hard ground again, and I utter a coarse peal of—Laughter.

At least, I say I do so. In point of fact, I have merely smiled. Twenty years ago, ten years ago, I should have laughed, and have professed to you that I had merely smiled. A very young man is not content to be very young, nor even a young man to be young: he wants to share the dignity of his elders. There is no dignity in laughter, there is much of it in smiles. Laughter is but a joyous surrender, smiles give token of mature criticism. It may be that in the early ages of this world there was far more laughter than is to be heard now, and that aeons hence laughter will be obsolete, and smiles universal—every one, always, mildly, slightly, smiling. But it is less useful to speculate as to mankind's past and future than to observe men. And you will have observed with me in the club-room that young men at most times look solemn, whereas old men or men of middle age mostly smile; and also that those young men do often laugh loud and long among themselves, while we others—the gayest and best of us in the most favourable circumstances—seldom achieve more than our habitual act of smiling. Does the sound of that laughter jar on us? Do we liken it to the crackling of thorns under a pot? Let us do so. There is no cheerier sound. But let us not assume it to be the laughter of fools because we sit quiet. It is absurd to disapprove of what one envies, or to wish a good thing were no more because it has passed out of our possession.

But (it seems that I must begin every paragraph by questioning the sincerity of what I have just said) *has* the gift of laughter been withdrawn from me? I protest that I do still, at the age of forty-seven, laugh often and loud and long. But not, I believe, so long and loud and often as in my less smiling youth. And I am proud, nowadays, of laughing, and grateful to any one who makes me laugh. That is a bad sign. I no longer take laughter as a matter of course. I realise, even after reading M. Bergson on it, how good a thing it is. I am qualified to praise it.

As to what is most precious among the accessories to the world we live in, different men hold different opinions. There are people whom the sea depresses, whom mountains exhilarate. Personally, I want the sea always —some not populous edge of it for choice; and with it sunshine, and wine, and a little music. My friend on the mountain yonder is of tougher fibre and sterner outlook, disapproves of the sea's laxity and instability, has no ear for music and no palate for the grape, and regards the sun as a rather enervating institution, like central heating in a house. What he likes is a grey day and the wind in his face; crags at a great altitude; and a flask of whisky. Yet I think that even he, if we were trying to determine from what inner sources mankind derives the greatest pleasure in life, would agree with me that only the emotion of love takes higher rank than the emotion of laughter. Both these emotions are partly mental, partly physical. It is said that the mental symptoms of love are wholly physical in origin. They are not the less ethereal for that. The physical sensations of laughter, on the other hand, are reached by a process whose starting-point is in the mind. They are not the less "gloriously of our clay." There is laughter that goes so far as to lose all touch with its motive, and to exist only, grossly, in itself. This is laughter at its best. A man to whom such laughter has often been granted may happen to die in a work-house. No matter. I will not admit that he has failed in life. Another man, who has never laughed thus, may be buried in Westminster Abbey, leaving more than a million pounds overhead. What then? I regard him as a failure.

Nor does it seem to me to matter one jot how such laughter is achieved.

Humour may rollick on high planes of fantasy or in depths of silliness. To many people it appeals only from those depths. If it appeal to them irresistibly, they are more enviable than those who are sensitive only to the finer kind of joke and not so sensitive as to be mastered and dissolved by it. Laughter is a thing to be rated according to its own intensity.

Many years ago I wrote an essay in which I poured scorn on the fun purveyed by the music halls, and on the great public for which that fun was quite good enough. I take that callow scorn back. I fancy that the fun itself was better than it seemed to me, and might not have displeased me if it had been wafted to me in private, in presence of a few friends. A public crowd, because of a lack of broad impersonal humanity in me, rather insulates than absorbs me. Amidst the guffaws of a thousand strangers I become unnaturally grave. If these people were the entertainment, and I the audience, I should be sympathetic enough. But to be one of them is a position that drives me spiritually aloof. Also, there is to me something rather dreary in the notion of going anywhere for the specific purpose of being amused. I prefer that laughter shall take me unawares. Only so can it master and dissolve me. And in this respect, at any rate, I am not peculiar. In music halls and such places, you may hear loud laughter, but—not see silent laughter, not see strong men weak, helpless, suffering, gradually convalescent, dangerously relapsing. Laughter at its greatest and best is not there.

To such laughter nothing is more propitious than an occasion that demands gravity. To have good reason for not laughing is one of the surest aids. Laughter rejoices in bonds. If music halls were schoolrooms for us, and the comedians were our schoolmasters, how much less talent would be needed for giving us how much more joy! Even in private and accidental intercourse, few are the men whose humour can reduce us, be we never so susceptible, to paroxysms of mirth. I will wager that nine tenths of the world's best laughter is laughter *at,* not *with.* And it is the people set in authority over us that touch most surely our sense of the ridiculous. Freedom is a good thing, but we lose through it golden moments. The schoolmaster to his pupils, the monarch to his courtiers, the editor to his staff— how priceless they are! Reverence is a good thing, and part of its value is that the more we revere a man, the more sharply are we struck by anything in him (and there is always much) that is incongruous with his greatness. And herein lies one of the reasons why as we grow older we laugh less. The men we esteemed so great are gathered to their fathers. Some of our coevals may, for aught we know, be very great, but good heavens! we can't esteem *them* so.

Of extreme laughter I know not in any annals a more satisfying example than one that is to be found in Moore's Life of Byron. Both Byron and Moore were already in high spirits when, on an evening in the spring of

1813, they went "from some early assembly" to Mr. Rogers' house in St. James's Place and were regaled there with an impromptu meal. But not high spirits alone would have led the two young poets to such excess of laughter as made the evening so very memorable. Luckily they both venerated Rogers (strange as it may seem to us) as the greatest of living poets. Luckily, too, Mr. Rogers was ever the kind of man, the coldly and quietly suave kind of man, with whom you don't take liberties, if you can help it —with whom, if you *can't* help it, to take liberties is in itself a most exhilarating act. And he had just received a presentation copy of Lord Thurlow's latest book, *Poems on Several Occasions.* The two young poets found in this elder's Muse much that was so execrable as to be delightful. They were soon, as they turned the pages, held in throes of laughter, laughter that was but intensified by the endeavours of their correct and nettled host to point out the genuine merits of his friend's work. And then suddenly—oh joy!—"we lighted," Moore records, "on the discovery that our host, in addition to his sincere approbation of some of this book's contents, had also the motive of gratitude for standing by its author, as one of the poems was a warm and, I need not add, well-deserved panegyric on himself. We were, however"—the narrative has an added charm from Tom Moore's demure care not to offend or compromise the still-surviving Rogers—"too far gone in nonsense for even this eulogy, in which we both so heartily agreed, to stop us. The opening line of the poem, was, as well as I can recollect, 'When Rogers o'er this labour bent'; and Lord Byron undertook to read it aloud;—but he found it impossible to get beyond the first two words. Our laughter had now increased to such a pitch that nothing could restrain it. Two or three times he began; but no sooner had the words 'When Rogers' passed his lips, than our fit burst out afresh,—till even Mr. Rogers himself, with all his feeling of our injustice, found it impossible not to join us; and we were, at last, all three in such a state of inextinguishable laughter, that, had the author himself been of our party, I question much whether he could have resisted the infection." The final fall and dissolution of Rogers, Rogers behaving as badly as either of them, is all that was needed to give perfection to this heart-warming scene. I like to think that on a certain night in spring, year after year, three ghosts revisit that old room and (without, I hope, inconvenience to Lord Northcliffe, who may happen to be there) sit rocking and writhing in the grip of that old shared rapture. Uncanny? Well, not more so than would have seemed to Byron and Moore and Rogers the notion that more than a hundred years away from them was some one joining in their laughter— as *I* do.

Alas, I cannot join in it more than gently. To imagine a scene, however vividly, does not give us the sense of being or even of having been, present at it. Indeed, the greater the glow of the scene reflected, the sharper is the

pang of our realisation that we were *not* there, and of our annoyance that
we weren't. Such a pang comes to me with special force whenever my
fancy posts itself outside the Temple's gate in Fleet Street, and there, at a
late hour of the night of May 10th, 1773, observes a gigantic old man
laughing wildly, but having no one with him to share and aggrandise his
emotion. Not that he is alone; but the young man beside him laughs only
in politeness and is inwardly puzzled, even shocked. Boswell has a keen,
an exquisitely keen, scent for comedy, for the fun that is latent in fine
shades of character; but imaginative burlesque, anything that borders on
lovely nonsense, he was not formed to savour. All the more does one revel
in his account of what led up to the moment when Johnson "to support
himself, laid hold of one of the posts at the side of the foot pavement, and
sent forth peals so loud that in the silence of the night his voice seemed to
resound from Temple Bar to Fleet Ditch."

No evening ever had an unlikelier ending. The omens were all for
gloom. Johnson had gone to dine at General Paoli's but was so ill that he
had to leave before the meal was over. Later he managed to go to Mr.
Chambers' rooms in the Temple. "He continued to be very ill" there, but
gradually felt better, and "talked with a noble enthusiasm of keeping up
the representation of respectable families," and was great on "the dignity
and propriety of male succession." Among his listeners, as it happened,
was a gentleman for whom Mr. Chambers had that day drawn up a will
devising his estate to his three sisters. The news of this might have been
expected to make Johnson violent in wrath. But no, for some reason he
grew violent only in laughter, and insisted thenceforth on calling that gentleman The Testator and chaffing him without mercy. "I daresay he thinks
he has done a mighty thing. He won't stay till he gets home to his seat in
the country, to produce this wonderful deed: he'll call up the landlord of
the first inn on the road; and after a suitable preface upon mortality and
the uncertainty of life, will tell him that he should not delay in making his
will; and Here, Sir, will he say, is *my* will, which I have just made, with the
assistance of one of the ablest lawyers in the kingdom; and he will read it
to him. He believes he has made this will; but he did not make it; you,
Chambers, made it for him. I hope you have had more conscience than to
make him say 'being of sound understanding!' ha, ha, ha! I hope he has
left me a legacy. I'd have his will turned into verse, like a ballad." These
flights annoyed Mr. Chambers, and are recorded by Boswell with the apology that he wishes his readers to be "acquainted with the slightest occasional characteristics of so eminent a man." Certainly, there is nothing
ridiculous in the fact of a man making a will. But this is the measure of
Johnson's achievement. He had created gloriously much out of nothing at
all. There he sat, old and ailing and unencouraged by the company, but
soaring higher and higher in absurdity, more and more rejoicing, and still

soaring and rejoicing after he had gone out into the night with Boswell, till at last in Fleet Street his paroxysms were too much for him and he could no more. Echoes of that huge laughter come ringing down the ages. But is there also perhaps a note of sadness for us in them? Johnson's endless sociability came of his inherent melancholy: he could not bear to be alone; and his very mirth was but a mode of escape from the dark thoughts within him. Of these the thought of death was the most dreadful to him, and the most insistent. He was forever wondering how death would come to him, and how he would acquit himself in the extreme moment. A later but not less devoted Anglican, meditating on his own end, wrote in his diary that "to die in church appears to be a great euthanasia, but not," he quaintly and touchingly added, "at a time to disturb worshippers." Both the sentiment here expressed and the reservation drawn would have been as characteristic of Johnson as they were of Gladstone. But to die of laughter—this, too, seems to me a great euthanasia; and I think that for Johnson to have died thus, that night in Fleet Street, would have been a grand ending to "a life radically wretched." Well, he was destined to out-live another decade; and, selfishly, who can wish such a life as his, or such a Life as Boswell's, one jot shorter?

Strange, when you come to think of it, that of all the countless folk who have lived before our time on this planet not one is known in history or in legend as having died of laughter. Strange, too, that not to one of all the characters in romance has such an end been allotted. Has it ever struck you what a chance Shakespeare missed when he was finishing the Second Part of King Henry the Fourth? Falstaff was not the man to stand cowed and bowed while the new young king lectured him off. Little by little, as Hal proceeded in that portentous allocution, the humour of the situation would have mastered old Sir John. His face, blank with surprise at first, would presently have glowed and widened, and his whole bulk have be-gun to quiver. Lest he should miss one word, he would have mastered himself. But the final words would have been the signal for release of all the roars pent up in him; the welkin would have rung; the roars, belike, would have gradually subsided in dreadful rumblings of more than utter-able or conquerable mirth. Thus and thus only might his life have been rounded off with dramatic fitness, *secundum ipsius naturam.* He never should have been left to babble of green fields and die "an it had been any christom child."

Falstaff is a triumph of comedic creation because we are kept laughing equally at and with him. Nevertheless, if I had the choice of sitting with him at the Boar's Head or with Johnson at the Turk's, I shouldn't hesitate for an instant. The agility of Falstaff's mind gains much of its effect by contrast with the massiveness of his body; but in contrast with Johnson's equal agility is Johnson's moral as well as physical bulk. His sallies "tell" the more startlingly because of the noble weight of character behind them: they are the better because *he* makes them. In Falstaff there isn't this final incongruity and element of surprise. Falstaff is but a sublimated sample of "the funny man." We cannot therefore, laugh so greatly with him as with Johnson. (Nor even *at* him; because we are not tickled so much by the weak points of a character whose points are all weak ones; also because we have no reverence trying to impose restraint upon us.) Still, Falstaff has indubitably the power to convulse us. I don't mean we ever are convulsed in reading Henry the Fourth. No printed page, alas, can thrill us to extremities of laughter. These are ours only if the mirthmaker be a living man whose jests we hear as they come fresh from his own lips. All I claim for Falstaff is that he would be able to convulse us if he were alive and accessible. Few, as I have said, are the humourists who can induce this state. To master and dissolve us, to give us the joy of being worn down and tired out with laughter, is a success to be won by no man save in virtue of a rare staying-power. Laughter becomes extreme only if it be consecutive. There must be no pauses for recovery. Touch-and-go humour, however happy, is not enough. The jester must be able to grapple his theme and hang on to it, twisting it this way and that, and making it yield magically all manner of strange and precious things, one after another, without pause. He must have invention keeping pace with utterance. He must be inexhaustible. Only so can he exhaust us.

I have a friend whom I would praise. There are many other of my friends to whom I am indebted for much laughter; but I do believe that if all of them sent in their bills to-morrow and all of them overcharged me not a little, the total of all those totals would be less appalling than that which looms in my own vague estimate of what I owe to Comus. Comus I call him here in observance of the line drawn between public and private virtue, and in full knowledge that he would of all men be the least glad to be quite personally thanked and laurelled in the market-place for the hours he has made memorable among his cronies. No one is so diffident as he, no one so self-postponing. Many people have met him again and again without faintly suspecting "anything much" in him. Many of his acquaintances—friends, too—relatives, even—have lived and died in the belief that he was quite ordinary. Thus is he the more greatly valued by his cronies. Thus do we pride ourselves on possessing some curious right quality to which alone he is responsive. But it would seem that either this asset of ours or its effect on him is intermittent. He can be dull and null enough with us sometimes—a mere asker of questions, or drawer of comparisons between this and that brand of cigarettes, or full expatiator on the merits of some new patent razor. A whole hour and more may be wasted in such humdrum and darkness. And then—something will have happened. There has come a spark in the murk; a flame now, presage of a radiance: Comus has begun. His face is a great part of his equipment. A cast of it might be somewhat akin to the comic mask of the ancients; but no cast could be worthy of it; mobility is the essence of it. It flickers and shifts in accord to the matter of his discourse; it contracts and it expands; is there anything its elastic can't express? Comus would be eloquent even were he dumb. And he is mellifluous. His voice, while he develops an idea or conjures up a scene, takes on a peculiar richness and unction. If he be describing an actual scene, voice and face are adaptable to those of the actual persons therein. But it is not in such mimicry that he excels. As a reporter he has rivals. For the most part, he moves on a higher plane than that of mere fact: he imagines, he creates, giving you not a person, but a type, a synthesis, and not what anywhere has been, but what anywhere might be—what, as one feels, for all the absurdity of it, just would be. He knows his world well, and nothing human is alien to him, but certain skeins of life have a special hold on him, and he on them. In his youth he wished to be a clergyman; and over the clergy of all grades and denominations his genius hovers and swoops and ranges with a special mastery. Lawyers he loves less; yet the legal mind seems to lie almost as wide-open to him as the sacerdotal; and the legal manner in all its phases he can unerringly burlesque. In the minds of journalists, diverse journalists, he is not less thoroughly at home, so that of the wild contingencies imagined by him there is none about which he cannot reel off an oral "leader" or "middle" in the likeliest style, and with as much ease as he can preach a High Church or Low Church sermon on it. Nor are his improvisations limited by prose. If a theme call for nobler treatment, he becomes an unflagging fountain of ludicrously adequate blank-verse. Or again, he may deliver himself in rhyme. There is no form of utterance that comes amiss to him for interpreting the human comedy, or for broadening the farce into which that comedy is turned by him. Nothing can stop him when once he is in the vein. No appeals move him. He goes from strength to strength while his audience is more and more piteously debilitated.

What a gift to have been endowed with! What a power to wield! And how often I have envied Comus! But this envy of him has never taken root in me. His mind laughs, doubtless, at his own conceptions; but not his body. And if you tell him something that you have been sure will convulse him you are likely to be rewarded with no more than a smile betokening that he sees the point. Incomparable laughter-giver, he is not much a laugher. He is vintner, not toper. I would therefore not change places with him. I am well content to have been his beneficiary during thirty years, and to be so for as many more as may be given us.

G. K. CHESTERTON

and a delicious contrast with the next writer V. Woolf. But — is he too "smily" — or blin[d]

G. K. Chesterton (1874–1936) *was one of the most popular and prolific British authors of his time. A man of enormous energy, industry, and communicative good spirits, he wrote some ninety books, including celebrated essay collections such as* All Things Considered, Tremendous Trifles, Come to Think of It, *and* The Uses of Diversity.

Chesterton had an essentially religious perspective, even before he converted formally to Roman Catholicism in 1922. His Father Brown mystery novels, as well as his books Heretics *and* Orthodoxy, *took the attitude that there is nothing stuffy about being religious, that it is indeed the highest kind of sanity. He had a mental pull toward paradox, the mystery of medieval Christianity, and the romance of church ritual. His whimsical imagination seemed able to imbue even the gritty realities of the modern world with a magical and romantic aura, as is demonstrated in the two essays that follow. This fantasy element helps explain why Borges, for instance, was a great fan of Chesterton's work. Another reason was Chesterton's sparkling, conversational, punning style. He can be a forceful arguer, with his cheerfully coercive, "favorite uncle" manner, but even when—or especially when —he tries to make us swallow something that seems wrong-headed or propagandistic, we will go along for the fun of the ride.*

A Piece of Chalk

I REMEMBER one splendid morning, all blue and silver, in the summer holidays, when I reluctantly tore myself away from the task of doing nothing in particular, and put on a hat of some sort and picked up a walking-stick, and put six very bright-coloured chalks in my pocket. I then went into the kitchen (which, along with the rest of the house, belonged to a very square and sensible old woman in a Sussex village), and asked the owner and occupant of the kitchen if she had any brown paper. She had a great deal; in fact, she had too much; and she mistook the purpose and the rationale of the existence of brown paper. She seemed to have an idea that if a person wanted brown paper he must be wanting to tie up parcels; which was the last thing I wanted to do; indeed, it is a thing which I have found to be beyond my mental capacity. Hence she dwelt very much on the varying qualities of toughness and endurance in the material. I explained to her that I only wanted to draw pictures on it, and that I did not want them to endure in the least; and that from my point of view, therefore, it was a question not of tough consistency, but of responsive surface, a thing comparatively irrelevant in a parcel. When she understood that I wanted to draw she offered to overwhelm me with note-paper, apparently supposing that I did my notes and correspondence on old brown paper wrappers from motives of economy.

I then tried to explain the rather delicate logical shade, that I not only liked brown paper, but liked the quality of brownness in paper, just as I liked the quality of brownness in October woods, or in beer, or in the peat-streams of the North. Brown paper represents the primal twilight of the first toil of creation, and with a bright-coloured chalk or two you can pick out points of fire in it, sparks of gold, and blood-red, and sea-green, like the first fierce stars that sprang out of divine darkness. All this I said (in an off-hand way) to the old woman; and I put the brown paper in my pocket along with the chalks, and possibly other things. I suppose every one must have reflected how primeval and how poetical are the things that one carries in one's pocket; the pocket-knife, for instance, the type of all human tools, the infant of the sword. Once I planned to write a book of poems entirely about the things in my pocket. But I found it would be too long; and the age of the great epics is past.

* * *

With my stick and my knife, my chalks and my brown paper, I went out on to the great downs. I crawled across those colossal contours that express the best quality of England, because they are at the same time soft and strong. The smoothness of them has the same meaning as the smoothness of great cart-horses, or the smoothness of the beech-tree; it declares in the teeth of our timid and cruel theories that the mighty are merciful. As my eye swept the landscape, the landscape was as kindly as any of its cottages, but for power it was like an earthquake. The villages in the immense valley were safe, one could see, for centuries; yet the lifting of the whole land was like the lifting of one enormous wave to wash them all away.

I crossed one swell of living turf after another, looking for a place to sit down and draw. Do not, for heaven's sake, imagine I was going to sketch from Nature. I was going to draw devils and seraphim, and blind old gods that men worshipped before the dawn of right, and saints in robes of angry crimson, and seas of strange green, and all the sacred or monstrous symbols that look so well in bright colours on brown paper. They are much better worth drawing than Nature; also they are much easier to draw. When a cow came slouching by in the field next to me, a mere artist might have drawn it; but I always get wrong in the hind legs of quadrupeds. So I drew the soul of the cow; which I saw there plainly walking before me in the sunlight; and the soul was all purple and silver, and had seven horns and the mystery that belongs to all the beasts. But though I could not with a crayon get the best out of the landscape, it does not follow that the landscape was not getting the best out of me. And this, I think, is the mistake that people make about the old poets who lived before Wordsworth, and were supposed not to care very much about Nature because they did not describe it much.

They preferred writing about great men to writing about great hills; but they sat on the great hills to write it. They gave out much less about Nature, but they drank in, perhaps, much more. They painted the white robes of their holy virgins with the blinding snow, at which they had stared all day. They blazoned the shields of their paladins with the purple and gold of many heraldic sunsets. The greenness of a thousand green leaves clustered into the live green figure of Robin Hood. The blueness of a score of forgotten skies became the blue robes of the Virgin. The inspiration went in like sunbeams and came out like Apollo.

But as I sat scrawling these silly figures on the brown paper, it began to dawn on me, to my great disgust, that I had left one chalk, and that a most exquisite and essential chalk, behind. I searched all my pockets, but I could not find any white chalk. Now, those who are acquainted with all the philosophy (nay, religion) which is typified in the art of drawing on brown paper, know that white is positive and essential. I cannot avoid remarking here upon a moral significance. One of the wise and awful truths which this brown-paper art reveals, is that, that white is a colour. It is not a mere absence of colour; it is a shining and affirmative thing, as fierce as red, as definite as black. When (so to speak) your pencil grows red-hot, it draws roses; when it grows white-hot, it draws stars. And one of the two or three defiant verities of the best religious morality, of real Christianity for example, is exactly the same thing; the chief assertion of religious morality is that white is a colour. Virtue is not the absence of vices or the avoidance of moral dangers; virtue is a vivid and separate thing, like pain or a particular smell. Mercy does not mean not being cruel or sparing people revenge or punishment; it means a plain and positive thing like the sun, which one has either seen or not seen. Chastity does not mean abstention from sexual wrong; it means something flaming, like Joan of Arc. In a word, God paints in many colours; but He never paints so gorgeously, I had almost said so gaudily, as when He paints in white. In a sense our age has realized this fact, and expressed it in our sullen costume. For if it were really true that white was a blank and colourless thing, negative and non-committal, then white would be used instead of black and grey for the funeral dress of this pessimistic period. We should see city gentlemen in frock coats of spotless silver satin, with top hats as white as wonderful arum lilies. Which is not the case.

Meanwhile I could not find my chalk.

I sat on the hill in a sort of despair. There was no town nearer than Chichester at which it was even remotely probable that there would be such a thing as an artist's colourman. And yet, without white, my absurd little pictures would be as pointless as the world would be if there were no good people in it. I stared stupidly round, racking my brain for expedients. Then I suddenly stood up and roared with laughter, again and again, so that the cows stared at me and called a committee. Imagine a man in the Sahara regretting that he had no sand for his hourglass. Imagine a gentleman in mid-ocean wishing that he had brought some salt water with him for his chemical experiments. I was sitting on an immense warehouse of white chalk. The landscape was made entirely out of white chalk. White chalk was piled mere miles until it met the sky. I stooped and broke a piece off the rock I sat on: it did not mark so well as the shop chalks do; but it gave the effect. And I stood there in a trance of pleasure, realizing that this Southern England is not only a grand peninsula, and a tradition and a civilization; it is something even more admirable. It is a piece of chalk.

On Running After One's Hat

I FEEL an almost savage envy on hearing that London has been flooded in my absence, while I am in the mere country. My own Battersea has been, I understand, particularly favored as a meeting of the waters. Battersea was already, as I need hardly say, the most beautiful of human localities. Now that it has the additional splendor of great sheets of water, there must be something quite incomparable in the landscape (or waterscape) of my romantic town. Battersea must be a vision of Venice. The boat that brought the meat from the butcher's must have shot along those lanes of rippling silver with the strange smoothness of a gondola. The greengrocer who brought cabbages to the corner of the Latchmere Road must have leant upon the oar with the unearthly grace of the gondolier. There is nothing so perfectly poetical as an island; and when a district is flooded it becomes an archipelago.

Some consider such romantic views of flood or fire slightly lacking in reality. But really this romantic view of such inconveniences is quite as practical as the other. The true optimist who sees in such things an opportunity for enjoyment is quite as logical and much more sensible than the ordinary "indignant Ratepayer" who sees in them an opportunity for grumbling. Real pain, as in the case of being burnt at Smithfield or having a toothache, is a positive thing; it can be supported, but scarcely enjoyed. But, after all, our toothaches are the exception, and as for being burnt at Smithfield, it only happens to us at the very longest intervals. And most of the inconveniences that make men swear or women cry are really sentimental or imaginative inconveniences—things altogether of the mind. For instance, we often hear grown-up people complaining of having to hang about a railway station and wait for a train? Did you ever hear a small boy complain of having to hang about a railway station and wait for a train? No; for to him to be inside a railway station is to be inside a cavern of wonder and a palace of poetical pleasures. Because to him the red light and the green light on the signal are like a new sun and new moon. Because to him when the wooden arm of the signal falls down suddenly, it is as if a great king had thrown down his staff as a signal and started a shrieking tournament of trains. I myself am of little boys' habit in this matter. They also serve who only stand and wait for the two-fifteen. Their meditations may be full of rich and fruitful things. Many of the most purple hours of my life have been passed at Clapham Junction, which is now, I suppose, under water. I have been there in many moods so fixed and mystical that the water might well have come up to my waist before I noticed it particularly. But, in the case of all such annoyances, as I have said, everything depends upon the emotional point of view. You can safely apply the test to almost every one of the things that are currently talked of as the typical nuisances of daily life.

For instance, there is a current impression that it is unpleasant to have to run after one's hat. Why should it be unpleasant to the well-ordered and pious mind? Not merely because it is running, and running exhausts one. The same people run much faster in games and sports. The same people run much more eagerly after an uninteresting little leather ball than they will after a nice silk hat. There is an idea that it is humiliating to run after one's hat; and when people say it is humiliating they mean that it is comic. It certainly is comic; but man is a very comic creature, and most of the things he does are comic—eating, for instance. And the most comic things of all are exactly the things that are most worth doing—such as making love. A man running after a hat is not half so ridiculous as a man running after a wife.

Now a man could, if he felt rightly in the matter, run after his hat with the manliest ardor and the most sacred joy. He might regard himself as a jolly huntsman pursuing a wild animal, for certainly no animal could be wilder. In fact, I am inclined to believe that hat-hunting on windy days will be the sport of the upper classes in the future. There will be a meet of ladies and gentlemen on some high ground on a gusty morning. They will be told that the professional attendants have started a hat in such-and-such a thicket, or whatever be the technical term. Notice that this employment will in the fullest degree combine sport with humanitarianism. The hunters would feel that they were not inflicting pain. Nay, they would feel that they were inflicting pleasure, rich, almost riotous pleasure, upon the people who were looking on. When last I saw an old gentleman running after his hat in Hyde Park, I told him that a heart so benevolent as his ought to be filled with peace and thanks at the thought of how much unaffected pleasure his every gesture and bodily attitude were at that moment giving to the crowd.

The same principle can be applied to every other typical domestic worry. A gentleman trying to get a fly out of the milk or a piece of cork out of his glass of wine often imagines himself to be irritated. Let him think for a moment of the patience of anglers sitting by dark pools, and let his soul be immediately irradiated with gratification and repose. Again, I have known some people of very modern views driven by their distress to the use of theological terms to which they attached no doctrinal significance, merely because a drawer was jammed tight and they could not pull it out. A friend of mine was particularly afflicted in this way. Every day his drawer was jammed, and every day in consequence it was something else that rhymes to it. But I pointed out to him that this sense of wrong was really subjective and relative; it rested entirely upon the assumption that the drawer could, should, and would come out easily. "But if," I said, "you picture to yourself that you are pulling against some powerful and oppressive enemy, the struggle will become merely exciting and not exasperating. Imagine that you are roping up a fellow creature out of an Alpine crevasse. Imagine even that you are a boy again and engaged in a tug-of-war between French and English." Shortly after saying this I left him; but I have no doubt at all that my words bore the best possible fruit. I have no doubt that every day of his life he hangs on to the handle of that drawer with a flushed face and eyes bright with battle, uttering encouraging shouts to himself, and seeming to hear all round him that roar of an applauding ring.

So I do not think it altogether fanciful or incredible to suppose that even the floods in London may be accepted and enjoyed poetically. Nothing beyond inconvenience seems really to have been caused by them; and inconvenience, as I have said, in only one aspect, and that the most unimaginative and accidental aspect of a really romantic situation. An adventure is only an inconvenience rightly considered. An inconvenience is only an adventure wrongly considered. The water that girdled the houses and shops of London must, if anything, have only increased their previous witchery and wonder. For as the Roman Catholic priest in the story said: "Wine is good with everything except water," and on a similar principle, water is good with everything except wine.

I find her savoring her depression beyond tedious.

defined how?

VIRGINIA WOOLF

Virginia Woolf (1882–1941) was one of the pioneers of modern fiction. She grew up in an intellectual climate, as the daughter of Leslie Stephen, a well-known man of letters, and was educated at home. Her mother died when Virginia was still a child—the first of many family deaths that would contribute to her lifelong melancholia and bouts of mental illness. She married another writer, Leonard Woolf, and they set up the Hogarth Press, which published new writing. They also drew around themselves a glittering company of London artists, writers, and intellectuals known as the Bloomsbury group, among them Lytton Strachey, E. M. Forster, John Maynard Keynes, Vita Sackville-West, Roger Fry, and Clive Bell.

Woolf, inspired by Dostoevsky and convinced that the realist novel dwelled too much on surface detail and did not capture the "myriad impressions" to which the mind was exposed, developed her own stream-of-consciousness technique in novels such as To the Lighthouse, Mrs. Dalloway, _and_ The Waves, _which plumbed the shifting consciousness and inner states of her characters. At the same time she was a prolific, important essayist, writing hundreds of book reviews and literary essays, the best of which were collected in her_ Common Reader. _In her literary criticism, Woolf worked out the theories and preferences that she employed in her fiction. She was also attracted to the mental freedom of the essay in and of itself, and wrote sympathetic appreciations of Montaigne, Hazlitt, and Addison._

Some of Woolf's most remarkable essay work was contained in book-length, extended meditations: A Room of One's Own (_an essential text for the women's movement_), Three Guineas, _and the achingly lovely, personal, unfinished memoir "A Sketch of the Past," in_ Moments of Being. _She also wrote a number of superb shorter personal essays, such as the two below,_

"Street Haunting" and "The Death of the Moth." Both show <u>her character-</u> *<u>istic movement toward reverie as well as her penchant for shifting angles</u>* *<u>of vision</u>. "Street Haunting," with its mobile, rhapsodic eye, exempli-* *fies Woolf's technique of darting, quicksilver leaps into different characters'* *consciousness. "The Death of the Moth," in contrast, is a still life, a* na-*ture morte.*

A writer fascinated with the boundary between life and death, whose aim *was to capture "a very vivid idea" of any subject, Virginia Woolf chose to* *drown herself rather than go on being incapacitated by severe depression.*

how self indulgent.

Street Haunting

A L O N D O N A D V E N T U R E

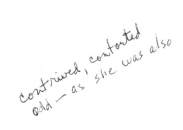

contrived, contorted *odd — as she was also*

N O O N E perhaps has ever felt passionately towards a lead pencil. But there are circumstances in which it can become supremely de-sirable to possess one; moments when we are set upon having an object, an excuse for walking half across London between tea and dinner. As the foxhunter hunts in order to preserve the breed of foxes, and the golfer plays in order that open spaces may be preserved from the builders, so when the desire comes upon us to go street rambling a pencil does for a pretext, and getting up we say: "Really I must buy a pencil," as if under cover of this excuse we could indulge safely in the greatest pleasure of town life in winter—rambling the streets of London.

The hour should be the evening and the season winter, for in winter the champagne brightness of the air and the sociability of the streets are grate-ful. We are not then taunted as in the summer by the longing for shade and solitude and sweet airs from the hayfields. The evening hour, too, gives us the irresponsibility which darkness and lamplight bestow. We are no longer quite ourselves. As we step out of the house on a fine evening between four and six, we shed the self our friends know us by and become part of that vast republican army of anonymous trampers, whose society is so agreeable after the solitude of one's own room. For there we sit sur-rounded by objects which perpetually express the oddity of our own tem-peraments and enforce the memories of our own experience. That bowl on the mantelpiece, for instance, was bought at Mantua on a windy day.

We were leaving the shop when the sinister old woman plucked at our skirts and said she would find herself starving one of these days, but, "Take it!" she cried, and thrust the blue and white china bowl into our hands as if she never wanted to be reminded of her quixotic generosity. So, guiltily, but suspecting nevertheless how badly we had been fleeced, we carried it back to the little hotel where, in the middle of the night, the innkeeper quarrelled so violently with his wife that we all leant out into the courtyard to look, and saw the vines laced about among the pillars and the stars white in the sky. The moment was stabilized, stamped like a coin indelibly among a million that slipped by imperceptibly. There, too, was the melancholy Englishman, who rose among the coffee cups and the little iron tables and revealed the secrets of his soul—as travellers do. All this— Italy, the windy morning, the vines laced about the pillars, the Englishman and the secrets of his soul—rise up in a cloud from the china bowl on the mantelpiece. And there, as our eyes fall to the floor, is that brown stain on the carpet. Mr. Lloyd George made that. "The man's a devil!" said Mr. Cummings, putting the kettle down with which he was about to fill the teapot so that it burnt a brown ring on the carpet.

But when the door shuts on us, all that vanishes. The shell-like covering which our souls have excreted to house themselves, to make for themselves a shape distinct from others, is broken, and there is left of all these wrinkles and roughnesses a central oyster of perceptiveness, an enormous eye. How beautiful a street is in winter! It is at once revealed and obscured. Here vaguely one can trace symmetrical straight avenues of doors and windows; here under the lamps are floating islands of pale light through which pass quickly bright men and women, who, for all their poverty and shabbiness, wear a certain look of unreality, an air of triumph, as if they had given life the slip, so that life, deceived of her prey, blunders on without them. But, after all, we are only gliding smoothly on the surface. The eye is not a miner, not a diver, not a seeker after buried treasure. It floats us smoothly down a stream; resting, pausing, the brain sleeps perhaps as it looks.

How beautiful a London street is then, with its islands of light, and its long groves of darkness, and on one side of it perhaps some tree-sprinkled, grass-grown space where night is folding herself to sleep naturally and, as one passes the iron railing, one hears those little cracklings and stirrings of leaf and twig which seem to suppose the silence of fields all round them, an owl hooting, and far away the rattle of a train in the valley. But this is London, we are reminded; high among the bare trees are hung oblong frames of reddish yellow light—windows; there are points of brilliance burning steadily like low stars—lamps; this empty ground, which holds the country in it and its peace, is only a London square, set about by offices and houses where at this hour fierce lights burn over maps, over documents, over desks where clerks sit turning with wetted forefinger the files of endless correspondences; or more suffusedly the firelight wavers and the lamplight falls upon the privacy of some drawing-room, its easy chairs, its papers, its china, its inlaid table, and the figure of a woman, accurately measuring out the precise number of spoons of tea which— She looks at the door as if she heard a ring downstairs and somebody asking, is she in?

But here we must stop peremptorily. We are in danger of digging deeper than the eye approves; we are impeding our passage down the smooth stream by catching at some branch or root. At any moment, the sleeping army may stir itself and wake in us a thousand violins and trumpets in response; the army of human beings may rouse itself and assert all its oddities and sufferings and sordidities. Let us dally a little longer, be content still with surfaces only—the glossy brilliance of the motor omnibuses; the carnal splendour of the butchers' shops with their yellow flanks and purple steaks; the blue and red bunches of flowers burning so bravely through the plate glass of the florists' windows.

For the eye has this strange property: it rests only on beauty; like a butterfly it seeks colour and basks in warmth. On a winter's night like this, when nature has been at pains to polish and preen herself, it brings back the prettiest trophies, breaks off little lumps of emerald and coral as if the whole earth were made of precious stone. The thing it cannot do (one is speaking of the average unprofessional eye) is to compose these trophies in such a way as to bring out the more obscure angles and relationships. Hence after a prolonged diet of this simple, sugary fare, of beauty pure and uncomposed, we become conscious of satiety. We halt at the door of the boot shop and make some little excuse, which has nothing to do with the real reason, for folding up the bright paraphernalia of the streets and withdrawing to some duskier chamber of the being where we may ask, as we raise our left foot obediently upon the stand: "What, then, is it like to be a dwarf?"

She came in escorted by two women who, being of normal size, looked like benevolent giants beside her. Smiling at the shop girls, they seemed to be disclaiming any lot in her deformity and assuring her of their protection. She wore the peevish yet apologetic expression usual on the faces of the deformed. She needed their kindness, yet she resented it. But when the shop girl had been summoned and the giantesses, smiling indulgently, had asked for shoes for "this lady" and the girl had pushed the little stand in front of her, the dwarf stuck her foot out with an impetuosity which seemed to claim all our attention. Look at that! Look at that! she seemed to demand of us all, as she thrust her foot out, for behold it was the shapely, perfectly proportioned foot of a well-grown woman. It was arched; it was aristocratic. Her whole manner changed as she looked at it resting on the stand. She looked soothed and satisfied. Her manner became full of self-confidence. She sent for shoe after shoe; she tried on pair after pair. She got up and pirouetted before a glass which reflected the foot only in yellow shoes, in fawn shoes, in shoes of lizard skin. She raised her little skirts and displayed her little legs. She was thinking that, after all, feet are the most important part of the whole person; women, she said to herself, have been loved for their feet alone. Seeing nothing but her feet, she imagined perhaps that the rest of her body was of a piece with those beautiful feet. She was shabbily dressed, but she was ready to lavish any money upon her shoes. And as this was the only occasion upon which she was not afraid of being looked at but positively craved attention, she was ready to use any device to prolong the choosing and fitting. Look at my feet, she seemed to be saying, as she took a step this way and then a step that way. The shop girl good-humouredly must have said something flattering, for suddenly her face lit up in ecstasy. But, after all, the giantesses, benevolent though they were, had their own affairs to see to; she must make up her mind; she must decide which to choose. At length, the pair was chosen and, as she walked out between her guardians, with the parcel swinging from her finger, the ecstasy faded, knowledge returned, the old peevishness, the old apology came back, and by the time she had reached the street again she had become a dwarf only.

But she had changed the mood; she had called into being an atmosphere which, as we followed her out into the street, seemed actually to create the humped, the twisted, the deformed. Two bearded men, brothers, apparently, stone-blind, supporting themselves by resting a hand on the head of a small boy between them, marched down the street. On they came with the unyielding yet tremulous tread of the blind, which seems to lend to their approach something of the terror and inevitability of the fate that has overtaken them. As they passed, holding straight on, the little convoy seemed to cleave asunder the passers-by with the momentum of its silence, its directness, its disaster. Indeed, the dwarf had started a hobbling grotesque dance to which everybody in the street now conformed: the stout lady tightly swathed in shiny sealskin; the feeble-minded boy sucking the silver knob of his stick; the old man squatted on a doorstep as if, suddenly overcome by the absurdity of the human spectacle, he had sat down to look at it—all joined in the hobble and tap of the dwarf's dance.

In what crevices and crannies, one might ask, did they lodge, this maimed company of the halt and the blind? Here, perhaps, in the top rooms of these narrow old houses between Holborn and Soho, where people have such queer names, and pursue so many curious trades, are gold beaters, accordion pleaters, cover buttons, or support life, with even great fantasticality, upon a traffic in cups without saucers, china umbrella handles, and highly-coloured pictures of martyred saints. There they lodge, and it seems as if the lady in the sealskin jacket must find life tolerable, passing the time of day with the accordion pleater, or the man who covers buttons; life which is so fantastic cannot be altogether tragic. They do not grudge us, we are musing, our prosperity; when, suddenly, turning the corner, we come upon a bearded Jew, wild, hunger-bitten, glaring out of his misery; or pass the humped body of an old woman flung abandoned on the step of a public building with a cloak over her like the hasty covering thrown over a dead horse or donkey. At such sights the nerves of the spine seem to stand erect; a sudden flare is brandished in our eyes; a question is asked which is never answered. Often enough these derelicts choose to lie not a stone's throw from theatres, within hearing of barrel organs, almost, as night draws on, within touch of the sequined cloaks and bright legs of diners and dancers. They lie close to those shop windows where commerce offers to a world of old women laid on door-steps, of blind men, of hobbling dwarfs, sofas which are supported by the gilt necks of proud swans; tables inlaid with baskets of many coloured fruit; sideboards paved with green marble the better to support the weight of boars' heads; and carpets so softened with age that their carnations have almost vanished in a pale green sea.

Passing, glimpsing, everything seems accidentally but miraculously sprinkled with beauty, as if the tide of trade which deposits its burden so punctually and prosaically upon the shores of Oxford Street had this night cast up nothing but treasure. With no thought of buying, the eye is sportive and generous; it creates; it adorns; it enhances. Standing out in the street, one may build up all the chambers of an imaginary house and furnish them at one's will with sofa, table, carpet. That rug will do for the hall. That alabaster bowl shall stand on a carved table in the window. Our merrymaking shall be reflected in that thick round mirror. But, having built and furnished the house, one is happily under no obligation to possess it; one can dismantle it in the twinkling of an eye, and build and furnish another house with other chairs and other glasses. Or let us indulge ourselves at the antique jewellers, among the trays of rings and the hanging necklaces. Let us choose those pearls, for example, and then imagine how, if we put them on, life would be changed. It becomes instantly between two and three in the morning; the lamps are burning very white in the deserted streets of Mayfair. Only motor-cars are abroad at this hour, and one has a sense of emptiness, of airiness, of secluded gaiety. Wearing pearls, wearing silk, one steps out on to a balcony which overlooks the gardens of sleeping Mayfair. There are a few lights in the bedrooms of great peers returned from Court, of silk-stockinged footmen, of dowagers who have pressed the hands of statesmen. A cat creeps along the garden wall. Love-making is going on sibilantly, seductively in the darker places of the room behind thick green curtains. Strolling sedately as if he were promenading a terrace beneath which the shires and counties of England lie sun-bathed, the aged Prime Minister recounts to Lady So-and-So with the curls and the emeralds the true history of some great crisis in the affairs of the land. We seem to be riding on the top of the highest mast of the tallest ship; and yet at the same time we know that nothing of this sort matters; love is not proved thus, nor great achievements completed thus; so that we sport with the moment and preen our feathers in it lightly, as we stand on the balcony watching the moonlit cat creep along Princess Mary's garden wall.

But what could be more absurd? It is, in fact, on the stroke of six; it is a winter's evening; we are walking to the Strand to buy a pencil. How, then, are we also on a balcony, wearing pearls in June? What could be more absurd? Yet it is nature's folly, not ours. When she set about her chief masterpiece, the making of man, she should have thought of one thing only. Instead, turning her head, looking over her shoulder, into each one of us she let creep instincts and desires which are utterly at variance with his main being, so that we are streaked, variegated, all of a mixture; the colours have run. Is the true self this which stands on the pavement in January, or that which bends over the balcony in June? Am I here, or am I there? Or is the true self neither this nor that, neither here nor there, but something so varied and wandering that it is only when we give the rein to its wishes and let it take its way unimpeded that we are indeed ourselves? Circumstances compel unity; for convenience' sake a man must be a whole. The good citizen when he opens his door in the evening must be banker, golfer, husband, father; not a nomad wandering the desert, a mystic staring at the sky, a debauchee in the slums of San Francisco, a soldier heading a revolution, a pariah howling with scepticism and solitude. When he opens his door, he must run his fingers through his hair and put his umbrella in the stand like the rest.

But here, none too soon, are the second-hand bookshops. Here we find anchorage in these thwarting currents of being; here we balance ourselves after the splendours and miseries of the streets. The very sight of the bookseller's wife with her foot on the fender, sitting beside a good coal fire, screened from the door, is sobering and cheerful. She is never reading, or only the newspaper; her talk, when it leaves bookselling, which it does so gladly, is about hats; she likes a hat to be practical, she says, as well as pretty. O no, they don't live at the shop; they live in Brixton; she must have a bit of green to look at. In summer a jar of flowers grown in her own garden is stood on the top of some dusty pile to enliven the shop. Books are everywhere; and always the same sense of adventure fills us. Second-hand books are wild books, homeless books; they have come together in vast flocks of variegated feather, and have a charm which the domesticated volumes of the library lack. Besides, in this random miscellaneous company we may rub against some complete stranger who will, with luck, turn into the best friend we have in the world. There is always a hope, as we reach down some greyish-white book from an upper shelf, directed by its air of shabbiness and desertion, of meeting here with a man who set out on horseback over a hundred years ago to explore the woollen market in the Midlands and Wales; an unknown traveller, who stayed at inns, drank his pint, noted pretty girls and serious customs, wrote it all down stiffly, laboriously for sheer love of it (the book was published at his own expense); was infinitely prosy, busy, and matter-of-fact, and so let flow in without his knowing it the very scent of hollyhocks and the hay together with such a portrait of himself as gives him forever a seat in the warm corner of the mind's inglenook. One may buy him for eighteen pence now. He is marked three and sixpence, but the bookseller's wife, seeing how shabby the covers are and how long the book has stood there since it was bought at some sale of a gentleman's library in Suffolk, will let it go at that.

Thus, glancing round the bookshop, we make other such sudden capricious friendships with the unknown and the vanished whose only record is, for example, this little book of poems, so fairly printed, so finely engraved, too, with a portrait of the author. For he was a poet and drowned untimely, and his verse, mild as it is and formal and sententious, sends forth still a frail fluty sound like that of a piano organ played in some back street resignedly by an old Italian organ-grinder in a corduroy jacket. There are travellers, too, row upon row of them, still testifying, indomitable spinsters that they were, to the discomforts that they endured and the sunsets they admired in Greece when Queen Victoria was a girl. A tour in Cornwall with a visit to the tin mines was thought worthy of voluminous record. People went slowly up the Rhine and did portraits of each other in Indian ink, sitting reading on deck beside a coil of rope; they measured the pyramids; were lost to civilization for years; converted Negroes in pestilential swamps. This packing up and going off, exploring deserts and catching fevers, settling in India for a lifetime, penetrating even to China and then returning to lead a parochial life at Edmonton, tumbles and tosses upon the dusty floor like an uneasy sea, so restless the English are, with the waves at their very door. The waters of travel and adventure seem to break upon little islands of serious effort and lifelong industry stood in jagged column upon the floor. In these piles of puce-bound volumes with gilt monograms on the back, thoughtful clergymen expound the gospels; scholars are to be heard with their hammers and their chisels chipping clear the ancient texts of Euripides and Aeschylus. Thinking, annotating, expounding goes on at a prodigious rate all around us and over everything, like a punctual, everlasting tide, washes the ancient sea of fiction. Innumerable volumes tell how Arthur loved Laura and they were sepa-

rated and they were unhappy and then they met and they were happy ever
after, as was the way when Victoria ruled these islands.

The number of books in the world is infinite, and one is forced to
glimpse and nod and move on after a moment of talk, a flash of understanding, as, in the street outside, one catches a word in passing and from
a chance phrase fabricates a lifetime. It is about a woman called Kate that
they are talking, how "I said to her quite straight last night . . . if you
don't think I'm worth a penny stamp, I said . . ." But who Kate is, and
to what crisis in their friendship that penny stamp refers, we shall never
know; for Kate sinks under the warmth of their volubility; and here, at the
street corner, another page of the volume of life is laid open by the sight
of two men consulting under the lamppost. They are spelling out the latest
wire from Newmarket in the stop press news. Do they think, then, that
fortune will ever convert their rags into fur and broadcloth, sling them
with watch-chains, and plant diamond pins where there is now a ragged
open shirt? But the main stream of walkers at this hour sweeps too fast to
let us ask such questions. They are wrapt, in this short passage from work
to home, in some narcotic dream, now that they are free from the desk,
and have the fresh air on their cheeks. They put on those bright clothes
which they must hang up and lock the key upon all the rest of the day,
and are great cricketers, famous actresses, soldiers who have saved their
country at the hour of need. Dreaming, gesticulating, often muttering a
few words aloud, they sweep over the Strand and across Waterloo Bridge
whence they will be slung in long rattling trains, to some prim little villa in
Barnes or Surbiton where the sight of the clock in the hall and the smell of
the supper in the basement puncture the dream.

But we are come to the Strand now, and as we hesitate on the curb, a
little rod about the length of one's finger begins to lay its bar across the
velocity and abundance of life. "Really I must—really I must"—that is it.
Without investigating the demand, the mind cringes to the accustomed
tyrant. One must, one always must, do something or other; it is not allowed one simply to enjoy oneself. Was it not for this reason that, some
time ago, we fabricated the excuse, and invented the necessity of buying
something? But what was it? Ah, we remember, it was a pencil. Let us go
then and buy this pencil. But just as we are turning to obey the command,
another self disputes the right of the tyrant to insist. The usual conflict
comes about. Spread out behind the rod of duty we see the whole breadth
of the river Thames—wide, mournful, peaceful. And we see it through the
eyes of somebody who is leaning over the Embankment on a summer
evening, without a care in the world. Let us put off buying the pencil; let
us go in search of this person—and soon it becomes apparent that this
person is ourselves. For if we could stand there where we stood six
months ago, should we not be again as we were then—calm, aloof, con-

tent? Let us try then. But the river is rougher and greyer than we remembered. The tide is running out to sea. It brings down with it a tug and two barges, whose load of straw is tightly bound down beneath tarpaulin covers. There is, too, close by us, a couple leaning over the balustrade with the curious lack of self-consciousness lovers have, as if the importance of the affair they are engaged on claims without question the indulgence of the human race. The sights we see and the sounds we hear now have none of the quality of the past; nor have we any share in the serenity of the person who, six months ago, stood precisely where we stand now. His is the happiness of death; ours the insecurity of life. He has no future; the future is even now invading our peace. It is only when we look at the past and take from it the element of uncertainty that we can enjoy perfect peace. As it is, we must turn, we must cross the Strand again, we must find a shop where, even at this hour, they will be ready to sell us a pencil.

It is always an adventure to enter a new room; for the lives and characters of its owners have distilled their atmosphere into it, and directly we enter it we breast some new wave of emotion. Here, without a doubt, in the stationer's shop people had been quarrelling. Their anger shot through the air. They both stopped; the old woman—they were husband and wife evidently—retired to a back room; the old man whose rounded forehead and globular eyes would have looked well on the frontispiece of some Elizabethan folio, stayed to serve us. "A pencil, a pencil," he repeated, "certainly, certainly." He spoke with the distraction yet effusiveness of one whose emotions have been roused and checked in full flood. He began opening box after box and shutting them again. He said that it was very difficult to find things when they kept so many different articles. He launched into a story about some legal gentleman who had got into deep waters owing to the conduct of his wife. He had known him for years; he had been connected with the Temple for half a century, he said, as if he wished his wife in the back room to overhear him. He upset a box of rubber bands. At last, exasperated by his incompetence, he pushed the swing door open and called out roughly: "Where d'you keep the pencils?" as if his wife had hidden them. The old lady came in. Looking at nobody, she put her hand with a fine air of righteous severity upon the right box. There were pencils. How then could he do without her? Was she not indispensable to him? In order to keep them there, standing side by side in forced neutrality, one had to be particular in one's choice of pencils; this was too soft, that too hard. They stood silently looking on. The longer they stood there, the calmer they grew; their heat was going down, their anger disappearing. Now, without a word said on either side, the quarrel was made up. The old man, who would not have disgraced Ben Jonson's title-page, reached the box back to its proper place, bowed profoundly his good-night to us, and they disappeared. She would get out her sewing; he would read his newspaper; the canary would scatter them impartially with seed. The quarrel was over.

In these minutes in which a ghost has been sought for, a quarrel composed, and a pencil bought, the streets had become completely empty. Life had withdrawn to the top floor, and lamps were lit. The pavement was dry and hard; the road was of hammered silver. Walking home through the desolation one could tell oneself the story of the dwarf, of the blind men, of the party in the Mayfair mansion, of the quarrel in the stationer's shop. Into each of these lives one could penetrate a little way, far enough to give oneself the illusion that one is not tethered to a single mind, but can put on briefly for a few minutes the bodies and minds of others. One could become a washerwoman, a publican, a street singer. And what greater delight and wonder can there be than to leave the straight lines of personality and deviate into those footpaths that lead beneath brambles and thick tree trunks into the heart of the forest where live those wild beasts, our fellow men?

That is true: to escape is the greatest of pleasures; street haunting in winter the greatest of adventures. Still as we approach our own doorstep again, it is comforting to feel the old possessions, the old prejudices, fold us round; and the self, which has been blown about at so many street corners, which has battered like a moth at the flame of so many inaccessible lanterns, sheltered and enclosed. Here again is the usual door; here the chair turned as we left it and the china bowl and the brown ring on the carpet. And here—let us examine it tenderly, let us touch it with reverence—is the only spoil we have retrieved from all the treasures of the city, a lead pencil.

The Death of the Moth (or, hers ?)

MOTHS THAT FLY BY DAY are not properly to be called moths; they do not excite that pleasant sense of dark autumn nights and ivy-blossom which the commonest yellow-underwing asleep in the shadow of the curtain never fails to rouse in us. They are hybrid creatures, neither gay like butterflies nor sombre like their own species.

Nevertheless the present specimen, with his narrow hay-coloured wings, fringed with a tassel of the same colour, seemed to be content with life. It was a pleasant morning, mid-September, mild, benignant, yet with a keener breath than that of the summer months. The plough was already scoring the field opposite the window, and where the share had been, the earth was pressed flat and gleamed with moisture. Such vigour came rolling in from the fields and the down beyond that it was difficult to keep the eyes strictly turned upon the book. The rooks too were keeping one of their annual festivities; soaring round the tree tops until it looked as if a vast net with thousands of black knots in it had been cast up into the air; which, after a few moments sank slowly down upon the trees until every twig seemed to have a knot at the end of it. Then, suddenly, the net would be thrown into the air again in a wider circle this time, with the utmost clamour and vociferation, as though to be thrown into the air and settle slowly down upon the tree tops were a tremendously exciting experience.

The same energy which inspired the rooks, the ploughmen, the horses, and even, it seemed, the lean bare-backed downs, sent the moth fluttering from side to side of his square of the window-pane. One could not help watching him. One was, indeed, conscious of a queer feeling of pity for him. The possibilities of pleasure seemed that morning so enormous and so various that to have only a moth's part in life, and a day moth's at that, appeared a hard fate, and his zest in enjoying his meagre opportunities to the full, pathetic. He flew vigorously to one corner of his compartment, and, after waiting there a second, flew across to the other. What remained for him but to fly to a third corner and then to a fourth? That was all he could do, in spite of the size of the downs, the width of the sky, the far-off smoke of houses, and the romantic voice, now and then, of a steamer out at sea. What he could do he did. Watching him, it seemed as if a fibre, very thin but pure, of the enormous energy of the world had been thrust into his frail and diminutive body. As often as he crossed the pane, I could fancy that a thread of vital light became visible. He was little or nothing but life.

Yet, because he was so small, and so simple a form of the energy that was rolling in at the open window and driving its way through so many narrow and intricate corridors in my own brain and in those of other human beings, there was something marvellous as well as pathetic about him. It was as if someone had taken a tiny bead of pure life and decking it as lightly as possible with down and feathers, had set it dancing and zig-zagging to show us the true nature of life. Thus displayed one could not get over the strangeness of it. One is apt to forget all about life, seeing it humped and bossed and garnished and cumbered so that it has to move with the greatest circumspection and dignity. Again, the thought of all that life might have been had he been born in any other shape caused one to view his simple activities with a kind of pity.

After a time, tired by his dancing apparently, he settled on the window ledge in the sun, and, the queer spectacle being at an end, I forgot about him. Then, looking up, my eye was caught by him. He was trying to resume his dancing, but seemed either so stiff or so awkward that he could only flutter to the bottom of the window-pane; and when he tried to fly across it he failed. Being intent on other matters I watched these futile attempts for a time without thinking, unconsciously waiting for him to resume his flight, as one waits for a machine, that has stopped momentarily, to start again without considering the reason of its failure. After perhaps a seventh attempt he slipped from the wooden ledge and fell, fluttering his wings, on to his back on the window sill. The helplessness of his attitude roused me. It flashed upon me that he was in difficulties; he could no longer raise himself; his legs struggled vainly. But, as I stretched out a pencil, meaning to help him to right himself, it came over me that the failure and awkwardness were the approach of death. I laid the pencil down again.

The legs agitated themselves once more. I looked as if for the enemy against which he struggled. I looked out of doors. What had happened there? Presumably it was mid-day, and work in the fields had stopped. Stillness and quiet had replaced the previous animation. The birds had taken themselves off to feed in the brooks. The horses stood still. Yet the power was there all the same, massed outside indifferent, impersonal, not attending to anything in particular. Somehow it was opposed to the little hay-coloured moth. It was useless to try to do anything. One could only watch the extraordinary efforts made by those tiny legs against an oncoming doom which could, had it chosen, have submerged an entire city, not merely a city, but masses of human beings; nothing, I knew had any chance against death. Nevertheless after a pause of exhaustion the legs fluttered again. It was superb this last protest, and so frantic that he succeeded at last in righting himself. One's sympathies, of course, were all on the side of life. Also, when there was nobody to care or to know, this gigantic effort on the part of an insignificant little moth, against a power of such magnitude, to retain what no one else valued or desired to keep, moved one strangely. Again, somehow, one saw life, a pure bead. I lifted the pencil again, useless though I knew it to be. But even as I did so, the unmistakable tokens of death showed themselves. The body relaxed, and instantly grew stiff. The struggle was over. The insignificant little creature now knew death. As I looked at the dead moth, this minute wayside triumph of so great a force over so mean an antagonist filled me with wonder. Just as life had been strange a few minutes before, so death was now as strange. The moth having righted himself now lay most decently and uncomplainingly composed. O yes, he seemed to say, death is stronger than I am.

GEORGE ORWELL

*Eric Blair (1903–1950), who used the pen name George Orwell, was born in India, where his father was a British civil servant. His family returned to England and sent him to a series of boarding schools (as described unforgettably in "Such, Such Were the Joys . . ."). He spent several years in Burma as a military policeman, after which he became so disgusted with imperialism and the class system that he renounced his former life and sought to remake himself, both as a writer and as a champion of the oppressed underdog. Whatever Orwell wrote about he made himself experience firsthand, courageously putting himself on the front line: he tasted poverty and the Depression (*Down and Out in Paris and London, The Road to Wigan Pier*), the fascist threat, and the Spanish Civil War (*Homage to Catalonia*). Orwell saw the 1930s as a period of historical crisis, to which writers were obligated to respond politically. His own politics included a humanist commitment to freedom and democratic socialism and a skepticism bordering on revulsion against most organized political groups, particularly those with a totalitarian bent. His strong anticommunist feelings were expressed in novels such as* Animal Farm *and* 1984, *while his distaste for cant and propagandistic deception is evident in his famous essay "Politics and the English Language."*

Orwell's essays, in their seeming transparency and plainspokenness, are among the most influential models of nonfiction prose in the modern era. Because his essay style sounds so persuasively natural in its clarity, simplicity, frankness, and directness, we sometimes forget the degree to which it is an artistic construction. Just as George Orwell was a made-up name, so the Orwell we feel so familiar with in the pages of his nonfiction—the honest observer, whose espousal of conscience and common decency is mediated by his own candid ambivalences—was to some extent a literary character (indeed, a more well-rounded character than any in his novels.) It is significant that Orwell, famous for his honesty, still needed to employ myth and mask; only in this way, perhaps, could he accommodate the "conscious double vision," as Raymond Williams put it, of insider and outsider, oppressor and oppressed, child and adult, attacker and lover of England.

According to Graham Good, Orwell's importance was that he "succeeded in making the art of the essay political. . . . [A] sense of urgency distinguished his work from the tone of calm, detached contemplation which is traditional in the essay from Montaigne onward. With Orwell the essay emerges from retirement; observation is no longer detached, but caught up in polemic. . . . He politicized the critical essay, and to a great degree also the travel essay and the autobiographical essay." At this historical remove, canonized by both left and right, Orwell has become a more elusive figure— "Saint George," at once vulnerable and aloof.

but: see p. 733 : S. R. Sanders — —
happily, NOT "detached"

Such, Such Were the Joys . . .

1

SOON AFTER I ARRIVED at Crossgates (not immediately, but after a week or two, just when I seemed to be settling into the routine of school life) I began wetting my bed. I was now aged eight, so that this was a reversion to a habit which I must have grown out of at least four years earlier.

Nowadays, I believe, bed-wetting in such circumstances is taken for granted. It is a normal reaction in children who have been removed from their homes to a strange place. In those days, however, it was looked on as a disgusting crime which the child committed on purpose and for which the proper cure was a beating. For my part I did not need to be told it was a crime. Night after night I prayed, with a fervour never previously attained in my prayers, "Please God, do not let me wet my bed! Oh, please God, do not let me wet my bed!" but it made remarkably little difference. Some nights the thing happened, others not. There was no volition about it, no consciousness. You did not properly speaking *do* the deed: you

merely woke up in the morning and found that the sheets were wringing
wet.

After the second or third offence I was warned that I should be beaten
next time, but I received the warning in a curiously roundabout way. One
afternoon, as we were filing out from tea, Mrs. Simpson, the headmaster's
wife, was sitting at the head of one of the tables chatting with a lady of
whom I know nothing, except that she was on an afternoon's visit to the
school. She was an intimidating, masculine-looking person wearing a riding habit, or something that I took to be a riding habit. I was just leaving
the room when Mrs. Simpson called me back, as though to introduce me
to the visitor.

Mrs. Simpson was nicknamed Bingo, and I shall call her by that name
for I seldom think of her by any other. (Officially, however, she was addressed as Mum, probably a corruption of the "Ma'am" used by public
school boys to their housemasters' wives.) She was a stocky square-built
woman with hard red cheeks, a flat top to her head, prominent brows and
deepset, suspicious eyes. Although a great deal of the time she was full of
false heartiness, jollying one along with mannish slang (*"Buck* up, old
chap!" and so forth), and even using one's Christian name, her eyes never
lost their anxious, accusing look. It was very difficult to look her in the
face without feeling guilty, even at moments when one was not guilty of
anything in particular.

"Here is a little boy," said Bingo, indicating me to the strange lady,
"who wets his bed every night. Do you know what I am going to do if you
wet your bed again?" she added, turning to me. "I am going to get the
Sixth Form to beat you."

The strange lady put on an air of being inexpressibly shocked, and
exclaimed "I-should-think-so!" And here occurred one of those wild, almost lunatic misunderstandings which are part of the daily experience of
childhood. The Sixth Form was a group of older boys who were selected
as having "character" and were empowered to beat smaller boys. I had
not yet learned of their existence, and I mis-heard the phrase "the Sixth
Form" as "Mrs. Form." I took it as referring to the strange lady—I
thought, that is, that her name was Mrs. Form. It was an improbable
name, but a child has no judgement in such matters. I imagined, therefore,
that it was *she* who was to be deputed to beat me. It did not strike me as
strange that this job should be turned over to a casual visitor in no way
connected with the school. I merely assumed that "Mrs. Form" was a
stern disciplinarian who enjoyed beating people (somehow her appearance
seemed to bear this out) and I had an immediate terrifying vision of her
arriving for the occasion in full riding kit and armed with a hunting whip.
To this day I can feel myself almost swooning with shame as I stood, a
very small, round-faced boy in short corduroy knickers, before the two

women. I could not speak. I felt that I should die if "Mrs. Form" were to
beat me. But my dominant feeling was not fear or even resentment: it was
simply shame because one more person, and that a woman, had been told
of my disgusting offence.

A little later, I forget how, I learned that it was not after all "Mrs.
Form" who would do the beating. I cannot remember whether it was that
very night that I wetted my bed again, but at any rate I did wet it again
quite soon. Oh, the despair, the feeling of cruel injustice, after all my
prayers and resolutions, at once again waking between the clammy sheets!
There was no chance of hiding what I had done. The grim statuesque
matron, Daphne by name, arrived in the dormitory specially to inspect my
bed. She pulled back the clothes, then drew herself up, and the dreaded
words seemed to come rolling out of her like a peal of thunder:

"REPORT YOURSELF to the headmaster after breakfast!"

I do not know how many times I heard that phrase during my early
years at Crossgates. It was only very rarely that it did not mean a beating.
The words always had a portentous sound in my ears, like muffled drums
or the words of the death sentence.

When I arrived to report myself, Bingo was doing something or other at
the long shiny table in the anteroom to the study. Her uneasy eyes
searched me as I went past. In the study Mr. Simpson, nicknamed Sim,
was waiting. Sim was a round-shouldered, curiously oafish-looking man,
not large but shambling in gait, with a chubby face which was like that of
an overgrown baby, and which was capable of good humour. He knew, of
course, why I had been sent to him, and had already taken a bone-handled
riding crop out of the cupboard, but it was part of the punishment of
reporting yourself that you had to proclaim your offence with your own
lips. When I had said my say, he read me a short but pompous lecture,
then seized me by the scruff of the neck, twisted me over and began
beating me with the riding crop. He had a habit of continuing his lecture
while he flogged you, and I remember the words "you dir-ty little boy"
keeping time with the blows. The beating did not hurt (perhaps as it was
the first time, he was not hitting me very hard), and I walked out feeling
very much better. The fact that the beating had not hurt was a sort of
victory and partially wiped out the shame of the bed-wetting. I was even
incautious enough to wear a grin on my face. Some small boys were hanging about in the passage outside the door of the ante-room.

"D'you get the cane?"

"It didn't hurt," I said proudly.

Bingo had heard everything. Instantly her voice came screaming after
me:

"Come here! Come here this instant! What was that you said?"

"I said it didn't hurt," I faltered out.

"How dare you say a thing like that? Do you think that is a proper thing to say? Go in and REPORT YOURSELF AGAIN!"

This time Sim laid on in real earnest. He continued for a length of time that frightened and astonished me—about five minutes, it seemed—ending up by breaking the riding crop. The bone handle went flying across the room.

"Look what you've made me do!" he said furiously, holding up the broken crop.

I had fallen into a chair, weakly snivelling. I remember that this was the only time throughout my boyhood when a beating actually reduced me to tears, and curiously enough I was not even now crying because of the pain. The second beating had not hurt very much either. Fright and shame seemed to have anesthetised me. I was crying partly because I felt that this was expected of me, partly from genuine repentance, but partly also because of a deeper grief which is peculiar to childhood and not easy to convey: a sense of desolate loneliness and helplessness, of being locked up not only in a hostile world but in a world of good and evil where the rules were such that it was actually not possible for me to keep them.

I knew that bed-wetting was (a) wicked and (b) outside my control. The second fact I was personally aware of, and the first I did not question. It was possible, therefore, to commit a sin without knowing that you committed it, without wanting to commit it, and without being able to avoid it. Sin was not necessarily something that you did: it might be something that happened to you. I do not want to claim that this idea flashed into my mind as a complete novelty at this very moment, under the blows of Sim's cane: I must have had glimpses of it even before I left home, for my early childhood had not been altogether happy. But at any rate this was the great, abiding lesson of my boyhood: that I was in a world where it was *not possible* for me to be good. And the double beating was a turning-point, for it brought home to me for the first time the harshness of the environment into which I had been flung. Life was more terrible, and I was more wicked, than I had imagined. At any rate, as I sat on the edge of a chair in Sim's study, with not even the self-possession to stand up while he stormed at me, I had a conviction of sin and folly and weakness, such as I do not remember to have felt before.

In general, one's memories of any period must necessarily weaken as one moves away from it. One is constantly learning new facts, and old ones have to drop out to make way for them. At twenty I could have written the history of my schooldays with an accuracy which would be quite impossible now. But it can also happen that one's memories grow sharper after a long lapse of time, because one is looking at the past with fresh eyes and can isolate and, as it were, notice facts which previously existed undifferentiated among a mass of others. Here are two things which in a sense I remembered, but which did not strike me as strange or interesting until quite recently. One is that the second beating seemed to me a just and reasonable punishment. To get one beating, and then to get another and far fiercer one on top of it, for being so unwise as to show that the first had not hurt—that was quite natural. The gods are jealous, and when you have good fortune you should conceal it. The other is that I accepted the broken riding crop as my own crime. I can still recall my feeling as I saw the handle lying on the carpet—the feeling of having done an ill-bred clumsy thing, and ruined an expensive object. *I* had broken it: so Sim told me, and so I believed. This acceptance of guilt lay unnoticed in my memory for twenty or thirty years.

So much for the episode of the bed-wetting. But there is one more thing to be remarked. This is that I did not wet my bed again—at least, I did wet it once again, and received another beating, after which the trouble stopped. So perhaps this barbarous remedy does work, though at a heavy price, I have no doubt.

2

Crossgates was an expensive and snobbish school which was in process of becoming more snobbish, and, I imagine, more expensive. The public school with which it had special connections was Harrow, but during my time an increasing proportion of the boys went on to Eton. Most of them were the children of rich parents, but on the whole they were the unaristocratic rich, the sort of people who live in huge shrubberied houses in Bournemouth or Richmond, and who have cars and butlers but not country estates. There were a few exotics among them—some South American boys, sons of Argentine beef barons, one or two Russians, and even a Siamese prince, or someone who was described as a prince.

Sim had two great ambitions. One was to attract titled boys to the school, and the other was to train up pupils to win scholarships at public schools, above all Eton. He did, towards the end of my time, succeed in getting hold of two boys with real English titles. One of them, I remember, was a wretched little creature, almost an albino, peering upwards out of weak eyes, with a long nose at the end of which a dewdrop always seemed to be trembling. Sim always gave these boys their titles when mentioning them to a third person, and for their first few days he actually addressed them to their faces as "Lord So-and-so." Needless to say he found ways of drawing attention to them when any visitor was being shown round the school. Once, I remember, the little fair-haired boy had a choking fit at dinner, and a stream of snot ran out of his nose onto his plate in a way horrible to see. Any lesser person would have been called a dirty little beast and ordered out of the room instantly: but Sim and Bingo laughed it off in a "boys will be boys" spirit.

All the very rich boys were more or less undisguisedly favoured. The school still had a faint suggestion of the Victorian "private academy" with its "parlour boarders," and when I later read about that kind of school in Thackeray I immediately saw the resemblance. The rich boys had milk and biscuits in the middle of the morning, they were given riding lessons once or twice a week, Bingo mothered them and called them by their Christian names, and above all they were never caned. Apart from the South Americans, whose parents were safely distant, I doubt whether Sim ever caned any boy whose father's income was much above £2,000 a year. But he was sometimes willing to sacrifice financial profit to scholastic prestige. Occasionally, by special arrangement, he would take at greatly reduced fees some boy who seemed likely to win scholarships and thus bring credit on the school. It was on these terms that I was at Crossgates myself: otherwise my parents could not have afforded to send me to so expensive a school.

I did not at first understand that I was being taken at reduced fees; it was only when I was about eleven that Bingo and Sim began throwing the fact in my teeth. For my first two or three years I went through the ordinary educational mill: then, soon after I had started Greek (one started Latin at eight, Greek at ten), I moved into the scholarship class, which was taught, so far as classics went, largely by Sim himself. Over a period of two or three years the scholarship boys were crammed with learning as cynically as a goose is crammed for Christmas. And with what learning! This business of making a gifted boy's career depend on a competitive examination, taken when he is only twelve or thirteen, is an evil thing at best, but there do appear to be preparatory schools which send scholars to Eton, Winchester, etc., without teaching them to see everything in terms of marks. At Crossgates the whole process was frankly a preparation for a sort of confidence trick. Your job was to learn exactly those things that would give an examiner the impression that you knew more than you did know, and as far as possible to avoid burdening your brain with anything else. Subjects which lacked examination-value, such as geography, were almost completely neglected, mathematics was also neglected if you were a "classical," science was not taught in any form—indeed it was so despised that even an interest in natural history was discouraged—and the books you were encouraged to read in your spare time were chosen with one eye on the "English Paper." Latin and Greek, the main scholarship subjects, were what counted, but even these were deliberately taught in a flashy, unsound way. We never, for example, read right through even a single book of a Greek or Latin author: we merely read short passages which were picked out because they were the kind of thing likely to be set as an "unseen translation." During the last year or so before we went up for our scholarships, most of our time was spent in simply working our way through the scholarship papers of previous years. Sim had sheaves of these in his possession, from every one of the major public schools. But the greatest outrage of all was the teaching of history.

There was in those days a piece of nonsense called the Harrow History Prize, an annual competition for which many preparatory schools entered. At Crossgates we mugged up every paper that had been set since the competition started. They were the kind of stupid question that is answered by rapping out a name or a quotation. Who plundered the Begams? Who was beheaded in an open boat? Who caught the Whigs bathing and ran away with their clothes? Almost all our historical teaching was on this level. History was a series of unrelated, unintelligible but—in some way that was never explained to us—important facts with resounding phrases tied to them. Disraeli brought peace with honour. Clive was astonished at his moderation. Pitt called in the New World to redress the balance of the Old. And the dates, and the mnemonic devices! (Did you know, for example, that the initial letters of "A black Negress was my aunt: there's her house behind the barn" are also the initial letters of the battles in the Wars of the Roses?) Bingo, who "took" the higher forms in history, revelled in this kind of thing. I recall positive orgies of dates, with the keener boys leaping up and down in their places in their eagerness to shout out the right answers, and at the same time not feeling the faintest interest in the meaning of the mysterious events they were naming.

"1587?"

"Massacre of St. Bartholomew!"

"1707?"

"Death of Aurangzeeb!"

"1713?"

"Treaty of Utrecht!"

"1773?"

"The Boston Tea Party!"

"1520?"

"Oo, Mum, please, Mum—"

"Please, Mum, please, Mum! Let me tell him, Mum!"

"Well; 1520?"

"Field of the Cloth of Gold!"

And so on.

But history and such secondary subjects were not bad fun. It was in "classics" that the real strain came. Looking back, I realise that I then worked harder than I have ever done since, and yet at the time it never seemed possible to make quite the effort that was demanded of one. We would sit round the long shiny table, made of some very pale-coloured, hard wood, with Sim goading, threatening, exhorting, sometimes joking, very occasionally praising, but always prodding, prodding away at one's mind to keep it up to the right pitch of concentration, as one might keep a sleepy person awake by sticking pins into him.

"Go on, you little slacker! Go on, you idle, worthless little boy! The whole trouble with you is that you're bone and horn idle. You eat too much, that's why. You wolf down enormous meals, and then when you come here you're half asleep. Go on, now, put your back into it. You're not *thinking*. Your brain doesn't sweat."

He would tap away at one's skull with his silver pencil, which, in my memory, seems to have been about the size of a banana, and which certainly was heavy enough to raise a bump: or he would pull the short hairs round one's ears, or, occasionally, reach out under the table and kick one's shin. On some days nothing seemed to go right, and then it would be: "All right, then, I know what you want. You've been asking for it the whole morning. Come along, you useless little slacker. Come into the study." And then whack, whack, whack, whack, and back one would come, red-wealed and smarting—in later years Sim had abandoned his riding crop in favour of a thin rattan cane which hurt very much more—to settle down to work again. This did not happen very often, but I do remember, more than once being led out of the room in the middle of a Latin sentence, receiving a beating and then going straight ahead with the same sentence, just like that. It is a mistake to think such methods do not work. They work very well for their special purpose. Indeed, I doubt whether classical education ever has been or can be successfully carried on without corporal punishment. The boys themselves believed in its efficacy. There was a boy named Beacham, with no brains to speak of, but evidently in acute need of a scholarship. Sim was flogging him towards the goal as one might do with a foundered horse. He went up for a scholarship at Uppingham, came back with a consciousness of having done badly, and a day or two later received a severe beating for idleness. "I wish I'd had that caning before I went up for the exam," he said sadly—a remark which I felt to be contemptible, but which I perfectly well understood.

The boys of the scholarship class were not all treated alike. If a boy were the son of rich parents to whom the saving of fees was not all-important, Sim would goad him along in a comparatively fatherly way, with jokes and digs in the ribs and perhaps an occasional tap with the pencil, but no hair-pulling and no caning. It was the poor but "clever" boys who suffered. Our brains were a gold-mine in which he had sunk money, and the dividends must be squeezed out of us. Long before I had grasped the nature of my financial relationship with Sim, I had been made to understand that I was not on the same footing as most of the other boys. In effect there were three castes in the school. There was the minority with an aristocratic or millionaire background, there were the children of the ordinary suburban rich, who made up the bulk of the school, and there were a few underlings like myself, the sons of clergymen, Indian civil servants, struggling widows and the like. These poorer ones were discouraged from going in for "extras" such as shooting and carpentry, and were humiliated over clothes and petty possessions. I never, for instance, succeeded in getting a cricket bat of my own, because "your parents wouldn't be able to afford it." This phrase pursued me throughout my schooldays. At Crossgates we were not allowed to keep the money we brought back with us, but had to "give it in" on the first day of term, and then from time to time were allowed to spend it under supervision. I and similarly placed boys were always choked off from buying expensive toys like model aeroplanes, even if the necessary money stood to our credit. Bingo, in particular, seemed to aim consciously at inculcating a humble outlook in the poorer boys. "Do you think that's the sort of thing a boy like you should buy?" I remember her saying to somebody—and she said this in front of the whole school; "You know you're not going to grow up with money, don't you? Your people aren't rich. You must learn to be sensible. Don't get above yourself!" There was also the weekly pocket-money, which we took out in sweets, dispensed by Bingo from a large table. The millionaires had sixpence a week, but the normal sum was threepence. I and one or two others were only allowed twopence. My parents had not given instructions to this effect, and the saving of a penny a week could not conceivably have made any difference to them: it was a mark of status. Worse yet was the detail of the birthday cakes. It was usual for each boy, on his birthday, to have a large iced cake with candles, which was shared out at tea between the whole school. It was provided as a matter of routine and went on his parents' bill. I never had such a cake, though my parents would have paid for it readily enough. Year after year, never daring to ask, I would miserably hope that this year a cake would appear. Once or twice I even rashly pretended to my companions that this time I *was* going to have a cake. Then came teatime, and no cake, which did not make me more popular.

Very early it was impressed upon me that I had no chance of a decent future unless I won a scholarship at a public school. Either I won my scholarship, or I must leave school at fourteen and become, in Sim's favourite phrase "a little office-boy at forty pounds a year." In my circumstances it was natural that I should believe this. Indeed, it was universally taken for granted at Crossgates that unless you went to a "good" public school (and only about fifteen schools came under this heading) you were ruined for life. It is not easy to convey to a grown-up person the sense of strain, of nerving oneself for some terrible, all-deciding combat, as the date of the examination crept nearer—eleven years old, twelve years old,

then thirteen, the fatal year itself! Over a period of about two years, I do
not think there was ever a day when "the exam," as I called it, was quite
out of my waking thoughts. In my prayers it figured invariably: and whenever I got the bigger portion of a wishbone, or picked up a horseshoe, or
bowed seven times to the new moon, or succeeded in passing through a
wishing-gate without touching the sides, then the wish I earned by doing
so went on "the exam" as a matter of course. And yet curiously enough I
was also tormented by an almost irresistible impulse *not* to work. There
were days when my heart sickened at the labours ahead of me, and I stood
stupid as an animal before the most elementary difficulties. In the holidays, also, I could not work. Some of the scholarship boys received extra
tuition from a certain Mr. Batchelor, a likeable, very hairy man who wore
shaggy suits and lived in a typical bachelor's "den"—booklined walls,
overwhelming stench of tobacco—somewhere in the town. During the
holidays Mr. Batchelor used to send us extracts from Latin authors to
translate, and we were supposed to send back a wad of work once a week.
Somehow I could not do it. The empty paper and the black Latin dictionary lying on the table, the consciousness of a plain duty shirked,
poisoned my leisure, but somehow I could not start, and by the end of the
holidays I would only have sent Mr. Batchelor fifty or a hundred lines.
Undoubtedly part of the reason was that Sim and his cane were far away.
But in term time, also, I would go through periods of idleness and stupidity when I would sink deeper and deeper into disgrace and even achieve a
sort of feeble defiance, fully conscious of my guilt and yet unable or unwilling—I could not be sure which—to do any better. Then Bingo or Sim
would send for me, and this time it would not even be a caning.

Bingo would search me with her baleful eyes. (What colour were those
eyes, I wonder? I remember them as green, but actually no human being
has green eyes. Perhaps they were hazel.) She would start off in her peculiar, wheedling, bullying style, which never failed to get right through
one's guard and score a hit on one's better nature.

"I don't think it's awfully decent of you to behave like this, is it? Do
you think it's quite playing the game by your mother and father to go on
idling your time away, week after week, month after month? Do you *want*
to throw all your chances away? You know your people aren't rich, don't
you? You know they can't afford the same things as other boys' parents.
How are they to send you to a public school if you don't win a scholarship? I know how proud your mother is of you. Do you *want* to let her
down?"

"I don't think he wants to go to a public school any longer," Sim would
say, addressing himself to Bingo with a pretence that I was not there. "I
think he's given up that idea. He wants to be a little office-boy at forty
pounds a year."

The horrible sensation of tears—a swelling in the breast, a tickling behind the nose—would already have assailed me. Bingo would bring out
her ace of trumps:

"And do you think it's quite fair to *us,* the way you're behaving? After
all we've done for you? You *do* know what we've done for you, don't
you?" Her eyes would pierce deep into me, and though she never said it
straight out, I did know. "We've had you here all these years—we even
had you here for a week in the holidays so that Mr. Batchelor could coach
you. We don't *want* to have to send you away, you know, but we can't
keep a boy here just to eat up our food, term after term. *I* don't think it's
very straight, the way you're behaving. Do you?"

I never had any answer except a miserable "No, Mum," or "Yes, Mum"
as the case might be. Evidently it was *not* straight, the way I was behaving.
And at some point or other the unwanted tear would always force its way
out of the corner of my eye, roll down my nose, and splash.

Bingo never said in plain words that I was a non-paying pupil, no doubt
because vague phrases like "all we've done for you" had a deeper emotional appeal. Sim, who did not aspire to be loved by his pupils, put it
more brutally, though, as was usual with him, in pompous language. "You
are living on my bounty" was his favourite phrase in this context. At least
once I listened to these words between blows of the cane. I must say that
these scenes were not frequent, and except on one occasion they did not
take place in the presence of other boys. In public I was reminded that I
was poor and that my parents "wouldn't be able to afford" this or that,
but I was not actually reminded of my dependent position. It was a final
unanswerable argument, to be brought forth like an instrument of torture
when my work became exceptionally bad.

To grasp the effect of this kind of thing on a child of ten or twelve, one
has to remember that the child has little sense of proportion or probability. A child may be a mass of egoism and rebelliousness, but it has not
accumulated experience to give it confidence in its own judgements. On
the whole it will accept what it is told, and it will believe in the most
fantastic way in the knowledge and power of the adults surrounding it.
Here is an example.

I have said that at Crossgates we were not allowed to keep our own
money. However, it was possible to hold back a shilling or two, and sometimes I used furtively to buy sweets which I kept hidden in the loose ivy
on the playing-field wall. One day when I had been sent on an errand I
went into a sweetshop a mile or more from the school and bought some
chocolates. As I came out of the shop I saw on the opposite pavement a
small sharp-faced man who seemed to be staring very hard at my school
cap. Instantly a horrible fear went through me. There could be no doubt
as to who the man was. He was a spy placed there by Sim! I turned away

unconcernedly, and then, as though my legs were doing it of their own accord, broke into a clumsy run. But when I got round the next corner I forced myself to walk again, for to run was a sign of guilt, and obviously there would be other spies posted here and there about the town. All that day and the next I waited for the summons to the study, and was surprised when it did not come. It did not seem to me strange that the headmaster of a private school should dispose of an army of informers, and I did not even imagine that he would have to pay them. I assumed that any adult, inside the school or outside, would collaborate voluntarily in preventing us from breaking the rules. Sim was all-powerful, and it was natural that his agents should be everywhere. When this episode happened I do not think I can have been less than twelve years old.

I hated Bingo and Sim, with a sort of shamefaced, remorseful hatred, but it did not occur to me to doubt their judgement. When they told me that I must either win a public school scholarship or become an office-boy at fourteen, I believed that those were the unavoidable alternatives before me. And above all, I believed Bingo and Sim when they told me they were my benefactors. I see now, of course, that from Sim's point of view I was a good speculation. He sank money in me, and he looked to get it back in the form of prestige. If I had "gone off," as promising boys sometimes do, I imagine that he would have got rid of me swiftly. As it was I won him two scholarships when the time came, and no doubt he made full use of them in his prospectuses. But it is difficult for a child to realise that a school is primarily a commercial venture. A child believes that the school exists to educate and that the schoolmaster disciplines him either for his own good, or from a love of bullying. Sim and Bingo had chosen to befriend me, and their friendship included canings, reproaches and humiliations, which were good for me and saved me from an office stool. That was their version, and I believed in it. It was therefore clear that I owed them a vast debt of gratitude. But I was *not* grateful, as I very well knew. On the contrary, I hated both of them. I could not control my subjective feelings, and I could not conceal them from myself. But it is wicked, is it not, to hate your benefactors? So I was taught, and so I believed. A child accepts the codes of behaviour that are presented to it, even when it breaks them. From the age of eight, or even earlier, the consciousness of sin was never far away from me. If I contrived to seem callous and defiant, it was only a thin cover over a mass of shame and dismay. All through my boyhood I had a profound conviction that I was no good, that I was wasting my time, wrecking my talents, behaving with monstrous folly and wickedness and ingratitude—and all this, it seemed, was inescapable, because I lived among laws which were absolute, like the law of gravity, but which it was not possible for me to keep.

3

No one can look back on his schooldays and say with truth that they were altogether unhappy.

I have good memories of Crossgates, among a horde of bad ones. Sometimes on summer afternoons there were wonderful expeditions across the Downs, or to Beachy Head, where one bathed dangerously among the chalk boulders and came home covered with cuts. And there were still more wonderful midsummer evenings when, as a special treat, we were not driven off to bed as usual but allowed to wander about the grounds in the long twilight, ending up with a plunge into the swimming bath at about nine o'clock. There was the joy of waking early on summer mornings and getting in an hour's undisturbed reading (Ian Hay, Thackeray, Kipling and H. G. Wells were the favourite authors of my boyhood) in the sunlit, sleeping dormitory. There was also cricket, which I was no good at but with which I conducted a sort of hopeless love affair up to the age of about eighteen. And there was the pleasure of keeping caterpillars—the silky green and purple puss-moth, the ghostly green poplar-hawk, the privet hawk, large as one's third finger, specimens of which could be illicitly purchased for sixpence at a shop in the town—and, when one could escape long enough from the master who was "taking the walk," there was the excitement of dredging the dew-ponds on the Downs for enormous newts with orange-coloured bellies. This business of being out for a walk, coming across something of fascinating interest and then being dragged away from it by a yell from the master, like a dog jerked onwards by the leash, is an important feature of school life, and helps to build up the conviction, so strong in many children, that the things you most want to do are always unattainable.

Very occasionally, perhaps once during each summer, it was possible to escape altogether from the barrack-like atmosphere of school, when Brown, the second master, was permitted to take one or two boys for an afternoon of butterfly hunting on a common a few miles away. Brown was a man with white hair and a red face like a strawberry, who was good at natural history, making models and plaster casts, operating magic lanterns, and things of that kind. He and Mr. Batchelor were the only adults in any way connected with the school whom I did not either dislike or fear. Once he took me into his room and showed me in confidence a plated, pearl-handled revolver—his "six-shooter," he called it—which he kept in a box under his bed. And oh, the joy of those occasional expeditions! The ride of two or three miles on a lonely little branch line, the afternoon of charging to and fro with large green nets, the beauty of the enormous dragon flies which hovered over the tops of the grasses, the sinister killing-bottle with its sickly smell, and then tea in the parlour of a pub with large slices of pale-coloured cake! The essence of it was in the railway journey, which seemed to put magic distances between yourself and school.

Bingo, characteristically, disapproved of these expeditions, though not actually forbidding them. "And have you been catching *little butterflies?*" she would say with a vicious sneer when one got back, making her voice as babyish as possible. From her point of view, natural history ("bug-hunting" she would probably have called it) was a babyish pursuit which a boy should be laughed out of as early as possible. Moreover it was somehow faintly plebeian, it was traditionally associated with boys who wore spectacles and were no good at games, it did not help you to pass exams, and above all it smelt of science and therefore seemed to menace classical education. It needed a considerable moral effort to accept Brown's invitation. How I dreaded that sneer of *little butterflies!* Brown, however, who had been at the school since its early days, had built up a certain independence for himself: he seemed able to handle Sim, and ignored Bingo a good deal. If it ever happened that both of them were away, Brown acted as deputy headmaster, and on those occasions, instead of reading the appointed lesson for the day at morning chapel, he would read us stories from the Apocrypha.

Most of the good memories of my childhood, and up to the age of about twenty, are in some way connected with animals. So far as Crossgates goes, it also seems, when I look back, that all my good memories are of summer. In winter your nose ran continually, your fingers were too numb to button your shirt (this was an especial misery on Sundays, when we wore Eton collars), and there was the daily nightmare of football—the cold, the mud, the hideous greasy ball that came whizzing at one's face, the gouging knees and trampling boots of the bigger boys. Part of the trouble was that in winter, after the age of about ten, I was seldom in good health, at any rate during term time. I had defective bronchial tubes and a lesion in one lung which was not discovered till many years later. Hence I not only had a chronic cough, but running was a torment to me. In those days, however, "wheeziness," or "chestiness," as it was called, was either diagnosed as imagination or was looked on as essentially a moral disorder, caused by overeating. "You wheeze like a concertina," Sim would say disapprovingly as he stood behind my chair: "You're perpetually stuffing yourself with food, that's why." My cough was referred to as a "stomach cough," which made it sound both disgusting and reprehensible. The cure for it was hard running, which, if you kept it up long enough, ultimately "cleared your chest."

It is curious, the degree—I will not say of actual hardship, but of squalor and neglect, that was taken for granted in upper-class schools of

that period. Almost as in the days of Thackeray, it seemed natural that a
little boy of eight or ten should be a miserable, snotty-nosed creature, his
face almost permanently dirty, his hands chapped, his nails bitten, his
handkerchief a sodden horror, his bottom frequently blue with bruises. It
was partly the prospect of actual physical discomfort that made the
thought of going back to school lie in one's breast like a lump of lead
during the last few days of the holidays. A characteristic memory of Crossgates is the astonishing hardness of one's bed on the first night of term.
Since this was an expensive school, I took a social step upwards by attending it, and yet the standard of comfort was in every way far lower than in
my own home, or indeed, than it would have been in a prosperous working-class home. One only had a hot bath once a week, for instance. The
food was not only bad, it was also insufficient. Never before or since have
I seen butter or jam scraped on bread so thinly. I do not think I can be
imagining the fact that we were underfed, when I remember the lengths
we would go in order to steal food. On a number of occasions I remember
creeping down at two or three o'clock in the morning through what
seemed like miles of pitch-dark stairways and passages—barefooted, stopping to listen after each step, paralysed with about equal fear of Sim,
ghosts and burglars—to steal stale bread from the pantry. The assistant
masters had their meals with us, but they had somewhat better food, and
if one got half a chance it was usual to steal left-over scraps of bacon rind
or fried potato when their plates were removed.

As usual, I did not see the sound commercial reason for this under-
feeding. On the whole I accepted Sim's view that a boy's appetite is a sort
of morbid growth which should be kept in check as much as possible. A
maxim often repeated to us at Crossgates was that it is healthy to get up
from a meal feeling as hungry as when you sat down. Only a generation
earlier than this it had been common for school dinners to start off with a
slab of unsweetened suet pudding, which, it was frankly said, "broke the
boys' appetites." But the under-feeding was probably less flagrant at preparatory schools, where a boy was wholly dependent on the official diet,
than at public schools, where he was allowed—indeed, expected—to buy
extra food for himself. At some schools, he would literally not have had
enough to eat unless he had bought regular supplies of eggs, sausages,
sardines, etc.; and his parents had to allow him money for this purpose. At
Eton, for instance, at any rate in College, a boy was given no solid meal
after mid-day dinner. For his afternoon tea he was given only tea and
bread and butter, and at eight o'clock he was given a miserable supper of
soup or fried fish, or more often bread and cheese, with water to drink.
Sim went down to see his eldest son at Eton and came back in snobbish
ecstasies over the luxury in which the boys lived. "They give them fried
fish for supper!" he exclaimed, beaming all over his chubby face. "There's

no school like it in the world." Fried fish! The habitual supper of the poorest of the working class! At very cheap boarding-schools it was no doubt worse. A very early memory of mine is of seeing the boarders at a grammar school—the sons, probably, of farmers and shopkeepers—being fed on boiled lights.

Whoever writes about his childhood must beware of exaggeration and self-pity. I do not want to claim that I was a martyr or that Crossgates was a sort of Dotheboys Hall. But I should be falsifying my own memories if I did not record that they are largely memories of disgust. The over-crowded, underfed, underwashed life that we led *was* disgusting, as I re-call it. If I shut my eyes and say "school," it is of course the physical surroundings that first come back to me: the flat playing-field with its cricket pavilion and the little shed by the rifle range, the draughty dormi-tories, the dusty splintery passages, the square of asphalt in front of the gymnasium, the raw-looking pinewood chapel at the back. And at almost every point some filthy detail obtrudes itself. For example, there were the pewter bowls out of which we had our porridge. They had overhanging rims, and under the rims there were accumulations of sour porridge, which could be flaked off in long strips. The porridge itself, too, contained more lumps, hairs and unexplained black things than one would have thought possible, unless someone were putting them there on purpose. It was never safe to start on that porridge without investigating it first. And there was the slimy water of the plunge bath—it was twelve or fifteen feet long, the whole school was supposed to go into it every morning, and I doubt whether the water was changed at all frequently—and the always-damp towels with their cheesy smell: and, on occasional visits in the win-ter, the murky sea-water of the local Baths, which came straight in from the beach and on which I once saw floating a human turd. And the sweaty smell of the changing-room with its greasy basins, and, giving on this, the row of filthy, dilapidated lavatories, which had no fastenings of any kind on the doors, so that whenever you were sitting there someone was sure to come crashing in. It is not easy for me to think of my school-days without seeming to breathe in a whiff of something cold and evil-smelling—a sort of compound of sweaty stockings, dirty towels, faecal smells blowing along corridors, forks with old food between the prongs, neck-of-mutton stew, and the banging doors of the lavatories and the echoing chamber-pots in the dormitories.

It is true that I am by nature not gregarious, and the W.C. and dirty-handkerchief side of life is necessarily more obtrusive when great numbers of human beings are crushed together in small space. It is just as bad in an army, and worse, no doubt, in a prison. Besides, boyhood is the age of disgust. After one has learned to differentiate, and before one has become hardened—between seven and eighteen, say—one seems always to be walking the tightrope over a cesspool. Yet I do not think I exaggerate the squalor of school life, when I remember how health and cleanliness were neglected, in spite of the hoo-ha about fresh air and cold water and keeping in hard training. It was common to remain constipated for days together. Indeed, one was hardly encouraged to keep one's bowels open, since the aperients tolerated were Castor Oil or another almost equally horrible drink called Liquorice Powder. One was supposed to go into the plunge bath every morning, but some boys shirked it for days on end, simply making themselves scarce when the bell sounded, or else slipping along the edge of the bath among the crowd, and then wetting their hair with a little dirty water off the floor. A little boy of eight or nine will not necessarily keep himself clean unless there is someone to see that he does it. There was a new boy named Hazel, a pretty, mother's darling of a boy, who came a little before I left. The first thing I noticed about him was the beautiful pearly whiteness of his teeth. By the end of that term his teeth were an extraordinary shade of green. During all that time, apparently, no one had taken sufficient interest in him to see that he brushed them.

But of course the differences between home and school were more than physical. That bump on the hard mattress, on the first night of term, used to give me a feeling of abrupt awakening, a feeling of: "This is reality, this is what you are up against." Your home might be far from perfect, but at least it was a place ruled by love rather than by fear, where you did not have to be perpetually on your guard against the people surrounding you. At eight years old you were suddenly taken out of this warm nest and flung into a world of force and fraud and secrecy, like a goldfish into a tank full of pike. Against no matter what degree of bullying you had no redress. You could only have defended yourself by sneaking, which, except in a few rigidly defined circumstances, was the unforgivable sin. To write home and ask your parents to take you away would have been even less thinkable, since to do so would have been to admit yourself unhappy and unpopular, which a boy will never do. Boys are Erewhonians: they think that misfortune is disgraceful and must be concealed at all costs. It might perhaps have been considered permissible to complain to your parents about bad food, or an unjustified caning, or some other ill-treatment inflicted by masters and not by boys. The fact that Sim never beat the richer boys suggests that such complaints were made occasionally. But in my own peculiar circumstances I could never have asked my parents to intervene on my behalf. Even before I understood about the reduced fees, I grasped that they were in some way under an obligation to Sim, and therefore could not protect me against him. I have mentioned already that throughout my time at Crossgates I never had a cricket bat of my own. I had been told this was because "your parents couldn't afford it." One day in the holidays, by some casual remark, it came out that they had provided ten shillings to buy me one: yet no cricket bat appeared. I did not protest to my parents, let alone raise the subject with Sim. How could I? I was dependent on him, and the ten shillings was merely a fragment of what I owed him. I realise now, of course, that it is immensely unlikely that Sim had simply stuck to the money. No doubt the matter had slipped his memory. But the point is that I assumed that he had stuck to it, and that he had a right to do so if he chose.

How difficult it is for a child to have any real independence of attitude could be seen in our behaviour towards Bingo. I think it would be true to say that every boy in the school hated and feared her. Yet we all fawned on her in the most abject way, and the top layer of our feelings towards her was a sort of guilt-stricken loyalty. Bingo, although the discipline of the school depended more on her than on Sim, hardly pretended to dispense justice. She was frankly capricious. An act which might get you a caning one day, might next day be laughed off as a boyish prank, or even commended because it "showed you had guts." There were days when everyone cowered before those deepset, accusing eyes, and there were days when she was like a flirtatious queen surrounded by courtier-lovers, laughing and joking, scattering largesse, or the promise of largesse ("And if you win the Harrow History Prize I'll give you a new case for your camera!"), and occasionally even packing three or four favoured boys into her Ford car and carrying them off to a teashop in town, where they were allowed to buy coffee and cakes. Bingo was inextricably mixed up in my mind with Queen Elizabeth, whose relations with Leicester and Essex and Raleigh were intelligible to me from a very early age. A word we all constantly used in speaking of Bingo was "favour." "I'm in good favour," we would say, or "I'm in bad favour." Except for the handful of wealthy or titled boys, no one was permanently in good favour, but on the other hand even the outcasts had patches of it from time to time. Thus, although my memories of Bingo are mostly hostile, I also remember considerable periods when I basked under her smiles, when she called me "old chap" and used my Christian name, and allowed me to frequent her private library, where I first made acquaintance with *Vanity Fair.* The high-water mark of good favour was to be invited to serve at table on Sunday nights when Bingo and Sim had guests to dinner. In clearing away, of course, one had a chance to finish off the scraps, but one also got a servile pleasure from standing behind the seated guests and darting deferentially forward when something was wanted. Whenever one had the chance to suck up, one did suck up, and at the first smile one's hatred turned into a sort of cringing love. I was always tremendously proud when I succeeded in making Bingo laugh. I have even, at her command, written *vers d'occasion,* comic verses to celebrate memorable events in the life of the school.

I am anxious to make it clear that I was not a rebel, except by force of circumstances. I accepted the codes that I found in being. Once, towards the end of my time, I even sneaked to Brown about a suspected case of homosexuality. I did not know very well what homosexuality was, but I knew that it happened and was bad, and that this was one of the contexts in which it was proper to sneak. Brown told me I was "a good fellow," which made me feel horribly ashamed. Before Bingo one seemed as helpless as a snake before a snake-charmer. She had a hardly varying vocabulary of praise and abuse, a whole series of set phrases, each of which promptly called forth the appropriate response. There was *"Buck* up, old chap!"*, which inspired one to paroxysms of energy; there was "Don't *be* such a fool!" (or, "It's path*eti*c, isn't it?"), which made one feel a born idiot; and there was "It isn't very straight of you, is it?", which always brought one to the brink of tears. And yet all the while, at the middle of one's heart, there seemed to stand an incorruptible inner self who knew that whatever one did—whether one laughed or snivelled or went into frenzies of gratitude for small favours—one's only true feeling was hatred.

4

I had learned early in my career that one can do wrong against one's will, and before long I also learned that one can do wrong without ever discovering what one has done or why it was wrong. There were sins that were too subtle to be explained, and there were others that were too terrible to be clearly mentioned. For example, there was sex, which was always smouldering just under the surface and which suddenly blew up into a tremendous row when I was about twelve.

At some preparatory schools homosexuality is not a problem, but I think that Crossgates may have acquired a "bad tone" thanks to the presence of the South American boys, who would perhaps mature a year or two earlier than an English boy. At that age I was not interested, so I do not actually know what went on, but I imagine it was group masturbation. At any rate, one day the storm suddenly burst over our heads. There were summonses, interrogations, confessions, floggings, repentances, solemn lectures of which one understood nothing except that some irredeemable sin known as "swinishness" or "beastliness" had been committed. One of the ringleaders, a boy named Horne, was flogged, according to eyewitnesses, for a quarter of an hour continuously before being expelled. His yells rang through the house. But we were all implicated, more or less, or felt ourselves to be implicated. Guilt seemed to hang in the air like a pall of smoke. A solemn, black-haired imbecile of an assistant master, who was later to be a Member of Parliament, took the older boys to a secluded room and delivered a talk on the Temple of the Body.

"Don't you realise what a wonderful thing your body is?" he said gravely. "You talk of your motor-car engines, your Rolls-Royces and Daimlers and so on. Don't you understand that no engine ever made is fit to be compared with your body? And then you go and wreck it, ruin it— for life!"

He turned his cavernous black eyes on me and added sadly:

"And you, whom I'd always believed to be quite a decent person after your fashion—you, I hear, are one of the very worst."

A feeling of doom descended upon me. So I was guilty too. I too had done the dreadful thing, whatever it was, that wrecked you for life, body and soul, and ended in suicide or the lunatic asylum. Till then I had hoped that I was innocent, and the conviction of sin which now took possession of me was perhaps all the stronger because I did not know what I had done. I was not among those who were interrogated and flogged, and it was not until the row was well over that I even learned about the trivial accident that had connected my name with it. Even then I understood nothing. It was not till about two years later that I fully grasped what that lecture on the Temple of the Body had referred to.

At this time I was in an almost sexless state, which is normal, or at any rate common, in boys of that age; I was therefore in the position of simultaneously knowing and not knowing what used to be called the Facts of Life. At five or six, like many children, I had passed through a phase of sexuality. My friends were the plumber's children up the road, and we used sometimes to play games of a vaguely erotic kind. One was called "playing at doctors," and I remember getting a faint but definitely pleasant thrill from holding a toy trumpet, which was supposed to be a stethoscope, against a little girl's belly. About the same time I fell deeply in love, a far more worshipping kind of love than I have ever felt for anyone since, with a girl named Elsie at the convent school which I attended. She seemed to me grown up, so I suppose she must have been fifteen. After that, as so often happens, all sexual feelings seemed to go out of me for many years. At twelve I knew more than I had known as a young child, but I understood less, because I no longer knew the essential fact that there is something pleasant in sexual activity. Between roughly seven and fourteen, the whole subject seemed to me uninteresting and, when for some reason I was forced to think of it, disgusting. My knowledge of the so-called Facts of Life was derived from animals, and was therefore distorted, and in any case was only intermittent. I knew that animals copulated and that human beings had bodies resembling those of animals: but that human beings also copulated I only knew, as it were reluctantly, when something, a phrase in the Bible perhaps, compelled me to remember it. Not having desire, I had no curiosity, and was willing to leave many questions unanswered. Thus, I knew in principle how the baby gets into the woman, but I did not know how it gets out again, because I had never followed the subject up. I knew all the dirty words, and in my bad moments I would repeat them to myself, but I did not know what the worst of them meant, nor want to know. They were abstractly wicked, a sort of verbal charm. While I remained in this state, it was easy for me to remain ignorant of any sexual misdeeds that went on about me, and to be hardly wiser even when the row broke. At most, through the veiled and terrible warnings of Bingo, Sim and all the rest of them, I grasped that the crime of which we were all guilty was somehow connected with the sexual organs. I had noticed, without feeling much interest, that one's penis sometimes stands up of its own accord (this starts happening to a boy long before he has any conscious sexual desires), and I was inclined to believe, or half-believe, that *that* must be the crime. At any rate, it was something to do with the penis—so much I understood. Many other boys, I have no doubt, were equally in the dark.

After the talk on the Temple of the Body (days later, it seems in retrospect: the row seemed to continue for days), a dozen of us were seated at the long shiny table which Sim used for the scholarship, under Bingo's lowering eye. A long, desolate wail rang out from a room somewhere above. A very small boy named Ronald, aged no more than about ten, who was implicated in some way, was being flogged, or was recovering from a flogging. At the sound, Bingo's eyes searched our faces, and settled on me.

"You see," she said.

I will not swear that she said, "You see what you have done," but that was the sense of it. We were all bowed down with shame. It was *our* fault. Somehow or other we had led poor Ronald astray: *we* were responsible for his agony and his ruin. Then Bingo turned upon another boy named Heath. It is thirty years ago, and I cannot remember for certain whether she merely quoted a verse from the Bible, or whether she actually brought out a Bible and made Heath read it; but at any rate the text indicated was:

"Who shall offend one of these little ones that believe in me, it were better for him that a millstone were hanged about his neck, and that he were drowned in the depth of the sea."

That, too, was terrible. Ronald was one of these little ones; we had offended him; it were better that a millstone were hanged about our necks and that we were drowned in the depth of the sea.

"Have you thought about that, Heath—have you thought what it means?" Bingo said. And Heath broke down into tears.

Another boy, Beacham, whom I have mentioned already, was similarly overwhelmed with shame by the accusation that he "had black rings round his eyes."

"Have you looked in the glass lately, Beacham?" said Bingo. "Aren't you ashamed to go about with a face like that? Do you think everyone doesn't know what it means when a boy has black rings round his eyes?"

Once again the load of guilt and fear seemed to settle down upon me. Had *I* got black rings round my eyes? A couple of years later I realised that these were supposed to be a symptom by which masturbators could be detected. But already, without knowing this, I accepted the black rings as a sure sign of depravity, *some* kind of depravity. And many times, even before I grasped the supposed meaning, I have gazed anxiously into the glass, looking for the first hint of that dreaded stigma, the confession which the secret sinner writes upon his own face.

These terrors wore off, or became merely intermittent, without affecting what one might call my official beliefs. It was still true about the mad-house and the suicide's grave, but it was no longer acutely frightening. Some months later it happened that I once again saw Horne, the ring-leader who had been flogged and expelled. Horne was one of the outcasts, the son of poor middle-class parents, which was no doubt part of the reason why Sim had handled him so roughly. The term after his expulsion he went on to South Coast College, the small local public school, which was hideously despised at Crossgates and looked upon as "not really" a public school at all. Only a very few boys from Crossgates went there, and Sim always spoke of them with a sort of contemptuous pity. You had no chance if you went to a school like that: at the best your destiny would be a clerkship. I thought of Horne as a person who at thirteen had already forfeited all hope of any decent future. Physically, morally and socially he was finished. Moreover I assumed that his parents had only sent him to South Coast College because after his disgrace no "good" school would have him.

During the following term, when we were out for a walk, we passed Horne in the street. He looked completely normal. He was a strongly built, rather good-looking boy with black hair. I immediately noticed that he looked better than when I had last seen him—his complexion, previously rather pale, was pinker—and that he did not seem embarrassed at meeting us. Apparently he was not ashamed either of having been ex-pelled, or of being at South Coast College. If one could gather anything from the way he looked at us as we filed past, it was that he was glad to have escaped from Crossgates. But the encounter made very little impres-sion on me. I drew no inference from the fact that Horne, ruined in body and soul, appeared to be happy and in good health. I still believed in the sexual mythology that had been taught me by Bingo and Sim. The myste-rious, terrible dangers were still there. Any morning the black rings might appear round your eyes and you would know that you too were among the lost ones. Only it no longer seemed to matter very much. These contradic-tions can exist easily in the mind of a child, because of its own vitality. It accepts—how can it do otherwise?—the nonsense that its elders tell it, but its youthful body, and the sweetness of the physical world, tell it another story. It was the same with Hell, which up to the age of about fourteen I officially believed in. Almost certainly Hell existed, and there were occasions when a vivid sermon could scare you into fits. But somehow it never lasted. The fire that waited for you was real fire, it would hurt in the same way as when you burnt your finger, and *for ever,* but most of the time you could contemplate it without bothering.

5

The various codes which were presented to you at Crossgates—religious, moral, social and intellectual—contradicted one another if you worked out their implications. The essential conflict was between the tradition of nineteenth-century asceticism and the actually existing luxury and snobbery of the pre-1914 age. On the one side were low-church Bible Christianity, sex puritanism, insistence on hard work, respect for academic distinction, disapproval of self-indulgence: on the other, contempt for "braininess" and worship of games, contempt for foreigners and the working class, an almost neurotic dread of poverty, and, above all, the assumption not only that money and privilege are the things that matter, but that it is better to inherit them than to have to work for them. Broadly, you were bidden to be at once a Christian and a social success, which is impossible. At the time I did not perceive that the various ideals which were set before us cancelled out. I merely saw that they were all, or nearly all, unattainable, so far as I was concerned, since they all depended not only on what you did but on what you *were.*

Very early, at the age of only ten or eleven, I reached the conclusion—no one told me this, but on the other hand I did not simply make it up out of my own head: somehow it was in the air I breathed—that you were no good unless you had £100,000. I had perhaps fixed on this particular sum as a result of reading Thackeray. The interest on £100,000 a year (I was in favour of a safe 4 per cent), would be £4,000, and this seemed to me the minimum income that you must possess if you were to belong to the real top crust, the people in the country houses. But it was clear that I could never find my way into that paradise, to which you did not really belong unless you were born into it. You could only *make* money, if at all, by a mysterious operation called "going into the City," and when you came out of the City, having won your £10,000, you were fat and old. But the truly enviable thing about the top-notchers was that they were rich while young. For people like me, the ambitious middle class, the examination passers, only a bleak, laborious kind of success was possible. You clambered upwards on a ladder of scholarships into the Home Civil Service or the Indian Civil Service, or possibly you became a barrister. And if at any point you "slacked" or "went off" and missed one of the rungs in the ladder, you became "a little office boy at forty pounds a year." But even if you climbed to the highest niche that was open to you, you could still only be an underling, a hanger-on of the people who really counted.

Even if I had not learned this from Sim and Bingo, I would have learned it from the other boys. Looking back, it is astonishing how intimately, intelligently snobbish we all were, how knowledgeable about names and addresses, how swift to detect small differences in accents and manners and the cut of clothes. There were some boys who seemed to drop money from their pores even in the bleak misery of the middle of a winter term. At the beginning and end of the term, especially, there was naively snobbish chatter about Switzerland, and Scotland with its ghillies and grouse moors, and "my uncle's yacht," and "our place in the country," and "my pony" and "my pater's touring car." There never was, I suppose, in the history of the world a time when the sheer vulgar fatness of wealth, without any kind of aristocratic elegance to redeem it, was so obtrusive as in those years before 1914. It was the age when crazy millionaires in curly top hats and lavender waistcoats gave champagne parties in rococo houseboats on the Thames, the age of diabolo and hobble skirts, the age of the "knut" in his grey bowler and cutaway coat, the age of *The Merry Widow,* Saki's novels, *Peter Pan* and *Where the Rainbow Ends,* the age when people talked about chocs and cigs and ripping and topping and heavenly, when they went for divvy weekends at Brighton and had scrumptious teas at the Troc. From the whole decade before 1914, there seems to breathe forth a smell of the more vulgar, un-grown-up kinds of luxury, a smell of brilliantine and crème de menthe and soft-centred chocolates—an atmosphere, as it were, of eating everlasting strawberry ices on green lawns to the tune of the Eton Boating Song. The extraordinary thing was the way in which everyone took it for granted that this oozing, bulging wealth of the English upper and upper-middle classes would last for ever, and was part of the order of things. After 1918 it was never quite the same again. Snobbishness and expensive habits came back, certainly, but they were self-conscious and on the defensive. Before the war the worship of money was entirely unreflecting and untroubled by any pang of conscience. The goodness of money was as unmistakable as the goodness of health or beauty, and a glittering car, a title or a horde of servants was mixed up in people's minds with the idea of actual moral virtue.

At Crossgates, in term time, the general bareness of life enforced a certain democracy, but any mention of the holidays, and the consequent competitive swanking about cars and butlers and country houses, promptly called class distinctions into being. The school was pervaded by a curious cult of Scotland, which brought out the fundamental contradiction in our standard of values. Bingo claimed Scottish ancestry, and she favoured the Scottish boys, encouraging them to wear kilts in their ancestral tartan instead of the school uniform, and even christened her youngest child by a Gaelic name. Ostensibly we were supposed to admire the Scots because they were "grim" and "dour" ("stern" was perhaps the key word), and irresistible on the field of battle. In the big schoolroom there was a steel engraving of the charge of the Scots Greys at Waterloo, all looking as though they enjoyed every moment of it. Our picture of Scotland was made up of burns, braes, kilts, sporrans, claymores, bagpipes, and the like, all somehow mixed up with the invigorating effects of porridge, Protestantism and a cold climate. But underlying this was something quite different. The real reason for the cult of Scotland was that only very rich people could spend their summers there. And the pretended belief in Scottish superiority was a cover for the bad conscience of the occupying English, who had pushed the Highland peasantry off their farms to make way for the deer forests, and then compensated them by turning them into servants. Bingo's face always beamed with innocent snobbishness when she spoke of Scotland. Occasionally she even attempted a trace of Scottish accent. Scotland was a private paradise which a few initiates could talk about and make outsiders feel small.

"You going to Scotland this hols?"

"Rather! We go every year."

"My pater's giving me a new gun for the twelfth. There's jolly good black game where we go. Get out, Smith! What are you listening for? You've never been in Scotland. I bet you don't know what a black-cock looks like."

Following on this, imitations of the cry of a black-cock, of the roaring of a stag, of the accent of "our ghillies," etc., etc.

And the questionings that new boys of doubtful social origin were sometimes put through—questionings quite surprising in their mean-minded particularity, when one reflects that the inquisitors were only twelve or thirteen!

"How much a year has your pater got? What part of London do you live in? Is that Knightsbridge or Kensington? How many bathrooms has your house got? How many servants do your people keep? Have you got a butler? Well, then, have you got a cook? Where do you get your clothes made? How many shows did you go to in the hols? How much money did you bring back with you?" etc., etc.

I have seen a little new boy, hardly older than eight, desperately lying his way through such a catechism:

"Have your people got a car?"

"Yes."

"What sort of car?"

"Daimler."

"How many horse-power?"

(Pause, and leap in the dark.) "Fifteen."

"What kind of lights?"

The little boy is bewildered.

"What kind of lights? Electric or acetylene?"

(A longer pause, and another leap in the dark.) "Acetylene."

"Coo! He says his pater's car's got acetylene lamps. They went out years ago. It must be as old as the hills."

"Rot! He's making it up. He hasn't got a car. He's just a navvy. Your pater's a navvy."

And so on.

By the social standards that prevailed about me, I was no good, and could not be any good. But all the different kinds of virtue seemed to be mysteriously interconnected and to belong to much the same people. It was not only money that mattered: there were also strength, beauty, charm, athleticism and something called "guts" or "character," which in reality meant the power to impose your will on others. I did not possess any of these qualities. At games, for instance, I was hopeless. I was a fairly good swimmer and not altogether contemptible at cricket, but these had no prestige value, because boys only attach importance to a game if it requires strength and courage. What counted was football, at which I was a funk. I loathed the game, and since I could see no pleasure or usefulness in it, it was very difficult for me to show courage at it. Football, it seemed to me, is not really played for the pleasure of kicking a ball about, but is a species of fighting. The lovers of football are large, boisterous, nobbly boys who are good at knocking down and trampling on slightly smaller boys. That was the pattern of school life—a continuous triumph of the strong over the weak. Virtue consisted in winning: it consisted in being bigger, stronger, handsomer, richer, more popular, more elegant, more unscrupulous than other people—in dominating them, bullying them, making them suffer pain, making them look foolish, getting the better of them in every way. Life was hierarchical and whatever happened was right. There were the strong, who deserved to win and always did win, and there were the weak, who deserved to lose and always did lose, everlastingly.

I did not question the prevailing standards, because so far as I could see there were no others. How could the rich, the strong, the elegant, the fashionable, the powerful, be in the wrong? It was their world, and the rules they made for it must be the right ones. And yet from a very early age I was aware of the impossibility of any *subjective* conformity. Always at the centre of my heart the inner self seemed to be awake, pointing out the difference between the moral obligation and the psychological *fact*. It was the same in all matters, worldly or other-worldly. Take religion, for instance. You were supposed to love God, and I did not question this. Till the age of about fourteen I believed in God, and believed that the accounts given of him were true. But I was well aware that I did not love him. On the contrary, I hated him, just as I hated Jesus and the Hebrew patriarchs. If I had sympathetic feelings towards any character in the Old Testament, it was towards such people as Cain, Jezebel, Haman, Agag, Sisera: in the New Testament my friends, if any, were Ananias, Caiaphas, Judas and Pontius Pilate. But the whole business of religion seemed to be strewn with psychological impossibilities. The Prayer Book told you, for example, to love God and fear him: but how could you love someone whom you feared? With your private affections it was the same. What you *ought* to feel was usually clear enough, but the appropriate emotion could not be commanded. Obviously it was my duty to feel grateful towards Bingo and Sim; but I was not grateful. It was equally clear that one ought to love one's father, but I knew very well that I merely disliked my own father, whom I had barely seen before I was eight and who appeared to me simply as a gruff-voiced elderly man forever saying "Don't." It was not that one did not want to possess the right qualities or feel the correct emotions, but that one could not. The good and the possible never seemed to coincide.

There was a line of verse that I came across, not actually while I was at Crossgates, but a year or two later, and which seemed to strike a sort of leaden echo in my heart. It was: "The armies of unalterable law." I understood to perfection what it meant to be Lucifer, defeated and justly defeated, with no possibility of revenge. The schoolmasters with their canes, the millionaires with their Scottish castles, the athletes with their curly hair —these were the armies of the unalterable law. It was not easy, at that date, to realise that in fact it *was* alterable. And according to that law I was damned. I had no money, I was weak, I was ugly, I was unpopular, I had a chronic cough, I was cowardly, I smelt. This picture, I should add, was not altogether fanciful. I was an unattractive boy. Crossgates soon made me so, even if I had not been so before. But a child's belief in its own shortcomings is not much influenced by facts. I believed, for example, that I "smelt," but this was based simply on general probability. It was notorious that disagreeable people smelt, and therefore presumably I did so too. Again, until after I had left school for good I continued to believe that I was preternaturally ugly. It was what my schoolfellows had told me, and I had no other authority to refer to. The conviction that it was *not possible* for me to be a success went deep enough to influence my actions till far into adult life. Until I was about thirty I always planned my life on the assumption not only that any major undertaking was bound to fail, but that I could only expect to live a few years longer.

But this sense of guilt and inevitable failure was balanced by something else: that is, the instinct to survive. Even a creature that is weak, ugly, cowardly, smelly and in no way justifiable still wants to stay alive and be happy after its own fashion. I could not invert the existing scale of values, or turn myself into a success, but I could accept my failure and make the best of it. I could resign myself to being what I was, and then endeavour to survive on those terms.

To survive, or at least to preserve any kind of independence, was essentially criminal, since it meant breaking rules which you yourself recognized. There was a boy named Johnny Hall who for some months oppressed me horribly. He was a big, powerful, coarsely handsome boy with a very red face and curly black hair, who was forever twisting somebody's arm, wringing somebody's ear, flogging somebody with a riding crop (he was a member of the Sixth Form), or performing prodigies of activity on the football field. Bingo loved him (hence the fact that he was habitually called by his Christian name), and Sim commended him as a boy who "had character" and could "keep order." He was followed about by a group of toadies who nicknamed him Strong Man.

One day, when we were taking off our overcoats in the changing-room, Hall picked on me for some reason. I "answered him back," whereupon he gripped my wrist, twisted it round, and bent my forearm back upon itself in a hideously painful way. I remember his handsome, jeering red face bearing down upon mine. He was, I think, older than I, besides being enormously stronger. As he let go of me a terrible, wicked resolve formed itself in my heart. I would get back on him by hitting him when he did not expect it. It was a strategic moment, for the master who had been "taking" the walk would be coming back almost immediately, and then there could be no fight. I let perhaps a minute go by, walked up to Hall with the most harmless air I could assume, and then, getting the weight of my body behind it, smashed my fist into his face. He was flung backwards by the blow and some blood ran out of his mouth. His always sanguine face turned almost black with rage. Then he turned away to rinse his mouth at the washing-basins.

"All right!" he said to me between his teeth as the master led us away.

For days after this he followed me about, challenging me to fight. Although terrified out of my wits, I steadily refused to fight. I said that the blow in the face had served him right, and there was an end of it. Curiously enough he did not simply fall upon me then and there, which public opinion would probably have supported him in doing. So gradually the matter tailed off, and there was no fight.

Now, I had behaved wrongly, by my own code no less than his. To hit him unawares was wrong. But to refuse to fight afterwards, knowing that if we fought he would beat me—that was far worse: it was cowardly. If I had refused because I disapproved of fighting, or because I genuinely felt the matter to be closed, it would have been all right; but I had refused merely because I was afraid. Even my revenge was made empty by that fact. I had struck the blow in a moment of mindless violence, deliberately not looking far ahead and merely determined to get my own back for once and damn the consequences. I had had time to realise that what I did was wrong, but it was the kind of crime from which you could get some satisfaction. Now all was nullified. There had been a sort of courage in the first act, but my subsequent cowardice had wiped it out.

The fact I hardly noticed was that although Hall formally challenged me to fight, he did not actually attack me. Indeed, after receiving that one blow he never oppressed me again. It was perhaps twenty years before I saw the significance of this. At the time I could not see beyond the moral dilemma that is presented to the weak in a world governed by the strong: Break the rules, or perish. I did not see that in that case the weak have the right to make a different set of rules for themselves; because, even if such an idea had occurred to me, there was no one in my environment who could have confirmed me in it. I lived in a world of boys, gregarious animals, questioning nothing, accepting the law of the stronger and avenging their own humiliations by passing them down to someone smaller. My situation was that of countless other boys, and if potentially I was more of a rebel than most, it was only because, by boyish standards, I was a poorer specimen. But I never did rebel intellectually, only emotionally. I had nothing to help me except my dumb selfishness, my inability—not, indeed, to despise myself, but to *dislike* myself—my instinct to survive.

It was about a year after I hit Johnny Hall in the face that I left Crossgates for ever. It was the end of a winter term. With a sense of coming out from darkness into sunlight I put on my Old Boy's tie as we dressed for the journey. I well remember the feeling of that brand-new silk tie round my neck, a feeling of emancipation, as though the tie had been at once a badge of manhood and an amulet against Bingo's voice and Sim's cane. I was escaping from bondage. It was not that I expected, or even intended, to be any more successful at a public school than I had been at Crossgates. But still, I was escaping. I knew that at a public school there would be more privacy, more neglect, more chance to be idle and self-indulgent and degenerate. For years past I had been resolved—unconsciously at first, but consciously later on—that when once my scholarship was won I would "slack off" and cram no longer. This resolve, by the way, was so fully carried out that between the ages of thirteen and twenty-two or -three I hardly ever did a stroke of avoidable work.

Bingo shook hands to say good-bye. She even gave me my Christian name for the occasion. But there was a sort of patronage, almost a sneer, in her face and in her voice. The tone in which she said good-bye was nearly the tone in which she had been used to say *little butterflies.* I had won two scholarships, but I was a failure, because success was measured not by what you did but by what you *were*. I was "not a good type of boy" and could bring no credit on the school. I did not possess character or courage or health or strength or money, or even good manners, the power to look like a gentleman.

"Good-bye," Bingo's parting smile seemed to say; "it's not worth quarrelling now. You haven't made much of a success of your time at Crossgates, have you? And I don't suppose you'll get on awfully well at a public school either. We made a mistake, really, in wasting our time and money on you. This kind of education hasn't much to offer to a boy with your background and outlook. Oh, don't think we don't understand you! We know all about those ideas you have at the back of your head, we know you disbelieve in everything we've taught you, and we know you aren't in the least grateful for all we've done for you. But there's no use in bringing it all up now. We aren't responsible for you any longer, and we shan't be seeing you again. Let's just admit that you're one of our failures and part without ill-feeling. And so, good-bye."

That at least was what I read into her face. And yet how happy I was, that winter morning, as the train bore me away with the gleaming new silk tie round my neck! The world was opening before me, just a little, like a grey sky which exhibits a narrow crack of blue. A public school would be better fun than Crossgates but at bottom equally alien. In a world where the prime necessities were money, titled relatives, athleticism, tailor-made clothes, neatly brushed hair, a charming smile, I was no good. All I had gained was a breathing-space. A little quietude, a little self-indulgence, a little respite from cramming—and then, ruin. What kind of ruin I did not know: perhaps the colonies or an office stool, perhaps prison or an early death. But first a year or two in which one could "slack off" and get the benefit of one's sins, like Doctor Faustus. It is the advantage of being thirteen that you can not only live in the moment, but do so with full consciousness, foreseeing the future and yet not caring about it. Next term I was going to Wellington. I had also won a scholarship at Eton, but was uncertain whether there would be a vacancy, and I was going to Wellington first. At Eton you had a room to yourself—a room which might even have a fire in it. At Wellington you had your own cubicle, and could make cocoa in the evenings. The privacy of it, the grown-upness! And there would be libraries to hang about in, and summer afternoons when you could shirk games and mooch about the countryside alone, with no master driving you along. Meanwhile there were the holidays. There was the .22 rifle that I had bought the previous holidays (the Crackshot, it was called, costing twenty-two and sixpence), and Christmas was coming next week. There were also the pleasures of overeating. I thought of some particularly voluptuous cream buns which could be bought for twopence each at a shop in our town. (This was 1916, and food-rationing had not yet started.) Even the detail that my journey-money had been slightly miscalculated, leaving about a shilling over—enough for an unforeseen cup of coffee and a cake or two somewhere on the way—was enough to fill me with bliss. There was time for a bit of happiness before the future closed in upon me. But I did know that the future was dark. Failure, failure, failure—failure behind me, failure ahead of me—that was by far the deepest conviction that I carried away.

6

All this was thirty years ago and more. The question is: Does a child at school go through the same kind of experiences nowadays?

The only honest answer, I believe, is that we do not with certainty know. Of course it is obvious that the present-day *attitude* towards education is enormously more humane and sensible than that of the past. The snobbishness that was an integral part of my own education would be almost unthinkable today, because the society that nourished it is dead. I recall a conversation that must have taken place about a year before I left Crossgates. A Russian boy, large and fair-haired, a year older than myself, was questioning me.

"How much a year has your father got?"

I told him what I thought it was, adding a few hundreds to make it sound better. The Russian boy, neat in his habits, produced a pencil and a small notebook and made a calculation.

"My father has over two hundred times as much money as yours," he announced with a sort of amused contempt.

That was in 1915. What happened to that money a couple of years later, I wonder? And still more I wonder, do conversations of that kind happen at preparatory schools now?

Clearly there has been a vast change of outlook, a general growth of "enlightenment," even among ordinary, unthinking middle-class people. Religious belief, for instance, has largely vanished, dragging other kinds of nonsense after it. I imagine that very few people nowadays would tell a child that if it masturbates it will end in the lunatic asylum. Beating, too, has become discredited, and has even been abandoned at many schools. Nor is the underfeeding of children looked on as a normal, almost meritorious act. No one now would openly set out to give his pupils as little food as they could do with, or tell them that it is healthy to get up from a meal as hungry as you sat down. The whole status of children has improved, partly because they have grown relatively less numerous. And the diffusion of even a little psychological knowledge has made it harder for parents and schoolteachers to indulge their aberrations in the name of discipline. Here is a case, not known to me personally, but known to someone I can vouch for, and happening within my own lifetime. A small girl, daughter of a clergyman, continued wetting her bed at an age when she should have grown out of it. In order to punish her for this dreadful deed, her father took her to a large garden party and there introduced her to the whole company as a little girl who wetted her bed: and to underline her wickedness he had previously painted her face black. I do not suggest that Bingo and Sim would actually have done a thing like this, but I doubt whether it would have much surprised them. After all, things do change. And yet—!

The question is not whether boys are still buckled into Eton collars on Sunday or told that babies are dug up under gooseberry bushes. That kind of thing is at an end, admittedly. The real question is whether it is still normal for a school child to live for years amid irrational terrors and lunatic misunderstandings. And here one is up against the very great difficulty of knowing what a child really feels and thinks. A child which appears reasonably happy may actually be suffering horrors which it cannot or will not reveal. It lives in a sort of alien under-water world which we can only penetrate by memory or divination. Our chief clue is the fact that we were once children ourselves, and many people appear to forget the atmosphere of their own childhood almost entirely. Think for instance of the unnecessary torments that people will inflict by sending a child back to school with clothes of the wrong pattern, and refusing to see that this matters! Over things of this kind a child will sometimes utter a protest, but a great deal of the time its attitude is one of simple concealment. Not to expose your true feelings to an adult seems to be instinctive from the age of seven or eight onwards. Even the affection that one feels for a child, the desire to protect and cherish it, is a cause of misunderstanding. One can love a child, perhaps, more deeply than one can love another adult, but is rash to assume that the child feels any love in return. Looking back on my own childhood, after the infant years were over, I do not believe that I ever felt love for any mature person, except my mother, and even her I did not trust, in the sense that shyness made me conceal most of my real feelings from her. Love, the spontaneous, unqualified emotion of love, was something I could only feel for people who were young. Towards people who were old—and remember that "old" to a child means over thirty, or even over twenty-five—I could feel reverence, respect, admiration or compunction, but I seemed cut off from them by a veil of fear and shyness mixed up with physical distaste. People are too ready to forget the child's *physical* shrinking from the adult. The enormous size of grown-ups, their ungainly, rigid bodies, their coarse wrinkled skins, their great relaxed eyelids, their yellow teeth, and the whiffs of musty clothes and beer and sweat and tobacco that disengage from them at every movement! Part of the reason for the ugliness of adults, in a child's eyes, is that the child is usually looking upwards, and few faces are at their best when seen from below. Besides, being fresh and unmarked itself, the child has impossibly high standards in the matter of skin and teeth and complexion. But the greatest barrier of all is the child's misconception about age. A child can hardly envisage life beyond thirty, and in judging people's ages it will make fantastic mistakes. It will think that a person of twenty-five is forty, that a person of forty is sixty-five, and so on. Thus, when I fell in love with Elsie I took her to be grown up. I met her again, when I was thirteen and she, I think, must have been twenty-three; she now seemed to me a middle-aged woman, somewhat past her best. And the child thinks of growing old as an almost obscene calamity, which for some mysterious reason will never happen to itself. All who have passed the age of thirty are joyless grotesques, endlessly fussing about things of no importance and staying alive without, so far as the child can see, having anything to live for. Only child life is real life. The schoolmaster who imagines he is loved and trusted by his boys is in fact mimicked and laughed at behind his back. An adult who does not seem dangerous nearly always seems ridiculous.

I base these generalisations on what I can recall of my own childhood outlook. Treacherous though memory is, it seems to me the chief means we have of discovering how a child's mind works. Only by resurrecting our own memories can we realise how incredibly distorted is the child's vision of the world. Consider this, for example. How would Crossgates appear to me now, if I could go back, at my present age, and see it as it was in 1915? What should I think of Bingo and Sim, those terrible, all-powerful monsters? I should see them as a couple of silly, shallow, ineffectual people, eagerly clambering up a social ladder which any thinking person could see to be on the point of collapse. I would be no more frightened of them than I would be frightened of a dormouse. Moreover, in those days they seemed to me fantastically old, whereas—though of this I am not certain—I imagine they must have been somewhat younger than I am now. And how would Johnny Hall appear, with his blacksmith's arms and his red, jeering face? Merely a scruffy little boy, barely distinguishable from hundreds of other scruffy little boys. The two sets of facts can lie side by side in my mind, because these happen to be my own memories. But it would be very difficult for me to see with the eyes of any other child, except by an effort of the imagination which might lead me completely astray. The child and the adult live in different worlds. If that is so, we cannot be certain that school, at any rate boarding school, is not still for many children as dreadful an experience as it used to be. Take away God, Latin, the cane, class distinctions and sexual taboos, and the fear, the hatred, the snobbery and the misunderstanding might still all be there. It will have been seen that my own main trouble was an utter lack of any sense of proportion or probability. This led me to accept outrages and believe absurdities, and to suffer torments over things which were in fact of no importance. It is not enough to say that I was "silly" and "ought to have known better." Look back into your own childhood and think of the nonsense you used to believe and the trivialities which could make you suffer. Of course my own case had its individual variations, but essentially it was that of countless other boys. The weakness of the child is that it starts with a blank sheet. It neither understands nor questions the society in which it lives, and because of its credulity other people can work upon it, infecting it with the sense of inferiority and the dread of offending against mysterious, terrible laws. It may be that everything that happened to me at Crossgates could happen in the most "enlightened" school, though perhaps in subtler forms. Of one thing, however, I do feel fairly sure, and that is that boarding schools are worse than day schools. A child has a better chance with the sanctuary of its home near at hand. And I think the characteristic faults of the English upper and middle classes may be partly due to the practice, general until recently, of sending children away from home as young as nine, eight or even seven.

I have never been back to Crossgates. In a way it is only within the last decade that I have really thought over my schooldays, vividly though their memory has haunted me. Nowadays, I believe, it would make very little impression on me to see the place again, if it still exists. And if I went inside and smelt again the inky, dusty smell of the big schoolroom, the rosiny smell of the chapel, the stagnant smell of the swimming bath and the cold reek of the lavatories, I think I should only feel what one invariably feels in revisiting any scene of childhood: How small everything has grown, and how terrible is the deterioration in myself!

IV

Other Cultures,
Other Continents

At last! "one of MY guys."

IVAN TURGENEV

Ivan Turgenev (1818–1883) is in the pantheon of great nineteenth-century Russian writers, along with Pushkin, Gogol, Tolstoy, Dostoevsky, and Chekhov. He was the leader of the Westernizing, progressive wing of Russian letters, as opposed to the more isolationist, mystically inclined Slavophiles, ✳ *such as Dostoevsky. Turgenev came early to an understanding of injustice, watching his cruel, domineering mother mistreat the peasants on her estate and everyone else around her. Indeed, his short story collection,* A Sportsman's Sketches, *is credited with helping to convince Alexander II to emancipate the serfs. Although Turgenev's fiction (*Fathers and Sons, Virgin Soil,* +2 here and others) grew out of a political analysis of the social conditions in Russia and an attempt to influence their direction, he was not a propagandist, preferring instead to practice the objective, observant, uninsistent storytelling associated with the French realist school. He spent a great deal of time in Paris, where he befriended many of the great writers of the day, such as Flaubert and George Sand; his career has come to embody cosmopolitanism and humaneness.*

Turgenev was a powerful and accomplished essayist—not surprising for a writer who elevated the literary sketch to an art. "The Execution of Tropmann," included in his Literary Reminiscences, *was one of his autobiographical sketches from Paris, written shortly after the event, when it was still fresh in his mind. Tropmann had been convicted of the murder of a man named Kink, his wife, and their six children, and was executed on January 19, 1870. Turgenev's essay—one of the strongest indictments of capital punishment ever written—is particularly effective because it implicates the writer in the barbarity of the deed, as a semi-unwilling voyeur to the carnival atmosphere of a public guillotining. The piece may thus be seen as a*

forerunner of the New Journalism, in which the very notion of journalistic neutrality is questioned and writers include themselves in the tale, letting subjective feelings color the report. It is interesting that Dostoevsky, who
✳ *detested Turgenev, mocked the writer's "squeamishness, about himself, about his own integrity and peace of mind, and that in the sight of a chopped off head!"—a willful misinterpretation of Turgenev's scruples as narcissism. The piece also belongs to the subgenre of description of an urban spectacle, to which Hazlitt and Lamb and many other nineteenth-century writers were attracted and which characterized the crowd as either benign or malevolent but in any case alive, with a will of its own.*

The Execution of Tropmann

1

IN JANUARY OF THE CURRENT YEAR (1870), while din-ing in Paris at the house of an old friend of mine, I received from M. Du Camp, the well-known writer and expert on the statistics of Paris, quite an unexpected invitation to be present at the execution of Tropmann —and not only at his execution: it was proposed that I should be admitted to the prison itself together with a small number of other privileged persons. The terrible crime committed by Tropmann has not yet been forgotten, but at that time Paris was interested in him and his impending execution as much as, if not more than, the recent appointment of the pseudo-Parliamentarian ministry of Olivier or the murder of Victor Noir, who fell at the hand of the afterwards surprisingly acquitted Prince P[ierre] Bonaparte. In the windows of all the photographers' and stationers' shops were exhibited whole rows of photographs showing a young fellow with a large forehead, dark eyes and puffy lips, the "famous" Pantin murderer (*de l'illustre assassin de Pantin*), and already for some evenings running thousands of workmen had gathered in the environs of the Roquette prison in the vain expectation of the erection of the guillotine, and dispersed only after midnight. Taken by surprise by M. Du Camp's proposal, I accepted it without giving it much thought. And having promised to arrive at the place fixed for our meeting—at the statue of Prince Eugene, on the boulevard of the same name, at 11 o'clock in the evening—I did not want to go back on my word. False pride prevented my doing so. . . . And what if they should think that I was a coward? As a punishment of myself—and as a lesson to others—I should now like to tell everything I saw. I intend to revive in my memory all the painful impressions of that night. It will not be only the reader's curiosity that will be satisfied: he may derive some benefit from my story.

2

A small crowd of people was already waiting for Du Camp and me at the statue of Prince Eugene. Among them was M. Claude, the police commissioner of Paris *(chef de la police de sûreté),* to whom Du Camp introduced me. The others were, like myself, privileged visitors, journalists, reporters, etc. Du Camp had warned me that we should probably have to spend a sleepless night in the office of the prison governor. The execution of condemned criminals takes place in winter at seven o'clock in the morning; but one has to be at the prison before midnight or one might not be able to push one's way through the crowd. There is only about half a mile from the statue of Prince Eugene to the Roquette prison, but so far I could see nothing in any way out of the ordinary. There were just a few more people on the boulevard than usual. One thing, though, one could not help noting: almost all the people were going—and some, especially women, running along—in the same direction: besides, all the cafés and pot-houses were ablaze with lights, which is very rare in the remote quarters of Paris, especially so late at night. The night was not foggy, but dull, damp without rain, and cold without frost, a typical French January night. M. Claude said that it was time to go, and off we went. He preserved the imperturbable cheerfulness of a man of affairs in whom such events did not arouse any feelings, except perhaps the desire to have done with his sad duty as soon as possible. M. Claude was a man of about fifty, of medium height, thick-set, broad-shouldered, with a round, closely cropped head and small, almost minute, features. Only his forehead and chin, and the back of his head, were extraordinarily broad; his unflinching energy came out in his dry and even voice, his pale, grey eyes, his short, strong fingers, in his muscular legs, and in all his unhurried but firm movements. He was said to be an expert at his profession, who inspired mortal terror in all thieves and murderers. Political crimes were not part of his duties. His assistant, M. J. . . . , whom Du Camp also greatly admired, looked like a kindly, almost sentimental man and his manners were much more refined. With the exception of these two gentlemen and perhaps Du Camp, we all felt a little awkward—or did it only seem to me to be so?—and a little ashamed, too, though we walked along jauntily—as though on a shooting expedition.

The nearer we came to the prison, the more crowded the streets became, though there were no real crowds as yet. No shouts could be heard, nor even any too loud conversations; it was evident that the "performance" had not yet commenced. Only the street urchins were already weaving round us; with their hands thrust in the pockets of their trousers and the peaks of their caps pulled over their eyes, they sauntered along with that special lolling, flitting gait, which can only be seen in Paris and which in the twinkling of an eye can be changed into a most quick run and the leaps of a monkey.

"There he is—there he is—it's him!" a few voices shouted around us.

"Why," Du Camp said to me suddenly, "you have been mistaken for the executioner!"

"A lovely beginning!" I thought.

The Paris executioner, *Monsieur de Paris,* whose acquaintance I made during that same night, is as tall and as grey as I.

But soon we came to a long, not too wide, square, bounded on two sides by two barrack-like buildings of grimy aspect and crude architecture: that was Roquette Square. On the left was the prison for young criminals (*prison des jeunes détenus)* and on the right—the house of the condemned prisoners (*maison de dépôt pour les condamnés),* or Roquette Prison.

3

A squad of soldiers was drawn up four deep right across the square, and about two hundred feet from it, another squad was also drawn up four deep. As a rule, no soldiers are present at an execution, but this time, in view of Tropmann's "reputation" and the present state of public opinion, excited by Noir's murder, the government thought it necessary to take special measures and not to leave the preservation of law and order to the police alone. The main gates of Roquette prison were exactly in the centre of the empty space, closed in by the soldiers. A few police sergeants walked slowly up and down before the gates; a young, rather fat police officer in an unusually richly embroidered cap (as it appeared the chief inspector of that quarter of the city) rushed upon our group with such insolence that it reminded me of the good old days in my beloved country, but recognizing his superiors, he calmed down. They let us into the small guard-room beside the gates with immense precautions, hardly opening the gates, and—after a preliminary examination and interrogation, took us across two inner courtyards, one large and another small, to the governor's lodgings. The governor, a tall, stalwart man, with a grey moustache and imperial, had the typical face of a French infantry officer, an aquiline nose, immobile, rapacious eyes and a tiny skull. He received us very politely and benignly; but even without his being aware of it, every gesture of his, every word of his, at once showed that he was "a reliable fellow" *(un gaillard solide),* an utterly loyal servant, who would not hesitate to carry out any order of his master. Indeed, he had proved his zeal in action: on the night of the *coup d'état* of December 2nd, he occupied with his battalion the printing works of the *Moniteur.* Like a real gentleman, he put the whole of his apartment at our disposal. It was on the second floor of the main building and consisted of four fairly well furnished rooms; in two of them a fire was lit in the fireplace. A small Italian greyhound with a dislocated leg and a mournful expression in her eyes, as though she, too, felt to be a prisoner, limped about, wagging her tail, from one rug to another. There were eight of us visitors; some of them I recognized from their photographs (Sardou, Albert Wolf), but I did not feel like talking to any of them. We all sat down on chairs in the drawing-room (Du Camp had gone out with M. Claude). It goes without saying that Tropmann became the subject of conversation and, as it were, the centre of all our thoughts. The prison governor told us that he had been asleep since nine o'clock in the evening and that he slept like a log; that he seemed to have guessed what had happened to his request for a reprieve; that he had implored him, the governor, to tell him the truth; that he kept insisting stubbornly that he had accomplices whom he refused to name; that he would probably lose his nerve at the decisive moment, but that he ate with appetite, did not read books, etc., etc. For our part, some of us wondered whether one ought to give credence to the words of a criminal who had proved himself to be an inveterate liar, went over the details of the murder, asked ourselves what the phrenologists would make of Tropmann's skull, raised the question of capital punishment—but all this was so lifeless, so dull, so platitudinous, that even those who spoke did not feel like carrying on. To talk of something else was rather embarrassing—impossible; impossible out of respect for death alone, for the man who was doomed to die. We were all overwhelmed by a feeling of irksome and wearisome—yes, wearisome-uneasiness: no one was really bored, but this dreary feeling was a hundred times worse than boredom! It seemed as though there would be no end to the night! As for me, there was one thing I was sure of, namely that I had no right to be where I was, that no psychological or philosophic considerations excused me. M. Claude came back and told us how the notorious Jude had slipped through his fingers and how he was still hoping to catch him if he was still alive. But suddenly we heard the heavy clatter of wheels and a few moments later we were informed that the guillotine had arrived. We all rushed out into the street—just as though we were glad of the news!

4

Before the prison gates stood a huge, closed van, drawn by three horses, harnessed one behind the other; another, two-wheeled van, a small and low one, which looked like an oblong box and was drawn by one horse, had stopped a little further off. (That one, as we learned later, was to convey the body of the executed man to the cemetery immediately after the execution.) A few workmen in short blouses were to be seen round the vans, and a tall man in a round hat, white necktie and a light overcoat thrown over his shoulders, was giving orders in an undertone. . . . That was the executioner. All the authorities—the prison governor, M. Claude, the district police inspector, and so on, were surrounding and greeting him. *"Ah, Monsieur Indric! bon soir, Monsieur Indric!"* (His real name is Heidenreich: he is an Alsatian.) Our group, too, walked up to him: *he* became for a moment the centre of our attention. There was a certain strained but respectful familiarity in the way he was treated by everybody. "We don't look down upon you for you are, after all, a person of importance!" Some of us, probably just to show off, even shook hands with him. (He had a pair of beautiful hands of remarkable whiteness.) I recalled a line from Pushkin's *Poltava:—*

> *The executioner . . .*
> *Playing with his white hands . . .*

M. Indric carried himself very simply, gently and courteously, but not without a touch of patriarchal gravity. It seemed that he felt that we regarded him that night as only second in importance after Tropmann, and, as it were, his first minister.

The workmen opened the big van and began taking out of it all the component parts of the guillotine, which they had to put up within fifteen feet of the prison gates.[1] Two lanterns began moving to and fro just above the ground, lighting up the polished cobblestones of the roadway with small, bright circles of light. I looked at my watch—it was only half past twelve! It had grown much duller and colder. There was already a great number of people about—and behind the lines of the soldiers, bordering the empty space in front of the prison, there rose the uninterrupted and confused din of human voices. I walked up to the soldiers: they stood motionless, drawing closer a little and breaking the original symmetry of

---

[1] The readers who wish to acquaint themselves not only with all the particulars of the "execution" but also with everything that comes before it, should consult M. Du Camp's excellent article: *La Prison de la Roquette* in the *Revue des deux Mondes,* No. 1, 1870.

their ranks. Their faces expressed nothing but cold and patiently submissive boredom; and even the faces I could discern behind the shakos and
uniforms of the soldiers and behind the three-cornered hats and tunics of
the policemen, the faces of the workmen and artisans, expressed almost
the same thing, only with the addition of a sort of indefinable irony. In
front, from behind the massively stirring and pressing crowd, one could
hear exclamations, like: *Ohé Tropmann! Ohé Lambert! Fallait pas qu'y
aille!* Shouts, shrill whistles. One could clearly make out some abusive
argument about a place, a fragment of a cynical song came creeping along
like a snake—and there was a sudden burst of loud laughter, instantly
caught up in the crowd and ending with a roar of coarse guffaws. The
"real business" had not yet begun; one could not hear the anti-dynastic
shouts everyone expected, nor the all too familiar menacing reverberations
of the Marseillaise.

I went back to the place near the slowly growing guillotine. A certain
gentleman, curly-headed and dark-faced, in a soft, grey hat, probably a
lawyer, was standing beside me haranguing two or three other gentlemen
in tightly buttoned up overcoats, waving the forefinger of his right hand
forcefully up and down, trying to prove that Tropmann was not a murderer, but a maniac. *"Un maniaque! Je vais vous le prouver! Suivez mon
raisonnement!"* he kept saying. *"Son mobile n'était pas l'assassinat, mais un
orgueil que je nommerais volontiers démesuré! Suivez mon raisonnement!"*
The gentlemen in the overcoats "followed his reasoning," but, judging by
their expressions, he scarcely convinced them; and the worker who sat on
the platform of the guillotine looked at him with undisguised contempt. I
returned to the prison governor's apartment.

5

A few of our "colleagues" had already gathered there. The courteous governor was regaling them with mulled wine. Again they started discussing
whether Tropmann was still asleep, what he ought to be feeling and
whether he could hear the noise of the people in spite of the distance of
his cell from the street, and so on. The governor showed us a whole heap
of letters addressed to Tropmann, who, as the governor assured us, refused to read them. Most of them seemed to be full of silly jokes, but there
were also some that were serious, in which he was conjured to repent and
confess everything; one Methodist clergyman sent a whole theological thesis on twenty pages; there were also small notes from ladies, who even
enclosed flowers—marguerites and immortelles—in some of them. The
prison governor told us that Tropmann had tried to get some poison from
the prison pharmacist and wrote a letter asking for it, which the pharma-

cist, of course, at once forwarded to the authorities. I could not help feeling that our worthy host was rather at a loss to explain to himself the interest we took in a man like Tropmann who, in his opinion, was a savage and disgusting animal, and almost ascribed it to the idle curiosity of civilian men of the world, the "idle rich." After a little talk we just crawled off into different corners. During the whole of that night we wandered about like condemned souls, *"comme des âmes en peine,"* as the French say; went into rooms, sat down side by side on chairs in the drawing room, inquired after Tropmann, glanced at the clock, yawned, went downstairs into the yard and into the street again, came back, again sat down. . . . Some told drawing room stories, exchanged trivial personal news, touched lightly on politics, the theatre, Noir's murder; others tried to crack jokes, to say something witty, but, somehow, it did not come off at all and—provoked a sort of unpleasant laughter, which was cut short immediately, and a sort of false approbation. I found a tiny sofa in the first room and, somehow or other, managed to lie down on it. I tried to sleep but, of course, did not sleep. I did not doze off for one moment.

The distant hollow noise of the crowd was getting louder, deeper and more and more unbroken. At three o'clock, according to M. Claude, who kept coming into the room, sitting down on a chair, falling asleep at once and disappearing again, summoned by one of his subordinates, there were already more than twenty-five thousand people gathered there. The noise struck me by its resemblance to the distant roar of the sea: the same sort of unending Wagnerian *crescendo,* not rising continuously, but with huge intervals between the ebb and flow; the shrill notes of women's and children's voices rose in the air like thin spray over this enormous rumbling noise; there was the brutal power of some elemental force discernible in it. It would grow quiet and die down for a moment, then the hubbub would start again, grow and swell, and in another moment it seemed about to strike, as though wishing to tear everything down, and then it would again retreat, grow quiet, and again swell—and there seemed to be no end to it. And what, I could not help asking myself, did this noise signify? Impatience, joy, malice? No! It did not serve as an echo of any separate, any human feeling. . . . It was simply the rumble and the roar of some elemental force.

6

At about three o'clock in the morning I must have gone out for the tenth time into the street. The guillotine was ready. Its two beams, separated by about two feet, with the slanting line of the connecting blade, stood out dimly and strangely rather than terribly against the dark sky. For some reason I imagined that those beams ought to be more distant from each other; their proximity lent the whole machine a sort of sinister shapeliness, the shapeliness of a long, carefully stretched out swan's neck. The large, dark-red wicker basket, looking like a suitcase, aroused a feeling of disgust in me. I knew that the executioners would throw the warm and still quivering dead body and the cut off head into that basket. . . . The mounted police *(garde municipale),* who had arrived a little earlier, took up their position in a large semi-circle before the façade of the prison; from time to time the horses neighed, gnawed at their bits and tossed their heads; large drops of froth showed up white on the road between their forelegs. The riders dozed sombrely beneath their bearskins, pulled over their eyes. The lines of the soldiers, cutting across the square and holding back the crowds, fell back further: now there were not two hundred but three hundred feet of empty space before the prison. I went up to one of those lines and gazed for a long time at the people crammed behind it; their shouting actually was elemental, that is, senseless. I still remember the face of a workman, a young fellow of about twenty: he stood there grinning, with his eyes fixed on the ground, just as though he were thinking of something amusing, then he would suddenly throw back his head, open his mouth wide and begin to shout in a drawn-out voice, without words, and then his head would again drop and he would start grinning again. What was going on inside that man? Why did he consign himself to such a painfully sleepless night, to an almost eight-hour long immobility? My ears did not catch any snatches of conversation; only occasionally there came through the unceasing uproar the piercing cry of a hawker selling a leaflet about Tropmann, about his life, his execution and even his "last words." . . . Or, again, an argument broke out somewhere far away, or there would be a hideous burst of laughter, or some women would start screaming. . . . This time I heard the Marseillaise, but it was sung only by five or six men, and that, too, with interruptions. The Marseillaise becomes significant only when thousands are singing it. *A bas Pierre Bonaparte!* someone shouted at the top of his voice. . . . Oo—oo —ah—ah! the crowd responded in an incoherent roar. In one place the shouts assumed the measured rhythm of a polka: one—two—three—four! one—two—three—four—to the well-known tune of *des lampions!* A heavy, rank breath of alcoholic fumes came from the crowd: a great deal of wine had been drunk by all those bodies; there were a great many drunken men there. It was not for nothing that the pot-houses glowed with red lights in the general background of this scene. The night had grown pitch-dark; the sky had become totally overcast and turned black. There were small clumps on the sparse trees, looming indistinctly out of the darkness like phantoms: those were street urchins who had climbed up on the trees and were sitting among the branches, whistling and screeching like birds. One of them had fallen down and, it is said, was fatally injured, having broken his spine, but he only aroused loud laughter, and that, too, for a short time.

On my way back to the prison governor's apartment, I passed the guillotine and saw on its platform the executioner surrounded by a small crowd of inquisitive people. He was carrying out a "rehearsal" for them; threw down the hinged plank, to which the criminal was fastened and which, as it fell, touched with its end the semi-circular slot between the beams; he let fall the knife, which ran down heavily and smoothly with a rapid, hollow roar, and so on. I did not stop to watch this "rehearsal," that is to say, I did not climb on to the platform: the feeling of some unknown transgression committed by myself, of some secret shame, was growing stronger and stronger inside me. . . . It is perhaps to this feeling that I must ascribe the fact that the horses, harnessed to the vans and calmly chewing the oats in their nosebags, seemed to me at that moment to be the only innocent creatures among us all.

Once more I went back to the solitude of my little sofa and once more I began to listen to the roar of the breakers on the sea-shore. . . .

7

Contrary to what is generally asserted, the *last* hour of waiting passes much more quickly than the first and, more especially, than the second or third. . . . So it happened this time. We were surprised at the news that it had struck six and that only one hour remained to the moment of execution. We had to go to Tropmann's cell in exactly half an hour: half past six. All traces of sleep at once disappeared from all the faces. I don't know what the others felt, but I felt terribly sick at heart. New figures appeared: a priest, a small, grey-haired little man with a thin little face flashed by in his long, black cassock with the ribbon of the Légion d'Honneur and a low, wide-brimmed hat. The prison governor prepared a sort of breakfast for us, *une collation;* huge cups of chocolate appeared on the round table in the drawing-room. . . . I did not even go near it, though our hospitable host advised me to fortify myself, "because the morning air might be harmful." To take food at that moment seemed— disgusting to me. Good Lord, a feast at such a time. "I have no right," I kept saying to myself for the hundredth time since the beginning of that night.

"Is *he* still asleep?" one of us asked, sipping his chocolate.

(They were all talking of Tropmann without referring to him by name: there could be no question of any other *him*.)

"Yes, he's asleep," replied the prison governor.

"In spite of this terrible racket?"

(The noise had, in fact, grown extraordinarily loud and turned into a kind of hoarse roar; the menacing chorus, no longer crescendo, rumbled on victoriously, gaily.)

"His cell is behind three walls," replied the prison governor.

M. Claude, whom the prison governor evidently treated as the most important person among us, looked at his watch and said: "Twenty past six."

We must, I expect, have all shuddered inwardly, but we just put on our hats and set off noisily after our guide.

"Where are you dining today?" a reporter asked in a loud voice.

But that struck us all as a little too unnatural.

8

We went out into the large prison courtyard; and there, in the corner on the right before a half-closed door, a sort of roll-call took place; then we were shown into a tall, narrow and entirely empty room with a leather stool in the centre.

"It is here that *la toilette du condamné* takes place," Du Camp whispered to me.

We did not all get in: there were only ten of us, including the prison governor, the priest, M. Claude and his assistant. During the next two or three minutes that we spent in that room (some kind of official documents were being signed there) the thought that we had no right to do what we were doing, that by being present with an air of hypocritical solemnity at the killing of a fellow human being, we were performing some odious, iniquitous farce—that thought flashed across my mind for the last time; as soon as we set off, again after M. Claude, along the wide stone corridor, dimly lit by two night-lights, I no longer felt anything except that now—now—this minute—this second. . . . We rapidly climbed two staircases into another corridor, walked through it, went down a narrow spiral staircase and found ourselves before an iron door. . . . Here!

The warder unlocked the door cautiously. It opened quietly—and we all went in quietly and in silence into a rather spacious room with yellow walls, a high barred window and a crumpled bed on which no one was lying. . . . The steady light of a large night lamp lit up all the objects in the room quite clearly.

I was standing a little behind the rest and, I remember, screwed up my eyes involuntarily; however, I saw at once, diagonally opposite me, a young, black-haired, black-eyed face, which, moving slowly from the left to right, gazed at us all with huge round eyes. That was Tropmann. He had woken up before our arrival. He was standing before the table on which he had just written a farewell (though rather trivial) letter to his mother. M. Claude took off his hat and went up to him.

"Tropmann," he said in his dry, soft, but peremptory voice, "we have come to inform you that your appeal for a reprieve has been dismissed and that the hour of retribution has come for you."

Tropmann turned his eyes on him, but they were no longer "huge"; he looked calmly, almost somnolently, and did not utter a word.

"My child," the priest exclaimed dully, going up to him from the other side, *"du courage!"*

Tropmann looked at him exactly as he had looked at M. Claude.

"I knew he wouldn't be afraid," said M. Claude in a confident tone, addressing us all. "Now when he has got over the first shock *(le premier choc)*, I can answer for him."

(So does a schoolmaster, wishing to cajole his pupil, tell him beforehand that he is "a clever fellow.")

"Oh, I'm not afraid *(Oh! je n'ai pas peur!)*," said Tropmann, addressing M. Claude again, "I'm not afraid!"

His voice, a pleasant, youthful baritone, was perfectly even.

The priest took a small bottle out of his pocket.

"Won't you have a drop of wine, my child?"

"Thank you, no," Tropmann replied politely, with a slight bow.

M. Claude addressed him again.

"Do you insist that you are not guilty of the crime for which you've been condemned?"

"I did not strike the blow! *(Je n'ai pas frappé!)*"

"But—? the prison governor interjected.

"I did not strike the blow!"

(For some time past Tropmann, as everyone knows, had asserted, contrary to his former depositions, that he did take the Kink family to the place where they had been butchered, but that they were murdered by his associates, and that even the injury on his hand was due to his attempt to save one of the small children. However, he had told as many lies during his trial as very few criminals have done before him.)

"And do you still assert that you had accomplices?"

"Yes."

"You can't name them, can you?"

"I can't and I won't. I won't," Tropmann raised his voice and his face flushed. It seemed as though he were going to be angry.

"Oh, all right, all right," M. Claude said hurriedly, as though implying that he had put his questions only as a formality and that there was something else that had to be done now. . . .

Tropmann had to undress.

Two warders went up to him and began taking off his prison strait-jacket *(camisole de force),* a kind of blouse of coarse bluish cloth, with belts and buckles behind, long sewn-up sleeves, to the ends of which strong pieces of tape were fastened near the thighs by the waist. Tropmann stood sideways, within two feet of me. Nothing prevented me from scrutinizing his face carefully. It could have been described as handsome but for the unpleasantly full lips, which made his mouth protrude a little too much and turn upwards funnel-like, just as with animals, and behind his lips were two rows of bad, sparse, fan-like teeth. He had thick, slightly wavy, dark hair, long eyebrows, expressive, protruding eyes, a wide clear forehead, a regular, slightly aquiline nose, little curls of black down on his chin. . . . If you happened to meet such a man outside prison and not in such surroundings, he would, no doubt, have made a good impression on you. Hundreds of such faces were to be seen among young factory workers, pupils of public institutions, etc. Tropmann was of medium height and of a youthfully thin and slender build. He looked to me like an overgrown boy, and, indeed, he was not yet twenty. He had a natural, healthy, slightly rosy complexion; he did not turn pale even at our entrance. . . . There could be no doubt that he really had slept all night. He did not raise his eyes and his breathing was regular and deep, like a man walking up a steep hill. Once or twice he shook his hair as though wishing to dismiss a troublesome thought, tossed back his head, threw a quick glance at the ceiling and heaved a hardly perceptible sigh. With the exception of those, almost momentary, movements, nothing in him disclosed, I won't say, fear, but even agitation or anxiety. We were all, I am sure, much paler and more agitated than he. When his hands were released from the sewn-up sleeves of the strait-jacket, he held up this strait-jacket in front of him, on his chest, with a pleased smile, while it was being undone at the back; little children behave like that when they are being undressed. Then he took off his shirt himself, put on another clean one, and carefully buttoned the neckband. . . . It was strange to see the free, sweeping movements of that naked body, those bare limbs against the yellowish background of the prison wall. . . .

Then he bent down and put on his boots, knocking loudly with his heels and soles against the floor and the wall to make sure his feet got into them properly. All this he did cheerfully and without any sign of constraint—almost gaily, just as though he had been invited to go for a walk. He was silent and—we were silent. We merely exchanged glances, shrugging our shoulders involuntarily with surprise. We were all struck by the simplicity of his movements, a simplicity which, like any other calm and natural manifestation of life, amounted almost to elegance. One of our colleagues, who met me by accident later during that day, told me that all during our stay in Tropmann's cell, he had kept imagining that it was not

1870, but 1794, that we were not ordinary citizens but Jacobins, and that we were taking to his execution not a common murderer but a marquis-legitimist, *un ci-devant, un talon rouge, monsieur!*

It has been observed that when people sentenced to death have their sentences read out to them, they either lapse into complete insensibility and, as it were, die and decompose beforehand, or show off and brazen it out; or else give themselves up to despair, weep, tremble and beg for mercy. . . . Tropmann did not belong to any of these categories—and that was why he puzzled even M. Claude himself. Let me say, by the way, that if Tropmann had begun to howl and weep, my nerves would certainly not have stood it and I should have run away. But at the sight of that composure, that simplicity and, as it were, modesty—all the feelings in me —the feelings of disgust for a pitiless murderer, a monster who cut the throats of little children while they were crying, *Maman! Maman!*, the feeling of compassion, finally, for a man whom death was about to swallow up, disappeared and dissolved in—a feeling of astonishment. What was sustaining Tropmann? Was it the fact that though he did not show off, he did "cut a figure" before *spectators,* gave us his last performance? Or was it innate fearlessness or vanity aroused by M. Claude's words, the pride of the struggle that had to be kept up to the end—or something else, some still undivined feeling? . . . That was a secret he took to the grave with him. Some people are still convinced that Tropmann was not in his right mind. (I have mentioned earlier the lawyer in the white hat, whom, incidentally, I never saw again.) The aimlessness, one might almost say, the absurdity of the annihilation of the entire Kink family serves to a certain extent as a confirmation of that point of view.

9

But presently he finished with his boots and—straightened out, shook himself—ready! *Again* they put the prison jacket on him. M. Claude asked us to go out and—leave Tropmann alone with the priest. We did not have to wait even two minutes in the corridor before his small figure with his head held up fearlessly appeared among us. His religious feelings were not very strong and he probably carried out the last rite of confession before the priest, absolving his sins, just as a rite. All of our group with Tropmann in the centre at once went up the narrow spiral staircase, which we had descended a quarter of an hour before, and—disappeared in pitch darkness: the night lamp on the staircase had gone out. It was an awful moment. We were all rushing upstairs, we could hear the rapid and harsh clatter of our feet on the iron steps, we trod on each other's heels, we knocked against each other's shoulders, one of us had his hat knocked off, someone behind me shouted angrily: *"Mais sacrédieu!* Light a candle! Let's have some light!" And there among us, together with us, in the pitch darkness was our victim, our prey—that unhappy man—and who of those who were pushing and scrambling upstairs was he? Would it not occur to him to take advantage of the darkness and with all his agility and the determination of despair to escape—where? Anywhere, to some remote corner of the prison—and just knock his head against a wall there! At least, he'd have killed himself. . . .

I do not know whether these "apprehensions" occurred to anyone else. . . . But they appeared to be in vain. Our whole group with the small figure in the middle emerged from the inside recess of the staircase into the corridor. Tropmann evidently belonged to the guillotine—and the procession set off towards it.

1 0

This procession could be called a flight. Tropmann walked in front of us with quick, resilient, almost bounding steps; he was obviously in a hurry, and we all hurried after him. Some of us, anxious to have a look at his face once more, even ran ahead to the right and the left of him. So we rushed across the corridor and ran down the other staircase, Tropmann jumping two steps at a time, ran across another corridor, jumped over a few steps and, at last, found ourselves in the tall room with the stool which I have mentioned and on which "the toilet of the condemned man" was to be completed. We entered through one door, and from the other door there appeared, walking importantly, in a white necktie and a black "suit," the executioner, looking for all the world like a diplomat or a protestant pastor. He was followed by a short, fat old man in a black coat, his first assistant, the hangman of Beauvais. The old man held a small leather bag in his hand. Tropmann stopped at the stool. Everyone took up a position round him. The executioner and his old assistant stood to the right of him, the prison governor and M. Claude to the left. The old man unlocked the key of the bag, took out a few white raw-hide straps, some of them long and some short, and kneeling with difficulty behind Tropmann, began hobbling his legs. Tropmann accidentally stepped on the end of one of those straps and the old man, trying to pull it out, muttered twice: *"Pardon, monsieur"* and, at last, touched Tropmann on the calf of the leg. Tropmann at once turned round and with his customary polite half-bow raised his foot and freed the strap. Meanwhile the priest was softly reading prayers in French out of a small book. Two other assistants came up, quickly removed the jacket from Tropmann, tied his hands behind him and began tying the straps round his whole body. The chief executioner

gave orders, pointing here and there with a finger. It seemed that there
were not enough holes in the straps for the tongues to go through: no
doubt, the man who made the holes had a fatter man in mind. The old
man at first searched in his bag, then fumbled about in all his pockets and,
having felt everything carefully, at last drew out from one of them a small,
crooked awl with which he began painfully to bore holes in the straps; his
unskilful fingers, swollen with gout, obeyed him badly, and, besides, the
hide was new and thick. He would make a hole, try it out—the tongue
would not go through: he had to bore a little more. The priest evidently
realised that things were not as they should be, and glancing stealthily
once or twice over his shoulder, began to draw out the words of the
prayers, so as to give the old man time to get things right. At last the
operation during which, I frankly confess, I was covered with cold sweat,
was finished and all the tongues went in where required. But then another
one started. Tropmann was asked to sit down on the stool, before which
he was standing, and the same gouty old man began cutting his hair. He
got out a pair of small scissors and, twisting his lips, carefully cut off at
first the collar of Tropmann's shirt, the shirt he had only just put on and
from which it would have been so easy to tear off the collar beforehand.
But the cloth was coarse and all in pleats and it resisted the none too
sharp blades. The chief executioner had a look and was dissatisfied: the
space left by the cut off piece was not big enough. He indicated with his
hand how much more he wanted cut off and the gouty old man set to
work again and cut out another big piece of cloth. The top and the back
was uncovered—the shoulder-blades became visible. Tropmann twitched
them slightly: it was cold in the room. Then the old man started on the
hair. Putting his puffy left hand on the head of Tropmann, who at once
bent it down obediently, he began cutting the hair with his right. Thick
strands of wiry, dark-brown hair slid over the shoulders and fell on the
floor; one of them rolled up to my boot. Tropmann kept bending his head
in the same obedient manner; the priest dragged out the words of the
prayers even more slowly. I could not take my eyes off those hands, once
stained with innocent blood, but now lying so helplessly one on top of the
other—and particularly that slender, youthful neck. . . . In my imagination I could not help seeing a line cut straight across it. . . . There, I
thought, a five-hundred-pound axe would in a few moments pass, smash-
ing the vertebrae and cutting through the veins and muscles, and yet the
body did not seem to expect anything of the kind: it was so smooth, so
white, so healthy. . . .

I could not help asking myself what that so obediently bent head was
thinking of at that moment. Was it holding on stubbornly and, as the
saying is, with clenched teeth, to one and the same thought: "I won't
break down!" Were all sorts of memories of the past, probably quite un-

important ones, flashing through it at that moment? Was the memory of the face of one of the members of the Kink family, twisted in the agony of death, passing through it? Or was it simply trying not to think—that head, and was merely repeating to itself: "That's nothing, that doesn't matter, we shall see, we shall see . . ." and would it go on repeating it till death came crashing down upon it—and there would be nowhere to recoil from it? . . .

And the little old man kept on cutting and cutting. . . . The hair crunched as it was caught up by the scissors. . . . At last this operation, too, was at an end. Tropmann got up quickly, shook his head. . . . Ordinarily, the condemned prisoners who are still able to speak at this moment address the governor of the prison with a last request, remind him of any money or debts they may leave behind, thank their warders, ask that a last note or a strand of hair should be sent to their relatives, send their regards for the last time—but Tropmann evidently was not an ordinary prisoner: he scorned such "sentimentalities" and did not utter a single word. He was silent. He waited. A short tunic was thrown over his shoulders. The executioner grasped his elbow. . . .

"Look here, Tropmann *(Voyons, Tropmann!),*" M. Claude's voice resounded in the death-like stillness, "soon, in another minute, everything will be at an end. Do you still persist in claiming that you had accomplices?"

"Yes, sir, I do persist *(Oui, monsieur, je persiste),*" answered Tropmann in the same pleasant, firm baritone voice, and he bent forward slightly, as though courteously apologising and even regretting that he could not answer otherwise.

"Eh bien! Allons!" said M. Claude, and we all set off; we went out into the large prison courtyard.

1 1

It was five to seven, but the sky hardly grew lighter and the same dull mist covered everything, concealing the contours of all objects. The roar of the crowd encompassed us by an unbroken, ear-splitting, thunderous wave as soon as we stepped over the threshold. Our small group, which had become thinner, for some of us had lagged behind, and I too, though walking with the others, kept myself a little apart, moved rapidly over the cobbled roadway of the courtyard straight to the gates. Tropmann minced along nimbly—his shackles interfered with his walk—and how small he suddenly appeared to me, almost a child! Suddenly the two halves of the gates, like some immense mouth of an animal, opened up slowly before us —and all at once, as though to the accompaniment of the great roar of the

overjoyed crowd which had at last caught sight of what it had been waiting for, the monster of the guillotine stared at us with its two narrow black
beams and its suspended axe.

I suddenly felt cold, so cold that I almost felt sick; it seemed to me that
this cold, too, rushed at us into the courtyard through those gates; my legs
gave way under me. However, I cast another glance at Tropmann. He
suddenly recoiled, tossing back his head and bending his knees, as though
someone hit him in the chest. "He's going to faint," someone whispered
in my ear. . . . But he recovered himself immediately and went forward
with a firm step. Those of us who wanted to see how his head would roll
off rushed past him into the street. . . . I had not enough courage for
that; with a sinking heart I stopped at the gates. . . .

I saw the executioner rise suddenly like a black tower on the left side of
the guillotine platform; I saw Tropmann, separated from the huddle of
people below, scrambling up the steps (there were ten of them—as many
as ten!); I saw him stopping and turning round; I heard him say: *"Dites à
Monsieur Claude!"*[1] I saw him appear above and two men pouncing on
him from the right and the left, like spiders on a fly; I saw him falling
forward suddenly and his heels kicking. . . .

But here I turned away and began to wait, the ground slowly rising and
falling under my feet. . . . And it seemed to me that I was waiting a
terribly long time.[2] I managed to notice that at Tropmann's appearance
the roar of the crowd seemed suddenly to roll up into a ball and—a
breathless hush fell over everything. . . . Before me stood a sentry, a
young red-cheeked fellow. . . . I just had time to see him looking in-
tently at me with dull perplexity and horror. . . . I even had time to
think that that soldier probably hailed from some god-forsaken village and
came from a decent, law-abiding family and—and the things he had to see
now! At last I heard a light knocking of wood on wood—that was the
sound made by the top part of the yoke with the slit for the passage of the
knife as it fell round the murderer's head and kept it immobile. . . .
Then something suddenly descended with a hollow growl and stopped
with an abrupt thud. . . . Just as though a huge animal had retched.
. . . I cannot think of any better comparison. I felt dizzy. Everything
swam before my eyes. . . .

Someone seized me by the arm. I looked up: it was M. Claude's assis-

---

[1] I did not hear the rest of the sentence. His last words were: *Dites à Monsieur Claude que je
persiste,* that is to say, tell M. Claude that I persist in claiming that I had accomplices. Tropmann
did not want to deprive himself of this last pleasure, this last satisfaction: to leave the sting of
doubt and reproach in the minds of his judges and the public.

[2] As a matter of fact, only *twenty* seconds passed between the time Tropmann put his foot on
the first step of the guillotine and the moment when his dead body was flung into the prepared
basket.

tant, M. J. . . . , whom my friend Du Camp, as I learnt afterwards, had asked to keep an eye on me.

"You are very pale," he said with a smile. "Would you like a drink of water?"

But I thanked him and went back to the prison courtyard, which seemed to me like a place of refuge from the horrors on the other side of the gates.

1 2

Our group assembled in the guard-house by the gates to take leave of the prison governor and wait for the crowds to disperse. I, too, went in there and learnt that, while lying on the plank, Tropmann suddenly threw his head sideways convulsively so that it did not fit into the semicircular hole. The executioners were forced to drag it there by the hair, and while they were doing it, Tropmann bit the finger of one of them—the chief one. I also heard that immediately after the execution, at the time when the body, thrown into the van, was being driven rapidly away, two men took advantage of the first moments of unavoidable confusion to force their way through the lines of the soldiers and, crawling under the guillotine, began wetting their handkerchiefs in the blood that had dripped through the chinks of the planks. . . .

But I listened to all that talk as though in a dream. I felt very tired—and I was not the only one to feel like that. They all looked tired, though they all obviously felt relieved, just as if a load had been removed from their backs. But not one of us, *absolutely no one looked like a man who realized that he had been present at the performance of an act of social justice:* everyone tried to turn away in spirit and, as it were, shake off the responsibility for this murder.

Du Camp and I said goodbye to the prison governor and went home. A whole stream of human beings, men, women and children, rolled past us in disorderly and untidy waves. Almost all of them were silent; only the labourers occasionally shouted to one another: "Where are you off to? And you?" and the street urchins greeted with whistling the "cocottes" who drove past. And what drunken, glum, sleepy faces! What an expression of boredom, fatigue, dissatisfaction, disappointment, dull, purposeless disappointment! I did not see many drunks, though: they had either been picked up already or quieted down themselves. The workaday life was receiving all these people once more into its bosom—and why, for the sake of what sensations, had they left its rut for a few hours? It is awful to think what is hidden there. . . .

About fifty yards from the prison we hailed a cab, got into it, and drove off.

On the way Du Camp and I discussed what we had seen and about which he had shortly before (in the January issue of *Revue des deux Mondes* already quoted by me) said so many weighty, sensible things. We talked of the unnecessary, senseless barbarism of all that medieval procedure, thanks to which the criminal's agony went on for half an hour (from twenty-eight minutes past six to seven o'clock), of the hideousness of all those undressings, dressings, hair-cutting, those journeys along corridors and up and down staircases. . . . By what right was all that done? How could such a shocking routine be allowed? And capital punishment itself —could it possibly be justified? We had seen the impression such a spectacle made on the common people: and, indeed, there was no trace of the so-called instructive spectacle at all. Scarcely one thousandth part of the crowd, no more than fifty or sixty people, could have seen anything in the semi-darkness of early morning at a distance of 150 feet and through the lines of soldiers and the cruppers of the horses. And the rest? What benefit, however small, could they have derived from that drunken, sleepless, idle, depraved night? I remembered the young labourer, who had been shouting senselessly and whose face I had studied for several minutes. Would he start work today as a man who hated vice and idleness more than before? And what about me? What did I get from it? A feeling of involuntary astonishment at a murderer, a moral monster, who could show his contempt for death. Can the law-giver desire such impressions? What "moral purpose" can one possibly talk about after so many refutations, confirmed by experience?

But I am not going to indulge in arguments: they would lead me too far. And, anyway, who is not aware of the fact that the question of capital punishment is one of the most urgent questions that humanity has to solve at this moment? I will be content and excuse my own misplaced curiosity if my account supplies a few arguments to those who are in favour of the abolition of capital punishment or, at least, the abolition of public executions.

Weimar, 1870.

—*Translated by David Magarshack*

LU HSUN

Lu Hsun (1881–1936) is considered by many to be the greatest modern Chinese writer. He once observed, speaking from experience, "I believe those who sink from prosperity to poverty probably come, in the process, to understand what the world is like." His first collection of short stories, Call to Arms, *and his volume of tender autobiographical sketches,* Dawn Blossoms Plucked at Dusk, *support this observation. Lu Hsun often wrote about his childhood in heartbreaking stories that he was, as he put it, "unable to erase from my memory." When his father became ill, he went almost daily to the pawnbroker's and then to the medicine shop. After his father died, he wanted to become a doctor and studied medicine in Japan, but he gave up that goal to pursue literature. His writings, which portray the poverty and suffering of common people and unemployed intellectuals, got him in trouble with the authorities while winning him the admiration of left-wing revolutionaries under Mao.*

Though Lu Hsun never actually joined the Communist party, being too protective of his aesthetic independence to submit to cadre discipline, he was celebrated after his death as a sort of exemplary cultural hero by the Maoists. With the communists' conquest of the mainland in 1948, his books were reprinted by the hundreds of thousands and became a standard part of the school curriculum. The irony is that his work is irreconcilably individual rather than collective in feeling, tinged as it is with loneliness and sadness, regret for selfish mistakes, and self-deprecating humor.

In the pieces printed below, written during Lu Hsun's final illness, we get a sense of his essay style, which is rooted in classical Chinese technique (see Ou-yang Hsiu) but adapted to modern times. With a nonchalance bordering on formlessness, the author records his thoughts, seemingly not caring

*whether they lead to something edifying or grotesque so long as they capture
the flow of mental life. The fact that he is writing from the perspective of a
dying man, of course, gives them added poignancy.*

This Too Is Life

T HIS, TOO, happens during illness.
   There are things which a healthy or a sick man ignores, either because he does not come across them or because they are too insignificant.
But a man just recovering from a serious illness experiences them. In my
case two good examples are the fearfulness of exhaustion and the comfort
of rest. I used often to boast that I did not know what it was to be tired.
In front of my desk there is a swivel-chair, and sitting there to write or
read carefully was work; beside it there is a wicker reclining chair, and
lying there to chat or skim through the papers was rest. I found no great
difference between the two, and often boasted of the fact. Now I know my
mistake. I found little difference because I was never tired, because I
never did any manual labour.

   A relative's son, after graduating from senior middle school, had to go
to a stocking factory as an apprentice. He was very unhappy about this,
and the work was so hard that he had virtually no rest the whole year
round. Too proud to slack, he stuck it for a year and more. Then one day
he collapsed and told his elder brother, "I've just no energy left."

   He never stood up again. He was sent home where he lay unwilling to
eat or drink, to stir or speak. A Protestant doctor fetched to examine him
said there was nothing organically wrong but the boy was completely worn
out. Since there was no cure for this either, what followed, naturally, was a
lingering death. I had two days like that, but for a different reason:
whereas he was tired out by work I was tired out by illness. I had literally
no desire for anything, as if nothing concerned me and all action would be
superfluous. I did not brood over death, but neither did I feel alive. This,
known as "the absence of all desire," is the first step towards death, and it
made some who loved me shed secret tears. But I took a turn for the
better when I wanted something to drink, and from time to time I looked

at the things around me—the walls and the flies. Only then did I feel tired enough to need rest.

To lie just as one pleases, stretching one's limbs and giving a huge yawn before settling into the most comfortable position to relax in every muscle, is sheer delight. I had never enjoyed this before. I doubt if the healthy and lucky have enjoyed it either.

The year before last, I remember, after another illness I wrote "Random Talk After Sickness" in five sections and gave it to *Literature;* but since the last four sections could not be published the first was printed alone. The article started clearly with a (1) but stopped abruptly without any (2) or (3) to follow, so that anyone who thought carefully must have been puzzled; but we cannot expect this thoughtfulness from every reader, nor even from every critic. And on the basis of the first section someone passed this judgement on me: "Lu Xun is in favour of illness." This time I may be spared, but to be on the safe side I had better announce here: "More is to follow."

Four or five days after I began to mend, waking in the night I called Guangping to wake her.

"Give me some water. And put the light on so that I can have a look round."

"What for?" She sounded rather alarmed, doubtless thinking I was raving.

"Because I want to live. Understand that? This, too, is life. I want to take a look round."

"Oh. . . ." She got up and gave me some tea, hesitated a little and quietly lay down again without putting on the light.

I knew she had not understood.

A street-lamp outside the window shed a glimmer of light in the room, and I had a quick look at the familiar walls and the angles between them, the familiar pile of books and the unbound pictures beside them, while outside night took its course, and all that infinite space, those innumerable people, were linked in some way with me. I breathed, I lived, I should live on. I began to feel more substantial and experienced an urge to action—but presently I fell asleep again.

The next morning when I looked round in the sunlight, sure enough, there were the familiar walls, the familiar piles of books . . . normally I would look at these too as a form of relaxation. But we tend to despise these things though they are one part of life, ranking them lower than drinking tea or scratching ourselves, or even counting them as nothing. We notice rare blossoms, not the branches and leaves. The biographer of a famous man generally does nothing but emphasize his peculiarities: how Li Bai wrote his poetry and became tipsy, how Napoleon fought his battles and went without sleep, not describing them when sober or asleep. In fact, a man who spends all his time getting tipsy or doing without sleep will certainly not live long. He can go without sleep or become tipsy sometimes because at other times he is sober and sleeps. Yet considering these normal events as the dregs of life, people will not spare them a glance.

So the men or happenings they see are like the elephant's leg which made the blind man groping round the elephant fancy it was shaped like a pillar. The ancient Chinese always liked to have "the whole." Even when making "black chicken pills" to cure women's disorders, they used the whole chicken, feathers, blood and all. This method may be rather ridiculous, yet the idea behind it is not a bad one.

The man who strips off the branches and leaves will never get blossoms and fruit.

Annoyed with Guangping for not putting on the light for me, I complained of her to everyone who called. By the time I was able to get about again, I looked through the magazines she had been reading. Sure enough, while I lay ill in bed quite a few distinguished journals had appeared. Though some still published "Beauty Tips," "An Old Tree Sheds Light" or "The Secrets of Nuns" in the back, the first pages had some rousingly heroic articles. Writers now have a "most vital theme": even Sai-jin-hua* who slept for a time with the German commander Waldersee during the Yi He Tuan Uprising has become canonized as a goddess in heaven to guard our realm.

Most admirable of all is the fact that the "Spring and Autumn" supplement of the *Shen Bao* which used to refer with such relish to the Empress Dowager and the Qing court, has also changed completely with the times. In the comments at the beginning of one number, we are even told that when eating melons we should think of our territory now carved up like a melon. Of course there is no gainsaying that at all times, in all places and on all occasions we should be patriotic. Still if I were to think like that while eating a melon, I doubt whether I could swallow it. Even if I made an effort and succeeded, I would probably have prolonged indigestion. And this may not be owing to my bad nervous state after illness. To my mind, a man who uses the melon as a simile when lecturing on our national disgrace, and the next moment cheerfully eats a melon absorbing its nourishment, is rather lacking in feeling. No lecture could have any effect on such a man.

Never having joined the volunteers myself, I can only guess at their feelings. But I ask myself: Does a soldier eating a melon make a point of

---

* A famous courtesan. During the occupation of Beijing by imperialist troops after the Yi He Tuan Movement, she became the mistress of Count Waldersee, the commander of the allied forces. She was believed to have intervened occasionally when the imperialist troops were looting and killing people.

eating and thinking at the same time? I doubt it. He probably just feels thirsty, wants a melon and finds it sweet, without giving a thought to any other high-sounding ideas. Eating the melon refreshes him and enables him to fight better than if he were thirsty; hence melon-eating does have something to do with resistance, but nothing to do with the rules on how to think laid down in Shanghai. If we ate and drank with long faces all the time, very soon we should have no appetite at all, and then what would become of our resistance?

Still there are men who will talk in this strange way, who will not even let you eat a melon normally. Actually a soldier's daily life is not entirely heroic; but when the whole of it is bound up with heroism, you have a real soldier.

August 23, 1936

Death

W HILE PREPARING A SELECTION of Käthe Kollwitz's works for publication, I asked Miss Agnes Smedley to write a preface. This struck me as most appropriate because the two of them were good friends. Soon the preface was ready, I had Mr. Mao Dun translate it, and it has now appeared in the Chinese edition. One passage in it reads:

> All these years Käthe Kollwitz—who never once used any title conferred on her—has made a great many sketches, pencil and ink drawings, woodcuts and etchings. When we study these, two dominant themes are evident: in her younger days her main theme was revolt, but in her later years it was motherly love, the protective maternal instinct, succour and death. All her works are pervaded by the idea of suffering, of tragedy, and a passionate longing to protect the oppressed.
>
> Once I asked her, "Why is it that instead of your former theme of revolt you now seem unable to shake off the idea of death?" She answered in tones of anguish, "It may be because I am growing older every day. . . ."

At that point I stopped to think. I estimated that it must have been in about 1910 that she first took death as her theme, when she was no more than forty-three or -four. I stop to think about it now because of my own age, of course. But a dozen or so years ago, as I recall, I did not have such a feeling about death. No doubt our lives have long been treated so casually as trifles of no consequence that we treat them lightly ourselves, not seriously as Europeans do. Some foreigners say that the Chinese are most afraid of death. But this is not true—actually, most of us die with no clear understanding of the meaning of death.

The general belief in a posthumous existence further strengthens the casual attitude towards death. As everyone knows, we Chinese believe in ghosts (more recently called "souls" or "spirits"); and since there are ghosts, after death we can at least exist as ghosts if not as men, which is better than nothing. But the imagined duration of this ghostly existence seems to vary according to one's wealth. The poor appear to believe that when they die their souls will pass into another body, an idea derived from Buddhism. Of course, transmigration in Buddhism is a complicated process, by no means so simple; but the poor are usually ignorant people who do not know this. That is why criminals condemned to death often show no fear when taken to the execution ground, but shout, "Twenty years from now I shall be a stout fellow again!" Moreover, according to popular belief a ghost wears the clothes he had on at the time of death; and since the poor have no good clothes and cannot therefore cut a fine figure as ghosts, it is far better for them to be reborn at once as naked babies. Did you ever see a new-born infant wearing a beggar's rags or a swimming-suit? No, never. Very well, then, that is a fresh start. Someone may object: If you believe in transmigration, in the next existence you may even be worse off or actually become a beast—what a fearful thought! But the poor don't seem to think that way. They firmly believe that they have not committed sins frightful enough to condemn them to becoming beasts: they have not had the position, power or money to commit such sins.

But neither do those men with position, power and money believe that they should become beasts. They either turn Buddhist in order to become saints, or advocate the study of the Confucian classics and a return to ancient ways in order to become Confucian sages. Just as in life they expect to be a privileged class, after death they expect to be exempt from transmigration. As for those who have a little money, though they also believe they should be exempt from transmigration, since they have no high ambitions or lofty plans they just wait placidly. Round about the age of fifty, they look for a burial place, buy a coffin, and burn paper money to open a bank account in the nether regions, expecting their sons and grandsons to sacrifice to them every year. This is surely much pleasanter than life on earth. If I were a ghost now, with filial descendants in the

world of men, I should not have to sell my articles one by one, or ask the
Beixin Publishing House for payment. I could simply lie at ease in my
cedarwood or fir coffin, while at every festival and at New Year a fine feast
and a pile of banknotes would be placed before me. That would be the
life!

Generally speaking, unlike the very rich and great, who are not bound
by the laws of the nether regions, the poor would like to be reborn at
once, while those comfortably-off would like to remain as ghosts for as
long as possible. The comfortably-off are willing to remain ghosts because
their life as ghosts (this sounds paradoxical but I can think of no better
way of expressing it) is the continuation of their life on earth and they are
not yet tired of it. Of course there are rulers in the nether regions who are
extremely strict and just; but they will make allowances for these ghosts
and accept presents from them too, just like good officials on earth.

Then there are others who are rather casual, who do not think much
about death even when they are dying, and I belong to this casual category. Thirty years ago as a medical student I considered the problem of
the existence of the soul, but did not know what to conclude. Later I
considered whether death was painful or not, and concluded that it varied
in different cases. And later still I stopped thinking about the matter and
forgot it. During the last ten years I have sometimes written a little about
the death of friends, but apparently I never thought of my own. In the last
two years I have been ill a great deal and usually for a considerable length
of time, which has often reminded me that I am growing older. Of course,
I have been constantly reminded of this fact by other writers owing to
their friendly or unfriendly concern.

Since last year, whenever I lay on my wicker chair recovering from
illness, I would consider what to do when I was well, what articles to
write, what books to translate or publish. My plans made, I would conclude, "All right—but I must hurry." This sense of urgency, which I never
had before, was due to the fact that unconsciously I had remembered my
age. But still I never thought directly of "death."

Not till my serious illness this year did I start thinking distinctly about
death. At first I treated my illness as in the past, relying on my Japanese
doctor, S——. Though not a specialist in tuberculosis, he is an elderly
man with a rich experience who studied medicine before me, is my senior,
and knows me very well—hence he talks frankly. Of course, however well
a doctor knows his patient, he still speaks with a certain reserve; but at
least he warned me two or three times, though I never paid any attention
and did not tell anyone. Perhaps because things had dragged on so long
and my last attack was so serious, some friends arranged behind my back
to invite an American doctor, D——, to see me. He is the only Western
specialist on tuberculosis in Shanghai. After his examination, although he

complimented me on my typically Chinese powers of resistance, he also announced that my end was near, adding that had I been a European I would already have been in my grave for five years. This verdict moved my soft-hearted friends to tears. I did not ask him to prescribe for me, feeling that since he had studied in the West he could hardly have learned how to prescribe for a patient five years dead. But Dr. D——'s diagnosis was in fact extremely accurate. I later had an X-ray photograph made of my chest which very largely bore out his findings.

Though I did not pay much attention to his announcement, it has influenced me a little: I spend all the time on my back, with no energy to talk or read and not enough strength to hold a newspaper. Since my heart is not yet "as tranquil as an old well," I am forced to think, and sometimes I think of death too. But instead of thinking that "twenty years from now I shall be a stout fellow again," or wondering how to prolong my stay in a cedarwood coffin, my mind dwells on certain trifles before death. It is only now that I am finally sure that I do not believe that men turn into ghosts. It occurred to me to write a will, and I thought: If I were a great nobleman with a huge fortune, my sons, sons-in-law, and others would have forced me to write a will long ago; whereas nobody has mentioned it to me. Still, I may as well leave one. I seem to have thought out quite a few items for my family, among which were:

1. Don't accept a cent from anyone for the funeral. This does not apply to old friends.
2. Get the whole thing over quickly, have me buried and be done with it.
3. Do nothing in the way of commemoration.
4. Forget me and live your own lives—if you don't, the more fools you.
5. When the child grows up, if he has no gifts let him take some small job to make a living. On no account let him become a writer or artist in name only.
6. Don't take other people's promises seriously.
7. Have nothing to do with people who injure others but who oppose revenge and advocate tolerance.

There were other items, too, but I have forgotten them. I remember also how during a fever I recalled that when a European is dying there is usually some sort of ceremony in which he asks pardon of others and pardons them. Now I have a great many enemies, and what should my answer be if some modernized person asked me my views on this? After some thought I decided: Let them go on hating me. I shall not forgive a single one of them either.

No such ceremony took place, however, and I did not draw up a will. I simply lay there in silence, struck sometimes by a more pressing thought: if this is dying, it isn't really painful. It may not be quite like this at the end, of course; but still, since this happens only once in a lifetime, I can take it. . . . Later, however, there came a change for the better. And now I am wondering whether this was really the state just before dying: a man really dying may not have such ideas. What it will be like, though, I still do not know.

September 5, 1936

—Translated by Yang Xianyi and Gladys Yang

JUNICHIRO TANIZAKI

Junichiro Tanizaki (1886–1965) is one of the giants of modern Japanese fiction. Born and raised in Tokyo, he fell early under the influence of Western "decadent" writers such as Baudelaire, Poe, and Wilde and tried to reconcile his young man's taste for the macabre and modern with an attraction to Japanese tradition, which deepened as he grew older. In 1923, while in his mid-thirties, he moved with his family to Osaka, thus distancing himself from the capital and his past as a "son of Tokyo." oh?

Tanizaki's work has a delightful spicy quality and is filled with brio, humor, and robust spirits—especially compared to his great, dour contemporary, Yasunari Kawabata. There is frequently also a touch of the perverse and a fascination with cruelty in Tanizaki, though somehow (as in the work of oh! *the filmmaker Luis Buñuel) the results manage to be liberating and pleasurable. His major works include* Naomi, Some Prefer Nettles, Seven Tales, The Key, Diary of a Mad Old Man, *and what is arguably the greatest Japanese novel of the twentieth century,* The Makioka Sisters. *A passionate antiquarian, Tanizaki also adapted the great eleventh-century classic* The Tale of Genji *into modern Japanese—a labor of love and ancestral respect.*

Tanizaki's magnificent personal essay "In Praise of Shadows" demonstrates all his characteristic traits: urbanity, wryness, learning, perversity, and *humanity, respect for tradition, innovative freshness, and a stimulating,* anti-fe *wide-ranging mind. The essay's structure keeps opening out like a series of rooms; indeed, reading it is like experiencing a piece of wonderfully complex domestic architecture. Perhaps its method of linked images also derives from* renga, *the long Japanese poem-chains composed of linked* haiku *or* tanka. *Just when you think the essay is coming to a standstill, it hooks on to another metaphor, another resonance. By the end, what began as a narrow meditation on the Japanese house has broadened to uncover the most sensitive connections between interiority, space, culture, ethnicity, body, eroticism, shadow, and human personality.* — and male negative evaluation of women.

In Praise of Shadows

W HAT INCREDIBLE PAINS the fancier of traditional architecture must take when he sets out to build a house in pure Japanese style, striving somehow to make electric wires, gas pipes, and water lines harmonize with the austerity of Japanese rooms—even someone who has never built a house for himself must sense this when he visits a teahouse, a restaurant, or an inn. For the solitary eccentric it is another matter, he can ignore the blessings of scientific civilization and retreat to some forsaken corner of the countryside; but a man who has a family and lives in the city cannot turn his back on the necessities of modern life— heating, electric lights, sanitary facilities—merely for the sake of doing things the Japanese way. The purist may rack his brain over the placement of a single telephone, hiding it behind the staircase or in a corner of the hallway, wherever he thinks it will least offend the eye. He may bury the wires rather than hang them in the garden, hide the switches in a closet or cupboard, run the cords behind a folding screen. Yet for all his ingenuity, his efforts often impress us as nervous, fussy, excessively contrived. For so accustomed are we to electric lights that the sight of a naked bulb beneath an ordinary milk glass shade seems simpler and more natural than any gratuitous attempt to hide it. Seen at dusk as one gazes out upon the countryside from the window of a train, the lonely light of a bulb under an old-fashioned shade, shining dimly from behind the white paper shoji of a thatch-roofed farmhouse, can seem positively elegant.

But the snarl and the bulk of an electric fan remain a bit out of place in a Japanese room. The ordinary householder, if he dislikes electric fans, can simply do without them. But if the family business involves the entertainment of customers in summertime, the gentleman of the house cannot afford to indulge his own tastes at the expense of others. A friend of mine, the proprietor of a Chinese restaurant called the Kairakuen, is a thorough-going purist in matters architectural. He deplores electric fans and long refused to have them in his restaurant, but the complaints from customers with which he was faced every summer ultimately forced him to give in.

I myself have had similar experiences. A few years ago I spent a great deal more money than I could afford to build a house. I fussed over every last fitting and fixture, and in every case encountered difficulty. There was the shoji: for aesthetic reasons I did not want to use glass, and yet paper alone would have posed problems of illumination and security. Much against my will, I decided to cover the inside with paper and the outside with glass. This required a double frame, thus raising the cost. Yet having gone to all this trouble, the effect was far from pleasing. The outside remained no more than a glass door; while within, the mellow softness of the paper was destroyed by the glass that lay behind it. At that point I was sorry I had not just settled for glass to begin with. Yet laugh though we may when the house is someone else's, we ourselves accept defeat only after having a try at such schemes.

Then there was the problem of lighting. In recent years several fixtures designed for Japanese houses have come on the market, fixtures patterned after old floor lamps, ceiling lights, candle stands, and the like. But I simply do not care for them, and instead searched in curio shops for old lamps, which I fitted with electric light bulbs.

What most taxed my ingenuity was the heating system. No stove worthy of the name will ever look right in a Japanese room. Gas stoves burn with a terrific roar, and unless provided with a chimney, quickly bring headaches. Electric stoves, though at least free from these defects, are every bit as ugly as the rest. One solution would be to outfit the cupboards with heaters of the sort used in streetcars. Yet without the red glow of the coals, the whole mood of winter is lost and with it the pleasure of family gatherings round the fire. The best plan I could devise was to build a large sunken hearth, as in an old farmhouse. In this I installed an electric brazier, which worked well both for boiling tea water and for heating the room. Expensive it was, but at least so far as looks were concerned I counted it one of my successes.

Having done passably well with the heating system, I was then faced with the problem of bath and toilet. My Kairakuen friend could not bear to tile the tub and bathing area, and so built his guest bath entirely of wood. Tile, of course, is infinitely more practical and economical. But when ceiling, pillars, and panelling are of fine Japanese stock, the beauty of the room is utterly destroyed when the rest is done in sparkling tile. The effect may not seem so very displeasing while everything is still new, but as the years pass, and the beauty of the grain begins to emerge on the planks and pillars, that glittering expanse of white tile comes to seem as incongruous as the proverbial bamboo grafted to wood. Still, in the bath utility can to some extent be sacrificed to good taste. In the toilet somewhat more vexatious problems arise.

Every time I am shown to an old, dimly lit, and, I would add, impeccably clean toilet in a Nara or Kyoto temple, I am impressed with the singular virtues of Japanese architecture. The parlor may have its charms, but the Japanese toilet truly is a place of spiritual repose. It always stands apart from the main building, at the end of a corridor, in a grove fragrant with leaves and moss. No words can describe that sensation as one sits in the dim light, basking in the faint glow reflected from the shoji, lost in meditation or gazing out at the garden. The novelist Natsume Sōseki counted his morning trips to the toilet a great pleasure, "a physiological delight" he called it. And surely there could be no better place to savor this pleasure than a Japanese toilet where, surrounded by tranquil walls and finely grained wood, one looks out upon blue skies and green leaves.

As I have said there are certain prerequisites: a degree of dimness, absolute cleanliness, and quiet so complete one can hear the hum of a mosquito. I love to listen from such a toilet to the sound of softly falling rain, especially if it is a toilet of the Kantō region, with its long, narrow windows at floor level; there one can listen with such a sense of intimacy to the raindrops falling from the eaves and the trees, seeping into the earth as they wash over the base of a stone lantern and freshen the moss about the stepping stones. And the toilet is the perfect place to listen to the chirping of insects or the song of the birds, to view the moon, or to enjoy any of those poignant moments that mark the change of the seasons. Here, I suspect, is where haiku poets over the ages have come by a great many of their ideas. Indeed one could with some justice claim that of all the elements of Japanese architecture, the toilet is the most aesthetic. Our forebears, making poetry of everything in their lives, transformed what by rights should be the most unsanitary room in the house into a place of unsurpassed elegance, replete with fond associations with the beauties of nature. Compared to Westerners, who regard the toilet as utterly unclean and avoid even the mention of it in polite conversation, we are far more sensible and certainly in better taste. The Japanese toilet is, I must admit, a bit inconvenient to get to in the middle of the night, set apart from the main building as it is; and in winter there is always a danger that one might catch cold. But as the poet Saitō Ryokū has said, "elegance is frigid." Better that the place be as chilly as the out-of-doors; the steamy heat of a Western-style toilet in a hotel is most unpleasant.

Anyone with a taste for traditional architecture must agree that the Japanese toilet is perfection. Yet whatever its virtues in a place like a temple, where the dwelling is large, the inhabitants few, and everyone helps with the cleaning, in an ordinary household it is no easy task to keep it clean. No matter how fastidious one may be or how diligently one may scrub, dirt will show, particularly on a floor of wood or tatami matting. And so here too it turns out to be more hygienic and efficient to install modern sanitary facilities—tile and a flush toilet—though at the price of destroying all affinity with "good taste" and the "beauties of nature." That burst of light from those four white walls hardly puts one in a mood to relish Sōseki's "physiological delight." There is no denying the cleanliness; every nook and corner is pure white. Yet what need is there to remind us so forcefully of the issue of our own bodies. A beautiful woman, no matter how lovely her skin, would be considered indecent were she to show her bare buttocks or feet in the presence of others; and how very crude and tasteless to expose the toilet to such excessive illumination. The cleanliness of what can be seen only calls up the more clearly thoughts of what cannot be seen. In such places the distinction between the clean and the unclean is best left obscure, shrouded in a dusky haze.

Though I did install modern sanitary facilities when I built my own house, I at least avoided tiles, and had the floor done in camphor wood. To that extent I tried to create a Japanese atmosphere—but was frustrated finally by the toilet fixtures themselves. As everyone knows, flush toilets are made of pure white porcelain and have handles of sparkling metal. Were I able to have things my own way, I would much prefer fixtures—both men's and women's—made of wood. Wood finished in glistening black lacquer is the very best; but even unfinished wood, as it darkens and the grain grows more subtle with the years, acquires an inexplicable power to calm and soothe. The ultimate, of course, is a wooden "morning glory" urinal filled with boughs of cedar; this is a delight to look at and allows not the slightest sound. I could not afford to indulge in such extravagances. I hoped I might at least have the external fittings made to suit my own taste, and then adapt these to a standard flushing mechanism. But the custom labor would have cost so much that I had no choice but to abandon the idea. It was not that I objected to the conveniences of modern civilization, whether electric lights or heating or toilets, but I did wonder at the time why they could not be designed with a bit more consideration for our own habits and tastes.

The recent vogue for electric lamps in the style of the old standing lanterns comes, I think, from a new awareness of the softness and warmth of paper, qualities which for a time we had forgotten; it stands as evidence of our recognition that this material is far better suited than glass to the Japanese house. But no toilet fixtures or stoves that are at all tasteful have yet come on the market. A heating system like my own, an electric brazier in a sunken hearth, seems to me ideal; yet no one ventures to produce even so simple a device as this (there are, of course, those feeble electric hibachi, but they provide no more heat than an ordinary charcoal hibachi); all that can be had ready-made are those ugly Western stoves.

There are those who hold that to quibble over matters of taste in the basic necessities of life is an extravagance, that as long as a house keeps out the cold and as long as food keeps off starvation, it matters little what they look like. And indeed for even the sternest ascetic the fact remains that a snowy day is cold, and there is no denying the impulse to accept the services of a heater if it happens to be there in front of one, no matter how cruelly its inelegance may shatter the spell of the day. But it is on occasions like this that I always think how different everything would be if we in the Orient had developed our own science. Suppose for instance that we had developed our own physics and chemistry: would not the techniques and industries based on them have taken a different form, would not our myriads of everyday gadgets, our medicines, the products of our industrial art—would they not have suited our national temper better than they do? In fact our conception of physics itself, and even the principles of chemistry, would probably differ from that of Westerners; and the facts we are now taught concerning the nature and function of light, electricity, and atoms might well have presented themselves in different form.

Of course I am only indulging in idle speculation; of scientific matters I know nothing. But had we devised independently at least the more practical sorts of inventions, this could not but have had profound influence upon the conduct of our everyday lives, and even upon government, religion, art, and business. The Orient quite conceivably could have opened up a world of technology entirely its own.

To take a trivial example near at hand: I wrote a magazine article recently comparing the writing brush with the fountain pen, and in the course of it I remarked that if the device had been invented by the ancient Chinese or Japanese it would surely have had a tufted end like our writing brush. The ink would not have been this bluish color but rather black, something like India ink, and it would have been made to seep down from the handle into the brush. And since we would have then found it inconvenient to write on Western paper, something near Japanese paper—even under mass production, if you will—would have been most in demand. Foreign ink and pen would not be as popular as they are; the talk of discarding our system of writing for Roman letters would be less noisy; people would still feel an affection for the old system. But more than that: our thought and our literature might not be imitating the West as they are, but might have pushed forward into new regions quite on their own. An insignificant little piece of writing equipment, when one thinks of it, has had a vast, almost boundless, influence on our culture.

* * *

But I know as well as anyone that these are the empty dreams of a novelist, and that having come this far we cannot turn back. I know that I am only grumbling to myself and demanding the impossible. If my complaints are taken for what they are, however, there can be no harm in considering how unlucky we have been, what losses we have suffered, in comparison with the Westerner. The Westerner has been able to move forward in ordered steps, while we have met superior civilization and have had to surrender to it, and we have had to leave a road we have followed for thousands of years. The missteps and inconveniences this has caused have, I think, been many. If we had been left alone we might not be much further now in a material way than we were five hundred years ago. Even now in the Indian and Chinese countryside life no doubt goes on much as it did when Buddha and Confucius were alive. But we would have gone only in a direction that suited us. We would have gone ahead very slowly, and yet it is not impossible that we would one day have discovered our own substitute for the trolley, the radio, the airplane of today. They would have been no borrowed gadgets, they would have been the tools of our own culture, suited to us.

One need only compare American, French, and German films to see how greatly nuances of shading and coloration can vary in motion pictures. In the photographic image itself, to say nothing of the acting and the script, there somehow emerge differences in national character. If this is true even when identical equipment, chemicals, and film are used, how much better our own photographic technology might have suited our complexion, our facial features, our climate, our land. And had we invented the phonograph and the radio, how much more faithfully they would reproduce the special character of our voices and our music. Japanese music is above all a music of reticence, of atmosphere. When recorded, or amplified by a loudspeaker, the greater part of its charm is lost. In conversation, too, we prefer the soft voice, the understatement. Most important of all are the pauses. Yet the phonograph and radio render these moments of silence utterly lifeless. And so we distort the arts themselves to curry favor for them with the machines. These machines are the inventions of Westerners, and are, as we might expect, well suited to the Western arts. But precisely on this account they put our own arts at a great disadvantage.

Paper, I understand, was invented by the Chinese; but Western paper is to us no more than something to be used, while the texture of Chinese paper and Japanese paper gives us a certain feeling of warmth, of calm and repose. Even the same white could as well be one color for Western paper and another for our own. Western paper turns away the light, while our paper seems to take it in, to envelop it gently, like the soft surface of a first snowfall. It gives off no sound when it is crumpled or folded, it is quiet and pliant to the touch as the leaf of a tree.

As a general matter we find it hard to be really at home with things that shine and glitter. The Westerner uses silver and steel and nickel tableware, and polishes it to a fine brilliance, but we object to the practice. While we do sometimes indeed use silver for teakettles, decanters, or saké cups, we prefer not to polish it. On the contrary, we begin to enjoy it only when the luster has worn off, when it has begun to take on a dark, smoky patina. Almost every householder has had to scold an insensitive maid who has polished away the tarnish so patiently waited for.

Chinese food is now most often served on tableware made of tin, a material the Chinese could only admire for the patina it acquires. When new it resembles aluminum and is not particularly attractive; only after long use brings some of the elegance of age is it at all acceptable. Then, as the surface darkens, the line of verse etched upon it gives a final touch of perfection. In the hands of the Chinese this flimsy, glittering metal takes on a profound and somber dignity akin to that of their red unglazed pottery.

The Chinese also love jade. That strange lump of stone with its faintly muddy light, like the crystallized air of the centuries, melting dimly, dully back, deeper and deeper—are not we Orientals the only ones who know its charms? We cannot say ourselves what it is that we find in this stone. It quite lacks the brightness of a ruby or an emerald or the glitter of a diamond. But this much we can say: when we see that shadowy surface, we think how Chinese it is, we seem to find in its cloudiness the accumulation of the long Chinese past, we think how appropriate it is that the Chinese should admire that surface and that shadow.

It is the same with crystals. Crystals have recently been imported in large quantities from Chile, but Chilean crystals are too bright, too clear. We have long had crystals of our own, their clearness always moderated, made graver by a certain cloudiness. Indeed, we much prefer the "impure" varieties of crystal with opaque veins crossing their depths. Even of glass this is true; for is not fine Chinese glass closer to jade or agate than to Western glass? Glassmaking has long been known in the Orient, but the craft never developed as in the West. Great progress has been made, however, in the manufacture of pottery. Surely this has something to do with our national character. We do not dislike everything that shines, but we do prefer a pensive luster to a shallow brilliance, a murky light that, whether in a stone or an artifact, bespeaks a sheen of antiquity.

Of course this "sheen of antiquity" of which we hear so much is in fact the glow of grime. In both Chinese and Japanese the words denoting this glow describe a polish that comes of being touched over and over again, a sheen produced by the oils that naturally permeate an object over long years of handling—which is to say grime. If indeed "elegance is frigid," it can as well be described as filthy. There is no denying, at any rate, that among the elements of the elegance in which we take such delight is a measure of the unclean, the unsanitary. I suppose I shall sound terribly defensive if I say that Westerners attempt to expose every speck of grime and eradicate it, while we Orientals carefully preserve and even idealize it. Yet for better or for worse we do love things that bear the marks of grime, soot, and weather, and we love the colors and the sheen that call to mind the past that made them. Living in these old houses among these old objects is in some mysterious way a source of peace and repose.

I have always thought that hospitals, those for the Japanese at any rate, need not be so sparkling white, that the walls, uniforms, and equipment might better be done in softer, more muted colors. Certainly the patients would be more reposed where they are able to lie on tatami matting surrounded by the sand-colored walls of a Japanese room. One reason we hate to go to the dentist is the scream of his drill; but the excessive glitter of glass and metal is equally intimidating. At a time when I was suffering from a severe nervous disorder, a dentist was recommended to me as having just returned from America with the latest equipment, but these tidings only made my hair stand on end. I chose instead to go to an old-fashioned dentist who maintained an office in an old Japanese house, a dentist of the sort found in small country towns. Antiquated medical equipment does have its drawbacks; but had modern medicine been developed in Japan we probably would have devised facilities and equipment for the treatment of the sick that would somehow harmonize with Japanese architecture. Here again we have to come off the loser for having borrowed.

There is a famous restaurant in Kyoto, the Waranjiya, one of the attractions of which was until recently that the dining rooms were lit by candlelight rather than electricity; but when I went there this spring after a long absence, the candles had been replaced by electric lamps in the style of old lanterns. I asked when this had happened, and was told that the change had taken place last year; several of their customers had complained that candlelight was too dim, and so they had been left no choice —but if I preferred the old way they should be happy to bring me a candlestand. Since that was what I had come for, I asked them to do so. And I realized then that only in dim half-light is the true beauty of Japanese lacquerware revealed. The rooms at the Waranjiya are about nine feet square, the size of a comfortable little tearoom, and the alcove pillars and ceilings glow with a faint smoky luster, dark even in the light of the lamp. But in the still dimmer light of the candlestand, as I gazed at the trays and bowls standing in the shadows cast by that flickering point of flame, I discovered in the gloss of this lacquerware a depth and richness like that of a still, dark pond, a beauty I had not before seen. It had not been mere chance, I realized, that our ancestors, having discovered lacquer, had conceived such a fondness for objects finished in it.

An Indian friend once told me that in his country ceramic tableware is still looked down upon, and that lacquerware is in far wider use. We, however, use ceramics for practically everything but trays and soup bowls; lacquerware, except in the tea ceremony and on formal occasions, is considered vulgar and inelegant. This, I suspect, is in part the fault of the much-vaunted "brilliance" of modern electric lighting. Darkness is an indispensible element of the beauty of lacquerware. Nowadays they make even a white lacquer, but the lacquerware of the past was finished in black, brown, or red, colors built up of countless layers of darkness, the inevitable product of the darkness in which life was lived. Sometimes a superb piece of black lacquerware, decorated perhaps with flecks of silver and gold—a box or a desk or a set of shelves—will seem to me unsettlingly garish and altogether vulgar. But render pitch black the void in which they stand, and light them not with the rays of the sun or electricity but rather a single lantern or candle: suddenly those garish objects turn somber, refined, dignified. Artisans of old, when they finished their works in lacquer and decorated them in sparkling patterns, must surely have had in mind dark rooms and sought to turn to good effect what feeble light there was. Their extravagant use of gold, too, I should imagine, came of understanding how it gleams forth from out of the darkness and reflects the lamplight.

Lacquerware decorated in gold is not something to be seen in a brilliant light, to be taken in at a single glance; it should be left in the dark, a part here and a part there picked up by a faint light. Its florid patterns recede into the darkness, conjuring in their stead an inexpressible aura of depth and mystery, of overtones but partly suggested. The sheen of the lacquer, set out in the night, reflects the wavering candlelight, announcing the drafts that find their way from time to time into the quiet room, luring one into a state of reverie. If the lacquer is taken away, much of the spell disappears from the dream world built by that strange light of candle and lamp, that wavering light beating the pulse of the night. Indeed the thin, impalpable, faltering light, picked up as though little rivers were running through the room, collecting little pools here and there, lacquers a pattern on the surface of the night itself.

Ceramics are by no means inadequate as tableware, but they lack the shadows, the depth of lacquerware. Ceramics are heavy and cold to the touch; they clatter and clink, and being efficient conductors of heat are not the best containers for hot foods. But lacquerware is light and soft to the touch, and gives off hardly a sound. I know few greater pleasures than holding a lacquer soup bowl in my hands, feeling upon my palms the weight of the liquid and its mild warmth. The sensation is something like that of holding a plump newborn baby. There are good reasons why lacquer soup bowls are still used, qualities which ceramic bowls simply do not possess. Remove the lid from a ceramic bowl, and there lies the soup, every nuance of its substance and color revealed. With lacquerware there is a beauty in that moment between removing the lid and lifting the bowl to the mouth when one gazes at the still, silent liquid in the dark depths of the bowl, its color hardly differing from that of the bowl itself. What lies within the darkness one cannot distinguish, but the palm senses the gentle movements of the liquid, vapor rises from within forming droplets on the rim, and the fragrance carried upon the vapor brings a delicate anticipation. What a world of difference there is between this moment and the moment when soup is served Western style, in a pale, shallow bowl. A moment of mystery, it might almost be called, a moment of trance.

Whenever I sit with a bowl of soup before me, listening to the murmur that penetrates like the far-off shrill of an insect, lost in contemplation of flavors to come, I feel as if I were being drawn into a trance. The experience must be something like that of the tea master who, at the sound of the kettle, is taken from himself as if upon the sigh of the wind in the legendary pines of Onoe.

It has been said of Japanese food that it is a cuisine to be looked at rather than eaten. I would go further and say that it is to be meditated upon, a kind of silent music evoked by the combination of lacquerware and the light of a candle flickering in the dark. Natsume Sōseki, in *Pillow of Grass,* praises the color of the confection yōkan; and is it not indeed a color to call forth meditation? The cloudy translucence, like that of jade; the faint, dreamlike glow that suffuses it, as if it had drunk into its very depths the light of the sun; the complexity and profundity of the color— nothing of the sort is to be found in Western candies. How simple and insignificant cream-filled chocolates seem by comparison. And when yōkan is served in a lacquer dish within whose dark recesses its color is scarcely distinguishable, then it is most certainly an object for meditation. You take its cool, smooth substance into your mouth, and it is as if the very darkness of the room were melting on your tongue; even undistinguished yōkan can then take on a mysteriously intriguing flavor.

In the cuisine of any country efforts no doubt are made to have the food harmonize with the tableware and the walls; but with Japanese food, a brightly lighted room and shining tableware cut the appetite in half. The dark miso soup that we eat every morning is one dish from the dimly lit houses of the past. I was once invited to a tea ceremony where miso was served; and when I saw the muddy, claylike color, quiet in a black lacquer bowl beneath the faint light of a candle, this soup that I usually take without a second thought seemed somehow to acquire a real depth, and to become infinitely more appetizing as well. Much the same may be said of soy sauce. In the Kyoto-Osaka region a particularly thick variety of soy is served with raw fish, pickles, and greens; and how rich in shadows is the viscous sheen of the liquid, how beautifully it blends with the darkness. White foods too—white miso, bean curd, fish cake, the white meat of fish —lose much of their beauty in a bright room. And above all there is rice. A glistening black lacquer rice cask set off in a dark corner is both beautiful to behold and a powerful stimulus to the appetite. Then the lid is briskly lifted, and this pure white freshly boiled food, heaped in its black container, each and every grain gleaming like a pearl, sends forth billows of warm steam—here is a sight no Japanese can fail to be moved by. Our cooking depends upon shadows and is inseparable from darkness.

I possess no specialized knowledge of architecture, but I understand that in the Gothic cathedral of the West, the roof is thrust up and up so as to place its pinnacle as high in the heavens as possible—and that herein is thought to lie its special beauty. In the temples of Japan, on the other hand, a roof of heavy tiles is first laid out, and in the deep, spacious shadows created by the eaves the rest of the structure is built. Nor is this true only of temples; in the palaces of the nobility and the houses of the common people, what first strikes the eye is the massive roof of tile or thatch and the heavy darkness that hangs beneath the eaves. Even at midday cavernous darkness spreads over all beneath the roof's edge, making entryway, doors, walls, and pillars all but invisible. The grand temples of Kyoto—Chion'in, Honganji—and the farmhouses of the remote countryside are alike in this respect: like most buildings of the past their roofs give the impression of possessing far greater weight, height, and surface than all that stands beneath the eaves.

In making for ourselves a place to live, we first spread a parasol to throw a shadow on the earth, and in the pale light of the shadow we put together a house. There are of course roofs on Western houses too, but they are less to keep off the sun than to keep off the wind and the dew; even from without it is apparent that they are built to create as few shadows as possible and to expose the interior to as much light as possible. If the roof of a Japanese house is a parasol, the roof of a Western house is no

more than a cap, with as small a visor as possible so as to allow the
sunlight to penetrate directly beneath the eaves. There are no doubt all
sorts of reasons—climate, building materials—for the deep Japanese
eaves. The fact that we did not use glass, concrete, and bricks, for instance, made a low roof necessary to keep off the driving wind and rain. A
light room would no doubt have been more convenient for us, too, than a
dark room. The quality that we call beauty, however, must always grow
from the realities of life, and our ancestors, forced to live in dark rooms,
presently came to discover beauty in shadows, ultimately to guide shadows
towards beauty's ends.

And so it has come to be that the beauty of a Japanese room depends
on a variation of shadows, heavy shadows against light shadows—it has
nothing else. Westerners are amazed at the simplicity of Japanese rooms,
perceiving in them no more than ashen walls bereft of ornament. Their
reaction is understandable, but it betrays a failure to comprehend the
mystery of shadows. Out beyond the sitting room, which the rays of the
sun can at best but barely reach, we extend the eaves or build on a veranda, putting the sunlight at still greater a remove. The light from the
garden steals in but dimly through paper-paneled doors, and it is precisely
this indirect light that makes for us the charm of a room. We do our walls
in neutral colors so that the sad, fragile, dying rays can sink into absolute
repose. The storehouse, kitchen, hallways, and such may have a glossy
finish, but the walls of the sitting room will almost always be of clay
textured with fine sand. A luster here would destroy the soft fragile beauty
of the feeble light. We delight in the mere sight of the delicate glow of
fading rays clinging to the surface of a dusky wall, there to live out what
little life remains to them. We never tire of the sight, for to us this pale
glow and these dim shadows far surpass any ornament. And so, as we
must if we are not to disturb the glow, we finish the walls with sand in a
single neutral color. The hue may differ from room to room, but the
degree of difference will be ever so slight; not so much a difference in
color as in shade, a difference that will seem to exist only in the mood of
the viewer. And from these delicate differences in the hue of the walls, the
shadows in each room take on a tinge peculiarly their own.

Of course the Japanese room does have its picture alcove, and in it a
hanging scroll and a flower arrangement. But the scroll and the flowers
serve not as ornament but rather to give depth to the shadows. We value a
scroll above all for the way it blends with the walls of the alcove, and thus
we consider the mounting quite as important as the calligraphy or painting. Even the greatest masterpiece will lose its worth as a scroll if it fails to
blend with the alcove, while a work of no particular distinction may blend
beautifully with the room and set off to unexpected advantage both itself
and its surroundings. Wherein lies the power of an otherwise ordinary

work to produce such an effect? Most often the paper, the ink, the fabric of the mounting will possess a certain look of antiquity, and this look of antiquity will strike just the right balance with the darkness of the alcove and room.

We have all had the experience, on a visit to one of the great temples of Kyoto or Nara, of being shown a scroll, one of the temple's treasures, hanging in a large, deeply recessed alcove. So dark are these alcoves, even in bright daylight, that we can hardly discern the outlines of the work; all we can do is listen to the explanation of the guide, follow as best we can the all-but-invisible brush strokes, and tell ourselves how magnificent a painting it must be. Yet the combination of that blurred old painting and the dark alcove is one of absolute harmony. The lack of clarity, far from disturbing us, seems rather to suit the painting perfectly. For the painting here is nothing more than another delicate surface upon which the faint, frail light can play; it performs precisely the same function as the sand-textured wall. This is why we attach such importance to age and patina. A new painting, even one done in ink monochrome or subtle pastels, can quite destroy the shadows of an alcove, unless it is selected with the greatest care.

A Japanese room might be likened to an inkwash painting, the paper-paneled shoji being the expanse where the ink is thinnest, and the alcove where it is darkest. Whenever I see the alcove of a tastefully built Japanese room, I marvel at our comprehension of the secrets of shadows, our sensitive use of shadow and light. For the beauty of the alcove is not the work of some clever device. An empty space is marked off with plain wood and plain walls, so that the light drawn into it forms dim shadows within emptiness. There is nothing more. And yet, when we gaze into the darkness that gathers behind the crossbeam, around the flower vase, beneath the shelves, though we know perfectly well it is mere shadow, we are overcome with the feeling that in this small corner of the atmosphere there reigns complete and utter silence; that here in the darkness immutable tranquility holds sway. The "mysterious Orient" of which Westerners speak probably refers to the uncanny silence of these dark places. And even we as children would feel an inexpressible chill as we peered into the depths of an alcove to which the sunlight had never penetrated. Where lies the key to this mystery? Ultimately it is the magic of shadows. Were the shadows to be banished from its corners, the alcove would in that instant revert to mere void.

This was the genius of our ancestors, that by cutting off the light from this empty space they imparted to the world of shadows that formed there a quality of mystery and depth superior to that of any wall painting or ornament. The technique seems simple, but was by no means so simply achieved. We can imagine with little difficulty what extraordinary pains were taken with each invisible detail—the placement of the window in the shelving recess, the depth of the crossbeam, the height of the threshold. But for me the most exquisite touch is the pale white glow of the shoji in the study bay; I need only pause before it and I forget the passage of time.

The study bay, as the name suggests, was originally a projecting window built to provide a place for reading. Over the years it came to be regarded as no more than a source of light for the alcove; but most often it serves not so much to illuminate the alcove as to soften the sidelong rays from without, to filter them through paper panels. There is a cold and desolate tinge to the light by the time it reaches these panels. The little sunlight from the garden that manages to make its way beneath the eaves and through the corridors has by then lost its power to illuminate, seems drained of the complexion of life. It can do no more than accentuate the whiteness of the paper. I sometimes linger before these panels and study the surface of the paper, bright, but giving no impression of brilliance.

In temple architecture the main room stands at a considerable distance from the garden; so dilute is the light there that no matter what the season, on fair days or cloudy, morning, midday, or evening, the pale, white glow scarcely varies. And the shadows at the interstices of the ribs seem strangely immobile, as if dust collected in the corners had become a part of the paper itself. I blink in uncertainty at this dreamlike luminescence, feeling as though some misty film were blunting my vision. The light from the pale white paper, powerless to dispel the heavy darkness of the alcove, is instead repelled by the darkness, creating a world of confusion where dark and light are indistinguishable. Have not you yourselves sensed a difference in the light that suffuses such a room, a rare tranquility not found in ordinary light? Have you never felt a sort of fear in the face of the ageless, a fear that in that room you might lose all consciousness of the passage of time, that untold years might pass and upon emerging you should find you had grown old and gray?

And surely you have seen, in the darkness of the innermost rooms of these huge buildings, to which sunlight never penetrates, how the gold leaf of a sliding door or screen will pick up a distant glimmer from the garden, then suddenly send forth an ethereal glow, a faint golden light cast into the enveloping darkness, like the glow upon the horizon at sunset. In no other setting is gold quite so exquisitely beautiful. You walk past, turning to look again, and yet again; and as you move away the golden surface of the paper glows ever more deeply, changing not in a flash, but growing slowly, steadily brighter, like color rising in the face of a giant. Or again you may find that the gold dust of the background, which until that moment had only a dull, sleepy luster, will, as you move past, suddenly gleam forth as if it had burst into flame.

How, in such a dark place, gold draws so much light to itself is a mystery to me. But I see why in ancient times statues of the Buddha were gilt with gold and why gold leaf covered the walls of the homes of the nobility. Modern man, in his well-lit house, knows nothing of the beauty of gold; but those who lived in the dark houses of the past were not merely captivated by its beauty, they also knew its practical value; for gold, in these dim rooms, must have served the function of a reflector. Their use of gold leaf and gold dust was not mere extravagance. Its reflective properties were put to use as a source of illumination. Silver and other metals quickly lose their gloss, but gold retains its brilliance indefinitely to light the darkness of the room. This is why gold was held in such incredibly high esteem.

I have said that lacquerware decorated in gold was made to be seen in the dark; and for this same reason were the fabrics of the past so lavishly woven of threads of silver and gold. The priest's surplice of gold brocade is perhaps the best example. In most of our city temples, catering to the masses as they do, the main hall will be brightly lit, and these garments of gold will seem merely gaudy. No matter how venerable a man the priest may be, his robes will convey no sense of his dignity. But when you attend a service at an old temple, conducted after the ancient ritual, you see how perfectly the gold harmonizes with the wrinkled skin of the old priest and the flickering light of the altar lamps, and how much it contributes to the solemnity of the occasion. As with lacquerware, the bold patterns remain for the most part hidden in darkness; only occasionally does a bit of gold or silver gleam forth.

I may be alone in thinking so, but to me it seems that nothing quite so becomes the Japanese skin as the costumes of the Nō theatre. Of course many are gaudy in the extreme, richly woven of gold and silver. But the Nō actor, unlike the Kabuki performer, wears no white powder. Whenever I attend the Nō I am impressed by the fact that on no other occasion is the beauty of the Japanese complexion set off to such advantage—the brownish skin with a flush of red that is so uniquely Japanese, the face like old ivory tinged with yellow. A robe woven or embroidered in patterns of gold or silver sets it off beautifully, as does a cloak of deep green or persimmon, or a kimono or divided skirt of a pure white, unpatterned material. And when the actor is a handsome young man with skin of fine texture and cheeks glowing with the freshness of youth, his good looks emerge as perfection, with a seductive charm quite different from a woman's. Here, one sees, is the beauty that made feudal lords lose themselves over their boy favorites.

Kabuki costumes, in the history plays and dance dramas, are no less colorful than Nō costumes; and Kabuki is commonly thought to have far greater sexual appeal than Nō. But to the adept the opposite is true. At first Kabuki will doubtless seem the more erotic and visually beautiful; but, whatever they may have been in the past, the gaudy Kabuki colors under the glare of the Western floodlamps verge on a vulgarity of which one quickly tires. And if this is true of the costumes it is all the more true of the makeup. Beautiful though such a face may be, it is after all made up; it has nothing of the immediate beauty of the flesh. The Nō actor performs with no makeup on his face or neck or hands. The man's beauty is his own; our eyes are in no way deceived. And so there is never that disappointment with the Nō actor that we feel upon seeing the unadorned face of the Kabuki actor who has played the part of a woman or handsome young man. Rather we are amazed how much the man's looks are enhanced by the gaudy costume of a medieval warrior—a man with skin like our own, in a costume we would not have thought would become him in the slightest.

I once saw Kongō Iwao play the Chinese beauty Yang Kuei-fei in the Nō play *Kōtei,* and I shall never forget the beauty of his hands showing ever so slightly from beneath his sleeves. As I watched his hands, I would occasionally glance down at my own hands resting on my knees. Again, and yet again, I looked back at the actor's hands, comparing them with my own; and there was no difference between them. Yet strangely the hands of the man on the stage were indescribably beautiful, while those on my knees were but ordinary hands. In the Nō only the merest fraction of the actor's flesh is visible—the face, the neck, the hands—and when a mask is worn, as for the role of Yang Kuei-fei, even the face is hidden; and so what little flesh can be seen creates a singularly strong impression. This was particularly true of Kongō Iwao; but even the hands of an ordinary actor —which is to say the hands of an average, undistinguished Japanese— have a remarkable erotic power which we would never notice were we to see the man in modern attire.

I would repeat that this is by no means true only of youthful or handsome actors. An ordinary man's lips will not ordinarily attract us; and yet on the Nō stage, the deep red glow and the moist sheen that come over them give a texture far more sensual than the painted lips of a woman. Chanting may keep the actor's lips constantly moist, but there is more to his beauty than this. Then again, the flush of red in the cheeks of a child actor can emerge with extraordinary freshness—an effect which in my experience is most striking against a costume in which green predominates. We might expect this to be true of a fair-skinned child; yet remarkably the reddish tinge shows to better effect on a dark-skinned child. For with the fair child the contrast between white and red is too marked, and the dark, somber colors of the Nō costume stand out too strongly, while against the brownish cheeks of the darker child the red is not so conspicuous, and costume and face complement each other beautifully. The perfect harmony of the yellow skin with garments of a subdued green or brown forces itself upon our attention as at no other time.

Were the Nō to be lit by modern floodlamps, like the Kabuki, this sense of beauty would vanish under the harsh glare. And thus the older the structure the better, for it is an essential condition of the Nō that the stage be left in the darkness in which it has stood since antiquity. A stage whose floor has acquired a natural gloss, whose beams and backdrop glow with a dark light, where the darkness beneath the rafters and eaves hangs above the actors' heads as if a huge temple bell were suspended over them—such is the proper place for Nō. Its recent ventures into huge auditoriums may have something to recommend them, but in such a setting the true beauty of the Nō is all but lost.

The darkness in which the Nō is shrouded and the beauty that emerges from it make a distinct world of shadows which today can be seen only on the stage; but in the past it could not have been far removed from daily life. The darkness of the Nō stage is after all the darkness of the domestic architecture of the day; and Nō costumes, even if a bit more splendid in pattern and color, are by and large those that were worn by court nobles and feudal lords. I find the thought fascinating: to imagine how very handsome, by comparison with us today, the Japanese of the past must have been in their resplendent dress—particularly the warriors of the fifteenth and sixteenth centuries. The Nō sets before us the beauty of Japanese manhood at its finest. What grand figures those warriors who traversed the battlefields of old must have cut in their full regalia emblazoned with family crests, the somber ground and gleaming embroidery setting off strong-boned faces burnished a deep bronze by wind and rain. Every devotee of the Nō finds a certain portion of his pleasure in speculations of this sort; for the thought that the highly colored world on the stage once existed just as we see it imparts to the Nō a historical fascination quite apart from the drama.

But the Kabuki is ultimately a world of sham, having little to do with beauty in the natural state. It is inconceivable that the beautiful women of old—to say nothing of the men—bore any resemblance to those we see on the Kabuki stage. The women of the Nō, portrayed by masked actors, are far from realistic; but the Kabuki actor in the part of a woman inspires not the slightest sense of reality. The failure is the fault of excessive lighting. When there were no modern floodlamps, when the Kabuki stage was lit by the meager light of candles and lanterns, actors must have been somewhat more convincing in women's roles. People complain that Kabuki actors are no longer really feminine, but this is hardly the fault of their talents or looks. If actors of old had had to appear on the bright stage of today, they would doubtless have stood out with a certain masculine harshness, which in the past was discreetly hidden by darkness. This was brought home to me vividly when I saw the aging Baikō in the role of the young Okaru. A senseless and extravagant use of lights, I thought, has destroyed the beauty of Kabuki.

A knowledgeable Osaka gentleman has told me that the Bunraku puppet theatre was for long lit by lamplight, even after the introduction of electricity in the Meiji era, and that this method was far more richly suggestive than modern lighting. Even now I find the puppets infinitely more real than the actors of female Kabuki parts. But in the dim lamplight, the hard lines of the puppet features softened, the glistening white of their faces muted—a chill comes over me when I think of the uncanny beauty the puppet theatre must once have had.

The female puppets consist only of a head and a pair of hands. The body, legs, and feet are concealed within a long kimono, and so the operators need only work their hands within the costume to suggest movements. To me this is the very epitome of reality, for a woman of the past did indeed exist only from the collar up and the sleeves out; the rest of her remained hidden in darkness. A woman of the middle or upper ranks of society seldom left her house, and when she did she shielded herself from the gaze of the public in the dark recesses of her palanquin. Most of her life was spent in the twilight of a single house, her body shrouded day and night in gloom, her face the only sign of her existence. Though the men dressed somewhat more colorfully than they do today, the women dressed more somberly. Daughters and wives of the merchant class wore astonishingly severe dress. Their clothing was in effect no more than a part of the darkness, the transition between darkness and face.

One thinks of the practice of blackening the teeth. Might it not have been an attempt to push everything except the face into the dark? Today this ideal of beauty has quite disappeared from everyday life, and one must go to an ancient Kyoto teahouse, such as the Sumiya in Shimabara, to find traces of it. But when I think back to my own youth in the old downtown section of Tokyo, and I see my mother at work on her sewing in the dim light from the garden, I think I can imagine a little what the old Japanese woman was like. In those days—it was around 1890—the Tokyo townsman still lived in a dusky house, and my mother, my aunts, my relatives, most women of their age, still blackened their teeth. I do not remember what they wore for everyday, but when they went out it was often in a gray kimono with a small, modest pattern.

My mother was remarkably slight, under five feet I should say, and I do not think that she was unusual for her time. I can put the matter strongly: women in those days had almost no flesh. I remember my mother's face and hands, I can clearly remember her feet, but I can remember nothing about her body. She reminds me of the statue of Kannon in the Chūgūji, whose body must be typical of most Japanese women of the past. The chest as flat as a board, breasts paperthin, back, hips, and buttocks forming an undeviating straight line, the whole body so lean and gaunt as to seem out of proportion with the face, hands, and feet, so lacking in substance as to give the impression not of flesh but of a stick—must not the traditional Japanese woman have had just such a physique? A few are still about—the aged lady in an old-fashioned household, some few geisha. They remind me of stick dolls, for in fact they are nothing more than poles upon which to hang clothes. As with the dolls their substance is made up of layer upon layer of clothing, bereft of which only an ungainly pole remains. But in the past this was sufficient. For a woman who lived in the dark it was enough if she had a faint, white face—a full body was unnecessary.

I suppose it is hard for those who praise the fleshly beauty we see under today's bright lights to imagine the ghostly beauty of those older women. And there may be some who argue that if beauty has to hide its weak points in the dark it is not beauty at all. But we Orientals, as I have suggested before, create a kind of beauty of the shadows we have made in out-of-the-way places. There is an old song that says "the brushwood we gather—stack it together, it makes a hut; pull it apart, a field once more." Such is our way of thinking—we find beauty not in the thing itself but in the patterns of shadows, the light and the darkness, that one thing against another creates.

A phosphorescent jewel gives off its glow and color in the dark and loses its beauty in the light of day. Were it not for shadows, there would be no beauty. Our ancestors made of woman an object inseparable from darkness, like lacquerware decorated in gold or mother-of-pearl. They hid as much of her as they could in shadows, concealing her arms and legs in the folds of long sleeves and skirts, so that one part and one only stood out—her face. The curveless body may, by comparison with Western women, be ugly. But our thoughts do not travel to what we cannot see. The unseen for us does not exist. The person who insists upon seeing her ugliness, like the person who would shine a hundred-candlepower light upon the picture alcove, drives away whatever beauty may reside there.

Why should this propensity to seek beauty in darkness be so strong only in Orientals? The West too has known a time when there was no electricity, gas, or petroleum, and yet so far as I know the West has never been disposed to delight in shadows. Japanese ghosts have traditionally had no feet; Western ghosts have feet, but are transparent. As even this trifle suggests, pitch darkness has always occupied our fantasies, while in the West even ghosts are as clear as glass. This is true too of our household implements: we prefer colors compounded of darkness, they prefer the colors of sunlight. And of silver and copperware: we love them for the burnish and patina, which they consider unclean, unsanitary, and polish to a glittering brilliance. They paint their ceilings and walls in pale colors to drive out as many of the shadows as they can. We fill our gardens with dense plantings, they spread out a flat expanse of grass.

But what produces such differences in taste? In my opinion it is this: we Orientals tend to seek our satisfactions in whatever surroundings we happen to find ourselves, to content ourselves with things as they are; and so darkness causes us no discontent, we resign ourselves to it as inevitable. If light is scarce then light is scarce; we will immerse ourselves in the darkness and there discover its own particular beauty. But the progressive Westerner is determined always to better his lot. From candle to oil lamp, oil lamp to gaslight, gaslight to electric light—his quest for a brighter light never ceases, he spares no pains to eradicate even the minutest shadow.

But beyond such differences in temperament, I should like to consider the importance of the difference in the color of our skin. From ancient times we have considered white skin more elegant, more beautiful than dark skin, and yet somehow this whiteness of ours differs from that of the white races. Taken individually there are Japanese who are whiter than Westerners and Westerners who are darker than Japanese, but their whiteness and darkness is not the same. Let me take an example from my own experience. When I lived on the Bluff in Yokohama I spent a good deal of my leisure in the company of foreign residents, at their banquets and balls. At close range I was not particularly struck by their whiteness, but from a distance I could distinguish them quite clearly from the Japanese. Among the Japanese were ladies who were dressed in gowns no less splendid than the foreigners', and whose skin was whiter than theirs. Yet from across the room these ladies, even one alone, would stand out unmistakably from amongst a group of foreigners. For the Japanese complexion, no matter how white, is tinged by a slight cloudiness. These women were in no way reticent about powdering themselves. Every bit of exposed flesh—even their backs and arms—they covered with a thick coat of white. Still they could not efface the darkness that lay below their skin. It was as plainly visible as dirt at the bottom of a pool of pure water. Between the fingers, around the nostrils, on the nape of the neck, along the spine—about these places especially, dark, almost dirty, shadows gathered. But the skin of the Westerners, even those of a darker complexion, had a limpid glow. Nowhere were they tainted by this gray shadow. From the tops of their heads to the tips of their fingers the whiteness was pure and unadulterated. Thus it is that when one of us goes among a group of Westerners it is like a grimy stain on a sheet of white paper. The sight offends even our own eyes and leaves none too pleasant a feeling.

We can appreciate, then, the psychology that in the past caused the white races to reject the colored races. A sensitive white person could not but be upset by the shadow that even one or two colored persons cast over a social gathering. What the situation is today I do not know, but at the time of the American Civil War, when persecution of Negroes was at its most intense, the hatred and scorn were directed not only at full-blooded Negroes, but at mulattos, the children of mulattos, and even the children of mulattos and whites. Those with the slightest taint of Negro blood, be it but a half, a quarter, a sixteenth, or a thirty-second, had to be ferreted out and made to suffer. Not even those who at a glance were indistinguishable from pure-blooded whites, but among whose ancestors two or three generations earlier there had been a Negro, escaped the searching gaze, no matter how faint the tinge that lay hidden beneath their white skin.

And so we see how profound is the relationship between shadows and the yellow races. Because no one likes to show himself to bad advantage, it is natural that we should have chosen cloudy colors for our food and clothing and houses, and sunk ourselves back into the shadows. I am not saying that our ancestors were conscious of the cloudiness in their skin. They cannot have known that a whiter race existed. But one must conclude that something in their sense of color led them naturally to this preference.

Our ancestors cut off the brightness on the land from above and created a world of shadows, and far in the depths of it they placed woman, marking her the whitest of beings. If whiteness was to be indispensible to supreme beauty, then for us there was no other way, nor do I find this objectionable. The white races are fair-haired, but our hair is dark; so nature taught us the laws of darkness, which we instinctively used to turn a yellow skin white. I have spoken of the practice of blackening the teeth, but was not the shaving of the eyebrows also a device to make the white face stand out? What fascinates me most of all, however, is that green, iridescent lipstick, so rarely used today even by Kyoto geisha. One can guess nothing of its power unless one imagines it in the low, unsteady light of a candle. The woman of old was made to hide the red of her mouth under green-black lipstick, to put shimmering ornaments in her hair; and so the last trace of color was taken from her rich skin. I know of nothing whiter than the face of a young girl in the wavering shadow of a lantern, her teeth now and then as she smiles shining a lacquered black through lips like elfin fires. It is whiter than the whitest white woman I can imagine. The whiteness of the white woman is clear, tangible, familiar, it is not this otherworldly whiteness. Perhaps the latter does not even exist. Perhaps it is only a mischievous trick of light and shadow, a thing of a moment only. But even so it is enough. We can ask for nothing more.

And while I am talking of this whiteness I want to talk also of the color of the darkness that enfolds it. I think of an unforgettable vision of darkness I once had when I took a friend from Tokyo to the old Sumiya teahouse in Kyoto. I was in a large room, the "Pine Room" I think, since destroyed by fire, and the darkness, broken only by a few candles, was of a richness quite different from the darkness of a small room. As we came in the door an elderly waitress with shaven eyebrows and blackened teeth was kneeling by a candle behind which stood a large screen. On the far side of the screen, at the edge of the little circle of light, the darkness seemed to fall from the ceiling, lofty, intense, monolithic, the fragile light of the candle unable to pierce its thickness, turned back as from a black wall. I wonder if my readers know the color of that "darkness seen by candlelight." It was different in quality from darkness on the road at night. It was a repletion, a pregnancy of tiny particles like fine ashes, each particle luminous as a rainbow. I blinked in spite of myself, as though to keep it out of my eyes.

Smaller rooms are the fashion now, and even if one were to use candles in them one would not get the color of that darkness; but in the old palace and the old house of pleasure the ceilings were high, the skirting corridors were wide, the rooms themselves were usually tens of feet long and wide, and the darkness must always have pressed in like a fog. The elegant aristocrat of old was immersed in this suspension of ashen particles, soaked in it, but the man of today, long used to the electric light, has forgotten that such a darkness existed. It must have been simple for specters to appear in a "visible darkness," where always something seemed to be flickering and shimmering, a darkness that on occasion held greater terrors than darkness out-of-doors. This was the darkness in which ghosts and monsters were active, and indeed was not the woman who lived in it, behind thick curtains, behind layer after layer of screens and doors—was she not of a kind with them? The darkness wrapped her round tenfold, twentyfold, it filled the collar, the sleeves of her kimono, the folds of her skirt, wherever a hollow invited. Further yet: might it not have been the reverse, might not the darkness have emerged from her mouth and those black teeth, from the black of her hair, like the thread from the great earth spider?

* * *

The novelist Takebayashi Musōan said when he returned from Paris a few years ago that Tokyo and Osaka were far more brightly lit than any European city; that even on the Champs Élysées there were still houses lit by oil lamps, while in Japan hardly a one remained unless in a remote mountain village. Perhaps no two countries in the world waste more electricity than America and Japan, he said, for Japan is only too anxious to imitate America in every way it can. That was some four or five years ago, before the vogue for neon signs. Imagine his surprise were he to come home today, when everything is so much brighter.

Yamamoto Sanehiko, president of the Kaizō publishing house, told me of something that happened when he escorted Dr. Einstein on a trip to Kyoto. As the train neared Ishiyama, Einstein looked out the window and remarked, "Now that is terribly wasteful." When asked what he meant, Einstein pointed to an electric lamp burning in broad daylight. "Einstein is a Jew, and so he is probably very careful about such things"—this was Yamamoto's interpretation. But the truth of the matter is that Japan wastes more electric light than any Western country except America.

This calls to mind another curious Ishiyama story. This year I had great trouble making up my mind where to go for the autumn moon-viewing. Finally, after much perplexed head-scratching, I decided on the Ishiyama Temple. The day before the full moon, however, I read in the paper that there would be loud-speakers in the woods at Ishiyama to regale the moon-viewing guests with phonograph records of the Moonlight Sonata. I canceled my plans immediately. Loud-speakers were bad enough, but if it could be assumed that they would set the tone, then there would surely be floodlights too strung all over the mountain. I remember another ruined moon-viewing, the year we took a boat on the night of the harvest full moon and sailed out over the lake of the Suma Temple. We put together a party, we had our refreshments in lacquered boxes, we set bravely out. But the margin of the lake was decorated brilliantly with electric lights in five colors. There was indeed a moon if one strained one's eyes for it.

So benumbed are we nowadays by electric lights that we have become utterly insensitive to the evils of excessive illumination. It does not matter all that much in the case of the moon, I suppose, but teahouses, restaurants, inns, and hotels are sure to be lit far too extravagantly. Some of this may be necessary to attract customers, but when the lights are turned on in summer even before dark it is a waste, and worse than the waste is the heat. I am upset by it wherever I go in the summer. Outside it will be cool, but inside it will be ridiculously hot, and more often than not because of lights too strong or too numerous. Turn some of them off and in no time at all the room is refreshingly cool. Yet curiously neither the guests nor the owner seem to realize this. A room should be brighter in winter, but dimmer in summer; it is then appropriately cool, and does not attract insects. But people will light the lights, then switch on an electric fan to combat the heat. The very thought annoys me.

One can endure a Japanese room all the same, for ultimately the heat escapes through the walls. But in a Western-style hotel circulation is poor, and the floors, walls, and ceilings drink in the heat and throw it back from every direction with unbearable intensity. The worst example, alas, is the Miyako Hotel in Kyoto, as anyone who has been in its lobby on a summer's evening should agree. It stands on high ground, facing north, commanding a view of Mount Hiei, Nyoigatake, the Kurodani pagoda, the forests, the green hills of Higashiyama—a splendidly fresh and clean view, all the more disappointing for being so. Should a person of a summer's evening set out to refresh himself among purple hills and crystal streams, to take in the cool breeze that blows through the tower on the heights, he will only find himself beneath a white ceiling dotted with huge milk glass lights, each sending forth a blinding blaze.

As in most recent Western-style buildings, the ceilings are so low that one feels as if balls of fire were blazing directly above one's head. "Hot" is no word for the effect, and the closer to the ceiling the worse it is—your head and neck and spine feel as if they were being roasted. One of these balls of fire alone would suffice to light the place, yet three or four blaze down from the ceiling, and there are smaller versions on the walls and pillars, serving no function but to eradicate every trace of shadow. And so the room is devoid of shadows. Look about and all you will see are white walls, thick red pillars, a garish floor done in mosaic patterns looking much like a freshly printed lithograph—all oppressively hot. When you enter from the corridor the difference in temperature is all too apparent. No matter how cool a breeze blows in, it is instantly transformed to hot wind.

I have stayed at the Miyako several times and think fondly of it. My warnings are given with the friendliest of intentions. It is a pity that so lovely a view, so perfect a place for enjoying the cool of a summer's night, should be utterly destroyed by electric lights. The Japanese quite aside, I cannot believe that Westerners, however much they may prefer light, can be other than appalled at the heat, and I have no doubt they would see immediately the improvement in turning down the lights. The Miyako is *FLW* by no means the only example. The Imperial Hotel, with its indirect lighting, is on the whole a pleasant place, but in summer even it might be a bit darker.

Light is used not for reading or writing or sewing but for dispelling the shadows in the farthest corners, and this runs against the basic idea of the Japanese room. Something is salvaged when a person turns off the lights at home to save money, but at inns and restaurants there is inevitably too much light in the halls, on the stairs, in the doorway, the gate, the garden.

The rooms and the water and stones outside become flat and shallow. There are advantages for keeping warm in the winter, I suppose, but in the summer, no matter to what isolated mountain resort a person flees to escape the heat, he has a disappointment waiting if it is an inn or hotel he is going to. I have found myself that the best way to keep cool is to stay at home, open the doors, and stretch out in the dark under a mosquito net.

I recently read a newspaper or magazine article about the complaints of old women in England. When they were young, they said, they respected their elders and took good care of them; but their own daughters care nothing at all for them, and avoid them as though they were somehow dirty. The morals of the young, they lamented, are not what they once were. It struck me that old people everywhere have much the same complaints. The older we get the more we seem to think that everything was better in the past. Old people a century ago wanted to go back two centuries, and two centuries ago they wished it were three centuries earlier. Never has there been an age that people have been satisfied with. But in recent years the pace of progress has been so precipitous that conditions in our own country go somewhat beyond the ordinary. The changes that have taken place since the Restoration of 1867 must be at least as great as those of the preceding three and a half centuries.

It will seem odd, I suppose, that I should go on in this vein, as if I too were grumbling in my dotage. Yet of this I am convinced, that the conveniences of modern culture cater exclusively to youth, and that the times *agreed* grow increasingly inconsiderate of old people. Let me take a familiar example: now that we cannot cross an intersection without consulting a traffic signal, old people can no longer venture confidently out into the streets. For someone sufficiently well-off to be driven about in an automobile there may be no problem, but on those rare occasions when I go into Osaka, it sets every nerve in my body on edge to cross from one side of the street to the other. If the signal is in the middle of the intersection it is easy enough to see it; but it is all but impossible to pick out a stop light that stands off to the side, where no one would ever expect to find it. If the intersection is broad, it is only too easy to confuse the light for facing traffic with the light for crossing traffic. It seemed to me the end of everything when the traffic policeman came to Kyoto. Now one must travel to such small cities as Nishinomiya, Sakai, Wakayama, or Fukuyama for the feel of Japan.

The same is true of food. In a large city it takes a concerted search to turn up a dish that will be palatable to an old person. Not long ago a newspaper reporter came to interview me on the subject of unusual foods, and I described to him the persimmon-leaf sushi made by the people who live deep in the mountains of Yoshino—and which I shall take the opportunity to introduce to you here. To every ten parts of rice one part of saké is added just when the water comes to a boil. When the rice is done it should be cooled thoroughly, after which salt is applied to the hands and the rice molded into bite-size pieces. At this stage the hands must be absolutely free of moisture, the secret being that only salt should touch the rice. Thin slices of lightly salted salmon are placed on the rice, and each piece is wrapped in a persimmon leaf, the surface of the leaf facing inward. Both the persimmon leaves and the salmon should be wiped with a dry cloth to remove any moisture. Then in a rice tub or sushi box, the interior of which is perfectly dry, the pieces are packed standing on end so that no space remains between them, and the lid is put in place and weighted with a heavy stone, as in making pickles. Prepared in the evening, the sushi should be ready to eat the next morning. Though the taste is best on the first day, it remains edible for two or three days. A slight bit of vinegar is sprinkled over each piece with a sprig of bitter nettle just before eating.

I learned of the dish from a friend who had been to Yoshino and found it so exceptionally good that he took the trouble to learn how to make it—but if you have the persimmon leaves and salted salmon it can be made anywhere. You need only remember to keep out every trace of moisture, and to cool the rice completely. I made some myself, and it was very good indeed. The oil of the salmon and the slight hint of salt give just the proper touch of seasoning to the rice, and the salmon becomes as soft as if it were fresh—the flavor is indescribable, and far better than the sushi one gets in Tokyo. I have become so fond of it that I ate almost nothing else this summer. What impressed me, however, was that this superb method of preparing salted salmon was the invention of poor mountain people. Yet a sampling of the various regional cuisines suggests that in our day country people have far more discriminating palates than city people, and that in this respect they enjoy luxuries we cannot begin to imagine.

And so as time goes by, old people give up the cities and retire to the country; and yet there is not much cause for hope there either, for country towns are year by year going the way of Kyoto, their streets strung with bright lights. There are those who say that when civilization progresses a bit further transportation facilities will move into the skies and under the ground, and that our streets will again be quiet, but I know perfectly well that when that day comes some new device for torturing the old will be invented. "Out of our way, old people," we say, and they have no recourse but to shrink back into their houses, to make whatever tidbits they can for themselves, and to enjoy their evening saké as best they can to the accompaniment of the radio.

But do not think that old people are the only ones to find fault. The author of the "Vox Populi Vox Dei" column in the Osaka *Asahi* recently castigated city officials who quite needlessly cut a swath through a forest and leveled a hill in order to build a highway through Minō Park. I was somewhat encouraged; for to snatch away from us even the darkness beneath trees that stand deep in the forest is the most heartless of crimes. At this rate every place of any beauty in Nara or in the suburbs of Kyoto and Osaka, as the price of being turned over to the masses, will be denuded of trees. But again I am grumbling.

I am aware of and most grateful for the benefits of the age. No matter what complaints we may have, Japan has chosen to follow the West, and there is nothing for her to do but move bravely ahead and leave us old ones behind. But we must be resigned to the fact that as long as our skin is the color it is the loss we have suffered cannot be remedied. I have written all this because I have thought that there might still be somewhere, possibly in literature or the arts, where something could be saved. I would call back at least for literature this world of shadows we are losing. In the mansion called literature I would have the eaves deep and the walls dark, I would push back into the shadows the things that come forward too clearly, I would strip away the useless decoration. I do not ask that this be done everywhere, but perhaps we may be allowed at least one mansion where we can turn off the electric lights and see what it is like without them.

—Translated by Thomas J. Harper
and Edward G. Seidenstricker

what an odd fellow — he & Brecht would have been a daunting pair. SAD.

WALTER BENJAMIN

Walter Benjamin (1892–1940) is now recognized as the greatest German literary critic, and one of the most important social critics, of the century. His throwaway insights are so rich that many lesser thinkers and academics have built whole careers by polishing his asides. The essay "The Work of Art in the Age of Mechanical Reproduction," about the influence of technology on art, has alone inspired a school of followers; and Benjamin's inexhaustibly suggestive writings on urbanism and the flâneur, that "connoisseur of the sidewalks," in his studies of Baudelaire and the Paris arcades, have changed the way we look at cities. Nevertheless, most of his fame has come about posthumously.

Impractical, a luftmensch, unhappy in love, Benjamin had a life that can only be called heartbreaking. Hoping for an academic career, he saw his brilliant dissertation rejected, partly because it was too difficult for his examiners to understand, partly because he was Jewish. This failure, perhaps fortunately for his later readers, threw him into a barely subsistent life as a free-lance essayist, reviewer, translator, and radio scriptwriter. He was also a passionate book collector (see "Unpacking My Library"), though he spent far more than he recouped as a sometime book dealer.

Alarmed at the growth of fascism in Germany, Benjamin resettled in Paris. Benjamin was attracted both to Marxism and Jewish mysticism; his intellectually powerful friends—the Judaic scholar Gershom Scholem, the communist playwright Bertolt Brecht, the Frankfurt School philosopher Theodor Adorno—each tried to pull him into their own orbits. Scholem wanted him to emigrate to Palestine to escape the Nazis; Adorno tried to get him to go to New York; but Benjamin was reluctant to leave Paris and his library, on which he so depended. Finally he fled with other refugees across the

Pyrenees on foot, but the border was unexpectedly (and temporarily) sealed off that day; in despair, he committed suicide.

    A strong case can be made for Benjamin as a literary artist—a poetic writer in the guise of a philosopher. Certainly this would explain both the evocative strangeness of his prose and his love of fragmentation, his obstinate shying away from philosophical systems and his attraction to belleslettres. Proust, Kafka, and the French surrealists were his acknowledged prose models. In the two essays below, we see Benjamin the personal essayist, drawing a self-mocking picture of himself as sad sack and schlemiel, the better to analyze his themes: the collecting obsession and the art of vision. "Hashish in Marseilles" is that rarity, an account of a drug experience that is cool, witty, surprising, and altogether unselfindulgent.

Unpacking My Library

A TALK ABOUT BOOK COLLECTING

I AM UNPACKING my library. Yes, I am. The books are not yet on the shelves, not yet touched by the mild boredom of order. I cannot march up and down their ranks to pass them in review before a friendly audience. You need not fear any of that. Instead, I must ask you to join me in the disorder of crates that have been wrenched open, the air saturated with the dust of wood, the floor covered with torn paper, to join me among piles of volumes that are seeing daylight again after two years of darkness, so that you may be ready to share with me a bit of the mood—it is certainly not an elegiac mood but, rather, one of anticipation—which these books arouse in a genuine collector. For such a man is speaking to you, and on closer scrutiny he proves to be speaking only about himself. Would it not be presumptuous of me if, in order to appear convincingly objective and down-to-earth, I enumerated for you the main sections or prize pieces of a library, if I presented you with their history or even their usefulness to a writer? I, for one, have in mind something less obscure, something more palpable than that; what I am really concerned with is giving you some insight into the relationship of a book collector to his possessions, into collecting rather than a collection. If I do this by elaborating on the various ways of acquiring books, this is something entirely arbitrary. This or any other procedure is merely a dam against the spring tide of memories which surges toward any collector as he contemplates his possessions. Every passion borders on the chaotic, but the collector's passion borders on the chaos of memories. More than that: the chance, the fate, that suffuse the past before my eyes are conspicuously present in the accustomed confusion of these books. For what else is this collection but a disorder to which habit has accommodated itself to such an extent that it can appear as order? You have all heard of people whom the loss of their books has turned into invalids, or of those who in order to acquire them became criminals. These are the very areas in which any order is a balancing act of extreme precariousness. "The only exact knowledge there is," said Anatole France, "is the knowledge of the date of publication and the format of books." And indeed, if there is a counterpart to the confusion of a library, it is the order of its catalogue.

Thus there is in the life of a collector a dialectical tension between the poles of disorder and order. Naturally, his existence is tied to many other things as well: to a very mysterious relationship to ownership, something about which we shall have more to say later; also, to a relationship to objects which does not emphasize their functional, utilitarian value—that is, their usefulness—but studies and loves them as the scene, the stage, of their fate. The most profound enchantment for the collector is the locking of individual items within a magic circle in which they are fixed as the final thrill, the thrill of acquisition, passes over them. Everything remembered and thought, everything conscious, becomes the pedestal, the frame, the base, the lock of his property. The period, the region, the craftsmanship, the former ownership—for a true collector the whole background of an item adds up to a magic encyclopedia whose quintessence is the fate of his object. In this circumscribed area, then, it may be surmised how the great physiognomists—and collectors are the physiognomists of the world of objects—turn into interpreters of fate. One has only to watch a collector handle the objects in his glass case. As he holds them in his hands, he seems to be seeing through them into their distant past as though inspired. So much for the magical side of the collector—his old-age image, I might call it.

Habent sua fata libelli: these words may have been intended as a general statement about books. So books like *The Divine Comedy,* Spinoza's *Ethics,* and *The Origin of Species* have their fates. A collector, however, interprets this Latin saying differently. For him, not only books but also copies of books have their fates. And in this sense, the most important fate of a copy is its encounter with him, with his own collection. I am not exaggerating when I say that to a true collector the acquisition of an old book is its rebirth. This is the childlike element which in a collector mingles with the element of old age. For children can accomplish the renewal of existence in a hundred unfailing ways. Among children, collecting is only one process of renewal; other processes are the painting of objects, the cutting out of figures, the application of decals—the whole range of childlike modes of acquisition, from touching things to giving them names. To renew the old world—that is the collector's deepest desire when he is driven to acquire new things, and that is why a collector of older books is closer to the wellsprings of collecting than the acquirer of luxury editions. How do books cross the threshold of a collection and become the property of a collector? The history of their acquisition is the subject of the following remarks.

Of all the ways of acquiring books, writing them oneself is regarded as the most praiseworthy method. At this point many of you will remember with pleasure the large library which Jean Paul's poor little schoolmaster Wutz gradually acquired by writing, himself, all the works whose titles interested him in book-fair catalogues; after all, he could not afford to buy them. Writers are really people who write books not because they are poor, but because they are dissatisfied with the books which they could buy but do not like. You, ladies and gentlemen, may regard this as a whimsical definition of a writer. But everything said from the angle of a real collector is whimsical. Of the customary modes of acquisition, the one most appropriate to a collector would be the borrowing of a book with its attendant non-returning. The book borrower of real stature whom we envisage here proves himself to be an inveterate collector of books not so much by the fervor with which he guards his borrowed treasures and by the deaf ear which he turns to all reminders from the everyday world of legality as by his failure to read these books. If my experience may serve as evidence, a man is more likely to return a borrowed book upon occasion than to read it. And the non-reading of books, you will object, should be characteristic of collectors? This is news to me, you may say. It is not news at all. Experts will bear me out when I say that it is the oldest thing in the world. Suffice it to quote the answer which Anatole France gave to a philistine who admired his library and then finished with the standard question, "And you have read all these books, Monsieur France?" "Not one-tenth of them. I don't suppose you use your Sèvres china every day?"

Incidentally, I have put the right to such an attitude to the test. For years, for at least the first third of its existence, my library consisted of no more than two or three shelves which increased only by inches each year. This was its militant age, when no book was allowed to enter it without the certification that I had not read it. Thus I might never have acquired a library extensive enough to be worthy of the name if there had not been an inflation. Suddenly the emphasis shifted; books acquired real value, or, at any rate, were difficult to obtain. At least this is how it seemed in Switzerland. At the eleventh hour I sent my first major book orders from there and in this way was able to secure such irreplaceable items as *Der blaue Reiter* and Bachofen's *Sage von Tanaquil,* which could still be obtained from the publishers at that time.

Well—so you may say—after exploring all these byways we should finally reach the wide highway of book acquisition, namely, the purchasing of books. This is indeed a wide highway, but not a comfortable one. The purchasing done by a book collector has very little in common with that done in a bookshop by a student getting a textbook, a man of the world buying a present for his lady, or a businessman intending to while away his next train journey. I have made my most memorable purchases on trips, as a transient. Property and possession belong to the tactical sphere. Collectors are people with a tactical instinct; their experience teaches them that when they capture a strange city, the smallest antique shop can be a fortress, the most remote stationery store a key position. How many cities have revealed themselves to me in the marches I undertook in the pursuit of books!

By no means all of the most important purchases are made on the premises of a dealer. Catalogues play a far greater part. And even though the purchaser may be thoroughly acquainted with the book ordered from a catalogue, the individual copy always remains a surprise and the order always a bit of a gamble. There are grievous disappointments, but also happy finds. I remember, for instance, that I once ordered a book with colored illustrations for my old collection of children's books only because it contained fairy tales by Albert Ludwig Grimm and was published at Grimma, Thuringia. Grimma was also the place of publication of a book of fables edited by the same Albert Ludwig Grimm. With its sixteen illustrations my copy of this book of fables was the only extant example of the early work of the great German book illustrator Lyser, who lived in Hamburg around the middle of the last century. Well, my reaction to the consonance of the names had been correct. In this case too I discovered the work of Lyser, namely *Linas Märchenbuch,* a work which has remained unknown to his bibliographers and which deserves a more detailed reference than this first one I am introducing here.

The acquisition of books is by no means a matter of money or expert knowledge alone. Not even both factors together suffice for the establishment of a real library, which is always somewhat impenetrable and at the same time uniquely itself. Anyone who buys from catalogues must have flair in addition to the qualities I have mentioned. Dates, place names, formats, previous owners, bindings, and the like: all these details must tell him something—not as dry, isolated facts, but as a harmonious whole; from the quality and intensity of this harmony he must be able to recognize whether a book is for him or not. An auction requires yet another set of qualities in a collector. To the reader of a catalogue the book itself must speak, or possibly its previous ownership if the provenance of the copy has been established. A man who wishes to participate at an auction must pay equal attention to the book and to his competitors, in addition to keeping a cool enough head to avoid being carried away in the competition. It is a frequent occurrence that someone gets stuck with a high purchase price because he kept raising his bid—more to assert himself than to acquire the book. On the other hand, one of the finest memories of a collector is the moment when he rescued a book to which he might never have given a thought, much less a wishful look, because he found it lonely and abandoned on the market place and bought it to give it its freedom— the way the prince bought a beautiful slave girl in *The Arabian Nights.* To a book collector, you see, the true freedom of all books is somewhere on his shelves.

To this day, Balzac's *Peau de chagrin* stands out from long rows of French volumes in my library as a memento of my most exciting experience at an auction. This happened in 1915 at the Rümann auction put up by Emil Hirsch, one of the greatest of book experts and most distinguished of dealers. The edition in question appeared in 1838 in Paris, Place de la Bourse. As I pick up my copy, I see not only its number in the Rümann collection, but even the label of the shop in which the first owner bought the book over ninety years ago for one-eightieth of today's price. "Papeterie I. Flanneau," it says. A fine age in which it was still possible to buy such a de luxe edition at a stationery dealer's! The steel engravings of this book were designed by the foremost French graphic artist and executed by the foremost engravers. But I was going to tell you how I acquired this book. I had gone to Emil Hirsch's for an advance inspection and had handled forty or fifty volumes; that particular volume had inspired in me the ardent desire to hold on to it forever. The day of the auction came. As chance would have it, in the sequence of the auction this copy of *La Peau de chagrin* was preceded by a complete set of its illustrations printed separately on India paper. The bidders sat at a long table; diagonally across from me sat the man who was the focus of all eyes at the first bid, the famous Munich collector Baron von Simolin. He was greatly interested in this set, but he had rival bidders; in short, there was a spirited contest which resulted in the highest bid of the entire auction—far in excess of three thousand marks. No one seemed to have expected such a high figure, and all those present were quite excited. Emil Hirsch remained unconcerned, and whether he wanted to save time or was guided by some other consideration, he proceeded to the next item, with no one really paying attention. He called out the price, and with my heart pounding and with the full realization that I was unable to compete with any of those big collectors I bid a somewhat higher amount. Without arousing the bidders' attention, the auctioneer went through the usual routine—

"Do I hear more?" and three bangs of his gavel, with an eternity seeming to separate each from the next—and proceeded to add the auctioneer's charge. For a student like me the sum was still considerable. The following morning at the pawnshop is no longer part of this story, and I prefer to speak about another incident which I should like to call the negative of an auction. It happened last year at a Berlin auction. The collection of books that was offered was a miscellany in quality and subject matter, and only a number of rare works on occultism and natural philosophy were worthy of note. I bid for a number of them, but each time I noticed a gentleman in the front row who seemed only to have waited for my bid to counter with his own, evidently prepared to top any offer. After this had been repeated several times, I gave up all hope of acquiring the book which I was most interested in that day. It was the rare *Fragmente aus dem Nachlass eines jungen Physikers* [Posthumous Fragments of a Young Physicist] which Johann Wilhelm Ritter published in two volumes at Heidelberg in 1810. This work has never been reprinted, but I have always considered its preface, in which the author-editor tells the story of his life in the guise of an obituary for his supposedly deceased unnamed friend—with whom he is really identical—as the most important sample of personal prose of German Romanticism. Just as the item came up I had a brain wave. It was simple enough: since my bid was bound to give the item to the other man, I must not bid at all. I controlled myself and remained silent. What I had hoped for came about: no interest, no bid, and the book was put aside. I deemed it wise to let several days go by, and when I appeared on the premises after a week, I found the book in the secondhand department and benefited by the lack of interest when I acquired it.

Once you have approached the mountains of cases in order to mine the books from them and bring them to the light of day—or, rather, of night —what memories crowd in upon you! Nothing highlights the fascination of unpacking more clearly than the difficulty of stopping this activity. I had started at noon, and it was midnight before I had worked my way to the last cases. Now I put my hands on two volumes bound in faded boards which, strictly speaking, do not belong in a book case at all: two albums with stick-in pictures which my mother pasted in as a child and which I inherited. They are the seeds of a collection of children's books which is growing steadily even today, though no longer in my garden. There is no living library that does not harbor a number of booklike creations from fringe areas. They need not be stick-in albums or family albums, autograph books or portfolios containing pamphlets or religious tracts; some people become attached to leaflets and prospectuses, others to handwriting facsimiles or typewritten copies of unobtainable books; and certainly periodicals can form the prismatic fringes of a library. But to get back to those albums: Actually, inheritance is the soundest way of acquiring a collection. For a collector's attitude toward his possessions stems from an owner's feeling of responsibility toward his property. Thus it is, in the highest sense, the attitude of an heir, and the most distinguished trait of a collection will always be its transmissibility. You should know that in saying this I fully realize that my discussion of the mental climate of collecting will confirm many of you in your conviction that this passion is behind the times, in your distrust of the collector type. Nothing is further from my mind than to shake either your conviction or your distrust. But one thing should be noted: the phenomenon of collecting loses its meaning as it loses its personal owner. Even though public collections may be less objectionable socially and more useful academically than private collections, the objects get their due only in the latter. I do know that time is running out for the type that I am discussing here and have been representing before you a bit *ex officio*. But, as Hegel put it, only when it is dark does the owl of Minerva begin its flight. Only in extinction is the collector comprehended.

Now I am on the last half-emptied case and it is way past midnight. Other thoughts fill me than the ones I am talking about—not thoughts but images, memories. Memories of the cities in which I found so many things: Riga, Naples, Munich, Danzig, Moscow, Florence, Basel, Paris; memories of Rosenthal's sumptuous rooms in Munich, of the Danzig Stockturm where the late Hans Rhaue was domiciled, of Süssengut's musty book cellar in North Berlin; memories of the rooms where these books had been housed, of my student's den in Munich, of my room in Bern, of the solitude of Iseltwald on the Lake of Brienz, and finally of my boyhood room, the former location of only four or five of the several thousand volumes that are piled up around me. O bliss of the collector, bliss of the man of leisure! Of no one has less been expected, and no one has had a greater sense of well-being than the man who has been able to carry on his disreputable existence in the mask of Spitzweg's "Bookworm." For inside him there are spirits, or at least little genii, which have seen to it that for a collector—and I mean a real collector, a collector as he ought to be— ownership is the most intimate relationship that one can have to objects. Not that they come alive in him; it is he who lives in them. So I have erected one of his dwellings, with books as the building stones, before you, and now he is going to disappear inside, as is only fitting.

—Translated by Harry Zohn

Hashish in Marseilles

PRELIMINARY REMARK: One of the first signs that hashish is beginning to take effect "is a dull feeling of foreboding; something strange, ineluctable is approaching . . . images and chains of images, long-submerged memories appear, whole scenes and situations are experienced; at first they arouse interest, now and then enjoyment, and finally, when there is no turning away from them, weariness and torment. By everything that happens, and by what he says and does, the subject is surprised and overwhelmed. His laughter, all his utterances happen to him like outward events. He also attains experiences that approach inspiration, illumination. . . . Space can expand, the ground tilt steeply, atmospheric sensations occur: vapor, an opaque heaviness of the air; colors grow brighter, more luminous; objects more beautiful, or else lumpy and threatening. . . . All this does not occur in a continuous development; rather, it is typified by a continual alternation of dreaming and waking states, a constant and finally exhausting oscillation between totally different worlds of consciousness; in the middle of a sentence these transitions can take place. . . . All this the subject reports in a form that usually diverges very widely from the norm. Connections become difficult to perceive, owing to the frequently sudden rupture of all memory of past events, thought is not formed into words, the situation can become so compulsively hilarious that the hashish eater for minutes on end is capable of nothing except laughing. . . . The memory of the intoxication is surprisingly clear." "It is curious that hashish poisoning has not yet been experimentally studied. The most admirable description of the hashish trance is by Baudelaire (*Les paradis artificiels*)." From Joël and Fränkel, "Der Haschisch-Rausch," *Klinische Wochenschrift,* 1926, vol. 5, p. 37.

Marseilles, July 29. At seven o'clock in the evening, after long hesitation, I took hashish. During the day I had been in Aix. With the absolute certainty, in this city of hundreds of thousands where no one knows me, of not being disturbed, I lie on the bed. And yet I am disturbed, by a little child crying. I think three-quarters of an hour have already passed. But it is only twenty minutes. . . . So I lie on the bed, reading and smoking. Opposite me always this view of the belly of Marseilles. The street I have so often seen is like a knife cut.

At last I left the hotel, the effects seeming nonexistent or so weak that the precaution of staying at home was unnecessary. My first port of call was the café on the corner of Cannebière and Cours Belsunce. Seen from the harbor, the one on the right, therefore not my usual café. What now? Only a certain benevolence, the expectation of being received kindly by people. The feeling of loneliness is very quickly lost. My walking stick begins to give me a special pleasure. One becomes so tender, fears that a shadow falling on the paper might hurt it. The nausea disappears. One reads the notices on the urinals. It would not surprise me if this or that person came up to me. But when no one does I am not disappointed, either. However, it is too noisy for me here.

Now the hashish eater's demands on time and space come into force. As is known, these are absolutely regal. Versailles, for one who has taken hashish, is not too large, or eternity too long. Against the background of these immense dimensions of inner experience, of absolute duration and immeasurable space, a wonderful, beatific humor dwells all the more fondly on the contingencies of the world of space and time. I feel this humor infinitely when I am told at the Restaurant Basso that the hot kitchen has just been closed, while I have just sat down to feast into eternity. Afterward, despite this, the feeling that all this is indeed bright, frequented, animated, and will remain so. I must note how I found my seat. What mattered to me was the view of the old port that one got from the upper floors. Walking past below, I had spied an empty table on the balcony of the second story. Yet in the end I only reached the first. Most of the window tables were occupied, so I went up to a very large one that had just been vacated. As I was sitting down, however, the disproportion of seating myself at so large a table caused me such shame that I walked across the entire floor to the opposite end to sit at a smaller table that became visible to me only as I reached it.

But the meal came later. First, the little bar on the harbor. I was again just on the point of retreating in confusion, for a concert, indeed a brass band, seemed to be playing there. I only just managed to explain to myself that it was nothing more than the blaring of car horns. On the way to the Vieux Port I already had this wonderful lightness and sureness of step that transformed the stony, unarticulated earth of the great square that I was crossing into the surface of a country road along which I strode at night like an energetic hiker. For at this time I was still avoiding the Cannebière, not yet quite sure of my regulatory functions. In that little harbor bar the hashish then began to exert its canonical magic with a primitive sharpness that I had scarcely felt until then. For it made me into a physiognomist, or at least a contemplator of physiognomies, and I underwent something unique in my experience: I positively fixed my gaze on the faces that I had around me, which were, in part, of remarkable coarseness or ugliness. Faces that I would normally have avoided for a twofold reason: I should neither have wished to attract their gaze nor endured their brutality. It was a very advanced post, this harbor tavern. (I believe it was the farthest accessible to me without danger, a circumstance I had gauged, in the trance, with the same accuracy with which, when utterly weary, one is able to fill a glass exactly to the brim without spilling a drop, as one can never do with sharp senses.) It was still sufficiently far from rue Bouterie, yet no bourgeois sat there; at the most, besides the true port proletariat, a few petit-bourgeois families from the neighborhood. I now suddenly understood how, to a painter—had it not happened to Rembrandt and many others?—ugliness could appear as the true reservoir of beauty, better than any treasure cask, a jagged mountain with all the inner gold of beauty gleaming from the wrinkles, glances, features. I especially remember a boundlessly animal and vulgar male face in which the "line of renunciation" struck me with sudden violence. It was above all men's faces that had begun to interest me. Now began the game, to be long maintained, of recognizing someone I knew in every face; often I knew the name, often not; the deception vanished as deceptions vanish in dreams: not in shame and compromised, but peacefully and amiably, like a being who has performed his service. Under these circumstances there was no question of loneliness. Was I my own company? Surely not so undisguisedly. I doubt whether that would have made me so happy. More likely this: I became my own most skillful, fond, shameless procurer, gratifying myself with the ambiguous assurance of one who knows from profound study the wishes of his employer. Then it began to take half an eternity until the waiter reappeared. Or, rather, I could not wait for him to appear. I went into the barroom and paid at the counter. Whether tips are usual in such taverns I do not know. But under other circumstances I should have given something in any case. Under hashish yesterday, however, I was on the stingy side; for fear of attracting attention by extravagance, I succeeded in making myself really conspicuous.

Similarly at Basso's. First I ordered a dozen oysters. The man wanted me to order the next course at the same time. I named some local dish. He came back with the news that none was left. I then pointed to a place in the menu in the vicinity of this dish, and was on the point of ordering each item, one after another, but then the name of the one above it caught my attention, and so on, until I finally reached the top of the list. This was not just from greed, however, but from an extreme politeness toward the dishes that I did not wish to offend by a refusal. In short, I came to a stop at a *pâté de Lyon*. Lion paste, I thought with a witty smile, when it lay clean on a plate before me, and then, contemptuously: This tender rabbit or chicken meat—whatever it may be. To my lionish hunger it would not have seemed inappropriate to satisfy itself on a lion. Moreover, I had tacitly decided that as soon as I had finished at Basso's (it was about half past ten) I should go elsewhere and dine a second time.

But first, back to the walk to Basso's. I strolled along the quay and read one after another the names of the boats tied up there. As I did so an incomprehensible gaiety came over me, and I smiled in turn at all the Christian names of France. The love promised to these boats by their names seemed wonderfully beautiful and touching to me. Only one of them, *Aero II,* which reminded me of aerial warfare, I passed by without cordiality, exactly as, in the bar that I had just left, my gaze had been obliged to pass over certain excessively deformed countenances.

Upstairs at Basso's, when I looked down, the old games began again. The square in front of the harbor was my palette, on which imagination mixed the qualities of the place, trying them out now this way, now that, without concern for the result, like a painter daydreaming on his palette. I hesitated before taking wine. It was a half bottle of Cassis. A piece of ice was floating in the glass. Yet it went excellently with my drug. I had chosen my seat on account of the open window, through which I could look down on the dark square. And as I did so from time to time, I noticed that it had a tendency to change with everyone who stepped onto it, as if it formed a figure about him that, clearly, had nothing to do with the square as he saw it but, rather, with the view that the great portrait painters of the seventeenth century, in accordance with the character of the dignitary whom they placed before a colonnade or a window, threw into a relief by this colonnade, this window. Later I noted as I looked down, "From century to century things grow more estranged."

Here I must observe in general: the solitude of such trances has its dark side. To speak only of the physical aspect, there was a moment in the harbor tavern when a violent pressure in the diaphragm sought relief through humming. And there is no doubt that truly beautiful, illuminating visions were not awakened. On the other hand, solitude works in these states as a filter. What one writes down the following day is more than an enumeration of impressions; in the night the trance cuts itself off from everyday reality with fine, prismatic edges; it forms a kind of figure and is more easily memorable. I should like to say: it shrinks and takes on the form of a flower.

To begin to solve the riddle of the ecstasy of trance, one ought to meditate on Ariadne's thread. What joy in the mere act of unrolling a ball of thread. And this joy is very deeply related to the joy of trance, as to that of creation. We go forward; but in so doing we not only discover the twists and turns of the cave, but also enjoy this pleasure of discovery against the background of the other, rhythmical bliss of unwinding the thread. The certainty of unrolling an artfully wound skein—is that not the joy of all productivity, at least in prose? And under hashish we are enraptured prose-beings in the highest power.

A deeply submerged feeling of happiness that came over me afterward, on a square off the Cannebière where rue Paradis opens onto a park, is more difficult to recall than everything that went before. Fortunately I find on my newspaper the sentence "One should scoop sameness from reality with a spoon." Several weeks earlier I had noted another, by Johannes V. Jensen, which appeared to say something similar: "Richard was a young man with understanding for everything in the world that was of the same kind." This sentence had pleased me very much. It enabled me now to confront the political, rational sense it had had for me earlier with the individual, magical meaning of my experience the day before. Whereas Jensen's sentence amounted, as I had understood it, to saying that things are as we know them to be, thoroughly mechanized and rationalized, the particular being confined today solely to nuances, my new insight was entirely different. For I saw only nuances, yet these were the same. I immersed myself in contemplation of the sidewalk before me, which, through a kind of unguent with which I covered it, could have been, precisely as these very stones, also the sidewalk of Paris. One often speaks of stones instead of bread. These stones were the bread of my imagination, which was suddenly seized by a ravenous hunger to taste what is the same in all places and countries. And yet I thought with immense pride of sitting here in Marseilles in a hashish trance; of who else might be sharing my intoxication this evening, how few. Of how I was incapable of fearing future misfortune, future solitude, for hashish would always remain. The music from a nearby nightclub that I had been following played a part in this stage. G. rode past me in a cab. It happened suddenly, exactly as, earlier, from the shadows of the boat, U. had suddenly, detached himself in the form of a harbor loafer and pimp. But there were not only known faces. Here, while I was in the state of deepest trance, two figures—citizens, vagrants, what do I know?—passed me as "Dante and Petrarch." "All men are brothers." So began a train of thought that I am no longer able to pursue. But its last link was certainly much less banal than its first and led on perhaps to images of animals.

"Barnabe," read the sign on a streetcar that stopped briefly at the square where I was sitting. And the sad confused story of Barnabas seemed to me no bad destination for a streetcar going into the outskirts of Marseilles. Something very beautiful was going on around the door of the dance hall. Now and then a Chinese in blue silk trousers and a glowing pink silk jacket stepped outside. He was the doorman. Girls displayed themselves in the doorway. My mood was free of all desire. It was amusing to see a young man with a girl in a white dress coming toward me and to be immediately obliged to think: "She got away from him in there in her shift, and now he is fetching her back. Well, well." I felt flattered by the thought of sitting here in a center of dissipation, and by "here" I did not mean the town but the little, not-very-eventful spot where I found myself. But events took place in such a way that the appearance of things touched me with a magic wand, and I sank into a dream of them. People and things behave at such hours like those little stage sets and people made of elder pith in the glazed tin-foil box, which, when the glass is rubbed, are electrified and fall at every movement into the most unusual relationships.

The music that meanwhile kept rising and falling, I called the rush switches of jazz. I have forgotten on what grounds I permitted myself to mark the beat with my foot. This is against my education, and it did not happen without inner disputation. There were times when the intensity of acoustic impressions blotted out all others. In the little bar, above all, everything was suddenly submerged in the noise of voices, not of streets. What was most peculiar about this din of voices was that it sounded entirely like dialect. The people of Marseilles suddenly did not speak good enough French for me. They were stuck at the level of dialect. The phenomenon of alienation that may be involved in this, which Kraus has formulated in the fine dictum "The more closely you look at a word the more distantly it looks back," appears to extend to the optical. At any rate I find among my notes the surprised comment "How things withstand the gaze."

The trance abated when I crossed the Cannebière and at last turned the corner to have a final ice cream at the little Café des Cours Belsunce. It was not far from the first café of the evening, in which, suddenly, the amorous joy dispensed by the contemplation of some fringes blown by the wind had convinced me that the hashish had begun its work. And when I recall this state I should like to believe that hashish persuades nature to permit us—for less egoistic purposes—that squandering of our own existence that we know in love. For if, when we love, our existence runs through nature's fingers like golden coins that she cannot hold and lets fall to purchase new birth thereby, she now throws us, without hoping or expecting anything, in ample handfuls to existence.

—Translated by Edmund Jephcott

JORGE LUIS BORGES

*Jorge Luis Borges (1899–1986) was one of the most original and influential of modern writers. Enormously learned, he seemed to draw inspiration more from books than raw experience; consequently, he has become one of the heroes of the school of metafiction. His major works—*Ficciones, The Aleph, Dreamtigers, The Book of Imaginary Beings*—show a penchant for fantasy, fiction about storytelling, and genre hybrids and laid the groundwork for literary postmodernism.*

Borges grew up in Buenos Aires and is associated with that city, which he portrayed in a dreamlike manner, as much as Kafka is associated with Prague. He anthologized Argentine literature while maintaining a lifelong love affair with English literature. He wrote important literary criticism; in a sense, everything he wrote, fiction and poetry included, was a kind of literary criticism—a part skeptical, part hopeful gloss on a fragmented text he pretended had passed into his hands. Not surprisingly, he loved essayists with imagination, particularly Robert Louis Stevenson and G. K. Chesterton.

"Blindness," from his collection Seven Nights, *is an example of an essay in the form of a lecture. It is also a moving meditation on the author's disability. Borges regarded his progressive blindness, the result of an inherited eye disease, not as entirely tragic but as an opportunity—as if this singular author, who always approached writing as a mysterious text to be deciphered, now saw the world itself as a shadowy, tantalizing palimpsest.*

Blindness

IN THE COURSE of the many lectures—too many lectures—I have given, I've observed that people tend to prefer the personal to the general, the concrete to the abstract. I will begin, then, by referring to my own modest blindness. Modest, because it is total blindness in one eye, but only partial in the other. I can still make out certain colors; I can still see blue and green. And yellow, in particular, has remained faithful to me. I remember when I was young I used to linger in front of certain cages in the Palermo zoo: the cages of the tigers and leopards. I lingered before the tigers' gold and black. Yellow is still with me, even now. I have written a poem entitled "The Gold of the Tigers," in which I refer to this friendship.

People generally imagine the blind as enclosed in a black world. There is, for example, Shakespeare's line: "Looking on darkness which the blind do see." If we understand *darkness* as *blackness,* then Shakespeare is wrong.

One of the colors that the blind—or at least this blind man—do *not* see is black; another is red. *Le rouge et le noir* are the colors denied us. I, who was accustomed to sleeping in total darkness, was bothered for a long time at having to sleep in this world of mist, in the greenish or bluish mist, vaguely luminous, which is the world of the blind. I wanted to lie down in darkness. The world of the blind is not the night that people imagine. (I should say that I am speaking for myself, and for my father and my grandmother, who both died blind—blind, laughing, and brave, as I also hope to die. They inherited many things—blindness, for example—but one does not inherit courage. I know that they were brave.)

The blind live in a world that is inconvenient, an undefined world from which certain colors emerge: for me, yellow, blue (except that the blue may be green), and green (except that the green may be blue). White has disappeared, or is confused with gray. As for red, it has vanished completely. But I hope some day—I am following a treatment—to improve and to be able to see that great color, that color which shines in poetry, and which has so many beautiful names in many languages. Think of *scharlach* in German, *scarlet* in English, *escarlata* in Spanish, *écarlate* in French. Words that are worthy of that great color. In contrast, *amarillo,* yellow, sounds weak in Spanish, in English it seems more like yellow. I think that in Old Spanish it was *amariello.*

I live in that world of colors, and if I speak of my own modest blindness, I do so, first, because it is not that perfect blindness which people imagine, and second, because it deals with me. My case is not especially dramatic. What is dramatic are those who suddenly lose their sight. In my case, that slow nightfall, that slow loss of sight, began when I began to see. It has continued since 1899 without dramatic moments, a slow nightfall that has lasted more than three quarters of a century. In 1955 the pathetic moment came when I knew I had lost my sight, my reader's and writer's sight.

In my life I have received many unmerited honors, but there is one which has made me happier than all the others: the directorship of the National Library. For reasons more political than literary, I was appointed by the Aramburu government.

I was named director of the library, and I returned to that building of which I had so many memories, on the Calle México in Monserrat, in the South of the city. I had never dreamed of the possibility of being director of the library. I had memories of another kind. I would go there with my father, at night. My father, a professor of psychology, would ask for some book by Bergson or William James, who were his favorite writers, or perhaps by Gustav Spiller. I, too timid to ask for a book, would look through some volume of the *Encyclopedia Britannica* or the German encyclopedias of Brockhaus or of Meyer. I would take a volume at random from the shelf and read. I remember one night when I was particularly rewarded, for I read three articles: on the Druids, the Druses, and Dryden—a gift of the letters *dr*. Other nights I was less fortunate.

I knew that Paul Groussac was in the building. I could have met him personally, but I was then quite shy; almost as shy as I am now. At the time, I believed that shyness was very important, but now I know that shyness is one of the evils one must try to overcome, that in reality to be shy doesn't matter—it is like so many other things to which one gives an exaggerated importance.

I received the nomination at the end of 1955. I was in charge of, I was told, a million books. Later I found out it was nine hundred thousand—a number that's more than enough. (And perhaps nine hundred thousand seems more than a million.)

Little by little I came to realize the strange irony of events. I had always imagined Paradise as a kind of library. Others think of a garden or of a palace. There I was, the center, in a way, of nine hundred thousand books in various languages, but I found I could barely make out the title pages and the spines. I wrote the "Poem of the Gifts," which begins:

> *No one should read self-pity or reproach*
> *into this statement of the majesty*

of God; who with such splendid irony
granted me books and blindness at one touch.

[tr. ALASTAIR REID]

Those two gifts contradicted each other: the countless books and the night, the inability to read them.

I imagined the author of that poem to be Groussac, for Groussac was also the director of the library and also blind. Groussac was more courageous than I: he kept his silence. But I knew that there had certainly been moments when our lives had coincided, since we both had become blind and we both loved books. He honored literature with books far superior to mine. But we were both men of letters, and we both passed through the library of forbidden books—one might say, for our darkened eyes, of blank books, books without letters. I wrote of the irony of God, and in the end I asked myself which of us had written that poem of a plural I and a single shadow.

At the time I ignored the fact that there had been another director of the library who was blind, José Mármol. Here appears the number three, which seals everything. Two is a mere coincidence; three a confirmation. A confirmation of a ternary order, a divine or theological confirmation.

Mármol was director of the library when it was on the Calle Venezuela. These days it is usual to speak badly of Mármol, or not to mention him at all. But we must remember that when we speak of the time of Rosas, we do not think of the admirable book by Ramos Mejia, *Rosas y su tiempo* (*"Rosas and his time"*), but of the era as it is described in Mármol's wonderfully gossipy novel, *La Amalia.* To bequeath the image of an age or of a country is no small glory.

We have, then, three people who shared the same fate. And, for me, the joy of returning to the Monserrat section, in the South. For everyone in Buenos Aires, the South is, in a mysterious way, the secret center of the city. Not the other, somewhat ostentatious center we show to tourists—in those days there was not that bit of public relations called the Barrio de San Telmo. But the South has come to be the modest secret center of Buenos Aires.

When I think of Buenos Aires, I think of the Buenos Aires I knew as a child: the low houses, the patios, the porches, the cisterns with turtles in them, the grated windows. That Buenos Aires was all of Buenos Aires. Now only the southern section has been preserved. I felt that I had returned to the neighborhood of my elders.

There were the books, but I had to ask my friends the names of them. I remembered a sentence from Rudolf Steiner, in his books on anthroposophy, which was the name he gave to his theosophy. He said that when something ends, we must think that something begins. His advice is salutory, but the execution is difficult, for we only know what we have lost, not what we will gain. We have a very precise image—an image at times shameless—of what we have lost, but we are ignorant of what may follow or replace it.

I made a decision. I said to myself: since I have lost the beloved world of appearances, I must create something else. At the time I was a professor of English at the university. What could I do to teach that almost infinite literature, that literature which exceeds the life of a man, and even generations of men? What could I do in four Argentine months of national holidays and strikes? I did what I could to teach the love of that literature, and I refrained as much as possible from dates and names.

Some female students came to see me. They had taken the exam and passed. (All students pass with me!) To the girls—there were nine or ten —I said: "I have an idea. Now that you have passed and I have fulfilled my obligation as a professor, wouldn't it be interesting to embark on the study of a language or a literature we hardly know?" They asked which language and which literature. "Well, naturally the English language and English literature. Let us begin to study them, now that we are free from the frivolity of the exams; let us begin at the beginning."

I remembered that at home there were two books I could retrieve. I had placed them on the highest shelf, thinking I would never use them. They were Sweet's *Anglo-Saxon Reader* and *The Anglo-Saxon Chronicle.* Both had glossaries. And so we gathered one morning in the National Library.

I thought: I have lost the visible world, but now I am going to recover another, the world of my distant ancestors, those tribes of men who rowed across the stormy northern seas, from Germany, Denmark, and the Low Countries, who conquered England, and after whom we name England— since *Angle-land,* land of the Angles, had previously been called the land of the Britons, who were Celts.

It was a Saturday morning. We gathered in Groussac's office, and we began to read. It was a situation that pleased and mortified us, and at the same time filled us with a certain pride. It was the fact that the Saxons, like the Scandinavians, used two runic letters to signify the two sounds of *th,* as in *thing* and *the.* This conferred an air of mystery to the page.

We were encountering a language which seemed different from English but similar to German. What always happens, when one studies a language, happened. Each one of the words stood out as though it had been carved, as though it were a talisman. For that reason the poems of a foreign language have a prestige they do not enjoy in their own language, for one hears, one sees, each one of the words individually. We think of the beauty, of the power, or simply of the strangeness of them.

We had good luck that morning. We discovered the sentence, "Julius

Caesar was the first Roman to discover England." Finding ourselves with
the Romans in a text of the North, we were moved. You must remember
we knew nothing of the language; each word was a kind of talisman we
unearthed. We found two words. And with those two words we became
almost drunk. (It's true that I was an old man and they were young
women—likely stages for inebriation.) I thought: "I am returning to the
language my ancestors spoke fifty generations ago; I am returning to that
language; I am reclaiming it. It is not the first time I speak it; when I had
other names this was the language I spoke." Those two words were the
name of London, *Lundenburh,* and the name of Rome, which moved us
even more, thinking of the light that had fallen on those northern islands,
Romeburh. I think we left crying, *"Lundenburh, Romeburh . . ."* in
the streets.

Thus I began my study of Anglo-Saxon, which blindness brought me.
And now I have a memory full of poetry that is elegiac, epic, Anglo-Saxon.

I had replaced the visible world with the aural world of the Anglo-
Saxon language. Later I moved on to the richer world of Scandinavian
literature: I went on to the Eddas and the sagas. I wrote *Ancient Germanic
Literature* and many poems based on those themes, but most of all I enjoyed it. I am now preparing a book on Scandinavian literature.

I did not allow blindness to intimidate me. And besides, my editor
made me an excellent offer: he told me that if I produced thirty poems in
a year, he would publish a book. Thirty poems means discipline, especially
when one must dictate every line, but at the same time it allows for a
sufficient freedom, as it is impossible that in one year there will not be
thirty occasions for poetry. Blindness has not been for me a total misfortune; it should not be seen in a pathetic way. It should be seen as a way of
life: one of the styles of living.

Being blind has its advantages. I owe to the darkness some gifts: the gift
of Anglo-Saxon, my limited knowledge of Icelandic, the joy of so many
lines of poetry, of so many poems, and of having written another book,
entitled, with a certain falsehood, with a certain arrogance, *In Praise
of Darkness.*

I would like to speak now of other cases, of illustrious cases. I will begin
with that obvious example of the friendship of poetry and blindness, with
the one who has been called the greatest of poets: Homer. (We know of
another blind Greek poet, Tamiris, whose work has been lost. Tamiris was
defeated in a battle with the muses, who broke his lyre and took away
his sight.)

Oscar Wilde had a curious hypothesis, one which I don't think is historically correct but which is intellectually agreeable. In general, writers try to
make what they say seem profound; Wilde was a profound man who tried
to seem frivolous. He wanted us to think of him as a conversationalist; he

wanted us to consider him as Plato considered poetry, as "that winged, fickle, sacred thing." Well, that winged, fickle, sacred thing called Oscar Wilde said that Antiquity had deliberately represented Homer as blind.

We do not know if Homer existed. The fact that seven cities vie for his name is enough to make us doubt his historicity. Perhaps there was no single Homer; perhaps there were many Greeks whom we conceal under the name of Homer. The traditions are unanimous in showing us a blind poet, yet Homer's poetry is visual, often splendidly visual—as was, to a far lesser degree, that of Oscar Wilde.

Wilde realized that his poetry was too visual, and he wanted to cure himself of that defect. He wanted to make poetry that was aural, musical —let us say like the poetry of Tennyson, or of Verlaine, whom he loved and admired so. Wilde said that the Greeks claimed that Homer was blind in order to emphasize that poetry must be aural, not visual. From that comes the *"de la musique avant toute chose"* of Verlaine and the symbolism contemporary to Wilde.

We may believe that Homer never existed, but that the Greeks imagined him as blind in order to insist on the fact that poetry is, above all, music; that poetry is, above all, the lyre; that the visual can or cannot exist in a poet. I know of great visual poets and great poets who are not visual —intellectual poets, mental ones—there's no need to mention names.

Let us go on to the example of Milton. Milton's blindness was voluntary. He knew from the beginning that he was going to be a great poet. This has occurred to other poets: Coleridge and De Quincey, before they wrote a single line, knew that their destiny was literary. I too, if I may mention myself, have always known that my destiny was, above all, a literary destiny—that bad things and some good things would happen to me, but that, in the long run, all of it would be converted into words. Particularly the bad things, since happiness does not need to be transformed: happiness is its own end.

Let us return to Milton. He destroyed his sight writing pamphlets in support of the execution of the king by Parliament. Milton said that he lost his sight voluntarily, defending freedom; he spoke of that noble task and never complained of being blind. He sacrificed his sight, and then he remembered his first desire, that of being a poet. They have discovered at Cambridge University a manuscript in which the young Milton proposes various subjects for a long poem.

"I might perhaps leave something so written to aftertimes, as they should not willingly let it die," he declared. He listed some ten or fifteen subjects, not knowing that one of them would prove prophetic: the subject of Samson. He did not know that his fate would, in a way, be that of Samson; that Samson, who had prophesied Christ in the Old Testament, also prophesied Milton, and with greater accuracy. Once he knew himself to be permanently blind, he embarked on two historical works, *A Brief History of Muscovia* and *A History of England,* both of which remained unfinished. And then the long poem *Paradise Lost*. He sought a theme that would interest all men, not merely the English. That subject was Adam, our common father.

He spent a good part of his time alone, composing verses, and his memory had grown. He would hold forty or fifty hendecasyllables of blank verse in his memory and then dictate them to whomever came to visit. The whole poem was written in this way. He thought of the fate of Samson, so close to his own, for now Cromwell was dead and the hour of the Restoration had come. Milton was persecuted and could have been condemned to death for having supported the execution of the king. But when they brought Charles II—son of Charles I, "The Executed"—the list of those condemned to death, he put down his pen and said, not without nobility, "There is something in my right hand which will not allow me to sign a sentence of death." Milton was saved, and many others with him.

He then wrote *Samson Agonistes*. He wanted to create a Greek tragedy. The action takes place in a single day, Samson's last. Milton thought on the similarity of destinies, since he, like Samson, had been a strong man who was ultimately defeated. He was blind. And he wrote those verses which, according to Landor, he punctuated badly, but which in fact had to be "Eyeless, in Gaza, at the mill, with the slaves"—as if the misfortunes were accumulating on Samson.

Milton has a sonnet in which he speaks of his blindness. There is a line one can tell was written by a blind man. When he has to describe the world, he says, "In this dark world and wide." It is precisely the world of the blind when they are alone, walking with hands outstretched, searching for props. Here we have an example—much more important than mine—of a man who overcomes blindness and does his work: *Paradise Lost, Paradise Regained, Samson Agonistes,* his best sonnets, part of *A History of England,* from the beginnings to the Norman Conquest. All of this was executed while he was blind, all of it had to be dictated to casual visitors.

The Boston aristocrat Prescott was helped by his wife. An accident, when he was a student at Harvard, had caused him to lose one eye and left him almost blind in the other. He decided that his life would be dedicated to literature. He studied, and learned, the literatures of England, France, Italy, and Spain. Imperial Spain offered him a world which was agreeable to his own rigid rejection of a democratic age. From an erudite he became a writer, and he dictated to his wife, who read to him, the histories of the conquest of Mexico and Peru, of the reign of the Catholic Kings and of Phillip II. It was a happy labor, almost impeccable, which took more than twenty years.

There are two examples which are closer to us. One I have already mentioned, Paul Groussac, who has been unjustly forgotten. People see him now as a French interloper in Argentina. It is said that his historical work has become dated, that today one makes use of greater documentation. But they forget that Groussac, like every writer, left two works: first, his subject, and second, the manner of its execution. Groussac revitalized Spanish prose. Alfonso Reyes, the greatest prose writer in Spanish in any era, once told me, "Groussac taught me how Spanish should be written." Groussac overcame his blindness and left some of the best pages in prose that have been written in our country. It will always please me to remember this.

Let us recall another example, one more famous than Groussac. In James Joyce we are also given a twofold work. We have those two vast and—why not say it?—unreadable novels, *Ulysses* and *Finnegans Wake*. But that is only half of his work (which also includes beautiful poems and the admirable *Portrait of an Artist as a Young Man*). The other half, and perhaps the most redeeming aspect (as they now say) is the fact that he took on the almost infinite English language. That language—which is statistically larger than all the others and offers so many possibilities for the writer, particularly in its concrete verbs—was not enough for him. Joyce, an Irishman, recalled that Dublin had been founded by Danish Vikings. He studied Norwegian—he wrote a letter to Ibsen in Norwegian—and then he studied Greek, Latin . . . He knew all the languages, and he wrote in a language invented by himself, difficult to understand but marked by a strange music. Joyce brought a new music to English. And he said, valorously (and mendaciously) that "of all the things that have happened to me, I think the least important was having been blind." Part of his vast work was executed in darkness: polishing the sentences in his memory, working at times for a whole day on a single phrase, and then writing it and correcting it. All in the midst of blindness or periods of blindness. In comparison, the impotence of Boileau, Swift, Kant, Ruskin, and George Moore was a melancholic instrument for the successful execution of their work; one might say the same of perversion, whose beneficiaries today have ensured that no one will ignore their names. Democritus of Abdera tore his eyes out in a garden so that the spectacle of reality would not distract him; Origen castrated himself.

I have enumerated enough examples. Some are so illustrious that I am ashamed to have spoken of my own personal case—except for the fact that people always hope for confessions and I have no reason to deny them mine. But, of course, it seems absurd to place my name next to those I have recalled.

I have said that blindness is a way of life, a way of life that is not entirely unfortunate. Let us recall those lines of the greatest Spanish poet, Fray Luis de León:

> *Vivir quiero conmigo,*
> *gozar quiero del bien que debo al cielo,*
> *a solas sin testigo,*
> *libre de amor, de celo,*
> *de odio, de esperanza, de recelo.*
>
> *[I want to live with myself,*
> *I want to enjoy the good that I owe to heaven,*
> *alone, without witnesses,*
> *free of love, of jealousy,*
> *of hate, of hope, of fear.]*

Edgar Allan Poe knew this stanza by heart.

For me, to live without hate is easy, for I have never felt hate. To live without love I think is impossible, happily impossible for each one of us. But the first part—"I want to live with myself,/ I want to enjoy the good that I owe to heaven"—if we accept that in the good of heaven there can also be darkness, then who lives more with themselves? Who can explore themselves more? Who can know more of themselves? According to the Socratic phrase, who can know himself more than the blind man?

A writer lives. The task of being a poet is not completed at a fixed schedule. No one is a poet from eight to twelve and from two to six. Whoever is a poet is one always, and continually assaulted by poetry. I suppose a painter feels that colors and shapes are besieging him. Or a musician feels that the strange world of sounds—the strangest world of art—is always seeking him out, that there are melodies and dissonances looking for him. For the task of an artist, blindness is not a total misfortune. It may be an instrument. Fray Luis de León dedicated one of his most beautiful odes to Francisco Salinas, a blind musician.

A writer, or any man, must believe that whatever happens to him is an instrument; everything has been given for an end. This is even stronger in the case of the artist. Everything that happens, including humiliations, embarrassments, misfortunes, all has been given like clay, like material for one's art. One must accept it. For this reason I speak in a poem of the ancient food of heroes: humiliation, unhappiness, discord. Those things are given to us to transform, so that we may make from the miserable circumstances of our lives things that are eternal, or aspire to be so.

If a blind man thinks this way, he is saved. Blindness is a gift. I have exhausted you with the gifts it has given me. It gave me Anglo-Saxon, it gave me some Scandinavian, it gave me a knowledge of a Medieval literature I had ignored, it gave me the writing of various books, good or bad, but which justified the moment in which they were written. Moreover, blindness has made me feel surrounded by the kindness of others. People always feel good will toward the blind.

I want to end with a line of Goethe: *"Alles Nahe werde fern,"* everything near becomes distant. Goethe was referring to the evening twilight. Everything near becomes distant. It is true. At nightfall, the things closest to us seem to move away from our eyes. So the visible world has moved away from my eyes, perhaps forever.

Goethe could be referring not only to twilight but to life. All things go off, leaving us. Old age is probably the supreme solitude—except that the supreme solitude is death. And "everything near becomes distant" also refers to the slow process of blindness, of which I hoped to show, speaking tonight, that it is not a complete misfortune. It is one more instrument among the many—all of them so strange—that fate or chance provide.

—Translated by Eliot Weinberger

previously unknown to me.

HUBERT BUTLER

*Now in his nineties, Hubert Butler (1900–   ) has been belatedly hailed
as a major Irish nonfiction writer.* His collected essays were recently reissued
in the trilogy Escape from the Anthill, The Children of Drancy, *and*
Grandmother and Wolfe Tone, *and a selected volume,* The Sub-Prefect
Should Have Held His Tongue, *was issued in 1990. Butler grew up in
Anglo-Irish farming society, and he has remained loyal to "the place where I
was born and where my father, grandfather and great-grandfather had lived
before me." His writing excavates, patiently, minutely, and realistically, the
layers of meaning that can be teased from the local.*

*As befits one who has witnessed Ireland's bloody history in this century,
Butler has a skeptical mistrust of generalities and ideologies. His is a vision
of "small co-operative communities," regional self-sufficiency, independence
from the cultural bullying of the metropolis and the homogenization of
tastes. Like Orwell, his moral sense seems to derive from a rock-solid decency, integrity, honesty, and tolerance of testy human difference. For all his
emphasis on staying close to home, he has traveled widely and lived in
Russia, Egypt, China, the United States, and the Balkans, and he has responded with exemplary personal involvement to the far-flung disasters of
history. During World War II, he helped settle Jewish refugees in Ireland; his
polemical essays alerted readers to the children rounded up by Nazis in
France and to the slaughter in Yugoslavia.*

*As a personal essayist, Butler has the ability to roam freely and fear-
lessly over immense autobiographical and historical terrain. His work,
notes R. F. Foster, "moves like a searchlight from that narrowly restricted
range [of localism], to take in and illuminate the largest questions imaginable. The subjects chosen may be travel, literature, philosophy, autobiogra-*

phy or (characteristically) move easily through all four inside a dozen pages. They are handled with wit, passion, humor and an almost offhand virtuosity of style."

Beside the Nore

I HAVE LIVED for most of my life on the Nore and own three fields upon its banks, some miles before it turns to the south-east and forces its way under Brandon Hill to join the Barrow above New Ross. In sixty years it has changed remarkably little. From a top window, looking across the river towards Blackstairs and Mount Leinster, I can still see the same stretch of cornfields, nut groves and mountain slopes. Beside the woods of Summerhill and Kilfane I can spot the round tower of Tullaherin and Kilbline, the sixteenth-century castle of the Shortalls. There is only one new cottage in sight.

This does not mean that we stagnate. The landscape is domestic and life is mainly prosperous but it has edged away from the rivers. The Nore, which traverses the county of Kilkenny, and passes through the city, and the Barrow, which skirts its eastern border, and all their tributaries gave up work and took to an easy life about a century ago. The mill wheels stopped turning and the roofs fell in on the millworkers' cottages, flags and duck-weed and king-cups choked the mill race and there is so much tranquil beauty around that some hope and many fear that the tourist agencies will soon discover us.

A century ago there were twenty-two flour mills, three large distilleries and four breweries on the Nore between Durrow and Inistioge. But industry had left the rivers long before I was born and as children we were constantly driving donkey carts down little lanes to riverside ruins beside which we bathed and fished and picnicked. And every ruin had its story and the tradition that these stories are worth recording, correcting, analysing has never died out.

Our riverside ruins are mostly not depressing, for many of their founders were original and complex men, whose lives gave evidence that vision and ingenuity can flourish here. Some of their industries did not survive them for long. They subsided gracefully after a generation or two but, like the flowers of summer, were fertile in their decay. Various economic causes can be alleged for their failure but often there is nothing to be said except that men grow old and have bored or stupid sons and that today there are many prosperous industries which would be more admirable as ruins covered with valerian and wild wall flowers.

One of our favourite picnic places was Annamult Woollen Factory, a very stylish and spacious ruin on the King's river just before it joins the Nore. Before the king-cups and the bullocks took over, it was in 1814 one of the most progressive factories in the British Isles. Its owners, Messrs Shaw and Nowlan, rivalled Robert Owen, the Utopian industrialist, in their concern for their 400 work people. The children all had free schooling and lesson books, their fathers and mothers had health insurance cards, and every Sunday they danced to the fiddle in the large courtyard. George Shaw and Timothy Nowlan were stern but just, and rather quizzical. (Shaw was, I believe, a great great uncle to George Bernard.) Employees who misbehaved were punished but not sacked. Sometimes the offender, dressed in a yellow jacket, was obliged to roll a stone round the courtyard in full view of the Sunday merrymakers. The factory, while it lasted, was hugely successful. The Prince Regent and all the employees of the Royal Dublin Society dressed themselves in its woollens and the fields around Annamult were white with a flock of 600 Merino sheep, vast bundles of wool with tiny faces, which the Prims, a famous Kilkenny family with Spanish relations, had imported from Spain.

The Marble Works at Maddoxtown, below Kilkenny, is another beautiful spot with proud memories. Children still hunt about among the loose strife and the willow herb for polished slabs, green Connemara, pink Midleton, and Kilkenny which is black with white flecks. William Colles, who invented special machinery for cutting and polishing by water power, was so clever that his neighbours thought him a necromancer. He almost succeeded in making dogs weave linen by turning wheels, and he invented an instrument, like an Aeolian harp, which played tunes as it floated down the Nore. His house and his manager's house, which face each other across the Bennettsbridge road, are still among the pleasantest of the old houses that decorate the banks of the Nore. Colles was a philosophical man; he wrote tragedies and to remind himself of the 'lapse of time' he had his portrait painted every seven years. His business had prospered in adversity for it was during the Napoleonic Wars, when foreign marble ceased to be imported, that he was able to flood the English market with his chimney pieces, punch bowls, buffets and vases. Then metal mantelpieces arrived and a few years ago all the blocks of marble that littered the river bank were bought by a firm which pounded them into a variegated paste, from which ten chimney pieces could be made as easily as Colles made one.

Maidenhall lies between Annamult and the Marble Works and the Grif-

fiths, who lived there 230 years ago, were such an original couple that I
have written of them separately. There are many beautiful little towns
along the Nore, but since 'each man kills the thing he loves' it is perhaps
unsafe to admire them. Their beauty depends on hump-backed bridges
and winding streets and large trees, all of which obstruct the motorist in
his race to progress. The curves of the bridge are now being straightened
with cement but often you can see the great stone slabs of the parapet
jutting out of the stream below the bridge.

All these little towns should have had their chroniclers, for one chroni-
cler attracts another and a village, conscious of its history, can resist the
tyranny of the government official. The Nore has not been as lucky as the
Barrow. I am sure that it was the O'Learys, hereditary scribes and bakers
of Graiguenamanagh on the Barrow, who attracted Sean O'Faolain to the
village in 1945. As editor of *The Bell* he stayed there for a week and
studied the town as a good teacher studies a child. How did it begin, how
was it going to develop? He found that it had been started by Wiltshire
monks, planted there by the Normans. For generations they had adhered
to their English ways, but had finally become assimilated. At the time of
the Reformation the last Abbot was one of the Kavanaghs and their descendants still own the beautiful woods along the river bank at Borris.
O'Faolain made a transparent map of the town, marking all its shops and
dwellings and offices and laid it over an outline map of the old Cistercian
Abbey. You can see how O'Leary's Bakery crept over the cloisters, how
the refectory became a Corn Store, and Denny's Pig Scales took over the
monks' cemetery. Everything changes, yet there is a core of continuity.
O'Faolain traces how the very same processes which eliminated typhus in
Graig and gave fresh water, sanitation and medical care, also almost destroyed the town. When the railways brought 'civilization,' the bargees,
the canal workers and the local craftsmen all became superfluous and got
on the trains themselves. In 1841 there were 2248 inhabitants, and in 1945
there were 844. And now? Are charabancs likely to be more beneficent
than the railways?

If Inistioge on the Nore is one of the loveliest of Irish villages, much of
the credit is due to William Tighe of Woodstock, the large house, whose
ruins lay till recently on the hill above it. For anyone who wants to know
about the Nore and the Barrow, his work, *A Statistical Survey of the
County Kilkenny, 1802,* is still indispensable. It has never been surpassed
and never will be, because the tribe to which he and Colles and Griffith
belonged, the rural polymaths, is now extinct. Tighe was a classical
scholar, an archaeologist, an economist, a sociologist, a politician (a passionate opponent of the Union). He knew the names of all the flowers and
all the fish of the two valleys of the Nore and the Barrow, in English, Irish
and Latin, and the price of potatoes in Goresbridge in 1798 and how

many 'unlicensed tippling houses' there were in Inistioge in 1800 (twenty-eight). He was a humane man and soberly recalls how melons and pineapples could be bought in Kilkenny while the poor children of Iverk went to school 'almost naked.'

He wrote a poem in four cantos called 'The Plants' about the Oak, the Rose, the Palm and the Vine. In the manner of Virgil's *Georgics* it is intended to be diverting as well as instructive. There are 150 pages of notes in Greek, Latin, Hebrew, French and Italian, and he lists 39 species of oak. He was specially interested in the oaks of Mamre, where Abraham, Isaac and Jacob were buried, and he built a small house near Woodstock in an oak grove and called it Mamre, the name by which it is still known.

His eighteenth-century archaeology once collided sensationally with the less adventurous kind which grew out of it. On Tory Hill, in south Kilkenny, there was a large stone slab inscribed with words which he copied scrupulously on a page of his *Statistical Survey* and interpreted as BELI DIVOSE.

(ƐLI CIVO)Ⴈ

He deduced from this that Baal and Dionysus were worshipped in Early Ireland. Nearly a generation later John O'Donovan, who was working on the Ordnance Survey, came up with a different explanation. He found people alive in Mullinavat who remembered hearing of Ned Connick, the carpenter, and how he had climbed up Tory Hill and carved his name on an ancient block of stone which had later been turned over.

Tighe had copied the inscription so conscientiously that it is only necessary to turn his page upside down and, making allowances for the roughness of the stone and Ned Connick's illiteracy, you can easily read:

ECONIC 1731

William Tighe's sister-in-law, Mary Tighe, whose effigy by Flaxman is housed behind the church at Inistioge, wrote a long poem called 'Psyche,' or the Legend of Love. She died young but, published after her death, 'Psyche' received considerable critical admiration. It is based on the story of Apuleius about the love of Cupid and Psyche.

The burning of Woodstock House, the home of poetry and learning, in 1922, was one of the saddest of Ireland's tragedies. But the beautiful plantations survived and there is scarcely in all Ireland a more charming walk than that which runs below the ruins along the Nore. On one side the river with its swans and water lilies, on the other the wooded cliffs and mossy glades sprinkled with ferns and frochans and foxgloves. ⛁

When I was young there were plenty of river picnics and neighbours visited each other by cot (long flat-bottomed boats which were used for net-fishing). It was every boy and girl's dream to take a cot to Inistioge, where the river becomes tidal. My brother and I once got as far as Thomastown and then our patience ran out and we walked to Inistioge and spent the night at a small hotel. There was a large stuffed white rabbit on a chest of drawers and at dawn we awoke scratching and observed two columns of insects advancing on us from the rabbit.

The hotel turned into a pub and small shops have come and gone but Inistioge is still the most beautiful and peaceful of villages. Not long ago I was sitting on a bench beside the bridge waiting for my grandchildren to come down the river by canoe from Maidenhall. I remember the red valerian, a broad bank of colour reflected on the dappled current. In such a place time stands still. The past comes close in disconnected fragments and I was thinking of the days when we were children and had dancing classes with the young Tighes at the Noreview Hotel in Thomastown; their mother, with my Aunt Harriet, used to run a Christian Science Reading Room opposite the Castle in Kilkenny, two spiders into whose web no fly ever came, and I remember when we went to Woodstock a side-car used to meet us at Thomastown station and the branches of the trees brushed our faces as we drove along.

The Tighes were friendly charming people who did not deserve the misfortunes that happened to them. When the war broke out Captain Tighe took his family to London, where he met his death in an accident that has never fully been explained. I do not believe they ever returned. In the spring of 1920 the Black and Tans took over Woodstock and patrolled the country at breakneck speed in their Crossley tenders. Then the Treaty came and they left as rapidly as they had come. It was an empty, undefended house that was finally destroyed.

Later in the afternoon an old man came and sat beside me, and I asked him what it was like when the Tans were in Woodstock. He was very ready to talk and afterwards I wrote down what he told me.

> They were in the village too [he said] and we had them in the house next door to us. They weren't too bad. They made us have a notice on all the doors with the names of the people in the house. I remember there was a young chap, Ned Brennan, maybe eight or nine, and they stuck him up on the pub counter and asked him to sing, and he sang 'Wrap the Green Flag Around Me'! He was a young chap, you see, and it was one of the songs he'd learnt. But the Tans just laughed and filled his pockets with pennies. When he came home his mother was very angry and said it was 'blood money' and wouldn't let him keep it.

The Tans had two spies going round the village [he went on] and didn't fourteen of our chaps chase after them so that the two jumped into the river. And our chaps shot one of them and the other got out and ran back to Woodstock to tell the Tans. And after that didn't the Tans burn O'Hanrahans' farm, oh, a big place with cow-sheds and barns and hay ricks. And they did nothing to save old Mrs. Hanrahan from burning, till Mrs. Newport of Ballygallon—she was an English-woman—came and blamed them for not getting her out, and they got her out and she took her to her own place.

I have always believed that local history is more important than national history. There should be an archive in every village, where stories such as the old man told me are recorded. Where life is fully and consciously lived in our own neighbourhood, we are cushioned a little from the impact of great far-off events which should be of only marginal concern to us.

Aunt Harriet

W HEN SHE GOT OLD AND ILL my grandmother grew frightened of being buried alive and she constantly asked for as-surance that she would be given an autopsy. It was a persistent fear. 'She's going on about old Topsy again,' my mother said once, when coming out of her room. My mother was under great strain and I was no use to her.

I was at Oxford and found it a place of such abundance that Ireland and everyone in it, particularly my relations, were diminished. I was inces-santly carping at them. In England we were nobody, while in Ireland, I maintained, if we gave it our first loyalty we could be somebody.

When Aunt Harriet, my father's sister, died, I went with my parents to keep Aunt Florence company at Lavistown. It is a small Georgian house with white Venetian blinds, built for the manager of the marble works by the founder William Colles. The marble works were still functioning in a desultory way just below Lavistown on the banks of the Nore. My father and mother slept in the big room over the dining-room where the coffin was laid on two chairs under the window. I slept in the small dressing-room off it.

Lavistown, which was four miles away from Maidenhall, was almost a second home to us; we were often there. I was very fond of Aunt Harriet, who superintended the cooking and the cook, Ellen, while Aunt Florence looked after the garden and the gardener, Donovan. We used to see more of Aunt Harriet because she had a bicycle, while Aunt Florence had to get Donovan to harness Maureen, the fat white pony. Aunt Harriet usually bicycled over with a cake in the basket on the handlebars and *The Christian Science Monitor* under it, for she was both a Christian Scientist and a Gaelic Leaguer. 'Well, chickabiddies!' she exclaimed when she saw us. The cake she gave to my mother, *The Christian Science Monitor* to us children, ostensibly because of the Children's page, but I'm sure she thought some effluence of her faith might reach us through it. The stories were usually about dressed-up rabbits, mice, bluebottles; more moral than Beatrix Potter but less entertaining. Any message they contained was lost on us, but I was offended on Aunt Harriet's behalf when my mother said, 'Anyway, it's good thick paper; wonderful for packing eggs.'

My mother said Aunt Harriet became a Christian Scientist because a certain Dr. Davis had failed to meet her under the clock on the platform at Kingsbridge Station in Dublin. She became a Gaelic Leaguer, I expect, because of the Cuffes who lived at Sheestown, a small house the other side of the Nore. Otway Cuffe was the brother and heir of the Earl of Desart, who lived at Desart Court about ten miles to the west. Mrs. Cuffe was the daughter of a Cornish nobleman and they had thrown all their hereditary prestige, which in those days was consider-able, into the Gaelic Revival, the development of a unique Irish civiliza-tion independent of politics. His sister-in-law, Lady Desart, had, as I have related, put her vast wealth largely at Otway Cuffe's disposal for the development of local industries. Though the bulk of the Unionists were sceptical, the Cuffes had many disciples. The Gaelic movement in-terested Aunt Harriet, while Aunt Florence was absorbed by home in-dustries and craft work, and they had a large framed photograph of Otway Cuffe in the dining-room at Lavistown.

All this might seem irrelevant to the story I have to tell about Aunt Harriet. It is a very brief story but nothing at all if I do not convey the closeness I felt to that body in the box. Love? Affection? Admiration? I think absolute involvement is the right phrase. She must have suspected in me, when I was quite small, some germ of heterodoxy of the kind she had nursed in herself. One day, when I was playing on the gravel at Lavistown, I fell and scraped my leg. I pointed out to Aunt Harriet that it was bleed-ing. 'It's nothing,' she said and put a piece of stamp paper on it. I pulled it off the moment she was out of sight and never told my mother, who would have been angry; Christian Science was unpopular in those days because a co-religionist of Aunt Harriet's, Mrs. Tighe of Woodstock, refused to have a doctor for her son and he died.

My two aunts went on sketching holidays every spring to Vernet les Bains but one summer Aunt Harriet went to Boston for some special celebration of Mary Baker Eddy, the great prophetess and heresiarch of Christian Science. My mother thought she might marry an elderly Christian Scientist there and feared for our prospects. We had always held that money that you inherit, unlike money that you earn, belongs to the family. We had forebears called Kingston who owned a shipyard in Cork and, when it closed, retained the ground rents of the buildings that went up on the quays beside the Lee. The ground rents passed on to their descendants, getting less and less with each generation, together with some good miniatures of themselves in a blue velvet frame by Frederick Buck of Cork. We got the miniatures and my aunts the ground rents.

Aunt Harriet came back much invigorated from Boston. She had been also to the Niagara Falls. Mrs. Eddy was dead at the time but she had seen her house and I think the cradle where she had been a baby. She had worshipped in the Mother Church of Christ Scientist and had not brought back a Christian Scientist husband. She would like to have told us more about Boston but everybody fidgetted uncomfortably when she started to talk of Mrs. Eddy and asked her feverishly about the Niagara Falls.

Aunt Harriet was the strictest sort of Christian Scientist. She never admitted to any illness. She never went to a dentist but let her teeth fall out so that her cheeks contracted round three or four solitary tusks. This did nothing for her appearance. Aunt Florence had frequent small illnesses and many visits from the doctor. There must have been some snappishness between the sisters but we children never heard a word of it. We squabbled as much as most families do, but confronted by the outside world we were loyal to each other.

In those days, the Sinn Feiners were in the habit of visiting people, two by two and often by night, asking them for money for 'dependents of the Irish Republicans.' They went to Lavistown one night and Aunt Harriet had looked out of her bedroom window and said reproachfully that she would give them nothing, that she had given up the Gaelic League when it had become political and when the Sinn Feiners had started a campaign of violence. After this little lecture they went away.

I told this to a friend of my own age who lived near by. 'I don't wonder,' she said, 'the Shinners got a shock and went off when Old Harriet poked her face out at them.' I took offence and told her she had no right to talk like that. She said pacifically: 'You should see my Aunt Eileen.'

*   *   *

I have left Aunt Harriet in her coffin a long way behind, but I am thinking of the memories she took with her; they were all unimportant but the past is a mosaic of tiny pieces, a fragment of a larger picture, Ireland in the twenties and the last days of the Anglo-Irish, and I will continue with more minutiae.

In the days before the War and the 1916 Rising, the more enlightened of the Anglo-Irish were trying desperately to identify themselves with Ireland. Aunt Harriet organized the first local Feis, an ancient festival of song and dance and miscellaneous junketting which centuries before took place at Tara. At the Kilkenny Feis there were competitions for Irish dancing and singing, lace-making, cake, jam, section honey and craft work. When it was all over Aunt Harriet was presented by the committee with a 'Tara' brooch, a richly ornamented safety pin with which the ancient Irish held their clothes together, mass produced from originals in the National Museum.

The Gaelic League was not 'political' in those days and even the British saw nothing against it. When Lady Aberdeen, Ireland's all but last Vice-Reine, came down to open our local concert hall, she defied the ridicule of the Anglo-Irish neighbours by dressing herself and the ladies of the party in emerald green with Tara brooches. She and her husband were very Scottish; he wore the Gordon tartan and they wrote a book called *We Twa*. They bred Aberdeen terriers and were Aberdonianly thrifty, and it was one of their aims to show how very Scottish one could be and yet loyal to the Crown. Why could not the Irish be the same? She entertained very little in the Vice-Regal Lodge, but started a campaign against tuberculosis with no political overtones, and motored all over Ireland trying with some success to introduce village nurses into every community.

Despite all this they were unpopular with both the more orthodox Gaels and ordinary Unionists; they were suspected of 'liberalism' which in Ireland was anathema to the traditional Unionist and one of our neighbours wrote a poem about them of which I can only remember one line: 'They cut the penny buns in half when Larkin came to tea.' (Larkin was a celebrated labour leader.)

The Cuffes and Aunt Florence and my mother all threw themselves into the crusade against tuberculosis (Aunt Harriet believed it was a delusion of the mind) and I think the Bennettsbridge village nurse was among the first in Ireland.

When Lord Aberdeen retired in 1915 he was made a Marquess and, conscious of his work for Ireland, he chose the title of Aberdeen and Tara, but the use of this most famous of all Irish placenames by a Scottish peer gave great offence. On leaving they sent photographs of themselves with an Aberdeen terrier beside them and one of the recipients wrote a letter which got great publicity: 'Thank you very much for the beautiful photograph of yourselves and your little dog Tara.' They changed Tara to Temair, which is a more ancient version of Tara but, as few knew this, no one objected.

Behind Lavistown is a big house, Leyrath, where Sir Charles Wheeler Cuffe, a distant relative of the Desarts, lived with his cousin Baroness Prochaska, an Austrianized Czech who was full of enthusiasm for home industries and handicrafts. She was very plain with projecting eyes and teeth and a gobbly Central European voice. I expect she knew the Czech language but only spoke it to her inferiors. She must have considered that the Anglo-Irish were a little like the Austro-Czechs, whose doom like theirs was only a few years away. She took up bee-keeping vigorously and prevailed on the County Council to appoint a Bee-Keeping Instructor. She had a row of hives at Leyrath with names like Peace, Love, Harmony. I don't know whether it was she or Otway Cuffe who was responsible for the Carpentry Instructor who travelled round the country villages. In Bennettsbridge he gave instruction to some twenty local boys in my father's barn once a week. I was taught with the other boys of my own age to make a small bracket on which to put a Holy Lamp. I was eight at the time and very class-conscious but had never learnt to say 'Please sir, can I leave the room?' And something awful happened that made the other boys titter and the Instructor pause to give me good advice. I thought of it with shame for months and months. This is the first time I've ever mentioned it.

The Baroness bought a horse-drawn coffee-van and got up every fair day at six a.m. and, joined sometimes by Aunt Florence, sometimes by Aunt Harriet or my elder sister, brought it to James's Green where the Kilkenny Fair was held. There they sold, very cheaply, tea, coffee and buns to the farmers, drovers and cattle-dealers. There was always a lot of money round the town on fair days, the pubs were crowded and there were men with plum-coloured faces walking unsteadily in the street. The coffee-van had an unacknowledged relevance to this. This went on for twenty years but the Baroness got ill and went to Auteven Cottage Hospital (this was one of Lady Desart's gifts to Kilkenny) and one day soon after that a lady, who was deputizing for her and had a less dominating character, was stopped, by order of the Corporation, and was not allowed in. The public-house keepers and other traders in Walkin Street, which led to the fair green, had put pressure on the Corporation. They claimed that they had a right to give drinks or proper breakfasts to drovers and that the coffee-van was depriving them of their livelihood. They said that the farmers were supporting the coffee-van because they were too mean to give their men the money for a proper breakfast.

Word of all this came to the Kilkenny Farmers' Union, an organization on which the Anglo-Irish landowners were well represented. A special meeting was held and they were all on the side of the Baroness and her coffee-van. And it was resolved that a message should be sent to her in hospital thanking her for her tireless work over the years and wishing her a speedy recovery. At the same time pressure was put on the Corporation to withdraw the veto on the coffee-van which the public-house keepers had forced them to make. The coffee-van continued as long as the Baroness lived but, when she died, it died with her.

I used to bicycle in with my father very early on the day of the Kilkenny Fair and we found the cattle from his two farms at Burnchurch and Drumherin waiting for us there, so it is not very difficult to revive all these memories, some of which are recorded in Aunt Florence's scrap book. It only slowly and sadly became apparent to my father that nature did not intend me to be a farmer. It was my younger brother, a small child then, who took over.

The Kilkenny Fair and the Kilkenny Farmers' Union ended long ago, as did the Instructors for Beekeeping and Carpentry, Lady Aberdeen's locally appointed nurse and her Women's National Health Association. I dare say they are not missed very much and have been replaced by something just as good, but some faculty of independent initiative, of overcoming apathy with an idea, has become rarer.

While Aunt Florence went to church in St. Canice's Cathedral, Kilkenny, Aunt Harriet stayed at home praying and reading Mrs. Eddy's *Science and Health with Key to the Scriptures.* Aunt Florence must have come back full of chat about the neighbours and their hats and the bishop's sermon. Did she have to suppress it all or did Aunt Harriet welcome this contact with the outside world?

I felt for her because at this time I was a very earnest Free Thinker, although I discovered at Oxford that my particular earnestness was twenty years out of date. I had the old nursery at the top of the house as my study and from there I could see my father and mother and two sisters setting off in the waggonette to Ennisnag church. I saw them turn down the avenue and eight minutes later I could see the top-hat of old Egan, the coachman (he sat on the box), appearing and disappearing and reappearing between the chestnut trees along the road and when it finally vanished I felt lonely but unyielding. Solitude was the price Aunt Harriet and I had to pay for our convictions. I did not change much but the world changed. In England people slipped out of faith and into indifference without mental or spiritual struggling. Earnest Rationalism like Lecky's and Bury's is the natural child of Irish Protestantism. It is the Catholic majority that keeps most of us defiantly Protestant.

Because of this, like a jelly that has stiffened inside its jelly-mould and slid out intact, I found myself accepting the Protestant ethos and bothering less about its dogma and mythology. We respect individualism and in particular 'the sacred right of private judgment,' as Grattan called it at the Convention of Dungannon in 1782. In Ireland it has played the same part in the life of the Irish Protestant as Authority has in the life of the Irish Catholic. It is frequently under attack and I have always done my best to defend it.

What was Lavistown like in January 1925? The house is still there but it has changed and I have to resurrect it by conjecture and present experience, not memory. The aconites might have been just out under the shelter of the big cypress tree that fell down many years ago, and a few tight buds of snowdrops perhaps, but the mauve crocuses, the small ones that seeded themselves under all the deciduous trees that lined the path to the garden and the back avenue, would only just have poked above the leaf mould.

The pony Maureen would have been there but would Ellen the cook? The tennis court would have been there and properly mown, and not the flat shaggy rectangle that survives still beside so many Irish country houses, recalling the days before 1922 when there were often tennis parties at different houses six days a week.

I remember the inside of the house better. Aunt Florence took in *The Queen* and used to enjoy discussing with us the Social Problem page. Aunt Harriet had a row of Irish books and Dinneen's Irish dictionary, and when I was sixteen she gave me William James's *Varieties of Religious Experience,* which did not interest me very much because I was proud to have no religious experience. It wasn't until years later that I discovered she had left a yellow ribbon in a chapter called 'The Religion of Healthy Mindedness' with a subsection on 'Mind Cure.'

I must come back to that night of 25 January 1925. We had a quiet low-voiced supper in the drawing-room opposite to the dining-room in which Aunt Harriet lay, and then we went to bed. I went first because I was in the little dressing-room. It was only the second time I had been in a house with a dead person (Granny had died the year before) and I took a long time to go to sleep, thinking of Aunt Harriet and all the things that had happened and not happened between us. It was a long chronicle of trivialities, letters I had not answered, copies of the *Monitor* with marked passages that I had not acknowledged, little openings for thoughtful conversations which I had gently closed.

Perhaps Aunt Harriet had access to some peace of mind, some freedom from pain which she had spent her life trying to share with us. But it was very difficult to think like this. It was another hour before I slept and at about four I was roused by a tapping sound. It came from the room below. It is only because my elder relations are all dead and I am an old man now, soon to go into a box myself, that I can write like this. Perhaps I should not for I have nothing interesting to relate, only what happened in my mind, and that is discreditable but not exciting.

If I could have gone downstairs directly from my room I know I would have, but to get down I had to go through my parents' room. They would certainly wake and I would put into their minds a horrifying thought, which it was my duty to confirm before expressing.

I spent the rest of the night wrestling with this problem even after the tapping had stopped. What worried me was the thought that in some supreme effort of faith she had half-conquered death, which like a wave in an ebbing tide had left her stranded half-alive on the foreshore.

I recalled Granny's fear of being buried alive. Would Aunt Harriet have woken up and not known whether she was already buried? And what could we do? Would I have to get Mr. Lewis the undertaker? Where did he live? Was there a hammer and a chisel in the house?

I got up as soon as I could and as I passed through my parents' room my mother said to my father: 'Did you hear that rapping in the night? It must have been the knob of the blind cord tapping on the window pane. There was a bit of wind.' 'Yes, I expect so,' my father said indifferently. When I got down, all was quiet and the blind cord did have a knob at the end of it but the wind had stopped and I could not convince myself that my mother's explanation was the correct one. She had never believed in Aunt Harriet's faith healing. 'She could have saved herself with something quite simple like cascara,' she had said. I seldom think of that night now, though I once used often to do so. It was not a question of being right or wrong in what I thought. I had envisaged a possibility and at all costs I should have tested it. It was the first of ten or fifteen grave mistakes that I think over in the wakeful nights. I wrote a poem about them, and then found that Yeats had written some lines that were more apposite.

> *Things said or done long years ago,*
> *Or things I did not do or say*
> *But thought that I might say or do,*
> *Weigh me down, and not a day*
> *But something is recalled,*
> *My conscience or my vanity appalled.*

In the daylight, commonsense prevailed. Aunt Harriet was self-effacing and considerate. She would sooner have gone through the ordeal of death a second time than be resurrected in a blaze of newspaper publicity. Very quickly the night vision of hands battering helplessly at unyielding wood was submerged. Mr. Lewis, the undertaker, arrived with the hearse and we took Aunt Florence with us to lunch at home and afterwards we met the hearse at Danesfort Cross and followed it to Burnchurch church, where my great-grandfather, once rector there, and all his family were buried. My mother said she had tried to find if there was some special Christian Science Burial Service and some special minister to perform it. Now it seems to me we did not try hard enough and that we should have urged her fellow believers to come down and do honour to their dead sister, who in a lonely way had been loyal to their principles.

Later still I felt that in view of the Cork ground rents it had been mean of us not to give my two aunts a tombstone to themselves. Instead we added their names as postscripts on the base of the tall cross put up to my Uncle Richard, who had caught cold and died after a tennis party in 1877 at the age of nineteen.

Forty years later, when I was in Boston, because of Aunt Harriet I went to the Mother Church of Christ Scientist and in a Christian Science Reading Room I found Mrs. Eddy's *Science and Health with Key to the Scriptures.* I was astonished. Mrs. Eddy took the offensive against philology.

'The dissection and definition of words,' she wrote, 'aside from their metaphysical content is not scientific.' Extracting the 'metaphysical' content from the name Adam, she writes: 'Divide it in half and it reads A dam, as the obstacle which the serpent Sin would impose between Man and his Creator,' and elsewhere she writes: 'Adam and his race are a dream of mortal mind because Cain went to live in the Land of Nod, the land of dreams and illusions.'

Was this the way Aunt Harriet and thousands of others reasoned? And yet I had to acknowledge that, as newspapers go, *The Christian Science Monitor* has many merits.

I learnt in Boston that Mary Baker Eddy had many enemies and critics there. One of them has related that some of the more ardent of her disciples thought she had conquered Death as well as Pain and that, when she proved to be mortal after all, one of them impersonated her and drove round Boston for several days in her well-known carriage till the faithful were ready to accept the truth.

Goodness often blossoms like roses on very rickety trellis-work, and beauty can grow out of nonsense. There are no grounds for supposing that one can live a life without pain and sadness, but is it wrong to believe that somehow, somewhere, this is possible?

Two years after Aunt Harriet, Aunt Florence eased herself out of life slowly and securely by many small illnesses. I got the Cork ground rents but after a few years the Post Office bought half the buildings on the site of the Kingston Shipyard and claimed to be exempt from ground rents. My two sisters got Lavistown. The gate lodge on the back avenue, where Donovan lived, belongs to my niece, who sold Lavistown to friends, who have made it a study centre. Students come there to learn about the flora and fauna of the Nore valley. The cows there produce special cheeses and the pigs special sausages. It is still a place where it is easier to believe in happiness than in pain.

E. M. CIORAN

E. M. Cioran (1911–   ) was born in Romania, the son of a Greek Ortho-dox priest. He has lived most of his life in Paris and writes exclusively in French, though his viewpoint remains that of an outsider, an émigré who speaks from the bitter Romanian perspective of a poor, regularly conquered homeland. Cioran is one of the great living masters of the philosophical essay. In his acidic writings (The Temptation to Exist, The Fall into Time, The New Gods, A Short History of Decay)*, he has taken on the mantle of Nietzsche, to write philosophy by aphorism and mini-essay and to destroy comfortable ideas. First he isolates and cauterizes the wounds of history with his corrosive intellect, then he cuts away all mental flab, false hopes, and shallow promises to expose the pus underneath. The satisfaction in reading Cioran comes from hearing the worst. Yet—and this is a tribute to his skill as a writer—exposure to his work can be revivifying. His despair has some-thing ecstatic and grimly funny about it, which we enjoy perhaps masochisti-cally, like a performance by a comic who insults the audience. Also, the very intransigence of Cioran's denial of easy solutions points to a spiritual yearn-ing that is deeply moving; this thirst that is never slaked is religious at the core. In "Some Blind Alleys: A Letter" Cioran takes on the emptiness of self-expression and literary ambition, thus cutting the legs out from under his own endeavors. It is also a strong example of the epistolary personal essay.*

Some Blind Alleys: A Letter

I HAD ALWAYS SUPPOSED, dear friend, that loving your province as you do, you were resolved upon the practice, there, of detachment, scorn, silence. Imagine, then, my surprise on hearing you say you were preparing a book about it! Instantaneously, I saw looming up within you a future monster: the author you will become. "Another one lost," I thought. Modestly, you refrained from asking the reasons for my disappointment; and I should have been incapable of giving them *viva voce*. "Another one lost, another one ruined *by his talent*," I kept murmuring to myself.

Penetrating the literary inferno, you will come to learn its artifices and its arsenic; shielded from the immediate, that caricature of yourself, you will no longer have any but formal experiences, indirect experiences; you will vanish into the Word. Books will be the sole object of your discussions. As for literary people, you will derive no benefit from them. But you will find this out too late, after having wasted your best years in a milieu without density or substance. The literary man? An indiscreet man, who devaluates his miseries, divulges them, tells them like so many beads: immodesty—the side-show of second-thoughts—is his rule; he *offers himself*. Every form of talent involves a certain shamelessness. Only sterility is truly distinguished—the man who effaces himself along with his secret, because he disdains to parade it: sentiments *expressed* are an agony for irony, a slap at humor.

To keep one's secret is the most fruitful of activities. It torments, erodes, *threatens* you. Even when confession is addressed to God, it is an outrage against ourselves, against the mainspring of our being. The apprehensions, shames, fears from which both religious and profane therapeutics would deliver us constitute a patrimony we should not allow ourselves to be dispossessed of, at any cost. We must defend ourselves against our healers and, even if we die for it, preserve our sicknesses and our sins. The confessional? a rape of conscience perpetrated in the name of heaven. And that other rape, psychological analysis! Secularized, prostituted, the confessional will soon be installed on our street corners: except for a couple of criminals, everyone aspires to have a public soul, a poster soul.

Drained by his fecundity, a phantom who has worn out his shadow, the man of letters diminishes with each word he writes. Only his vanity is inexhaustible; if it were psychological, it would have limits: those of the self. But it is cosmic or demonic: it submerges him. His "work" obsesses him; he continually alludes to it, as if, on our planet, there were nothing outside himself which deserved attention or curiosity. Woe to anyone with the impudence or bad taste to discuss anything but his productions! You will understand, then, how one day, leaving a literary luncheon, I saw the necessity for a Saint Bartholomew's Day Massacre of men of letters.

[margin note: only men?]

Voltaire was the first literary man to erect his incompetence into a procedure, a method. Before him, the writer, content to be tangent to events, was more modest: plying his trade in a limited sector, he followed his own nose and kept it clean. Nothing of the journalist about him, at most he was interested in the anecdotic aspect of certain solitudes: his indiscretion was *ineffectual.*

With our braggart, things change. None of the subjects which intrigued his times escaped his sarcasm, his half-knowledge, his craving for controversy, his universal vulgarity. In Voltaire, everything was impure except his style . . . Profoundly superficial, without any sensibility for the *intrinsic,* for the interest reality offers in itself, he inaugurated in letters our ideological gossip. His mania for chatter, for indoctrinating, his porter's-lodge wisdom, were to make him the prototype, the model of the *littérateur.* Since he said everything about himself, and since he exploited to the last drop the resources of his nature, he no longer troubles us: we read him and move on. On the other hand, in the case of a Pascal we feel sure he has not told us all there is to say; even when he irritates us, he is never, for us, *an author.*

To write books is to have a certain relation with original sin. For what is a book if not a loss of innocence, an act of aggression, a repetition of our Fall? To publish one's taints in order to amuse or exasperate! A barbarism with respect to our intimacy, a profanation, a defilement. And a temptation. I know what I am talking about, and I speak—advisedly. At least I have the excuse of hating my actions, of performing them without believing in them. You are more honest: you will write books and you will believe in them, you will believe in the reality of words, in those childish and indecent fictions. From the depths of my disgust, everything literary looks to me like a chastisement; I shall try to forget my life for fear of discussing it; or else, unable to accede to that absolute of disillusion, I shall condemn myself to a morose frivolity. Shards of instinct, nonetheless, compel me to cling to words. Silence is unbearable: what strength it takes to settle into the concision of the Inexpressible! It is easier to renounce bread than speech. Unfortunately, the verbal turns to verbiage, to literature. Even thought that way tends, ever ready to spread out, to puff up; to check it with a period, to contract it into an epigram or a witticism is to counter its expansion, its natural movement, its impulse toward dilution, toward inflation. Whence our systems, whence our philosophies. This obsession with brevity paralyzes the mind's progress, for the mind needs words *en masse,* without which, turned upon itself, it ruminates upon its impotence. If thinking is an art of repeating, of discrediting the essential, it is because the mind is a pedant. And an enemy of any form of wit, of all those who are obsessed with paradox and arbitrary definitions. Horrified by banality, by "the universally valid," they address themselves to the accidental side of things, to matters "obvious" to no one. Preferring an approximative but piquant formula to an evident but insipid reasoning, they aspire to no particular accuracy and amuse themselves at the expense of "truths." Reality does not hold up—why should they take seriously the theories that try to prove its solidarity? In everything, they are paralyzed by the fear of boring or of being bored. This fear, if you are subject to it, will comprise all your undertakings. You try to write; immediately there looms up before you the image of your reader . . . And you lay down your pen. The notion you want to develop is too much for you: what is the use of examining it, of getting to the heart of the matter? Couldn't a single phrase, a formula translate it? Besides, how set forth what you already know? If you are obsessed by a verbal economy, you can neither read nor reread any book without detecting its artifices and its redundancies. You finally discover that even the author you continually return to pads his sentences, hoards pages and collapses on an idea in order to flatten it, to stretch it out. Poem, novel, essay, play—everything seems too long. The writer—it is his function—always says more than he has to say: he swells his thought and swathes it with words. All that subsists of a work are two or three *moments:* lightning in the lumber room. Shall I tell you what I really think? Every word is a word *de trop.* Yet the question is: to write. Let us write . . . , let us dupe each other.

Boredom dismantles the mind, renders it superficial, out at the seams, saps it from within and dislocates it. Once ennui has seized you, it will accompany you to every encounter, as it has accompanied me for as long as I can remember. I know no moment when it was not here, beside me, in the air, in my words and in those of others, on my face and on all faces. It is both mask and substance, façade and reality. I cannot imagine myself, living or dead, without it. Boredom has made me into a speechifier ashamed of raising his voice, a theoretician for the senile and the adolescent, for metaphysical menopauses, a vestige of a creature, a hallucinated clown. Whatever share of Being was dispensed to me is being eroded by ennui, and if a few scraps remain it is only because boredom requires some substance on which to act . . . The Void in action, it ransacks brains and reduces them to a heap of fractured concepts. No idea which it leaves *in touch* with any other, which it fails to isolate and grind down, so that the mind's activity is debased into a series of discontinuous moments.

Notions, sentiments, sensations in tatters, such is the effect of its passage. It would make a saint into an amateur, a Hercules into a rag. Boredom is a sickness that extends *farther* than space; you must flee it, or entertain merely meaningless projects, like mine when it drives me to the wall. I dream then of an acid thought which might insinuate itself into things and disorganize them, perforate them, come out the other side—of a book whose syllables, attacking the paper, would suppress literature and readers alike, of a book that would be both carnival and apocalypse of Letters, an ultimatum to the pestilence of the Word.

I find it hard to understand your ambition to make a name for yourself in an age when the epigone is *de rigueur.* A comparison is inevitable. On the philosophical and literary level, Napoleon had rivals who were his equals: Hegel by the excess of his system, Byron by his unbuttoned liberty, Goethe by a mediocrity *without precedent.* Today, it would be futile to elicit the literary pendant to the adventurers, the tyrants of the century. If, politically, we have given proof of an unprecedented insanity, in the domain of the mind only tiny destinies fidget; no conqueror *by the pen:* nothing but monsters, hysterics, simply *cases.* We do not have, and I fear never shall have, the *oeuvre* of our undoing, a Don Quixote in hell. The more the times distend, the more literature shrinks. And it is as pygmies that we shall be engulfed by the Unparalleled.

Judging from appearances, in order to revive our aesthetic illusions we require an *askesis* of several centuries, an ordeal by silence, an age of non-literature. For the moment, it remains for us to corrupt every genre, to drive them to the extremes which deny them, to undo what was marvelously done. If, in this enterprise, we show some concern for perfection, perhaps we shall manage to create a new type of vandalism . . .

Placed outside of style, incapable of harmonizing our debacles, we no longer define ourselves in relation to Greece: it has ceased to be our guideline, our nostalgia or our remorse; it has been extinguished within us . . . But so has the Renaissance.

From Hölderlin and Keats to Walter Pater, the nineteenth century was able to oppose its opacities and to counter them with the image of a mirific antiquity, a cure by light—in short, Paradise. A forged paradise, it goes without saying. What matters is that it was aspired to, even if only to combat modernity and its grimaces. One could devote oneself to another age, and cling to it with all the violence of regret. The past still *functioned.*

We no longer have a past; or rather, there is nothing left of the past which is our own; no longer a chosen country, no lying salvation, no refuge in yore. Our prospects? Impossible to disentangle them: *we are barbarians without a future.* Expression not being of a stature to measure itself against events, to fabricate books and appear proud of doing so constitutes a spectacle eminently pathetic: what necessity impels a writer who has produced fifty books to write still one more? Why this proliferation, this fear of being forgotten, this debased coquetry? Only the literature of need deserves our indulgence these days, produced by the slave, the drudge of the pen. In any case, there is no longer anything *to construct,* neither in literature nor philosophy. Only people who live by them, materially I mean, should take them up. We are entering a period of broken forms, of creations in reverse. Anyone can flourish now. I am scarcely anticipating. Barbarism is accessible to all: it is sufficient to develop a taste for it. Blithely, we shall dissolve the centuries.

What your book will be, I can guess only too well. You live in the provinces: insufficiently corrupted, possessed of pure anxieties, you are unaware how much any "sentiment" dates. The inner drama is reaching its end. How dare a man venture once again upon a work that begins with the "soul," with a prehistoric infinite?

And then, there is the matter of tone. Yours—I'm afraid—will be of the "noble," "reassuring" variety, tainted with common sense, proportion, or elegance. Get it through your head that a book should address itself to our incivism, to our singularities, to our lofty turpitudes, and that a "humane" writer who sacrifices to ideas which are too acceptable signs his own literary death warrant.

Examine the minds which manage to intrigue us: far from taking the way of the world into consideration, they defend *indefensible* positions. If they are lifelike, at least, it is thanks to their limitations, to the passion of their sophistries: the concessions which they have made to "reason" disappoint us, irritate us. Discretion is deadly to genius; ruinous to talent. You will understand, dear friend, why I have apprehensions about your complicities with the "humane."

As though to give yourself a certain "positive" assurance, which harbored as well a suspicion of superiority, you have often reproached me for what you call my "appetite for destruction." You should know that I destroy nothing: I record, I record the *imminent,* the thirst of a world which is canceling itself out and which, upon the wreck of its appearances, races toward the unknown and the incommensurable, toward a spasmodic style. I know one mad old woman who expects her house to fall to pieces from one minute to the next; she spends her days and her nights on the alert; creeping from room to room, ears cocked for every sound, she is furious that the *event* takes so long to occur. In a larger context, the old woman's behavior is our own. We count on a collapse, even though we do not think about it. It will not always be this way; one can even foresee that the fear of ourselves, result of a more general fear, will constitute the basis of education, the principle of future pedagogies. I believe in the future of the terrible. You, my dear friend, are so little prepared for it that you are about to enter literature. I have no qualifications to discourage you; at least I should like you to proceed without illusions. Temper the author champing within you, adopt for your own, with suitable enlargement, this remark of Saint John Climacus: "Nothing procures so many crowns for the monk as discouragement."

If, upon further reflection, I have shown some complacency in destroying, it was, contrary to what you think, always at my own expense. One does not destroy, save as one destroys *oneself.* I have hated myself in all the objects of my hatreds, I have imagined miracles of annihilation, pulverized my hours, tested the gangrenes of the intellect. Initially an instrument or a method, skepticism ultimately took up residence inside me, became my physiology, the fate of my body, my visceral principle, the disease I can neither cure nor die of. I incline—it is only too true—toward things stripped of any chance of ending or surviving. So you will understand why I have always been concerned with the West. This concern seemed to you absurd or gratuitous. "The West—you aren't even part of it," you pointed out. Is it my fault if my greed for misery has not found another object? Where else will I find so persistent a will to fail? I envy the West the dexterity with which it manages to die out. When I would fortify my disappointments, I turn my mind toward this theme of an inexhaustible negative richness. And if I open some history of France, England, Spain, or Germany, the contrast between what they were and what they are gives me, besides a certain vertigo, the pride of having discovered, at last, the axioms of twilight.

I am far from trying to pervert your hopes: life will take care of that. Like everyone else, you will proceed from one forfeiture to the next. At your age, I had the advantage of knowing some people in a position to initiate me, to make me blush for my illusions; they truly educated me. Without them, should I have had the courage to face or to endure the years? By imposing *their* bitterness, they prepared me for my own. Armed with great ambitions, they set out to conquer some glory or other. Failure awaited them. Delicacy, lucidity, sloth? I could not tell you which virtue cut across their plans. They belonged to that category of individuals whom one meets in capital cities, living by expedients, always looking for a situation they reject as soon as it is found. From their remarks I learned more than from all the rest of my associations. Most of them carried a book inside them, the book of their setbacks; tempted by the demon of literature, they nonetheless withstood it, so subjugated were they by their defeats, so full of disaster were their lives. They are commonly called "failures." They form a type of man apart, which I shall attempt to describe to you, at the risk of simplifying him. A voluptuary of fiasco, he seeks his own diminution in everything, never gets past the preliminaries of his future, nor crosses the threshold of any enterprise. Rivaling the angels in *abulia,* he meditates upon the secret of action, and takes but one initiative:

that of abandon. His faith, if he has any, serves him as a pretext for new capitulations, for a degradation glimpsed and longed for: he collapses into God . . . If he reflects upon the "mystery," it is to show others to what lengths he carries his indignity. He inhabits his convictions like a worm in the fruit; he founders with them and recovers only to rouse against himself whatever melancholies he has left. If he smothers his gifts, it is because he so loves his lassitude; he advances toward his past, retraces his steps *in the name of his talents.*

You will be surprised to learn that he proceeds in this way only because he has adopted a rather odd attitude with regard to his enemies. Let me explain. When we are in the mood to be effective, we know that our enemies cannot keep us from placing ourselves at the center of their attention and of their interest. They prefer us to themselves, they take our affairs to heart. In our turn we are concerned with them, we watch over their health, as over their hatred, which alone permits us to sustain a few illusions about ourselves. They save us, belong to us—they are our own. With regard to his enemies, *the failure* reacts differently. Not knowing how to preserve them, he ends up losing interest in them, minimizing them, no longer taking them seriously. A detachment with the gravest consequences. In vain will he attempt, later, to goad them on, to waken the slightest curiosity about him, to provoke their indiscretion or their rage; in vain, too, will he attempt to rouse them to pity his condition, to conserve or quicken their rancor. With no one *against whom* to affirm himself, he will be imprisoned in solitude and sterility. A solitude and sterility I prized so highly among these defeated men responsible, as I have said, for my education. Among others, they revealed to me the stupidities inherent in the cult of Truth . . . I shall never forget my comfort when it ceased to be my business. A master of every error, I could at last explore a world of appearances, of frivolous enigmas. Nothing more to pursue, except the pursuit of nothing. The Truth? An adolescent fad or a symptom of senility. Yet out of some trace of nostalgia or some craving for slavery, I still seek it, unconsciously, stupidly. A second's inattention is enough for me to relapse into the oldest, the most absurd of prejudices.

I am destroying myself, certainly; meanwhile, in this asthmatic climate that convictions create in a world of oppressed men, I breathe; I breathe in my fashion. Some day, who knows? you may experience this pleasure of aiming at an idea, firing at it, seeing it there, prone, before you, and then beginning the exercise again on another, on all; this longing to lean over someone, to divert him from his old appetites, his old vices, in order to impose new and more noxious ones upon him, until he dies of them; to set yourself against an age or a civilization, to fling yourself upon time and martyrize its moments; then to turn against yourself, to torment your memories and your ambitions and, destroying your breath, to infect the air in order to suffocate all the better . . . , some day perhaps you will know this form of breathing which is deliverance from self and from everything. Then you will be able to commit yourself to anything without adhering to it.

My purpose was to put you on guard against the Serious, against that sin which nothing redeems. In exchange, I wanted to offer you . . . futility. Now—why conceal it?—futility is the most difficult thing in the world, I mean a futility that is conscious, acquired, deliberate. In my presumption, I hoped to achieve it by the practice of skepticism. Yet skepticism adapts itself to our character, follows our defects and our passions, even our follies; skepticism personalizes itself. (There are as many skepticisms as there are temperaments.) Doubt waxes by all that weakens or opposes it; it is a sickness within another sickness, an obsession within obsession. If you pray, it rises to the level of your prayer; it oversees your delirium, even as it imitates it; in the middle of your vertigo, you will doubt—vertiginously. Thus, to abolish the Serious, skepticism itself is of no avail; nor, alas, is poetry. The older I grow, the more I realize that I have counted too much on poetry. I have loved it at the expense of my health; I anticipated succumbing to my worship of it. Poetry! the word itself once led me to imagine a thousand universes and now no longer wakens in my mind anything but a vision of singsong and nullity, of fetid mysteries and affectations. It is only fair to add that I have made the mistake of frequenting a good number of poets. With very few exceptions, they were uselessly solemn, infatuated, or odious, monsters, specialists, tormentors, and martyrs of the adjective whose dilettantism, lucidity, and intellectual sensibility I had vastly overestimated. Is futility, then, no more than an "ideal"? That is what I must fear, that is what I shall never be resigned to. Each time I catch myself assigning some importance to things, I incriminate my mind, I challenge it and suspect it of some weakness, of some depravity. I try to wrest myself from everything, to raise myself by uprooting myself; in order to become futile, we must sever our roots, must become metaphysically *alien.*

In order to justify your ties, and as though impatient to bear the burden of them, you claimed one day that it was easy for me to float, to flourish in thin air because, coming from a country without history, nothing *weighed* upon me. I acknowledge the advantage of belonging to a minor country, of living without a background, with the unconcern of a tumbler, an idiot or a saint, or with the detachment of that serpent which, coiled around itself, survives without food for years on end, as if it were some god of inanition or else concealed, beneath the suavity of its hebetude, some hideous sun.

Without any tradition to encumber me, I cultivate a curiosity about that displacement which will soon be the universal fate. By will or by force, we shall all suffer an historical eclipse, the imperative of confusion. Already we are being canceled out in the sum of our divergences from ourselves. By constantly denying itself, our mind has lost its center, diffused in *attitudes,* in metamorphoses as futile as they are inevitable. Whence the indecency and the mobility of our behavior. Our unbelief and even our faith are marked by it.

To attack God, to seek to dethrone Him, to supplant Him, is an exploit in bad taste, the performance of an envious man who takes a vain satisfaction in coming to grips with a unique and uncertain Enemy. Whatever form it takes, atheism presumes a lack of manners, as does, for converse reasons, apologetics; for is it not an indelicacy as well as a hypocritical charity, an impiety to do battle in order to sustain God, to assure Him, whatever the cost, a—longevity? The love or the hate we bear Him reveals not so much the quality of our anxieties as the grossness of our cynicism.

We are responsible for this state of affairs only in part. From Tertullian to Kierkegaard, by accentuating the absurdity of faith, Christianity has created an undercurrent which, now appearing in broad daylight, has overflowed the Church. What believer, in his fits of lucidity, does not consider himself a servant of the Irrational? God was to suffer for it. Hitherto we granted Him our virtues; we dared not lend Him our vices. Humanized, He resembles us now: none of our defects is alien to Him. Never have the broadening of theology and the thirst for anthropomorphism been carried so far. This modernization of Heaven marks its end. How can we venerate an advanced God, an up-to-date God? To His misfortune, He will not soon recover His "infinite transcendence."

"Beware," you might argue, "beware what you call a 'failure of manners.' You are only denouncing atheism the better to sacrifice to it."

Upon myself I am only too aware of the stigmata of my time: I cannot leave God in peace; along with the snobs, I entertain myself by repeating that He is dead, as if that had any meaning. By such impertinence we hope to despatch our solitudes, and the supreme phantom which inhabits them. In reality, as they increase they merely bring us closer to what haunts them.

When Nothingness invades me and, according to an Oriental formula, I attain to the "vacuity of the void," it so happens that, crushed by such an extremity, I fall back on God, if only out of a desire to trample my doubts underfoot, to contradict myself and, multiplying my *frissons,* to seek in Him a stimulant. The experience of the Void is the unbeliever's mystic temptation, his possibility for prayer, his moment of plenitude. At our limits, a God appears, or something that serves his turn.

* * *

We are far from literature: but far only in appearance. These are only words, sins of the Word. I recommended to you the dignity of skepticism: here I am prowling around the Absolute. A technique of contradiction? Recall, instead, Flaubert's words: "I am a mystic and I believe in nothing." I see it as the adage of our age, of an age infinitely intense, and without substance. There exists a voluptuousness which is all our own: the voluptuousness of conflict *as such.* Convulsive minds, fanatics of the improbable, drawn between dogma and aporia, we are as ready to leap into God *out of rage* as we are resolved not to vegetate in Him.

Only the professional heretic, the man rejected by vocation, is contemporary, at once the spew and panic of our orthodoxies. In the past, you were defined by the values to which you subscribed; today, by those you repudiate. Without the pomp of negation, man is a pauper, a lamentable "creator," incapable of fulfilling his destiny as a capitalist of collapse, an amateur of the crash. Wisdom? Never was any period so free of it—in other words, never was man more himself: a being refractory to wisdom. A traitor to zoology, an animal *astray,* man rebels against nature, even as the heretic against tradition. The heretic is thus man to the second degree. Every innovation is his doing. His passion: to find himself at the origin, at the point of departure of anything and everything. Even when he is humble, he aspires to make others feel the effects of his humility and believes that a religious, philosophical, or political system is worth the trouble of being broken or renewed: to put oneself at the heart of a rupture is all he asks. Hating equilibrium and the sluggishness of institutions, he shoulders them aside to hasten their end.

The wise man, the sage, is hostile to the new. Disabused, he abdicates: that is his form of protest. Proud enough to isolate himself in the *norm,* he asserts himself by *retreat.* To what does he aspire? To surmount or neutralize his contradictions. If he succeeds, he proves that they lacked vigor, that he had transcended before truly facing them. Instinct failing, it is easy for him to be master of himself, to pontificate in the anemia of his serenity.

Once we are carried away by ourselves, we realize that it is not in our power to stop, to cool off our contradictions or conjure them away. They guide us, stimulate us and kill us. The sage, rising above them, accommodates himself to them, does not suffer from them, *gains* nothing by dying. In other periods, he was a model; for us, he is no more than a failure of biology, an anomaly without attraction.

You defame wisdom, because you cannot accede to it, because it is "forbidden" you, you may be thinking. In fact it is certain that is what you are thinking. To which I answer that it is too *late* to be wise, that in any case it would serve no purpose, for the same abyss will engulf us all, wise and foolish alike, sane and mad. I acknowledge, moreover, that I am the sage I shall never be . . . Every formula for salvation acts upon me like a poison: it defeats me, augments my difficulties, aggravates my relations with others, irritates my wounds and, instead of exercising a salutary virtue upon the economy of my days, plays a mortal role in them. Yes, every wisdom acts upon me like a *toxin*. No doubt you are also thinking that I am too much "in step" with this age, that I am making too many concessions to it. In fact, I applaud and deny it with all the passion and incoherence I possess. It gives me the sensation of a last act, hypostatized. Must we deduce from this that it will never end, that this interminable coda will merely perpetuate its incompletion? Nothing of the kind. I foresee what will happen, and to enhance such knowledge we need merely reread Saint Jerome's letter after the sack of Rome by Alaric. It expresses the astonishment and the uneasiness of a man who, from the periphery of an empire, contemplates its disintegration and its inertia. Consider this document: it is your epitaph, anticipated. I do not know if it is legitimate to speak of the end of man; but I am certain of the fall of all the fictions by which we have lived until today. Let us say that history is finally revealing its night side, and, to remain in the realm of the unspecific, that a world is destroying itself. Well then, in the hypothesis that I alone can keep this from happening, I shall make no gesture, I shall not raise my little finger. Man attracts and appalls me, I love and hate him with a vehemence which condemns me to passivity. I cannot imagine how to go about saving him from his fatality. How naive we must be to blame or defend him! Lucky those who entertain toward him a clear and distinct sentiment: they will perish *saved*.

To my shame, I confess that there was a time when I too belonged to that category of happy beings. Man's fate touched me to the quick, though in another fashion. I must have been about twenty, your age. "A humanist" in reverse, I supposed—in my still intact pride—that to become the enemy of the human race was the highest dignity to which one might aspire. Eager to cover myself with ignominy, I envied all who exposed themselves to the world's sarcasm and spittle and who, accumulating shame upon shame, missed no occasion for solitude. I came thus to idealize Judas because, refusing to endure any longer the anonymity of dedication, he sought to singularize himself by treason. It was not out of venality, I chose to think, but ambition that he *gave Jesus away*. He dreamed of equaling him, of counterbalancing him in evil; in good, with such a competitor, there was no way for Judas to distinguish himself. Since the honor of being crucified was forbidden him, he was able to make the tree of Aceldama a replica of the Cross. All my thoughts followed him on the road to that hanging, while I too prepared to sell my idols. I envied his infamies, the courage it took to make himself execrated. What a torment to be ordinary, a man among men! Turning to the monks meditating night and day on their seclusion, I imagined them mulling over crimes and outrages that were more or less aborted. Every solitary, I told myself, is suspect: a *pure* being does not isolate himself. To seek the intimacy of a cell, one must have a heavy conscience; one must be afraid of one's conscience. I regretted bitterly that the history of monasticism had been undertaken by straightforward minds, as incapable of conceiving the need to be odious to oneself as of experiencing that melancholy which moves mountains . . . A raving hyena, I anticipated making myself hateful to every creature, forcing them to league together against me, crushing them or being crushed by them. In other words, I was ambitious . . . Since then, by dint of modulations, my illusions were to lose their virulence and creep modestly toward disgust, ambiguity, and bewilderment.

At the end of these deliberations, I cannot help repeating that it is hard for me to discern the place you seek to occupy in our time; in order to inscribe yourself within the age, have you enough flexibility, enough of a thirst for inconsistency? Your sense of balance presages nothing very helpful here. As you are, you have a long way to go. In order to liquidate your past, your innocence, you require an initiation into vertigo. Simple enough for those who understand that fear, grafted onto matter, causes it to make that leap of which we are in a sense the final reverberation. There is no such thing as time, there is only that fear which develops and disguises itself as moments . . . , which is here, inside us and outside us, omnipresent and invisible, the mystery of our silences and our screams, of our prayers and our blasphemies. Now, it is precisely in the twentieth century that this fear is approaching its apogee, full blown, proud of its conquests and its successes. Neither our frenzies nor our cynicism had hoped for as much. And it is no longer surprising that we are so far from Goethe, the last citizen of the cosmos, the last grand *naïf*. His "mediocrity" joins nature's. The least *déraciné* of minds: a friend of the elements. Opposed to all that he was, for us it is a necessity and almost a duty to be unfair to him, to shatter him within us, to shatter *ourselves* . . .

If you lack the power to demoralize yourself along with the age, to go as low and as far, do not complain of being misunderstood by it. Above all, do not suppose yourself to be a precursor: there will be no "light" in this century. Hence if you insist upon contributing some innovation, prospect your nights or despair of your career.

In any case, do not accuse me of having used a peremptory tone with you. My convictions are pretexts: what right do I have to impose them on you? The same is not true of my vacillations; those I do not invent, I believe in them, I believe in them despite myself. Hence it is in good faith, and regretfully, that I have inflicted upon you this lesson in perplexity.

—*Translated by Richard Howard*

ROLAND BARTHES

Roland Barthes (1915–1980) was a <u>French literary and cultural critic</u> and a <u>leading exponent of semiotics, the science of signs and symbols</u> and their role in culture and society. In his famous essay collection, Mythologies, *he turned his bemused, demystifying intelligence on everything from wrestling to car ads to the face of Garbo, seeking to penetrate the subtle messages within the world around us. He was among the <u>first to assume that popular culture has an immense shaping influence on individual development</u>. <u>There is a subversive agenda in Barthes' work</u>: he would like to burrow from within, to <u>decompose what he calls "bourgeois consciousness"—the owning classes' manipulation of the platitudes of mass culture</u>. But, believer in paradox that he is, he understands how impossible it may be to analyze the status quo without being part of it and to some extent abetting it.*

Barthes was the most seductive and accessible literary stylist of the recent generation of French structuralists and deconstructionists, who have shaken up the intellectual scene. By his own acknowledgment <u>he was less a philosopher than an essayist</u>—and an increasingly personal one at that. In his fascinating autobiographical work, Roland Barthes by Roland Barthes, *he <u>fragments himself into a mosaic of revealing, partial glimpses</u>. For instance: "As a child, I was often and intensely bored. This evidently began very early, it has continued my whole life, in gusts (increasingly rare, it is true, thanks to work and friends), and <u>it has always been noticeable to others</u>. A panic boredom, to the point of distress: like the kind I feel in panel discussions, lectures, parties among strangers, group amusements: wherever boredom* can *be seen. Might boredom be my form of hysteria?" It is characteristic of Barthes that he writes so <u>intimately about both boredom and joy</u> (the Barthean* jouissance, *with its connotation in*

French of orgasm) as though they were opposite but connected ends of the same seesaw.

The piece below, "Leaving the Movie Theater," shows Barthes characteristically analyzing the borderline moments surrounding immersion in pleasure. As so often with this writer, who swims like a fish between third- and first-person descriptions of himself, he takes a common occurrence in daily life and invests it with elegance and mystery. Some would say mystification: it is yet another paradox that the great demystifier often left incense clouds in his wake, and the promise of a meaning just *beyond our grasp.* But that is part of the charm of Barthes' writing.

Leaving the Movie Theater

THERE IS SOMETHING TO CONFESS: your speaker likes to *leave* a movie theater. Back out on the more or less empty, more or less brightly lit sidewalk (it is invariably at night, and during the week, that he *goes*), and heading uncertainly for some café or other, he walks in silence (he doesn't like discussing the film he's just seen), a little dazed, wrapped up in himself, feeling the cold—he's *sleepy,* that's what he's thinking, his body has become something *sopitive,* soft, limp, and he feels a little disjointed, even (for a moral organization, relief comes only from this quarter) irresponsible. In other words, obviously, he's coming out of hypnosis. And hypnosis (an old psychoanalytic device—one that psychoanalysis nowadays seems to treat quite condescendingly) means only one thing to him: the most venerable of powers: healing. And he thinks of music: isn't there such a thing as hypnotic music? The castrato Farinelli, whose *messa di voce* was "as incredible for its duration as for its emission," relieved the morbid melancholy of Philip V of Spain by singing him the same aria every night for fourteen years.

This is often how he leaves a movie theater. How does he go in? Except for the—increasingly frequent—case of a specific cultural quest (a selected, sought-for, *desired* film, object of a veritable preliminary alert), he goes to movies as a response to idleness, leisure, free time. It's as if, even before he went into the theater, the classic conditions of hypnosis were in force: vacancy, want of occupation, lethargy; it's not in front of the film and because of the film that he *dreams off*—it's without knowing it, even before he becomes a spectator. There is a "cinema situation," and this situation is pre-hypnotic. According to a true metonymy, the darkness of the theater is prefigured by the "twilight reverie" (a prerequisite for hypnosis, according to Breuer-Freud) which precedes it and leads him from street to street, from poster to poster, finally burying himself in a dim, anonymous, indifferent cube where that festival of affects known as a film will be presented.

What does the "darkness" of the cinema mean? (Whenever I hear the word *cinema,* I can't help thinking *hall,* rather than *film.*) Not only is the dark the very substance of reverie (in the pre-hypnoid meaning of the term); it is also the "color" of a diffused eroticism; by its human condensation, by its absence of worldliness (contrary to the cultural *appearance* that has to be put in at any "legitimate theater"), by the relaxation of postures (how many members of the cinema audience slide down into their seats as if into a bed, coats or feet thrown over the row in front!), the movie house (ordinary model) is a site of availability (even more than cruising), the inoccupation of bodies, which best defines modern eroticism —not that of advertising or strip-tease, but that of the big city. It is in this urban dark that the body's freedom is generated; this invisible work of possible affects emerges from a veritable cinematographic cocoon; the movie spectator could easily appropriate the silkworm's motto: *Inclusum labor illustrat;* it is because I am enclosed that I work and glow with all my desire.

In this darkness of the cinema (anonymous, populated, numerous—oh, the boredom, the frustration of so-called private showings!) lies the very fascination of the film (any film). Think of the contrary experience: on television, where films are also shown, no fascination; here darkness is erased, anonymity repressed; space is familiar, articulated (by furniture, known objects), tamed: the eroticism—no, to put it better, to get across the particular kind of lightness, of unfulfillment we mean: the eroticization of the place is foreclosed: television *doomed* us to the Family, whose household instrument it has become—what the hearth used to be, flanked by its communal kettle.

In that opaque cube, one light: the film, the screen? Yes, of course. But also (especially?), visible and unperceived, that dancing cone which pierces the darkness like a laser beam. This beam is minted, according to the rotation of its particles, into changing figures; we turn our face toward the *currency* of a gleaming vibration whose imperious jet brushes our skull, glancing off someone's hair, someone's face. As in the old hypnotic experiments, we are fascinated—without seeing it head-on—by this shining site, motionless and dancing.

It's exactly as if a long stem of light had outlined a keyhole, and then we all peered, flabbergasted, through that hole. And nothing in this ecstasy is provided by sound, music, words? Usually—in current productions—the audio protocol can produce no *fascinated* listening; conceived to reinforce the *lifelikeness* of the anecdote, sound is merely a supplementary instrument of representation; it is meant to integrate itself unobtrusively into the object shown, it is in no way detached from this object; yet it would take very little in order to separate this sound track: one displaced or magnified sound, the grain of a voice milled in our eardrums, and the fascination begins again; for it never comes except from artifice, or better still: from the *artifact*—like the dancing beam of the projector—which comes from overhead or to the side, blurring the scene shown by the screen *yet without distorting its image* (its *gestalt,* its meaning).

For such is the narrow range—at least for me—in which can function the fascination of film, the cinematographic hypnosis: I must be in the story (there must be verisimilitude), but I must also be *elsewhere:* a slightly disengaged image-repertoire, that is what I must have—like a scrupulous, conscientious, organized, in a word *difficult* fetishist, that is what I require of the film and of the situation in which I go looking for it.

The film image (including the sound) is what? A *lure.* I am confined with the image as if I were held in that famous dual relation which establishes the image-repertoire. The image is there, in front of me, for me: coalescent (its signified and its signifier melted together), analogical, total, pregnant; it is a perfect lure: I fling myself upon it like an animal upon the scrap of "lifelike" rag held out to him; and, of course, it sustains in me the misreading attached to Ego and to image-repertoire. In the movie theater, however far away I am sitting, I press my nose against the screen's mirror, against that "other" image-repertoire with which I narcissistically identify myself (it is said that the spectators who choose to sit as close to the screen as possible are children and movie buffs); the image captivates me, captures me: I am *glued* to the representation, and it is this glue which established the *naturalness* (the pseudo-nature) of the filmed scene (a glue prepared with all the ingredients of "technique"); the Real knows only distances, the Symbolic knows only masks; the image alone (the image-repertoire) is *close,* only the image is *"true"* (can produce the resonance of truth). Actually, has not the image, statutorily, all the characteristics of the *ideological?* The historical subject, like the cinema spectator I am imagining, is also *glued* to ideological discourse: he experiences its coalescence, its analogical security, its naturalness, its "truth": it is a lure (*our* lure, for who escapes it?); the Ideological would actually be the image-repertoire of a period of history, the Cinema of a society; like the film which lures its clientele, it even has its photograms; is not the stereotype a fixed image, a quotation to which our language is glued? And in the commonplace have we not a dual relation: narcissistic and maternal?

How to come unglued from the mirror? I'll risk a pun to answer: by *taking off* (in the aeronautical and narcotic sense of the term). Of course, it is still possible to conceive of an art which will break the dual circle, the fascination of film, and loosen the glue, the hypnosis of the lifelike (of the analogical), by some recourse to the spectator's critical vision (or listening); is this not what the Brechtian alienation-effect involves? Many things can help us to "come out of" (imaginary and/or ideological) hypnosis: the very methods of an epic art, the spectator's culture or his ideological vigilance; contrary to classical hysteria, the image-repertoire vanishes once one observes that it exists. But there is another way of going to the movies (besides being armed by the discourse of counter-ideology); by letting oneself be fascinated *twice over,* by the image and by its surroundings—as if I had two bodies at the same time: a narcissistic body which gazes, lost, into the engulfing mirror, and a perverse body, ready to fetishize not the image but precisely what exceeds it: the texture of the sound, the hall, the darkness, the obscure mass of the other bodies, the rays of light, entering the theater, leaving the hall; in short, in order to distance, in order to "take off," I complicate a "relation" by a "situation." What I use to distance myself from the image—that, ultimately, is what fascinates me: I am hypnotized by a distance; and this distance is not critical (intellectual); it is, one might say, an amorous distance: would there be, in the cinema itself (and taking the word at its etymological suggestion) a possible bliss of *discretion?*

—Translated by Richard Howard

NATALIA GINZBURG

Natalia Ginzburg (1916–1991) is now valued as a major Italian writer of the second half of the twentieth century. She spent most of her life in the city of Turin, where she befriended the novelist Cesare Pavese and was married to Leone Ginzburg. Her husband, a scholar of Russian literature and a leader of the antifascist underground, was killed by the Nazis in 1944. She herself endured great suffering and poverty during the war, and raised her children by herself. After the war she worked for the prestigious publishing house Enaudi, married the scholar Gabriele Baldini, the model for "he" in "He and I," and began writing her books. Family Sayings, *an autobiographical novel, won the coveted Strega Prize.*

Ginzburg's deceptively plain style, with its homey domestic details, every-day images, and singsong speech, effectively conveys sophisticated ideas and mature wisdom in an unintimidating manner. In her essay collection, The Little Virtues, *the author writes about herself as if she were an ordinary girl, wife, mother, widow, with a peasant's stubbornness and endurance. Her aesthetic and humanist viewpoint seems to have been fashioned in the same crucible as postwar neorealist Italian movies. Even her writing gift is brought down to earth, as in this passage from the essay "My Vocation":*

> *When I write something I usually think it is very important and that I am a very fine writer. I think this happens to everyone. But there is one corner of my mind in which I know very well what I am, which is a small, a very small writer. I swear I know it. But that doesn't matter much to me. Only, I don't want to think about names: I can see that if I am asked 'a small writer like who?' it would sadden me to think of the names of other small writers. I prefer to think that no one has ever been*

like me, however small, however much a mosquito or a flea of a writer I
may be. The important thing is to be convinced that this really is your
vocation, your profession, something you will do all your life.

The following essay, "He and I," captures the seesaw of human compan-
ionship and love with a patience and sensitivity to interconnectedness that it
is hard to imagine a male essayist attempting, much less equaling.

AH! Lopate finally sees himself without magnifocation

He and I

H E   A L W A Y S   F E E L S   H O T, I always feel cold. In the summer
when it really is hot he does nothing but complain about how hot
he feels. He is irritated if he sees me put a jumper on in the evening.

He speaks several languages well; I do not speak any well. He manages
—in his own way—to speak even the languages that he doesn't know.

He has an excellent sense of direction, I have none at all. After one day
in a foreign city he can move about in it as thoughtlessly as a butterfly. I
get lost in my own city; I have to ask directions so that I can get back
home again. He hates asking directions; when we go by car to a town we
don't know he doesn't want to ask directions and tells me to look at the
map. I don't know how to read maps and I get confused by all the little
red circles and he loses his temper.

He loves the theatre, painting, music, especially music. I do not understand music at all, painting doesn't mean much to me and I get bored
at the theatre. I love and understand one thing in the world and that
is poetry.

He loves museums, and I will go if I am forced to but with an unpleasant sense of effort and duty. He loves libraries and I hate them.

He loves travelling, unfamiliar foreign cities, restaurants. I would like to
stay at home all the time and never move.

All the same I follow him on his many journeys. I follow him to museums, to churches, to the opera. I even follow him to concerts, where I fall
asleep.

Because he knows the conductors and the singers, after the performance is over he likes to go and congratulate them. I follow him down long corridors lined with the singers' dressing-rooms and listen to him talking to people dressed as cardinals and kings.

He is not shy; I am shy. Occasionally however I have seen him be shy. With the police when they come over to the car armed with a notebook and pencil. Then he is shy, thinking he is in the wrong.

And even when he doesn't think he is in the wrong. I think he has a respect for established authority. I am afraid of established authority, but he isn't. He respects it. There is a difference. When I see a policeman coming to fine me I immediately think he is going to haul me off to prison. He doesn't think about prison; but, out of respect, he becomes shy and polite.

During the Montesi trial, because of his respect for established authority, we had very violent arguments.

He likes tagliatelle, lamb, cherries, red wine. I like minestrone, bread soup, omelettes, green vegetables.

He often says I don't understand anything about food, that I am like a great strong fat friar—one of those friars who devour soup made from greens in the darkness of their monasteries; but he, oh he is refined and has a sensitive palate. In restaurants he makes long inquiries about the wines; he has them bring two or three bottles then looks at them and considers the matter, and slowly strokes his beard.

There are certain restaurants in England where the waiter goes through a little ritual: he pours some wine into a glass so that the customer can test whether he likes it or not. He used to hate this ritual and always prevented the waiter from carrying it out by taking the bottle from him. I used to argue with him about this and say that you should let people carry out their prescribed tasks.

And in the same way he never lets the usherette at the cinema direct him to his seat. He immediately gives her a tip but dashes off to a completely different place from the one she shows him with her torch.

At the cinema he likes to sit very close to the screen. If we go with friends and they look for seats a long way from the screen, as most people do, he sits by himself in the front row. I can see well whether I am close to the screen or far away from it, but when we are with friends I stay with them out of politeness; all the same it upsets me because I could be next to him two inches from the screen, and when I don't sit next to him he gets annoyed with me.

We both love the cinema, and we are ready to see almost any kind of film at almost any time of day. But he knows the history of the cinema in great detail; he remembers old directors and actors who have disappeared and been forgotten long ago, and he is ready to travel miles into the most distant suburbs in search of some ancient silent film in which an actor

appears—perhaps just for a few seconds—whom he affectionately associates with memories of his early childhood. I remember one Sunday afternoon in London; somewhere in the distant suburbs on the edge of the
countryside they were showing a film from the 1930s, about the French
Revolution, which he had seen as a child, and in which a famous actress of
that time appeared for a moment or two. We set off by car in search of the
street, which was a very long way off; it was raining, there was a fog, and
we drove for hour after hour through identical suburbs, between rows of
little grey houses, gutters and railings; I had the map on my knees and I
couldn't read it and he lost his temper; at last, we found the cinema and
sat in the completely deserted auditorium. But after a quarter of an hour,
immediately after the brief appearance of the actress who was so important to him, he already wanted to go; I on the other hand, after seeing so
many streets, wanted to see how the film finished. I don't remember
whether we did what he wanted or what I wanted; probably what he
wanted, so that we left after a quarter of an hour, also because it was late
—though we had set off early in the afternoon it was already time for
dinner. But when I begged him to tell me how the film ended I didn't get
a very satisfactory answer; because, he said, the story wasn't at all important, the only thing that mattered was those few moments, that actress's
curls, gestures, profile.

I never remember actors' names, and as I am not good at remembering
faces it is often difficult for me to recognize even the most famous of
them. This infuriates him; his scorn increases as I ask him whether it was
this one or that one; "You don't mean to tell me," he says, "You don't
mean to tell me that you didn't recognize William Holden!"

And in fact I didn't recognize William Holden. All the same, I love the
cinema too; but although I have been seeing films for years I haven't been
able to provide myself with any sort of cinematic education. But he has
made an education of it for himself and he does this with whatever attracts
his curiosity; I don't know how to make myself an education out of anything, even those things that I love best in life; they stay with me as scattered images, nourishing my life with memories and emotions but without
filling the void, the desert of my education.

He tells me I have no curiosity, but this is not true. I am curious about a
few, a very few, things. And when I have got to know them I retain
scattered impressions of them, or the cadence of phrase, or a word. But
my world, in which these completely unrelated (unless in some secret fashion unbeknown to me) impressions and cadences rise to the surface, is a
sad, barren place. His world, on the other hand, is green and populous
and richly cultivated; it is a fertile, well-watered countryside in which
woods, meadows, orchards and villages flourish.

Everything I do is done laboriously, with great difficulty and uncertainty. I am very lazy, and if I want to finish anything it is absolutely essential that I spend hours stretched out on the sofa. He is never idle, and is always doing something; when he goes to lie down in the afternoons he takes proofs to correct or a book full of notes; he wants us to go to the cinema, then to a reception, then to the theatre—all on the same day. In one day he succeeds in doing, and in making me do, a mass of different things, and in meeting extremely diverse kinds of people. If I am alone and try to act as he does I get nothing at all done, because I get stuck all afternoon somewhere I had meant to stay for half an hour, or because I get lost and cannot find the right street, or because the most boring person and the one I least wanted to meet drags me off to the place I least wanted to go to.

If I tell him how my afternoon has turned out he says it is a completely wasted afternoon and is amused and makes fun of me and loses his temper; and he says that without him I am good for nothing. *and she stays?*

I don't know how to manage my time; he does.

He likes receptions. He dresses casually, when everyone is dressed formally; the idea of changing his clothes in order to go to a reception never enters his head. He even goes in his old raincoat and crumpled hat; a woollen hat which he bought in London and which he wears pulled down over his eyes. He only stays for half an hour; he enjoys chatting with a glass in his hand for half an hour; he eats lots of *hors d'oeuvres,* and I eat almost none because when I see him eating so many I feel that I at least must be well-mannered and show some self-control and not eat too much; after half an hour, just as I am beginning to feel at ease and to enjoy myself, he gets impatient and drags me away.

I don't know how to dance and he does.

I don't know how to type and he does.

I don't know how to drive. If I suggest that I should get a licence too he disagrees. He says I would never manage it. I think he likes me to be dependent on him for some things.

I don't know how to sing and he does. He is a baritone. Perhaps he would have been a famous singer if he had studied singing.

Perhaps he would have been a conductor if he had studied music. When he listens to records he conducts the orchestra with a pencil. And he types and answers the telephone at the same time. He is a man who is able to do many things at once.

He is a professor and I think he is a good one.

He could have been many things. But he has no regrets about those professions he did not take up. I could only ever have followed one profession—the one I chose and which I have followed almost since childhood. And I don't have any regrets either about the professions I did not take up, but then I couldn't have succeeded at any of them.

I write stories, and for many years I have worked for a publishing house.

I don't work badly, or particularly well. All the same I am well aware of the fact that I would have been unable to work anywhere else. I get on well with my colleagues and my boss. I think that if I did not have the support of their friendship I would soon have become worn out and unable to work any longer.

For a long time I thought that one day I would be able to write screenplays for the cinema. But I never had the opportunity, or I did not know how to find it. Now I have lost all hope of writing screenplays. He wrote screenplays for a while, when he was younger. And he has worked in a publishing house. He has written stories. He has done all the things that I have done and many others too.

He is a good mimic, and does an old countess especially well. Perhaps he could also have been an actor.

Once, in London, he sang in a theatre. He was Job. He had to hire evening clothes; and there he was, in his evening clothes, in front of a kind of lectern; and he sang. He sang the words of Job; the piece called for something between speaking and singing. And I, in my box, was dying of fright. I was afraid he would get flustered, or that the trousers of his evening clothes would fall down.

He was surrounded by men in evening clothes and women in long dresses, who were the angels and devils and other characters in Job.

It was a great success, and they said that he was very good.

If I loved music I would love it passionately. But I don't understand it, and when he persuades me to go to concerts with him my mind wanders off and I think of my own affairs. Or I fall sound asleep.

I like to sing. I don't know how to sing and I sing completely out of tune; but I sing all the same—occasionally, very quietly, when I am alone. I know that I sing out of tune because others have told me so; my voice must be like the yowling of a cat. But I am not—in myself—aware of this, and singing gives me real pleasure. If he hears me he mimics me; he says that my singing is something quite separate from music, something invented by me.

When I was a child I used to yowl tunes I had made up. It was a long wailing kind of melody that brought tears to my eyes.

It doesn't matter to me that I don't understand painting or the figurative arts, but it hurts me that I don't love music, and I feel that my mind suffers from the absence of this love. But there is nothing I can do about it, I will never understand or love music. If I occasionally hear a piece of music that I like I don't know how to remember it; and how can I love something that I can't remember?

It is the words of a song that I remember. I can repeat words that I love over and over again. I repeat the tune that accompanies them too, in my own yowling fashion, and I experience a kind of happiness as I yowl.

When I am writing it seems to me that I follow a musical cadence or rhythm. Perhaps music was very close to my world, and my world could not, for whatever reason, make contact with it.

In our house there is music all day long. He keeps the radio on all day. Or plays records. Every now and again I protest a little and ask for a little silence in which to work; but he says that such beautiful music is certainly conducive to any kind of work.

He has bought an incredible number of records. He says that he owns one of the finest collections in the world.

In the morning when he is still in his dressing gown and dripping water from his bath, he turns the radio on, sits down at the typewriter and begins his strenuous, noisy, stormy day. He is superabundant in everything; he fills the bath to overflowing, and the same with the teapot and his cup of tea. He has an enormous number of shirts and ties. On the other hand he rarely buys shoes.

His mother says that as a child he was a model of order and precision; apparently once, on a rainy day, he was wearing white boots and white clothes and had to cross some muddy streams in the country—at the end of his walk he was immaculate and his clothes and boots had not one spot of mud on them. There is no trace in him of that former immaculate little boy. His clothes are always covered in stains. He has become extremely untidy.

But he scrupulously keeps all the gas bills. In drawers I find old gas bills, which he refuses to throw away, from houses we left long ago.

I also find old, shrivelled Tuscan cigars, and cigarette holders made from cherry wood.

I smoke a brand of king-size, filterless cigarettes called *Stop,* and he smokes his Tuscan cigars.

I am very untidy. But as I have got older I have come to miss tidiness, and I sometimes furiously tidy up all the cupboards. I think this is because I remember my mother's tidiness. I rearrange the linen and blanket cupboards and in the summer I reline every drawer with strips of white cloth. I rarely rearrange my papers because my mother didn't write and had no papers. My tidiness and untidiness are full of complicated feelings of regret and sadness. His untidiness is triumphant. He has decided that it is proper and legitimate for a studious person like himself to have an untidy desk.

He does not help me get over my indecisiveness, or the way I hesitate before doing anything, or my sense of guilt. He tends to make fun of every tiny thing I do. If I go shopping in the market he follows me and spies on me. He makes fun of the way I shop, of the way I weigh the oranges in my hand unerringly choosing, he says, the worst in the whole market; he ridicules me for spending an hour over the shopping, buying onions at one stall, celery at another and fruit at another. Sometimes he does the shopping to show me how quickly he can do it; he unhesitatingly buys everything from one stall and then manages to get the basket delivered to the house. He doesn't buy celery because he cannot abide it.

And so—more than ever—I feel I do everything inadequately or mistakenly. But if I once find out that he has made a mistake I tell him so over and over again until he is exasperated. I can be very annoying at times.

His rages are unpredictable, and bubble over like the head on beer. My rages are unpredictable too, but his quickly disappear whereas mine leave a noisy nagging trail behind them which must be very annoying—like the complaining yowl of a cat.

Sometimes in the midst of his rage I start to cry, and instead of quietening him down and making him feel sorry for me this infuriates him all the more. He says my tears are just play-acting, and perhaps he is right. Because in the middle of my tears and his rage I am completely calm.

I never cry when I am really unhappy.

There was a time when I used to hurl plates and crockery on the floor during my rages. But not any more. Perhaps because I am older and my rages are less violent, and also because I dare not lay a finger on our plates now; we bought them one day in London, in the Portobello Road, and I am very fond of them.

The price of those plates, and of many other things we have bought, immediately underwent a substantial reduction in his memory. He likes to think he did not spend very much and that he got a bargain. I know the price of that dinner service—it was £16, but he says £12. And it is the same with the picture of King Lear that is in our dining room, and which he also bought in the Portobello Road (and then cleaned with onions and potatoes); now he says he paid a certain sum for it, but I remember that it was much more than that.

Some years ago he bought twelve bedside mats in a department store. He bought them because they were cheap, and he thought he ought to buy them; and he bought them as an argument against me because he considered me to be incapable of buying things for the house. They were made of mud-coloured matting and they quickly became very unattractive; they took on a corpse-like rigidity and were hung from a wire line on the kitchen balcony, and I hated them. I used to remind him of them, as an example of bad shopping; but he would say that they had cost very little indeed, almost nothing. It was a long time before I could bring myself to throw them out—because there were so many of them, and because just as I was about to get rid of them it occurred to me that I could use them for rags. He and I both find throwing things away difficult; it must be a kind

of Jewish caution in me, and the result of my extreme indecisiveness; in
him it must be a defence against his impulsiveness and open-handedness.

He buys enormous quantities of bicarbonate of soda and aspirins.

Now and again he is ill with some mysterious ailment of his own; he
can't explain what he feels and stays in bed for a day completely wrapped
up in the sheets; nothing is visible except his beard and the tip of his red
nose. Then he takes bicarbonate of soda and aspirins in doses suitable for
a horse, and says that I cannot understand because I am always well, I am
like those great fat strong friars who go out in the wind and in all weathers
and come to no harm; he on the other hand is sensitive and delicate and
suffers from mysterious ailments. Then in the evening he is better and
goes into the kitchen and cooks himself tagliatelle.

When he was a young man he was slim, handsome and finely built; he
did not have a beard but long, soft moustaches instead, and he looked like
the actor Robert Donat. He was like that about twenty years ago when I
first knew him, and I remember that he used to wear an elegant kind of
Scottish flannel shirt. I remember that one evening he walked me back to
the *pensione* where I was living; we walked together along the *Via Nazionale*. I already felt that I was very old and had been through a great deal
and had made many mistakes, and he seemed a boy to me, light years
away from me. I don't remember what we talked about on that evening
walking along the *Via Nazionale;* nothing important, I suppose, and the
idea that we would become husband and wife was light years away from
me. Then we lost sight of each other, and when we met again he no longer
looked like Robert Donat, but more like Balzac. When we met again he
still wore his Scottish shirts but on him now they looked like garments for
a polar expedition; now he had his beard and on his head he wore his
ridiculous crumpled woollen hat; everything about him put you in mind of
an imminent departure for the North Pole. Because, although he always
feels hot, he has the habit of dressing as if he were surrounded by snow,
ice and polar bears; or he dresses like a Brazilian coffee-planter, but he
always dresses differently from everyone else.

If I remind him of that walk along the *Via Nazionale* he says he remembers it, but I know he is lying and that he remembers nothing; and I
sometimes ask myself if it was us, these two people, almost twenty years
ago on the *Via Nazionale,* two people who conversed so politely, so ur-
banely, as the sun was setting; who chatted a little about everything perhaps and about nothing; two friends talking, two young intellectuals out
for a walk; so young, so educated, so uninvolved, so ready to judge one
another with kind impartiality; so ready to say goodbye to one another for
ever, as the sun set, at the corner of the street.

—Translated by Dick Davis

CARLOS FUENTES

Carlos Fuentes (1928–   ) is a celebrated Mexican novelist (The Death of Artemio Cruz, Terra Nostra, The Old Gringo) and the author of several volumes of nonfiction, including his virtuoso book of selected essays, Myself with Others. *"How I Started to Write," from that collection, focuses on a favorite theme of the personal essay: the crystallization of a personal and professional self. But Fuentes' piece is about more than just the acquisition of vocation; it is also a study of ethnic identity and its complex role in the creative individual's development—a subject of particular importance in our era.*

As one learns from the essay, Fuentes was the son of a Mexican diplomat and grew up in the United States. His sense of Mexican tradition was therefore not automatic but had to be intentionally and self-consciously acquired. At first Mexico came to him from books and movies; later, through city wanderings, sexual adventures, and friendships. Fuentes remains the arch-cosmopolite, at home as much in Paris, New York, and Rome as in Mexico City. His essays reflect the viewpoint of a polyglot intellectual afloat in world culture; he draws from the Japanese filmmaker Mizoguchi and the Czech writer Milan Kundera as readily as from fellow Latin Americans Gárcia Marquez and Borges.

Fuentes has championed the maximalist, all-assimilating, encyclopedic approach of Cervantes and Diderot. Another of his models is Erasmus, the Renaissance scholar who did so much to spread a universal humanist culture in the sixteenth century. Fuentes may be seen as an Erasmian figure at the crossroads of late twentieth-century culture, mediating between the industrial West and the Third World, synthesizing and articulating the latest pluralist/modernist international perspectives. While some critics consider his oh?

*novels more glib than profound, his power and confidence in handling the
essay genre are indisputable. Here the charms of Fuentes' restless, absorbent,
critical intelligence, his warm loyalties, and his wide experience are placed in
their most attractive setting.*

How I Started to Write

1

I WAS BORN on November 11, 1928, under the sign I would have
chosen, Scorpio, and on a date shared with Dostoevsky, Crommelynck,
and Vonnegut. My mother was rushed from a steaming-hot movie house
in those days before Colonel Buendía took his son to discover ice in the
tropics. She was seeing King Vidor's version of *La Bohème* with John
Gilbert and Lillian Gish. Perhaps the pangs of my birth were provoked by
this anomaly: a silent screen version of Puccini's opera. Since then, the
operatic and the cinematographic have had a tug-of-war with my words, as
if expecting the Scorpio of fiction to rise from silent music and blind
images.

All this, let me add to clear up my biography, took place in the sweltering heat of Panama City, where my father was beginning his diplomatic
career as an attaché to the Mexican legation. (In those days, embassies
were established only in the most important capitals—no place where the
mean average year-round temperature was perpetually in the nineties.)
Since my father was a convinced Mexican nationalist, the problem of
where I was to be born had to be resolved under the sign, not of Scorpio,
but of the Eagle and the Serpent. The Mexican legation, however, though
it had extraterritorial rights, did not have even a territorial midwife; and
the Minister, a fastidious bachelor from Sinaloa by the name of Ignacio
Norris, who resembled the poet Quevedo as one pince-nez resembles another, would have none of me suddenly appearing on the legation parquet,
even if the Angel Gabriel had announced me as a future Mexican writer of
some, albeit debatable, merit.

So if I could not be born in a fictitious, extraterritorial Mexico, neither
would I be born in that even more fictitious extension of the United States
of America, the Canal Zone, where, naturally, the best hospitals were. So,

between two territorial fictions—the Mexican legation, the Canal Zone—and a mercifully silent close-up of John Gilbert, I arrived in the nick of time at the Gorgas Hospital in Panama City at eleven that evening.

The problem of my baptism then arose. As if the waters of the two neighboring oceans touching each other with the iron fingertips of the canal were not enough, I had to undergo a double ceremony: my religious baptism took place in Panama, because my mother, a devout Roman Catholic, demanded it with as much urgency as Tristram Shandy's parents, although through less original means. My national baptism took place a few months later in Mexico City, where my father, an incorrigible Jacobin and priest-eater to the end, insisted that I be registered in the civil rolls established by Benito Juárez. Thus, I appear as a native of Mexico City for all legal purposes, and this anomaly further illustrates a central fact of my life and my writing: I am Mexican by will and by imagination.

All this came to a head in the 1930s. By then, my father was counselor of the Mexican Embassy in Washington, D.C., and I grew up in the vibrant world of the American thirties, more or less between the inauguration of Citizen Roosevelt and the interdiction of Citizen Kane. When I arrived here, Dick Tracy had just met Tess Truehart. As I left, Clark Kent was meeting Lois Lane. You are what you eat. You are also the comics you peruse as a child. *if any?*

At home, my father made me read Mexican history, study Mexican geography, and understand the names, the dreams and defeats of Mexico: a nonexistent country, I then thought, invented by my father to nourish my infant imagination with yet another marvelous fiction: a land of Oz with a green cactus road, a landscape and a soul so different from those of the United States that they seemed a fantasy.

A cruel fantasy: the history of Mexico was a history of crushing defeats, whereas I lived in a world, that of my D.C. public school, which celebrated victories, one victory after another, from Yorktown to New Orleans to Chapultepec to Appomattox to San Juan Hill to Belleau Wood: had this nation never known defeat? Sometimes the names of United States victories were the same as the names of Mexico's defeats and humiliations: Monterrey. Veracruz. Chapultepec. Indeed: from the Halls of Montezuma to the shores of Tripoli. In the map of my imagination, as the United States expanded westward, Mexico contracted southward. Miguel Hidalgo, the father of Mexican independence, ended up with his head on exhibit on a lance at the city gates of Chihuahua. Imagine George and Martha beheaded at Mount Vernon.

To the south, sad songs, sweet nostalgia, impossible desires. To the north, self-confidence, faith in progress, boundless optimism. Mexico, the imaginary country, dreamed of a painful past; the United States, the real country, dreamed of a happy future.

The French equate intelligence with rational discourse, the Russians with intense soul-searching. For a Mexican, intelligence is inseparable from maliciousness—in this, as in many other things, we are quite Italian: *furberia,* roguish slyness, and the cult of appearances, *la bella figura,* are Italianate traits present everywhere in Latin America: Rome, more than Madrid, is our spiritual capital in this sense.

For me, as a child, the United States seemed a world where intelligence was equated with energy, zest, enthusiasm. The North American world blinds us with its energy; we cannot see ourselves, we must see *you.* The United States is a world full of cheerleaders, prize-giving, singin' in the rain: the baton twirler, the Oscar awards, the musical comedies cannot be repeated elsewhere; in Mexico, the Hollywood statuette would come dipped in poisoned paint; in France, Gene Kelly would constantly stop in his steps to reflect: *Je danse, donc je suis.*

Many things impressed themselves on me during those years. The United States—would you believe it?—was a country where things worked, where nothing ever broke down: trains, plumbing, roads, punctuality, personal security seemed to function perfectly, at least at the eye level of a young Mexican diplomat's son living in a residential hotel on Washington's Sixteenth Street, facing Meridian Hill Park, where nobody was then mugged and where our superb furnished seven-room apartment cost us 110 pre-inflation dollars a month. Yes, in spite of all the problems, the livin' seemed easy during those long Tidewater summers when I became perhaps the first and only Mexican to prefer grits to guacamole. I also became the original Mexican Calvinist: an invisible taskmaster called Puritanical Duty shadows my every footstep: I shall not deserve anything unless I work relentlessly for it, with iron discipline, day after day. Sloth is sin, and if I do not sit at my typewriter every day at 8 a.m. for a working day of seven to eight hours, I will surely go to hell. No *siestas* for me, alas and alack and *hélas* and *ay-ay-ay:* how I came to envy my Latin brethren, unburdened by the Protestant work ethic, and why must I, to this very day, read the complete works of Hermann Broch and scribble in my black notebook on a sunny Mexican beach, instead of lolling the day away and waiting for the coconuts to fall?

But the United States in the thirties went far beyond my personal experience. The nation that Tocqueville had destined to share dominance over half the world realized that, in effect, only a continental state could be a modern state; in the thirties, the U.S.A. had to decide *what to do* with its new worldwide power, and Franklin Roosevelt taught us to believe that the first thing was for the United States to show that it was capable of living up to its ideals. I learned then—my first political lesson—that this is your true greatness, not, as was to be the norm in my lifetime, material wealth, not arrogant power misused against weaker peoples, not ignorant ethnocentrism burning itself out in contempt for others.

As a young Mexican growing up in the U.S., I had a primary impression of a nation of boundless energy, imagination, and the will to confront and solve the great social issues of the times without blinking or looking for scapegoats. It was the impression of a country identified with its own highest principles: political democracy, economic well-being, and faith in its human resources, especially in that most precious of all capital, the renewable wealth of education and research.

Franklin Roosevelt, then, restored America's self-respect in this essential way, not by macho posturing. I saw the United States in the thirties lift itself by its bootstraps from the dead dust of Oklahoma and the gray lines of the unemployed in Detroit, and this image of health was reflected in my daily life, in my reading of Mark Twain, in the images of movies and newspapers, in the North American capacity for mixing fluffy illusion and hard-bitten truth, self-celebration and self-criticism: the madcap heiresses played by Carole Lombard coexisted with the Walker Evans photographs of hungry, old-at-thirty migrant mothers, and the nimble tread of the feet of Fred Astaire did not silence the heavy stomp of the boots of Tom Joad.

My school—a public school, nonconfessional and coeducational—reflected these realities and their basically egalitarian thrust. I believed in the democratic simplicity of my teachers and chums, and above all I believed I was, naturally, in a totally unselfconscious way, a part of that world. It is important, at all ages and in all occupations, to be "popular" in the United States; I have known no other society where the values of "regularity" are so highly prized. I was popular, I was "regular." Until a day in March—March 18, 1938. On that day, a man from another world, the imaginary country of my childhood, the President of Mexico, Lázaro Cárdenas, nationalized the holdings of foreign oil companies. The headlines in the North American press denounced the "communist" government of Mexico and its "red" president; they demanded the invasion of Mexico in the sacred name of private property, and Mexicans, under international boycott, were invited to drink their oil.

Instantly, surprisingly, I became a pariah in my school. Cold shoulders, aggressive stares, epithets, and sometimes blows. Children know how to be cruel, and the cruelty of their elders is the surest residue of the malaise the young feel toward things strange, things other, things that reveal our own ignorance or insufficiency. This was not reserved for me or for Mexico: at about the same time, an extremely brilliant boy of eleven arrived from Germany. He was a Jew and his family had fled from the Nazis. I shall always remember his face, dark and trembling, his aquiline nose and deep-set, bright eyes with their great sadness; the sensitivity of his hands and the strangeness of it all to his American companions. This young man, Hans Berliner, had a brilliant mathematical mind and he walked and saluted like a Central European; he wore short pants and high woven stockings, Tyrolean jackets and an air of displaced courtesy that infuriated the popular, regular, feisty, knickered, provincial, Depression-era little sons of bitches at Henry Cooke Public School on Thirteenth Street N.W.

The shock of alienation and the shock of recognition are sometimes one and the same. What was different made others afraid, less of what was different than of themselves, of their own incapacity to recognize themselves in the alien.

I discovered that my father's country was real. And that I belonged to it. Mexico was my identity yet I lacked an identity; Hans Berliner suffered more than I—headlines from Mexico are soon forgotten; another great issue becomes all-important for a wonderful ten days' media feast—yet he had an identity as a Central European Jew. I do not know what became of him. Over the years, I have always expected to see him receive a Nobel Prize in one of the sciences. Surely, if he lived, he integrated himself into North American society. I had to look at the photographs of President Cárdenas: he was a man of another lineage; he did not appear in the repertory of glossy, seductive images of the salable North American world. He was a mestizo, Spanish and Indian, with a faraway, green, and liquid look in his eyes, as if he were trying to remember a mute and ancient past.

Was that past mine as well? Could I dream the dreams of the country suddenly revealed in a political act as something more than a demarcation of frontiers on a map or a hillock of statistics in a yearbook? I believe I then had the intuition that I would not rest until I came to grips myself with that common destiny which depended upon still another community: the community of time. The United States had made me believe that we live only for the future; Mexico, Cárdenas, the events of 1938, made me understand that only in an act of the present can we make present the past as well as the future: to be a Mexican was to identify a hunger for being, a desire for dignity rooted in many forgotten centuries and in many centuries yet to come, but rooted here, now, in the instant, in the vigilant time of Mexico I later learned to understand in the stone serpents of Teotihuacán and in the polychrome angels of Oaxaca.

Of course, as happens in childhood, all these deep musings had no proof of existence outside an act that was, more than a prank, a kind of affirmation. In 1939, my father took me to see a film at the old RKO-Keith in Washington. It was called *Man of Conquest* and it starred Richard Dix as Sam Houston. When Dix/Houston proclaimed the secession of the Republic of Texas from Mexico, I jumped on the theater seat and proclaimed on my own and from the full height of my nationalist ten years, "Viva México! Death to the gringos!" My embarrassed father hauled me out of the theater, but his pride in me could not resist leaking my first rebellious act to the *Washington Star*. So I appeared for the first time in a newspaper and became a child celebrity for the acknowledged ten-day span. I read Andy Warhol *avant l'air-brush:* Everyone shall be famous for at least five minutes.

In the wake of my father's diplomatic career, I traveled to Chile and entered fully the universe of the Spanish language, of Latin American politics and its adversities. President Roosevelt had resisted enormous pressures to apply sanctions and even invade Mexico to punish my country for recovering its own wealth. Likewise, he did not try to destabilize the Chilean radicals, communists, and socialists democratically elected to power in Chile under the banners of the Popular Front. In the early forties, the vigor of Chile's political life was contagious: active unions, active parties, electoral campaigns all spoke of the political health of this, the most democratic of Latin American nations. Chile was a politically verbalized country. It was no coincidence that it was also the country of the great Spanish-American poets Gabriela Mistral, Vicente Huidobro, Pablo Neruda.

I only came to know Neruda and became his friend many years later. This King Midas of poetry would write, in his literary testament rescued from a gutted house and a nameless tomb, a beautiful song to the Spanish language. The Conquistadors, he said, took our gold, but they left us their gold: they left us our words. Neruda's gold, I learned in Chile, was the property of all. One afternoon on the beach at Lota in southern Chile, I saw the miners as they came out, mole-like, from their hard work many feet under the sea, extracting the coal of the Pacific Ocean. They sat around a bonfire and sang, to guitar music, a poem from Neruda's *Canto General.* I told them that the author would be thrilled to know that his poem had been set to music.

What author? they asked me in surprise. For them, Neruda's poetry had no author, it came from afar, it had always been sung, like Homer's. It was the poetry, as Croce said of the *Iliad,* "d'un popolo intero poetante," of an entire poetizing people. It was the document of the original identity of poetry and history.

I learned in Chile that Spanish could be the language of free men, I was also to learn in my lifetime, in Chile in 1973, the fragility of both our language and our freedom when Richard Nixon, unable to destroy American democracy, merrily helped to destroy Chilean democracy, the same thing Leonid Brezhnev had done in Czechoslovakia.

An anonymous language, a language that belongs to us all, as Neruda's poem belonged to those miners on the beach, yet a language that can be kidnapped, impoverished, sometimes jailed, sometimes murdered. Let me summarize this paradox: Chile offered me and the other writers of my generation in Santiago both the essential fragility of a cornered language, Spanish, and the protection of the Latin of our times, the lingua franca of the modern world, the English language. At the Grange School, under the awesome beauty of the Andes, José Donoso and Jorge Edwards, Roberto Torretti, the late Luis Alberto Heyremans, and myself, by then all budding amateurs, wrote our first exercises in literature within this mini-Britannia. We all ran strenuous cross-country races, got caned from time to time, and recuperated while reading Swinburne; and we were subjected to huge doses of rugby, Ruskin, porridge for breakfast, and a stiff upper lip in military defeats. But when Montgomery broke through at El Alamein, the assembled school tossed caps in the air and hip-hip-hoorayed to death. In South America, clubs were named after George Canning and football teams after Lord Cochrane; no matter that English help in winning independence led to English economic imperialism, from oil in Mexico to railways in Argentina. There was a secret thrill in our hearts: our Spanish conquerors had been beaten by the English; the defeat of Philip II's invincible Armada compensated for the crimes of Cortés, Pizarro, and Valdivia. If Britain was an empire, at least she was a democratic one.

In Washington, I had begun writing a personal magazine in English, with my own drawings, book reviews, and epochal bits of news. It consisted of a single copy, penciled and crayonned, and its circulation was limited to our apartment building. Then, at age fourteen, in Chile, I embarked on a more ambitious project, along with my schoolmate Roberto Torretti: a vast Caribbean saga that was to culminate in Haiti on a hilltop palace (Sans Souci?) where a black tyrant kept a mad French mistress in a garret. All this was set in the early nineteenth century and in the final scene (Shades of Jane Eyre! Reflections on Rebecca! Fans of Joan Fontaine!) the palace was to burn down, along with the world of slavery.

But where to begin? Torretti and I were, along with our literary fraternity at The Grange, avid readers of Dumas *père*. A self-respecting novel, in our view, had to start in Marseilles, in full view of the Chateau d'If and the martyrdom of Edmond Dantès. But we were writing in Spanish, not in French, and our characters had to speak Spanish. But, what Spanish? My Mexican Spanish, or Roberto's Chilean Spanish? We came to a sort of compromise: the characters would speak like Andalusians. This was probably a tacit homage to the land from which Columbus sailed.

The Mexican painter David Alfaro Siqueiros was then in Chile, painting the heroic murals of a school in the town of Chillán, which had been devastated by one of Chile's periodic earthquakes. He had been implicated in a Stalinist attempt on Trotsky's life in Mexico City and his commission to paint a mural in the Southern Cone was a kind of honorary exile. My father, as chargé d'affaires in Santiago, where his mission was to press the proudly independent Chileans to break relations with the Berlin-Rome Axis, rose above politics in the name of art and received Siqueiros regularly for lunch at the Mexican Embassy, which was a delirious mansion, worthy of William Beckford's follies, built by an enriched Italian tailor called Fallabella, on Santiago's broad Pedro de Valdivia Avenue.

This Gothic grotesque contained a Chinese room with nodding Buddhas, an office in what was known as Westminster Parliamentary style, Napoleonic lobbies, Louis XV dining rooms, Art Deco bedrooms, a Florentine loggia, many busts of Dante, and, finally, a vast Chilean vineyard in the back.

It was here, under the bulging Austral grapes, that I forced Siqueiros to sit after lunch and listen to me read our by then 400-page-long opus. As he drowsed off in the shade, I gained and lost my first reader. The novel, too, was lost; Torretti, who now teaches philosophy of science at the University of Puerto Rico, has no copy; Siqueiros is dead, and, besides, he slept right through my reading. I myself feel about it like Marlowe's Barabbas about fornication: that was in another country, and, besides, the wench is dead. Yet the experience of writing this highly imitative melodrama was not lost on me; its international setting, its self-conscious search for language (or languages, rather) were part of a constant attempt at a breakthrough in my life. My upbringing taught me that cultures are not isolated, and perish when deprived of contact with what is different and challenging. Reading, writing, teaching, learning, are all activities aimed at introducing civilizations to each other. No culture, I believed unconsciously ever since then, and quite consciously today, retains its identity in isolation; identity is attained in contact, in contrast, in breakthrough.

Rhetoric, said William Butler Yeats, is the language of our fight with others; poetry is the name of our fight with ourselves. My passage from English to Spanish determined the concrete expression of what, before, in Washington, had been the revelation of an identity. I wanted to write and I wanted to write in order to show myself that my identity and my country were real: now, in Chile, as I started to scribble my first stories, even publishing them in school magazines, I learned that I must in fact write in Spanish.

The English language, after all, did not need another writer. The English language has always been alive and kicking, and if it ever becomes drowsy, there will always be an Irishman . . .

In Chile I came to know the possibilities of our language for giving wing to freedom and poetry. The impression was enduring; it links me forever to that sad and wonderful land. It lives within me, and it transformed me into a man who knows how to dream, love, insult, and write only in Spanish. It also left me wide open to an incessant interrogation: What happened to this universal language, Spanish, which after the seventeenth century ceased to be a language of life, creation, dissatisfaction, and personal power and became far too often a language of mourning, sterility, rhetorical applause, and abstract power? Where were the threads of my tradition, where could I, writing in mid-twentieth century in Latin America, find the direct link to the great living presences I was then starting to read, my lost Cervantes, my old Quevedo, dead because he could not tolerate one more winter, my Góngora, abandoned in a gulf of loneliness?

At sixteen I finally went to live permanently in Mexico and there I found the answers to my quest for identity and language, in the thin air of a plateau of stone and dust that is the negative Indian image of another highland, that of central Spain. But, between Santiago and Mexico City, I spent six wonderful months in Argentina. They were, in spite of their brevity, so important in this reading and writing of myself that I must give them their full worth. Buenos Aires was then, as always, the most beautiful, sophisticated, and civilized city in Latin America, but in the summer of 1944, as street pavements melted in the heat and the city smelled of cheap wartime gasoline, rawhide from the port, and chocolate éclairs from the *confiterías,* Argentina had experienced a succession of military coups: General Rawson had overthrown President Castillo of the cattle oligarchy, but General Ramírez had then overthrown Rawson, and now General Farrell had overthrown Ramírez. A young colonel called Juan Domingo Perón was General Farrell's up-and-coming Minister of Labor, and I heard an actress by the name of Eva Duarte play the "great women of history" on Radio Belgrano. A stultifying hack novelist who went by the pen name Hugo Wast was assigned to the Ministry of Education under his real name, Martínez Zuviría, and brought all his anti-Semitic, undemocratic, pro-fascist phobias to the Buenos Aires high-school system, which I had suddenly been plunked into. Coming from the America of the New Deal, the ideals of revolutionary Mexico, and the politics of the Popular Front in Chile, I could not stomach this, rebelled, and was granted a full summer of wandering around Buenos Aires, free for the first time in my life, following my preferred tango orchestras—Canaro, D'Arienzo, and Anibal Troilo, alias Pichuco—as they played all summer long in the Renoir-like shade and light of the rivers and pavilions of El Tigre and Maldonado. Now the comics were in Spanish: Mutt and Jeff were Benitín y Eneas. But Argentina had its own comic-book imperialism: through the magazines *Billiken* and *Patoruzú,* all the children of Latin America knew from the crib that "las Malvinas son Argentinas."

Two very important things happened. First, I lost my virginity. We lived in an apartment building on the leafy corner of Callao and Quintana, and after 10 a.m. nobody was there except myself, an old and deaf Polish doorkeeper, and a beautiful Czech woman, aged thirty, whose husband was a film producer. I went up to ask her for her *Sintonía,* which was the radio guide of the forties, because I wanted to know when Evita was doing Joan of Arc. She said that had passed, but the next program was Madame Du Barry. I wondered if Madame Du Barry's life was as interesting as Joan of Arc's. She said it was certainly less saintly, and, besides, it could be emulated. How? I said innocently. And thereby my beautiful apprenticeship. We made each other very happy. And also very sad: this was not the liberty of love, but rather its libertine variety: we loved in hiding. I was too young to be a real sadist. So it had to end.

The other important thing was that I started reading Argentine literature, from the gaucho poems to Sarmiento's *Memories of Provincial Life* to Cané's *Juvenilia* to Güiraldes's *Don Segundo Sombra* to . . . to . . . to— and this was as good as discovering that Joan of Arc was also sexy—to Borges. I have never wanted to meet Borges personally because he belongs to that summer in B.A. He belongs to my personal discovery of Latin American literature.

2

Latin American extremes: if Cuba is the Andalusia of the New World, the Mexican plateau is its Castile. Parched and brown, inhabited by suspicious cats burnt too many times by foreign invasions, Mexico is the sacred zone of a secret hope: the gods shall return.

Mexican space is closed, jealous, and self-contained. In contrast, Argentine space is open and dependent on the foreign: migrations, exports, imports, words. Mexican space was vertically sacralized thousands of years ago. Argentine space patiently awaits its horizontal profanation.

I arrived on the Mexican highland from the Argentine pampa when I was sixteen years old. As I said, it was better to study in a country where the Minister of Education was Jaime Torres Bodet than in a country where he was Hugo Wast. This was not the only contrast, or the most important one. A land isolated by its very nature—desert, mountain, chasm, sea, jungle, fire, ice, fugitive mists, and a sun that never blinks—Mexico is a multi-level temple that rises abruptly, blind to horizons, an arrow that wounds the sky but refuses the dangerous frontiers of the land, the canyons, the sierras without a human footprint, whereas the pampa is nothing if not an eternal frontier, the very portrait of the horizon, the sprawling flatland of a latent expansion awaiting, like a passive lover, the vast and rich overflow from that concentration of the transitory represented by the commercial metropolis of Buenos Aires, what Ezequiel Martínez Estrada called Goliath's head on David's body.

A well-read teenager, I had tasted the literary culture of Buenos Aires, then dominated by *Sur* magazine and Victoria Ocampo's enlightened mixture of the cattle oligarchy of the Pampas and the cultural clerisy of Paris, a sort of Argentinian cosmopolitanism. It then became important to appreciate the verbal differences between the Mexican culture, which, long before Paul Valéry, knew itself to be mortal, and the Argentine culture, founded on the optimism of powerful migratory currents from Europe, innocent of sacred stones or aboriginal promises. Mexico, closed to immigration by the TTT—the Tremendous Texas Trauma that in 1836 cured us once and for all of the temptation to receive Caucasian colonists because they had airport names like Houston and Austin and Dallas—devoted its population to breeding like rabbits. Blessed by the Pope, Coatlicue, and Jorge Negrete, we are, all eighty million of us, Catholics in the Virgin Mary, misogynists in the stone goddesses, and *machistas* in the singing, pistol-packing *charro*.

The pampa goes on waiting: twenty-five million Argentinians today; scarcely five million more than in 1945, half of them in Buenos Aires.

Language in Mexico is ancient, old as the oldest dead. The eagles of the Indian empire fell, and it suffices to read the poems of the defeated to understand the vein of sadness that runs through Mexican literature, the feeling that words are identical to a farewell: "Where shall we go to now, O my friends?" asks the Aztec poet of the Fall of Tenochtitlán: "The smoke lifts; the fog extends. Cry, my friends. Cry, oh cry." And the contemporary poet Xavier Villaurrutia, four centuries later, sings from the bed of the same lake, now dried up, from its dry stones:

> *In the midst of a silence deserted as a street before the crime*
> *Without even breathing so that nothing may disturb my death*
> *In this wall-less solitude*
> *When the angels fled*
> *In the grave of my bed I leave my bloodless statue.*

A sad, underground language, forever being lost and recovered. I soon learned that Spanish as spoken in Mexico answered to six unwritten rules:

* Never use the familiar *tu*—thou—if you can use the formal you— *usted.*
* Never use the first-person possessive pronoun, but rather the second-person, as in "This is *your* home."
* Always use the first-person singular to refer to your own troubles, as in "Me fue del carajo, mano." But use the first-person plural when referring to your successes, as in "During our term, we distributed three million acres."
* Never use one diminutive if you can use five in a row.
* Never use the imperative when you can use the subjunctive.
* And only then, when you have exhausted these ceremonies of communication, bring out your verbal knife and plunge it deep into the other's heart: "Chinga a tu madre, cabrón."

The language of Mexicans springs from abysmal extremes of power and impotence, domination and resentment. It is the mirror of an overabundance of history, a history that devours itself before extinguishing and then regenerating itself, phoenix-like, once again. Argentina, on the contrary, is a tabula rasa, and it demands a passionate verbalization. I do not know another country that so fervently—with the fervor of Buenos Aires, Borges would say—opposes the silence of its infinite space, its physical and mental pampa, demanding: Please, *verbalize* me! Martin Fierro, Carlos Gardel, Jorge Luis Borges: reality must be captured, desperately, in the verbal web of the gaucho poem, the sentimental tango, the metaphysical tale: the pampa of the gaucho becomes the garden of the tango becomes the forked paths of literature.

What is forked? What is said.

What is said? What is forked.

Everything: Space. Time. Language. History. Our history. The history of Spanish America.

I read *Ficciones* as I flew north on a pontoon plane, courtesy of Pan American Airways. It was wartime, we had to have priority; all cameras were banned, and glazed plastic screens were put on our windows several minutes before we landed. Since I was not an Axis spy, I read Borges as we splashed into Santos, saying that the best proof that the Koran is an Arab book is that not a single camel is mentioned in its pages. I started thinking that the best proof that Borges is an Argentinian is in everything he has to evoke because it isn't there, as we glided into an invisible Rio de Janeiro. And as we flew out of Bahia, I thought that Borges invents a world because he needs it. I need, therefore I imagine.

By the time we landed in Trinidad, "Funes the Memorious" and "Pierre Ménard, Author of Don Quixote" had introduced me, without my being aware, to the genealogy of the serene madmen, the children of Erasmus. I did not know then that this was the most illustrious family of modern fiction, since it went, backwards, from Pierre Ménard to Don Quixote himself. During two short lulls in Santo Domingo (then, horrifyingly, called Ciudad Trujillo) and Port-au-Prince, I had been prepared by Borges to encounter my wonderful friends Toby Shandy, who reconstructs in his miniature cabbage patch the battlefields of Flanders he was not able to experience historically; Jane Austen's Catherine Moreland and Gustave Flaubert's Madame Bovary, who like Don Quixote believe in what they read; Dickens's Mr. Micawber, who takes his hopes to be realities; Dostoevsky's Myshkin, an idiot because he gives the benefit of the doubt to the good possibility of mankind; Pérez Galdós's Nazarín, who is mad because he believes that each human being can daily be Christ, and who is truly St. Paul's madman: "Let him who seems wise among you become mad, so that he might truly become wise."

As we landed at Miami airport, the glazed windows disappeared once and for all and I knew that, like Pierre Ménard, a writer must always face the mysterious duty of literally reconstructing a spontaneous work. And so I met my tradition: *Don Quixote* was a book waiting to be written. The history of Latin America was a history waiting to be lived.

3

When I finally arrived in Mexico, I discovered that my father's imaginary country was real, but more fantastic than any imaginary land. It was as real as its physical and spiritual borders: Mexico, the only frontier between the industrialized and the developing worlds; the frontier between my country and the United States, but also between all of Latin America and the United States, and between the Catholic Mediterranean and the Protestant Anglo-Saxon strains in the New World.

It was with this experience and these questions that I approached the gold and mud of Mexico, the imaginary, imagined country, finally real but only real if I saw it from a distance that would assure me, because of the very fact of separation, that my desire for reunion with it would be forever urgent, and only real if I wrote it. Having attained some sort of perspective, I was finally able to write a few novels where I could speak of the scars of revolution, the nightmares of progress, and the perseverance of dreams.

I wrote with urgency because my absence became a destiny, yet a shared destiny: that of my own body as a young man, that of the old body of my country, and that of the problematic and insomniac body of my language. I could, perhaps, identify the former without too much trouble: Mexico and myself. But the language belonged to us all, to the vast community that writes and talks and thinks in Spanish. And without this language I could give no reality to either myself or my land. Language thus became the center of my personal being and of the possibility of forming my own destiny and that of my country into a shared destiny.

But nothing is shared in the abstract. Like bread and love, language and ideas are shared with human beings. My first contact with literature was sitting on the knees of Alfonso Reyes when the Mexican writer was ambassador to Brazil in the earlier thirties. Reyes had brought the Spanish classics back to life for us; he had written the most superb books on Greece; he was the most lucid of literary theoreticians; in fact, he had translated all of Western culture into Latin American terms. In the late forties, he was living in a little house the color of the *mamey* fruit, in Cuernavaca. He would invite me to spend weekends with him, and since I was eighteen and a night prowler, I kept him company from eleven in the morning, when Don Alfonso would sit in a café and toss verbal bouquets at the girls strolling around the plaza that was then a garden of laurels and not, as it has become, of cement. I do not know if the square, ruddy man seated at the next table was a British consul crushed by the nearness of the volcano; but if Reyes, enjoying the spectacle of the world, quoted Lope de Vega and Garcilaso, our neighbor the *mescal* drinker would answer, without looking at us, with the more somber *stanze* of Marlowe and John Donne. Then we would go to the movies in order, Reyes said, to bathe in contemporary epic, and it was only at night that he would start scolding me: You have not read Stendhal yet? The world didn't start five minutes ago, you know.

He could irritate me. I read, against his classical tastes, the most modern, the most strident books, without understanding that I was learning his lesson: there is no creation without tradition; the "new" is an inflection on a preceding form; novelty is always a variation on the past. Borges said that Reyes wrote the best Spanish prose of our times. He taught me that culture had a smile, that the intellectual tradition of the whole world was ours by birthright, and that Mexican literature was important because it was literature, not because it was Mexican.

One day I got up very early (or maybe I came in very late from a binge) and saw him seated at five in the morning, working at his table, amid the aroma of the jacaranda and the bougainvillea. He was a diminutive Buddha, bald and pink, almost one of those elves who cobble shoes at night while the family sleeps. He liked to quote Goethe: Write at dawn, skim the cream of the day, then you can study crystals, intrigue at court, and make love to your kitchen maid. Writing in silence, Reyes did not smile. His world, in a way, ended on a funereal day in February 1913 when his insurrectionist father, General Bernardo Reyes, fell riddled by machine-gun bullets in the Zócalo in Mexico City, and with him fell what was left of Mexico's Belle Epoque, the long and cruel peace of Porfirio Díaz.

The smile of Alfonso Reyes had ashes on its lips. He had written, as a response to history, the great poem of exile and distance from Mexico: the poem of a cruel Iphigenia, the Mexican Iphigenia of the valley of Anáhuac:

> *I was another, being myself;*
> *I was he who wanted to leave.*
> *To return is to cry. I do not repent of this wide world.*
> *It is not I who return,*
> *But my shackled feet.*

My father had remained in Buenos Aires as Mexican chargé d'affaires, with instructions to frown on Argentina's sympathies toward the Axis. My mother profited from his absence to enroll me in a Catholic school in

Mexico City. The brothers who ruled this institution were preoccupied with something that had never entered my head: sin. At the start of the school year, one of the brothers would come before the class with a white lily in his hand and say: "This is a Catholic youth before kissing a girl." Then he would throw the flower on the floor, dance a little jig on it, pick up the bedraggled object, and confirm our worst suspicions: "This is a Catholic boy after . . ."

Well, all this made life very tempting. Retrospectively, I would agree with Luis Buñuel that sex without sin is like an egg without salt. The priests at the Colegio Francés made sex irresistible for us; they also made leftists of us by their constant denunciation of Mexican liberalism and especially of Benito Juárez. The sexual and political temptations became very great in a city where provincial mores and sharp social distinctions made it very difficult to have normal sexual relationships with young or even older women.

All this led, as I say, to a posture of rebellion that for me crystallized in the decision to be a writer. My father, by then back from Argentina, sternly said, Okay, go out and be a writer, but not at my expense. I became a very young journalist at the weekly *Siempre,* but my family pressured me to enter law school, or, in the desert of Mexican literature, I would literally die of hunger and thirst. I was sent to visit Alfonso Reyes in his enormous library-house, where he seemed more diminutive than ever, ensconced in a tiny corner he saved for his bed among the Piranesi-like perspective of volume piled upon volume. He said to me: "Mexico is a very formalistic country. If you don't have a title, you are nobody: *nadie, ninguno.* A title is like the handle on a cup; without it, no one will pick you up. You must become a *licenciado,* a lawyer; then you can do whatever you please, as I did."

So I entered the School of Law at the National University, where, as I feared, learning tended to be by rote. The budding explosion in the student population was compounded by cynical teachers who would spend the whole hour of class taking attendance on the two hundred students of civil law, from Aguilar to Zapata. But there were great exceptions of true teachers who understood that the law is inseparable from culture, from morality, and from justice. Foremost among these were the exiles from defeated Republican Spain, who enormously enriched Mexican universities, publishing houses, the arts, and the sciences. Don Manuel Pedroso, former dean of the University of Seville, made the study of law compatible with my literary inclinations. When I would bitterly complain about the dryness and boredom of learning the penal or mercantile codes by heart, he would counter: "Forget the codes. Read Dostoevsky, read Balzac. There's all you have to know about criminal or commercial law." He also made me see that Stendhal was right that the best model for a well-structured novel is the Napoleonic Code of Civil Law. Anyway, I found that culture consists of connections, not of separations: to specialize is to isolate.

Sex was another story, but Mexico City was then a manageable town of one million people, beautiful in its extremes of colonial and nineteenth-century elegance and the garishness of its exuberant and dangerous nightlife. My friends and I spent the last years of our adolescence and the first of our manhood in a succession of cantinas, brothels, strip joints, and silver-varnished nightclubs where the bolero was sung and the mambo danced; whores, mariachis, magicians were our companions as we struggled through our first readings of D. H. Lawrence and Aldous Huxley, James Joyce and André Gide, T. S. Eliot and Thomas Mann. Salvador Elizondo and I were the two would-be writers of the group, and if the realistic grain of *La Región Más Transparente* (*Where the Air Is Clear*) was sown in this, our rather somnambulistic immersion in the spectral nightlife of Mexico City, it is also true that the cruel imagination of an instant in Elizondo's *Farabeuf* had the same background experience. We would go to a whorehouse oddly called El Buen Tono, choose a poor Mexican girl who usually said her name was Gladys and she came from Guadalajara, and go to our respective rooms. One time, a horrible scream was heard and Gladys from Guadalajara rushed out, crying and streaming blood. Elizondo, in the climax of love, had slashed her armpit with a razor.

Another perspective, another distance for approximation, another possibility of sharing a language. In 1950 I went to Europe to do graduate work in international law at the University of Geneva. Octavio Paz had just published two books that had changed the face of Mexican literature, *Libertad Bajo Palabra* and *El Laberinto de la Soledad.* My friends and I had read those books aloud in Mexico, dazzled by a poetics that managed simultaneously to renew our language from within and to connect it to the language of the world.

At age thirty-six, Octavio Paz was not very different from what he is today. Writers born in 1914, like Paz and Julio Cortázar, surely signed a Faustian pact at the very mouth of hell's trenches; so many poets died in that war that someone had to take their place. I remember Paz in the so-called existentialist nightclubs of the time in Paris, in discussion with the very animated and handsome Albert Camus, who alternated philosophy and the boogie-woogie in La Rose Rouge. I remember Paz in front of the large windows of a gallery on the Place Vendôme, reflecting Max Ernst's great postwar painting "Europe after the Rain," and the painter's profile as an ancient eagle; and I tell myself that the poetics of Paz is an art of civilizations, a movement of encounters. Paz the poet meets Paz the thinker, because his poetry is a form of thought and his thought is a form of poetry; and as a result of this meeting, an encounter of civilizations takes place. Paz introduces civilizations to one another, makes them presentable before it is too late, because behind the wonderful smile of Camus, fixed forever in the absurdity of death, behind the bright erosion of painting by Max Ernst and the crystals of the Place Vendôme, Octavio and I, when we met, could hear the voice of *el poeta Libra,* Ezra, lamenting the death of the best, "for an old bitch gone in the teeth, for a botched civilization."

Octavio Paz has offered civilizations the mirror of their mortality, as Paul Valéry did, but also the reflection of their survival in an epidemic of meetings and erotic risks. In the generous friendship of Octavio Paz, I learned that there were no privileged centers of culture, race, or politics; that nothing should be left out of literature, because our time is a time of deadly reduction. The essential orphanhood of our time is seen in the poetry and thought of Paz as a challenge to be met through the renewed flux of human knowledge, of all human knowledge. We have not finished thinking, imagining, acting. It is still possible to know the world; we are unfinished men and women.

> I am not at the crossroads;
> > to choose
> is to go wrong.

For my generation in Mexico, the problem did not consist in discovering our modernity but in discovering our tradition. The latter was brutally denied by the comatose, petrified teaching of the classics in Mexican secondary schools: one had to bring Cervantes back to life in spite of a school system fatally oriented toward the ideal of universities as sausage factories; in spite of the more grotesque forms of Mexican nationalism of the time. A Marxist teacher once told me it was un-Mexican to read Kafka; a fascist critic said the same thing (this has been Kafka's Kafkian destiny everywhere), and a rather sterile Mexican author gave a pompous lecture at the Bellas Artes warning that readers who read Proust would proustitute themselves.

To be a writer in Mexico in the fifties, you had to be with Alfonso Reyes and with Octavio Paz in the assertion that Mexico was not an isolated, virginal province but very much part of the human race and its cultural tradition; we were all, for good or evil, contemporary with all men and women.

In Geneva, I regained my perspective. I rented a garret overlooking the beautiful old square of the Bourg-du-Four, established by Julius Caesar as the Forum Boarium two millennia ago. The square was filled with coffeehouses and old bookstores. The girls came from all over the world; they were beautiful, and they were independent. When they were kissed, one did not become a sullied lily. We had salt on our lips. We loved each other, and I also loved going to the little island where the lake meets the river, to spend long hours reading. Since it was called Jean-Jacques Rousseau Island, I took along my volume of the *Confessions.* Many things came together then. A novel was the transformation of experience into history. The modern epic had been the epic of the first-person singular, of the I, from St. Augustine to Abélard to Dante to Rousseau to Stendhal to Proust. Joyce de-Joyced fiction: Here comes everybody! But H.C.E. did not collectively save the degraded Ego from exhaustion, self-doubt, and, finally, self-forgetfulness. When Odysseus says that he is nonexistent, we know and he knows that he is disguised; when Beckett's characters proclaim their nonbeing, we know that "the fact is notorious": they are no longer disguised. Kafka's man has been forgotten; no one can remember K the land surveyor; finally, as Milan Kundera tells us, nobody can remember Prague, Czechoslovakia, history.

I did not yet know this as I spent many reading hours on the little island of Rousseau at the intersection of Lake Geneva and the Rhône River back in 1951. But I vaguely felt that there was something beyond the exploration of the self that actually made the idea of human personality possible if the paths beyond it were explored. Cervantes taught us that a book is a book is a book: Don Quixote does not invite us into "reality" but into an act of the imagination where all things are real: the characters are active psychological entities, but also the archetypes they herald and always the figures from whence they come, which were unimaginable, unthinkable, like Don Quixote, before they became characters first and archetypes later.

Could I, a Mexican who had not yet written his first book, sitting on a bench on an early spring day as the *bise* from the Jura Mountains quieted down, have the courage to explore for myself, with my language, with my tradition, with my friends and influences, that region where the literary figure bids us consider it in the uncertainty of its gestation? Cervantes did it in a precise cultural situation: he brought into existence the modern world by having Don Quixote leave his secure village (a village whose name has been, let us remember, forgotten) and take to the open roads, the roads of the unsheltered, the unknown, and the different, there to lose what he read and to gain what we, the readers, read in him.

The novel is forever traveling Don Quixote's road, from the security of the analogous to the adventure of the different and even the unknown. In my way, this is the road I wanted to travel. I read Rousseau, or the adventures of the I; Joyce and Faulkner, or the adventures of the We; Cervantes, or the adventures of the You he calls the Idle, the Amiable Reader: you. And I read, in a shower of fire and in the lightning of enthusiasm, Rimbaud. His mother asked him what a particular poem was about. And he answered: "I have wanted to say what it says there, literally and in all other senses." This statement of Rimbaud's has been an inflexible rule for me and for what we are all writing today; and the present-day vigor of the literature of the Hispanic world, to which I belong, is not alien to this Rimbaudian approach to writing: Say what you mean, literally and in all other senses.

I think I imagined in Switzerland what I would try to write someday, but first I would have to do my apprenticeship. Only after many years would I be able to write what I then imagined; only years later, when I not only knew that I had the tools with which to do it, but also, and equally important, when I knew that if I did not write, death would not do it for me. You start by writing to live. You end by writing so as not to die. Love is the marriage of this desire and this fear. The women I have loved I have desired for themselves, but also because I feared myself.

4

My first European experience came to a climax in the summer of 1950. It was a hot, calm evening on Lake Zurich, and some wealthy Mexican friends had invited me to dinner at the elegant Baur-au-Lac Hotel. The summer restaurant was a floating terrace on the lake. You reached it by a gangplank, and it was lighted by paper lanterns and flickering candles. As I unfolded my stiff white napkin amid the soothing tinkle of silver and glass, I raised my eyes and saw the group dining at the next table.

Three ladies sat there with a man in his seventies. This man was stiff and elegant, dressed in double-breasted white serge and immaculate shirt and tie. His long, delicate fingers sliced a cold pheasant, almost with daintiness. Yet even in eating he seemed to me unbending, with a ramrod-back, military bearing. His aged face showed "a growing fatigue," but the pride with which his lips and jaws were set sought desperately to hide the fact, while the eyes twinkled with "the fiery play of fancy."

As the carnival lights of that summer's night in Zurich played with a fire of their own on the features I now recognized, Thomas Mann's face was a theater of implicit, quiet emotions. He ate and let the ladies do the talking; he was, in my fascinated eyes, a meeting place where solitude gives birth to beauty unfamiliar and perilous, but also to the perverse and the illicit. Thomas Mann had managed, out of this solitude, to find the affinity "between the personal destiny of [the] author and that of his contemporaries in general." Through him, I had imagined that the products of this solitude and of this affinity were named art (created by one) and civilization (created by all). He spoke so surely, in *Death in Venice,* of the "tasks imposed upon him by his own ego and the European soul" that as I, paralyzed with admiration, saw him there that night I dared not conceive of such an affinity in our own Latin American culture, where the extreme demands of a ravaged, voiceless continent often killed the voice of the self and made a hollow political monster of the voice of the society, or killed it, giving birth to a pitiful, sentimental dwarf.

Yet, as I recalled my passionate reading of everything he wrote, from *Blood of the Walsungs* to *Dr. Faustus,* I could not help but feel that, in spite of the vast differences between his culture and ours, in both of them literature in the end asserted itself through a relationship between the visible and the invisible worlds of narration. A novel should "gather up the threads of many human destinies in the warp of a single idea"; the I, the You, and the We were only separate and dried up because of a lack of imagination. Unbeknownst to him, I left Thomas Mann sipping his demitasse as midnight approached and the floating restaurant bobbed slightly and the Chinese lanterns quietly flickered out. I shall always thank him for silently teaching me that, in literature, you know only what you imagine.

The Mexico of the forties and fifties I wrote about in *La Región Más Transparente* was an imagined Mexico, just as the Mexico of the eighties and nineties I am writing about in *Cristóbal Nonato (Christopher Unborn)* is totally imagined. I fear that we would know nothing of Balzac's Paris and Dickens's London if they, too, had not invented them. When in the spring of 1951 I took a Dutch steamer back to the New World, I had with me the ten Bible-paper tomes of the Pléiade edition of Balzac. This phrase of his has been a central creed of mine: "Wrest words from silence and ideas from obscurity." The reading of Balzac—one of the most thorough and metamorphosing experiences of my life as a novelist—taught me that one must exhaust reality, transcend it, in order to reach, to try to reach, that absolute which is made of the atoms of the relative: in Balzac, the marvelous worlds of *Séraphita* or *Louis Lambert* rest on the commonplace worlds of *Père Goriot* and *César Birotteau.* Likewise, the Mexican reality of *Where the Air Is Clear* and *The Death of Artemio Cruz* existed only to clash with my imagination, my negation, and my perversion of the facts, because, remember, I had learned to imagine Mexico before I ever knew Mexico.

This was, finally, a way of ceasing to tell what I understood and trying to tell, behind all the things I knew, the really important things: what I did not know. *Aura* illustrates this stance much too clearly, I suppose. I prefer to find it in a scene set in a cantina in *A Change of Skin,* or in a taxi drive in *The Hydra Head.* I never wanted to resolve an enigma, but to point out that there *was* an enigma.

I always tried to tell my critics: Don't classify me, read me. I'm a writer, not a genre. Do not look for the purity of the novel according to some nostalgic canon, do not ask for generic affiliation but rather for a dialogue, if not for the outright abolition, of genre; not for one language but for many languages at odds with one another; not, as Bakhtin would put it, for unity of style but for *heteroglossia,* not for monologic but for dialogic imagination. I'm afraid that, by and large, in Mexico at least, I failed in this enterprise. Yet I am not disturbed by this fact, because of what I have just said: language is a shared and sharing part of culture that cares little about formal classifications and much about vitality and connection, for culture itself perishes in purity or isolation, which is the deadly wages of perfection. Like bread and love, language is shared with others. And human beings share a tradition. There is no creation without tradition. No one creates from nothing.

I went back to Mexico, but knew that I would forever be a wanderer in search of perspective: this was my real baptism, not the religious or civil ceremonies I have mentioned. But no matter where I went, Spanish would be the language of my writing and Latin America the culture of my language.

Neruda, Reyes, Paz; Washington, Santiago de Chile, Buenos Aires, Mexico City, Paris, Geneva; Cervantes, Balzac, Rimbaud, Thomas Mann: only with all the shared languages, those of my places and friends and masters, was I able to approach the fire of literature and ask it for a few sparks.

Strange, powerful, poetic
Lopate could use some of
this dignity

WOLE SOYINKA

Wole Soyinka (1934–) is a Nigerian playwright, novelist, essayist, and poet. He is best known for his innovative work in the theater, where he has mixed African folklore and mythology with Western absurdist techniques in plays such as A Dance in the Forests, The Strong Breed, Kongi's Harvest, *and* The Road.

During the Nigerian civil war (1967–1969), Soyinka was imprisoned without charge or trial. The Man Died: Prison Notes *is a searing account of that period, particularly impressive because Soyinka continued to experiment with literary techniques in telling the story of his incarceration while living through it. "Why Do I Fast?" conveys the author's strength and utter conviction to remain true to his ideals, without, however, minimizing the inner stress and fear that the self would break down that the situation threatened. Soyinka has also written an enchanting classic of African autobiography,* Ake: The Years of Childhood. *In 1986 he was awarded the Nobel Prize for literature.*

odd contrast w/ this essay

Why Do I Fast?

W H Y do I fast? I do not mean, why do I fast now? I have settled that in terms of continuing conflict. But why do I fast at all? Why have I, at any given time, suddenly decided—I must now do without food for some time? Perhaps I ought to settle that in my mind before I am trapped in a fatal demand of my own self-indulgence.

Yes, self-indulgence. A sensual self-indulgence. It is important to separate the area of will-power from the drugged immersion in rainbow-tinted ether. For I suspect that it is the truly sensual that take easily to fasting.

I have read of, but never experienced even a nearness of the sensation of freezing to death. I understand that after a while the body ceases to feel pain, sinks blissfully into sleep. Rest. I think fasting must be like that. It begins with that critical hump which is in fact a very brief passage and occurs during the first three days. The body either succumbs at this point or afterwards condemns the very thought of food. I find it best to provoke this hump as early as possible. When the decision to fast is taken, I dwell on the next meal in my mind, I let my body crave it and I let the food come to me. I am hungry. I open the dishes and sniff, I dwell on the tasting, the mastication, the swallowing. I salivate. I dwell on my body's satisfaction, the heavy body-contented sleep that must follow if I fill my hunger from this plenitude. A fierce protest commences in the pit of the stomach and I let it rage. Armed with the power of my veto, I stand aside and enjoy the violent conflict, waiting for my cue to thump the gavel. The moment arrives and I cover the food with a slow deliberate motion saying: This taste cannot die. I have known it and will know it again. Taste is selectiveness, choice. I am denied choice and thus all taste is rendered non-existent. Pleasure also is choice; it is fulfilment and choice. My existence is a crippled one, it debases fulfilment by restricting fields of fulfilment. To take pleasure in the granted area of fulfilment is self-betrayal. To eat without pleasure is to betray my nature. From now on I will not betray my nature.

Sometimes a day or two later the stomach devils come out again to play. But I view their antics with dispassionate interest. Food cannot tempt me but I wonder sometimes what I would do if I had, within reach, vitamin pills. I do after all entertain fears of the gut-walls collapsing, of unfed enzymes atrophying and dying, of perpetual damages done to the body by excess. I know it is wiser to take a glass of orange juice a day but I am not capable of the compromise. Orange juice is too close to food. Vitamin pills on the other hand do not seem insiduous saboteurs of will-power; that test has luckily never come. So I accept only a glass of water each day, sipped at intervals. I ensure that I do not exceed the one glass a day.

The body achieves, of course, true weightlessness. I am blown about by the lightest breeze, by the lightest lyrical thought or metaphor. The body is like an onion and I watch the flesh peel off, layer by layer, layer by layer. And this is the risk, it is this condition that begins the danger of self-indulgence. For, by the fourth day the will is no longer involved. I become hungry for the show-down, the moment when I must choose between death or surrender. I resent even the glass of water and begin to cheat. Each day it gets lesser by a fraction. Once, for a whole day I did not drink at all. In the morning I said, I shall drink at noon. At noon I began to cheat, procrastinating until I decided I shall drink an entire cupful when the sun goes down. I lay in bed until dark, then said, I did not see the sun go down.

What do I do all day? I watch light motes in the air. When eyes are shut a whole universe of colours fills the dome of darkness behind the eyelids. In extreme fasts the open eye is treated to the same display on a lighter, vaster scale. The air is broken up in swirls of coloured dots. Each speck of dust in a sunbeam is a fiery planet in the galaxy, its motion sedately plotted, imbued with immense significance. In the muting of sounds which overtakes the senses the mind drifts easily into transcendental moods, wiping out environment, reality, fragmenting slowly till it becomes one with specks of dust in ether.

Only sunsets prove unbearable, for while sounds are muted, colours are intensified, and the sunsets turn raw, cannibalistic, fanged and blooded as if the drooling demon of day is sinking its teeth in the lap of a loud lascivious courtesan, reeking of gore. Not so the storm-clouds with their copper rims and light golden depths hinting of caverns beyond the passages of dieties. The stars fade into nothingness; only the silence exists that brought them forth.

Rejoicing, I watch my body waste. I identify but do not prohibit the human satisfaction which comes from the pain and fear, the concern and incredulity in their eyes as the gaolers prowl round, on orders to report the slightest hint of weakening. Something in me, a glee I recognize as profoundly human laughs and condescends when a warder stops and says, "Please, this is not possible. You must stop." The Grand Seer enters . . . "I have come to beg you. I ask you to think of your family, your wife, your children." I protest—but I am well and strong. "You cannot see yourself. I can. We all do. You don't know what you look like. You are a living skeleton." *in 10 days?*

It is strange, but the effect they all have on me is to resent even that cup of water. Each time the Grand Seer has turned up I have thrown the rest away. His concern adds to the growing sense of superhumanity. I need neither drink nor food. Soon I shall need no air.

The hallucinations, the brief fainting spells in which walls, earth and sky move suddenly about me I accept and control. And so I know it is no illusion when one night I detect the motion of a terrestrial object among the stars. Seeking beyond stars into that pool of silence I fasten suddenly on this fluid speck, sedate and self-assured in its predetermined orbit. Another hallucination? The passage was brief since I could only follow its motion through my barred window. Yet I am so certain that I wait again the following day and the next. And remember its identity. A heavenly body but a human satellite. The immensity of the moment—the moment of certainty—becomes imperishable. Locked and barred from a more direct communion, a human assertiveness has reached me through the cosmos, a proud, inextinguishable promethean spark among dead bodies, astral wraiths, failed deities, tinsel decorations in barren space. Sign, probe and question I accept you, incandescent human dare. Extension of my restless eye and mind I claim you and absorb you. I transmit you, pore of my skin, electronic core of my will, prowl . . . prowl . . .

Tenth day of fast. By day a speck of dust on a sun-beam. By night a slow shuttle in the cosmos. Night . . .

A clear night, and the moon pouring into my cell. I thought, a shroud? I have returned again and again to this night of the greatest weakness and lassitude, to the hours of lying still on the stark clear-headed acceptance of the thought that said: it is painless. The body weakens and breath slows to a stop. Gone was the fear that a life-urge might make me retreat at this moment. I held no direct thought of death, only of the probable end of a course of action, I felt the weakness in the joints of my bones and within in the bone itself. A dry tongue that rasped loosely in the mouth. I felt a great repose in me, an enervating peace of the world and the universe within me, a peace that truly "passeth all understanding." I wrote . . .

> *I anoint my flesh*
> *Thought is hallowed in the lean*
> *Oil of solitude*
> *I call you forth, all, upon*
> *Terraces of light. Let the dark*
> *Withdraw*
>
> *I anoint my voice*
> *And let it sound hereafter*
> *Or dissolve upon its lonely passage*

In your void. Voices new
Shall rouse the echoes when
Evil shall again arise

I anoint my heart
Within its flame I lay
Spent ashes of your hate—
Let evil die.

No one came on the eleventh day. I thought the gaoler when he peeped in my cell looked wary, even frightened. I mistook the cause. It had happened. It was happening, happening even then. I understood now why the Seer had laid waste their paradise. I understood when they stormed into my Crypt the following day, the twelfth, questioning and threatening. I wedged myself between door and wall for support, seeking to disguise my weakness. It was a long way, a long height from which to cast down my gaze and understand. The sounds, the words, the gestures were plain and yet remote. The presence of strange faces, and the Grand Seer among them concerned me crucially but did not touch me. I saw and pitied his bafflement. They paused often waiting, pauses of increasing desperation. I watched them hang upon my silence yet I could only think, But what is it? What do you want of me? Why should you want of me?

I need nothing. I feel nothing. I desire nothing.

Were these new kingdoms which that sage hermit sought, the kingdoms of nothing? Or did he speak, as being replete in his own being, spurning all exterior augmentation?

SARA SULERI

Sara Suleri (1953–   ) was born and raised in Pakistan and now teaches English at Yale University. She is the author of both a critical study, The Rhetoric of English India, *and a marvelous memoir in the form of interlocking personal essays,* Meatless Days. *Just as she is the product of two cultures (a Muslim father and a Welsh mother), so her essay writing straddles two worlds, Lahore and New Haven, in two voices—the storyteller who renders her past in juicy, lively detail and the cool, trained analyst of texts and narratives (including her own memories). The themes of displacement and of yearning for a return to "mother's milk" receive her keen, wry scrutiny.*

In a sense, Suleri belongs to the roving, postcolonialist, postmodernist impulse, shared by Salman Rushdie, Michael Ondaatje, and others, which is shaking up literature with rambunctious mixings of genres, learned mockeries of political power, and maximalist merger of Western and Third World aesthetics. But she also has the traditional essayist's ability to write classically elegant, compact, conversational, aphoristic prose that keeps reaching for wisdom and balance, with impressive success.

Meatless Days

I HAD STRONGLY HOPED that they would say sweetbreads instead of testicles, but I was wrong. The only reason it had become a question in my mind was Tillat's fault, of course: she had come visiting from Kuwait one summer, arriving in New Haven with her three children, all of them designed to constitute a large surprise. As a surprise it worked wonderfully, leaving me reeling with the shock of generation that attends on infants and all the detail they manage to accrue. But the end of the day would come at last, and when the rhythm of their sleep sat like heavy peace upon a room, then Tillat and I could talk. Our conversations were meals, delectable, but fraught with a sense of prior copyright, because each of us was obliged to talk too much about what the other did not already know. Speaking over and across the separation of our lives, we discovered that there was an internal revenue involved in so much talking, so much listening. One evening my sister suddenly remembered to give me a piece of information that she had been storing up, like a squirrel, through the long desert months of the previous year. Tillat at twenty-seven had arrived at womanhood with comparatively little fuss—or so her aspect says—and her astonishing recall of my mother's face has always seemed to owe more to faithfulness than to the accident of physiognomy. "Sara," said Tillat, her voice deep with the promise of surprise, "do you know what *kapura* are?" I was cooking and a little cross. "Of course I do," I answered with some affront. "They're sweetbreads, and they're cooked with kidneys, and they're very good." Natives should always be natives, exactly what they are, and I felt irked to be so probed around the issue of my own nativity. But Tillat's face was kindly with superior knowledge. "Not sweetbread," she gently said. "They're testicles, that's what *kapura* really are." Of course I refused to believe her, went on cooking, and that was the end of that.

The babies left, and I with a sudden spasm of free time watched that organic issue resurface in my head—something that had once sat quite simply inside its own definition was declaring independence from its name and nature, claiming a perplexity that I did not like. And, too, I needed different ways to be still thinking about Tillat, who had gone as completely as she had arrived, and deserved to be reproached for being such an unreliable informant. So, the next time I was in the taut companionship of

Pakistanis in New York, I made a point of inquiring into the exact status of *kapura* and the physiological location of its secret, first in the animal and then in the meal. Expatriates are adamant, entirely passionate about such matters as the eating habits of the motherland. Accordingly, even though I was made to feel that it was wrong to strip a food of its sauce and put it back into its bodily belonging, I certainly received an unequivocal response: *kapura,* as naked meat, equals a testicle. Better, it is tantamount to a testicle neatly sliced into halves, just as we make no bones about asking the butcher to split chicken breasts in two. "But," and here I rummaged for the sweet realm of nomenclature, "couldn't *kapura* on a lazy occasion also accommodate something like sweetbreads, which is just a nice way of saying that pancreas is not a pleasant word to eat?" No one, however, was interested in this finesse. "Balls, darling, balls," someone drawled, and I knew I had to let go of the subject.

Yet I was shocked. It was my mother, after all, who had told me that sweetbreads are sweetbreads, and if she were wrong on that score, then how many other simple equations had I now to doubt? The second possibility that occurred to me was even more unsettling: maybe my mother knew that sweetbreads are testicles but had cunningly devised a ruse to make me consume as many parts of the world as she could before she set me loose in it. The thought appalled me. It was almost as bad as attempting to imagine what the slippage was that took me from nipple to bottle and away from the great letdown that signifies lactation. What a falling off! How much I must have suffered when so handed over to the shoddy metaphors of Ostermilk and Babyflo. Gosh, I thought, to think that my mother could do that to me. For of course she must have known, in her Welsh way, that sweetbreads could never be simply sweetbreads in Pakistan. It made me stop and hold my head over that curious possibility: what else have I eaten on her behalf?

I mulled over that question for days, since it wantonly refused to disappear after it had been posed: instead, it settled in my head and insisted on being reformulated, with all the tenacity of a query that actually expects to be met with a reply. My only recourse was to make lists, cramped and strictly alphabetical catalogs of all the gastronomic wrongs I could blame on my mother; but somehow by the time I reached *T* and "tripe," I was always interrupted and had to begin again. Finally it began to strike me as a rather unseemly activity for one who had always enjoyed a measure of daughterly propriety, and I decided that the game was not to be played again but discarded like table scraps. For a brief span of time I felt free, until some trivial occasion—a dinner, where chicken had been cleverly cooked to resemble veal—caused me to remind my friends of that obsolete little phrase, "mutton dressed up as lamb," which had been such a favorite of my mother's. Another was "neither flesh nor fowl," and as I

chatted about the curiousness of those phrases, I suddenly realized that
my friends had fallen away and my only audience was the question itself,
heaving up its head again and examining me with reproach and some
scorn. I sensed that it would be unwise to offer another list to this triumphant interlocutor, so I bowed my head and knew what I had to do. In
order to submit even the most imperfect answer, I had to go back to
where I belonged and—past a thousand different mealtimes—try to re-
construct the parable of the *kapura*.

Tillat was not around to hear me sigh and wonder where I should possibly begin. The breast would be too flagrant and would make me too
tongue-tied, so I decided instead to approach the *kapura* in a mildly devious way, by getting at it through its mate. To the best of my knowledge I
had never seen *kapura* cooked outside the company of kidney, and so for
Tillat's edification alone I tried to begin with the story of the kidney,
which I should have remembered long ago, not twenty-five years after its
occurrence. We were living in Lahore, in the 9-T Gulberg house, and in
those days our cook was Qayuum. He had a son and two daughters with
whom we were occasionally allowed to play: his little girl Munni I specially
remember because I liked the way her hair curled and because of all the
times that she was such a perfect recipient of fake *pan*. *Pan,* an adult
delicacy of betel leaf and nut, can be quite convincingly replicated by a
mango leaf stuffed with stones: Ifat, my older sister, would fold such beautifully simulated *pan* triangles that Munni would thrust them into her
mouth each time—and then burst into tears. I find it odd today to imagine
how that game of guile and trust could have survived even a single repetition, but I recollect it distinctly as a weekly ritual, with us waiting in
fascination for Munni to get streetwise, which she never did. Instead, she
cried with her mouth wide open and would run off to her mother with
little pebbles falling out of her mouth, like someone in a fairy tale.

Those stones get linked to kidneys in my head, as part of the chain
through which Munni got the better of me and anticipated the story I
really intend to tell. It was an evil day that led her father Qayuum to buy
two water buffalo, tethering them at the far end of the garden and making
my mother beam at the prospect of such fresh milk. My older brother
Shahid liked pets and convinced me that we should beam too, until he
and I were handed our first overpowering glasses of buffalo milk. Of milks
it is certainly the most oceanic, with archipelagoes and gulf streams of
cream emitting a pungent, grassy odor. Trebly strong is that smell at milking-time, which my mother beamingly suggested we attend. She kept away
herself, of course, so she never saw the big black cows, with their ominous
glassy eyes, as they shifted from foot to foot. Qayuum pulled and pulled at
their white udders and, in a festive mood, called up the children one by
one to squirt a steaming jet of milk into their mouths. When my turn

came, my mother, not being there, did not see me run as fast as I could
away from the cows and the cook, past the vegetable garden and the
goldfish pond, down to the farthermost wall, where I lay down in the grass
and tried to faint, but couldn't.

I knew the spot from prior humiliations, I admit. It was where I had
hidden twice in the week when I was caught eating cauliflower and was
made to eat kidney. The cauliflower came first—it emerged as a fragrant
little head in the vegetable garden, a bumpy vegetable brain that looked
innocent and edible enough to make me a perfect victim when it called. In
that era my greatest illicit joy was hastily chawing off the top of each new
cauliflower when no one else was looking. The early morning was my
favorite time, because then those flowers felt firm and crisp with dew. I
would go to the vegetable patch and squat over the cauliflowers as they
came out one by one, hold them between my knees, and chew as many
craters as I could into their jaunty tightness. Qayuum was crushed. "There
is an animal, Begum Sahib," he mourned to my mother, "like a savage in
my garden. *Maro! Maro!*" To hear him made me nervous, so the following
morning I tried to deflect attention from the cauliflowers by quickly pulling out all the little radishes while they were still pencil-thin: they lay on
the soil like a pathetic accumulation of red herrings. That was when
Munni caught me. *"Abba Ji!"* she screamed for her father like a train
engine. Everybody came running, and for a while my squat felt frozen to
the ground as I looked up at an overabundance of astonished adult faces.
"What are you doing, Sara *Bibi?*" the driver finally and gently asked.
"Smelling the radishes," I said in a baby and desperate defiance, "so that
the animal can't find the cauliflower." "Which one?" "The new cauliflower." "Which animal, *bibi ji,* you naughty girl?" "The one that likes to
eat the cauliflower that I like to smell." And when they laughed at me, I
did not know where to put my face for shame.

They caught me out that week, two times over, because after I had been
exposed as the cauliflower despoiler and had to enter a new phase of
penitence, Qayuum the cook insisted on making me eat kidney. *"Kirrnee,"*
he would call it with a glint in his eye, *"kirrnee."* My mother quite agreed
that I should learn such discipline, and the complicated ritual of endurance they imposed did make me teach myself to take a kidney taste without dwelling too long on the peculiarities of kidney texture. I tried to be
unsurprised by the mushroom pleats that constitute a kidney's underbelly
and by the knot of membrane that holds those kidney folds in place. One
day Qayuum insisted that only kidneys could sit on my plate, mimicking
legumes and ignoring their thin and bloody juices. Wicked Ifat came into
the room and waited till I had started eating; then she intervened. "Sara,"
said Ifat, her eyes brimming over with wonderful malice, "do you know
what kidneys do?" I aged, and my meal regressed, back to its vital belong-

ing in the world of function. "Kidneys make pee, Sara," Ifat told me, "That's what they do, they make pee." And she looked so pleased to be able to tell me that; it made her feel so full of information. Betrayed by food, I let her go, and wept some watery tears into the kidney juice, which was designed anyway to evade cohesion, being thin and in its nature inexact. Then I ran out to the farthermost corner of the garden, where I would later go to hide my shame of milking-time in a retch that refused to materialize.

Born the following year, Tillat would not know that cautionary tale. Nor would she know what Ifat did when my father called from Lady Willingdon Hospital in Lahore to repeat that old phrase, "It is a girl." "It's a girl!" Ifat shouted, as though simply clinching for the world the overwhelming triumph of her will. Shahid, a year my senior, was found half an hour later sobbing next to the goldfish pond near the vegetable garden, for he had been banking on the diluting arrival of a brother. He must have been upset, because when we were taken to visit my mother, he left his penguin—a favorite toy—among the old trees of the hospital garden, where we had been sent to play. I was still uncertain about my relation to the status of this new baby: my sister was glad that it was a girl, and my brother was sad that it wasn't a boy, but we all stood together when penguiny was lost.

It is to my discredit that I forgot this story, both of what the kidney said and what it could have told to my still germinating sister. Had I borne something of those lessons in mind, it would have been less of a shock to have to reconceive the *kapura* parable; perhaps I'd have been prepared for more skepticism about the connection between kidneys and sweetbreads —after all, they fall into no logical category of togetherness. The culinary humor of kidneys and testicles stewing in one another's juices is, on the other hand, very fine: I wish I had had the imagination to intuit all the unwonted jokes people tell when they start cooking food. I should have remembered all those nervously comic edges, and the pangs, that constitute most poignancies of nourishment. And so, as an older mind, I fault myself for not having the wits to recognize what I already knew. I must have always known exactly what *kapura* are, because the conversation they provoked came accompanied with shocks of familiarity that typically attend a trade of solid information. What I had really wanted to reply, first to Tillat and then to my Pakistani friends, was: yes, of course, who do you think I am, what else could they *possibly be?* Anyone with discrimination could immediately discern the connection between *kapura* and their namesake: the shape is right, given that we are now talking about goats; the texture involves a bit of a bounce, which works; and the taste is altogether too exactly what it is. So I should have kept in mind that, alas, we know the flavor of each part of the anatomy: that much imagination belongs to everyone's palate. Once, when my sisters and I were sitting in a sunny winter garden, Tillat began examining some ants that were tumbling about the blades of grass next to her chair. She looked acute and then suddenly said, "How very sour those little ants must be." Ifat declared that she had always thought the same herself, and though I never found out how they arrived at this discovery, I was impressed by it, their ability to take the world on their tongues.

So poor Irfani, how much his infant taste buds must have colored his perception of the grimness of each day. Irfan was born in London, finally another boy, but long after Shahid had ceased looking for playmates in the home. It now strikes me as peculiar that my parents should choose to move back to Pakistan when Farni was barely a year old, and to decide on June, that most pitiless month, in which to return to Lahore. The heat shriveled the baby, giving his face an expression of slow and bewildered shock, which was compounded by the fact that for the next year there was very little that the child could eat. Water boiled ten times over would still retain virulence enough to send his body into derangements, and goat's milk, cow's milk, everything liquid seemed to convey malevolence to his minuscule gut. We used to scour the city for aging jars of imported baby-food; these, at least, he would eat, though with a look of profound mis-trust—but even so, he spent most of the next year with his body in violent rebellion against the idea of food. It gave his eyes a gravity they have never lost.

Youngster he was, learning lessons from an infant's intuition to fear food, and to some degree all of us were equally watchful for hidden trick-eries in the scheme of nourishment, for the way in which things would always be missing or out of place in Pakistan's erratic emotional market. Items of security—such as flour or butter or cigarettes or tea—were al-ways vanishing, or returning in such dubiously shiny attire that we could barely stand to look at them. We lived in the expectation of threatening surprise: a crow had drowned in the water tank on the roof, so for a week we had been drinking dead-crow water and couldn't understand why we felt so ill; the milkman had accidentally diluted our supply of milk with paraffin instead of water; and those were not pistachios, at all, in a tub of Hico's green ice cream. Our days and our newspapers were equally full of disquieting tales about adulterated foods and the preternaturally keen eye that the nation kept on such promiscuous blendings. I can understand it, the fear that food will not stay discrete but will instead defy our categories of expectation in what can only be described as a manner of extreme belligerence. I like order to a plate, and know the great sense of failure that attends a moment when what is potato to the fork is turnip to the mouth. It's hard, when such things happen.

So, long before the *kapura* made its comeback in my life, we in Pakistan were bedmates with betrayal and learned how to take grim satisfaction from assessing the water table of our outrage. There were both lean times and meaty times, however; occasionally, body and food would sit happily at the same side of the conference table. Take, for example, Ramzan, the Muslim month of fasting, often recollected as the season of perfect meals. Ramzan, a lunar thing, never arrives at the same point of time each year, coming instead with an aura of slight and pleasing dislocation. Somehow it always took us by surprise: new moons are startling to see, even by accident, and Ramzan's moon betokened a month of exquisite precision about the way we were to parcel out our time. On the appointed evenings we would rake the twilight for that possible sliver, and it made the city and body both shudder with expectation to spot that little slip of a moon that signified Ramzan and made the sky historical. How busy Lahore would get! Its minarets hummed, its municipalities pulled out their old air-raid sirens to make the city noisily cognizant: the moon had been sighted, and the fast begun.

I liked it, the waking up an hour before dawn to eat the prefast meal and chat in whispers. For three wintry seasons I would wake up with Dadi, my grandmother, and Ifat and Shahid: we sat around for hours making jokes in the dark, generating a discourse of unholy comradeship. The food itself, designed to keep the penitent sustained from dawn till dusk, was insistent in its richness and intensity, with bread dripping clarified butter, and curried brains, and cumin eggs, and a peculiarly potent vermicelli, soaked overnight in sugar and fatted milk. And if I liked the getting up at dawn, then Dadi completely adored the eating of it all. I think she fasted only because she so enjoyed the *sehri* meal and that mammoth infusion of food at such an extraordinary hour. At three in the morning the rest of us felt squeamish about linking the deep sleep dreams we had just conducted and so much grease—we asked instead for porridge—but Dadi's eating was a sight to behold and admire. She hooted when the city's sirens sounded to tell us that we should stop eating and that the fast had now begun: she enjoyed a more direct relation with God than did petty municipal authorities and was fond of declaiming what Muhammad himself had said in her defense. He apparently told one of his contemporaries that *sehri* did not end until a white thread of light described the horizon and separated the landscape from the sky. In Dadi's book that thread could open into quite an active loom of dawning: the world made waking sounds, the birds and milkmen all resumed their proper functions, but Dadi's regal mastication—on the last brain now— declared it still was night.

I stopped that early rising years before Tillat and Irfan were old enough to join us, before Ifat ran away to get married, and before my father returned to ritual and overtook his son Shahid's absent place. So my memories of it are scant, the fast of the faithful. But I never lost my affection for the twilight meal, the dusky *iftar* that ended the fast after the mosques had lustily rung with the call for the *maghrib* prayer. We'd start eating dates, of course, in order to mimic Muhammad, but then with what glad eyes we'd welcome the grilled liver and the tang of pepper in the orange juice. We were happy to see the spinach leaves and their fantastical shapes, deftly fried in the lightest chick-pea batter, along with the tenderness of fresh fruit, most touching to the palate. There was a curious invitation about the occasion, converting what began as an act of penance into a godly and obligatory cocktail hour that provided a fine excuse for company and affability. When we lived in Pakistan, that little swerve from severity into celebration happened often. It certainly was true of meatless days.

The country was made in 1947, and shortly thereafter the government decided that two days out of each week would be designated as meatless days, in order to conserve the national supply of goats and cattle. Every Tuesday and Wednesday the butchers' shops would stay firmly closed, without a single carcass dangling from the huge metal hooks that lined the canopies under which the butchers squatted, selling meat, and without the open drains at the side of their narrow street ever running with a trace of blood. On days of normal trade, blood would briskly flow, carrying with it flotillas of chicken feathers, and little bits of sinew and entrail, or a bladder full and yellow that a butcher had just bounced deftly into the drain. On meatless days that world emptied into a skeletal remain: the hot sun came to scorch away all the odors and liquids of slaughter and shriveled on the chopping blocks the last curlicues of anything organic, making them look both vacant and precise.

As a principle of hygiene I suppose it was a good idea although it really had very little to do with conservation: the people who could afford to buy meat, after all, were those who could afford refrigeration, so the only thing the government accomplished was to make some people's Mondays very busy indeed. The Begums had to remember to give the cooks thrice as much money; the butchers had to produce thrice as much meat; the cooks had to buy enough flesh and fowl and other sundry organs to keep an averagely carnivorous household eating for three days. A favorite meatless day breakfast, for example, consisted of goat's head and feet cooked with spices into a rich and ungual sauce—remarkable, the things that people eat. And so, instead of creating an atmosphere of abstention in the city, the institution of meatless days rapidly came to signify the imperative behind the acquisition of all things fleshly. We thought about beef, which is called "big meat," and we thought about mutton, "little meat," and then we collectively thought about chicken, the most coveted of them all.

But here I must forget my American sojourn, which has taught me to look on chicken as a notably undignified bird, with pimply skin and pockets of fat tucked into peculiar places and unnecessarily meaty breasts. Those meatless day fowls, on the other hand, were a thing apart. Small, not much bigger than the average quail, they had a skin that cooked to the texture of rice paper, breaking even over the most fragrant limbs and wings. Naturally we cherished them and lavished much care on trying to obtain the freshest of the crop. Once I was in Karachi with my sister Nuz when the thought that she had to engage in the social ferocity of buying chickens was making her quite depressed. We went anyway, with Nuz assuming an alacrity that had nothing to do with efficiency and everything to do with desperation. Nuz stood small and dark in the chicken-monger's shop, ordered her birds, paid for them, and then suddenly remembered her housewifely duty. "Are they fresh?" she squawked, clutching at them, "Can you promise me they're fresh?" The chicken-monger looked at her with some perplexity. "But Begum Sahib," he said gently, "they're alive."

"Oh," said Nuz, "so they are," and calmed down immediately. I have always admired her capacity to be reassured by the world and take without a jot of embarrassment any comfort it is prepared to offer. So I thought she had forgotten about the issue of freshness as we drove home (with the dejected chickens tied up in a rope basket on the back seat) and the Karachi traffic grew lunchtime crazed. But "Oh," she said again, half an hour later, "So a fresh chicken is a dead chicken." "Not too dead," I replied. It made us think of meatless days as some vast funeral game, where Monday's frenetic creation of fresh things beckoned in the burial meals of Tuesday and Wednesday. "Food," Nuz said with disgust—"It's what you bury in your body." To make her feel less alone, we stopped at Shezan's on the way home, to get her an adequate supply of marzipan; for she eats nothing but sweet things. Food she'll cook—wonderful *Sindi* tastes, exotic to my palate—but sugar is the only thing Nuz actually wants to taste.

Irfan was the same about birds. He preferred to grow them rather than eat them. There was a time when he had a hundred doves on the roof of the Khurshid Alam Road house, which was quite a feat, considering that they'd had to be kept a strict secret from my father. Papa hated doves, associating them with the effete gambling of Deccan princedoms or with Trafalgar Square and his great distaste of the English ability to combine rain and pigeon droppings. So Irfan built dovecote after dovecote on our roof, while Papa had no idea of the commerce and exchange beneath which he was living. When he stayed at home to write, every sound would send him snarling, so then he heard with passionate hatred the long and low dove murmurings. He groaned and pulled his hair to think that his rooftop could actually be hospitable to pigeons: every evening he would dispatch Irfan to stand on the flat brick roof that was designed for summer sleep beneath the stars, so that he could shoo the birds away before they even dreamed of cooing. Since twilight was the hour when Farni preferred to feed the doves, life between him and Papa was perfect for a while. But then things fell apart. One afternoon Papa suddenly remembered that Irfan was at school and felt it incumbent on himself to gather as much information as he could about the academic progress of his youngest child, the renegade. In the evenings two tutors would come to coach Irfan in Urdu and math, and to them my father turned for an assessment of his son. "Too unhappy!" wailed the math master, "Today just too sad!" Papa bridled with defensiveness, asking for more specific fact. "Cat, sir, cat," mourned the Urdu teacher, "Cat has eaten up his fifty doves." The math master shook his head in commiseration, and Papa later liked to claim that his mind went from "bats in the belfry" through every possible idiomatic permutation he could give to cats and doves, until—only just realizing he had heard a literal truth—he stared from one face to the next, like a man aghast with knowledge.

Am I wrong, then, to say that my parable has to do with nothing less than the imaginative extravagance of food and all the transmogrifications of which it is capable? Food certainly gave us a way not simply of ordering a week or a day but of living inside history, measuring everything we remembered against a chronology of cooks. Just as Papa had his own yardstick—a word he loved—with which to measure history and would talk about the Ayub era, or the second martial law, or the Bhutto regime, so my sisters and I would place ourselves in time by remembering and naming cooks. "In the Qayuum days," we'd say, to give a distinctive flavor to a particular anecdote, or "in the Allah Ditta era." And our evocations only get more passionate now that cooks are a dying breed in Pakistan and have left us for the more ample kitchens of the gulf states and the more cramped but lucrative spaces of the Curries in a Hurry at Manchester and Leeds. There is something nourishing about the memory of all those shadow dynasties: we do not have to subsist only on the litany that begins, "After General Ayub came General Yahya; after the Bhutto years came General Zulu Haq," but can also add; "Qayuum begat Shorty and his wife; and they begat the Punjabi poet only called Khansama; he begat Ramzan and Karam Dad the bearer; Ramzan begat Tassi-Passi, and he begat Allah Ditta, meanest of them all."

We were always waiting for Allah Ditta to die. He was a good cook and a mean man who announced the imminence of his death for years, though he ended up surviving nearly half of the family. Still, he was useful. My mother was a nervous cook—probably because her mother had been a stern woman about such decorum—and was glad to be able to turn everything over to Allah Ditta and take refuge instead in the university. It is odd to recall that her precise mind could see a kitchen as an empty space;

I think she had given suck so many times and had engaged in so many umbilical connections that eating had become syncopated in her head to that miraculous shorthand. Not that pregnancy was a mystical term in her lexicon: on the contrary, the idea would make her assume a fastidious and pained expression. So she absolutely understood when Ifat, large with Ayesha this time, wafted into the house and murmured, "Do you know what it is like to have something kicking at you all the time and realize that you can never kick it back?" Mamma, never one to state the obvious, would look up pleadingly at that, as though the obvious was so much with us anyway that we all deserved to be spared its articulation. Or she would utter one of her curious archaisms: "Don't fret, child," she'd say, "don't fret."

But Ifat was good at fretting, apt at creating an aura of comfort by being able to characterize precisely the details of anything that could be discomforting to her. And so the state of pregnancy could on occasion make her eyes abstract, as she looked down at herself and vaguely said, "I've eaten too much, I've eaten too much." "There's too much body about the business," she once told me, "and too much of it is your own." Later, when Ayesha was born, a girl with blue unfurling fingers, the baby still would not permit my sister to empty into peace. She refused to eat enough, bloating her mother's breasts into helpless engorgement. So Ifat lay in bed, surrounded by such instruments of torture as breast pumps and expressers and her great facility for imprecation. Expressing letters rather than breasts was my normal ken, and it hurt to watch the meticulousness with which she set about relieving her body of that extraneous liquid. It was worse than a dentist, and for hours we implored her to take respite, but Ifat would not stop until her ferocious fever turned to sweat and her face was as white as in labor. Then she slept, waking once out of a dream like a beautiful gaunt owl to look at me oddly and say, "Mamma fed me once." In the morning the infant ate, and when Ifat's breasts lost their raging heat, it was as though stiffness could leave the entire household, erect as we had been to her distress. "Ordinary pumps again," she breathed, "they're mine again, at last." We smiled at that. Hard to believe, today, that those machines are gone for good.

For Ifat always was a fine source of stories about the peculiarities of food, particularly on the points of congruence between the condition of pregnancy and the circumstance of cooking, since both teeter precariously between the anxieties of being overdone and being underdone. When I left Pakistan, I had to learn how to cook—or, better—how to conceive of a kitchen as a place where I actually could be private. Now I like to cook, although I remain fascinated by my deep-seated inability to boil an egg exactly to the point that I would like to see it boiled, which seems like such an easy accomplishment of the efficient. I have finally come to the realization that I must feel slightly peculiar about eggs, because I am un-easy until they have been opened up and the flagrant separation between yolk and egg can be whisked into some yellow harmony. When I simply try to boil an egg, I've noticed, I am sure to give it an unconsciously advertent crack, so that the humming water suddenly swirls with some-thing viscous, and then I have to eat my eggs with gills and frills. Not that I very frequently boil an egg: once in five years, perhaps. I can distinctly remember the last occasion: it was when I was about to be visited by the tallest man in my acquaintance, in the days when I still used to tolerate such things.

He was a curious chap, whose bodily discomfort with the world was most frequently expressed in two refrains: one was "Not enough food!" and the second, "Too much food!" During the era of our association, I rapidly learned that the one intimacy we had to eschew above all others was the act of making meals and eating them alone. We could eat in restaurants and public places, surrounded by the buffer of other tables and strangers' voices, but for the two of us to be making and taking a meal on our own was such a fearful thought that the physical largess at my side would break into a myriad of tiny quakes. It was revelatory for me, who had never before watched someone for whom a dining table was so mark-edly more of a loaded domestic space than was a bed, but I was not totally averse to this new logic. It exercised my imagination to devise oblique methods of introducing food into my house, free-floating and aimless items that could find their way into anyone's mouth with such studied carelessness that they could do no damage to the integrity of a flea. I felt as though I were still in Sussex, putting out a saucer of milk and goodwill for the hedgehogs in the garden and then discreetly vanishing before they froze into prickles of shyness and self-dismay. "What is it, after all, be-tween food and the body?" I asked one day in an exasperation of pain, and never got an answer in reply.

Tom and Tillat tried to behave like friends; they cooked together in a way I liked—but with me the man was so large that he could conceive of himself only in bits, always conscious of how segments of his body could go wandering off, tarsals and metatarsals heedlessly autonomous. Such dissipation made him single-minded. He never worried about the top of his head, because he had put it behind him. His mother chose his glasses for him. His desires made him merely material: he looked at himself just as a woman looks when her infant takes its first tremulous step into the upright world, melting her into a modesty of consternation and pride. And his left hand could never see what his right hand was doing, for they were too far apart, occupying as they did remote hemispheres of control. Perhaps I should have been able to bring those bits together, but such a narrative was not available to me, not after what I knew of storytelling.

Instead, we watched the twist through which food became our staple metaphor, suggesting that something of the entire event had—against our will —to do with hunger. "You do not have the backbone of a shrimp," I mourned, gazing up at the spread-sheet of that man mountain. "You have a head the size of a bowl of porridge and a brain the size of a pea." This was in a restaurant. I was surprised beyond measure when that big head bent back and wept, a quick summer shower of tears. By the time he left, all surfaces were absolutely dry.

In any event, rain in America has never felt to me like a condition of glad necessity, and Tom and I will never know the conversations that we might have had on something like the twelfth of August in Lahore, for nothing can approximate what the monsoons make available in happy possibility. I think it was the smell that so intoxicated us after those dreary months of nostril-scorching heat, the smell of dust hissing at the touch of rain and then settling down, damply placid on the ground. People could think of eating again: after the first rains, in July, they gave themselves over to a study of mangoes, savoring in high seriousness the hundred varieties of that fruit. When it rained in the afternoons, children were allowed to eat their mangoes in the garden, stripped naked and dancing about, first getting sticky with mango juice and then getting slippery with rain. In our time such games drove Ifat and Shahid and me quite manic in our merriment, while Mamma sat reading on a nearby monsoon veranda to censor us if we transgressed too far. Years later, Tillat and I served a similar function when Ifat left her children with us—we sat on the veranda, letting them play in the rain. Ifat would have rushed off to shop or to do something equally important, while her children would long for Irfan, whom they loved boisterously, to come back from school. Mamma, on such afternoons, would not be there. It returns as a poignancy to me, that I have forgotten where Mamma could possibly be on such an occasion.

She was not there on the afternoon when, after the rains had whetted our appetites, I went out with my old friends Nuzhat Ahmad and Ayla, as the three of us often did, in a comradeship of girlhood. We went driving to Bagh-e-Jinnah, formerly known as Lawrence Gardens, located opposite the Governor's House along the Mall in Lahore. We were trying to locate the best *gol guppa* vendor in town and stopped by to test the new stand in Lawrence Gardens. *Gol guppas* are a strange food: I have never located an equivalent to them or their culinary situation. They are an outdoor food, a passing whim, and no one would dream of recreating their frivolity inside her own kitchen. A *gol guppa* is a small hollow oval of the lightest pastry that is dipped into a fiery liquid sauce made of tamarind and cayenne and lemon and cold water. It is evidently a food invented as a joke, in a moment of good humor. We stopped the car next to some tall jaman trees

(which many years before Shahid and I loved to climb) and enjoyed ourselves a great deal, until a friendly elbow knocked the bowl of *gol guppa*
sauce all over my lap. It gave me a new respect for foodstuffs, for never
has desire brought me to quite such an instantaneous effect. My groin's
surprise called attention to passageways that as a rule I am only theoreti-
cally aware of owning, all of which folded up like a concertina in protest
against such an explosive aeration. For days after, my pupils stayed di-
lated, while my interiors felt gaunt and hollow-eyed.

I retold this ten-year-old episode to Tillat when she came visiting,
shortly after she had hit me over the head with her testicles-equal-*kapura*
tale. I was trying to cheer her up and distract her from the rather obvious
fact that, once again, her children were refusing to eat. "Do you know
how much happier my life would be if my children would eat?" Tillat
wailed, and there was little I could say to deny it. "It's your fault, Tatty," I
said consolingly, "your body manufactured chocolate milk." Certainly
those children had a powerful impulse toward chocolate: it was deranging,
to pull out the Cadbury's for breakfast. It gave Tillat a rather peculiar
relation to food: it made her a good cook but a somewhat stern one, as
though she were always waiting for her meals to undergo a certain neurotic collapse. One day she turned quite tragic, cooking for some visitors
of mine, when the *shami kebabs* she was frying obstinately refused to
cohere into their traditional shape. I did not expect Tillat's moonface to
look so wracked, as though the secret of all things lay in that which made
the *shami* cling to the *kebab*. "Never mind, Tillat. We'll just call them
Kuwaiti *kebabs* and then no one will know they look peculiar." Of course
I was right, and the meal was most satisfactory.

I missed Tillat's children when they left. There are too many of them, of
course—all of my siblings have had too many. Each year I resolve afresh
that my quota of aunthood is full, that I no longer am going to clutter my
head with new names, new birthdays. But then something happens, like
finding in the mail another photograph of a new baby, and against my will
they draw me in again. I did not see Ifat's children for four years after she
had died, and when Tillat and I visited them in Rawalpindi, in the pink
house on the hill, Ayesha, the youngest, whispered to her paternal grandmother, "My aunts smell like my mother." When she repeated that to me,
it made me tired and grave. Tillat and I slept for ten hours that night,
drowning in a sleep we could not forestall, attempting to waken and then
falling back exhausted into another dreamless hour.

I described that sleep to Shahid, wondering about it, during one of our
rare encounters. I was trying to imagine what it would be like not to meet
his children again, since in those days he had lost them. We talked about
that, he and I, walking through the benign winter of a London afternoon,
while the light was failing in irregular slashes. I always feel quiet to be

walking at his side, glad to notice all the ways his face has taken age and yet remains the same. That face and I occupied the same playpen, ate sand out of the same sandbox together. I had not seen him for two years, which made me tender when we met, talking about how we could not see Surraya and Karim, his children. "I'll tell you what it's like, Sara," Shahid said. Then he stopped still and looked at me. "It's like the thing that a lush forgets, which is the absence of extremity."

All at once I felt relieved my mother was not there to overhear such conversation. I was glad that I had never seen, could no longer see, the cast her face would surely have taken hearing that sentence from her son. I wanted her to be put where she should be put, away from all of this, back in a bed where she need not have to know the desperate sleep Tillat and I had slept, hour after hour of reaching for the shoreline only to be pulled back into unending night. It was almost her reproach that I wished to be spared, the quiet voice that would look up and say, "Honestly, you children." I was afraid she would tell us that we were just as careless with our children as we had been with our books or our toys or our clothes, and I did not want to hear her proven right. The chagrin of the thought perplexed me as Shahid and I walked on, until I suddenly remembered the chagrin on Barkat the washerman's face when he was three days late in bringing back our school uniforms. Mamma's Urdu was an erratic thing, with sudden moments of access into idioms whose implications would throw her audience into gasps of surprise. When Barkat's recalcitrance kept her children denuded of clean white starched shirts and dresses to wear to school each day, Mamma's Urdu took a deep breath and opened the nearest idiomatic door, which sent her unknowing into the great precisions of classic amorous discourse. Barkat did not know where to look in his chagrin when Mamma gazed at him and said, her reproach as clear as a bell, "Barkat, how could you cause me such exquisite pain?" I reminded Shahid of that story. It made us laugh from Connaught Court to Edgware Road.

Tillat has three children, none of whom my mother ever saw, and I missed them after they left New Haven. I could not forget the way Tillat's three-year-old and only daughter, called Heba, broke my heart when she refused to swallow food. She sat at a table putting food in her mouth and growing chipmunk cheeks: we would try to ignore them as long as we could, but Heba knew how nervous we were getting, that we would soon break down and let her spit her mouthfuls out, whereupon she could resume her lovely jabber as though no grief had transpired at all. She ravaged me, but somehow it was consoling to be so readily available to pain and to observe in her manner and her face some ancient lineaments of my own. One day she startled me by confidentially saying that her brother Omi has a penis, but she has blood. When I asked her what she meant, "I looked inside to see," she answered, and glanced at me pragmatically. It made me glad for her that she had had such introspective courage to knock at the door of her body and insist it let her in. Heba has large eyes, as black as grapes, and hands that she wields like an Indian dancer. "Why don't you like me, Omi?" she would ask relentlessly. "I'm nice, too." It drove her elder brother into furies of rage. "I don't like you! I don't!" Omi shouted, while Heba looked at him with curiosity. Watching over her baby patience, I realized I need not worry about her, that child who was busy adding herself to the world and would not rest until it had made her properly welcome, long after she had forgotten me.

It reminds me that I am glad to have washed my hands of my sister Ifat's death and can think of her now as a house I once rented but which is presently inhabited by people I do not know. I miss her body, of course, and how tall she was, with the skull of a leopard and the manner of a hawk. But that's aesthetic, and aside from it, Ifat is just a repository of anecdotes for me, something I carry around without noticing, like lymph. One morning last year I woke myself up at dawn to escape the involutions of a dream that held me like a tax collector in a place where I did not want to be. For a moment I could not remember what city I was in, or what bedroom, until everything became lucid as I realized that Ifat was dead at last. "Darling, what a nosebleed," I found myself saying before I slept again and paid my dues.

Thus Nuz was right, absolutely right, when she wrote to me in her sprawling handwriting that looks so much like Karachi and said indignantly, "Of course my hair is going to fall out, what do you expect, when life is so full of stress? Now I wear a wig and look smarter than ever." Then she added, with the uncanny knowledge only Nuz can muster, "People are only good for light conversation." I liked the way that phrase lingered, born as it was from Nuzzi's unwitting capacity for the lingering phrase. The last time I was in London, I never saw Shahid's face light up so brightly as when he showed me a card that read, in florid script, "Greetings from Pakistan," beneath the image of some bustling Pathan dancers. Inside it Nuz had written, "Dearest Shahid, I am so sorry to hear of your divorce, my mother has had a brain hemorrhage and I am completely shattered, Merry Christmas and Happy New Year. Love, Nuz." Nuzzi's mother was my father's first wife, and also his cousin, so I suppose she can count as a relative of ours although we have never met. Luckily she made a miraculous recovery before Nuz went completely bald.

My own mother would hate it that we could laugh at such a tale. Such merriment made her look at her progeny with suspicion, unable to accept that she could ever whelp this mordant laughter. When Ifat was pregnant with Alia, I remember how worried Mamma looked one day when she came across Ifat's first child, little Tunsi-boy, telling his nurse that Ama had eaten another baby so he'd have a brother or a sister soon. "So they think you eat them up!" I was full of exclamation when Ifat told me this story, which made us laugh in poignant glee. Mamma came into the room and looked at us in a growing recognition of dismay. "Perhaps you do," she quietly said.

Five years later, I wish I had understood and remembered my mother's reprimand during the week she finally died. Sitting in the American Midwest, I thought of all my brothers and sisters, who watched my mother die in the jaunty dawn of a March day and who—fatigued and uncaring of the delicious respite of the dateline—gave me eight hours when Mamma was still historically alive. In a Lahore dawn on the ninth of March my mother's body failed to register on the hospital's gray screens; I in America was informed on the eighth, so technically I had a few more hours of my mother's life to savor before I needed to consign her into the ground. It made me secretly angry that such a reticent woman could choose to do something so rash and declarative as to die in such a double-handed way.

And then, when I was trying to move away from the raw irritability of grief, I dreamed a dream that left me reeling. It put me in London, on the pavement of some unlovely street, an attempted crescent of vagrant houses. A blue van drove up: I noticed it was a refrigerated car and my father was inside it. He came to tell me that we must put my mother in her coffin, and he opened the blue hatch of the van to make me reach inside, where it was very cold. What I found were hunks of meat wrapped in cellophane, and each of them felt like Mamma, in some odd way. It was my task to carry those flanks across the street and to fit them into the coffin at the other side of the road, like pieces in a jigsaw puzzle. Although my dream will not let me recall how many trips I made, I know my hands felt cold. Then, when my father's back was turned, I found myself engaged in rapid theft—for the sake of Ifat and Shahid and Tillat and all of us, I stole away a portion of that body. It was a piece of her foot I found, a small bone like a knuckle, which I quickly hid inside my mouth, under my tongue. Then I and the dream dissolved, into an extremity of tenderness.

It is hard to believe today that I thought the dream too harsh a thing. As parable, the *kapura* does not dare to look much further. It wishes to take the taste of my imagination only quite so far and, like my mother, makes me trebly entranced; had I really been perplexed at such a simple thing? Or perhaps my mind had designed me to feel rudely tender. I had eaten, that was all, and woken to a world of meatless days.

V

The American Scene

HENRY DAVID THOREAU

↓ d. @ 45

Henry David Thoreau (1817–1862) is one of the seminal figures in American literature. His stubborn insistence on living one's own life and fighting free of the pressures of materialism and conformity have had a profound influence on writers that followed him, from Whitman to the Beats to members of the current school of nature writing such as Edward Hoagland, Wendell Berry, and Annie Dillard. Taking a leaf from his mentor-friend Emerson's essay "Self-Reliance," Thoreau began building a cabin in Massachusetts, raising his own food, and writing about the experience in a journal that ultimately became his classic, Walden. *He defended his prickly individualism, articulating in the essay "Civil Disobedience" the political notion that a person must follow his conscience rather than the dictates of the state.*

As a writer he also went his own way, helping to shape modern American prose with his forthright utterances. Though Thoreau asserted that his writing style was merely an outgrowth of what he had to say, he was in fact a virtuoso literary artist. His sentences are long—some extremely long, building on themselves with expansive delight and a reluctance to close—yet clear at every moment. There is a fluid movement between general comment and personal testimony; Thoreau will pull back with a "For my part" just when you think he is getting too speculatively woolly. His descriptions are vivid and filled with sharp sensory detail.

In the piece below, he fixes on a subject that is close to the very nature of essay writing: walking. An essay is akin to taking a mental stroll. Thoreau loved excursions of all kinds. Here he celebrates the free-flowing, unstructured nature of the walk, a kind of basic research of the mind, which he connects with the virtue of wilderness and keeping some land uncultivated. His conviction that "in wildness is the preservation of the world" has become the central insight of present ecological theory.

Walking

I WISH to speak a word for Nature, for absolute freedom and wildness, as contrasted with a freedom and culture merely civil,—to regard man as an inhabitant, or a part and parcel of Nature, rather than a member of society. I wish to make an extreme statement, if so I may make an emphatic one, for there are enough champions of civilization: the minister and the school-committee, and every one of you will take care of that.

I have met with but one or two persons in the course of my life who understood the art of Walking, that is, of taking walks,—who had a genius, so to speak, for *sauntering:* which word is beautifully derived "from idle people who roved about the country, in the Middle Ages, and asked charity, under pretence of going *à la Sainte Terre,*" to the Holy Land, till the children exclaimed, "There goes a *Sainte-Terrer,*" a Saunterer,—a Holy-Lander. They who never go to the Holy Land in their walks, as they pretend, are indeed mere idlers and vagabonds; but they who do go there are saunterers in the good sense, such as I mean. Some, however, would derive the word from *sans terre,* without land or a home, which, therefore, in the good sense, will mean, having no particular home, but equally at home everywhere. For this is the secret of successful sauntering. He who sits still in a house all the time may be the greatest vagrant of all; but the saunterer, in the good sense, is no more vagrant than the meandering river, which is all the while sedulously seeking the shortest course to the sea. But I prefer the first, which, indeed, is the most probable derivation. For every walk is a sort of crusade, preached by some Peter the Hermit in us, to go forth and reconquer this Holy Land from the hands of the Infidels.

It is true, we are but faint-hearted crusaders, even the walkers, nowadays, who undertake no persevering, never-ending enterprises. Our expeditions are but tours, and come round again at evening to the old hearthside from which we set out. Half the walk is but retracing our steps. We should go forth on the shortest walk, perchance, in the spirit of undying adventure, never to return,—prepared to send back our embalmed hearts only as relics to our desolate kingdoms. If you are ready to leave father and mother, and brother and sister, and wife and child and friends, and never see them again,—if you have paid your debts, and made your will, and settled all your affairs, and are a free man, then you are ready for a walk.

To come down to my own experience, my companion and I, for I sometimes have a companion, take pleasure in fancying ourselves knights of a new, or rather an old, order,—not Equestrians or Chevaliers, not Ritters or riders, but Walkers, a still more ancient and honorable class, I trust. The chivalric and heroic spirit which once belonged to the Rider seems now to reside in, or perchance to have subsided into, the Walker,—not the Knight, but Walker Errant. He is a sort of fourth estate, outside of Church and State and People.

We have felt that we almost alone hereabouts practised this noble art; though, to tell the truth, at least, if their own assertions are to be received, most of my townsmen would fain walk sometimes, as I do, but they cannot. No wealth can buy the requisite leisure, freedom, and independence, which are the capital in this profession. It comes only by the grace of God. It requires a direct dispensation from Heaven to become a walker. You must be born into the family of the Walkers. *Ambulator nascitur, non fit.* Some of my townsmen, it is true, can remember and have described to me some walks which they took ten years ago, in which they were so blessed as to lose themselves for half an hour in the woods; but I know very well that they have confined themselves to the highway ever since, whatever pretensions they may make to belong to this select class. No doubt they were elevated for a moment as by the reminiscence of a previous state of existence, when even they were foresters and outlaws.

> *"When he came to grene wode,*
> *In a mery mornynge,*
> *There he herde the notes small*
> *Of byrdes mery syngynge.*

> *"It is ferre gone, sayd Robyn,*
> *That I was last here;*
> *Me lyste a lytell for to shote*
> *At the donne dere."*

I think that I cannot preserve my health and spirits, unless I spend four hours a day at least,—and it is commonly more than that,—sauntering through the woods and over the hills and fields, absolutely free from all worldly engagements. You may safely say, A penny for your thoughts, or a thousand pounds. When sometimes I am reminded that the mechanics and shopkeepers stay in their shops not only all the forenoon, but all the afternoon too, sitting with crossed legs, so many of them,—as if the legs were made to sit upon, and not to stand or walk upon,—I think that they deserve some credit for not having all committed suicide long ago.

I, who cannot stay in my chamber for a single day without acquiring some rust, and when sometimes I have stolen forth for a walk at the eleventh hour of four o'clock in the afternoon, too late to redeem the day, when the shades of night were already beginning to be mingled with the daylight, have felt as if I had committed some sin to be atoned for,—I confess that I am astonished at the power of endurance, to say nothing of the moral insensibility, of my neighbors who confine themselves to shops and offices the whole day for weeks and months, ay, and years almost together. I know not what manner of stuff they are of,—sitting there now at three o'clock in the afternoon, as if it were three o'clock in the morning. Bonaparte may talk of the three-o'clock-in-the-morning courage, but it is nothing to the courage which can sit down cheerfully at this hour in the afternoon over against one's self whom you have known all the morning, to starve out a garrison to whom you are bound by such strong ties of sympathy. I wonder that about this time, or say between four and five o'clock in the afternoon, too late for the morning papers and too early for the evening ones, there is not a general explosion heard up and down the street, scattering a legion of antiquated and house-bred notions and whims to the four winds for an airing,—and so the evil cure itself.

How womankind, who are confined to the house still more than men, stand it I do not know; but I have ground to suspect that most of them do not *stand* it at all. When, early in a summer afternoon, we have been shaking the dust of the village from the skirts of our garments, making haste past those houses with purely Doric or Gothic fronts, which have such an air of repose about them, my companion whispers that probably about these times their occupants are all gone to bed. Then it is that I appreciate the beauty and the glory of architecture, which itself never turns in, but forever stands out and erect, keeping watch over the slumberers.

No doubt temperament, and, above all, age, have a good deal to do with it. As a man grows older, his ability to sit still and follow indoor occupations increases. He grows vespertinal in his habits as the evening of life approaches, till at last he comes forth only just before sundown, and gets all the walk that he requires in half an hour.

But the walking of which I speak has nothing in it akin to taking exercise, as it is called, as the sick take medicine at stated hours,—as the swinging of dumb-bells or chairs; but is itself the enterprise and adventure of the day. If you would get exercise, go in search of the springs of life. Think of a man's swinging dumb-bells for his health, when those springs are bubbling up in far-off pastures unsought by him!

Moreover, you must walk like a camel, which is said to be the only beast which ruminates when walking. When a traveller asked Wordsworth's servant to show him her master's study, she answered, "Here is his library, but his study is out of doors."

Living much out of doors, in the sun and wind, will no doubt produce a certain roughness of character,—will cause a thicker cuticle to grow over some of the finer qualities of our nature, as on the face and hands, or as severe manual labor robs the hands of some of their delicacy of touch. So staying in the house, on the other hand, may produce a softness and smoothness, not to say thinness of skin, accompanied by an increased sensibility to certain impressions. Perhaps we should be more susceptible to some influences important to our intellectual and moral growth, if the sun had shone and the wind blown on us a little less; and no doubt it is a nice matter to proportion rightly the thick and thin skin. But methinks that is a scurf that will fall off fast enough,—that the natural remedy is to be found in the proportion which the night bears to the day, the winter to the summer, thought to experience. There will be so much the more air and sunshine in our thoughts. The callous palms of the laborer are conversant with finer tissues of self-respect and heroism, whose touch thrills the heart, than the languid fingers of idleness. That is mere sentimentality that lies abed by day and thinks itself white, far from the tan and callus of experience.

When we walk, we naturally go to the fields and woods: what would become of us, if we walked only in a garden or a mall? Even some sects of philosophers have felt the necessity of importing the woods to themselves, since they did not go to the woods. "They planted groves and walks of Platanes," where they took *subdiales ambulationes* in porticos open to the air. Of course it is of no use to direct our steps to the woods, if they do not carry us thither. I am alarmed when it happens that I have walked a mile into the woods bodily, without getting there in spirit. In my afternoon walk I would fain forget all my morning occupations and my obligations to society. But it sometimes happens that I cannot easily shake off the village. The thought of some work will run in my head, and I am not where my body is,—I am out of my senses. In my walks I would fain return to my senses. What business have I in the woods, if I am thinking of something out of the woods? I suspect myself, and cannot help a shudder, when I find myself so implicated even in what are called good works, —for this may sometimes happen.

My vicinity affords many good walks; and though for so many years I have walked almost every day, and sometimes for several days together, I have not yet exhausted them. An absolutely new prospect is a great happiness, and I can still get this any afternoon. Two or three hours' walking will carry me to as strange a country as I expect ever to see. A single farmhouse which I had not seen before is sometimes as good as the dominions of the King of Dahomey. There is in fact a sort of harmony discoverable between the capabilities of the landscape within a circle of ten miles' radius, or the limits of an afternoon walk, and the threescore years and ten of human life. It will never become quite familiar to you.

Nowadays almost all man's improvements, so called, as the building of houses, and the cutting down of the forest and of all large trees, simply deform the landscape, and make it more and more tame and cheap. A people who would begin by burning the fences and let the forest stand! I saw the fences half consumed, their ends lost in the middle of the prairie, and some worldly miser with a surveyor looking after his bounds, while heaven had taken place around him, and he did not see the angels going to and fro, but was looking for an old post-hole in the midst of paradise. I looked again, and saw him standing in the middle of a boggy, stygian fen, surrounded by devils, and he had found his bounds without a doubt, three little stones, where a stake had been driven, and looking nearer, I saw that the Prince of Darkness was his surveyor.

I can easily walk ten, fifteen, twenty, any number of miles, commencing at my own door, without going by any house, without crossing a road except where the fox and the mink do: first along by the river, and then the brook, and then the meadow and the wood-side. There are square miles in my vicinity which have no inhabitant. From many a hill I can see civilization and the abodes of man afar. The farmers and their works are scarcely more obvious than woodchucks and their burrows. Man and his affairs, church and state and school, trade and commerce, and manufactures and agriculture, even politics, the most alarming of them all,—I am pleased to see how little space they occupy in the landscape. Politics is but a narrow field, and that still narrower highway yonder leads to it. I sometimes direct the traveller thither. If you would go to the political world, follow the great road,—follow that market-man, keep his dust in your eyes, and it will lead you straight to it; for it, too, has its place merely, and does not occupy all space. I pass from it as from a bean-field into the forest, and it is forgotten. In one half-hour I can walk off to some portion of the earth's surface where a man does not stand from one year's end to another, and there, consequently, politics are not, for they are but as the cigar-smoke of a man.

The village is the place to which the roads tend, a sort of expansion of the highway, as a lake of a river. It is the body of which roads are the arms and legs,—a trivial or quadrivial place, the thoroughfare and ordinary of travellers. The word is from the Latin *villa*, which, together with *via*, a way, or more anciently *ved* and *vella*, Varro derives from *veho*, to carry, because the villa is the place to and from which things are carried. They who got their living by teaming were said *vellaturam facere*. Hence, too, apparently, the Latin word *vilis* and our vile; also *villain*. This suggests what kind of degeneracy villagers are liable to. They are wayworn by the travel that goes by and over them, without travelling themselves.

Some do not walk at all; others walk in the highways; a few walk across lots. Roads are made for horses and men of business. I do not travel in them much, comparatively, because I am not in a hurry to get to any tavern or grocery or livery-stable or depot to which they lead. I am a good horse to travel, but not from choice a roadster. The landscape-painter uses the figures of men to mark a road. He would not make that use of my figure. I walk out into a Nature such as the old prophets and poets, Menu, Moses, Homer, Chaucer, walked in. You may name it America, but it is not America: neither Americus Vespucius, nor Columbus, nor the rest were the discoverers of it. There is a truer account of it in mythology than in any history of America, so called, that I have seen.

However, there are a few old roads that may be trodden with profit, as if they led somewhere now that they are nearly discontinued. There is the Old Marlborough Road, which does not go to Marlborough now, me-thinks, unless that is Marlborough where it carries me. I am the bolder to speak of it here, because I presume that there are one or two such roads in every town.

THE OLD MARLBOROUGH ROAD.

> *Where they once dug for money,*
> *But never found any;*
> *Where sometimes Martial Miles*
>   *Singly files,*
>   *And Elijah Wood,*
>   *I fear for no good:*
> *No other man,*
> *Save Elisha Dugan,—*
> *O man of wild habits,*
> *Partridges and rabbits,*
> *Who hast no cares*
> *Only to set snares,*
> *Who liv'st all alone,*
> *Close to the bone,*
> *And where life is sweetest*
> *Constantly eatest.*

When the spring stirs my blood
  With the instinct to travel,
  I can get enough gravel
On the Old Marlborough Road.
    Nobody repairs it,
    For nobody wears it;
    It is a living way,
    As the Christians say.
Not many there be
  Who enter therein,
Only the guests of the
  Irishman Quin.
What is it, what is it,
  But a direction out there,
And the bare possibility
  Of going somewhere?
    Great guide-boards of stone,
    But travellers none;
    Cenotaphs of the towns
    Named on their crowns.
    It is worth going to see
    Where you might *be.*
    What king
    Did the thing,
    I am still wondering;
    Set up how or when,
    By what selectmen,
    Gourgas or Lee,
    Clark or Darby?
    They're a great endeavor
    To be something forever;
    Blank tablets of stone,
    Where a traveller might groan,
    And in one sentence
    Grave all that is known;
    Which another might read,
    In his extreme need.
    I know one or two
    Lines that would do,
    Literature that might stand
    All over the land,
    Which a man could remember
    Till next December,

And read again in the spring,
After the thawing.
If with fancy unfurled
You leave your abode,
You may go round the world
By the Old Marlborough Road.

At present, in this vicinity, the best part of the land is not private property; the landscape is not owned, and the walker enjoys comparative freedom. But possibly the day will come when it will be partitioned off into so-called pleasure-grounds, in which a few will take a narrow and exclusive pleasure only,—when fences shall be multiplied, and man-traps and other engines invented to confine men to the *public* road, and walking over the surface of God's earth shall be construed to mean trespassing on some gentleman's grounds. To enjoy a thing exclusively is commonly to exclude yourself from the true enjoyment of it. Let us improve our opportunities, then, before the evil days come.

What is it that makes it so hard sometimes to determine whither we will walk? I believe that there is a subtile magnetism in Nature, which, if we unconsciously yield to it, will direct us aright. It is not indifferent to us which way we walk. There is a right way; but we are very liable from heedlessness and stupidity to take the wrong one. We would fain take that walk, never yet taken by us through this actual world, which is perfectly symbolical of the path which we love to travel in the interior and ideal world; and sometimes, no doubt, we find it difficult to choose our direction, because it does not yet exist distinctly in our idea.

When I go out of the house for a walk, uncertain as yet whither I will bend my steps, and submit myself to my instinct to decide for me, I find, strange and whimsical as it may seem, that I finally and inevitably settle southwest, toward some particular wood or meadow or deserted pasture or hill in that direction. My needle is slow to settle,—varies a few degrees, and does not always point due southwest, it is true, and it has good authority for this variation, but it always settles between west and south-southwest. The future lies that way to me, and the earth seems more unexhausted and richer on that side. The outline which would bound my walks would be, not a circle, but a parabola, or rather like one of those cometary orbits which have been thought to be non-returning curves, in this case opening westward, in which my house occupies the place of the sun. I turn round and round irresolute sometimes for a quarter of an hour, until I decide, for a thousandth time, that I will walk into the southwest or west. Eastward I go only by force; but westward I go free. Thither no business leads me. It is hard for me to believe that I shall find fair land-scapes or sufficient wildness and freedom behind the eastern horizon. I am not excited by the prospect of a walk thither; but I believe that the forest which I see in the western horizon stretches uninterruptedly toward the setting sun, and there are no towns nor cities in it of enough conse-quence to disturb me. Let me live where I will, on this side is the city, on that the wilderness, and ever I am leaving the city more and more, and withdrawing into the wilderness. I should not lay so much stress on this fact, if I did not believe that something like this is the prevailing tendency of my countrymen. I must walk toward Oregon, and not toward Europe. And that way the nation is moving, and I may say that mankind progress from east to west. Within a few years we have witnessed the phenomenon of a southeastward migration, in the settlement of Australia; but this af-fects us as a retrograde movement, and, judging from the moral and physi-cal character of the first generation of Australians, has not yet proved a successful experiment. The eastern Tartars think that there is nothing west beyond Thibet. "The world ends there," say they, "beyond there is noth-ing but a shoreless sea." It is unmitigated East where they live.

We go eastward to realize history and study the works of art and litera-ture, retracing the steps of the race; we go westward as into the future, with a spirit of enterprise and adventure. The Atlantic is a Lethean stream, in our passage over which we have had an opportunity to forget the Old World and its institutions. If we do not succeed this time, there is perhaps one more chance for the race left before it arrives on the banks of the Styx; and that is in the Lethe of the Pacific, which is three times as wide.

I know not how significant it is, or how far it is an evidence of singular-ity, that an individual should thus consent in his pettiest walk with the general movement of the race; but I know that something akin to the migratory instinct in birds and quadrupeds,—which, in some instances, is known to have affected the squirrel tribe, impelling them to a general and mysterious movement, in which they were seen, say some, crossing the broadest rivers, each on its particular chip, with its tail raised for a sail, and bridging narrower streams with their dead,—that something like the *furor* which affects the domestic cattle in the spring, and which is referred to a worm in their tails,—affects both nations and individuals, either pe-rennially or from time to time. Not a flock of wild geese cackles over our town, but it to some extent unsettles the value of real estate here, and, if I were a broker, I should probably take that disturbance into account.

> "Than longen folk to gon on pilgrimages,
> And palmeres for to seken strange strondes."

Every sunset which I witness inspires me with the desire to go to a West as distant and as fair as that into which the sun goes down. He appears to migrate westward daily, and tempt us to follow him. He is the Great Western Pioneer whom the nations follow. We dream all night of those mountain-ridges in the horizon, though they may be of vapor only, which were last gilded by his rays. The island of Atlantis, and the islands and gardens of the Hesperides, a sort of terrestrial paradise, appear to have been the Great West of the ancients, enveloped in mystery and poetry. Who has not seen in imagination, when looking into the sunset sky, the gardens of the Hesperides, and the foundation of all those fables?

Columbus felt the westward tendency more strongly than any before. He obeyed it, and found a New World for Castile and Leon. The herd of men in those days scented fresh pastures from afar.

> *"And now the sun had stretched out all the hills,*
> *And now was dropped into the western bay;*
> *At last he rose, and twitched his mantle blue;*
> *To-morrow to fresh woods and pastures new."*

Where on the globe can there be found an area of equal extent with that occupied by the bulk of our States, so fertile and so rich and varied in its productions, and at the same time so habitable by the European, as this is? Michaux, who knew but part of them, says that "the species of large trees are much more numerous in North America than in Europe; in the United States there are more than one hundred and forty species that exceed thirty feet in height; in France there are but thirty that attain this size." Later botanists more than confirm his observations. Humboldt came to America to realize his youthful dreams of a tropical vegetation, and he beheld it in its greatest perfection in the primitive forests of the Amazon, the most gigantic wilderness on the earth, which he has so eloquently described. The geographer Guyot, himself a European, goes farther,— farther than I am ready to follow him; yet not when he says,—"As the plant is made for the animal, as the vegetable world is made for the animal world, America is made for the man of the Old World. . . . The man of the Old World sets out upon his way. Leaving the highlands of Asia, he descends from station to station towards Europe. Each of his steps is marked by a new civilization superior to the preceding, by a greater power of development. Arrived at the Atlantic, he pauses on the shore of this unknown ocean, the bounds of which he knows not, and turns upon his footprints for an instant." When he has exhausted the rich soil of Europe, and reinvigorated himself, "then recommences his adventurous career westward as in the earliest ages." So far Guyot.

From this western impulse coming in contact with the barrier of the Atlantic sprang the commerce and enterprise of modern times. The younger Michaux, in his "Travels West of the Alleghanies in 1802," says that the common inquiry in the newly settled West was, " 'From what part of the world have you come?' As if these vast and fertile regions would naturally be the place of meeting and common country of all the inhabitants of the globe."

To use an obsolete Latin word, I might say, *Ex Oriente lux; ex Occidente FRUX.* From the East light; from the West fruit.

Sir Francis Head, an English traveller and a Governor-General of Canada, tells us that "in both the northern and southern hemispheres of the New World, Nature has not only outlined her works on a larger scale, but has painted the whole picture with brighter and more costly colors than she used in delineating and in beautifying the Old World. . . . The heavens of America appear infinitely higher, the sky is bluer, the air is fresher, the cold is intenser, the moon looks larger, the stars are brighter, the thunder is louder, the lightning is vivider, the wind is stronger, the rain is heavier, the mountains are higher, the rivers longer, the forests bigger, the plains broader." This statement will do at least to set against Buffon's account of this part of the world and its productions.

Linnaeus said long ago, "Nescio quae facies *laeta, glabra* plantis Americanis: I know not what there is of joyous and smooth in the aspect of American plants;" and I think that in this country there are no, or at most very few, *Africanae bestiae,* African beasts, as the Romans called them, and that in this respect also it is peculiarly fitted for the habitation of man. We are told that within three miles of the centre of the East-Indian city of Singapore, some of the inhabitants are annually carried off by tigers; but the traveller can lie down in the woods at night almost anywhere in North America without fear of wild beasts.

These are encouraging testimonies. If the moon looks larger here than in Europe, probably the sun looks larger also. If the heavens of America appear infinitely higher, and the stars brighter, I trust that these facts are symbolical of the height to which the philosophy and poetry and religion of her inhabitants may one day soar. At length, perchance, the immaterial heaven will appear as much higher to the American mind, and the intimations that star it as much brighter. For I believe that climate does thus react on man,—as there is something in the mountain-air that feeds the spirit and inspires. Will not man grow to greater perfection intellectually as well as physically under these influences? Or is it unimportant how many foggy days there are in his life? I trust that we shall be more imaginative, that our thoughts will be clearer, fresher, and more ethereal, as our sky,—our understanding more comprehensive and broader, like our plains,—our intellect generally on a grander scale, like our thunder and lightning, our rivers and mountains and forests,— and our hearts shall even correspond in breadth and depth and grandeur to our inland seas. Perchance there will appear to the traveller something, he knows not what, of *laeta* and *glabra,* of joyous and serene, in our very faces. Else to what end does the world go on, and why was America discovered?

To Americans I hardly need to say,—

"Westward the star of empire takes its way."

As a true patriot, I should be ashamed to think that Adam in paradise was more favorably situated on the whole than the backwoodsman in this country.

Our sympathies in Massachusetts are not confined to New England; though we may be estranged from the South, we sympathize with the West. There is the home of the younger sons, as among the Scandinavians they took to the sea for their inheritance. It is too late to be studying Hebrew; it is more important to understand even the slang of to-day.

Some months ago I went to see a panorama of the Rhine. It was like a dream of the Middle Ages. I floated down its historic stream in something more than imagination, under bridges built by the Romans, and repaired by later heroes, past cities and castles whose very names were music to my ears, and each of which was the subject of a legend. There were Ehren-breitstein and Rolandseck and Coblentz, which I knew only in history. They were ruins that interested me chiefly. There seemed to come up from its waters and its vine-clad hills and valleys a hushed music as of Crusaders departing for the Holy Land. I floated along under the spell of enchantment, as if I had been transported to an heroic age, and breathed an atmosphere of chivalry.

Soon after, I went to see a panorama of the Mississippi, and as I worked my way up the river in the light of to-day, and saw the steamboats wooding up, counted the rising cities, gazed on the fresh ruins of Nauvoo, beheld the Indians moving west across the stream, and, as before I had looked up the Moselle now looked up the Ohio and the Missouri, and heard the legends of Dubuque and of Wenona's Cliff,—still thinking more of the future than of the past or present,—I saw that this was a Rhine stream of a different kind; that the foundations of castles were yet to be laid, and the famous bridges were yet to be thrown over the river; and I felt that *this was the heroic age itself,* though we know it not, for the hero is commonly the simplest and obscurest of men.

The West of which I speak is but another name for the Wild; and what I have been preparing to say is, that in Wildness is the preservation of the World. Every tree sends its fibres forth in search of the Wild. The cities import it at any price. Men plough and sail for it. From the forest and wilderness come the tonics and barks which brace mankind. Our ancestors were savages. The story of Romulus and Remus being suckled by a wolf is not a meaningless fable. The founders of every State which has risen to eminence have drawn their nourishment and vigor from a similar wild source. It was because the children of the Empire were not suckled by the wolf that they were conquered and displaced by the children of the Northern forests who were.

I believe in the forest, and in the meadow, and in the night in which the corn grows. We require an infusion of hemlock-spruce or arborvitae in our tea. There is a difference between eating and drinking for strength and from mere gluttony. The Hottentots eagerly devour the marrow of the koodoo and other antelopes raw, as a matter of course. Some of our Northern Indians eat raw the marrow of the Arctic reindeer, as well as various other parts, including the summits of the antlers, as long as they are soft. And herein, perchance, they have stolen a march on the cooks of Paris. They get what usually goes to feed the fire. This is probably better than stall-fed beef and slaughter-house pork to make a man of. Give me a wildness whose glance no civilization can endure,—as if we lived on the marrow of koodoos devoured raw.

There are some intervals which border the strain of the wood-thrush, to which I would migrate,—wild lands where no settler has squatted; to which, methinks, I am already acclimated.

The African hunter Cummings tells us that the skin of the eland, as well as that of most other antelopes just killed, emits the most delicious perfume of trees and grass. I would have every man so much like a wild antelope, so much a part and parcel of Nature, that his very person should thus sweetly advertise our senses of his presence, and remind us of those parts of Nature which he most haunts. I feel no disposition to be satirical, when the trapper's coat emits the odor of musquash even; it is a sweeter scent to me than that which commonly exhales from the merchant's or the scholar's garments. When I go into their wardrobes and handle their vestments, I am reminded of no grassy plains and flowery meads which they have frequented, but of dusty merchants' exchanges and libraries rather.

A tanned skin is something more than respectable, and perhaps olive is a fitter color than white for a man,—a denizen of the woods. "The pale white man!" I do not wonder that the African pitied him. Darwin the naturalist says, "A white man bathing by the side of a Tahitian was like a plant bleached by the gardener's art, compared with a fine, dark green one, growing vigorously in the open fields."

Ben Jonson exclaims,—

"How near to good is what is fair!"

So I would say,—

How near to good is what is wild!

Life consists with wildness. The most alive is the wildest. Not yet subdued to man, its presence refreshes him. One who pressed forward incessantly and never rested from his labors, who grew fast and made infinite demands on life, would always find himself in a new country or wilderness, and surrounded by the raw material of life. He would be climbing over the prostrate stems of primitive forest-trees.

Hope and the future for me are not in lawns and cultivated fields, not in towns and cities, but in the impervious and quaking swamps. When, formerly, I have analyzed my partiality for some farm which I had contemplated purchasing, I have frequently found that I was attracted solely by a few square rods of impermeable and unfathomable bog,—a natural sink in one corner of it. That was the jewel which dazzled me. I derive more of my subsistence from the swamps which surround my native town than from the cultivated gardens in the village. There are no richer parterres to my eyes than the dense beds of dwarf andromeda (*Cassandra calyculata*) which cover these tender places on the earth's surface. Botany cannot go farther than tell me the names of the shrubs which grow there,—the high-blueberry, panicled andromeda, lamb-kill, azalea, and rhodora,—all standing in the quaking sphagnum. I often think that I should like to have my house front on this mass of dull red bushes, omitting other flower plots and borders, transplanted spruce and trim box, even gravelled walks,—to have this fertile spot under my windows, not a few imported barrow-fulls of soil only to cover the sand which was thrown out in digging the cellar. Why not put my house, my parlor, behind this plot, instead of behind that meagre assemblage of curiosities, that poor apology for a Nature and Art, which I call my front-yard? It is an effort to clear up and make a decent appearance when the carpenter and mason have departed, though done as much for the passer-by as the dweller within. The most tasteful front-yard fence was never an agreeable object of study to me; the most elaborate ornaments, acorn-tops, or what not, soon wearied and disgusted me. Bring your sills up to the very edge of the swamp, then, (though it may not be the best place for a dry cellar,) so that there be no access on that side to citizens. Front-yards are not made to walk in, but, at most, through, and you could go in the back way.

Yes, though you may think me perverse, if it were proposed to me to dwell in the neighborhood of the most beautiful garden that ever human art contrived, or else of a Dismal swamp, I should certainly decide for the swamp. How vain, then, have been all your labors, citizens, for me!

My spirits infallibly rise in proportion to the outward dreariness. Give me the ocean, the desert or the wilderness! In the desert, pure air and solitude compensate for want of moisture and fertility. The traveller Burton says of it,—"Your *morale* improves; you become frank and cordial, hospitable and single-minded. . . . In the desert, spirituous liquors excite only disgust. There is a keen enjoyment in a mere animal existence." They who have been travelling long on the steppes of Tartary say,—"On reëntering cultivated lands, the agitation, perplexity, and turmoil of civilization oppressed and suffocated us; the air seemed to fail us, and we felt every moment as if about to die of asphyxia." When I would recreate myself, I seek the darkest wood, the thickest and most interminable, and, to the citizen, most dismal swamp. I enter a swamp as a sacred place,—a *sanctum sanctorum.* There is the strength, the marrow of Nature. The wild-wood covers the virgin mould,—and the same soil is good for men and for trees. A man's health requires as many acres of meadow to his prospect as his farm does loads of muck. There are the strong meats on which he feeds. A town is saved, not more by the righteous men in it than by the woods and swamps that surround it. A township where one primitive forest waves above, while another primitive forest rots below,—such a town is fitted to raise not only corn and potatoes, but poets and philosophers for the coming ages. In such a soil grew Homer and Confucius and the rest, and out of such a wilderness comes the Reformer eating locusts and wild honey.

To preserve wild animals implies generally the creation of a forest for them to dwell in or resort to. So it is with man. A hundred years ago they sold bark in our streets peeled from our own woods. In the very aspect of those primitive and rugged trees, there was, methinks, a tanning principle which hardened and consolidated the fibres of men's thoughts. Ah! already I shudder for these comparatively degenerate days of my native village, when you cannot collect a load of bark of good thickness,—and we no longer produce tar and turpentine.

The civilized nations—Greece, Rome, England—have been sustained by the primitive forests which anciently rotted where they stand. They survive as long as the soil is not exhausted. Alas for human culture! little is to be expected of a nation, when the vegetable mould is exhausted, and it is compelled to make manure of the bones of its fathers. There the poet sustains himself merely by his own superfluous fat, and the philosopher comes down on his marrow-bones.

It is said to be the task of the American "to work the virgin soil," and that "agriculture here already assumes proportions unknown everywhere else." I think that the farmer displaces the Indian even because he redeems the meadow, and so makes himself stronger and in some respects more natural. I was surveying for a man the other day a single straight line one hundred and thirty-two rods long, through a swamp, at whose entrance might have been written the words which Dante read over the entrance to the infernal regions,—"Leave all hope, ye that enter,"—that is, of ever getting out again; where at one time I saw my employer actually up to his neck and swimming for his life in his property, though it was still winter. He had another similar swamp which I could not survey at all, because it was completely under water, and nevertheless, with regard to a third swamp, which I did *survey* from a distance, he remarked to me, true to his instincts, that he would not part with it for any consideration, on account of the mud which it contained. And that man intends to put a girdling ditch round the whole in the course of forty months, and so redeem it by the magic of his spade. I refer to him only as the type of a class.

The weapons with which we have gained our most important victories, which should be handed down as heirlooms from father to son, are not the sword and the lance, but the bush-whack, the turf-cutter, the spade, and the bog-hoe, rusted with the blood of many a meadow, and begrimed with the dust of many a hard-fought field. The very winds blew the Indian's cornfield into the meadow, and pointed out the way which he had not the skill to follow. He had no better implement with which to intrench himself in the land than a clam-shell. But the farmer is armed with plough and spade.

In Literature it is only the wild that attracts us. Dulness is but another name for tameness. It is the uncivilized free and wild thinking in "Hamlet" and the "Iliad," in all the Scriptures and Mythologies, not learned in the schools, that delights us. As the wild duck is more swift and beautiful than the tame, so is the wild—the mallard—thought, which 'mid falling dews wings its way above the fens. A truly good book is something as natural, and as unexpectedly and unaccountably fair and perfect, as a wild flower discovered on the prairies of the West or in the jungles of the East. Genius is a light which makes the darkness visible, like the lightning's flash, which perchance shatters the temple of knowledge itself,—and not a taper lighted at the hearth-stone of the race, which pales before the light of common day.

English literature, from the days of the minstrels to the Lake Poets,— Chaucer and Spenser and Milton, and even Shakespeare, included,— breathes no quite fresh and in this sense wild strain. It is an essentially tame and civilized literature, reflecting Greece and Rome. Her wilderness is a green wood,—her wild man a Robin Hood. There is plenty of genial love of Nature, but not so much of Nature herself. Her chronicles inform us when her wild animals, but not when the wild man in her, became extinct.

The science of Humboldt is one thing, poetry is another thing. The poet to-day, notwithstanding all the discoveries of science, and the accumulated learning of mankind, enjoys no advantage over Homer.

Where is the literature which gives expression to Nature? He would be a poet who could impress the winds and streams into his service, to speak for him; who nailed words to their primitive senses, as farmers drive down stakes in the spring, which the frost has heaved; who derived his words as often as he used them,—transplanted them to his page with earth adhering to their roots; whose words were so true and fresh and natural that they would appear to expand like the buds at the approach of spring, though they lay half-smothered between two musty leaves in a library,—ay, to bloom and bear fruit there, after their kind, annually, for the faithful reader, in sympathy with surrounding Nature.

I do not know of any poetry to quote which adequately expresses this yearning for the Wild. Approached from this side, the best poetry is tame. I do not know where to find in any literature, ancient or modern, any account which contents me of that Nature with which even I am acquainted. You will perceive that I demand something which no Augustan nor Elizabethan age, which no *culture,* in short, can give. Mythology comes nearer to it than anything. How much more fertile a Nature, at least, has Grecian mythology its root in than English literature! Mythology is the crop which the Old World bore before its soil was exhausted, before the fancy and imagination were affected with blight; and which it still bears, wherever its pristine vigor is unabated. All other literatures endure only as the elms which overshadow our houses; but this is like the great dragon-tree of the Western Isles, as old as mankind, and, whether that does or not, will endure as long; for the decay of other literatures makes the soil in which it thrives.

The West is preparing to add its fables to those of the East. The valleys of the Ganges, the Nile, and the Rhine, having yielded their crop, it remains to be seen what the valleys of the Amazon, the Plate, the Orinoco, the St. Lawrence, and the Mississippi will produce. Perchance, when, in the course of ages, American liberty has become a fiction of the past,—as it is to some extent a fiction of the present,—the poets of the world will be inspired by American mythology.

The wildest dreams of wild men, even, are not the less true, though they may not recommend themselves to the sense which is most common among Englishmen and Americans to-day. It is not every truth that recommends itself to the common sense. Nature has a place for the wild clematis as well as for the cabbage. Some expressions of truth are reminiscent,—others merely *sensible,* as the phrase is,—others prophetic. Some forms of disease, even, may prophesy forms of health. The geologist has discovered that the figures of serpents, griffins, flying dragons, and other fanciful embellishments of heraldry, have their prototypes in the forms of fossil species which were extinct before man was created, and hence "indicate a faint and shadowy knowledge of a previous state of organic existence."

The Hindoos dreamed that the earth rested on an elephant, and the elephant on a tortoise, and the tortoise on a serpent; and though it may be an unimportant coincidence, it will not be out of place here to state, that a fossil tortoise has lately been discovered in Asia large enough to support an elephant. I confess that I am partial to these wild fancies, which transcend the order of time and development. They are the sublimest recreation of the intellect. The partridge loves peas, but not those that go with her into the pot.

In short, all good things are wild and free. There is something in a strain of music, whether produced by an instrument or by the human voice,—take the sound of a bugle in a summer night, for instance,—which by its wildness, to speak without satire, reminds me of the cries emitted by wild beasts in their native forests. It is so much of their wildness as I can understand. Give me for my friends and neighbors wild men, not tame ones. The wildness of the savage is but a faint symbol of the awful ferity with which good men and lovers meet.

I love even to see the domestic animals reassert their native rights,— any evidence that they have not wholly lost their original wild habits and vigor; as when my neighbor's cow breaks out of her pasture early in the spring and boldly swims the river, a cold, gray tide, twenty-five or thirty rods wide, swollen by the melted snow. It is the buffalo crossing the Mississippi. This exploit confers some dignity on the herd in my eyes,—already dignified. The seeds of instinct are preserved under the thick hides of cattle and horses, like seeds in the bowels of the earth, an indefinite period.

Any sportiveness in cattle is unexpected. I saw one day a herd of a dozen bullocks and cows running about and frisking in unwieldly sport, like huge rats, even like kittens. They shook their heads, raised their tails, and rushed up and down a hill, and I perceived by their horns, as well as by their activity, their relation to the deer tribe. But, alas! a sudden loud *Whoa!* would have damped their ardor at once, reduced them from venison to beef, and stiffened their sides and sinews like the locomotive. Who but the Evil One has cried, "Whoa!" to mankind? Indeed, the life of cattle, like that of many men, is but a sort of locomotiveness; they move a side at a time, and man, by his machinery, is meeting the horse and the ox half-way. Whatever part the whip has touched is thenceforth palsied. Who would ever think of a *side* of any of the supple cat tribe, as we speak of a *side* of beef?

I rejoice that horses and steers have to be broken before they can be made the slaves of men, and that men themselves have some wild oats still left to sow before they become submissive members of society. Undoubtedly, all men are not equally fit subjects for civilization; and because the majority, like dogs and sheep, are tame by inherited disposition, this is no reason why the others should have their natures broken that they may be reduced to the same level. Men are in the main alike, but they were made several in order that they might be various. If a low use is to be served, one man will do nearly or quite as well as another; if a high one, individual excellence is to be regarded. Any man can stop a hole to keep the wind away, but no other man could serve so rare a use as the author of this illustration did. Confucius says,—"The skins of the tiger and the leopard, when they are tanned, are as the skins of the dog and the sheep tanned." But it is not the part of a true culture to tame tigers, any more than it is to make sheep ferocious; and tanning their skins for shoes is not the best use to which they can be put.

When looking over a list of men's names in a foreign language, as of military officers, or of authors who have written on a particular subject, I am reminded once more that there is nothing in a name. The name Menschikoff, for instance, has nothing in it to my ears more human than a whisker, and it may belong to a rat. As the names of the Poles and Russians are to us, so are ours to them. It is as if they had been named by the child's rigmarole,—*Iery wiery ichery van, tittle-tol-tan.* I see in my mind a herd of wild creatures swarming over the earth, and to each the herdsman has affixed some barbarous sound in his own dialect. The names of men are of course as cheap and meaningless as *Bose* and *Tray,* the names of dogs.

Methinks it would be some advantage to philosophy, if men were named merely in the gross, as they are known. It would be necessary only to know the genus and perhaps the race or variety, to know the individual. We are not prepared to believe that every private soldier in a Roman army had a name of his own,—because we have not supposed that he had a character of his own. At present our only true names are nicknames. I knew a boy who, from his peculiar energy, was called "Buster" by his playmates, and this rightly supplanted his Christian name. Some travellers tell us that an Indian had no name given him at first, but earned it, and his name was his fame; and among some tribes he acquired a new name with every new exploit. It is pitiful when a man bears a name for convenience merely, who has earned neither name nor fame.

I will not allow mere names to make distinctions for me, but still see men in herds for all them. A familiar name cannot make a man less strange to me. It may be given to a savage who retains in secret his own wild title earned in the woods. We have a wild savage in us, and a savage name is perchance somewhere recorded as ours. I see that my neighbor, who bears the familiar epithet William, or Edwin, takes it off with his jacket. It does not adhere to him when asleep or in anger, or aroused by any passion or inspiration. I seem to hear pronounced by some of his kin at such a time his original wild name in some jaw-breaking or else melodious tongue.

Here is this vast, savage, howling mother of ours, Nature, lying all around, with such beauty, and such affection for her children, as the leopard; and yet we are so early weaned from her breast to society, to that culture which is exclusively an interaction of man on man,—a sort of breeding in and in, which produces at most a merely English nobility, a civilization destined to have a speedy limit.

In society, in the best institutions of men, it is easy to detect a certain precocity. When we should still be growing children, we are already little men. Give me a culture which imports much muck from the meadows, and deepens the soil,—not that which trusts to heating manures, and improved implements and modes of culture only!

Many a poor sore-eyed student that I have heard of would grow faster, both intellectually and physically, if, instead of sitting up so very late, he honestly slumbered a fool's allowance.

There may be an excess even of informing light. Niépce, a Frenchman, discovered "actinism," that power in the sun's rays which produces a chemical effect,—that granite rocks, and stone structures, and statues of metal, "are all alike destructively acted upon during the hours of sunshine, and, but for provisions of Nature no less wonderful, would soon perish under the delicate touch of the most subtile of the agencies of the universe." But he observed that "those bodies which underwent this change during the daylight possessed the power of restoring themselves to their original conditions during the hours of night, when this excitement was no longer influencing them." Hence it has been inferred that "the hours of darkness are as necessary to the inorganic creation as we know night and sleep are to the organic kingdom." Not even does the moon shine every night, but gives place to darkness.

I would not have every man nor every part of a man cultivated, any more than I would have every acre of earth cultivated: part will be tillage, but the greater part will be meadow and forest, not only serving an immediate use, but preparing a mould against a distant future, by the annual decay of the vegetation which it supports.

There are other letters for the child to learn than those which Cadmus invented. The Spaniards have a good term to express this wild and dusky knowledge,—*Gramática parda*, tawny grammar,—a kind of mother-wit derived from that same leopard to which I have referred.

We have heard of a Society for the Diffusion of Useful Knowledge. It is said that knowledge is power; and the like. Methinks there is equal need of a Society for the Diffusion of Useful Ignorance, what we will call Beautiful Knowledge, a knowledge useful in a higher sense: for what is most of our boasted so-called knowledge but a conceit that we know something, which robs us of the advantage of our actual ignorance? What we call knowledge is often our positive ignorance; ignorance our negative knowledge. By long years of patient industry and reading of the newspapers,—for what are the libraries of science but files of newspapers?—a man accumulates a myriad facts, lays them up in his memory, and then when in some spring of his life he saunters abroad into the Great Fields of thought, he, as it were, goes to grass like a horse, and leaves all his harness behind in the stable. I would say to the Society for the Diffusion of Useful Knowledge, sometimes,—Go to grass. You have eaten hay long enough. The spring has come with its green crop. The very cows are driven to their country pastures before the end of May; though I have heard of one unnatural farmer who kept his cow in the barn and fed her on hay all the year round. So, frequently, the Society for the Diffusion of Useful Knowledge treats its cattle.

A man's ignorance sometimes is not only useful, but beautiful,—while his knowledge, so called, is oftentimes worse than useless, besides being ugly. Which is the best man to deal with,—he who knows nothing about a subject, and, what is extremely rare, knows that he knows nothing, or he who really knows something about it, but thinks that he knows all?

My desire for knowledge is intermittent; but my desire to bathe my head in atmospheres unknown to my feet is perennial and constant. The highest that we can attain to is not Knowledge, but Sympathy with Intelligence. I do not know that this higher knowledge amounts to anything more definite than a novel and grand surprise on a sudden revelation of the insufficiency of all that we called Knowledge before,—a discovery that there are more things in heaven and earth than are dreamed of in our philosophy. It is the lighting up of the mist by the sun. Man cannot *know* in any higher sense than this, any more than he can look serenely and with impunity in the face of sun: Ὡς τί νοων,οὐ κεῖνον νοήσεις,—"You will not perceive that, as perceiving a particular thing," say the Chaldean Oracles.

There is something servile in the habit of seeking after a law which we may obey. We may study the laws of matter at and for our convenience, but a successful life knows no law. It is an unfortunate discovery certainly, that of a law which binds us where we did not know before that we were bound. Live free, child of the mist,—and with respect to knowledge we are all children of the mist. The man who takes the liberty to live is superior to all the laws, by virtue of his relation to the law-maker. "That is active duty," says the Vishnu Purana, "which is not for our bondage; that is knowledge which is for our liberation: all other duty is good only unto weariness; all other knowledge is only the cleverness of an artist."

* * *

It is remarkable how few events or crises there are in our histories; how little exercised we have been in our minds; how few experiences we have had. I would fain be assured that I am growing apace and rankly, though my very growth disturb this dull equanimity,—though it be with struggle through long, dark, muggy nights or seasons of gloom. It would be well, if all our lives were a divine tragedy even, instead of this trivial comedy or farce. Dante, Bunyan, and others, appear to have been exercised in their minds more than we: they were subjected to a kind of culture such as our district schools and colleges do not contemplate. Even Mahomet, though many may scream at his name, had a good deal more to live for, ay, and to die for, than they have commonly.

When, at rare intervals, some thought visits one, as perchance he is walking on a railroad, then indeed the cars go by without his hearing them. But soon, by some inexorable law, our life goes by and the cars return.

> *"Gentle breeze, that wanderest unseen,*
> *And bendest the thistles round Loira of storms,*
> *Traveller of the windy glens,*
> *Why hast thou left my ear so soon?"*

While almost all men feel an attraction drawing them to society, few are attracted strongly to Nature. In their relation to Nature men appear to me for the most part, notwithstanding their arts, lower than the animals. It is not often a beautiful relation, as in the case of the animals. How little appreciation of the beauty of the landscape there is among us! We have to be told that the Greeks called the world $Κόσμος$, Beauty, or Order, but we do not see clearly why they did so, and we esteem it at best only a curious philological fact.

For my part, I feel that with regard to Nature I live a sort of border life, on the confines of a world into which I make occasional and transitional and transient forays only, and my patriotism and allegiance to the State into whose territories I seem to retreat are those of a moss-trooper. Unto a life which I call natural I would gladly follow even a will-o'-the-wisp through bogs and sloughs unimaginable, but no moon nor fire-fly has shown me the causeway to it. Nature is a personality so vast and universal that we have never seen one of her features. The walker in the familiar fields which stretch around my native town sometimes finds himself in another land than is described in their owners' deeds, as it were in some far-away field on the confines of the actual Concord, where her jurisdiction ceases, and the idea which the word Concord suggests ceases to be suggested. These farms which I have myself surveyed, these bounds which I have set up, appear dimly still as through a mist; but they have no chemistry to fix them; they fade from the surface of the glass; and the picture which the painter painted stands out dimly from beneath. The world with which we are commonly acquainted leaves no trace, and it will have no anniversary.

I took a walk on Spaulding's Farm the other afternoon. I saw the setting sun lighting up the opposite side of a stately pine wood. Its golden rays straggled into the aisles of the wood as into some noble hall. I was impressed as if some ancient and altogether admirable and shining family had settled there in that part of the land called Concord, unknown to me,—to whom the sun was servant,—who had not gone into society in the village,—who had not been called on. I saw their park, their pleasure-ground, beyond through the wood, in Spaulding's cranberry-meadow. The pines furnished them with gables as they grew. Their house was not obvious to vision; the trees grew through it. I do not know whether I heard the sounds of a suppressed hilarity or not. They seemed to recline on the sunbeams. They have sons and daughters. They are quite well. The farmer's cart-path, which leads directly through their hall, does not in the least put them out,—as the muddy bottom of a pool is sometimes seen through the reflected skies. They never heard of Spaulding, and do not know that he is their neighbor,—notwithstanding I heard him whistle as he drove his team through the house. Nothing can equal the serenity of their lives. Their coat of arms is simply a lichen. I saw it painted on the pines and oaks. Their attics were in the tops of the trees. They are of no politics. There was no noise of labor. I did not perceive that they were weaving or spinning. Yet I did detect, when the wind lulled and hearing was done away, the finest imaginable sweet musical hum,—as of a distant hive in May, which perchance was the sound of their thinking. They had no idle thoughts, and no one without could see their work, for their industry was not as in knots and excrescences embayed.

But I find it difficult to remember them. They fade irrevocably out of my mind even now while I speak and endeavor to recall them, and recollect myself. It is only after a long and serious effort to recollect my best thoughts that I become again aware of their cohabitancy. If it were not for such families as this, I think I should move out of Concord.

We are accustomed to say in New England that few and fewer pigeons visit us every year. Our forests furnish no mast for them. So, it would seem, few and fewer thoughts visit each growing man from year to year, for the grove in our minds is laid waste,—sold to feed unnecessary fires of ambition, or sent to mill, and there is scarcely a twig left for them to perch on. They no longer build nor breed with us. In some more genial season, perchance, a faint shadow flits across the landscape of the mind, cast by the *wings* of some thought in its vernal or autumnal migration, but, looking up, we are unable to detect the substance of the thought itself. Our winged thoughts are turned to poultry. They no longer soar, and they attain only to a Shanghai and Cochin-China grandeur. Those *gra-a-ate thoughts,* those *gra-a-ate men* you hear of!

We hug the earth,—how rarely we mount! Methinks we might elevate ourselves a little more. We might climb a tree, at least. I found my account in climbing a tree once. It was a tall white pine, on the top of a hill; and though I got well pitched, I was well paid for it, for I discovered new mountains in the horizon which I had never seen before,—so much more of the earth and the heavens. I might have walked about the foot of the tree for threescore years and ten, and yet I certainly should never have seen them. But, above all, I discovered around me,—it was near the end of June,—on the ends of the topmost branches only, a few minute and delicate red cone-like blossoms, the fertile flower of the white pine looking heavenward. I carried straightway to the village the topmost spire, and showed it to stranger jurymen who walked the streets,—for it was court-week,—and to farmers and lumber-dealers and wood-choppers and hunters, and not one had ever seen the like before, but they wondered as at a star dropped down. Tell of ancient architects finishing their works on the tops of columns as perfectly as on the lower and more visible parts! Nature has from the first expanded the minute blossoms of the forest only toward the heavens, above men's heads and unobserved by them. We see only the flowers that are under our feet in the meadows. The pines have developed their delicate blossoms on the highest twigs of the wood every summer for ages, as well over the heads of Nature's red children as of her white ones; yet scarcely a farmer or hunter in the land has ever seen them.

Above all, we cannot afford not to live in the present. He is blessed over all mortals who loses no moment of the passing life in remembering the past. Unless our philosophy hears the cock crow in every barn-yard within our horizon, it is belated. That sound commonly reminds us that we are growing rusty and antique in our employments and habits of thought. His philosophy comes down to a more recent time than ours. There is something suggested by it that is a newer testament,—the gospel according to this moment. He has not fallen astern; he has got up early, and kept up early, and to be where he is to be in season, in the foremost rank of time. It is an expression of the health and soundness of Nature, a brag for all the world,—healthiness as of a spring burst forth, a new fountain of the Muses, to celebrate this last instant of time. Where he lives no fugitive slave laws are passed. Who has not betrayed his master many times since last he heard that note?

The merit of this bird's strain is in its freedom from all plaintiveness. The singer can easily move us to tears or to laughter, but where is he who can excite in us a pure morning joy? When, in doleful dumps, breaking the awful stillness of our wooden sidewalk on a Sunday, or, perchance, a watcher in the house of mourning, I hear a cockerel crow far or near, I think to myself, "There is one of us well, at any rate,"—and with a sudden gush return to my senses.

We had a remarkable sunset one day last November. I was walking in a meadow, the source of a small brook, when the sun at last, just before setting, after a cold gray day, reached a clear stratum in the horizon, and the softest, brightest morning sunlight fell on the dry grass and on the stems of the trees in the opposite horizon, and on the leaves of the shrub-oaks on the hill-side, while our shadows stretched long over the meadow eastward, as if we were the only motes in its beams. It was such a light as we could not have imagined a moment before, and the air also was so warm and serene that nothing was wanting to make a paradise of that meadow. When we reflected that this was not a solitary phenomenon, never to happen again, but that it would happen forever and ever an infinite number of evenings, and cheer and reassure the latest child that walked there, it was more glorious still.

The sun sets on some retired meadow, where no house is visible, with all the glory and splendor that it lavishes on cities, and perchance, as it has never set before,—where there is but a solitary marsh-hawk to have his wings gilded by it, or only a musquash looks out from his cabin, and there is some little black-veined brook in the midst of the marsh, just beginning to meander, winding slowly round a decaying stump. We walked in so pure and bright a light, gilding the withered grass and leaves, so softly and serenely bright, I thought I had never bathed in such a golden flood, without a ripple or a murmur to it. The west side of every wood and rising ground gleamed like the boundary of Elysium, and the sun on our backs seemed like a gentle herdsman driving us home at evening.

So we saunter toward the Holy Land, till one day the sun shall shine more brightly than ever he has done, shall perchance shine into our minds and hearts, and light up our whole lives with a great awakening light, as warm and serene and golden as on a bank-side in autumn.

More Ho- Hum

H . L . MENCKEN

Though he wrote books on philosophy and linguistics, Henry Louis Mencken (1880–1956) viewed himself primarily as a newspaperman and was undoubtedly the greatest writer among practicing American journalists. Born in Baltimore, a city to which he remained loyal, he worked most of his life for the Baltimore Sun; *many of his noted essays (such as "On Being an American") originated as newspaper columns. Particularly famous were his coverage of the Scopes "monkey" trial, which pitted evolutionists against fundamentalists, and his dispatches on political conventions.*

Mencken had a satiric eye for hypocrisy, sanctimony, and fraudulence. In his widely read magazines, The Smart Set *and* The American Mercury, *he helped shape the consciousness of a generation of educated readers. A provocateur and gadfly, mercilessly puncturing the American middle class (which he called the "booboisie"), he managed to get away with insulting the public and espousing unpopular views, partly because his affection for America was still so palpable underneath the digs, and partly because he wrote so entertainingly that his readers could not help being amused. Mencken gathered his pieces into collections that he called* Prejudices. *Some of his "prejudices" now seem close to bigotry, but he was a complex, contradictory man, a freethinker and a champion of minority causes. He enjoyed life and wrote enthusiastically about eating clams, listening to music, and watching prize fights.* ⁊

Mencken's sentences could be hard-hitting and blunt or employ ornate vocabulary, often as comic counterpoint to the lowly subjects (political skullduggery, baldness) he was writing about. While he was more of a social commentator than a pure personal essayist, everything he wrote had a personal, idiosyncratic stamp, and he frequently made himself a character in his writings. After his death, it was feared that his work might become dated, as so much of it was pinned to topical material; but now it appears we will always read Mencken, for the felicities of his heightened style and the pugnacity of his persona. His influence today can be seen in such elegant essay stylists as Gore Vidal, Murray Kempton, and Joan Didion.

On Being an American

1

A PPARENTLY there are those who begin to find it disagreeable. One of them unburdened his woes in this place last Tuesday, under the heading of "Is America Fit to Live In?" Let me confess at once that his elegy filled me with great astonishment. I had labored under the impression that this Republic was wholly satisfactory to all 100% Americans —that any proposal to fumigate and improve it was as personally offensive to them as a proposal to improve the looks of their wives. Yet here was a 100% American ranting against it like a Bolshevik on a soap box. And here was I, less than ½ of 1% American by volume, standing aghast. A curious experience, indeed. Can it be that all the 100% Americans are preparing to throw up their hands and move out, leaving the land that the Fathers sweated and bled for to us Huns?

God forbid! I'd as lief have some poor working girl (mistaking the street number) leave twins on my doorstep. No one would weep saltier tears than I when the huge fleet of Mayflowers sailed away, bound for some land of liberty. For what makes America charming is precisely the Americans—that is, those above 50%, those above proof. They are, by long odds, the most charming people that I have ever encountered in this world. They have the same charm that one so often notes in a young girl, say of seventeen or eighteen, and perhaps it is grounded upon the same qualities; artlessness, great seriousness, extreme self-consciousness, a fresh and innocent point of view, a disarming and ingratiating ignorance. They are culturally speaking the youngest of white races, and they have all the virtues that go with youngness. It is easy to excite them. It is easy to fool them. But it is very hard to dislike them.

Perhaps there is something deeper than the qualities I have rehearsed. I grope for it vaguely, and decide that it is probably a naïve fidelity to good intentions. The Americans do everything with the best of motives, and with all the solemnity that goes therewith. And they get the reward that the jocose gods invariably bestow. I recall a scene in a low burlesque show, witnessed for hire in my days as a dramatic critic. A chorus girl executes a fall on the stage, and Krausemeyer, the Swiss comedian, rushes to her aid. As he stoops painfully to pick her up, Irving Rabinovitz, the Zionist comedian, fetches him a fearful clout across the cofferdam with a slapstick. Here, in brief, is the history of the United States, particularly in recent years. Say what you will against it, I maintain to the last that it is diverting—that it affords stimulating entertainment to a civilized man.

2

Where, indeed, is there a better show in the world? Where has there been a better show since the Reformation? It goes on daily, not in three rings, but in three hundred rings, and in each one of them whole battalions of acrobats tie themselves into fabulous knots, and the handsomest gals in Christendom pirouette upon the loveliest and most skittish horses, and clowns of unbelievable limberness and humor perform inordinate monkey-shines. Consider, for example, the current campaign for the Presidency. Would it be possible to imagine anything more stupendously grotesque—a deafening, nerve-wracking battle to the death between Tweedledum and Tweedledee—the impossible, with fearful snorts, gradually swallowing the inconceivable? I defy anyone to match it elsewhere on this earth. In other lands, at worst, there are at least issues, ideas, personalities. Somebody says something intelligible, and somebody replies. It is important to somebody that the thing go this way or that way. But here, having perfected democracy, we lift the whole combat to a gaudy symbolism, to a disembodied transcendentalism, to metaphysics, that sweet nirvana. Here we load a pair of palpably tin cannons with blank cartridges charged with talcum-powder, and so let fly. Here one may howl over the show without an uneasy reminder that some one is being hurt.

I hold that this exhibition is peculiarly American—that nowhere else on this disreputable ball has the art of the sham-battle been developed to such fineness. Two late experiences in point. A few weeks back a Berlin paper reprinted an article of mine from the *Evening Sunpaper,* with an explanatory preface. In this preface the editor was at pains to explain that no intelligent man in the United States regarded the result of an election as important, and to warn the Germans against getting into feverish sweats over such combats. Last week I had dinner with an Englishman. From cocktails to bromo seltzer he bewailed the political lassitude of the English populace—its growing indifference to the whole political buffoonery. Here we have two typical foreign attitudes; the Germans make politics too harsh and implacable, and the English take politics too lightly. Both attitudes make for bad shows. Observing a German election, one is uncomfortably harassed and stirred up; observing an English election, one falls asleep. In the United States the thing is better done. Here it is purged of all menace, all sinister quality, all genuine significance—and stuffed with such gorgeous humors, such extravagant imbecilities, such uproarious farce that one comes to the end of it with one's midriff in tatters.

3

But feeling better for the laugh. As the 100% *pleurour* said last Tuesday, the human soul craves joy. It is necessary to happiness, to health. Well, here is the land of joy. Here the show never stops. What could be more steadily mirth-provoking than the endless battle of the Puritans to make this joy unlawful and impossible? The effort is itself a greater joy to one standing on the sidelines than any or all of the joys that it combats. If I had to choose between hanging Dr. Kelly and closing all of the theatres in Baltimore, I'd surely shut up the theatres, for nine times out of ten their laborious struggles to amuse me merely bore me, whereas Dr. Kelly fetches me every time. He is, it seems to me, the eternal American, ever moved by good intentions, ever lifting me to yells with the highest of motives, ever stooping à la Krausemeyer to pick up a foundered chorus girl and ever getting a thumping clout from the Devil.

I am sinful, and such spectacles delight me. If the slapstick were a sash-weight the show would be cruel, and I'd probably go to the rescue of Dr. Kelly. As it is I know that he is not hurt. On the contrary, it does him good: it helps to get him into Heaven. As for me, it helps to divert me from my sorrows, of which there are many. More, it makes me a better American. One man likes the republic because it pays better wages than Bulgaria. Another because it has laws to keep him sober, pious and faithful to his wife. Another because the Woolworth Building is higher than the cathedral at Chartres. Another because Roosevelt could not leave the job to his son. Another because, living here, he can read the New York *Journal.* Another because there is a warrant out for him somewhere else. Me, I like it because it amuses me. I never get tired of the show. It is worth every cent it costs.

4

I have never heard of such a show in any other country. Perhaps one goes on in Russia, but, as the European *Advocatus Diaboli* said last Tuesday, it is difficult to be happy when one is hungry. Here one always gets plenty to eat, even in the midst of war, and, despite Prohibition, quite enough to drink. I remember many postprandial felicities, inconceivable in Europe, Asia, Africa or Oceania. Four nights, for example, at the Billy Sunday circus; one night in particular. I had got down a capital dinner, with three or four coffin-varnish cocktails and half a bottle of Beni Carlo. (Ah, those days!) Proceeding to the holy place, I witnessed the incomparable spectacle of a governor of Maryland, the president of a bank and the president of the Western Maryland Railroad moaning and puffing in a bull-ring together. Match it in Europe if you can! I defy you to name the country. The governor, prefect, lord lieutenant, *Oberpräsident* of an ancient and imperial province sobbing out his sins in the presence of 20,000 neckstretchers, the while a florid man with an elkhorn mustache played "Throw Out the Lifeline" on a trombone!

Another memory. The other day, in New York, I gave ear to a publisher soured and made hopeless by the incessant forays of the Comstocks—*The "Genius"* and *Jurgen* suppressed out of hand, half a dozen other good books killed abornin', the national letters hamstrung and knee-haltered by a violent arbitrary and unintelligible despotism. That night I went to the Winter Garden to see the new show. During the first part, 40 or 50 head of girls with their legs bare marched down a runway into the audience, passing within four or five centimetres of my popping eyes. During the second part two comedians came out and began to make jokes about what Havelock Ellis calls inversion. Revolve the thing in your mind. Here was I, an innocent young yokel, forbidden by law to read *Jurgen,* and yet it was quite lawful to beguile me with a herd of half-naked vampires and to divert me with jests proper only to banquets of internes at the Phipps Clinic! After the show I met Ernest A. Boyd. He told me that he had a fearful beer thirst and would gladly give $5 for a *Humpen* of 2³⁄4%. I raised him $1, but we found that malt was forbidden. But down in Greenwich Village we found plenty of 100-proof Scotch at 65 cents a drink.

5

Let the 100% viewer-with-alarm stay his tears. If this is not joy, then what is?

Ho Hom

ROBERT BENCHLEY

Robert Benchley (1889–1945) was a popular American humorist, essayist, drama critic, and movie actor. A member of the group of Algonquin wits, which included Dorothy Parker and George S. Kaufman, Benchley possessed a seemingly bottomless ability to turn daily life and its stubborn, minor irritations into entertaining commentary. His skill is deceptively simple; the economical speed with which he could summon a recognizable persona and animate it on the page is something many essayists today would give a great deal for. Like Max Beerbohm and James Thurber, Benchley could zero in on human foibles with a cartoonist's panache.

  Not only did Benchley write fifteen books of humorous essays, including Of All Things, My Ten Years in a Quandary *and* How They Grew, *and* Benchley Beside Himself, *he also created and starred in forty-six movie shorts (such as* Sex Life of the Polyp *and* How to Sleep*), which usually satirized educational or how-to demonstrations with mock-professorial drollness. The readiness with which Benchley made fun of himself, deriving laughs from his alleged physical ordinariness, may be seen in the characteristically light-toned "My Face," which nevertheless brushes against the disturbing, uncanny quality of all doppelgänger literature.*

My Face

MERELY AS AN OBSERVER of natural phenomena, I am fascinated by my own personal appearance. This does not mean that I am *pleased* with it, mind you, or that I can even tolerate it. I simply have a morbid interest in it.

Each day I look like someone, or some*thing,* different. I never know what it is going to be until I steal a look in the glass. (Oh, I don't suppose you really could call it stealing. It belongs to me, after all.)

One day I look like Wimpy, the hamburger fancier in the Popeye the Sailor saga. Another day it may be Wallace Beery. And a third day, if I have let my mustache get out of hand, it is Bairnsfather's Old Bill. And not until I peek do I know what the show is going to be.

Some mornings, if I look in the mirror soon enough after getting out of bed, there is no resemblance to any character at all, either in or out of fiction, and I turn quickly to look behind me, convinced that a stranger has spent the night with me and is peering over my shoulder in a sinister fashion, merely to frighten me. On such occasions, the shock of finding that I am actually possessor of the face in the mirror is sufficient to send me scurrying back to bed, completely unnerved.

All this is, of course, very depressing, and I often give off a low moan at the sight of the new day's metamorphosis, but I can't seem to resist the temptation to learn the worst. I even go out of my way to look at myself in store-window mirrors, just to see how long it will take me to recognize myself. If I happen to have on a new hat, or am walking with a limp, I sometimes pass right by my reflection without even nodding. Then I begin to think: "You must have given off *some* visual impression into that mirror. You're not a disembodied spirit yet—I hope."

And I go back and look again, and, sure enough, the strange-looking man I thought was walking just ahead of me in the reflection turns out to have been my own image all the time. It makes a fellow stop and think, I can tell you.

This almost masochistic craving to offend my own aesthetic sense by looking at myself and wincing also comes out when snapshots or class photographs are being passed around. The minute someone brings the envelope containing the week's grist of vacation prints from the drug-store developing plant, I can hardly wait to get my hands on them. I try to dissemble my eagerness to examine those in which I myself figure, but there is a greedy look in my eye which must give me away.

The snapshots in which I do not appear are so much dross in my eyes, but I pretend that I am equally interested in them all.

"This is very good of Joe," I say, with a hollow ring to my voice, sneaking a look at the next print to see if I am in it.

Ah! Here, at last, is one in which I show up nicely. By "nicely" I mean "clearly." Try as I will to pass it by casually, my eyes rivet themselves on that corner of the group in which I am standing. And then, when the others have left the room, I surreptitiously go through the envelope again, just to gaze my fill on the slightly macabre sight of Myself as others see me.

In some pictures I look even worse than I had imagined. On what I call my "good days," I string along pretty close to form. But day in and day out, in mirror or in photograph, there is always that slight shock of surprise which, although unpleasant, lends a tang to the adventure of peeking. I never can quite make it seem possible that this is really Poor Little Me, the Little Me I know so well and yet who frightens me so when face to face.

My only hope is that, in this constant metamorphosis which seems to be going on, a winning number may come up sometime, if only for a day. Just what the final outcome will be, it is hard to predict. I may settle down to a constant, plodding replica of Man-Mountain Dean in my old age, or change my style completely and end up as a series of Bulgarian peasant types. I may just grow old along with Wimpy.

But whatever is in store for me, I shall watch the daily modulations with an impersonal fascination not unmixed with awe at Mother Nature's gift for caricature, and will take the bitter with the sweet and keep a stiff upper lip.

As a matter of fact, my upper lip is pretty fascinating by itself, in a bizarre sort of way.

JAMES THURBER

James Thurber (1894–1961) is one of the most beloved American humorists. Along with his contemporaries Ring Lardner, Dorothy Parker, Robert Benchley, and S. J. Perelman, he helped inject wit, whimsy, and inspired nonsense into American essay prose. Thurber grew up in Columbus, Ohio, and many of his pieces are about boyhood in that less-than-metropolis and his eccentric family. Coming east, he began what was to be a lifelong association with The New Yorker, *where he served for a while under Harold Ross as managing editor (see Thurber's memoir,* The Years with Ross) *and later as a perennial contributor, helping to set, along with his friend E. B. White, the magazine's tone. Thurber and White collaborated on a droll spoof of marriage manuals,* Is Sex Necessary? *Thurber's humor frequently derived from the battle between the sexes, and his portraits of domineering women and meek men left no doubt which sex he thought to be the weaker.*

Like Max Beerbohm, Thurber was a gifted cartoonist, and the illustrations that dot his books bring to mind the slightly loony, surreal, antiheroic, dog-ridden atmosphere known as "Thurberesque." He had an uncanny ability to take any written form in modern life, from the questionnaire to the how-to book, and satirize it in a few pages. The title of the following piece, "The Secret Life of James Thurber," simultaneously parodies celebrity autobiographies and his own famous story "The Secret Life of Walter Mitty," which charts the distance between the common man's rich fantasy life and pedestrian reality. As demonstrated here, Thurber's humor is partly situational and partly linguistic: his sentences have a runaway giddiness.

The Secret Life of James Thurber

I HAVE ONLY dipped here and there into Salvador Dali's "The Secret Life of Salvador Dali" (with paintings by Salvador Dali and photographs of Salvador Dali), because anyone afflicted with what my grandmother's sister Abigail called "the permanent jumps" should do no more than skitter through such an autobiography, particularly in these melancholy times.

One does not have to skitter far before one comes upon some vignette which gives the full shape and flavor of the book: the youthful dreamer of dreams biting a sick bat or kissing a dead horse, the slender stripling going into man's estate with the high hope and fond desire of one day eating a live but roasted turkey, the sighing lover covering himself with goat dung and aspic that he might give off the true and noble odor of the ram. In my flying trip through Dali I caught other glimpses of the great man: Salvador adoring a seed ball fallen from a plane tree, Salvador kicking a tiny playmate off a bridge, Salvador caressing a crutch, Salvador breaking the old family doctor's glasses with a leather-thonged mattress-beater. There would appear to be only two things in the world that revolt him (and I don't mean a long-dead hedgehog). He is squeamish about skeletons and grasshoppers. Oh, well, we all have our idiosyncrasies.

Señor Dali's memoirs have set me to thinking. I find myself muttering as I shave, and on two occasions I have swung my crutch at a little neighbor girl on my way to the post office. Señor Dali's book sells for six dollars. My own published personal history (Harper & Brothers, 1933) sold for $1.75. At the time I complained briefly about this unusual figure, principally on the ground that it represented only fifty cents more than the price asked for a book called "The Adventures of Horace the Hedgehog," published the same month. The publishers explained that the price was a closely approximated vertical, prefigured on the basis of profitable ceiling, which in turn was arrived at by taking into consideration the effect on diminishing returns of the horizontal factor.

In those days all heads of business firms adopted a guarded kind of double talk, commonly expressed in low, muffled tones, because nobody knew what was going to happen and nobody understood what had. Big business had been frightened by a sequence of economic phenomena which had clearly demonstrated that our civilization was in greater danger of being turned off than of gradually crumbling away. The upshot of it all was that I accepted the price of $1.75. In so doing, I accepted the state of the world as a proper standard by which the price of books should be fixed. And now, with the world in ten times as serious a condition as it was in 1933, Dali's publishers set a price of six dollars on his life story. This brings me to the inescapable conclusion that the price-fixing principle, in the field of literature, is not global but personal. The trouble, quite simply, is that I told too much about what went on in the house I lived in and not enough about what went on inside myself.

Let me be the first to admit that the naked truth about me is to the naked truth about Salvador Dali as an old ukulele in the attic is to a piano in a tree, and I mean a piano with breasts. Señor Dali has the jump on me from the beginning. He remembers and describes in detail what it was like in the womb. My own earliest memory is of accompanying my father to a polling booth in Columbus, Ohio, where he voted for William McKinley.

It was a drab and somewhat battered tin shed set on wheels, and it was filled with guffawing men and cigar smoke; all in all, as far removed from the paradisiacal placenta of Salvador Dali's first recollection as could well be imagined. A fat, jolly man dandled me on his knee and said that I would soon be old enough to vote against William Jennings Bryan. I thought he meant that I could push a folded piece of paper into the slot of the padlocked box as soon as my father was finished. When this turned out not to be true, I had to be carried out of the place kicking and screaming. In my struggles I knocked my father's derby off several times. The derby was not a monstrously exciting love object to me, as practically everything Salvador encountered was to him, and I doubt, if I had that day to live over again, that I could bring myself, even in the light of exotic dedication as I now know it, to conceive an intense and perverse affection for the derby. It remains obstinately in my memory as a rather funny hat, a little too large in the crown, which gave my father the appearance of a tired, sensitive gentleman who had been persuaded against his will to take part in a game of charades.

We lived on Champion Avenue at the time, and the voting booth was on Mound Street. As I set down these names, I begin to perceive an essential and important difference between the infant Salvador and the infant me. This difference can be stated in terms of environment. Salvador was brought up in Spain, a country colored by the legends of Hannibal, El Greco, and Cervantes. I was brought up in Ohio, a region steeped in the tradition of Coxey's Army, the Anti-Saloon League, and William Howard Taft. It is only natural that the weather in little Salvador's soul should have been stirred by stranger winds and enveloped in more fantastic mists than

the weather in my own soul. But enough of mewling apology for my lack-
lustre early years. Let us get back to my secret life, such as it was, stopping
just long enough to have another brief look at Señor Dali on our way.

Salvador Dali's mind goes back to a childhood half imagined and half real,
in which the edges of actuality were sometimes less sharp than the edges
of dream. He seems somehow to have got the idea that this sets him off
from Harry Spencer, Charlie Doakes, I. Feinberg, J. J. McNaboe, Willie
Faulkner, Herbie Hoover, and me. What Salvie had that the rest of us
kids didn't was the perfect scenery, characters, and costumes for his desperate little rebellion against the clean, the conventional, and the comfortable. He put perfume on his hair (which would have cost him his life in,
say, Bayonne, N.J., or Youngstown, Ohio), he owned a lizard with two
tails, he wore silver buttons on his shoes, and he knew, or imagined he
knew, little girls named Galuchka and Dullita. Thus he was born halfway
along the road to paranoia, the soft Poictesme of his prayers, the melting
Oz of his oblations, the capital, to put it so that you can see what I am
trying to say, of his heart's desire. Or so, anyway, it must seem to a native
of Columbus, Ohio, who, as a youngster, bought his twelve-dollar suits at
the F. & R. Lazarus Co., had his hair washed out with Ivory soap, owned
a bull terrier with only one tail, and played (nicely and a bit diffidently)
with little girls named Irma and Betty and Ruby.

   Another advantage that the young Dali had over me, from the standpoint of impetus toward paranoia, lay in the nature of the adults who
peopled his real world. There was, in Dali's home town of Figueras, a
family of artists named Pitchot (musicians, painters, and poets), all of
whom adored the ground that the *enfant terrible* walked on. If one of
them came upon him throwing himself from a high rock—a favorite relaxation of our hero—or hanging by his feet with his head immersed in a pail
of water, the wild news was spread about the town that greatness and
genius had come to Figueras. There was a woman who put on a look of
maternal interest when Salvador threw rocks at her. The mayor of the
town fell dead one day at the boy's feet. A doctor in the community (not
the one he had horsewhipped) was seized of a fit and attempted to beat
him up. (The contention that the doctor was out of his senses at the time
of the assault is Dali's, not mine.)

   The adults around me when I was in short pants were neither so glamorous nor so attentive. They consisted mainly of eleven maternal great-
aunts, all Methodists, who were staunch believers in physic, mustard plas-
ters, and Scripture, and it was part of their dogma that artistic tendencies
should be treated in the same way as hiccups or hysterics. None of them
was an artist, unless you can count Aunt Lou, who wrote sixteen-stress

verse, with hit-and-miss rhymes, in celebration of people's birthdays or on the occasion of great national disaster. It never occurred to me to bite a bat in my aunts' presence or to throw stones at them. There was one escape, though: my secret world of idiom.

Two years ago my wife and I, looking for a house to buy, called on a firm of real-estate agents in New Milford. One of the members of the firm, scrabbling through a metal box containing many keys, looked up to say, "The key to the Roxbury house isn't here." His partner replied, "It's a common lock. A skeleton will let you in." I was suddenly once again five years old, with wide eyes and open mouth. I pictured the Roxbury house as I would have pictured it as a small boy, a house of such dark and nameless horrors as have never crossed the mind of our little bat-biter.

It was of sentences like that, nonchalantly tossed off by real-estate dealers, great-aunts, clergymen, and other such prosaic persons that the enchanted private world of my early boyhood was made. In this world, businessmen who phoned their wives to say that they were tied up at the office sat roped to their swivel chairs, and probably gagged, unable to move or speak, except somehow, miraculously, to telephone; hundreds of thousands of businessmen tied to their chairs in hundreds of thousands of offices in every city of my fantastic cosmos. An especially fine note about the binding of all the businessmen in all the cities was that whoever did it always did it around five o'clock in the afternoon.

Then there was the man who left town under a cloud. Sometimes I saw him all wrapped up in the cloud, and invisible, like a cat in a burlap sack. At other times it floated, about the size of a sofa, three or four feet above his head, following him wherever he went. One could think about the man under the cloud before going to sleep; the image of him wandering around from town to town was a sure soporific.

Not so the mental picture of a certain Mrs. Huston, who had been terribly cut up when her daughter died on the operating table. I could see the doctors too vividly, just before they set upon Mrs. Huston with their knives, and I could hear them. "Now, Mrs. Huston, will we get up on the table like a good girl, or will we have to be put there?" I could usually fight off Mrs. Huston before I went to sleep, but she frequently got into my dreams, and sometimes she still does.

I remember the grotesque creature that came to haunt my meditations when one evening my father said to my mother, "What did Mrs. Johnson say when you told her about Betty?" and my mother replied, "Oh, she was all ears." There were many other wonderful figures in the secret, surrealist landscapes of my youth: the old lady who was always up in the air, the husband who did not seem to be able to put his foot down, the man who lost his head during a fire but was still able to run out of the house yelling, the young lady who was, in reality, a soiled dove. It was a world that, of necessity, one had to keep to oneself and brood over in silence, because it would fall to pieces at the touch of words. If you brought it out into the light of actual day and put it to the test of questions, your parents would try to laugh the miracles away, or they would take your temperature and put you to bed. (Since I always ran a temperature, whenever it was taken, I was put to bed and left there all alone with Mrs. Huston.)

Such a world as the world of my childhood is, alas, not year-proof. It is a ghost that, to use Henley's words, gleams, flickers, vanishes away. I think it must have been the time my little Cousin Frances came to visit us that it began surely and forever to dissolve. I came into the house one rainy dusk and asked where Frances was. "She is," said our cook, "up in the front room crying her heart out." The fact that a person could cry so hard that his heart would come out of his body, as perfectly shaped and glossy as a red velvet pincushion, was news to me. For some reason I had never heard the expression, so common in American families whose hopes and dreams run so often counter to attainment. I went upstairs and opened the door of the front room. Frances, who was three years older than I, jumped up off the bed and ran past me, sobbing, and down the stairs.

My search for her heart took some fifteen minutes. I tore the bed apart and kicked up the rugs and even looked in the bureau drawers. It was no good. I looked out the window at the rain and the darkening sky. My cherished mental image of the man under the cloud began to grow dim and fade away. I discovered that, all alone in a room, I could face the thought of Mrs. Huston with cold equanimity. Downstairs, in the living room, Frances was still crying. I began to laugh.

Ah there, Salvador!

F. SCOTT FITZGERALD

*F. Scott Fitzgerald (1896–1940) is considered one of the great American fiction writers of the twentieth century. His novels (*This Side of Paradise, The Beautiful and the Damned, The Great Gatsby, Tender Is the Night*) helped define the Jazz Age. He and his wife, Zelda, symbolized in many people's minds the glittering, party-loving, bored, expatriate "lost generation" of the 1920s, and their subsequent bouts with alcoholism and mental illness came to seem an inevitable payment for the myth that attached to them.*

It should be noted that in his fine early short stories, Fitzgerald already frequently used a commentating narrator whose gift for generalization and conversational confiding was essayistic in manner. Between 1931 and 1937 he wrote a wonderful series of personal essays, mostly for Esquire *magazine, which were collected in book form shortly after his death by his friend Edmund Wilson. The title piece, "The Crack-Up," sounded a new note in American autobiographical essays. Mordant, candid, hard-bitten, and purged of the sentimentality and nimbus of glamour usually associated with Fitzgerald's name, it gave a convincing, grisly account of hitting bottom. Fitzgerald's ability to take his best and worst experiences and distill them into hard-won wisdom, in a prose style full of zest and shrewd, entertaining self-amusement, show what a natural talent he had for the personal essay, and how much further he might have gone with it if he had not died at age forty-four.*

The Crack-Up

Brilliant, vulnerable + clear view of his mental shattering. RARE ... as he was

1.

OF COURSE ALL LIFE is a process of breaking down, but the blows that do the dramatic side of the work—the big sudden blows that come, or seem to come, from outside—the ones you remember and blame things on and, in moments of weakness, tell your friends about, don't show their effect all at once. There is another sort of blow that comes from within—that you don't feel until it's too late to do anything about it, until you realize with finality that in some regard you will never be as good a man again. The first sort of breakage seems to happen quick —the second kind happens almost without your knowing it but is realized suddenly indeed.

Before I go on with this short history, let me make a general observation —the test of a first-rate intelligence is the ability to hold two opposed ideas in the mind at the same time, and still retain the ability to function. One should, for example, be able to see that things are hopeless and yet be determined to make them otherwise. This philosophy fitted on to my early adult life, when I saw the improbable, the implausible, often the "impossible," come true. Life was something you dominated if you were any good. Life yielded easily to intelligence and effort, or to what proportion could be mustered of both. It seemed a romantic business to be a successful literary man—you were not ever going to be as famous as a movie star but what note you had was probably longer-lived—you were never going to have the power of a man of strong political or religious convictions but you were certainly more independent. Of course within the practice of your trade you were forever unsatisfied—but I, for one, would not have chosen any other.

As the twenties passed, with my own twenties marching a little ahead of them, my two juvenile regrets—at not being big enough (or good enough) to play football in college, and at not getting overseas during the war— resolved themselves into childish waking dreams of imaginary heroism that were good enough to go to sleep on in restless nights. The big problems of life seemed to solve themselves, and if the business of fixing them was difficult, it made one too tired to think of more general problems.

Life, ten years ago, was largely a personal matter. I must hold in balance the sense of the futility of effort and the sense of the necessity to struggle; the conviction of the inevitability of failure and still the determination to "succeed"—and, more than these, the contradiction between the dead hand of the past and the high intentions of the future. If I could do this through the common ills—domestic, professional and personal—then the ego would continue as an arrow shot from nothingness to nothingness with such force that only gravity would bring it to earth at last.

For seventeen years, with a year of deliberate loafing and resting out in the center—things went on like that, with a new chore only a nice prospect for the next day. I was living hard, too, but: "Up to forty-nine it'll be all right," I said. "I can count on that. For a man who's lived as I have, that's all you could ask."

—And then, ten years this side of forty-nine, I suddenly realized that I had prematurely cracked.

2.

Now a man can crack in many ways—can crack in the head—in which case the power of decision is taken from you by others! or in the body, when one can but submit to the white hospital world; or in the nerves. William Seabrook in an unsympathetic book tells, with some pride and a movie ending, of how he became a public charge. What led to his alcoholism or was bound up with it, was a collapse of his nervous system. Though the present writer was not so entangled—having at the time not tasted so much as a glass of beer for six months—it was his nervous reflexes that were giving way—too much anger and too many tears.

Moreover, to go back to my thesis that life has a varying offensive, the realization of having cracked was not simultaneous with a blow, but with a reprieve.

Not long before, I had sat in the office of a great doctor and listened to a grave sentence. With what, in retrospect, seems some equanimity, I had gone on about my affairs in the city where I was then living, not caring much, not thinking how much had been left undone, or what would become of this and that responsibility, like people do in books; I was well insured and anyhow I had been only a mediocre caretaker of most of the things left in my hands, even of my talent.

But I had a strong sudden instinct that I must be alone. I didn't want to see any people at all. I had seen so many people all my life—I was an average mixer, but more than average in a tendency to identify myself, my ideas, my destiny, with those of all classes that I came in contact with. I was always saving or being saved—in a single morning I would go through the emotions ascribable to Wellington at Waterloo. I lived in a world of inscrutable hostiles and inalienable friends and supporters.

But now I wanted to be absolutely alone and so arranged a certain insulation from ordinary cares.

It was not an unhappy time. I went away and there were fewer people. I found I was good-and-tired. I could lie around and was glad to, sleeping or dozing sometimes twenty hours a day and in the intervals trying resolutely not to think—instead I made lists—made lists and tore them up, hundreds of lists: of cavalry leaders and football players and cities, and popular tunes and pitchers, and happy times, and hobbies and houses lived in and how many suits since I left the army and how many pairs of shoes (I didn't count the suit I bought in Sorrento that shrunk, nor the pumps and dress shirt and collar that I carried around for years and never wore, because the pumps got damp and grainy and the shirt and collar got yellow and starch-rotted). And lists of women I'd liked, and of the times I had let myself be snubbed by people who had not been my betters in character or ability.

—And then suddenly, surprisingly, I got better.

—And cracked like an old plate as soon as I heard the news.

That is the real end of this story. What was to be done about it will have to rest in what used to be called the "womb of time." Suffice it to say that after about an hour of solitary pillow-hugging, I began to realize that for two years my life had been a drawing on resources that I did not possess, that I had been mortgaging myself physically and spiritually up to the hilt. What was the small gift of life given back in comparison to that?—when there had once been a pride of direction and a confidence in enduring independence.

I realized that in those two years, in order to preserve something—an inner hush maybe, maybe not—I had weaned myself from all the things I used to love—that every act of life from the morning tooth-brush to the friend at dinner had become an effort. I saw that for a long time I had not liked people and things, but only followed the rickety old pretense of liking. I saw that even my love for those closest to me was become only an attempt to love, that my casual relations—with an editor, a tobacco seller, the child of a friend, were only what I remembered I *should* do, from other days. All in the same month I became bitter about such things as the sound of the radio, the advertisements in the magazines, the screech of tracks, the dead silence of the country—contemptuous at human softness, immediately (if secretively) quarrelsome toward hardness—hating the night when I couldn't sleep and hating the day because it went toward night. I slept on the heart side now because I knew that the sooner I could tire that out, even a little, the sooner would come that blessed hour of nightmare which, like a catharsis, would enable me to better meet the new day.

There were certain spots, certain faces I could look at. Like most Middle Westerners, I have never had any but the vaguest race prejudices—I always had a secret yen for the lovely Scandinavian blondes who sat on porches in St. Paul but hadn't emerged enough economically to be part of what was then society. They were too nice to be "chickens" and too quickly off the farmlands to seize a place in the sun, but I remember going round blocks to catch a single glimpse of shining hair—the bright shock of a girl I'd never know. This is urban, unpopular talk. It strays afield from the fact that in these latter days I couldn't stand the sight of Celts, English, Politicians, Strangers, Virginians, Negroes (light or dark), Hunting People, or retail clerks, and middlemen in general, all writers (I avoided writers very carefully because they can perpetuate trouble as no one else can)—and all the classes as classes and most of them as members of their class . . .

Trying to cling to something, I liked doctors and girl children up to the age of about thirteen and well-brought-up boy children from about eight years old on. I could have peace and happiness with these few categories of people. I forgot to add that I liked old men—men over seventy, sometimes over sixty if their faces looked seasoned. I liked Katharine Hepburn's face on the screen, no matter what was said about her pretentiousness, and Miriam Hopkins' face, and old friends if I only saw them once a year and could remember their ghosts.

All rather inhuman and undernourished, isn't it? Well, that, children, is the true sign of cracking up.

It is not a pretty picture. Inevitably it was carted here and there within its frame and exposed to various critics. One of them can only be described as a person whose life makes other people's lives seem like death —even this time when she was cast in the usually unappealing role of Job's comforter. In spite of the fact that this story is over, let me append our conversation as a sort of postscript:

"Instead of being so sorry for yourself, listen—" she said. (She always says "Listen," because she thinks while she talks—*really* thinks.) So she said: "Listen. Suppose this wasn't a crack in you—suppose it was a crack in the Grand Canyon."

"The crack's in me," I said heroically.

"Listen! The world only exists in your eyes—your conception of it. You can make it as big or as small as you want to. And you're trying to be a little puny individual. By God, if I ever cracked, I'd try to make the world crack with me. Listen! The world only exists through your apprehension of it, and so it's much better to say that it's not you that's cracked—it's the Grand Canyon."

"Baby et up all her Spinoza?"

"I don't know anything about Spinoza. I know—" She spoke, then, of old woes of her own, that seemed, in the telling, to have been more dolorous than mine, and how she had met them, over-ridden them, beaten them.

I felt a certain reaction to what she said, but I am a slow-thinking man,

and it occurred to me simultaneously that of all natural forces, vitality is
the incommunicable one. In days when juice came into one as an article
without duty, one tried to distribute it—but always without success; to
further mix metaphors, vitality never "takes." You have it or you haven't
it, like health or brown eyes or honor or a baritone voice. I might have
asked some of it from her, neatly wrapped and ready for home cooking
and digestion, but I could never have got it—not if I'd waited around for
a thousand hours with the tin cup of self-pity. I could walk from her door,
holding myself very carefully like cracked crockery, and go away into the
world of bitterness, where I was making a home with such materials as are
found there—and quote to myself after I left her door:

*"Ye are the salt of the earth. But if the salt hath lost its savour, wherewith
shall it be salted?"*

Matthew 5-13.

3. Handle With Care

IN A PREVIOUS ARTICLE this writer told about his realization
that what he had before him was not the dish that he had ordered for
his forties. In fact—since he and the dish were one, he described himself
as a cracked plate, the kind that one wonders whether it is worth preserving. Your editor thought that the article suggested too many aspects without regarding them closely, and probably many readers felt the same way
—and there are always those to whom all self-revelation is contemptible,
unless it ends with a noble thanks to the gods for the Unconquerable Soul.

But I had been thanking the gods too long, and thanking them for
nothing. I wanted to put a lament into my record, without even the background of the Euganean Hills to give it color. There weren't any
Euganean hills that I could see.

Sometimes, though, the cracked plate has to be retained in the pantry,
has to be kept in service as a household necessity. It can never again be
warmed on the stove nor shuffled with the other plates in the dishpan; it
will not be brought out for company, but it will do to hold crackers late at
night or to go into the ice box under left-overs . . .

Hence this sequel—a cracked plate's further history.

Now the standard cure for one who is sunk is to consider those in
actual destitution or physical suffering—this is an all-weather beatitude for
gloom in general and fairly salutory day-time advice for everyone. But at
three o'clock in the morning, a forgotten package has the same tragic

importance as a death sentence, and the cure doesn't work—and in a real dark night of the soul it is always three o'clock in the morning, day after day. At that hour the tendency is to refuse to face things as long as possible by retiring into an infantile dream—but one is continually startled out of this by various contacts with the world. One meets these occasions as quickly and carelessly as possible and retires once more back into the dream, hoping that things will adjust themselves by some great material or spiritual bonanza. But as the withdrawal persists there is less and less chance of the bonanza—one is not waiting for the fade-out of a single sorrow, but rather being an unwilling witness of an execution, the disintegration of one's own personality . . .

Unless madness or drugs or drink come into it, this phase comes to a dead-end, eventually, and is succeeded by a vacuous quiet. In this you can try to estimate what has been sheared away and what is left. Only when this quiet came to me, did I realize that I had gone through two parallel experiences.

The first time was twenty years ago, when I left Princeton in junior year with a complaint diagnosed as malaria. It transpired, through an X-ray taken a dozen years later, that it had been tuberculosis—a mild case, and after a few months of rest I went back to college. But I had lost certain offices, the chief one was the presidency of the Triangle Club, a musical comedy idea, and also I dropped back a class. To me college would never be the same. There were to be no badges of pride, no medals, after all. It seemed on one March afternoon that I had lost every single thing I wanted —and that night was the first time that I hunted down the spectre of womanhood that, for a little while, makes everything else seem unimportant.

Years later I realized that my failure as a big shot in college was all right —instead of serving on committees, I took a beating on English poetry; when I got the idea of what it was all about, I set about learning how to write. On Shaw's principle that "If you don't get what you like, you better like what you get," it was a lucky break—at the moment it was a harsh and bitter business to know that my career as a leader of men was over.

Since that day I have not been able to fire a bad servant, and I am astonished and impressed by people who can. Some old desire for personal dominance was broken and gone. Life around me was a solemn dream, and I lived on the letters I wrote to a girl in another city. A man does not recover from such jolts—he becomes a different person and, eventually, the new person finds new things to care about.

The other episode parallel to my current situation took place after the war, when I had again over-extended my flank. It was one of those tragic loves doomed for lack of money, and one day the girl closed it out on the basis of common sense. During a long summer of despair I wrote a novel instead of letters, so it came out all right, but it came out all right for a different person. The man with the jingle of money in his pocket who married the girl a year later would always cherish an abiding distrust, an animosity, toward the leisure class—not the conviction of a revolutionist but the smouldering hatred of a peasant. In the years since then I have never been able to stop wondering where my friends' money came from, nor to stop thinking that at one time a sort of *droit de seigneur* might have been exercised to give one of them my girl.

For sixteen years I lived pretty much as this latter person, distrusting the rich, yet working for money with which to share their mobility and the grace that some of them brought into their lives. During this time I had plenty of the usual horses shot from under me—I remember some of their names—*Punctured Pride, Thwarted Expectation, Faithless, Show-off, Hard Hit, Never Again.* And after awhile I wasn't twenty-five, then not even thirty-five, and nothing was quite as good. But in all these years I don't remember a moment of discouragement. I saw honest men through moods of suicidal gloom—some of them gave up and died; others adjusted themselves and went on to a larger success than mine; but my morale never sank below the level of self-disgust when I had put on some unsightly personal show. Trouble has no necessary connection with discouragement —discouragement has a germ of its own, as different from trouble as arthritis is different from a stiff joint.

When a new sky cut off the sun last spring, I didn't at first relate it to what had happened fifteen or twenty years ago. Only gradually did a certain family resemblance come through—an over-extension of the flank, a burning of the candle at both ends; a call upon physical resources that I did not command, like a man over-drawing at his bank. In its impact this blow was more violent than the other two but it was the same in kind—a feeling that I was standing at twilight on a deserted range, with an empty rifle in my hands and the targets down. No problem set—simply a silence with only the sound of my own breathing.

In this silence there was a vast irresponsibility toward every obligation, a deflation of all my values. A passionate belief in order, a disregard of motives or consequences in favor of guess work and prophecy, a feeling that craft and industry would have a place in any world—one by one, these and other convictions were swept away. I saw that the novel, which at my maturity was the strongest and supplest medium for conveying thought and emotion from one human being to another, was becoming subordinated to a mechanical and communal art that, whether in the hands of Hollywood merchants or Russian idealists, was capable of reflecting only the tritest thought, the most obvious emotion. It was an art in which words were subordinate to images, where personality was worn down to the inevitable low gear of collaboration. As long past as 1930, I had a hunch that the talkies would make even the best selling novelist as archaic as silent pictures. People still read, if only Professor Canby's book of the month—curious children nosed at the slime of Mr. Tiffany Thayer in the drugstore libraries—but there was a rankling indignity, that to me had become almost an obsession, in seeing the power of the written word subordinated to another power, a more glittering, a grosser power . . .

I set that down as an example of what haunted me during the long night—this was something I could neither accept nor struggle against, something which tended to make my efforts obsolescent, as the chain stores have crippled the small merchant, an exterior force, unbeatable—

(I have the sense of lecturing now, looking at a watch on the desk before me and seeing how many more minutes—).

Well, when I had reached this period of silence, I was forced into a measure that no one ever adopts voluntarily: I was impelled to think. God, was it difficult! The moving about of great secret trunks. In the first exhausted halt, I wondered whether I had ever thought. After a long time I came to these conclusions, just as I write them here:

1. That I had done very little thinking, save within the problems of my craft. For twenty years a certain man had been my intellectual conscience. That was Edmund Wilson.

2. That another man represented my sense of the "good life," though I saw him once in a decade, and since then he might have been hung. He is in the fur business in the Northwest and wouldn't like his name set down here. But in difficult situations I had tried to think what *he* would have thought, how *he* would have acted.

3. That a third contemporary had been an artistic conscience to me —I had not imitated his infectious style, because my own style, such as it is, was formed before he published anything, but there was an awful pull toward him when I was on a spot.

4. That a fourth man had come to dictate my relations with other people when these relations were successful: how to do, what to say. How to make people at least momentarily happy (in opposition to Mrs. Post's theories of how to make everyone thoroughly uncomfortable with a sort of systematized vulgarity). This always confused me and made me want to go out and get drunk, but this man had seen the game, analyzed it and beaten it, and his word was good enough for me.

5. That my political conscience had scarcely existed for ten years save as an element of irony in my stuff. When I became again concerned with the system I should function under, it was a man

much younger than myself who brought it to me, with a mixture
of passion and fresh air.

So there was not an "I" any more—not a basis on which I could orga-
nize my self-respect—save my limitless capacity for toil that it seemed I
possessed no more. It was strange to have no self—to be like a little boy
left alone in a big house, who knew that now he could do anything he
wanted to do, but found that there was nothing that he wanted to do—
(The watch is past the hour and I have barely reached my thesis. I have
some doubts as to whether this is of general interest, but if anyone wants
more, there is plenty left, and your editor will tell me. If you've had
enough, say so—but not too loud, because I have the feeling that someone, I'm not sure who, is sound asleep—someone who could have helped
me to keep my shop open. It wasn't Lenin, and it wasn't God.)

4 . Pasting It Together

I HAVE SPOKEN in these pages of how an exceptionally optimistic
young man experienced a crack-up of all values, a crack-up that he
scarcely knew of until long after it occurred. I told of the succeeding
period of desolation and of the necessity of going on, but without benefit
of Henley's familiar heroics, "my head is bloody but unbowed." For a
check-up of my spiritual liabilities indicated that I had no particular head
to be bowed or unbowed. Once I had had a heart but that was about all I
was sure of.

This was at least a starting place out of the morass in which I
floundered: "I felt—therefore I was." At one time or another there had
been many people who had leaned on me, come to me in difficulties or
written me from afar, believed implicitly in my advice and my attitude
toward life. The dullest platitude monger or the most unscrupulous Ras-
putin who can influence the destinies of many people must have some
individuality, so the question became one of finding why and where I had
changed, where was the leak through which, unknown to myself, my enthusiasm and my vitality had been steadily and prematurely trickling away.

One harassed and despairing night I packed a brief case and went off a
thousand miles to think it over. I took a dollar room in a drab little town
where I knew no one and sunk all the money I had with me in a stock of
potted meat, crackers and apples. But don't let me suggest that the change
from a rather overstuffed world to a comparative asceticism was any Re-

search Magnificent—I only wanted absolute quiet to think out why I had developed a sad attitude toward sadness, a melancholy attitude toward melancholy and a tragic attitude toward tragedy—*why I had become identified with the objects of my horror or compassion.*

Does this seem a fine distinction? It isn't: identification such as this spells the death of accomplishment. It is something like this that keeps insane people from working. Lenin did not willingly endure the sufferings of his proletariat, nor Washington of his troops, nor Dickens of his London poor. And when Tolstoy tried some such merging of himself with the objects of his attention, it was a fake and a failure. I mention these because they are the men best known to us all.

It was dangerous mist. When Wordsworth decided that "there had passed away a glory from the earth," he felt no compulsion to pass away with it, and the Fiery Particle Keats never ceased his struggle against t. b. nor in his last moments relinquished his hope of being among the English poets.

My self-immolation was something sodden-dark. It was very distinctly not modern—yet I saw it in others, saw it in a dozen men of honor and industry since the war. (I heard you, but that's too easy—there were Marxians among these men.) I had stood by while one famous contemporary of mine played with the idea of the Big Out for half a year; I had watched when another, equally eminent, spent months in an asylum unable to endure any contact with his fellow men. And of those who had given up and passed on I could list a score.

This led me to the idea that the ones who had survived had made some sort of clean break. This is a big word and is no parallel to a jail-break when one is probably headed for a new jail or will be forced back to the old one. The famous "Escape" or "run away from it all" is an excursion in a trap even if the trap includes the south seas, which are only for those who want to paint them or sail them. A clean break is something you cannot come back from; that is irretrievable because it makes the past cease to exist. So, since I could no longer fulfill the obligations that life had set for me or that I had set for myself, why not slay the empty shell who had been posturing at it for four years? I must continue to be a writer because that was my only way of life, but I would cease any attempts to be a person—to be kind, just or generous. There were plenty of counterfeit coins around that would pass instead of these and I knew where I could get them at a nickel on the dollar. In thirty-nine years an observant eye has learned to detect where the milk is watered and the sugar is sanded, the rhinestone passed for diamond and the stucco for stone. There was to be no more giving of myself—all giving was to be outlawed henceforth under a new name, and that name was Waste.

The decision made me rather exuberant, like anything that is both real and new. As a sort of beginning there was a whole shaft of letters to be tipped into the waste basket when I went home, letters that wanted something for nothing—to read this man's manuscript, market this man's poem, speak free on the radio, indite notes of introduction, give this interview, help with the plot of this play, with this domestic situation, perform this act of thoughtfulness or charity.

The conjuror's hat was empty. To draw things out of it had long been a sort of sleight of hand, and now, to change the metaphor, I was off the dispensing end of the relief roll forever.

The heady villainous feeling continued.

I felt like the beady-eyed men I used to see on the commuting train from Great Neck fifteen years back—men who didn't care whether the world tumbled into chaos tomorrow if it spared their houses. I was one with them now, one with the smooth articles who said:

"I'm sorry but business is business." Or:

"You ought to have thought of that before you got into this trouble." Or:

"I'm not the person to see about that."

And a smile—ah, I would get me a smile. I'm still working on that smile. It is to combine the best qualities of a hotel manager, an experienced old social weasel, a headmaster on visitors' day, a colored elevator man, a pansy pulling a profile, a producer getting stuff at half its market value, a trained nurse coming on a new job, a body-vender in her first rotogravure, a hopeful extra swept near the camera, a ballet dancer with an infected toe, and of course the great beam of loving kindness common to all those from Washington to Beverly Hills who must exist by virtue of the contorted pan.

The voice too—I am working with a teacher on the voice. When I have perfected it the larynx will show no ring of conviction except the conviction of the person I am talking to. Since it will be largely called upon for the elicitation of the word "Yes," my teacher (a lawyer) and I are concentrating on that, but in extra hours. I am learning to bring into it that polite acerbity that makes people feel that far from being welcome they are not even tolerated and are under continual and scathing analysis at every moment. These times will of course not coincide with the smile. This will be reserved exclusively for those from whom I have nothing to gain, old worn-out people or young struggling people. They won't mind—what the hell, they get it most of the time anyhow.

But enough. It is not a matter of levity. If you are young and you should write asking to see me and learn how to be a sombre literary man writing pieces upon the state of emotional exhaustion that often overtakes writers in their prime—if you should be so young and so fatuous as to do this, I would not do so much as acknowledge your letter, unless you were related to someone very rich and important indeed. And if you were dying of starvation outside my window, I would go out quickly and give you the smile and the voice (if no longer the hand) and stick around till somebody raised a nickel to phone for the ambulance, that is if I thought there would be any copy in it for me.

I have now at last become a writer only. The man I had persistently tried to be became such a burden that I have "cut him loose" with as little compunction as a Negro lady cuts loose a rival on Saturday night. Let the good people function as such—let the overworked doctors die in harness, with one week's "vacation" a year that they can devote to straightening out their family affairs, and let the underworked doctors scramble for cases at one dollar a throw; let the soldiers be killed and enter immediately into the Valhalla of their profession. That is their contract with the gods. A writer need have no such ideals unless he makes them for himself, and this one has quit. The old dream of being an entire man in the Goethe-Byron-Shaw tradition, with an opulent American touch, a sort of combination of J. P. Morgan, Topham Beauclerk and St. Francis of Assisi, has been relegated to the junk heap of the shoulder pads worn for one day on the Princeton freshman football field and the overseas cap never worn overseas.

So what? This is what I think now: that the natural state of the sentient adult is a qualified unhappiness. I think also that in an adult the desire to be finer in grain than you are, "a constant striving" (as those people say who gain their bread by saying it) only adds to this unhappiness in the end —that end that comes to our youth and hope. My own happiness in the past often approached such an ecstasy that I could not share it even with the person dearest to me but had to walk it away in quiet streets and lanes with only fragments of it to distil into little lines in books—and I think that my happiness, or talent for self-delusion or what you will, was an exception. It was not the natural thing but the unnatural—unnatural as the Boom; and my recent experience parallels the wave of despair that swept the nation when the Boom was over.

I shall manage to live with the new dispensation, though it has taken some months to be certain of the fact. And just as the laughing stoicism which has enabled the American Negro to endure the intolerable conditions of his existence has cost him his sense of the truth—so in my case there is a price to pay. I do not any longer like the postman, nor the grocer, nor the editor, nor the cousin's husband, and he in turn will come to dislike me, so that life will never be very pleasant again, and the sign *Cave Canem* is hung permanently just above my door. I will try to be a correct animal though, and if you throw me a bone with enough meat on it I may even lick your hand.

Is Lopate saying White was phoney? How condescending— How arrogant

E. B. WHITE

Elwin Brooks White (1899–1985) was considered by many the preeminent American essayist of his time. He helped keep the essay form alive during a period when public interest in it had waned. In 1925 he joined the staff of The New Yorker, *and he maintained a lifelong association with that magazine. The persona that he created in his essays and "Talk of the Town" pieces—a friendly, gentlemanly family man, curious about nature and city life, undidactic, modest, civic-minded, mildly nostalgic and elegiac—set the* ✳ *tone for that periodical. At times White's persona threatens to become irksomely bland in its genial self-effacement, but his intelligence and humor save the day.*

White's revision of William Strunk, Jr.'s, The Elements of Style *propounded standards for a clear, clean, spare, modern American prose, which not only governed his own writing but had an enormous influence on generations of college students and journalists. He was noted as well for his juvenile classics,* Charlotte's Web *and* Stuart Little. *Yet a dozen essays of his, most notably "Once More to the Lake," "The Ring of Time," "Here Is New York," "Death of a Pig," "Sootfall and Fallout" (which spurred the ecology movement), "The World of Tomorrow," and "Afternoon of an American Boy," constitute his most lasting contribution to literature. The examples below show how ambitious a reach White's essays had—formally, emotionally, philosophically, and politically—behind their deceptively unassuming tone.*

Once More to the Lake

August 1941

ONE SUMMER, along about 1904, my father rented a camp on a lake in Maine and took us all there for the month of August. We all got ringworm from some kittens and had to rub Pond's Extract on our arms and legs night and morning, and my father rolled over in a canoe with all his clothes on; but outside of that the vacation was a success and from then on none of us ever thought there was any place in the world like that lake in Maine. We returned summer after summer—always on August 1 for one month. I have since become a salt-water man, but sometimes in summer there are days when the restlessness of the tides and the fearful cold of the sea water and the incessant wind that blows across the afternoon and into the evening make me wish for the placidity of a lake in the woods. A few weeks ago this feeling got so strong I bought myself a couple of bass hooks and a spinner and returned to the lake where we used to go, for a week's fishing and to revisit old haunts.

I took along my son, who had never had any fresh water up his nose and who had seen lily pads only from train windows. On the journey over to the lake I began to wonder what it would be like. I wondered how time would have marred this unique, this holy spot—the coves and streams, the hills that the sun set behind, the camps and the paths behind the camps. I was sure that the tarred road would have found it out, and I wondered in what other ways it would be desolated. It is strange how much you can remember about places like that once you allow your mind to return into the grooves that lead back. You remember one thing, and that suddenly reminds you of another thing. I guess I remembered clearest of all the early mornings, when the lake was cool and motionless, remembered how the bedroom smelled of the lumber it was made of and of the wet woods whose scent entered through the screen. The partitions in the camp were thin and did not extend clear to the top of the rooms, and as I was always the first up I would dress softly so as not to wake the others, and sneak out into the sweet outdoors and start out in the canoe, keeping close along the shore in the long shadows of the pines. I remembered being very careful never to rub my paddle against the gunwale for fear of disturbing the stillness of the cathedral.

The lake had never been what you would call a wild lake. There were cottages sprinkled around the shores, and it was in farming country although the shores of the lake were quite heavily wooded. Some of the cottages were owned by nearby farmers, and you would live at the shore and eat your meals at the farmhouse. That's what our family did. But although it wasn't wild, it was a fairly large and undisturbed lake and there were places in it that, to a child at least, seemed infinitely remote and primeval.

I was right about the tar: it led to within half a mile of the shore. But when I got back there, with my boy, and we settled into a camp near a farmhouse and into the kind of summertime I had known, I could tell that it was going to be pretty much the same as it had been before—I knew it, lying in bed the first morning, smelling the bedroom and hearing the boy sneak quietly out and go off along the shore in a boat. I began to sustain the illusion that he was I, and therefore, by simple transposition, that I was my father. This sensation persisted, kept cropping up all the time we were there. It was not an entirely new feeling, but in this setting it grew much stronger. I seemed to be living a dual existence. I would be in the middle of some simple act, I would be picking up a bait box or laying down a table fork, or I would be saying something, and suddenly it would be not I but my father who was saying the words or making the gesture. It gave me a creepy sensation.

We went fishing the first morning. I felt the same damp moss covering the worms in the bait can, and saw the dragonfly alight on the tip of my rod as it hovered a few inches from the surface of the water. It was the arrival of this fly that convinced me beyond any doubt that everything was as it always had been, that the years were a mirage and that there had been no years. The small waves were the same, chucking the rowboat under the chin as we fished at anchor, and the boat was the same boat, the same color green and the ribs broken in the same places, and under the floorboards the same fresh-water leavings and débris—the dead helgramite, the wisps of moss, the rusty discarded fishhook, the dried blood from yesterday's catch. We stared silently at the tips of our rods, at the dragonflies that came and went. I lowered the tip of mine into the water, tentatively, pensively dislodging the fly, which darted two feet away, poised, darted two feet back, and came to rest again a little farther up the rod. There had been no years between the ducking of this dragonfly and the other one— the one that was part of memory. I looked at the boy, who was silently watching his fly, and it was my hands that held his rod, my eyes watching. I felt dizzy and didn't know which rod I was at the end of.

We caught two bass, hauling them in briskly as though they were mackerel, pulling them over the side of the boat in a businesslike manner without any landing net, and stunning them with a blow on the back of the head. When we got back for a swim before lunch, the lake was exactly where we had left it, the same number of inches from the dock, and there

was only the merest suggestion of a breeze. This seemed an utterly enchanted sea, this lake you could leave to its own devices for a few hours
and come back to, and find that it had not stirred, this constant and
trustworthy body of water. In the shallows, the dark, water-soaked sticks
and twigs, smooth and old, were undulating in clusters on the bottom
against the clean ribbed sand, and the track of the mussel was plain. A
school of minnows swam by, each minnow with its small individual
shadow, doubling the attendance, so clear and sharp in the sunlight. Some
of the other campers were in swimming, along the shore, one of them with
a cake of soap, and the water felt thin and clear and unsubstantial. Over
the years there had been this person with the cake of soap, this cultist, and
here he was. There had been no years.

Up to the farmhouse to dinner through the teeming, dusty field, the
road under our sneakers was only a two-track road. The middle track was
missing, the one with the marks of the hooves and the splotches of dried,
flaky manure. There had always been three tracks to choose from in
choosing which track to walk in; now the choice was narrowed down to
two. For a moment I missed terribly the middle alternative. But the way
led past the tennis court, and something about the way it lay there in the
sun reassured me; the tape had loosened along the backline, the alleys
were green with plantains and other weeds, and the net (installed in June
and removed in September) sagged in the dry noon, and the whole place
steamed with midday heat and hunger and emptiness. There was a choice
of pie for dessert, and one was blueberry and one was apple, and the
waitresses were the same country girls, there having been no passage of
time, only the illusion of it as in a dropped curtain—the waitresses were
still fifteen; their hair had been washed, that was the only difference—they
had been to the movies and seen the pretty girls with the clean hair.

Summertime, oh, summertime, pattern of life indelible, the fade-proof
lake, the woods unshatterable, the pasture with the sweetfern and the
juniper forever and ever, summer without end; this was the background,
and the life along the shore was the design, the cottagers with their innocent and tranquil design, their tiny docks with the flagpole and the American flag floating against the white clouds in the blue sky, the little paths
over the roots of the trees leading from camp to camp and the paths
leading back to the outhouses and the can of lime for sprinkling, and at
the souvenir counters at the store the miniature birch-bark canoes and the
postcards that showed things looking a little better than they looked. This
was the American family at play, escaping the city heat, wondering
whether the newcomers in the camp at the head of the cove were "common" or "nice," wondering whether it was true that the people who drove
up for Sunday dinner at the farmhouse were turned away because there
wasn't enough chicken.

It seemed to me, as I kept remembering all this, that those times and those summers had been infinitely precious and worth saving. There had been jollity and peace and goodness. The arriving (at the beginning of August) had been so big a business in itself, at the railway station the farm wagon drawn up, the first smell of the pine-laden air, the first glimpse of the smiling farmer, and the great importance of the trunks and your father's enormous authority in such matters, and the feel of the wagon under you for the long ten-mile haul, and at the top of the last long hill catching the first view of the lake after eleven months of not seeing this cherished body of water. The shouts and cries of the other campers when they saw you, and the trunks to be unpacked, to give up their rich burden. (Arriving was less exciting nowadays, when you sneaked up in your car and parked it under a tree near the camp and took out the bags and in five minutes it was all over, no fuss, no loud wonderful fuss about trunks.)

Peace and goodness and jollity. The only thing that was wrong now, really, was the sound of the place, an unfamiliar nervous sound of the outboard motors. This was the note that jarred, the one thing that would sometimes break the illusion and set the years moving. In those other summertimes all motors were inboard; and when they were at a little distance, the noise they made was a sedative, an ingredient of summer sleep. They were one-cylinder and two-cylinder engines, and some were make-and-break and some were jump-spark, but they all made a sleepy sound across the lake. The one-lungers throbbed and fluttered, and the twin-cylinder ones purred and purred, and that was a quiet sound, too. But now the campers all had outboards. In the daytime, in the hot mornings, these motors made a petulant, irritable sound; at night, in the still evening when the afterglow lit the water, they whined about one's ears like mosquitoes. My boy loved our rented outboard, and his great desire was to achieve single-handed mastery over it, and authority, and he soon learned the trick of choking it a little (but not too much), and the adjustment of the needle valve. Watching him I would remember the things you could do with the old one-cylinder engine with the heavy flywheel, how you could have it eating out of your hand if you got really close to it spiritually. Motorboats in those days didn't have clutches, and you would make a landing by shutting off the motor at the proper time and coasting in with a dead rudder. But there was a way of reversing them, if you learned the trick, by cutting the switch and putting it on again exactly on the final dying revolution of the flywheel, so that it would kick back against compression and begin reversing. Approaching a dock in a strong following breeze, it was difficult to slow up sufficiently by the ordinary coasting method, and if a boy felt he had complete mastery over his motor, he was tempted to keep it running beyond its time and then reverse it a few feet from the dock. It took a cool nerve, because if you threw the switch a twentieth of a second too soon you would catch the flywheel when it still had speed enough to go up past center, and the boat would leap ahead, charging bull-fashion at the dock.

We had a good week at the camp. The bass were biting well and the sun shone endlessly, day after day. We would be tired at night and lie down in the accumulated heat of the little bedrooms after the long hot day and the breeze would stir almost imperceptibly outside and the smell of the swamp drift in through the rusty screens. Sleep would come easily and in the morning the red squirrel would be on the roof, tapping out his gay routine. I kept remembering everything, lying in bed in the mornings—the small steamboat that had a long rounded stern like the lip of a Ubangi, and how quietly she ran on the moonlight sails, when the older boys played their mandolins and the girls sang and we ate doughnuts dipped in sugar, and how sweet the music was on the water in the shining night, and what it had felt like to think about girls then. After breakfast we would go up to the store and the things were in the same place—the minnows in a bottle, the plugs and spinners disarranged and pawed over by the youngsters from the boys' camp, the Fig Newtons and the Beeman's gum. Outside, the road was tarred and cars stood in front of the store. Inside, all was just as it had always been, except there was more Coca-Cola and not so much Moxie and root beer and birch beer and sarsaparilla. We would walk out with the bottle of pop apiece and sometimes the pop would backfire up our noses and hurt. We explored the streams, quietly, where the turtles slid off the sunny logs and dug their way into the soft bottom; and we lay on the town wharf and fed worms to the tame bass. Everywhere we went I had trouble making out which was I, the one walking at my side, the one walking in my pants.

One afternoon while we were there at that lake a thunderstorm came up. It was like the revival of an old melodrama that I had seen long ago with childish awe. The second-act climax of the drama of the electrical disturbance over a lake in America had not changed in any important respect. This was the big scene, still the big scene. The whole thing was so familiar, the first feeling of oppression and heat and a general air around camp of not wanting to go very far away. In mid-afternoon (it was all the same) a curious darkening of the sky, and a lull in everything that had made life tick; and then the way the boats suddenly swung the other way at their moorings with the coming of a breeze out of the new quarter, and the premonitory rumble. Then the kettle drum, then the snare, then the bass drum and cymbals, then crackling light against the dark, and the gods grinning and licking their chops in the hills. Afterward the calm, the rain steadily rustling in the calm lake, the return of light and hope and spirits, and the campers running out in joy and relief to go swimming in the rain, their bright cries perpetuating the deathless joke about how they were getting simply drenched, and the children screaming with delight at the new sensation of bathing in the rain, and the joke about getting drenched linking the generations in a strong indestructible chain. And the comedian who waded in carrying an umbrella.

When the others went swimming, my son said he was going in, too. He pulled his dripping trunks from the line where they had hung all through the shower and wrung them out. Languidly, and with no thought of going in, I watched him, his hard little body, skinny and bare, saw him wince slightly as he pulled up around his vitals the small, soggy, icy garment. As he buckled the swollen belt, suddenly my groin felt the chill of death.

The Ring of Time

16 yrs th
story of the Lake

Fiddler Bayou, March 22, 1956

A FTER THE LIONS had returned to their cages, creeping angrily through the chutes, a little bunch of us drifted away and into an open doorway nearby, where we stood for a while in semidarkness, watching a big brown circus horse go harumphing around the practice ring. His trainer was a woman of about forty, and the two of them, horse and woman, seemed caught up in one of those desultory treadmills of afternoon from which there is no apparent escape. The day was hot, and we kibitzers were grateful to be briefly out of the sun's glare. The long rein, or tape, by which the woman guided her charge counterclockwise in his dull career formed the radius of their private circle, of which she was the revolving center; and she, too, stepped a tiny circumference of her own, in order to accommodate the horse and allow him his maximum scope. She had on a short-skirted costume and a conical straw hat. Her legs were bare and she wore high heels, which probed deep into the loose tanbark and kept her ankles in a state of constant turmoil. The great size and meekness of the horse, the repetitious exercise, the heat of the afternoon, all exerted a hypnotic charm that invited boredom; we spectators were experiencing a languor—we neither expected relief nor felt entitled to any. We had paid a dollar to get into the grounds, to be sure, but we had got our dollar's worth a few minutes before, when the lion trainer's whiplash had got caught around a toe of one of the lions. What more did we want for a dollar?

Behind me I heard someone say, "Excuse me, please," in a low voice. She was halfway into the building when I turned and saw her—a girl of sixteen or seventeen, politely threading her way through us onlookers who blocked the entrance. As she emerged in front of us, I saw that she was barefoot, her dirty little feet fighting the uneven ground. In most respects she was like any of two or three dozen showgirls you encounter if you wander about the winter quarters of Mr. John Ringling North's circus, in Sarasota—cleverly proportioned, deeply browned by the sun, dusty, eager, and almost naked. But her grave face and the naturalness of her manner gave her a sort of quick distinction and brought a new note into the gloomy octagonal building where we had all cast our lot for a few moments. As soon as she had squeezed through the crowd, she spoke a word or two to the older woman, whom I took to be her mother, stepped to the ring, and waited while the horse coasted to a stop in front of her. She gave the animal a couple of affectionate swipes on his enormous neck and then swung herself aboard. The horse immediately resumed his rocking canter, the woman goading him on, chanting something that sounded like "Hop! Hop!"

In attempting to recapture this mild spectacle, I am merely acting as recording secretary for one of the oldest of societies—the society of those who, at one time or another, have surrendered, without even a show of resistance, to the bedazzlement of a circus rider. As a writing man, or secretary, I have always felt charged with the safekeeping of all unexpected items of worldly or unworldly enchantment, as though I might be held personally responsible if even a small one were to be lost. But it is not easy to communicate anything of this nature. The circus comes as close to being the world in microcosm as anything I know; in a way, it puts all the rest of show business in the shade. Its magic is universal and complex. Out of its wild disorder comes order; from its rank smell rises the good aroma of courage and daring; out of its preliminary shabbiness comes the final splendor. And buried in the familiar boasts of its advance agents lies the modesty of most of its people. For me the circus is at its best before it has been put together. It is at its best at certain moments when it comes to a point, as through a burning glass, in the activity and destiny of a single performer out of so many. One ring is always bigger than three. One rider, one aerialist, is always greater than six. In short, a man has to catch the circus unawares to experience its full impact and share its gaudy dream.

The ten-minute ride the girl took achieved—as far as I was concerned, who wasn't looking for it, and quite unbeknownst to her, who wasn't even striving for it—the thing that is sought by performers everywhere, on whatever stage, whether struggling in the tidal currents of Shakespeare or bucking the difficult motion of a horse. I somehow got the idea she was just cadging a ride, improving a shining ten minutes in the diligent way all serious artists seize free moments to hone the blade of their talent and keep themselves in trim. Her brief tour included only elementary postures and tricks, perhaps because they were all she was capable of, perhaps because her warmup at this hour was unscheduled and the ring was not rigged for a real practice session. She swung herself off and on the horse several times, gripping his mane. She did a few knee-stands—or whatever they are called—dropping to her knees and quickly bouncing back up on her feet again. Most of the time she simply rode in a standing position, well aft on the beast, her hands hanging easily at her sides, her head erect, her straw-colored ponytail lightly brushing her shoulders, the blood of exertion showing faintly through the tan of her skin. Twice she managed a one-foot stance—a sort of ballet pose, with arms outstretched. At one point the neck strap of her bathing suit broke and she went twice around the ring in the classic attitude of a woman making minor repairs to a garment. The fact that she was standing on the back of a moving horse while doing this invested the matter with a clownish significance that perfectly fitted the spirit of the circus—jocund, yet charming. She just rolled the strap into a neat ball and stowed it inside her bodice while the horse rocked and rolled beneath her in dutiful innocence. The bathing suit proved as self-reliant as its owner and stood up well enough without benefit of strap.

The richness of the scene was in its plainness, its natural condition—of horse, of ring, of girl, even to the girl's bare feet that gripped the bare back of her proud and ridiculous mount. The enchantment grew not out of anything that happened or was performed but out of something that seemed to go round and around and around with the girl, attending her, a steady gleam in the shape of a circle—a ring of ambition, of happiness, of youth. (And the positive pleasures of equilibrium under difficulties.) In a week or two, all would be changed, all (or almost all) lost: the girl would wear makeup, the horse would wear gold, the ring would be painted, the bark would be clean for the feet of the horse, the girl's feet would be clean for the slippers that she'd wear. All, all would be lost.

As I watched with the others, our jaws adroop, our eyes alight, I became painfully conscious of the element of time. Everything in the hideous old building seemed to take the shape of a circle, conforming to the course of the horse. The rider's gaze, as she peered straight ahead, seemed to be circular, as though bent by force of circumstance; then time itself began running in circles, and so the beginning was where the end was, and the two were the same, and one thing ran into the next and time went round and around and got nowhere. The girl wasn't so young that she did not know the delicious satisfaction of having a perfectly behaved body and the fun of using it to do a trick most people can't do, but she was too young to know that time does not really move in a circle at all. I thought: "She will never be as beautiful as this again"—a thought that made me acutely unhappy—and in a flash my mind (which is too much of a busybody to suit me) had projected her twenty-five years ahead, and she was now in the center of the ring, on foot, wearing a conical hat and high-heeled shoes, the image of the older woman, holding the long rein, caught in the treadmill of an afternoon long in the future. "She is at that enviable moment in life [I thought] when she believes she can go once around the ring, make one complete circuit, and at the end be exactly the same age as at the start." Everything in her movements, her expression, told you that for her the ring of time was perfectly formed, changeless, predictable, without beginning or end, like the ring in which she was traveling at this moment with the horse that wallowed under her. And then I slipped back into my trance, and time was circular again—time, pausing quietly with the rest of us, so as not to disturb the balance of a performer.

Her ride ended as casually as it had begun. The older woman stopped the horse, and the girl slid to the ground. As she walked toward us to leave, there was a quick, small burst of applause. She smiled broadly, in surprise and pleasure; then her face suddenly regained its gravity and she disappeared through the door.

It has been ambitious and plucky of me to attempt to describe what is indescribable, and I have failed, as I knew I would. But I have discharged my duty to my society; and besides, a writer, like an acrobat, must occasionally try a stunt that is too much for him. At any rate, it is worth reporting that long before the circus comes to town, its most notable performances have already been given. Under the bright lights of the finished show, a performer need only reflect the electric candle power that is directed upon him; but in the dark and dirty old training rings and in the makeshift cages, whatever light is generated, whatever excitement, whatever beauty, must come from original sources—from internal fires of professional hunger and delight, from the exuberance and gravity of youth. It is the difference between planetary light and the combustion of stars.

The South is the land of the sustained sibilant. Everywhere, for the appreciative visitor, the letter "s" insinuates itself in the scene: in the sound of sea and sand, in the singing shell, in the heat of sun and sky, in the sultriness of the gentle hours, in the siesta, in the stir of birds and insects.

In contrast to the softness of its music, the South is also cruel and hard and prickly. A little striped lizard, flattened along the sharp green bayonet of a yucca, wears in its tiny face and watchful eye the pure look of death and violence. And all over the place, hidden at the bottom of their small sandy craters, the ant lions lie in wait for the ant that will stumble into their trap. (There are three kinds of lions in this region: the lions of the circus, the ant lions, and the Lions of the Tampa Lions Club, who roared their approval of segregation at a meeting the other day—all except one, a Lion named Monty Gurwit, who declined to roar and thereby got his picture in the paper.)

The day starts on a note of despair: the sorrowing dove, alone on its telephone wire, mourns the loss of night, weeps at the bright perils of the unfolding day. But soon the mockingbird wakes and begins an early rehearsal, setting the dove down by force of character, running through a few slick imitations, and trying a couple of original numbers into the bargain. The redbird takes it from there. Despair gives way to good humor. The Southern dawn is a pale affair, usually, quite different from our northern daybreak. It is a triumph of gradualism; night turns to day imperceptibly, softly, with no theatrics. It is subtle and undisturbing. As the first light seeps in through the blinds I lie in bed half awake, despairing with the dove, sounding the A for the brothers Alsop. All seems lost, all seems sorrowful. Then a mullet jumps in the bayou outside the bedroom window. It falls back into the water with a smart smack. I have asked several people why the mullet incessantly jump and I have received a variety of answers. Some say the mullet jump to shake off a parasite that annoys them. Some say they jump for the love of jumping—as the girl on the horse seemed to ride for the love of riding (although she, too, like all artists, may have been shaking off some parasite that fastens itself to the creative spirit and can be got rid of only by fifty turns around a ring while standing on a horse).

In Florida at this time of year, the sun does not take command of the day until a couple of hours after it has appeared in the east. It seems to carry no authority at first. The sun and the lizard keep the same schedule; they bide their time until the morning has advanced a good long way before they come fully forth and strike. The cold lizard waits astride his warming leaf for the perfect moment; the cold sun waits in his nest of clouds for the crucial time.

On many days, the dampness of the air pervades all life, all living. Matches refuse to strike. The towel, hung to dry, grows wetter by the hour. The newspaper, with its headlines about integration, wilts in your hand and falls limply into the coffee and the egg. Envelopes seal themselves. Postage stamps mate with one another as shamelessly as grasshoppers. But most of the time the days are models of beauty and wonder and comfort, with the kind sea stroking the back of the warm sand. At evening there are great flights of birds over the sea, where the light lingers; the gulls, the pelicans, the terns, the herons stay aloft for half an hour after land birds have gone to roost. They hold their ancient formations, wheel and fish over the Pass, enjoying the last of day like children playing outdoors after suppertime.

To a beachcomber from the North, which is my present status, the race problem has no pertinence, no immediacy. Here in Florida I am a guest in two houses—the house of the sun, the house of the State of Florida. As a guest, I mind my manners and do not criticize the customs of my hosts. It gives me a queer feeling, though, to be at the center of the greatest social crisis of my time and see hardly a sign of it. Yet the very absence of signs seems to increase one's awareness. Colored people do not come to the public beach to bathe, because they would not be made welcome there; and they don't fritter away their time visiting the circus, because they have other things to do. A few of them turn up at the ballpark, where they occupy a separate but equal section of the left-field bleachers and watch Negro players on the visiting Braves team using the same bases as the white players, instead of separate (but equal) bases. I have had only two small encounters with "color." A colored woman named Viola, who had been a friend of my wife's sister years ago, showed up one day with some laundry of ours that she had consented to do for us, and with the bundle she brought a bunch of nasturtiums, as a sort of natural accompaniment to the delivery of clean clothes. The flowers seemed a very acceptable thing and I was touched by them. We asked Viola about her daughter, and she said she was at Kentucky State College, studying voice.

The other encounter was when I was explaining to our cook, who is from Finland, the mysteries of bus travel in the American Southland. I showed her the bus stop, armed her with a timetable, and then, as a matter of duty, mentioned the customs of the Romans. "When you get on the bus," I said, "I think you'd better sit in one of the front seats—the seats in back are for colored people." A look of great weariness came into her face, as it does when we use too many dishes, and she replied, "Oh, I know—isn't it silly!"

Her remark, coming as it did all the way from Finland and landing on this sandbar with a plunk, impressed me. The Supreme Court said nothing about silliness, but I suspect it may play more of a role than one might suppose. People are, if anything, more touchy about being thought silly than they are about being thought unjust. I note that one of the arguments in the recent manifesto of Southern Congressmen in support of the doctrine of "separate but equal" was that it had been founded on "common sense." The sense that is common to one generation is uncommon to the next. Probably the first slave ship, with Negroes lying in chains on its decks, seemed commonsensical to the owners who operated it and to the planters who patronized it. But such a vessel would not be in the realm of common sense today. The only sense that is common, in the long run, is the sense of change—and we all instinctively avoid it, and object to the passage of time, and would rather have none of it.

The Supreme Court decision is like the Southern sun, laggard in its early stages, biding its time. It has been the law in Florida for two years now, and the years have been like the hours of the morning before the sun has gathered its strength. I think the decision is as incontrovertible and warming as the sun, and, like the sun, will eventually take charge.

But there is certainly a great temptation in Florida to duck the passage of time. Lying in warm comfort by the sea, you receive gratefully the gift of the sun, the gift of the South. This is true seduction. The day is a circle —morning, afternoon, and night. After a few days I was clearly enjoying the same delusion as the girl on the horse—that I could ride clear around the ring of day, guarded by wind and sun and sea and sand, and be not a moment older.

M . F . K . FISHER

Mary Frances Kennedy Fisher (1908–1992) has an enigmatic place in American letters, being perhaps <u>undervalued as a serious writer</u> and overvalued, or at least overmystified, as a cult figure. Many regard her as the patron saint and paragon of modern food writing. She herself said, "I do not consider myself a food writer." Yet a good deal of her output was for magazines such as Food and Wine *and* Gourmet. *Certainly food was her primary subject matter, and her achievement was to use this seemingly mundane concern as a metaphor <u>for the analysis of human appetite, disappointment, and rapture.</u> Her most personal (and best) book,* The Gastronomical Me, *gives us glimpses of <u>a rather hard life</u>—the <u>failure of her first marriage,</u> the illness and death of her beloved second husband, the cowardly behavior of many Europeans during World War II—through the scrim of an education in eating. As she said once in an interview, "One has to live, you know. You can't just die from grief or anything. You don't die. You might as well eat well, have a good glass of wine, a good tomato." It is this <u>stoical realism</u> that fleshes out her epicurean search and gives it depth.*

Stylistically, Fisher had a taste for aphorisms, sentences of compressed wit that boldly cut through any dithering. Sometimes the reader is left hungry for more of her life—intentionally so. She practiced a discipline of restraint and omission, creating essentially <u>an oblique, dignified, detached persona</u> rather than a chatty, confessional one. Nonetheless, she could be disarmingly and alarmingly honest. Her very satisfying personal essays about cooking, which appeared originally in The New Yorker *and were collected in* With Bold Knife and Fork, *display a casual erudition and an anecdotal warmth. Fisher translated Brillat-Savarin's* The Physiology of Taste, *and her writing was increasingly informed by a historical perspective on food preparation.*

W. H. Auden once called her the best American prose stylist alive, a compliment that seems in retrospect more provocative than considered; but there is no question that her writing is of a very high order and gives pleasure even to those who don't especially care about food. (*as Lopate wasn't*)

Once a Tramp, Always . . .

T HERE IS A MISTAKEN IDEA, ancient but still with us, that an overdose of anything from fornication to hot chocolate will teach restraint by the very results of its abuse. A righteous and worried father, feeling broad-minded and full of manly understanding, will urge a rich cigar upon his fledgling and almost force him to be sick, to show him how to smoke properly. Another, learning that his sons have been nipping dago red, will chain them psychologically to the dinner table and drink them under it, to teach them how to handle their liquor like gentlemen. Such methods are drastic and of dubious worth, I think. People continue to smoke and to drink, and to be excessive or moderate according to their own needs. Their good manners are a matter more of innate taste than of outward training.

Craving—the actual and continued need for something—is another matter. Sometimes it lasts for one's lifetime. There is no satisfying it, except temporarily, and that can spell death or ruin. At least three people I know very well, children of alcoholic parents, were literally born drunk, and after sad experience they face the hideous fact that one more nip will destroy them. But they dream of it. Another of my friends dreams of chocolate, and is haunted by sensory fantasies of the taste and smell of chocolate, and occasionally talks of chocolate the way some people talk of their mistresses, but one Hershey bar would damn him and his liver too. (Members of A.A. pray to God daily to keep them from taking that First Drink. A first candy bar can be as dangerous.) These people choose to live, no matter how cautiously, because they know that they can never be satisfied. For them real satiety, the inner spiritual kind, is impossible. They are, although in a noble way, cheating: an *honest* satyr will risk death from exhaustion, still happily aware that there will always be more women in the world than he can possibly accommodate.

Somewhere between the extremes of putative training in self-control and unflagging discipline against wild cravings lie the sensual and voluptuous gastronomical favorites-of-a-lifetime, the nostalgic yearnings for flavors once met in early days—the smell or taste of a gooseberry pie on a summer noon at Peachblow Farm, the whiff of anise from a Marseille bar. Old or moderately young, of any sex, most of us can forgo the analyst's couch at will and call up some such flavors. It is better thus. Kept verbal, there is small danger of indigestion, and in truth, a gooseberry pie can be a horror (those pale beady acid fruits, the sugar never masking their mean acidity, the crust sogging . . . my father rhapsodized occasionally about the ones at Peachblow and we tried to recapture their magic for him, but it was impossible). And a glass of *pastis* at the wrong time and with the wrong people can turn into a first-class emetic, no matter how it used to make the mind and body rejoice in Provence. Most people like to talk, once steered onto the right track, about their lifetime favorites in food. It does not matter if they have only dreamed of them for the past countless decades: favorites remain, and mankind is basically a faithful bunch of fellows. If you loved Gaby Deslys or Fanny Brice, from no matter how far afar, you still can and do. And why not? There is, in this happily insatiable fantasizing, no saturation point, no moment at which the body must cry: *Help!*

Of course, the average person has not actually possessed a famous beauty, and it is there that gastronomy serves as a kind of surrogate, to ease our longings. One does not need to be a king or mogul to indulge most, if at all, of his senses with the heady enjoyment of a dish—speaking in culinary terms, that is. I myself, to come right down to it, have never been in love from afar, except perhaps for a handful of fleeting moments when a flickering shot of Wallace Reid driving over a cliff would make me feel queer. I know of women who have really mooned, and for years, over some such glamorous shadow, and it is highly possible that my own immunity is due to my sensual satisfaction, even vicarious, in such things as potato chips and Beluga caviar. This realization is cruelly matter-of-fact to anyone of romantic sensitivity, and I feel vaguely apologetic about it. At the same time, I am relieved. I am free from any regrets that Clark Marlon Barrymore has never smiled at me. I know that even though I eat potato chips perhaps once every three years, I can, whenever I wish to, tap an almost unlimited fountain of them not five hundred feet from my own door. It is not quite the same thing with caviar, of course, and I have dug into a one-pound tin of it, fresh and pearly gray, not more than eight or nine times in my life. But I know that for a while longer the Acipensers of the Black and Caspian seas will be able to carry out their fertility rites and that I may even partake again of their delectable fruits. Meanwhile, stern about potato chips on the one hand and optimistic about Beluga on the other, I can savor with my mind's palate their strange familiarity.

It is said that a few connoisseurs, such as old George Saintsbury, can recall *physically* the bouquet of certain great vintages a half century after tasting them. I am a mouse among elephants now, but I can say just as surely that this minute, in a northern California valley, I can taste-smell-hear-see and then feel between my teeth the potato chips I ate slowly one November afternoon in 1936, in the bar of the Lausanne Palace. They were uneven in both thickness and color, probably made by a new apprentice in the hotel kitchen, and almost surely they smelled faintly of either chicken or fish, for that was always the case there. They were a little too salty, to encourage me to drink. They were ineffable. I am still nourished by them. That is probably why I can be so firm about not eating my way through barrels, tunnels, mountains more of them here in the land where they hang like square cellophane fruit on wire trees in all the grocery stores, to tempt me sharply every time I pass them.

As for the caviar, I can wait. I know I cannot possibly, *ever,* eat enough of it to satisfy my hunger, my unreasonable lust, so I think back with what is almost placidity upon the times I could attack a tub of it and take five minutes or so for every small voluptuous mouthful. Again, why not? Being carnal, such dreams are perforce sinful in some vocabularies. Other ways of thinking might call them merely foolish, or Freudian "substitutes." That is all right; I know that I can cultivate restraint, or accept it patiently when it is thrust upon me—just as I know that I can walk right down Main Street this minute and buy almost as many Macadamia nuts as I would like to eat, and certainly enough to make me feel very sick for a time, but that I shan't do so.

I have some of the same twinges of basic craving for those salty gnarled little nuts from Hawaii as the ones I keep ruthlessly at bay for the vulgar fried potatoes and the costly fish eggs. Just writing of my small steady passion for them makes my mouth water in a reassuringly controlled way, and I am glad there are dozens of jars of them in the local goodies shoppe, for me not to buy. I cannot remember when I first ate a Macadamia, but I was hooked from that moment. I think it was about thirty years ago. The Prince of Wales was said to have invested in a ranch in Hawaii which raised them in small quantities, so that the name stuck in my mind because *he* did, but I doubt that royal business cunning had much to do with my immediate delectation. The last time I ate one was about four months ago, in New York. I surprised my *belle-soeur* and almost embarrassed myself by letting a small moan escape me when she put a bowl of them beside my chair; they were beautiful—so lumpy, Macadamian, salty, golden! And I ate one, to save face. One. I can still sense its peculiar crispness and its complete Macadamianimity. How fortunate I am!

Many of the things we batten on in our fantasies are part of our childhoods, although none of mine has been, so far in this list. I was perhaps twenty-three when I first ate almost enough caviar—not to mention any caviar at all that I can now remember. It was one of the best, brightest days of my whole life with my parents, and lunching in the quiet back room at the Café de la Paix was only a part of the luminous whole. My mother ate fresh foie gras, sternly forbidden to her liver, but she loved the cathedral at Strasbourg enough to risk almost any kind of retribution, and this truffled slab was so plainly the best of her lifetime that we all agreed it could do her nothing but good, which it did. My father and I ate caviar, probably Sevruga, with green-black smallish beads and a superb challenge of flavor for the iced grassy vodka we used to cleanse our happy palates. We ate three portions apiece, tacitly knowing it could never happen again that anything would be quite so mysteriously perfect in both time and space. The headwaiter sensed all this, which is, of course, why he was world-known, and the portions got larger, and at our third blissful command he simply put the tin in its ice bowl upon our table. It was a regal gesture, like being tapped on the shoulder with a sword. We bowed, served ourselves exactly as he would have done, grain for grain, and had no need for any more. It was reward enough to sit in the almost empty room, chaste rococo in the slanting June sunlight, with the generous tub of pure delight between us, Mother purring there, the vodka seeping slyly through our veins, and real wood strawberries to come, to make us feel like children again and not near-gods. That was a fine introduction to what I hope is a reasonably long life of such occasional bliss.

As for potato chips, I do not remember them earlier than my twenty-first year, when I once ate stupidly and well of them in a small, stylish restaurant in Germany, where we had to wait downstairs in the tavern while our meal was being readied to eat upstairs. Beside me on a table was a bowl of exquisitely fresh and delicate chips, and when we finally sat down I could not face the heavily excellent dinner we had ordered. I was ashamed of my gluttony, for it is never commendable, even when based on ignorance. Perhaps *that* is why I am so stern today about not eating many of the devilish temptations?

There is one other thing I know I shall never get enough of—champagne. I cannot say when I drank my first prickly, delicious glass of it. I was raised in Prohibition, which meant that my father was very careful about his bootleggers, but the general adult drinking stayed around pinch-bottle Scotch as safest in those days, and I think I probably started my lifelong affair with Dom Pérignon's discovery in 1929, when I first went to France. It does not matter. I would gladly ask for the same end as a poor peasant's there, who is given a glass of champagne on his deathbed to cheer him on his way.

I used to think, in my Russian-novel days, that I would cherish a lover who managed through thick and thin, snow and sleet, to have a bunch of

Parma violets on my breakfast tray each morning—also rain or shine,
Christmas or August, and onward into complete Neverland. Later, I
shifted my dream plan—a split of cold champagne, one half hour *before*
the tray! Violets, sparkling wine, and trays themselves were as nonexistent
as the lover(s), of course, but once again, why not? By now, I sip a mug of
vegetable broth and count myself fortunate, while my mind's nose and
eyes feast on the pungency of the purple blossoms, and the champagne
stings my sleepy tongue . . . and on feast days I drink a little glass of
California "dry Sauterne" from the icebox . . . and it is much easier to
get out of bed to go to work if there is not that silly tray there.

Mayonnaise, real mayonnaise, good mayonnaise, is something I can
dream of any time, almost, and not because I ate it when I was little but
because I did not. My maternal grandmother, whose Victorian neuroses
dictated our family table tastes until I was about twelve, found salads
generally suspect but would tolerate the occasional serving of some watery
lettuce in a dish beside each plate (those crescents one still sees now and
then in English and Swiss boardinghouses and the mansions of American
Anglophiles). On it would be a dab or lump or blob, depending on the
current cook, of what was quietly referred to as Boiled Dressing. It
seemed dreadful stuff—enough to harm one's soul.

I do not have my grandmother's own recipe, although I am sure she
seared it into many an illiterate mind in her kitchens, but I have found an
approximation, which I feel strangely forced to give. It is from Miss
Parloa's *New Cook Book,* copyrighted in Boston in 1880 by Estes and
Lauriat:

> Three eggs, one tablespoon each of sugar, oil and salt, a scant table-
> spoonful of mustard, a cupful of milk and one of vinegar. Stir oil,
> mustard, salt and sugar in a bowl until perfectly smooth. Add the
> eggs, and beat well; then add the vinegar, and finally the milk. Place
> the bowl in a basin of boiling water, and stir the dressing until it
> thickens like soft custard. . . . The dressing will keep two weeks if
> bottled tightly and put in a cool place.

On second thought, I think Grandmother's receipt, as I am sure it was
called, may have used one egg instead of three, skimped on the sugar and
oil, left out the mustard, and perhaps eliminated the milk as well. It was a
kind of sour whitish gravy and. . . . Yes! Patience is its own reward; I
have looked in dozens of cookbooks without finding her abysmal secret,
and now I have it: she did not use eggs at all, but *flour.* That is it. Flour
thickened the vinegar—no need to waste eggs and sugar . . . Battle
Creek frowned on oil, and she spent yearly periods at that health resort
. . . mustard was a heathen spice . . . salt was cheap, and good cider

vinegar came by the gallon. . . . And (here I can hear words as clearly as I can see the limp wet lettuce under its load of Boiled Dressing): "Salad is roughage and a French idea."

As proof of the strange hold childhood remembrance has on us, I think I am justified to print once, and only once, my considered analysis of the reason I must live for the rest of my life with an almost painful craving for mayonnaise made with fresh eggs and lemon juice and good olive oil:

Grandmother's Boiled Dressing

> 1 cup cider vinegar
> Enough flour to make thin paste
> Salt to taste

Mix well, boil slowly fifteen minutes or until done, and serve with wet shredded lettuce.

Unlike any other recipe I have ever given, this one has never been tested and never shall be, nor is it recommended for anything but passing thought.

Some of the foods that are of passionate interest in childhood, as potently desirable as drink to a toper, with time lose everything but a cool intellectuality. For about three years, when I was around six, we sometimes ate hot milk toast for Sunday night supper, but made with rich cocoa, and I would start waiting for the next time as soon as I had swallowed the last crumbly buttery brown spoonful of it. I am thankful I need have no real fear of ever being faced with another bowl of the stuff, but equally happy that I can still understand how its warmth and savor satisfied my senses then. I feel much the same grateful relief when I conjure, no matter how seldom, the four or five years when I was in boarding schools and existed—sensually, at least—from one private slow orgy to the next, of saltines and Hershey bars, bite for bite.

There is one concoction, or whatever it should be called, that I was never allowed to eat, and that I dreamed of almost viciously for perhaps seventeen years, until I was about twenty-two and married. I made it then and ate every bit of it and enjoyed it enormously and have never tasted it since, except in the happy reaches of my gastronomical mind. And not long ago, when I found a distinctly literary reference to it, I beamed and glowed. I love the reality of Mark Twain almost as much as I love the dream image of this dish, and when he included it, just as I myself would have, in a list of American foods he planned to eat—"a modest, private affair," all to himself—I could hardly believe the miraculous coincidence: my ambrosia, my god's!

In *A Tramp Abroad,* Twain grouses about the food he found in Europe in 1878 (even a god can sound a little limited at times) and makes a list of the foods he has missed the most and most poignantly awaits on his return. It starts out "Radishes," which is indeed either blind or chauvinistic, since I myself always seem to eat five times as many of them when I am a tramp abroad as when I am home. He then names eighty separate dishes and ends, "All sorts of American pastry. Fresh American Fruits. . . . Ice water." Love is *not* blind, and I do feel sorry about a certain lack of divinity in this utterance, but my faith and loyalty are forever strengthened by items 57 and 58: "Mashed Potatoes. Catsup."

These two things were printed on the same line, and I feel—in fact, I *know*—that he meant "Mashed Potatoes *and* Catsup," or perhaps "Mashed Potatoes *with* Catsup." This certainty springs from the fact that there is, in my own mind and plainly in his, an affinity there. The two belong together. I have known this since I was about five, or perhaps even younger. I have proved it—only once, but very thoroughly. I am willing to try to again, preferably in "a modest, private affair, all to myself," but in public if I should ever be challenged.

We often ate mashed potatoes at home. Grandmother liked what my mother secretly scoffed at as "slip-and-go-easies": custards, junkets, strained stewed tomatoes, things like that, with mashed potatoes, of course, at the head of the list as a necessity alongside any decent cut of meat. But—and here is the secret, perhaps, of my lifelong craving—we were never allowed to taste catsup. Never. It was spicy and bad for us, and "common" in bottles. (This is an odd fact, chronologically, for all the housekeepers of my beldam's vintage prided themselves on their special receipts for "ketchups," made of everything from oysters to walnuts and including the plentiful love apple.)

I remember that once when Grandmother was gone off to a religious convention, Mother asked each of us what we would most like to eat before the awesome Nervous Stomach took over our menus again. My father immediately said he would pick a large salad of watercress from the Rio Hondo and make a dressing of olive oil and wine vinegar—a double cock-snoot, since olive oil was an exotic smelly stuff kept only to rub on the navels of the new babies that seemed to arrive fairly often, and watercress grew along the banks of a stream that might well be . . . er . . . *used* by cows. When my turn came, I said, "Mashed potatoes and catsup." I forget exactly what went on next, except that Father was for letting me eat all I wanted of the crazy mixture and I never did get to. Ah, well . . . I loved watercress, too, and whatever forbidden fruits we bit into during that and similar gastric respites, and I did not need to stop dreaming.

My one deliberate challenge to myself was delicious. I was alone, which seems to be indicated for many such sensual rites. The potatoes were light, whipped to a firm cloud with rich hot milk, faintly yellow from ample butter. I put them in a big warmed bowl, made a dent about the size of a respectable coffee cup, and filled it to the brim with catsup from a large, full, *vulgar* bottle that stood beside my table mat where a wineglass would be at an ordinary, commonplace, everyday banquet. Mine was, as I have said, delicious. I would, as I have also said, gladly do it again if I were dared to. But I prefer to nourish myself with the knowledge that it is not impossible (potato chips), not too improbable (fresh Beluga caviar). And now I am sharing it with a friend. I could not manage to serve forth to Mark Twain the "Sheep-head and croakers, from New Orleans," or the "Prairie hens, from Illinois," that he dreamed of in European boarding-houses ninety years ago, but mashed potatoes *with* catsup are ready to hand when he says the word.

MARY McCARTHY

Mary McCarthy (1912–1989) was equally celebrated in her time as a novelist (The Group, The Company She Keeps) *and a nonfiction writer, though it is probably her essays and memoirs that will endure. Her greatest literary creation was herself, "Mary McCarthy," the testy, worldly, sharp-tongued, and unillusioned first-person character who narrates her best work. This includes her wonderful autobiography,* Memoirs of a Catholic Girlhood, *and her fine essays and travel writings, most notably* On the Contrary *and* Venice Observed.

After a difficult childhood, in which she suffered the deaths of her parents and was farmed out to indifferent, cruel relatives, McCarthy was "saved" by a good education at an Episcopal seminary and Vassar College. While still a young woman, she burst on the American intellectual scene and attracted attention with her fiercely critical and polemical pieces. She is associated with the time when literary quarterlies such as The Partisan Review, Commentary, *and* Encounter *exercised allure and engaged political, artistic, and personal matters with equal energy. Her appreciation for European intellectual life helped to bring an air of cosmopolitanism to American culture.*

McCarthy's writing style is lucid, carefully crafted, shrewd, ironic, and candid. She is unafraid to make herself look bad when it suits the narrative, as we see in "My Confession." She does not appeal to her readers for sympathy so much as she implicates us in the heady apportionment of guilt and innocence—hers and everyone else's.

My Confession

Fall, 1953

E VERY AGE has a keyhole to which its eye is pasted. Spicy court-memoirs, the lives of gallant ladies, recollections of an ex-nun, a monk's confession, an atheist's repentance, true-to-life accounts of prostitution and bastardy gave our ancestors a penny peep into the forbidden room. In our own day, this type of sensational fact-fiction is being produced largely by ex-Communists. Public curiosity shows an almost prurient avidity for the details of political defloration, and the memoirs of ex-Communists have an odd resemblance to the confessions of a white slave. Two shuddering climaxes, two rendezvous with destiny, form the poles between which these narratives vibrate: the first describes the occasion when the subject was seduced by Communism; the second shows him wresting himself from the demon embrace. Variations on the form are possible. Senator McCarthy, for example, in his book, *McCarthyism, the Fight for America,* uses a tense series of flashbacks to dramatize his encounter with Communism: the country lies passive in Communism's clasp; he is given a tryst with destiny in the lonely Arizona hills, where, surrounded by "real Americans without any synthetic sheen," he attains the decision that will send him down the long marble corridors to the Senate Caucus Room to bare the shameful commerce.

The diapason of choice plays, like movie music, round today's apostle to the Gentiles: Whittaker Chambers on a park bench and, in a reprise, awake all night at a dark window, facing the void. These people, unlike ordinary beings, are shown the true course during a lightning storm of revelation, on the road to Damascus. And their decisions are lonely decisions, silhouetted against a background of public incomprehension and hostility.

I object. I have read the reminiscences of Mr. Chambers and Miss Bentley. I too have had a share in the political movements of our day, and my experience cries out against their experience. It is not the facts I balk at—I have never been an espionage agent—but the studio atmosphere of sublimity and purpose that enfolds the facts and the chief actor. When Whittaker Chambers is mounted on his tractor, or Elizabeth Bentley, alone, is meditating her decision in a white New England church, I have the sense that they are on location and that, at any moment, the director will call "Cut." It has never been like that for me; events have never waited, like extras, while I toiled to make up my mind between good and evil. In fact, I have never known these mental convulsions, which appear quite strange to me when I read about them, even when I do not question the author's sincerity.

Is it really so difficult to tell a good action from a bad one? I think one usually knows right away or a moment afterward, in a horrid flash of regret. And when one genuinely hesitates—or at least it is so in my case—it is never about anything of importance, but about perplexing trivial things, such as whether to have fish or meat for dinner, or whether to take the bus or subway to reach a certain destination, or whether to wear the beige or the green. The "great" decisions—those I can look back on pensively and say, "That was a turning-point"—have been made without my awareness. Too late to do anything about it, I discover that I have chosen. And this is particularly striking when the choice has been political or historic. For me, in fact, the mark of the historic is the nonchalance with which it picks up an individual and deposits him in a trend, like a house playfully moved by a tornado. My own experience with Communism prompts me to relate it, just because it had this inadvertence that seems to me lacking in the true confessions of reformed Communists. Like Stendhal's hero, who took part in something confused and disarrayed and insignificant that he later learned was the Battle of Waterloo, I joined the anti-Communist movement without meaning to and only found out afterward, through others, the meaning or "name" assigned to what I had done. This occurred in the late fall of 1936.

Three years before, I had graduated from college—Vassar, the same college Elizabeth Bentley had gone to—without having suffered any fracture of my political beliefs or moral frame. All through college, my official political philosophy was royalism; though I was not much interested in politics, it irritated me to be told that "you could not turn the clock back." But I did not see much prospect for kingship in the United States (unless you imported one, like the Swedes), and, *faute de mieux,* I awarded my sympathies to the Democratic Party, which I tried to look on as the party of the Southern patriciate. At the same time, I had an aversion to Republicans—an instinctive feeling that had been with me since I was a child of eight pedaling my wagon up and down our cement driveway and howling "Hurray for Cox" at the Republican neighbors who passed by. I disliked businessmen and business attitudes partly, I think, because I came from a professional (though Republican) family and had picked up a disdain for businessmen as being beneath us, in education and general culture. And the anti-Catholic prejudice against Al Smith during the 1928 election, the tinkling amusement at Mrs. Smith's vulgarity, democratized me a little in spite of myself: I was won by Smith's plebeian charm, the big coarse nose, and rubbery politician's smile.

But this same distrust of uniformity made me shrink, in 1932, from the sloppily dressed Socialist girls at college who paraded for Norman Thomas and tirelessly argued over "Cokes"; their eager fellowship and scrawled placards and heavy personalities bored me—there was something, to my mind, deeply athletic about this socialism. It was a kind of political hockey played by big, gaunt, dyspeptic girls in pants. It startled me a little, therefore, to learn that in an election poll taken of the faculty, several of my favorite teachers had voted for Thomas; in them, the socialist faith appeared rather charming, I decided—a gracious and attractive oddity, like the English Ovals they gave you when you came for tea. That was the winter Hitler was coming to power and, hearing of the anti-Jewish atrocities, I had a flurry of political indignation. I wrote a prose-poem that dealt, in a mixed-up way, with the Polish Corridor and the Jews. This poem was so unlike me that I did not know whether to be proud of it or ashamed of it when I saw it in a college magazine. At this period, we were interested in surrealism and automatic writing, and the poem had a certain renown because it had come out of my interior without much sense or order, just the way automatic writing was supposed to do. But there my political development stopped.

The depression was closer to home; in New York I used to see apple-sellers on the street corners, and, now and then, a bread line, but I had a very thin awareness of mass poverty. The depression was too close to home to awaken anything but curiosity and wonder—the feelings of a child confronted with a death in the family. I was conscious of the suicides of stockbrokers and businessmen, and of the fact that some of my friends had to go on scholarships and had their dress allowances curtailed, while their mothers gaily turned to doing their own cooking. To most of us at Vassar, I think, the depression was chiefly an upper-class phenomenon.

My real interests were literary. In a paper for my English Renaissance seminar, I noted a resemblance between the Elizabethan puritan pundits and the school of Marxist criticism that was beginning to pontificate about proletarian literature in the *New Masses*. I disliked the modern fanatics, cold, envious little clerics, equally with the insufferable and ridiculous Gabriel Harvey—Cambridge pedant and friend of Spenser—who tried to introduce the rules of Latin quantity into English verse and vilified a true poet who had died young, in squalor and misery. I really hated absolutism and officiousness of any kind (I preferred my kings martyred) and was pleased to be able to recognize a Zeal-of-the-Land-Busy in proletarian dress. And it was through a novel that I first learned, in my senior year, about the Sacco-Vanzetti case. The discovery that two innocent men had been executed only a few years back while I, oblivious, was in boarding school, gave me a disturbing shock. The case was still so near that I was tantalized by a feeling that it was not too late to do something—try still another avenue, if Governor Fuller and the Supreme Court obdurately would not be moved. An unrectified case of injustice has a terrible way of lingering, restlessly, in the social atmosphere like an unfinished equation. I went on to the Mooney case, which vexed not only my sense of equity but my sense of plausibility—how was it possible for the prosecution to lie so, in broad daylight, with the whole world watching?

When in May, 1933, however, before graduation, I went down to apply for a job at the old *New Republic* offices, I was not drawn there by the magazine's editorial policy—I hardly knew what it was—but because the book-review section seemed to me to possess a certain elegance and independence of thought that would be hospitable to a critical spirit like me. And I was badly taken aback when the book-review editor, to whom I had been shunted—there was no job—puffed his pipe and remarked that he would give me a review if I could show him that I was either a genius or starving. "I'm not starving," I said quickly; I knew I was not a genius and I was not pleased by the suggestion that I would be taking bread from other people's mouths. I did not think this a fair criterion and in a moment I said so. In reply, he put down his pipe, shrugged, reached out for the material I had brought with me, and half-promised, after an assaying glance, to send me a book. My notice finally appeared; it was not very good, but I did not know that and was elated. Soon I was reviewing novels and biographies for both the *New Republic* and the *Nation* and preening myself on the connection. Yet, whenever I entered the *New Republic*'s waiting room, I was seized with a feeling of nervous guilt toward the shirtsleeved editors upstairs and their busy social conscience, and, above all, toward the shabby young men who were waiting too and who had, my bones told me, a better claim than I to the book I hoped to take away with me. They looked poor, pinched, scholarly, and supercilious, and I did not know which of these qualities made me, with my clicking high heels and fall "ensemble," seem more out of place.

I cannot remember the moment when I ceased to air my old royalist convictions and stuffed them away in an inner closet as you do a dress or an ornament that you perceive strikes the wrong note. It was probably at the time when I first became aware of Communists as a distinct entity. I had known about them, certainly, in college, but it was not until I came to New York that I began to have certain people, celebrities, pointed out to me as Communists and to turn my head to look at them, wonderingly. I had no wish to be one of them, but the fact that they were there—an unreckoned factor—made my own political opinions take on a protective coloration. This process was accelerated by my marriage—a week after graduation—to an actor and playwright who was in some ways very much like me. He was the son of a Minnesota normal school administrator who had been the scapegoat in an academic scandal that had turned him out of his job and reduced him, for a time, when my husband was nine or ten, to selling artificial limbs and encyclopedia sets from door to door. My husband still brooded over his father's misfortune, like Hamlet or a character in Ibsen, and this had given his nature a sardonic twist that inclined him to behave like a paradox—to follow the mode and despise it, live in a Beekman Place apartment while lacking the money to buy groceries, play bridge with society couples and poker with the stage electricians, dress in the English style and carry a walking stick while wearing a red necktie.

He was an odd-looking man, prematurely bald, with a tense, arresting figure, a broken nose, a Standard English accent, and wry, circumflexed eyebrows. There was something about him both baleful and quizzical; whenever he stepped on the stage he had the ironic air of a symbol. This curious appearance of his disqualified him for most Broadway roles; he was too young for character parts and too bald for juveniles. Yet just this disturbing ambiguity—a Communist painter friend did a drawing of him that brought out a resemblance to Lenin—suited the portentous and equivocal atmosphere of left-wing drama. He smiled dryly at Marxist terminology, but there was social anger in him. During the years we were married, the only work he found was in productions of "social" significance. He played for the Theatre Union in *The Sailors of Cattaro,* about a mutiny in the Austrian fleet, and in *Black Pit,* about coal miners; the following year, he was in *Winterset* and Archibald MacLeish's *Panic*—the part of a blind man in both cases. He wrote revue sketches and unproduced plays, in a mocking, despairing, but none the less radical vein; he directed the book of a musical called *Americana* that featured the song, "Brother, Can You Spare a Dime?" I suppose there was something in him of both the victim and the leader, an undertone of totalitarianism; he was very much interested in the mythic qualities of leadership and talked briskly about a Farmer-Labor party in his stage English accent. Notions of the superman and the genius flickered across his thoughts. But this led him, as it happened, away from politics, into sheer personal vitalism, and it was only in plays that he entered "at the head of a mob." In personal life he was very winning, but that is beside the point here.

The point is that we both, through our professional connections, began to take part in a left-wing life, to which we felt superior, which we laughed at, but which nevertheless was influencing us without our being aware of it. If the composition of the body changes every seven years, the composition of our minds during the seven years changed, so that though our thoughts looked the same to us, inside we had been altered, like an old car which has had part after part replaced in it under the hood.

We wore our rue with a difference; we should never have considered joining the Communist Party. We were not even fellow-travelers; we did not sign petitions or join "front" groups. We were not fools, after all, and were no more deceived by the League against War and Fascism, say, than by a Chinatown bus with a carload of shills aboard. It was part of our metropolitan sophistication to know the truth about Communist fronts. We accepted the need for social reform, but we declined to draw the "logical" inference that the Communists wanted us to draw from this. We argued with the comrades backstage in the dressing rooms and at literary cocktail parties; I was attacked by a writer in the *New Masses*. We knew about Lovestoneites and Trotskyites, even while we were ignorant of the labor theory of value, the law of uneven development, the theory of permanent revolution *vs.* socialism in one country, and so on. "Lovestone is a Lovestoneite!" John wrote in wax on his dressing-room mirror, and on his door in the old Civic Repertory he put up a sign: "Through these portals pass some of the most beautiful tractors in the Ukraine."

The comrades shrugged and laughed, a little unwillingly. They knew we were not hostile but merely unserious, politically. The comrades who knew us best used to assure us that our sophistication was just an armor; underneath, we must care for the same things they did. They were mistaken, I am afraid. Speaking for myself, I cannot remember a single broad altruistic emotion visiting me during that period—the kind of emotion the simpler comrades, with their shining eyes and exalted faces, seemed to have in copious secretion. And yet it was true: we were not hostile. We marched in May Day parades, just for the fun of it, and sang, "Hold the Fort, for We Are Coming," and *"Bandiera Rossa,"* and "The Internationale," though we always bellowed "The *Socialist* International shall be the human race," instead of "The International Soviet," to pique the Communists in our squad. We took part in evening clothes in a consumers' walk-out at the Waldorf to support a waiters' strike—the Communists had nothing to do with this—and we grew very excited (we did have negative feelings) when another young literary independent was arrested and booked. During a strike at a department store, John joined the sympathetic picketing and saw two of his fellow actors carried off in the Black Maria; they missed a matinee and set off a controversy about what was the *first* responsibility of a Communist playing in a proletarian drama. We went once or twice to a class for actors in Marxism, just to see what was up; we went to a debate on Freud and/or Marx, to a debate on the execution of the hundred and four White Guards following Kirov's assassination.

Most ex-Communists nowadays, when they write their autobiographies or testify before Congressional committees, are at pains to point out that their actions were very, very bad and their motives very, very good. I would say the reverse of myself, though without the intensives. I see no reason to disavow my actions, which were perfectly all right, but my motives give me a little embarrassment, and just because I cannot disavow them: that fevered, contentious, trivial show-off in the May Day parade is still recognizably me.

We went to dances at Webster Hall and took our uptown friends. We went to parties to raise money for the sharecroppers, for the Theatre Union, for the *New Masses.* These parties generally took place in a borrowed apartment, often a sculptor's or commercial artist's studio; you paid for your drinks, which were dispensed at a long, wet table; the liquor was dreadful; the glasses were small, and there was never enough ice. Long-haired men in turtle-necked sweaters marched into the room in processions and threw their overcoats on the floor, against the wall, and sat on them; they were only artists and bit-actors, but they gave these affairs a look of gangsterish menace, as if the room were guarded by the goons of the future. On couches with wrinkled slipcovers, little spiky-haired girls, like spiders, dressed in peasant blouses and carapaced with Mexican jewelry, made voracious passes at baby-faced juveniles; it was said that they "did it for the Party," as a recruiting effort. Vague, soft-faced old women with dust mops of whitish hair wandered benevolently about seeking a listener; on a sofa against a wall, like a deity, sat a bearded scion of an old Boston family, stiff as a post. All of us, generally, became very drunk; the atmosphere was horribly sordid, with cigarette burns on tables, spilled drinks, ashes everywhere, people passed out on the bed with the coats or necking, you could not be sure which. Nobody cared what happened because there was no host or hostess. The fact that a moneyed person had been simple enough to lend the apartment seemed to make the guests want to desecrate it, to show that they were exercising not a privilege but a right.

Obviously, I must have hated these parties, but I went to them, partly because I was ashamed of my own squeamishness, and partly because I had a curiosity about the Communist men I used to see there, not the actors or writers, but the higher-ups, impresarios and theoreticians—dark, smooth-haired owls with large white lugubrious faces and glasses. These were the spiritual directors of the Communist cultural celebrities and they moved about at these parties like so many monks or abbés in a worldly salon. I had always liked to argue with the clergy, and I used to argue with these men, who had the air, as they stood with folded arms, of listening not to a disagreement but to a confession. Whenever I became tight, I would bring up (oh, *vino veritas*) the Czar and his family. I did not see why they all had had to be killed—the Czar himself, yes, perhaps, and the

Czarina, but not the young girls and the children. I knew the answer, of course (the young Czarevitch or one of his sisters might have served as a rallying point for the counter-revolutionary forces), but still I gazed hopefully into these docents' faces, seeking a trace of scruple or compassion. But I saw only a marmoreal astuteness. The question was of bourgeois origin, they said with finality.

The next morning I was always bitterly ashamed. I had let these omniscient men see the real me underneath, and the other me squirmed and gritted her teeth and muttered, Never, never, *never* again. And yet they had not convinced me—there was the paradox. The superiority I felt to the Communists I knew had, for me at any rate, good grounding; it was based on their lack of humor, their fanaticism, and the slow drip of cant that thickened their utterance like a nasal catarrh. *And yet* I was tremendously impressed by them. They made me feel petty and shallow; they had, shall I say, a daily ugliness in their life that made my pretty life tawdry. I think all of us who moved in that ambience must have felt something of the kind, even while we laughed at them. When John and I, for instance, would say of a certain actor, "He is a Party member," our voices always contained a note of respect. This respect might be mixed with pity, as when we saw some blue-eyed young profile, fresh from his fraternity and his C average, join up because a sleazy girl had persuaded him. The literary Communists I sincerely despised because I was able to judge the quality of the work they published and see their dishonesty and contradictions; even so, when I beheld them in person, at a Webster Hall dance, I was troubled and felt perhaps I had wronged them—perhaps there was something in them that my vision could not perceive, as some eyes cannot perceive color.

People sometimes say that they envied the Communists because they were so "sure." In my case, this was not exactly it; I was sure, too, intellectually speaking, as far as I went. That is, I had a clear mind and was reasonably honest, while many of the Communists I knew were pathetically fogged up. In any case, my soul was not particularly hot for certainties.

And yet in another way I did envy the Communists, or, to be more accurate, wonder whether I ought to envy them. I could not, I saw, be a Communist because I was not "made that way." Hence, to be a Communist was to possess a sort of privilege. And this privilege, like all privileges, appeared to be a source of power. Any form of idiocy or aberration can confer this distinction on its owner, at least in our age, which aspires to a "total" experience; in the thirties it was the Communists who seemed fearsomely to be the happy few, not because they had peace or certitude but because they were a mutation—a mutation that threatened, in the words of their own anthem, to become the human race.

There was something arcane in every Communist, and the larger this area was the more we respected him. That was why the literary Communists, who operated in the open, doing the hatchet work on artists' reputations, were held in such relatively low esteem. An underground worker rated highest with us; next were the theoreticians and oracles; next were the activists, who mostly worked, we heard, on the waterfront. Last came the rank and file, whose work consisted of making speeches, distributing leaflets, attending Party and faction meetings, joining front organizations, marching in parades and demonstrations. These people we dismissed as uninteresting not so much because their work was routine but because the greater part of it was visible. In the same way, among individual comrades, we looked up to those who were close-lipped and stern about their beliefs and we disparaged the more voluble members—the forensic little actors who tried to harangue us in the dressing rooms. The idea of a double life was what impressed us: the more talkative comrades seemed to have only one life, like us; but even they, we had to remind ourselves, had a secret annex to their personality, which was signified by their Party name. It is hard not to respect somebody who has an alias.

Of fellow-travelers, we had a very low opinion. People who were not willing to "go the whole way" filled us with impatient disdain. The only fellow-travelers who merited our notice were those of whom it was said: the Party prefers that they remain on the outside. I think some fellow-travelers circulated such stories about themselves deliberately, in order to appear more interesting. There was another type of fellow-traveler who let it be known that they stayed out of the Party because of some tiny doctrinal difference with Marxism. This tiny difference magnified them enormously in their own eyes and allowed them to bear gladly the accusation of cowardice. I knew one such person very well—a spruce, ingratiating swain, the heir to a large fortune—and I think it was not cowardice but a kind of pietistic vanity. He felt he cut more of a figure if he seemed to be doing the Party's dirty work gratuitously, without compulsion, like an oblate.

In making these distinctions (which were the very distinctions the Party made), I had no idea, of course, that I was allowing myself to be influenced by the Party in the field where I was most open to suasion—the field of social snobbery. Yet in fact I was being deterred from forming any political opinions of my own, lest I find I was that despised article, a "mere" socialist or watery liberal, in the same way that a young snob coming to college and seeing who the "right" people are will strive to make no friends rather than be caught with the wrong ones.

For me, the Communist Party was *the* party, and even though I did not join it, I prided myself on knowing that it was the pinnacle. It is only now that I see the social component in my attitude. At the time, I simply supposed that I was being clear-sighted and logical. I used to do research and typing for a disgruntled middle-aged man who was a freak for that day—an anti-Communist Marxist—and I was bewildered by his anti-Party bias. While we were drinking hot tea, Russian style, from glasses during the intervals of our work, I would try to show him his mistake. "Don't you think it's rather futile," I expostulated, "to criticize the Party the way you do, from the outside? After all, it's the *only* working-class Party, and if *I* were a Marxist I would join it and try to reform it." Snorting, he would raise his small deep-set blue eyes and stare at me and then try patiently to show me that there was no democracy in the Party. I listened disbelievingly. It seemed to me that it would just be a question of converting first one comrade and then another to your point of view till gradually you had achieved a majority. And when my employer assured me that they would throw you out if you tried that, my twenty-three-year-old wisdom cocked an eyebrow. I thought I knew what was the trouble: he was a pathologically lazy man and his growling criticisms of the Party were simply a form of malingering, like the aches and pains he used to manufacture to avoid working on an article. A real revolutionary who was not afraid of exertion would get into the Party and fight.

The curious idea that being critical of the Party was a compelling reason for joining it must have been in the air, for the same argument was brought to bear on me in the summer of 1936—the summer my husband and I separated and that I came closest to the gravitational pull of the Communist world. Just before I went off to Reno, there was a week in June when I stayed in Southampton with the young man I was planning to marry and a little Communist organizer in an old summer house furnished with rattan and wicker and Chinese matting and mother-of-pearl and paper fans. We had come there for a purpose. The little organizer had just been assigned a car—a battered old Ford roadster that had been turned over to the Party for the use of some poor organizer; it may have been the very car that figured in the Hiss case. My fiancé, who had known him for years, perhaps from the peace movement, was going to teach him to drive. We were all at a pause in our lives. The following week our friend was supposed to take the car to California and do propaganda work among the migrant fruit-pickers; I was to go to Reno; my fiancé, a vivacious young bachelor, was to conquer his habits of idleness and buckle down to a serious job. Those seven days, therefore, had a special, still quality, like the days of a novena you make in your childhood; a part of each of them was set aside for the Party's task. It was early in June; the musty house that belonged to my fiancé's parents still had the winter-smell of mice and old wood and rust and mildew. The summer colony had not yet arrived; the red flag, meaning that it was dangerous to swim, flew daily on the beach; the roads were nearly empty. Every afternoon we would take the old car, canvas flapping, to a deserted stretch of straight road in the dunes, where the neophyte could take the wheel.

He was a large-browed, dwarfish man in his late thirties, with a deep widow's peak, a bristly short mustache, and a furry western accent—rather simple, open-natured, and cheerful, the sort of person who might have been a small-town salesman or itinerant newspaperman. There was an energetic, hopeful innocence about him that was not confined to his political convictions—he could *not* learn to drive. Every day the same thing happened; he would settle his frail yet stocky figure trustingly in the driver's seat, grip the wheel, step on the starter, and lose control of the car, which would shoot ahead in first or backward in reverse for a few perilous feet till my fiancé turned off the ignition; Ansel always mistook the gas for the brake and forgot to steer while he was shifting gears.

It was clear that he would never be able to pass the driver's test at the county seat. In the evenings, to make up to him for his oncoming disappointment (we smiled when he said he could start without a license), we encouraged him to talk about the Party and tried to take an intelligent interest. We would sit by the lamp and drink and ask questions, while he smoked his short pipe and from time to time took a long draught from his highball, like a man alone musing in a chair.

And finally one night, in the semi-dark, he knocked out his pipe and said to me: "You're very critical of the Party. Why don't you join it?" A thrill went through me, but I laughed, as when somebody has proposed to you and you are not sure whether they are serious. "I don't think I'd make very good material." "You're wrong," he said gravely. "You're just the kind of person the Party needs. You're young and idealistic and independent." I broke in: "I thought independence was just what the Party didn't want." "The Party needs criticism," he said. "But it needs it from the inside. If people like you who agree with its main objectives would come in and criticize, we wouldn't be so narrow and sectarian." "You admit the Party is narrow?" exclaimed my fiancé. "Sure, I admit it," said Ansel, grinning. "But it's partly the fault of people like Mary who won't come in and broaden us." And he confided that he himself made many of the same criticisms I did, but he made them from within the Party, and so could get himself listened to. "The big problem of the American Party," said Ansel, puffing at his pipe, "is the smallness of the membership. People say we're ruled from Moscow; I've never seen any sign of it. But let's suppose it's true, for the sake of argument. This just means that the American Party isn't big enough yet to stand on its own feet. A big, indigenous party couldn't be ruled from Moscow. The will of the members would have to rule it, just as their dues and contributions would support it." "That's where I come in, I suppose?" I said, teasing. "That's where you come in," he calmly agreed. He turned to my fiancé. "Not you," he said. "You won't have the time to give to it. But for Mary I think it would be an interesting experiment."

An interesting experiment . . . I let the thought wander through my mind. The subject recurred several times, by the lamplight, though with no particular urgency. Ansel, I thought (and still think), was speaking sincerely and partly in my own interest, almost as a spectator, as if he would be diverted to see how I worked out in the Party. All this gave me quite a new sense of Communism and of myself too; I had never looked upon my character in such a favorable light. And as a beneficiary of Ansel's charity, I felt somewhat ashamed of the very doubt it raised: the suspicion that he might be blind to the real facts of inner Party life. I could admire where I could not follow, and, studying Ansel, I decided that I admired the Communists and would probably be one, if I were the person he thought me. Which I was afraid I was not. For me, such a wry conclusion is always uplifting, and I had the feeling that I mounted in understanding when Sunday morning came and I watched Ansel pack his sturdy suitcase and his briefcase full of leaflets into the old roadster. He had never yet driven more than a few yards by himself, and we stood on the front steps to await what was going to happen: he would not be able to get out of the driveway, and we would have to put him on the train and return the car to the Party when we came back to New York. As we watched, the car began to move; it picked up speed and grated into second, holding to the middle of the road as it turned out of the driveway. It hesitated and went into third: Ansel was driving! Through the back window we saw his figure hunched over the wheel; the road dipped and he vanished. We had witnessed a miracle, and we turned back into the house, frightened. All day we sat waiting for the call that would tell us there had been an accident, but the day passed without a sound, and by nightfall we accepted the phenomenon and pictured the little car on the highway, traveling steadily west in one indefatigable thrust, not daring to stop for gas or refreshment, lest the will of the driver falter.

This parting glimpse of Ansel through the car's back window was, as it turned out, ultimate. Politically speaking, we reached a watershed that summer. The first Moscow trial took place in August. I knew nothing of this event because I was in Reno and did not see the New York papers. Nor did I know that the Party line had veered to the right and that all the fellow-travelers would be voting, not for Browder as I was now prepared to do (if only I remembered to register), but for Roosevelt. Isolated from these developments in the mountain altitudes, I was blossoming, like a

lone winter rose overlooked by the frost, into a revolutionary thinker of
the pure, uncompromising strain. The detached particles of the past three
years' experience suddenly "made sense," and I saw myself as a radical.

"Book Bites Mary," wrote back a surprised literary editor when I sent
him, from Reno, a radiant review of a novel about the Paris Commune
that ended with the heroine sitting down to read the *Communist Manifesto*. In Seattle, when I came to stay with my grandparents, I found a
strike on and instantly wired the *Nation* to ask if I could cover it. Every
night I was off to the Labor Temple or a longshoreman's hall while my
grandparents took comfort from the fact that I seemed to be against Roosevelt, the Democrats, and the Czars of the A. F. of L.—they did not quite
grasp my explanation, that I was criticizing "from the left."

Right here, I come up against a puzzle: why didn't I take the *next step?*
But it is only a puzzle if one thinks of me not as a concrete entity but as a
term in a logical operation: you agree with the Communist Party; *ergo,* you
join it. I reasoned that way but I did not behave so. There was something
in me that capriciously resisted being a term in logic, and the very fact that
I cannot elicit any specific reason why I did not join the Party shows that I
was never really contemplating it, though I can still hear my own voice,
raised very authoritatively at a cafeteria table at the Central Park Zoo,
pointing out to a group of young intellectuals that if we were serious we
would join the Communists.

This was in September and I was back in New York. The Spanish Civil
War had begun. The pay-as-you-go parties were now all for the Loyalists,
and young men were volunteering to go and fight in Spain. I read the
paper every morning with tears of exaltation in my eyes, and my sympathies rained equally on Communists, Socialists, Anarchists, and the brave
Catholic Basques. My heart was tense and swollen with popular-front solidarity. I applauded the Lincoln Battalion, protested non-intervention, hurried into Wanamaker's to look for cotton-lace stockings: I was boycotting
silk on account of Japan in China. I was careful to smoke only union-made
cigarettes; the white package with Sir Walter Raleigh's portrait came
proudly out of my pocketbook to rebuke Chesterfields and Luckies.

It was a period of intense happiness; the news from the battlefront was
often encouraging and the practice of virtue was surprisingly easy. I
moved into a one-room apartment on a crooked street in Greenwich Village and exulted in being poor and alone. I had a part-time job and read
manuscripts for a publisher; the very riskiness of my situation was zestful
—I had decided not to get married. The first month or so was scarifyingly
lonely, but I survived this, and, starting early in November, I began to feel
the first stirrings of popularity. A new set of people, rather smart and

moneyed, young Communists with a little "name," progressive hosts and
modernist hostesses, had discovered me. The fact that I was poor and
lived in such a funny little apartment increased the interest felt: I was
passed from hand to hand, as a novelty, like Gulliver among the Brob-
dingnagians. During those first days in November, I was chiefly conscious
of what a wonderful time I was starting to have. All this while, I had
remained ignorant of the fissure that was opening. Nobody, I think, had
told me of the trial of Zinoviev and Kamenev—the trial of the sixteen—or
of the new trial that was being prepared in Moscow, the trial of Pyatakov
and Radek.

Then, one afternoon in November, I was taken to a cocktail party, in
honor of Art Young, the old *Masses* cartoonist, whose book, *The Best of
Art Young,* was being published that day. It was the first publisher's party
I had ever been to, and my immediate sensation was one of disappointment: nearly all these people were strangers and, to me, quite unattractive.
Art Young, a white-haired little kewpie, sitting in a corner, was pointed
out to me, and I turned a respectful gaze on him, though I had no clear
idea who he was or how he had distinguished himself. I presumed he was
a veteran Communist, like a number of the stalwarts in the room, survivors of the old *Masses* and the *Liberator.* Their names were whispered to
me and I nodded; this seemed to be a commemorative occasion, and the
young men hovered in groups around the old men, as if to catch a word
for posterity. On the outskirts of certain groups I noticed a few poorly
dressed young men, bolder spirits, nervously flexing their lips, framing
sentences that would propel them into the conversational center, like actors with a single line to speak.

The solemnity of these proceedings made me feel terribly ill at ease. It
was some time before I became aware that it was not just me who was
nervous: the whole room was under a constraint. Some groups were avoiding other groups, and now and then an arrow of sarcasm would wing like
a sniper's bullet from one conversation to another.

I was standing, rather bleakly, by the refreshment table, when a question was thrust at me: did I think Trotsky was entitled to a hearing? It was
a novelist friend of mine, dimple-faced, shaggy-headed, earnest, with a
whole train of people, like a deputation, behind him. Trotsky? I glanced
for help at a sour little man I had been talking with, but he merely
shrugged. My friend made a beckoning gesture and a circle closed in.
What had Trotsky done? Alas, I had to ask. A tumult of voices proffered
explanations. My friend raised a hand for silence. Leaning on the table, he
supplied the background, speaking very slowly, in his dragging, disconso-
late voice, like a schoolteacher wearied of his subject. Trotsky, it appeared,
had been accused of fostering a counter-revolutionary plot in the Soviet
Union—organizing terrorist centers and conspiring with the Gestapo to

murder the Soviet leaders. Sixteen old Bolsheviks had confessed and implicated him. It had been in the press since August.

I blushed; everybody seemed to be looking at me strangely. I made a violent effort to take in what had been said. The enormity of the charge dazed me, and I supposed that some sort of poll was being taken and that I was being asked to pronounce on whether Trotsky was guilty or innocent. I could tell from my friend's low, even, melancholy tone that he regarded the charges as derisory. "What do you want me to say?" I protested. "I don't know anything about it." "Trotsky denies the charges," patiently intoned my friend. "He declares it's a GPU fabrication. Do you think he's entitled to a hearing?" My mind cleared. "Why, of course." I laughed—were there people who would say that Trotsky was *not* entitled to a hearing? But my friend's voice tolled a rebuke to this levity. "She says Trotsky is entitled to his day in court."

The sour little man beside me made a peculiar, sucking noise. "You disagree?" I demanded, wonderingly. "I'm smart," he retorted. "I don't let anybody ask me. You notice, he doesn't ask me?" "Shut up, George," said my novelist friend impatiently. "I'm asking *her*. One thing more, Mary," he continued gravely. "Do you believe that Trotsky should have the right of asylum?" The right of asylum! I looked for someone to share my amusement—were we in ancient Greece or the Middle Ages? I was sure the U.S. government would be delighted to harbor such a distinguished foreigner. But nobody smiled back. Everybody watched dispassionately, as for form's sake I assented to the phrasing: yes, Trotsky, in my opinion, was entitled to the right of asylum.

I went home with the serene feeling that all these people were slightly crazy. *Right of asylum, his day in court!*—in a few hours I had forgotten the whole thing.

Four days later I tore open an envelope addressed to me by something that called itself "Committee for the Defense of Leon Trotsky," and idly scanned the contents. "We demand for Leon Trotsky the right of a fair hearing and the right of asylum." Who were these demanders, I wondered, and, glancing down the letterhead, I discovered my own name. I sat down on my unmade studio couch, shaking. How dared they help themselves to my signature? This was the kind of thing the Communists were always being accused of pulling; apparently, Trotsky's admirers had gone to the same school. I had paid so little heed to the incident at the party that a connection was slow to establish itself. Reading over the list of signers, I recognized "names" that had been present there and remembered my novelist-friend going from person to person, methodically polling. . . .

How were they feeling, I wondered, when they opened their mail this morning? My own feelings were crisp. In two minutes I had decided to withdraw my name and write a note of protest. Trotsky had a right to a hearing, but I had a right to my signature. For even if there had been a legitimate misunderstanding (it occurred to me that perhaps I had been the only person there not to see the import of my answers), nothing I had said committed me to Trotsky's *defense.*

The "decision" was made, but according to my habit I procrastinated. The severe letter I proposed to write got put off till the next day and then the next. Probably I was not eager to offend somebody who had been a good friend to me. Nevertheless, the letter would undoubtedly have been written, had I been left to myself. But within the next forty-eight hours the phone calls began. People whom I had not seen for months or whom I knew very slightly telephoned to advise me to get off the newly formed Committee. These calls were not precisely threatening. Indeed, the caller often sounded terribly weak and awkward, as if he did not like the mission he had been assigned. But they were peculiar. For one thing, they usually came after nightfall and sometimes quite late, when I was already in bed. Another thing, there was no real effort at persuasion: the caller stated his purpose in standardized phrases, usually plaintive in tone (the Committee was the tool of reaction, and all liberal people should dissociate them-selves from its activities, which were an unwarranted intervention in the domestic affairs of the Soviet Union), and then hung up, almost immedi-ately, before I had a proper chance to answer. Odd too—the voices were not those of my Communist friends but of the merest acquaintances. These people who admonished me to "think about it" were not people whose individual opinions could have had any weight with me. And when I did think about it, this very fact took on an ominous and yet to me absurd character: I was not being appealed to personally but imperson-ally warned.

Behind these phone calls there was a sense of the Party wheeling its forces into would-be disciplined formations, like a fleet or an army maneu-vering. This, I later found, was true: a systematic telephone campaign was going on to dislodge members from the Committee. The phone calls gen-erally came after dark and sometimes (especially when the recipient was elderly) in the small hours of the morning. The more prominent signers got anonymous messages and threats.

And in the morning papers and the columns of the liberal magazines I saw the results. During the first week, name after name fell off the Com-mittee's letterhead. Prominent liberals and literary figures issued state-ments deploring their mistake. And a number of people protested that their names had been used without permission. . . .

There, but for the grace of God, went I, I whispered, awestruck, to myself, hugging my guilty knowledge. Only Heaven—I plainly saw—by making me dilatory had preserved me from joining this sorry band. Here was the occasion when I should have been wrestling with my conscience or standing, floodlit, at the crossroads of choice. But in fact I was only aware that I had had a providential escape. I had been saved from having to decide about the Committee; *I* did not decide it—the Communists with their pressure tactics took the matter out of my hands. We all have an instinct that makes us side with the weak, if we do not stop to reason about it, the instinct that makes a householder shield a wounded fugitive without first conducting an inquiry into the rights and wrongs of his case. Such "decisions" are simple reflexes; they do not require courage; if they did, there would be fewer of them. When I saw what was happening, I rebounded to the defense of the Committee without a single hesitation—it was nobody's business, I felt, how I happened to be on it, and if anybody had asked me, I should have lied without a scruple.

Of course, I did not foresee the far-reaching consequences of my act—how it would change my life. I had no notion that I was now an anti-Communist, where before I had been either indifferent or pro-Communist. I did, however, soon recognize that I was in a rather awkward predicament—not a moral quandary but a social one. I knew nothing about the cause I had espoused; I had never read a word of Lenin or Trotsky, nothing of Marx but the *Communist Manifesto,* nothing of Soviet history; the very names of the old Bolsheviks who had confessed were strange and almost barbarous in my ears. As for Trotsky, the only thing that made me think that he might be innocent was the odd behavior of the Communists and the fellow-traveling liberals, who seemed to be infuriated at the idea of a free inquiry. All around me, in the fashionable Stalinist circles I was now frequenting, I began to meet with suppressed excitement and just-withheld disapproval. Jeweled lady-authors turned white and shook their bracelets angrily when I came into a soirée; rising young men in publishing or advertising tightened their neckties dubiously when I urged them to examine the case for themselves; out dancing in a night club, tall, collegiate young Party members would press me to their shirt-bosoms and tell me not to be silly, honey.

And since I seemed to meet more Stalinists every day, I saw that I was going to have to get some arguments with which to defend myself. It was not enough, apparently, to say you were for a fair hearing; you had to rebut the entire case of the prosecution to get anybody to incline an ear in your direction. I began to read, headlong, the literature on the case—the pamphlets issued by Trotsky's adherents, the verbatim report of the second trial published by the Soviet Union, the "bourgeois" press, the Communist press, the radical press. To my astonishment (for I had scarcely dared think it), the trials did indeed seem to be a monstrous frame-up. The defendant, Pyatakov, flew to Oslo to "conspire" with Trotsky during a winter when, according to the authorities, no planes landed at the Oslo airfield; the defendant, Holtzmann, met Trotsky's son, Sedov, in 1936, at the Hotel Bristol in Copenhagen, which had burned down in 1912; the witness, Romm, met Trotsky in Paris at a time when numerous depositions testified that he had been in Royan, among clouds of witnesses, or on the way there from the south of France.

These were only the most glaring discrepancies—the ones that got in the newspapers. Everywhere you touched the case something crumbled. The carelessness of the case's manufacture was to me its most terrifying aspect; the slovenly disregard for credibility defied credence, in its turn. How did they dare? I think I was more shaken by finding that I was on the right side than I would have been the other way round. And yet, except for a very few people, nobody seemed to mind whether the Hotel Bristol had burned down or not, whether a real plane had landed, whether Trotsky's life and writings were congruent with the picture given of him in the trials. When confronted with the facts of the case, people's minds sheered off from it like jelly from a spoon.

Anybody who has ever tried to rectify an injustice or set a record straight comes to feel that he is going mad. And from a social point of view, he *is* crazy, for he is trying to undo something that is finished, to unravel the social fabric. That is why my liberal friends looked so grave and solemn when I would press them to come to a meeting and listen to a presentation of the facts—for them this was a Decision, too awful to be considered lightly. The Moscow trials were a historical fact and those of us who tried to undo them were uneasily felt to be crackpots, who were trying to turn the clock back. And of course the less we were listened to, the more insistent and earnest we became, even while we realized we were doing our cause harm. It is impossible to take a moderate tone under such conditions. If I admitted, though, to being a little bit hipped on the subject of Trotsky, I could sometimes gain an indulgent if flickering attention —the kind of attention that stipulates, "She's a bit off but let's hear her story." And now and then, by sheer chance, one of my hearers would be arrested by some stray point in my narrative; the disparaging smile would slowly fade from his features, leaving a look of blank consternation. He would go off and investigate for himself, and in a few days, when we met again, he would be a crackpot too.

Most of us who became anti-Communists at the time of the trials were drawn in, like me, by accident and almost unwillingly. Looking back, as on a love affair, a man could say that if he had not had lunch in a certain restaurant on a certain day, he might not have been led to ponder the facts of the Moscow trials. Or not then at any rate. And had he pondered them at a later date, other considerations would have entered and his conversion would have had a different style. On the whole, those of us who became anti-Communists during that year, 1936–37, have remained liberals—a thing that is less true of people of our generation who were converted earlier or later. A certain doubt of orthodoxy and independence of mass opinion was riveted into our anti-Communism by the heat of that period. As soon as I make this statement, exceptions leap into my mind, but I think as a generalization it will stand. Those who became anti-Communist earlier fell into two classes: the experts and those to whom any socialist ideal was repugnant. Those whose eyes were opened later, by the Nazi-Soviet pact, or still later, by God knows what, were left bruised and full of self-hatred or self-commiseration, because they had palliated so much and truckled to a power-center; to them, Communism's chief sin seems to be that it deceived *them,* and their public atonement takes on both a vindicating and a vindictive character.

We were luckier. Our anti-Communism came to us neither as the fruit of a special wisdom nor as a humiliating awakening from a prolonged deception, but as a natural event, the product of chance and propinquity. One thing followed another, and the will had little to say about it. For my part, during that year, I realized, with a certain wistfulness, that it was too late for me to become any kind of Marxist. Marxism, I saw, from the learned young men I listened to at Committee meetings, was something you had to take up young, like ballet dancing.

So, I did not try to be a Marxist or a Trotskyite, though for the first time I read a little in the Marxist canon. But I got the name of being a Trotskyite, which meant, in the end, that I saw less of the conventional Stalinists I had been mingling with and less of conventional people generally. (My definition of a conventional person was quite broad: it included anyone who could hear of the Moscow trials and maintain an unruffled serenity.) This, then, was a break or a rupture, not very noticeable at first, that gradually widened and widened, without any conscious effort on my part, sometimes to my regret. This estrangement was not marked by any definite stages; it was a matter of tiny choices. Shortly after the Moscow trials, for instance, I changed from the *Herald Tribune* to the *Times;* soon I had stopped doing crossword puzzles, playing bridge, reading detective stories and popular novels. I did not "give up" these things; they departed from me, as it were, on tiptoe, seeing that my thoughts were elsewhere.

To change from the *Herald Tribune* to the *Times,* is not, I am aware, as serious a step as breaking with international Communism when you have been its agent; and it occurs to me that Mr. Chambers and Miss Bentley might well protest the comparison, pointing out that they were profoundly dedicated people, while I was a mere trifler, that their decisions partook of the sublime, where mine descended to the ridiculous—as Mr. Chambers says, he was ready to give his life for his beliefs. Fortunately (though I could argue the point, for we all give our lives for our beliefs, piecemeal or whole), I have a surprise witness to call for my side, who did literally die for his political views.

I am referring to Trotsky, the small, frail, pertinacious old man who wore whiskers, wrinkles, glasses, shock of grizzled hair, like a gleeful disguise for the erect young student, the dangerous revolutionary within him. Nothing could be more alien to the convulsed and tormented moonscapes of the true confessions of ex-Communists than Trotsky's populous, matter-of-fact recollections set out in *My Life.* I have just been rereading this volume, and though I no longer subscribe to its views, which have certainly an authoritarian and doctrinaire cast that troubles me today, nevertheless I experience a sense of recognition here that I cannot find in the pages of our own repentant "revolutionaries." The old man remained unregenerate; he never admitted that he had sinned. That is probably why nobody seems to care for, or feel apologetic to, his memory. It is an interesting point—and relevant, I think, to my story—that many people today actually have the impression that Trotsky died a natural death.

In a certain sense, this is perfectly true. I do not mean that he lived by violence and therefore might reasonably be expected to die by violence. He was a man of words primarily, a pamphleteer and orator. He was armed, as he said, with a pen and peppered his enemies with a fusillade of articles. Hear the concluding passages of his autobiography: "Since my exile, I have more than once read musings in the newspapers on the subject of the 'tragedy' that has befallen me. I know no *personal* tragedy. I know the change of two chapters of revolution. One American paper which published an article of mine accompanied it with a profound note to the effect that in spite of the blows the author had suffered, he had, as evidenced by his article, preserved his clarity of reason. I can only express my astonishment at the Philistine attempt to establish a connection between the power of reasoning and a government post, between mental balance and the present situation. I do not know, and never have known, of any such connection. In prison, with a book or pen in my hand, I experienced the same sense of deep satisfaction that I did at mass-meetings of the revolution. I felt the mechanics of power as an inescapable burden, rather than as a spiritual satisfaction."

This was not a man of violence. Nevertheless, one can say that he died a natural death—a death that was in keeping with the open manner of his life. There was nothing arcane in Trotsky; that was his charm. Like an ordinary person he was hospitably open to hazard and accident. In his autobiography, he cannot date the moment when he became a socialist.

One factor in his losing out in the power-struggle at the time of Lenin's death was his delay in getting the telegram that should have called him home from the Caucasus, where he was convalescent, to appear at Lenin's funeral—*had* he got the telegram, the outcome perhaps would have been different. Or again, perhaps not. It may be that the whims of chance are really the importunities of design. But if there is a Design, it aims, in real lives, like the reader's or mine or Trotsky's, to look natural and fortuitous; that is how it gets us into its web.

Trotsky himself, looking at his life in retrospect, was struck, as most of us are on such occasions, by the role chance had played in it. He tells how one day, during Lenin's last illness, he went duck-shooting with an old hunter in a canoe on the River Dubna, walked through a bog in felt boots —only a hundred steps—and contracted influenza. This was the reason he was ordered to Sukhu for the cure, missed Lenin's funeral, and had to stay in bed during the struggle for primacy that raged that autumn and winter. "I cannot help noting," he says, "how obligingly the accidental helps the historical law. Broadly speaking, the entire historical process is a refraction of historical law through the accidental. In the language of biology, one might say that the historical law is realized through the natural selection of accidents." And with a touch of quizzical gaiety he sums up the problem as a Marxian: "One can foresee the consequences of a revolution or a war, but it is impossible to foresee the consequences of an autumn shooting-trip for wild ducks." This shrug before the unforeseen implies an acceptance of consequences that is a far cry from penance and prophecy. Such, it concedes, is life. *Bravo,* old sport, I say, even though the hall is empty.

*name is unknown to me.
Let's leave it @ that.
A tedious self-announced
"failure"*

SEYMOUR KRIM

Seymour Krim (1922–1989) was born and raised in Manhattan, where he lived for most of his life, and his persona is that of the quintessential New Yorker: street-smart, neurotic, ambitious, self-mocking, manic yet depressed or downbeat. His mother and father both died young, and he carried with him an orphan's hunger for love. He began as a literary critic, in awe of the giants of modernism and American fiction; but his essays became more and more personal, and he evolved a unique, hipster prose style that was shot through with the then-contemporary influences of bebop, action painting, and Beat Generation writing. Krim's mission was to bring to essay writing the excitement and ecstatic rush that Kerouac and Ginsberg had developed in fiction and poetry—to make of the essay a "ride." He would dive in like a jazz soloist, already on a high note, and try to ascend from there by feeding in harrowing confessions, unresolved contradictions, and riffs of gnarled insight.

Krim also saw the New Journalism as a major breakthrough, allowing the nonfiction writer to discard the mask of neutrality and "to insert himself into these events through his writing, to become an actor upon them instead of a helpless observer, to try and influence the making of history itself with his art so that he can save himself as a man." In his three essay collections, Views of a Near-Sighted Cannoneer, Shake It for the World, Smartass, *and* You and Me, *he practiced "laying it on the line," as he called it, with gut-wrenching, naked pieces about his own nervous breakdowns, sexual hungers, and envy of those who had "made it." Failure—both his own and that of the American dream—was a major theme of Krim's. James Wolcott noted, "His willingness to face failure first thing in the morning is what gives Krim's writing its tremendous tender sense of fraternity. . . . It may be lonely at the top, but it's crowded at the bottom." Ironically, part of Krim's sense of failure came from never having realized his youthful ambition, to write big American novels; essay writing seemed to him something of a compromise, a minor art. Had he valued it more highly, he might have realized what a genuine success he was.*

For My Brothers and Sisters
in the Failure Business*

W E A R E A L L V I C T I M S of the imagination in this country. The American Dream may sometimes seem like a dirty joke these days, but it was internalized long ago by our fevered little minds and it remains to haunt us as we fumble with the unglamorous pennies of life during the illusionless middle years. At 51, believe it or not, or believe it and pity me if you are young and swift, I still don't know truly "what I want to be." I've published several serious books. I rate an inch in *Who's Who in America*. I teach at a so-called respected university. But in that profuse upstairs delicatessen of mine I'm as open to every wild possibility as I was at 13, although even I know that the chances of acting them out diminish with each heartbeat.

One life was never quite enough for what I had in mind.

At 50 my father was as built-in as a concrete foundation and at 55 he was crushed out of existence by the superstructure of his life. I have no

---

*America to me was and is the dream of my life. I cannot separate my private self from it. I have become a pessimist because I live in a time so hard on people, including me, that I sometimes wish I hadn't been born into all this. Not only to spare me more bum trips but to free me from my knowledge of other people's situations. I have never really learned how to live. I improvise—and fuck up anyway. But through it all I owe so unfathomably much of whatever I am to being American that I couldn't conceive of my being alive in any other dress. It is what I want. Yes. I think the time must come soon if mankind is going to find life possible when this romance with country has to be junked for the sake of everyone else. This world is made up of individuals—what my friend at the liquor store, Vinnie Porrazzo, calls God's children—not separate governments. But until we become a state equal to every other one, I want to be a decent patriot; maybe afterwards, too, on a smaller scale. That's all I've ever really wanted. I'm homesick for that sweet land of liberty and not only the pursuit of happiness but the fulfillment of it. Not to die for my country, I've already done it too often, but to live for it. Oh, I'll tell you, I'll make a mean mother of a patriot. I want America to know this kid was here.—S.K.

superstructure except possibly in my head. I literally live alone with my fierce dreams, and my possessions are few. My father knew where he stood or thought he did, having originally come from an iron-cross Europe, but I only know that I stand on today with a silent prayer that tomorrow will bring to me my revelation and miraculize me.

That's because I come from America, which has to be the classic, ultimate, then-they-broke-the-mold incubator of not knowing who you are until you find out. I have never really found out and I expect what remains of my life to be one long search party for the final me. I don't kid myself that I'm alone in this, hardly, and I don't really think that the great day will ever come when I hold a finished me in my fist and say here you are, congratulations. I'm talking primarily about the expression of that me in the world, the shape it takes, the profile it zings out, the "work" it does.

You may sometimes think everyone lives in the crotch of the pleasure principle these days except you, but you have company, friend. I live under the same pressures you do. It is still your work or role that finally gives you your definition in our society, and the thousands upon thousands of people who I believe are like me are those who have never found the professional skin to fit the riot in their souls. Many never will. I think what I have to say here will speak for some of their secret life and for that other sad America you don't hear too much about. This isn't presumption so much as a voice of scars and stars talking. I've lived it and will probably go on living it until they take away my hotdog.

Consider (as the noble Dickens used to say about just such a lad as I) a boy at the turn of the 30s growing up in this land without parents, discipline, any religion to speak of, yet with a famished need that almost unconsciously filled the vacuum where the solid family heart should be, the dizzying spectacle of his senses. America was my carnival at an earlier age than most and I wanted to be everything in it that turned me on, like a youth bouncing around crazed on a boardwalk. I mean literally everything. I was as unanchored a kid as you can conceive of, an open fuse-box of blind yearning, and out of what I now assume was unimaginable loneliness and human hunger I greedily tried on the personalities of every type on the national scene as picked up through newspapers, magazines, movies, radio, and just nosing around.

And what a juicy parade through any inexperienced and wildly applauding mind America was then, what a nonstop variety show of heroes, adventurers, fabulous kinds of human beings to hook on to if you were totally on your own without any guidance and looking for your star in a society that almost drove you batty with desire. In my earnest role-playing the philosophical tramp and the cool millionaire-playboy were second nature to me, as were the style and stance of ballplayers, barnstorming pilots, polar explorers, radio personalities (how can I ever forget you, gorgeous-voiced Ted Husing?), generals, bridge-building engineers, treasure-hunters, crooners, inventors. I wanted to be and actually was Glenn Cunningham, Joe E. Penner, Kid Chocolate, Chandu the Magician, Eugene O'Neill, a Gangbuster. If you're old enough, tick off the names of the rotogravure big-shots of the time and see Seymour impersonating them in his private magic theater. And later on when I had lost my adolescent shame and knew myself to be a freak of the imagination, even wallowed in it, I identified with women like Amelia Earhart and even the hot ripe early pinup girl, Iris Adrian, and transvestited my mind to see the world through their long lashes and tough lace. Democracy means democracy of the fantasy life, too, there are no cops crouching in the corridors of the brain. Dr. Freud's superego hasn't been able to pull its old country rank over here, even though it's tried like a mother, or should I say a father?

But my point is this: what a great fitting-room for experimentation, a huge sci-fi lab for making the self you wanted, America was for those of us who needed models, forms, shapes we could throw ourselves into. Obviously, everyone from my generation didn't chuck caution out the window even if they felt the lure, as I did, of a new make-your-own-lifesize-man era. Some of my more realistic contemporaries narrowed it all down early and became the comparative successes they are today. Whether it's making a lot of money selling scrap in a junkyard (Ed Feinberg) or writing thrillers for connoisseurs of kinkiness (Patricia Highsmith), they all had to focus clearly, work hard. As traps and frustrations of 51 close down around me, with all the small defects and petty hurts that sometimes seem to choke away all thoughts of the unique Homeric journey of the inner person in America, everyone's inner person, I salute them for achieving some of what they wanted. Nobody gets it all. But I salute anyone in this bewildering dreamland of a nation who has managed to cut through the wilderness of tangled trails to some definite cabin of achievement and reward.

Yet those of us who have never really nailed it down, who have charged through life from enthusiasm to enthusiasm, from new project to new project, even from personality-revolution to personality-revolution, have a secret also. I'm sorry to say it isn't the kind that desperate people can use to improve themselves, like those ads in the newspaper. Sadly enough, it is the kind that people in my seven-league but very leaky boots often take to psychiatrists, hoping to simplify their experience because they can't cope with the murderous tangle of it. But for those of us who have lived through each twist and turn, the psychiatry sessions, the occasional abyss, the endless review of our lives to see where we went wrong, and then come to see our natures as strange and special manifestations of a time and place that will never come again, there is a wonder in it that almost makes up for the beating we are beginning to take at the hands of the professional heavyweight world.

Our secret is that we still have an epic longing to be more than what we are, to multiply ourselves, to integrate all the identities and action-fantasies we have experienced, above all to keep experimenting with our lives all the way to Forest Lawn to see how much we can make real out of that prolific American Dream machine within. Let me say it plainly: Our true projects have finally been ourselves. It's as if we had taken literally the old cornball Land of Opportunity slogan and incorporated it into the pit of the being instead of the space around us; and fallen so much in love with the ongoing excitement of becoming, even the illusion of becoming, that our pants often fall down and reveal our dirty skivvies and skinny legs. The laughter hurts, believe me, but it doesn't stop us for very long. We were hooked early.

What it comes down to is that the America of the pioneer has been made subjective by us. The endless rolling back of the frontier goes on within our heads all the time. We are the updated Daniel Boones of American inner-space. Each of our lives, for those of us in this country-wide fraternity, seems to us a novel or a play or a movie in itself, draining our energy but then at other moments lifting us up to spectacular highs, yet always moving, the big wagon-train of great new possibilities always crushing on. The fact that all of this is private doesn't make it any less real. What it does do is make us ache with hopelessness at times as to how to find a vocation for this private super-adventure serial out on the streets of life.

I know for a fact that I wanted to become a novelist in my teens just so that I could be all these different personalities and events that it was physically impossible for me to be any other way. As a matter of fact, I feel that the writing of the realistic/romantic novel in America (and they were usually one and the same, with the hairy details just used to tack down the sweep of imagination) came out of these basic human needs to transcend the one body and temperament you were born with in order to mingle imaginatively with a cast of thousands that could only exist in a monster-country like ours. Others wanted to become actors for much the same reason, to impersonate all the people they could not be, but in my case I wanted to compose the script itself so that I could participate in the minds as well as the outward actions of characters who were all extensions of myself and my own mad love affair with the fabulous diversity of this society.

I never accepted the discipline or, finally, the belief in a pure fiction separate from myself and never became the marvelous novelist of my teenage ambition. But I was an inward one, just as so many young kids today shoot movies in their heads with themselves as the leading character. I think it was just an accident of history that made me good at words instead of the sounds and pictures which are the newest language, but I feel little superiority at being able to pitch a word or two compared to those like myself in other ways who are tongue-tied. What unites us all is that we never knew except in bits and pieces how to find a total expression, appreciated by our peers, in which we could deliver ourselves of all the huge and contradictory desires we felt within. The country was too rich and confusing for us to want to be one thing at the expense of another. We were the victims of our enormous appreciation of it all.

Even though, with words coming easily to me, I began in my 20s that long string of never totally satisfying jobs as Office of War Information rewrite man, assistant pulp editor, motion-picture publicity writer, motion-picture script reader, book reviewer, finally editor of a magazine, I was always looking past them. When I heard a great black blues singer, I wanted to incorporate that sound in me and even tried singing in Greenwich Village. When I saw a handsome movie star close up, I thought that was my birthright also and went to a plastic surgeon to try and make me look more like this example of male beauty. When I had saturated myself with the brilliant records of Lenny Bruce and Lord Buckley, I thought that I too should improvise in a nightclub and even played a small engagement in the Midwest to painfully act this dream out. Whatever I saw that was good in others and which I didn't possess, I tried literally to add to my nature, graft on to the living flesh. It seemed to me, and I'm sure to those like me who haven't yet spoken, that American society was essentially a launching pad for the endless development of the Self.

We cared more about trying to enlarge and extend the boundaries of being what we were, of demonically sucking all of the country's possibilities into ourselves, than we did about perfecting a single craft or profession. As I've said, it was a beautiful, breathless eagerness for all the life we could hold inside, packed layer on layer like a bulging quart container of ice cream. Granted that in a way it was the most rank kind of selfishness and self-absorption, yet this too was forecast and made part of the national inheritance in 1870 when Walt Whitman chanted, "One's-self I sing —a simple, separate person; yet utter the word Democratic, the word En-Masse." That's what this democracy was for us, a huge supermarket of mass man where we could take a piece here and a piece there to make our personalities for ourselves instead of putting up with what was given at the beginning.

But this lovely idea became for some of us a tragedy, or at least a terrible confusion that wasn't counted on at the beginning. When do you stop making a personality? When do you stop fantasizing an endless you and try to make it with what you've got? The answer is never, really. You keep adding and subtracting from that creation which is yourself until the last moment. Once begun, it is not a habit that can be given up easily. Some people who started off this risky life-game with high hopes found that after a while they were unable to live with the self they began with and unable to come close to the self, or selves, they desired to be. They live in pain, and some are no longer living at all, having found it too bitter to take.

In my own case, because of the fluency with words, I was able to express my own longings and desires with personal statements in print as the years went by, and thus I wasn't as completely frustrated as those other dreamers I know who have run the gamut of jobs and flings at movies, writing, dancing, politics, and yet have never found a home to match their imaginations. Simply put, they never found a form to contain them, or have only caught it momentarily, and then it was gone.

During my 20s and 30s, even into my 40s, it was exhilarating to learn and be involved at this and then that steaming source—the *Partisan Review* brigade of radical intellectuals, then the Beat Generation, then a wonderful fling at daily newspaper reporting on the New York *Herald Tribune,* then the breakthrough (to my mind) of the New Journalism. I was confident as are all American nomads of the jeweled highways of the imagination that there would be a sudden confluence of all the roads at some fated point and then I would put it all together with a gorgeous thunderclap. No soap. Actually all of this *can* conceivably happen, but the mathematics are against you as time goes on. Yet time is just that factor we don't want to hear about until it elbows us in the nose.

We know all along that time is squeezing us into a corner while we mentally rocket to each new star that flares across our sky, and yet we can't help ourselves. We forget that our contemporaries are building up wealth of one kind or another, reputations, consistency, credit in the world, and that it counts for more as age settles down around all of us, the very age we have denied or ignored. In a way, those of us who have lived higher in the mind than on the sidewalk making and revising our salad of possibilities have stayed younger than we should have. We have even been sealed off from our own image as it's seen by others.

Yet each one of us sooner or later gets the elbow that reminds us that the "real world" we have postponed making a deal with, in fact played with like Chaplin kicking the globe around in *The Great Dictator,* has been evaluating us with a different set of standards than the ones we have been applying to ourselves. If we have been snotty towards ordinary success, proud and mysterious as we followed the inner light, even making thoughtless cracks about those who settle for little, then the day always comes when our own inability to put it all together is seen by another who wants to cut us down to size and our lives suddenly explode in our faces. . . .

I was living in Europe at the time, where the attitude towards personal success and failure is much less of a real distinction than over here because of the evenhanded wounds of recent history. Everyone was badly hurt by the war. Even today one man or woman's fate counts for less than some kind of minimum well-being for masses of people who are trapped by political and economic circumstances beyond their control and must learn to live, cheerfully if possible, without much hope for large personal triumphs. It is a relief for Americans who come from a society that glorifies individual achievement to the aching and breaking point to live over there for a while, and try to recuperate from the American heat in a different psychological climate. In fact many of our permanent expatriates are just the kind of people I have been talking about all through this communication, a band who have never found themselves by our official standards and perhaps never will, but who can live more at peace beyond our shores with less money and less strain than at home.

I, too, had been unkinked in this easier, we're-all-fucked-together-so-let's-make-the-best-of-it environment, self-lulled into thinking I was as rich and potential a human gold mine as I always believed—as all of us in my camp want to believe—when the dirty American word "failure" winged its way across the water and hit me where it hurts. . . . It suddenly and brutally defined to me the price I had paid for my bid to be everything that proposed itself to my imagination. Maybe I never had a choice, and would have been an uncertain performer at whatever I did, but my decision to aim at the stars had been a conscious one and this was the way it was being weighed on the common man's do-it-or-shut-up scale. . . .

But if you are a proud, searching "failure" in this society, and we can take ironic comfort in the fact that there are hundreds of thousands of us, then it is smart and honorable to know what you attempted and why you are now vulnerable to the body blows of those who once saw you robed in the glow of your vision and now only see an unmade bed and a few unwashed cups on the bare wooden table of a gray day. What we usually refuse to acknowledge in our increasingly defensive posture is that we chose our royal inner trip out of an excess of blind faith, out of a reach beyond what we might have had if our desires had been less grandiose. I can't really criticize this, I think it is inherent in the American mystique to want to go all the way to the limit of your imagination, but if we are straight about it we must accept that we are in large part responsible for the jam we are now in.

In my own situation I know only too well that from childhood and adolescence on I clutched at the habit of dreaming up a glittering future, always, instead of putting my head down and slugging my way through the present. I must confess that in an almost reflexive sense I still find myself doing this childish number, as do so many of those other poor lovely romantics who are like me. It's a primitive method so native to us by now that it is part of us. What was once a psychological choice when we were young, in other words, has now become for many of us a habit as hard to kick as junk. The handy magic of relying on the future, on tomorrow, to knit together all the parts of a self that we hoarded up for a lifetime can't be stopped at this late date, or won't be stopped, because our frame of mind was always that of a long-odds gambler. One day it would all pay off. But for most of us, I'm afraid that day will never come—the original hopes, their extravagant range and spaciousness, and yes, their lack of specific clarity and specific definition, were beyond translation into deed. They dramatized our lives for a good long while and then turned slightly sour when people began to ask for proof.

For a minority, and I still believe this, the special form they seek to pull it all together will unexpectedly click into place after years of turning the key this way and that. And as for myself, I am lucky I guess in that I can write about this very phenomenon that I live while others who experience it just as toughly, maybe even more so, are without the words to tell you what they have gone through. Maybe that is my "revelation," the final "me," my purpose in the schemelessness of things after looking so strenuously in all directions and being so discontented with what I can apparently do without strain.

But this is a poor second to what I wanted and I will never be satisfied with sketching my own portrait and that of those like me when it was action we finally craved, after all those dress rehearsals in the mind, and not self-analysis. America worked on us too hard, when you get right down to it. We imaginatively lived out all the mythic possibilities, all the personal turn-on of practically superhuman accomplishment, stimulated by the fables of the media. We were the perfect big-eyed consumers of this country's four-color ad to the universe, wanting to be one tempting thing and then another and ending up, most of us, with little but the sadly smiling hope that time would somehow solve our situation. When I've been brave, I've told my friends who share my plight that this is no longer a true possibility to hang on to. Time will most likely repeat itself. We will most likely repeat ourselves. Most of my friends agree, with that hard twinkle in the eye that unites all of us who have earned it.

But you cannot separate us from the deepest promise of the country as it was lived within by very sensitive poets without a tongue, so to speak, and perhaps the ultimate failure of the country. This last is not an easy thing to say, even in a time in which America-baiting is the rage. Like most of us in the failure business, I am, we are, patriots so outrageously old-fashioned that we incorporated the spirit of the country in our very heads, took literally its every invitation to the greatest kind of self-fulfillment ever known. There's something beautiful about being an American sucker, even if you pay for it with tears and worse. We were millionaires of the spirit for at least 20 adult years before we felt the lowering of the boom, and in the last analysis it is the spirit, the attitude within, a quality of soul, that this country has to offer to history much more than its tangible steel and the bright blood too often accompanying it. . . .

JAMES BALDWIN

James Baldwin (1924–1987) was the greatest American essayist in the second half of the twentieth century. *His nonfiction collections, especially* Notes of a Native Son, Nobody Knows My Name, *and* The Fire Next Time, *perfected a unique style of maximum tension which yoked together two opposites, tenderness and ferocity. In Baldwin's hands, as in Orwell's,* ✱ *the essay lost its stigma of benign, bellletristic coziness and became a matter of life and death.*

*Racism was Baldwin's central theme; he used it as a searchlight to uncover the world's sorrow and the failure and persistence of love. Though an ambitious novelist (*Go Tell It on the Mountain, Giovanni's Room, Another Country*) and playwright, Baldwin left his most lasting literary achievement in his essays.*

He began as a boy preacher in Harlem, and his writing style was clearly marked by the rolling-voiced, call-and-response excitement of the African- ✱ *American church. The other dominant influence was the qualifying, burrowing, analytical prose of Henry James—and, by extension, the high style of New York quarterlies such as* Partisan Review, *which he mastered at a precocious age. His essays seem a battleground between these early influences: the analytical and the oracular. Some of the weakest passages occur when Baldwin starts sermonizing without a proper argument to back him up, bullying his readers, say, to love one another more. Still, there is something admirable about his always reaching for a higher emotional pitch.*

Baldwin's apocalyptic book-length essay The Fire Next Time *created a great stir when it came out. It now seems a masterpiece, but it also marks the beginning of the tendentious rodomontade that was to mar his later work. The longer that Baldwin, who emigrated to Europe, stayed abroad, the more rhetoric he seemed to need to paper over his weakening grasp on daily American life. And yet, if his later essays fall off, they still contain more stimulating bits and interesting passages than almost anyone else's. Bravely, maybe foolhardily, Baldwin challenged the notion of the well-made essay with expanding galaxies ("No Name in the Street," "The Devil Finds Work") that keep shooting off in different directions, collecting eloquence, digressions, and juicy subthemes even as they ultimately fail to cohere.*

priggy bias ↗

Notes of a Native Son

1

ON THE TWENTY-NINTH OF JULY, in 1943, my father died. On the same day, a few hours later, his last child was born. Over a month before this, while all our energies were concentrated in waiting for these events, there had been, in Detroit, one of the bloodiest race riots of the century. A few hours after my father's funeral, while he lay in state in the undertaker's chapel, a race riot broke out in Harlem. On the morning of the third of August, we drove my father to the graveyard through a wilderness of smashed plate glass.

The day of my father's funeral had also been my nineteenth birthday. As we drove him to the graveyard, the spoils of injustice, anarchy, discontent, and hatred were all around us. It seemed to me that God himself had devised, to mark my father's end, the most sustained and brutally dissonant of codas. And it seemed to me, too, that the violence which rose all about us as my father left the world had been devised as a corrective for the pride of his eldest son. I had declined to believe in that apocalypse which had been central to my father's vision; very well, life seemed to be saying, here is something that will certainly pass for an apocalypse until the real thing comes along. I had inclined to be contemptuous of my father for the conditions of his life, for the conditions of our lives. When his life had ended I began to wonder about that life and also, in a new way, to be apprehensive about my own.

I had not known my father very well. We had got on badly, partly because we shared, in our different fashions, the vice of stubborn pride.

When he was dead I realized that I had hardly ever spoken to him. When he had been dead a long time I began to wish I had. It seems to be typical of life in America, where opportunities, real and fancied, are thicker than anywhere else on the globe, that the second generation has no time to talk to the first. No one, including my father, seems to have known exactly how old he was, but his mother had been born during slavery. He was of the first generation of free men. He, along with thousands of other Negroes, came North after 1919 and I was part of that generation which had never seen the landscape of what Negroes sometimes call the Old Country.

He had been born in New Orleans and had been a quite young man there during the time that Louis Armstrong, a boy, was running errands for the dives and honky-tonks of what was always presented to me as one of the most wicked of cities—to this day, whenever I think of New Orleans, I also helplessly think of Sodom and Gomorrah. My father never mentioned Louis Armstrong, except to forbid us to play his records; but there was a picture of him on our wall for a long time. One of my father's strong-willed female relatives had placed it there and forbade my father to take it down. He never did, but he eventually maneuvered her out of the house and when, some years later, she was in trouble and near death, he refused to do anything to help her.

He was, I think, very handsome. I gather this from photographs and from my own memories of him, dressed in his Sunday best and on his way to preach a sermon somewhere, when I was little. Handsome, proud, and ingrown, "like a toenail," somebody said. But he looked to me, as I grew older, like pictures I had seen of African tribal chieftains: he really should have been naked, with warpaint on and barbaric mementos, standing among spears. He could be chilling in the pulpit and indescribably cruel in his personal life and he was certainly the most bitter man I have ever met; yet it must be said that there was something else in him, buried in him, which lent him his tremendous power and, even, a rather crushing charm. It had something to do with his blackness, I think—he was very black—with his blackness and his beauty, and with the fact that he knew that he was black but did not know that he was beautiful. He claimed to be proud of his blackness but it had also been the cause of much humiliation and it had fixed bleak boundaries to his life. He was not a young man when we were growing up and he had already suffered many kinds of ruin; in his outrageously demanding and protective way he loved his children, who were black like him and menaced, like him; and all these things sometimes showed in his face when he tried, never to my knowledge with any success, to establish contact with any of us. When he took one of his children on his knee to play, the child always became fretful and began to cry; when he tried to help one of us with our homework the absolutely unabating tension which emanated from him caused our minds and our tongues to become paralyzed, so that he, scarcely knowing why, flew into a rage and the child, not knowing why, was punished. If it ever entered his head to bring a surprise home for his children, it was, almost unfailingly, the wrong surprise and even the big watermelons he often brought home on his back in the summertime led to the most appalling scenes. I do not remember, in all those years, that one of his children was ever glad to see him come home. From what I was able to gather of his early life, it seemed that this inability to establish contact with other people had always marked him and had been one of the things which had driven him out of New Orleans. There was something in him, therefore, groping and tentative, which was never expressed and which was buried with him. One saw it most clearly when he was facing new people and hoping to impress them. But he never did, not for long. We went from church to smaller and more improbable church, he found himself in less and less demand as a minister, and by the time he died none of his friends had come to see him for a long time. He had lived and died in an intolerable bitterness of spirit and it frightened me, as we drove him to the graveyard through those unquiet, ruined streets, to see how powerful and overflowing this bitterness could be and to realize that this bitterness now was mine.

When he died I had been away from home for a little over a year. In that year I had had time to become aware of the meaning of all my father's bitter warnings, had discovered the secret of his proudly pursed lips and rigid carriage: I had discovered the weight of white people in the world. I saw that this had been for my ancestors and now would be for me an awful thing to live with and that the bitterness which had helped to kill my father could also kill me.

He had been ill a long time—in the mind, as we now realized, reliving instances of his fantastic intransigence in the new light of his affliction and endeavoring to feel a sorrow for him which never, quite, came true. We had not known that he was being eaten up by paranoia, and the discovery that his cruelty, to our bodies and our minds, had been one of the symptoms of his illness was not, then, enough to enable us to forgive him. The younger children felt, quite simply, relief that he would not be coming home anymore. My mother's observation that it was he, after all, who had kept them alive all these years meant nothing because the problems of keeping children alive are not real for children. The older children felt, with my father gone, that they could invite their friends to the house without fear that their friends would be insulted or, as had sometimes happened with me, being told that their friends were in league with the devil and intended to rob our family of everything we owned. (I didn't fail to wonder, and it made me hate him, what on earth we owned that anybody else would want.)

His illness was beyond all hope of healing before anyone realized that he was ill. He had always been so strange and had lived, like a prophet, in such unimaginably close communion with the Lord that his long silences which were punctuated by moans and hallelujahs and snatches of old songs while he sat at the living-room window never seemed odd to us. It was not until he refused to eat because, he said, his family was trying to poison him that my mother was forced to accept as a fact what had, until then, been only an unwilling suspicion. When he was committed, it was discovered that he had tuberculosis and, as it turned out, the disease of his mind allowed the disease of his body to destroy him. For the doctors could not force him to eat, either, and, though he was fed intravenously, it was clear from the beginning that there was no hope for him.

In my mind's eye I could see him, sitting at the window, locked up in his terrors; hating and fearing every living soul including his children who had betrayed him, too, by reaching toward the world which had despised him. There were nine of us. I began to wonder what it could have felt like for such a man to have had nine children whom he could barely feed. He used to make little jokes about our poverty, which never, of course, seemed very funny to us; they could not have seemed very funny to him, either, or else our all too feeble response to them would never have caused such rages. He spent great energy and achieved, to our chagrin, no small amount of success in keeping us away from the people who surrounded us, people who had all-night rent parties to which we listened when we should have been sleeping, people who cursed and drank and flashed razor blades on Lenox Avenue. He could not understand why, if they had so much energy to spare, they could not use it to make their lives better. He treated almost everybody on our block with a most uncharitable asperity and neither they, nor, of course, their children were slow to reciprocate.

The only white people who came to our house were welfare workers and bill collectors. It was almost always my mother who dealt with them, for my father's temper, which was at the mercy of his pride, was never to be trusted. It was clear that he felt their very presence in his home to be a violation: this was conveyed by his carriage, almost ludicrously stiff, and by his voice, harsh and vindictively polite. When I was around nine or ten I wrote a play which was directed by a young, white schoolteacher, a woman, who then took an interest in me, and gave me books to read and, in order to corroborate my theatrical bent, decided to take me to see what she somewhat tactlessly referred to as "real" plays. Theater-going was forbidden in our house, but, with the really cruel intuitiveness of a child, I suspected that the color of this woman's skin would carry the day for me. When, at school, she suggested taking me to the theater, I did not, as I might have done if she had been a Negro, find a way of discouraging her, but agreed that she should pick me up at my house one evening. I then, very cleverly, left all the rest to my mother, who suggested to my father, as I knew she would, that it would not be very nice to let such a kind woman make the trip for nothing. Also, since it was a schoolteacher, I imagine that my mother countered the idea of sin with the idea of "education," which word, even with my father, carried a kind of bitter weight.

Before the teacher came my father took me aside to ask *why* she was coming, what *interest* she could possibly have in our house, in a boy like me. I said I didn't know but I, too, suggested that it had something to do with education. And I understood that my father was waiting for me to say something—I didn't quite know what; perhaps that I wanted his protection against this teacher and her "education." I said none of these things and the teacher came and we went out. It was clear, during the brief interview in our living room, that my father was agreeing very much against his will and that he would have refused permission if he had dared. The fact that he did not dare caused me to despise him: I had no way of knowing that he was facing in that living room a wholly unprecedented and frightening situation.

Later, when my father had been laid off from his job, this woman became very important to us. She was really a very sweet and generous woman and went to a great deal of trouble to be of help to us, particularly during one awful winter. My mother called her by the highest name she knew: she said she was a "christian." My father could scarcely disagree but during the four or five years of our relatively close association he never trusted her and was always trying to surprise in her open, Midwestern face the genuine, cunningly hidden, and hideous motivation. In later years, particularly when it began to be clear that this "education" of mine was going to lead me to perdition, he became more explicit and warned me that my white friends in high school were not really my friends and that I would see, when I was older, how white people would do anything to keep a Negro down. Some of them could be nice, he admitted, but none of them were to be trusted and most of them were not even nice. The best thing was to have as little to do with them as possible. I did not feel this way and I was certain, in my innocence, that I never would.

But the year which preceded my father's death had made a great change in my life. I had been living in New Jersey, working in defense plants, working and living among southerners, white and black. I knew about the South, of course, and about how southerners treated Negroes and how they expected them to behave, but it had never entered my mind that anyone would look at me and expect *me* to behave that way. I learned in New Jersey that to be a Negro meant, precisely, that one was never looked at but was simply at the mercy of the reflexes the color of one's skin caused in other people. I acted in New Jersey as I had always acted, that is as though I thought a great deal of myself—I had to *act* that way—with results that were, simply, unbelievable. I had scarcely arrived before I had earned the enmity, which was extraordinarily ingenious, of all my superiors and nearly all my co-workers. In the beginning, to make matters worse, I simply did not know what was happening. I did not know what I had done, and I shortly began to wonder what *anyone* could possibly do, to bring about such unanimous, active, and unbearably vocal hostility. I knew about jim crow but I had never experienced it. I went to the same self-service restaurant three times and stood with all the Princeton boys before the counter, waiting for a hamburger and coffee; it was always an extraordinarily long time before anything was set before me; but it was not until the fourth visit that I learned that, in fact, nothing had ever been set before me: I had simply picked something up. Negroes were not served there, I was told, and they had been waiting for me to realize that I was always the only Negro present. Once I was told this, I determined to go there all the time. But now they were ready for me and, though some dreadful scenes were subsequently enacted in that restaurant, I never ate there again.

It was the same story all over New Jersey, in bars, bowling alleys, diners, places to live. I was always being forced to leave, silently, or with mutual imprecations. I very shortly became notorious and children giggled behind me when I passed and their elders whispered or shouted—they really believed that I was mad. And it did begin to work on my mind, of course; I began to be afraid to go anywhere and to compensate for this I went places to which I really should not have gone and where, God knows, I had no desire to be. My reputation in town naturally enhanced my reputation at work and my working day became one long series of acrobatics designed to keep me out of trouble. I cannot say that these acrobatics succeeded. It began to seem that the machinery of the organization I worked for was turning over, day and night, with but one aim: to eject me. I was fired once, and contrived, with the aid of a friend from New York, to get back on the payroll; was fired again, and bounced back again. It took a while to fire me for the third time, but the third time took. There were no loopholes anywhere. There was not even any way of getting back inside the gates.

That year in New Jersey lives in my mind as though it were the year during which, having an unsuspected predilection for it, I first contracted some dread, chronic disease, the unfailing symptom of which is a kind of blind fever, a pounding in the skull and fire in the bowels. Once this disease is contracted, one can never be really carefree again, for the fever, without an instant's warning, can recur at any moment. It can wreck more important things than race relations. There is not a Negro alive who does not have this rage in his blood—one has the choice, merely, of living with it consciously or surrendering to it. As for me, this fever has recurred in me, and does, and will until the day I die.

My last night in New Jersey, a white friend from New York took me to the nearest big town, Trenton, to go to the movies and have a few drinks. As it turned out, he also saved me from, at the very least, a violent whipping. Almost every detail of that night stands out very clearly in my memory. I even remember the name of the movie we saw because its title impressed me as being so patly ironical. It was a movie about the German occupation of France, starring Maureen O'Hara and Charles Laughton and called *This Land Is Mine.* I remember the name of the diner we walked into when the movie ended: it was the "American Diner." When we walked in the counterman asked what we wanted and I remember answering with the casual sharpness which had become my habit: "We want a hamburger and a cup of coffee, what do you think we want?" I do not know why, after a year of such rebuffs, I so completely failed to anticipate his answer, which was, of course, "we don't serve Negroes here." This reply failed to discompose me, at least for the moment. I made some sardonic comment about the name of the diner and we walked out into the streets.

This was the time of what was called the "brownout," when the lights in all American cities were very dim. When we reentered the streets something happened to me which had the force of an optical illusion, or a nightmare. The streets were very crowded and I was facing north. People were moving in every direction but it seemed to me, in that instant, that all of the people I could see, and many more than that, were moving toward me, against me, and that everyone was white. I remember how their faces gleamed. And I felt, like a physical sensation, a click at the nape of my neck as though some interior string connecting my head to my body had been cut. I began to walk. I heard my friend call after me, but I ignored him. Heaven only knows what was going on in his mind, but he had the good sense not to touch me—I don't know what would have happened if he had—and to keep me in sight. I don't know what was going on in my mind, either; I certainly had no conscious plan. I wanted to do something to crush these white faces, which were crushing me. I walked for perhaps a block or two until I came to an enormous, glittering, and fashionable restaurant in which I knew not even the intercession of the Virgin would cause me to be served. I pushed through the doors and took the first vacant seat I saw, at a table for two, and waited.

I do not know how long I waited and I rather wonder, until today, what I could possibly have looked like. Whatever I looked like, I frightened the waitress who shortly appeared, and the moment she appeared all of my fury flowed toward her. I hated her for her white face, and for her great, astounded, frightened eyes. I felt that if she found a black man so frightening I would make her fright worthwhile.

She did not ask me what I wanted, but repeated, as though she had learned it somewhere, "We don't serve Negroes here." She did not say it with the blunt, derisive hostility to which I had grown so accustomed, but, rather, with a note of apology in her voice, and fear. This made me colder and more murderous than ever. I felt I had to do something with my hands. I wanted her to come close enough for me to get her neck between my hands.

So I pretended not to have understood her, hoping to draw her closer. And she did step a very short step closer, with her pencil poised incongruously over her pad, and repeated the formula: ". . . don't serve Negroes here."

Somehow, with the repetition of that phrase, which was already ringing in my head like a thousand bells of a nightmare, I realized that she would never come any closer and that I would have to strike from a distance. There was nothing on the table but an ordinary watermug half full of water, and I picked this up and hurled it with all my strength at her. She ducked and it missed her and shattered against the mirror behind the bar. And, with that sound, my frozen blood abruptly thawed, I returned from wherever I had been, I *saw,* for the first time, the restaurant, the people with their mouths open, already, as it seemed to me, rising as one man, and I realized what I had done, and where I was, and I was frightened. I rose and began running for the door. A round, potbellied man grabbed me by the nape of the neck just as I reached the doors and began to beat me about the face. I kicked him and got loose and ran into the streets. My friend whispered, *"Run!"* and I ran.

My friend stayed outside the restaurant long enough to misdirect my pursuers and the police, who arrived, he told me, at once. I do not know what I said to him when he came to my room that night. I could not have said much. I felt, in the oddest, most awful way, that I had somehow betrayed him. I lived it over and over and over again, the way one relives an automobile accident after it has happened and one finds oneself alone and safe. I could not get over two facts, both equally difficult for the imagination to grasp, and one was that I could have been murdered. But the other was that I had been ready to commit murder. I saw nothing very clearly but I did see this: that my life, my *real* life, was in danger, and not from anything other people might do but from the hatred I carried in my own heart.

2

I had returned home around the second week in June—in great haste because it seemed that my father's death and my mother's confinement were both but a matter of hours. In the case of my mother, it soon became clear that she had simply made a miscalculation. This had always been her tendency and I don't believe that a single one of us arrived in the world, or has since arrived anywhere else, on time. But none of us dawdled so intolerably about the business of being born as did my baby sister. We sometimes amused ourselves, during those endless, stifling weeks, by picturing the baby sitting within in the safe, warm dark, bitterly regretting the necessity of becoming a part of our chaos and stubbornly putting it off as long as possible. I understood her perfectly and congratulated her on showing such good sense so soon. Death, however, sat as purposefully at my father's bedside as life stirred within my mother's womb and it was harder to understand why he so lingered in that long shadow. It seemed that he had bent, and for a long time, too, all of his energies toward dying. Now death was ready for him but my father held back.

All of Harlem, indeed, seemed to be infected by waiting. I had never before known it to be so violently still. Racial tensions throughout this country were exacerbated during the early years of the war, partly because the labor market brought together hundreds of thousands of ill-prepared people and partly because Negro soldiers, regardless of where they were born, received their military training in the south. What happened in defense plants and army camps had repercussions, naturally, in every Negro ghetto. The situation in Harlem had grown bad enough for clergymen, policemen, educators, politicians, and social workers to assert in one breath that there was no "crime wave" and to offer, in the very next breath, suggestions as to how to combat it. These suggestions always seemed to involve playgrounds, despite the fact that racial skirmishes were occurring in the playgrounds, too. Playground or not, crime wave or not, the Harlem police force had been augmented in March, and the unrest grew—perhaps, in fact, partly as a result of the ghetto's instinctive hatred of policemen. Perhaps the most revealing news item, out of the steady parade of reports of muggings, stabbings, shootings, assaults, gang wars, and accusations of police brutality, is the item concerning six Negro girls who set upon a white girl in the subway because, as they all too accurately put it, she was stepping on their toes. Indeed she was, all over the nation.

I had never before been so aware of policemen, on foot, on horseback, on corners, everywhere, always two by two. Nor had I ever been so aware of small knots of people. They were on stoops and on corners and in doorways, and what was striking about them, I think, was that they did not seem to be talking. Never, when I passed these groups, did the usual sound of a curse or a laugh ring out and neither did there seem to be any hum of gossip. There was certainly, on the other hand, occurring between them communication extraordinarily intense. Another thing that was striking was the unexpected diversity of the people who made up these groups. Usually, for example, one would see a group of sharpies standing on the street corner, jiving the passing chicks; or a group of older men, usually, for some reason, in the vicinity of a barber shop, discussing baseball scores, or the numbers, or making rather chilling observations about women they had known. Women, in a general way, tended to be seen less often together—unless they were church women, or very young girls, or prostitutes met together for an unprofessional instant. But that summer I saw the strangest combinations: large, respectable, churchly matrons standing on the stoops or the corners with their hair tied up, together with a girl in sleazy satin whose face bore the marks of gin and the razor, or heavy-set, abrupt, no-nonsense older men, in company with the most disreputable and fanatical "race" men, or these same "race" men with the sharpies, or these sharpies with the churchly women. Seventh Day Adventists and Methodists and Spiritualists seemed to be hobnobbing with Holyrollers and they were all, alike, entangled with the most flagrant disbelievers; something heavy in their stance seemed to indicate that they had all, incredibly, seen a common vision, and on each face there seemed to be the same strange, bitter shadow.

The churchly women and the matter-of-fact, no-nonsense men had children in the Army. The sleazy girls they talked to had lovers there, the sharpies and the "race" men had friends and brothers there. It would have demanded an unquestioning patriotism, happily as uncommon in this country as it is undesirable, for these people not to have been disturbed by the bitter letters they received, by the newspaper stories they read, not to have been enraged by the posters, then to be found all over New York, which described the Japanese as "yellow-bellied Japs." It was only the "race" men, to be sure, who spoke ceaselessly of being revenged—how this vengeance was to be exacted was not clear—for the indignities and dangers suffered by Negro boys in uniform; but everybody felt a directionless, hopeless bitterness, as well as that panic which can scarcely be suppressed when one knows that a human being one loves is beyond one's reach, and in danger. This helplessness and this gnawing uneasiness does something, at length, to even the toughest mind. Perhaps the best way to sum all this up is to say that the people I knew felt, mainly, a peculiar kind of relief when they knew that their boys were being shipped out of the south, to do battle overseas. It was, perhaps, like feeling that the most dangerous part of a dangerous journey had been passed and that now, even if death should come, it would come with honor and without the complicity of their countrymen. Such a death would be, in short, a fact with which one could hope to live.

It was on the twenty-eighth of July, which I believe was a Wednesday, that I visited my father for the first time during his illness and for the last time in his life. The moment I saw him I knew why I had put off this visit so long. I had told my mother that I did not want to see him because I hated him. But this was not true. It was only that I *had* hated him and I wanted to hold on to this hatred. I did not want to look on him as a ruin: it was not a ruin I had hated. I imagine that one of the reasons people cling to their hates so stubbornly is because they sense, once hate is gone, that they will be forced to deal with pain.

We traveled out to him, his older sister and myself, to what seemed to be the very end of a very Long Island. It was hot and dusty and we wrangled, my aunt and I, all the way out, over the fact that I had recently begun to smoke and, as she said, to give myself airs. But I knew that she wrangled with me because she could not bear to face the fact of her brother's dying. Neither could I endure the reality of her despair, her unstated bafflement as to what had happened to her brother's life, and her own. So we wrangled and I smoked and from time to time she fell into a heavy reverie. Covertly, I watched her face, which was the face of an old woman; it had fallen in, the eyes were sunken and lightless; soon she would be dying, too.

In my childhood—it had not been so long ago—I had thought her beautiful. She had been quick-witted and quick-moving and very generous with all the children and each of her visits had been an event. At one time one of my brothers and myself had thought of running away to live with her. Now she could no longer produce out of her handbag some unexpected and yet familiar delight. She made me feel pity and revulsion and fear. It was awful to realize that she no longer caused me to feel affection. The closer we came to the hospital the more querulous she became and at the same time, naturally, grew more dependent on me. Between pity and guilt and fear I began to feel that there was another me trapped in my skull like a jack-in-the-box who might escape my control at any moment and fill the air with screaming.

She began to cry the moment we entered the room and she saw him lying there, all shriveled and still, like a little black monkey. The great, gleaming apparatus which fed him and would have compelled him to be still even if he had been able to move brought to mind, not beneficence, but torture; the tubes entering his arm made me think of pictures I had seen when a child, of Gulliver, tied down by the pygmies on that island. My aunt wept and wept, there was a whistling sound in my father's throat; nothing was said; he could not speak. I wanted to take his hand, to say something. But I do not know what I could have said, even if he could have heard me. He was not really in that room with us, he had at last really embarked on his journey; and though my aunt told me that he said he was going to meet Jesus, I did not hear anything except that whistling in his throat. The doctor came back and we left, into that unbearable train again, and home. In the morning came the telegram saying that he was dead. Then the house was suddenly full of relatives, friends, hysteria, and confusion and I quickly left my mother and the children to the care of those impressive women, who, in Negro communities at least, automatically appear at times of bereavement armed with lotions, proverbs, and patience, and an ability to cook. I went downtown. By the time I returned, later the same day, my mother had been carried to the hospital and the baby had been born.

3

For my father's funeral I had nothing black to wear and this posed a nagging problem all day long. It was one of those problems, simple, or impossible of solution, to which the mind insanely clings in order to avoid the mind's real trouble. I spent most of that day at the downtown apartment of a girl I knew, celebrating my birthday with whisky and wondering what to wear that night. When planning a birthday celebration one naturally does not expect that it will be up against competition from a funeral and this girl had anticipated taking me out that night, for a big dinner and a nightclub afterwards. Sometime during the course of that long day we decided that we would go out anyway, when my father's funeral service was over. I imagine I decided it, since, as the funeral hour approached, it became clearer and clearer to me that I would not know what to do with myself when it was over. The girl, stifling her very lively concern as to the possible effects of the whisky on one of my father's chief mourners, concentrated on being conciliatory and practically helpful. She found a black shirt for me somewhere and ironed it and, dressed in the darkest pants and jacket I owned, and slightly drunk, I made my way to my father's funeral.

The chapel was full, but not packed, and very quiet. There were, mainly, my father's relatives, and his children, and here and there I saw faces I had not seen since childhood, the faces of my father's one-time friends. They were very dark and solemn now, seeming somehow to suggest that they had known all along that something like this would happen. Chief among the mourners was my aunt, who had quarreled with my father all his life; by which I do not mean to suggest that her mourning was insincere or that she had not loved him. I suppose that she was one of the few people in the world who had, and their incessant quarreling proved precisely the strength of the tie that bound them. The only other person in the world, as far as I knew, whose relationship to my father rivaled my aunt's in depth was my mother, who was not there.

It seemed to me, of course, that it was a very long funeral. But it was, if anything, a rather shorter funeral than most, nor, since there were no overwhelming, uncontrollable expressions of grief, could it be called—if I dare to use the word—successful. The minister who preached my father's funeral sermon was one of the few my father had still been seeing as he neared his end. He presented to us in his sermon a man whom none of us had ever seen—a man thoughtful, patient, and forbearing, a Christian inspiration to all who knew him, and a model for his children. And no doubt the children, in their disturbed and guilty state, were almost ready to believe this; he had been remote enough to be anything and, anyway, the shock of the incontrovertible, that it was really our father lying up there in that casket, prepared the mind for anything. His sister moaned and this grief-stricken moaning was taken as corroboration. The other faces held a dark, noncommittal thoughtfulness. This was not the man they had known, but they had scarcely expected to be confronted with *him;* this was, in a sense deeper than questions of fact, the man they had not known, and the man they had not known may have been the real one. The real man, whoever he had been, had suffered and now he was dead: this was all that was sure and all that mattered now. Every man in the chapel hoped that when his hour came he, too, would be eulogized, which is to say forgiven, and that all of his lapses, greeds, errors, and strayings from the truth would be invested with coherence and looked upon with charity. This was perhaps the last thing human beings could give each other and it was what they demanded, after all, of the Lord. Only the Lord saw the midnight tears, only He was present when one of His children, moaning and wringing hands, paced up and down the room. When one slapped one's child in anger the recoil in the heart reverberated through heaven and became part of the pain of the universe. And when the children were hungry and sullen and distrustful and one watched them, daily, growing wilder, and further away, and running headlong into danger, it was the Lord who knew what the charged heart endured as the strap was laid to the backside; the Lord alone who knew what one would have said if one had had, like the Lord, the gift of the living word. It was the Lord who knew of the impossibility every parent in that room faced: how to prepare the child for the day when the child would be despised and how to *create* in the child—by what means?—a stronger antidote to this poison than one had found for oneself. The avenues, side streets, bars, billiard halls, hospitals, police stations, and even the playgrounds of Harlem—not to mention the houses of correction, the jails, and the morgue—testified to the potency of the poison while remaining silent as to the efficacy of whatever antidote, irresistibly raising the question of whether or not such an antidote existed; raising, which was worse, the question of whether or not an antidote was desirable; perhaps poison should be fought with poison. With these several schisms in the mind and with more terrors in the heart than could be named, it was better not to judge the man who had gone down under an impossible burden. It was better to remember: *Thou knowest this man's fall; but thou knowest not his wrassling.*

While the preacher talked and I watched the children—years of changing their diapers, scrubbing them, slapping them, taking them to school, and scolding them had had the perhaps inevitable result of making me love them, though I am not sure I knew this then—my mind was busily breaking out with a rash of disconnected impressions. Snatches of popular songs, indecent jokes, bits of books I had read, movie sequences, faces, voices, political issues—I thought I was going mad; all these impressions suspended, as it were, in the solution of the faint nausea produced in me by the heat and liquor. For a moment I had the impression that my alcoholic breath, inefficiently disguised with chewing gum, filled the entire chapel. Then someone began singing one of my father's favorite songs and, abruptly, I was with him, sitting on his knee, in the hot, enormous, crowded church which was the first church we attended. It was the Abyssinian Baptist Church on 138th Street. We had not gone there long. With this image, a host of others came. I had forgotten, in the rage of my growing up, how proud my father had been of me when I was little. Apparently, I had had a voice and my father had liked to show me off before the members of the church. I had forgotten what he had looked like when he was pleased but now I remembered that he had always been grinning with pleasure when my solos ended. I even remembered certain expressions on his face when he teased my mother—had he loved her? I would never know. And when had it all begun to change? For now it seemed that he had not always been cruel. I remembered being taken for a haircut and scraping my knee on the footrest of the barber's chair and I remembered my father's face as he soothed my crying and applied the stinging iodine. Then I remembered our fights, fights which had been of the worst possible kind because my technique had been silence.

I remembered the one time in all our life together when we had really spoken to each other.

It was on a Sunday and it must have been shortly before I left home. We were walking, just the two of us, in our usual silence, to or from church. I was in high school and had been doing a lot of writing and I was, at about this time, the editor of the high school magazine. But I had also been a Young Minister and had been preaching from the pulpit. Lately, I had been taking fewer engagements and preached as rarely as possible. It was said in the church, quite truthfully, that I was "cooling off."

My father asked me abruptly, "You'd rather write than preach, wouldn't you?"

I was astonished at his question—because it was a real question. I answered, "Yes."

That was all we said. It was awful to remember that that was all we had ever said.

The casket now was opened and the mourners were being led up the aisle to look for the last time on the deceased. The assumption was that the family was too overcome with grief to be allowed to make this journey alone and I watched while my aunt was led to the casket and, muffled in black, and shaking, led back to her seat. I disapproved of forcing the children to look on their dead father, considering that the shock of his death, or, more truthfully, the shock of death as a reality, was already a little more than a child could bear, but my judgment in this matter had been overruled and there they were, bewildered and frightened and very small, being led, one by one, to the casket. But there is also something very gallant about children at such moments. It has something to do with their silence and gravity and with the fact that one cannot help them. Their legs, somehow, seem *exposed,* so that it is at once incredible and terribly clear that their legs are all they have to hold them up.

I had not wanted to go to the casket myself and I certainly had not wished to be led there, but there was no way of avoiding either of these forms. One of the deacons led me up and I looked on my father's face. I cannot say that it looked like him at all. His blackness had been equivocated by powder and there was no suggestion in that casket of what his power had or could have been. He was simply an old man dead, and it was hard to believe that he had ever given anyone either joy or pain. Yet, his life filled that room. Further up the avenue his wife was holding his newborn child. Life and death so close together, and love and hatred, and right and wrong, said something to me which I did not want to hear concerning man, concerning the life of man.

After the funeral, while I was downtown desperately celebrating my birthday, a Negro soldier, in the lobby of the Hotel Braddock, got into a fight with a white policeman over a Negro girl. Negro girls, white policemen, in or out of uniform, and Negro males—in or out of uniform—were part of the furniture of the lobby of the Hotel Braddock and this was certainly not the first time such an incident had occurred. It was destined, however, to receive an unprecedented publicity, for the fight between the policeman and the soldier ended with the shooting of the soldier. Rumor, flowing immediately to the streets outside, stated that the soldier had been shot in the back, an instantaneous and revealing invention, and that the soldier had died protecting a Negro woman. The facts were somewhat different—for example, the soldier had not been shot in the back, and was not dead, and the girl seems to have been as dubious a symbol of womanhood as her white counterpart in Georgia usually is, but no one was interested in the facts. They preferred the invention because this invention expressed and corroborated their hates and fears so perfectly. It is just as well to remember that people are always doing this. Perhaps many of those legends, including Christianity, to which the world clings began their conquest of the world with just some such concerted surrender to distortion. The effect, in Harlem, of this particular legend was like the effect of a lit match in a tin of gasoline. The mob gathered before the doors of the Hotel Braddock simply began to swell and to spread in every direction, and Harlem exploded.

The mob did not cross the ghetto lines. It would have been easy, for example, to have gone over Morningside Park on the west side or to have crossed the Grand Central railroad tracks at 125th Street on the east side, to wreak havoc in white neighborhoods. The mob seems to have been mainly interested in something more potent and real than the white face, that is, in white power, and the principal damage done during the riot of the summer of 1943 was to white business establishments in Harlem. It might have been a far bloodier story, of course, if, at the hour the riot began, these establishments had still been open. From the Hotel Braddock the mob fanned out, east and west along 125th Street, and for the entire length of Lenox, Seventh, and Eighth avenues. Along each of these avenues, and along each major side street—116th, 125th, 135th, and so on—bars, stores, pawnshops, restaurants, even little luncheonettes had been smashed open and entered and looted—looted, it might be added, with more haste than efficiency. The shelves really looked as though a bomb had struck them. Cans of beans and soup and dog food, along with toilet paper, corn flakes, sardines and milk tumbled every which way, and abandoned cash registers and cases of beer leaned crazily out of the splintered windows and were strewn along the avenues. Sheets, blankets, and clothing of every description formed a kind of path, as though people had dropped them while running. I truly had not realized that Harlem *had* so many stores until I saw them all smashed open; the first time the word *wealth* ever entered my mind in relation to Harlem was when I saw it scattered in the streets. But one's first, incongruous impression of plenty was countered immediately by an impression of waste. None of this was doing anybody any good. It would have been better to have left the plate glass as it had been and the goods lying in the stores.

It would have been better, but it would also have been intolerable, for Harlem had needed something to smash. To smash something is the ghetto's chronic need. Most of the time it is the members of the ghetto who smash each other, and themselves. But as long as the ghetto walls are standing there will always come a moment when these outlets do not work. That summer, for example, it was not enough to get into a fight on Lenox Avenue, or curse out one's cronies in the barber shops. If ever, indeed, the violence which fills Harlem's churches, pool halls, and bars erupts outward in a more direct fashion, Harlem and its citizens are likely to vanish in an apocalyptic flood. That this is not likely to happen is due to a great many reasons, most hidden and powerful among them the Negro's real relation to the white American. This relation prohibits, simply, anything as uncomplicated and satisfactory as pure hatred. In order really to hate white people, one has to blot so much out of the mind—and the heart—that this hatred itself becomes an exhausting and self-destructive pose. But this does not mean, on the other hand, that love comes easily: the white world is too powerful, too complacent, too ready with gratuitous humiliation, and, above all, too ignorant and too innocent for that. One is absolutely forced to make perpetual qualifications and one's own reactions are always canceling each other out. It is this, really, which has driven so many people mad, both white and black. One is always in the position of having to decide between amputation and gangrene. Amputation is swift but time may prove that the amputation was not necessary—or one may delay the amputation too long. Gangrene is slow, but it is impossible to be sure that one is reading one's symptoms right. The idea of going through life as a cripple is more than one can bear, and equally unbearable is the risk of swelling up slowly, in agony, with poison. And the trouble, finally, is that the risks are real even if the choices do not exist.

"But as for me and my house," my father had said, "we will serve the Lord." I wondered, as we drove him to his resting place, what this line had meant for him. I had heard him preach it many times. I had preached it once myself, proudly giving it an interpretation different from my father's. Now the whole thing came back to me, as though my father and I were on our way to Sunday school and I were memorizing the golden text: *And if it seem evil unto you to serve the Lord, choose you this day whom you will serve; whether the gods which your fathers served that were on the other side of the flood, or the gods of the Amorites, in whose land ye dwell: but as for me and my house, we will serve the Lord.* I suspected in these familiar lines a meaning which had never been there for me before. All of my father's texts and songs, which I had decided were meaningless, were arranged before me at his death like empty bottles, waiting to hold the meaning which life would give them for me. This was his legacy: nothing is ever escaped. That bleakly memorable morning I hated the unbelievable streets and the Negroes and whites who had, equally, made them that way. But I knew that it was folly, as my father would have said, this bitterness was folly. It was necessary to hold on to the things that mattered. The dead man mattered, the new life mattered; blackness and whiteness did not matter; to believe that they did was to acquiesce in one's own destruction. Hatred, which could destroy so much, never failed to destroy the man who hated and this was an immutable law.

It began to seem that one would have to hold in the mind forever two ideas which seemed to be in opposition. The first idea was acceptance, the acceptance, totally without rancor, of life as it is, and men as they are: in the light of this idea, it goes without saying that injustice is a commonplace. But this did not mean that one could be complacent, for the second idea was of equal power: that one must never, in one's own life, accept these injustices as commonplace but must fight them with all one's strength. This fight begins, however, in the heart and it now had been laid to my charge to keep my own heart free of hatred and despair. This intimation made my heart heavy and, now that my father was irrecoverable, I wished that he had been beside me so that I could have searched his face for the answers which only the future would give me now.

Alas, Poor Richard

1. Eight Men

U NLESS A WRITER is extremely old when he dies, in which case he has probably become a neglected institution, his death must always seem untimely. This is because a real writer is always shifting and changing and searching. The world has many labels for him, of which the most treacherous is the label of Success. But the man behind the label knows defeat far more intimately than he knows triumph. He can never be absolutely certain that he has achieved his intention.

This tension and authority—the authority of the frequently defeated—are in the writer's work, and cause one to feel that, at the moment of his death, he was approaching his greatest achievements. I should think that guilt plays some part in this reaction, as well as a certain unadmitted relief. Guilt, because of our failure in a relationship, because it is extremely difficult to deal with writers as people. Writers are said to be extremely egotistical and demanding, and they are indeed, but that does not distinguish them from anyone else. What distinguishes them is what James once described as a kind of "holy stupidity." The writer's greed is appalling. He wants, or seems to want, everything and practically everybody; in another sense, and at the same time, he needs no one at all; and families, friends, and lovers find this extremely hard to take. While he is alive, his work is fatally entangled with his personal fortunes and misfortunes, his personality, and the social facts and attitudes of his time. The unadmitted relief, then, of which I spoke has to do with a certain drop in the intensity of our bewilderment, for the baffling creator no longer stands between us and his works.

He does not, but many other things do, above all our own preoccupations. In the case of Richard Wright, dead in Paris at fifty-two, the fact that he worked during a bewildering and demoralizing era in Western history makes a proper assessment of his work more difficult. In *Eight Men,* the earliest story, "The Man Who Saw the Flood," takes place in the Deep South and was first published in 1937. One of the two previously unpublished stories in the book, "Man, God Ain't Like That," begins in Africa, achieves its hideous resolution in Paris, and brings us, with an ironical and fitting grimness, to the threshold of the 1960s. It is because of this story, which is remarkable, and "Man of All Work," which is a masterpiece, that I cannot avoid feeling that Wright, as he died, was acquiring a new tone, and a less uncertain esthetic distance, and a new depth.

Shortly after we learned of Richard Wright's death, a Negro woman who was rereading *Native Son* told me that it meant more to her now than it had when she had first read it. This, she said, was because the specific social climate which had produced it, or with which it was identified, seemed archaic now, was fading from our memories. Now, there was only the book itself to deal with, for it could no longer be read, as it had been read in 1940, as a militant racial manifesto. Today's racial manifestoes were being written very differently, and in many different languages; what mattered about the book now was how accurately or deeply the life of Chicago's South Side had been conveyed.

I think that my friend may prove to be right. Certainly, the two oldest stories in this book, "The Man Who Was Almost a Man," and "The Man Who Saw the Flood," both Depression stories, both occurring in the South, and both, of course, about Negroes, do not seem dated. Perhaps it is odd, but they did not make me think of the 1930s, or even, particularly, of Negroes. They made me think of human loss and helplessness. There is a dry, savage, folkloric humor in "The Man Who Was Almost a Man." It tells the story of a boy who wants a gun, finally manages to get one, and, by a hideous error, shoots a white man's mule. He then takes to the rails, for he would have needed two years to pay for the mule. There is nothing funny about "The Man Who Saw the Flood," which is as spare and moving an account as that delivered by Bessie Smith in "Backwater Blues."

It is strange to begin to suspect, now, that Richard Wright was never, really, the social and polemical writer he took himself to be. In my own relations with him, I was always exasperated by his notions of society,

politics, and history, for they seemed to me utterly fanciful. I never believed that he had any real sense of how a society is put together. It had
not occurred to me, and perhaps it had not occurred to him, that his
major interests as well as his power lay elsewhere. Or perhaps it *had* occurred to me, for I distrusted his association with the French intellectuals,
Sartre, de Beauvoir, and company. I am not being vindictive toward them
or condescending toward Richard Wright when I say that it seemed to me
that there was very little they could give him which he could use. It has
always seemed to me that ideas were somewhat more real to them than
people; but anyway, and this is a statement made with the very greatest
love and respect, I always sensed in Richard Wright a Mississippi picka-
ninny, mischievous, cunning, and tough. This always seemed to be at the
bottom of everything he said and did, like some fantastic jewel buried in
high grass. And it was painful to feel that the people of his adopted country were no more capable of seeing this jewel than were the people of his
native land, and were in their own way as intimidated by it.

Even more painful was the suspicion that Wright did not want to know
this. The meaning of Europe for an American Negro was one of the things
about which Richard Wright and I disagreed most vehemently. He was
fond of referring to Paris as the "city of refuge"—which it certainly was,
God knows, for the likes of us. But it was not a city of refuge for the
French, still less for anyone belonging to France; and it would not have
been a city of refuge for us if we had not been armed with American
passports. It did not seem worthwhile to me to have fled the native fantasy
only to embrace a foreign one. (Someone, some day, should do a study in
depth of the role of the American Negro in the mind and life of Europe,
and the extraordinary perils, different from those of America but not less
grave, which the American Negro encounters in the Old World.)

But now that the storm of Wright's life is over, and politics is ended
forever for him, along with the Negro problem and the fearful conundrum
of Africa, it seems to have been the tough and intuitive, the genuine Richard Wright, who was being recorded all along. It now begins to seem, for
example, that Wright's unrelentingly bleak landscape was not merely that
of the Deep South, or of Chicago, but that of the world, of the human
heart. The landscape does not change in any of these stories. Even the
most good-natured performance this book contains, good-natured by
comparison only, "Big Black Good Man," takes place in Copenhagen in
the winter, and in the vastly more chilling confines of a Danish hotel-
keeper's fears.

In "Man of All Work," a tight, raging, diamond-hard exercise in irony,
a Negro male who cannot find a job dresses himself up in his wife's

clothes and hires himself out as a cook. ("Who," he demands of his horrified, bedridden wife, "ever looks at us colored folks anyhow?") He gets
the job, and Wright uses this incredible situation to reveal, with beautiful
spite and accuracy, the private lives of the master race. The story is told
entirely in dialogue, which perfectly accomplishes what it sets out to do,
racing along like a locomotive and suggesting far more than it states.

The story, without seeming to, goes very deeply into the demoraliza-
tion of the Negro male and the resulting fragmentization of the Negro
family which occurs when the female is forced to play the male role of
breadwinner. It is also a maliciously funny indictment of the sexual terror and hostility of American whites: and the horror of the story is increased by its humor.

"Man, God Ain't Like That" is a fable of an African's discovery of
God. It is a far more horrible story than "Man of All Work," but it too
manages its effects by a kind of Grand Guignol humor, and it too is an
unsparing indictment of the frivolity, egotism, and wrongheadedness of
white people—in this case, a French artist and his mistress. It, too, is told
entirely in dialogue and recounts how a French artist traveling through
Africa picks up an African servant, uses him as a model, and, in order to
shock and titillate his jaded European friends, brings the African back to
Paris with him.

Whether or not Wright's vision of the African sensibility will be recognized by Africans, I do not know. But certainly he has managed a frightening and truthful comment on the inexorably mysterious and dangerous
relationships between ways of life, which are also ways of thought. This
story and "Man of All Work" left me wondering how much richer our
extremely poor theater might now be if Wright had chosen to work in it.

But "The Man Who Killed a Shadow" is something else again; it is
Wright at the mercy of his subject. His great forte, it now seems to me,
was an ability to convey inward states by means of externals: "The Man
Who Lived Underground," for example, conveys the spiritual horror of a
man and a city by a relentless accumulation of details, and by a series of
brief, sharply cut-off tableaus, seen through chinks and cracks and key-
holes. The specifically sexual horror faced by a Negro cannot be dealt
with in this way. "The Man Who Killed a Shadow" is a story of rape and
murder, and neither the murderer nor his victim ever comes alive. The
entire story seems to be occurring, somehow, beneath cotton. There are
many reasons for this. In most of the novels written by Negroes until
today (with the exception of Chester Himes's *If He Hollers Let Him Go*)
there is a great space where sex ought to be; and what usually fills this
space is violence.

*   *   *

This violence, as in so much of Wright's work, is gratuitous and compulsive. It is one of the severest criticisms than can be leveled against his work. The violence is gratuitous and compulsive because the root of the violence is never examined. The root is rage. It is the rage, almost literally the howl, of a man who is being castrated. I do not think that I am the first person to notice this, but there is probably no greater (no more misleading) body of sexual myths in the world today than those which have proliferated around the figure of the American Negro. This means that he is penalized for the guilty imagination of the white people who invest him with their hates and longings, and is the principal target of their sexual paranoia. Thus, when in Wright's pages a Negro male is found hacking a white woman to death, the very gusto with which this is done, and the great attention paid to the details of physical destruction reveal a terrible attempt to break out of the cage in which the American imagination has imprisoned him for so long.

In the meantime, the man I fought so hard and who meant so much to me, is gone. First America, then Europe, then Africa failed him. He lived long enough to find all of the terms on which he had been born become obsolete; presently, all of his attitudes seemed to be historical. But as his life ended, he seems to me to have been approaching a new beginning. He had survived, as it were, his own obsolescence, and his imagination was beginning to grapple with that darkest of all dark strangers for him, the African. The depth thus touched in him brought him a new power and a new tone. He had survived exile on three continents and lived long enough to begin to tell the tale.

2 . The Exile

I was far from imagining, when I agreed to write this memoir, that it would prove to be such a painful and difficult task. What, after all, can I really say about Richard . . . ? Everything founders in the sea of what might have been. We might have been friends, for example, but I cannot honestly say that we were. There might have been some way of avoiding our quarrel, our rupture; I can only say that I failed to find it. The quarrel having occurred, perhaps there might have been a way to have become reconciled. I think, in fact, that I counted on this coming about in some mysterious, irrevocable way, the way a child dreams of winning, by means of some dazzling exploit, the love of his parents.

However, he is dead now, and so we never shall be reconciled. The debt I owe him can now never be discharged, at least not in the way I hoped to be able to discharge it. In fact, the saddest thing about our relationship is that my only means of discharging my debt to Richard was to become a writer; and this effort revealed, more and more clearly as the years went on, the deep and irreconcilable differences between our points of view.

This might not have been so serious if I had been older when we met. . . . If I had been, that is, less uncertain of myself, and less monstrously egotistical. But when we met, I was twenty, a carnivorous age; he was then as old as I am now, thirty-six; he had been my idol since high school, and I, as the fledgling Negro writer, was very shortly in the position of his protégé. This position was not really fair to either of us. As writers we were about as unlike as any two writers could possibly be. But no one can read the future, and neither of us knew this then. We were linked together, really, because both of us were black. I had made my pilgrimage to meet him because he was the greatest black writer in the world for me. In *Uncle Tom's Children,* in *Native Son,* and, above all, in *Black Boy,* I found expressed, for the first time in my life, the sorrow, the rage, and the murderous bitterness which was eating up my life and the lives of those around me. His work was an immense liberation and revelation for me. He became my ally and my witness, and alas! my father.

I remember our first meeting very well. It was in Brooklyn; it was winter. I was broke, naturally, shabby, hungry, and scared. He appeared from the depths of what I remember as an extremely long apartment. Now his face, voice, manner, figure are all very sadly familiar to me. But they were a great shock to me then. It is always a shock to meet famous men. There is always an irreducible injustice in the encounter, for the famous man cannot possibly fit the image which one has evolved of him. My own image of Richard was almost certainly based on Canada Lee's terrifying stage portrait of Bigger Thomas. Richard was not like that at all. His voice was light and even rather sweet, with a southern melody in it; his body was more round than square, more square than tall; and his grin was more boyish than I had expected, and more diffident. He had a trick, when he greeted me, of saying, "Hey, boy!" with a kind of pleased, surprised expression on his face. It was very friendly, and it was also, faintly, mockingly conspiratorial—as though we were two black boys, in league against the world, and had just managed to spirit away several loads of watermelon.

We sat in the living room and Richard brought out a bottle of bourbon and ice and glasses. Ellen Wright was somewhere in the back with the baby, and made only one brief appearance near the end of the evening. I did not drink in those days, did not know how to drink, and I was terrified that the liquor, on my empty stomach, would have the most disastrous consequences. Richard talked to me, or, rather, drew me out on the subject of the novel I was working on then. I was so afraid of falling off my

chair and so anxious for him to be interested in me, that I told him far
more about the novel than I, in fact, knew about it, madly improvising,
one jump ahead of the bourbon, on all the themes which cluttered up my
mind. I am sure that Richard realized this, for he seemed to be amused by
me. But I think he liked me. I know that I liked him, then, and later, and
all the time. But I also know that, later on, he did not believe this.

He agreed, that night, to read the sixty or seventy pages I had done on
my novel as soon as I could send them to him. I didn't dawdle, naturally,
about getting the pages in the mail, and Richard commented very kindly
and favorably on them, and his support helped me to win the Eugene F.
Saxton Fellowship. He was very proud of me then, and I was puffed up
with pleasure that he was proud, and was determined to make him
prouder still.

But this was not to be, for, as so often happens, my first real triumph
turned out to be the herald of my first real defeat. There is very little
point, I think, in regretting anything, and yet I do, nevertheless, rather
regret that Richard and I had not become friends by this time, for it might
have made a great deal of difference. We might at least have caught a
glimpse of the difference between my mind and his; and if we could have
argued about it then, our quarrel might not have been so painful later. But
we had not become friends mainly, indeed, I suppose, because of this very
difference, and also because I really was too young to be his friend and
adored him too much and was too afraid of him. And this meant that
when my first wintry exposure to the publishing world had resulted in the
irreparable ruin—carried out by me—of my first novel, I scarcely knew
how to face anyone, let alone Richard. I was too ashamed of myself and I
was sure that he was ashamed of me, too. This was utter foolishness on my
part, for Richard knew far more about first novels and fledgling novelists
than that; but I had been out for his approval. It simply had not occurred
to me in those days that anyone *could* approve of me if I had tried for
something and failed. The young think that failure is the Siberian end of
the line, banishment from all the living, and tend to do what I then did—
which was to hide.

I, nevertheless, did see him a few days before he went to Paris in 1946.
It was a strange meeting, melancholy in the way a theater is melancholy
when the run of the play is ended and the cast and crew are about to be
dispersed. All the relationships so laboriously created now no longer exist,
seem never to have existed; and the future looks gray and problematical
indeed. Richard's apartment—by this time, he lived in the Village, on
Charles Street—seemed rather like that, dismantled, everything teetering
on the edge of oblivion; people rushing in and out, friends, as I supposed,
but alas, most of them were merely admirers; and Richard and I seemed
really to be at the end of *our* rope, for he had done what he could for me,

and it had not worked out, and now he was going away. It seemed to me that he was sailing into the most splendid of futures, for he was going, of all places! to France, and he had been invited there by the French government. But Richard did not seem, though he was jaunty, to be overjoyed. There was a striking sobriety in his face that day. He talked a great deal about a friend of his, who was in trouble with the U.S. Immigration authorities, and was about to be, or already had been, deported. Richard was not being deported, of course, he was traveling to a foreign country as an honored guest; and he was vain enough and young enough and vivid enough to find this very pleasing and exciting. Yet he knew a great deal about exile, all artists do, especially American artists, especially American Negro artists. He had endured already, liberals and literary critics to the contrary, a long exile in his own country. He must have wondered what the real thing would be like. And he must have wondered, too, what would be the unimaginable effect on his daughter, who could now be raised in a country which would not penalize her on account of her color.

And that day was very nearly the last time Richard and I spoke to each other without the later, terrible warfare. Two years later, I, too, quit America, never intending to return. The day I got to Paris, before I even checked in at a hotel, I was carried to the Deux Magots, where Richard sat, with the editors of *Zero* magazine. "Hey, boy!" he cried, looking more surprised and pleased and conspiratorial than ever, and younger and happier; I took this meeting as a good omen, and I could not possibly have been more wrong.

I later became rather closely associated with *Zero* magazine, and wrote for them the essay called "Everybody's Protest Novel." On the day the magazine was published, and before I had seen it, I walked into the Brasserie Lipp. Richard was there, and he called me over. I will never forget that interview, but I doubt that I will ever be able to recreate it.

Richard accused me of having betrayed him, and not only him but all American Negroes by attacking the idea of protest literature. It simply had not occurred to me that the essay could be interpreted in that way. I was still in that stage when I imagined that whatever was clear to me had only to be pointed out to become immediately clear to everyone. I was young enough to be proud of the essay and, sad and incomprehensible as it now sounds, I really think that I had rather expected to be patted on the head for my original point of view. It had not occurred to me that this point of view, which I had come to, after all, with some effort and some pain, could be looked on as treacherous or subversive. Again, I had mentioned Richard's *Native Son* at the end of the essay because it was the most important and most celebrated novel of Negro life to have appeared in America. Richard thought that I had attacked it, whereas, as far as I was concerned, I had scarcely even criticized it. And Richard thought that I was trying to destroy his novel and his reputation; but it had not entered my mind that either of these *could* be destroyed, and certainly not by me. And yet, what made the interview so ghastly was not merely the foregoing or the fact that I could find no words with which to defend myself. What made it most painful was that Richard was right to be hurt, I was wrong to have hurt him. He saw clearly enough, far more clearly than I had dared to allow myself to see, what I had done: I had used his work as a kind of springboard into my own. His work was a road-block in my road, the sphinx, really, whose riddles I had to answer before I could become myself. I thought confusedly then, and feel very definitely now, that this was the greatest tribute I could have paid him. But it is not an easy tribute to bear and I do not know how I will take it when my time comes. For, finally, Richard was hurt because I had not given him credit for any human feelings or failings. And indeed I had not, he had never really been a human being for me, he had been an idol. And idols are created in order to be destroyed.

This quarrel was never really patched up, though it must be said that, over a period of years, we tried. "What do you mean, *protest!*" Richard cried. *"All* literature is protest. You can't name a single novel that isn't protest." To this I could only weakly counter that all literature might be protest but all protest was not literature. "Oh," he would say then, looking, as he so often did, bewilderingly juvenile, "here you come again with all that art for art's sake crap." This never failed to make me furious, and my anger, for some reason, always seemed to amuse him. Our rare, best times came when we managed to exasperate each other to the point of helpless hilarity. "Roots," Richard would snort, when I had finally worked my way around to this dreary subject, "what———roots! Next thing you'll be telling me is that all colored folks have rhythm." Once, one evening, we managed to throw the whole terrifying subject to the winds, and Richard, Chester Himes, and myself went out and got drunk. It was a good night, perhaps the best I remember in all the time I knew Richard. For he and Chester were friends, they brought out the best in each other, and the atmosphere they created brought out the best in me. Three absolutely tense, unrelentingly egotistical, and driven people, free in Paris but far from home, with so much to be said and so little time in which to say it!

And time was flying. Part of the trouble between Richard and myself, after all, was that I was nearly twenty years younger and had never seen the South. Perhaps I can now imagine Richard's odyssey better than I could then, but it is only imagination. I have not, in my own flesh, traveled, and paid the price of such a journey, from the Deep South to Chicago to New York to Paris; and the world which produced Richard Wright has vanished and will never be seen again. Now, it seems almost in the twinkling of an eye, nearly twenty years have passed since Richard and I sat nervously over bourbon in his Brooklyn living room. These years have seen nearly all of the props of the Western reality knocked out from under it, all of the world's capitals have changed, the Deep South has changed, and Africa has changed.

For a long time, it seems to me, Richard was cruelly caught in this high wind. His ears, I think, were nearly deafened by the roar, all about him, not only of falling idols but of falling enemies. Strange people indeed crossed oceans, from Africa and America, to come to his door; and he really did not know who these people were, and they very quickly sensed this. Not until the very end of his life, judging by some of the stories in his last book, *Eight Men,* did his imagination really begin to assess the century's new and terrible dark stranger. Well, he worked up until the end, died, as I hope to do, in the middle of a sentence, and his work is now an irreducible part of the history of our swift and terrible time. Whoever He may be, and wherever you may be, may God be with you, Richard, and may He help me not to fail that argument which you began in me.

3. Alas, Poor Richard

And my record's clear today, the church brothers and sisters used to sing, *for He washed my sins away, And that old account was settled long ago!* Well, so, perhaps it was, for them; they were under the illusion that they could read their records right. I am far from certain that I am able to read my own record at all, I would certainly hesitate to say that I am able to read it right. And, as for accounts, it is doubtful that I have ever really "settled" an account in my life.

Not that I haven't tried. In my relations with Richard, I was always trying to set the record "straight," to "settle" the account. This is but another way of saying that I wanted Richard to see me, not as the youth I had been when he met me, but as a man. I wanted to feel that he had accepted me, had accepted my right to my own vision, my right, as his equal, to disagree with him. I nourished for a long time the illusion that this day was coming. One day, Richard would turn to me, with the light of sudden understanding on his face, and say, "Oh, *that's* what you mean." And then, so ran the dream, a great and invaluable dialogue would have begun. And the great value of this dialogue would have been not only in its power to instruct all of you, and the ages. Its great value would have been in its power to instruct me, its power to instruct Richard: for it would have been nothing less than that so universally desired, so rarely achieved reconciliation between spiritual father and spiritual son.

Now, of course, it is not Richard's fault that I felt this way. But there is not much point, on the other hand, in dismissing it as simply my fault, or my illusion. I had identified myself with him long before we met: in a sense by no means metaphysical, his example had helped me to survive. He was black, he was young, he had come out of the Mississippi nightmare and the Chicago slums, and he was a writer. He proved it could be done—proved it to me, and gave me an arm against all those others who assured me it could *not* be done. And I think I had expected Richard, on the day we met, somehow, miraculously, to understand this, and to rejoice in it. Perhaps that sounds foolish, but I cannot honestly say, not even now, that I really think it is foolish. Richard Wright had a tremendous effect on countless numbers of people whom he never met, multitudes whom he now will never meet. This means that his responsibilities and his hazards were great. I don't think that Richard ever thought of me as one of his responsibilities—*bien au contraire!*—but he certainly seemed, often enough, to wonder just what he had done to deserve me.

Our reconciliation, anyway, never took place. This was a great loss for me. But many of our losses have a compensating gain. In my efforts to get through to Richard, I was forced to begin to wonder exactly why he held himself so rigidly against me. I could not believe—especially if one grants *my* reading of our relationship—that it could be due only to my criticism of his work. It seemed to me then, and it seems to me now, that one really needs those few people who take oneself and one's work seriously enough to be unimpressed by the public hullabaloo surrounding the former or the uncritical solemnity which menaces the latter from the instant that, for whatever reason, it finds itself in vogue.

No, it had to be more than that—the more especially as his attitude toward me had not, it turned out, been evolved for my particular benefit. It seemed to apply, with equal rigor, against a great many others. It applied against old friends, incontestably his equals, who had offended him, always, it turned out, in the same way: by failing to take his word for all the things he imagined, or had been led to believe, his word could cover. It applied against younger American Negroes who felt that Joyce, for example, not he, was the master; and also against younger American Negroes who felt that Richard did not know anything about jazz, or who insisted that the Mississippi and the Chicago he remembered were not precisely the Mississippi and the Chicago that they knew. It applied against Africans who refused to take Richard's word for Africa, and it applied against Algerians who did not feel that Paris was all that Richard had it cracked up to be. It applied, in short, against anyone who seemed to threaten Richard's system of reality. As time went on, it seemed to me that these people became more numerous and that Richard had fewer and fewer friends. At least, most of those people whom I had known to be friends of Richard's seemed to be saddened by him, and, reluctantly, to drift away. He's been away too long, some of them said. He's cut himself off from his roots. I resisted this judgment with all my might, more for my own sake than for Richard's, for it was far too easy to find this judgment used against myself. For the same reason I defended Richard when an African told me, with a small, mocking laugh, *I believe he thinks he's white*. I did *not* think I had been away too long: but I could not fail to begin, however unwillingly, to wonder about the uses and hazards of expatriation. I did not think I was white, either, or I did not *think* I thought so. But the Africans might think I did, and who could blame them? In their eyes, and in terms of my history, I could scarcely be considered the purest or most dependable of black men.

And I think that it was at about this point that I began to watch Richard as though he were a kind of object lesson. I could not help wondering if he, when facing an African, felt the same awful tension between envy and despair, attraction and revulsion. I had always been considered very dark, both Negroes and whites had despised me for it, and I had despised myself. But the Africans were much darker than I; I was a paleface among them, and so was Richard. And the disturbance thus created caused all of my extreme ambivalence about color to come floating to the surface of my mind. The Africans seemed at once simpler and more devious, more directly erotic and at the same time more subtle, and they were proud. If they had ever despised themselves for their color, it did not show, as far as I could tell. I envied them and feared them—feared that they had good reason to despise me. What did Richard feel? And what did Richard feel about other American Negroes abroad?

For example: one of my dearest friends, a Negro writer now living in Spain, circled around me and I around him for months before we spoke. One Negro meeting another at an all-white cocktail party, or at that larger cocktail party which is the American colony in Europe, cannot but wonder how the other got there. The question is: Is he for real? or is he kissing ass? Almost all Negroes, as Richard once pointed out, are almost always acting, but before a white audience—which is quite incapable of judging their performance: and even a "bad nigger" is, inevitably, giving something of a performance, even if the entire purpose of his performance is to terrify or blackmail white people.

Negroes know about each other what can here be called family secrets, and this means that one Negro, if he wishes, can "knock" the other's "hustle"—can give his game away. It is still not possible to overstate the price a Negro pays to climb out of obscurity—for it is a *particular* price, involved with being a Negro; and the great wounds, gouges, amputations, losses, scars, endured in such a journey cannot be calculated. But even this is not the worst of it, since he is really dealing with two hierarchies, one white and one black, the latter modeled on the former. The higher he rises, the less is his journey worth, since (unless he is extremely energetic and anarchic, a genuinely "bad nigger" in the most positive sense of the term) all he can possibly find himself exposed to is the grim emptiness of the white world—which does not live by the standards it uses to victimize him—and the even more ghastly emptiness of black people who wish they were white. Therefore, one "exceptional" Negro watches another "exceptional" Negro in order to find out if he knows how vastly successful and bitterly funny the hoax has been. Alliances, in the great cocktail party of the white man's world, are formed, almost purely, on this basis, for if both of you can laugh, you have a lot to laugh about. On the other hand, if only one of you can laugh, one of you, inevitably, is laughing at the other.

In the case of my new-found friend, Andy, and I, we were able, luckily, to laugh together. We were both baffled by Richard, but still respectful and fond of him—we accepted from Richard pronouncements and attitudes which we would certainly never have accepted from each other, or from anyone else—at the time Richard returned from wherever he had been to film *Native Son.* (In which, to our horror, later abundantly justified, he himself played Bigger Thomas.) He returned with a brainstorm, which he outlined to me one bright, sunny afternoon, on the terrace of the Royal St. Germain. He wanted to do something to protect the rights of American Negroes in Paris; to form, in effect, a kind of pressure group which would force American businesses in Paris, and American government offices, to hire Negroes on a proportional basis.

This seemed unrealistic to me. How, I asked him, in the first place, could one find out how many American Negroes there were in Paris? Richard quoted an approximate, semi-official figure, which I do not remember, but I was still not satisfied. Of this number, how many were looking for jobs? Richard seemed to feel that they spent most of their time being turned down by American bigots, but this was not really my impression. I am not sure I said this, though, for Richard often made me feel that the word "frivolous" had been coined to describe me. Nevertheless, my objections made him more and more impatient with me, and I began to wonder if I were not guilty of great disloyalty and indifference concerning the lot of American Negroes abroad. (I find that there is something helplessly sardonic in my tone now, as I write this, which also handicapped me on that distant afternoon. Richard, more than anyone I have ever known, brought this tendency to the fore in me. I always wanted to kick him, and say, "Oh, come off it, baby, ain't no white folks around now, let's tell it like it *is.*")

Still, most of the Negroes I knew had *not* come to Paris to look for work. They were writers or dancers or composers, they were on the GI Bill, or fellowships, or more mysterious shoestrings, or they worked as jazz musicians. I did not know anyone who doubted that the American hiring system remained in Paris exactly what it had been at home—but how was one to prove this, with a handful, at best, of problematical Negroes, scattered throughout Paris? Unlike Richard, I had no reason to suppose that any of them even *wanted* to work for Americans—my evidence, in fact, suggested that this was just about the last thing they wanted to do. But, even if they did, and even if they were qualified, how could one *prove* that So-and-So had not been hired by TWA *because* he was a Negro? I had found this almost impossible to do at home. Isn't this, I suggested, the kind of thing which ought to be done from Washington? Richard, however, was not to be put off, and he had made me feel so guilty that I agreed to find out how many Negroes were then working for the ECA.

There turned out to be two or three or four, I forget how many. In any case, we were dead, there being no way on earth to prove that there should have been six or seven. But we were all in too deep to be able to turn back now, and, accordingly, there was a pilot meeting of this extraordinary organization, quite late, as I remember, one evening, in a private room over a bistro. It was in some extremely inconvenient part of town, and we all arrived separately or by twos. (There was some vague notion, I think, of defeating the ever-present agents of the CIA, who certainly ought to have had better things to do, but who, quite probably, on the other hand, didn't.) We may have defeated pursuit on our way there, but there was certainly no way of defeating detection as we arrived: slinking casually past the gaping mouths and astounded eyes of a workingman's bistro, like a disorganized parade, some thirty or forty of us, through a back door, and up the stairs. My friend and I arrived a little late, perhaps a little drunk, and certainly on a laughing jag, for we felt that we had been trapped in one of the most improbable and old-fashioned of English melodramas.

But Richard was in his glory. He was on the platform above us, I think he was alone there; there were only Negroes in the room. The results of the investigations of others had proved no more conclusive than my own —one could certainly not, on the basis of our findings, attack a policy or evolve a strategy—but this did not seem to surprise Richard, or, even, to disturb him. It was decided, since we could not be a pressure group, to form a fellowship club, the purpose of which would be to get to know the French, and help the French to get to know us. Given our temperaments, neither Andy nor myself felt any need to join a club for this, we were getting along just fine on our own; but, somewhat to my surprise, we did not know many of the other people in the room, and so we listened. If it were only going to be a social club, then, obviously, the problem, as far as we were concerned, was over.

Richard's speech, that evening, made a great impact on me. It frightened me. I felt, but suppressed the feeling, that he was being mightily condescending toward the people in the room. I suppressed the feeling because most of them did not, in fact, interest me very much; but I was still in that stage when I felt guilty about not loving every Negro that I met. Still, perhaps for this very reason, I could not help resenting Richard's aspect and Richard's tone. I do not remember how his speech began, but I will never forget how it ended. News of this get-together, he told us, had caused a great stir in Parisian intellectual circles. Everyone was filled with wonder (as well they might be) concerning the future of such a group. A great many white people had wished to be present, Sartre, de Beauvoir, Camus—"and," said Richard, *"my own wife.* But I told them, before I can allow you to come, we've got to prepare the Negroes to receive you!"

This revelation, which was uttered with a smile, produced the most strained, stunned, uneasy silence. I looked at Andy, and Andy looked at me. There was something terribly funny about it, and there was something not funny at all. I rather wondered what the probable response would have been had Richard dared make such a statement in, say, a Negro barbershop; rather wondered, in fact, what the probable response would have been had anyone else dared make such a statement to anyone in the room, under different circumstances. ("Nigger, I been receiving white folks all my life—prepare *who?* Who you think you going to *prepare?"*) It seemed to me, in any case, that the preparation ought, at least, to be conceived of as mutual: there was no reason to suppose that Parisian intellectuals were more "prepared" to "receive" American Negroes than American Negroes were to receive them—rather, all things considered, the contrary.

This was the extent of my connection with the Franco-American Fellowship Club, though the club itself, rather anemically, seemed to drag on for some time. I do not know what it accomplished—very little, I should imagine; but it soon ceased to exist because it had never had any reason to come into existence. To judge from complaints I heard, Richard's interest in it, once it was—roughly speaking—launched, was minimal. He told me once that it had cost him a great deal of money—this referred, I think, to some disastrous project, involving a printer's bill, which the club had undertaken. It seemed, indeed, that Richard felt that, with the establishment of this club, he had paid his dues to American Negroes abroad, and at home, and forever; had paid his dues, and was off the hook, since they had once more proved themselves incapable of following where he led. For yet one or two years to come, young Negroes would cross the ocean and come to Richard's door, wanting his sympathy, his help, his time, his money. God knows it must have been trying. And yet, they could not possibly have taken up more of his time than did the dreary sycophants by whom, as far as I could tell, he was more and more surrounded. Richard and I, of course, drifted farther and farther apart—our dialogues became too frustrating and too acrid—but, from my helplessly sardonic distance, I could only make out, looming above what seemed to be an indescribably cacophonous parade of mediocrities, and a couple of the world's most empty and pompous black writers, the tough and loyal figure of Chester Himes. There was a noticeable chill in the love affair which had been going on between Richard and the French intellectuals. He had always made American intellectuals uneasy, and now they were relieved to discover that he bored them, and even more relieved to say so. By this time he had managed to estrange himself from almost all of the younger American Negro writers in Paris. They were often to be found in the same café, Richard compulsively playing the pinball machine, while they, spitefully and deliberately, refused to acknowledge his presence. Gone were the days when he had only to enter a café to be greeted with the American Negro equivalent of *"cher maître"* ("Hey, Richard, how you making it, my man? Sit down and tell me something."), to be seated at a table, while all the bright faces turned toward him. The brightest faces were now turned from him, and among these faces were the faces of the Africans and the Algerians. They did not trust him—and their distrust was venomous because they felt that he had promised them so much. When the African said to me, "I believe he thinks he's white," he meant that Richard cared more about his safety and comfort than he cared about the black condition. But it was to this condition, at least in part, that he owed his safety and comfort and power and fame. If one-tenth of the suffering which obtained (and obtains) among Africans and Algerians in Paris had been occurring in Chicago, one could not help feeling that Richard would have raised the roof. He never ceased to raise the roof, in fact, as far as the American color problem was concerned. But time passes quickly. The American Negroes had discovered that Richard did not really know much about the present dimensions and complexity of the Negro problem here, and, profoundly, did not want to know. And one of the reasons that he did not want to know was that his real impulse toward American Negroes, individually, was to despise them. They, therefore, dismissed his rage and his public pronouncements as an unmanly reflex; as for the Africans, at least the younger ones, they knew he did not know them and did not want to know them, and they despised *him*. It must have been extremely hard to bear, and it was certainly very frightening to watch. I could not help feeling: *Be careful. Time is passing for you, too, and this may be happening to you one day.*

For who has not hated his black brother? Simply *because* he is black, *because* he is brother. And who has not dreamed of violence? That fantastical violence which will drown in blood, wash away in blood, not only generation upon generation of horror, but which will also release the individual horror, carried everywhere in the heart. Which of us has overcome his past? And the past of a Negro is blood dripping down through leaves, gouged-out eyeballs, the sex torn from its socket and severed with a knife. But this past is not special to the Negro. This horror is also the past, and the everlasting potential, or temptation, of the human race. If we do not know this, it seems to me, we know nothing about ourselves, nothing about each other; to have accepted this is also to have found a source of strength—source of all our power. But one, must first accept this paradox, with joy.

The American Negro has paid a hidden, terrible price for his slow climbing to the light; so that, for example, Richard was able, at last, to live in Paris exactly as he would have lived, had he been a white man, here, in America. This may seem desirable, but I wonder if it is. Richard paid the price such an illusion of safety demands. The price is a turning away from, an ignorance of, all of the powers of darkness. This sounds mystical, but it is not; it is a hidden fact. It is the failure of the moral imagination of Europe which has created the forces now determined to overthrow it. No European dreamed, during Europe's heyday, that they were sowing, in a dark continent, far away, the seeds of a whirlwind. It was not dreamed, during the Second World War, that Churchill's ringing words to the English were overheard by English slaves—who, now, coming in their thousands to the mainland, menace the English sleep. It is only now, in America, and it may easily be too late, that any of the anguish, to say nothing of the rage, with which the American Negro has lived so long begins, dimly, to trouble the public mind. The suspicion has been planted—and the principal effect, so far, here, has been panic—that perhaps the world is darker and therefore more real than we have allowed ourselves to believe.

Time brought Richard, as it has brought the American Negro, to an extraordinarily baffling and dangerous place. An American Negro, however deep his sympathies, or however bright his rage, ceases to be simply a black man when he faces a black man from Africa. When I say simply a black man, I do not mean that being a black man is simple, anywhere. But I am suggesting that one of the prices an American Negro pays—or can pay—for what is called his "acceptance" is a profound, almost ineradicable self-hatred. This corrupts every aspect of his living, he is never at peace again, he is out of touch with himself forever. And, when he faces an African, he is facing the unspeakably dark, guilty, erotic past which the Protestant fathers made him bury—for their peace of mind, and for their power—but which lives in his personality and haunts the universe yet. What an African, facing an American Negro sees, I really do not yet know; and it is too early to tell with what scars and complexes the African has come up from the fire. But the war in the breast between blackness and whiteness, which caused Richard such pain, need not be a war. It is a war which just as it denies both the heights and the depths of our natures, takes, and has taken, visibly, and invisibly, as many white lives as black ones. And, as I see it, Richard was among the most illustrious victims of this war. This is why, it seems to me, he eventually found himself wandering in a no-man's-land between the black world and the white. It is no longer important to be white—thank heaven—the white face is no longer invested with the power of this world; and it is devoutly to be hoped that it will soon no longer be important to be black. The experience of the American Negro, if it is ever faced and assessed, makes it possible to hope for such a reconciliation. The hope and the effect of this fusion in the breast of the American Negro is one of the few hopes we have of surviving the wilderness which lies before us now.

superficial, tedious, precious
Ho Hum

GORE VIDAL

Gore Vidal (1925–) is one of America's major essayists as well as a distinguished novelist and playwright. Born into a prominent Washington family—his grandfather was a U.S. senator, his father a pioneering figure in commercial aviation—Vidal has always been fascinated with politics, and even ran for public office several times. Like H. L. Mencken, one of his influences, he has happily played gadfly, satirist, and polemicist, though his mockery of the Republic's "know-nothingism" is from a more consistently progressive-left viewpoint than that of the Baltimore sage. Vidal has a patrician love and knowledge of history rare in American writers, as his historical novels (Burr; Lincoln; Washington, D.C.) attest. This historical sense also colors his approach to the essay, a form to which he has devoted nine volumes, including the massive, collected United States: Essays 1952–1992. *He is a master of the elegant, lucid, unbuttoned nonfiction prose style.*

    "Some Memories of the Glorious Bird and an Earlier Self" is characteristic of Vidal's "review-essay" method: he will generally take a newly published book (in this case, Tennessee Williams' memoirs) as a point of departure for a wider meditation on a subject. Often he will bring in personal experiences that bear on the public figure or topic. Although he keeps a tight rein on his private life and is rarely confessional per se, he does reveal, in flashes, a good deal about his life and character. "Some Memories . . ." is a good example of what might be called a double portrait, of Williams and the author. The self-portrait has the effect of bringing into sharper relief the singularities of his sometime friend. Also noteworthy is the judicious balance with which Vidal reveals Williams' cultural limitations and self-promotions without in any way demeaning his achievement as a playwright.

Some Memories of the Glorious Bird and an Earlier Self

"I PARTICULARLY LIKE New York on hot summer nights when all the . . . uh, superfluous people are off the streets." Those were, I think, the first words Tennessee addressed to me; then the foggy blue eyes blinked, and a nervous chuckle filled the moment's silence before I said whatever I said.

Curtain rising. The place: an apartment at the American Academy in Rome. Occasion: a party for some newly arrived Americans, among them Frederic Prokosch, Samuel Barber. The month: March 1948. The day: halcyon. What else could a March day be in the golden age?

I am pleased that I can remember so clearly my first meeting with the Glorious Bird, as I almost immediately called him for reasons long since forgotten (premonition, perhaps, of the eventual take-off and flight of youth's sweet bird?). Usually, I forget first meetings, excepting always those solemn audiences granted by the old and famous when I was young and green. I recall vividly every detail of André Gide's conversation and appearance, including the dark velvet beret he wore in his study at 1 bis rue Vaneau. I recall even more vividly my visits to George Santayana in his cell at the Convent of the Blue Nuns. All these audiences, meetings, introductions took place in that *anno mirabilis* 1948, a year that proved to be the exact midpoint between the end of the Second World War and the beginning of what looks to be a permanent cold war. At the time, of course, none of us knew where history had placed us.

At that first meeting I thought Tennessee every bit as ancient as Gide and Santayana. After all, I was twenty-two. He was thirty-seven; but claimed to be thirty-three on the sensible ground that the four years he had spent working for a shoe company did not count. Now he was the most celebrated American playwright. *A Streetcar Named Desire* was still running in New York when we met that evening in a flat overlooking what was, in those days, a quiet city where hardly anyone was superfluous unless it was us, the first group of American writers and artists to arrive in Rome after the war.

In 1946 and 1947 Europe was still out-of-bounds for foreigners. But by 1948 the Italians had begun to pull themselves together, demonstrating once more their astonishing ability to cope with disaster which is so perfectly balanced by their absolute inability to deal with success.

Rome was strange to all of us. For one thing, Italy had been sealed off not only by war but by Fascism. Since the early thirties few English or American artists knew Italy well. Those who did included mad Ezra, gentle Max, spurious B.B. and, of course, the Anglo-American historian Harold (now Sir Harold) Acton, in stately residence at Florence. By 1948 Acton had written supremely well about both the Bourbons of Naples and the later Medici of Florence; unfortunately, he was—is—prone to the writing of memoirs. And so, wanting no doubt to flesh out yet another chapter in the ongoing story of a long and marvelously uninteresting life, Acton came down to Rome to look at the new invaders. What he believed he saw and heard, he subsequently published in a little volume called *More Memoirs of an Aesthete,* a work to be cherished for its quite remarkable number of unaesthetic misprints and misspellings.

"After the First World War American writers and artists had emigrated to Paris; now they pitched upon Rome." So Acton begins. "According to Stendhal, the climate was enough to gladden anybody, but this was not the reason: one of them explained to me that it was the facility of finding taxis, and very little of Rome can be seen from a taxi. Classical and Romantic Rome was no more to them than a picturesque background. Tennessee Williams, Victor [he means Frederic] Prokosch and Gore Vidal created a bohemian annexe to the American Academy. . . ." Liking Rome for its many taxis is splendid stuff and I wish I had said it. Certainly whoever did was putting Acton on, since the charm of Rome—1948—was the lack of automobiles of any kind. But Acton is just getting into stride. More to come.

Toward the end of March Tennessee gave a party to inaugurate his new flat in the Via Aurora (in the golden age even the street names were apt). Somehow or other, Acton got himself invited to the party. I remember him floating like some large pale fish through the crowded room; from time to time, he would make a sudden lunge at this or that promising bit of bait while Tennessee, he tells us, "wandered as a lost soul among the guests he assembled in an apartment which might have been in New York. . . . Neither he nor any of the group I met with him spoke Italian, yet he had a typically Neapolitan protégé who could speak no English."

At this time Tennessee and I had been in Rome for only a few weeks and French, not Italian, was the second language of the reasonably well-educated American of that era. On the other hand, Prokosch knew Italian, German, and French; he also bore with becoming grace the heavy weight of a Yale doctorate in Middle English. But to Acton the author of *The Asiatics,* the translator of Hölderlin and Louise Labé was just another barbarian whose works "fell short of his perfervid imagination, [he] had the dark good looks of an advertiser of razor blades. . . ." Happily, "Gore Vidal, the youngest in age, aggressively handsome in a clean-limbed sophomore style, had success written all over him. . . . His candour was engaging but he was slightly on the defensive, as if he anticipated an attack on his writings or his virtue." Well, the young G.V. wasn't so dumb: seeing the old one-two plainly in the middle distance, he kept sensibly out of reach.

"A pudgy, taciturn, moustached little man without any obvious distinction." Thus Acton describes Tennessee. He then zeroes in on the "protégé" from Naples, a young man whom Acton calls "Pierino." Acton tells us that Pierino had many complaints about Tennessee and his friends, mostly due to the language barrier. The boy was also eager to go to America. Acton tried to discourage him. Even so, Pierino was enthralled. " 'You are the first *galantuomo* who has spoken to me this evening.' " After making a date to see the *galantuomo* later on that evening, Pierino split. Acton then told Tennessee, "as tactfully as I could, that his young protégé felt neglected. . . . [Tennessee] rubbed his chin thoughtfully and said nothing, a little perplexed. There was something innocently childish about his expression." It does not occur to the memoirist that Tennessee might have been alarmed at his strange guest's bad manners. "Evidently he was not aware that Pierino wanted to be taken to America and I have wondered since whether he took him there, for that was my last meeting with Tennessee Williams." It must be said that Acton managed to extract quite a lot of copy out of a single meeting. To put his mind at rest, Tennessee did take Pierino to America and Pierino is now a married man and doing, as they say, well.

"This trifling episode illustrated the casual yet condescending attitude of certain foreigners towards the young Italians they cultivated on account of their Latin charm without any interest in their character, aspirations or desires." This sentiment or sentimentality could be put just as well the other way around and with far more accuracy. Italian trade has never had much interest in the character, aspirations or desires of those to whom they rent their ass. When Acton mediates upon The Italian Boy, a sweet and sickly hypocrisy clouds his usually sharp prose and we are in E. M. Forsterland where the lower orders (male) are worshiped, and entirely misunderstood. But magnum of sour grapes to one side, Acton is by no means inaccurate. Certainly he got right Tennessee's indifference to place, art, history. The Bird seldom reads a book and the only history he knows is his own; he depends, finally, on a romantic genius to get him through life. Above all, he is a survivor, never more so than now in what he calls his "crocodile years."

I picked up Tennessee's *Memoirs* with a certain apprehension. I looked myself up in the Index; read the entries and found some errors, none grave. I started to read; was startled by the technique he had chosen. Some years ago, Tennessee told me that he had been reading (that is to say, looking at) my "memoir in the form of a novel" *Two Sisters.* In this book I alternated sections describing certain events in 1948 with my every-day life while writing the book. Memory sections I called *Then.* The day-by-day descriptions I called *Now.* At the time Tennessee found *Two Sisters* interesting because he figured in it. He must also have found it technically interesting because he has serenely appropriated my form and has now no doubt forgotten just how the idea first came to him to describe the day-to-day life of a famous beleaguered playwright acting in an off-Broadway production of the failing play *Small Craft Warnings* while, in alternating sections, he recalls the early days not only of Tennessee Williams but of one Thomas Lanier Williams, who bears only a faint familial resemblance to the playwright we all know from a thousand and one altogether too candid interviews.

There is a foreword and, like all forewords, it is meant to disarm. Un-fortunately, it armed me to the teeth. During the 1973 tryout of a play in New Haven, Tennessee was asked to address some Yale drama students. Incidentally, the style of the foreword is unusually seductive, the old mas-ter at his most beguiling: self-pity and self-serving kept in exquisite bal-ance by the finest comic style since S. L. Clemens.

"I found myself entering (through a door marked EXIT) an auditorium considerably smaller than the Shubert but containing a more than propor-tionately small audience. I would say roughly about two-score and ten, not including a large black dog which was resting in the lap of a male student in the front row. . . . The young faces before me were uniformly inex-pressive of any kind of emotional reaction to my entrance. . . ." I am surprised that Tennessee was surprised. The arrogance and self-satisfac-tion of drama students throughout Academe are among the few constants in a changing world. Any student who has read Sophocles in translation is, demonstrably, superior to Tennessee Williams in the untidy flesh. These dummies reflect of course the proud mediocrity of their teachers, who range, magisterially, through something called "world drama" where evolution works only backward. Teachers and taught are to be avoided.

"I am not much good at disguising my feelings, and after a few mo-ments I abandoned all pretense of feeling less dejection than I felt." The jokes did not work. So "I heard myself describing an encounter, then quite recent, with a fellow playwright in the Oak Room Bar at Manhat-tan's Plaza Hotel." It was with "my old friend Gore Vidal. I had em-braced him warmly. However, Mr. Vidal is not a gentleman to be dis-armed by a cordial embrace, and when, in response to his perfunctory inquiries about the progress of rehearsals . . . I told him . . . all seemed a dream come true after many precedent nightmares, he smiled at me with a sort of rueful benevolence and said 'Well, Bird, it won't do much good, I'm afraid, you've had too much bad personal exposure for anything to help you much anymore.'

"Well, then, for the first time, I could see a flicker of interest in the young faces before me. It may have been the magic word Vidal or it may have been his prophecy of my professional doom." Asked if the prognosis was accurate, Tennessee looked at the black dog and said, "Ask the dog."

An unsettling anecdote. I have no memory of the Plaza meeting. I am also prone, when dining late, to suffer from what Dorothy Parker used grimly to refer to as "the frankies," or straight talk for the other person's good like frankly-that-child-would-not-have-been-born-mongoloid-if-you-hadn't. . . . An eyewitness, however, assures me that I did not say what Tennessee attributes to me. Yet his paranoia always has some basis in reality. I have an uncomfortable feeling that I was probably thinking what I did not say and what he later thought I did say. When it comes to something unspoken, the Bird has a sharp ear.

It is hard now to realize what a bad time of it Tennessee used to have from the American press. During the forties and fifties the anti-fag battalions were everywhere on the march. From the high lands of *Partisan Review* to the middle ground of *Time* magazine, envenomed attacks on real or suspected fags never let up. A *Time* cover story on Auden was killed when the managing editor of the day was told that Auden was a fag. From 1945 to 1961 *Time* attacked with unusual ferocity everything produced or published by Tennessee Williams. "Fetid swamp" was the phrase most used to describe his work. But, in *Time,* as well as in time, all things will come to pass. The Bird is now a beloved institution.

Today, at sixty-four, Tennessee has the same voracious appetite for work and for applause that he had at twenty-four. More so, I would suspect, since glory is a drug more addictive than any other as heroes have known from Achilles on (Donald Wyndham's *roman à clef* about Tennessee bore the apt title *The Hero Continues).* But fashions in the theater change. The superstar of the forties and fifties fell on bad times, and that is the burden of these memoirs. In sharp detail we are told how the hero came into being. Less sharply, Tennessee describes the bad days when the booze and the pills caused him to hallucinate; to slip out of a world quite bad enough as it is into nightmare land. "I said to my friend Gore, 'I slept through the sixties,' and he said, 'You didn't miss a thing.'" Tennessee often quotes this exchange. But he leaves out the accompanying caveat: "If you missed the sixties, Bird, God knows what you are going to do with the seventies."

But of course life is not divided into good and bad decades; it is simply living. For a writer, life is, again simply, writing and in these memoirs the old magician can still create a world. But since it is hardly news to the Bird that we are for the night, the world he shows us is no longer the Romantic's lost Eden but Prospero's island where, at sunset, magicians often enjoy revealing the sources of their rude magic, the tricks of a trade.

Not that a magician is honor-bound to tell the whole truth. For in-

stance: "I want to admit to you that I undertook this memoir for merce-
nary reasons. It is actually the first piece of work, in the line of writing,
that I have undertaken for material profit." The sniffy tone is very much
that of St. Theresa scrubbing floors. Actually, Tennessee is one of the
richest of living writers. After all, a successful play will earn its author a
million or more dollars and Tennessee has written quite a few successful
plays. Also, thirteen of his works have been made into films.

Why the poor-mouthing? Because it has always been the Bird's tactic to
appear in public flapping what looks to be a pathetically broken wing. By
arousing universal pity, he hopes to escape predators. In the old days
before a play opened on Broadway, the author would be asked to write a
piece for the Sunday *New York Times* drama section. Tennessee's pieces
were always thrilling; sometimes horrendous. He would reveal how that
very morning he had coughed up blood with his sputum. But, valiantly, he
had gone on writing, knowing the new play would be his last work, ever
. . . By the time the Bird had finished working us over, only Louis
Kronenberger at *Time* had the heart to attack him.

But now that Tennessee's physical and mental health are good (he
would deny this instantly; "I have had, in recent days, a series of palpita-
tions of the variety known as terminal"), only the cry of poverty will, he
thinks, act as lightning conductor and insure him a good press for the
Memoirs. Certainly he did not write this book for the $50,000 advance. As
always, fame is the spur. Incidentally, he has forgotten that in the past he
did write for money when he was under contract to MGM and worked on
a film called *Marriage Is a Private Affair,* starring Lana Turner and James
Craig (unless of course Tennessee now sees in this movie that awesome
moral grandeur first detected by the film critic Myra Breckinridge).

The *Memoirs* start briskly. Tennessee is a guest at a country house in
Wiltshire near Stonehenge. On the grounds of the estate is a "stone which
didn't quite make it to Henge." He looks himself up in *Who's Who.*
Broods on his past; shifts back and forth in time. *Now* and *Then.* The
early days are fascinating to read about even though the Williams family is
already known to every playgoer not only from *The Glass Menagerie* but
also from the many other plays and stories in which appear, inexorably,
Rose the Sister, Edwina the Mother, Dakin the Brother, Cornelius the
Father, Reverend Dakin the Grandfather, as well as various other relatives
now identified for the first time. He also tells us how he was hooked by
the theater when some St. Louis amateurs put on a play he had written. "I
knew that writing was my life, and its failure would be my death. . . ."

I have never known any writer with the exception of the artistically
gifted and humanly appalling Carson McCullers who cared so much about
the opinion of those condemned to write for newspapers. Uneasily confronting a truly remarkable hunger for absolute praise and total notice,
Tennessee admits that, when being interviewed, he instinctively "hams it

up in order to provide 'good copy.' The reason? I guess a need to convince the world that I do indeed still exist and to make this fact a matter of public interest and amusement." Fair enough, Bird. But leave your old friends out.

"This book is a sort of catharsis of puritanical guilt feelings, I suppose. 'All good art is an indiscretion.' Well, I can't assure you that this book will be art, but it is bound to be an indiscretion, since it deals with my adult life. . . .

"Of course I could devote this whole book to a discussion of the art of drama, but wouldn't that be a bore?

"It would bore me to extinction, I'm afraid, and it would be a very, very short book, about three sentences to the page with extremely wide margins. The plays speak for themselves."

A wise choice: the plays do speak for themselves and Tennessee's mind is not, to say the least, at home with theory. Most beautifully, the plays speak for themselves. Not only does Tennessee have a marvelous comedic sense but his gloriously outrageous dramatic effects can be enormously satisfying. He makes poetic (without quotes) the speech of those half-educated would-be genteel folk who still maintain their babble in his head. Only on those rare occasions when he tries to depict educated or upper-class people does he falter. Somewhat reproachfully, he told me that he had been forced several times to use a dictionary while reading *Two Sisters.*

What, I asked, was one of the words you had to look up? "Solipsistic," he said. Tennessee's vocabulary has never been large (I note that he still thinks "eclectic" means "esoteric"). But then he is not the sort of writer who sees words on the page; rather he hears them in his head and when he is plugged into the right character, the wrong word never sounds.

"Life that winter in Rome: a golden dream, and I don't just mean Raffaello (Acton's "Pierino") and the mimosa and total freedom of life. Stop there: What I do mean is the total freedom of life and Raffaello and the mimosa. . . ." That season we were, all of us, symbolically, out of jail. Free of poverty and hack work, Tennessee had metamorphosed into the Glorious Bird while I had left behind me three years in the wartime army and a near-fatal bout with hepatitis. So it was, at the beginning of that golden dream, we met.

Tennessee's version: "[Gore] had just published a best-seller, called *The City and the Pillar,* which was one of the first homosexual novels of consequence. I had not read it but I knew that it had made the best-seller lists and that it dealt with a 'forbidden subject.' " Later, Tennessee actually read the book (the only novel of mine he has ever been able to get through) and said, "You know you spoiled it with that ending. You didn't know what a good book you had." Fair comment.

"Gore was a handsome kid, about twenty-four *[sic],* and I was quite

taken by his wit as well as his appearance." Incidentally, I am mesmerized
by the tributes to my beauty that keep cropping up in the memoirs of the
period. At the time nobody reliable thought to tell me. In fact, it was my
impression that I was not making out as well as most people because, with
characteristic malice, Nature had allowed Guy Madison and not me to
look like Guy Madison.

"We found that we had interests in common and we spent a lot of time
together. Please don't imagine that I am suggesting that there was a romance." I don't remember whether or not I ever told Tennessee that I had
actually seen but not met him the previous year. He was following me up
Fifth Avenue while I, in turn, was stalking yet another quarry. I recognized
him: he wore a blue bow tie with white polka dots. In no mood for literary
encounters, I gave him a scowl and he abandoned the chase just north of
Rockefeller Center. I don't recall how my own pursuit ended. We walked
a lot in the golden age.

"I believe we also went to Florence that season and were entertained by
that marvelous old aesthete Berenson." No, that was someone else. "And
then one afternoon Gore took me to the Convent of the Blue Nuns to
meet the great philosopher and essayist, by then an octogenarian and
semi-invalid, Santayana." I had to drag Tennessee to meet Santayana. Neither had heard of the other. But Tennessee did stare at the old man with
great interest. Afterward, the Bird remarked, "Did you notice how he said
'in the days when I had secretaries, *young men?*' "

In the *Memoirs* Tennessee tells us a great deal about his sex life, which
is one way of saying nothing about oneself. Details of this body and that
body tend to blur on the page as they do in life. Tennessee did not get
around to his first homosexual affair until he was well into his twenties, by
which time he had achieved several mature as well as sexually meaningful
and life-enhancing heterosexual relationships. Except he wasn't really all
that enhanced by these "mature" relationships. Lust for the male set his
nerves to jangling. Why was he such a late-developer? Well, this was close
to half a century ago, and Tennessee was the product of that Southern
puritan environment where all sex was sin and unnatural sex was peculiarly horrible.

I think that the marked difference between my attitude toward sex and
that of Tennessee made each of us somewhat startling to the other. I never
had the slightest guilt or anxiety about what I always took to be a normal
human appetite. He was—and is—guilt-ridden, and although he tells us
that he believes in no afterlife, he is still too much the puritan not to
believe in sin. At some deep level Tennessee truly believes that the
homosexualist is wrong and that the heterosexualist is right. Given this all-
pervading sense of guilt, he is drawn in both life and work to the idea of
expiation, of death.

Tennessee tells of his affair with a dancer named Kip. But Kip left him; got married; died young. Then Tennessee was drawn to a pseudonymous lover in New Orleans; that affair ended in drink and violence. For a number of years Tennessee lived with an Italo-American, Frank Merlo. Eventually they fell out. They were reunited when Frank was dying of cancer. Frank's last days were sufficiently horrifying to satisfy any puritan's uneasy conscience while, simultaneously, justifying the romantic's extreme vision of the world: "I shall but love thee better after death."

The other line running through Tennessee's emotional life is what I call the Monster Women. Surrogate mothers one might say if Tennessee's own mother, Miss Edwina, were not so implacably in this world, even as I write these lines. Currently convinced that the blacks signal to one another during the long St. Louis nights by clanging the lids of the trash cans, Miss Edwina is every inch the Amanda of *The Glass Menagerie.* In fact, so powerful is Tennessee's creation that in the presence of Miss Edwina one does not listen to her but only to what he has made of her.

"I had forty gentlemen callers that day," she says complacently. We are having dinner in the restaurant of the Robert Clay Hotel in Miami. Delicately she holds a fork with a shrimp on it. Fork and shrimp proceed slowly to her mouth while Tennessee and I stare, hypnotized not only by the constant flow of conversation but by the never-eaten shrimp for just as she is about to take the first bite, yet another anecdote wells up from deep inside her . . . ah, *solipsistic* brain and the fork returns to the plate, the shrimp untouched. "Tom, remember when that little dog took the hat with the plume and ran all 'round the yard . . . ?" This is also from *The Glass Menagerie.* Tennessee nervously clears his throat. Again the shrimp slowly rises to the wide straight mouth which resembles nothing so much as the opening to a miniature letter box—one designed for engraved invitations only. But once again the shrimp does not arrive. "Tom, do you remember . . . ?"

Tennessee clears his throat again. *"Mother, eat your shrimp."*

"Why," counters Miss Edwina, "do you keep making that funny sound in your throat?"

"Because, Mother, when you destroy someone's life you must expect certain nervous disabilities."

Yet Tennessee went on adding even more grotesque ladies than Miss Edwina to his life. I could never take any of them from Carson McCullers to Jane Bowles to Anna Magnani. Yes, yes, yes, they were superb talents all. Part of the artistic heritage of the twentieth century. I concede their talent, their glory, their charm—for Tennessee but not for me. Carson spoke only of her work. Of its greatness. The lugubrious Southern sing-song voice never stopped: "Did ya see muh lovely play? Did ya lahk muh lovely play? Am Ah gonna win the Pew-litzuh prahzz?" Jane ("the finest writer of fiction we have in the States") Bowles was more original. She thought and talked a good deal about food and made powerful scenes in restaurants. The best that one could say of Magnani was that she liked dogs. When Marlon Brando agreed to act with her in the film of Tennessee's *Orpheus Descending,* he warned, "When I do a scene with her, I'm going to carry a rock in each hand."

I don't know what Tennessee gets from the Monster Women, but if they give him solace nothing else matters. Certainly he has a huge appetite for the grotesque not only in art but in life. In fact, he is dogged by the grotesque. Once, in the airport at Miami, we were stopped by a plump middle-aged man who had known Tennessee whom he called Tom from the old days in St. Louis. The man seemed perfectly ordinary. He talked to Tennessee about friends they had in common. Then I noticed that the man was carrying a large string bag containing two roast turkeys and a half dozen loaves of bread. "What," I asked, "is that?" The man gave us a knowing wink. "Well, I got me two roast turkeys in there. And also these loaves of bread *because you know about the food in Miami.*" Then he was gone. It would seem that the true artist need never search for a subject; the subject always knows where to find him.

It is curious how friends actually regard one another—or think they do—when memoir-time rolls around, and the boneyard beckons. A figure of some consequence in our far-off golden age was the composer-novelist Paul Bowles. From time to time over the years, Tennessee has bestowed a number of Walter Winchell-ish Orchids on Paul as well as on Jane (I fear that a lifetime on Broadway has somewhat corrupted the Bird's everyday speech and prose although nothing, happily, can affect the authenticity of those voices in his head). Certainly Bowles was an early hero of Tennessee's.

But now let us see what Bowles makes of Tennessee in *his* memoir *Without Stopping.* "One morning when we were getting ready to leave for the beach" (this was Acapulco, 1940), "someone arrived at the door and asked to see me. It was a round-faced, sun-burned young man in a big floppy sombrero and a striped sailor sweater, who said his name was Tennessee Williams, that he was a playwright, and that Lawrence Langner of the Theatre Guild had told him to look me up. I asked him to come in and installed him in a hammock, explaining that we had to hurry to the beach with friends. I brought him books and magazines and rum and coke, and told him to ask the servants for sandwiches if he got hungry. Then we left. Seven hours later we got back to the house and found our visitor lying contentedly in the hammock, reading. We saw him again each day until he left."

Paul Bowles used to quote Virgil Thomson's advice to a young music critic: Never intrude your personal opinions when you write music criticism. "The words that you use to describe what you've heard will be the criticism." Bowles on Tennessee demonstrates a mastery of the unsaid. Needless to say, Tennessee read what Bowles had written about him. Now watch the Bird as he strikes . . .

"It was there in Acapulco that summer that I first met Jane and Paul Bowles. They were staying at a pension in town and Paul was, as ever, upset about the diet and his stomach. The one evening that we spent together that summer was given over almost entirely to the question of what he could eat in Acapulco that he could digest, and poor little Janie kept saying, 'Oh, Bubbles, if you'd just stick to cornflakes and fresh fruit!' and so on and so on. None of her suggestions relieved his dyspeptic humor.

"I thought them a very odd and charming couple." I think I give Tennessee that round, on points. But Bowles's prose still remains the perfect model for judgment by indirection even though, like Tennessee, he occasionally gets the facts wrong. Bowles writes: "Gore had just played a practical joke on Tennessee and Truman Capote which he recounted to me in dialect, as it were. He had called Tennessee on the telephone and, being a stupendous mimic, had made himself into Truman for the occasion. Then, complete with a snigger, he induced Tennessee to make uncomplimentary remarks about Gore's writing."

This is a curious variation on the actual story. A number of times I would ring Tennessee, using Capote's voice. The game was to see how long it would take him to figure out that it was not Capote. One day I rang and spoke to what I thought was Tennessee. But it was Frank Merlo, newly installed in the flat. I had not got beyond my imitable whine, "This is *Tru*man," when Frank began to attack Tennessee. I broke the connection. Frank never knew whether or not I had repeated his complaints to Tennessee. I did not. But years later I did tell Bowles the story.

Back to 1948: "In those days Truman was about the best companion you could want," writes Tennessee. "He had not turned bitchy. Well, he had not turned *maliciously* bitchy. But he was full of fantasies and mischief." That summer Capote arrived in Paris where Tennessee and I were staying at the Hôtel de l'Université ("A raffish hotel but it suited Gore and me perfectly as there was no objection to young callers"), and Capote would keep us entranced with mischievous fantasies about the great. Apparently, the very sight of him was enough to cause lifelong heterosexual men to tumble out of unsuspected closets. When Capote refused to surrender his virtue to the drunken Errol Flynn, "Errol threw *all* my suitcases out of the window of the Beverly Wilshire Hotel!" I should note here that the young Capote was no less attractive in his person then than he is today.

When Tennessee and I would exchange glances during these stories,

Capote would redouble his efforts. Did we know that Albert Camus was in love with him? Yes, Camus! Madly in love. Recently Capote's biographer told me that the Capote-Camus connection might well prove to be a key chapter. No doubt it will also provide a startling footnote to the life story of Camus, a man known until now as a womanizer. Then Capote showed us a gold and amethyst ring. "From André Gide," he sighed. Happily, I was able to check that one out. A few days later I called on Gide in the company of my English publisher. "How," I asked in my best Phillips Exeter French, "did you find Truman Capote?" "Who?" Gide asked. I suspect that it was then, in the fabulous summer of '48, that the nonfiction novel was born.

To return again to 1948, I have a bit more to report on that season.

"Frankie and I had been out late one evening and when we returned to the apartment the transom on the front door was open and from within came the voice of Truman Capote, shrill with agitation. . . . In the apartment were Truman, Gore Vidal, and a female policeman. . . . It seemed that Truman and Gore, still on friendly terms at this point, had got a bit drunk together and had climbed in through the transom of the apartment to wait for me and Frankie."

Before this story petrifies into literary history, let me amend the record. Tennessee, an actress, and I came back to Tennessee's flat to find Capote and a friend in the clutches of the law. They had indeed been caught entering the flat. But by the time we arrived, Capote had matters well under control. Plainclotheswoman and plainclothesman were listening bug-eyed to Capote, who was telling them *every*thing about the private lives of Mr. and Mrs. Charles Chaplin.

Tennessee's asides on the various personages who have come his way are often amusing, sometimes revelatory. He describes a hilarious dinner with the Russian performer Yevtushenko, who saw fit to lecture Tennessee on commercialism, sexual perversion, and the responsibilities of art while swilling expensive wine. Tennessee admired Dylan Thomas until he actually met him and received "this put-down: 'How does it feel to make all that Hollywood money?' " There was also the snub from Sartre. Tennessee gave a party at the Hôtel de l'Université, hoping that Sartre would come. Instead the Master sat a few blocks away at a café, and for several hours he made a point of *not* coming to the party despite the pleas of various emissaries.

Tennessee omits to mention a splendid lunch given us at the Grand Véfour by Jean Cocteau, who wanted the French rights to *A Streetcar Named Desire* for Jean Marais to act in. I came along as translator. Marais looked beautiful but sleepy. Cocteau was characteristically brilliant. He spoke no English but since he could manage an occasional "th" sound as well as the final "g," he often gave the impression that he was speaking

English. Tennessee knew no French. He also had no clear idea just who Cocteau was, while Cocteau knew nothing about Tennessee except that he had written a popular American play with a splendid part in it for his lover Marais. Between Tennessee's solemn analyses of the play and Cocteau's rhetoric about theater (the long arms flailed like semaphores denoting some dangerous last junction), no one made any sense at all except Marais who broke his long silence to ask, apropos the character Stanley Kowalski, "Will I have to use a Polish accent?"

Although Marais and Cocteau broke up soon afterward, Cocteau did the play without Marais. Cocteau's adaptation was, apparently, a gorgeous mess. Naked black youths writhed through beaded curtains while Arletty, miscast as Blanche, struck attitudes among peacock feathers.

The situation of a practicing playwright in the United States is not a happy one, to understate (or bowles) the matter. Broadway is more and more an abandoned parcel of real estate. Except for a native farce or two and a handful of "serious" plays imported from the British Isles, Broadway is noted chiefly for large and usually bad musicals. During the theater season of 1947–48 there were 43 straight plays running on Broadway. In 1974–75 there were 18, mostly imported. Adventurous plays are now done off-Broadway and sometimes off-off . . . where our memoirist ended up as a performer in *Small Craft Warnings.*

Unique among writers, the American playwright must depend upon the praise of journalists who seldom know very much about anything save the prejudices of their employers. With the collapse of a half dozen newspapers in the last third of a century, the success of a play now depends almost entirely upon the good will of the critic for *The New York Times.* The current reviewer is an amiable and enthusiastic Englishman who knows a good deal about ballet but not so much about the social and political nuances of his adopted land. Yet at sixty-four Tennessee Williams is still trying to curry favor with the press. Of *Small Craft Warnings,* "Clive Barnes" (in *The New York Times)* "was cautiously respectful. With the exception of Leonard Harris, I disregard TV reviews. I suppose they were generally negative."

Then Tennessee has second thoughts. And a new paragraph: "To say that I disregard TV reviews is hardly the total truth. How could I disregard any review which determines the life or death of a production?" How indeed? Yet after thirty years of meaningless praise and equally meaningless abuse, it is no wonder that Tennessee is a bit batty. On those rare occasions when Tennessee's literary peers have got around to looking at his work, the result has been depressing: witness, Mary McCarthy's piece "A Streetcar Named Success."

There have been complaints that these *Memoirs* tell us too much about Tennessee's sex life and too little about his art. Personally, I find the candor about his sex life interesting if not illuminating. At the worst, it will feed that homophobia which is too much a part of the national psyche. Yet perhaps it is better to write this sort of thing oneself rather than leave it to others to invent.

Recently that venerable vendor of book-chat Alfred Kazin wrote, "Vidal gets more literary mileage out of his sex life than anyone since Oscar Wilde and Jean Cocteau." This struck me as breathtakingly wrong. First, neither Wilde nor Cocteau ever exploited his sex life for "mileage." Each was reticent in public. Eventually the law revealed the private life of the first, while friends (and an ambiguous sort of unsigned memoir) revealed the life of the second. The book-chat writer does mention the admittedly too many interviews I've lately given to magazines like *Playboy* where sex is always a Solemn and Sacred subject and where I, too, am Solemn but never personal. As evidence of my seeking mileage he quotes the rather lame " 'In youth I never missed a trick . . . I tried everything . . . I could no more go to bed with somebody whose work I admired than I could . . . well, make love to a mirror. Fame in others switches off desire.' " Not, I would say, the most prurient of giveaway lines. Except in *Two Sisters,* a memoir done with mirrors, I have not used myself as a subject for private analysis on the ground that since we live in a time where the personality of the writer is everything and what he writes is nothing, only a fool would aid the enemy by helping to trivialize life, work.

A columnist reports that Tennessee was obliged to cut his *Memoirs* in half because of the "filth." I hope that we are given that other half one day; and I doubt that there will be much "filth," only indiscretions which ought to be interesting. After all, Tennessee has known or come across a great many of our time's movers and shakers. I say "come across" because for a long period he was . . . well, inattentive. Sometimes the stupefying combination of Nembutal and vodka (now abandoned) addled him. I was present when Edna Ferber (yes, Edna Ferber) came over to our table at a restaurant and introduced herself. With considerable charm, she told Tennessee how much she admired him. He listened to her with eyes that had narrowed to what Miss Ferber would have described as "mere slits." As she walked away, the Bird hissed, "Why is that woman attacking me?"

Tennessee is the sort of writer who does not develop; he simply continues. By the time he was an adolescent he had his themes. Constantly he plays and replays the same small but brilliant set of cards. I am not aware that any new information (or feeling?) has got through to him in the twenty-eight years since our Roman spring. In consequence, we have drifted apart. "Gore no longer receives me," said the Bird to one of his innumerable interviewers; and he put this down to my allegedly glamorous social life. But the reason for the drifting apart is nothing more than difference of temperament. I am a compulsive learner of new things while the Bird's occasional and sporadic responses to the world outside the proscenium arch have not been fortunate. "Castro was, after all, a gentleman," he announced after an amiable meeting with the dictator. Tell that to the proscribed fags of Cuba.

Tennessee's much publicized conversion to Roman Catholicism took place during the time of his great confusion. Shortly after the Bird was received into the arms of Mother Church, a Jesuit priest rang him up and asked if he would like an audience with the Pope? a meeting with the head of the Jesuit order? Oh yes. Yes! Tennessee was delighted. The next morning the priest arrived to take Tennessee to the Vatican where, presumably, the Pope was waiting on tenterhooks to examine the Church's latest haul. Unfortunately, Tennessee had forgotten all about the audience. He would have to beg off, he said; he was just not up to the Pope that day. The priest was stunned. The Pope's reaction has not been recorded.

The Jesuits, however, are made of tougher material. The secretary of the Black Pope rang to say that since a cocktail party had been arranged, Mr. Williams was going to be there, or else. The Bird was present. Almost immediately, he began to ham it up about God. Now if there is anything a Jesuit likes less than chat of God, it is having to listen to the religious enthusiasm of a layman. Trying to deflect Tennessee from what was fast turning into a Billy Graham exhortation about God and goodness, one of the Jesuits asked, "How do you start to write a play, Mr. Williams?" The Bird barely paused in his glorious ascent. "I start," he said sharply, "with a sentence." He then told the assembled members of the Society of Jesus that ever since becoming a Roman Catholic, he had felt a divine presence constantly with him. The Jesuits shifted uneasily at this. Like the old trouper he is, the Bird then paused abruptly in midflight in order to see just what effect he was having. After a moment of embarrassed silence, one of the Jesuits asked, timidly, "Is this presence a *warm* presence?"

"There is," said the Bird firmly, "no temperature."

But despite the "conversion," Tennessee now writes, "I am unable to believe that there is anything but permanent oblivion after death. . . . For me, what is there but to feel beneath me the steadily rising current of mortality and to summon from my blood whatever courage is native to it, and once there was a great deal." As he ends the Memoirs, he thinks back upon Hart Crane, whose legend has always haunted him. But though a romantic, Tennessee is no Crane. For one thing, it is too late to choose an abrupt death at sea. For another, art is too beguiling and difficult: "life is made up of moment-to-moment occurrences in the nerves and the perceptions, and try as you may, you can't commit them to the actualities of your own history."

But Tennessee continues to try. Now he has invited the world to take a close look at him, more or less as he is (the lighting of course has been carefully arranged, and he is not one to confuse an Entrance with an Exit). The result should be gratifying. The Glorious Bird is not only recognized but applauded in the streets. When he came to sign copies of the *Memoirs* in a large Manhattan bookstore, nearly a thousand copies were sold and the store had to be shut because of overcrowding. The resemblance to the latter days of Judy Garland would be disquieting were it not for the happy fact that since Tennessee cannot now die young he will probably not die at all (his grandfather lived for almost a century). In any case, artists who continue to find exhilarating the puzzles art proposes never grow bored and so have no need of death.

As for life? Well, that is a hard matter. But it was always a hard matter for those of us born with a sense of the transiency of these borrowed atoms that make up our corporeal being.

"I need," Tennessee writes with sudden poignancy, "somebody to laugh with." Well, don't we all, Bird? Anyway, be happy that your art has proved to be one of those stones that really did make it to Henge, enabling future magicians to gauge from its crafty placement not only the dour winter solstice of our last days but the summer solstice, too—the golden dream, the mimosa, the total freedom, and all that lovely time unspent now spent.

OK – but why "knuckle under" as a child? make one's own "label" – fear? of what?

ADRIENNE RICH

Adrienne Rich (1929–   ), an acclaimed poet and essayist, is the author of numerous poetry volumes, including Diving into the Wreck, *which won the National Book Award in poetry;* Of Woman Born, *a nonfiction study of motherhood as an institution; and several essay collections, including* Of Lies, Secrets and Silence *and* Blood, Bread and Poetry. *Rich has often taken the domestic as a starting point for an examination of global suffering and injustice. Her investigation of her own experiences as a dutiful daughter, wife, and mother contributed to her evolution into an antiwar activist and lesbian feminist. She has thoughtfully explored the connections among the personal, the aesthetic, and the political.*

Rich's prose style has a certain austere, plain, obstinate, puritanically serious quality, bordering on dour; it is as though verbal flashiness were equated in her mind with insincerity, and levity with irresponsibility. What makes the best of her essays so effective is that you feel she is really trying to work something out, going around and around the problem until it yields some hard-won truth. Her commitment to the struggle for clarity is quite moving, and because she has a first-rate mind, the insights she arrives at can be rigorously forceful. In the essay below, she uncovers, layer by layer, her ambivalence about being a Jew (or half-Jew) and a woman, using her own specific circumstances to illuminate the more universal issue of divided identities.

Split at the Root

AN ESSAY ON JEWISH IDENTITY

F OR ABOUT FIFTEEN MINUTES I have been sitting chin in
hand in front of the typewriter, staring out at the snow. Trying to be
honest with myself, trying to figure out why writing this seems to me so
dangerous an act, filled with fear and shame, and why it seems so necessary. It comes to me that in order to write this I have to be willing to do
two things: I have to claim my father, for I have my Jewishness from him
and not from my gentile mother; and I have to break his silence, his
taboos; in order to claim him I have in a sense to expose him.

And there is of course the third thing: I have to face the sources and the
flickering presence of my own ambivalence as a Jew; the daily, mundane
anti-Semitisms of my entire life.

These are stories I have never tried to tell before. Why now? Why, I
asked myself sometime last year, does this question of Jewish identity float
so impalpably, so ungraspably, around me, a cloud I can't quite see the
outlines of, which feels to me without definition?

And yet I've been on the track of this longer than I think.

In a long poem written in 1960, when I was thirty-one years old, I described myself as "Split at the root, neither Gentile nor Jew, Yankee nor
Rebel."* I was still trying to have it both ways: to be neither/nor, trying to
live (with my Jewish husband and three children more Jewish in ancestry
than I) in the predominantly gentile Yankee academic world of Cambridge, Massachusetts.

But this begins, for me, in Baltimore, where I was born in a hospital in
the Black ghetto, whose lobby contained an immense, white marble statue
of Christ.

My father was then a young teacher and researcher in the department of
pathology at the Johns Hopkins Medical School, one of the very few Jews
to attend or teach at that institution. He was from Birmingham, Alabama;
his father, Samuel, was an immigrant from Austria-Hungary and his
mother, Hattie Rice, a Sephardic Jew from Vicksburg, Mississippi. My

---

* "Readings of History" in Adrienne Rich, *Snapshots of a Daughter-in-Law*. W. W. Norton,
New York, 1967, pp. 36–40.

grandfather had had a shoe store in Birmingham, which did well enough to allow him to retire comfortably, and to leave my grandmother, on his death, a small income. The only souvenirs of my grandfather, Samuel Rich, were his ivory flute, which lay on our living-room mantel and was not to be played with; his thin gold pocket-watch, which my father wore; and his Hebrew prayer book, which I discovered among my father's books in the course of reading my way through his library. In this prayer book there was a newspaper clipping about my grandparents' wedding, which took place in a synagogue.

My father, Arnold, was sent in adolescence to a military school in the Tennessee mountains, a place for training white Southern Christian gentlemen. I suspect that there were few if any other Jewish boys at Colonel Bingham's. Or at "Mr. Jefferson's university," in Charlottesville, where he studied as an undergraduate. With whatever conscious forethought, Samuel and Hattie sent their son into the dominant Southern WASP culture, to become an "exception," to enter the professional class. Never, in describing these experiences, did he ever speak of having suffered—from loneliness, cultural alienation, or outsiderhood. I never heard him use the word "anti-Semitism."

It was only in college, when I read a poem by Karl Shapiro beginning: "To hate the Negro and avoid the Jew / is the curriculum" that it flashed on me that there was an untold side to my father's story of his student years. He looked recognizably Jewish, was short and slender in build with dark wiry hair and deepset eyes, high forehead, and curved nose.

My mother is a gentile. In Jewish law I cannot count myself a Jew. If it is true that "We think back through our mothers if we are women" (Virginia Woolf)—and I myself have affirmed this—then even according to lesbian theory, I cannot (or need not?) count myself a Jew.

The white Southern Protestant woman, the gentile, has always been there for me to peel back into. That's a whole piece of history in itself, for my gentile grandmother and my mother were also frustrated artists and intellectuals, a lost writer and a lost composer between them. Readers and annotators of books, note-takers, my mother a good pianist still, in her eighties. But there was also the obsession with ancestry, with "background," the Southern talk of family, not as people you would necessarily know and depend on, but as heritage, the guarantee of "good breeding." There was the inveterate romantic heterosexual fantasy, the mother telling the daughter how to attract men (my mother often used the word "fascinate"); the assumption that relations between the sexes could only be romantic, that it was in the woman's interest to cultivate "mystery," conceal her actual feelings. Survival tactics, of a kind, I think today, knowing what I know about the white woman's sexual role in the Southern racist scenario. Heterosexuality as protection, but also drawing white women deeper into collusion with white men.

It would be easy to push away and deny the gentile in me: that white Southern woman, that social Christian. At different times in my life, I suppose, I have wanted to push away one or the other burden of inheritance, to say merely, *I am a woman; I am a lesbian.* If I call myself a Jewish lesbian do I thereby try to shed some of my Southern gentile guilt, my white woman's culpability? If I call myself only through my mother, is it because I pass more easily through a world where being a lesbian often seems like outsiderhood enough?

According to Nazi logic, my two Jewish grandparents would have made me a *Mischling, first-degree:* non-exempt from the Final Solution.

The social world in which I grew up was Christian virtually without needing to say so; Christian imagery, music, language, symbols, assumptions everywhere. It was also a genteel, white middle-class world in which "common" was a term of deep opprobrium. "Common" white people might speak of "niggers"; *we* were taught never to use that word; *we* said "Negroes" (even as we accepted segregation, the eating taboo, the assumption that Black people were simply of a separate species). Our language was more polite, distinguishing us from the "rednecks," or the lynch mob mentality. So charged with negative meaning was even the word "Negro" that as children we were taught never to use it in front of Black people. We were taught that any mention of skin color in the presence of colored people was treacherous forbidden ground. In a parallel way, the word "Jew" was not used by polite gentiles. I sometimes heard my best friend's father, a Presbyterian minister, allude to "the Hebrew people," or "people of the Jewish faith." The world of acceptable folk was white, gentile (christian, really) and had "ideals" (which colored people, white "common" people, were not supposed to have). "Ideals" and "manners" included not hurting someone's feelings by calling her or him a Negro or a Jew—naming the hated identity. This is the mental framework of the 1930s and 1940s in which I was raised.

(Writing this I feel, dimly, like the betrayer: of my father, who did not speak the word; of my mother, who must have trained me in the messages; of my caste and class; of my whiteness itself.)

Two memories: I am in a play-reading at school, of *The Merchant of Venice.* Whatever Jewish law says, I am quite sure I was *seen* as Jewish (with a reassuringly gentile mother) in that double-vision that bigotry allows. I am the only Jewish girl in the class and I am playing Portia. As always, I read my part aloud for my father the night before, and he tells me to convey, with my voice, more scorn and contempt with the word "Jew": "Therefore, Jew. . . ." I have to say the word out, and say it loudly. I was encouraged to pretend to be a non-Jewish child acting a non-Jewish character who has to speak the word "Jew" emphatically. Such a child would not have had trouble with the part. But *I* must have had trouble with the part, if only because the word itself was really taboo. I can see that there was a kind of terrible, bitter bravado about my father's way of handling this. And who would not dissociate from Shylock in order to identify with Portia? As a Jewish child who was also a female I loved Portia—and, like every other Shakespearean heroine, she proved a treacherous role model.

A year or so later I am in another play, *The School for Scandal,* in which a notorious spendthrift is described as having "many excellent friends . . . among the Jews." In neither case was anything explained, either to me or to the class at large about this scorn for Jews and the disgust surrounding Jews and money. Money, when Jews wanted it, had it, or lent it to others, seemed to take on a peculiar nastiness, and Jews and money had some peculiar and unspeakable relation.

At this same school—in which we had christian hymns and prayers, and read aloud through the Bible morning after morning—I gained the impression that Jews were in the Bible and mentioned in English literature, had been persecuted centuries ago by the wicked Inquisition, but that they seemed not to exist in everyday life. These were the 1940s and we were told a great deal about the Battle of Britain, the noble French Resistance fighters, the brave, starving Dutch—but I did not learn of the resistance of the Warsaw Ghetto until I left home.

I was sent to the Episcopal church, baptized, and confirmed, and attended it for about five years, though without belief. That religion seemed to have little to do with belief or commitment; it was liturgy that mattered, not moral passion. Neither of my parents ever entered that church, and my father would not enter *any* church for any reason —wedding or funeral. Nor did I enter a synagogue until I left Baltimore. When I came home from church, for a while, my father insisted on reading aloud to me from Thomas Paine's *The Age of Reason*—a diatribe against institutional religion. Thus, he explained, I would have a balanced view of these things, a choice. He—they—did not give me the choice to be a Jew. My mother explained to me when I was filling out forms for college that if any question was asked about "religion" I should put down "Episcopalian" rather than "none"—to seem to have no religion was, she implied, dangerous.

But it was white social christianity, rather than any particular christian sect, that the world was founded on. The very word "christian" was used as a synonym for virtuous, just, peaceloving, generous, etc. etc.* The norm was christian: "religion: none" was indeed not acceptable. Anti-Semitism was so intrinsic as not to have a name. I don't recall exactly being taught that the Jews killed Jesus; "Christ-killer" seems too strong a term for the bland Episcopal vocabulary; but certainly we got the impression that the Jews had been caught out in a terrible mistake, failing to recognize the true Messiah, and were thereby less advanced in moral and spiritual sensibility. The Jews had actually allowed *moneylenders in the Temple* (again, the unexplained obsession with Jews and money). They were of the past, archaic, primitive as older (and darker) cultures are supposed to be primitive: Christianity was lightness, fairness, peace on earth, and combined the feminine appeal of "the meek shall inherit the earth" with the masculine stride of "Onward, Christian Soldiers."

Sometime in 1946, while still in high school, I read in the newspaper that a theatre in Baltimore was showing films of the Allied liberation of the Nazi concentration camps. Alone, I went downtown after school one afternoon and watched the stark, blurry but unmistakable newsreels. When I try to go back and touch the pulse of that girl of sixteen, growing up in many ways so precocious and so ignorant, I am overwhelmed by a memory of despair, a sense of inevitability, more enveloping than any I had ever known. Anne Frank's diary and many other personal narratives of the Holocaust were still unknown or unwritten. But it came to me that every one of those piles of corpses, mountains of shoes and clothing, had contained, simply, individuals, who had believed, as I now believed of myself, that they were meant to live out a life of some kind of meaning, that the world possessed some kind of sense and order; yet *this* had happened to them. And I, who believed my life was intended to be so interesting and meaningful, was connected to those dead by something—not just mortality but a taboo name, a hated identity. Or was I—did I really have to be? Writing this now, I feel belated rage, that I was so impoverished by the family and social worlds I lived in, that I had to try to figure out by myself what this did indeed mean for me. That I had never been taught about resistance, only about passing. That I had no language for anti-Semitism itself.

When I went home and told my parents where I had been, they were not pleased. I felt accused of being morbidly curious, not healthy, sniffing around death for the thrill of it. And since, at sixteen, I was often not sure of the sources of my feelings or of my motives for doing what I did, I

---

* In a similar way the phrase "that's white of you" implied that you were behaving with the superior decency and morality expected of white, but not of Black people.

probably accused myself as well. One thing was clear: there was nobody in my world with whom I could discuss those films. Probably at the same time I was reading accounts of the camps in magazines and newspapers; what I remember was the films, and having questions that I could not even phrase: such as, are those men and women "them" or "us"?

To be able to ask even the child's astonished question *Why do they hate us so?* means knowing how to say "we." The guilt of not knowing, the guilt of perhaps having betrayed my parents, or even those victims, those survivors, through mere curiosity—these also froze in me for years the impulse to find out more about the Holocaust.

1947: I left Baltimore to go to college in Cambridge, Massachusetts, left (I thought) the backward, enervating South for the intellectual, vital North. New England also had for me some vibration of higher moral rectitude, of moral passion even, with its seventeenth-century Puritan inner scrutiny, its Abolitionist righteousness, Colonel Shaw and his Black Civil War regiment depicted in granite on Boston Common, its nineteenth-century literary "flowering." At the same time, I found myself, at Radcliffe, among Jewish women. I used to sit for hours over coffee with what I thought of as the "real" Jewish students, who told me about middle-class Jewish culture in America. I described my background—for the first time to strangers—and they took me on, some with amusement at my illiteracy, some arguing that I could never marry into a strict Jewish family, some convinced I didn't "look Jewish," others that I did. I learned the names of holidays and foods, which surnames are Jewish and which are "changed names"; about girls who had had their noses "fixed," their hair straightened. For these young Jewish women, students in the late 1940s, it was acceptable, perhaps even necessary, to strive to look as gentile as possible, but they stuck proudly to being Jewish; expected to marry a Jew, have children, keep the holidays, carry on the culture.

I felt I was testing a forbidden current, that there was danger in these revelations. I bought a reproduction of a Chagall portrait of a rabbi in striped prayer-shawl and hung it on the wall of my room. I was admittedly young and trying to educate myself, but I was also doing something that *is* dangerous: I was flirting with identity.

One day that year I was in a small shop where I had bought a dress with a too-long skirt. The shop employed a seamstress who did alterations, and she came in to pin up the skirt on me. I am sure that she was a recent immigrant, a survivor. I remember a short, dark woman wearing heavy glasses, with an accent so foreign I could not understand her words.

Something about her presence was very powerful and disturbing to me. After marking and pinning up the skirt she sat back on her knees, looked up at me, and asked in a hurried whisper: "You Jewish?" Eighteen years of training in assimilation sprang into the reflex by which I shook my head, rejecting her, and muttered, "No."

What was I actually saying "no" to? She was poor, older, struggling with a foreign tongue, anxious; she had escaped the death that had been intended for her, but I had no imagination of her possible courage and foresight, her resistance; I did not see in her a heroine who had perhaps saved many lives including her own. I saw the frightened immigrant, the seamstress hemming the skirts of college girls, the wandering Jew. But I was an American college girl, having her skirt hemmed. And I was frightened myself, I think, because she had recognized me ("It takes one to know one," my friend Edie at Radcliffe had said) even if I refused to recognize myself or her; even if her recognition was sharpened by loneliness, or the need to feel safe with me.

But why should she have felt safe with me? I myself was living in a false sense of safety.

There are betrayals in my life that I have known at the very moment were betrayals: this was one of them. There are other betrayals committed so repeatedly, so mundanely, that they leave no memory trace behind: only a growing residue of misery, of dull, accreted self-hatred. Often these take the form not of words but of silence. Silence before the joke at which everyone is laughing: the anti-woman joke, the racist joke, the anti-Semitic joke. Silence and then amnesia. Blocking it out when the oppressor's language starts coming from the lips of one we admire, whose courage and eloquence have touched us: *She didn't really mean that: he didn't really say that.* But the accretions build up out of sight, like scale inside a kettle.

1948: I come home from my freshman year at college flaming with new insights, new information. I am the daughter who has gone out into the world, to the pinnacle of intellectual prestige, Harvard, fulfilling my father's hopes for me, but also exposed to dangerous influences. I have already been reproved for attending a rally for Henry Wallace and the Progressive Party. I challenged my father: "Why haven't you told me that I am Jewish? Why do you never talk about being a Jew?" He answered measuredly, "You know that I have never denied that I am a Jew. But it's not important to me. I am a scientist, a Deist. I have no use for organized religion. I choose to live in a world of many kinds of people. There are Jews I admire and others whom I despise. I am a person, not simply a Jew." The words are as I remember them, not perhaps exactly as spoken. But that was the message. And it contained enough truth—as all denial drugs itself on partial truth—so that it remained for the time being unanswerable, even though it left me high and dry, split at the root, gasping for clarity, for air.

At that time Arnold Rich was living in suspension, waiting to be appointed to the professorship of pathology at Johns Hopkins. The appointment was delayed for years, no Jew ever having held a professorial chair in that medical school. And he wanted it badly. It must have been a very bitter time for him, since he had believed so greatly in the redeeming power of excellence, of being the most brilliant, inspired man for the job. With enough excellence, you could presumably make it stop mattering that you were Jewish; you could become the *only* Jew in the gentile world, a Jew so "civilized," so far from "common," so attractively combining Southern gentility with European cultural values that no one would ever confuse you with the raw, "pushy" Jews of New York, the "loud, hysterical" refugees from Eastern Europe, the "overdressed" Jews of the urban South.

We—my sister, mother, and I—were constantly urged to speak quietly in public, to dress without ostentation, to repress all vividness or spontaneity, to assimilate with a world which might see us as too flamboyant. I suppose that my mother, pure gentile though she was, could be seen as acting "common" or "Jewish" if she laughed too loudly or spoke aggressively. My father's mother, who lived with us half the year, was a model of circumspect behavior, dressed in dark blue or lavender, retiring in company, ladylike to an extreme, wearing no jewelry except a good gold chain, a narrow brooch, a string of pearls. A few times, within the family, I saw her anger flare, felt the passion she was repressing. But when Arnold took us out to a restaurant, or on a trip, the Rich women were always tuned down to some WASP level my father believed, surely, would protect us all —maybe also make us unrecognizable to the "real Jews" who wanted to seize us, drag us back to the *shtetl,* the ghetto, in its many manifestations.

For, yes: that *was* a message—that some Jews would be after you, once they "knew," to rejoin them, to re-enter a world that was messy, noisy, unpredictable, maybe poor—"even though," as my mother once wrote me, criticizing my largely Jewish choice of friends in college: "some of them will be the most brilliant, fascinating people you'll ever meet." I wonder if that isn't one message of assimilation—of America—that the unlucky or the unachieving want to pull you backward, that to identify with them is to court downward mobility, lose the precious chance of passing, of token existence. There was always, within this sense of Jewish identity, a strong class discrimination. Jews might be "fascinating" as individuals but came with huge unruly families who "poured chicken soup over everyone's head" (in the phrase of a white Southern male poet). Anti-Semitism could thus be justified by the bad behavior of certain Jews; and if you did not effectively deny family and community, there would always be a cousin claiming kinship with you, who was the "wrong kind" of Jew.

I have always believed his attitude toward other Jews depended on who they were. . . . It was my impression that Jews of this background looked down on Eastern European Jews, including Polish Jews and Russian Jews, who generally were not as well educated. This from a letter written to me recently by a gentile who had worked in my father's department, whom I had asked about anti-Semitism there and in particular regarding my father. This informant also wrote me that it was hard to perceive anti-Semitism in Baltimore because the racism made so much more intense an impression: *I would almost have to think that Blacks went to a different heaven than the whites, because the bodies were kept in a separate morgue, and some white persons did not even want blood transfusions from Black donors.* My father's mind was racist and misogynist, yet as a medical student he noted in his journal that Southern male chivalry stopped at the point of any white man in a streetcar giving his seat to an old, weary, Black woman standing in the aisle. Was this a Jewish insight—an outsider's insight, even though the outsider was striving to be on the inside?

Because what isn't named is often more permeating than what is, I believe that my father's Jewishness profoundly shaped my own identity, and our family existence. They were shaped both by external anti-Semitism and my father's self-hatred, and by his Jewish pride. What Arnold did, I think, was call his Jewish pride something else: achievement, aspiration, genius, idealism. Whatever was unacceptable got left back under the rubric of Jewishness, or the "wrong kind" of Jews: uneducated, aggressive, loud. The message I got was that we were really superior: nobody else's father had collected so many books, had traveled so far, knew so many languages. Baltimore was a musical city, but for the most part, in the families of my school friends, culture was for women. My father was an amateur musician, read poetry, adored encyclopaedic knowledge. He prowled and pounced over my school papers, insisting I use "grown-up" sources; he criticized my poems for faulty technique and gave me books on rhyme and metre and form. His investment in my intellect and talent was egotistical, tyrannical, opinionated and terribly wearing. He taught me nevertheless to believe in hard work, to mistrust easy inspiration, to write and rewrite; to feel that I *was* a person of the book, even though a woman; to take ideas seriously. He made me feel, at a very young age, the power of language, and that I could share in it.

The Riches were proud, but we also had to be very careful. Our behavior had to be more impeccable than other people's. Strangers were not to be trusted, nor even friends; family issues must never go beyond the family; the world was full of potential slanderers, betrayers, *people who could not understand.* Even within the family, I realize that I never in my whole life knew what he was really feeling. Yet he spoke—monologued—with driving intensity. You could grow up in such a house mesmerized by the local electricity, the crucial meanings assumed by the merest things. This used to seem to me a sign that we were all living on some high emotional plane. It was a difficult force-field for a favored daughter to disengage from.

Easy to call that intensity Jewish; and I have no doubt that passion is one of the qualities required for survival over generations of persecution. But what happens when passion is rent from its original base, when the white gentile world is softly saying: "Be more like us and you can be almost one of us"? What happens when survival seems to mean closing off one emotional artery after another? His forebears in Europe had been forbidden to travel, or expelled from one country after another, had special taxes levied on them if they left the city walls, had been forced to wear special clothes and badges, restricted to the poorest neighborhoods. He had wanted to be a "free spirit," to travel widely among "all kinds of people." Yet in his prime of life he lived in an increasingly withdrawn world, in his house up on a hill in a neighborhood where Jews were not supposed to be able to buy property, depending almost exclusively on interactions with his wife and daughters to provide emotional connectedness. In his home, he created a private defense system so elaborate that even as he was dying my mother felt unable to talk freely with his colleagues, or others who might have helped her.

I imagine that the loneliness of the "only," the token, often doesn't feel like loneliness but like a kind of dead echo chamber. Certain things that ought to, don't resonate. Somewhere Beverly Smith writes of women of color "inspiring the behavior" in each other. When there's nobody to "inspire the behavior," act out of the culture, there is an atrophy, a dwindling, which is partly invisible.

I was married in 1953, in the Hillel House at Harvard, under a portrait of Albert Einstein. My parents refused to come. I was marrying a Jew, of the "wrong kind" from an Orthodox Eastern European background. Brooklyn-born, he had gone to Harvard, changed his name, was both indissolubly connected to his childhood world, and terribly ambivalent about it. My father saw this marriage as my having fallen prey to the Jewish family, Eastern European division.

Like many women I knew in the fifties, living under a then-unquestioned heterosexual imperative, I married in part because I knew no better way to disconnect from my first family. I married a "real Jew" who was himself almost equally divided between a troubled yet ingrained Jewish identity, and the pull toward Yankee approval, assimilation. But at least he was not adrift as a single token in a gentile world. We lived in a world where there was much intermarriage, where a certain "Jewish flavor" was accepted within the dominant gentile culture. People talked glibly of "Jewish self-hatred" but anti-Semitism was rarely identified. It was as if you could have it both ways, identity and assimilation, without having to think about it very much.

I was moved and gratefully amazed by the affection and kindliness my husband's parents showed me, the half-*shiksa*. I longed to embrace that family, that new and mysterious Jewish world. It was never a question of conversion—my husband had long since ceased being observant—but of a burning desire to do well, please these new parents, heal the split-consciousness in which I had been raised, and, of course, to belong. In the big sunny apartment on Eastern Parkway, the table would be spread on Saturday afternoons with a white or embroidered cloth and plates of coffee-cake, sponge-cake, *mohn*-cake, cookies, for a family gathering where everyone ate and drank—coffee, milk, cake—and later the talk eddied among the women still around the table or in the kitchen, while the men ended up in the living-room watching the ball-game. I had never known this kind of family, in which mock insults were cheerfully exchanged, secrets whispered in corners among two or three, children and grandchildren boasted about, and the new daughter-in-law openly inspected. I was profoundly attracted by all this, including the punctilious observance of *kashruth,* the symbolism lurking behind daily kitchen tasks. I saw it all as quintessentially and authentically Jewish, and thus I objectified both the people and the culture. My unexamined anti-Semitism allowed me to do this. But also, I had not yet recognized that as a woman I stood in a particular and equally unexamined relationship to the Jewish family and to Jewish culture.

There were several years during which I did not see, and barely communicated with my parents. At the same time, my father's personality haunted my life. Such had been the force of his will in our household that for a long time I felt I would have to pay in some terrible way for having disobeyed him. When finally we were reconciled, and my husband and I and our children began to have some minimal formal contact with my parents, the obsessional power of Arnold's voice or handwriting had given way to a dull sense of useless anger and pain. I wanted him to cherish and approve of me not as he had when I was a child, but as the woman I was, who had her own mind and had made her own choices. This, I finally realized, was not to be; Arnold demanded absolute loyalty, absolute submission to his will. In my separation from him, in my realization at what a price that once-intoxicating approval had been bought, I was learning in concrete ways a great deal about patriarchy, in particular how the "special" woman, the favored daughter, is controlled and rewarded.

Arnold Rich died in 1968 after a long deteriorating illness; his mind had gone and he had been losing his sight for years. It was a year of intensifying political awareness for me, the Martin Luther King and Robert Kennedy assassinations, the Columbia University strike. But it was not that these events and the meetings and demonstrations that surrounded them, pre-empted the time of mourning for my father; I had been mourning a long time for an early, primary, and intense relationship, by no means always benign, but in which I had been ceaselessly made to feel that what I did with my life, the choices I made, the attitudes I held, were of the utmost consequence.

Sometimes in my thirties, on visits to Brooklyn, I sat on Eastern Parkway, a baby-stroller at my feet: one of many rows of young Jewish women on benches with children in that neighborhood. I used to see the Lubavitcher Hassidim—then beginning to move into the Crown Heights neighborhood—walking out on shabbas, the women in their *sheitels* a little behind the men. My father-in-law pointed them out as rather exotic—too old-country, perhaps, too unassimilated even for his devout sense of Jewish identity. It took many years for me to understand—partly because I understood so little about class in America—how in my own family, and in the very different family of my in-laws, there were degrees and hierarchies of assimilation which looked askance upon each other—and also geographic lines of difference, as between Southern Jews and New York Jews, whose manners and customs varied along class as well as regional lines.

I had three sons before I was thirty, and during those years I often felt that to be a Jewish woman, a Jewish mother, was to be perceived in the Jewish family as an entirely physical being, a producer and nourisher of children. The experience of motherhood was eventually to radicalize me; but before that I was encountering the institution of motherhood most directly in a Jewish cultural version; and I felt rebellious, moody, defensive, unable to sort out what was Jewish from what was simply motherhood, or female destiny. (I lived in Cambridge, not Brooklyn, but there, too, restless, educated women sat on benches with baby-strollers, half-stunned, not by Jewish cultural expectations, but by the American cultural expectations of the 1950s).

My children were taken irregularly to Seders, to Bar Mitzvahs, and to special services in their grandfather's temple. Their father lit Hanukkah candles while I stood by, having relearned each year the English meaning of the Hebrew blessing. We all celebrated a secular, liberal Christmas. I read aloud from books about Esther and the Maccabees and Moses, and also from books about Norse goblins and Chinese grandmothers and Celtic dragon-slayers. Their father told stories of his boyhood in Brooklyn, his grandmother in the Bronx who had to be visited on the subway every week, of misdeeds in Hebrew school, of being a bright Jewish kid at Boys' High. In the permissive liberalism of academic Cambridge, you could raise your children to be vaguely or distinctly Jewish as you would, but Christian myth and calendar organized the year. My sons grew up knowing far more about the existence and concrete meaning of Jewish culture than I had. But I don't recall sitting down with them and telling them that millions of people like themselves, many of them children, had been rounded up and murdered in Europe in their parents' lifetime. Nor was I able to tell them that they came in part out of the rich, thousand-year-old, Ashkenazic culture of Eastern Europe, which the Holocaust destroyed; or that they came from a people whose secular tradition had included a hatred of oppression and a willingness to fight for justice—an anti-racist, a socialist, and even sometimes a feminist vision. I could not tell them these things because they were still too blurred in outline in my own mind.

The emergence of the Civil Rights movement in the sixties I remember as lifting me out of a sense of personal frustration and hopelessness. Reading James Baldwin's early essays, in the fifties, had stirred me with a sense that apparently "given" situations like racism could be analyzed and described and that this could lead to action, to change. Racism had been so utter and implicit a fact of my childhood and adolescence, had felt so central among the silences, negations, cruelties, fears, superstitions of my early life, that somewhere among my feelings must have been the hope that if Black people could become free, of the immense political and social burdens they were forced to bear, I too could become free, of all the ghosts and shadows of my childhood, named and unnamed. When "the Movement" began, it felt extremely personal to me. And it was often Jews who spoke up for the justice of the cause, Jewish civil rights lawyers who were traveling South; it was two young Jews who were found murdered with a young Black man in Mississippi. Schwerner, Goodman, Chaney.

Moving to New York in the mid-sixties meant almost immediately being plunged into the debate over community control of public schools, in which Black and Jewish teachers and parents were often on opposite sides of extremely militant barricades. It was easy as a white liberal to deplore and condemn the racism of middle-class Jewish parents or angry Jewish schoolteachers, many of them older women; to displace our own racism onto them; or to feel it as too painful to think about. The struggle for

Black civil rights had such clarity about it for me: I knew that segregation was wrong, that unequal opportunity was wrong, I knew that segregation in particular was more than a set of social and legal rules, it meant that even "decent" white people lived in a network of lies and arrogance and moral collusion. In the world of Jewish assimilationist and liberal politics which I knew best, however, things were far less clear to me, and anti-Semitism went almost unmentioned. It was even possible to view anti-Semitism as a reactionary agenda, a concern of *Commentary* magazine or, later, the Jewish Defense League. Most of the political work I was doing in the late 1960s was on racial issues, in particular as a teacher in the City University during the struggle for Open Admissions. The white colleagues I thought of as allies were, I think, mostly Jewish. Yet it was easy to see other New York Jews, who had climbed out of poverty and exploitation through the public school system and the free city colleges, as now trying to block Black and Puerto Rican students trying to do likewise. I didn't understand then that I was living between two strains of Jewish social identity: the Jew as radical visionary and activist who understands oppression firsthand; and the Jew as part of America's devouring plan in which the persecuted, called to assimilation, learn that the price is to engage in persecution.

And indeed, there *was* intense racism among Jews as well as white gentiles in the City University, part of the bitter history of Jews and Blacks which James Baldwin had described much earlier, in his 1948 essay on "The Harlem Ghetto";* part of the divide-and-conquer script still being rehearsed by those of us who have the least to gain from it.

By the time I left my marriage, after seventeen years and three children, I had become identified with the women's liberation movement. It was an astonishing time to be a woman of my age. In the 1950s, seeking a way to grasp the pain I seemed to be feeling most of the time, to set it in some larger context, I had read all kinds of things, but it was James Baldwin and Simone de Beauvoir who had described the world—though differently—in terms that made the most sense to me. By the end of the sixties there were two political movements, one already meeting severe repression, one just emerging—which addressed those descriptions of the world.

And there was, of course, a third movement, or a movement-within-a-movement—the early lesbian manifestos, the new visibility and activism of lesbians everywhere. I had known very early on that the women's movement was not going to be a simple walk across an open field; that it would pull on every fibre of my existence; that it would mean going back and

---

* *Notes of a Native Son.* Beacon Press, 1955.

searching the shadows of my consciousness. Reading *The Second Sex* in 1950s isolation as an academic housewife had felt less dangerous than reading "The Myth of Vaginal Orgasm" or "Woman-Identified Woman" in a world where I was in constant debate and discussion with women over every aspect of our lives that we could as yet name. De Beauvoir had placed "The Lesbian" on the margins, and there was little in her book to suggest the power of woman-bonding. But the passion of debating ideas with women was an erotic passion for me, and the risking of self with women that was necessary in order to win some truth out of the lies of the past was also erotic. The suppressed lesbian I had been carrying in me since adolescence began to stretch her limbs and her first full-fledged act was to fall in love with a Jewish woman.

Some time during the early months of that relationship, I dreamed that I was arguing feminist politics with my lover. *Of course,* I said to her in this dream, *if you're going to bring up the Holocaust against me, there's nothing I can do.* If, as I believe, I was both myself and her in this dream, it spoke of the split in my consciousness. I had been, more or less, a Jewish heterosexual woman; but what did it mean to be a Jewish lesbian? What did it mean to feel myself, as I did, both anti-Semite and Jew? And, as a feminist, how was I charting for myself the oppressions within oppression?

The earliest feminist papers on Jewish identity that I read were critiques of the patriarchal and misogynist elements in Judaism, or of the caricaturing of Jewish women in literature by Jewish men. I remember hearing Judith Plaskow give a paper called "Can a Woman Be a Jew?" (her conclusion was, "yes, but . . ."). I was soon after in correspondence with a former student who had emigrated to Israel, was a passionate feminist, and wrote me at length of the legal and social constraints on women there, the stirrings of contemporary Israeli feminism, and the contradictions she felt in her daily life. With the new politics, activism, literature of a tumultuous feminist movement around me, a movement which claimed universality though it had not yet acknowledged its own racial, class, and ethnic perspectives, or its fears of the differences among women—I pushed aside for one last time thinking further about myself as a Jewish woman. I saw Judaism, simply, as yet another strand of patriarchy; if asked to choose I might have said (as my father had said in other language): *I am a woman, not a Jew.* (But, I always added mentally, if Jews had to wear yellow stars again, I too would wear one. As if I would have the choice to wear it or not.)

Sometimes I feel I have seen too long from too many disconnected angles: white, Jewish, anti-Semite, racist, anti-racist, once-married, lesbian, middle-class, feminist, exmatriate Southerner, *split at the root:* that I will never bring them whole. I would have liked, in this essay, to bring together the meanings of anti-Semitism and racism as I have experienced them and as I believe they intersect in the world beyond my life. But I'm not able to do this yet. I feel the tension as I think, make notes: *if you really look at the one reality, the other will waver and disperse.* Trying in one week to read Angela Davis and Lucy Dawidowicz;* trying to hold throughout a feminist, a lesbian, perspective—what does this mean? Nothing has trained me for this. And sometimes I feel inadequate to make any statement as a Jew: I feel the history of denial within me like an injury, a scar—for assimilation has affected my perceptions, those early lapses in meaning, those blanks, are with me still. My ignorance can be dangerous to me, and to others.

Yet we can't wait for the undamaged to make our connections for us; we can't wait to speak until we are wholly clear and righteous. There is no purity, and, in our lifetimes, no end to this process.

This essay, then, has no conclusions: it is another beginning, for me. Not just a way of saying, in 1982 Right-wing America, *I too will wear the yellow star.* It's a moving into accountability, enlarging the range of accountability. I know that in the rest of my life, the next half-century or so, every aspect of my identity will have to be engaged. The middle-class white girl taught to trade obedience for privilege. The Jewish lesbian raised to be a heterosexual gentile. The woman who first heard oppression named and analyzed in the Black civil rights struggle. The woman with three sons, the feminist who hates male violence. The woman limping with a cane, the woman who has stopped bleeding, are also accountable. The poet who knows that beautiful language can lie, that the oppressor's language sometimes sounds beautiful. The woman trying, as part of her resistance, to clean up her act.

---

* Angela Y. Davis, *Women, Race and Class.* Random House, 1981; Lucy S. Dawidowicz, *The War Against the Jews* 1933–1945 (1975), Bantam Books, 1979.

Here's an odd one — he openly displays it.

EDWARD HOAGLAND

Edward Hoagland (1932–   ) is generally acknowledged to be one of the leading American essayists of the current era. He began writing essays in 1968 and has remained faithful to this barely remunerative form with a steadfastness matched by few of his generation. His essay collections include The Courage of Turtles, Walking the Dead Diamond River, Red Wolves and Black Bears, The Tugman's Passage, Heart's Desire, *and* Balancing Acts. *He has also written several novels, most notably* Seven Rivers West.

A disciple of Thoreau, Hoagland has written extensively on nature; his descriptions have the rapt, observant character and serene appreciation of a professional woodsman or navigator. He is also a great wanderer, willing to go anywhere and bring back a report, in travel writing of a superior order. A native New Yorker, he has what he calls a "city rat" side as well, and is one of the few ecologically minded nature writers who does not feel called upon to attack urban life while extolling the virtues of rural solitude.

Hoagland, like the classical personal essayists before him, utilizes the eccentricities and flaws in his character to bring an essay alive. In the two examples below, we see the Hoagland persona first in an amiable, caring vein ("The Courage of Turtles"), then in a more biting, confessional aspect ("The Threshold and the Jolt of Pain"). These essays also demonstrate the characteristic qualities of Hoagland's prose style: densely textured, imagistic sentences that reach a lyricism that one normally associates with the prose poem.

The Courage of Turtles

1ST line is a grabber

T URTLES ARE A KIND of bird with the governor turned low.
With the same attitude of removal, they cock a glance at what is
going on, as if they need only to fly away. Until recently they were also a
case of virtue rewarded, at least in the town where I grew up, because,
being humble creatures, there were plenty of them. Even when we still
had a few bobcats in the woods the local snapping turtles, growing up to
forty pounds, were the largest carnivores. You would see them through
the amber water, as big as greeny wash basins at the bottom of the pond,
until they faded into the inscrutable mud as if they hadn't existed at all.

When I was ten I went to Dr. Green's Pond, a two-acre pond across the
road. When I was twelve I walked a mile or so to Taggart's Pond, which
was lusher, had big water snakes and a waterfall; and shortly after that I
was bicycling way up to the adventuresome vastness of Mud Pond, a lake-
sized body of water in the reservoir system of a Connecticut city, possessed of cat-backed little islands and empty shacks and a forest of pines
and hardwoods along the shore. Otters, foxes, and mink left their prints
on the bank; there were pike and perch. As I got older, the estates and
forgotten back lots in town were parceled out and sold for nice prices, yet,
though the woods had shrunk, it seemed that fewer people walked in the
woods. The new residents didn't know how to find them. Eventually, exploring, they did find them, and it required some ingenuity and doubling
around on my part to go for eight miles without meeting someone. I was
grown by now, I lived in New York, and that's what I wanted to do on the
occasional weekends when I came out.

Since Mud Pond contained drinking water I had felt confident nothing
untoward would happen there. For a long while the developers stayed
away, until the drought of the mid-1960s. This event, squeezing the edges
in, convinced the local water company that the pond really wasn't a necessity as a catch basin, however; so they bulldozed a hole in the earthen
dam, bulldozed the banks to fill in the bottom, and landscaped the flow of
water that remained to wind like an English brook and provide a domestic
view for the houses which were planned. Most of the painted turtles of
Mud Pond, who had been inaccessible as they sunned on their rocks,
wound up in boxes in boys' closets within a matter of days. Their footsteps in the dry leaves gave them away as they wandered forlornly. The
snappers and the little musk turtles, neither of whom leave the water ex-

cept once a year to lay their eggs, dug into the drying mud for another siege of hot weather, which they were accustomed to doing whenever the pond got low. But this time it was low for good; the mud baked over them and slowly entombed them. As for the ducks, I couldn't stroll in the woods and not feel guilty, because they were crouched beside every stagnant pothole, or were slinking between the bushes with their heads tucked into their shoulders so that I wouldn't see them. If they decided I had, they beat their way up through the screen of trees, striking their wings dangerously, and wheeled about with that headlong, magnificent velocity to locate another poor puddle.

I used to catch possums and black snakes as well as turtles, and I kept dogs and goats. Some summers I worked in a menagerie with the big personalities of the animal kingdom, like elephants and rhinoceroses. I was twenty before these enthusiasms began to wane, and it was then that I picked turtles as the particular animal I wanted to keep in touch with. I was allergic to fur, for one thing, and turtles need minimal care and not much in the way of quarters. They're personable beasts. They see the same colors we do and they seem to see just as well, as one discovers in trying to sneak up on them. In the laboratory they unravel the twists of a maze with the hot-blooded rapidity of a mammal. Though they can't run as fast as a rat, they improve on their errors just as quickly, pausing at each crossroads to look left and right. And they rock rhythmically in place, as we often do, although they are hatched from eggs, not the womb. (A common explanation psychologists give for our pleasure in rocking quietly is that it recapitulates our mother's heartbeat *in utero.*)

Snakes, by contrast, are dryly silent and priapic. They are smooth movers, legalistic, unblinking, and they afford the humor which the humorless do. But they make challenging captives; sometimes they don't eat for months on a point of order—if the light isn't right, for instance. Alligators are sticklers too. They're like war-horses, or German shepherds, and with their bar-shaped, vertical pupils adding emphasis, they have the *idée fixe* of eating, eating, even when they choose to refuse all food and stubbornly die. They delight in tossing a salamander up towards the sky and grabbing him in their long mouths as he comes down. They're so eager that they get the jitters, and they're too much of a proposition for a casual aquarium like mine. Frogs are depressingly defenseless: that moist, extensive back, with the bones almost sticking through. Hold a frog and you're holding its skeleton. Frogs' tasty legs are the staff of life to many animals—herons, raccoons, ribbon snakes—though they themselves are hard to feed. It's not an enviable role to be the staff of life, and after frogs you descend down the evolutionary ladder a big step to fish.

* * *

Turtles cough, burp, whistle, grunt and hiss, and produce social judgments. They put their heads together amicably enough, but then one drives the other back with the suddenness of two dogs who have been conversing in tones too low for an onlooker to hear. They pee in fear when they're first caught, but exercise both pluck and optimism in trying to escape, walking for hundreds of yards within the confines of their pen, carrying the weight of that cumbersome box on legs which are cruelly positioned for walking. They don't feel that the contest is unfair; they keep plugging, rolling like sailorly souls—a bobbing, infirm gait, a brave, sea-legged momentum—stopping occasionally to study the lay of the land. For me, anyway, they manage to contain the rest of the animal world. They can stretch out their necks like a giraffe, or loom underwater like an apocryphal hippo. They browse on lettuce thrown on the water like a cow moose which is partly submerged. They have a penguin's alertness, combined with a build like a brontosaurus when they rise up on tiptoe. Then they hunch and ponderously lunge like a grizzly going forward.

Baby turtles in a turtle bowl are a puzzle in geometrics. They're as decorative as pansy petals, but they are also self-directed building blocks, propping themselves on one another in different arrangements, before upending the tower. The timid individuals turn fearless, or vice versa. If one gets a bit arrogant he will push the others off the rock and afterwards climb down into the water and cling to the back of one of those he has bullied, tickling him with his hind feet until he bucks like a bronco. On the other hand, when this same milder-mannered fellow isn't exerting himself, he will stare right into the face of the sun for hours. What could be more lionlike? And he's at home in or out of the water and does lots of metaphysical tilting. He sinks and rises, with an infinity of levels to choose from; or, elongating himself, he climbs out on the land again to perambulate, sits boxed in his box, and finally slides back in the water, submerging into dreams.

I have five of these babies in a kidney-shaped bowl. The hatchling, who is a painted turtle, is not as large as the top joint of my thumb. He eats chicken gladly. Other foods he will attempt to eat but not with sufficient perseverance to succeed because he's so little. The yellow-bellied terrapin is probably a yearling, and he eats salad voraciously, but no meat, fish, or fowl. The Cumberland terrapin won't touch salad or chicken but eats fish and all of the meats except for bacon. The little snapper, with a black crenellated shell, feasts on any kind of meat, but rejects greens and fish. The fifth of the turtles is African. I acquired him only recently and don't know him well. A mottled brown, he unnerves the greener turtles, dragging their food off to his lairs. He doesn't seem to want to be green—he bites the algae off his shell, hanging meanwhile at daring, steep, head-first angles.

The snapper was a Ferdinand until I provided him with deeper water. Now he snaps at my pencil with his downturned and fearsome mouth, his swollen face like a napalm victim's. The Cumberland has an elliptical red mark on the side of his green-and-yellow head. He is benign by nature and ought to be as elegant as his scientific name *(Pseudemys scripta elegans)*, except he has contracted a disease of the air bladder which has permanently inflated it; he floats high in the water at an undignified slant and can't go under. There may have been internal bleeding, too, because his carapace is stained along its ridge. Unfortunately, like flowers, baby turtles often die. Their mouths fill up with a white fungus and their lungs with pneumonia. Their organs clog up from the rust in the water, or diet troubles, and, like a dying man's, their eyes and heads become too prominent. Toward the end, the edge of the shell becomes flabby as felt and folds around them like a shroud.

While they live they're like puppies. Although they're vivacious, they would be a bore to be with all the time, so I also have an adult wood turtle about six inches long. Her top shell is the equal of any seashell for sculpturing, even a Cellini shell; it's like an old, dusty, richly engraved medallion dug out of a hillside. Her legs are salmon-orange bordered with black and protected by canted, heroic scales. Her plastron—the bottom shell— is splotched like a margay cat's coat, with black ocelli on a yellow background. It is convex to make room for the female organs inside, whereas a male's would be concave to help him fit tightly on top of her. Altogether, she exhibits every camouflage color on her limbs and shells. She has a turtleneck neck, a tail like an elephant's, wise old pachydermous hind legs, and the face of a turkey—except that when I carry her she gazes at the passing ground with a hawk's eyes and mouth. Her feet fit to the fingers of my hand, one to each one, and she rides looking down. She can walk on the floor in perfect silence, but usually she lets her plastron knock portentously, like a footstep, so that she resembles some grand, concise, slow-moving id. But if an earthworm is presented, she jerks swiftly ahead, poises above it, and strikes like a mongoose, consuming it with wild vigor. Yet she will climb on my lap to eat bread or boiled eggs.

If put into a creek, she swims like a cutter, nosing forward to intercept a strange turtle and smell him. She drifts with the current to go downstream, maneuvering behind a rock when she wants to take stock, or sinking to the nether levels, while bubbles float up. Getting out, choosing her path, she will proceed a distance and dig into a pile of humus, thrusting herself to the coolest layer at the bottom. The hole closes over her until it's as small as a mouse's hole. She's not as aquatic as a musk turtle, not quite as terrestrial as the box turtles in the same woods, but because of her versatility she's marvelous, she's everywhere. And though she breathes the way we breathe, with scarcely perceptible movements of her chest, sometimes instead she pumps her throat ruminatively, like a pipe smoker sucking and puffing. She waits and blinks, pumping her throat, turning her head, then sets off like a loping tiger in slow motion, hurdling the jungly lumber, the pea vine and twigs. She estimates angles so well that when she rides over the rocks, sliding down a drop-off with her rugged front legs extended, she has the grace of a rodeo mare.

But she's well off to be with me rather than at Mud Pond. The other turtles have fled—those that aren't baked into the bottom. Creeping up the brooks to sad, constricted marshes, burdened as they are with that box on their backs, they're walking into a setup where all their enemies move thirty times faster than they. It's like the nightmare most of us have whimpered through, where we are weighted down disastrously while trying to flee; fleeing our home ground, we try to run.

I've seen turtles in still worse straits. On Broadway, in New York, there is a penny arcade which used to sell baby terrapins that were scrawled with bon mots in enamel paint, such as KISS ME BABY. The manager turned out to be a wholesaler as well, and once I asked him whether he had any larger turtles to sell. He took me upstairs to a loft room devoted to the turtle business. There were desks for the paper work and a series of racks that held shallow tin bins atop one another, each with several hundred babies crawling around in it. He was a smudgy-complexioned, bespectacled, serious fellow and he did have a few adult terrapins, but I was going to school and wasn't actually planning to buy; I'd only wanted to see them. They were aquatic turtles, but here they went without water, presumably for weeks, lurching about in those dry bins like handicapped citizens, living on gumption. An easel where the artist worked stood in the middle of the floor. She had a palette and a clip attachment for fastening the babies in place. She wore a smock and a beret, and was homely, short, and eccentric-looking, with funny black hair, like some of the ladies who show their paintings in Washington Square in May. She had a cold, she was smoking, and her hand wasn't very steady, although she worked quickly enough. The smile that she produced for me would have looked giddy if she had been happier, or drunk. Of course the turtles' doom was sealed when she painted them, because their bodies inside would continue to grow but their shells would not. Gradually, invisibly, they would be crushed. Around us their bellies—two thousand belly shells—rubbed on the bins with a mournful, momentous hiss.

Somehow there were so many of them I didn't rescue one. Years later, however, I was walking on First Avenue when I noticed a basket of living turtles in front of a fish store. They were as dry as a heap of old bones in the sun; nevertheless, they were creeping over one another gimpily, doing their best to escape. I looked and was touched to discover that they appeared to be wood turtles, my favorites, so I bought one. In my apartment

I looked closer and realized that in fact this was <u>a diamondback terrapin</u>, which was bad news. Diamondbacks are tidewater turtles from brackish estuaries, and I had no seawater to keep him in. He spent his days thumping interminably against the baseboards, pushing for an opening through the wall. He drank thirstily but would not eat and had none of the hearty, accepting qualities of wood turtles. He was morose, paler in color, sleeker and more Oriental in the carved ridges and rings that formed his shell. Though I felt sorry for him, finally I found his unrelenting presence exasperating. I carried him, struggling in a paper bag, across town to the Morton Street Pier on the Hudson River. It was August but gray and windy. He was very surprised when I tossed him in; for the first time in our association, I think, he was afraid. He looked afraid as he bobbed about on top of the water, looking up at me from ten feet below. Though we were both accustomed to his resistance and rigidity, seeing him still pitiful, I recognized <u>that I must have done the wrong thing</u>. At least the river was salty, but it was also bottomless; the waves were too rough for him, and the tide was coming in, bumping him against the pilings underneath the pier. Too late, I realized that he wouldn't be able to swim to a peaceful inlet in New Jersey, even if he could figure out which way to swim. But since, short of diving in after him, there was nothing I could do, I walked away.

The Threshold and the Jolt of Pain

LIKE MOST BOYS in their teens, I wondered once in a while how I would take torture. Badly, I thought. Later I thought not so badly, as I saw myself under the pressures of danger or emergency, once when a lion cub grabbed my hand in its mouth and I wrestled its lips for half a minute with my free hand. Another summer when I fought forest fires in a crew of Indians in the West, we stood up under intense heat and thirst, watching the flames crackle toward us irresistibly while we waited to see whether the fire lines that we had cut were going to hold. I've climbed over the lip of a high waterfall; I've scratched inside a hippopotamus's capacious jaws; I faced a pistol one day in Wyoming with some

degree of fortitude. However, I knew that all this élan would vanish if my
sex organs were approached. The initiation to join the Boy Scouts in our
town was to have one's balls squeezed, so I never joined. Even to have my
knuckle joints ground together in a handshake contest reduces me to
quick surrender—something about bone on bone. I steered clear of the
BB-gun fights in my neighborhood, and I could be caught in a chase and
tied up easily by someone slower who yelled as if he were gaining ground,
so I made friends with most of the toughies as a defensive measure.

As a boy I was much given to keeping pets and showering care on them,
but I had a sadistic streak as well. In boarding school my roommate got
asthma attacks when he was jumped on, and I always backed away laughing when his tormentors poured into the room. There was another nice
boy whom I seldom picked on myself, and with sincere horror I watched a
game grip the Florentine fancy of our corridor. Divided in teams, we
would push him back and forth as a human football from goal to goal.
The crush at the center, where he was placed, was tremendous, and
though no one remembered, I'd invented the game.

My first love affair was with a Philadelphian, a woman of twenty-seven.
That is, she was the first woman I slept with. She was a love in the sense
that she loved me; I was close and grateful to her but didn't love her—I'd
loved one girl earlier whom I hadn't slept with. She lived in one of those
winsome houses that they have down there, with a tiled backyard and
three floors, one room to each floor. We wandered along the waterfront
and spent Saturdays at the street market, which is the largest and visually
the richest street market in the United States. I was not an ogre to her, but
I did by stages develop the habit of beating her briefly with my belt or
hairbrush before we made love, a practice which I have foregone ever
since. It may be indicative of the preoccupations of the 1950s that I worried less about this than about any tendencies I may have had toward
being homosexual; but the experience gives me a contempt for pornogra-
phy of that arch gruesome genre, quite in vogue nowadays as psychological "exploration," where whipping occurs but the flesh recovers its sheen
overnight and the whippee doesn't perhaps hang her(him)self, propelling
the whipper into the nervous breakdown which he is heading for.

Seeing eventual disaster ahead, I didn't go deeply into this vein of sensation, just as I was shrewd enough as a boy not to be picked on often or
to suffer more than a few accidents. Once I ran my hand through an apple
crusher on a relative's farm, and once I imitated a child's stutter at summer camp, thereby—or so I imagined (remembering what was supposed
to happen to you if you crossed your eyes)—picking up the malady at the
age of six. Almost my only pangs, then, were this stutter, which still remains in my mouth. It may strike other people as more than a spasm, but
to me it's a spasm of pain of a kind which I haven't time for, or time to

regard as anything else. It's like someone who has a lesion or twist in his small intestine, which hurts him abruptly and of which he is hardly aware otherwise. The well-grooved wince I make in shaking the words out seems to keep my face pliant and reasonably young.

Somerset Maugham described his bitter discovery when he was a boy that prayer was no help: he woke up next morning still clamped to his adamant stutter. I was more of a pantheist; I kept trusting to the efficacy of sleep itself, or to the lilting lift that caused birds to fly. Also I went to a bunch of speech therapists. At the Ethical Culture School in New York, for example, a woman taught me to stick my right hand in my pocket and, with that hidden hand, to write down over and over the first letter of the word I was stuttering on. This was intended to distract me from stuttering, and it did for a week or two. The trouble was that watching me play pocket pool that way was more unsettling to other people than the ailment it was meant to cure. At a camp in northern Michigan I was trained by a team from the university to speak so slowly that in effect I wasn't speaking at all; I talked with the gradualism of a flower growing—so absurdly tardy a process that my mind unhinged itself from what was going on. In Cambridge, Massachusetts, a young fellow from the University of Iowa—and oh, how *he* stuttered—took the most direct approach. He got me to deliberately imitate myself, which was hard on me since I was already terribly tired of stuttering, and to stare, as well, at the people whom I was talking to in order to find out what their reactions were. I found out, for one thing, that some of my friends and about a fifth of the strangers I met smiled when the difficulty occurred, though they generally turned their heads to the side or wiped their mouths with one hand to hide the smile. Thereafter, life seemed simpler if I avoided looking at anybody, whoever he was, when I was stuttering badly, and I wasn't so edgily on the alert to see if I'd spit inadvertently.

Not that I lacked understanding for the smilers, though, because for many years I too had had the strange impulse, hardly controllable, to smile if somebody bumped his head on a low door lintel or received sad news. The phenomenologists say this is a form of defense. It goes with childhood especially, and I stopped indulging in it one night in Boston when I was in a police patrol wagon. A friend and I had been out for a walk, he was hit by a car, and as he woke from unconsciousness during the ride to the hospital and asked what had happened, I found myself grinning down at him while I answered. A few weeks later I was walking past an apartment building just as a rescue squad carried out a would-be suicide. He was alive, on a stretcher. When our eyes touched he smiled impenetrably, but I didn't smile back.

As a stutterer, I learned not to write notes. You put yourself at someone's mercy more when you write him a note than if you just stand there like a rhinoceros and snort. I could write a *Stutterer's Guide to Europe,* too: the titters in old Vienna, the knowing English remembering their King, the raw scorching baitings I met with in Greece, surrounded sometimes like a muzzled bear. The fourth means of effecting a cure I heard about was based on the fact that stutterers are able to sing without stuttering; hence, the victim should swing one of his arms like a big pendulum and talk in time to this—which again was a worse fate than the impediment. Though I didn't try it, I was sent to a lady voice teacher who laid my hand on her conspicuous chest so that I could "feel her breathe." For just that moment the lessons worked wonderfully; if I wasn't speechless I spoke in a rush.

Stammering (a less obtrusive word I used to prefer) apparently is not unattractive to women. It's a masculine encumbrance; five times as many men as women suffer from it. I was seldom alone while I was in Europe, and once or twice girls told me by way of a pick-me-up that they'd loved someone "for" his stutter. When I went into my seizures at parties, if a woman didn't step back she stepped forward, whereas the men did neither. The female instinct does not apply nearly so favorably to other afflictions. In our glib age the stutterer has even been considered a kind of contemporary hero, a presumed honest man who is unable to gab with the media people. Beyond the particular appeal of this image, it does seem to suit a writer. Publishers are fastidious types and some whom I've met have sidled away in distress from my flabbering face as soon as they could, but they probably remembered my name if they caught it. The purity image or Billy Budd stuff didn't intrigue them, just the hint of compulsion and complexity. Though I don't greatly go for either picture, in social terms I've thought of my stutter as a sort of miasma behind the Ivy League–looking exterior. People at parties take me for William Buckley until I begin, so I keep my mouth shut and smile prepossessingly as long as I can.

Being in these vocal handcuffs made me a desperate, devoted writer at twenty. I worked like a dog, choosing each word. I wrote two full-length novels in iambic meter and a firehose style. Three hundred review copies of the second of these were sent out, but I received, I think, only three reviews. This was new pain, a man's career pain, with its attendant stomach trouble and neck and back cramps. A couple of years after that I got divorced from my first wife, and bawled like a half-butchered bull for an hour, rolled up on the floor of my apartment, while the two homosexuals next door listened in silence close to the wall, wondering what they ought to do. It was a purge, but the pain of that experience I remember best was an earlier scene. I'd announced to my wife, whom I loved and still love, my belief that we needed to separate. The next time we talked she crossed the room to my chair, knelt down beside me, and asked what was going to become of each of us. That is the most painful splinter in my life, the most painful piece of the past. With variations the ache was prolonged through many fugitive suppers. In fact we still meet, holding hands and laughing at each other's jokes until we feel tears.

Who knows which qualities are godly? Pain probably makes us a bit godly, though, as tender love does. It makes us rue and summarize; it makes us bend and yield up ourselves. Pain is a watchdog medically, telling us when to consult a doctor, and then it's the true-blue dog at the bedside who rivals the relatives for fidelity. Last summer my father died of cancer. We had made peace, pretty much, a few years before. Although he had opposed my desire to be a writer, he ended up trying to write a book too, and he turned over to me at the last an old family history which he'd been hiding, partly because it mentioned a lot of muteness among my ancestors and partly in order to prevent my exploiting the stories. My voice and my liberal opinions grew a little more clarion in the household during the months he was dying. From a selfish standpoint, I suppose I was almost ready for him to die, but I was very earnestly sorry for every stage of rough handling involved in the process and for his own overriding regret that his life was cut off. Having lost our frank fear of death along with our faith in an afterlife, we have all adopted our fear of pain as a feeble alternative. Our regret, too, is magnified. When he was in discomfort I stuttered a great deal, but when he was not, when he was simply reminiscing or watching TV, I stuttered scarcely a bit. Then, as he was actually dying, during our last interview, he turned on the bed and asked me something. My answer was blocked in my mouth and his face went rigid with more pain than mine. He was startled because in the exigencies of dying he had forgotten that my infirmity was still there unhealed. He straightened, shutting his eyes, not wanting to end his life seeing it. Nevertheless, he'd often told me that it was my problems he loved me for rather than for my successes and sleekness. He loved my sister for being waiflike and my mother for being on occasion afraid she was mentally ill.

We were quite hardy while the months passed. Mother and he lay side by side on the bed clasping hands. Because of the pills, until nearly the end he was not suffering pain of the magnitude he had dreaded. The last couple of days there was a tossing, pitching, horrific pain, but the body more than the mind was responding—the body attempting to swallow its tongue. What I remember, therefore, of death's salutation to my father was that it came as a tickler, making his withered body twitch, touching him here and touching him there, wasting his tissues away like white wax, while his head on the headrest above looked down and watched; or he'd shoot an acute glance at me from out of the hunching amalgam of pricks, jactitation, and drug-induced torpor. Death tickled him in a gradual crescendo, taking its time, and, with his ironic attorney's mind, he was amused. His two satisfactions were that he was privy to its most intimate preparations, everything just-so and fussy, and that at last the long spiky battling within the family was over and done. The new summer blossomed. In mid-June I saw what is meant by "a widow's tears." They flow in a flood of tremulous vulnerability, so that one thinks they will never stop.

Most severe on the physiologists' scale of pain is that of childbirth. It's also the worst that I've seen. A year had gone by since I'd left the army and quit visiting my Philadelphia friend. She came to New York, looked me up, discovered me vomiting, thin as a rail because of woman trouble, and moved in with me on the Upper West Side, spooning in food and mothering me. Then, at about the time I perked up, she told me that she had got pregnant by a chap back in Philadelphia.

We drew out our savings and started for San Francisco, that vainglorious, clam-colored city. In her yellow convertible, with my English setter and her cocker spaniel, we drove through the South and through Texas, taking Highway 80 because it was the autumn and cold. I remember that whenever we stopped by the side of the road in Mississippi to let the dogs pee, and I shouted if one of them dawdled, any black woman or man who happened to be close by would turn to see what I wanted, quite naturally, as if I had called. It was a grueling trip. I'd begun vomiting again after my friend told me she was pregnant, and she was suffering mysterious pains in that region between her legs, which no druggist would touch. But we reached Russian Hill and established ourselves in one of the local apartment hotels. For a while during the seven-month wait this living arrangement didn't work out and she moved to a Florence Crittenton Home and I went to the beach, but we ended the period together. At six one morning I drove her up to a whelk-pink hospital on a breezy hill and sat in the labor room for eight hours, watching the blue grid of stretch marks on her anguished stomach: awful pain. She jolted and screamed, sucking gas from a cup, squeezing my hand and falling asleep between the throes. It took me three days to stop shaking, though it was a normal delivery throughout, and she, by the mental safety catch which women have, had blocked off most of the memory by the time she was wheeled to her room asleep. I'm ashamed to say that I'd spanked her a little the night before, not realizing it was the night before: I never spanked her again.

The contract she'd signed obliged my friend to relinquish the baby girl to the Home for three weeks, after which she could appropriate her completely as her own. I was privileged to keep her breasts flowing during those weeks, a luxury that would have been fitting for Zeus; and, to the astonishment of the Home, as soon as the interval expired we showed up for the child. This was so rare that they wondered whether we were kidnappers. Then we drove East. The baby acquired a stepfather before she was out of her infancy and is now about ten.

So, pain is a packet of chiseling tools. Women in labor make no bones about protesting its severity. Neither does a dying man once he has stopped lingering with the living—thinking of the memories of his behavior which he is leaving his children, for instance. It's when we have no imperative purpose in front of our sufferings that we think about "bearing up"; "bearing up" is converted to serve as a purpose. Pain, love, boredom, and glee, and anticipation or anxiety—these are the pilings we build our lives from. In love we beget more love and in pain we beget more pain. Since we must like it or lump it, we like it. And why not, indeed?

WENDELL BERRY

Wendell Berry (1934–   ) was born in Kentucky and is inextricably associated with that landscape. After living in New York and California for several years, he returned to his native soil, not only to write but to farm. He wrote about the decision: "That summer I began to see, however dimly, that one of my ambitions, perhaps my governing ambition, was to belong fully to this place, to belong as the thrushes and the herons and the muskrats belonged, to be altogether at home here. That is still my ambition. But now I have come to see that it proposes an enormous labor. It is a spiritual ambition, like goodness. The wild creatures belong to the place by nature, but as a man I can belong to it only by understanding and by virtue. It is an ambition I cannot hope to succeed in wholly, but I have come to believe that it is the most worthy of all." This passage conveys some of Berry's upright, puritanical sternness as well as the biblical poetry, syntactical suppleness, and rhetorical resources of his language. He rarely shows humor, or even irony; but then, saints are rarely funny, and Wendell Berry, in his lifelong efforts to protect the earth's ecological balance, is something of a saint; certainly his fellow nature writers regard him as such.

Berry's farming experience has given him the insights to write knowledgeably and technically about agriculture and animal husbandry. His many essay collections, including The Long-Legged House, A Continuous Harmony, The Unsettling of America, Recollected Essays *(a selection),* Gift of Good Land, Standing by Words, *and* Home Economics, *amply demonstrate his dedication to the essay form, although he has also written novels and poetry. The piece below, "An Entrance to the Woods," highlights his extraordinary sensitivity in feeling out a threshold, a transition into nature. (As such, it bears comparison with Barthes' "Leaving the Movie Theater," which is also about the phenomenology of transitions.)*

An Entrance to the Woods

O N   A   F I N E   S U N N Y   A F T E R N O O N at the end of September I leave my work in Lexington and drive east on I-64 and the Mountain Parkway. When I leave the Parkway at the little town of Pine Ridge I am in the watershed of the Red River in the Daniel Boone National Forest. From Pine Ridge I take Highway 715 out along the narrow ridgetops, a winding tunnel through the trees. And then I turn off on a Forest Service Road and follow it to the head of a foot trail that goes down the steep valley wall of one of the tributary creeks. I pull my car off the road and lock it, and lift on my pack.

It is nearly five o'clock when I start walking. The afternoon is brilliant and warm, absolutely still, not enough air stirring to move a leaf. There is only the steady somnolent trilling of insects, and now and again in the woods below me the cry of a pileated woodpecker. Those, and my footsteps on the path, are the only sounds.

From the dry oak woods of the ridge I pass down into the rock. The foot trails of the Red River Gorge all seek these stony notches that little streams have cut back through the cliffs. I pass a ledge overhanging a sheer drop of the rock, where in a wetter time there would be a waterfall. The ledge is dry and mute now, but on the face of the rock below are the characteristic mosses, ferns, liverwort, meadow rue. And here where the ravine suddenly steepens and narrows, where the shadows are long-lived and the dampness stays, the trees are different. Here are beech and hemlock and poplar, straight and tall, reaching way up into the light. Under them are evergreen thickets of rhododendron. And wherever the dampness is there are mosses and ferns. The faces of the rock are intricately scalloped with veins of ironstone, scooped and carved by the wind.

Finally from the crease of the ravine I am following there begins to come the trickling and splashing of water. There is a great restfulness in the sounds these small streams make; they are going down as fast as they can, but their sounds seem leisurely and idle, as if produced like gemstones with the greatest patience and care.

A little later, stopping, I hear not far away the more voluble flowing of the creek. I go on down to where the trail crosses and begin to look for a camping place. The little bottoms along the creek here are thickety and weedy, probably having been kept clear and cropped or pastured not so long ago. In the more open places are little lavender asters, and the even smaller-flowered white ones that some people call beeweed or farewell-summer. And in low wet places are the richly flowered spikes of great lobelia, the blooms an intense startling blue, exquisitely shaped. I choose a place in an open thicket near the stream, and make camp.

It is a simple matter to make camp. I string up a shelter and put my air mattress and sleeping bag in it, and I am ready for the night. And supper is even simpler, for I have brought sandwiches for this first meal. In less than an hour all my chores are done. It will still be light for a good while, and I go over and sit down on a rock at the edge of the stream.

And then a heavy feeling of melancholy and lonesomeness comes over me. This does not surprise me, for I have felt it before when I have been alone at evening in wilderness places that I am not familiar with. But here it has a quality that I recognize as peculiar to the narrow hollows of the Red River Gorge. These are deeply shaded by the trees and by the valley walls, the sun rising on them late and setting early; they are more dark than light. And there will often be little rapids in the stream that will sound, at a certain distance, exactly like people talking. As I sit on my rock by the stream now, I could swear that there is a party of campers coming up the trail toward me, and for several minutes I stay alert, listening for them, their voices seeming to rise and fall, fade out and lift again, in happy conversation. When I finally realize that it is only a sound the creek is making, though I have not come here for company and do not want any, I am inexplicably sad.

These are haunted places, or at least it is easy to feel haunted in them, alone at nightfall. As the air darkens and the cool of the night rises, one feels the immanence of the wraiths of the ancient tribesmen who used to inhabit the rock houses of the cliffs; of the white hunters from east of the mountains; of the farmers who accepted the isolation of these nearly inaccessible valleys to crop the narrow bottoms and ridges and pasture their cattle and hogs in the woods; of the seekers of quick wealth in timber and ore. For though this is a wilderness place, it bears its part of the burden of human history. If one spends much time here and feels much liking for the place, it is hard to escape the sense of one's predecessors. If one has read of the prehistoric Indians whose flint arrowpoints and pottery and hominy holes and petroglyphs have been found here, then every rock shelter and clifty spring will suggest the presence of those dim people who have disappeared into the earth. Walking along the ridges and the stream bottoms, one will come upon the heaped stones of a chimney, or the slowly filling depression of an old cellar, or will find in the spring a japonica bush or periwinkles or a few jonquils blooming in a thicket that used to be a dooryard. Wherever the land is level enough there are abandoned

fields and pastures. And nearly always there is the evidence that one follows in the steps of the loggers.

That sense of the past is probably one reason for the melancholy that I
feel. But I know that there are other reasons.

One is that, though I am here in body, my mind and my nerves too are
not yet altogether here. We seem to grant to our high-speed roads and our
airlines the rather thoughtless assumption that people can change places as
rapidly as their bodies can be transported. That, as my own experience
keeps proving to me, is not true. In the middle of the afternoon I left off
being busy at work, and drove through traffic to the freeway, and then for
a solid hour or more I drove sixty or seventy miles an hour, hardly aware
of the country I was passing through, because on the freeway one does not
have to be. The landscape has been subdued so that one may drive over it
at seventy miles per hour without any concession whatsoever to one's
whereabouts. One might as well be flying. Though one is in Kentucky one
is not experiencing Kentucky; one is experiencing the highway, which
might be in nearly any hill country east of the Mississippi.

Once off the freeway, my pace gradually slowed, as the roads became
progressively more primitive, from seventy miles an hour to a walk. And
now, here at my camping place, I have stopped altogether. But my mind is
still keyed to seventy miles an hour. And having come here so fast, it is
still busy with the work I am usually doing. Having come here by the
freeway, my mind is not so fully here as it would have been if I had come
by the crookeder, slower state roads; it is incalculably farther away than it
would have been if I had come all the way on foot, as my earliest predecessors came. When the Indians and the first white hunters entered this
country they were altogether here as soon as they arrived, for they had
seen and experienced fully everything between here and their starting
place, and so the transition was gradual and articulate in their consciousness. Our senses, after all, were developed to function at foot speeds; and
the transition from foot travel to motor travel, in terms of evolutionary
time, has been abrupt. The faster one goes, the more strain there is on the
senses, the more they fail to take in, the more confusion they must tolerate
or gloss over—and the longer it takes to bring the mind to a stop in the
presence of anything. Though the freeway passes through the very heart of
this forest, the motorist remains several hours' journey by foot from what
is living at the edge of the right-of-way.

But I have not only come to this strangely haunted place in a short time
and too fast. I have in that move made an enormous change: I have departed from my life as I am used to living it, and have come into the
wilderness. It is not fear that I feel; I have learned to fear the everyday
events of human history much more than I fear the everyday occurrences

of the woods; in general, I would rather trust myself to the woods than to any government that I know of. I feel, instead, an uneasy awareness of severed connections, of being cut off from all familiar places and of being a stranger where I am. What is happening at home? I wonder, and I know I can't find out very easily or very soon.

Even more discomforting is a pervasive sense of unfamiliarity. In the places I am most familiar with—my house, or my garden, or even the woods near home that I have walked in for years—I am surrounded by associations; everywhere I look I am reminded of my history and my hopes; even unconsciously I am comforted by any number of proofs that my life on the earth is an established and a going thing. But I am in this hollow for the first time in my life. I see nothing that I recognize. Everything looks as it did before I came, as it will when I am gone. When I look over at my little camp I see how tentative and insignificant it is. Lying there in my bed in the dark tonight, I will be absorbed in the being of this place, invisible as a squirrel in his nest.

Uneasy as this feeling is, I know it will pass. Its passing will produce a deep pleasure in being here. And I have felt it often enough before that I have begun to understand something of what it means:

Nobody knows where I am. I don't know what is happening to anybody else in the world. While I am here I will not speak, and will have no reason or need for speech. It is only beyond this lonesomeness for the places I have come from that I can reach the vital reality of a place such as this. Turning toward this place, I confront a presence that none of my schooling and none of my usual assumptions have prepared me for: the wilderness, mostly unknowable and mostly alien, that is the universe. Perhaps the most difficult labor for my species is to accept its limits, its weakness and ignorance. But here I am. This wild place where I have camped lies within an enormous cone widening from the center of the earth out across the universe, nearly all of it a mysterious wilderness in which the power and the knowledge of men count for nothing. As long as its instruments are correct and its engines run, the airplane now flying through this great cone is safely within the human freehold; its behavior is as familiar and predictable to those concerned as the inside of a man's living room. But let its instruments or its engines fail, and at once it enters the wilderness where nothing is foreseeable. And these steep narrow hollows, these cliffs and forested ridges that lie below, are the antithesis of flight.

Wilderness is the element in which we live encased in civilization, as a mollusk lives in his shell in the sea. It is a wilderness that is beautiful, dangerous, abundant, oblivious of us, mysterious, never to be conquered or controlled or second-guessed, or known more than a little. It is a wilderness that for most of us most of the time is kept out of sight, camouflaged, by the edifices and the busyness and the bothers of human society.

And so, coming here, what I have done is strip away the human facade that usually stands between me and the universe, and I see more clearly where I am. What I am able to ignore much of the time, but find undeniable here, is that all wildernesses are one: there is a profound joining between this wild stream deep in one of the folds of my native country and the tropical jungles, the tundras of the north, the oceans and the deserts. Alone here, among the rocks and the trees, I see that I am alone also among the stars. A stranger here, unfamiliar with my surroundings, I am aware also that I know only in the most relative terms my whereabouts within the black reaches of the universe. And because the natural processes are here so little qualified by anything human, this fragment of the wilderness is also joined to other times; there flows over it a nonhuman time to be told by the growth and death of the forest and the wearing of the stream. I feel drawing out beyond my comprehension perspectives from which the growth and the death of a large poplar would seem as continuous and sudden as the raising and the lowering of a man's hand, from which men's history in the world, their brief clearing of the ground, will seem no more than the opening and shutting of an eye.

And so I have come here to enact—not because I want to but because, once here, I cannot help it—the loneliness and the humbleness of my kind. I must see in my flimsy shelter, pitched here for two nights, the transience of capitols and cathedrals. In growing used to being in this place, I will have to accept a humbler and a truer view of myself than I usually have.

A man enters and leaves the world naked. And it is only naked—or nearly so—that he can enter and leave the wilderness. If he walks, that is; and if he doesn't walk it can hardly be said that he has entered. He can bring only what he can carry—the little that it takes to replace for a few hours or a few days an animal's fur and teeth and claws and functioning instincts. In comparison to the usual traveler with his dependence on machines and highways and restaurants and motels—on the economy and the government, in short—the man who walks into the wilderness is naked indeed. He leaves behind his work, his household, his duties, his comforts —even, if he comes alone, his words. He immerses himself in what he is not. It is a kind of death.

The dawn comes slow and cold. Only occasionally, somewhere along the creek or on the slopes above, a bird sings. I have not slept well, and I waken without much interest in the day. I set the camp to rights, and fix breakfast, and eat. The day is clear, and high up on the points and ridges to the west of my camp I can see the sun shining on the woods. And suddenly I am full of an ambition: I want to get up where the sun is; I want to sit still in the sun up there among the high rocks until I can feel its warmth in my bones.

I put some lunch into a little canvas bag, and start out, leaving my jacket so as not to have to carry it after the day gets warm. Without my jacket, even climbing, it is cold in the shadow of the hollow, and I have a long way to go to get to the sun. I climb the steep path up the valley wall, walking rapidly, thinking only of the sunlight above me. It is as though I have entered into a deep sympathy with those tulip poplars that grow so straight and tall out of the shady ravines, not growing a branch worth the name until their heads are in the sun. I am so concentrated on the sun that when some grouse flush from the undergrowth ahead of me, I am thunderstruck; they are already planing down into the underbrush again before I can get my wits together and realize what they are.

The path zigzags up the last steepness of the bluff and then slowly levels out. For some distance it follows the backbone of a ridge, and then where the ridge is narrowest there is a great slab of bare rock lying full in the sun. This is what I have been looking for. I walk out into the center of the rock and sit, the clear warm light falling unobstructed all around. As the sun warms me I begin to grow comfortable not only in my clothes, but in the place and the day. And like those light-seeking poplars of the ravines, my mind begins to branch out.

Southward, I can hear the traffic on the Mountain Parkway, a steady continuous roar—the corporate voice of twentieth-century humanity, sustained above the transient voices of its members. Last night, except for an occasional airplane passing over, I camped out of reach of the sounds of engines. For long stretches of time I heard no sounds but the sounds of the woods.

Near where I am sitting there is an inscription cut into the rock:

A · J · SARGENT
fEB · 24 · 1903

Those letters were carved there more than sixty-six years ago. As I look around me I realize that I can see no evidence of the lapse of so much time. In every direction I can see only narrow ridges and narrow deep hollows, all covered with trees. For all that can be told from this height by looking, it might still be 1903—or, for that matter, 1803 or 1703, or 1003. Indians no doubt sat here and looked over the country as I am doing now; the visual impression is so pure and strong that I can almost imagine myself one of them. But the insistent, the overwhelming, evidence of the time of my own arrival is in what I can hear—that roar of the highway off there in the distance. In 1903 the continent was still covered by a great ocean of silence, in which the sounds of machinery were scattered at wide intervals of time and space. Here, in 1903, there were only the natural sounds of the place. On a day like this, at the end of September, there would have been only the sounds of a few faint crickets, a woodpecker now and then, now and then the wind. But today, two-thirds of a century later, the continent is covered by an ocean of engine noise, in which silences occur only sporadically and at wide intervals.

From where I am sitting in the midst of this island of wilderness, it is as though I am listening to the machine of human history—a huge flywheel building speed until finally the force of its whirling will break it in pieces, and the world with it. That is not an attractive thought, and yet I find it impossible to escape, for it has seemed to me for years now that the doings of men no longer occur within nature, but that the natural places which the human economy has so far spared now survive almost accidentally within the doings of men. This wilderness of the Red River now carries on its ancient processes *within* the human climate of war and waste and confusion. And I know that the distant roar of engines, though it may *seem* only to be passing through this wilderness, is really bearing down upon it. The machine is running now with a speed that produces blindness—as to the driver of a speeding automobile the only thing stable, the only thing not a mere blur on the edge of the retina, is the automobile itself—and the blindness of a thing with power promises the destruction of what cannot be seen. That roar of the highway is the voice of the American economy; it is sounding also wherever strip mines are being cut in the steep slopes of Appalachia, and wherever cropland is being destroyed to make roads and suburbs, and wherever rivers and marshes and bays and forests are being destroyed for the sake of industry or commerce.

No. Even here where the economy of life is really an economy—where the creation is yet fully alive and continuous and self-enriching, where whatever dies enters directly into the life of the living—even here one cannot fully escape the sense of an impending human catastrophe. One cannot come here without the awareness that this is an island surrounded by the machinery and the workings of an insane greed, hungering for the world's end—that ours is a "civilization" of which the work of no builder or artist is symbol, nor the life of any good man, but rather the bulldozer, the poison spray, the hugging fire of napalm, the cloud of Hiroshima.

Though from the high vantage point of this stony ridge I see little hope that I will ever live a day as an optimist, still I am not desperate. In fact, with the sun warming me now, and with the whole day before me to wander in this beautiful country, I am happy. A man cannot despair if he can imagine a better life, and if he can enact something of its possibility. It is only when I am ensnarled in the meaningless ordeals and the ordeals of meaninglessness, of which our public and political life is now so productive, that I lose the awareness of something better, and feel the despair of having come to the dead end of possibility.

Today, as always when I am afoot in the woods, I feel the possibility, the reasonableness, the practicability of living in the world in a way that would enlarge rather than diminish the hope of life. I feel the possibility of a frugal and protective love for the creation that would be unimaginably more meaningful and joyful than our present destructive and wasteful economy. The absence of human society, that made me so uneasy last night, now begins to be a comfort to me. I am afoot in the woods. I am alive in the world, this moment, without the help or the interference of any machine. I can move without reference to anything except the lay of the land and the capabilities of my own body. The necessities of foot travel in this steep country have stripped away all superfluities. I simply could not enter into this place and assume its quiet with all the belongings of a family man, property holder, etc. For the time, I am reduced to my irreducible self. I feel the lightness of body that a man must feel who has just lost fifty pounds of fat. As I leave the bare expanse of the rock and go in under the trees again, I am aware that I move in the landscape as one of its details.

Walking through the woods, you can never see far, either ahead or behind, so you move without much of a sense of getting anywhere or of moving at any certain speed. You burrow through the foliage in the air much as a mole burrows through the roots in the ground. The views that open out occasionally from the ridges afford a relief, a recovery of orientation, that they could never give as mere "scenery," looked at from a turnout at the edge of a highway.

The trail leaves the ridge and goes down a ravine into the valley of a creek where the night chill has stayed. I pause only long enough to drink the cold clean water. The trail climbs up onto the next ridge.

It is the ebb of the year. Though the slopes have not yet taken on the bright colors of the autumn maples and oaks, some of the duller trees are already shedding. The foliage has begun to flow down the cliff faces and the slopes like a tide pulling back. The woods is mostly quiet, subdued, as if the pressure of survival has grown heavy upon it, as if above the growing warmth of the day the cold of winter can be felt waiting to descend.

At my approach a big hawk flies off the low branch of an oak and out over the treetops. Now and again a nuthatch hoots, off somewhere in the woods. Twice I stop and watch an ovenbird. A few feet ahead of me there is a sudden movement in the leaves, and then quiet. When I slip up and examine the spot there is nothing to be found. Whatever passed there has disappeared, quicker than the hand that is quicker than the eye, a shadow fallen into a shadow.

In the afternoon I leave the trail. My walk so far has come perhaps three-quarters of the way around a long zigzagging loop that will eventually bring me back to my starting place. I turn down a small unnamed branch of the creek where I am camped, and I begin the loveliest part of the day. There is nothing here resembling a trail. The best way is nearly always to follow the edge of the stream, stepping from one stone to another. Crossing back and forth over the water, stepping on or over rocks and logs, the way ahead is never clear for more than a few feet. The stream accompanies me down, threading its way under boulders and logs and over little falls and rapids. The rhododendron overhangs it so closely in places that I can go only by stooping. Over the rhododendron are the great dark heads of the hemlocks. The streambanks are ferny and mossy. And through this green tunnel the voice of the stream changes from rock to rock; subdued like all the other autumn voices of the woods, it seems sunk in a deep contented meditation on the sounds of *l.*

The water in the pools is absolutely clear. If it weren't for the shadows and ripples you would hardly notice that it is water; the fish would seem to swim in the air. As it is, where there is no leaf floating, it is impossible to tell exactly where the plane of the surface lies. As I walk up on a pool the little fish dart every which way out of sight. And then after I sit still a while, watching, they come out again. Their shadows flow over the rocks and leaves on the bottom. Now I have come into the heart of the woods. I am far from the highway and can hear no sound of it. All around there is a grand deep autumn quiet, in which a few insects dream their summer songs. Suddenly a wren sings way off in the underbrush. A redbreasted nuthatch walks, hooting, headfirst down the trunk of a walnut. An ovenbird walks out along the limb of a hemlock and looks at me, curious. The little fish soar in the pool, turning their clean quick angles, their shadows seeming barely to keep up. As I lean and dip my cup in the water, they scatter. I drink, and go on.

When I get back to camp it is only the middle of the afternoon or a little after. Since I left in the morning I have walked something like eight miles. I haven't hurried—have mostly poked along, stopping often and looking around. But I am tired, and coming down the creek I have got both feet wet. I find a sunny place, and take off my shoes and socks and set them to dry. For a long time then, lying propped against the trunk of a tree, I read and rest and watch the evening come.

All day I have moved through the woods, making as little noise as possible. Slowly my mind and my nerves have slowed to a walk. The quiet of the woods has ceased to be something that I observe; now it is something that I am a part of. I have joined it with my own quiet. As the twilight draws on I no longer feel the strangeness and uneasiness of the evening before. The sounds of the creek move through my mind as they move through the valley, unimpeded and clear.

When the time comes I prepare supper and eat, and then wash kettle and cup and spoon and put them away. As far as possible I get things ready for an early start in the morning. Soon after dark I go to bed, and I sleep well.

I wake long before dawn. The air is warm and I feel rested and wide awake. By the light of a small candle lantern I break camp and pack. And then I begin the steep climb back to the car.

The moon is bright and high. The woods stands in deep shadow, the light falling soft through the openings of the foliage. The trees appear immensely tall, and black, gravely looming over the path. It is windless and still; the moonlight pouring over the country seems more potent than the air. All around me there is still that constant low singing of the insects. For days now it has continued without letup or inflection, like ripples on water under a steady breeze. While I slept it went on through the night, a shimmer on my mind. My shoulder brushes a low tree overhanging the path and a bird that was asleep on one of the branches startles awake and flies off into the shadows, and I go on with the sense that I am passing near to the sleep of things.

In a way this is the best part of the trip. Stopping now and again to rest, I linger over it, sorry to be going. It seems to me that if I were to stay on, today would be better than yesterday, and I realize it was to renew the life of that possibility that I came here. What I am leaving is something to look forward to.

stylistically interesting — *but so*
totally focused on me—me—me— &
what do we learn??

JOAN DIDION

Joan Didion (1934–   ) has been a major figure in the revival of the con-
temporary American essay. Her pieces began appearing in mass magazines in
the sixties, and she was a key practitioner of that decade's New Journalism,
which combined reportage with personal, subjective disclosure. A novelist
(Play It as It Lays, A Book of Common Prayer) as well as an essayist,
Didion has shown an uncanny ability to create atmosphere on the page. Like
Raymond Chandler, she captured, through telling detail, the sun-desolate,
alienated side of suburban California's pleasure principle; unlike Chandler,
however, her ominous mood-setting was in the service not of murder mys-
tery but of something more unsettling: an existential questioning whether
any meaningful story can be made of our lives. In her three essay collections,
Slouching Toward Bethlehem, The White Album, and After Henry, she
perfected the technique of gathering disparate fragments to convey the ran-
domness and absence of narrative coherence in contemporary life. One of the
things that makes her essays so fascinating is her will as a formalist to
keep them structurally tight, even as she obstinately denies that the pieces
"add up."

"Goodbye to All That," her early, bittersweet memoir of New York, has
echoes of F. Scott Fitzgerald's "My Lost City" in its elegiac rhythms and its
conflation of the author's and Gotham's loss of youth. The end of innocence
—disenchantment—is a frequent Didion motif, but its positive side, she
implies, is the acquisition of worldliness, so necessary to a country she sees
as imperially naive. Didion has written extensive political commentary, usu-
ally critical of the power structure. A fastidious prose stylist, she has pro-
duced work that has grown in syntactical complexity and intellectual density
over the years, sometimes to the point of mannerism. But like Lamb,

Mencken, and Vidal, she is not afraid of being mannered or irritating; she rather celebrates her crabby, migrainous persona, as in the lovely personal essay "In Bed."

Goodbye to All That

How many miles to Babylon?
Three score miles and ten—
Can I get there by candlelight?
Yes, and back again—
If your feet are nimble and light
You can get there by candlelight.

I T I S E A S Y to see the beginnings of things, and harder to see the ends. I can remember now, with a clarity that makes the nerves in the back of my neck constrict, when New York began for me, but I cannot lay my finger upon the moment it ended, can never cut through the ambiguities and second starts and broken resolves to the exact place on the page where the heroine is no longer as optimistic as she once was. When I first saw New York I was twenty, and it was summertime, and I got off a DC-7 at the old Idlewild temporary terminal in a new dress which had seemed very smart in Sacramento but seemed less smart already, even in the old Idlewild temporary terminal, and the warm air smelled of mildew and some instinct, programmed by all the movies I had ever seen and all the songs I had ever heard sung and all the stories I had ever read about New York, informed me that it would never be quite the same again. In fact it never was. Some time later there was a song on all the jukeboxes on the upper East Side that went "but where is the schoolgirl who used to be me," and if it was late enough at night I used to wonder that. I know now that almost everyone wonders something like that, sooner or later and no matter what he or she is doing, but one of the mixed blessings of being twenty and twenty-one and even twenty-three is the conviction that nothing like this, all evidence to the contrary notwithstanding, has ever happened to anyone before.

Of course it might have been some other city, had circumstances been different and the time been different and had I been different, might have been Paris or Chicago or even San Francisco, but because I am talking about myself I am talking here about New York. That first night I opened my window on the bus into town and watched for the skyline, but all I could see were the wastes of Queens and the big signs that said MIDTOWN TUNNEL THIS LANE and then a flood of summer rain (even that seemed remarkable and exotic, for I had come out of the West where there was no summer rain), and for the next three days I sat wrapped in blankets in a hotel room air-conditioned to 35° and tried to get over a bad cold and a high fever. It did not occur to me to call a doctor, because I knew none, and although it did occur to me to call the desk and ask that the air conditioner be turned off, I never called, because I did not know how much to tip whoever might come—was anyone ever so young? I am here to tell you that someone was. All I could do during those three days was talk long-distance to the boy I already knew I would never marry in the spring. I would stay in New York, I told him, just six months, and I could see the Brooklyn Bridge from my window. As it turned out the bridge was the Triborough, and I stayed eight years.

In retrospect it seems to me that those days before I knew the names of all the bridges were happier than the ones that came later, but perhaps you will see that as we go along. Part of what I want to tell you is what it is like to be young in New York, how six months can become eight years with the deceptive ease of a film dissolve, for that is how those years appear to me now, in a long sequence of sentimental dissolves and old-fashioned trick shots—the Seagram Building fountains dissolve into snowflakes, I enter a revolving door at twenty and come out a good deal older, and on a different street. But most particularly I want to explain to you, and in the process perhaps to myself, why I no longer live in New York. It is often said that New York is a city for only the very rich and the very poor. It is less often said that New York is also, at least for those of us who came there from somewhere else, a city for only the very young.

I remember once, one cold bright December evening in New York, suggesting to a friend who complained of having been around too long that he come with me to a party where there would be, I assured him with the bright resourcefulness of twenty-three, "new faces." He laughed literally until he choked, and I had to roll down the taxi window and hit him on the back. "New faces," he said finally, "don't tell me about *new faces.*" It seemed that the last time he had gone to a party where he had been promised "new faces," there had been fifteen people in the room, and he had already slept with five of the women and owed money to all but two of the men. I laughed with him, but the first snow had just begun to fall and the big Christmas trees glittered yellow and white as far as I could see up Park Avenue and I had a new dress and it would be a long while before I would come to understand the particular moral of the story.

It would be a long while because, quite simply, I was in love with New York. I do not mean "love" in any colloquial way, I mean that I was in love with the city, the way you love the first person who ever touches you and never love anyone quite that way again. I remember walking across Sixty-second Street one twilight that first spring, or the second spring, they were all alike for a while. I was late to meet someone but I stopped at Lexington Avenue and bought a peach and stood on the corner eating it and knew that I had come out of the West and reached the mirage. I could taste the peach and feel the soft air blowing from a subway grating on my legs and I could smell lilac and garbage and expensive perfume and I knew that it would cost something sooner or later—because I did not belong there, did not come from there—but when you are twenty-two or twenty-three, you figure that later you will have a high emotional balance, and be able to pay whatever it costs. I still believed in possibilities then, still had the sense, so peculiar to New York, that something extraordinary would happen any minute, any day, any month. I was making only $65 or $70 a week then ("Put yourself in Hattie Carnegie's hands," I was advised without the slightest trace of irony by an editor of the magazine for which I worked), so little money that some weeks I had to charge food at Bloomingdale's gourmet shop in order to eat, a fact which went unmentioned in the letters I wrote to California. I never told my father that I needed money because then he would have sent it, and I would never know if I could do it by myself. At that time making a living seemed a game to me, with arbitrary but quite inflexible rules. And except on a certain kind of winter evening—six-thirty in the Seventies, say, already dark and bitter with a wind off the river, when I would be walking very fast toward a bus and would look in the bright windows of brownstones and see cooks working in clean kitchens and imagine women lighting candles on the floor above and beautiful children being bathed on the floor above that—except on nights like those, I never felt poor; I had the feeling that if I needed money I could always get it. I could write a syndicated column for teenagers under the name "Debbi Lynn" or I could smuggle gold into India or I could become a $100 call girl, and none of it would matter.

Nothing was irrevocable; everything was within reach. Just around every corner lay something curious and interesting, something I had never before seen or done or known about. I could go to a party and meet someone who called himself Mr. Emotional Appeal and ran The Emotional Appeal Institute or Tina Onassis Blandford or a Florida cracker who was then a regular on what he called "the Big C," the Southampton–El Morocco circuit ("I'm well-connected on the Big C, honey," he would tell me over collard greens on his vast borrowed terrace), or the widow of the celery king of the Harlem market or a piano salesman from Bonne Terre, Missouri, or someone who had already made and lost two fortunes in Midland, Texas. I could make promises to myself and to other people and there would be all the time in the world to keep them. I could stay up all night and make mistakes, and none of it would count.

You see I was in a curious position in New York: it never occurred to me that I was living a real life there. In my imagination I was always there for just another few months, just until Christmas or Easter or the first warm day in May. For that reason I was most comfortable in the company of Southerners. They seemed to be in New York as I was, on some indefinitely extended leave from wherever they belonged, disinclined to consider the future, temporary exiles who always knew when the flights left for New Orleans or Memphis or Richmond or, in my case, California. Someone who lives always with a plane schedule in the drawer lives on a slightly different calendar. Christmas, for example, was a difficult season. Other people could take it in stride, going to Stowe or going abroad or going for the day to their mothers' places in Connecticut; those of us who believed that we lived somewhere else would spend it making and cancelling airline reservations, waiting for weatherbound flights as if for the last plane out of Lisbon in 1940, and finally comforting one another, those of us who were left, with the oranges and mementos and smoked-oyster stuffings of childhood, gathering close, colonials in a far country.

Which is precisely what we were. I am not sure that it is possible for anyone brought up in the East to appreciate entirely what New York, the idea of New York, means to those of us who came out of the West and the South. To an Eastern child, particularly a child who has always had an uncle on Wall Street and who has spent several hundred Saturdays first at F. A. O. Schwarz and being fitted for shoes at Best's and then waiting under the Biltmore clock and dancing to Lester Lanin, New York is just a city, albeit *the* city, a plausible place for people to live. But to those of us who came from places where no one had heard of Lester Lanin and Grand Central Station was a Saturday radio program, where Wall Street and Fifth Avenue and Madison Avenue were not places at all but abstractions ("Money," and "High Fashion," and "The Hucksters"), New York was no mere city. It was instead an infinitely romantic notion, the mysterious nexus of all love and money and power, the shining and perishable dream itself. To think of "living" there was to reduce the miraculous to the mundane; one does not "live" at Xanadu.

In fact it was difficult in the extreme for me to understand those young women for whom New York was not simply an ephemeral Estoril but a real place, girls who bought toasters and installed new cabinets in their apartments and committed themselves to some reasonable future. I never bought any furniture in New York. For a year or so I lived in other people's apartments; after that I lived in the Nineties in an apartment furnished entirely with things taken from storage by a friend whose wife had moved away. And when I left the apartment in the Nineties (that was when I was leaving everything, when it was all breaking up) I left everything in it, even my winter clothes and the map of Sacramento County I had hung on the bedroom wall to remind me who I was, and I moved into a monastic four-room floor-through on Seventy-fifth Street. "Monastic" is perhaps misleading here, implying some chic severity; until after I was married and my husband moved some furniture in, there was nothing at all in those four rooms except a cheap double mattress and box springs, ordered by telephone the day I decided to move, and two French garden chairs lent me by a friend who imported them. (It strikes me now that the people I knew in New York all had curious and self-defeating sidelines. They imported garden chairs which did not sell very well at Hammacher Schlemmer or they tried to market hair straighteners in Harlem or they ghosted exposés of Murder Incorporated for Sunday supplements. I think that perhaps none of us was very serious, *engagé* only about our most private lives.)

All I ever did to that apartment was hang fifty yards of yellow theatrical silk across the bedroom windows, because I had some idea that the gold light would make me feel better, but I did not bother to weight the curtains correctly and all that summer the long panels of transparent golden silk would blow out the windows and get tangled and drenched in the afternoon thunderstorms. That was the year, my twenty-eighth, when I was discovering that not all of the promises would be kept, that some things are in fact irrevocable and that it had counted after all, every evasion and every procrastination, every mistake, every word, all of it.

That is what it was all about, wasn't it? Promises? Now when New York comes back to me it comes in hallucinatory flashes, so clinically detailed that I sometimes wish that memory would effect the distortion with which it is commonly credited. For a lot of the time I was in New York I used a perfume called *Fleurs de Rocaille,* and then *L'Air du Temps,* and now the slightest trace of either can short-circuit my connections for the rest of the day. Nor can I smell Henri Bendel jasmine soap without falling back into the past, or the particular mixture of spices used for boiling crabs. There were barrels of crab boil in a Czech place in the Eighties where I once shopped. Smells, of course, are notorious memory stimuli, but there are other things which affect me the same way. Blue-and-white striped sheets. Vermouth cassis. Some faded nightgowns which were new in 1959 or 1960, and some chiffon scarves I bought about the same time.

I suppose that a lot of us who have been young in New York have the same scenes on our home screens. I remember sitting in a lot of apartments with a slight headache about five o'clock in the morning. I had a friend who could not sleep, and he knew a few other people who had the same trouble, and we would watch the sky lighten and have a last drink with no ice and then go home in the early morning light, when the streets were clean and wet (had it rained in the night? we never knew) and the few cruising taxis still had their headlights on and the only color was the red and green of traffic signals. The White Rose bars opened very early in the morning; I recall waiting in one of them to watch an astronaut go into space, waiting so long that at the moment it actually happened I had my eyes not on the television screen but on a cockroach on the tile floor. I liked the bleak branches above Washington Square at dawn, and the monochromatic flatness of Second Avenue, the fire escapes and the grilled storefronts peculiar and empty in their perspective.

It is relatively hard to fight at six-thirty or seven in the morning without any sleep, which was perhaps one reason we stayed up all night, and it seemed to me a pleasant time of day. The windows were shuttered in that apartment in the Nineties and I could sleep a few hours and then go to work. I could work then on two or three hours' sleep and a container of coffee from Chock Full O' Nuts. I liked going to work, liked the soothing and satisfactory rhythm of getting out a magazine, liked the orderly progression of four-color closings and two-color closings and black-and-white closings and then The Product, no abstraction but something which looked effortlessly glossy and could be picked up on a newsstand and weighed in the hand. I liked all the minutiae of proofs and layouts, liked working late on the nights the magazine went to press, sitting and reading *Variety* and waiting for the copy desk to call. From my office I could look across town to the weather signal on the Mutual of New York Building and the lights that alternately spelled out TIME and LIFE above Rockefeller Plaza; that pleased me obscurely, and so did walking uptown in the mauve eight o'clocks of early summer evenings and looking at things, Lowestoft tureens in Fifty-seventh Street windows, people in evening clothes trying to get taxis, the trees just coming into full leaf, the lambent air, all the sweet promises of money and summer.

Some years passed, but I still did not lose that sense of wonder about New York. I began to cherish the loneliness of it, the sense that at any given time no one need know where I was or what I was doing. I liked walking, from the East River over to the Hudson and back on brisk days, down around the Village on warm days. A friend would leave me the key to her apartment in the West Village when she was out of town, and sometimes I would just move down there, because by that time the telephone was beginning to bother me (the canker, you see, was already in the rose) and not many people had that number. I remember one day when someone who did have the West Village number came to pick me up for lunch there, and we both had hangovers, and I cut my finger opening him a beer and burst into tears, and we walked to a Spanish restaurant and drank Bloody Marys and _gazpacho_ until we felt better. I was not then guilt-ridden about spending afternoons that way, because I still had all the afternoons in the world.

And even that late in the game I still liked going to parties, all parties, bad parties, Saturday-afternoon parties given by recently married couples who lived in Stuyvesant Town, West Side parties given by unpublished or failed writers who served cheap red wine and talked about going to Guadalajara, Village parties where all the guests worked for advertising agencies and voted for Reform Democrats, press parties at Sardi's, the worst kinds of parties. You will have perceived by now that I was not one to profit by the experience of others, that it was a very long time indeed before I stopped believing in new faces and began to understand the lesson in that story, which was that it is distinctly possible to stay too long at the Fair.

I could not tell you when I began to understand that. All I know is that it was very bad when I was twenty-eight. Everything that was said to me I seemed to have heard before, and I could no longer listen. I could no longer sit in little bars near Grand Central and listen to someone complaining of his wife's inability to cope with the help while he missed another train to Connecticut. I no longer had any interest in hearing about the advances other people had received from their publishers, about plays which were having second-act trouble in Philadelphia, or about people I would like very much if only I would come out and meet them. I had already met them, always. There were certain parts of the city which I had to avoid. I could not bear upper Madison Avenue on weekday mornings (this was a particularly inconvenient aversion, since I then lived just fifty or sixty feet east of Madison), because I would see women walking Yorkshire terriers and shopping at Gristede's, and some Veblenesque gorge would rise in my throat. I could not go to Times Square in the afternoon, or to the New York Public Library for any reason whatsoever. One day I could not go into a Schrafft's; the next day it would be Bonwit Teller.

I hurt the people I cared about, and insulted those I did not. I cut myself off from the one person who was closer to me than any other. I cried until I was not even aware when I was crying and when I was not, cried in elevators and in taxis and in Chinese laundries, and when I went to the doctor he said only that I seemed to be depressed, and should see a "specialist." He wrote down a psychiatrist's name and address for me, but I did not go.

Instead I got married, which as it turned out was a very good thing to do but badly timed, since I still could not walk on upper Madison Avenue in the mornings and still could not talk to people and still cried in Chinese laundries. I had never before understood what "despair" meant, and I am not sure that I understand now, but I understood that year. Of course I could not work. I could not even get dinner with any degree of certainty, and I would sit in the apartment on Seventy-fifth Street paralyzed until my husband would call from his office and say gently that I did not have to get dinner, that I could meet him at Michael's Pub or at Toots Shor's or at Sardi's East. And then one morning in April (we had been married in January) he called and told me that he wanted to get out of New York for a while, that he would take a six-month leave of absence, that we would go somewhere.

It was three years ago that he told me that, and we have lived in Los Angeles since. Many of the people we knew in New York think this a curious aberration, and in fact tell us so. There is no possible, no adequate answer to that, and so we give certain stock answers, the answers everyone gives. I talk about how difficult it would be for us to "afford" to live in New York right now, about how much "space" we need. All I mean is that I was very young in New York, and that at some point the golden rhythm was broken, and I am not that young any more. The last time I was in New York was in a cold January, and everyone was ill and tired. Many of the people I used to know there had moved to Dallas or had gone on Antabuse or had bought a farm in New Hampshire. We stayed ten days, and then we took an afternoon flight back to Los Angeles, and on the way home from the airport that night I could see the moon on the Pacific and smell jasmine all around and we both knew that there was no longer any point in keeping the apartment we still kept in New York. There were years when I called Los Angeles "the Coast," but they seem a long time ago.

In Bed

THREE, FOUR, sometimes five times a month, I spend the day in bed with a migraine headache, insensible to the world around me. Almost every day of every month, between these attacks, I feel the sudden irrational irritation and flush of blood into the cerebral arteries which tell me that migraine is on its way, and I take certain drugs to avert its arrival. If I did not take the drugs, I would be able to function perhaps one day in four. The physiological error called migraine is, in brief, central to the given of my life. When I was 15, 16, even 25, I used to think that I could rid myself of this error by simply denying it, character over chemistry. "Do you have headaches *sometimes? frequently? never?*" the application forms would demand. "Check one." Wary of the trap, wanting whatever it was that the successful circumnavigation of that particular form could bring (a job, a scholarship, the respect of mankind and the grace of God), I would check one. *"Sometimes,"* I would lie. That in fact I spent one or two days a week almost unconscious with pain seemed a shameful secret, evidence not merely of some chemical inferiority but of all my bad attitudes, unpleasant tempers, wrongthink.

For I had no brain tumor, no eyestrain, no high blood pressure, nothing wrong with me at all: I simply had migraine headaches, and migraine headaches were, as everyone who did not have them knew, imaginary. I fought migraine then, ignored the warnings it sent, went to school and later to work in spite of it, sat through lectures in Middle English and presentations to advertisers with involuntary tears running down the right side of my face, threw up in washrooms, stumbled home by instinct, emptied ice trays onto my bed and tried to freeze the pain in my right temple, wished only for a neurosurgeon who would do a lobotomy on house call, and cursed my imagination.

It was a long time before I began thinking mechanistically enough to accept migraine for what it was: something with which I would be living, the way some people live with diabetes. Migraine is something more than the fancy of a neurotic imagination. It is an essentially hereditary complex of symptoms, the most frequently noted but by no means the most unpleasant of which is a vascular headache of blinding severity, suffered by a surprising number of women, a fair number of men (Thomas Jefferson had migraine, and so did Ulysses S. Grant, the day he accepted Lee's surrender), and by some unfortunate children as young as two years old. (I had my first when I was eight. It came on during a fire drill at the Columbia School in Colorado Springs, Colorado. I was taken first home and then to the infirmary at Peterson Field, where my father was stationed. The Air Corps doctor prescribed an enema.) Almost anything can trigger a specific attack of migraine: stress, allergy, fatigue, an abrupt change in barometric pressure, a contretemps over a parking ticket. A flashing light. A fire drill. One inherits, of course, only the predisposition. In other words I spent yesterday in bed with a headache not merely because of my bad attitudes, unpleasant tempers and wrongthink, but because both my grandmothers had migraine, my father has migraine and my mother has migraine.

No one knows precisely what it is that is inherited. The chemistry of migraine, however, seems to have some connection with the nerve hormone named serotonin, which is naturally present in the brain. The amount of serotonin in the blood falls sharply at the onset of migraine, and one migraine drug, methysergide, or Sansert, seems to have some effect on serotonin. Methysergide is a derivative of lysergic acid (in fact Sandoz Pharmaceuticals first synthesized LSD-25 while looking for a migraine cure), and its use is hemmed about with so many contraindications and side effects that most doctors prescribe it only in the most incapacitating cases. Methysergide, when it is prescribed, is taken daily, as a preventive; another preventive which works for some people is old-fashioned ergotamine tartrate, which helps to constrict the swelling blood vessels during the "aura," the period which in most cases precedes the actual headache.

Once an attack is under way, however, no drug touches it. Migraine gives some people mild hallucinations, temporarily blinds others, shows up not only as a headache but as a gastrointestinal disturbance, a painful sensitivity to all sensory stimuli, an abrupt overpowering fatigue, a stroke-like aphasia, and a crippling inability to make even the most routine connections. When I am in a migraine aura (for some people the aura lasts fifteen minutes, for others several hours), I will drive through red lights, lose the house keys, spill whatever I am holding, lose the ability to focus my eyes or frame coherent sentences, and generally give the appearance of being on drugs, or drunk. The actual headache, when it comes, brings with it chills, sweating, nausea, a debility that seems to stretch the very limits of endurance. That no one dies of migraine seems, to someone deep into an attack, an ambiguous blessing.

My husband also has migraine, which is unfortunate for him but fortunate for me: perhaps nothing so tends to prolong an attack as the accusing eye of someone who has never had a headache. "Why not take a couple of aspirin," the unafflicted will say from the doorway, or "I'd have a headache, too, spending a beautiful day like this inside with all the shades drawn." All of us who have migraine suffer not only from the attacks themselves but from this common conviction that we are perversely refusing to cure ourselves by taking a couple of aspirin, that we are making ourselves sick, that we "bring it on ourselves." And in the most immediate sense, the sense of why we have a headache this Tuesday and not last Thursday, of course we often do. There certainly is what doctors call a "migraine personality," and that personality tends to be ambitious, inward, intolerant of error, rather rigidly organized, perfectionist. "You don't look like a migraine personality," a doctor once said to me. "Your hair's messy. But I suppose you're a compulsive housekeeper." Actually my house is kept even more negligently than my hair, but the doctor was right nonetheless: perfectionism can also take the form of spending most of a week writing and rewriting and not writing a single paragraph.

But not all perfectionists have migraine, and not all migrainous people have migraine personalities. We do not escape heredity. I have tried in most of the available ways to escape my own migrainous heredity (at one point I learned to give myself two daily injections of histamine with a hypodermic needle, even though the needle so frightened me that I had to close my eyes when I did it), but I still have migraine. And I have learned now to live with it, learned when to expect it, how to outwit it, even how to regard it, when it does come, as more friend than lodger. We have reached a certain understanding, my migraine and I. It never comes when I am in real trouble. Tell me that my house is burned down, my husband has left me, that there is gunfighting in the streets and panic in the banks, and I will not respond by getting a headache. It comes instead when I am fighting not an open guerrilla war with my own life, during weeks of small household confusions, lost laundry, unhappy help, canceled appointments, on days when the telephone rings too much and I get no work done and the wind is coming up. On days like that my friend comes uninvited.

And once it comes, now that I am wise in its ways, I no longer fight it. I lie down and let it happen. At first every small apprehension is magnified, every anxiety a pounding terror. Then the pain comes, and I concentrate only on that. Right there is the usefulness of migraine, there in that imposed yoga, the concentration on the pain. For when the pain recedes, ten or twelve hours later, everything goes with it, all the hidden resentments, all the vain anxieties. The migraine has acted as a circuit breaker, and the fuses have emerged intact. There is a pleasant convalescent euphoria. I open the windows and feel the air, eat gratefully, sleep well. I notice the particular nature of a flower in a glass on the stair landing. I count my blessings.

tedious

ANNIE DILLARD

Annie Dillard (1945–   ) came to essays through poetry, and her prose has the unmistakable imprint of a trained poet. When she writes about a tomcat with bloody paws ("And some mornings I'd wake in daylight to find my body covered with paw prints in blood; I looked as though I'd been painted with roses"), there is the bounce of poetic rhythm, the weight of the sudden, arresting image, the semicolon functioning like an end-stop in verse, and the hush that surrounds much contemporary American poetry. Dillard is fascinated with silence, with the muteness of things, and her work surges up from that mystery and returns to it. Teaching a Stone to Talk, *the title of one of her essay collections, could serve for all.*

She grew up in Pittsburgh, as described in her attractive memoir, An American Childhood. *Her first prose book,* Pilgrim at Tinker Creek, *appeared in 1974 and made her an instant celebrity. Her reputation was consolidated by* Holy the Firm. *Dillard is a self-described seeker, a pilgrim on a mission to retrieve a sense of ecstatic wonder before the natural world. The religious aspect of her essays links her to the tradition of the Christian literary sermon. It must be said that sometimes her calls to wonder become programmatic and saccharine. But when she is at the top of her form, as in the essay below, "Seeing," her writing is truly magical. It has the freedom and the power to move outward in giddy, imaginative directions. As Donald Hall noted, "Her mind combines qualities not often found together: an almost insatiable curiosity about details of the natural world, science, and thought together with a spiritual appetite, a visionary's or mystic's seeking through religious study and meditation. Combining these qualities, she becomes a major writer of American prose."*

Seeing

W HEN I WAS SIX or seven years old, growing up in Pittsburgh, I used to take a precious penny of my own and hide it for someone else to find. It was a curious compulsion; sadly, I've never been seized by it since. For some reason I always "hid" the penny along the same stretch of sidewalk up the street. I would cradle it at the roots of a sycamore, say, or in a hole left by a chipped-off piece of sidewalk. Then I would take a piece of chalk, and, starting at either end of the block, draw huge arrows leading up to the penny from both directions. After I learned to write I labeled the arrows: SURPRISE AHEAD or MONEY THIS WAY. I was greatly excited, during all this arrow-drawing, at the thought of the first lucky passer-by who would receive in this way, regardless of merit, a free gift from the universe. But I never lurked about. I would go straight home and not give the matter another thought, until, some months later, I would be gripped again by the impulse to hide another penny.

It is still the first week in January, and I've got great plans. I've been thinking about seeing. There are lots of things to see, unwrapped gifts and free surprises. The world is fairly studded and strewn with pennies cast broadside from a generous hand. But—and this is the point—who gets excited by a mere penny? If you follow one arrow, if you crouch motionless on a bank to watch a tremulous ripple thrill on the water and are rewarded by the sight of a muskrat kit paddling from its den, will you count that sight a chip of copper only, and go your rueful way? It is dire poverty indeed when a man is so malnourished and fatigued that he won't stoop to pick up a penny. But if you cultivate a healthy poverty and simplicity, so that finding a penny will literally make your day, then, since the world is in fact planted in pennies, you have with your poverty bought a lifetime of days. It is that simple. What you see is what you get.

I used to be able to see flying insects in the air. I'd look ahead and see, not the row of hemlocks across the road, but the air in front of it. My eyes would focus along that column of air, picking out flying insects. But I lost interest, I guess, for I dropped the habit. Now I can see birds. Probably some people can look at the grass at their feet and discover all the crawling creatures. I would like to know grasses and sedges—and care. Then my least journey into the world would be a field trip, a series of happy recognitions. Thoreau, in an expansive mood, exulted, "What a rich book might be made about buds, including, perhaps, sprouts!" It would be nice to think so. I cherish mental images I have of three perfectly happy people. One collects stones. Another—an Englishman, say—watches clouds. The third lives on a coast and collects drops of seawater which he examines microscopically and mounts. But I don't see what the specialist sees, and so I cut myself off, not only from the total picture, but from the various forms of happiness.

Unfortunately, nature is very much a now-you-see-it, now-you-don't affair. A fish flashes, then dissolves in the water before my eyes like so much salt. Deer apparently ascend bodily into heaven; the brightest oriole fades into leaves. These disappearances stun me into stillness and concentration; they say of nature that it conceals with a grand nonchalance, and they say of vision that it is a deliberate gift, the revelation of a dancer who for my eyes only flings away her seven veils. For nature does reveal as well as conceal: now-you-don't-see-it, now-you-do. For a week last September migrating red-winged blackbirds were feeding heavily down by the creek at the back of the house. One day I went out to investigate the racket; I walked up to a tree, an Osage orange, and a hundred birds flew away. They simply materialized out of the tree. I saw a tree, then a whisk of color, then a tree again. I walked closer and another hundred blackbirds took flight. Not a branch, not a twig budged: the birds were apparently weightless as well as invisible. Or, it was as if the leaves of the Osage orange had been freed from a spell in the form of red-winged blackbirds; they flew from the tree, caught my eye in the sky, and vanished. When I looked again at the tree the leaves had reassembled as if nothing had happened. Finally I walked directly to the trunk of the tree and a final hundred, the real diehards, appeared, spread, and vanished. How could so many hide in the tree without my seeing them? The Osage orange, unruffled, looked just as it had looked from the house, when three hundred red-winged blackbirds cried from its crown. I looked downstream where they flew, and they were gone. Searching, I couldn't spot one. I wandered downstream to force them to play their hand, but they'd crossed the creek and scattered. One show to a customer. These appearances catch at my throat; they are the free gifts, the bright coppers at the roots of trees.

It's all a matter of keeping my eyes open. Nature is like one of those line drawings of a tree that are puzzles for children: Can you find hidden in the leaves a duck, a house, a boy, a bucket, a zebra, and a boot? Specialists can find the most incredibly well-hidden things. A book I read when I was young recommended an easy way to find caterpillars to rear: you simply find some fresh caterpillar droppings, look up, and there's your caterpillar. More recently an author advised me to set my mind at ease about those piles of cut stems on the ground in grassy fields. Field mice make them; they cut the grass down by degrees to reach the seeds at the head. It seems that when the grass is tightly packed, as in a field of ripe grain, the blade won't topple at a single cut through the stem; instead, the cut stem simply drops vertically, held in the crush of grain. The mouse severs the bottom again and again, the stem keeps dropping an inch at a time, and finally the head is low enough for the mouse to reach the seeds. Meanwhile, the mouse is positively littering the field with its little piles of cut stems into which, presumably, the author of the book is constantly stumbling.

If I can't see these minutiae, I still try to keep my eyes open. I'm always on the lookout for antlion traps in sandy soil, monarch pupae near milkweed, skipper larvae in locust leaves. These things are utterly common, and I've not seen one. I bang on hollow trees near water, but so far no flying squirrels have appeared. In flat country I watch every sunset in hopes of seeing the green ray. The green ray is a seldom-seen streak of light that rises from the sun like a spurting fountain at the moment of sunset; it throbs into the sky for two seconds and disappears. One more reason to keep my eyes open. A photography professor at the University of Florida just happened to see a bird die in midflight; it jerked, died, dropped, and smashed on the ground. I squint at the wind because I read Steward Edward White: "I have always maintained that if you looked closely enough you could *see* the wind—the dim, hardly-made-out, fine debris fleeing high in the air." White was an excellent observer, and devoted an entire chapter of *The Mountains* to the subject of seeing deer: "As soon as you can forget the naturally obvious and construct an artificial obvious, then you too will see deer."

But the artificial obvious is hard to see. My eyes account for less than one percent of the weight of my head; I'm bony and dense; I see what I expect. I once spent a full three minutes looking at a bullfrog that was so unexpectedly large I couldn't see it even though a dozen enthusiastic campers were shouting directions. Finally I asked, "What color am I looking for?" and a fellow said, "Green." When at last I picked out the frog, I saw what painters are up against: the thing wasn't green at all, but the color of wet hickory bark.

The lover can see, and the knowledgeable. I visited an aunt and uncle at a quarter-horse ranch in Cody, Wyoming. I couldn't do much of anything useful, but I could, I thought, draw. So, as we all sat around the kitchen table after supper, I produced a sheet of paper and drew a horse. "That's one lame horse," my aunt volunteered. The rest of the family joined in: "Only place to saddle that one is his neck"; "Looks like we better shoot the poor thing, on account of those terrible growths." Meekly, I slid the pencil and paper down the table. Everyone in that family, including my three young cousins, could draw a horse. Beautifully. When the paper came back it looked as though five shining, real quarter horses had been corraled by mistake with a papier-mâché moose; the real horses seemed to gaze at the monster with a steady, puzzled air. I stay away from horses now, but I can do a creditable goldfish. The point is that I just don't know what the lover knows; I just can't see the artificial obvious that those in the know construct. The herpetologist asks the native, "Are there snakes in that ravine?" "Nosir." And the herpetologist comes home with, yessir, three bags full. Are there butterflies on that mountain? Are the bluets in bloom, are there arrowheads here, or fossil shells in the shale?

Peeping through my keyhole I see within the range of only about thirty percent of the light that comes from the sun; the rest is infrared and some little ultraviolet, perfectly apparent to many animals, but invisible to me. A nightmare network of ganglia, charged and firing without my knowledge, cuts and splices what I do see, editing it for my brain. Donald E. Carr points out that the sense impressions of one-celled animals are *not* edited for the brain: "This is philosophically interesting in a rather mournful way, since it means that only the simplest animals perceive the universe as it is."

A fog that won't burn away drifts and flows across my field of vision. When you see fog move against a backdrop of deep pines, you don't see the fog itself, but streaks of clearness floating across the air in dark shreds. So I see only tatters of clearness through a pervading obscurity. I can't distinguish the fog from the overcast sky; I can't be sure if the light is direct or reflected. Everywhere darkness and the presence of the unseen appalls. We estimate now that only one atom dances alone in every cubic meter of intergalactic space. I blink and squint. What planet or power yanks Halley's Comet out of orbit? We haven't seen that force yet; it's a question of distance, density, and the pallor of reflected light. We rock, cradled in the swaddling band of darkness. Even the simple darkness of night whispers suggestions to the mind. Last summer, in August, I stayed at the creek too late.

Where Tinker Creek flows under the sycamore log bridge to the tear-shaped island, it is slow and shallow, fringed thinly in cattail marsh. At this spot an astonishing bloom of life supports vast breeding populations of insects, fish, reptiles, birds, and mammals. On windless summer evenings I stalk along the creek bank or straddle the sycamore log in absolute stillness, watching for muskrats. The night I stayed too late I was hunched on the log staring spellbound at spreading, reflected stains of lilac on the water. A cloud in the sky suddenly lighted as if turned on by a switch; its reflection just as suddenly materialized on the water upstream, flat and floating, so that I couldn't see the creek bottom, or life in the water under the cloud. Downstream, away from the cloud on the water, water turtles smooth as beans were gliding down with the current in a series of easy, weightless push-offs, as men bound on the moon. I didn't know whether to trace the progress of one turtle I was sure of, risking sticking my face in one of the bridge's spider webs made invisible by the gathering dark, or take a chance on seeing the carp, or scan the mudbank in hope of seeing a muskrat, or follow the last of the swallows who caught at my heart and trailed it after them like streamers as they appeared from directly below, under the log, flying upstream with their tails forked, so fast.

But shadows spread, and deepened, and stayed. After thousands of years we're still strangers to darkness, fearful aliens in an enemy camp with our arms crossed over our chests. I stirred. A land turtle on the bank, startled, hissed the air from its lungs and withdrew into its shell. An uneasy pink here, an unfathomable blue there, gave great suggestion of lurking beings. Things were going on. I couldn't see whether that sere rustle I heard was a distant rattlesnake, slit-eyed, or a nearby sparrow kicking in the dry flood debris slung at the foot of a willow. Tremendous action roiled the water everywhere I looked, big action, inexplicable. A tremor welled up beside a gaping muskrat burrow in the bank and I caught my breath, but no muskrat appeared. The ripples continued to fan upstream with a steady, powerful thrust. Night was knitting over my face an eyeless mask, and I still sat transfixed. A distant airplane, a delta wing out of nightmare, made a gliding shadow on the creek's bottom that looked like a stingray cruising upstream. At once a black fin slit the pink cloud on the water, shearing it in two. The two halves merged together and seemed to dissolve before my eyes. Darkness pooled in the cleft of the creek and rose, as water collects in a well. Untamed, dreaming lights flickered over the sky. I saw hints of hulking underwater shadows, two pale splashes out of the water, and round ripples rolling close together from a blackened center.

At last I stared upstream where only the deepest violet remained of the cloud, a cloud so high its underbelly still glowed feeble color reflected from a hidden sky lighted in turn by a sun halfway to China. And out of that violet, a sudden enormous black body arced over the water. I saw only a cylindrical sleekness. Head and tail, if there was a head and tail, were both submerged in cloud. I saw only one ebony fling, a headlong dive to darkness; then the waters closed, and the lights went out.

I walked home in a shivering daze, up hill and down. Later I lay openmouthed in bed, my arms flung wide at my sides to steady the whirling darkness. At this latitude I'm spinning 836 miles an hour round the earth's axis; I often fancy I feel my sweeping fall as a breakneck arc like the dive of dolphins, and the hollow rushing of wind raises hair on my neck and the side of my face. In orbit around the sun I'm moving 64,800 miles an hour. The solar system as a whole, like a merry-go-round unhinged, spins, bobs, and blinks at the speed of 43,200 miles an hour along a course set east of Hercules. Someone has piped, and we are dancing a tarantella until the sweat pours. I open my eyes and I see dark, muscled forms curl out of water, with flapping gills and flattened eyes. I close my eyes and I see stars, deep stars giving way to deeper stars, deeper stars bowing to deepest stars at the crown of an infinite cone.

"Still," wrote van Gogh in a letter, "a great deal of light falls on everything." If we are blinded by darkness, we are also blinded by light. When too much light falls on everything, a special terror results. Peter Freuchen describes the notorious kayak sickness to which Greenland Eskimos are prone. "The Greenland fjords are peculiar for the spells of completely quiet weather, when there is not enough wind to blow out a match and the water is like a sheet of glass. The kayak hunter must sit in his boat without stirring a finger so as not to scare the shy seals away. . . . The sun, low in the sky, sends a glare into his eyes, and the landscape around moves into the realm of the unreal. The reflex from the mirror-like water hypnotizes him, he seems to be unable to move, and all of a sudden it is as if he were floating in a bottomless void, sinking, sinking, and sinking. . . . Horror-stricken, he tries to stir, to cry out, but he cannot, he is completely paralyzed, he just falls and falls." Some hunters are especially cursed with this panic, and bring ruin and sometimes starvation to their families.

Sometimes here in Virginia at sunset low clouds on the southern or northern horizon are completely invisible in the lighted sky. I only know one is there because I can see its reflection in still water. The first time I discovered this mystery I looked from cloud to no-cloud in bewilderment, checking my bearings over and over, thinking maybe the ark of the covenant was just passing by south of Dead Man Mountain. Only much later did I read the explanation: polarized light from the sky is very much weakened by reflection, but the light in clouds isn't polarized. So invisible clouds pass among visible clouds, till all slide over the mountains; so a greater light extinguishes a lesser as though it didn't exist.

In the great meteor shower of August, the Perseid, I wail all day for the shooting stars I miss. They're out there showering down, committing hara-kiri in a flame of fatal attraction, and hissing perhaps at last into the ocean. But at dawn what looks like a blue dome clamps down over me like a lid on a pot. The stars and planets could smash and I'd never know. Only a piece of ashen moon occasionally climbs up or down the inside of the dome, and our local star without surcease explodes on our heads. We have really only that one light, one source for all power, and yet we must turn away from it by universal decree. Nobody here on the planet seems aware of this strange, powerful taboo, that we all walk about carefully averting our faces, this way and that, lest our eyes be blasted forever.

Darkness appalls and light dazzles; the scrap of visible light that doesn't hurt my eyes hurts my brain. What I see sets me swaying. Size and distance and the sudden swelling of meanings confuse me, bowl me over. I straddle the sycamore log bridge over Tinker Creek in the summer. I look at the lighted creek bottom: snail tracks tunnel the mud in quavering curves. A crayfish jerks, but by the time I absorb what has happened, he's gone in a billowing smokescreen of silt. I look at the water: minnows and shiners. If I'm thinking minnows, a carp will fill my brain till I scream. I look at the water's surface: skaters, bubbles, and leaves sliding down. Suddenly, my own face, reflected, startles me witless. Those snails have been tracking my face! Finally, with a shuddering wrench of the will, I see clouds, cirrus clouds. I'm dizzy, I fall in. This looking business is risky.

Once I stood on a humped rock on nearby Purgatory Mountain, watching through binoculars the great autumn hawk migration below, until I discovered that I was in danger of joining the hawks on a vertical migration of my own. I was used to binoculars, but not, apparently, to balancing on humped rocks while looking through them. I staggered. Everything advanced and receded by turns; the world was full of unexplained foreshortenings and depths. A distant huge tan object, a hawk the size of an elephant, turned out to be the browned bough of a nearby loblolly pine. I followed a sharp-shinned hawk against a featureless sky, rotating my head unawares as it flew, and when I lowered the glass a glimpse of my own looming shoulder sent me staggering. What prevents the men on Palomar from falling, voiceless and blinded, from their tiny, vaulted chairs?

I reel in confusion; I don't understand what I see. With the naked eye I can see two million light-years to the Andromeda galaxy. Often I slop some creek water in a jar and when I get home I dump it in a white china bowl. After the silt settles I return and see tracings of minute snails on the bottom, a planarian or two winding round the rim of water, roundworms shimmying frantically, and finally, when my eyes have adjusted to these dimensions, amoebae. At first the amoebae look like muscae volitantes, those curled moving spots you seem to see in your eyes when you stare at a distant wall. Then I see the amoebae as drops of water congealed, bluish, translucent, like chips of sky in the bowl. At length I choose one individual and give myself over to its idea of an evening. I see it dribble a grainy foot before it on its wet, unfathomable way. Do its unedited sense impressions include the fierce focus of my eyes? Shall I take it outside and show it Andromeda, and blow its little endoplasm? I stir the water with a finger, in case it's running out of oxygen. Maybe I should get a tropical aquarium with motorized bubblers and lights, and keep this one for a pet. Yes, it would tell its fissioned descendants, the universe is two feet by five, and if you listen closely you can hear the buzzing music of the spheres.

Oh, it's mysterious lamplit evenings, here in the galaxy, one after the other. It's one of those nights when I wander from window to window, looking for a sign. But I can't see. Terror and a beauty insoluble are a ribband of blue woven into the fringes of garments of things both great and small. No culture explains, no bivouac offers real haven or rest. But it could be that we are not seeing something. Galileo thought comets were an optical illusion. This is fertile ground: since we are certain that they're not, we can look at what our scientists have been saying with fresh hope. What if there are *really* gleaming, castellated cities hung upside-down over the desert sand? What limpid lakes and cool date palms have our caravans always passed untried? Until, one by one, by the blindest of leaps, we light on the road to these places, we must stumble in darkness and hunger. I turn from the window. I'm blind as a bat, sensing only from every direction the echo of my own thin cries.

I chanced on a wonderful book by Marius von Senden, called *Space and Sight*. When Western surgeons discovered how to perform safe cataract operations, they ranged across Europe and America operating on dozens of men and women of all ages who had been blinded by cataracts since birth. Von Senden collected accounts of such cases; the histories are fascinating. Many doctors had tested their patients' sense perceptions and ideas of space both before and after the operations. The vast majority of patients, of both sexes and all ages, had, in von Senden's opinion, no idea of space whatsoever. Form, distance, and size were so many meaningless syllables. A patient "had no idea of depth, confusing it with roundness." Before the operation a doctor would give a blind patient a cube and a sphere; the patient would tongue it or feel it with his hands, and name it correctly. After the operation the doctor would show the same objects to the patient without letting him touch them; now he had no clue whatsoever what he was seeing. One patient called lemonade "square" because it pricked on his tongue as a square shape pricked on the touch of his hands. Of another postoperative patient, the doctor writes, "I have found in her no notion of size, for example, not even within the narrow limits which she might have encompassed with the aid of touch. Thus when I asked her to show me how big her mother was, she did not stretch out her hands, but set her two index-fingers a few inches apart." Other doctors reported their patients' own statements to similar effect. "The room he was in . . . he knew to be but part of the house, yet he could not conceive that the whole house could look bigger"; "Those who are blind from birth . . . have no real conception of height or distance. A house that is a mile away is thought of as nearby, but requiring the taking of a lot of steps. . . . The elevator that whizzes him up and down gives no more sense of vertical distance than does the train of horizontal."

For the newly sighted, vision is pure sensation unencumbered by meaning: "The girl went through the experience that we all go through and forget, the moment we are born. She saw, but it did not mean anything but a lot of different kinds of brightness." Again, "I asked the patient what he could see; he answered that he saw an extensive field of light, in which everything appeared dull, confused, and in motion. He could not distinguish objects." Another patient saw "nothing but a confusion of forms and colours." When a newly sighted girl saw photographs and paintings, she asked, " 'Why do they put those dark marks all over them?' 'Those aren't dark marks,' her mother explained, 'those are shadows. That is one of the ways the eye knows that things have shape. If it were not for shadows many things would look flat.' 'Well, that's how things do look,' Joan answered. 'Everything looks flat with dark patches.' "

But it is the patients' concepts of space that are most revealing. One patient, according to his doctor, "practiced his vision in a strange fashion; thus he takes off one of his boots, throws it some way off in front of him, and then attempts to gauge the distance at which it lies; he takes a few steps towards the boot and tries to grasp it; on failing to reach it, he moves on a step or two and gropes for the boot until he finally gets hold of it." "But even at this stage, after three weeks' experience of seeing," von Senden goes on, " 'space,' as he conceives it, ends with visual space, i.e., with colour-patches that happen to bound his view. He does not yet have the notion that a larger object (a chair) can mask a smaller one (a dog), or that the latter can still be present even though it is not directly seen."

In general the newly sighted see the world as a dazzle of color-patches. They are pleased by the sensation of color, and learn quickly to name the colors, but the rest of seeing is tormentingly difficult. Soon after his operation a patient "generally bumps into one of these colour-patches and observes them to be substantial, since they resist him as tactual objects do. In walking about it also strikes him—or can if he pays attention—that he is continually passing in between the colours he sees, that he can go past a visual object, that a part of it then steadily disappears from view; and that in spite of this, however he twists and turns—whether entering the room from the door, for example, or returning back to it—he always has a visual space in front of him. Thus he gradually comes to realize that there is also a space behind him, which he does not see."

The mental effort involved in these reasonings proves overwhelming for many patients. It oppresses them to realize, if they ever do at all, the tremendous size of the world, which they had previously conceived of as something touchingly manageable. It oppresses them to realize that they have been visible to people all along, perhaps unattractively so, without their knowledge or consent. A disheartening number of them refuse to use their new vision, continuing to go over objects with their tongues, and lapsing into apathy and despair. "The child can see, but will not make use of his sight. Only when pressed can he with difficulty be brought to look at objects in his neighbourhood; but more than a foot away it is impossible to bestir him to the necessary effort." Of a twenty-one-year-old girl, the doctor relates, "Her unfortunate father, who had hoped for so much from this operation, wrote that his daughter carefully shuts her eyes whenever she wishes to go about the house, especially when she comes to a staircase, and that she is never happier or more at ease than when, by closing her eyelids, she relapses into her former state of total blindness." A fifteen-year-old boy, who was also in love with a girl at the asylum for the blind, finally blurted out, "No, really, I can't stand it any more; I want to be sent back to the asylum again. If things aren't altered, I'll tear my eyes out."

Some do learn to see, especially the young ones. But it changes their lives. One doctor comments on "the rapid and complete loss of that striking and wonderful serenity which is characteristic only of those who have never yet seen." A blind man who learns to see is ashamed of his old habits. He dresses up, grooms himself, and tries to make a good impression. While he was blind he was indifferent to objects unless they were edible; now, "a sifting of values sets in . . . his thoughts and wishes are mightily stirred and some few of the patients are thereby led into dissimulation, envy, theft and fraud."

On the other hand, many newly sighted people speak well of the world, and teach us how dull is our own vision. To one patient, a human hand, unrecognized, is "something bright and then holes." Shown a bunch of grapes, a boy calls out, "It is dark, blue and shiny. . . . It isn't smooth, it has bumps and hollows." A little girl visits a garden. "She is greatly astonished, and can scarcely be persuaded to answer, stands speechless in front of the tree, which she only names on taking hold of it, and then as 'the tree with the lights in it.' " Some delight in their sight and give themselves over to the visual world. Of a patient just after her bandages were removed, her doctor writes, "The first things to attract her attention were her own hands; she looked at them very closely, moved them repeatedly to and fro, bent and stretched the fingers, and seemed greatly astonished at the sight." One girl was eager to tell her blind friend that "men do not really look like trees at all," and astounded to discover that her every visitor had an utterly different face. Finally, a twenty-two-year-old girl was dazzled by the world's brightness and kept her eyes shut for two weeks. When at the end of that time she opened her eyes again, she did not recognize any objects, but, "the more she now directed her gaze upon everything about her, the more it could be seen how an expression of gratification and astonishment overspread her features; she repeatedly exclaimed: 'Oh God! How beautiful!' "

I saw color-patches for weeks after I read this wonderful book. It was summer; the peaches were ripe in the valley orchards. When I woke in the morning, color-patches wrapped round my eyes, intricately, leaving not one unfilled spot. All day long I walked among shifting color-patches that parted before me like the Red Sea and closed again in silence, transfigured, whenever I looked back. Some patches swelled and loomed, while others vanished utterly, and dark marks flitted at random over the whole dazzling sweep. But I couldn't sustain the illusion of flatness. I've been around for too long. Form is condemned to an eternal danse macabre with meaning: I couldn't unpeach the peaches. Nor can I remember ever having seen without understanding; the color-patches of infancy are lost. My brain then must have been smooth as any balloon. I'm told I reached for the moon; many babies do. But the color-patches of infancy swelled as meaning filled them; they arrayed themselves in solemn ranks down distances which unrolled and stretched before me like a plain. The moon rocketed away. I live now in a world of shadows that shape and distance color, a world where space makes a kind of terrible sense. What gnosticism is this, and what physics? The fluttering patch I saw in my nursery window—silver and green and shape-shifting blue—is gone; a row of Lombardy poplars takes its place, mute, across the distant lawn. That humming oblong creature pale as light that stole along the walls of my room at night, stretching exhilaratingly around the corners, is gone, too, gone the night I ate of the bittersweet fruit, put two and two together and puckered forever my brain. Martin Buber tells this tale: "Rabbi Mendel once boasted to his teacher Rabbi Elimelekh that evenings he saw the angel who rolls away the light before the darkness, and mornings the angel who rolls away the darkness before the light. 'Yes,' said Rabbi Elimelekh, 'in my youth I saw that too. Later on you don't see these things any more.' "

Why didn't someone hand those newly sighted people paints and brushes from the start, when they still didn't know what anything was? Then maybe we all could see color-patches too, the world unraveled from reason, Eden before Adam gave names. The scales would drop from my eyes; I'd see trees like men walking; I'd run down the road against all orders, hallooing and leaping.

* * *

Seeing is of course very much a matter of verbalization. Unless I call my attention to what passes before my eyes, I simply won't see it. It is, as Ruskin says, "not merely unnoticed, but in the full, clear sense of the word, unseen." My eyes alone can't solve analogy tests using figures, the ones which show, with increasing elaborations, a big square, then a small square in a big square, then a big triangle, and expect me to find a small triangle in a big triangle. I have to say the words, describe what I'm seeing. If Tinker Mountain erupted, I'd be likely to notice. But if I want to notice the lesser cataclysms of valley life, I have to maintain in my head a running description of the present. It's not that I'm observant; it's just that I talk too much. Otherwise, especially in a strange place, I'll never know what's happening. Like a blind man at the ball game, I need a radio.

When I see this way I analyze and pry. I hurl over logs and roll away stones; I study the bank a square foot at a time, probing and tilting my head. Some days when a mist covers the mountains, when the muskrats won't show and the microscope's mirror shatters, I want to climb up the blank blue dome as a man would storm the inside of a circus tent, wildly, dangling, and with a steel knife claw a rent in the top, peep, and, if I must, fall.

But there is another kind of seeing that involves a letting go. When I see this way I sway transfixed and emptied. The difference between the two ways of seeing is the difference between walking with and without a camera. When I walk with a camera, I walk from shot to shot, reading the light on a calibrated meter. When I walk without a camera, my own shutter opens, and the moment's light prints on my own silver gut. When I see this second way I am above all an unscrupulous observer.

It was sunny one evening last summer at Tinker Creek; the sun was low in the sky, upstream. I was sitting on the sycamore log bridge with the sunset at my back, watching the shiners the size of minnows who were feeding over the muddy sand in skittery schools. Again and again, one fish, then another turned for a split second across the current and flash! the sun shot out from its silver side. I couldn't watch for it. It was always just happening somewhere else, and it drew my vision just as it disappeared: flash, like a sudden dazzle of the thinnest blade, a sparking over a dun and olive ground at chance intervals from every direction. Then I noticed white specks, some sort of pale petals, small, floating from under my feet on the creek's surface, very slow and steady. So I blurred my eyes and gazed towards the brim of my hat and saw a new world. I saw the pale white circles roll up, roll up, like the world's turning, mute and perfect, and I saw the linear flashes, gleaming silver, like stars being born at random down a rolling scroll of time. Something broke and something opened. I filled up like a new wineskin. I breathed an air like light; I saw a light like water. I was the lip of a fountain the creek filled forever; I was ether, the leaf in the zephyr; I was flesh-flake, feather, bone.

When I see this way I see truly. As Thoreau says, I return to my senses. I am the man who watches the baseball game in silence in an empty stadium. I see the game purely; I'm abstracted and dazed. When it's all over and the white-suited players lope off the green field to their shadowed dugouts, I leap to my feet; I cheer and cheer.

But I can't go out and try to see this way. I'll fail, I'll go mad. All I can do is try to gag the commentator, to hush the noise of useless interior babble that keeps me from seeing just as surely as a newspaper dangled before my eyes. The effort is really a discipline requiring a lifetime of dedicated struggle; it marks the literature of saints and monks of every order East and West, under every rule and no rule, discalced and shod. The world's spiritual geniuses seem to discover universally that the mind's muddy river, this ceaseless flow of trivia and trash, cannot be dammed, and that trying to dam it is a waste of effort that might lead to madness. Instead you must allow the muddy river to flow unheeded in the dim channels of consciousness; you raise your sights; you look along it, mildly, acknowledging its presence without interest and gazing beyond it into the realm of the real where subjects and objects act and rest purely, without utterance. "Launch into the deep," says Jacques Ellul, "and you shall see."

The secret of seeing is, then, the pearl of great price. If I thought he could teach me to find it and keep it forever I would stagger barefoot across a hundred deserts after any lunatic at all. But although the pearl may be found, it may not be sought. The literature of illumination reveals this above all: although it comes to those who wait for it, it is always, even to the most practiced and adept, a gift and a total surprise. I return from one walk knowing where the killdeer nests in the field by the creek and the hour the laurel blooms. I return from the same walk a day later scarcely knowing my own name. Litanies hum in my ears; my tongue flaps in my mouth Ailinon, alleluia! I cannot cause light; the most I can do is try to put myself in the path of its beam. It is possible, in deep space, to sail on solar wind. Light, be it particle or wave, has force: you rig a giant sail and go. The secret of seeing is to sail on solar wind. Hone and spread your spirit till you yourself are a sail, whetted, translucent, broadside to the merest puff.

*   *   *

When her doctor took her bandages off and led her into the garden, the girl who was no longer blind saw "the tree with the lights in it." It was for this tree I searched through the peach orchards of summer, in the forests of fall and down winter and spring for years. Then one day I was walking along Tinker Creek thinking of nothing at all and I saw the tree with the lights in it. I saw the backyard cedar where the mourning doves roost charged and transfigured, each cell buzzing with flame. I stood on the grass with the lights in it, grass that was wholly fire, utterly focused and utterly dreamed. It was less like seeing than like being for the first time seen, knocked breathless by a powerful glance. The flood of fire abated, but I'm still spending the power. Gradually the lights went out in the cedar, the colors died, the cells unflamed and disappeared. I was still ringing. I had been my whole life a bell, and never knew it until at that moment I was lifted and struck. I have since only very rarely seen the tree with the lights in it. The vision comes and goes, mostly goes, but I live for it, for the moment when the mountains open and a new light roars in spate through the crack, and the mountains slam.

RICHARD SELZER

Richard Selzer (1928–   ) grew up in Troy, New York, and studied medicine. He described his coming-of-age in an affecting memoir, Down from Troy. *A practicing surgeon, Selzer is one of the new wave of literary scientists-clinicians (Stephen Jay Gould, Lewis Thomas, F. Gonzalez-Crussi, Oliver Sacks) who have brought a wealth of knowledge about the natural world to the essay form. What sets Selzer apart from these others is his willingness to write much more personally, even confessionally, about his feelings, reactions, and motives, in the tradition of the idiosyncratic first-person essay. He is also steeped in the sound of old English prose and relishes antiquarian diction and syntax; in Selzer one hears echoes of Sir Thomas Browne's* Urn Burial, Burton's Anatomy of Melancholy, *Montaigne, Lamb, and Hazlitt.*

Mortal Lessons: Notes on the Art of Surgery was Selzer's first essay collection, and it contains astonishing arias to the body and disease. One of these, "The Knife," proceeds by proposing a series of metaphors (religious, sexual, equine, and so on) for the surgeon's tool, until the object is surrounded by multiple, contradictory meanings. The author makes a synecdochic identification with his scalpel (a later collection was called Confessions of a Knife). *Selzer's capacity for giddy wonderment, even in such sobering confines as the operating theater, may strike some readers as self-indulgent or a kind of tasteless black humor, but he keeps tight control over his prose, and his compassion never falters. Ultimately, his descriptions have the tonic effect of making us look realistically at the impermanence and sturdiness of flesh.*

The Knife

O NE HOLDS THE KNIFE as one holds the bow of a cello or a tulip—by the stem. Not palmed nor gripped nor grasped, but lightly, with the tips of the fingers. The knife is not for pressing. It is for drawing across the field of skin. Like a slender fish, it waits, at the ready, then, go! It darts, followed by a fine wake of red. The flesh parts, falling away to yellow globules of fat. Even now, after so many times, I still marvel at its power—cold, gleaming, silent. More, I am still struck with a kind of dread that it is I in whose hand the blade travels, that my hand is its vehicle, that yet again this terrible steel-bellied thing and I have conspired for a most unnatural purpose, the laying open of the body of a human being.

A stillness settles in my heart and is carried to my hand. It is the quietude of resolve layered over fear. And it is this resolve that lowers us, my knife and me, deeper and deeper into the person beneath. It is an entry into the body that is nothing like a caress; still, it is among the gentlest of acts. Then stroke and stroke again, and we are joined by other instruments, hemostats and forceps, until the wound blooms with strange flowers whose looped handles fall to the sides in steely array.

There is sound, the tight click of clamps fixing teeth into severed blood vessels, the snuffle and gargle of the suction machine clearing the field of blood for the next stroke, the litany of monosyllables with which one prays his way down and in: *clamp, sponge, suture, tie, cut.* And there is color. The green of the cloth, the white of the sponges, the red and yellow of the body. Beneath the fat lies the fascia, the tough fibrous sheet encasing the muscles. It must be sliced and the red beef of the muscles separated. Now there are retractors to hold apart the wound. Hands move together, part, weave. We are fully engaged, like children absorbed in a game or the craftsmen of some place like Damascus.

Deeper still. The peritoneum, pink and gleaming and membranous, bulges into the wound. It is grasped with forceps, and opened. For the first time we can see into the cavity of the abdomen. Such a primitive place. One expects to find drawings of buffalo on the walls. The sense of trespassing is keener now, heightened by the world's light illuminating the organs, their secret colors revealed—maroon and salmon and yellow. The vista is sweetly vulnerable at this moment, a kind of welcoming. An arc of the liver shines high and on the right, like a dark sun. It laps over the pink sweep of the stomach, from whose lower border the gauzy omentum is draped, and through which veil one sees, sinuous, slow as just-fed snakes, the indolent coils of the intestine.

You turn aside to wash your gloves. It is a ritual cleansing. One enters this temple doubly washed. Here is man as microcosm, representing in all his parts the earth, perhaps the universe.

I must confess that the priestliness of my profession has ever been impressed on me. In the beginning there are vows, taken with all solemnity. Then there is the endless harsh novitiate of training, much fatigue, much sacrifice. At last one emerges as celebrant, standing close to the truth lying curtained in the Ark of the body. Not surplice and cassock but mask and gown are your regalia. You hold no chalice, but a knife. There is no wine, no wafer. There are only the facts of blood and flesh.

And if the surgeon is like a poet, then the scars you have made on countless bodies are like verses into the fashioning of which you have poured your soul. I think that if years later I were to see the trace from an old incision of mine, I should know it at once, as one recognizes his pet expressions.

But mostly you are a traveler in a dangerous country, advancing into the moist and jungly cleft your hands have made. Eyes and ears are shuttered from the land you left behind; mind empties itself of all other thought. You are the root of groping fingers. It is a fine hour for the fingers, their sense of touch so enhanced. The blind must know this feeling. Oh, there is risk everywhere. One goes lightly. The spleen. No! No! Do not touch the spleen that lurks below the left leaf of the diaphragm, a manta ray in a coral cave, its bloody tongue protruding. One poke and it might rupture, exploding with sudden hemorrhage. The filmy omentum must not be torn, the intestine scraped or denuded. The hand finds the liver, palms it, fingers running along its sharp lower edge, admiring. Here are the twin mounds of the kidneys, the apron of the omentum hanging in front of the intestinal coils. One lifts it aside and the fingers dip among the loops, searching, mapping territory, establishing boundaries. Deeper still, and the womb is touched, then held like a small muscular bottle—the womb and its earlike appendages, the ovaries. How they do nestle in the cup of a man's hand, their power all dormant. They are frailty itself.

There is a hush in the room. Speech stops. The hands of the others, assistants and nurses, are still. Only the voice of the patient's respiration remains. It is the rhythm of a quiet sea, the sound of waiting. Then you speak, slowly, the terse entries of a Himalayan climber reporting back.

"The stomach is okay. Greater curvature clean. No sign of ulcer. Pylorus, duodenum fine. Now comes the gall-bladder. No stones. Right kidney, left, all right. Liver . . . uh-oh."

Your speech lowers to a whisper, falters, stops for a long, long moment, then picks up again at the end of a sigh that comes through your mask like a last exhalation.

"Three big hard ones in the left lobe, one on the right. Metastatic deposits. Bad, bad. Where's the primary? Got to be coming from somewhere."

The arm shifts direction and the fingers drop lower and lower into the pelvis—the body impaled now upon the arm of the surgeon to the hilt of the elbow.

"Here it is."

The voice goes flat, all business now.

"Tumor in the sigmoid colon, wrapped all around it, pretty tight. We'll take out a sleeve of the bowel. No colostomy. Not that, anyway. But, God, there's a lot of it down there. Here, you take a feel."

You step back from the table, and lean into a sterile basin of water, resting on stiff arms, while the others locate the cancer.

When I was a small boy, I was taken by my father, a general practitioner in Troy, New York, to St. Mary's Hospital, to wait while he made his rounds. The solarium where I sat was all sunlight and large plants. It smelled of soap and starch and clean linen. In the spring, clouds of lilac billowed from the vases; and in the fall, chrysanthemums crowded the magazine tables. At one end of the great high-ceilinged, glass-walled room was a huge cage where colored finches streaked and sang. Even from the first, I sensed the nearness of that other place, the Operating Room, knew that somewhere on these premises was that secret dreadful enclosure where *surgery* was at that moment happening. I sat among the cut flowers, half drunk on the scent, listening to the robes of the nuns brush the walls of the corridor, and felt the awful presence of *surgery*.

Oh, the pageantry! I longed to go there. I feared to go there. I imagined surgeons bent like storks over the body of the patient, a circle of red painted across the abdomen. Silence and dignity and awe enveloped them, these surgeons; it was the bubble in which they bent and straightened. Ah, it was a place I would never see, a place from whose walls the hung and suffering Christ turned his affliction to highest purpose. It is thirty years since I yearned for that old Surgery. And now I merely break the beam of an electric eye, and double doors swing open to let me enter, and as I enter, always, I feel the surging of a force that I feel in no other place. It is as though I am suddenly stronger and larger, heroic. Yes, that's it!

The operating room is called a theatre. One walks onto a set where the cupboards hold tanks of oxygen and other gases. The cabinets store steel cutlery of unimagined versatility, and the refrigerators are filled with bags of blood. Bodies are stroked and penetrated here, but no love is made.

Nor is it ever allowed to grow dark, but must always gleam with a grotesque brightness. For the special congress into which patient and surgeon enter, the one must have his senses deadened, the other his sensibilities restrained. One lies naked, blind, offering; the other stands masked and gloved. One yields; the other does his will.

I said no love is made here, but love happens. I have stood aside with lowered gaze while a priest, wearing the purple scarf of office, administers Last Rites to the man I shall operate upon. I try not to listen to those terrible last questions, the answers, but hear, with scorching clarity, the words that formalize the expectation of death. For a moment my resolve falters before the resignation, the *attentiveness,* of the other two. I am like an executioner who hears the cleric comforting the prisoner. For the moment I am excluded from the centrality of the event, a mere technician standing by. But it is only for the moment.

The priest leaves, and we are ready. Let it begin.

Later, I am repairing the strangulated hernia of an old man. Because of his age and frailty, I am using local anesthesia. He is awake. His name is Abe Kaufman, and he is a Russian Jew. A nurse sits by his head, murmuring to him. She wipes his forehead. I know her very well. Her name is Alexandria, and she is the daughter of Ukrainian peasants. She has a flat steppe of a face and slanting eyes. Nurse and patient are speaking of blintzes, borscht, piroshki—Russian food that they both love. I listen, and think that it may have been her grandfather who raided the shtetl where the old man lived long ago, and in his high boots and his blouse and his fury this grandfather pulled Abe by his side curls to the ground and stomped his face and kicked his groin. Perhaps it was that ancient kick that caused the hernia I am fixing. I listen to them whispering behind the screen at the head of the table. I listen with breath held before the prism of history.

"Tovarich," she says, her head bent close to his.

He smiles up at her, and forgets that his body is being laid open.

"You are an angel," the old man says.

One can count on absurdity. There, in the midst of our solemnities, appears, small and black and crawling, an insect: The Ant of the Absurd. The belly is open; one has seen and felt the catastrophe within. It seems the patient is already vaporizing into angelhood in the heat escaping therefrom. One could warm one's hands in that fever. All at once that ant is there, emerging from beneath one of the sterile towels that border the operating field. For a moment one does not really see it, or else denies the sight, so impossible it is, marching precisely, heading briskly toward the open wound.

Drawn from its linen lair, where it snuggled in the steam of the great sterilizer, and survived, it comes. Closer and closer, it hurries toward the incision. Ant, art thou in the grip of some fatal *ivresse?* Wouldst hurtle over these scarlet cliffs into the very boil of the guts? Art mad for the reek we handle? Or in some secret act of formication engaged?

The alarm is sounded. An ant! An ant! And we are unnerved. Our fear of defilement is near to frenzy. It is not the mere physical contamination that we loathe. It is the evil of the interloper, that he scurries across our holy place, and filthies our altar. He *is* disease—that for whose destruction we have gathered. Powerless to destroy the sickness before us, we turn to its incarnation with a vengeance, and pluck it from the lip of the incision in the nick of time. Who would have thought an ant could move so fast?

Between thumb and forefinger, the intruder is crushed. It dies as quietly as it lived. Ah, but now there is death in the room. It is a perversion of our purpose. Albert Schweitzer would have spared it, scooped it tenderly into his hand, and lowered it to the ground.

The corpselet is flicked into the specimen basin. The gloves are changed. New towels and sheets are placed where it walked. We are pleased to have done something, if only a small killing. The operation resumes, and we draw upon ourselves once more the sleeves of office and rank. Is our reverence for life in question?

In the room the instruments lie on trays and tables. They are arranged precisely by the scrub nurse, in an order that never changes, so that you can reach blindly for a forceps or hemostat without looking away from the operating field. The instruments lie *thus!* Even at the beginning, when all is clean and tidy and no blood has been spilled, it is the scalpel that dominates. It has a figure the others do not have, the retractors and the scissors. The scalpel is all grace and line, a fierceness. It grins. It is like a cat—to be respected, deferred to, but which returns no amiability. To hold it above a belly is to know the knife's force—as though were you to give it slightest rein, it would pursue an intent of its own, driving into the flesh, a wild energy.

In a story by Borges, a deadly knife fight between two rivals is depicted. It is not, however, the men who are fighting. It is the knives themselves that are settling their own old score. The men who hold the knives are mere adjuncts to the weapons. The unguarded knife is like the unbridled war-horse that not only carries its helpless rider to his death, but tramples all beneath its hooves. The hand of the surgeon must tame this savage thing. He is a rider reining to capture a pace.

So close is the joining of knife and surgeon that they are like the Centaur—the knife, below, all equine energy, the surgeon, above, with his delicate art. One holds the knife back as much as advances it to purpose. One is master of the scissors. One is partner, sometimes rival, to the knife.

In a moment it is like the long red fingernail of the Dragon Lady. Thus does the surgeon curb in order to create, restraining the scalpel, governing it shrewdly, setting the action of the operation into a pattern, giving it form and purpose.

It is the nature of creatures to live within a tight cuirass that is both their constriction and their protection. The carapace of the turtle is his fortress and retreat, yet keeps him writhing on his back in the sand. So is the surgeon rendered impotent by his own empathy and compassion. The surgeon cannot weep. When he cuts the flesh, his own must not bleed. Here it is all work. Like an asthmatic hungering for air, longing to take just one deep breath, the surgeon struggles not to feel. It is suffocating to press the feeling out. It would be easier to weep or mourn—for you know that the lovely precise world of proportion contains, just beneath, *there,* all disaster, all disorder. In a surgical operation, a risk may flash into reality: the patient dies . . . of *complication.* The patient knows this too, in a more direct and personal way, and he is afraid.

And what of that *other,* the patient, you, who are brought to the operating room on a stretcher, having been washed and purged and dressed in a white gown? Fluid drips from a bottle into your arm, diluting you, leaching your body of its personal brine. As you wait in the corridor, you hear from behind the closed door the angry clang of steel upon steel, as though a battle were being waged. There is the odor of antiseptic and ether, and masked women hurry up and down the halls, in and out of rooms. There is the watery sound of strange machinery, the tinny beeping that is the transmitted heartbeat of yet another *human being.* And all the while the dreadful knowledge that soon you will be taken, laid beneath great lamps that will reveal the secret linings of your body. In the very act of lying down, you have made a declaration of surrender. One lies down gladly for sleep or for love. But to give over one's body and will for surgery, to *lie down* for it, is a yielding of more than we can bear.

Soon a man will stand over you, gowned and hooded. In time the man will take up a knife and crack open your flesh like a ripe melon. Fingers will rummage among your viscera. Parts of you will be cut out. Blood will run free. Your blood. All the night before you have turned with the presentiment of death upon you. You have attended your funeral, wept with your mourners. You think, "I should never have had surgery in the springtime." It is too cruel. Or on a Thursday. It is an unlucky day.

Now it is time. You are wheeled in and moved to the table. An injection is given. "Let yourself go," I say. "It's a pleasant sensation," I say. "Give in," I say.

Let go? Give in? When you know that you are being tricked into the hereafter, that you will end when consciousness ends? As the monstrous silence of anesthesia falls discourteously across your brain, you watch your soul drift off.

Later, in the recovery room, you awaken and gaze through the thickness of drugs at the world returning, and you guess, at first dimly, then surely, that you have not died. In pain and nausea you will know the exultation of death averted, of life restored.

What is it, then, this thing, the knife, whose shape is virtually the same as it was three thousand years ago, but now with its head grown detachable? Before steel, it was bronze. Before bronze, stone—then back into unremembered time. Did man invent it or did the knife precede him here, hidden under ages of vegetation and hoofprints, lying in wait to be discovered, picked up, used?

The scalpel is in two parts, the handle and the blade. Joined, it is six inches from tip to tip. At one end of the handle is a narrow notched prong upon which the blade is slid, then snapped into place. Without the blade, the handle has a blind, decapitated look. It is helpless as a trussed maniac. But slide on the blade, click it home, and the knife springs instantly to life. It is headed now, edgy, leaping to mount the fingers for the gallop to its feast.

Now is the moment from which you have turned aside, from which you have averted your gaze, yet toward which you have been hastened. Now the scalpel sings along the flesh again, its brute run unimpeded by germs or other frictions. It is a slick slide home, a barracuda spurt, a rip of embedded talon. One listens, and almost hears the whine—nasal, high, delivered through that gleaming metallic snout. The flesh splits with its own kind of moan. It is like the penetration of rape.

The breasts of women are cut off, arms and legs sliced to the bone to make ready for the saw, eyes freed from sockets, intestines lopped. The hand of the surgeon rebels. Tension boils through his pores, like sweat. The flesh of the patient retaliates with hemorrhage, and the blood chases the knife wherever it is withdrawn.

Within the belly a tumor squats, toadish, fungoid. A gray mother and her brood. The only thing it does not do is croak. It too is hacked from its bed as the carnivore knife lips the blood, turning in it in a kind of ecstasy of plenty, a gluttony after the long fast. It is just for this that the knife was created, tempered, heated, its violence beaten into paper-thin force.

At last a little thread is passed into the wound and tied. The monstrous booming fury is stilled by a tiny thread. The tempest is silenced. The operation is over. On the table, the knife lies spent, on its side, the bloody meal smear-dried upon its flanks. The knife rests.

And waits.

PHILLIP LOPATE

Phillip Lopate (1943–   ) is the author of two essay collections, Bachelor-hood *and* Against Joie de Vivre, *as well as two novels, two volumes of poetry, and a nonfiction account of his work as a writer in the schools,* Being with Children. *His characteristic subjects include city life, the disorders of love and friendship, movies, families, neurotic resistance, and rationalization. Modesty forbids the editor of this anthology from assessing his prowess as an essay writer—though it did not prevent him from including the following entry. About it, he has this to say: "I wrote 'Against Joie de Vivre' after reading a good deal of Montaigne, particularly his later essays. It was my attempt to do something in a large, quasi-philosophical vein. Of course the central proposition is nonsensical—no one can be against the joy of life, really—and I knew that at the time, but I wanted to push a prejudice, or dark impulse, of mine as far as it would go, and see where it would take me."*

Against Joie de Vivre

[handwritten annotation: Sarcasm abounds. why? ← / is HE bitter?]

OVER THE YEARS I have developed a distaste for the spectacle of *joie de vivre,* the knack of knowing how to live. Not that I disapprove of all hearty enjoyment of life. A flushed sense of happiness can overtake a person anywhere, and one is no more to blame for it than the Asiatic flu or a sudden benevolent change in the weather (which is often joy's immediate cause). No, what rankles me is the stylization of this private condition into a bullying social ritual.

The French, who have elevated the picnic to their highest rite, are probably most responsible for promoting this smugly upbeat, flaunting style. It took the French genius for formalizing the informal to bring sticky sacramental sanctity to the baguette, wine, and cheese. A pure image of sleeveless *joie de vivre* Sundays can also be found in Renoir's paintings. Weekend satyrs dance and wink, leisure takes on a bohemian stripe. A decent writer, Henry Miller, caught the French malady and ran back to tell us of *pissoirs* in the Paris streets (why this should have impressed him so, I've never figured out).

But if you want a double dose of *joie de vivre,* you need to consult a later, hence more stylized, version of the French myth of pagan happiness: those *Family of Man* photographs of endlessly kissing lovers, snapped by Doisneau and Boubat, or Cartier-Bresson's icon of the proud tyke carrying bottles of wine. If Cartier-Bresson and his disciples are excellent photographers for all that, it is in spite of their occasionally rubbing our noses in a tediously problematic "affirmation of life."

Though it is traditionally the province of the French, the whole Mediterranean is a hotbed of professional *joie de vivrism,* which they have gotten down to a routine like a crack *son et lumière* display. The Italians export *dolce far niente* as aggressively as tomato paste. For the Greeks, a Zorba dance to life has supplanted classical antiquities as their main touristic lure. Hard to imagine anything as stomach-turning as being forced to participate in such an oppressively robust, folknik effusion. Fortunately, the country has its share of thin, nervous, bitter types, but Greeks do exist who would clutch you to their joyfully stout bellies and crush you there. The *joie de vivrist* is an incorrigible missionary who presumes that everyone wants to express pro-life feelings in the same stereotyped manner.

A warning: since I myself have a large store of nervous discontent (some would say hostility), I am apt to be harsh in my secret judgments of others, seeing them as defective because they are not enough like me. From moment to moment, the person I am with often seems too shrill, too bland, too something-or-other to allow my own expansiveness to swing into stage center. "Feeling no need to drink, you will promptly despise a drunkard" (Kenneth Burke). So it goes with me, which is why I am not a literary critic. I have no faith that my discriminations in taste are anything but the picky awareness of what will keep me stimulated, based on the peculiar family and class circumstances that formed me. But the knowledge that my discriminations are skewed and not always universally desirable doesn't stop me in the least from making them, just as one never gives up a negative first impression, no matter how many times it is contradicted. A believer in astrology (to cite another false system), having guessed that someone is a Sagittarius, and then told he is a Scorpio, says "Scorpio— yes, of course!" without missing a beat, or relinquishing confidence in his ability to tell people's signs, or in his idea that the person is somehow secretly Sagittarian.

1. The Houseboat

I remember exactly when my dislike for *joie de vivre* began to crystallize. It was 1969. We had gone to visit an old Greek painter on his houseboat in Sausalito. Old Vartas's vitality was legendary, and it was considered a spiritual honor to meet him, like getting an audience with the pope. Each Sunday he had a sort of open house, or open boat.

My "sponsor," Frank, had been many times to the houseboat, furnishing Vartas with record albums, since the old painter had a passion for San Francisco rock bands. Frank told me that Vartas had been a pal of Henry Miller's and I, being a writer of Russian descent, would love him. I failed to grasp the syllogism, but, putting aside my instinct to dislike anybody I have been assured I will adore, I prepared myself to give the man a chance.

Greeting us on the gangplank was an old man with thick, lush, white hair and snowy eyebrows, his face reddened from the sun. As he took us into the houseboat cabin he told me proudly that he was seventy-seven years old, and gestured toward the paintings that were spaced a few feet apart on the floor, leaning against the wall. They were celebrations of the blue Aegean, boats moored in ports, whitewashed houses on a hill, painted in primary colors and decorated with collaged materials: mirrors, burlap, Life Saver candies. These sunny little canvases with their talented innocence, third-generation spirit of Montmartre, bore testimony to a love of life so unbending as to leave an impression of rigid narrow-mindedness as extreme as any Savonarola's. Their rejection of sorrow was total. They were the sort of festive paintings that sell at high-rent Madison Avenue galleries specializing in European *schlock*.

Then I became aware of three young, beautiful women, bare-shoul-dered, wearing white pajama pants, each with long blond hair falling onto a sky-blue halter—unmistakably suggesting the Three Graces. They lived with him on the houseboat, I was told, giving no one knew what compen-sation for their lodgings. Perhaps their only payment was to feed his vanity in front of outsiders. The Greek painter smiled with the air of an old fox around the trio. For their part, the women obligingly contributed their praises of Vartas's youthful zip, which of course was taken by some guests as double entendre for undiminished sexual prowess. The Three Graces also gathered the food offerings of the visitors to make a midday meal.

Then the boat, equipped with a sail, was launched to sea. I must admit it gave me a spoilsport's pleasure when the winds turned becalmed. We could not move. Aboard were several members of the Bay Area's French colony, who dangled their feet over the sides, passed around bunches of grapes, and sang what I imagined were Gallic camping songs. The French know boredom, so they would understand how to behave in such a situa-tion. It has been my observation that many French men and women sta-tioned in America have the attitude of taking it easy, slumming at a health resort, and nowhere more so than in California. The *émigré* crew included a securities analyst, an academic sociologist, a museum administrator and his wife, a modiste: on Vartas's boat, they all got drunk and carried on like redskins, noble savages off Tahiti.

Joie de vivre requires a *soupçon* of the primitive. But since the illusion of the primitive soon palls and has nowhere to go, it becomes necessary to make new initiates. A good part of the day, in fact, was taken up with regulars interpreting to first-timers like myself certain mores pertaining to the houseboat, as well as offering tidbits about Vartas's Rabelaisian views of life. Here everyone was encouraged to do what he willed. (How much could you do on a becalmed boat surrounded by strangers?) No one had much solid information about their host's past, which only increased the privileged status of those who knew at least one fact. Useless to ask the object of this venerating speculation, since Vartas said next to nothing (adding to his impressiveness) when he was around, and disappeared be-low for long stretches of time.

In the evening, after a communal dinner, the new Grateful Dead record Frank had brought was put on the phonograph, and Vartas danced, first by himself, then with all three Graces, bending his arms in broad, hooking sweeps. He stomped his foot and looked around scampishly at the guests for appreciation, not unlike an organ-grinder and his monkey. Imagine, if you will, a being whose generous bestowal of self-satisfaction invites and is willing to receive nothing but flattery in return, a person who has managed to make others buy his somewhat senile projection of indestructibility as a Hymn to Life. In no sense could he be called a charlatan; he delivered what he promised, an incarnation of *joie de vivre,* and if it was shallow, it was also effective, managing even to attract an enviable "harem" (which was what really burned me).

A few years passed.

Some Dutch TV crew, ever on the lookout for exotic bits of Americana that would make good short subjects, planned to do a documentary about Vartas as a sort of paean to eternal youth. I later learned from Frank that Vartas died before the shooting could be completed. A pity, in a way. The home movie I've run off in my head of the old man is getting a little tattered, the colors splotchy, and the scenario goes nowhere, lacks point. All I have for sure is the title: *The Man Who Gave* Joie de Vivre *a Bad Name.*

"Ah, what a twinkle in the eye the old man has! He'll outlive us all." So we speak of old people who bore us, when we wish to honor them. We often see projected onto old people this worship of the life force. It is not the fault of the old if they then turn around and try to exploit our misguided amazement at their longevity as though it were a personal tour de force. The elderly, when they are honest with themselves, realize they have done nothing particularly to be proud of in lasting to a ripe old age, and then carrying themselves through a thousand more days. Yet you still hear an old woman or man telling a bus driver with a chuckle, "Would you believe that I am eighty-four years old!" As though they should be patted on the back for still knowing how to talk, or as though they had pulled a practical joke on the other riders by staying so spry and mobile. Such insecure, wheedling behavior always embarrasses me. I will look away rather than meet the speaker's eyes and be forced to lie with a smile, "Yes, you are remarkable," which seems condescending on my part and humiliating to us both.

Like children forced to play the cute part adults expect of them, some old people must get confused trying to adapt to a social role of indeterminate standards, which is why they seem to whine: "I'm doing all right, aren't I—for my age?" It is interesting that society's two most powerless groups, children and the elderly, have both been made into sentimental symbols. In the child's little hungry hands grasping for life, joined to the old person's frail slipping fingers hanging on to it, you have one of the commonest advertising metaphors for intense appreciation. It is enough to show a young child sleeping in his or her grandparent's lap to procure *joie de vivre* overload.

2 . The Dinner Party

I am invited periodically to dinner parties and brunches—and I go, because I like to be with people and oblige them, even if I secretly cannot share their optimism about these events. I go, not believing that I will have fun, but with the intent of observing people who think a *dinner party* a good time. I eat their fancy food, drink the wine, make my share of entertaining conversation, and often leave having had a pleasant evening, which does not prevent me from anticipating the next invitation with the same bleak lack of hope. To put it in a nutshell, I am an ingrate.

Although I have traveled a long way from my proletarian origins and talk, dress, act, and spend money like a perfect little bourgeois, I hold on to my poor-boy's outrage at the "decadence" (meaning dull entertainment style) of the middle and upper-middle classes; or, like a model Soviet moviegoer watching scenes of prerevolutionary capitalists gorging themselves on caviar, I am appalled, but I dig in with the rest.

Perhaps my uneasiness with dinner parties comes from the simple fact that not a single dinner party was given by my solitudinous parents the whole time I was growing up, and I had to wait until my late twenties before learning the ritual. A spy in the enemy camp, I have made myself a patient observer of strange customs. For the benefit of other late-starting social climbers, this is what I have observed.

As everyone should know, the ritual of the dinner party begins away from the table. Usually in the living room, cheeses and walnuts are set out, to start the digestive juices flowing. Here introductions between strangers are also made. Most dinner parties contain at least a few guests who have been unknown to each other before that evening, but who the host and/or hostess envision would enjoy meeting. These novel pairings and their interactions add spice to the postmortem: Who got along with whom? The lack of prior acquaintanceship also ensures that the guests will have to rely on and go through the only people known to everyone, the host and hostess, whose absorption of this helplessly dependent attention is one of the main reasons for throwing dinner parties.

Although an after-work "leisure activity," the dinner party is in fact a celebration of professional identity. Each of the guests has been preselected as in a floral bouquet; and in certain developed forms of this ritual there is usually a cunning mix of professions. Yet the point is finally not so much diversity as commonality; what remarkably shared attitudes and interests these people from different vocations demonstrate by conversing intelligently, or at least glibly, on the topics that arise. Naturally, a person cannot discourse too technically about one's line of work, so he or she picks precisely those themes that invite overlap. The psychiatrist laments the new breed of egoless, narcissistic patient who keeps turning up in his office (a beach bum who lacks the work ethic); the college professor bemoans the shoddy intellectual backgrounds and self-centered ignorance of his students; and the bookseller parodies the customer who pronounced Sophocles to rhyme with "bifocals." The dinner party is thus an exercise in locating ignorance—elsewhere. Whoever is present is *ipso facto* part of that beleaguered remnant of civilized folk fast disappearing from earth.

Or think of a dinner party as a club of revolutionaries, a technocratic elite whose social interactions that night are a dry run for some future takeover of the state. These are the future cabinet members (now only a shadow cabinet, alas) meeting to practice for the first time. How well they get on! "The time will soon be ripe, my friends. . . ." If this is too fanciful for you, then compare the dinner party to a utopian community, a Brook Farm supper club, in which only the best and most useful community members are chosen to participate. The smugness begins as soon as one enters the door, since one is already part of the chosen few. And from then on, every mechanical step in dinner-party process is designed to augment the atmosphere of group *amour-propre.* This is not to say that there won't be one or two people in an absolute torment of exclusion, too shy to speak up, or suspecting that when they do their contributions fail to carry the same weight as those of the others. The group's all-purpose drone of self-contentment ignores these drowning people—cruelly inattentive in one sense but benign in another: it invites them to join the shared ethos of success any time they are ready.

The group is asked to repair to the table. Once again they find themselves marveling at a shared perception of life. How delicious the fish soup! How cute the stuffed tomatoes! What did you use in this green sauce? Now comes much talk of ingredients, and credit is given where credit is due. It is Jacques who made the salad. It was Mamie who brought the homemade bread. Everyone pleads with the hostess to sit down, not to work so hard—an empty formula whose hypocrisy bothers no one. Who else is going to put the butter dish on the table? For a moment all become quiet, except for the sounds of eating. This corresponds to the part in a church service that calls for silent prayer.

I am saved from such culinary paganism by the fact that food is largely an indifferent matter to me. I rarely think much about what I am putting in my mouth. Though my savage, illiterate palate has inevitably been educated to some degree by the many meals I have shared with people who care enormously about such things, I resist going any further. I am superstitious that the day I send back a dish at a restaurant, or make a complicated journey somewhere just for a meal, that day I will have sacrificed my freedom and traded in my soul for a lesser god.

I don't expect the reader to agree with me. That's not the point. Unlike the behavior called for at a dinner party, I am not obliged, sitting at my typewriter, to help procure consensus every moment. So I am at liberty to declare, to the friend who once told me that dinner parties were one of the only opportunities for intelligently convivial conversations to take place in this cold, fragmented city, that she is crazy. The conversation at dinner parties is of a mind-numbing caliber. No discussion of any clarifying rigor—be it political, spiritual, artistic, or financial—can take place in a context where fervent conviction of any kind is frowned upon, and the desire to follow through a sequence of ideas must give way every time to the impressionistic, breezy flitting from topic to topic. Talk must be bubbly but not penetrating. Illumination would only slow the flow. Some hit-and-run remark may accidentally jog an idea loose, but in such cases it is better to scribble a few words down on the napkin for later than attempt to "think" at a dinner party.

What do people talk about at such gatherings? The latest movies, the priciness of things, word processors, restaurants, muggings and burglaries, private versus public schools, the fool in the White House (there have been so many fools in a row that this subject is getting tired), the undeserved reputations of certain better-known professionals in one's field, the fashions in investments, the investments in fashion. What is traded at the dinner-party table is, of course, class information. You will learn whether you are in the avant-garde or rear guard of your social class, or, preferably, right in step.

As for Serious Subjects, dinner-party guests have the latest *New Yorker* in-depth piece to bring up. People who ordinarily would not spare a moment worrying about the treatment of schizophrenics in mental hospitals, the fate of Great Britain in the Common Market, or the disposal of nuclear wastes suddenly find their consciences orchestrated in unison about these problems, thanks to their favorite periodical—though a month later they have forgotten all about it and are on to something new.

The dinner party is a suburban form of entertainment. Its spread in our big cities represents an insidious Fifth Column suburbanization of the metropolis. In the suburbs it becomes necessary to be able to discourse knowledgeably about the heart of the city, but from the viewpoint of a day-shopper. Dinner-party chatter is the communicative equivalent of roaming around shopping malls.

Much thought has gone into the ideal size for a dinner party—usually with the hostess arriving at the figure eight. Six would give each personality too much weight; ten would lead to splintering side discussions; eight is the largest number still able to force everyone into the same compulsively congenial conversation. My own strength as a conversationalist comes out less in groups of eight than one-to-one, which may explain my resistance to dinner parties. At the table, unfortunately, any engrossing *tête-à-tête* is frowned upon as antisocial. I often find myself in the frustrating situation of being drawn to several engaging people in among the bores, and wishing I could have a private conversation with each, without being able to do more than signal across the table a wry recognition of that fact. "Some other time, perhaps," we seem to be saying with our eyes, all evening long.

Later, however—to give the devil his due—when guests and hosts retire from the table back to the living room, the strict demands of group participation may be relaxed, and individuals allowed to pair off in some form of conversational intimacy. But one must be ever on the lookout for the group's need to swoop everybody together again for one last demonstration of collective fealty.

The first to leave breaks the communal spell. There is a sudden rush to the coat closet, the bathroom, the bedroom, as others, under the protection of the first defector's original sin, quit the Party apologetically. The utopian dream has collapsed: left behind are a few loyalists and insomniacs, swillers of a last cognac. "Don't leave yet," begs the host, knowing what a sense of letdown, pain, and self-recrimination awaits. Dirty dishes are, if anything, a comfort: the faucet's warm gush serves to stave off the moment of anesthetized stock-taking—Was that really necessary?—in the sobering silence that follows a dinner party.

3. Joie's Doppelgänger

I have no desire to rail against the Me Generation. We all know that the current epicurean style of the Good Life, from light foods to running shoes, is a result of market research techniques developed to sell "spot" markets, and, as such, a natural outgrowth of consumer capitalism. I may not like it, but I can't pretend that my objections are the result of a high-minded Laschian political analysis. Moreover, my own record of activism is not so noticeably impressive that I can lecture the Sunday brunchers to roll up their sleeves and start fighting social injustices instead of indulging themselves.

No, if I try to understand the reasons for my antihedonistic biases I must admit that they come from somewhere other than idealism. It's odd, because there seems to be a contradiction between the curmudgeonly feeling inside me and my periodically strong appetite for life. I am reminded of my hero, William Hazlitt, with his sarcastic, grumpy disposition on the one hand, and his capacity for "gusto" (his word, not Schlitz's) on the other. With Hazlitt, one senses a fanatically tenacious defense of individuality and independence against some unnamed bully stalking him. He had trained himself to be a connoisseur of vitality, and got irritated when life was not filled to the brim. I am far less irritable—before others; I will laugh if there is the merest *anything* to laugh at. But it is a tense, pouncing pleasure, not one that will allow me to sink into undifferentiated relaxation. The prospect of a long day at the beach makes me panic. There is no harder work I can think of than taking myself off to somewhere pleasant, where I am forced to stay for hours and "have fun." Taking it easy, watching my personality's borders loosen and dissolve, arouse an unpleasantly floating giddiness. I don't even like water beds. Fear of Freud's "oceanic feeling," I suppose—I distrust anything that will make me pause long enough to be put in touch with my helplessness.

The other repugnance I experience around *joie de vivrism* is that I associate its rituals with depression. All these people sitting around a pool, drinking margaritas—they're not really happy, they're depressed. Perhaps I am generalizing too much from my own despair in such situations. Drunk, sunbaked, stretched out in a beach chair, I am unable to ward off the sensation of being utterly alone, unconnected, cut off from the others.

An article in the Science section of the *Times* about depression (they seem to run one every few months) described the illness as a pattern of "learned helplessness." Dr. Martin Seligman of the University of Pennsylvania described his series of experiments: "At first mild electrical shocks were given to dogs, from which they were unable to escape. In a second set of experiments, dogs were given shocks from which they could escape —but they didn't try. They just lay there, passively accepting the pain. It seemed that the animals' inability to control their experiences had brought them to a state resembling clinical depression in humans."

Keep busy, I always say. At all costs avoid the trough of passivity, which leads to the Slough of Despond. Someone (a girlfriend, who else?) once accused me of being intolerant of the depressed way of looking at the world, which had its own intelligence and moral integrity, both obviously unavailable to me. It's true. I don't like the smell of depression (it has a smell, a very distinct one, something fetid like morning odors), and I stay away from depressed characters whenever possible. Except when they happen to be my closest friends or family members. It goes without saying that I am also, for all my squeamishness, attracted to depressed people, since they seem to know something I don't. I wouldn't rule out the possibility that the brown-gray logic of depression *is* the truth. In another experiment (also reported in the *Time*'s Science section), pitting "optimists" against clinically diagnosed "depressives" on their self-perceived abilities to effect outcomes according to their wills, researchers tentatively concluded that depressed people may have a more realistic, clear-sighted view of the world.

Nevertheless, what I don't like about depressives sometimes is their chummy I-told-you-so smugness, like Woody Allen fans who treat anhedonia as a vanguard position.

And for all that, depressives make the most rabid converts to *joie de vivre*. The reason for this is that *joie de vivre* and depression are not opposites but relatives of the same family, practically twins. When I see *joie de vivre* rituals, I always notice, like a TV ghost, depression right alongside it. I knew a man, dominated by a powerful father, who thought he had come out of a long depression occasioned, in his mind, by his divorce. Whenever I met him he would say that his life was getting better and better. Now he could run long distances, he was putting healthy food into his system, he was more physically fit at forty than he had been at twenty-five; now he had dates, he was going out with three different women, he had a good therapist, he was looking forward to renting a bungalow in better woods than the previous summer. . . . I don't know whether it was his tone of voice when he said this, his sagging shoulders, or what, but I always had an urge to burst into tears. If only he had admitted he was miserable I could have consoled him outright instead of being embarrassed to notice the deep hurt in him, like a swallowed razor cutting him from inside. And his pain still stunk up the room like in the old days, that sour cabbage smell was in his running suit, yet he wouldn't let on, he thought the smell was gone. The therapist had told him to forgive himself, and he had gone ahead and done it, the poor *schnook*. But tell me: Why would anyone need such a stylized, disciplined regimen of enjoyment if he were not depressed?

4. In the Here and Now

The argument of both the hedonist and the guru is that if we were but to open ourselves to the richness of the moment, to concentrate on the feast before us, we would be filled with bliss. I have lived in the present from time to time, and I can tell you that it is much overrated. Occasionally, as a holiday from stroking one's memories or brooding about future worries, I grant you, it can be a nice change of pace. But to "be here now," hour after hour, would never work. I don't even approve of stories written in the present tense. As for poets who never use a past participle, they deserve the eternity they are striving for.

Besides, the present has a way of intruding whether you like it or not. Why should I go out of my way to meet it? Let it splash on me from time to time, like a car going through a puddle, and I, on the sidewalk of my solitude, will salute it grimly like any other modern inconvenience.

If I attend a concert, obviously not to listen to the music but to find a brief breathing space in which to meditate on the past and future, I realize that there may be moments when the music invades my ears and I am forced to pay attention to it, note after note. I believe I take such intrusions gracefully. The present is not always an unwelcome guest, so long as it doesn't stay too long and cut into my remembering or brooding time.

Even for survival, it's not necessary to focus one's full attention on the present. The instincts of a pedestrian crossing the street in a reverie will usually suffice. Alertness is all right as long as it is not treated as a promissory note on happiness. Anyone who recommends attention to the moment as a prescription for grateful wonder is telling only half the truth. To be happy one must pay attention, but to be unhappy one must also have paid attention.

Attention, at best, is a form of prayer. Conversely, as Simone Weil said, prayer is a way of focusing attention. All religions recognize this when they ask their worshipers to repeat the name of their God, a devotional practice that draws the practitioner into a trancelike awareness of the present, and the objects around oneself. With one part of the soul one praises God, and with the other part one expresses a hunger, a dissatisfaction, a desire for more spiritual contact. Praise must never stray too far from longing, that longing which takes us implicitly beyond the present.

I was about to say that the very act of attention implies longing, but this is not necessarily true. Attention is not always infused with desire; it can settle on us most placidly once desire has been momentarily satisfied, like after the sex act. There are also periods following overwork, when the exhausted slave-body is freed and the eyes dilate to register with awe the lights of the city; one is too tired to desire anything else.

Such moments are rare. They form the basis for a poetic appreciation of the beauty of the world. However, there seems no reliable way to invoke or prolong them. The rest of the time, when we are not being edgy or impatient, we are often simply *disappointed,* which amounts to a confession that the present is not good enough. People often try to hide their disappointment—just as Berryman's mother told him not to let people see that he was bored, because it suggested that he had no "inner resources." But there is something to be said for disappointment.

This least respected form of suffering, downgraded to a kind of petulance, at least accurately measures the distance between hope and reality. And it has its own peculiar satisfactions: Why else do we return years later to places where we had been happy, if not to savor the bittersweet pleasures of disappointment? "For as you well know: while a single disappointment may elicit tears, a repeated disappointment will evoke a smile" (Musil).

Moreover, disappointment is the flip side of a strong, predictive feeling for beauty or appropriate civility or decency: only those with a sense of order and harmony can be disappointed.

We are told that to be disappointed is immature, in that it presupposes unrealistic expectations, whereas the wise man meets each moment head-on without preconceptions, with freshness and detachment, grateful for anything it offers. However, this pernicious teaching ignores everything we know of the world. If we continue to expect what turns out to be not forthcoming, it is not because we are unworldly in our expectations, but because our very worldliness has taught us to demand of an unjust world that it behave a little more fairly. The least we can do, for instance, is to register the expectation that people in a stronger position be kind and not cruel to those in a weaker one, knowing all the while that we will probably be disappointed.

The truth is, most wisdom is embittering. The task of the wise person cannot be to pretend with false naïveté that every moment is new and unprecedented, but to bear the burden of bitterness that experience forces on us with as much uncomplaining dignity as strength will allow. Beyond that, all we can ask of ourselves is that bitterness not cancel out our capacity still to be surprised.

5. Making Love

If it is true that I have the tendency to withhold sympathy from those pleasures or experiences that fall outside my capabilities, the opposite is also true: I admire immoderately those things I cannot do. I've always gone out with women who swam better than I did. It's as if I were asking them to teach me how to make love. Though I know how to make love (more or less), I have never fully shaken that adolescent boy's insecurity that there was more to it than I could ever imagine, and that I needed a full-time instructress. For my first sexual experiences, in fact, I chose older women. Later, when I slept with women my own age and younger, I still tended to take the stylistic lead from them, adapting myself to each one's rhythm and ardor, not only because I wanted to be "responsive," but because I secretly thought that women—any woman—understood love-making in a way that I did not. In bed I came to them as a student, and I have made them pay later, in other ways, for letting them see me thus. Sex has always been so impromptu, so out of my control, so different each time, that even when I became the confident bull in bed I was dismayed by this sudden power, itself a form of powerlessness because so unpredictable.

Something Michel Leiris wrote in his book *Manhood,* has always stuck with me: "It has been some time, in any case, since I have ceased to consider the sexual act as a simple matter, but rather as a relatively exceptional act, necessitating certain inner accommodations that are either particularly tragic or particularly exalted, but very different, in either case, from what I regard as my usual disposition."

The transformation from a preoccupied urban intellectual to a sexual animal involves, at times, an almost superhuman strain. To find in one's bed a living, undulating woman of God knows what capacities and secret desires may seem too high, too formal, too ridiculous or blissful an occasion—even without the shock to an undernourished heart like mine of an injection of undiluted affection, if the woman proves loving as well.

Most often, I simply do what the flood allows me to, improvising here or there like a man tying a white flag to a raft that is being swiftly swept along, a plea for love or forgiveness. But as for artistry, control, enslavement through my penis, that's someone else. Which is not to say that there weren't women who were perfectly happy with me as a lover. In those cases, there was some love between us outside of bed: the intimacy was much more intense because we had something big to say to each other before we ever took off our clothes, but which could now be said only with our bodies.

With other women, whom I cared less about, I was sometimes a dud. I am not one of those men who can force themselves to make love passionately or athletically when their affections are not engaged. From the perplexity of wide variations in my experiences I have been able to tell myself that I am neither a good nor a bad lover, but one who responds differently according to the emotions present. A banal conclusion; maybe a true one.

It does not do away, however, with some need to have my remaining insecurities about sexual ability laid to rest. I begin to suspect that all my fancy distrust of hedonism comes down to a fear of being judged in this one category: Do I make love well? Every brie and wine picnic, every tanned body relaxing on the beach, every celebration of *joie de vivre* carries a sly wink of some missed sexual enlightenment that may be too threatening to me. I am like the prudish old maid who blushes behind her packages when she sees sexy young people kissing.

When I was twenty I married. My wife was the second woman I had ever slept with. Our marriage was the recognition that we suited one another remarkably well as company—could walk and talk and share insights all day, work side by side like Chinese peasants, read silently together like graduate students, tease each other like brother and sister, and when at night we found our bodies tired, pull the covers over ourselves and become lovers. She was two years older than I, but I was good at faking maturity; and I found her so companionable and trustworthy and able to take care of me that I could not let such a gold mine go by.

Our love life was mild and regular. There was a sweetness to sex, as befitted domesticity. Out of the surplus energy of late afternoons I would find myself coming up behind her sometimes as she worked in the kitchen, taking her away from her involvements, leading her by the hand into the bedroom. I would unbutton her blouse. I would stroke her breasts, and she would get a look in her eyes of quiet intermittent hunger, like a German shepherd being petted; she would seem to listen far off; absentmindedly daydreaming, she would return my petting, stroke my arm with distracted patience like a mother who has something on the stove, trying to calm her weeping child. I would listen, too, to guess what she might be hearing, bird calls or steam heat. The enlargement of her nipples under my fingers fascinated me. Goose bumps either rose on her skin where I touched or didn't, I noted with scientific interest, a moment before getting carried away by my own eagerness. Then we were undressing, she was doing something in the bathroom, and I was waiting on the bed, with all the consciousness of a sun-mote. I was large and ready, the proud husband, waiting to receive my treasure. . . .

I remember our favorite position was with her on top, me on the bottom, upthrusting and receiving. Distraction, absentmindedness, return, calm exploration marked our sensual life. To be forgetful seemed the highest grace. We often achieved perfection.

Then I became haunted with images of seductive, heartless cunts. It was the era of the miniskirt, girl-women, Rudi Gernreich bikinis and Tiger Morse underwear, see-through blouses, flashes of flesh that invited the hand to go creeping under and into costumes. I wanted my wife to be more glamorous. We would go shopping for dresses together; she would complain that her legs were wrong for the new fashions. Or she would come home proudly with a bargain pink and blue felt minidress, bought for three dollars at a discount store, which my aching heart would tell me missed the point completely.

She, too, became dissatisfied with the absence of furtive excitement in our marriage. She wanted to seduce me, like a stranger on a plane. But I was too easy, so we ended up seducing others. Then we turned back to each other and with one last desperate attempt, before the marriage fell to pieces, each sought in the other a plasticity of sensual forms, like the statuary in an Indian temple. In our lovemaking I tried to believe that the body of one woman was the body of all women; all I achieved was a groping to distance lovingly familiar forms into those of anonymous erotic succubi. The height of this insanity, I remember, was one evening in the park when I pounded my wife's lips with kisses in an effort to provoke something between us like "hot passion." My eyes closed, I practiced a repertoire of French tongue-kisses on her. I shall never forget her frightened silent appeal that I stop, because I had turned into someone she no longer recognized.

But we were young, and so, dependent on each other, like orphans. By the time I left, at twenty-five, I knew I had been a fool, and had ruined everything, but I had to continue being a fool because it had been my odd misfortune to have stumbled onto kindness and tranquillity too quickly.

I moved to California in search of an earthly sexual paradise, and that year I tried hardest to make my peace with *joie de vivre*. I was sick but didn't know it—a diseased animal, Nietzsche would say. I hung around Berkeley's campus, stared up at the Campanile tower; I sat on the grass watching coeds younger than I and, pretending that I was still going to university (no deeper sense of being a fraud obtainable), I tried to grasp the rhythms of carefree youth; I blended in at rallies, I stood at the fringes of be-ins, watching new rituals of communal love, someone being passed through the air hand to hand. But I never "trusted the group" enough to let myself be the guinea pig; or if I did, it was only with the proud stubborn conviction that nothing could change me—though I also wanted to change. Swearing I would never learn transcendence, I hitchhiked and climbed mountains. I went to wine-tasting festivals and accepted the wine jug from hippie gypsies in a circle around a beach campfire without first wiping off the lip. I registered for a Free School course in human sexual response just to get laid, and when that worked, I was shocked, and took up with someone else. There were many women in those years who got naked with me. I smoked grass with them, and as a sign of faith I took psychedelic drugs; we made love in bushes and beach houses, as though hacking through jungles with machetes to stay in touch with our ecstatic genitals while our minds soared off into natural marvels. Such experiences taught me, I will admit, how much romantic feeling can transform the body whose nerve tendrils are receptive to it. Technicolor fantasies of one girlfriend as a senorita with flowers in her impossibly wavy hair would suddenly pitch and roll beneath me, and the bliss of touching her naked suntanned breast and the damp black pubic hairs was too unthinkably perfect to elicit anything but abject gratitude. At such moments I have held the world in my hands and known it. I was coming home to the body of Woman, those globes and grasses that had launched me. In the childish fantasy accompanying one sexual climax, under LSD, I was hitting a home run and the Stars and Stripes flying in the background of my mind's eye as I "slid into home" acclaimed the patriotic rightness of my seminal release. For once I had no guilt about how or when I ejaculated.

If afterward, when we came down, there was often a sour air of disenchantment and mutual prostitution, that does not take away from the legacy, the rapture of those moments. If I no longer use drugs—in fact, have become somewhat antidrug—I think I still owe them something for showing me how to recognize the all-embracing reflex. At first I needed drugs to teach me about the stupendousness of sex. Later, without them, there would be situations—after a lovely talk or coming home from a party in a taxi—when I would be overcome by amorous tropism toward the woman with me. The appetite for flesh that comes over me at such moments, and the pleasure there is in finally satisfying it, seems so just that I always think I have stumbled into a state of blessed grace. That it can never last, that it is a trick of the mind and the blood, are rumors I push out of sight.

To know rapture is to have one's whole life poisoned. If you will forgive a ridiculous analogy, a tincture of rapture is like a red bandana in the laundry that runs and turns all the white wash pink. We should just as soon stay away from any future ecstatic experiences that spoil everyday living by comparison. Not that I have any intention of stopping. Still, if I will have nothing to do with religious mysticism, it is probably because I sense a susceptibility in that direction. Poetry is also dangerous; all quickening awakenings to Being extract a price later.

Are there people who live under such spells all the time? Was this the secret of the idiotic smile on the half-moon face of the painter Vartas? The lovers of life, the robust Cellinis, the Casanovas? Is there a technique to hedonism that will allow the term of rapture to be indefinitely extended? I don't believe it. The hedonist's despair is still that he is forced to make do with the present. Who knows about the success rate of religious mystics? In any case, I could not bring myself to state that what I am waiting for is God. Such a statement would sound too grandiose and presumptuous, and make too great a rupture in my customary thinking. But I can identify with the pre- if not the post-stage of what Simone Weil describes:

"The soul knows for certain only that it is hungry. The important thing is that it announces its hunger by crying. A child does not stop crying if we suggest to it that perhaps there is no bread. It goes on crying just the same. The danger is not lest the soul should doubt whether there is any bread, but lest, by a lie, it should persuade itself that it is not hungry."

So much for *joie de vivre.* It's too compensatory. I don't really know what I'm waiting for. I know only that until I have gained what I want from this life, my expressions of gratitude and joy will be restricted to variations of a hunter's alertness. I give thanks to a nip in the air that clarifies the scent. But I think it hypocritical to pretend satisfaction while I am still hungry.

SCOTT RUSSELL SANDERS

Scott Russell Sanders (1945–   ) is one of the most devoted and consistent practitioners of the personal essay in America. His collections The Paradise of Bombs *and* Secrets of the Universe *have earned him a following among fans of the essay, and his work appears regularly in* Harper's, The Georgia Review, *and best-essay anthologies. Sanders grew up in Tennessee and Ohio (he lived near a munitions factory), and settled in Bloomington, Indiana, where he teaches at the University at Indiana. He has written extensively about sense of place* (In Limestone Country, Staying Put) *and is an accomplished nature writer.*

The essay below, "Under the Influence," is about his response not to landscape, however, but to his father's alcoholism. As such, it may be seen as part of a burgeoning literature about the afflictions of substance abuse and the scars left on the children of addicts. Sanders threads his way through this minefield, so susceptible to cliché and victimized self-pity, with exemplary honesty, feeling, and willingness to take responsibility. His quiet midwestern modesty and sense of privacy, seemingly at odds with an autobiographical genre that normally attracts flamboyant, self-dramatizing egotists, accounts for some of the essay's tension—as though he would rather not write about himself, but the form demands it. The reflective personal essayist is obliged to dig deep into his psyche and reveal the results, and Sanders shows he is equal to the challenge.

✶✶
Under the Influence

MY FATHER DRANK. He drank as a gut-punched boxer gasps for breath, as a starving dog gobbles food—compulsively, secretly, in pain and trembling. I use the past tense not because he ever quit drinking but because he quit living. That is how the story ends for my father, age sixty-four, heart bursting, body cooling and forsaken on the linoleum of my brother's trailer. The story continues for my brother, my sister, my mother, and me, and will continue so long as memory holds.

In the perennial present of memory, I slip into the garage or barn to see my father tipping back the flat green bottles of wine, the brown cylinders of whiskey, the cans of beer disguised in paper bags. His Adam's apple bobs, the liquid gurgles, he wipes the sandy-haired back of a hand over his lips, and then, his bloodshot gaze bumping into me, he stashes the bottle or can inside his jacket, under the workbench, between two bales of hay, and we both pretend the moment has not occurred.

"What's up, buddy?" he says, thick-tongued and edgy.

"Sky's up," I answer, playing along.

"And don't forget prices," he grumbles. "Prices are always up. And taxes."

In memory, his white 1951 Pontiac with the stripes down the hood and the Indian head on the snout jounces to a stop in the driveway; or it is the 1956 Ford station wagon, or the 1963 Rambler shaped like a toad, or the sleek 1969 Bonneville that will do 120 miles per hour on straightaways; or it is the robin's-egg blue pickup, new in 1980, battered in 1981, the year of his death. He climbs out, grinning dangerously, unsteady on his legs, and we children interrupt our game of catch, our building of snow forts, our picking of plums, to watch in silence as he weaves past into the house, where he slumps into his overstuffed chair and falls asleep. Shaking her head, our mother stubs out the cigarette he has left smoldering in the ashtray. All evening, until our bedtimes, we tiptoe past him, as past a snoring dragon. Then we curl in our fearful sheets, listening. Eventually he wakes with a grunt, Mother slings accusations at him, he snarls back, she yells, he growls, their voices clashing. Before long, she retreats to their bedroom, sobbing—not from the blows of fists, for he never strikes her, but from the force of words.

Left alone, our father prowls the house, thumping into furniture, rummaging in the kitchen, slamming doors, turning the pages of the newspaper with a savage crackle, muttering back at the late-night drivel from television. The roof might fly off, the walls might buckle from the pressure of his rage. Whatever my brother and sister and mother may be thinking on their own rumpled pillows, I lie there hating him, loving him, fearing him, knowing I have failed him. I tell myself he drinks to ease an ache that gnaws at his belly, an ache I must have caused by disappointing him somehow, a murderous ache I should be able to relieve by doing all my chores, earning A's in school, winning baseball games, fixing the broken washer and the burst pipes, bringing in money to fill his empty wallet. He would not hide the green bottles in his tool box, would not sneak off to the barn with a lump under his coat, would not fall asleep in the daylight, would not roar and fume, would not drink himself to death, if only I were perfect.

I am forty-two as I write these words, and I know full well now that my father was an alcoholic, a man consumed by disease rather than by disappointment. What had seemed to me a private grief is in fact a public scourge. In the United States alone some ten or fifteen million people share his ailment, and behind the doors they slam in fury or disgrace, countless other children tremble. I comfort myself with such knowledge, holding it against the throb of memory like an ice pack against a bruise. There are keener sources of grief: poverty, racism, rape, war. I do not wish to compete for a trophy in suffering. I am only trying to understand the corrosive mixture of helplessness, responsibility, and shame that I learned to feel as the son of an alcoholic. I realize now that I did not cause my father's illness, nor could I have cured it. Yet for all this grown-up knowledge, I am still ten years old, my own son's age, and as that boy I struggle in guilt and confusion to save my father from pain.

Consider a few of our synonyms for *drunk:* tipsy, tight, pickled, soused, and plowed; stoned and stewed, lubricated and inebriated, juiced and sluiced; three sheets to the wind, in your cups, out of your mind, under the table, lit up, tanked up, wiped out; besotted, blotto, bombed, and buzzed; plastered, polluted, putrified; loaded or looped, boozy, woozy, fuddled, or smashed; crocked and shit-faced, corked and pissed, snockered and sloshed.

It is a mostly humorous lexicon, as the lore that deals with drunks—in jokes and cartoons, in plays, films, and television skits—is largely comic. Aunt Matilda nips elderberry wine from the sideboard and burps politely during supper. Uncle Fred slouches to the table glassy-eyed, wearing a lamp shade for a hat and murmuring, "Candy is dandy but liquor is quicker." Inspired by cocktails, Mrs. Somebody recounts the events of her day in a fuzzy dialect, while Mr. Somebody nibbles her ear and croons a bawdy song. On the sofa with Boyfriend, Daughter giggles, licking gin from her lips, and loosens the bows in her hair. Junior knocks back some brews with his chums at the Leopard Lounge and stumbles home to the wrong house, wonders foggily why he cannot locate his pajamas, and crawls naked into bed with the ugliest girl in school. The family dog slurps from a neglected martini and wobbles to the nursery, where he vomits in Baby's shoe.

It is all great fun. But if in the audience you notice a few laughing faces turn grim when the drunk lurches on stage, don't be surprised, for these are the children of alcoholics. Over the grinning mask of Dionysus, the leering mask of Bacchus, these children cannot help seeing the bloated features of their own parents. Instead of laughing, they wince, they mourn. Instead of celebrating the drunk as one freed from constraints, they pity him as one enslaved. They refuse to believe *in vino veritas,* having seen their befuddled parents skid away from truth toward folly and oblivion. And so these children bite their lips until the lush staggers into the wings.

My father, when drunk, was neither funny nor honest; he was pathetic, frightening, deceitful. There seemed to be a leak in him somewhere, and he poured in booze to keep from draining dry. Like a torture victim who refuses to squeal, he would never admit that he had touched a drop, not even in his last year, when he seemed to be dissolving in alcohol before our very eyes. I never knew him to lie about anything, ever, except about this one ruinous fact. Drowsy, clumsy, unable to fix a bicycle tire, throw a baseball, balance a grocery sack, or walk across the room, he was stripped of his true self by drink. In a matter of minutes, the contents of a bottle could transform a brave man into a coward, a buddy into a bully, a gifted athlete and skilled carpenter and shrewd businessman into a bumbler. No dictionary of synonyms for *drunk* would soften the anguish of watching our prince turn into a frog.

Father's drinking became the family secret. While growing up, we children never breathed a word of it beyond the four walls of our house. To this day, my brother and sister rarely mention it, and then only when I press them. I did not confess the ugly, bewildering fact to my wife until his wavering walk and slurred speech forced me to. Recently, on the seventh anniversary of my father's death, I asked my mother if she ever spoke of his drinking to friends. "No, no, never," she replied hastily. "I couldn't bear for anyone to know."

The secret bores under the skin, gets in the blood, into the bone, and stays there. Long after you have supposedly been cured of malaria, the fever can flare up, the tremors can shake you. So it is with the fevers of shame. You swallow the bitter quinine of knowledge, and you learn to feel pity and compassion toward the drinker. Yet the shame lingers in your marrow, and, because of the shame, anger.

For a long stretch of my childhood we lived on a military reservation in Ohio, an arsenal where bombs were stored underground in bunkers, vintage airplanes burst into flames, and unstable artillery shells boomed nightly at the dump. We had the feeling, as children, that we played in a mine field, where a heedless footfall could trigger an explosion. When Father was drinking, the house, too, became a mine field. The least bump could set off either parent.

The more he drank, the more obsessed Mother became with stopping him. She hunted for bottles, counted the cash in his wallet, sniffed at his breath. Without meaning to snoop, we children blundered left and right into damning evidence. On afternoons when he came home from work sober, we flung ourselves at him for hugs, and felt against our ribs the telltale lump in his coat. In the barn we tumbled on the hay and heard beneath our sneakers the crunch of buried glass. We tugged open a drawer in his workbench, looking for screwdrivers or crescent wrenches, and spied a gleaming six-pack among the tools. Playing tag, we darted around the house just in time to see him sway on the rear stoop and heave a finished bottle into the woods. In his good night kiss we smelled the cloying sweetness of Clorets, the mints he chewed to camouflage his dragon's breath.

I can summon up that kiss right now by recalling Theodore Roethke's lines about his own father in "My Papa's Waltz":

> *The whiskey on your breath*
> *Could make a small boy dizzy;*
> *But I hung on like death:*
> *Such waltzing was not easy.*

Such waltzing was hard, terribly hard, for with a boy's scrawny arms I was trying to hold my tipsy father upright.

For years, the chief source of those incriminating bottles and cans was a grimy store a mile from us, a cinder block place called Sly's, with two gas pumps outside and a moth-eaten dog asleep in the window. A strip of flypaper, speckled the year round with black bodies, coiled in the doorway. Inside, on rusty metal shelves or in wheezing coolers, you could find pop and Popsicles, cigarettes, potato chips, canned soup, raunchy postcards, fishing gear, Twinkies, wine, and beer. When Father drove anywhere on errands, Mother would send us kids along as guards, warning us not to let him out of our sight. And so with one or more of us on board, Father would cruise up to Sly's, pump a dollar's worth of gas or plump the tires with air, and then, telling us to wait in the car, he would head for that fly-spangled doorway.

Dutiful and panicky, we cried, "Let us go in with you!"

"No," he answered. "I'll be back in two shakes."

"Please!"

"No!" he roared. "Don't you budge, or I'll jerk a knot in your tails!"

So we stayed put, kicking the seats, while he ducked inside. Often, when he had parked the car at a careless angle, we gazed in through the window and saw Mr. Sly fetching down from a shelf behind the cash register two green pints of Gallo wine. Father swigged one of them right there at the counter, stuffed the other in his pocket, and then out he came, a bulge in his coat, a flustered look on his red face.

Because the Mom and Pop who ran the dump were neighbors of ours, living just down the tar-blistered road, I hated them all the more for poisoning my father. I wanted to sneak in their store and smash the bottles and set fire to the place. I also hated the Gallo brothers, Ernest and Julio, whose jovial faces shone from the labels of their wine, labels I would find, torn and curled, when I burned the trash. I noted the Gallo brothers' address, in California, and I studied the road atlas to see how far that was from Ohio, because I meant to go out there and tell Ernest and Julio what they were doing to my father, and then, if they showed no mercy, I would kill them.

While growing up on the back roads and in the country schools and cramped Methodist churches of Ohio and Tennessee, I never heard the word *alcoholism,* never happened across it in books or magazines. In the nearby towns, there were no addiction treatment programs, no community mental health centers, no Alcoholics Anonymous chapters, no therapists. Left alone with our grievous secret, we had no way of understanding Father's drinking except as an act of will, a deliberate folly or cruelty, a moral weakness, a sin. He drank because he chose to, pure and simple. Why our father, so playful and competent and kind when sober, would choose to ruin himself and punish his family, we could not fathom.

Our neighborhood was high on the Bible, and the Bible was hard on drunkards. "Woe to those who are heroes at drinking wine, and valiant men in mixing strong drink," wrote Isaiah. "The priest and the prophet reel with strong drink, they are confused with wine, they err in vision, they stumble in giving judgment. For all tables are full of vomit, no place is without filthiness." We children had seen those fouled tables at the local truck stop where the notorious boozers hung out, our father occasionally among them. "Wine and new wine take away the understanding," declared the prophet Hosea. We had also seen evidence of that in our father, who could multiply seven-digit numbers in his head when sober, but when drunk could not help us with fourth-grade math. Proverbs warned: "Do not look at wine when it is red, when it sparkles in the cup and goes down smoothly. At the last it bites like a serpent, and stings like an adder. Your eyes will see strange things, and your mind utter perverse things." Woe, woe.

Dismayingly often, these biblical drunkards stirred up trouble for their own kids. Noah made fresh wine after the flood, drank too much of it, fell asleep without any clothes on, and was glimpsed in the buff by his son Ham, whom Noah promptly cursed. In one passage—it was so shocking we had to read it under our blankets with flashlights—the patriarch Lot fell down drunk and slept with his daughters. The sins of the fathers set their children's teeth on edge.

Our ministers were fond of quoting St. Paul's pronouncement that drunkards would not inherit the kingdom of God. These grave preachers assured us that the wine referred to during the Last Supper was in fact grape juice. Bible and sermons and hymns combined to give us the impression that Moses should have brought down from the mountain another stone tablet, bearing the Eleventh Commandment: Thou shalt not drink.

The scariest and most illuminating Bible story apropos of drunkards was the one about the lunatic and the swine. Matthew, Mark, and Luke each told a version of the tale. We knew it by heart: When Jesus climbed out of his boat one day, this lunatic came charging up from the graveyard, stark naked and filthy, frothing at the mouth, so violent that he broke the strongest chains. Nobody would go near him. Night and day for years this madman had been wailing among the tombs and bruising himself with stones. Jesus took one look at him and said, "Come out of the man, you unclean spirits!" for he could see that the lunatic was possessed by demons. Meanwhile, some hogs were conveniently rooting nearby. "If we have to come out," begged the demons, "at least let us go into those swine." Jesus agreed. The unclean spirits entered the hogs, and the hogs rushed straight off a cliff and plunged into a lake. Hearing the story in Sunday school, my friends thought mainly of the pigs. (How big a splash did they make? Who paid for the lost pork?) But I thought of the redeemed lunatic, who bathed himself and put on clothes and calmly sat at the feet of Jesus, restored—so the Bible said—to "his right mind."

When drunk, our father was clearly in his wrong mind. He became a stranger, as fearful to us as any graveyard lunatic, not quite frothing at the mouth but fierce enough, quick-tempered, explosive; or else he grew maudlin and weepy, which frightened us nearly as much. In my boyhood despair, I reasoned that maybe he wasn't to blame for turning into an ogre. Maybe, like the lunatic, he was possessed by demons. I found support for my theory when I heard liquor referred to as "spirits," when the newspapers reported that somebody had been arrested for "driving under the influence," and when church ladies railed against that "demon drink."

If my father was indeed possessed, who would exorcise him? If he was a sinner, who would save him? If he was ill, who would cure him? If he suffered, who would ease his pain? Not ministers or doctors, for we could not bring ourselves to confide in them; not the neighbors, for we pretended they had never seen him drunk; not Mother, who fussed and pleaded but could not budge him; not my brother and sister, who were only kids. That left me. It did not matter that I, too, was only a child, and a bewildered one at that. I could not excuse myself.

On first reading a description of delirium tremens—in a book on alcoholism I smuggled from the library—I thought immediately of the frothing lunatic and the frenzied swine. When I read stories or watched films about grisly metamorphoses—Dr. Jekyll becoming Mr. Hyde, the mild husband changing into a werewolf, the kindly neighbor taken over by a brutal alien —I could not help seeing my own father's mutation from sober to drunk. Even today, knowing better, I am attracted by the demonic theory of drink, for when I recall my father's transformation, the emergence of his ugly second self, I find it easy to believe in possession by unclean spirits. We never knew which version of Father would come home from work, the true or the tainted, nor could we guess how far down the slope toward cruelty he would slide.

How far a man *could* slide we gauged by observing our back-road neighbors—the out-of-work miners who had dragged their families to our corner of Ohio from the desolate hollows of Appalachia, the tightfisted farmers, the surly mechanics, the balked and broken men. There was, for example, whiskey-soaked Mr. Jenkins, who beat his wife and kids so hard we could hear their screams from the road. There was Mr. Lavo the wino, who fell asleep smoking time and again, until one night his disgusted wife bundled up the children and went outside and left him in his easy chair to burn; he awoke on his own, staggered out coughing into the yard, and pounded her flat while the children looked on and the shack turned to ash. There was the truck driver, Mr. Sampson, who tripped over his son's tricycle one night while drunk and got so mad that he jumped into his semi and drove away, shifting through the dozen gears, and never came back. We saw the bruised children of these fathers clump onto our school bus, we saw the abandoned children huddle in the pews at church, we saw the stunned and battered mothers begging for help at our doors.

Our own father never beat us, and I don't think he ever beat Mother, but he threatened often. The Old Testament Yahweh was not more terrible in his wrath. Eyes blazing, voice booming, Father would pull out his belt and swear to give us a whipping, but he never followed through, never needed to, because we could imagine it so vividly. He shoved us, pawed us with the back of his hand, as an irked bear might smack a cub, not to injure, just to clear a space. I can see him grabbing Mother by the hair as she cowers on a chair during a nightly quarrel. He twists her neck back until she gapes up at him, and then he lifts over her skull a glass quart bottle of milk, the milk running down his forearm, and he yells at her, "Say just one more word, one goddamn word, and I'll shut you up!" I fear she will prick him with her sharp tongue, but she is terrified into silence, and so am I, and the leaking bottle quivers in the air, and milk slithers through the red hair of my father's uplifted arm, and the entire scene is there to this moment, the head jerked back, the club raised.

When the drink made him weepy, Father would pack a bag and kiss each of us children on the head, and announce from the front door that he was moving out. "Where to?" we demanded, fearful each time that he would leave for good, as Mr. Sampson had roared away for good in his diesel truck. "Someplace where I won't get hounded every minute," Father would answer, his jaw quivering. He stabbed a look at Mother, who might say, "Don't run into the ditch before you get there," or, "Good riddance," and then he would slink away. Mother watched him go with arms crossed over her chest, her face closed like the lid on a box of snakes. We children bawled. Where could he go? To the truck stop, that den of iniquity? To one of those dark, ratty flophouses in town? Would he wind up sleeping under a railroad bridge or on a park bench or in a cardboard box, mummied in rags, like the bums we had seen on our trips to Cleveland and Chicago? We bawled and bawled, wondering if he would ever come back.

He always did come back, a day or a week later, but each time there was a sliver less of him.

In Kafka's *The Metamorphosis,* which opens famously with Gregor Samsa waking up from uneasy dreams to find himself transformed into an insect, Gregor's family keep reassuring themselves that things will be just fine again, "When he comes back to us." Each time alcohol transformed our father, we held out the same hope, that he would really and truly come back to us, our authentic father, the tender and playful and competent man, and then all things would be fine. We had grounds for such hope. After his weepy departures and chapfallen returns, he would sometimes go weeks, even months without drinking. Those were glad times. Joy banged inside my ribs. Every day without the furtive glint of bottles, every meal without a fight, every bedtime without sobs encouraged us to believe that such bliss might go on forever.

Mother was fooled by just such a hope all during the forty-odd years she knew this Greeley Ray Sanders. Soon after she met him in a Chicago delicatessen on the eve of World War II, and fell for his butter-melting Mississippi drawl and his wavy red hair, she learned that he drank heavily. But then so did a lot of men. She would soon coax or scold him into breaking the nasty habit. She would point out to him how ugly and foolish it was, this bleary drinking, and then he would quit. He refused to quit during their engagement, however, still refused during the first years of marriage, refused until my sister came along. The shock of fatherhood sobered him, and he remained sober through my birth at the end of the war and right on through until we moved in 1951 to the Ohio arsenal, that paradise of bombs. Like all places that make a business of death, the arsenal had more than its share of alcoholics and drug addicts and other varieties of escape artists. There I turned six and started school and woke into a child's flickering awareness, just in time to see my father begin sneaking swigs in the garage.

He sobered up again for most of a year at the height of the Korean War, to celebrate the birth of my brother. But aside from that dry spell, his only breaks from drinking before I graduated from high school were just long enough to raise and then dash our hopes. Then during the fall of my senior year—the time of the Cuban missile crisis, when it seemed that the nightly explosions at the munitions dump and the nightly rages in our household might spread to engulf the globe—Father collapsed. His liver, kidneys, and heart all conked out. The doctors saved him, but only by a hair. He stayed in the hospital for weeks, going through a withdrawal so terrible that Mother would not let us visit him. If he wanted to kill himself, the doctors solemnly warned him, all he had to do was hit the bottle again. One binge would finish him.

Father must have believed them, for he stayed dry for the next fifteen years. It was an answer to prayer, Mother said, it was a miracle. I believe it was a reflex of fear, which he sustained over the years through courage and pride. He knew a man could die from drink, for his brother Roscoe had. We children never laid eyes on doomed Uncle Roscoe, but in the stories Mother told us he became a fairy-tale figure, like a boy who took the wrong turning in the woods and was gobbled up by the wolf.

The fifteen-year dry spell came to an end with Father's retirement in the spring of 1978. Like many men, he gave up his identity along with his job. One day he was a boss at the factory, with a brass plate on his door and a reputation to uphold; the next day he was a nobody at home. He and Mother were leaving Ontario, the last of the many places to which his job had carried them, and they were moving to a new house in Mississippi, his childhood stomping grounds. As a boy in Mississippi, Father sold Coca-Cola during dances while the moonshiners peddled their brew in the parking lot; as a young blade, he fought in bars and in the ring, seeking a state Golden Gloves championship; he gambled at poker, hunted pheasants, raced motorcycles and cars, played semiprofessional baseball, and, along with all his buddies—in the Black Cat Saloon, behind the cotton gin, in the woods—he drank. It was a perilous youth to dream of recovering.

After his final day of work, Mother drove on ahead with a car full of begonias and violets, while Father stayed behind to oversee the packing. When the van was loaded, the sweaty movers broke open a six-pack and offered him a beer.

"Let's drink to retirement!" they crowed. "Let's drink to freedom! to fishing! hunting! loafing! Let's drink to a guy who's going home!"

At least I imagine some such words, for that is all I can do, imagine, and I see Father's hand trembling in midair as he thinks about the fifteen sober years and about the doctors' warning, and he tells himself *Goddamnit, I am a free man,* and *Why can't a free man drink one beer after a lifetime of hard work?* and I see his arm reaching, his fingers closing, the can tilting to his lips. I even supply a label for the beer, a swaggering brand that promises on television to deliver the essence of life. I watch the amber liquid pour down his throat, the alcohol steal into his blood, the key turn in his brain.

Soon after my parents moved back to Father's treacherous stomping ground, my wife and I visited them in Mississippi with our five-year-old daughter. Mother had been too distraught to warn me about the return of the demons. So when I climbed out of the car that bright July morning and saw my father napping in the hammock, I felt uneasy, for in all his sober years I had never known him to sleep in daylight. Then he lurched upright, blinked his bloodshot eyes, and greeted us in a syrupy voice. I was hurled back helpless into childhood.

"What's the matter with Papaw?" our daughter asked.

"Nothing," I said. "Nothing!"

Like a child again, I pretended not to see him in his stupor, and behind my phony smile I grieved. On that visit and on the few that remained before his death, once again I found bottles in the workbench, bottles in the woods. Again his hands shook too much for him to run a saw, to make his precious miniature furniture, to drive straight down back roads. Again he wound up in the ditch, in the hospital, in jail, in treatment centers. Again he shouted and wept. Again he lied. "I never touched a drop," he swore. "Your mother's making it up."

I no longer fancied I could reason with the men whose names I found on the bottles—Jim Beam, Jack Daniels—nor did I hope to save my father by burning down a store. I was able now to press the cold statistics about alcoholism against the ache of memory: ten million victims, fifteen million, twenty. And yet, in spite of my age, I reacted in the same blind way as I had in childhood, ignoring biology, forgetting numbers, vainly seeking to erase through my efforts whatever drove him to drink. I worked on their place twelve and sixteen hours a day, in the swelter of Mississippi summers, digging ditches, running electrical wires, planting trees, mowing grass, building sheds, as though what nagged at him was some list of chores, as though by taking his worries on my shoulders I could redeem him. I was flung back into boyhood, acting as though my father would not drink himself to death if only I were perfect.

I failed of perfection; he succeeded in dying. To the end, he considered himself not sick but sinful. "Do you want to kill yourself?" I asked him. "Why not?" he answered. "Why the hell not? What's there to save?" To the end, he would not speak about his feelings, would not or could not give a name to the beast that was devouring him.

In silence, he went rushing off the cliff. Unlike the biblical swine, however, he left behind a few of the demons to haunt his children. Life with him and the loss of him twisted us into shapes that will be familiar to other sons and daughters of alcoholics. My brother became a rebel, my sister retreated into shyness, I played the stalwart and dutiful son who would hold the family together. If my father was unstable, I would be a rock. If he squandered money on drink, I would pinch every penny. If he wept when drunk—and only when drunk—I would not let myself weep at all. If he roared at the Little League umpire for calling my pitches balls, I would throw nothing but strikes. Watching him flounder and rage, I came to dread the loss of control. I would go through life without making anyone mad. I vowed never to put in my mouth or veins any chemical that would banish my everyday self. I would never make a scene, never lash out at the ones I loved, never hurt a soul. Through hard work, relentless work, I would achieve something dazzling—in the classroom, on the basketball floor, in the science lab, in the pages of books—and my achievement would distract the world's eyes from his humiliation. I would become a worthy sacrifice, and the smoke of my burning would please God.

It is far easier to recognize these twists in my character than to undo them. Work has become an addiction for me, as drink was an addiction for my father. Knowing this, my daughter gave me a placard for the wall: WORKAHOLIC. The labor is endless and futile, for I can no more redeem myself through work than I could redeem my father. I still panic in the face of other people's anger, because his drunken temper was so terrible. I shrink from causing sadness or disappointment even to strangers, as though I were still concealing the family shame. I still notice every twitch of emotion in the faces around me, having learned as a child to read the weather in faces, and I blame myself for their least pang of unhappiness or anger. In certain moods I blame myself for everything. Guilt burns like acid in my veins.

I am moved to write these pages now because my own son, at the age of ten, is taking on himself the griefs of the world, and in particular the griefs of his father. He tells me that when I am gripped by sadness he feels responsible; he feels there must be something he can do to spring me from depression, to fix my life. And that crushing sense of responsibility is exactly what I felt at the age of ten in the face of my father's drinking. My son wonders if I, too, am possessed. I write, therefore, to drag into the light what eats at me—the fear, the guilt, the shame—so that my own children may be spared.

I still shy away from nightclubs, from bars, from parties where the solvent is alcohol. My friends puzzle over this, but it is no more peculiar than for a man to shy away from the lions' den after seeing his father torn apart. I took my own first drink at the age of twenty-one, half a glass of burgundy. I knew the odds of my becoming an alcoholic were four times higher than for the sons of nonalcoholic fathers. So I sipped warily.

I still do—once a week, perhaps, a glass of wine, a can of beer, nothing stronger, nothing more. I listen for the turning of a key in my brain.

GAYLE PEMBERTON

Gayle Pemberton (1948–   ) grew up in Minnesota, took her B.A. from the University of Michigan and her Ph.D. from Harvard, and has taught at numerous universities. She is the associate director of African-American studies at Princeton University. Pemberton's first essay collection, The Hottest Water in Chicago, *established her as a virtuoso of the personal essay. The book's subtitle,* On Family, Race, Time, and American Culture, *announced the themes that she braided both within each piece and throughout the whole. The book has a remarkable coherence, unified as it is by the essayist's strong, self-aware persona. Possibly the most singular African-American essayist to have appeared on the scene since the death of James Baldwin, Pemberton inherits from Baldwin a complex understanding of the intersections between personal and political, and a desire to convey a solitary experience and viewpoint without sacrificing her solidarity with the African-American community.*

Pemberton's portraits of her middle-class black family are particularly compelling: the striving, civic-minded architect father, the glamorous, movie-loving mother, the sister with whom the narrator alternately identifies and competes, the opinionated, judgmental grandmother. In her work, family is both safe haven and problematic coccoon. The world outside, beckoning mysteriously, also inflicts subtle and gross wounds of racism and sexism, which Pemberton describes precisely and unsentimentally.

Do He Have Your Number, Mr. Jeffrey?

D URING THE FALL of 1984 I worked for three weekends as a
caterer's assistant in Southern California. Like lots of others seeking
their fortunes in L.A., I was working by day as a temporary typist in a
Hollywood film studio. I was moonlighting with the caterer because, like
lots of others, I was going broke on my typist's wages.

Though the job was not particularly enjoyable, the caterer and her husband were congenial, interesting people who certainly would have become
good friends of mine had I stayed in California. I spent my three weekends in basic scullery work—wiping and slicing mushrooms, mixing bat-
ters, peeling apples, tomatoes, and cucumbers, drying plates, glasses, and
cutlery. Greater responsibilities would have come with more experience,
but I had brushed off California's dust before I learned any real catering
secrets or professional gourmet techniques.

One exhausting dinner party, given by a rich man for his family and
friends, turned out to be among the reasons I brushed off that California
dust. This dinner was such a production that our crew of five arrived the
day before to start preparing. The kitchen in this house was larger than
some I've seen in fine French restaurants. Our caterer was one of a new
breed of gourmet cooks who do all preparation and cooking at the
client's home—none of your cold-cut or warming-tray catering. As a result, her clients had a tendency to have loads of money and even more
kitchen space.

Usually her staff was not expected to serve the meal, but on this occasion we did. I was directed to wear stockings and black shoes and I was
given a blue-patterned apron dress, with frills here and there, to wear.
Clearly, my academic lady-banker pumps were out of the question, so I
invested in a pair of trendy black sneakers—which cost me five dollars less
than what I earned the entire time I worked for the caterer. Buying the
sneakers was plainly excessive but I told myself they were a necessary
expense. I was not looking forward to wearing the little French serving-
girl uniform, though. Everything about it and me were wrong, but I had
signed on and it would have been unseemly and downright hostile to
jump ship.

One thing I liked about the caterer was her insistence that her crew not
be treated as servants—that is, we worked for her and took orders from

her, not from the clients, who might find ordering us around an embold-
ening and socially one-upping experience. She also preferred to use crystal
and china she rented, keeping her employees and herself safe from a client's rage in case a family heirloom should get broken. But on this occasion, her client insisted that we use his Baccarat crystal. We were all made
particularly nervous by his tone. It was the same tone I heard from a
mucky-muck at my studio typing job: cold, arrogant, a matter-of-fact "you
are shit" attitude that is well known to nurses and secretaries.

I had never served a dinner before that one—that is, for strangers,
formally. I had mimed serving festive meals for friends, but only in a
lighthearted way. And, when I was a child, my family thought it a good
exercise in etiquette—not to mention in labor savings—to have me serve
at formal dinners. "It's really fun, you know," they would say. I never
handled the good china, though.

I didn't mind cutting up mushrooms or stirring sauce in some foul rich
man's kitchen for pennies, but I certainly didn't like the idea of serving at
this one's table. I saw our host hold up one of his goblets to a guest,
showing off the fine line and texture. There were too many conflicting
images for me to be content with the scene. He was working hard on his
image for his guests; I was bothered by the way I looked to myself and by
what I might have looked like to the assembled crew, guests, and host. I
couldn't get the idea of black servility to white power out of my mind.

The food was glorious. I recall serving quenelles at one point, followed
by a consommé brunoise, a beef Wellington with a carrot and herb based
sauce that I stirred for a short eternity, vegetables with lemon butter, and
a variety of mouth-watering pastries for dessert. We worked throughout
the meal, topping up wine and coffee, removing plates, bumping into each
other. As long as I was doing this absurd thing I decided to make some
kind of mental work attend it. I made the entire scene a movie, and as I
served I created a silent voice-over. At one point, after the quenelles and
the entrée and before the coffee, the table of eight sat discussing literature
—a discussion of the "what'd you think of . . ." variety. My professorial
ears pricked up. I discovered that one member of the party had actually
read the book in question, while a few others had skimmed condensed
versions in a magazine. My voice-over could have vied, I thought, with the
shrillest Bolshevik propaganda ever written.

PEMBERTON (VOICE-OVER)

(haughtily)

You self-satisfied, rich, feeble-brained, idiotic, priggish, filthy mag-
gots! You, you sit here talking literature—why, you don't even know
what the word means. This is high intellectual discourse for you, isn't

it? High, fine. You are proud to say, "I thought the theme honest."
What, pray tell, is an honest theme? It might be better to consider the
dishonesty of your disgusting lives. Why, here I am, a Ph.D in literature, listening to this garbage, making a pittance, while you illiterate
pig-running-dogs consume food and non-ideas with the same relish.

Oh, I did go on. My script was melodramatic, with great soliloquies,
flourishes, and, for verisimilitude, an eastern European accent. My come-
uppance came as I dried the last of the Baccarat goblets. The crystal, no
doubt responding to the dissonance and intensity of my sound track, shattered as I held it in my hand. The rest of the crew said they'd never seen
anyone look as sick as I did at that moment. The goblet was worth more
than the price of my trendy sneakers and my night's work combined. I
decided to go home.

I drove slowly back to my room near Culver City; it was well past
midnight. I had the distinct sense that I was the only sober driver on the
Santa Monica Freeway that night, but given the weaving pattern of my
driving—to avoid the other weavers—I fully expected to be picked up and
jailed. Then, some alcohol residue from the broken goblet would have
transported itself magically into my bloodstream to make me DWI, just as
the goblet had reacted to my thoughts and sacrificed itself in the name of
privilege, money, and mean-spiritedness. I made it home, feeling woozy as
I left my car.

I didn't have to pay for the goblet; the caterer did. She was insured. I
worked another party for her—another strange collection of people, but a
more festive occasion—and I didn't have to wear the French maid's outfit.
I got to stand happily behind a buffet, helping people serve themselves. I
think back on my catering experience the way people do who, once something's over, say that they're glad they did it—like lassoing a bull, riding
him, then busting ribs and causing permanent sacroiliac distress. The job
was just one of many I've had to take to make me believe I could survive
when it was obvious that I was going further and further into the hole. I
never had more than ten dollars in my wallet the entire time I lived in
L.A., and not much more than that in the bank. Perhaps there's something about L.A. that makes working unlikely jobs—jobs your parents
send you to college to keep you from having to do—all right and reasonable, since very little makes sense there anyway, and surviving means belly-
ing up to the illusion bar and having a taste with everyone else.

L.A. has been like that for a long time. It did not occur to me that
night, as I moved from one dinner guest to another dressed in that ludicrous outfit, that I might have created some other kind of scenario—
linking what I was doing to what my mother had done nearly fifty years
before, probably no farther than ten miles away.

* * *

It was in the middle thirties, Los Angeles. My mother's employers supplied her with a beige uniform with a frilled bib, short puff sleeves, and a narrow, fitted waist. The skirt of the dress was narrow, stopping just below the knee. She wore seamed stockings and low pumps, black. And her job, as far as she could ascertain, was to just be, nothing else. The couple who employed her—the husband wrote screenplays—had no children, and did not require her services to either cook or clean. I suppose they thought that having a maid was a requirement of their social position. So, Mother got the job. She is fair-skinned, and at that time she wore her dark, wavy hair long, in large curls that gathered just below her neck. I've seen pictures from those days and see her most enviable figure, an old-fashioned size ten, held up by long legs that, doubtless, were enhanced by the seamed stockings and pumps. Her employers were quite proud of her and thought she looked, they said, "just like a little French girl." When I was very young and filled with important questions, Mother explained to me that she thought it "damned irritating that whites who knew full well who they were hiring and talking to went to such lengths to try to make blacks into something else. If they wanted a little French girl, why didn't they go out and get one?" Ah, the days before *au pairs*. Well, I knew the answer to that one too.

Mother had moved to L.A. with her mother. Nana had decided to leave Papa, tired of his verbal abusiveness and profligacy. There were various cousins in California, and I am sure the appeal of the West and new beginnings at the start of the Depression made the choice an easy one. Both of my parents told me that they didn't feel the Depression all that much; things had never been financially good and little changed for them after Wall Street fell. The timing seemed right to Nana. Her other daughter, my aunt, had recently married. My mother had finished her third year at the university and, I bet, got an attack of wanderlust. She went with Nana to help her—and also to get some new air. The circumstances accommodated themselves.

I remember my shock when I learned that Mother had worked as a maid. I had always known that she had lived in California, but as a child, it never occurred to me that she would have had to "do something" there. It was not so much that my middle-class feathers were ruffled by the revelation as that I found it difficult to see her in a role that, on screen at least, was so demeaning and preposterous. Mother simply did not fit the stereotype I had been fed. And, to make matters worse, Grandma had taken pains to inform my sister and me when we were little girls that we should avoid—at all costs—rooming with whites in college or working in their homes. Her own stints as a dance-hall matron had convinced her, she said, that whites were the filthiest people on earth. The thought of my mother cleaning up after them made me want to protect her, to undo the necessity for that kind of work by some miraculous feat of time travel, to rescue her from the demeaning and the dirty.

Mother's attitude about her past employment was more pragmatic, of course. She explained to me—as if I didn't know—that there were really no avenues for black women apart from "service," as it was called, prostitution, and, perhaps, schoolteaching. Nana had no higher education and Mother's was incomplete, so service was the only route they could take. Mother also assured me that she had not cleaned unimaginable filth, but rather, with nothing else to do, had sat all day long reading novels, memorably *Anthony Adverse* by Hervey Allen, a big best-seller of 1934. My image of Mother became brighter, but in some ways more curious: there she was, imagined as a French maid by her employers, but really a black coed, lolling around a Los Angeles home reading *Anthony Adverse.* That's one far cry from Butterfly McQueen as Prissy in *Gone with the Wind.*

All good things must come to an end, as they say, and Mother's job did one day. She had been dating a man, she says, "who was very handsome, looked Latin, like Cesar Romero, but he was black too." Talk about images. He arrived to pick her up for a date as she got off work. He inquired after her at the front door—oops—and there went the job. Seems the little French maid's Spanish-looking boyfriend should have realized that no matter what black might appear to be, it better not act other than what it was. A slip in racial protocol, a lost novel-reading employ. "So it went," Mother said. After that incident she decided to look for a different kind of work and she began selling stockings for the Real Silk Hosiery Company, door-to-door.

Mother was lucky. I suspect that she and Nana might have had a tougher time if they had been brown-skinned, for contrary to many images from movies, white employers—if they were going to hire blacks at all— preferred the lighter-skinned variety. This was true of professions as diverse as chorus girls, maids, schoolteachers, waitresses, and shop clerks, an implied greater worth as blackness disappears drop by drop into ginger, to mocha, to "high yellow," to white. This scale was intraracially internalized too, making a shambles of black life from the earliest slave days to the present. These gradations also made color-line crossing a popular black sport, particularly since white America seemed to be at once so secure and satisfied in its whiteness and so ignorant of who's who and who's what. Blacks existed only as whites saw them, blackness affirming white racial self-consciousness and nothing else. This is what Ralph Ellison's invisibility is all about; it is what we have all lived.

In the evenings and on weekends, Mother and Nana used to go to the movies; they both were hooked and on location for Hollywood's Golden

Age. I love movies too. It is on the gene, as I frequently remind myself as I sit watching a vintage B from the forties for the fifth time or so when I ought to be reading a book. A major chunk of my misspent youth involved watching them. When I should have been reading, or studying mathematics, or learning foreign languages—like my more successful academic friends—I was hooked on three-reelers.

During my youth Mother was my partner in all this. When I was in kindergarten and first grade on half-day shifts, I never missed a morning movie. When we watched together I would barrage her with important questions: "Who is that?" "Is he dead?" "Is she dead?" "Who was she married to?" "Is this gonna be sad?" Mother was never wrong, except once. We were watching an early Charles Bickford movie and I asked the standard heady question: "Is he dead?" Mother said, "Oh, Lord, yes. He died years ago." Several years later I came home triumphantly from a drive-in and announced that I had seen Bickford in *The Big Country* and that he looked just fine and alive to me.

Of course, hopeless romanticism is the disease that can be caught from the kind of movie-going and movie-watching my mother and I have done. There she was, with her mother, frequently a part of the crowd being held behind the barricades at Hollywood premieres, sighing and pointing with agitation as gowned and white-tied stars glided from limousines into rococo movie-houses. Both she and Nana read screen magazines—the forerunners to our evening news programs—that detailed the romantic, hedonistic public and private exploits of Hollywood's royalty. It was a time when my mother, as French maid reading *Anthony Adverse,* had to wait only a few months before the novel burst onto the screen, with glorious illusionary history and Frederic March swashbuckling his way into the hearts of screaming fans. The stars were part of the studio system and could be counted on to appear with frequency, even if the roles appeared to be the same and only the titles, and a few plot twists, changed. (I am convinced, for example, that the 1934 *Imitation of Life* was remade as *Mildred Pierce* in 1945, the major change being that the relatively good daughter of the former becomes the monster of the latter. Louise Beavers and Fredi Washington in the black theme of *Imitation of Life* only slightly alter the major plot.)

Mother's was the perfect generation to see Hollywood movies when they were fresh, new, and perhaps more palpable than they are now—when comedies of remarriage, as Stanley Cavell calls them, and historical adventures and melodramas dominated the screen, when westerns and political dramas were self-consciously mythologizing the American past and present, and when young French maids and their mothers, along with the impoverished, the disillusioned, the lost, and even the comfortable and secure, could sit before the silver screen and see a different world pro-

jected than the one they lived in. And they could dream. Mother loves to
sketch faces and clothing, using an artistic talent inherited from Papa. She
marveled at the stars and their sculpted (sometimes) faces, and would
draw from memory the costume designs that made the likes of Edith
Head, Cecil Beaton, and Irene famous.

Hopeless romanticism was the threat, but neither Nana nor Mother—
nor I completely—succumbed to it. They never confused reality with anything they saw on either the big or the small screen. And they taught me
what they believed. They both warned me, in different ways and at different times, to be wary of the type of people who wake up to a new world
every day (and I've met some)—people with no memory, ingenuous, incapable of seeing either the implications or the connections between one
event and another, people who willingly accept what the world makes of
them on a Tuesday, forget as night falls, and wake up on Wednesday ready
to make the same mistakes. It might have been some of that ingenuous-
ness that produced my feelings of discomfort when I learned that Mother
had been a maid, and she understood how I felt.

My mother always deplored the depiction of blacks on screen. She saw
their roles as demeaning and designed to evoke either cheap sentimentality, cheap laughter, or cheap feelings of superiority in the white audiences
they were aimed at. And, although she says she didn't see many of them,
Mother loathed the all-black B movies Hollywood made for the "colored"
audience, where the stereotypes were broader and more offensive to her,
and where the musical interludes did no justice to real talent, she said, but
trivialized it. She even hated musical interludes featuring black performers
in the standard white A and B movies. She was—and still is—cold to
arguments that say talented black performers needed to take any work
they could get, and that black audiences were encouraged and happy to
see black Hollywood stars no matter what they were doing. Mother countered that Hattie McDaniel's acceptance speech, when she won an Oscar
for her role as Mammy in *Gone with the Wind,* was written for her, and
that McDaniel was denied the status of eating dinner with her peers
that night.

We have talked about all of this many, many times, particularly when I
have felt it necessary to sort out my own complex and conflicting reactions
to Hollywood movies. Like Mother, I have seen as nothing but illusion the
world projected on the screen. But as Michael Wood notes in *America in
the Movies:* "All movies mirror reality in some way or other. There are no
escapes, even in the most escapist pictures. . . . The business of films is
the business of dreams . . . but then dreams are scrambled messages
from waking life, and there is truth in lies, too." Mother may have recoiled
from black images on screen because they affirmed a reality she did not
like. She could suspend her disbelief at white characters and their predica-

ments, she could enter the dream worlds of aristocrats and chorus girls living happily ever after, or dying romantic, drawn-out deaths, because there was some measure of inner life given these portrayals. The audience demanded some causal foundation to acts ranging from heroism and self-sacrifice to murder, duplicity, and pure cussedness. But black characters on screen, no matter how polished their roles, were ultimately as invisible as she was in her own role as French maid—a projection only of what the white world wanted to see, robbed of the implication of inner lives, nothing but glorified surfaces that really said everything about whiteness and nothing at all about blackness. It didn't matter to Mother if the characters were maids or butlers, lawyers or doctors, simpletons or singers. I knew there was an inner life, a real person in my mother—passionate and shy, lacking self-confidence but projecting intense intelligence and style—and that she had no business being anybody's French girl. The "truth in lies" was that Hollywood rent from us our human dignity while giving us work, as it sought to defuse and deflect our real meaning—a potentially dangerous meaning—in American life.

Mother found these invisible blacks painful to watch because they were so effective as images created in white minds. These complex feelings are on the gene too. I find Shirley Temple movies abominable, notwithstanding the dancing genius of Bill "Bojangles" Robinson. In *The Little Colonel* young Shirley has just been given a birthday party; there are hats and horns and all sorts of scrubbed white children celebrating with her. At some moment—I refuse to watch the film again to be precise—she gets up and takes part of her cake to a group of dusty and dusky children who are waiting outside in the backyard of the house. The only reason for their existence is to be grateful for the crumbs and to sing a song. There can be no other motivation, no reason to exist at all, except to show the dear Little Colonel's largesse and liberal-mindedness, befitting someone not quite to the manor born but clearly on her way to the manor life.

I was watching an Alfred Hitchcock festival not long ago. Hitchcock films are some of Mother's favorites. She likes the illusions and twists of plots, the scrambling of images light and dark. I realized that I hadn't seen *Rear Window* since I was a little girl, and that at the time I hadn't understood much of what had taken place in the movie. I was very interested in it this time around. There was James Stewart, as Jeffries, in the heaviest makeup ever, with his blue eyes almost enhanced out of his face, looking at evil Raymond Burr through binoculars in the apartment across the way. I was letting the film take me where it would; I created an *explication de texte,* noting how the film raises questions about voyeurism and images. Indeed, Stewart, in looking at the world from his temporary infirmity, is only content when he places a narrative line on the lives of the people on the other side of his binoculars. He is, in a sense, reacting to images and attempting to order them—as we all do.

At a crucial moment in the movie, Stewart realizes that he is in danger. The evil wife-murderer and dismemberer, Burr, knows that Stewart has figured out the crime. Stewart hobbles to the telephone, trying to reach his friend, Wendell Corey. Corey isn't in, but Stewart gets the babysitter on the line—who speaks in a vaudevillian black accent. He asks her to have Corey call him when he returns. The babysitter asks, "Do he have your number, Mr. Jeffrey?"

I called my mother to tell her that I had an interesting bit of trivia from *Rear Window*. She became angry when she heard it, said she was appalled. "He should have been ashamed of himself," she said of Hitchcock. Into the white world of *Rear Window* and questions of imagery, it was necessary to place a familiar black image—and this time it didn't even have a face.

Mother and Nana left L.A. in 1937. Working in service and selling silk stockings could not provide enough money for them to survive. They went back to the frozen North. Mother married in 1939; Nana returned to Papa and stayed with him until he died in 1967.

Nana and Papa both moved to L.A. in 1950, Papa then a semi-retired architect. They had a beautiful home on West Fourth Avenue. It was right in the middle of a two-block area that became part of the Santa Monica Freeway. One morning, on my way to a catering job, I drove my car as far as I could, to the fence above the freeway. I got out and thought long and hard about what had been lost—beyond a house, of course, but their lives gone, part of my youth as a little girl visiting in summers, and dreams about what life could be in the semi-tropical paradise of Southern California where they made dreams that seduced the whole world.

✓RICHARD RODRIGUEZ

Richard Rodriguez (1944–   ) is one of the most distinctive and impressive voices in contemporary American essay writing. He grew up in Sacramento, California, was educated in Catholic schools, and was a "scholarship boy," the favorite minority student at college and graduate school, until this preferential treatment began to dismay him, and he opted out of an academic career for one as a writer. His debut book of interlocking autobiographical essays, Hunger of Memory, *charted his inevitable alienation as an educated second-generation son from his warm Mexican immigrant parents. It caused a great deal of talk, partly because of the controversial skeptical positions he took regarding affirmative action and bilingualism and partly because of the exceptionally mature, polished, reflective style of the writing. Indeed, the book's subtitle,* The Education of Richard Rodriguez, *seems intentionally to echo an earlier stylist of American prose, Henry Adams. Rodriguez himself has readily acknowledged George Orwell's influence. Orwellian, certainly, are the interrogations of conscience and the attempt to write moral essays that combine personal honesty with a political and social dimension.*

Rodriguez's second collection, Days of Obligation, *confirmed both his importance as an essayist and his prickly singularity. In pieces such as "Late Victorians," he detaches himself from the sentimental clichés and comforts of group identity (whether ethnic or sexual), while at the same time castigating himself for remaining an observer, sitting on the fence. "Late Victorians" is also a masterly portrait of a city (San Francisco), a time, and a plague. It exemplifies the mosaic technique of constructing a coherent essay from the seemingly fragmented materials of daily life.*

Late Victorians

S T. A U G U S T I N E writes from his cope of dust that we are rest-less hearts, for earth is not our true home. Human unhappiness is evidence of our immortality. Intuition tells us we are meant for some other city.

Elizabeth Taylor, quoted in a magazine article of twenty years ago, spoke of cerulean Richard Burton days on her yacht, days that were never-theless undermined by the elemental private reflection: This must end.

On a Sunday in summer, ten years ago, I was walking home from the Latin mass at St. Patrick's, the old Irish parish downtown, when I saw thousands of people on Market Street. It was the Gay Freedom Day parade—not the first, but the first I ever saw. Private lives were becoming public. There were marching bands. There were floats. Banners blocked single lives thematically into a processional mass, not unlike the consor-tiums of the blessed in Renaissance paintings, each saint cherishing the apparatus of his martyrdom: GAY DENTISTS. BLACK AND WHITE LOVERS. GAYS FROM BAKERSFIELD. LATINA LESBIANS. From the foot of Market Street they marched, east to west, following the mythic American path toward optimism.

I followed the parade to Civic Center Plaza, where flags of routine nations yielded sovereignty to a multitude. Pastel billows flowed over all.

Five years later, another parade. Politicians waved from white con-vertibles. "Dykes on Bikes" revved up, thumbs-upped. But now banners bore the acronyms of death. AIDS. ARC. Drums were muffled as passing, plum-spotted young men slid by on motorized cable cars.

Though I am alive now, I do not believe an old man's pessimism is necessarily truer than a young man's optimism simply because it comes after. There are things a young man knows that are true and are not yet in the old man's power to recollect. Spring has its sappy wisdom. Lonely teenagers still arrive in San Francisco aboard Greyhound buses. The city can still seem, by comparison with where they came from, paradise.

*   *   *

Four years ago on a Sunday in winter—a brilliant spring afternoon—I was jogging near Fort Point while overhead a young woman was, with difficulty, climbing over the railing of the Golden Gate Bridge. Holding down her skirt with one hand, with the other she waved to a startled spectator (the newspaper next day quoted a workman who was painting the bridge) before she stepped onto the sky.

To land like a spilled purse at my feet.

Serendipity has an eschatological tang here. Always has. Few American cities have had the experience, as we have had, of watching the civic body burn even as we stood, out of body, on a hillside, in a movie theater. Jeanette MacDonald's loony scatting of "San Francisco" has become our go-to-hell anthem. San Francisco has taken some heightened pleasure from the circus of final things. To Atlantis, to Pompeii, to the Pillar of Salt, we add the Golden Gate Bridge, not golden at all, but rust red. San Francisco toys with the tragic conclusion.

For most of its brief life, San Francisco has entertained an idea of itself as heaven on earth, whether as Gold Town or City Beautiful or the Haight-Ashbury.

San Francisco can support both comic and tragic conclusions because the city is geographically *in extremis,* a metaphor for the farthest-flung possibility, a metaphor for the end of the line. Land's end.

To speak of San Francisco as land's end is to read the map from one direction only—as Europeans would read it or as the East Coast has always read. In my lifetime San Francisco has become an Asian city. To speak, therefore, of San Francisco as land's end is to betray parochialism. My parents came here from Mexico. They saw San Francisco as the North. The West was not west for them. They did not share the Eastern traveler's sense of running before the past—the darkening time zone, the lowering curtain.

I cannot claim for myself the memory of a skyline such as the one César saw. César came to San Francisco in middle age; César came here as to some final place. He was born in South America; he had grown up in Paris; he had been everywhere, done everything; he assumed the world. Yet César was not condescending toward San Francisco, not at all. Here César saw revolution, and he embraced it.

Whereas I live here because I was born here. I grew up ninety miles away, in Sacramento. San Francisco was the nearest, the easiest, the inevitable city, since I needed a city. And yet I live here surrounded by people for whom San Francisco is the end of quest.

I have never looked for utopia on a map. Of course I believe in human advancement. I believe in medicine, in astrophysics, in washing machines. But my compass takes its cardinal point from tragedy. If I respond to the metaphor of spring, I nevertheless learned, years ago, from my Mexican father, from my Irish nuns, to count on winter. The point of Eden for me, for us, is not approach but expulsion.

After I met César in 1984, our friendly debate concerning the halcyon properties of San Francisco ranged from restaurant to restaurant. I spoke of limits. César boasted of freedoms.

It was César's conceit to add to the gates of Jerusalem, to add to the soccer fields of Tijuana, one other dreamscape hoped for the world over. It was the view from a hill, through a mesh of tram wires, of an urban neighborhood in a valley. The vision took its name from the protruding wedge of a theater marquee. Here César raised his glass without discretion: To the Castro.

There were times, dear César, when you tried to switch sides, if only to scorn American optimism, which, I remind you, had already become your own. At the high school where César taught, teachers and parents had organized a campaign to keep kids from driving themselves to the junior prom, in an attempt to forestall liquor and death. Such a scheme momentarily reawakened César's Latin skepticism.

Didn't the Americans know? (His tone exaggerated incredulity.) Teenagers will crash into lampposts on their way home from proms, and there is nothing to be done about it. You cannot forbid tragedy.

By California standards I live in an old house. But not haunted. There are too many tall windows, there is too much salty light, especially in winter, though the windows rattle, rattle in summer when the fog flies overhead, and the house creaks and prowls at night. I feel myself immune to any confidence it seeks to tell.

To grow up homosexual is to live with secrets and within secrets. In no other place are those secrets more closely guarded than within the family home. The grammar of the gay city borrows metaphors from the nineteenth-century house. "Coming out of the closet" is predicated upon family laundry, dirty linen, skeletons.

I live in a tall Victorian house that has been converted to four apartments; four single men.

Neighborhood streets are named to honor nineteenth-century men of action, men of distant fame. Clay. Jackson. Scott. Pierce. Many Victorians in the neighborhood date from before the 1906 earthquake and fire.

Architectural historians credit the gay movement of the 1970s with the urban restoration of San Francisco. Twenty years ago this was a borderline neighborhood. This room, like all the rooms of the house, was painted headache green, apple green, boardinghouse green. In the 1970s, homosexuals moved into black and working-class parts of the city, where they were perceived as pioneers or as block-busters, depending.

Two decades ago, some of the least expensive sections of San Francisco were wooden Victorian sections. It was thus a coincidence of the market that gay men found themselves living within the architectural metaphor for family. No other architecture in the American imagination is more evocative of family than the Victorian house. In those same years—the 1970s—and within those same Victorian houses, homosexuals were living rebellious lives to challenge the foundations of domesticity.

Was "queer-bashing" as much a manifestation of homophobia as a reaction against gentrification? One heard the complaint, often enough, that gay men were as promiscuous with their capital as otherwise, buying, fixing up, then selling and moving on. Two incomes, no children, described an unfair advantage. No sooner would flower boxes begin to appear than an anonymous reply was smeared on the sidewalk out front: KILL FAGGOTS.

The three- or four-story Victorian house, like the Victorian novel, was built to contain several generations and several classes under one roof, behind a single oaken door. What strikes me at odd moments is the confidence of Victorian architecture. Stairs, connecting one story with another, describe the confidence that bound generations together through time—confidence that the family would inherit the earth. The other day I noticed for the first time the vestige of a hinge on the topmost newel of the staircase. This must have been the hinge of a gate that kept infants upstairs so many years ago.

If Victorian houses assert a sturdy optimism by day, they are also associated in our imaginations with the Gothic—with shadows and cobwebby gimcrack, long corridors. The nineteenth century was remarkable for escalating optimism even as it excavated the backstairs, the descending architecture of nightmare—Freud's labor and Engels's.

I live on the second story, in rooms that have been rendered as empty as Yorick's skull—gutted, unrattled, in various ways unlocked—added skylights and new windows, new doors. The hallway remains the darkest part of the house.

This winter the hallway and lobby are being repainted to resemble an eighteenth-century French foyer. Of late we had walls and carpet of Sienese red; a baroque mirror hung in an alcove by the stairwell. Now we are to have enlightened austerity—black-and-white marble floors and faux masonry. A man comes in the afternoons to texture the walls with a sponge and a rag and to paint white mortar lines that create an illusion of permanence, of stone.

The renovation of Victorian San Francisco into dollhouses for libertines may have seemed, in the 1970s, an evasion of what the city was actually becoming. San Francisco's rows of storied houses proclaimed a multigenerational orthodoxy, all the while masking the city's unconventional soul. Elsewhere, meanwhile, domestic America was coming undone.

Suburban Los Angeles, the prototype for a new America, was characterized by a more apparently radical residential architecture. There was, for example, the work of Frank Gehry. In the 1970s, Gehry exploded the nuclear-family house, turning it inside out intellectually and in fact. Though, in a way, Gehry merely completed the logic of the postwar suburban tract house—with its one story, its sliding glass doors, Formica kitchen, two-car garage. The tract house exchanged privacy for mobility. Heterosexuals opted for the one-lifetime house, the freeway, the birth-control pill, minimalist fiction.

The age-old description of homosexuality is of a sin against nature. Moralistic society has always judged emotion literally. The homosexual was sinful because he had no kosher place to stick it. In attempting to drape the architecture of sodomy with art, homosexuals have lived for thousands of years against the expectations of nature. Barren as Shakers and, interestingly, as concerned with the small effect, homosexuals have made a covenant against nature. Homosexual survival lay in artifice, in plumage, in lampshades, sonnets, musical comedy, couture, syntax, religious ceremony, opera, lacquer, irony.

I once asked Byron, an interior decorator, if he had many homosexual clients. *"Mais non,"* said he, flexing his eyelids. "Queers don't need decorators. They were born knowing how. All this ASID stuff—tests and regulations—as if you can confer a homosexual diploma on a suburban housewife by granting her a discount card."

A knack? The genius, we are beginning to fear in an age of AIDS, is irreplaceable—but does it exist? The question is whether the darling affinities are innate to homosexuality or whether they are compensatory. Why have so many homosexuals retired into the small effect, the ineffectual career, the stereotype, the card shop, the florist? *Be gentle with me?* Or do homosexuals know things others do not?

This way power lay. Once upon a time, the homosexual appropriated to himself a mystical province, that of taste. Taste, which is, after all, the insecurity of the middle class, became the homosexual's licentiate to challenge the rule of nature. (The fairy in his blood, he intimated.)

Deciding how best to stick it may be only an architectural problem or a question of physics or of engineering or of cabinetry. Nevertheless, society's condemnation forced the homosexual to find his redemption outside nature. *We'll put a little skirt here.* The impulse is not to create but to re-create, to sham, to convert, to sauce, to rouge, to fragrance, to prettify. No effect is too small or too ephemeral to be snatched away from nature, to be ushered toward the perfection of artificiality. *We'll bring out the highlights there.* The homosexual has marshaled the architecture of the straight world to the very gates of Versailles—that great Vatican of fairyland—beyond which power is tyrannized by leisure.

In San Francisco in the 1980s, the highest form of art became interior decoration. The glory hole was thus converted to an eighteenth-century foyer.

I live away from the street, in a back apartment, in two rooms. I use my bedroom as a visitor's room—the sleigh bed tricked up with shams into a sofa—whereas I rarely invite anyone into my library, the public room, where I write, the public gesture.

I read in my bedroom in the afternoon because the light is good there, especially now, in winter, when the sun recedes from the earth.

There is a door in the south wall that leads to a balcony. The door was once a window. Inside the door, inside my bedroom, are twin green shutters. They are false shutters, of no function beyond wit. The shutters open into the room; they have the effect of turning my apartment inside out.

A few months ago I hired a man to paint the shutters green. I wanted the green shutters of Manet—you know the ones I mean—I wanted a weathered look, as of verdigris. For several days the painter labored, rubbing his paints into the wood and then wiping them off again. In this way he rehearsed for me decades of the ravages of weather. Yellow enough? Black?

The painter left one afternoon, saying he would return the next, leaving behind his tubes, his brushes, his sponges and rags. He never returned. Someone told me he has AIDS.

A black woman haunts California Street between the donut shop and the cheese store. She talks to herself—a debate, wandering, never advancing. Pedestrians who do not know her give her a wide berth. Somebody told me her story; I don't know whether it's true. Neighborhood merchants tolerate her presence as a vestige of dispirited humanity clinging to an otherwise dispiriting progress of "better" shops and restaurants.

Repainted façades extend now from Jackson Street south into what was once the heart of the "Mo"—black Fillmore Street. Today there are watercress sandwiches at three o'clock where recently there had been loud-mouthed kids, hole-in-the-wall bars, pimps. Now there are tweeds and perambulators, matrons and nannies. Yuppies. And gays.

The gay-male revolution had greater influence on San Francisco in the 1970s than did the feminist revolution. Feminists, with whom I include lesbians—such was the inclusiveness of the feminist movement—were pre-occupied with career, with escape from the house in order to create a sexually democratic city. Homosexual men sought to reclaim the house, the house that traditionally had been the reward for heterosexuality, with all its selfless tasks and burdens.

Leisure defined the gay-male revolution. The gay political movement began, by most accounts, in 1969 with the Stonewall riots in New York City, whereby gay men fought to defend the nonconformity of their leisure.

It was no coincidence that homosexuals migrated to San Francisco in the 1970s, for the city was famed as a playful place, more Catholic than Protestant in its eschatological intuition. In 1975, the state of California legalized consensual homosexuality, and about that same time Castro Street, southwest of downtown, began to eclipse Polk Street as the homosexual address in San Francisco. Polk Street was a string of bars. The Castro was an entire district. The Castro had Victorian houses and churches, bookstores and restaurants, gyms, dry cleaners, supermarkets, and an elected member of the Board of Supervisors. The Castro supported baths and bars, but there was nothing furtive about them. On Castro Street the light of day penetrated gay life through clear plate-glass windows. The light of day discovered a new confidence, a new politics. Also a new look—a noncosmopolitan, Burt Reynolds, butch-kid style: beer, ball games, Levi's, short hair, muscles.

Gay men who lived elsewhere in the city, in Pacific Heights or in the Richmond, often spoke with derision of "Castro Street clones," describing the look, or scorned what they called the ghettoization of homosexuality. To an older generation of homosexuals, the blatancy of Castro Street threatened the discreet compromise they had negotiated with a tolerant city.

As the Castro district thrived, Folsom Street, south of Market, also began to thrive, as if in contradistinction to the utopian Castro. Folsom Street was a warehouse district of puddled alleys and deserted corners. Folsom Street offered an assortment of leather bars—an evening's regress to the outlaw sexuality of the fifties, the forties, the nineteenth century, and so on—an eroticism of the dark, of the Reeperbahn, or of the guardsman's barracks.

The Castro district implied that sexuality was more crucial, that homosexuality was the central fact of identity. The Castro district, with its ice-cream parlors and hardware stores, was the revolutionary place.

Into which carloads of vacant-eyed teenagers from other districts or from middle-class suburbs would drive after dark, cruising the neighborhood for solitary victims.

The ultimate gay-basher was a city supervisor named Dan White, ex-cop, ex-boxer, ex-fireman, ex–altar boy. Dan White had grown up in the Castro district; he recognized the Castro revolution for what it was. Gays had achieved power over him. He murdered the mayor and he murdered the homosexual member of the Board of Supervisors.

Katherine, a sophisticate if ever there was one, nevertheless dismisses two men descending the aisle at the Opera House: "All so sleek and smooth-jowled and silver-haired—they don't seem real, poor darlings. It must be because they don't have children."

Lodged within Katherine's complaint is the perennial heterosexual annoyance with the homosexual's freedom from childrearing, which does not so much place the homosexual beyond the pale as it relegates the homosexual outside "responsible" life.

It was the glamour of gay life, after all, as much as it was the feminist call to career, that encouraged heterosexuals in the 1970s to excuse themselves from nature, to swallow the birth-control pill. Who needs children? The gay bar became the paradigm for the singles bar. The gay couple became the paradigm for the selfish couple—all dressed up and everywhere to go. And there was the example of the gay house in illustrated life-style magazines. At the same time that suburban housewives were looking outside the home for fulfillment, gay men were reintroducing a new generation in the city—heterosexual men and women—to the complaisancies of the barren house.

Puritanical America dismissed gay camp followers as yuppies; the term means to suggest infantility. Yuppies were obsessive and awkward in their materialism. Whereas gays arranged a decorative life against a barren state, yuppies sought early returns—lives that were not to be all toil and spin. Yuppies, trained to careerism from the cradle, wavered in their pursuit of the Northern European ethic—indeed, we might now call it the pan-Pacific ethic—in favor of the Mediterranean, the Latin, the Catholic, the Castro, the Gay.

The international architectural idioms of Skidmore, Owings & Merrill, which defined the skyline of the 1970s, betrayed no awareness of any street-level debate concerning the primacy of play in San Francisco or of any human dramas resulting from urban redevelopment. The repellent office tower was a fortress raised against the sky, against the street, against the idea of a city. Offices were hives where money was made, and damn all.

In the 1970s, San Francisco divided between the interests of downtown and the pleasures of the neighborhoods. Neighborhoods asserted idiosyncrasy, human scale, light. San Francisco neighborhoods perceived downtown as working against their influence in determining what the city should be. Thus neighborhoods seceded from the idea of a city.

The gay movement rejected downtown as representing "straight" conformity. But was it possible that heterosexual Union Street was related to Castro Street? Was it possible that either was related to the Latino Mission district? Or to the Sino-Russian Richmond? San Francisco, though complimented worldwide for holding its center, was in fact without a vision of itself entire.

In the 1980s, in deference to the neighborhoods, City Hall would attempt a counterreformation of downtown, forbidding "Manhattanization." Shadows were legislated away from parks and playgrounds. Height restrictions were lowered beneath an existing skyline. Design, too, fell under the retrojurisdiction of the city planner's office. The Victorian house was presented to architects as a model of what the city wanted to uphold and to become. In heterosexual neighborhoods, one saw newly built Victorians. Downtown, postmodernist prescriptions for playfulness advised skyscrapers to wear party hats, buttons, comic mustaches. Philip Johnson yielded to the dollhouse impulse to perch angels atop one of his skyscrapers.

I can see downtown from my bedroom window. But days pass and I do not leave the foreground for the city. Most days my public impression of San Francisco is taken from Fillmore Street, from the anchorhold of the Lady of the Donut Shop.

She now often parades with her arms crossed over her breasts in an "X," the posture emblematic of prophecy. And yet gather her madness where she sits on the curb, chain-smoking, hugging her knees, while I disappear down Fillmore Street to make Xerox copies, to mail letters, to rent a video, to shop for dinner. I am soon pleased by the faint breeze from the city, the slight agitation of the homing crowds of singles, so intent upon the path of least resistance. I admire the prosperity of the corridor, the shop windows that beckon inward toward the perfected lifestyle, the little way of the City of St. Francis.

Turning down Pine Street, I am recalled by the prickly silhouette of St. Dominic's Church against the scrim of the western sky. I turn, instead, into the Pacific Heights Health Club.

In the 1970s, like a lot of men and women in this city, I joined a gym. My club, I've even caught myself calling it.

In the gay city of the 1970s, bodybuilding became an architectural preoccupation of the upper middle class. Bodybuilding is a parody of labor, a useless accumulation of the laborer's bulk and strength. No useful task is accomplished. And yet there is something businesslike about habitués, and the gym is filled with the punch-clock logic of the workplace. Machines clank and hum. Needles on gauges toll spent calories.

The gym is at once a closet of privacy and an exhibition gallery. All four walls are mirrored.

I study my body in the mirror. Physical revelation—nakedness—is no longer possible, cannot be desired, for the body is shrouded in meat and wears itself.

The intent is some merciless press of body against a standard, perfect mold. Bodies are "cut" or "pumped" or "buffed" as on an assembly line in Turin. A body becomes so many extrovert parts. Delts, pecs, lats, traps.

I harness myself in a Nautilus cage.

Lats become wings. For the gym is nothing if not the occasion for transcendence. From homosexual to autosexual . . .

I lift weights over my head, baring my teeth like an animal with the strain.

. . . to nonsexual. The effect of the overdeveloped body is the miniaturization of the sexual organs—of no function beyond wit. Behold the ape become Blakean angel, revolving in an empyrean of mirrors.

The nineteenth-century mirror over the fireplace in my bedroom was purchased by a decorator from the estate of a man who died last year of AIDS. It is a top-heavy piece, confusing styles. Two ebony-painted columns support a frieze of painted glass above the mirror. The frieze depicts three bourgeois graces and a couple of free-range cherubs. The lake of the mirror has formed a cataract, and at its edges it is beginning to corrode.

Thus the mirror that now draws upon my room owns some bright curse, maybe—some memory not mine.

As I regard this mirror, I imagine St. Augustine's meditation slowly hardening into syllogism, passing down through centuries to confound us: evil is the absence of good.

We have become accustomed to figures disappearing from our landscape. Does this not lead us to interrogate the landscape?

With reason do we invest mirrors with the superstition of memory, for they, though glass, though liquid captured in a bay, are so often less fragile than we are. They—bright ovals, or rectangles, or rounds—bump down unscathed, unspilled through centuries, whereas we . . .

The man in the red baseball cap used to jog so religiously on Marina Green. By the time it occurs to me that I have not seen him for months, I realize he may be dead—not lapsed, not moved away. People come and go in the city, it's true. But in San Francisco death has become as routine an explanation for disappearance as Mayflower Van Lines.

AIDS, it has been discovered, is a plague of absence. Absence opened in the blood. Absence condensed into the fluid of passing emotion. Absence shot through opalescent tugs of semen to deflower the city.

And then AIDS, it was discovered, is a nonmetaphorical disease, a disease like any other. Absence sprang from substance—a virus, a hairy bubble perched upon a needle, a platter of no intention served round: fever, blisters, a death sentence.

At first I heard only a few names—names connected, perhaps, with the right faces, perhaps not. People vaguely remembered, as through the cataract of this mirror, from dinner parties or from intermissions. A few articles in the press. The rumored celebrities. But within months the slow beating of the blood had found its bay.

One of San Francisco's gay newspapers, the *Bay Area Reporter,* began to accept advertisements from funeral parlors and casket makers, inserting them between the randy ads for leather bars and tanning salons. The *Reporter* invited homemade obituaries—lovers writing of lovers, friends remembering friends and the blessings of unexceptional life.

Peter. Carlos. Gary. Asel. Perry. Nikos.

Healthy snapshots accompany each annal. At the Russian River. By the Christmas tree. Lifting a beer. In uniform. A dinner jacket. A satin gown.

He was born in Puerto La Libertad, El Salvador.

He attended Apple Valley High School, where he was their first male cheerleader.

From El Paso. From Medford. From Germany. From Long Island.

I moved back to San Francisco in 1979. Oh, I had had some salad days elsewhere, but by 1979 I was a wintry man. I came here in order not to be distracted by the ambitions or, for that matter, the pleasures of others but to pursue my own ambition. Once here, though, I found the company of men who pursued an earthly paradise charming. Skepticism became my demeanor toward them—I was the dinner-party skeptic, a firm believer in Original Sin and in the limits of possibility.

Which charmed them.

He was a dancer.

He settled into the interior-design department of Gump's, where he worked until his illness.

He was a teacher.

César, for example.

César had an excellent mind. César could shave the rind from any assertion to expose its pulp and jelly. But César was otherwise ruled by pulp. César loved everything that ripened in time. Freshmen. Bordeaux. César could fashion liturgy from an artichoke. Yesterday it was not ready (cocking his head, rotating the artichoke in his hand over a pot of cold water).

Tomorrow will be too late (Yorick's skull). Today it is perfect (as he lit the fire beneath the pot). We will eat it now.

If he's lucky, he's got a year, a doctor told me. If not, he's got two.

The phone rang. AIDS had tagged a friend. And then the phone rang again. And then the phone rang again. Michael had tested positive. Adrian, well, what he had assumed were shingles . . . Paul was back in the hospital. And César, dammit, César, even César, especially César.

That winter before his death, César traveled back to South America. On his return to San Francisco, he described to me how he had walked with his mother in her garden—his mother chafing her hands as if she were cold. But it was not cold, he said. They moved slowly. Her summer garden was prolonging itself this year, she said. The cicadas will not stop singing.

When he lay on his deathbed, César said everyone else he knew might get AIDS and die. He said I would be the only one spared—"spared" was supposed to have been chased with irony, I knew, but his voice was too weak to do the job. "You are too circumspect," he said then, wagging his finger upon the coverlet.

So I was going to live to see that the garden of earthly delights was, after all, only wallpaper—was that it, César? Hadn't I always said so? It was then I saw that the greater sin against heaven was my unwillingness to embrace life.

César said he found paradise at the baths. He said I didn't understand. He said if I had to ask about it, I might as well ask if a wife will spend eternity with Husband #1 or Husband #2.

The baths were places of good humor, that was Number One; there was nothing demeaning about them. From within cubicles men would nod at one another or not, but there was no sting of rejection, because one had at last entered a region of complete acceptance. César spoke of floating from body to body, open arms yielding to open arms in an angelic round.

The best night. That's easy, he said, the best night was spent in the pool with an antiques dealer—up to their necks in warm water—their two heads bobbing on an ocean of chlorine green, bawling Noël Coward songs.

But each went home alone?

Each satisfied, dear, César corrected. And all the way home San Francisco seemed to him balmed and merciful, he said. He felt weightlessness of being, the pavement under his step as light as air.

It was not as in some Victorian novel—the curtains drawn, the pillows plumped, the streets strewn with sawdust. It was not to be a matter of

custards in covered dishes, steaming possets, *Try a little of this, my dear.*
Or gathering up the issues of *Architectural Digest* strewn about the bed.
Closing the biography of Diana Cooper and marking its place. Or the
unfolding of discretionary screens, morphine, parrots, pavilions.

César experienced agony.

Four of his high-school students sawed through a Vivaldi quartet in the
corridor outside his hospital room, prolonging the hideous garden.

*In the presence of his lover Gregory and friends, Scott passed from this
life. . . .*

He died peacefully at home in his lover Ron's arms.

*Immediately after a friend led a prayer for him to be taken home and
while his dear mother was reciting the 23rd Psalm, Bill peacefully took his
last breath.*

I stood aloof at César's memorial, the kind of party he would enjoy,
everyone said. And so for a time César lay improperly buried, unconvinc-
ingly resurrected in the conditional: would enjoy. What else could they
say? César had no religion beyond aesthetic bravery.

Sunlight remains. Traffic remains. Nocturnal chic attaches to some discovered restaurant. A new novel is reviewed in *The New York Times.* And
the mirror rasps on its hook. The mirror is lifted down.

A priest friend, a good friend, who out of naïveté plays the cynic,
tells me—this is on a bright, billowy day; we are standing outside—"It's
not as sad as you may think. There is at least spectacle in the death of
the young. Come to the funeral of an old lady sometime if you want to
feel an empty church."

I will grant my priest friend this much: that it is easier, easier on me, to
sit with gay men in hospitals than with the staring old. Young men talk as
much as they are able.

But those who gather around the young man's bed do not see Chatter-
ton. This doll is Death. I have seen people caressing it, staring Death
down. I have seen people wipe its tears, wipe its ass; I have seen people
kiss Death on his lips, where once there were lips.

*Chris was inspired after his own diagnosis in July 1987 with the truth and
reality of how such a terrible disease could bring out the love, warmth, and
support of so many friends and family.*

Sometimes no family came. If there was family, it was usually Mother.
Mom. With her suitcase and with the torn flap of an envelope in her hand.

Brenda. Pat. Connie. Toni. Soledad.

Or parents came but then left without reconciliation, some preferring to
say "cancer."

But others came. They walked Death's dog. They washed his dishes.
They bought his groceries. They massaged his poor back. They changed
his bandages. They emptied his bedpan.

Men who sought the aesthetic ordering of existence were recalled to nature. Men who aspired to the mock-angelic settled for the shirt of hair. The gay community of San Francisco, having found freedom, consented to necessity—to all that the proud world had for so long held up to them, withheld from them, as "real humanity."

And if gays took care of their own, they were not alone. AIDS was a disease of the entire city. Nor were Charity and Mercy only male, only gay. Others came. There were nurses and nuns and the couple from next door, co-workers, strangers, teenagers, corporations, pensioners. A community was forming over the city.

Cary and Rick's friends and family wish to thank the many people who provided both small and great kindnesses.

He was attended to and lovingly cared for by the staff at Coming Home Hospice.

And the saints of this city have names listed in the phone book, names I heard called through a microphone one cold Sunday in Advent as I sat in Most Holy Redeemer Church. It might have been any of the churches or community centers in the Castro district, but it happened at Most Holy Redeemer at a time in the history of the world when the Roman Catholic Church pronounced the homosexual a sinner.

A woman at the microphone called upon volunteers from the AIDS Support Group to come forward. Throughout the church, people stood up, young men and women, and middle-aged and old, straight, gay, and all of them shy at being called. Yet they came forward and assembled in the sanctuary, facing the congregation, grinning self-consciously at one another, their hands hidden behind them.

I am preoccupied by the fussing of a man sitting in the pew directly in front of me—in his seventies, frail, his iodine-colored hair combed forward and pasted upon his forehead. Fingers of porcelain clutch the pearly beads of what must have been his mother's rosary. He is not the sort of man any gay man would have chosen to become in the 1970s. He is probably not what he himself expected to become. Something of the old dear about him, wizened butterfly, powdered old pouf. Certainly he is what I fear becoming. And then he rises, this old monkey, with the most beatific dignity, in answer to the microphone, and he strides into the sanctuary to take his place in the company of the Blessed.

So this is it—this, what looks like a Christmas party in an insurance office, and not as in Renaissance paintings, and not as we had always thought, not some flower-strewn, some sequined curtain call of grease-painted heroes gesturing to the stalls. A lady with a plastic candy cane pinned to her lapel. A Castro clone with a red bandana exploding from his hip pocket. A perfume-counter lady with an Hermès scarf mantled upon her shoulder. A black man in a checkered sports coat. The pink-haired punkess with a jewel in her nose. Here, too, is the gay couple in middle age; interchangeable plaid shirts and corduroy pants. Blood and shit and Mr. Happy Face. These know the weight of bodies.

Bill died.

. . . Passed on to heaven.

. . . Turning over in his bed one night and then gone.

These learned to love what is corruptible, while I, barren skeptic, reader of St. Augustine, curator of the earthly paradise, inheritor of the empty mirror, I shift my tailbone upon the cold, hard pew.

SELECTED BIBLIOGRAPHY

I. Works About the Essay

The following texts should help supply a way of thinking about the personal essay within the larger literary category of the essay form.

ADORNO, THEODOR. "The Essay as Form," *Notes to Literature,* Vol. 1. New York: Columbia University Press, 1991.
  A meaty philosophical look at the essay, by one of the major figures of the Frankfurt School.

BURTRYM, ALEXANDER J., ed. *Essays on the Essay: Redefining the Genre.* Athens: University of Georgia Press, 1989.
  An indispensable, if uneven, collection of pieces by scholars and practitioners on essayists and their work, which grew out of a conference on the subject.

DOBRÉE, BONAMY. *English Essayists.* London: Collins, 1956.
  An elegantly slender, breezily learned survey of the essay through one national tradition.

GOOD, GRAHAM. *The Observing Self: Rediscovering the Essay.* London and New York: Routledge, 1988.
  Intelligent, solid analyses of the essay as a genre, with chapters devoted to Montaigne, Bacon, Johnson, Hazlitt, James, Woolf, Eliot, and Orwell. Excellent.

HAZLITT, WILLIAM. "On the Periodical Essayists," *Lectures on the English Comic Writers.* New York: Doubleday Dolphin.
  Short but pungent, and fascinating.

LUKACS, GEORG. "On the Nature and Form of the Essay," *Soul and Form.* Cambridge, Mass.: MIT Press, 1974.
  A pathbreaking, densely thoughtful meditation on the essay form by the great Hungarian literary critic.

II. Pertinent Books by Authors Featured in this Anthology

ADDISON, JOSEPH, and STEELE, RICHARD. *Selected Essays from the Tatler, the Spectator, & the Guardian.* Daniel McDonald, ed. New York: Macmillan, 1973.

————. *Selections from the Tatler and the Spectator.* New York: Penguin, 1982.

BALDWIN, JAMES. *The Price of the Ticket: Collected Nonfiction, 1948–1985.* New York: St. Martin's, 1985.
> This huge, wonderful volume contains all of Baldwin's essays. In addition, certain collections as they first appeared may be obtained individually, as follows: *Notes of a Native Son* (Beacon Press); *The Fire Next Time, No Name in the Street,* and *The Devil Finds Work* (Dell Books).

BARTHES, ROLAND. *Roland Barthes.* New York: Hill and Wang, 1977.

————. *The Rustle of Language.* New York: Hill and Wang, 1986.

BEERBOHM, MAX. *Selected Prose.* Boston: Little, Brown, 1970.

BENCHLEY, ROBERT. *The Benchley Roundup.* Chicago: University of Chicago Press, 1983.

BENJAMIN, WALTER. *Illuminations.* New York: Schocken, 1969.

————. *Reflections.* New York: Schocken, 1986.

BERRY, WENDELL. *Recollected Essays, 1965–1980.* San Francisco: North Point, 1981.

BORGES, JORGE LUIS. *The Aleph and Other Stories, 1933–1969.* New York: Dutton, 1978.
> Includes the long "Autobiographical Essay."

————. *Seven Nights.* New York: New Directions, 1984.

BUTLER, HUBERT. *The Sub-Prefect Should Have Held His Tongue, and Other Essays.* New York: Viking Penguin, 1991.

CHESTERTON, G. K. *Collected Works* (15 vols.). New York: Ignatius Press, 1986– .

————. *Orthodoxy.* New York: Doubleday, 1973.

CIORAN, E. M. *The Temptation to Exist.* New York: Seaver Books, 1986.

COWLEY, ABRAHAM. *Essays, Plays, & Sundry Verses.* Reprint of 1906 edition. New York: Somerset.

DIDION, JOAN. *Slouching Toward Bethlehem.* New York: Farrar, Straus and Giroux, 1990.

————. *The White Album.* New York: Farrar, Straus and Giroux, 1990.

DILLARD, ANNIE. *The Annie Dillard Library: Living by Fiction, An American Childhood, Holy the Firm, Pilgrim at Tinker's Creek, Teaching a Stone to Talk.* New York: Harper Collins, 1989.

EDGEWORTH, MARIA. *Castle Rackrent.* New York: Norton, 1965.

————. *The Meridian Anthology of Early Women Writers: British Literary Women from Aphra Behn to Maria Edgeworth, 1660–1800.* Katharine M. Rogers and William McCarthy, eds. New York: Meridian, 1987.

FISHER, M. F. K. *The Art of Eating.* New York: Macmillan, 1990.

———. *With Bold Knife and Fork.* New York: Putnam, 1979.

FITZGERALD, F. SCOTT. *The Crack-Up.* New York: New Directions, 1956.

FUENTES, CARLOS. *Myself with Others: Selected Essays.* New York: Farrar, Straus and Giroux, 1990.

GINZBURG, NATALIA. *The Little Virtues.* New York: Arcade, 1989.

HAZLITT, WILLIAM. *Selected Writings.* Ronald Blythe, ed. London: Penguin, 1970.

———. *Selected Writings.* Jon Cook, ed. Oxford: Oxford University Press, 1991.

HOAGLAND, EDWARD. *Balancing Acts.* New York: Simon & Schuster, 1992.

———. *Heart's Desire: The Best of Edward Hoagland.* New York: Summit, 1988.

HSIU, OU-YANG. *The Literary Works of Ou-yang Hsiu.* Cambridge, England: Cambridge University Press, 1984.

———. *Love and Time.* Port Townsend, Washington: Copper Canyon Press, 1989.

HSUN, LU. *Selected Stories of Lu Hsun.* New York: Norton, 1977.

———. *Selected Works.* Beijing: Foreign Language Press, 1989.

JOHNSON, SAMUEL. *Selected Essays from the Rambler, Adventurer & Idler.* New Haven: Yale University Press, 1968.

KENKO. *Essays in Idleness: The Tsurezuregusa of Kenko.* New York: Columbia University Press, 1972.

KRIM, SEYMOUR. *What's This Cat's Story? The Best of Seymour Krim.* New York: Paragon House, 1991.

LAMB, CHARLES. *Essays of Elia and Last Essays of Elia.* Oxford: Oxford University Press, 1987.

LOPATE, PHILLIP. *Bachelorhood.* New York: Poseidon, 1989.

———. *Against Joie de Vivre.* New York: Poseidon, 1991.

McCARTHY, MARY. *Memories of a Catholic Girlhood.* New York: Harcourt Brace Jovanovich, 1972.

———. *On the Contrary.* New York: Hippocrene, 1976.

MENCKEN, H. L. *A Mencken Chrestomathy.* New York: Pantheon, 1982.

———. *Prejudices.* James T. Farrell, ed. New York: Random House, 1958.

———. *The Impossible H. L. Mencken.* New York: Anchor, 1991.
 The "chrestomathy" is a vast personal choice by Mencken himself. *Prejudices* is a selective, "top hits" collection. The third, *The Impossible H. L. Mencken,* is a generous selection of his best newspaper stories.

MONTAIGNE, MICHEL DE. *The Complete Essays.* Donald M. Frame, tr. Stanford, Calif.: Stanford University Press, 1958.

————. *The Complete Essays.* M. A. Screech, tr. New York: Viking Penguin, 1992. The Frame translation has been standard for decades; it is ripe, stately, and elegant. The new Screech translation is a little faster and more colloquial. I prefer the Frame by a hair, possibly because I am used to it, but both are good.

ORWELL, GEORGE. *Collected Essays* (3 vols). New York: Harcourt Brace Jovanovich, 1968.

————. *A Collection of Essays.* New York: Harvest/HBJ, 1970.

PEMBERTON, GAYLE. *The Hottest Water in Chicago.* New York: Anchor, 1993.

PLUTARCH. *Moralia,* Vols. 1–15. Cambridge, Mass.: Harvard University Press.

————. *Selected Essays on Love, the Family, and the Good Life.* Moses Hadas, tr. New York: Mentor, 1957.

RICH, ADRIENNE. *Blood, Bread & Poetry: Selected Prose, 1979–1985.* New York: Norton, 1986.

————. *On Lies, Secrets & Silence: Selected Prose, 1966–1978.* New York: Norton, 1979.

RODRIGUEZ, RICHARD. *Days of Obligation: An Argument with My Mexican Father.* New York: Viking Penguin, 1992.

————. *Hunger of Memory: The Education of Richard Rodriguez.* Boston: David Godine, 1982.

SANDERS, SCOTT RUSSELL. *The Paradise of Bombs.* New York: Touchstone, 1988.

————. *Secrets of the Universe.* Boston: Beacon, 1992.

SELZER, RICHARD. *Mortal Lessons: Notes of the Art of Surgery.* New York: Simon & Schuster, 1987.

————. *Down from Troy: A Doctor Comes of Age.* New York: William Morrow, 1992.

SENECA. *The Stoic Philosophy of Seneca: Essays and Letters.* Moses Hadas, tr. New York: Norton, 1958.

————. *Letters from a Stoic.* Robin Campbell, tr. New York: Penguin Classics, 1969. I prefer the Hadas translation, which has more of the condensation and snap of Seneca's sentences, but the Campbell is easier to come by and has many fine pieces not in the Hadas selection.

SHONAGON, SEI. *The Pillow Book.* Ivan Morris, tr. New York: Columbia University Press, 1991.

SOYINKA, WOLE. *Ake: The Years of Childhood.* New York: Vintage, 1989.

———. *The Man Died: Prison Notes.* New York: Farrar, Straus and Giroux, 1988.

STEVENSON, ROBERT LOUIS. *The Lantern-Bearers and Other Essays.* Farrar, Straus and Giroux, 1988.

SULERI, SARA. *Meatless Days.* Chicago: University of Chicago Press, 1991.

TANIZAKI, JUNICHIRO. *Childhood Years: A Memoir.* Tokyo & New York: Kodansha, 1988.

———. *In Praise of Shadows.* Thomas J. Harper and Edward G. Seidensticker, tr. New Haven: Leete's Island, 1977.

THOREAU, HENRY DAVID. *Essays of Thoreau.* Richard Dillman, ed. Durham: North Carolina University Press, 1991.

———. *The Variorum Walden.* New York: Twayne Publishers, 1962.

THURBER, JAMES. *The Thurber Carnival.* New York: Harper Colophon, 1975.

TURGENEV, IVAN. *Turgenev's Literary Reminiscences.* New York: Farrar, Straus and Giroux, 1958.

———. *A Sportsman's Notebook.* New York: Ecco, 1986.

VIDAL, GORE. *United States: Essays 1952–1992.* New York: Random House, 1993.

WHITE, E. B. *Essays of E. B. White.* New York: Harper & Row, 1979.

WOOLF, VIRGINIA. *Collected Essays of Virginia Woolf* (6 vols.). New York: Harcourt Brace Jovanovich, 1987– .

———. *The Death of the Moth and Other Essays.* New York: Harcourt Brace Jovanovich, 1979.

———. *Moments of Being.* New York: Harcourt Brace Jovanovich, 1985.

III. Suggested Further Reading

The writers in this section are first-rate essayists who could not be included in this anthology for reasons of space or other considerations (see the Introduction for the rationale for selection).

ABBEY, EDWARD. *Slumgullion Stew: An Edward Abbey Reader.* New York: E. P. Dutton, 1984.

BACON, FRANCIS. *The Essays.* New York: Penguin, 1985.

BAKER, RUSSELL. *So This Is Depravity.* New York: Congdon & Lattes, 1980.

BLY, CAROL. *Letters from the Country.* New York: Harper & Row, 1981.

BRODSKY, JOSEPH. *Less than One: Selected Essays.* New York: Farrar, Straus and Giroux, 1986.

BROWNE, SIR THOMAS. *The Religio Medici and Other Writings.* New York: Everyman's Library, 1931.

BROYARD, ANATOLE. *Intoxicated by My Illness.* New York: Clarkson Potter, 1992.

BURTON, ROBERT. *Anatomy of Melancholy.* New York: Tudor Publishing Company, 1938.

CICERO. *Selected Works.* New York: Penguin Classics, 1960.

——. *On the Good Life.* New York: Penguin Classics, 1971.

CROUCH, STANLEY. *Notes of a Hanging Judge.* New York: Oxford University Press, 1990.

DAVENPORT, GUY. *The Geography of the Imagination.* New York: Pantheon, 1992.

DE QUINCEY, THOMAS. *Selected Writings.* New York: Random House, 1937.

EARLY, GERALD. *Tuxedo Junction: Essays on American Culture.* New York: Ecco, 1989.

EHRLICH, GRETEL. *The Solace of Open Spaces.* New York: Viking, 1985.

EISLEY, LOREN. *The Night Country.* New York: Scribner's, 1971.

EMERSON, RALPH WALDO. *Essays and Lectures.* New York: Library of America, 1983.

EPSTEIN, JOSEPH. *The Middle of My Tether: Familiar Essays.* New York: Norton, 1983.

ERASMUS. *Erasmus on His Times: A Shortened Version of "The Adages."* Cambridge, England: Cambridge University Press, 1980.

GASS, WILLIAM. *Habitations of the Word: Essays.* New York: Simon & Schuster, 1985.

GOMBROWICZ, WITOLD. *Diary,* vol. 1. Evanston, Ill.: Northwestern University Press, 1988.

GONZALEZ-CRUSSI, F. *Notes of an Anatomist.* New York: Harcourt Brace Jovanovich, 1985.

GRAVES, JOHN. *From a Limestone Ledge.* New York: Knopf, 1980.

HADAS, RACHEL. *Living in Time.* New Brunswick, N.J.: Rutgers University Press, 1990.

HARDWICK, ELIZABETH. *A View of My Own.* New York: Ecco, 1982.

HARRISON, BARBARA GRIZZUTI. *The Astonishing World.* New York: Ticknor & Fields, 1992.

HOLM, BILL. *Coming Home Crazy.* Minneapolis: Milkweed Editions, 1990.

JAMES, C. L. R. *The C. L. R. James Reader.* Cambridge, Mass.: Blackwell, 1992.

LAWRENCE, D. H. *D. H. Lawrence and Italy: Twilight in Italy, Sea and Sardinia, Etruscan Places.* New York: Viking Penguin, 1985.

LEOPARDI, GIACOMO. *The Moral Essays.* New York: Columbia University Press, 1983.

LEVI, PRIMO. *Other People's Trades.* New York: Summit, 1989.

LIEBLING, A. J. *Between Meals.* San Francisco: North Point, 1986.

MAIRS, NANCY. *Plaintext.* New York: Harper & Row, 1987.

MAMET, DAVID. *Some Freaks.* New York: Viking, 1989.

MORLEY, CHRISTOPHER. *Christopher Morley's New York.* New York: Fordham University Press, 1988.

MUSIL, ROBERT. *Posthumous Papers of a Living Author.* Hygiene, Col.: Eridanos Press, 1987.

NKOSI, LEWIS. *Home and Exile.* London: Longman, 1983.

OZICK, CYNTHIA. *Art and Ardor.* New York: Knopf, 1983.

PERRIN, NOEL. *First Person Rural: Essays of a Sometime Farmer.* New York: Penguin, 1980.

POLLAN, MICHAEL. *Second Nature.* New York: Atlantic Monthly Press, 1991.

SCHWARTZ, DELMORE. *The Ego Is Always at the Wheel.* New York: New Directions, 1986.

SHEED, WILFRED. *Essays in Disguise.* New York: Knopf, 1990.

SONTAG, SUSAN. *Under the Sign of Saturn.* New York: Vintage, 1981.

UPDIKE, JOHN. *Self-Consciousness.* New York: Knopf, 1989.

WARSHOW, ROBERT. *The Immediate Experience.* New York: Anchor, 1964.